# HARTLEPOOL UNITED

## THE COMPLETE RECORD

# HARTLEPOOL UNITED

## THE COMPLETE RECORD

MALCOLM ERRINGTON

First published in Great Britain in 2012 by
DB Publishing, an imprint of JMD Media Ltd



ISBN 978-1-78091-030-7

Printed and bound by Copytech (UK) Ltd, Peterborough

# Contents

# Biblography

*The definitive Hartlepool United* by Gordon Small, Association of Football Statisticians.
*A Tenner and a Box of Kippers* by Jonathan Strange, Tempus Publishing, 2006.
*Hartlepool United: In the Beginning 1908 to 1921* by Colin Foster, Katcha Publishing, 2005.
*A Century of 'Poolies'* by Colin Foster, MRT Publishing, 2008.
*Up the Pools* by Neil Watson and Roy Kelly, Ords Ltd, 1991.
*Hartlepool United* by Ed Law, Breedon Books Publishing, 1989.
*Football League Players Records 1888 to 1939* by Michael Joyce, SoccerData, 2004.
The PFA Premier and Football League Players Records 1946 to 2005 by Barry J. Hugman, Queen Anne Press, 2005.
*Rothmans/Sky Football Yearbooks 1970 to 2009* by Jack Rollin and others, Various publishers, 1970 to 2009.
*Soccer at War 1939 to 1945* by Jack Rollin, Headline Book Publishing, 1985.
*Hotbed of Soccer* by Arthur Appleton, Rupert Hart-Davis, 1960.
*Soccer Who's Who* by Maurice Galsworthy, The Sportsmans Book Club, 1965.
*With Clough by Taylor* by Peter Taylor, Sidgwick and Jackson, 1980.
Breedon Books Complete Record series – Various clubs 1988 to date.
The Times Newspaper Archive.

Reference Websites
www.inthemadcrowd.co.uk
www.poolstats.co.uk

# ACKNOWLEDGEMENTS

This book would not have been possible without the help and support of numerous individuals, some of whom I know personally, and others who I have never met and yet were only too willing help on a practical level and offer advice and encouragement from a distance. I accept that some of the details contained herein will contradict previous publications and widely held opinions and beliefs. My defence is that I have conscientiously cross referenced my original sources to other reputable publications and documents (birth and death certificates) to satisfy myself as to the validity of the published material.

Regarding particular help and support I am grateful for the unfailing courtesy of the staff of Hartlepool Central Library in providing access to the archives of the local newspaper archives, the *Hartlepool Mail* and to Bob Watson for his interest and input into the detail of this book as well as allowing unrestricted access to his library of football books. Special thanks to the late Ken Johnson, Hartlepool's all-time leading goalscorer, for providing personal background and archive material. To Michael Davage for his patience in providing personal details on many of the players and to Gordon Small and Colin Foster, fellow authors on the club's history, for their support and encouragement. Also my thanks go to Alan Bushnell for the autographed Manchester United programme, Rob Robinson for the photographs of his late father, George Park of Edinburgh St Bernards for the image and information on Davy Gordon, and Eric Paylor of the *Middlesbrough Evening Gazette* for his help. Finally the *Hartlepool Mail* for consenting to the publication of many of the photographs contained herein.

I must also make mention of the staff and management of DB Publishing. Without initial encouragement and support from Steve Caron this book would never have been published.

And finally, leaving the best till last, my wonderful wife Margaret who has put up with this marathon undertaking with her usual patience and forbearance, even when my offer of a trip out to such places as Durham and Morpeth was merely an excuse to visit the local Births & Deaths Registry Office.

# Introduction

To the reader expecting a football club history recounting championships, Cup wins and famous international players, this volume will be a disappointment. This is not a journal of playing triumphs and star players watched by massive crowds and intense media coverage. This is a history of a football club which for most of my lifetime has carried the disparaging label 'Cinderella club' and has survived a record number of re-election applications to rightly celebrate its recent centenary and unbroken membership of the Football League since 1921. It is a matter of opinion whether the words of a former manager that being in charge of Hartlepool United 'is the hardest job in football' still hold true today.

I first watched Hartlepools United (as they were then called) in 1954 as a nine-year-old, taken as a treat on the birthday of a school friend. Two goals by Tommy McGuigan were enough to beat Port Vale, the runaway leaders of the Third Division North, in front of a crowd of over 8,500. My first memory of a 'big game' came the next year with the FA Cup tie against Nottingham Forest in January 1955 which attracted a then record crowd of 17,200 crammed, like myself, into the 'Vic' to witness a thrilling draw. These were the days before mass television coverage, when supporters relied on the Saturday night football 'Green Un' to keep abreast of news and match reports of their local team. Hartlepools were well served in that respect by Charlie Summerbell, a legend in local football journalism, who wrote under the nom de plume, 'Sentinel'.

As the austerity of the immediate post-war era gave way to the 'swinging sixties', 'Pools fortunes went into reverse with multiple re-election applications (automatic relegation was still some years away) and one financial crisis after another. The arrival of the charismatic Brian Clough, who worked tirelessly promoting the club to the Hartlepool public, arrested this trend and paved the way for a first-ever promotion in 1968 which saw crowds return. Another innovation in this era was the introduction of floodlit mid-week League games, which sadly coincided with relegation, resulting in a short-lived upturn in fortunes, and a long struggle for survival then ensued.

With the benefit of hindsight, it now seems a minor miracle that the club not only survived the traumatic events of the 1970s and 1980s, when attendances reached an all-time low, but also managed to retain their Football League status. Much of the credit for this must go to long-serving manager Billy Horner who by shrewdly signing players from non-League football and developing youngsters who were later sold on, usually at ridiculously low transfer fees by naive chairmen, managed to keep Hartlepool United in business. It speaks volumes for the fortunes of the club in this era that one of the few positives was the demolition of the dilapidated wooden Clarence Road stand following the Bradford fire tragedy, although it was to be some years before a new structure was in place.

The arrival of ebullient Gary Gibson as chairman coincided with a thrilling promotion in 1991, with a team containing the likes of Joe Allon, Rob McKinnon and Paul Dalton.

Gibson further strengthened the side with record signing Andy Saville, a proven goalscorer at this level. Despite this and the quality of the visiting opposition, the sceptical Hartlepool public never quite took to the chairman and his team, and attendances remained well below expectations, with the result that star players were transferred followed by the inevitable relegation back to the bottom tier of the Football League.

The sale of the club by Gibson in 1994 to popular local businessman Harold Hornsey galvanised local support, and the building of the Cyril Knowles stand, complete with private hospitality boxes, transformed the club's image and brought a new generation of supporter to the Victoria Park, as it was now named. The latter part of the decade saw two further major developments at local and national level. Firstly, the transfer of ownership to the Increased Oil Recovery company under the stewardship of Ken Hodcroft, and the appointment of Chris Turner as manager, resulted in the club reaching new heights, with promotions and Play-offs a regular feature of Hartlepool United's seasons. Secondly, the advent of Sky Sports Television and the regular coverage of the game at all levels. This has proved a mixed blessing as the extra revenue from live games and share of the lucrative television contract has to be balanced against the explosion in players wages (at all levels) and the advent of the 'armchair supporter' who solely watches the leading Premiership clubs and never attends a live game.

Hartlepool United, its players, supporters, officials, and employees have much to be thankful for in a period of great uncertainty and global recession. By sound management both on and off the field of play the club has avoided the financial pitfalls of over ambition and reckless spending. Not only has Hartlepool United made progress in a material way with the continuing improvements at the Victoria Park (you can now be married there), but it has also continued to progress on the field of play and looks forward to the 2010–11 season, with a record fourth successive campaign in the third tier of English Football.

Anyone who does not regard this as real progress should talk to a Luton Town or Grimsby Town supporter – teams which during the lifetime of this writer once featured in the top tier of English football and now languish outside the Football League.

# The History of Hartlepool United Football Club

## The Birth of a Football Club

On 5 June 1908 a limited liability company was registered under the name 'The Hartlepools United Football and Athletic Club Company Ltd' with a share capital of 2,000 shares of £1 each, thereby creating a professional football club.

Prior to this date, the people of the Hartlepools had been raised on the two amateur football codes, association and rugby. The rugby code flourished in the area, through the two principal clubs, Hartlepool Rovers, formed in 1879, and West Hartlepool, formed in 1881, who forged a rivalry which continues to this day. Originally West Hartlepool Rugby Club played at the Victoria Ground, their home since 1886; however, financial difficulties caused the club to disband briefly, and it was at this point that the professional football club was formed and took over the venue. The amateurs continued to play in the Northern League, and a ground-sharing arrangement was reached to play both sets of fixtures on the Victoria Ground, the amateurs having lost the right to continue playing at their Park Road ground.

The West Hartlepool Amateur Football Club had distinguished itself by winning the FA Amateur Cup in 1905, defeating Clapton Orient 3–2 in the Final at Shepherds Bush in front of a near-capacity crowd with the overwhelming majority supporting the London side. This was a major achievement and stimulated debate among the supporters of the association game and the wider public of the Hartlepools as to whether the two towns could support a professional football team.

The amateurs of West Hartlepool continued to hold their own in the Northern League and finished the 1907–08 season in the top five, averaging attendances at their Park Road ground of over 1,500; however, storm clouds were gathering over the West Hartlepool Rugby Club, and they ended the season in serious financial difficulties, with their Victoria Road ground in need of major repairs. They folded on 28 April 1908, and after weeks of rumours a professional football club was formed registered under the name of 'The Hartlepools United Football and Athletic Club Company Limited'.

Several prominent local individuals, including former vice-presidents of the rugby club, Messrs R. Martin and W. Paterson, along with former committee member W.J. Coates, were elected to the new board of Hartlepools United. Their first task was to appoint a manager, and in this they made a wise choice. Alfred Ernest Priest was born in South Bank and earned League Championship and FA Cup-winners' medals with Sheffield United as well as

1908 FA Cup tie against West Hartlepool. Smith (arm raised) scores the winning goal.

playing for England. He joined from neighbours Middlesbrough, where he was an assistant coach, and immediately appointed himself captain for the club's first season as a professional side.

The new club of Hartlepools United was elected to the North Eastern League for the 1908–09 season, and the directors entered into a ground-sharing arrangement with the West Hartlepool amateurs who, having lost the right to play at their Park Road venue, needed a new home. The first match on 2 September 1908 was a friendly against a Newcastle United side including several first-team players. They recorded a resounding 6–0 victory, which set them up for their first competitive game in the North Eastern League away to Hebburn Argyle. After an opening draw, the stage was set the following Saturday for the inaugural League fixture at the Victoria Ground against Seaham White Star. A crowd estimated to be 5,000 turned up to witness a disappointing goalless draw before results improved with wins in the next three home games.

The good form of the professional team was matched by the amateurs in the Northern League, and the Hartlepools were soon to experience the magic of the FA Cup when the two sides were drawn against each other in the first qualifying round. Strictly speaking, United were the away side for what turned out to be a memorable football occasion, witnessed by a crowd of over 7,000. The spectators saw a hard-fought contest in which the amateurs matched their professional opponents before narrowly losing.

Hartlepools United finished the 1908–09 season in a highly respectable fourth place in the North Eastern League, attracting several attendances of 5,000 plus. Joshie Fletcher was ever present throughout the campaign, scoring 27 League goals in a season which was, in all aspects, judged a success. Fred Priest limited his appearances as the season wore on to concentrate on his managerial duties. At the end of the season the club embarked on a tour

Hartlepool United 1909 Durham Senior Cup winners. Back row, left to right: J. Spoors (trainer), T. Hegarty, F. Mearns, R. Hegarty, A.E. Priest (manager). Middle row: S. Tweddle, J. Hand, W. Ledger, C. Smith. Front row: F. Tweddle, J. Fletcher, F. Edgley, T. Brown, W. Roberts.

of Germany with 12 players, to play against Hamburg and Bremen (now Werder Bremen), winning both games in convincing fashion. 'Pools' hosts were fulsome in their praise of Fred Priest and his players, who returned to West Hartlepool in high spirits, having not only enjoyed their football, but also the fine weather and lavish hospitality.

The 1909–10 season saw another top-four finish and resounding wins of 10–0 and 12–0 over Hebburn Argyle and Workington respectively. In the latter game centre-forward Jack Hogg scored nine goals! The season was blighted, however, by the death of Frank Edgley at the premature age of 28 years. Edgley was already ill when he travelled to Germany, and his last game for the club was on 22 January 1910, a 5–1 victory over Sunderland Royal Rovers. If the season had been a success for United, the opposite was true of the amateurs of 'West'. After a difficult season in the Northern League, which included a 9–1 defeat against Crook Town, they bowed to the inevitable after their final League game against Stockton, which attracted a mere 200 spectators, and disbanded.

During the close season Hartlepools United made their first application to join the Football League when representatives from the club visited 26 of the 40 League clubs to petition support for the application. The rest were petitioned by a letter, signed by Councillor Paterson, club president, and Councillor Martin, honorary secretary. This outlined the club's case in the most optimistic terms, even claiming that the Victoria Ground could accommodate 14,000 spectators, with ready scope for further expansion! Harsh reality set in when only one vote was received in the ballot, which elected Huddersfield Town to Division Two of the Football League.

Frank Edgley with the Durham Senior Cup.

James Hogg, scorer of nine goals in the 12–0 rout of Workington, April 1910.

Hartlepools United reached the near summit of the North Eastern League in the 1910–11 season when Fred Priest's side finished third, with only the second XIs of Newcastle United and Sunderland, both major clubs during this period, above them. Key to this success was Joshie Fletcher, who played every game and contributed 15 goals. The season also saw the formation of the club's first reserve side, which was admitted to the Wearside League, playing as Hartlepools United 'A'. They acquitted themselves well, finishing third out of 13 clubs and winning 14 of their 24 fixtures. In the close season the club made a second application to join the Football League, only to see Grimsby Town, relegated the previous season, return to the Second Division.

After three consecutive top-four finishes, it was perhaps inevitable that results would decline in the 1911–12 season, which was to prove Fred Priest's last as manager. Early exits in both the FA Cup, to North Shields Adelaide, and the Durham Senior Cup, to Darlington, saw a decline in support which meant a third application to join the Football League was out of the question. The final home game of the season against Spennymoor United attracted a meagre 500 spectators.

Percy Humphreys succeeded Fred Priest as player-manager in June 1912. Humphreys had had a successful playing career with Queen's Park Rangers, Notts County, Leicester Fosse, Chelsea and Tottenham Hotspur, as well as winning an England cap. He made 28 appearances during the season, scoring 11 goals, and demonstrated his versatility by appearing in the centre-half and centre-forward positions. There was some compensation to the indifferent League form in the FA Cup when, after qualifying victories over Houghton Rovers, Wingate Albion, Sunderland Rovers and Castleford, a first-ever appearance in the competition proper was thwarted by Gainsborough Trinity. Inevitably, the moderate League form affected attendances, and so the directors took the decision to postpone applications for Football League membership indefinitely. Humphreys left the club at the end of the season and retired from playing due to persistent knee injuries. The directors decided to continue with the player-manager, however, and shortly before the 1913–14 season appointed Jack Manners in the role.

Jack Manners had made over 200 appearances for West Bromwich Albion, his only club. He made 31 League and Cup appearances, scoring four goals as 'Pools improved to seventh position in the North Eastern League. The following season, 1914–15, saw Manners maintain the club's position in circumstances that tested every professional club in the country. Following the outbreak of World War One in the August, the Football Association took the bold decision to continue with the fixtures for the season, despite strong opposition from many quarters. Despite all clubs, including Hartlepools United, fulfilling their fixtures, there was understandable scepticism on the part of the paying public, as was evidenced by the fall in attendances. This, in turn, led to a fall in income, which brought many clubs to the verge of ruin and affected their prospects for years to come. With an escalation in hostilities during the summer of 1915, the Football Association had no choice but to abandon the League programme, with the result that no football was played at the Victoria Ground for four years.

Despite the ending of the 'Great War' in November 1918, the military authorities still occupied the Victoria Ground in August 1919, the date set for the resumption of League football. Responding to the challenge, the directors arranged for the club's home fixtures for the 1919–20 season to be played at the West Hartlepool Expansion ground at Foggy Furze. Jack Manners resumed his managerial duties and his hastily assembled team – which included 10 'guest' players (only goalkeeper Gill was local) – resumed competitive football on 30 August 1919 with a North Eastern League fixture against Ashington. The initial impact of so many 'guests' resulted in a 10-game run without a win before a more settled side started to produce results. The impact of this can be judged from the 38 players used to fulfil a 34-game fixture list! Taking everything into account, Manners did well to see his side finish in ninth position.

Harry Thoms, who played in both the North Eastern and Football Leagues for Hartlepools.

Jack Manners retired as player-manager at the end of the season and left on good terms, with the club making a presentation to recognise his efforts in re-establishing professional football in the Hartlepools following the deprivations of the war years. A few days after Manners's departure Cecil Potter joined from Hull City in the player-manager role. Potter spent the majority of his playing career with Norwich City and appeared for Tottenham Hotspur before the war. He arrived at the right time, as during the summer the Football League announced the creation of a new Division Three for the 1920–21 season. Before Hartlepools United had a chance to enthuse over the prospect of League football, it was announced that the new division would be comprised entirely of southern clubs! In the end Grimsby Town was the sole 'northern' representative, fuelling speculation that a further division based on regional representation would be added the following season.

In January 1921 a meeting took place in Manchester between Football League officials and representatives of clubs wishing to be considered for membership of the Northern Section of the Third Division. Hartlepools United were one of 30 clubs represented who agreed to detailed enquiries into their finances, ground facilities and playing personnel. The United directors made a sound case, stating that the capacity of the Victoria Ground was in excess of 10,000 and planned improvements would increase that to over 16,000. Ground facilities, although described as basic, compared favourably to other applicant clubs and finances were sound. The one concern was the playing strength and recent results.

Potter's team had made a slow start to the 1920–21 season, winning only one of the opening 10 League games. A 10-game FA Cup campaign which eventually finished in defeat at Swansea revived the season and improved League results after Christmas, eventually resulting in a satisfactory ninth-placed finish. Central to this improvement was the form of Jimmy Lister, who scored 18 goals in 20 appearances, and the League momentum gained in the second half of the season, together with the Cup run, stood the club in good stead in its campaign to join the new Third Division North.

On 12 March 1921 the club received the news that it had been elected to the Third Division North of the Football League. Within days of the news, Cecil Potter relinquished his playing responsibilities to become secretary-manager, a role which would allow him to concentrate on strengthening the playing staff for the coming season, Hartlepools United's debut in the Football League.

## Into the Football League and 'Europe'

The new Third Division North initially comprised 20 clubs from a list of 30 applicants including north-east clubs Ashington, Darlington and Durham City. Among those to miss out were Blyth Spartans and West Stanley, who both finished above Hartlepools in their final North Eastern League season.

The Third Division North of the Football League 'kicked-off' on Saturday 27 August 1921, with Hartlepools travelling to Wrexham, previously of the Birmingham & District League, and fielding the following side: Gill, Crilly, Thoms, Dougherty, Hopkins, Short, Kessler, Mulholland, Lister, Robertson and Donald. In front of a reported 10,000 spectators 'Pools established a 2–0 half-time lead, with goals from Mulholland and Lister. Despite a strong second-half rally by the home side, no further goals were scored, resulting in Hartlepools recording a memorable victory on their Football League debut.

The fixture lists of the early seasons usually reversed the previous week's games, so Wrexham were the first League visitors to the Victoria Ground the following Saturday. Any thoughts that a repeat of the first game's result was on the cards were quickly dispelled by a Wrexham side who had learned the lessons of the defeat, going on to earn a hard-fought 1–0 victory courtesy of a Reg Leck goal in front of another estimated 10,000 crowd.

Despite winning their next home game against Southport with a Jimmy Lister goal, the first in the Football League by a home player at the Victoria Ground, Hartlepools struggled to come to terms with the demands of League football. No goals were scored in the next four games, and the encouragement of a four-goal home victory over Halifax Town was only succeeded by another four-game goalless streak.

Although results were relatively modest, attendances held up well and supporters were rewarded with a turn around in form, beginning on Boxing Day with a victory over Stalybridge Celtic. Six wins in the next eight games followed, culminating in a resounding 7–0 win over hapless Chesterfield in which George Crowther scored the club's first-ever Football League hat-trick. After this triumph, the remaining fixtures brought six further wins to give the club a top-four finish with 42 points from 38 games. Stockport County were the first champions of the new Third Division North on 56 points, with Darlington and Grimsby Town second and third respectively, both on 50 points, making 'Pools a distant fourth.

During the close season, the club embarked on a five-match tour of Spain, with Cecil Potter in charge of a virtually full-strength squad of players. Five games were played over a nine-day period in May, three against Racing Club Santander and two against Oviedo. Despite the heat and travelling involved, Potter's team excelled themselves, winning four and only suffering a single defeat on the day after an eight-hour train journey to play an Oviedo side that included several 'guest' players. Potter himself had the distinction of accepting an invitation from the Santander club to play for them in the third game against his side. For the record the following played on the tour: Bratt, Chesser, Crilly, Dougherty, Gill, Harris, Longmore, Nicholson, Pentland, Potter, Robertson and Rowe.

Hartlepools United's debut season in the Football League could be considered a relative success in playing terms, despite a failure to score in 15 games. Peter Robertson was the leading scorer with 12 goals in 26 games. Also the use of 34 players, 15 of whom played less than 10 games apiece, suggested that much work needed to be done on the management side, and it was no surprise when David Gordon replaced Cecil Potter, who joined Derby County in July 1922.

Despite the satisfactory playing record and consistent support, and an estimated crowd of over 11,000 attending the Darlington game, the club lost money on the season. Factors such as a trade depression and the size of the playing staff with too many full-time professionals took their toll financially, and it was obvious the new manager would have to be more prudent in the second season. David Gordon, despite having a successful playing career with Hull City, had only limited management experience, having previously been secretary-manager of Scottish club Hibernian.

The optimism of the inaugural League season was not maintained in 1922–23. A poor start, which saw only one win in the first six games, was exacerbated by a run of seven games without a win during November and December, culminating in a heavy defeat at Darlington on Christmas Day. Emphatic wins against the eventual champions Nelson and Stalybridge Celtic early in the New Year were quickly followed by an eight-game losing streak, resulting in attendances falling below the 3,000 mark. A final League position of 15th with 32 points from 38 games was only two points better than Ashington, who had to apply for re-election. Despite the appointment of a new manager, the playing staff reduced only marginally, with 31 players making League appearances and only Tommy Yews appearing in over 30 games. No player managed double figures in goals, with Lowe Braidford top scoring with nine in 29 appearances.

Ted Smith played 63 games at left-back between 1923 and 1925 before joining Newport County.

The following season, 1923–24, resulted in what was to become almost a ritual for the club in the coming seasons, applying for re-election to the Football League. The season began brightly,

Billy Cowell made 87 appearances in goal between 1924 and 1926.

however, with 'Pools winning their opening two games, only to be followed by a solitary victory in the succeeding 12, which included a run of five games without a goal. Twenty games were lost, nine at home, and only 33 goals were scored in 38 games. A total of 25 points was the same as Barrow, who finished bottom on goal average. By the end of a dismal season, attendances had dropped below 2,000, and the optimism of the previous two campaigns completely evaporated. Manager Gordon used 32 players, including an Egyptian, Tewfik Abdallah, during the season, with Billy Smith top scoring with nine goals in 27 games. Smith also scored a remarkable seven goals in the 10–1 rout of St Peters Albion in an FA Cup qualifying tie.

After successfully applying for re-election, the 1924–25 season continued the trend set previously, with United struggling at the bottom of the League. This was reflected in attendances, with fewer than 2,000 spectators attending the games against Nelson and Durham City. Despite using 30 players, manager Gordon finally had an ever present in versatile winger Ernie Butler. Smith again top scored with 12 goals in only 17 appearances.

If League form was a major disappointment, the club enjoyed an FA Cup run which culminated in them playing in the first round proper for the first time against the holders Newcastle United at St James' Park. To reach this stage they lodged an appeal against an ineligible player following defeat at Ashington. This was upheld and Ashington were expelled from the competition. Home wins against Bishop Auckland and St Albans City set up the dream tie. In front of a crowd of 36,632, easily a record for any Hartlepools United game at the time, and facing opposition that included nine members of the Cup-winning side, 'Pools gave a sterling account of themselves. Superbly marshalled by their captain, Charlie Storer, the home side only took the lead just before half-time with a Neil Harris goal. The visitors started the second half positively but conceded further goals to McDonald, Cowan and McKenzie before Cec Hardy scored a late consolation.

Despite the relative success of the Cup run, results in the League continued to disappoint and David Gordon was eventually replaced as manager by Jack Manners, who started his second spell in charge on 25 October 1925. Manners's previous spell with Hartlepools United had been in the North Eastern League days, and his appointment was influenced by the financial constraints imposed on the club.

For the 1925–26 season the Football Association made one of the most important changes to the game's laws by amending the offside rule requirement of three players between the goal and the scorer to two. This had an immediate impact on the game in general, and Hartlepools United in particular when they lost their first game at Rochdale 6–0.

Results rapidly improved, with five wins in the next six games before a temporary downturn following the change of manager saw a seven-game unbeaten run over the Christmas and New Year period, which culminated in a record 9–3 win over Walsall.

The season ended with a final League position of sixth, with 44 points from 42 games and 82 goals scored. For the first time in their League career United had the benefit of a settled side with only 22 players used, four of whom made only one appearance each. Three players were ever present: goalkeeper Billy Cowell, right-back Tom Lilley and centre-forward Harry Wensley, who top scored with 21 goals, the first Hartlepools player to break the 20-goal barrier in a League season.

Sadly, this improvement was not maintained during the following season, 1926–27. A poor start, with only two wins in the opening eight games, saw attendances plummet, with barely 1,200 fans turning up for the visit of Bradford Park Avenue in November. Results improved over the Christmas and New Year period before a record defeat 7–2 to Accrington Stanley at the beginning of February. Attendances for the next three home games were below 3,000 and the final home game against New Brighton, a 4–0 win, only attracted 1,983 diehard fans to witness Jack Manners' last game in charge. A final League position of 17th reflected a loss of form of several key players, and 26 appeared during the

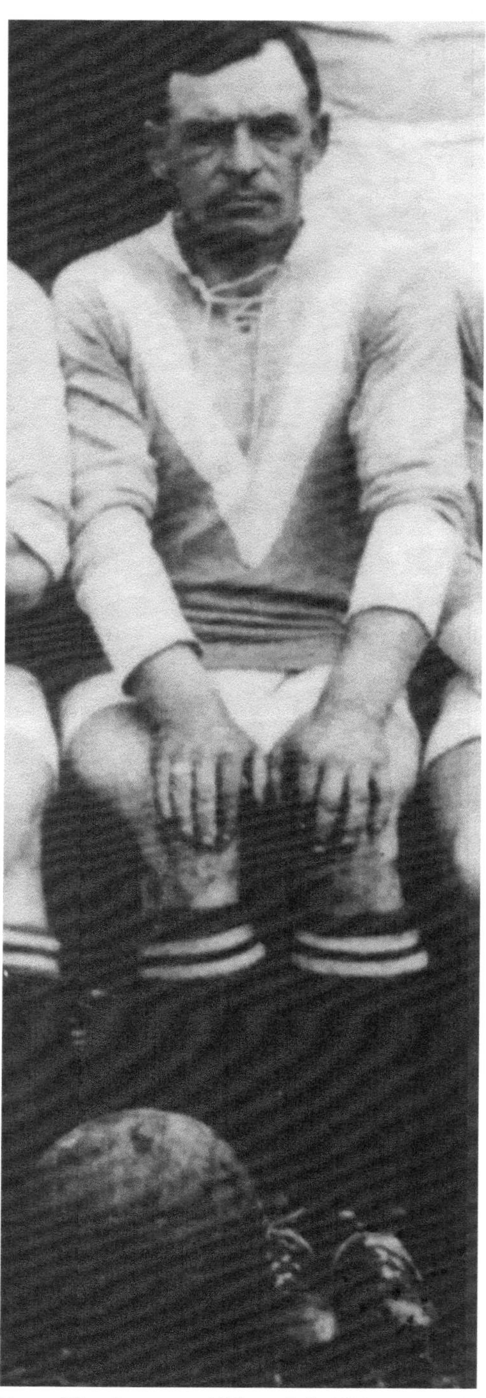

Harry Wensley scored 37 goals in 76 League appearances between 1925 and 1927.

Ernie Butler joined from Queen's Park Rangers and later played for Durham City.

campaign. Once again Wensley was leading scorer with a highly creditable 16 goals in 34 games.

Bill Norman, formerly in charge of Blackpool, replaced Manners as manager only 10 days before the kick-off of the 1927–28 season, yet he still managed a winning start in his opening two games. Subsequent results were mixed until Bill Robinson was selected at centre-forward against Nelson in early November. Despite a 4–2 defeat, with Robinson scoring both goals, the number nine embarked on a goalscoring run which culminated in 28 League goals in 33 appearances, a record to this day. Robinson also had the 'distinction' of becoming the only 'Pools player to score a hat-trick and finish on the losing side when Nelson won 5–4 at the Vic. The new manager used 25 players in attaining a marginally improved 15th-place League finish, which failed to impress the Hartlepools public despite Robinson's goalscoring heroics. By the end of the season, attendances had once again dropped below the 2,000 mark.

The 1928–29 season, which ultimately resulted in a second re-election application, is perhaps best remembered for the introduction to professional football of W.G. 'Ginger' Richardson. Born in Framwellgate Moor, he joined 'Pools aged 20 years old from the United Bus Company FC, having previously played for Horden Wednesday. Richardson made 29 appearances, scoring 19 goals, before signing for West Bromwich Albion in the June. At the Hawthorns he was nicknamed 'Ginger' and became a goalscoring legend, setting a club record which still stands of 39 League goals in

W.G. 'Ginger' Richardson scored 19 goals in his debut season and went on to England fame with West Bromwich Albion.

the 1935–36 season, culminating in his selection for England. His other major triumph for the Albion was to score both goals in the 1931 FA Cup Final victory over local rivals Birmingham City. Despite the attraction of such a talented young player in the team, United were unable to break the cycle of defeats and remained in the bottom two places after the New Year until the season's end. In all they conceded a record 112 League goals, 74 of which came in 21 away games. Ashington eventually finished bottom with 23 points, three fewer than 'Pools, and paid the price by being replaced by York City.

## A Life of Depression On and Off the Pitch

The early optimism of entry into the Football League had now dissipated, as attendances confirmed. From an average gate of 7,239 in their first season, 'Pools had seen a steady decline to less than half that figure, 3,360, by the end of the season. Clearly drastic action was required for the next season, 1929–30, if a repeat was to be avoided.

It arrived in the commanding form of Frank Barson, a former England international who spent the prime of his career with Manchester United. His other clubs included Barnsley, Aston Villa, with whom he had won an FA Cup-winners' medal, and Watford. An insight into Barson's style can be gleaned from his disciplinary record which, in an era before yellow cards and commonplace sendings off, included four suspensions. Despite his regular brushes with authority he was considered the complete centre-half, with tactical sense to compliment his superb physical play. It was a major coup for the club to sign a player of Barson's stature. In reality he made only nine appearances during the season, scoring two goals, but his influence spread to the rest of the team

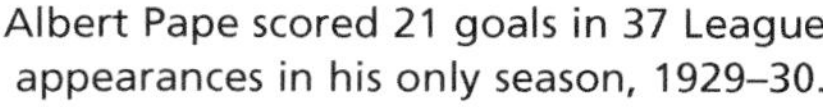

Albert Pape scored 21 goals in 37 League appearances in his only season, 1929–30.

Josh Hewitt scored 55 goals in 117 games between 1930 and 1934.

and results improved dramatically. A final placing of eighth bore testimony to the upturn in fortunes, with 13 victories at home including a win against the eventual champions Port Vale in front of 7,473 fans. Ironically, 'Pools also suffered their heaviest home defeat to date, an 8–2 reverse to Rochdale, for whom the quaintly named Tommy Tippett scored six goals. Albert Pape top scored with 21 goals in 37 appearances, which included a scoring run of five consecutive games.

Whatever improvement was made, it quickly evaporated during the 1930–31 season when a third re-election application was only avoided by a superior goal average over Rochdale. Another poor start, which produced only one win in the first nine games, set the tone for the season. Despite Harry Simmons scoring five goals against Wigan Borough in a 6–1 romp on New Year's Day to set a new individual record, the attendance nadir was reached in early March when 'Pools' first sub-1,000 gate was recorded against Crewe Alexandra, when only 853 diehards turned up to see a 2–0 win. Simmons finished the season as leading scorer with 17 League goals in 31 appearances, with no other player reaching double figures.

The remedy in terms of securing a consistent goalscorer for the long term came in the form of Johnny Wigham. Wigham was a Jarrow schoolteacher who was playing for Hebburn Colliery, and he was to become a regular for Hartlepools United up to the outbreak of World War Two. In his debut season, 1931–32, he contributed 13 goals in 24 games, although Sydney Lumley was leading scorer with 18 League goals.

Jimmy Hamilton as a player in 1932.

Such consistency brought about an improvement in results and subsequent League position. A finish of 13th may not seem meteoric; however, compared to the previous season it was highly satisfactory. This was despite a defence that conceded 100 League goals, including seven games when five or more goals were let in. One record that still stands was set in the home fixture against York City when both Joss Hewitt and Bobby Dixon, playing at centre-half, recorded hat-tricks in a 7–2 win, the only time that two Hartlepools players have scored hat-tricks in the same game.

Jacky Carr had joined Hartlepools during the season as a player-coach, having previously played for Middlesbrough and Blackpool. An England international, he played for Middlesbrough in their Second Division Championship seasons of 1927 and 1929 and came with a reputation as a schemer and provider rather than a goalscorer. This was borne out by his solitary goal in his 10 games for the club that season. He assumed the role of acting manager following Bill Norman's demise and a strong finish to the campaign saw him confirmed in the role.

If Carr's first priority was to strengthen the defence, and the signing of Jack O'Donnell confirmed that, then the 1932–33 season was to be remarkable in terms of the volume of goals (203) recorded in a League season of 42 games. Despite scoring 87, their best total to date, they conceded a staggering 116, 87 of which came in away games. Not surprisingly, they only managed one away victory, yet despite this they still finished a respectable 14th thanks to a sound home record which included 15 victories. For the first time four players, Hewitt (23 goals), Wigham (15 goals), Pedwell (15 goals) and Dixon (11 goals), reached double figures. Steve Bowron was ever present, and despite the mixed results only 21 players were used during the season. This total included four goalkeepers: Owbridge, Wilks, Tremain and Rivers, suggesting that the lack of a reliable custodian was a major factor in the defensive problems.

The following season, 1933–34, saw a modest improvement both in a final League position of 11th and in the number of goals conceded, 93. For the third consecutive season no goalless draws featured in the League results, with the goalscoring heroics of Hewitt (20 goals), Pedwell (18 goals), Wigham (15 goals) and Hardy (12 goals) the major contributors. In an early season purple patch Joss Hewitt scored in five consecutive games. Attendances, however, remained stubbornly below the 4,000 mark, with a season's average of 3,687. The final home game against Rotherham United attracted a mere 1,083 to witness a convincing victory.

Manager Carr was now only too aware of what the first priority was – to strengthen his defence. Ossie Park was recruited from Newcastle United, for whom he had played 43 games, and Jack Proctor was signed from New Delavel to add much-needed stability to a rearguard that had conceded over 200 League goals in the past two seasons. This to some extent had the desired effect, as the 'goals against' column shrank to a mere 78 for the 1934–35 season. For only the fourth time in their League career 'Pools managed to score more goals (80) than they conceded, thanks largely to the goalscoring exploits of Duncan Lindsay (21 goals) and Albert Bonass (20 goals). Paradoxically, given the positive goals difference, 'Pools actually finished a place lower than the previous season, in 12th, with home gates averaging a lowly 3,114. Such attendances had a severe impact on gate receipts, and by the end of the season the club's accumulated debt stood at £6,562.

During the close season Jacky Carr left to manage Tranmere Rovers and was succeeded by former player and captain Jimmy Hamilton. Hamilton left his role of player-coach at Gateshead to join his former club, where it was hoped his Army background would instill method and discipline into the Hartlepools side. The 1935–36 season was to be a success on several fronts, with the highest League finish since 1930, reaching the third round of the FA Cup for the first time, a new record attendance of 15,064 and, most importantly of all, a financial profit for the first time in five seasons. Johnny Wigham was well to the fore with 16 goals in 31 starts and the defence continued to improve, with the 'goals against' column a respectable 61.

The FA Cup adventure began with a narrow win at Mansfield, before a second replay was required to overcome Halifax Town at St James' Park in which Johnny Wigham scored a hat-trick. The third round saw 'Pools drawn at home to First Division opposition for the first time against Grimsby Town. Public interest was intense, and despite poor weather over 15,000 crammed into the Victoria Ground. The home side were not overawed by their more illustrious opponents, despite being reduced to 10 men when goalkeeper Jimmy Mittel was

Hartlepools United in their 'sunday best', 1934.

Hartlepools United, 1935. Back row, left to right: J. Hamilton (manager), G. Brown, J. Proctor, J. Mittell, W. Allison, R. Mill, J. Wigham. Front row: A. Thompson, L, Hardy, O. Park, A. Robertson, A. Barras.

carried off. Dick Hardy, a right-winger, took over in goal and Mittel returned to play on the wing. Wigham was outstanding, with strong support coming from Bonass and Robertson and the rest of the team. The First Division side were reported as happy to settle for a goalless draw to take the tie to a replay. As so often happens with higher League opposition, they were a different proposition on their own ground, and so it proved on this occasion. Despite 'Pools' best efforts, the experience of international players such as Glover and Bestall told, and the home side ran out 4–1 winners. Grimsby went on to reach the semi-final, losing to eventual winners Arsenal.

The relative success encouraged the club's directors to sanction an audacious signing for the coming season in Sam English. English, an Irish international, made his name with Glasgow Rangers and Liverpool. While at Rangers he was involved in the tragic incident which resulted in John Thompson, the Celtic goalkeeper, sustaining a depressed fracture of the skull from which he died. Although no blame was attached to English for the accident, the memory of it was to affect the rest of his playing career.

With a settled squad of players, only 21 were used throughout the 1936–37 season, and with a solid home record which recorded 16 wins, 'Pools improved to finish a creditable sixth. After a strong start which saw only one defeat in the first seven games, a record League attendance of 12,220 turned up for the Chester game at the start of November which was narrowly lost.

A few weeks later, 'Pools visited Darlington for a match full of incident and goals. In the first half they recovered from a two-goal deficit to equalise before the home side restored the advantage by half-time, 4–2. Again 'Pools equalised before Darlington scored a fifth goal, which the home crowd thought was the winner, only for Johnny Wigham to equalise yet again in the dying moments to level the scores at 5–5. The Hartlepools public responded well to the improvement in both play and position by recording an average attendance of 5,740 – the best since the inaugural season. Another stand-out result in a high-scoring campaign was the 8–2 defeat at Mansfield which saw Ted Harston score seven goals for the Field Mill side.

Following his success in terms of both results and finances, Jimmy Hamilton now embarked on a radical new course by signing experienced players from senior professional clubs. Previously the core of the team was drawn from local amateur teams and professionals with strong north-east connections, with the odd 'star' signing as described. Now goalkeeper Alan Taylor and Ernie Thomas of Tottenham Hotspur and Ernest Curtis, a Welsh international from Birmingham City, arrived at the Victoria Ground. While the club directors deserved credit for bringing what they thought was class and experience to supplement a squad of players that had progressed to a top-six place, they were to learn – as others have since – that such policies do not guarantee success.

The 1937–38 season was to be a major disappointment, with re-election only avoided by a superior goal average to Barrow. For this 'Pools had a seven-game unbeaten run at the end of the season to thank, as none of the 'star' signings were successful, with Curtis only managing a single goal in his 16 appearances. The settled side of the previous two seasons was dismantled as 32 players were used by Hamilton, 12 of whom managed fewer than six appearances apiece. Despite the alarming drop in form, attendances held up well and averaged over 5,000 for the second successive season.

If diehard 'Poolies' thought the bottom had been reached, they were mistaken; the 1938–39 season was to finish in a third application for re-election after a dismal campaign. The pattern was set in the first five games, which resulted in five defeats without a solitary goal being scored. Results went from bad to worse as Hamilton introduced 21 new faces in a futile attempt to find a winning combination. The legacy of disrupting a settled, successful side with 'star' signings had well and truly come home to roost. The 'goals against' column was back in the stratosphere with 94, a 2–8 drubbing at Chester being the worst result of this awful season.

Not surprisingly, the Annual General Meeting of the Football League held to determine re-election was a low-key affair,

Jack Brown was the oldest debutant at the age of 38 years 6 months, against Gateshead in 1937.

given the prevailing circumstances and absence of a strong alternative candidate. Consequently, United (38 votes) were re-elected, along with Accrington Stanley (29 votes). Shrewsbury Town (22 votes) were their nearest challengers.

Preparations for the 1939–40 season were totally overshadowed by a public realisation that a major conflict with Germany was about to start. Despite this, the Football League issued full fixture lists, and the programme kicked-off on 26 August with 'Pools playing a draw at home to Barrow. A defeat at Gateshead four days later was followed by another draw at Crewe on 2 September before war was declared the following day. The next week the government announced the cancellation of all sporting events and the Football League declared that results for the 1939–40 season should be expunged from the record.

The outbreak of World War Two and subsequent cancellation of the League programme brought to an end the first phase in Hartlepools United's Football League history. In the 18 seasons since joining the Football League in 1921 the club had achieved a best finish of fourth in the first season, and four other top-10 placings. Set against this were three re-election applications and two narrow escapes by goal average. In the FA Cup they reached the third round only once, in 1935–36, when they lost in a replay to Grimsby Town of the First Division, the home tie attracting a record crowd to that point of 15,064.

Six managers held the hot seat during this period, with Jimmy Hamilton having the longest tenure. Attendances fell from an average of 7,239 in the first season to 4,164 by the outbreak of war, with a low of 3,020 in 1926–27. The top players earned about £5 10 shillings a week during the season (no pay in the summer) and admission of 1 shilling was charged to adults. Many people were prevented from attending simply because they could not afford the admission fee in an era of high unemployment and virtually no financial support from the government.

The leading figure in the club during these difficult years was W.J. 'Bill' Yeats, who became chairman in 1924, succeeding R. Stonehouse. The contribution this public-spirited gentleman made to the club can never be underestimated, particularly during the war years following the departure of Jimmy Hamilton. In this he was supported by another legendary 'Pools 'backroom boy', Frank S. Perryman, who became secretary in 1930 and guided the club financially through the war years and into the immediate peacetime period until his retirement in 1961. Bill Yeats remained as chairman until 1952, a total of 28 years' service, far longer than any other holder of the post.

## The War Years and the Resumption of League Football

Following the cessation of League football, the authorities quickly realised that a regional form of professional football would have beneficial effect on a population being fed a daily war news diet of defeats and disasters.

The remainder of the 1939–40 season saw Hartlepools United in the North-East Regional League, formed on the basis of location rather than status, so Newcastle United and Middlesbrough were included, with fixtures played on a home and away basis. United's

Raich Carter, a distinguished wartime guest.

experience of this compromise was not a happy one, with only six of 20 games won. Most registered professionals were required for the war effort, and all clubs relied on guest players who found it impossible to make any sort of long-term commitment. The most notable of these 'guests' was Raich Carter, Sunderland's Championship and FA Cup-winning captain. Understandably, attendances were low and it was no surprise when, following the departure of manager Jimmy Hamilton in June 1940, the directors decided against continuing in the regional League.

This decision created a major void as the Victoria Ground was requisitioned for military purposes and received little or no maintenance for the next three years. It was on the initiative of chairman Bill Yeats that Hartlepools United made an application to re-join the Football League's regional competition for the 1943–44 season. In this they were greatly helped by Darlington's successful application, as the League's management was keen to retain an equal number of clubs in the competition. 'Pools' application was accepted in the July, despite the club being without a manager or playing staff. There was also the small matter of the Victoria Ground, having been used for a variety of purposes in the previous three years, being what the local press reported as 'very much the worse for wear'. The new season was scheduled to start on 28 August.

Bill Yeats realised that if the club was to restart professional football it would have to employ an experienced manager with a reputation for managing clubs on a shoestring budget. In the same month as his club's application was accepted, Yeats offered the post of manager to 56-year-old Fred Westgarth, then in charge of Bradford City. Despite an improved contract from the Yorkshire club, Westgarth, a north-east man, decided to take on what he described as 'the hardest job in football'.

The week preceding the opening game against Middlesbrough saw club officials, including the chairman, with voluntary support, work overtime to prepare both the ground and pitch for the game. The East Stand was the major problem as it had been reduced to a shell and its wooden supports were rotted away. Only the turnstiles on the Clarence Road side of the ground were deemed to be in working order to admit supporters. The pitch was not cut and rolled until the Monday, being best described as in 'fairly good condition'.

Fred Westgarth's hastily assembled team for the Middlesbrough game was no different in this respect, and he was signing players almost up to the kick-off of the first game. For the record, with their registered club in the case of 'guests', this was his first team: Heywood (Sunderland), Tabram (Swansea), Milne (Rochdale), Scott (Brentford), Barrett (West Ham), Daniels, Mullen, Robinson (Charlton), Bamford (Swansea), Scrimshaw, Adams (Tottenham). The side included three internationals: Barratt (England), Scott (England) and Bamford (Wales). A crowd of 2,584 was entertained by the Old Operatic Band prior to the kick-off, and they saw an open and exciting game. Just before half-time, Scrimshaw headed the only goal to give Hartlepools United a narrow victory in their first competitive game for three years.

The Football League North consisted of 50 clubs, with each side playing games on a home and away basis against local area

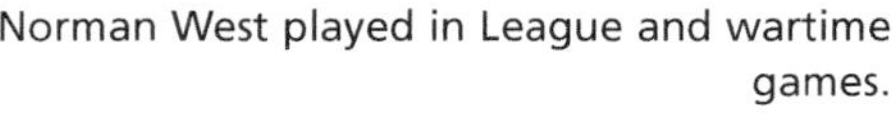

Norman West played in League and wartime games.

Leo Harden, who scored the first goal on the resumption of League football.

opposition. The impact of guest players can be judged by the first Championship, which was completed on Christmas Day. 'Pools had used 31 players to complete the opening 22 fixtures, with local player Jack Howe of Derby County guesting in two games. Howe later won an FA Cup-winners' medal and played in three full internationals for England.

A highly creditable 10th-place finish compared favourably with Newcastle United's 39th placing. The format of the Wartime Leagues continued the following season, 1944–45, which saw a decline in the final position to 37th. A consolation was the attendances for the League War Cup ties, which saw 11,869 watch Darlington and nearly 10,000 at both the Newcastle and Sunderland games.

The 1945–46 season saw the restructuring of Leagues towards a more conventional format, albeit still on a regional basis to save on travel costs. 'Pools played in the Third Division North East, finishing bottom. The FA Cup also resumed on a two-leg, home and away basis for the only time. United were drawn against Gateshead and, unable to play guest players, suffered an embarrassing 8–3 aggregate defeat, which suggested much work needed to be done by the manager before the resumption of the 1946–47 Football League season.

In common with every other club in the country, the new season heralded the restart of competitive League football. It speaks volumes for the amount of team rebuilding that Fred Westgarth undertook for the start of the new season that only centre-forward Jack Price had played for 'Pools before the war. Of the other 25 players who appeared that season, all were making their Football League debuts for the club and only Billy Brown was ever present. This was a major factor as 'Pools struggled in the early games of the season, winning only four of their first 16 matches. Attendances were also affected by the dreadful winter of 1947, with several games postponed due to snow-bound pitches and sub-zero temperatures. Before the harsh weather set in, however, record League attendances were recorded both at home, with 12,800 for Rotherham United, and away, with a staggering 30,064 turning up at Hull City on Boxing Day. The season finished with 'Pools in 13th place, having averaged 7,556 at home games, a creditable figure given the atrocious weather which prevailed throughout the winter.

The start of the 1947–48 season saw the team kitted out in the fondly remembered blue-and-white halved shirts with black shorts. If supporters hoped for better results for their team in the new strip, they were to be disappointed. No wins were recorded in the first six games, and the low point came at Gateshead on Christmas Day with a seven-goal hiding. Despite this result, a lack of goals was the main problem, with blank returns in 16 games and three players, Isaac, Richardson and Sloan, sharing the dubious distinction of being top scorer with a meagre seven goals apiece. Results improved somewhat in the New Year, and a strong end-of-season run with five wins in the final eight games saw the team finish in 19th position, with gates averaging 7,803, slightly up on the previous season. Thirty players were used during the season, with Hughes at centre-half making 39 League appearances.

The 1948–49 season began with a stunning 6–1 home victory against Rochdale in front of over 10,000 spectators. Sadly, only five more games were won prior to the New Year, and although the second half of the season showed a slight improvement, a finish of 16th place was not something to celebrate. Westgarth employed 26 players during the season, with goalkeeper Rimmington and Hughes ever presents. Watty Moore, who was to set the club appearances record, made his debut at centre-forward against Wrexham at the Victoria Ground and scored in a 2–2 draw.

Two highlights of the campaign were the games against Hull City, which featured the legendary Raich Carter, formerly of Sunderland and England. The home match attracted a record League crowd for the Victoria Ground of 17,118, while the return at Boothferry Park saw 35,357 spectators present. Hull won both games 2–0, and the attendances were testimony to the popularity of Carter during his time as player-manager of the Humberside club. Following the Hull game the club's precarious financial position was bolstered by the transfer of Fred Richardson to Barnsley for the substantial fee of £5,000. This must have been particularly galling for supporters, as Richardson had contributed nine goals in 12 games and home attendances, despite results, were averaging 11,803 up to the point of his departure.

The trend continued the following season, 1949–50, of playing almost as many different players as League points accrued, 29 players earning 33 points to finish in a lowly 18th position. The defence was the problem, with 80 goals against including a spell in October when 17 were conceded in three consecutive games, against Rotherham (five), Carlisle (five) and Mansfield (seven). The plus points for the season were attendances, with 10 League gates in excess of 10,000, five of which came at home. The season also saw the debut of 18-year-old Ken Johnson, who scored on his debut in a 3–0 home victory over Bradford City. Johnson's career was to span three decades until his retirement in 1964 as the club's all-time leading League goalscorer.

Fred Jarrie played only three games before joining Crook Town and winning an FA Amateur Cup-winners' medal.

The major triumph for Hartlepools United to this point in their history is that they managed to survive despite the financial problems and three re-election

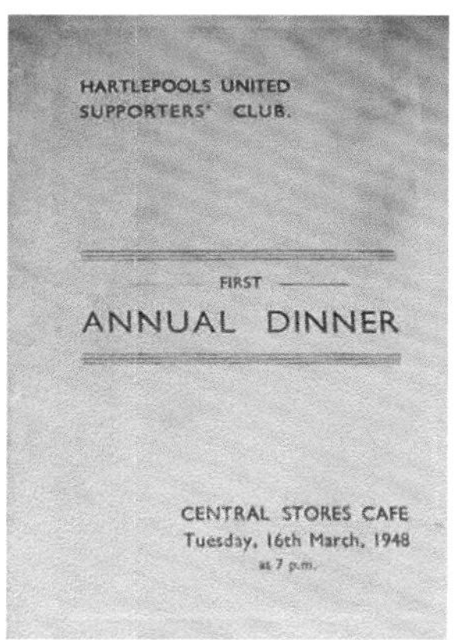
HARTLEPOOLS UNITED
SUPPORTERS' CLUB.
FIRST
ANNUAL DINNER
CENTRAL STORES CAFE
Tuesday, 16th March, 1948
at 7 p.m.

1948 HUFCSA first annual dinner.

applications. Under the leadership of Bill Yeats and his two lieutenants, Fred Westgarth on the playing side and Frank Perryman in charge of finance and administration, the club was served by pragmatic individuals who recognised that they were in for the long haul. To this end Westgarth began a process of developing from within, supported by players with strong north-east ties, which was ultimately to make his team a real power in their division and respected opponents in the FA Cup.

## The Making of a Team to be Proud of

A settled side was finally beginning to emerge by the 1950–51 season, as was evidenced by the 22 players used, six of whom played in three or fewer games. Tommy McGuigan, signed from Ayr United, made an immediate impact and missed only four games all season. It took time, however, for the side to settle and only two wins were recorded in the first 15 games. A six-goal triumph against Barrow in November was the prelude to a steady improvement, which resulted in a 16th-place finish. The season's highlight came in March when Darlington were thrashed 6–1 and Joe Willetts achieved the rare feat of scoring three times from the penalty spot. This form was maintained in the next home game against Rotherham United, the League leaders and champions in waiting. A strong team performance saw 'Pools win 3–1 in front of nearly 9,000 spectators. Eric Wildon was leading goalscorer for the campaign with 26 goals in 44 League appearances, which included four goals against Wrexham and hat-tricks against Barrow and Bradford Park Avenue in successive home games.

Real progress was made in 1951–52 as the team consolidated further and crowds improved, 12,225 watching Gateshead during a strong start in which four of the first seven fixtures were won. Only 20 players were used during a season in which 'Pools finished ninth, with Moore and Willetts ever present, and Burnett missing only one game. Wildon again top scored with 19 goals in 39 appearances. Another cause for satisfaction was the FA Cup performances when, after defeating Rhyl and Watford, United travelled to Burnley, then a major First Division side, and despite losing narrowly by a single goal in front of 38,608 spectators earned widespread praise for their performance. Goalkeeper 'Berry' Brown was singled out for praise following an outstanding display, having no chance with Les Shannon's decisive goal. This was the beginning of a succession of prime Cup fixtures which were to illuminate the forthcoming seasons for supporters.

The progress of the previous season was not maintained in 1952–53, however, as another poor start saw only two wins in the opening eight games despite a settled side. Only 19 players were used all season, with Willetts again ever present and Moore and McGuigan only missing one each. The fact that Wildon top-scored with a mere 11 goals in 31

Jackie Newton, Ken Johnson and Tommy McGuigan in training.

appearances highlighted where the problem lay, with 'Pools goalless in 14 matches. In an effort to remedy the lack of goals Westgarth re-signed Fred Richardson from Chester for a £1,000 transfer fee, but he only managed four goals in 27 appearances. The performance of the season came in early March against the eventual champions Oldham Athletic. For only the third time in the campaign 'Pools scored four goals, with their opponents managing only a single reply in front of a crowd of 9,421. Despite the lack of progress in the League, 'Pools continued to enjoy solid support with an average home attendance of 8,074, slightly down on the previous season.

The following season, 1953–54, saw another disappointing League campaign ultimately

Tommy McGuigan scores against Southport in 1953.

result in an 18th-place finish. No wins in the first nine games set the tone, only to be relieved by six consecutive home wins which included a 6–0 trouncing of Rochdale with four goals by Leo Harden. 'Pools, however, exceeded expectations in the Cup. A home draw against Mansfield Town in the first round gave no hint of future success; but, a 3–0 victory in the replay was 'rewarded' with a visit to Northampton Town. In front of 18,772 spectators 'Pools took the lead through Harden before the home side levelled late in the game. The replay at the Vic attracted a 12,169 crowd and went to extra-time before a Linacre goal set up a third-round tie. Once again the draw favoured the opposition and United travelled to the Potteries to face Stoke City of the Second Division. Despite taking the lead through Richardson, Stoke were the better side and used the heavy pitch to good advantage as 'Pools tired in the second half. A 6–2 defeat was considered harsh by many fans and a reflection of the players' fitness levels in the absence of a full-time professional coach.

Fred Westgarth's strategy of bringing on local talent, supplemented by shrewd free-transfer signings to form a settled side, finally came to fruition during the 1954–55 season. Of the 19 players used, Moore was an ever-present, with Newton and Stamper both missing only one game each. Indeed, the most problematic position appeared to be goalkeeper, with three custodians, Brown, Dyson and Taylor, tried. Nineteen clean sheets testified to a change of style, particularly as McGuigan top scored with 18 goals, the only player to achieve double figures.

If the joy of finishing fifth, the club's best finish since the inaugural 1921–22 season, was not enough for their long-suffering supporters, 'Pools again exceeded expectations in the FA Cup. The campaign, which saw 10,000-plus attendances at every game, began with home wins against Chesterfield and Aldershot before the third-round tie against

Chelsea's goalkeeper Robertson watches a shot go wide with Wicks in support.

The 1954 Hartlepools United Durham Senior Cup-winning team. Back row, left to right: F. Perryman (secretary), N. Westgarth (trainer), W. Linacre, F. Richardson, J. Newton, W. Moore, A. Corbett, G. Taylor, B. Brown, F. Stamper, J. Smith, R. Thompson, J. McLaughlin, F. Westgarth (manager). Front row: K. Johnson, E. Wildon, J. Willets, T. McGuigan, L. Harden.

Darlington ended a 1–1 draw, Harden equalising in the second half. The replay at Feethams was played on a frozen pitch and, according to contemporary reports, was a 'hard fought' contest. Darlington took a two-goal lead before a second-half fightback saw the experienced Richardson score twice to earn a second replay. The teams replayed again at neutral Ayresome Park, where goals from Richardson and a Newton penalty extended United's unbeaten run to a record 18 games.

For the first time in their history Hartlepools United participated in the fourth round of the FA Cup, drawn at home against Nottingham Forest, then in the Second Division. The all-ticket tie attracted 17,200 spectators, and they saw a thrilling game, with the home side the stronger in the first half. Shortly after half-time Scott scored for Forest, and a long period of sustained pressure by 'Pools followed, culminating in an equaliser from a Newton penalty after a goal-bound shot by Johnson was handled. Despite all their efforts, 'Pools could not find a winner, and a replay was required at the City Ground. Again, the so-called underdogs dominated proceedings in front of over 20,000 fans without turning their superiority into goals. In an action-packed first half, with Linacre outstanding, Kelly gave Forest the lead from the penalty spot after Thompson had fouled Scott. Barely three minutes later 'Pools were awarded a penalty following a handling offence by McKinley, but Newton shot wide. The second half saw further 'Pools pressure finally rewarded when Stamper scored following a goalmouth scramble. In a frantic finish, with Linacre and Luke having shots saved, no further goals resulted. Extra-time was required, with Forest finally prevailing in the 114th minute through centre-forward Wilson.

Fred Westgarth was determined to build on the progress achieved the previous season by adding Billy Anderson, Joe Rayment and Billy Robinson to his staff for the 1955–56 campaign. The results of his team-building were evidenced by the 21 players used. Five made six or fewer appearances, with Thompson, Lumley and Moore ever present. Over 10,000 fans saw a 3–0 opening victory over Darlington before being brought back down to earth with heavy defeats at Workington and Stockport. These proved temporary setbacks, however, and 'Pools recovered to finish fourth with a 6–1 Boxing Day victory over Crewe Alexandra a stand-out performance. Ken Johnson scored four times in this game and finished the season as leading scorer with 21 goals in 30 appearances. A final position of fourth equalled 'Pools' best-ever placing, and average home attendances of nearly 8,000 testified to the team's popularity.

The FA Cup campaign began at home to local rivals Gateshead, and a 3–0 victory was followed by a narrow 2–1 win at Chesterfield to put United once again in the hat for the third round. Having missed out on a home glamour tie in previous seasons, the home draw against reigning League champions Chelsea was ample compensation. Chelsea had won their first-ever title the previous season by matching the direct, physical style of the leading post-war sides such as Arsenal and Wolverhampton Wanderers. Unlike today, they were not considered a 'glamour' side, and this was evident in the way they approached the Cup tie. Despite 'Pools' best efforts in front of 16,862 spectators, they could not match their opponents' physical style of play, and despite the closeness of the 1–0 scoreline Chelsea controlled the game after Moore's 23rd-minute own-goal following an error by Jim Dyson. The sense of anticlimax was reflected in the attendance of only 3,851 the following Saturday for the game against Wrexham, which resulted in a 3–2 victory.

Hartlepools United,1956–57. Back row, left to right: T. McGuigan, R. Lumley, F. Stamper, R. Guthrie, W. Anderson, R. Thompson, K. Johnson. Front row: W. Robinson, J. Cameron, W. Moore, G. Luke.

So to the 1956–57 season, during which Hartlepools United were to rewrite their record books. The season certainly began with a bang. Ten wins in the opening 12 games, with 38 goals scored by eight different players, resulted in attendances regularly topping the 10,000 mark. The United team appeared unstoppable, with Ralph Guthrie from Arsenal and Newcastle's Ken Waugh added to the playing staff. A poor spell during October and November saw a run of eight games without a win in the League before the rot was stopped against non-League Selby Town in the first round of the FA Cup. League form was rediscovered in time to take on another non-League side, Blyth Spartans, at Croft Park. In a physical game on a difficult pitch 'Pools managed to prevail 1–0, thanks to a Johnson goal.

This win put Westgarth's team into the draw for the third round once again. Having drawn the reigning Football League champions at home in the third round the previous season, a punter could have had long odds on it happening again, yet that is precisely what happened. Hartlepools United were drawn at home to Manchester United, the reigning League Champions and current First Division leaders. An all-ticket record crowd of 17,264 crammed into the Vic to witness a memorable game. The visitors, nicknamed the Busby Babes due to their youthful age and appearance, cruised into a three-goal lead within 30 minutes. A heavy defeat for the home side looked inevitable, particularly as Ken Johnson was injured and little more than a passenger. It was a surprise when Frank Stamper pulled a goal back just before half-time following a mix-up in the Manchester defence.

The game was totally different after the break, with the home side playing like men possessed. Johnson headed a spectacular second before Jackie Newton scored with a strong

THIS IS THE OFFICIAL PROGRAMME OF

MANCHESTER UNITED

FOOTBALL CLUB LIMITED

OLD TRAFFORD - MANCHESTER - Telephone: TRA 1661

Chairman: H. P. HARDMAN, Esq.

Directors: Dr. W. MACLEAN, G. E. WHITTAKER, Esq., J. ALAN GIBSON, Esq., W. H. PETHERBRIDGE, Esq.

Manager: MATT BUSBY Secretary: W. R. CRICKMER

Editor: DAVID W. WICKS

*Advertisement and editorial enquiries should be addressed to the "United Review", Sidney F. Wicks Ltd., Cheetwood House, 21 Newton Street, Manchester 1. Telephone: CENtral 9047/8*

VOLUME XVIII, No. 14. 12th JANUARY 1957

**MATT BUSBY TALKING**

What a fight, and what a fright! At Hartlepools, in the cup-tie, you would have said it was all over when United were three goals in the lead after 35 minutes' play. But we reckoned without a wonderful fight-back by the Third Division club. It was a splendid game, however, played on a very heavy ground and with rain falling for most of the time. Hartlepools rubbed one goal off before the interval, and had equalised by the 67th minute of the match. Then came United's winning goal at 4-3 with 10 minutes left for play.

I would like to pay tribute not only to the Hartlepools team for their gallant, and brilliant challenge, but to the home spectators who, while wildly enthusiastic, as you may imagine, never deviated from the course of true sportsmanship, and, at the end, quite freely admitted that United had been the better team. That was echoed in the Board Room, and when I spoke, on the telephone, to Mr. Fred Westgarth, the Hartlepools manager, who was ill in bed, I assured him that he had every reason to be delighted with the play of his team and that United were certainly worried by the trend of events after the interval. Well played, Hartlepools! We shall never forget your grand struggle and very clean play. You deserved a replay!

**OUR COVER PICTURE.**

**United v. Chelsea**

**Result 3-0**

Centre-forward Taylor (third from left) scores his second and United's third goal. Chelsea 'keeper Matthews is well beaten as are full-backs P. and J. Sillett.

We acknowledge the courtesy of the "Daily Mail" in allowing us to print this picture.

FORD ....think of NUNNS
MAIN DEALERS
H. E. NUNN & CO. LTD., 282 BURY NEW ROAD, MANCHESTER 7
Telephone: BROughton 2201


PAGE TWO

Matt Busby's programme notes on 'Pools Cup tie.

drive from 20 yards. Manchester United were badly rattled and took time to reorganise and compose themselves; however, by this stage 'Pools' biggest enemy was probably the heavy pitch, and in a thrilling finale Whelan scored the winner for the Babes.

The excitement of the Manchester United visit, throughout the build-up, the game itself and the aftermath, was overshadowed by the illness of Fred Westgarth and his death the following month. Within days his team travelled to Derby County, their principal rivals for promotion, and lost 2–0 in front of 24,644 fans. Mixed results followed, and a highest-ever finish of second was not enough to secure promotion, as only the champions were elevated.

During this momentous season 'Pools had numerous highlights:

- **Highest-ever League position – second.**
- **Record number of League goals scored – 90.**
- **Record home attendance of 17,264 against Manchester United in the FA Cup.**
- **Three players were ever present: Ralph Guthrie, Ray Thompson and Watty Moore, Moore for the third consecutive season.**
- **Ken Johnson scored 26 League and Cup goals in 45 games. It was the second successive season in which he scored more than 20 goals.**
- **21 attendances, including Cup ties, in excess of 10,000, of which 11 were at home.**
- **Record average home attendance of 9,627.**

## A New Manager and a New League

The 1957–58 season was to be the last with the Third Division organised on a regional north-south basis. The Football League had decided to restructure into four national divisions, with the top 12 clubs from the two regional Leagues comprising the new Third Division. As a club with serious ambitions to gain promotion to the Second Division, never mind the Third, the prospect of finishing lower than mid-table was not something the club's management and supporters were thinking about as the new season approached.

Following the demise of Fred Westgarth in February, the directors wisely took their time in appointing a replacement. Fred's son had filled the breach to the end of the season, and a general feeling that the time had come for a complete change prevailed. Ray Middleton was appointed manager on 17 May 1957 at the age of 37 years. Born in Boldon Colliery, he played as a goalkeeper, first for Washington Colliery Welfare and North Shields before signing as a professional at the age of 17 years with Chesterfield, where he spent 14 seasons and appeared in 500 consecutive games. In 1951 he was transferred to Derby County for a £10,000 fee, spending three successful seasons there which also saw him play in England B and FA representative games.

Initially Middleton relied on the squad of players he inherited, which appeared a sound policy when five of the first six games were won and 17 goals scored. A particularly memorable victory was the 5–1 thrashing of Darlington, which the local paper described as a 'gala performance', all the goals being scored in the second half. The crowd of 14,876 was a record for a mid-week game; indeed, the first four home games all attracted gates of over

10,000. The next three games were lost, however, and a run of mixed results culminated in an horrendous 7–0 defeat by Rochdale in early November resulting in Ralph Guthrie, Ray Thompson and Watty Moore being dropped. The next four games, with Moore restored, were won, including a 5–0 FA Cup win over Prescot Cables. This run took 'Pools to third in the League, but unfortunately any hopes of yet another Cup adventure were dispelled in the second-round defeat by Stockport County. The Cup exit heralded the start of a poor run of League results which produced only three wins in the next 20 games to leave 'Pools struggling in the wrong half of the division. Matters were not helped by the absences of leading scorer Peter Thompson and influential winger George Luke. Understandably, attendances were affected by the team's performances, with barely 3,000 fans turning up for the Stockport game in March.

As the unhappy season progressed Middleton started to mould the side in his style and the appearances of familiar faces started to diminish. Ken Waugh was an ever-present at right-back, leaving Jock Cameron and Ray Thompson to share the left-back duties. Jackie Newton's appearances became less frequent as a young half-back, Tommy Burlison, signed from Lincoln City, took over as first choice. Ken Johnson was in competition with Jackie Smith and Peter Thompson for the number-nine shirt. Anderson and Robinson made only infrequent appearances.

By Easter 'Pools' fate looked consigned to the new Fourth Division; however, two wins and a draw over the holiday period gave renewed hope of a top-half finish. The crunch came in the last match at home to the new champions, Scunthorpe United. A crowd of over 8,000 saw a hard-fought contest, with Scunthorpe winning a narrow 2–1 victory. 'Pools finished a lowly 17th in their final Division Three North season with 44 points. This, however, should be viewed in the context that Stockport County finished ninth with 47 points and a win in their final game would have ensured qualification to the new Third Division.

The 1958–59 season heralded Hartlepools United's debut in the new Fourth Division with a home fixture against Shrewsbury Town. Defeat in front of a healthy crowd of 7,344 was offset two days later when Bradford Park Avenue were convincingly beaten 3–0, with Anderson scoring 'Pools' first goal in the new League from the penalty spot. Heavy home defeats to Port Vale, the ultimate champions, and York suggested that Middleton had made too many changes too quickly. A run of 10 games with only a single win sent 'Pools plummeting down the division, along with attendances, which by now were below the 4,000 mark. A good March, in which three games were won, was a prelude to arguably the most amazing game ever played at the Victoria Ground.

Barrow arrived for the game on 4 April firmly rooted at the bottom of the table and certainties to apply for re-election. They had yet to play 'Pools that season as the away fixture was scheduled for the 21st. A respectable crowd of 4,126 turned up, and from the first whistle it was apparent that the visitors had little appetite for the contest. Goals came at regular intervals to such an extent that 'Pools had a staggering 7–0 advantage by half-time. Despite Kemp replying for the visitors, three further goals made the final score 10–1, a club and Fourth Division record. Contemporary reports suggested 'Pools should have won by an even greater margin given the feebleness of the opposition! The season ended on a high note with a 2–1 victory over League runners-up Coventry City, with Terry MacGregor scoring his first goal for the club.

The 1959–60 season was to be a watershed in the post-war era of the club as the hard-won achievements of the Westgarth years were finally swept away. An opening 3–0 home win over Aldershot was quickly followed by a depressing run of results which reached a nadir during November and December when 11 games without a win meant that Ray Middleton lost his job. His replacement, Bill Robinson, a native of Whitburn, had been assistant manager at West Ham United and was signed on a three-year contract, yet he failed to halt the inevitable decline which resulted in a bottom-place finish with 109 goals conceded. Only 59 goals were scored, of which Harry Clark (21 goals) and Jackie Smith (17 goals) contributed nearly two-thirds. In the penultimate home game against Carlisle United, a 2–1 defeat in front of 3,603 spectators, Watty Moore played the last of his 472 games for the club. On 5 May, after completion of the League programme, Moore appeared in his benefit match with most of the leading figures from the legendary Westgarth team, which many north-east football commentators felt had been broken up too hastily. Results from recent seasons certainly supported this view.

The inevitable application for re-election resulted in a controversy which still lingers in north-east football circles to this day. The other League applicants were Oldham Athletic, Southport and Gateshead, along with Peterborough United, who had an impressive record in the Midland League and more importantly had achieved national recognition with a run of giant-killing results in the FA Cup competition. Of the League clubs, Southport had made the most applications – seven, three in the last four seasons.

When the result of the ballot was announced, Peterborough were duly elected with 35 votes at the expense of Gateshead, who only managed 18 compared to Hartlepools United's 34. The Gateshead officials were shell-shocked by the rejection, which laid down a marker and proved that traditional clubs could not rely forever on the 'old pals act' at the expense of ambitious non-League clubs with well-appointed grounds. It was later reported that a major factor in the rejection of the Tyneside club was the poor state of their Redheugh ground and the surrounding greyhound track; although the fact that Gateshead had the lowest average attendance (3,412) of all Football League clubs that season could not be ignored.

## The Not-so-Swinging Sixties

The dire financial situation at the club only allowed Bill Robinson to retain nine full-time professionals for the 1960–61 season. Jackie Smith, a popular player who was ever present the previous season, was transferred to Watford, and Scott, who made 43 appearances, went to York in exchange for George Patterson, a wing-half. George Lackenby was signed from relegated Gateshead to replace Watty Moore and Bobby Lumley returned to 'Pools, also from the Tyneside club. To support the meagre professional resources, local players such as Bobby Folland, Alan Melville, Barry Parkes and Gordon Lithgo made appearances during the season with varying degrees of success.

The first visitors of the season were newly elected Peterborough United, who arrived for a Monday night game. In front of a surprising crowd of 10,784 they demonstrated just what the League had been missing by recording a comfortable victory, with Terry Bly, their prolific goalscorer, claiming both goals. This set the tone for Peterborough's debut League season and they went on to win promotion in fine style, finishing the season as champions. For 'Pools, after the consolation of a 5–0 win against local rivals Darlington, the season went from bad to worse. A run of 12 League games without a win in the New Year sealed their fate and only Chester were below them by a single point at the season's end. The form of local players Bobby Folland and Barry Parkes provided welcome relief from the monotonous run of defeats. Folland scored all five goals in a 5–1 victory over Oldham Athletic in April, only the second 'Pools player to achieve this feat, and Parkes contributed seven goals in 11 games, including a hat-trick against Northampton Town.

Another key feature of this season was the introduction of the Football League Cup, programmed to balance the traditional FA Cup schedule, which was mainly played in the second half of the season. Hence Hartlepools United's first game in the competition was away to Oldham Athletic on Tuesday 11 October. If the League authorities thought the new competition would match the FA Cup in terms of interest and support, they were to be sadly mistaken. A lowly crowd of 3,630 turned up to watch what was described as a 'scrappy game', with the home side claiming a 2–1 victory. Ken Johnson scored United's first goal in the new competition.

Despite the success of newly elected Peterborough United, no serious contenders were put forward to challenge the four clubs applying for re-election: Exeter City, Barrow, Chester and, of course, Hartlepools United. Thus they were all re-elected unopposed.

The 1961–62 season surprised even the most disillusioned supporter by actually being worse for the club, while in the same season a number of memorable events occurred, one in particular which is best forgotten. Manager Robinson continued with his policy, dictated by financial constraints, of supporting a core of experienced professionals with outstanding local talent. A real find was Johnny Edgar from York City, who scored 20 goals in 40 starts in his debut season despite the problems around him. 'Pools' season went from bad to worse in the second half of the campaign when they failed to win in a 13-game spell. This included their worst-ever League defeat, 10–1 at Wrexham, in which three players, Wyn Davies, Roy Ambler and Roy Barnes, each scored hat-tricks, a unique event in Football League history. This result condemned the club in most people's eyes to relegation, particularly as Oxford United were campaigning strongly for League status and had the backing of many southern clubs. Once again, however, luck intervened. On the same day that Wrexham inflicted that record defeat, Accrington Stanley lost heavily at Crewe. The following week the Lancashire club took the unprecedented step of resigning from the Football League with the season still in progress.

Accrington had allowed their debts to accumulate to £60,000 and were clearly unable to fulfil their obligations, both on and off the pitch. There was no shortage of clubs willing to play their remaining fixtures, North Shields and Nelson among them, but the League decided otherwise and Stanley's playing record for the season to date was expunged. The upshot of this was that at the end of the season a vacancy existed in the Fourth Division and Oxford

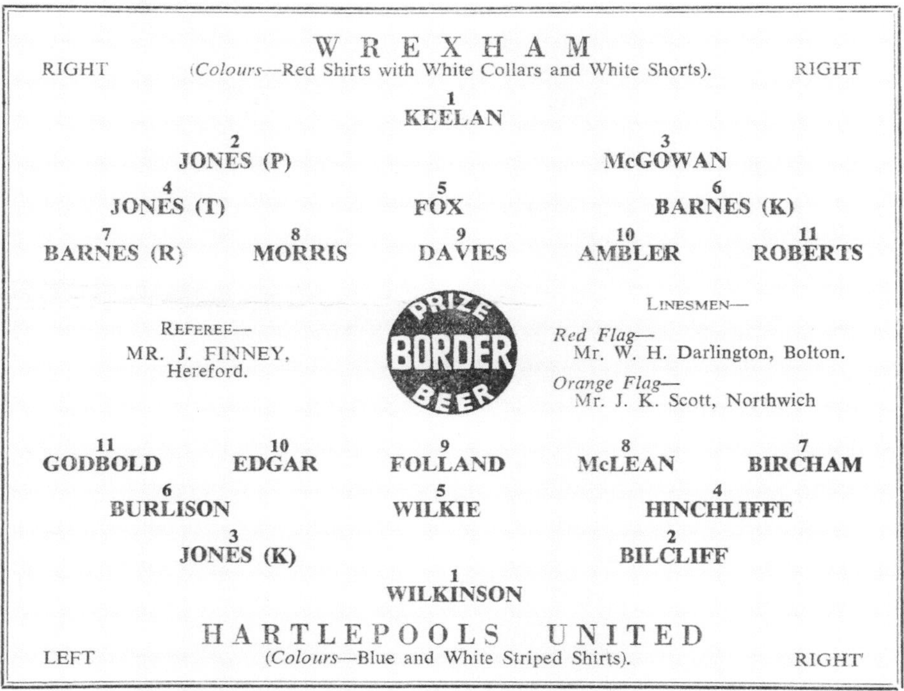

WREXHAM

RIGHT (*Colours*—Red Shirts with White Collars and White Shorts). RIGHT

1 KEELAN

2 JONES (P) 3 McGOWAN

4 JONES (T) 5 FOX 6 BARNES (K)

7 BARNES (R) 8 MORRIS 9 DAVIES 10 AMBLER 11 ROBERTS

REFEREE—
MR. J. FINNEY, Hereford.

PRIZE BORDER BEER

LINESMEN—
*Red Flag*—
Mr. W. H. Darlington, Bolton.
*Orange Flag*—
Mr. J. K. Scott, Northwich

11 GODBOLD 10 EDGAR 9 FOLLAND 8 McLEAN 7 BIRCHAM

6 BURLISON 5 WILKIE 4 HINCHLIFFE

3 JONES (K) 2 BILCLIFF

1 WILKINSON

HARTLEPOOLS UNITED

LEFT (*Colours*—Blue and White Striped Shirts). RIGHT

The team line ups from the record 10–1 defeatagainst Wrexham in March 1962.

United, the Southern League champions, were duly elected. The three clubs applying for re-election, Chester, Doncaster Rovers and Hartlepools United, had no opposition given the unique circumstances and were automatically returned for another term.

In May 1962 the directors decided yet another change of manager was required and Bill Robinson duly left. In July they appointed Allenby Chilton, a former England international who enjoyed great success with Manchester United in the immediate post-war years, winning League Championship and FA Cup-winners' medals. Originally from Seaham Colliery, he had managed Grimsby Town and latterly Wigan Athletic, then a non-League side, with some success as well as scouting for 'Pools. One can only assume that the Hartlepools board made clear the dire financial situation to Chilton before he signed for them, or he was keen to test his managerial skills with a League club in his native North East. Either way, it is difficult to see how either party could reasonably expect an improvement by continuing with predominately the same squad of players.

So the 1962–63 season was thus a continuation of the depressing saga of decline which began with the ending of the Westgarth era. With the Fourth Division restored to 24 clubs, 'Pools managed to finish bottom with only seven wins to show for their efforts. They were seven points adrift of second-bottom Bradford City and managed to concede 104 goals, despite being managed by a former England centre-half! Matters were made even worse when the club in the close season reported a record loss of £22,403 on the financial year ended 31 July 1962. To put the sum into context, gate receipts for the 1961–62 season only amounted to £10,146, and the declared loss included contributions from the supporters' association totalling £17,500!

Clearly United could not continue in this vein, and Allenby Chilton was relieved of his duties in April to be replaced by Bobby Gurney. Gurney was a popular figure in north-east football, having played in the Sunderland League Championship and FA Cup-winning sides of the 1930s. Born at Silksworth, he managed Peterborough United and Darlington before becoming chief scout for Leeds United. Hartlepools brought him from Horden Colliery to become their 13th manager.

Gurney fronted the club delegation that went cap in hand to the Football League meeting to make a fourth consecutive application for re-election. A low-key meeting, with no serious candidate for promotion, merely voted for the status quo. It did not escape attention, however, that within the past seven seasons the club's average attendance had fallen from almost 10,000 to less than 4,000. The lack of quality players was a major factor, and the failure to develop local talent, as in the previous decade, resulted in a gap in class which was widening with every passing season.

At this juncture in the history of Hartlepools United, a character emerges who will always be associated with the period, Ernest Ord. Ord was a local businessman who acquired a considerable fortune in local trade during the immediate post-war years. His small stature belied a tenacious and ambitious personality, and he was used to getting his own way. He succeeded Norman Hope as chairman and immediately set about restoring the club's fortunes, or so he hoped. His first major act was to sign Ambrose Fogarty from Sunderland for a substantial fee, reported by the local press to be £10,000, to be paid in instalments. Fogarty had been an integral member of the fine Sunderland team of the early 1960s and was still an Irish international. It was considered a major coup for 'Pools that they had been able to attract such a prominent player, still in his relative prime.

## The Betting Scandal

The severe winter of 1962–63 resulted in major disruptions to the lives of the public in general, and sport in particular. The early months of 1963 saw virtually no football played with the consequence that players, hardly overpaid in this era, had to survive on basic pay without the opportunity for earning the bonuses that supplemented their low income.

This created an environment in which the desire to make up for lost earnings led to the formation of a network of players from all levels of the professional game to influence the results and bet on matches involving their teams. At the heart of this conspiracy was Jimmy Gauld, a Mansfield Town player who had previously played for Charlton Athletic, Everton, Plymouth Argyle and Swindon Town. Gauld was now in the veteran stage of his career and saw the opportunity to make money from games which he hoped would draw little attention to the result.

One such game was the Hartlepools United versus Mansfield Town Division Four game on 13 May 1963, which saw the visitors well placed for promotion against the struggling home side. Despite the gap in their respective League positions, 'Pools stormed into a two-goal lead before Mansfield rallied and eventually won 4–3. John Brown, the United centre-forward, scored twice during the game. It later emerged in *The People* newspaper that Hartlepools player Andy Fraser had taken money to influence the result, along with accusations that his teammates John Brown, Derek McLean and Norman Oakley were also implicated. Fraser admitted the charge, which was denied by the other three players. Under pressure from Ernest Ord to substantiate the accusations against Brown, McLean and Oakley, *The People* failed to respond, with the result that their reputations remained unblemished.

In September 1963, as further revelations appeared in *The People*, former Hartlepools captain Ken Thomson admitted betting on games involving his club, although he denied deliberately underperforming to influence the result. He told magistrates he needed the money to go to university after he finished playing football. Thomson was suspended from the game for life.

The prosecution and imprisonment of Gauld in May 1964 revealed how far the betting scandal had permeated English football when David Layne, Peter Swan and Tony Kay were found guilty of match-fixing in First Division games involving Sheffield Wednesday. Kay, who was by then an Everton player having been transferred for £56,000, was also a current England international. He, along with Layne and Swan, was sent to prison and banned for life.

The accusations continued in *The People* throughout the summer of 1964, with allegations made against former Hartlepools United captain Ray Bilcliff, among others. Bilcliff had given the club sterling service in the latter part of his career, and there was genuine dismay when he returned from a family holiday at chairman Ord's request to answer the allegations, which he strongly denied. Once again, *The People* failed to provide evidence to support their revelations, and as public interest waned in the story they quietly dropped the issue.

## The Arrival and Departure of Local Heroes

Ambrose, or Amby, Fogarty had joined the club in November 1963 in the middle of yet another awful run. Of the 18 League games played prior to his arrival only three were won, and his debut at Stockport resulted in another defeat. His home debut was another matter, however, as 'Pools introduced local player Terry Francis for the visit of Bradford Park Avenue. The match was a triumph for Francis as he recorded a hat-trick on his League debut, thereby joining a select band of players who have achieved this distinction. The final score in no way flattered the home side, and the 5,632 fans attracted by the signing of Fogarty went home happy for the first time in many a day.

This was to prove a false dawn, however, and results quickly returned to what had become the norm with only a further six wins recorded by the season's end. Inevitably a fifth successive application for re-election was required and successfully made. By now many impartial observers were convinced the 'Gateshead effect' was working in 'Pools' favour, as there appeared to be some reluctance on the part of the Football League hierarchy to deprive the North East, still considered the 'hotbed of soccer' in many quarters, of another League club.

At the end of the season local hero Ken Johnson, the club's leading scorer, shared a joint benefit with Tom Burlison. Over 11,000 fans turned up to pay to see a gala football occasion as a Hartlepools All-Star XI, which included Wilf Mannion, Bobby Mitchell and Jack Howe, lost 6–3 to a full strength Sunderland side captained by Charlie Hurley. This took place a few weeks after chairman Ernest Ord suspended Johnson for 14 days for what the local paper described as a 'dressing room disagreement'. Five days later, Ord was forced into a humiliating climb-down by rescinding the suspension.

Bobby Gurney vacated the managerial hot seat in January 1964 to be replaced on a temporary basis by Alvan Williams. Aged only 31, Williams was the complete opposite of his immediate predecessors, who were football veterans. He joined Hartlepools initially as trainer from Bangor City, having previously played as a professional with Bury, Wrexham, Bradford Park Avenue and Exeter City. Williams set about completely reshaping the playing squad, with an improvement in away results his top priority. The fact that he only used 19 players throughout the 1964–65 League campaign is testimony to his success in a short period of time.

Overnight, United took on a more stable look, with a solid defence comprising Ken Simpkins ever present in goal, Storton and Marshall at full-back, Morrell or Brass at right-half, and Fox and Harrison the centre-backs. In attack, Bannister played on both wings, Fogarty at inside-right, Peter Thompson at centre-forward scoring 16 goals, and Wright and Bradley forming the left-wing partnership. If there was a disappointment it was with Terry Francis, who failed to build on his impressive start and made only four appearances.

Hartlepools United, 1964. Back row, left to right: P. Gordon (trainer), S. Storton, K. Simpkins, R. Brass, A. Fox, E. Harrison, W. Marshall, A. Williams (manager). Front row: H. Hamilton, C. Wright, P. Thompson, T. Francis, N. Bannister.

With a settled side, results improved but, typical of 'Pools, they made their fans wait. No wins in the first five games suggested a continuation of previous seasons, but three successive wins changed the mood. In early October the visit of high-flying Millwall recalled happier days as a crowd of 10,734 saw a home victory by a solitary Peter Thompson goal. The recovery was not yet complete, however, as 10 home games were drawn, and only four wins on the road confirmed that Alvan Williams still had work to do to complete the turn-around. But a final League position of 15th was highly acceptable compared to the embarrassments of previous seasons. At least Hartlepools United's name did not feature on the re-election ballot sheet.

It was perhaps inevitable that even modest success for the perennial strugglers would attract attention to the man who was responsible for the improvement. At the end of the season Southend offered Alvan Williams their manager's job, and he left, taking his assistant Peter Gordon with him. He thus became the first Hartlepools manager in the post-war era to achieve personal promotion by joining a bigger club.

Having seen real progress under Williams, a young ambitious manager, the directors reverted to type by appointing Geoff Twentyman, a former Liverpool player, as his successor for the 1965–66 season. He arrived from Carlisle United, having previously been player-manager of Irish side Ballymena United.

This was the season in which the Football Association finally bowed to pressure from both within the game and from the general public to allow a substitute to replace an injured player. Throughout the 1950s a number of high-profile games, particularly FA Cup Finals, had been ruined as a spectacle when a series of players received injuries which either required them to leave the field or to continue in a severely reduced capacity. Despite the introduction of substitutes in internationals, including those involving England, the governing authority stubbornly refused to sanction the change. Eventually common sense prevailed and the revolutionary change was implemented for the 1965–66 season. In common with the majority of managers, Geoff Twentyman took his time before taking advantage of the new concessionary rule. He waited until the fifth game of the season, a five-goal defeat at Aldershot, before introducing Bryan Drysdale in place of the injured Peter Thompson. Despite his distinguished playing career with Liverpool, Twentyman was unable to make any impression at the Victoria Ground, and his brief spell as manager lasted only 13 games. After a run of five defeats in six games with only two goals scored, the directors recognised that they had made a mistake with his appointment, and he left in October 1965.

## When I Tell You to Do Something Young Man, You Do It!

The short reign of Geoff Twentyman convinced United's board that the best way forward was with a young ambitious manager who was looking to make a name for himself after his playing days. The success of Alvan Williams underpinned this philosophy, and so the search began for a suitable candidate.

Brian Clough retired as a player due to an injury sustained while playing for Sunderland in a vital promotion game against Bury at Roker Park. A collision with the Bury goalkeeper caused a complete tear to the cruciate and medial knee ligaments. After missing the rest of the season, Clough attempted a three-game comeback the following campaign, but it was obvious his playing career was over. He remained at Roker Park until July 1965 when he was relieved of his post as youth-team coach without explanation. On being offered the job as manager of Hartlepools United by Ernest Ord on a salary of £2,500, a record for the club, he telephoned Peter Taylor with the comment 'I've been offered the managership of Hartlepools, and I don't fancy it. But if you come, I'll consider it.'

Clough was recommended to Ernest Ord by the legendary former Sunderland and England forward Len Shackleton, who wrote a highly regarded column for the *Sunday People* newspaper. Shackleton's theory was that two men, the right two, could build a club faster than one, and in his former Middlesbrough colleague Peter Taylor, Clough had found the right man. The bad news for chairman Ord was that this meant another relatively expensive employee on the payroll; however, the dynamic duo joined 'Pools despite their misgivings, realising even at that early stage that it was to be merely a stepping stone to greater things.

Clough began by winning his first three games, including an FA Cup tie at home to Workington. Hard reality then took over, and a winless run of seven games culminated in a six-goal hammering at Tranmere Rovers. The rest of the season then settled into a pattern of win a few, lose a few, to finish a respectable 18th given the dreadful start. Clough's first managerial signing was Tony Parry, a wing half-back from Burton Albion who was getting interest from First Division clubs. In what was to become his trademark in years to come, Clough persuaded the player to join his club confident in the knowledge that better times were just ahead. Parry was to become a firm favourite with the Victoria Ground faithful with his wholehearted displays and sportsmanlike behaviour. Another Burton player quickly followed in goalkeeper Les Green, who replaced Ken Simpkins.

The restructuring of the club continued apace with the creation of an effective scouting system, with regional scouts paid by results. Clough himself galvanised support by appearing

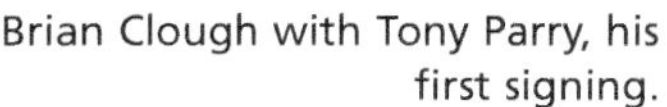
Brian Clough with Tony Parry, his first signing.

throughout the town in working men's clubs and other social outlets. His commitment to the cause was underpinned by his decision to live in the town, on the new Fens Estate, and take lessons for a public service vehicle licence so he could drive the team bus in an emergency.

Clough added players of the calibre of John Gill, a stopper-style centre-half, and Albert Broadbent, a skilful inside-forward, to add strength and guile to the goalscoring talents of Ernie Phythian and Jimmy Mulvaney. With Ambrose Fogarty still an influence, the 1966–67 season began with a draw at Aldershot, followed by a 2–1 home win against Wrexham in front of 5,664 spectators. Attendances held up as results, particularly at home, improved, and a crowd of 9,586 witnessed a narrow defeat to Southend in January. A final position of eighth could have been improved further with a stronger finish to the season as only two of the last seven games were won. Ernie Phythian was outstanding throughout with 26 goals in all games, ably supported by Jimmy Mulvaney, who scored 19 goals in 37 League appearances. The precocious talent of 16-year-old John McGovern, 'Pools' youngest-ever player, was introduced and he made a creditable 33 appearances following his League debut in the final game of the previous season.

At this point Len Shackleton enters the story again. A great football man, he was only too aware of the talent Brian Clough possessed for management and how perfectly his partnership with Peter Taylor dovetailed. Following the dismissal of Tim Ward, he telephoned Sam Longson, the chairman of Derby County, and suggested their names. Longson later admitted that Clough and Taylor had never entered his mind as possible candidates, but given Shackleton's stature in the game he put them at the top of his list. Initially Brian Clough was reluctant to leave. Although he was not contracted to the club, his north-east roots kept telling him to stay and continue with the job he had started. The key issue, as always, was money. At Hartlepools his transfer budget was £7,000, £4,000 of which went on the acquisition of John Gill from Mansfield Town. Sam Longson was offering a staggering £70,000 at Derby in an attempt to restore the Midlands club to former glories. With a heavy heart he telephoned John Curry, who had succeeded Ord as chairman, and resigned. The rest, as they say, is history.

## Promotion and Relegation

Chairman John Curry had the unenviable task prior to the start of the 1967–68 season of finding a new manager. His first choice was Peter Taylor, who made it clear he intended to join Clough at Derby once the contract formalities were sorted out. Brian Clough's final duty as manager was to issue a retained list, which contained few surprises: Brian Grant and Joe Livingstone, along with part-timer John Bates, were released, thereby ensuring that the new manager would inherit a strong squad, a luxury afforded to few of his predecessors.

John Curry's choice was 41-year-old Welshman Angus McLean, who was trainer-coach at Hull City. He had extensive experience of the game and brought John Simpson with him as his assistant. Chairman Curry remarked to the press that he was pleased to have filled the vacant posts 'with a minimum of fuss'.

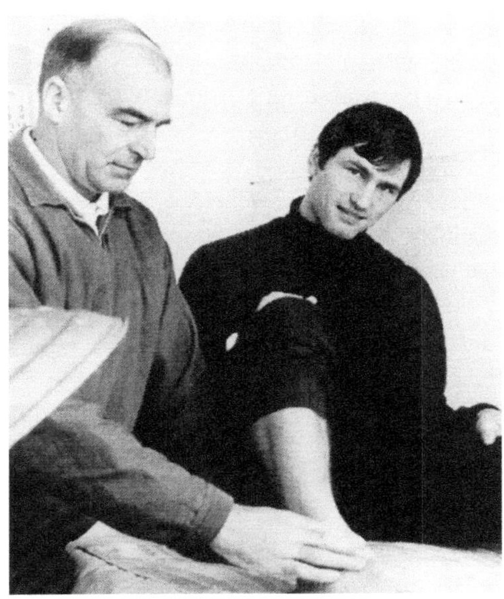
John Simpson and Terry Bell.

McLean's first signing was a 31-year-old goalkeeper from Notts County, George Smith, who had 323 games to his credit. Defenders Wilson Hepplewhite, from Carlisle, and 19-year-old Alan Goad, who was yet to make his League debut, soon followed. The new manager promised a more attacking approach than his predecessor, particularly in away games.

After a series of warm-up matches against Scottish side Queen of the South, and more familiar opposition in Carlisle United, Whitley Bay and Billingham Synthonia, the League campaign began at home with a solid 2–0 win over Brentford with goals from the dynamic duo, Ernie Phythian and Jimmy Mulvaney. Following a narrow away win at Bradford Park Avenue with a Wright goal, a sequence of six games followed without a win, of which four were goalless. The last of these saw the introduction of Terry Bell on a regular basis in place of Mulvaney. Despite a home victory over Barnsley with two Phythian goals, the next four games failed to produce success.

This sequence saw only one League victory in 11 games and understandably raised major questions about the team's promotion credentials. Further interest was generated in the poorly-regarded Football League Cup, when after a first-round victory over Bradford City, 'Pools were drawn away to Derby County, managed by Brian Clough. Clough was reported as being delighted with the draw and hoped for a 30,000 attendance for the sake of his old club. In the event a commendable 17,810 fans turned up to witness a comfortable 4–0 triumph for the home team, which included John O'Hare and Kevin Hector in the forward line at a combined cost of £65,000.

The run was finally ended with successive victories over Newport County and Bradford City, in which Jimmy Mulvaney played his last games for the club. Popular with supporters and a natural goalscorer who formed a dynamic partnership with Ernie Phythian, his departure to Barrow for a £2,000 transfer fee was not considered great business by McLean. The team for the Newport game included goalkeeper Ken Simpkins selected at centre-forward, a position he was to play in another five times, who contributed one goal. While it is not unique for a contracted goalkeeper to be selected for an outfield position, the selection of a custodian with international honours (Simpkins was a Welsh Under-23 international) to lead a forward line of fellow professionals is surely without parallel in the Football League.

Results then began to stabilise, with wins and defeats broadly in line, before McLean made the signing that lit the blue touch paper of promotion. Bobby Cummings, signed from Darlington for a £1,500 fee, had been a major part of Newcastle United's 1964–65 Second Division Championship side and had a reputation as a natural goalscorer. His debut against

Wrexham saw him partnered with local boy Peter Blowman, who scored twice in a 3–0 win, the other goal a Phythian penalty. A heavy reverse at promotion rivals Barnsley the following week was to be the final defeat of the season as United embarked on a 16-game run which included 11 victories. Cummings contributed nine goals in this sequence with strong support coming from Bell, McGovern and Wright. The final home games against Chesterfield and Swansea Town both attracted attendances of over 11,000 as Hartlepools United finally laid to rest the ghosts of the past and achieved their first promotion by finishing third with 60 points behind champions Luton Town (66 points) and Barnsley (61 points).

A major factor in their success was the improvement in away form, as promised by McLean, which saw 10 games won. Only one game was lost at home to Southend early in the season, and a mere 12 goals were conceded at the Vic. McLean used 24 players in the season, with Smith and Drysdale each missing only one game. Terry Bell finished as leading goalscorer with 14 in 36 games, followed by Ernie Phythian, who struck 11 in 32 appearances, his final one against Crewe in the promotion run-in. He left at the end of the season to emigrate to South Africa to continue his football career at the behest of Roy Bailey, the former Ipswich Town goalkeeper, who had settled there.

Although promotion was eventually won, Gus McLean complained throughout the season, both in his programme notes and in press interviews, about the lack of support through the turnstiles. Attendances that began in the 8,000 range quickly fell to barely half that figure during the poor run in September and October. At one point McLean claimed there was little interest in the town and continually lamented the lack of money. A crowd of over 9,000 saw the Boxing Day derby against Darlington, only for the next three home games to attract sub-5,000 attendances. Once the promotion run-in began, however, crowds improved dramatically. Although the manager was understandably keen to claim the credit for the promotion success, many supporters believed then, as now, that he merely benefited from a squad inherited from his predecessor Brian Clough. To an extent this is true, but he has to be given credit for the signings of George Smith and Bobby Cummings and the introduction of 17-year-old Peter Blowman, who were so vital to the ultimate triumph.

Bobby Cummings signs for 'Pools.

# A New Name, Same Old Failings

On 1 April 1967 the towns of West Hartlepool and Hartlepool amalgamated to create a single borough, Hartlepool. By the end of the 1967–68 season the club directors decided that the town's football club, in order to be representative of the 'new' town, should be renamed Hartlepool Association Football Club. So the club began the new season not only with an enhanced status, but also with a new name.

McLean promised attacking football and goals for the new season, 1968–69, in the Third Division. Despite sharing eight goals with Dundee United in a pre-season friendly, harsh reality soon set in when the League campaign started against Bournemouth at home in front of a healthy crowd of 6,971. A 1–1 draw was the prelude to a run of five games that produced only a single goal and included a seven-goal thrashing by Reading. With no money made available in the close season, the manager had to rely on the promotion-winning squad of players in the opening games. Worse was to come when John McGovern left to join Clough at Derby County in a £7,000 deal. Despite this windfall McLean, now on a five-year contract, was given little money to spend. His next signing, following McGovern's departure, was 22-year-old Ron Young, a winger from Hull City, for a £4,000 fee.

The new signing's influence paid immediate dividends when, at the seventh time of asking, United finally won at home to Watford with goals from Young on his debut and a Cummings penalty. The next five games brought three draws and two defeats, with only a single goal scored. The home game against Barrow in early October which ended in a disastrous defeat was witnessed by barely 3,000 spectators. Clearly the lack of goals and consequent victories, so bullishly promised by the manager, was taking its inevitable toll on support. By the New Year 'Pools were fourth bottom of Division Three with 19 points from 23 games (two points for a win). Following a heavy reverse against Rotherham, both John Sheridan and Bobby Cummings were put on the transfer list.

A five-game unbeaten run in March, which saw Terry Bell score four goals in three games, failed to impress the Victoria Ground faithful, and only 2,754 turned up to witness a fine 2–0 win over Reading, revenge for the heavy defeat earlier in the season. In the end it was the lack of goals that sealed 'Pools' fate. Despite losing only one of their last seven games, four were goalless and a final total of 19 draws and only 40 goals scored, less than one a game, told its own story. United finished third bottom with 39 points, virtually a point a goal, losing 17 games, the same number as Tranmere, who finished in seventh position.

McLean promised an immediate return, stating that his squad of players was too good for the Fourth Division. Sentinel, the local football correspondent, writing in the *Hartlepool Mail* following the final match against Crewe, a 0–0 draw in front of only 2,035 fans, remarked that 'this was Hartlepool's final appearance as a Third Division side for the time being...'

# Re-elections and a League Cup Run

During the close season Bryan Drysdale, the club's best player in the eyes of both the manager and most supporters, was transferred to Bristol City for a reported £15,000 transfer fee. This was a far cry from the £40,000 McLean had valued him at a few months earlier and was an indication of the parlous state of the finances at the Victoria Ground. Barely 3,000 turned up for the opening game of the 1969–70 season to witness a goalless draw against Brentford; however, the season surprisingly took a turn for the better when Scunthorpe United were beaten in the Football League Cup, a competition 'Pools had very little pedigree in, and Derby County were drawn at home in the second round. This meant a return for Brian Clough and Peter Taylor and their team, now a First Division side. Nearly 8,000 turned up to see Hartlepool give a strong account of themselves against quality opposition, which included two former players, Les Green and John McGovern. They were supported by Derby legends Roy McFarland, Dave Mackay, John O'Hare, Kevin Hector and Alan Hinton. The home side defended stoutly throughout the first half before Derby took command after the break with three goals, Terry Bell managing a consolation goal in a match full of entertaining football.

Only two wins in the first 14 games preceded the final visit of Bradford Park Avenue in October as they ultimately finished bottom and failed to be re-elected, being replaced by Cambridge United. 'Pools had a rare success that afternoon, with Terry Bell scoring a hat-trick and new signing Harry Kirk from Darlington adding a brace. The dramatic fall in attendances (only 1,824 saw the Southend game in mid-December) prompted chairman John Curry to take what he described as 'extreme measures'. This meant the sale of Terry Bell to Reading for £8,000 in February, and the re-election die was well and truly cast when the final seven games were lost without a single goal scored. The lack of goals was reflected in blank score sheets in 22 League games, nearly half the season's fixtures.

McLean resigned as manager immediately following the final game, citing 'restrictive conditions' as the reason. He claimed that John Curry had wished to reduce his reported £8,000-a-year salary, generous for a manager of a Fourth Division club, and he no longer felt able to continue. His assistant John Simpson was immediately appointed manager and began the inevitable rebuilding process for the start of the 1970–71 season.

Within a week of his appointment Simpson placed seven players on free transfers – goalkeeper George Smith, full-back Bob Dobbing, half-backs Tommy Lee and Andy McCluskey, and forwards Derek Tail, Peter Blowman and Malcolm Thompson. Of these Peter Blowman was especially unlucky to have played for the club in a period when the lack of an experienced, consistent goalscorer would have benefited his development. To replace them, Simpson turned to former Sunderland players Nick Sharkey and George Herd, as well as Malcolm Clarke, Peter Barlow, Malcolm Dawes and Ralph Wright, all from Third and Fourth Division clubs.

One win in the first nine games, 2–1 at home to Barrow, was not an auspicious start for the new manager. During this sequence Harry Kirk achieved the 'distinction' of being the first Hartlepool substitute to score when he netted a consolation goal in the defeat at

Stockport. A narrow home win against Notts County in front of a meagre 2,772 spectators was the prelude to a nine-game run without a win, and the club was clearly in trouble despite a Christmas rally which produced three wins and a draw. During this spell further misery was heaped on long-suffering supporters when 'Pools suffered the indignity of a first-round FA Cup defeat to Rhyl from the Cheshire League.

In the New Year, with attendances barely above the 1,000 mark, Hartlepool Council's Finance Committee, under the chairmanship of Alderman J.A. Pounder, met with club officials to discuss the ever-worsening financial position. Alderman Pounder expressed sympathy for the club while at the same time requiring guarantees to support any financial assistance the council might offer. At the beginning of March the committee announced immediate aid of £10,000 to relieve the current crisis, a sum which probably saved the club from extinction. This was in addition to £40,000-worth of buildings and ground upgrades which the council had previously financed through an increase in the rent for the Victoria Ground.

John Simpson resigned a few days after the announcement of the council's loan, to be immediately replaced by the former Sunderland full-back Len Ashurst in a player-manager role. Ashurst arrived too late in the season to save 'Pools from a 10th re-election application, yet despite having a pretty thin playing record, with only six goals scored away from home, they survived along with Newport County, each polling 33 votes. This was taken as a clear signal that the League's patience was understandably wearing thin.

Len Ashurst's first campaign as manager began with a home win, 3–1 against Reading. The Hartlepool public failed to respond to their council's munificence and a crowd of 2,470, low for the opening game, saw two Ellis penalties and a Young goal seal the win. Ironically, nearly 6,000 turned up four days later to watch a goalless draw against Barnsley in the little-regarded Football League Cup, with the return at Oakwell attracting 9,577 to witness a narrow home win in extra-time. These displays encouraged supporters to the next two home games, Southend (5,479) and Darlington (7,156), in which 'Pools were unable to record a victory. Following a six-goal thrashing at Brentford, only two of the next 12 games were won, and they were once again firmly rooted in the bottom four.

At this point in the season the FA Cup, not normally a major feature of United's recent seasons, came into play. An easy first-round home win over Scarborough was followed by another tie against non-League opposition in the second round, away to Boston United.

The home side comprised part-time players, many of whom were in the veteran stage. Despite this, they competed fiercely and took the lead through their player-manager Jim Smith. A second goal galvanised 'Pools into action, but Bobby Veart's late strike was no consolation, and yet again they were the victims of a Cup giant-killing act. It may be assumed that they had no further interest in the competition, yet nothing could be further from the truth.

Non-League Hereford United had battled their way through the qualifying games to reach the third round and were rewarded with a dream tie, away to Newcastle United, the sort of draw the Hartlepools directors would have given their back teeth for. After a draw at St James' Park, and in the full glare of national press and television coverage, Hereford triumphed in the replay at their Edgar Street ground, 2–1 after extra-time. Their equalising goal by part-timer Ronnie Radford is still shown as the best televised goal ever on the BBC's *Match of the Day* programme. Strong public support virtually guaranteed Hereford's election to the

Willie Waddell scored vital goals in the ultimately successful re-election battle.

Football League several weeks in advance of the season's end and subsequent voting. In most people's minds it was odds on who would be relegated to accommodate the new club, Hartlepool FC.

In a perverse way, Hereford's Cup exploits (they eventually lost to West Ham United) helped galvanise Hartlepool. With no doubt in the manager's mind that a bottom-four finish meant relegation, Ashurst responded by selling the popular Tony Parry to Derby for £5,000 and bringing in Willie Waddell, who was to contribute vital goals in the run-in. A victory at Newport County, with goals from Ashurst and Sharkey, was a prelude to a six-game run that included only one defeat. An Easter campaign which brought successive home wins and improved support against Stockport County and high-flying Scunthorpe United was abruptly halted by fellow strugglers Barrow. After four wins in the next five games, the crunch came at, of all places, Feethams.

This was a game 'Pools simply had to win to ensure their League status, and an estimated 5,000 'Poolies' made the short trip to Darlington. In front of nearly 9,000 partisan fans Darlington had the better of the first half and deservedly led at the break. Hartlepool staged a spirited second-half recovery, with Bill Green equalising before Willie Waddell scored the winner, provoking scenes of jubilation among the visiting supporters. This result not only guaranteed their League status, but also ensured they finished above Darlington! In the final analysis it was another perennial struggler, Barrow, that made way for ambitious Hereford United, even though Crewe finished bottom, eight points below them. The message from the Football League was now clear – anyone who continues to make re-election applications will be thrown out.

Len Ashurst decided that in the absence of a proven goalscorer and the money to buy one, the 1972–73 campaign would have to be based on a mean defence. In this his task was to be greatly helped by goalkeeper Barry Watling, a new signing from Notts County on the inevitable free transfer. Watling was to be ever present throughout the season, only conceding 51 League goals, just three more than champions Southport. It was no surprise that all the problems lay with an attack that could only manage 34 goals all season, with John Coyne top scorer with a meagre nine from 41 games, the majority coming at centre-forward. Ten home games were drawn, six finished scoreless and the aggregate goals at home only totalled 32, 17 scored by the home side. During the season Ashurst recruited Tony Toms as trainer to replace George Herd, who left the previous season. Toms, a former commando, was primarily a fitness coach who took the players on 'survival' training on the North Yorkshire Moors. His methods met with mixed reactions from players and fans alike,

Hartlepool FC, 1972–73. Back row, left to right: N. Warnock, G. Potter, J. Coyne, W. Green, B. Watling, A. Goad, J. Honour, R. Smith, W. Waddell. Front row: J. Kelly, R. Young, B. Conlan, M. Dawes, R. Veart, M. Spelman.

and their merits were thrown into question as 'Pools faded towards the end of the season, failing to win any of the last eight games. Their final placing of 20th not only avoided the need to apply for re-election – they had a five-point cushion over Crewe – but they also had the satisfaction of seeing rivals Darlington finish rock bottom.

The close season saw the inevitable departures, including Neil Warnock who, while never reaching great heights as a player, later enjoyed a successful career as a manager, including a spell with Sheffield United in the FA Premier League. Warnock was followed by Bobby Smith, Ron Young and more importantly Bill Green, who joined Carlisle United for a reported £15,000 fee. Recognising that goals were now the number-one priority, Ashurst added both strength and guile to his attack with the signings of Malcolm Moore, Kevin McMahon and Alan Gauden. They were to contribute 30 goals in all games throughout the 1973–74 campaign and give sterling service to the club.

Another poor start with only two wins in the first 15 League games saw 'Pools in familiar territory, 91st in the Football League and knocked out of the Cup by another non-League side, Altrincham. The pre-Christmas weekend, never the best in terms of attendances, saw a meagre crowd of 844 witness a convincing win over Scunthorpe United. This was 'Pools' first post-war League gate of less than 1,000 and inevitably placed even more pressure on the financial position. The club's directors blamed everything from the weather to Christmas shopping, while the manager lamented injuries to key players. Better results, however, were just around the corner.

The Scunthorpe result marked the beginning of a turnaround which saw only three defeats in 20 games with 31 goals scored, including convincing wins over Stockport (3–0), Mansfield (4–0), Workington (3–0) and Doncaster (3–0). Throughout this spell the three new men, Moore, McMahon and Gauden, all contributed vital goals, thus repaying the manager's faith in them. This run of results contributed to Ashurst winning the Fourth Division's Manager of the Month award, the first time such an accolade had come to a Hartlepool manager.

The Stockport game was the first ever to be played at the Victoria Ground on a Sunday. HM Government, recognising a desire among the general public for access to sporting events as well as retail facilities on the Sabbath, was gradually relaxing the laws. A curious feature of these regulations was that in order to charge admission on a Sunday the public were entitled to free entry if they so wished. Therefore, the club had to open a turnstile that gave entry without payment, although it was later reported that very few of the 5,747 who attended made use of it.

The Easter period began with 'Pools in the dizzy heights of eighth position, only to fall away in their last seven games after failing to register a single victory; however, a final position of 11th was highly satisfactory given the traumas of recent seasons. The estimable Barry Watling was again ever present in goal throughout the campaign, and Ashurst called upon only 20 players, proving yet again the benefit of a settled side.

A fact of life in the lower divisions of the Football League is that success, however modest, attracts attention. So it was with the manager and his fitness trainer. Having assembled a balanced squad of players on a shoestring budget and finished in the top half of the League, it was inevitable that a club from a higher division would come calling. It was therefore no surprise when Len Ashurst and Tony Toms were offered the same roles at Third Division Gillingham, which they accepted. The Hartlepool board then turned to former Newcastle United, Coventry, Oxford United and Darlington player Ken Hale, who had coaching experience with Halifax Town.

The 1974–75 season was to be memorable for an exciting and extended run in the much-maligned Football League Cup. Introduced in 1960 as an 'early season' Cup competition, it failed to capture the public's imagination in the way the premier Cup competition did. Matters were made worse by the Football League's initial decision to make entry optional, meaning that the likes of Manchester United and Liverpool did not compete in the early years. Finals were played on a two-leg, home and away basis, which saw the likes of Norwich City and Rotherham United compete for what was being promoted as a major event. The paying public were not impressed, and only the decision to give the competition a Wembley Final in 1967 revived its prospects.

After a comfortable opening home win against Newport County in the League, 'Pools played their first match in the Football League Cup at Workington and triumphed 2–1, with goals from McMahon and Gauden. The second round saw them drawn away to Third

Action from the 1974 League Cup tie against Aston Villa.

Division Bournemouth, and everyone thought that would be the end of another abortive Cup campaign. At this stage it is as well to remind the reader that Cup ties were played to a finish irrespective of how many games were required to produce a winner. Penalty shoot-outs and golden goals were in the future. A draw at Dean Court courtesy of a Gauden strike was followed by the sides sharing four goals at the Vic a week later. United returned to the south coast five days later and repeated the first result with a Moore goal before the sides met for a fourth time, with the home side prevailing through a Ward strike in front of nearly 7,000 spectators.

Enthusiasm for the competition had been tempered by the knowledge that Hartlepool's opponents in the third round were to be Blackburn Rovers, leaders of the Third Division and in the ascendancy due to the munificence of their benefactor, Jack Walker. Yet another draw resulted, with 'Pools matching the Lancashire club and taking an early lead through Moore. Eventually Blackburn equalised and everyone imagined that they would prevail in the replay and that the run was over. Nothing could have been further from the truth. In front of 11,145 at Ewood Park the whole team gave an excellent account of themselves, playing football way above that expected of a mid-table Fourth Division side. Goals from George Potter and Kevin McMahon earned a 2–1 victory, which set up a fourth-round tie against Second Division Aston Villa.

By now the League Cup run had captured the imagination of the Hartlepool public, and a record attendance for a floodlight match at the Victoria Ground (12,305) turned up to witness a thrilling 1–1 draw, with Malcolm Moore scoring for 'Pools. The replay was a one-sided affair as Villa triumphed 6–1 to end 'Pools' Cup adventure, which had lasted a staggering nine games.

In the League results were mixed, with 'Pools never rising above 12th position and eventually finishing one place lower. Despite record attendances in League Cup games, the bread and butter of the Fourth Division failed to ignite the public's interest – as an average gate for the season of 2,635 testified. Malcolm Moore, the hero of the League Cup campaign, was ever present throughout the season and contributed 19 goals in total. He was admirably supported by Alan Goad, Barry Watling and Bobby Smith, who each missed only one game.

The 1975–76 campaign began with three drawn games followed by two defeats, before success was finally tasted at Southport in front of barely 1,000 spectators. United's form, after

John Simpson attends to Alan Goad's injury.

an initial struggle, revived dramatically in late autumn with seven wins in nine games, thereby providing the catalyst for an overdue run in the FA Cup. After a comfortable first-round victory over Stockport, sterner resistance was met in non-League Marine, who battled out a draw on their ground. The replay was an entertaining affair, with Malcolm Moore scoring a hat-trick in a 6–3 victory.

The draw for the ever-glamorous third round presented Hartlepool with a dream tie away to Manchester City, at the time one of the country's most attractive teams. Over 26,000, many from Hartlepool, attended the match, which was played in perfect conditions with the formidable home side at full strength. From the outset it was clear the visitors would be no match for the First Division side, and early goals from Oakes and Tueart quickly put paid to any thoughts the travelling supporters may have entertained of an upset. Despite City's supremacy, which was eventually reflected in a 6–0 scoreline, the match was remembered for an ugly incident involving Denis Tueart and George Potter midway through the second half. Potter, more in frustration than malice, kicked out at Tueart, who responded with a deliberate head-butt which fractured the player's cheekbone. Potter required extensive treatment before being stretchered from the field, with the referee indicating he had been sent off. Tueart was also dismissed. The incident left a bad taste all round, particularly as Potter was hospitalised until he was well enough to travel.

The resounding FA Cup defeat was a prelude to a League run of 13 games without a win before a rally over the Easter period resulted in a mid-table, 14th-place finish. During the season Ernest Ord briefly returned once again as chairman to stabilise the finances in succession to Thomas Aird. Ord's final spell as chairman was to last a mere three weeks before he stood down in favour of local farmer Vince Barker. A new chapter in the history of Hartlepool FC was about to begin.

## New Chairman, New Name, Same Old Failings

Vince Barker's first full season as chairman was to see a return to the dreaded re-election campaign, which many supporters had hoped the club had left in the past. A dreadful start, with no win in the opening 10 League games, resulted in the inevitable departure of manager Ken Hale. Hale's replacement was first-team coach Billy Horner, who had managed Darlington and had an extensive playing career with Middlesbrough.

Horner initially stopped the rot and endeared himself to both the chairman and fans by signing Malcolm Poskett from Whitby Town. Poskett, a former Hartlepool player, was an instant success, scoring a hat-trick against Torquay in only his sixth appearance. A few weeks later he scored within 34 seconds of the kick-off in a three-goal victory over Scunthorpe. Despite Poskett's heroics, the team struggled, and a seven-game winless run towards the end of the season resulted in an 11th re-election application. Bottom side Workington Town, making their fourth successive application, were the unlucky club to be rejected in favour of Southern League Wimbledon.

Following the successful application for re-election, Barker and his board of directors took the sensible decision to restore 'United' to the club's name, nine years after it was dropped. Following the amalgamation of the two towns in 1967, it was no longer appropriate to pluralize the name, so Hartlepool United was the logical choice.

If Hartlepool United's long-suffering supporters thought a new name would bring about a change in their club's fortunes, they were to be sadly mistaken. As ever, finance was the root cause of the problems, which were only resolved by two pieces of good fortune. The 1977–78 season began in the now usual pattern of more losses than wins before Poskett hit top form as a prelude to another run in the FA Cup.

After victories over Tranmere Rovers and Runcorn, the third-round draw threw up a home tie against Second Division Crystal Palace, who were managed by Terry Venables. In view of their League form, few 'experts' gave 'Pools a chance against a team and a manager ultimately destined for greater things. Yet on the day they fully deserved their victory thanks to two Bob Newton goals and an excellent all-round team performance. The fourth-round draw paired United with Bobby Robson's Ipswich Town at Portman Road. Ipswich fielded arguably their all-time finest side and were too strong all round for a United team that never gave up despite the 4–1 scoreline. The quality of the opposition can be gauged by the fact that they went on to win the FA Cup, defeating Arsenal in the Final.

A few days after the Cup exit, chairman Barker accepted a £60,000 offer from Brighton for Malcolm Poskett, easily a record fee for a Hartlepool player. This had a disastrous effect on results for the rest of the season, which included an eight-goal defeat by Swansea,

Keith Houchen and Bob Newton v Aldershot 1979.

Hartlepool United, 1979. Back row, left to right: G. Smith (player-coach), M. Fagan, M. Lawrence, W. Ayre, G. Richardson, T. Ramshaw, S. Brooks, K. Houchen, G. Larkin, D. Loadwick, W. Maddren (coach). Front row: W. Goldthorpe, M. Garry, P. O'Mari, J. Linacre, P. Staff, W. Horner (manager), D. Norton, A. Duncan, G. Normanton, R. Hogan.

resulting in a 12th application for re-election. One statistic of note belonged to centre-half Billy Ayre, who played all 46 League games and top scored with 12 goals, all from open play.

As in the previous year a strong candidate, Wigan Athletic, was seeking election to the Football League. On the first ballot Southport, members since 1921, received the same number of votes as Wigan, who finally prevailed on a second vote. Hartlepool United supporters were left to speculate about how many more re-election applications would be successful.

Clearly an improvement was required the following season, 1978–79, and despite an opening-day home defeat by Doncaster Rovers only one of the next eight League games was lost. A major factor in the improvement was the developing talent of Keith Houchen, who brought goals and a physical presence to the attack. As well as enjoying improved League form which brought Billy Horner a Manager of the Month award, the FA Cup once again brought top-class opposition to the Victoria Ground in the form of Leeds United. After narrow one-goal wins against Grimsby and Crewe, 'Pools were rewarded with a home third-round tie against the Yorkshire giants. Despite the presence of a reported 16,000 crowd, the home team were no match for First Division opponents and suffered an embarrassing defeat. This set the tone for the remainder of the season with a run of 16 games without a win before a late rally secured a respectable 13th position. In the final away game at Halifax, Mark Lawrence scored all four goals in a 4–2 victory.

Horner continued with the nucleus of the squad which had broken the re-election sequence, with Billy Ayre, Keith Houchen and Bob Newton at the heart of his team's efforts. The emergence of talented youngsters such as Mark Lawrence, John Linacre and Roy Hogan gave cause for genuine optimism, which remained unfulfilled throughout a disappointing 1979–80 campaign that resulted in a 19th-place finish, a mere two points above a re-election place.

Such promise was nearly fulfilled the next season, 1980–81, when despite first-round exits from both Cup competitions 'Pools' League form up to Christmas saw them riding high in third place. A major influence on the improvement was Bobby Kerr, Sunderland's Cup-winning captain, who went on to play in every game. Houchen contributed 17 League goals and was ably supported by Newton with 10. The promotion challenge faded in February with five successive defeats followed by a 'win one, lose one' sequence through to the end of the season. A ninth-place finish, 'Pools' first top-10 placing since the 1968 promotion season, did not impress everyone, however, with attendances barely averaging 3,000.

The 1981–82 season saw the introduction of the Football League Associate Members' Cup for clubs from the Third and Fourth Divisions. Initially it was played on a group basis prior to the start of the League programme, and Hartlepool United made an inauspicious start by losing their three games 1–0. This set the tone for the League campaign, with inconsistent form ensuring another season of mid-table mediocrity, which in some quarters was considered an improvement. A rare highlight was a Keith Houchen hat-trick inside 25 minutes at Peterborough, with the sides sharing eight goals. Such feats do not pass unnoticed, however, and it was no surprise when the talented striker moved to Orient for a £25,000 fee, which chairman Barker used to settle a tax demand from the Inland Revenue. By the end of the season attendances had fallen to the 1,200 mark as the Hartlepool public grew understandably tired of the continued failure of the club to raise standards both on and off the pitch.

## A Game and a Club in Decline

After the relative success of the previous two League campaigns, results took a dramatic turn for the worse during the 1982–83 season. A combination of factors contributed to the decline, which was to end in another re-election application. Money, as ever, was at the root of the problem, combined with chairman Barker's long-running campaign to acquire ownership of the Victoria Ground from the local council. Matters were not helped by the chairman's policy of accepting derisory offers for key players which, while providing short-term relief, exacerbated the problem in the long term. The one bright spot in a dismal season was the emergence of the supremely talented 20-year-old Andrew Linighan, who made 45 League appearances. A new low was reached on the pitch at Torquay when three players were sent off, Roy Hogan for one foul too many, along with Kevin Johnson and Rob Smith for 'a heated exchange of words'!

Towards the end of the season manager Billy Horner was made the scapegoat for the team's failings and was replaced by John Duncan, formerly of Tottenham Hotspur, in the April. Duncan only stayed until the end of the season, a mere nine games, before resigning following another successful re-election application. The penultimate home game against Colchester on a bank holiday attracted a mere 804 spectators. If die-hard fans thought that their team had reached rock bottom, however, then they were very much mistaken.

# Team Line-up

## ALDERSHOT V HARTLEPOOL UNITED

| ALDERSHOT | HARTLEPOOL UNITED |
|---|---|
| *Colours:* Red and Blue | *Colours:* Yellow |
| 1 Glen JOHNSON | 1 Eddie BLACKBURN |
| 2 Paul SHRUBB | 2 Philip BROWN |
| 3 Peter SCOTT | 3 Barry STIMPSON |
| 4 Les BRILEY | 4 Frankie BAGG |
| 5 Mark WHITLOCK | 5 Andy LINIGAN |
| 6 Manny ANDRUSZEWSKI | 6 Bill SPOWART |
| 7 Brian LUCAS | 7 Mark CAGE |
| 8 Dale BANTON | 8 Arthur PICKERING |
| 9 Mark SANFORD | 9 Roy HOGAN |
| 10 Ian McDONALD | 10 Paul DOBSON |
| 11 Stuart ROBINSON | 11 Alan WRIGHT |
| 12 | 12 |
| *Manager:* Len Walker | *Manager:* Billy Horner |

## Ball Donors

M. Grant, Esq. (Lottery Agent No. 1357)
N. O. Warren, Esq., Alton
Sandell Perkins Ltd., Guildford (2)
Mrs. Pullen, Farncombe
Barclays Bank PLC (2)
W. W. Baggs & Son (Landscape Contractors)
Peter Gough, *New Inn*, Hawley
R. H. Lamarre, Esq.
Edgar Jerome, Ltd.
M. H. Garrood, Esq.
E. Grenham, Sheldon's Bakeries (F'boro) Ltd.
Rev. Michael Pusey
J. E. Robinson, Esq.
Alexander Job
Matthew Job
W. Wheatley, Esq. (2)
J. B. Dunham, Esq.
B. G. Oliver, Esq.
An Anonymous Donor
In memory of Sonny Farrar
Mr. Paul Clarke

SURRIDGE COBBLER

***The Aldershot Football Club are indebted to those who have generously donated match balls.***

## Match Officials

***Referee:***
**A. R. GLASSON** (Salisbury)

***Linesmen:***
**N. S. BUTLER** (East Molesey)
*RED FLAG*

**J. F. HILL** (Redhill)
*YELLOW FLAG*

TONY GLASSON commenced refereeing whilst serving in Cyprus in 1958 and, via Wiltshire and Western Leagues, was appointed to the Football League Line and through to the Full List in 1973.

He has refereed two F.A. Amateur Cup quarter-finals, was linesman to the Anglo-Italian Cup and European Championship (Belgium v France) in 1974. Reserve official in 1978 for the England v Italy international. Refereed Chelsea's matches against New York Cosmos and Moscow Dynamos, and the 1981 Jersey Cup Final.

A married man, with four sons, he is a building surveyor, and is interested in architectural design work and gardening. His ambition is to officiate at Wembley.

'Pools 'joke' team in the 1983 Aldershot programme.

Mick Docherty was appointed manager for the 1983–84 season in succession to Duncan and came with a genuine footballing pedigree. His father Tommy played for Arsenal and Scotland and had managed at the highest level, Chelsea and Manchester United being among his many clubs. Mick Docherty's playing career was primarily with Burnley and

Sunderland, and he had a brief spell as caretaker manager of the latter. He was to set new standards as having the worst record of any Hartlepool manager, with a solitary win in his 21 League and Cup games in charge. His departure in December paved the way for the return, in a caretaker capacity, of Billy Horner, who immediately set about recalling players released by his two predecessors. After a brief rally, Horner was unable to prevent a 14th, and final, application for re-election, with supporters understandably voting with their feet. A mere 790 dedicated souls attended the penultimate home game against Stockport County, Hartlepool United's lowest-ever home attendance for a League game.

At the beginning of 1984 the club was presented with a £29,000 tax demand by the Inland Revenue. Before an offer from the players to forgo a month's wages could be taken up, John Smart, a Tyneside businessman, joined the board to relieve the financial pressures. As practical evidence of his support, Smart entered into the club's first sponsorship deal, which saw the players wear shirts with his company 'New County' printed on the front. By the end of the season Vince Barker's position became untenable, particularly in the light of falling attendances, and in June Smart duly became chairman. His immediate tasks were to confirm Horner as manager and lead a successful re-election campaign. For the first time in many a long day, supporters looked forward to a new season with a modest degree of optimism.

During the close season Andrew Linighan was transferred to Leeds United for £60,000, thereby setting the club up for the new campaign free from financial pressures. Linighan was to enjoy a successful career with, among others, Norwich and Arsenal, winning an FA Cup-winners' medal with the latter. Billy Horner strengthened his squad with the signings of Kevin Dixon, Alan Stevenson, Graeme Hedley and Les Mutrie for the 1984–85 campaign.

After failing to record a win in their first six League games, United embarked on a nine-game unbeaten run which took them to the dizzy heights of the top six, winning Horner his second Manager of the Month award. As so often happens, on winning this accolade the manager saw his team's form dip dramatically in the New Year, with the end result of a 19th-place League finish. The FA Cup was a welcome distraction, with a first-round victory over once-mighty Derby County, now a Third Division side, in front of over 7,000 fans. This was bettered in attendance terms when over 8,500 turned out to witness the second-round tie against York City. Predictably, 'Pools failed to rise to the challenge, and the visitors recorded a comfortable victory with goals from John MacPhail and Keith Houchen.

Despite the lowly finish, chairman Smart continued to back his manager and

Bob Newton in his second spell with the club.

Kevin Dixon scores the winning goal in the 2–1 FA Cup defeat of Derby County.

the close season saw an arrival in the form of Alan Shoulder from Newcastle United, and the return of the popular Bob Newton. Also signed were two players whose names were to become synonymous with Hartlepool United, Brian Honour and Keith Nobbs. The 1985–86 season began with a bang, and by November 'Pools were second after a 12-game run which included nine wins. With Alan Shoulder in sparkling form and an unbeaten run in January, it seemed nothing could stop Hartlepool United gaining their second promotion.

Then the fates intervened in the form of the weather and an inspector from the local council. Four postponements in February created a fixture backlog which stretched a small playing staff to the limit and beyond. March and April saw a nine-game winless run as three games a week were played to make up the lost ground, which in turn wrecked their promotion chances. Worse was to follow when the Vic's capacity was reduced to 2,100 following a safety inspection which declared the roof coverings on the Town and Rink end

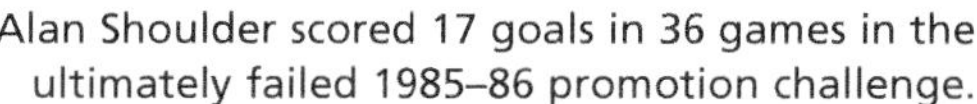
Alan Shoulder scored 17 goals in 36 games in the ultimately failed 1985–86 promotion challenge.

stands unsafe. The end result was that barely 2,000-strong crowds attended the final home games, a sad end to a season that had promised so much.

Prior to the 1986–87 League campaign, chairman John Smart and Billy Horner were photographed toasting an anticipated promotion success following the progress of the previous season. If ever there was a case of 'pride coming before a fall' this was it, as none of the opening eight League games were won, resulting in Horner being replaced by his assistant, former player John Bird. Ironically for Horner, he had brought his successor to the Victoria Ground in 1980 from Newcastle United, and the new manager boasted an impressive playing career of almost 500 League appearances. He was, however, to have an unhappy relationship with his chairman, who at one point resigned after disagreements with fellow directors.

On the playing field, results in no way matched expectations as an 18th-place League finish indicated. One of the few consolations in a season of underachievement was the form of Rob McKinnon, who only missed one game. The uneasy truce between Smart and Bird continued throughout the close season, although the pair contrived to make one of Hartlepool United's best-ever signings when Paul Baker arrived from Carlisle United on a free transfer.

Baker made an immediate impact, scoring 25 goals in all competitions and forming a highly effective partnership with Andy Toman, who contributed 20. Their goalscoring feats ensured an entertaining season, with runs in both the FA Cup and the Sherpa Van Trophy Cup competitions. These games compensated for the inconsistent League form, which began with a poor start, improved to such an extent that John Bird twice won the Manager of the Month award and then fell away dramatically, with none of the final eight League games won. Even so, a 16th-place finish was scant reward for a season that had held such hope.

After losing narrowly to First Division Luton Town at home in the third round of the FA Cup, 'Pools embarked on a run in the Sherpa Van Trophy. Following wins over Mansfield, Doncaster and Carlisle, the draw threw up Sunderland at Roker Park. Few people gave the Fourth Division underdogs a chance, yet on a windswept night they surprised everyone with a narrow win courtesy of a Brian Honour goal direct from a corner-kick. With talk of Wembley in the air, the draw presented a home semi-final tie against Preston North End. On the night, however, the Third Division side were too strong, with Nigel Jemson scoring both their goals and David Brown, son of Berry, in outstanding form in the visitors' goal.

In preparation for the new season the club arranged a pre-season game against Manchester United, who had previously played a single game at Victoria Park in 1957, the classic FA Cup tie featuring the famous 'Busby Babes' side. Twenty years had elapsed since their last Championship success, and despite finishing runners-up to Liverpool the previous season there was much speculation about the future of their manager, Alex Ferguson. In the event, a crowd of just over 2,000 saw 'Pools turn on the style in a stunning 6–0 win, with Kevin Dixon scoring a hat-trick. The visiting side contained eight internationals, including Norman Whiteside, Viv Anderson, Alan Brazil and Paul McGrath, yet were totally outplayed and never seriously threatened a reply. Goalkeeper Chris Turner, later to manage 'Pools, has since recalled the atmosphere in the dressing room following the woeful display, as Ferguson went into his now famous 'hairdryer' mode.

If ever success was to prove a double-edged sword, so it was with Hartlepool United at the start of the 1988–89 season, when five of the opening six League games were won, taking John Bird's side to second in the League. York City, having sacked Bobby Saxton for a poor start to the season, made Bird the proverbial 'offer he could not refuse', taking Alan Little with him. Chairman Smart immediately turned to his friend Bob Moncur, the former Newcastle United and Scotland captain, who had managerial experience with Hearts, Carlisle and Plymouth. On the surface it appeared an inspired choice as Moncur was popular with football fans throughout the North East; however, his love of the sea and sailing was to be a major cause for concern before too long.

Within weeks of his arrival Moncur brought Joe Allon to the Victoria Ground to add pace and goals to compliment the more powerful approach of Paul Baker. If fans thought this partnership would be allowed to blossom they were mistaken, as after only two games the manager switched Baker to a role in central-defence, preferring Simon Grayson in the forward position. Once again compensation for inconsistent League form was found in an FA Cup run. After home wins against Wigan, Notts County and Bristol City, the fourth-round draw saw the visit of Bournemouth for the only tie featuring a north-east club.

A crowd of over 6,000 saw a hard-fought contest which ended in a draw after Luther Blissett equalised from the penalty spot following Brian Honour's goal. The replay at Dean Court, with an estimated 1,000 'Poolies' supporting their team, was an entertaining affair, with Bournemouth taking a two-goal lead through own-goals by Baker and Moverley. Joe Allon pulled one back before Cooke restored the two-goal advantage for the hosts, only for Toman to reduce the deficit once again to a single goal. Two further goals for the home side gave the 5–2 scoreline an unrealistic look on a night when fate decreed that a first-ever fifth-round FA Cup appearance, against Manchester United no less, was not to be.

Hartlepool United, 1989. Back row, left to right: B. Honour, S. Grayson, W. Stokes, R. Moverley, R. McKinnon, A. Barrass, P. Dalton. Middle row: K. Nobbs, P. Baker, G. Henderson (physio), B. Robson (assistant manager), J. Craggs (coach), J. Allon, D. Stackle. Front row: M. Robson, K. Davies, P. Ogden, P. Atkinson, J. Tinkler, R. Doig, S. Plaskett.

The 1988–89 season saw the introduction of automatic relegation to the Football Conference for the side finishing in 24th position. Many fans and observers wondered why it had taken so long to introduce this eminently sensible rule and banish forever the re-election campaigns, of which Hartlepool United with a record 14 successful applications were the experts. In the event, despite a modest 19th-place finish, 'Pools were never in any danger of finishing bottom, a fate that befell neighbours Darlington, with Maidstone United having the distinction of being the first club to achieve automatic promotion.

## A New Chairman and Manager and a Promotion

The start of the 1989–90 season was to set new standards of ineptitude in the running of a professional football club. The root of the problem lay in chairman John Smart agreeing to Bob Moncur participating in a boating competition, the timing of which coincided with his team's pre-season preparations. Inevitably 'Pools suffered a heavy four-goal defeat at Halifax in the opening game, with the travelling supporters making their views known to Smart in plain terms in the car park following the game. Moncur's response was to give debuts to a group of promising youth players, Don Hutchison among them, who were simply not ready for the demands of the professional game. Two League wins in the opening 19 games signalled the end for both men, and after a protracted boardroom wrangle Smart stood down and Gary Gibson became the new chairman.

Tony Barratt scores a rare goal against Hereford in October 1989.

The peerless Paul Gascoigne in League Cup action against Pools at White Hart Lane.

Gibson, after initially agreeing to continue with Moncur, rightly decided that only a new manager could restore order to the Victoria Ground. In this he chose wisely, appointing the former Tottenham and England player Cyril Knowles to the hot seat. Knowles had previously managed Darlington and Torquay United and brought a wealth of knowledge of the clubs and players of the lower divisions. This was reflected in his first signings, Paul Olsson and Ian Bennyworth, who made an immediate impact over the Christmas period in convincing wins over Scarborough and Grimsby. The New Year heralded a resounding 5–0 defeat of Stockport in which Baker scored four times, followed by a seven-game unbeaten run in March which saw a second successive 19th-place finish. Throughout the season Moncur and Knowles used 44 players, of whom only McKinnon was ever present, with Allon, Dalton and Tinkler missing only a single game each.

In the media-driven atmosphere in which the game is played today it is often easy to forget that many triumphs are earned over a 46-game season and not in the first minute of the opening game. So it was with Hartlepool United's 1990–91 campaign, which began with a victory at Chesterfield only to be followed by a draw and four defeats, all goalless. Amazingly Joe Allon, who was to break goalscoring records throughout the season, did not register his first League goal until game seven, a narrow win over Aldershot. To add further distraction to the inconsistent League form, 'Pools reached the second round of the Football League Cup and drew Tottenham Hotspur, who included England World Cup heroes Gary Lineker and Paul Gascoigne in their ranks. Despite a five-goal defeat in the first leg at White Hart Lane, a capacity attendance turned out at the Vic to watch the stars. In the event only Gascoigne played (as a second-half substitute), and a sterling performance by United kept the scoreline to a respectable 2–1 defeat, with Paul Dalton scoring a superb individual goal.

October began with the League table showing a familiar story – Hartlepool United in 23rd position. Back-to-back wins over Aldershot and Maidstone relieved the pressure, and they finished the month in the top 10 following further victories over Peterborough and Hereford. November brought a narrow defeat at promotion-chasing Northampton before four successive League wins and an FA Cup success at Runcorn, with the prolific Allon scoring a hat-trick. The club received a boost of a more material kind with the transfer of Don Hutchison to Liverpool for a club record fee of £175,000, which was particularly welcome as attendances still barely rose above the 2,000 mark. The New Year brought four wins in six games before form stumbled in February with only a single success before events took a dramatic turn for the worse.

Following the mid-week defeat at Scunthorpe, Cyril Knowles complained of suffering from headaches and double vision. He was admitted to hospital on the morning of the home game against Torquay United and never took charge of a Hartlepool United game again. The club's chief executive Alan Murray immediately took over the managerial duties. A draw against Torquay was followed by defeat at Lincoln and at this stage anything could have happened to the season.

In the event a team that included Rob McKinnon, John MacPhail, Brian Honour, Joe Allon, Paul Baker and Paul Dalton rose to the occasion and embarked on a run which saw 11 of the final 16 games of the season won, with 31 goals scored, as 'Pools stormed to an automatic promotion place. Allon was magnificent, scoring 35 goals overall, ably supported by Baker and Dalton with all three players ever present throughout the League campaign. The final game at home to Northampton Town attracted a near 7,000 gate as the Hartlepool public finally gave the team the support they deserved. On a day of high drama, with five clubs contesting three promotion places, United gave their fans something to cheer about by storming to victory with goals from Dalton, Allon and Baker to finish third a single point behind the champions, Darlington.

The jubilation of promotion was tempered by the sad news of Cyril Knowles's untimely death in August 1991 shortly after the start of the new season. Chairman Gary Gibson had appointed Alan Murray as manager on a permanent basis following the promotion success, and his first priority during the summer was to replace the ebullient Joe Allon, who had joined Chelsea in a reported £300,000 deal.

The promotion to Division Three gave both Gibson and Murray problems previously not faced by their many predecessors. This was to be the final season of the old Football League structure of four divisions, with the FA Premier League, sponsored by Sky Sports television, scheduled for its debut in the 1992–93 season. Already, several clubs in the Third Division with ambitious chairmen recognised the potential of the new Premier League and were making plans to gain promotions to the new top tier of English football, among them Reading, Birmingham City, Wigan Athletic, Fulham and Bolton Wanderers. This was the quality of opposition that faced Hartlepool United at the start of the 1991–92 campaign. With Joe Allon the only major departure from the promotion-winning side, Alan Murray

1991 promotion celebrations.

decided to open the season with virtually the same team apart from goalkeeper Martin Hodge, who was acquired from Leicester City.

After an opening-day loss at Torquay, the first home game in front of a meagre 2,858 spectators saw United turn on the style in a 2–0 victory over Reading. Results in the first half of the season exceeded all expectations with notable wins over Birmingham, Wigan and Fulham during an eight-game unbeaten run. To cap it all 'Pools had Cup runs in both competitions, which only ended in replay defeats to Crystal Palace and Ipswich Town. Despite the positive results and quality of the opposition, average League attendances by the New Year were a mere 3,624, with the chairman understandably perplexed as to what else was required to attract more support.

Matters were not helped when the hugely popular Rob McKinnon returned to his native Scotland with Motherwell for a six-figure fee. Chairman Gibson responded by signing Lenny Johnrose from Blackburn Rovers and, in March, Andy Saville from Barnsley for a club record fee. He must have felt that fate was against him, however, when Saville was injured on his debut against Darlington and played no further part for the rest of the season. Perhaps understandably, results fell away in the second half of the season, although a final position of 11th was highly satisfactory in the circumstances. Special mention must be made of midfielder Paul Olsson, who played in all 58 League and Cup games, setting a shining example for commitment and consistency.

Thanks to the shenanigans of the marketing men Hartlepool United were 'promoted' to Division Two of the Football League for the 1992–93 season. Despite the departure of several key members of the promotion-winning side, they began magnificently, losing only once in their opening 11 League games to occupy second place in the table. Despite a dip in form, they still occupied a top-four place when Premiership Crystal Palace visited Victoria Park for a third-round FA Cup tie on the first Saturday of January.

'Pools had qualified for the plum tie following victories over Doncaster and Southport and for the first time at the Vic the BBC's *Match of the Day* cameras were present to record events. In front of a near-capacity crowd United excelled themselves by matching their illustrious opponents every step of the way. Stephen Jones in particular deserved praise for a string of superb saves that kept the Premership side's forwards at bay. As the game headed for a draw Nicky Southall was fouled in the penalty area and an ice cool Andy Saville converted the resulting penalty to record Hartlepool United's first victory over a side from the top tier of English football.

Andy Saville, record £60,000 signing, in 1992.

The Cup win was followed by two goalless draws before the fourth-round tie against Sheffield United. In front of over 20,000 fans at Bramall Lane, the players again raised their game against higher opposition before losing to an Alan Cork goal. For manager Alan Murray this was to be as good as it got, as his team then went 18 League games without a win, failing to score in a staggering 11 consecutive matches. Following a home defeat to Bournemouth in front of barely 2,000 spectators, he was sacked by chairman Gary Gibson and replaced by Viv Busby. At the time United were still in a comfortable mid-table position and the chairman's decision appeared premature. After briefly flirting with relegation, four wins in the closing games of the season ensured a comfortable 16th-place League position – still, this was a disappointment in a season that had begun so well.

The 1993–94 season was destined to be a struggle from the first game as Viv Busby attempted to fashion a team lacking the key players who had contributed to the success of recent campaigns. The departure of Andy Saville the previous March left the team without a natural goalscorer as well as a talismanic figure on the pitch. Despite the best efforts of Keith Houchen and Colin West, they only managed 13 League goals in a season destined for relegation long before the visit of Plymouth Argyle in the final game, which resulted in an 8–1 humiliation, Hartlepool United's record home defeat.

Viv Busby's tenure as manager was terminated by chairman Gibson with the League season only 17 games old and the club in turmoil on and off the pitch. Payment of players' wages had become a major issue as boardroom unrest resulted in two directors attempting to oust Gibson and take over the club. The move failed and resulted in nine players being placed on the transfer list as an economy measure! Busby's record of eight wins and 23 defeats in a 42-match spell tells only part of the story, and he left with several senior players praising his coaching methods.

Busby's replacement John MacPhail took over the hot seat in a player-manager capacity. Unable to strengthen the playing staff, MacPhail had little alternative than to work with the existing players. One change was in goal, where Tim Carter was dropped in favour of Steven Jones, who played in the remaining 28 games. MacPhail was to win only one of his first 19 games before a three-match winning run gave some respectability to his record – only for the record home defeat by Plymouth to effectively seal his fate.

One interesting event in the closing stages of the season was the attendance for the visit of Burnley of the future Prime Minister Tony Blair, accompanied by his press secretary Alistair Campbell and Peter Mandelson, MP for Hartlepool. Campbell, a lifelong Burnley supporter, must have been mortified, as the struggling home side turned on a champagne display for their distinguished visitor, winning 4–1.

## Cometh the Hour, Cometh the Man

At the beginning of August 1994 Gary Gibson sold his majority shareholding to local businessman Harold Hornsey, and an air of optimism prevailed among supporters that better days were just over the horizon. Hornsey immediately began a tour of the local working men's clubs to galvanise support for the club. In his early days as chairman he was

Harold Hornsey, chairman from 1994 to 1997.

personally required to support the club with £20,000 a week to maintain its existence pending the payment of monies due from the Football League.

MacPhail continued as player-manager for the start of the 1994–95 season, which saw barely 3,000 turn up for the first home game against local rivals Darlington. 'Pools won a poor game through a Chris Lynch goal, only for the next three games, all goalless, to be lost. Despite the chairman's best efforts to promote the club, attendances had already slumped to barely 2,000 and the axe inevitably fell on the manager. It later emerged that MacPhail had been dismissed for a breach of contract regarding his continuing relationship with Gary Gibson, although he was allowed to remain in a playing capacity.

Harold Hornsey took his time finding a successor and in the interim appointed Billy Horner as caretaker manager, a situation that lasted for five games throughout September. At the end of the month Hornsey announced that David McCreery was to return in a player-manager role. Initially the change appeared to work, particularly as Keith Houchen rediscovered his goalscoring form before a 12-game League run without a win, coupled with a six-goal humiliation at Port Vale in the FA Cup, saw United flirting with relegation. A late rally was not enough to save McCreery's job, and he was replaced by Houchen with three games of the season remaining. In the final analysis a League position of 18th could have been much worse, and the new chairman was left to reflect that much work, both on and off the field, was still to be done.

Despite the problems on the pitch, a major event took place in July 1995 with the opening of the new Clarence Road stand, which cost £650,000 and was named in honour of former manager, the late Cyril Knowles. If the chairman thought the improved facility would attract support back to the newly renamed Victoria Park he was mistaken, however, as attendances barely reached the 2,000 mark for the opening games of the season. One bright spot was the first-round Football League Cup victory over Scarborough, which saw United win their first-ever penalty shoot-out after the two-legged tie finished 1–1. Their reward was a tie against Arsenal for the second year in succession, which attracted a near 5,000 crowd.

League results, however, continued to be a concern, despite the form of Steven Howard, who was signed from Tow Law. In October former fans' favourite Joe Allon returned to the scene of his previous triumphs, signing from Lincoln City for a £50,000 transfer fee. Allon's return coincided unfortunately with an eight-game winless run and a home defeat to Darlington in the first round of the FA Cup competition. Results improved in the second half of the season despite the lack of goals; 17 League games were scoreless, an alarming statistic for a side that included Keith Houchen, Joe Allon, Steve Halliday, Paul Conlon and a young Steven Howard in its ranks. After major investments in both the playing staff and facilities, chairman Hornsey was entitled to expect better than a 20th-place League finish and average crowds of barely 2,000.

The 1996–97 campaign began on a positive note with two wins, before mixed results in September were the prelude to a run of seven defeats and a draw followed by an FA Cup exit to York City, resulting in the inevitable departure of Keith Houchen. The final straw was the home defeat by bottom club Brighton which left 'Pools in 23rd position. Harold Hornsey acted quickly in naming the veteran Mick Tait as manager and saw an immediate improvement in results, with four of the next six games won, resulting in a welcome move up the table.

This proved to be another false dawn, however, as a nine-game winless run in the New Year brought the club to the brink of relegation. Hornsey had no alternative but to sanction an influx of new faces if his club was to remain in the Football League. The final day for transfers, 27 March, saw almost unprecedented transfer activity as Mick Tait signed no fewer than five players. Darren Knowles and Richard Lucas joined from Scarborough, Jon Cullen from non-League Morpeth Town, former favourite Paul Baker from Scunthorpe and local boy Michael Brown on loan from Manchester City.

All five started the League game two days later against Colchester United, a 1–0 win, the first victory in nine games. Three wins and a draw in the remaining six fixtures guaranteed the club's League safety, with the highlight being a 2–1 win at Darlington courtesy of goals from Michael Brown and Joe Allon. Despite the understandable relief at preserving their League status, 'Pools had finished a lowly 20th for a second successive season, and doubts were beginning to surface about whether chairman Hornsey had the resources to move the club forward.

## Towards the New Millennium

The start of the 1997–98 season was notable for two events. Firstly, 'Pools lost only one of their opening nine League games and, secondly, at the end of September Harold Hornsey sold his majority shareholding to Increased Oil Recovery Ltd (IOR), an Aberdeen-based business owned by Norwegian millionaire Berge Larsen. Hornsey issued a statement emphasising the new owner's long-term commitment and agreeing to work alongside the IOR director Ken Hodcroft to provide continuity. In their first game under IOR ownership, United continued their good form by beating Shrewsbury Town 2–1 at home with goals by Denny Ingram and Jon Cullen, watched by a crowd of 2,253. The rollercoaster ride which was to change the club, both in terms of public perception and playing achievement, had begun.

Following IOR's acquisition of the club, steady progress was made to enter the New Year in sixth position. A major influence on the improvement in results was Norwegian international Jan-Ove Pedersen who, despite scoring only once in 17 League appearances, created numerous chances for others. His departure coincided with a slump in form, with only three of the remaining 19 League games won and a consequent decline in attendances to below the 2,000 mark. In the final analysis a League position of 17th was scant reward for a promising start, with defender Darren Knowles ever present.

Hopes were high that the new owners would make an impact for the 1998–99 campaign when three of the opening four League games were won. The away fixture at Halifax on 4 September saw Hartlepool United make their debut in a live televised game on Sky Sports. Unfortunately the match was marred by crowd trouble among both sets of supporters and resulted in a 2–1 defeat for the visitors with Chris Beech scoring 'Pools' first-ever live televised goal. This defeat was the prelude to a poor run of results which saw only four further League wins by the New Year and a place in the dreaded relegation zone. Chairman Hodcroft's response was to back the signing of north-east footballing legend Peter Beardsley for the remainder of the season, proof positive that IOR were prepared to invest in the team. While Beardsley's presence gave everyone a lift, results did not improve, resulting in the dismissal of Mick Tait and the appointment in a caretaker capacity of Paul Baker and Brian Honour as joint managers. Despite initial success against Rochdale and Halifax, the popular pair were passed over for the permanent job when Chris Turner was appointed manager on 24 February with 'Pools in 22nd position in Division Three.

The arrival of Chris Turner coincided with further team strengthening, which saw the return of Rob McKinnon on loan and signings Gary Strodder, Chris Freestone, Gary Jones and Chris Westwood, who was to have such an impact in future seasons. The greatly strengthened team, rock bottom at the start of April, won four and drew two of their final eight games to finish 22nd and avoid relegation to the Conference. The manner of the 'great escape' left no one in any doubt that the people now in charge of Hartlepool United were setting their sights higher than relegation campaigns.

## Play-offs and Promotions

The 1999–2000 season, with the new millennium on the horizon, was hailed by the local press as the start of a new era for the club. This was greeted with familiar scepticism by long-suffering supporters, and early results reflected this as only one of the opening seven League games was won. Chris Turner steadily moulded the team towards his style of play, introducing Martin Hollund, Chris Westwood, Sam Shilton and Colin West into a side that already included Darren Knowles, Mickey Barron, Graeme Lee, Tommy Miller and Paul Stephenson.

Twelve League games were won by the New Year, moving 'Pools into the previous uncharted territory of the Play-off places, five points behind leaders Rotherham United. A mini-slump in February saw a drop to eighth place before a strong run-in restored the Play-off place with a final League position of seventh. Paul Stephenson was ever present and Tommy Miller top-scored with 14 goals.

Fate decreed that Hartlepool United were to play their first-ever Play-offs against neighbours Darlington, with the first leg at the Vic. After seasons of underachievement the prospect of a Wembley Play-off Final was the stuff of dreams for supporters. Unfortunately, the occasion seemed to affect the players, and a near-capacity crowd saw the visitors record a 2–0 victory, with their second goal coming from a Gabbiadini penalty after Martin Hollund was sent off for a professional foul on Glen Naylor. The return at Feethams was televised live at Victoria Park, with a crowd of several thousand witnessing a narrow 1–0 victory for the Quakers. So 'Pools' first-ever taste of the Play-offs ended in disappointment, and the question on all supporters' lips was 'is this a one-off?'

Hopes were high that the 2000–01 campaign would go one better than a Play-off place and result in a long-awaited promotion. Early results, however, mirrored the previous season, with only two League wins in the opening nine games as Chris Turner introduced Anthony Williams, Paul Arnison and Mark Tinkler to his side. An unbeaten 21-game run took the team into the Play-off places a mere three points behind third-placed Cardiff City. Three successive defeats ended hopes of automatic promotion, followed by a strong finish in fourth position, earning a Play-off tie against seventh-placed Blackpool and the added pressure of being favourites for the Final.

As ever in football, things are never that simple and a highly motivated Blackpool side, inspired by a Brett Ormerod brace, won the home leg 2–0. This gave 'Pools a mountain to climb in the return, and Ormerod again scored twice in Blackpool's resounding 3–1 triumph. Despite the disappointment of a second Play-off failure, United could look back on the season with satisfaction, particular highlights being Chris Westwood and Tommy Miller who were ever-presents, with the latter contributing 16 League goals, a total only bettered by Kevin Henderson.

Hartlepool United appeared better placed for the start of the 2001–02 season than in living memory. The stable management team of Chris Turner and Colin West were in charge of a playing squad which included Mickey Barron, Graeme Lee, Chris Westwood, Mark Tinkler, Kevin Henderson, Paul Stephenson, Anthony Williams and a young Adam Boyd. The question was who would replace Tommy Miller, transferred in the close season to Ipswich Town for a club record £750,000, as the midfield playmaker? The answer came from Cambridge United in the form of Richie Humphreys on a free transfer. Humphreys, a former England Under-21 international, had started his career with his home-town club Sheffield Wednesday. Despite his undoubted footballing ability he only managed to start 55 games in six seasons, which included loan spells at Scunthorpe and Cardiff. If anyone had any doubts about his commitment to the cause of Hartlepool United they were to be proved very much mistaken over the coming seasons.

The campaign began as a reprise of the previous two seasons with only a single win in the opening nine League games. Towards the end of this run Chris Turner pulled another master stroke in the transfer market when he persuaded the vastly experienced Gordon Watson to join and add much needed firepower to the attack. Results improved in the New Year and, following a 5–1 demolition of Southend, 'Pools entered the top 10 a mere four points from a Play-off position. The season ended on a high with six wins in the last seven games, which included a 7–1 rout of a demoralised Swansea side and a final position of seventh, making a hat-trick of Play-off campaigns.

Pools' opponents in their third successive Play-off tie were Cheltenham Town, who had also finished the season strongly and only missed automatic promotion by a point. Over

Swansea 7–1 scorers Darryl Clarke, Adam Boyd, Kevin Henderson, Eifion Williams, Gordon Watson.

7,000 packed Victoria Park for the first leg, which saw the home side dominate the first half and lead through an Eifion Williams goal on the stroke of half-time. Cheltenham defended stoutly for most of the second period and were rewarded with an equaliser in the closing minutes. The second leg at Whaddon Road again saw United dominate proceedings and take a first-half lead through Paul Arnison. Cheltenham equalised within minutes to conclude the scoring, and the tie remained deadlocked after extra-time. The penalty shoot-out was a tense affair, with Paul Stephenson missing the second kick and Cheltenham taking a 3–1 lead. Duff missed for the home side before Watson and Henderson levelled at 4–4, only for Richie Humphreys to miss the fifth kick and hand victory to Cheltenham 5–4.

Three successive seasons resulting in the Play-offs had totally transformed the public perception of Hartlepool United with a consequent increase in support both at Victoria Park and within the local and national media. It was with understandable optimism that supporters welcomed the start of the 2002–03 campaign, which unlike the previous terms started with a bang as 'Pools won six of the opening nine League fixtures with only a single defeat. This run, which included a 4–1 demolition of Darlington in front of over 6,000 fans, took United to the top of the League, three points clear of Rochdale.

Despite the loss of Gordon Watson through injury following the Darlington game, no team seemed capable of stopping the 'Pools juggernaut as Eifion Williams took over the role of top scorer, with solid contributions also coming from Mark Tinkler and Richie Humphreys. A run of six wins in seven games through October and November consolidated the position at the top before the inevitable happened.

It was apparent to everyone that the progress the club was making under Chris Turner's management would attract attention from clubs with a higher profile, and so it turned out

Hartlepool Mayor Stuart Drummond with his alter ego H'angus the club mascot, 2002.

when Sheffield Wednesday made their former player the proverbial 'offer too good to refuse'. Turner left Victoria Park with the best wishes of all concerned, and attention quickly turned to his successor. Chairman Ken Hodcroft, refusing to make a panic appointment, initially placed Turner's assistant Colin West in charge on a caretaker basis. West was in charge for two games, a win and a draw, before the surprise announcement that Mike Newell, previously reserve-team coach at Tranmere Rovers, was to be appointed manager until the end of the season. West left soon afterwards to rejoin Chris Turner at Hillsborough.

Newell took over a team that was four points clear at the top Division Three. If supporters thought the new management would result in a change of League fortunes they were mistaken, as 'Pools went on an 11-match unbeaten run in the New Year to lengthen their lead over Rushden & Diamonds to 12 points. It appeared nothing could stop their march to the title other than a run of eight games which only produced a single victory. By this stage the lead was down to a single point with five games remaining. A convincing home win over Leyton Orient was followed by a four-goal drubbing at Scunthorpe with a win and a draw in the final home games of the season. This left United requiring a win in the final game at, of all places, Rushden & Diamonds, to claim their first-ever title. In a tense atmosphere Rushden took a first-half lead, and it was not until the 90th minute that Chris Westwood levelled the scores, which was enough for the hosts to claim the title.

Despite finishing runners-up, and thereby gaining automatic promotion, Hartlepool United could look back on the season with much pride. The departure of Chris Turner did not upset the team, which continued its winning ways until the final stages, with Anthony Williams, Chris Westwood and Richie Humphreys ever-presents and Eifion Williams top-scoring with 15 goals. Average attendances of nearly 5,000 were the highest for 35 years and well up on the previous season. A surprising postscript to the campaign was the departure of Mike Newell who, for unspecified reasons, did not have his contract renewed by chairman Ken Hodcroft.

The chairman surprised everyone at the beginning of June with his choice of Neale Cooper as Newell's successor. Cooper had previous management experience with Forfar Athletic and Ross County and faced an immediate problem with the departure of Graeme Lee to Chris Turner's Sheffield Wednesday on a free transfer. Lee's replacement Michael Nelson came from Bury and proved to be a hugely popular signing with the supporters, allowing the team to continue to function at a high level of performance.

The 2003–04 Division Two campaign started with a surprise victory at Peterborough followed by a run of eight games with only one defeat, which included an 8–1 demolition of Grimsby Town. By Christmas United were comfortably placed in 10th position, a mere two points off a Play-off place. The FA Cup added to the season by producing a glamour draw against Sunderland at the Stadium of Light in the third round after wins over non-League Whitby Town and Burton Albion. The second-round tie was broadcast live by the BBC, no doubt due to the presence of Nigel Clough, son of Brian, as Burton manager. The game was watched by his father, Hartlepool United's most celebrated manager, and he must have had mixed feelings about the visitors' narrow win courtesy of a Joel Porter goal. Declining interviews, Brian Clough left the ground quietly after what was to be one of his last public appearances.

The third-round tie at Sunderland attracted a crowd of over 40,000, the highest attendance for a Hartlepool United game at that time, to witness the hosts struggle to overcome a determined and well-organised 'Pools side who only succumbed to a fine piece of individual skill from Julio Arca in the second half. A return to League action saw a strengthening of results with a sequence of five successive wins in April setting up a tense end to the campaign. In the final analysis a sixth-place finish and a Play-off place was just reward for a memorable season in which Ritchie Humphreys was again ever present and Eifion Williams retained the top-scorer position, with strong support coming from a developing Adam Boyd.

United's opponents in the Play-offs were Bristol City, who were managed by Danny Wilson. A near-capacity crowd filled the Vic for the first leg under the spotlight of the Sky Sports cameras. City scored in their first attack and set their stall out to defend the lead. They succeeded until late in the game when Joel Porter equalised from Adam Boyd's pass. The return at Ashton Gate was also televised by Sky and was watched by an 18,000-plus crowd. They witnessed a classic encounter between two well-matched sides. After a goalless first half, Tony Sweeney gave 'Pools the lead on the hour mark with a brilliant goal. With every player in blue and white giving his all to the cause, they held the lead until two minutes from time when Goodfellow equalised for City. To make matters worse, Roberts added a second in injury time to give the hosts a victory they scarcely deserved. So United lost their fourth Play-off semi-final in five years, and a feeling prevailed among supporters that the club was destined never to reach a Final. So to the 2004–05 season…

Neale Cooper placed the emphasis firmly on attack for his second season in charge. A stable defence with Jim Provett in goal, later replaced by Dimi Konstantopoulos; Mickey Barron, Matty Robson and Hugh Robertson sharing the full-back berths; ultra-reliable central-defenders Mickey Nelson and Chris Westwood; a midfield containing Mark Tinkler, Tony Sweeney, Ritchie Humphreys and Gavin Strachan; and the goalscoring potential of Eifion Williams, Joel Porter and Adam Boyd, added up to one of Hartlepool United's strongest-ever squads.

'Pools fans.

Adam Boyd scores v Sheffield Wednesday, April 2005.

A steady start based on home wins and away defeats saw United in ninth place at the end of November, a mere point off a Play-off place. A run of 11 games with only a single defeat improved the League position to fifth by the end of February. The winning streak was rudely interrupted in March with four consecutive defeats, which included a 6–4 home loss to struggling Wrexham for whom Juan Ugarte scored five, a record for a visiting player. Despite winning only two of their remaining nine fixtures, 'Pools held on to finish sixth, a single point above Bristol City, and earn a Play-off place in League One for the first time. After the penultimate League fixture the club made the dramatic announcement that Neale Cooper had left his post as manager 'by mutual agreement' and that his assistant Martin Scott would be in charge of the team to the end of the season.

Martin Scott's first and only priority on taking over as manager was to prepare the side for the Play-off semi-final against third-placed Tranmere Rovers, with the first leg at

Victoria Park. His team used the home advantage to good effect, completely dominating the first half, and it was no surprise when an in-form Adam Boyd gave them the lead. Rovers rallied strongly after half-time, only to fall further behind when Boyd scored his second with a stunning shot from 20 yards. This result gave 'Pools their first Play-off victory at the ninth attempt.

The second leg at Prenton Park saw the home side completely dominate the first half without scoring. The turning point came after half-time when Mickey Barron went off injured and Tranmere scored within minutes of his departure. With Konstantopoulos in commanding form it appeared United would hold out, only for Beresford to bring Rovers level with only minutes remaining. Extra-time was an anti-climax as two tired teams played out the remaining minutes and prepared for the penalty shoot-out. Taylor missed Tranmere's first penalty, only for this to be cancelled out by Mark Tinkler with 'Pools' second effort. Both teams exchanged successful kicks until Tranmere's seventh penalty was saved by Konstantopoulos. In a frenzied atmosphere Ritchie Humphreys calmly stepped up to slot the ball home and send Hartlepool United into their first-ever Play-off Final.

Ritchie Humphreys coolly converts the winning penalty in the Play-off semi-final shootout against Tranmere.

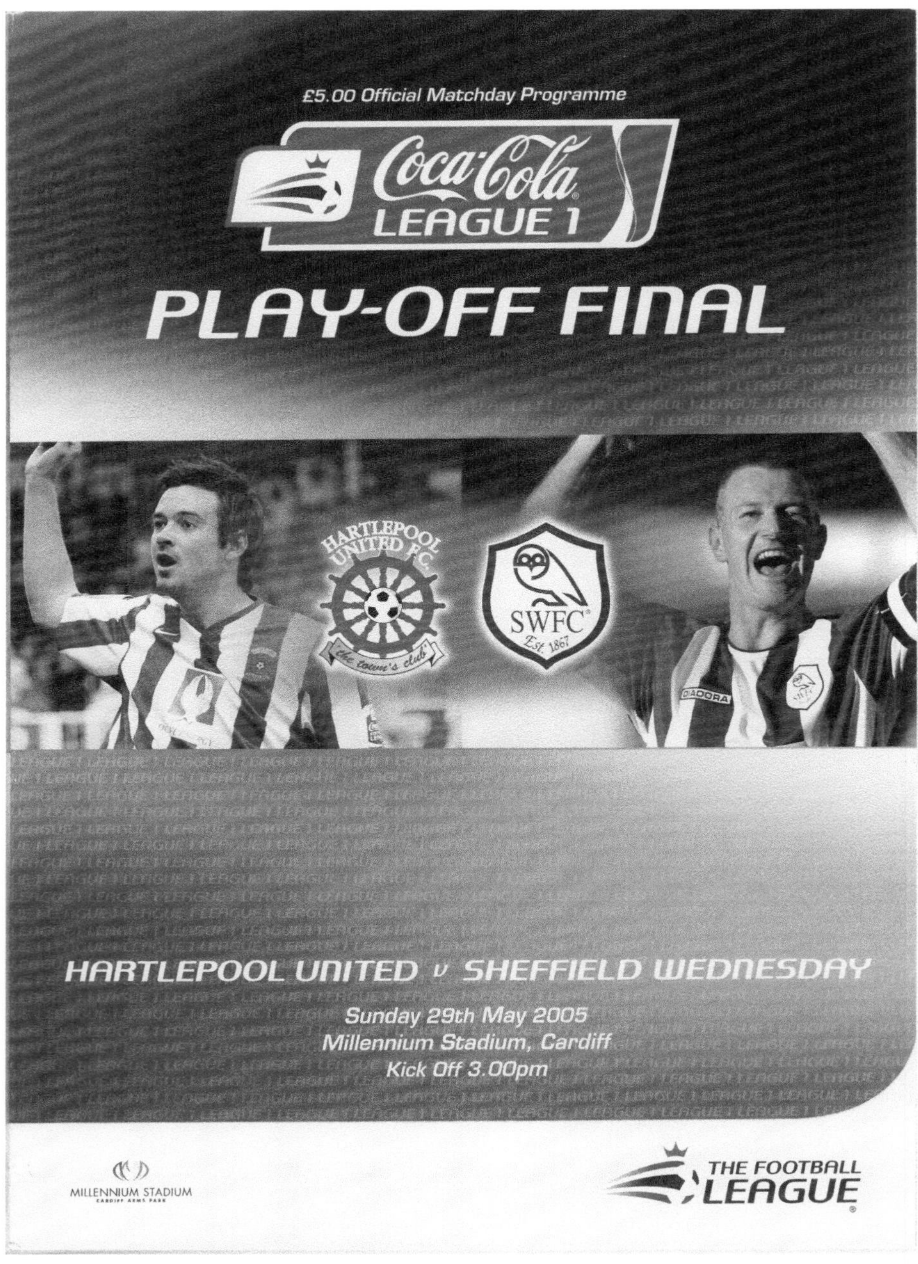


2005 Sheffield Wednesday Play-off Final programme.

The League One Final was played at the Millennium Stadium, Cardiff, against Sheffield Wednesday in front of 59,808 spectators, of which at least one third were supporting Hartlepool United. After Wednesday had taken the lead on the stroke of half-time, second-half goals from Williams and Daly gave United the advantage, which they never looked like losing. The game swung on a marginal decision, which not only gave Wednesday a penalty, but also resulted in the dismissal of Chris Westwood for a professional foul, as the referee Mr Crossley saw it. On a hot sunny May afternoon the burden of playing extra-time a man short was too much even for 'Pools and two late goals settled the game in Sheffield's favour, which gave the final scoreline a totally unrealistic look.

In the summer chairman Ken Hodcroft confirmed Martin Scott as manager and players and supporters looked forward with understandable optimism to the new campaign. One of the manager's first tasks was to return to his former club Sunderland and sign Ben Clark as replacement for Chris Westwood, who joined Walsall during the close season.

The 2005–06 season began with Mark Tinkler, Mickey Barron and Joel Porter on the injured list, and their collective absence was sorely missed in the early weeks of the season when only two of the opening 11 League games were won. Wins were cancelled out by losses through to the New Year with 'Pools in 16th position, a mere four points above the relegation zone. Things then went from bad to worse with a resounding 3–0 home defeat to Blackpool, which resulted in a drop into the bottom four. At the end of the game Martin Scott was allegedly involved in a fraças with some of his players, which carried on into the dressing room. There was understandable criticism from both supporters and the local press about results and the conduct of players and manager, which resulted in Scott being relieved of his position within a few days.

Paul Stephenson, Hartlepool United youth-team coach, agreed to manage the team through to the end of the season and give the chairman time to find a suitable manager. In order to strengthen the club's football management Chris Turner returned to Victoria Park in February 2006 as director of football with responsibility for pre-season planning, participation in tournaments and Football League issues. The chairman's statement stressed that his role would not entail responsibility for first-team affairs.

Stephenson was unable to prevent the inevitable relegation with only two wins in the final 14 League games, and along with the supporters he saw seven seasons of uninterrupted progress disappear in a matter of weeks. In such a climate it speaks volumes for the professionalism and commitment of Dimi Konstantopoulos and Ritchie Humphreys that they played in all 46 League games.

## Triumph and Tragedy

On 14 June 2006 the club announced that Danny Wilson had been appointed manager in succession to Martin Scott. Wilson, a Northern Ireland international, had previously managed Barnsley, Sheffield Wednesday, Bristol City and MK Dons, and the appointment was well received by supporters and public alike. Recognising that the team had underperformed in the previous campaign, the new manager relied on the squad of players he inherited for the 2006–07 season. When early results produced only one win in the opening seven League games alarm bells were ringing with 'Pools 19th in League

Two. The introduction of Gary Liddle and Willie Boland acted as the catalyst for a change in fortunes with four wins in five games. October passed without a victory, and a home defeat to Barnet saw 'Pools firmly entrenched in the lower half of the table in 16th position.

In an effort to kick-start the season, Danny Wilson signed Daryl Duffy and Andy Monkhouse, a striker and a winger, on loan. On 18 November 'Pools won a narrow 2–1 victory at Accrington, with goals from Eifion Williams and Ritchie Humphreys, to begin a record 23-game unbeaten run that did not end until 7 April at Barnet. A match at Accrington was the start of nine successive wins and was the only game in that sequence in which a goal was conceded. Unable to extend Daryl Duffy's loan spell, Wilson signed the vastly experienced Richie Barker from Mansfield for a club record £100,000 transfer fee to maintain the momentum.

By the New Year, United had moved into the top six and had leaders Walsall firmly in their sights, attaining pole position on 20 February with a 3–2 win over Macclesfield Town at the Vic, and they consolidated their position in the coming games. By the time of the Barnet fixture they were eight points clear of second-placed Walsall with six games to go. Wins over Accrington and Wycombe, the latter confirming promotion, consolidated 'Pools' position at the top before a draw and a loss against Notts County and Rochdale left them requiring victory over Bristol Rovers to clinch the League Two Championship.

With a capacity home crowd behind them all seemed well when Joel Porter scored on the half-hour mark after sustained pressure. The second half was a different story as Rovers equalised with a penalty and pressed for a winner to claim a Play-off place. Five minutes from time Lambert scored the goal that broke the hearts of everyone concerned and meant they had to settle for runners'-up medals. It was a testimony to the progress made by the club over the past several years that finishing second and claiming promotion was viewed as a failure in the eyes of many supporters.

Danny Wilson spent the close season reshaping his squad of players following several high-profile departures, the most significant of which was that of Dimi Konstantopoulos, a free agent, who signed for Coventry City. Eifion Williams, Darrell Clarke, Darren Williams and Mark Tinkler were released and Mickey Barron was appointed reserve-team coach.

To address the balance, Jan Budtz and Aaran Lee-Barratt joined to fill the goalkeeping positions, along with highly rated Scottish Under-21 defender, Jamie McCunnie. Godwin Antwi-Birago, a central-defender, arrived on a season's loan from Liverpool, and experienced players Ian Moore and Robbie Elliott both joined from Leeds United. This influx saw seven players make their Hartlepool League debuts in the opening League One fixture at Luton, a disappointing 2–1 loss. Four wins in the next seven games included a single defeat at Leeds in front of 26,877 spectators. At this point 'Pools were fourth in the table, and when the next away game saw a resounding 4–2 win at high-flying Leyton Orient hopes were high of a promotion campaign.

As so often happens, sport can mirror life with its triumphs and tragedies. On 19 October a Hartlepool United player, 20-year-old Michael Maidens, was enjoying an

Michael Maidens.

evening with his friends when the car he was travelling in was involved in an accident on a Teesside road, which resulted in his death. This had a devastating effect, not only on his family and close friends, but also on his club and teammates. The Football League immediately agreed to the cancellation of the away fixture at Swansea and the following days saw a huge tide of public sympathy for the young player and his family.

The tragic death of Michael Maidens had an understandable impact on performances on the pitch, with only one of the next six League games won. Successive home wins against Tranmere and Crewe brought some relief before a six-game winless streak brought United within four points of a relegation place. The major problem was away from the Vic, with nine defeats already recorded in a season barely past the halfway stage. One highlight was the visit of the Sky Sports cameras for the home game against Bournemouth, which unfortunately turned out to be a disappointment as the sides played out a tame draw.

Danny Wilson's response was to sign Alan Thompson, a former England international, from Leeds United on loan, release Ian Moore for 'personal reasons' and place Anthony Sweeney on the transfer list! His decisions seemed vindicated with a decisive 4–0 win over struggling Luton as the team embarked on a winning home run which saw 19 goals scored and mid-table respectability restored. Away form remained the problem, with a narrow win at Oldham at the beginning of March only 'Pools' fourth win in 18 attempts on the road.

Any outside chance the club had of finishing in a Play-off place effectively ended with a 3–1 home defeat to League leaders Swansea City. Despite the advantage of a Liddle goal in less than a minute, the visitors recovered to lead by half-time thanks to a marginal penalty award against Ben Clark. Despite their best efforts, 'Pools could not find an equaliser and Swansea added a third goal late in the game. This effectively marked the end of 'Pools' season, as the final fixtures were played in an atmosphere of uncertainty with several players out of contract at the end of the season. Ritchie Humphreys, as ever, was a consistent performer, only missing a single League game, a total matched by the rock of the defence, Michael Nelson. Humphreys's service was recognised by supporters with his third Player of the Year award and the ultimate accolade of Player of the Century when he came top in a poll featuring prominent players from the club's history.

Manager Wilson's retained list contained no surprises, with Robbie Elliott, Ali Gibb, Michael Rae and Stephen Turnbull released and Godwin Antwi-Birago returning to Liverpool after his season-long loan deal.

The 2008–09 campaign began with a stunning 4–2 victory over Colchester United, with James Brown in impressive form, scoring twice. An even more impressive result quickly followed, with a three-goal demolition of Championship side Scunthorpe United in the Carling Cup. The next two League games were lost before 'Pools surprised everybody in their second-round Carling Cup tie by beating Premiership West Bromwich Albion 3–1 after extra-time, only their second-ever victory over a side from the top flight. League form remained inconsistent, however, and the Carling Cup adventure ended honourably at Leeds in a narrow defeat.

At the beginning of October, Danny Wilson pulled off a major transfer coup by signing Kevin Kyle from Coventry on a month's loan deal. Kyle, a strong, physical centre-forward, had cost the Light Blues £600,000 when he moved from Sunderland. His presence made an immediate impact, and four consecutive wins took 'Pools up to ninth in the table, two points off the top six. This proved to be a false dawn as only two of the next 18 League games were won and James Brown suffered a serious injury which kept him sidelined for the rest of the season.

During this spell Hartlepool United parted company with their manager, Danny Wilson. Chris Turner, director of sport, immediately took over responsibility for the day-to-day management of the players and team affairs. Only days before the departure of Danny Wilson, Hartlepool United chairman Ken Hodcroft reported a loss of £1.6 million for the previous season at the club's Annual General Meeting, drawing attention to the decline in attendances for the current season of nearly 1,000 on average. He concluded his statement by adding that talks with Hartlepool Borough Council on the acquisition of Victoria Park were progressing 'slowly but surely'.

Despite the inconsistent League form and financial problems, Hartlepool United embarked on an FA Cup run that surpassed the expectations of even the most optimistic of supporters. After a narrow first-round victory over Brighton in a replay, United travelled to the Fylde coast to earn a place in the third round with a hard-fought 3–2 victory after the hosts had led in the opening period. 'Pools had their prayers answered when they were paired at home to Premiership Stoke City, a strong, physical team with a direct approach to the game. Despite their obvious physical advantages, the visitors, who began the game with several reserves, were matched every step of the way and the only surprise was that it took until the 49th minute for Micky Nelson to open the scoring. The Stoke manager Tony Pulis quickly introduced experienced substitutes following this reverse, but it made little difference and David Foley's spectacular strike was the icing on the cake for the home supporters.

The draw for the fourth round was again kind to Hartlepool as for the first time in their history they played successive home ties against sides from the top tier. This time West Ham United were the visitors for the first-ever fixture between the two clubs. Such was the interest in the tie that not only a near 7,000 crowd, but also a national television audience, saw an accomplished West Ham take control at the end of the first half with two goals, one a highly dubious penalty award. Despite 'Pools' best efforts in the second period, they were unable to reduce the deficit and the Hammers emerged worthy winners.

With the culmination of the Cup run, Chris Turner's attention turned to the League and survival in the third flight of English football. Liam Henderson, Daniel Nardiello and

Rune Lange were loan signings designed to add more firepower to an attack that had become over-reliant on Joel Porter. Some gloss was taken off the arrival of the new recruits when Porter announced that he would be returning to his native Australia at the end of the season to play for Gold Coast United.

United were finding wins hard to come by, and it took a surprise win at Swindon Town, courtesy of a late Ben Clark penalty, to break the sequence. Ironically, Swindon were now managed by Danny Wilson, himself in the middle of a battle for League One survival. After the Swindon success 'Pools managed a mere three wins from their final 13 games and only survived courtesy of a surprise 3–2 victory at Yeovil thanks to a Joel Porter brace, his final goals for the club, and a stunning Nardiello header. With several players out of contract at the end of a frustrating season, it was apparent that new faces would be introduced before the next campaign.

Within days of the season's end, Hartlepool United announced the signing of former favourite Adam Boyd on a free transfer from Leyton Orient. The popular Joel Porter, whom Boyd replaced, was rightly named Player of the Season in time for him to receive the award prior to his return to Australia.

## The Return of an Old Favourite and an Influx of New Faces

Chris Turner wasted no time in adding to his playing squad following the acquisition of Adam Boyd. Leon McSweeney, Peter Hartley, Neil Austin, Scott Flinders, Jon Andre Fredriksen, Denis Behan, Steve Haslam and Colin Larkin all arrived before the opening fixture at Milton Keynes Dons which saw six players make their Hartlepool debuts. A creditable goalless draw was followed by two home defeats before a welcome win at Gillingham saw Turner's team pick up three points at the fourth attempt. Further wins at Oldham and Swindon were cancelled out by poor home form which saw only two of the opening seven fixtures won.

The mixed start had a major impact on attendances with just over 3,000 witnessing a goalless draw against Brentford in early October. Worse followed in the FA Cup when non-League Kettering Town, managed by former Hartlepool player Mark Cooper, deservedly won 1–0 in front of a mere 2,645 crowd. Two wins in the next eight games saw attendances slump to a nine year low for the visit of Yeovil Town and the gap between the 'haves and have nots' of League One was clearly demonstrated on Boxing Day at Leeds when 30,191 saw the home side win 3–1 after 'Pools had taken an early lead through Armann Bjornsson, another new signing. This attendance was the second highest for a Football League featuring Hartlepool United.

The New Year brought little respite for Chris Turner as MK Dons strolled to a 5–0 victory at 'The Vic' with former player Jermaine Easter scoring and tormenting the defence all afternoon. This result proved a watershed for many supporters and criticism of the management became both vocal and written with a steady stream of letters featuring in the local press. With attendances the lowest in League One and his team threatened with relegation Chris Turner's response was to bring in Joe Gamble, a midfield player from Cork City, and Roy O'Donovan, a centre-forward from Sunderland.

A spirited two-all draw against high-flying Leeds was followed by convincing home wins over Carlisle and Southend, with O'Donovan scoring a hat-trick, to settle the nerves of supporters. Further wins over Leyton Orient and Brighton appeared to have banished the relegation threat only for it to emerge that United had fielded an ineligible player in the latter game, namely Gary Liddle.

It emerged following the Brighton game that Liddle had received his 10th booking of the season at Orient and should have served an immediate two match ban. Despite protests from the manager that notification was not received until the day after the Brighton match the Football League ruled that the club and player were guilty and deducted three points as well as fining Gary Liddle. This put the club in real danger of relegation and it is to the credit of Chris Turner and his players that they lost only once in their last five games, gaining a point in a goalless draw at Brentford to avoid the dreaded drop by virtue of a superior goal difference to Gillingham, the second successive season Hartlepool United have narrowly avoided relegation.

Chris Turner's 'retained list' contained surprises in the release of the stalwart Ben Clark and Ritchie Jones, an energetic albeit inconsistent midfield player, as well as releasing several fringe players. He offered contract extensions to fans favourite Ritchie Humphreys along with James Brown, Sam Collins, Tony Sweeney and promising teenager Billy Gruelich. It remained to be seen how the playing squad would fare in the coming season in an increasingly competitive League One given the current level of home support – the lowest in the division.

Before training began for the 2010–11 season Chris Turner pulled a surprise by sacking Colin West as reserve team manager, effectively his assistant for almost three years. Within days the highly experienced Mick Wadsworth was appointed as first team coach in place of West. After several players were trialled in preseason friendlies Turner offered contracts to Evan Horwood, Fabian Yantorno and Paul Murray, the latter a 33-year-old midfield player on an initial monthly contract. The season began in promising fashion with a point at Rochdale in a goalless draw before 'Pools upset the form book by convincingly beating Sheffield United of the Championship in the first round of the Football League Cup. A 2–2 draw followed against Swindon Town before yet another bombshell was dropped by chairman Ken Hodcroft – the departure of Chris Turner.

The club announced via its website that Chris Turner had resigned his job as Director of Sport with immediate effect. In a terse statement reference was made to the 12 players recruited over the past year and the three point deduction which nearly saw the club relegated. No mention of past achievements and thanks for service was made. The statement went on to confirm that Mick Wadsworth, newly appointed coach, would act as temporary manager for the impending visit to Yeovil.

A number of factors undoubtedly contributed to Chris Turner's downfall in particular the signing of a number of players on two year contracts, reputedly on the highest wages in 'Pools history, who simply failed to make their mark. The 'Liddlegate affair' which saw a three point deduction, as well as a £15,000 fine, brought the club to within a hairsbreadth of relegation and merely tarnished Turner's reputation further. The appointment of the vastly experienced Mick Wadsworth as coach for the new season merely added to the speculation that Turner's days were numbered despite an unbeaten start to the season.

In a later statement chairman Ken Hodcroft also announced that Russ Green had resigned his post as chief executive with immediate effect. In contrast to the Chris Turner announcement the chairman praised Green for his eight years of service and wished him well for the future.

Mick Wadsworth's tenure in charge started on a positive note with a convincing 2–0 win at Yeovil before reality set in with a vengeance. A three-goal defeat in the League Cup at home to Premiership Wigan could be excused only for worse to quickly follow with a 0–5 defeat at Victoria Park to promotion favourites Sheffield Wednesday. A four game winless run was ended with a narrow win against Walsall before Carlisle inflicted another humiliating home defeat, this time by a four goal margin. Wadsworth's response was to drop Adam Boyd and Denis Behan, replacing them with Colin Larkin and James Brown. The changes had the desired effect as only two games were lost in a 14 match run through to the New Year which saw 'Pools rise to within three points of a Play-off place with two games in hand.

During this spell 'Pools suffered the indignity of staging possibly the shortest game in Football League history when the fixture against Leyton Orient was abandoned after only two minutes 50 seconds of play due to adverse weather conditions. The referee, Carl Boyeson, decided to start with a pitch already saturated and heavy rain falling with no prospect of respite. Within minutes of the abandonment the club announced that ticket stubs would remain valid for the rearranged game and supporters unable to attend would receive a full refund, a small consolation to the hardy souls who turned out on such a dreadful night.

Despite the improvement in League form 'Pools made heavy weather of non-League Vauxhall Motors in the first round of the FA Cup. After a goalless draw at The Vic, notable only for Ritchie Humphrey's first ever dismissal, a James Brown goal in the replay was sufficient to earn a second round tie at home to Yeovil Town. After a postponement due to the continuing wintry weather the tie took place in front of 'Pools lowest FA Cup gate since joining the Football League in 1921, a mere 1,914 which included 42 dedicated away fans. Despite the lowly attendance both teams played their part in an entertaining game which saw 'Pools win 4–2 with Tony Sweeney scoring a hat-trick. This spell of relative success was enough to earn Mick Wadsworth the December League One Manager of the Month award with the consistent Sam Collins named Player of the Month.

The adage that monthly awards prove to be a mixed blessing was quickly confirmed as 'Pools form fell away in the New Year with FA Cup defeat at Watford followed by a six match winless League run which effectively ended all hopes of challenging for the Play-offs. The remaining games of the season produced a mixed bag of results with the only highlight being Ritchie Humphreys appearance as a late substitute at Exeter which took him past the legendary Wattie Moore's record which had stood since 1964. 'Pools final

League One position of 16th was a fair reflection of a season of variable results and performances. Tony Sweeney was rightly voted the fans Player of the Year receiving over half of the votes cast.

Mick Wadsworth's retained list contained few surprises as he released most of the overpaid failures largely responsible for Chris Turner's departure namely – Armann Bjornsson, Denis Behan, Leon McSweeney, Michael MacKay, Joe Gamble and Fabian Yantorno.

## The Best £100 Offer Ever Made by Any Football Club

Russ Green had returned to the Victoria Park in January after a sabbatical and he surprised the Hartlepool public in general and the football world at large in July by announcing an offer of a £100 adult season ticket for the 2011–12 campaign, provided sales of 4,000 were achieved. The offer, rightly welcomed and strongly promoted by the local press and media, was an outstanding success and the club declared on the closing date that sales of 5,674 had been achieved, proof positive that supporters will back their team provided realistic prices are charged. As a further incentive 'Pools sprang another surprise by announcing the signing of Nolberto Solano for the coming season. The former Newcastle United and Peru player had an association with Mick Wadsworth during their time on Tyneside and this was a factor in persuading the player to sign.

The 2011–12 campaign started with a hugely successful testimonial game against Sunderland for the long serving Ritchie Humphreys, now holder of Hartlepool United's appearances record. On a glorious summer evening 5,757 fans turned up to witness a celebration of the legendary player's career against a strong Sunderland side which played a full part in the evening's entertainment.

A few days later, 'Pools League One campaign got underway against promotion favourites Milton Keynes Dons. Goals from Adam Boyd and James Brown twice gave United the lead only for the hosts to earn a draw with a late goal. The performance, rather than the result, suggested that better days lay ahead for the club. A first-round defeat to Sheffield United in the League Cup courtesy of a penalty shoot-out was the forerunner to three consecutive draws before a winning streak of five games culminating in a win at Bournemouth took 'Pools up to third place in League One and established a new club record start to a season of nine games without defeat. Results coupled with home attendances averaging nearly 5,300 gave grounds for renewed optimism.

The arrival at Victoria Park in early October of promotion favourites Sheffield Wednesday saw the record start come to an end in front of a capacity crowd. Despite the narrowness of the single goal scoreline the visitors were the stronger side as the home forwards struggled to make an impact. A week later 'Pools television hoodoo struck again when the visit to Meadow Lane in front of the Sky Sports cameras saw Notts County record a comfortable three goal victory. Another home defeat, to Wycombe Wanderers, was balanced by victory at Chesterfield only for the next two games at The Vic to be lost, making four consecutive home defeats. Four points from the next two away games (Leyton Orient draw, Scunthorpe win) were a prelude to further home losses to Yeovil and Preston which resulted in Mick Wadsworth's departure.

Opinions were divided on the merits of Wadsworth's sacking. On the one hand he had seen his team set a new record for an unbeaten start to a season while on the other he was in a run of six consecutive home League defeats. The local press speculated that the presence of IOR owner Bengt Larsson at the Preston game, a dire 1–0 defeat, was a major influence on the decision. A club statement announced that Mickey Barron would take temporary charge of the first team pending the appointment of a new 'manager'. Barron's temporary three game tenure all resulted in defeats including two at home before the club surprised almost everyone associated with it, press and supporters alike, by announcing that Neale Cooper was to return as 'manager' in all but name.

Since leaving 'Pools Neale Cooper had spells with Gillingham and Peterhead, a Scottish club with whom he enjoyed some success. His appointment as first team coach was widely welcomed by home supporters who had grown frustrated by the run of home defeats and the apparent lack of commitment by some established players. His first game back in charge was a home defeat, the eighth successive, to relegation threatened Scunthorpe who won more comfortably than the 2–1 scoreline suggests. Cooper's response to this display was to drop Adam Boyd and play 17-year-old Luke James at centre-forward in the next game against Rochdale, at home. James responded by scoring the second goal in a 2–0 win which made him 'Pools youngest ever goalscorer and finally ended the depressing run of home defeats.

Despite the win over Rochdale the manager quickly recognized that major changes would be required to the playing squad to bring the overall standard up to the level he required. Two draws followed, the second a highly commendable performance at Hillsborough against Sheffield Wednesday, before 'Pools turned in their best home performance of the season, 4–0 against Calisle which raised hopes of a challenge for a Play-off place.

Such optimism however could not be maintained and an embarrassing five goal defeat to bottom club Wycombe Wanderers brought all concerned at Victoria Park back to earth. The remaining fixtures brought more defeats than victories as goals almost completely dried up. The final game against champions Charlton Athletic at the Valley saw travelling 'Poolies' adopt 'smurf' outfits as a contribution to the party atmosphere, one which won widespread praise at a national level as an excellent example of how the game of football should be.

Following the final game which saw 'Pools finish 13th in League One Neale Cooper published his 'retained list' which saw several players released. Most prominent was Adam Boyd who had only managed six goals in his 31 appearances, albeit 18 of which were as a substitute. James Brown was another expected departure as his injury hit career restricted his appearances over the past two seasons. Steve Haslem, Colin Larkin and Nobby Solano, the latter a high profile preseason signing, also said farewell to Victoria Park. In an interview with the *Hartlepool Mail* Neale Cooper stated his intention to use the funds generated by the departures to bring in 'better players' and he backed his words within days by signing Jonathan Franks, a 22-year-old attacking midfield player from neighbours Middlesbrough.

# Victoria Park Story

Hartlepool United is one of the few established Football League clubs who have only played at one venue throughout their long and often chequered history. In many ways the history of Victoria Park, or the Vic as it is known locally, mirrors that of the football team, with long periods of decline interrupted by brief spells of revival until the present-day situation of solid foundations providing a basis for further progress.

## A Home for Both Football Codes

The Victoria Ground, as it was originally called, was the home of West Hartlepool Rugby Football Club, who purchased the land from the North-Eastern Railway Company in the 1880s. The rugby club initially played in the Foggy Furze area on a temporary basis, and the desire to find a permanent home near the town centre resulted in the purchase of a piece of land from the railway company.

The site was bordered by Clarence Road to the east and what was then Hart Road, now Raby Road, to the west, with the Clarence Cricket Ground, home of West Hartlepool Cricket Club, immediately to the south. The area to the north remained largely undeveloped for some years. The site of the cricket ground was later occupied by the Greyhound Stadium with the rugby football field at its centre. This was used by the reformed West Hartlepool Rugby Club until the late 1960s prior to their move to a new ground at Brierton Lane, with the site now occupied by a Morrisons supermarket.

The land, originally part of a large quarry, was little more than a collection of dilapidated allotments and tumbledown sheds. The rugby club cleared and levelled the site in order to develop a football ground with a level playing surface complete with stands and players' changing rooms. This was completed in 1886, the year of Queen Victoria's Jubilee, and the ground was named in her honour.

West Hartlepool Amateur Football Club had formed in 1881, the same year as West Hartlepool Rugby Football Club, and originally played in the Northumberland & Durham Association, which included the Sunderland club, later to become a major force in English football. In 1883 they became founder members of the Durham Association and within the decade had joined the Northern League. Although they were now an established side, they struggled to attract support, primarily due to the lack of a permanent ground. The highlight for the amateur team was undoubtedly winning the FA Amateur Cup in 1905 against Clapton Orient by 3–2. This was achieved in front of a near capacity crowd at Shepherd's Bush, the overwhelming majority of whom supported the London club.

Despite Durham County successfully hosting the Rugby County Championship finals at the ground in 1905 and again in 1907, by the end of the following season West Hartlepool RFC were in severe financial difficulties, with major repairs required at the Victoria Ground. The rugby club folded on 28 April 1908 and within a few days it was announced that a professional association football club was to be formed, and 'The Hartlepools United Football and Athletic Club Company Limited' was duly registered on 1 June 1908.

The directors, led by Chairman William Paterson, were to state in a later application (1910) to join the Football League that only £400 of capital had been spent acquiring the ground and affecting necessary repairs, that it had a capacity for 14,000 spectators with scope for expansion and was only three minutes' walk from the railway station!

## A Suitable Stage for Professional Football

Hartlepools United successfully applied to join the North-Eastern League for the 1908–09 season as well as agreeing to the amateur club, West Hartlepool, playing their home games in the Northern League at the Victoria Ground. The amateurs had previously played at a site in Park Road, but the ground-sharing arrangement lasted only a few seasons before the amateur club folded through lack of support.

Hartlepools United's first game at the ground on 2 September 1908 was against a Newcastle United side described as a 'Reserve XI'. Despite containing several first-team players in what was to be a Championship-winning season, the visitors were humbled by a resounding 6–0 defeat.

After drawing their first competitive game away at Hebburn on 5 September, the stage was set for the inaugural home League game against Seaham White Star a week later. A crowd estimated at 3,000, each paying four pence admission, saw a disappointing goalless draw. The following week the amateur side, West Hartlepool, recorded an emphatic 7–1 victory against Scarborough in a Northern League fixture.

A home victory for the professional side was not to be long delayed, as on 26 September goals from Edgley and Fletcher gave 'Pools a 2–0 success over North Shields. A week later the town was gripped, not for the last time, with Cup fever when the professionals were drawn against the amateurs of 'West' in an FA Cup qualifying round. Officially it was a home tie for the amateurs, but as the clubs shared the Victoria Ground it hardly mattered. On 3 October 1908 an estimated crowd of 7,000 saw the professionals eventually prevail 2–1 in a keenly contested game.

## A Town and a Club Under Bombardment

The advent of World War One in August 1914 was a defining point in the history of football, and all clubs, great and small, were affected by the outcome. The Football Association, the guardian of the game, immediately announced that all first-class fixtures would continue for the 1914–15 season. While this was seen as a bold decision to provide a degree of 'normality' during the conflict, it imposed a heavy financial burden on clubs. Despite continuing to charge the standard admission of sixpence, half for soldiers, the club recorded a loss of £500, a huge sum of money at the time. During the close season the Football Association finally bowed to the inevitable, and professional football was suspended throughout the remainder of the conflict.

The Great War, as it came to be known, caused much damage and suffering to the people of Hartlepool, as was evidenced by the bombardment by German warships in December 1914. Hartlepools United were no different in this respect having had their ground, requisitioned by the military with all the consequent damage and upheaval that entailed. To make matters worse, on the night of 27 November 1916 a German Zeppelin, in flames from persistent artillery fire, jettisoned its remaining bombs as it headed seawards. Two of the bombs shattered the Clarence Road stand and caused considerable damage to the infrastructure of the ground. At the cessation of hostilities the club claimed £2,500 compensation from the German government, a claim that they persisted with for some years only to find that the response was even more of the same in the next World War.

During the war years a variety of different events took place at the Vic to raise funds for the war effort and local charities. Aside from the inevitable football matches, some involving ladies' teams, military tournaments and events took place offering bayonet training, tug of war, horseback wrestling and three-legged races, all with the laudable intentions of 'boosting morale'. The impact on the playing surface can only be imagined with such a diverse series of activities. The military occupation eventually came to an end in May 1919 and the board began negotiations regarding repairs and maintenance to the ground. Tenders were submitted for internal work and repairs to the boundary fencing with a request they be given 'urgent consideration'.

Football resumed on 25 October 1919 against Sunderland Reserves with both the usual entrances on the Clarence Road and Mill House sides in operation, the game resulting in a draw. The return to the Vic was not without problems in terms of the playing surface as deteriorating weather in the New Year damaged the turf, and supporters were requested not to cross the pitch at the half-time interval via the medium of the local press. In an attempt to improve the quality of the surface the club placed advertisements advising the public that cinders and ballast could be tipped on the ground as a beneficial means of enrichment.

Another frustration for the directors at this time was the age-old problem of spectators finding innovative ways of watching the games without paying. Given the struggle the directors had had to make the ground fit for the resumption of games, this was a valid grievance on their part. Central to the issue was access from the Quoits Club (now the Raglan Quoits Club) at the Gasworks end of the ground. Such was the level of abuse, that public opinion was firmly with the club in the matter of a levy of 2s 6d for each transgression, such monies to be paid into the ground development fund.

## A Ground Fit for the Football League?

On 20 May 1920 a meeting took place in Manchester to discuss the formation and membership of the new Division Three. Central to the Hartlepools application was the Victoria Ground and its playing facilities. Hartlepools United's chairman, Alderman William Coates, outlined the issues regarding the military occupation and the outstanding compensation for the air damage and issues arising from the occupation. He mentioned the generosity of Councillor Salmon, whose company had provided the external railings to enclose the ground. In total the club had a debt outstanding of £650 for putting the ground in order. A further £214 had been paid for Army huts left inside the Victoria Ground. Mr Walker, the Football Association representative, acknowledged the efforts made by the club and offered to meet with Colonel Kentish of the British Army in an attempt to resolve the compensation issue once and for all. His influence was clear when on 24 June 1920 a cheque for £1,200 was received from the military in full and final settlement, notwithstanding the claim on the German government for air-raid damage.

In January 1921 the club received a questionnaire circulated to all clubs interested in joining the new Third Division North. Basically, it required details of ground condition and capacity, gate receipts, funding and indebtedness. Once again the issue of compensation from the German government was raised, and in the absence of any progress the only avenue left open to the club was its shareholders. At a follow-up meeting in March the League Management Committee agreed that given the expenditure of considerable sums of money by the clubs there was a 'moral obligation' to proceed with the new Division Three North. Shortly after this meeting, Hartlepools United received the eagerly anticipated news that they were elected to the new League for the 1921–22 season.

The accounts at the end of the 1921 season revealed a healthy profit of £527, which was earmarked, along with additional sums, for the further improvement of the Victoria Ground in preparation for League football. Such provision included the erection of a temporary stand on the Clarence Road side of the ground. This became the infamous wooden structure, with a seating capacity of 900, which would remain until it was rightly condemned in 1985 following the Bradford City fire tragedy.

On 3 September 1921 the first Football League fixture was held at the Victoria Ground, Hartlepools United versus Wrexham. Contemporary reports estimated the attendance at 10,000 to see the visitors win a keenly contested game 1–0. The next home game two weeks later against Southport resulted in a 1–0 home win, with Jimmy Lister scoring the first-ever League goal at the Vic.

The interwar years were relatively quiet in terms of ground developments. A notable football occasion was the visit of Grimsby Town, the first side from Division One to play a competitive match at the Victoria Ground, in an FA Cup third-round tie in front of a record attendance of 15,064. The game, which ended in a goalless draw, was nearly called off on the eve of the game when severe gales blew the roof off the Clarence Road stand. Not for the last time were urgent repairs quickly affected to allow the game to proceed.

On 26 August 1939 the final game before the cancellation of the Football League programme due to the outbreak of World War Two was played against Barrow, which ended a 1–1 draw in front of a crowd of 6,380, few of whom realised that it would be almost six years to the day before League football would return to the Vic.

## A Battle for Survival for Club and Country

Hartlepools United continued to play at the Victoria Ground throughout the 1939–40 season in the hastily formed North-East Division which included, among others, Newcastle

United, Sunderland and Middlesbrough. Such games were popular given the circumstances, and interest was heightened by the inclusion, for all sides, of 'guest' players. This lasted until the end of the season when the directors took the decision to cease all playing activity, thereby parting company with their manager, Jimmy Hamilton, and the entire professional staff.

In the intervening period the Vic was requisitioned by the military authorities and used for a variety of purposes. Organised football resumed on 28 August 1943 on the initiative of Hartlepools long-serving chairman William Yeats, who brokered a successful application to join the Football League North Championship. At this point the club was without a manager and a team, and there was also the small matter of the overall condition of the Victoria Ground, especially the pitch which was described in the local press as 'very much the worse for wear'.

Following the appointment of Fred Westgarth as manager in July 1943, attention focused on making the ground fit for playing a game of football. The week preceding the opening game against Middlesbrough saw club officials, including the chairman, with voluntary support, work overtime to prepare both the ground and pitch for the game. The East Stand was the major problem as it had been reduced to a shell and its wooden supports were rotted away. Only the turnstiles on the Clarence Road side were deemed to be in working order to admit supporters. The pitch was not cut and rolled until the Monday before the game, being best described as in 'fairly good condition'. Westgarth's hastily assembled team played Middlesbrough in the first game, a 1–0 win in front of 2,584 paying spectators.

Hartlepools United continued to play in the wartime League and Cup competitions with attendances of up to 9,000 for the games against strong Newcastle United and Sunderland sides. In the 1945–46 Third Division North Cup competition, after beating Crewe in the first round a crowd of over 8,000 saw the first leg of the second round against Southport, evidence of the strong local interest that remained in the game. The long-awaited resumption of the Football League programme on 31 August 1946 saw a crowd of 7,259 attend a Division Three North game against Barrow, which ended a 1–1 draw. Ironically, this was the same opponents and scoreline as the final game before the outbreak of war.

## The Post-war Boom Years

The resumption of football following World War Two prompted an upsurge in interest from which every club benefited. Within weeks Hartlepools attracted an attendance of over 12,000 for the visit of Rotherham United, and they played in front of over 30,000 at Hull. This pattern was followed in the coming seasons with a record Football League attendance of 17,118 at the Victoria Ground in October 1948. The following season saw Hartlepools United play nearly half their League games in front of attendances in excess of 10,000. An incident on 10 December 1949 provided testimony to the interest when the FA Cup tie against Norwich City continued despite the local fire brigade being called to attend to a fire at the rear of the Clarence Road stand. It took several minutes to extinguish the blaze, during which time play continued with the majority of the 11,144 crowd unaware of the commotion.

The Clarence Road stand in the 1950s with the '10 minute' flag.

It was not only Football League and FA Cup ties that attracted large crowds in this era. In the 1952–53 season the West Hartlepool Schoolboys team distinguished themselves, and the town, by reaching the quarter-finals of the English Schools Trophy. In doing so they defeated Manchester Schools in front of over 12,000 spectators before topping that attendance in the drawn game against Chesterfield Schools, which attracted a staggering 14,000, one of the

Action from the 1950s, with the Mill House stand and terracing in the background.

highest-ever attendances at the Victoria Ground. The schoolboys eventually lost the replay against Chesterfield, who finished as runners-up in the Final to Swansea.

Such enthusiasm for football at all levels persuaded chairman Harold Sargeant, in June 1954, to make a pledge to replace the old Mill House stand and install new dressing rooms. This seemed a sensible proposition as 'Pools FA Cup successes resulted in record attendances against Nottingham Forest (17,200) in 1955, which was topped by the visit of Manchester United in 1957 (17,246). In-between, Chelsea attracted over 16,000 in the 1956 competition.

Progress was finally made on the first improvements since World War Two when in the close season of 1957 the old wooden stand on the Mill House side of the ground was demolished and new terracing and barriers constructed along the length of the ground. The terracing at both the Rink and Town ends was also extended, resulting in the club's long-serving secretary, Frank Perryman, informing both press and public that the Victoria Ground now had capacity for 22,000 spectators!

While this may have been a rare show of optimism on the part of Mr Perryman, the early-season League game against Darlington attracted a record midweek attendance of 14,876 spectators. 'Pools won 5–1 with all the goals coming in the second half. The halcyon days of the immediate post-war era drew to a close when, on 4 April 1959, Hartlepool United registered their record victory with a 10–1 triumph over a hapless Barrow side with 4,126 in attendance.

## The Club and the Council, Chapter 1

The 1960s saw a number of proposals for the redevelopment of the Victoria Ground, beginning with an anonymous Durham company presenting outline plans in 1965 for a new grandstand, social club and cafeteria. As in the past there was much discussion and precious little action. Words were, however, translated into effect in November 1966 when, on the initiative of chairman Ernest Ord, floodlights were installed at the Victoria Ground at a cost of £15,000. West Hartlepool Council provided the capital sum, with the cost to be recovered by a substantial increase in the club's annual rental. The first-ever floodlit match at the Victoria Ground took place on 6 January 1967 when Southend were the visitors, Ernie Phythian scoring in a 1–2 defeat which attracted a 9,586 crowd.

The 1970s heralded a new era in the history of the club and the Victoria Ground. The decade began with the opening, on 1 August 1970, of the new Mill House stand, costing £30,000. This was officially opened with a pre-season friendly game against Scottish side Raith Rovers. 'Pools won 2–1 with two goals from Nicky Sharkey in front of 1,884 spectators. To finance the new stand the now Hartlepool Borough Council again granted a substantial loan towards the cost, with the club paying further rental increases to finance the capital cost.

The rest of the decade saw a string of highs and lows in Hartlepool United's fortunes as both the club and the game in general evolved to meet the challenges of a changing social environment. A major 'low' took place on 22 December 1973 when a mere 844 spectators, a record low (at the time) for a League game, saw Scunthorpe United beaten 3–0.

In response to widespread public demand, 3 February 1974 saw a 'high' – the first Sunday game to be played at the Victoria Ground. A crowd of 5,747, some of whom took advantage of a 'free gate' as required by the regulations, saw a convincing victory over Stockport County. This was followed in the November when a record attendance for a floodlit game of 12,305 spectators, paying gate receipts of £5,000, witnessed the fourth-round Football League Cup tie against Aston Villa which finished a 1–1 draw.

## The Club and the Council, Chapter 2

Encouraged by such relative successes, the directors led by chairman Vince Barker made Hartlepool Borough Council an offer in January 1977 of £24,000 to buy back the Victoria Ground. This was initially rejected by the council, who in October proposed that the club buy the ground for £60,000 on a 99-year lease. The club accepted this proposal in principle and negotiations began. Progress appeared to have been made when, in February 1978, chairman Barker stated his intention to pay cash for the ground and the council approved outline planning permission for ground improvements. By April the club cleared their rent arrears and the council passed planning permission for a new gymnasium, social club and changing rooms.

The New Year, 1979, heralded problems both on and off the field, when 'Pools crashed out of the FA Cup 2–6 to Leeds United in front of a reported 16,000 crowd. Within a month, Barker, frustrated by the lack of progress, accused the council of delaying tactics, threatening drastic action if the sale was delayed any longer. The following February the two parties met with the result that Hartlepool United agreed to forego any rights to compensation, apart from the provision of a boundary wall that was to be erected when the new road on the Clarence Road side of the ground was built.

The long-running saga escalated still further in July 1980 when chairman Barker accused the council of reneging on the sale price for the ground. Although neither party released any figures, a sum of £30,000 was believed to be the difference in the valuation. Barker then threatened to move the club out of the town in protest at what he continued to describe as the council's 'delaying tactics'. This turned into an all-out crisis the following March when Hartlepool Council placed a time limit on the finalisation of the sale following a string of queries from the club. At this point Barker threatened to move the club to Scarborough, having declined offers of financial help from local businessmen Harold Hornsey and Frank Owbridge. Both the Scarborough chairman, Don Robinson, and Graeme Kelly, secretary to the Football League, declined to comment on the proposal.

This effectively marked the end of this sorry chapter in the long-running saga of the ownership of Victoria Park. Thankfully, focus returned to matters on the football pitch with the ground staging, in November 1981, an FA Cup first-round tie between Horden Colliery Welfare and Blackpool, due to Horden's ground being declared unsuitable for the game. Blackpool won the tie 1–0 in front of a crowd of 4,465.

Understandable frustration among supporters with events both on and off the field of play was evidenced by a number of games that produced record low attendances during the

The Clarence Road Stand, a dismal sight in 1982.

early 1980s. The decline of public interest in football was not unique to Hartlepool United, however, and a series of tragic events at football grounds at home and abroad focussed attention on the general state of the national game, from the Prime Minister Margaret Thatcher down through all levels of government and the public at large.

## A Game and a Ground in Intensive Care

At the beginning of April 1985 a survey by officials from Hartlepool Borough Council declared the much-maligned East Stand on the Clarence Road side of the ground to be unsafe due to serious rot at both ends of the wooden structure. The club was asked to confirm that the necessary insurance cover was in place to protect spectators in the event of a serious incident. After some negotiation, the club was allowed to keep the stand open for the remaining home games, pending a long-term solution.

Chairman John Smart begins the demolition of the Clarence Road stand in the 1985 close season.

The tragic events at Bradford City, where the main stand caught fire, killing spectators, acted as the catalyst for finally bringing the curtain down on the infamous East Stand. Chairman John Smart personally led the demolition team in clearing the site in order to provide a formation of 'temporary' portakabins which provided dressing rooms and office accommodation, which in the opinion of many were little improvement, notwithstanding the safety aspect.

Following the demolition of the Clarence Road stand, the playing area was moved several feet towards the Mill House side, and ambitious plans announced for the redevelopment of that side of the ground with luxury changing rooms, players' and sponsors' lounges, management and office accommodation, and a club shop. Despite backing from the local brewery Camerons, the response from Hartlepool Council was to announce plans for a hypermarket on the Vic, with a counter proposal that the club move to a brand new 'super' stadium on vacant land on the outskirts of town. By the end of the season no one was surprised to learn that both proposals had been abandoned.

In February 1986 the club and its supporters suffered a further blow when the capacity of the Victoria Ground was drastically reduced to a mere 2,100 after the roofing cover on both the Rink and Town ends was declared unsafe and had to be demolished. This came at a time when attendances were regularly in excess of 3,000. Local neighbours Middlesbrough generously offered the use of Ayresome Park until work could be carried out restoring the capacity, but chairman John Smart declined the offer, citing his commitment to the fans.

The start of the 1986–87 season saw an event take place at the Vic which is rare in the annals of Football League history, when the ground hosted two League games on the same day. The background to this extraordinary event was the plight of near neighbours Middlesbrough, then a Third Division club, who had declared themselves bankrupt. A rescue package by a consortium of Teesside businessmen did not materialise in time for the padlocks to be removed from the gates of Ayresome Park, so in order to fulfil their opening-day fixture they were given permission to play at the Victoria Ground.

On the 23 August 1986, Hartlepool United kicked-off at 3.00pm in front of a crowd of 2,800 against Cardiff City in a Division Four fixture resulting in a 1–1 draw, Tony Smith scoring. This was then followed by Middlesbrough against Port Vale, a Division Three contest that attracted 3,456 spectators and finished 2–2, with Archie Stephens scoring both Boro goals. Ironically, 'Pools then played Middlesbrough three days later in a home, first-round, first-leg Littlewoods Cup tie which also finished a 1–1 draw.

## The Club and the Council, Chapter 3

In November 1986, Hartlepool Council informed the club that they were not prepared to sell them the ground, thereby reducing by 50 per cent any grants that may potentially have been forthcoming from the Football Grounds Improvement Trust. Consequently, the club was unable to effect necessary improvements to the Town and Rink ends, resulting in fans continuing to stand without any cover from the elements.

The following February the club surprised everyone by announcing plans for a super stadium incorporating leisure facilities costing nearly £9 million. The board, led by chairman John Smart, announced optimistically that the money would come from local business and corporate sponsorship and was greeted with some scepticism by the press and fans alike. In the end it came, predictably, to nothing and probably did more harm than good with supporters who continued to suffer sub-standard facilities. A small crumb of comfort was provided during the 1988 close season when work finally got underway on the Rink End stand, incorporating a new roof and the provision of seating.

The 1990s opened on a note of optimism with a new chairman, Gary Gibson, a custom-built social facility for fans – 'The Corner Flag' – and a promotion. All this was followed on 2 January 1993 with a victory over Premier League Crystal Palace in the third round of the FA Cup. For the first time a Hartlepool United game was featured on the BBC's *Match of the Day* programme and attracted national media plaudits for the stirring manner of the victory.

Following three eventful seasons in Division Two, the 1993–94 campaign saw relegation return with another unwanted record. In the final game of the season, a demoralised team conceded a record home defeat, 8–1 to Plymouth Argyle. Despite the disappointment of relegation, the arrival of local businessman Harold Hornsey as chairman heralded the beginning of a new era in the history of Hartlepool United.

## Enter the People's Hero

Harold Hornsey, widely respected in the local community, immediately made his intentions clear regarding the development of the Victoria Ground. With public opinion firmly on his side, Hartlepool Council recognised the need to move forward, and work began on the re-development of the Clarence Road side of the ground. In July 1995 the new Clarence Road stand, costing £650,000, was officially opened by chairman Hornsey and named in honour of former manager, the late Cyril Knowles. The stand was funded by a grant of £490,000 from the Football Trust and other grants from Hartlepool Council and City Challenge. To provide further evidence of the chairman's good intentions, the Town End was re-roofed and re-terraced by local company Expamet under a sponsorship deal, to provide cover on all four sides. To recognise these developments, the ground was renamed Victoria Park, a change which reflected the extent of the modernisation.

The progress made in the profile and perception of Hartlepool United with the ground improvements attracted attention from other quarters, and in September 1997 Harold Hornsey accepted an offer from the Increased Oil Recovery Company (IOR) to take over the club. Hornsey issued a statement in which he emphasised the new owner's long-term commitment and its ability to take Hartlepool United forward. He further stated that he would continue to work alongside the IOR directors to help put their ideas into practice, thereby ensuring a smooth transition with the new owners.

September 1998 saw an event considered previously unlikely when West Hartlepool Rugby Football Club returned to the Vic after an absence of 90 years to play their Allied Dunbar Premiership fixtures for the coming season. The move was necessitated by their Brierton Lane ground being acquired by a local builder for a housing development. The

The Town End under attack from Leeds in 2010.

first Premiership game of professional rugby at the ground took place on 12 September against London Irish, watched by several thousand spectators. The visitors recorded a 44–20 victory in what was to turn out to be a difficult season for 'West'.

Following the departure of West Hartlepool from their Brierton Lane ground and its subsequent re-development, Hartlepool United acquired the rugby club's corporate hospitality suites and installed them in the Cyril Knowles stand to provide, for the first time ever at Victoria Park, executive-style facilities for supporters and their guests.

## The Dawn of a New Era

The new millennium heralded a previously unheard of development with the live television coverage of Hartlepool United home games. This move was predominately initiated by the new medium of subscription television, pioneered in the United Kingdom by Sky Television. As the popularity of the FA Premier League gathered momentum, public interest in all clubs within the structure of the Football League also increased with a corresponding rise in media coverage.

Following 'Pools success in reaching their first-ever Play-off semi-final in the 1999–2000 season, the club made arrangements to install a large screen to take relayed televised pictures of the Division Three second-leg Play-off game against Darlington live from their Feethams ground on 18 May. A substantial crowd paid ground admission to witness 'Pools lose 0–1.

The Victoria Park faithful did not have to wait long for a live televised game when the Sky Sports cameras arrived at the ground in August 2001 to cover the Football League Cup first-round tie against Nottingham Forest. Unfortunately 'Pools failed to do themselves justice on this occasion, and a strong Forest side ran out convincing winners.

Cyril Knowles stand present day.

Further Play-off success resulted in the 2003–04 first-leg semi-final against Bristol City on 15 May being televised live, again by Sky Sports, and with the policy established of televising all Play-off games live, the following season's semi-final against Tranmere Rovers was also broadcast.

The start of the 2006–07 season saw the club enter into a shirt sponsorship deal with the world famous Nike organisation, which not only provided a new strip and associated leisure wear, but also a new club shop at the rear of the main office complex, providing a dedicated facility for supporters, open on a daily basis.

As live Sky Sports football coverage was further extended to all competitions, the first home FA Cup game to be televised was a first-round replay against Rochdale on 20 November, with 'Pools finally winning through on a penalty shoot-out. The final piece in the television jigsaw was completed the following season, 2007–08, when a live Football League broadcast from Victoria Park saw Hartlepool entertain Bournemouth in a drawn League One game on 18 November.

Victoria Park from the air.

In September 2007 IOR celebrated the 10th anniversary of their takeover from Harold Hornsey. Chairman throughout that time, Ken Hodcroft, paid tribute to the progress made with five Play-off campaigns, two promotions and a solitary relegation. He expressed optimism for the future and confirmed IOR's long-term commitment with the wish to see Hartlepool Council finally agree to the sale of Victoria Park to maintain the momentum.

In response to the chairman's comments, a council committee, chaired by Councillor Robbie Payne and including Councillors Jackson, Hargreaves and Tumilty, met in November to discuss Hartlepool United's proposal to take over the ownership of Victoria Park. The following month, in presenting his Annual Report, Ken Hodcroft confirmed that negotiations for the purchase of the Victoria Ground were ongoing and he expected further meetings with Hartlepool Council representatives early in 2008.

Boxing Day saw Leeds United play their first-ever League game at Victoria Park in front of a record attendance, since the ground was redeveloped and renamed, of 7,784. The game ended a 1–1 draw after Michael Nelson had given 'Pools the lead, only for Beckford to equalise for the visitors in the last minute.

Towards the end of the season the *Hartlepool Mail* reported that further talks had been held between the club and council regarding the sale of Victoria Park. Councillor Robbie Payne, chairman of the Hartlepool United Executive Committee, reported that the club had outlined its plans for the future development of the ground. Another council member, Victor Tumilty, felt that 'real' progress had now been made towards achieving a satisfactory outcome for both the club and the town. Club chairman Ken Hodcroft later commented in his Annual Report that talks were progressing 'slowly but surely'.

Despite the lack of tangible progress with Hartlepool Council, IOR continued to invest in improvements to the facilities and ground at Victoria Park, including the provision of a 'Centenary Suite', opened by Alan Shearer, to recognise the club's 100-year anniversary, and an electronic scoreboard in the corner of the Expamet and Mill House stands. Added to these improvements, the club continued to receive plaudits about the immaculate playing surface maintained by award-winning groundsman David Brown, which compared favourably with the pitches at the homes of more illustrious Premiership neighbours.

The 2008–09 season was distinguished by the arrival at Victoria Park of three teams with Premiership status. In August West Bromwich Albion arrived in the second round of the Carling Cup and were the victims of the shock of the round when 'Pools deservedly won 3–1 in extra-time. The third round of the FA Cup saw another home tie against top-flight opposition in the form of Stoke City, who were similarly dispatched 2–0 with goals from Nelson and Foley, the latter a contender for goal of the season. This win brought West Ham United to Victoria Park for their first-ever visit. Gianfranco Zola paid 'Pools the compliment of playing a full-strength side, and their class showed in a comfortable 2–0 victory. The game was shown live on television at the peak Saturday lunchtime viewing slot.

Tangible evidence that the club continued to maintain momentum in the provision of 'off-the-field' facilities to supporters and public alike came on Friday 25 September 2009 when Linda Longstaff and Frank Bujnowski became the first couple to be married in the Centenary Suite following the granting of a wedding licence to the club.

# IOR AND VICTORIA PARK – AN END TO THE SAGA?

In early November Hartlepool Council's Executive committee charged with the responsibility of negotiating the sale of the Victoria Park to the club, held another meeting with the club's representatives. Chaired by Councillor Robbie Payne, it was reported that the Council were committed to the reaching an agreement as part of an overall package providing greater leisure provision across the whole Mill House site.

By March 2010 the *Hartlepool Mail* was reporting that at a recent Council meeting it was agreed 'in principle' that the Victoria Park should be sold back to the club. Councillor Payne commented that all members of the committee were quite clear that they wished to pursue a sale and reach a conclusion acceptable to both parties as quickly as possible, adding that the Council has a duty to get best value for the town's taxpayers and therefore it is vital a realistic valuation is agreed with the club.

After six months deliberation Hartlepool Borough Council formally rejected the club's latest offer to buy the Victoria Park and adjacent land. Councillor Payne, chairman of the committee, described the club's offer of £50,000 as derisory further commenting that the figure was barely one tenth of the council's valuation and his committee owed a duty to the town and ratepayers to achieve a commercial valuation for the valuable site. A spokesman for Hartlepool United expressed 'extreme disappointment' at the decision. Mayor Stuart Drummond was quoted as hoping both parties could continue negotiations and reach a mutually advantageous agreement.

At the Annual General Meeting of Hartlepool United Football Club Ltd in December chairman Ken Hodcroft gave a wide ranging review of the club's activities and financial circumstances embarking on a lengthy criticism of Hartlepool Council over its failure to sell the Victoria Park to IOR, a company of which he is managing director. He claimed the council's valuation of £650,000 was totally unrealistic and failed to recognise the contribution of IOR over many years. The chairman ended with a veiled threat that the company would have to re-evaluate its 'economic model' in respect of future investment if it did not own the Victoria Park.

A year later, with little progress on the sale of the ground Ken Hodcroft again commented at the club's Annual General Meeting that negotiations with Hartlepool Council were ongoing while hinting that a positive outcome may not be far away. The *Hartlepool Mail* had reported prior to the AGM that Hartlepool Council, in conjunction with the club and other interested parties, commissioned an independent report on the future development of the Mill House site and the economic benefits of the football club to the town and its residents.

The eagerly anticipated report was published in March 2012 and enthusiastically received by Mayor Stuart Drummond and his cabinet members. Its main proposals encompassed the redevelopment of the Rink End stand to possibly incorporating a hotel and a complete rebuild or refurbishment of the Mill House leisure centre to provide an attractive proposition for investment from both public and private sectors. Gus Robinson Developments, a local company, indicated its willingness to be the preferred developer for the site. Also involved was Camerons Brewery, owner of the Mill House public house, who remained supportive of the developments overall goals.

The key issue was the transfer of the Victoria Park to Hartlepool United which required the approval of the full council. The club currently pays an annual rent of £18,000 to the council under the terms of the lease and the latest valuation of £625,000 would be waived under the proposals. Any such transfer would be conditional on the club committing to the development plan and any such agreement would also include a covenant that the land must always be used as a football ground. Mayor Drummond concluded his statement by reiterating, somewhat optimistically, the need to increase the capacity of the Victoria Park, particularly if promotion to the Championship, the second tier of English football, was ever achieved.

It remains to be seen if such a deal is finally concluded and the ownership reverts back to Hartlepool United thereby allowing the club's munificent owners, IOR Ltd, to continue with development of the Victoria Park to the long term benefit of the town, the club's supporters, and the team management and players.

# Matches to Remember

## *Match to Remember 1* **27 August 1921**

## Wrexham 0 Hartlepools United 2

The eagerly awaited inaugural games of the newly formed Third Division North of the Football League saw Hartlepools United make the long journey to Wrexham to begin, for both clubs, a sequence which was to continue unbroken in that League until its dissolution in 1958.

A crowd of over 8,000 was present at the Racecourse Ground for the start of the historic encounter, and they saw Hartlepools win the toss and elect to play towards the Town goal with the wind in their favour.

Straight from the kick-off Wrexham nearly scored, but Tom Crilly robbed Edwards of the ball. Hartlepools then enjoyed a period of possession with Kessler giving Simpson no end of trouble with his dazzling wing play. Foster was next to test the home defence when he got in a shot from a free-kick, but Hopkins was on hand to clear.

Then it was Wrexham's turn to exert some pressure, with Ernie Lloyd going close; however, just when Wrexham's game was showing some promise, their downfall began. Robert Griffiths made a faulty clearance that let Mulholland through. He played a quick one-two with Kessler, and with Godding coming out to meet him, Mulholland lifted the ball over the goalkeeper and into the net for Hartlepools' first goal after 20 minutes.

Wrexham made a determined effort to equalise, but while pushing forward they were caught out at the back as Kessler outpaced Griffiths to play the ball into the middle for Lister, who gave Godding no chance. The score, however, was disallowed due to Lister being adjudged to be in an offside position.

After Noel Edwards went close for Wrexham, Hartlepools again went on the attack. From a throw-in they found the unmarked Lister, who raced forward and shot past Godding for Hartlepools' second goal five minutes from half-time.

William 'Tot' Hopkins.

Tom Crilly.

**Half-time: Wrexham 0 Hartlepools United 2**
After the interval, Donald shot just wide for the visitors before Wrexham rallied with Burton, passing inside to Bert Goode, who put in one of his characteristic drives, which was too high on this occasion.

The home side now settled down and it was not long afterwards that Bill Cotton got into a promising goalscoring position, only to come into contact with Bert Goode, resulting in his shot going well over the crossbar.

Within minutes there was an almost identical chance, but this time the inside-forwards got in a mix-up and the Hartlepool defence cleared. Shortly afterwards Gill made a commanding clearance from a testing free-kick from the Wrexham left wing.

Wrexham's forwards continued to attack with both Burton and Cotton going close, but Gill was again equal to their efforts. Matthew Burton again sent a ball across the goalmouth and United rallied. Robertson and Lister seemed to have a clear run at goal but Simpson got across and cleared.

Wrexham's last chance came five minutes from the end, but once again the home forwards failed to capitalise on the chance and the United defence cleared upfield to safety.

**Full-time: Wrexham 0 Hartlepools United 2**
**Wrexham:** Godding, Ellis, Simpson, Mathais, Foster, Griffiths, Burton, Goode, Cotton, Edwards, Lloyd.
**Hartlepools United:** Gill, Crilly, Thomas, Dougherty, Hopkins, Short, Kessler, Mulholland, Lister, Robertson, Donald.
*Scorers:* Mulholland (20 mins), Lister (40 mins).
*Referee:* J. Cahill (Liverpool).
*Attendance:* 10,000 (estimate).

---

## *Match to Remember 2* — **10 January 1925**

# Newcastle United 4 Hartlepools United 1

After comfortable home wins against amateurs Bishop Auckland and St Albans in the earlier rounds, Hartlepools United reached the first round proper of the FA Cup for the first time in their history. If club officials and players hoped for a 'plum draw' they were not to be disappointed as they were matched against the Cup holders, Newcastle United of the

The Hartlepool United team that faced Newcastle United.

First Division. To add further spice to the tie, the Tyneside club were in the middle of a 12-match unbeaten League run which was to take them to the top of the division, while their opponents were second bottom of Division Three North.

A crowd of 36,632, paying £2,229, was present on a glorious fine day as Charlie Storer led the visitors out, preceded by a mascot dressed in blue and white. The home team attacked from the kick-off with Seymour crossing for Harris to head goalward, only for Cowell to save brilliantly at the expense of a corner. Storer was in superb form, marshalling his defence and repeatedly winning the ball in the tackle to set his forwards on the attack. As the game settled down, Syd Hardy combined with Alec Cook to set up centre-forward Smith, only for his shot to be saved by Bradley in the home goal. Newcastle replied with a Hudspeth effort, which was saved at the second attempt by Cowell.

Newcastle continued to play a fast, attacking game which revolved around their international centre-forward Neil Harris. At times it appeared that he wanted to win the game on his own with his long-range shooting; however, his efforts were finally rewarded five minutes from half-time when he headed Seymour's accurate pass home.

**Half-time: Newcastle United 1 Hartlepools United 0**

The second half began with both sides having an equal share of the play. After 55 minutes Newcastle increased their lead when McDonald scored a fine solo goal

Tom Lilley.

following a free-kick. The Magpies now dominated the play and after Cowan had added a third, McKenzie scored the goal of the game with a magnificent 30-yard drive, which was too powerful for Cowell. Despite these reverses the visitors never gave up and gained a consolation goal in the 87th minute when Syd Hardy scored.

In the post-match report the *Newcastle Journal* paid tribute to the visitors' efforts, describing the game as 'Cup tie football of a high standard'.

**Full-time: Newcastle United 4 Hartlepools United 1**
**Newcastle United:** Bradley, Hampson, Hudspeth, McKenzie, Spencer, Gibson, Irwin, Cowan, Harris, McDonald, Seymour.
*Scorers:* Harris, McDonald, Cowan, McKenzie.
**Hartlepools United:** Cowell, Lilley, Allen, Young, Storer, Jobson, S. Hardy, C. Hardy, T.P. Smith, Butler, Cook.
*Scorer:* S. Hardy.
*Referee:* J.W.D. Fowler.
*Attendance:* 36,632.

---

## *Match to Remember 3* **23 January 1926**

# Hartlepools United 9 Walsall 3

The change to the offside law in 1925 whereby the number of opponents required between attacker and goal was reduced from three to two brought about an immediate and dramatic increase in the number of goals in League games. Hartlepools United felt the impact on the opening day of the season with a 6–0 defeat at Rochdale before responding positively to the change and finishing in sixth position, scoring 82 goals, 59 of them at home. The highlight of the season was the visit of struggling Walsall, 'Pools' 14th home League game, which had seen them score in every one up to that point.

Jack Foster, the home captain, won the toss and elected to play with the advantage of strong breeze. The early exchanges were fairly even, with Wensley prominent for the home side forcing a corner which was eventually cleared. After 10 minutes Cec Hardy opened the scoring with a first-time shot, and within two minutes Best added a second following a goalmouth scramble. Walsall appeared demoralised by the early reverses and, following a strong run by Lilley, Wensley diverted his cross-shot past a startled Wait in the Walsall goal. Such was 'Pools' dominance that the game was being played totally in Walsall's half, with Foster, the home centre-half, joining in the attack on several occasions.

Eventually the visitors took advantage of slack defending and Felix reduced the arrears in the 21st minute. 'Pools almost replied within a minute but Syd Hardy's effort was disallowed for offside. It hardly mattered, as shortly afterwards another home corner saw Foster's header rebound from the crossbar to Cec Hardy, who scored his second goal. Walsall looked demoralised as they failed to come to terms with the strong wind, Sid Hardy

Cec Hardy scored a hat-trick against Walsall.

adding a fifth goal from another corner. Some relief finally came for the visitors just before half-time when Crockford took advantage of a sleepy home defence to reduce the arrears.

**Half-time: Hartlepools United 5 Walsall 2**
The second half was a mirror image of the first, despite Walsall having the wind in their favour. Carr (twice), Cec Hardy and Sid Hardy added to the home team's tally against totally demoralised opponents. The visitors finally gained some small consolation through Crockford, who scored his second goal of the afternoon by taking advantage of another lapse by the lackadaisical home defence in which goalkeeper Cowell was equally to blame.

The final score was both a record victory and aggregate score for Hartlepools United in the Football League.

**Full-time: Hartlepools United 9 Walsall 3**
**Hartlepools United:** Cowell, Lilley, Kell, Jobson, Foster, Richardson, Best, Carr, Wensley, C. Hardy, S. Hardy.
*Scorers:* C. Hardy (3), Best, Wensley, S. Hardy (2), Carr (2).
**Walsall:** Wait, Groves, Smith, Holt, Adams, Binks, Felix, Clark, Crockford, Alcock, Lawley.
*Scorers:* Felix, Crockford (2).
*Referee:* H. Hopkinson (Rochdale).
*Attendance:* 3,358.

---

## *Match to Remember 4* — **11 January 1936**

# Hartlepools United 0 Grimsby Town 0

Hartlepools United won through to the third round of the FA Cup after a three-game struggle against Halifax Town, which finally ended with a 4–1 victory at St James' Park, with Johnny Wigham scoring a hat-trick. Their reward was a home tie against First Division Grimsby Town, the first such opponents at the Victoria Ground from the top tier of English Football.

The game caught the public's imagination in a way not previously experienced by the Hartlepools club. The 15,064 attendance, paying gate receipts of £815, was a record for the ground at the time, and that was after overnight gales had damaged the roof of the Clarence

Jimmy Mittell (right) was injured against Grimsby and Dick Hardy (below) took over in goal.

Road stand. Grimsby fielded probably their best-ever side, which included Pat Glover and Jackie Bestall, both international forwards at the peak of their careers.

Ossie Park won the toss for the home side and the game began in bright sunshine. The visitors started the stronger with Glover, Craven and Lewis prominent in their early attacks. Jimmy Mittel then saved bravely at the feet of Glover before 'Pools forced two corners in quick succession, both of which were scrambled clear. In all the excitement play had to be held up a few minutes for a collapsed barrier which threatened to let the crowd on the pitch. The police quickly restored the situation only for tragedy to strike in the playing sense when Mittel was injured saving at Baldry's feet and stunned in the process. After treatment by the touchline he was carried on a stretcher to the dressing room.

With no substitutes allowed the home side re-organised, with Dick Hardy taking over in goal, making an already difficult task almost impossible. Mittel returned shortly afterwards with three stitches in his hand and took Hardy's place on the right wing. Hardy then distinguished himself by saving Buck's thunderous drive and clearing a loose ball before Lewis had time to take advantage.

**Half-time: Hartlepools United 0 Grimsby Town 0**

The second half saw the whole Hartlepools team draw on hidden reserves of stamina, none more so than Johnny Wigham who tried everything to escape the attentions of Betmead. Grimsby had a great chance to win the tie when Allison twice failed to clear from Craven, leaving Glover in the clear only for stand-in goalkeeper Hardy to make a spectacular save. The Cup tie ended with even honours and the referee, Mr Noble, earned praise for the tact and firmness with which he controlled the game.

**Full-time: Hartlepools United 0 Grimsby Town 0**

**Hartlepools United:** Mittel, Proctor, Allison, Brown, Park, Heward, Hardy, Hill, Wigham, Hill, Bonass.

**Grimsby Town:** Tweedy, Kelly, Hodgson, Hall, Betmead, Buck, Baldry, Bestall, Glover, Craven, Lewis.

*Referee:* A. Noble (Sheffield).

*Attendance:* 15,064.

WATCH THE 'POOLS DOCKER !
in
Football Mail
(THE GREEN 'UN)
Get that Saturday Green 'Un
habit all the year round

You will be sure to "SCORE"
IF YOU MAKE
SAGE'S
Your Shopping "GOAL" for this Season.
SPORTS GOODS, FANCY & TRAVEL GOODS
FOUNTAIN PENS and BOOK SHOP— 4-6 LYNN St.

THE
WELCUT
TAILORS
LIMITED
Athenaeum Buildings,
LYNN STREET—
Branches at Darlington, Bishop Auckland, Stockton and Wallsend.
UNBEATABLE
HOME
or
AWAY
Phone - - 3636

TEAMS FOR SATURDAY, 29th JANUARY, 1955. Kick off 2-45 p.m.

F.A. CUP—FOURTH ROUND

HARTLEPOOLS UNITED Nº 2980

Right Wing 1—Taylor Left Wing
2—Cameron 3—Thompson
4—Newton 5—Moore 6—Stamper
7—Linacre 8—Johnson, K. 9—Richardson 10—McGuigan 11—Luke

Referee: Mr. A. Holland (Barnsley)
Linesmen: Mr. J. Brass - - Red; Mr. J. E. Thacker - Gold

11—Small 10—Barrett 9—Wilson 8—Holder 7—Scott
6—Burkitt 5—McKinlay 4—Morley
3—Thomas 2—Whare
Left Wing 1—Farmer Right Wing

NOTTINGHAM FOREST

ANDREW C. WATT
LIMITED
Leading Agents for Ronson Lighters
TOBACCO BLENDERS
and
PIPE SPECIALISTS
20 CHURCH STREET

HESLOP & HALL LTD.
ANDREW STREET PHONE 4167-8
CENTRAL HEATING ENGINEERS
PLUMBING & ELECTRICAL ENGINEERS
LEADED LIGHT MANUFACTURERS,
GLAZING CONTRACTORS.

A. WALKER
FOR
SMALL MEAT PRODUCTS
Wholesale enquiries to: 60 RABY ROAD Phone 4514

Nottingham Forest programme.

---

## *Match to Remember 5* — 29 January 1955

# Hartlepools United 1 Nottingham Forest 1

Following their hard-fought victory over Darlington at the third attempt, Hartlepools United reached the fourth round of the FA Cup for the first time and were rewarded with a home draw against Nottingham Forest of the Second Division. Although the opposition were not from the top tier, the Cup tie caught the imagination of the Hartlepools public to such an extent that a record crowd of 17,200 packed into the 'Vic' to witness a thrilling encounter.

From the kick-off the visitors took the initiative with their fast and skilful play which had the 'Pools defence at full stretch. Centre-forward Wilson, supported by wingers Scott and Small, continually threatened throughout a first half, which saw only 'keeper George Taylor stand between them and a rout. Their failure to find the net took its toll as the half wore on and 'Pools came into the game through sheer grit and determination.

**Half-time: Hartlepools United 0 Nottingham Forest 0**

Within minutes of the restart the visitors finally scored when Scott took a pass from Wilson and converted the chance in fine style. If many of the record crowd expected this to be the

Forest's Thomas handles Johnson's shot to concede the penalty.

start of a rout they were mistaken as 'Pools mounted a determined fight-back with Tommy McGuigan probing and creating chances from himself and others, including Linacre and Richardson. The latter almost scored with a diving header from a Luke cross. At this point only Forest 'keeper Farmer stood between the home forwards and the goal their play deserved.

The pressure finally told in the 75th minute when a goal-bound shot by Johnson was fisted away by Forest's left-back Thomas, with Farmer beaten. In a tense atmosphere Newton calmly scored with the penalty, shooting firmly to the top corner of Farmer's left side.

The remaining minutes were all 'Pools' as they battled for a winner, which they deserved for their second-half performance. Forest, looking distinctly ragged, held on in a game which was played in a sporting spirit and without a single incident.

**Full-time: Hartlepools United 1 Nottingham Forest 1**
**Hartlepools United:** Taylor, Cameron, Thompson, Newton, Moore, Stamper, Linacre, Johnson, Richardson, McGuigan, Luke.
*Scorer:* Newton penalty (75 mins).
**Nottingham Forest:** Farmer, Whare, Thomas, Morley, McKinley, Burkitt, Scott, Barrett, Wilson, Holder, Small.
*Scorer:* Scott (48 mins).
*Referee:* A. Holland (Barnsley).
*Attendance:* 17,200.

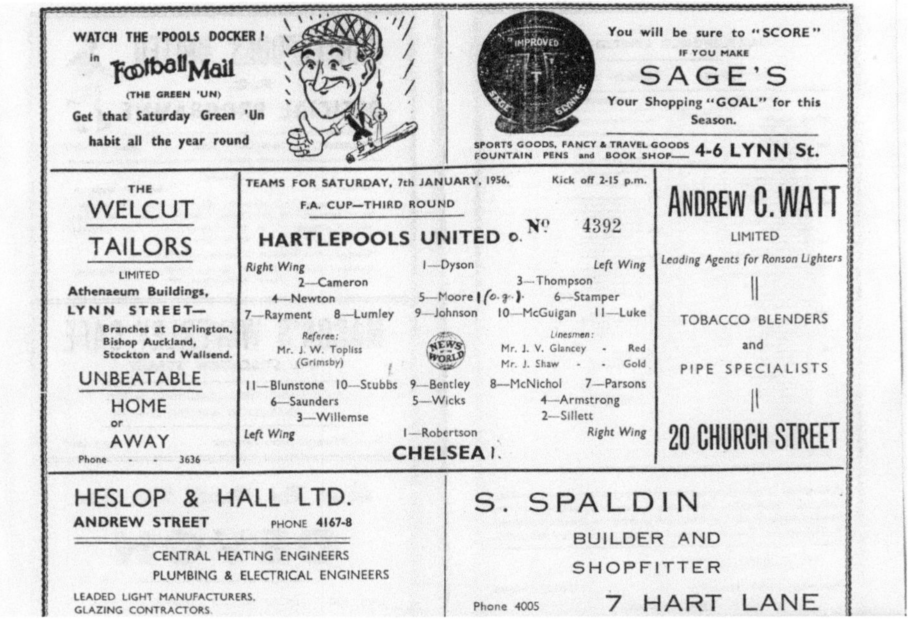

WATCH THE 'POOLS DOCKER !
in
FootballMail
(THE GREEN 'UN)
Get that Saturday Green 'Un
habit all the year round

You will be sure to "SCORE"
IF YOU MAKE
SAGE'S
Your Shopping "GOAL" for this Season.
SPORTS GOODS, FANCY & TRAVEL GOODS
FOUNTAIN PENS and BOOK SHOP— 4-6 LYNN St.

THE
WELCUT
TAILORS
LIMITED
Athenaeum Buildings,
LYNN STREET—
Branches at Darlington, Bishop Auckland, Stockton and Wallsend.
UNBEATABLE
HOME
or
AWAY
Phone - - 3636

TEAMS FOR SATURDAY, 7th JANUARY, 1956. Kick off 2-15 p.m.
F.A. CUP—THIRD ROUND
No 4392

HARTLEPOOLS UNITED 0.

Right Wing — Left Wing
1—Dyson
2—Cameron 3—Thompson
4—Newton 5—Moore 1 (o.g.) 6—Stamper
7—Rayment 8—Lumley 9—Johnson 10—McGuigan 11—Luke

Referee: Mr. J. W. Topliss (Grimsby)
Linesmen: Mr. J. V. Glancey - Red; Mr. J. Shaw - - Gold

11—Blunstone 10—Stubbs 9—Bentley 8—McNichol 7—Parsons
6—Saunders 5—Wicks 4—Armstrong
3—Willemse 2—Sillett
1—Robertson
Left Wing — Right Wing

CHELSEA 1.

ANDREW C. WATT
LIMITED
Leading Agents for Ronson Lighters
TOBACCO BLENDERS
and
PIPE SPECIALISTS
20 CHURCH STREET

HESLOP & HALL LTD.
ANDREW STREET PHONE 4167-8
CENTRAL HEATING ENGINEERS
PLUMBING & ELECTRICAL ENGINEERS
LEADED LIGHT MANUFACTURERS,
GLAZING CONTRACTORS.

S. SPALDIN
BUILDER AND
SHOPFITTER
Phone 4005 7 HART LANE

Hartlepool v Chelsea programme.

## *Match to Remember 6* — 7 January 1956

# Hartlepools United 0 Chelsea 1

After defeating Gateshead and Chesterfield in the first two rounds of the FA Cup, Hartlepools United were given a plum home tie against the reigning Football League champions Chelsea. The directors immediately announced the game was to be all-ticket for the first-ever visit of the reigning champions to the Victoria Ground for a competitive game.

A crowd of over 16,000 welcomed the visitors, who were at full strength apart from Dicks in place of Armstrong, who had taken ill during the previous evening. Chelsea won the toss and elected to attack the Rink End against a 'Pools side wearing shirts borrowed, from Arsenal due to the clash of traditional blue and white colours. This arrangement was facilitated by Fred Westgarth through his long-standing friendship with Tom Whittaker, the Arsenal manager.

From the outset it was apparent that the visitors were a physically stronger side, with Willemse and Wicks prominent in the early exchanges. 'Pools' first threat came from a Luke cross, which Johnson laid back to Newton, whose hard low dive was blocked by Saunders. After a Johnson effort was saved in fine style by Robertson it became apparent that for all 'Pools effort and enthusiasm the champions were the stronger side, and after an opening 20 minutes in which the home side were the equals of their more illustrious opponents, Chelsea took the lead.

Willemse and Robertson halt another Hartlepool attack.

After Dyson had saved smartly from Bentley, Blunstone advanced down the left wing and crossed, more in hope than anticipation. Dyson, aware of the presence of Parsons, chose to fist the ball rather than catch it. The ball struck Moore on the chest and gently rolled into the goal with the goalkeeper completely wrong-footed.

The home side regrouped following this piece of misfortune and continued to battle away at a Chelsea defence which looked as strong and formidable as a brick wall. Towards

Willemse clears from Joe Rayment.

half-time the Blues nearly scored again when a Bentley header completely beat Dyson only to miss by inches. The half-time break came with the champions well in control.

**Half-time: Hartlepools United 0 Chelsea 1**

The second half continued where the first left off, with the home side making determined efforts to score against a well drilled, highly organised side which was content to sit back and defend their lead. As the game wore on the superior fitness of the visitors began to tell, with Wicks outstanding, and despite 'Pools' best efforts they could not breech the visitors' defence. Long before the final whistle the home supporters resigned themselves to the inevitable and the game finished without any last-minute drama.

**Full-time: Hartlepools United 0 Chelsea 1**

**Hartlepools United:** Dyson, Cameron, Thompson, Newton, Moore, Stamper, Rayment, Lumley, Johnson, McGuigan, Luke.

**Chelsea:** Robertson, Sillett, Willemse, Dicks, Wicks, Saunders, Parsons, McNichol, Bentley, Stubbs, Blunstone.

*Scorer:* Moore own-goal (23 mins).

*Referee:* J.W. Topliss (Grimsby).

*Attendance:* 16,862.

---

## *Match to Remember 7* **5 January 1957**

# Hartlepools United 3 Manchester United 4

Following the visit of Chelsea in the third round of the FA Cup the previous season, Hartlepools United hardly dare hope for another home draw against the reigning Football League champions, having won through hard-fought ties against Selby Town and Blyth Spartans. Yet that is what happened with the visit of Manchester United, the celebrated 'Busby Babes'.

As with Chelsea, the Hartlepools directors immediately declared the tie all-ticket with a doubling of admission prices. Despite this and poor weather, a record attendance of 17,264 paid £3,470 to witness a classic Cup encounter. The visitors were at full strength in contrast to their hosts, who made enforced changes due to Bobby Lumley's freak accident during a 'head tennis' exhibition at a local theatre, with Frank Stamper moving to inside-forward and Billy Anderson covering the wing half-back position.

From the kick-off Manchester United attacked at a pace which belied the muddy conditions and it was no surprise when Whelan gave them the lead after seven minutes, quickly followed by a second goal from the impressive Berry a minute later. Despite the speed and power of their opponents, 'Pools responded positively with Johnson proving a handful for Mark Jones. In spite of the home side's best efforts they fell further behind in the 32nd minute when Taylor scored from a Berry pass. Further woe befell 'Pools when

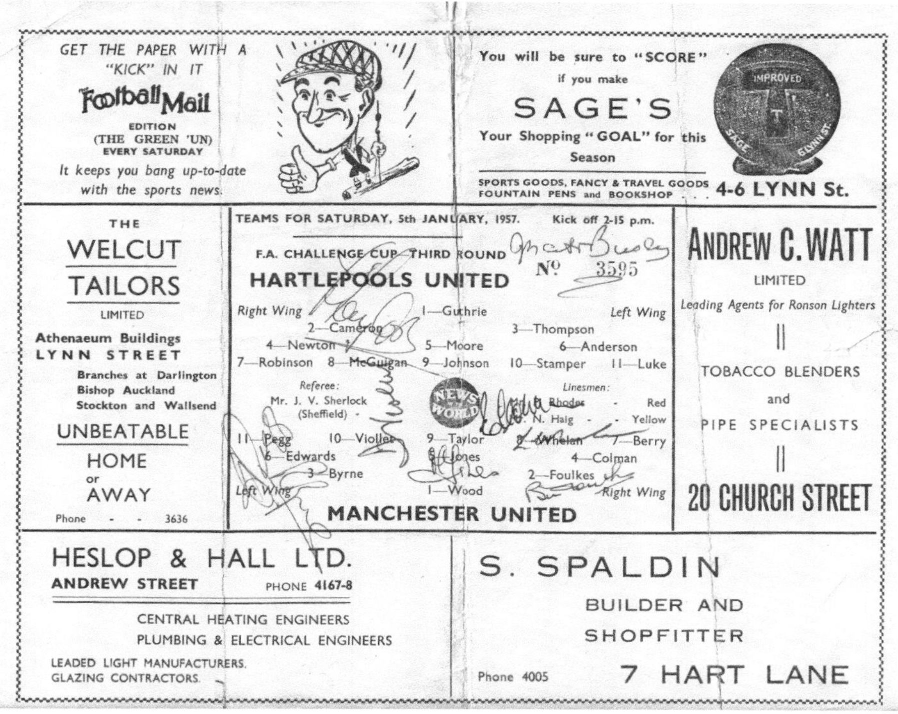

GET THE PAPER WITH A "KICK" IN IT

Football Mail

EDITION (THE GREEN 'UN) EVERY SATURDAY

It keeps you bang up-to-date with the sports news.

You will be sure to "SCORE" if you make

SAGE'S

Your Shopping "GOAL" for this Season

SPORTS GOODS, FANCY & TRAVEL GOODS FOUNTAIN PENS and BOOKSHOP . . . 4-6 LYNN St.

THE WELCUT TAILORS LIMITED

Athenaeum Buildings LYNN STREET

Branches at Darlington Bishop Auckland Stockton and Wallsend

UNBEATABLE HOME or AWAY

Phone - - 3636

TEAMS FOR SATURDAY, 5th JANUARY, 1957. Kick off 2-15 p.m.

F.A. CHALLENGE CUP—THIRD ROUND

Nº 3595

HARTLEPOOLS UNITED

Right Wing — Left Wing

1—Guthrie

2—Cameron 3—Thompson

4—Newton 5—Moore 6—Anderson

7—Robinson 8—McGuigan 9—Johnson 10—Stamper 11—Luke

Referee: Mr. J. V. Sherlock (Sheffield)

Linesmen: Mr. B. Rhodes - Red; N. Haig - Yellow

11—Pegg 10—Viollet 9—Taylor 8—Whelan 7—Berry

6—Edwards 5—Jones 4—Colman

3—Byrne 2—Foulkes

1—Wood

Left Wing — Right Wing

MANCHESTER UNITED

ANDREW C. WATT LIMITED

Leading Agents for Ronson Lighters

TOBACCO BLENDERS and PIPE SPECIALISTS

20 CHURCH STREET

HESLOP & HALL LTD.

ANDREW STREET PHONE 4167-8

CENTRAL HEATING ENGINEERS

PLUMBING & ELECTRICAL ENGINEERS

LEADED LIGHT MANUFACTURERS. GLAZING CONTRACTORS.

S. SPALDIN

BUILDER AND SHOPFITTER

Phone 4005 7 HART LANE

Manchester United programme signed by Matt Busby and players.

Johnson was injured and left the field for treatment before some relief was forthcoming with a goal by Stamper following a mistake by Byrne. The first half ended with Guthrie making a fine save from Berry, who continued to be a major threat.

**Half-time: Hartlepools United 1 Manchester United 3**

Hartlepools were forced to re-organise for the second half due to Johnson's injury, with Robinson playing a central role and the injured centre-forward moving to the right wing.

Newton's low drive equalises the score at 3–3.

These changes unsettled the visitors' defence and it was no surprise when an unmarked Johnson reduced the arrears with a header from Luke's cross. This goal galvanised the home supporters and, in a frenzy of excitement, Newton levelled the scores with a low drive through a packed penalty area. Both sides tired in the heavy conditions as they searched for a winner and after Guthrie had saved from Berry the ball broke to Whelan, who restored the visitors' lead after 76 minutes. In the closing minutes Johnson cut in and shot into the side netting as 'Pools pressed for an equaliser, and the match ended with the home side on the attack, forcing Ray Wood to punch clear from a corner.

**Full-time: Hartlepools United 3 Manchester United 4**
**Hartlepools United:** Guthrie, Cameron, Thompson, Newton, Moore, Anderson, Robinson, McGuigan, Johnson, Stamper, Luke.
*Scorers:* Stamper (35 mins), Johnson (53 mins), Newton (65 mins).
**Manchester United:** Wood, Foulkes, Byrne, Colman, Woods, Edwards, Berry, Whelan, Taylor, Viollett, Pegg.
*Scorers:* Whelan (7 mins), Berry (8 mins), Taylor (32 mins), Whelan (76 mins).
*Referee:* J.V. Sherlock (Sheffield).
*Attendance:* 17,264.

---

## *Match to Remember 8* **26 August 1957**

# Hartlepools United 5 Darlington 1

The opening home game of the 1957–58 season saw local rivals Darlington visit the Victoria Ground for a mid-week fixture. Hartlepools had won their first game of the season the previous Saturday, 2–1 at Accrington, and their new manager, Ray Middleton, was looking to build on this success despite key players missing through injury.

The combination of a warm sunny evening, kick-off 6.30pm, and the opening of the new Mill House terracing attracted a record crowd to the Victoria Ground for a mid-week game of 14,876, which included a strong contingent from Darlington. If they were expecting fireworks from the first whistle they were disappointed as the opening half was a sterile affair, with the visitors' tough tackling disrupting the normally smooth play of the home forwards, with Luke particularly out of form. When a chance did fall to Willis, playing in place of the injured Rayment, his weak effort was easily saved by Tennant. The half ended in stalemate with both sides struggling to find their form and defences well in control.

**Half-time: Hartlepools United 0 Darlington 0**
The opening to the second half was in direct contrast to what had gone on earlier. Almost immediately Jackie Smith converted a cross past Tennant to give 'Pools the lead. This goal transformed the home side's forwards as they found the extra yard of pace to unsettle

The Hartlepool United players who stormed to victory over Darlington. Back row: N. Westgarth (trainer), W. Anderson, K. Waugh, J. Newton, R. Guthrie, F. Stamper, R. Thompson, J. Smith, F. Perryman (secretary). Front row: J. Rayment, R. Lumley, K. Johnson, W. Moore, G. Willis, T. McGuigan, G. Luke.

Darlington's previously untroubled defence. Central to these attacks was Bobby Lumley, who added a second within seven minutes of the opener, and a third after 65 minutes. With centre-forward Smith working tirelessly to unsettle the Darlington defenders it fell to winger Willis to complete the home scoring with strikes in the 68th and 73rd minutes. Darlington, to their credit, never gave up in the face of such an onslaught and gained a small consolation five minutes from time when Harbertson scored.

Despite the home forwards grabbing the headlines, 'Pools defence also played its part, with Guthrie, Waugh and the ultra-reliable Moore in commanding form. 'Pools captain Moore never allowed the visitors' highly regarded centre-forward Tulip to become a major threat.

**Full-time: Hartlepools United 5 Darlington 1**
**Hartlepools United:** Guthrie, Waugh, Thompson, Newton, Moore, Stamper, Willis, Lumley, Smith, McGuigan, Luke.
*Scorers:* Smith (47 mins), Lumley (54 mins), Lumley (65 mins), Willis (68 min), Willis (73 mins).
**Darlington:** Tennant, Storey, Henderson, Neale, Greener, Rutherford, Forster, Harbertson, Tulip, Morton, Moran.
*Scorer:* Harbertson (85 mins).
*Referee:* L. Howarth (Beverley).
*Attendance:* 14,876.

## *Match to Remember 9* **4 April 1959**

# Hartlepools United 10 Barrow 1

The 1958–59 season saw the introduction of the new League structure, with Hartlepools United placed in the Fourth Division following a disappointing final Division Three North campaign which resulted in a lowly 17th-place finish.

With the team in transition under Ray Middleton results did not match expectations, and by the time bottom club Barrow arrived the home side were hardly better off, languishing in 22nd position. Despite this a crowd of over 4,000 turned up to witness what was to be not only a record victory for Hartlepools United but also a record for the newly formed Fourth Division.

From the kick-off the Barrow defence struggled to cope with the home attacks, and it took only eight minutes for Harry Clark to open the scoring. The visitors somehow managed to hold on until the 19th minute when centre-forward Smith added a second. After a half-hour of total home domination George Luke added a third, before Smith completed his hat-trick with goals in the 34th and 38 minutes. The visitors' defence, with the exception of goalkeeper Heys, was now a complete shambles and further goals from Scott and Langland completed the first-half scoring, four goals having come in a 10-minute spell.

**Half-time: Hartlepools United 7 Barrow 0**

After a quiet opening to the second half, the unthinkable happened when Kemp pulled one back for Barrow after 55 minutes. This sparked the home forwards back into action against the inept visiting defence, with only over-eagerness preventing further goals. Eventually Luke hammered in his second and goal number eight of the game, to be followed a few minutes later by Clark scoring his second. As if to add insult to injury, Marsden, the visitors' centre-half, then scored through his own-goal seven minutes from time despite a despairing dive by Heys, Barrow's shell-shocked goalkeeper.

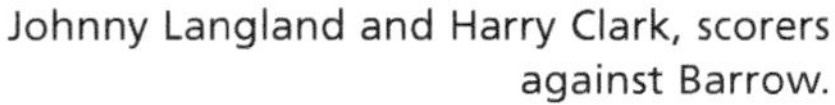

Johnny Langland and Harry Clark, scorers against Barrow.

**Full-time: Hartlepools United 10 Barrow 1**

**Hartlepools United:** Oakley, Cameron, Waugh, Johnson, Moore, Anderson, Scott, Langland, Smith, Clark, Luke.

*Scorers:* Clark (8 mins), Smith (19 mins), Luke (30 mins), Smith (34 mins), Smith (38 mins), Scott (42 mins), Langland (44 mins), Luke (65 mins), Clark (79 mins), Marsden own-goal (83 mins).

**Barrow:** Heys, Simpson, Jackson, Proctor, Marsden, Murray, King, McIlvenney, Purdon, Keen, Kemp.

*Scorer:* Kemp (55 mins).

*Referee:* A.W. Luty (Leeds).

*Attendance:* 4,126.

---

## *Match to Remember 10* — **30 October 1965**

# Bradford City 1 Hartlepools United 3

Brian Clough's first game as a manager unsurprisingly produced a drama even before a ball was kicked. His team sheet included Alan Fox at centre-half, who on the eve of the match was transferred to Bradford City for £3,500, thereby requiring the new manager to make

Clough's first team against Bradford City. Ashworth replaced Fox, who had been transferred to Bradford.

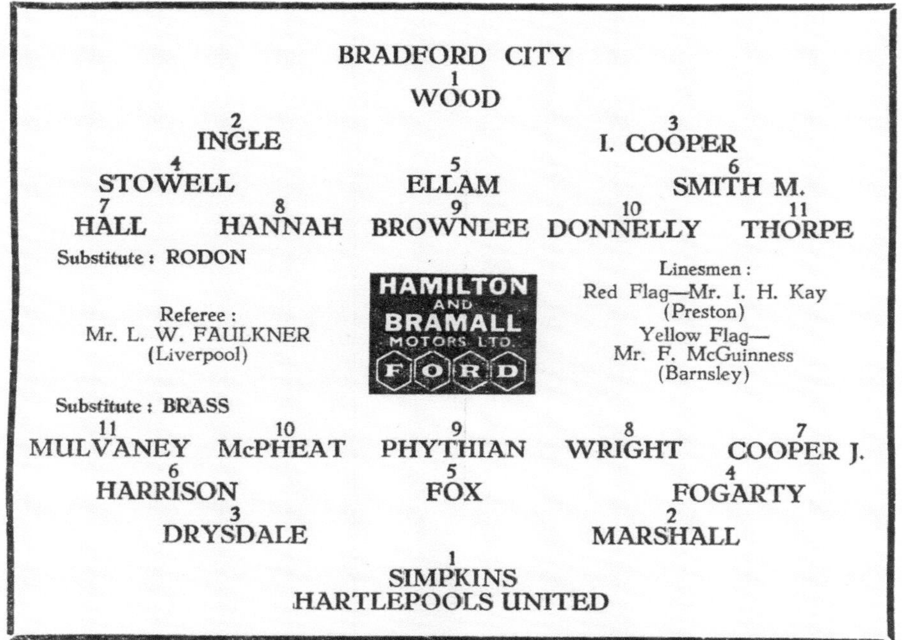

BRADFORD CITY

1 WOOD

2 INGLE — 3 I. COOPER

4 STOWELL — 5 ELLAM — 6 SMITH M.

7 HALL — 8 HANNAH — 9 BROWNLEE — 10 DONNELLY — 11 THORPE

Substitute : RODON

Referee : Mr. L. W. FAULKNER (Liverpool)



Linesmen : Red Flag—Mr. I. H. Kay (Preston) Yellow Flag—Mr. F. McGuinness (Barnsley)

Substitute : BRASS

11 MULVANEY — 10 McPHEAT — 9 PHYTHIAN — 8 WRIGHT — 7 COOPER J.

6 HARRISON — 5 FOX — 4 FOGARTY

3 DRYSDALE — 2 MARSHALL

1 SIMPKINS

HARTLEPOOLS UNITED

Jimmy Mulvaney scored two goals against Bradford City.

several changes to the original line up chosen by the directors before his appointment. This was Hartlepools' seventh away game of the season, and in the previous six they had scored only a single goal and earned a solitary point, evidence of the task facing Clough. Both teams were propping up the Fourth Division, with Bradford in bottom place with six points from 13 games and 'Pools a mere two points better off.

Ambrose Fogarty won the toss for the visitors and the match started on a heavy pitch following persistent overnight rain in front of a meagre crowd of barely 2,000. Bradford had the better of the early exchanges, hitting the post and dictating the play before 'Pools responded in a positive manner. After 21 minutes a Mulvaney free-kick found Cliff Wright, who scored from 10 yards. This was only Hartlepools' second away League goal in the season to date. Even better was to come when Jimmy Mulvaney, who had a fine game, scored a second goal from a tight angle after 35 minutes. Bradford replied almost immediately when Ellam scored with a spectacular half volley which gave Simpkins no chance.

**Half-time: Bradford City 1 Hartlepools United 2**

The second half continued with the visitors dominating the game. Phythian in particular was giving Fox, his opposite number, recently signed from Hartlepools, a hard time. It was no surprise when, late in the game, Mulvaney added a third goal following a Phythian run past three defenders. Both Mulvaney and McPheat went close to adding a fourth goal in the final minutes. This win lifted 'Pools up to the heady heights of 22nd place, and so began the career of one of football's most illustrious managers.

**Full-time: Bradford City 1 Hartlepools United 3**

**Bradford City:** Wood, Ingle, Cooper, Stowell, Fox, Smith, Hall, Hannah, Donnelly, Ellam, Thorpe.

*Scorer:* Ellam (36 mins).

**Hartlepools United:** Simpkins, Marshall, Drysdale, Fogarty, Harrison, Ashworth, Cooper, Wright, Phythian, McPheat, Mulvaney.

*Scorers:* Wright (21 mins), Mulvaney (35 mins), Mulvaney (84 mins).

*Referee:* L.W. Faulkner (Liverpool).

*Attendance:* 2,373.

## *Match to Remember 11* **6 May 1968**

# Swansea Town 0 Hartlepools United 2

Hartlepool were on the verge of their first-ever promotion when they played Swansea Town in the penultimate game of the 1967–68 season. The team was on a 14-game unbeaten run which had taken them into the promotion places when they arrived at the Vetch Field needing a win to ensure Third Division football at the 'Vic' the following season. Their previous game against struggling Exeter City had finished goalless, and with Bradford City surprisingly dropping a point at home, 'Pools needed two points from their last two games to secure a long-awaited promotion. By a quirk of the fixture list, both matches were against Swansea Town.

The match did not get off to an auspicious start as both teams had to change in a nearby Army drill hall due to Swansea's main stand having burnt down during the season. Unperturbed by the unfamiliar facilities, 'Pools made a storming start which saw them take the lead within the first 10 minutes, with Cliff Wright winning the ball from Slee and passing to Bobby Cummings, who scored from just inside the penalty area. The home side, however, were determined to make life difficult for the visitors, with the veteran Welsh international Ivor Allchurch in superb form with his prompting and passing which required the 'Pools defence, expertly marshalled by John Gill, to be at the top of their game.

The 1968 promotion squad discuss tactics with Gus McLean.

**Half-time: Swansea Town 0 Hartlepools United 1**

Any hopes that the home team had of spoiling the promotion party were dispelled just after the hour mark, when McGovern's corner was volleyed by Wright against a post, only for Wilson Hepplewhite to slam home the rebound. Swansea, however, refused to give in and a strong rally saw goal-bound efforts from Humphries and Allchurch blocked on the goalline by, firstly, Drysdale and then Bircumshaw.

With Sheridan and Parry in dominant form, the latter having a strong penalty appeal refused, the remaining minutes were played out without any further alarms for the visitors. At the final whistle the small band of loyal fans which had made the long journey to South Wales celebrated their team's first-ever promotion in style.

**Full-time: Swansea Town 0 Hartlepools United 2**

**Swansea Town:** Hayes, R. Evans, Gomersall, Screen, Slee, Lawrence, Humphries, Williams, Todd, I. Allchurch, B. Evans.

*Substitute:* Thomas for Todd (71 mins).

**Hartlepools United:** Smith, Bircumshaw, Drysdale, Sheridan, Gill, Parry, McGovern, Bell, Cummings, Wright, Hepplewhite.

*Scorers:* Cummings (9 mins), Hepplewhite (69 mins).

*Referee:* D. Nippard (Bournemouth).

*Attendance:* 3,491.

---

## *Match to Remember 12* **12 November 1974**

# Hartlepool 1 Aston Villa 1

Hartlepool played a staggering seven games to reach the fourth round of the Football League Cup for the first time. After disposing of Workington, they required four matches to beat Bournemouth and finally progressed against Blackburn Rovers after a replay against them at Ewood Park. Their opponents, Aston Villa, were ultimately destined to win the trophy, beating Norwich City in the Final as well as gaining promotion to the First Division as runners-up to Manchester United.

Given the pedigree of the opposition, it was no surprise that a crowd of 12,305 paying gate receipts of £5,000, a record attendance for the Victoria Ground for a floodlight game, turned up to witness a classic Cup tie. From the kick-off the illustrious visitors took control in the early stages before 'Pools rallied and had strong appeals for a penalty when Gauden was brought down by Brown. On the half hour Malcolm Moore missed a glorious chance for the home side, and shortly afterwards Villa's veteran defender Aitken scored with a powerful shot, which gave Watling no chance. After this reverse both the home team and their supporters became a little subdued as the visitors seemed content to hold on to their advantage. Despite the best efforts of centre-forward Malcolm Moore, 'Pools were unable to create any clear-cut chances and the interval offered a welcome respite for the home team.

Aston Villa centre-half Nicholl clears a 'Pools attack.

**Half-time: Hartlepool 0 Aston Villa 1**
If the first half had belonged to the First Division side, the second most definitely belonged to a rejuvenated Hartlepool. From the restart 'Pools threw everything into attack with the visitors forced to defend in depth, with only a lone forward in the home half of the field. After several near misses the pressure finally paid off on the hour mark when, from Shoulder's free-kick, Moore deflected the ball wide of Cumbes to level the score. 'Pools, urged on by a capacity crowd, maintained the pressure up to the final whistle without quite managing to deliver a knock-out blow.

**Full-time: Hartlepool 1 Aston Villa 1**
**Hartlepool:** Watling, R. Smith, Shoulder, Dawes, Goad, Potter, Honour, Gauden, Moore, McMahon, Spelman.
*Scorer:* Moore (60 mins).
**Aston Villa:** Cumbes, Robson, Aitken, Ross, Nicholl, Brown, Graydon, Little, Campbell, Hamilton, Carrodus.
*Scorer:* Aitken (33 mins).
*Referee:* M. Lowe (Sheffield).
*Attendance:* 12,305.

---

## *Match to Remember 13* **7 January 1978**

# Hartlepool United 2 Crystal Palace 1

Following early rounds victories over Tranmere Rovers and Runcorn, 'Pools were rewarded with a third-round FA Cup tie at home to Crystal Palace of the Second Division. Despite 'Pools' 23rd position in Division Four and their record of never having beaten a side from

Derrick Downing and Malcolm Poskett, who both played major roles in the FA Cup defeat of Crystal Palace.

the top two divisions in the FA Cup, the tie attracted national attention. Palace were dubbed by the London press 'the team of the 80s', having won the FA Youth Cup the previous season, and they were managed by the flamboyant Terry Venables in the early stages of a career which was to embrace Tottenham Hotspur, Barcelona and England.

The game started with Palace pressing for an early goal to settle any pre-match nerves. This duly arrived after nine minutes when Chatterton scored from a defence-splitting pass by Swindlehurst. Many home supporters in the near 10,000 crowd must have feared the worst, only for their fears to be allayed a few minutes later by Bob Newton, who took advantage of some slack marking in the Palace defence to equalise with a shot from 15 yards. Before the visitors had time to recover from this setback, a move involving Malone, Gibb and Poskett resulted in Newton heading home to give 'Pools the lead after 18 minutes. For several minutes the home side pressed for a third goal with Poskett having a effort disallowed for offside and Gibb missing a sitter with the goal at his mercy. Gradually Palace came back into the game, and the half-time whistle brought an end to a classic half of Cup tie football.

**Half-time: Hartlepool United 2 Crystal Palace 1**

The start of the second half saw a different Palace side as they dominated the early exchanges, no doubt galvanised by a few words of wisdom from Terry Venables. During this period Eddie Edgar was outstanding in the home goal, making brilliant saves from Swindlehurst and Hinshelwood. The home crowd rallied behind their team, and as the half wore on the absence of an equaliser caused frustrations for the visitors, which resulted in a loss of control and, eventually, the game.

Hartlepool had won a famous victory, their first against opposition from the second tier of English football and only the second time in their history they reached the fourth round. The result caused many media commentators to label it 'the shock of the round'.

**Full-time: Hartlepool United 2 Crystal Palace 1**
**Hartlepool United:** Edgar, Malone, Creamer, Gibb, Ayre, Smith, McMordie, Downing, Newton, Poskett, Bielby.
*Scorers:* Newton (14 mins), Newton (18 mins).
**Crystal Palace:** Burns, Hinshelwood, Sansom, Holder, Cannon, Gilbert, Nicholas, Chatterton, Swindlehurst, Bourne, Silkman.
*Scorer:* Chatterton (9 mins).
*Referee:* D. Richardson (Great Harwood).
*Attendance:* 9,502.

---

## *Match to Remember 14* **11 May 1991**

# Hartlepool United 3 Northampton Town 1

Hartlepool United's 1990–91 promotion challenge went to the final game of the season in what was one of the tightest contests for the coveted top-four places in recent years. On the final Saturday of the season only one point separated Darlington, Blackpool, Stockport County, Peterborough United and 'Pools, who had an inferior goal difference to their four rivals. Hence they needed to beat Northampton Town, who still had a chance of a Play-off place themselves, and hope one of the others dropped points.

A capacity crowd of nearly 7,000 packed into the 'Vic' for what was to be an afternoon of high drama. The home side started in determined fashion, pressing for an early goal to calm the nerves of supporters who had become accustomed to being let down on the big occasion. United attacked in force with Allon, Baker and Dalton prominent in the early exchanges. It was the latter who took on the visitors' defence in the 17th minute and scored a trademark goal. The crowd went wild, expecting more goals from the potent home strike-force, only to see the visitors reassert themselves and press for an equaliser. It came as no surprise that just before the half-time whistle Brown levelled the scores, which it had to be said was a fair reflection of the overall first-half play.

**Half-time: Hartlepool United 1 Northampton Town 1**
The second half began with the capacity crowd aware that Blackpool, managed by Billy Ayre, were losing at Walsall and that a win would guarantee 'Pools' promotion. Nevertheless, the visitors had no intention of letting up as their Play-off hopes were still very much alive. A tense opening to the final 45 minutes of the season saw both teams reluctant to take risks, with Wilson forcing a fine save from Kevin Poole. On the hour mark the Allon–Baker partnership – which was to total 40 League goals for the campaign – took the game by the scruff of the neck.

Paul Dalton scores the first goal against Northampton.

First Joe Allon restored 'Pools' advantage following a McKinnon corner, and hardly before the cheers had died down Paul Baker stormed through the heart of the visitors' defence and put the game beyond doubt. The timing and manner of these goals knocked the stuffing out of Northampton and the remaining minutes were played in a carnival atmosphere as the crowd celebrated only their club's second-ever promotion.

**Full-time: Hartlepool United 3 Northampton Town 1**
**Hartlepool United:** Poole, Nobbs, McKinnon, Tupling, MacPhail, Bennyworth, Allon, Olsson, Baker, Honour, Dalton.
*Scorers:* Dalton (17 mins), Allon (61 mins), Baker (64 mins).
**Northampton Town:** Gleasure, Williams, Wilson, Terry, Angus, Quow, Campbell, Bell, Adcock, Barnes, Brown.
*Scorer:* Brown (44 mins).
*Referee:* L. Dilkes (Mosley).
*Attendance:* 6,957.

---

## *Match to Remember 15* **2 January 1993**

# Hartlepool United 1 Crystal Palace 0

Following first and second-round victories over Doncaster Rovers and Southport respectively in the FA Cup, 'Pools were rewarded with a third-round home tie against Steve Coppell's Crystal Palace, founder members of the newly formed FA Premier League. The draw was greeted with some trepidation by home supporters as the previous season the sides had met in the Football League Cup, and after a creditable draw at the 'Vic', United were comprehensively beaten in the replay, 6–1 at Selhurst Park. A near capacity crowd was present to witness 'Pools' first-ever appearance on the BBC's *Match of the Day* programme, which earned the club a £12,000 match fee. It was also chairman Gary Gibson's 38th birthday.

Both sides made a cautious start before Steve Jones, 'Pools' teenage goalkeeper, made a brave save at the feet of Thomas. The home side came more into the game with Andy Saville prominent in attack, supported by Nicky Southall who had an effort blocked by Thomas. Palace then forced three corners in succession which were eventually cleared, and as half-time approached Olsson lifted the home supporters' spirits, bringing a fine save from Nigel Martyn.

**Half-time: Hartlepool United 0 Crystal Palace 0**

The second half continued in the same vein as the first with neither side prepared to commit to all out attack. The visitors seemed content to hold out for a draw and even a Johnrose header which flashed just wide did not alter their tactics. 'Pools now had the advantage, at least territorially, and committed more players forward in search of a goal. Three successive corners were forced and only partially cleared when the ball broke to Nicky Southall inside the penalty area. Although not directly threatening Martyn's goal, Shaw rushed at the home player and made contact, which resulted in Southall going to ground. Dermot Gallacher, a hugely experienced referee, had a perfect view of the incident and did not hesitate in awarding a penalty. Despite vehement protests from the visitors, the coolest man inside Victoria Ground, Andy Saville, stepped up and placed a perfect penalty-kick low inside Martyn's right-hand post.

The goal came after 82 minutes and despite the time remaining the Palace players seemed demoralised by the penalty award. 'Pools played out the final minutes without further alarms to record their first victory over opposition from the top tier of English football.

Andy Saville's penalty v Crystal Palace.

**Full-time: Hartlepool United 1 Crystal Palace 0**

**Hartlepool United:** Jones, R. Cross, P. Cross, Gilchrist, MacPhail, Emerson, Johnrose, Olsson, Saville, Honour, Southall.

*Scorer:* Saville penalty (82 mins).

**Crystal Palace:** Martyn, Humphrey, Shaw, Coleman, Young, Bowry, Osborn, Thomas, Armstrong, Rodger, McGoldrick.

*Referee:* D. Gallagher (Oxfordshire).

*Attendance:* 6,721.

---

## *Match to Remember 16* **13 September 2003**

# Hartlepool United 8 Grimsby Town 1

Grimsby Town arrived at Victoria Park on this late summer evening to face a Hartlepool side which had lost only one of their opening League games and recorded a victory over Sheffield Wednesday in the League Cup. Balanced against this impressive record, however, was the previous home game against Oldham which had finished goalless.

Neale Cooper made his attacking intentions clear with his team selection which saw Gabbiadini, Robinson and Williams for a three-pronged attack against a Grimsby side which included player-manager Paul Groves and former 'Pools youth-team goalkeeper Aidan Davison.

From the outset it was obvious the 'The Mariners' would struggle to hold a fluent home team, whose approach was to attack, attack, attack. The only surprise was it took until the 19th minute for the first goal when the hapless Groves headed Strachan's free-kick past his own

'Pools goalscorers – Eifion Williams, Marco Gabbiadini, Paul Robinson, Ritchie Humphreys and Gavin Strachan.

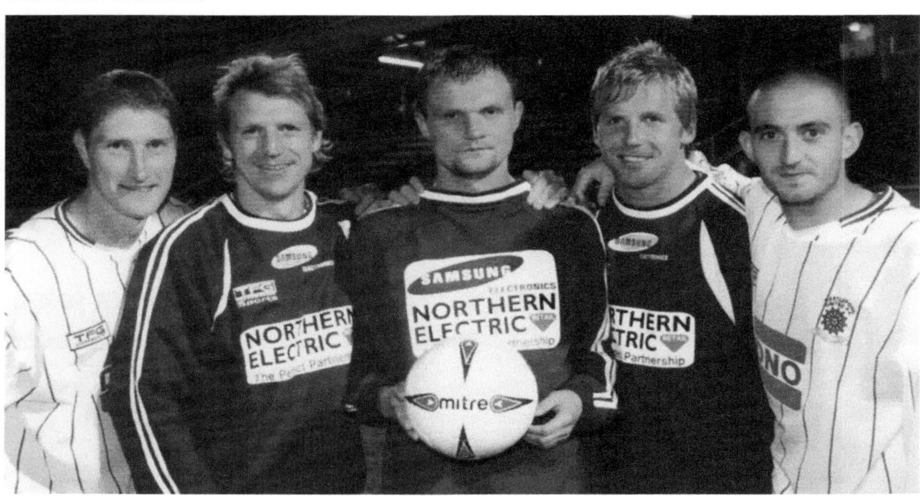

goalkeeper. Worse followed a minute later when Gabbiadini was hauled back by Ford and Paul Robinson calmly side-footed the resulting penalty home. Grimsby's woes increased eight minutes later as Gavin Strachan took advantage of another infringement and fired the free-kick inside Davison's near post. A mere three minutes later goal number four arrived when Barron and Robinson combined to set Richie Humphreys up to score with a trademark finish.

**Half-time: Hartlepool United 4 Grimsby Town 0**

The opening to the second half saw the visitors offer some resistance, with Jon Rowan taking advantage of some slack marking. This merely served to galvanise the home attack once more and Robinson took Robson's through ball in his stride to score a fifth goal. There was still 30 minutes remaining when Marco Gabbiadini added his name to the score sheet, turning Robinson's cross home from close range. Eifion Williams added a seventh goal after Robinson unselfishly passed to the Welshman rather than attempt a shot himself. The striker had his reward minutes later when debutant Ryan McCann and Darrell Clarke combined to set Robinson up for a simple goal, which completed his deserved hat-trick. This goal gave 'Pools their biggest win since the record victory over Barrow in 1959.

A postscript to the game was the plight of some Grimsby fans who understandably exited the ground early only to find that their coach had broken down, thereby delaying their departure from Victoria Park!

**Full-time: Hartlepool United 8 Grimsby Town 1**

**Hartlepool United:** Provett, Barron, Westwood, Nelson, Robson, Strachan, Tinkler, Humphreys, Williams, Gabbiadini, Robinson.

*Substitutes:* Clarke for Strachan (70 mins), McCann for Gabbiadini (72 mins), Easter for Robinson (81 mins).

*Scorers:* Groves own-goal (19 mins), Robinson penalty (20 mins), Strachan (28 mins), Humphreys (31 mins), Robinson (56 mins), Gabbiadini (60 mins), Williams (68 mins), Robinson (80 mins).

**Grimsby Town:** Davison, Crowe, Ford, Crane, Barnard, Cas, Groves, Campbell, Hockless, Rowan, Boulding.

*Substitutes:* Nimmo for Rowan (61 mins), Soames for Boulding (76 mins).

*Scorer:* Rowan (48 mins).

*Referee:* S. Mathieson (Cheshire).

*Attendance:* 5,583.

---

## *Match to Remember 17* — 3 May 2003

# Rushden & Diamonds 1 Hartlepool United 1

Hartlepool United travelled to Nene Park, home of Rushden & Diamonds, accompanied by over 1,600 travelling supporters needing a win to clinch their first-ever Championship

Graeme Lee had a goal disallowed against Rushden & Diamonds.

trophy at any level. To give the game added spice the hosts only needed to avoid defeat to secure their first title in only their second season in the Football League.

After a tentative opening by both teams Rushden gradually gained the upper hand, with Onandi Lowe stretching both Lee and Westwood with pace and aerial power. Anthony Williams then saved well from Bignot and Hall before he was beaten in the 29th minute by the latter from 10 yards. The home side continued to press and Barron made a timely block on a goal-bound shot by Gray. As half-time approached 'Pools saw Lee booked for a mis-timed tackle on Lowe and the injured Watson replaced by Henderson.

**Half-time: Rushden & Diamonds 1 Hartlepool United 0**
'Pools made a determined start to the second half, with Eifion Williams twice forcing saves from Turley before Lee headed home a Humphreys throw, only for the referee to disallow the effort for a foul on goalkeeper Turley by Henderson.

Both sides continued to attack and Rushden almost scored a second when Lowe's header hit the crossbar and bounced down on the goalline. Shortly after the hour mark 'Pools thought they had equalised, only for Lee's header to be disallowed following a foul by Henderson on Turley. Substitute Easter replaced Clarke and immediately won a corner. Hunter cleared the resulting cross only for the visitors to exert more pressure. With only minutes remaining Lee's powerful 25-yard shot was saved by Turley at the expense of a corner. From the resulting kick Chris Westwood headed home from 10 yards to bring the scores level, and there was just time for a final flourish when Tinkler's header was well saved. The draw saw Rushden clinch the Third Division Championship and Hartlepool promoted as runners-up.

**Full-time: Rushden & Diamonds 1 Hartlepool United 1**
**Rushden & Diamonds:** Turley, Edwards, Bignot, Hunter, Underwood, Hall, Bell, Burgess, Gray, Darby, Lowe.
*Scorer:* Hall (29 mins).
**Hartlepool United:** A. Williams, Barron, Robinson, Lee, Westwood, Tinkler, Clark, Humphreys, E. Williams, Watson, Smith.
*Substitutes:* Henderson for Watson (45 mins), Easter for Clarke (78 mins).
*Scorer:* Westwood (89 mins).
*Referee:* L. Cable (Surrey).
*Attendance:* 6,291.

## *Match to Remember 18* **29 May 2005**

# Hartlepool United 2 Sheffield Wednesday 4 (after extra-time)

The League One Play-off Final at Cardiff's Millennium Stadium was the climax to a momentous season which saw Hartlepool United continue to progress both in terms of results on the pitch and overall advancement in the broader footballing sense.

'Pools reached the Play-off Final after a tense two-leg tie against Tranmere Rovers in which there was little to choose between two well-matched teams. 'Pools took a 2–0 lead to Prenton Park after the first leg, only to see it evaporate in the closing minutes of normal time. A penalty shoot-out was required to decide which club went to Cardiff. 'Pools eventually prevailed 6–5, with Richie Humphreys converting the deciding penalty.

On a glorious sunny afternoon Martin Scott led Hartlepool United out to face Sheffield Wednesday for the biggest game in their 97-year history. Records were being set even before the game started as an all-ticket crowd of 59,808, easily the biggest for any game involving 'Pools, settled in their seats to watch the drama unfold.

After a tentative start 'Pools settled down, and Brunt tested Konstantopolous with a low drive. On the half hour Martin Scott was forced into a change when Butler, a surprise choice, was injured in a clash with Whelan and was replaced by Williams. Shortly afterwards Porter, receiving a Nelson pass, went close with a chip over the Wednesday crossbar. A few minutes later, following a corner, Boyd fired over from Sweeney's pass. In the second minute of added time Rocastle made the run from which McGovern, receiving Peacock's pass, fired home from close range to give Wednesday the lead.

PLAY-OFF FINAL

League 1 Play-Off Final Squads

| Hartlepool United | | Sheffield Wednesday | |
| --- | --- | --- | --- |
| Manager: Martin Scott | | Manager: Paul Sturrock | |
| Jim Provett | 1 | 1 | David Lucas |
| Mickey Barron | 2 | 2 | Lee Bullen |
| Hugh Robertson | 3 | 3 | Paul Heckingbottom |
| Mark Tinkler | 4 | 4 | Graeme Lee |
| Michael Nelson | 5 | 5 | Steve Adams |
| Chris Westwood | 6 | 6 | Glenn Whelan |
| Darrell Clarke | 7 | 7 | Jon-Paul McGovern |
| Ritchie Humphreys | 8 | 8 | Matthew Hamshaw |
| Eifion Williams | 9 | 9 | Steven MacLean |
| Adam Boyd | 10 | 10 | Lee Peacock |
| Gavin Strachan | 11 | 11 | Chris Brunt |
| Joel Porter | 14 | 12 | Patrick Collins |
| Antony Sweeney | 15 | 14 | Rory McArdle |
| Jon Daly | 16 | 16 | Richard Wood |
| Ben Clark | 17 | 17 | Richard Evans |
| Matty Robson | 18 | 18 | Alex Bruce |
| Jon Brackstone | 19 | 19 | Paul Smith |
| Steven Istead | 20 | 20 | Lewis McMahon |
| Dimitrios Konstantopoulos | 21 | 21 | Chris Adamson |
| Darren Craddock | 22 | 22 | James Quinn |
| Graham Low | 24 | 23 | Craig Rocastle |
| Andrew Appleby | 25 | 24 | Zigor Aranalde |
| David Foley | 26 | 25 | Drew Talbot |
| James Brown | 28 | 26 | Danny Reet |
| Michael Maidens | 29 | 27 | Graham Barrett |
| Stephen Turnbull | 30 | 28 | Ross Greenwood |
| Thomas Butler | 32 | 30 | Liam Needham |
| Steve Howey | 42 | 31 | Adam Proudlock |
| | | 33 | Robert Poulter |
| | | 34 | Luke Foster |
| | | 39 | Tommy Spurr |

Officials
Referee: **Phil Crossley** (Kent)
Assistant Referees: **Darren Cann** (Norfolk), **Andrew Halliday** (North Yorkshire)
Fourth Official: **Andre Marriner** (West Midlands)

If you require more copies of today's official souvenir programme, you can order them direct from **ProgrammeMaster** on **08700 20 20 20** or visit **www.programmemaster.com**

90 THE FOOTBALL LEAGUE WWW.FOOTBALL-LEAGUE.CO.

The Play-off Final teams.

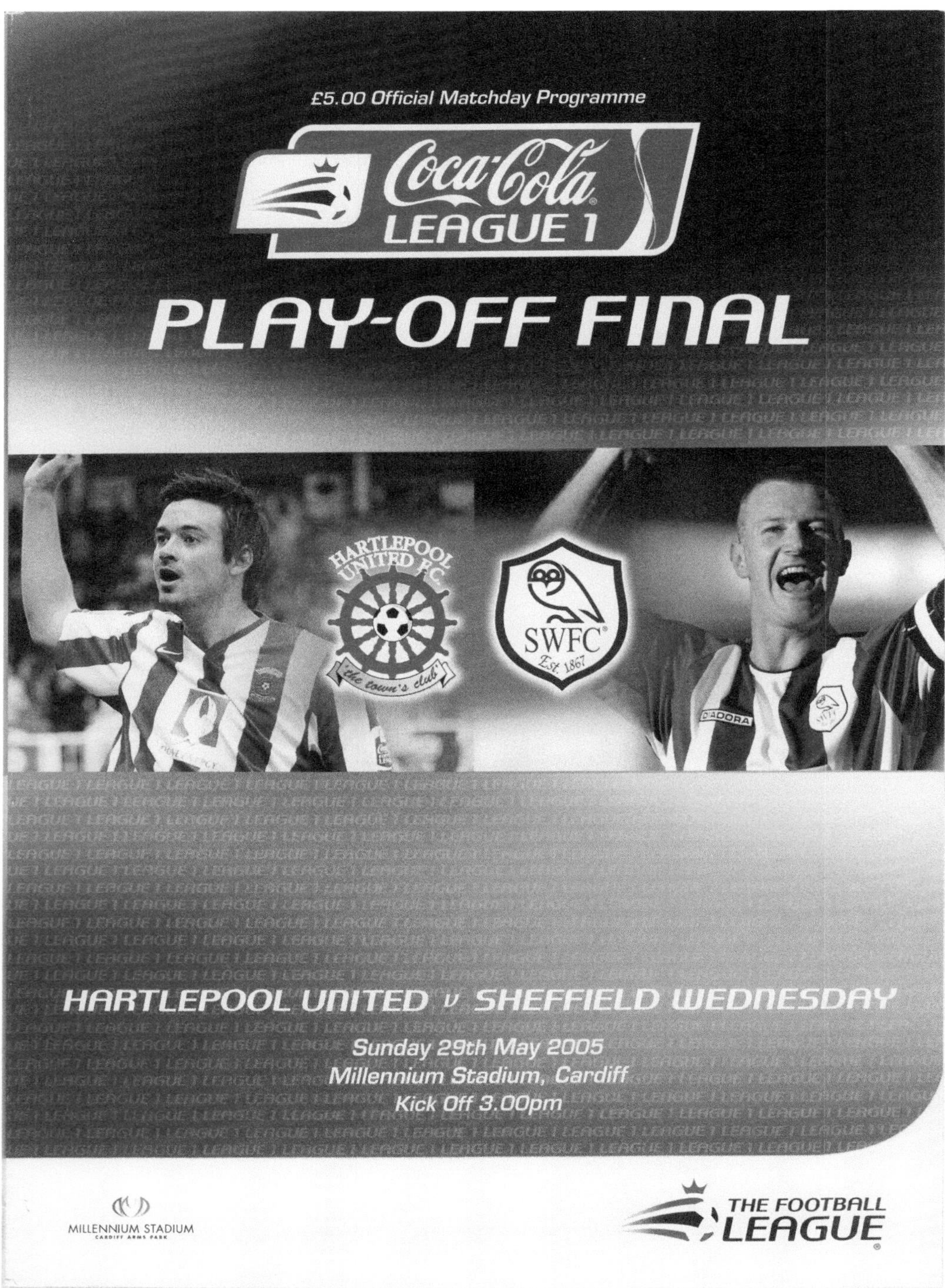


2005 Play-off programme.

Eifion Williams celebrates his equalising goal.

**Half-time: Hartlepool United 0 Sheffield Wednesday 1**

Hartlepool started the second half with a bang, equalising after 63 seconds when a Humphreys throw eluded Boyd only to run on to Eifion Williams, who scored from three yards. Robson and Sweeney then had shots go narrowly wide before McGovern's goal-bound shot was blocked by Robson as the tempo of the game increased. After 69 minutes Jon Daly replaced the tiring Porter, and within a minute he gave 'Pools the lead from Strachan's free-kick. The goal stunned Wednesday and manager Sturrock's response was a triple substitution to bring a halt to 'Pools' momentum. The pivotal moment of the game arrived in the 82nd minute as Wednesday became increasingly desperate. Talbot chased a through ball and outpaced Westwood with Konstantopolous about to dive at the attacker's feet. Westwood appeared to make minimal contact with Talbot, who went to ground, and despite being several yards behind the play, referee Crossley immediately pointed to the penalty spot and sent Westwood off. MacLean scored from the penalty spot to leave 'Pools a player down and no more substitutes available. Just before the end of 90 minutes Nelson blocked Wood's close-range effort, making extra-time inevitable.

**Full-time: Hartlepool United 2 Sheffield Wednesday 2**

Within four minutes the normally reliable Nelson made a slip which allowed Whelan to run through, round Konstantopolous and score in an open goal. The effort of playing a man short on a hot May afternoon took its toll and 'Pools were restricted to a 40-yard effort from Richie Humphreys in their search for an equaliser.

**Extra-time half-time: Hartlepool United 2 Sheffield Wednesday 3**

In the second period of extra-time Wednesday were content to play a game of keep ball as the Hartlepool players expended every last ounce of energy in search of an equaliser. In the final minute of what had been a classic Play-off Final, Talbot found the energy to outpace Robson and Strachan and shoot beyond Konstantopolous to give the scoreline a grossly flattering look in Wednesday's favour.

**Extra-time full-time: Hartlepool United 2 Sheffield Wednesday 4**
**Hartlepool Unted:** Konstantopolous, Barron, Nelson, Westwood, Robson, Strachan, Butler, Sweeney, Humphreys, Porter, Boyd.
*Substitutes:* Williams for Butler (31 mins), Craddock for Barron (61 mins), Daly for Porter (69 mins).
*Scorers:* Williams (47 mins), Daly (71 mins).
**Sheffield Wednesday:** Lucas, Bullen, Heckinbottom, Wood, Bruce, Whelan, McGovern, Brunt, Rocastle, Peacock, Quinn.
*Substitutes:* Collins for Bruce, Talbot for Peacock, MacLean for Quinn (all 77 mins).
*Scorers:* McGovern (45 mins), MacLean penalty (82 mins), Whelan (94 mins), Talbot (120 mins).
*Referee:* P. Crossley (Kent).
*Attendance:* 59,808.

---

## *Match to Remember 19* — 14 April 2007

# Wycombe Wanderers 0 Hartlepool United 1

Hartlepool United made a rapid return to League One when they overcame a stubborn Wycombe Wanderers side to record their 21st win in 26 games, a sequence that included only a single defeat. Their visit to Adams Park against a side which still entertained Play-off ambitions provided a stiff test for a 'Pools team which had suffered a rare defeat in its previous away game against Barnet.

In front of an estimated 1,000 travelling supporters 'Pools had the better of a scrappy first half of few chances. Barker went closest with an overhead-kick which hit a post and Batista saved Eifion Williams follow-up. The half ended with Gary Liddle shooting narrowly wide from 20 yards. Wycombe's best effort came when Doherty and Mooney set up a chance for McGleish, only for the excellent Konstantopolous to avert the danger.

**Half-time: Wycombe Wanderers 0 Hartlepool United 0**
Wycombe started the second half strongly with Jermaine Easter, a former 'Pools player, bringing a smart save from Konstantopolous when through on goal. The substitution of Eifion Williams by Joel Porter nearly paid immediate dividends, with Batista saving well from the Australian. Shortly afterwards, with 'Pools in the ascendancy, both Liddle and Foley (on for Brown) went close before the breakthrough finally came.

With the game entering the closing stages, clever inter-play by Porter and Monkhouse resulted in the latter crossing for Richie Barker to direct a diving header beyond Batista and give 'Pools the victory they so richly deserved – and with it promotion. The win left them

The players celebrate promotion with a win at Wycombe Wanderers. Standing: W. Boland, M. Barron, A. Gibb, G. Liddle, J. Brown, B. Clark, J. Provett, D. Williams, M. Nelson, D. Konstantopoulus, L. Bullock. On the ground: R. Humphreys, J. Porter, E. Williams, D. Foley, R. Baker.

two points clear of Walsall at the top of the table with three games to go, none of which were won and resulted in a final position of second, runners-up to champions Walsall.

**Full-time: Wycombe Wanderers 0 Hartlepool United 1**
**Wycombe Wanderers:** Batista, Stockley, Golbourne, Doherty, Christon, Martin, Grant, Bloomfield, Mooney, Easter, McGleish.
*Substitutes:* Oakes for Doherty (31 mins), Torres for McGleish (61 mins), Onibuje for Christon (76 mins).
**Hartlepool United:** Konstantopolous, D. Williams, Humphreys, Liddle, Nelson, Clark, Brown, Boland, E. Williams, Barker, Monkhouse.
*Substitutes:* Foley for Brown (64 mins), Porter for Williams (69 mins).
*Scorer:* Barker (81 mins).
*Referee:* A. D'Urso (Essex).
*Attendance:* 5,540.

---

## *Match to Remember 20* **3 January 2009**

# Hartlepool United 2 Stoke City 0

Premiership Stoke City arrived at Victoria Park as clear favourites to progress to the fourth round of the FA Cup against a Hartlepool side which had won only one of their previous nine League games. The home side had only once beaten a Premiership team in the

Michael Nelson outjumps the much-vaunted Stoke defence to head the first goal.

competition, Crystal Palace in 1993, and were clearly the underdogs against a Stoke team which came with a reputation for physical and direct tactics, notably the long throw-ins of Rory Delap.

On a cold, clear afternoon the visitors almost scored in the opening minutes when Sonko headed Whelan's cross against a post and Robson cleared off the line. 'Pools came under further pressure when both Sweeney and Mackay were injured and had to be substituted as Stoke continued to press for a goal, with Tonge's low shot testing Lee-Barratt. As half-time approached Simonsen saved well from Robson following a deflection off Sonko, with the home side continuing to match their Premiership opponents in all phases of the game.

**Half-time: Hartlepool United 0 Stoke City 0**

Within minutes of the restart Victoria Park was set alight by Michael Nelson heading home Robson's free-kick in classic centre-half fashion at the far post. Stoke responded by sending on experienced forwards Lawrence and Kitson to bolster their attack and find an equaliser. They made little impact, however, as 'Pools continued to dictate the game, resulting in David Foley sealing victory in the 76 minute with a thunderous 25-yard drive that gave Simonsen no chance. The visitors briefly rallied with Delap, their best player, beating

McCunnie before shooting narrowly wide from a good position. This proved to be their final effort and the game ended with 'Pools comfortably in control of the closing minutes.

In post match interviews, Tony Pulis, the Stoke manager, was generous in his praise, stating 'It was Hartlepool's day and we will take the defeat on the chin'.

**Full-time: Hartlepool United 2 Stoke City 0**
**Hartlepool United:** Lee-Barratt, Sweeney, Humphreys, Clark, Nelson, Collins, Liddle, Jones, Porter, Mackay, Robson.
*Substitutes:* McCunnie for Sweeney (17 mins), Foley for Mackay (33 mins), Monkhouse for Jones (90 mins).
*Scorers:* Nelson (49 mins), Foley (76 mins).
**Stoke City:** Simonsen, Davies, Dickinson, Olofinjana, Shawcross, Sonko, Soares, Whelan, Pericard, Tonge, Delap.
*Substitutes:* Lawrence for Soares (54 mins), Kitson for Olofinjana (54 mins), Wilkinson for Davies (71 mins).
*Referee:* M. Halsey (Lancashire).
*Attendance:* 5,367.

# Top 100 Players

## ALLON, Joseph Ball

**(1988–90 and 1995–97)**

Centre-forward/Outside-right, 5ft 11in, 11st 2lb
Born: Gateshead, 12 November 1966
Signed from: Swansea City, 27 October 1988, £10,000
Transferred: Chelsea, 14 August 1991, £300,000
Re-signed: Lincoln City, 9 October 1995, £50,000
Career: Newcastle United, Swansea City, Hartlepool United, Chelsea, Port Vale (loan), Brentford, Southend United (loan), Port Vale, Lincoln City, Hartlepool United
Debut: v Hereford United, 29 October 1988
Appearances: League: 164+4 apps, 67 gls; FA Cup: 7+1 apps, 5 gls; FL Cup: 8 apps, 4 gls; Other: 10 apps, 3 gls. Total: 189+5 apps, 79 gls

Joe Allon rewrote 'Pools record books during the 1990–91 promotion season by becoming the first, and, to date, only player to break the 30-goal barrier in all competitions, totalling 35 goals in all 55 games played. He also equalled Billy Robinson's record of 28 League goals in a season, set in 1927–28. A key member of the promotion side, he formed a formidable striking partnership with Paul Baker, which was a major factor in the team's success.

Gateshead-born Allon joined Newcastle United as an apprentice and was a member of the 1985 FA Youth Cup-winning side, which included Paul Gascoigne and Paul Stephenson. He made his First Division debut the same season against Stoke City, going on to make nine senior appearances for the Tyneside club and scoring two goals before being released by manager Willie McFaul.

Joe Allon was signed by Bobby Moncur following a promising loan spell for a bargain £10,000 transfer fee from Swansea City in October 1988. His first full season, 1989–90, yielded 17 goals in 45 League appearances, but a quiet start to the following campaign, when he took seven games to score, nearly resulted in Cyril Knowles transferring him to Scarborough. Only Allon's refusal to move kept him at the Vic and the rest, as they say, is history.

Allon's final tally of 28 League goals during the promotion season and several awards, including the Hennessy Cognac North East Player of the Year, brought him to the notice of Chelsea, who paid a £300,000 transfer fee for his services, a record for a 'Pools player at the time. Despite a relatively short career at Stamford Bridge he made a lasting impression on their supporters before making the short journey to join Brentford, where he enjoyed another successful season with 19 goals in 45 games.

After spells at Southend, Port Vale and Lincoln he rejoined Hartlepool in 1995, making a further 56 League appearances and reclaiming the club's top scorer spot in the 1995–96 season. A knee injury forced his retirement from playing in August 1997 and he initially pursued a career in the media before joining the coaching staff at Leeds United in 2007.

## ANDERSON, William Boston

**(1956–61)**

Wing half-back, 5ft 8in, 10st 9lb
Born: Sunderland, 28 March 1935
Signed from: Barnsley, 16 February 1956, free transfer
Transferred: South Shields, August 1961
Career: Silksworth Juniors, Barnsley, Hartlepools United, South Shields
Debut: v Chesterfield, 3 March 1956
Appearances: League: 179 apps, 11 gls; FA Cup: 8 apps, 0 gls; Total: 187 apps, 11 gls

A native of Sunderland, at the age of 18 Billy Anderson was signed by Barnsley in September 1952 from local side Silksworth Juniors, going on to make six appearances for the Oakwell side in three seasons as well as representing the British Army while on National Service.

Originally signed by Fred Westgarth in February 1956 as a cover for the wing-half positions, he played in 33 consecutive games following his debut at Chesterfield in the March of that year. Anderson started the following season as a first choice, but

lost his place following a run of poor results. It was Bobby Lumley's freak injury that led to a recall in December 1956, resulting in his appearance in the epic Manchester United Cup game.

Initially he was left out by Ray Middleton, playing only 19 games in the new manager's first season before re-establishing himself following Frank Stamper's retirement. Thereafter he gave the club sterling service through into the early 1960s, making 48 League and Cup appearances during 1958–59 season, including 'Pools' record 10–1 victory against Barrow.

On leaving the Victoria Ground Billy Anderson followed the well-worn path to Simonside Hall, home of South Shields, to join former 'Pools favourites George Luke and Billy Robinson. In May 1964 he returned to the Victoria Ground to play in the Johnson-Burlison testimonial game alongside north-east footballing legends Wilf Mannion and Bobby Mitchell.

## AYRE, William

**(1977–81)**

Centre-half, 5ft 10in, 12st 1lb
Born: Crookhill, 7 May 1952
Died: Southport, 16 April 2002
Signed from: Scarborough, 1 August 1977, £2,500
Transferred: Halifax Town, January 1981, free transfer
Career: Scarborough, Hartlepool United, Halifax Town, Mansfield Town, Halifax Town
Debut: v Torquay United, 20 August 1977
Appearances: League: 141 apps, 27 gls; FA Cup: 8 apps, 1 gl; FL Cup: 6 apps, 0 gls; Total: 155 apps, 28 gls

Billy Ayre was a bargain £2,500 signing by manager Billy Horner from Scarborough, for whom he appeared in two FA Trophy-winning Finals in 1976 and 1977, winning the supporters' Player of the Year award for the second triumph. While with the Conference side he taught art and physical education at St Leonard's RCVA Comprehensive School in Durham.

Ayre, described by the local press as 'battle hardened', was brought in to provide stability to a defence which had conceded over 50 goals in away games the previous season. His first term, 1977–78, saw him not only ever present in 53 League and Cup games, but also finishing as leading goalscorer with a highly creditable 12 goals, all of which were scored from open play.

He played in over 40 games in each of the next two seasons, continuing to contribute vital goals as 'Pools lifted themselves above the re-election zone. The arrival of John Bird restricted his appearances and he signed for Halifax Town in January 1981, playing 95 League games at the Shay in two spells between 1981 and 1984. In between Ayre also had a spell with Mansfield Town, for whom he played 67 games.

Billy Ayre initially entered management with Halifax Town in October 1984 on a caretaker basis before Mick Jones took over. In December 1986 he became manager on a permanent basis, and after four years he joined Blackpool, initially as assistant to Graham Carr and later as manager.

Ayre took the Bloomfield Road side on a record-breaking run, losing only five of the remaining 30 games to reach a Play-off Final with Torquay United. Despite losing in a penalty shoot-out, Ayre's side continued their revival the following season and promotion was deservedly gained against Scunthorpe United, again in a penalty shoot-out in the Play-off Final. Following a disappointing campaign the following season he was sacked by flamboyant chairman Owen Oyston to be replaced by Sam Allardyce.

Ayre was later involved in management roles at Scarborough, Southport, Swansea City and Cardiff City before joining Bury as a coach. It was with the latter club that he was working when he died prematurely of lymph node cancer shortly before his 50th birthday in April 2002, leaving a wife and two children. His popularity with the Victoria Park faithful was fully demonstrated when he was voted Player of the 1970s at the club's Player of the Century awards in 2008.

## BAKER, David Paul

**(1987–91 and 1996–98)**

Centre-forward, 6ft 1in, 12st 10lb

Born: Newcastle upon Tyne, 5 January 1963

Signed from: Carlisle United, 1 August 1987, free transfer

Transferred: Motherwell, 10 March 1992, £75,000

Re-signed: Scunthorpe United, 27 March 1997, undisclosed

Transferred: Carlisle United, 1 August 1999, free transfer

Career: Bishop Auckland, Southampton, Carlisle United, Hartlepool United, Motherwell, Gillingham, York City, Torquay United, Scunthorpe United, Hartlepool United, Carlisle United

Debut: v Newport County, 15 August 1987
Appearances: League: 217+15 apps, 76 gls; FA Cup: 16 apps, 6 gls; FL Cup: 14 apps, 5 gls; Other: 16 apps, 5 gls. Total: 263+15 apps, 92 gls

Paul Baker experienced every emotion in his Hartlepool United career as he went from hero to zero and back to hero again. Signed by John Bird from Carlisle United on a free transfer, after a spell as a trainee with Southampton, he was an instant success, scoring 25 goals in all competitions in the 1987–88 season.

The arrival of Bobby Moncur following Bird's departure to York City saw the new manager convert Baker to a central-defender, with the inevitable consequences for both his, and the team's, goals tally. This frustration was further increased by a 19th-place League finish, which in no way reflected the potential of the playing squad, particularly as Moncur had signed Joe Allon and belatedly reverted Baker back to centre-forward.

The beginning of the following season, 1989–90, saw 'Pools in desperate straits due to a complete lack of pre-season preparation, with Moncur playing Baker in defence and attack, even filling the right-back role in the final days of the manager's unsuccessful term of office. The timely arrival of Cyril Knowles soon put an end to this nonsense and Baker's 15 League goals – he scored only two in his first 16 games – in partnership with Joe Allon ensured 'Pools eventually finished in 19th position, having been down and out prior to Knowles's arrival.

The following season, 1990–91, saw Baker, now captain, at the height of his powers, when in partnership with Joe Allon the team stormed to promotion success with the pair contributing 40 League goals to the success. The next term in Division Three saw him continue to

score regularly against higher level opposition, with the inevitable result that Scottish club Motherwell signed him in March for £75,000. Despite this, he still managed 13 goals in 29 League appearances, making him joint top scorer with Paul Dalton for the season.

After a mere nine League appearances for Motherwell, scoring a single goal, Baker signed for Gillingham for another sizeable fee and later had spells with York, Torquay and Scunthorpe. He was re-signed by Mick Tait in March 1997 to partner Joe Allon for the final games of a relegation battle which was ultimately avoided thanks to their goals in the final five games, which brought three wins and a draw. Continuing to play in the early part of the 1997–98 season, he briefly shared the managerial duties with Brian Honour following the departure of Mick Tait.

The appointment of Chris Turner in February 1999 saw Baker briefly revert back to player status and he finally left the club at the end of the season, signing for Carlisle United in the August for the 1999–2000 campaign and appearing on occasion with Rob McKinnon and Steve

Halliday. After spells with Bedlington Terriers, Durham City, Blyth Spartans and Arbroath, he was employed in a coaching capacity at the East Durham & Houghall Community College. In September 2005 Baker became manager of Newcastle Benfield for the next two years before moving in a similar capacity to Newcastle Blue Star and later scouting for Norwich City. He continued his association with Hartlepool United by playing in the annual Northern Master tournament.

## BARRON, Michael James

**(1996–2008)**

Defender, 5ft 11in, 11st 10lb
Born: Chester-le-Street, 22 December 1974
Signed from: Middlesbrough, 8 July 1997, free transfer (loan, 6 September 1996)
Transferred: Retired
Career: Middlesbrough, Hartlepool United
Debut: v Hereford United, 7 September 1996
Appearances: League: 315+10 apps, 3 gls; Play-off: 11 apps, 0 gls; FA Cup: 13+1 apps, 1 gl; FL Cup: 8+1 apps, 0 gls; Other: 15 apps, 0 gls. Total: 362+12 apps, 4 gls

Mickey Barron started his career as a youth trainee with Middlesbrough, with whom he made three League appearances, one in the Premiership. He initially joined 'Pools on loan at the start of the 1996–97 season, making 16 League appearances, mainly as a central-defender. It was Mick Tait who signed him on permanently during the close season, surely one of Hartlepool's best-ever deals, and he went on to make 33 League appearances, with his new manager unsure as to his best position.

During the next nine seasons Mickey Barron was to be at the heart of the renaissance of Hartlepool United Football Club, for the most part as captain. His exemplary behaviour, both on and off the pitch, set an example to players and

supporters alike which had a profound impact on the way the club was perceived in the new millennium. Evidence of his popularity with the fans were his successive Player of the Year awards in 1998 and 1999.

The arrival of Chris Turner saw Barron establish himself at the heart of the first 'Pools team to reach the Play-offs and, despite losing to Darlington, continue this fine form for the next two seasons, which both culminated in Play-off losses, to Blackpool and Cheltenham Town respectively. The 2002–03 campaign saw 'Pools take Division Three by storm, with Barron only missing four League games, and the club narrowly lost the title in the final game. His leadership remained unaffected by managerial changes as 'Pools gained a Division Two Play-off place, which paired them against Bristol City, After a draw at the Vic, Sweeney gave 'Pools the lead only for the hosts to prevail with two late goals. Mickey Barron played himself to a standstill in the second leg as Hartlepool went within a few minutes of their first Play-off Final. Such a Final was only just round the corner, and, despite missing most of the League campaign, Barron played in the Play-off games including the epic Final against Sheffield Wednesday.

He managed only 15 League appearances during the 2005–06 season under new manager Martin Scott. Hartlepool United's unexpected fall from grace could undoubtedly be attributed in some way to his lack of appearances and presence on the field of play. After 10 years devoted service the club awarded Mickey Barron a testimonial year, which included a game against Leeds United. He was appointed club captain for the 2007–08 season and retired from playing in January 2008 to become youth-team coach in succession to Paul Stephenson.

At the time of his retirement Mickey Barron had achieved seventh place in Hartlepool United's all-time list of appearances, testimony to his service to the club.

## BELL, Terence John

**(1966–70)**

Centre-forward, 5ft 10in, 10st 10lb
Born: Sherwood, 1 August 1944
Signed from: Nuneaton Borough, 1 July 1966
Transferred: Reading, 1 March 1970, £10,000
Career: Burton Albion, Nottingham Forest, Manchester City, Portsmouth, Nuneaton Borough, Hartlepools United, Reading, Aldershot
Debut: v Bradford City, 17 September 1966
Appearances: League: 111+6 apps, 34 gls; FA Cup: 4 apps, 3 gls; FL Cup: 2 apps, 1 gl; Total: 117+6 apps, 38 gls

Terry Bell was signed by Brian Clough from non-League Nuneaton Borough to provide additional goalscoring support to Ernie Phythian. Originally with Burton Albion, where Peter Taylor was manager, Bell had brief spells with Nottingham Forest, Manchester City and Portsmouth without managing a single game, hence his decision to revert to non-League football.

As with so many players throughout his managerial career, Brian Clough recognised potential others could not see and converted Bell from a midfield player to a goalscoring forward; although by the player's own admission Peter Taylor had major reservations about his ability to score goals in professional football.

After a quiet start to his 'Pools career, with only one goal in 14 full appearances spread over his debut season, Bell emerged as the trump card in the promotion season, when in partnership with Phythian and latterly Bobby Cummings he finished top scorer with 14 goals in 37 League appearances.

Like the rest of the team Bell struggled in the higher division and it was obvious his talents needed experienced support which was not forthcoming due to the usual financial constraints. Following the inevitable relegation, he continued to score goals in a struggling side and, despite his transfer in March 1970, he still finished as leading scorer with 12 goals in 30 consecutive appearances.

Terry Bell's transfer to Reading for a £10,000 fee, necessitated by financial pressures, proved a success for both club and player, and he was voted the Royals' Player of the Year in his first season. After four years and 20 goals in 87 League appearances he moved to Aldershot in July 1973, scoring a creditable 49 goals in 124 games.

After finishing playing in 1977, Bell joined Wokingham FC in a player/commercial manager role, leaving after a dispute with the board of directors. He was later employed as a sales executive in the airport services industry and now lives in retirement in Reading.

## BIRCUMSHAW, Anthony

**(1966–71)**

Defender, 5ft 11in, 12st 8lb
Born: Mansfield, 8 February 1945
Signed from: Notts County, 1 July 1966, free transfer
Transferred: May 1971, Nuneaton Borough, free transfer
Career: Notts County, Hartlepool United, Nuneaton Borough
Debut: v Bradford City, 17 September 1966
Appearances: League: 182+3 apps, 11 gls; FA Cup: 7 apps, 0 gls; FL Cup: 2 apps, 0 gls; Total: 191+3 apps, 11 gls

Tony Bircumshaw was signed from Notts County, for whom he had the distinction of being their youngest-ever player when he made his League debut on 3 April 1961 against Brentford aged 16 years 54 days, a record which still stands.

After 148 League appearances for the Meadow Lane club he was signed by Brian Clough on a free transfer, making 34 appearances in his debut season at the Victoria Ground. He immediately formed an impressive full-back partnership with Bryan Drysdale, which was to be a key factor in the 1967–68 promotion season. Indeed, 'Pools' relatively poor start could be attributed to Bircumshaw missing several early games during a winless six-game sequence. In total he went on to make 34 League appearances in the first promotion campaign, 31 of them in partnership with Drysdale.

The difficult 1968–69 season in the Third Division saw Bircumshaw maintain the high standards of the previous campaign, still in partnership with Bryan Drysdale. Despite the pressure of a relegation battle, 'Pools only conceded 29 goals at home, a testimony to the quality of the defence. Following Drysdale's transfer to Bristol City in the close season, Bircumshaw continued to be a model of consistency, missing only six League games in Gus McLean's final season, which was to end with another application for re-election. His final season, 1971–72, was another struggle with first John Simpson and latterly Len Ashurst attempting to raise the team above the re-election zone,

ultimately without success. Appearing in 39 League games, he contributed a creditable six goals, only two less than leading scorer Nicky Sharkey.

Tony Bircumshaw was released by Ashurst at the end of the season and returned to his Midlands roots, signing for Nuneaton Borough before retiring from football to work with his brother Peter, a former professional footballer, in the family business. He later worked for an insurance firm and scouted for Nottingham Forest.

## BIRD, John Charles

**(1980–85)**

Centre-half, 6ft 0in, 12st 0lb

Born: Rossington near Doncaster, 9 June 1948

Signed from: Newcastle United, 1 July 1980, free transfer

Transferred: Retired

Career: Doncaster United, Doncaster Rovers, Preston North End, Newcastle United, Hartlepool United

Debut: v Wigan Athletic, 16 August 1980

Appearances: League: 139+2 apps, 16 gls; FA Cup: 4 apps, 0 gls; FL Cup: 6 apps, 0 gls; Other: 4 apps, 0 gls. Total: 153+2 apps, 16 gls

John Bird signed for his home-town club Doncaster Rovers from local side Doncaster United while still a teenager and went on to make 50 League appearances for the South Yorkshire side before joining Preston North End in March 1971 in a £6,000 deal. Over the next four seasons he established his reputation as a strong, determined centre-half, making 166 League appearances for the Deepdale club and scoring nine goals. His transfer to Newcastle United in August 1975 for a £60,000 fee resulted in the resignation of Bobby Charlton, the Preston manager. After five seasons and 87 League

appearances with the Tyneside club he was signed by Billy Horner on a free transfer in the summer of 1980.

Bird's first season, 1980–81, saw him miss only a single League game, scoring four goals, in a campaign which promised much until a run of poor results ended in a ninth-place finish. The following season saw him form a central-defensive partnership with a young Andrew Linighan, which served 'Pools well for the next two seasons despite disappointing League form. Linighan's outstanding form eventually resulted in him taking over the number-five shirt from his older partner, leaving Bird to develop his coaching skills as Billy Horner's assistant. In a five-year spell as a player at the Victoria Ground John Bird made 138 League appearances, scoring a creditable 15 goals.

John Bird was appointed manager of Hartlepool United by chairman John Smart after a poor start to the 1986–87 season. His relationship with Smart was never an easy one and, after building a side to challenge for promotion, he accepted an offer to manage York City in October 1988. He initially had some success, rescuing the Minstermen from a disastrous start to finish in a respectable mid-table position. His first full season,

1989–90, resulted in another mid-table finish in 13th place, and when his side declined to a lowly 21st at the end of the 1990–91 campaign he lost his job. He later coached at Doncaster Rovers and in February 1994 became manager of struggling Halifax Town. After two years of continual struggle at the Shay he decided to retire from football to concentrate on his passion, painting.

John Bird is probably unique among professional footballers in that he is now an accomplished artist with his own studio at Bawtry, near Doncaster. Already holding exhibitions while at Newcastle United, his paintings have sold worldwide to prominent individuals and corporations. In 2006 he was one of 25 artists selected to participate in the 'Drawings for Turner' project, and his representation of a Turner sketch was part of the exhibition.

## BLACKBURN, Edwin Huitson

**(1983–87)**

Goalkeeper, 5ft 9in, 10st 5lb
Born: Houghton-le-Spring, 18 April 1957
Signed from: York City, 10 January 1983, free transfer
Transferred: Halmstads BK, free transfer
Career: Hull City, York City, Hartlepool United, Halmstads BK (Sweden)
Debut: v Peterborough United, 12 January 1983
Appearances: League: 161 apps, 0 gls; FA Cup: 3 apps, 0 gls; FL Cup: 6 apps, 0 gls; Other: 5 apps, 0 gls. Total: 175 apps, 0 gls

Eddie Blackburn was signed by Billy Horner from York City, who had paid Hull £6,000 for his services, in January 1983, following the sudden departure of John Watson. Blackburn had made 87 appearances in the previous two seasons for the Minster Men and was generally regarded as a reliable custodian despite his

lack of inches, being elected Clubman of the Year in 1981. His arrival at the Victoria Ground coincided with a major slump in 'Pools' fortunes, which saw a mere four wins in his first 20 appearances through to the end of the season.

In the following season, 1983–84, despite results declining even further, Blackburn made 41 League appearances, a total bettered only by Andrew Linighan. The arrival of Alan Stevenson limited his chances the following term before he re-established himself as the first-choice custodian following Stevenson's appointment as commercial manager. Throughout the 1985–86 season he was ever present during the League campaign, which saw a massive improvement in 'Pools' form, resulting in a final position of seventh. His last season, 1986–87, again was a testimony to his consistency as he missed only one League game. He was surprisingly released by John Bird at the end of the season on a free transfer and joined Swedish side Halmstads BK on a two-year contract which was ended prematurely due to a serious ankle injury.

## BONASS, Albert Edward

**(1934–36)**

Outside-left, 5ft 9in, 11st 0lb
Born: York, 1 January 1912
Died: Tockwith, 9 October 1945
Signed from: York City, August 1934, free transfer
Transferred: Chesterfield, August 1936, free transfer
Career: Dringhouses, York Wednesday, Darlington, York City, Hartlepools United, Chesterfield, Queen's Park Rangers
Debut: Walsall, 25 August 1934
Appearances: League: 77 apps, 31 gls; FA Cup: 9 apps, 4 gls; Other: 3 apps, 1 gl. Total: 89 apps, 36 gls

Albert Bonass was an orthodox outside-left who played for non-League Dringhouses and York Wednesday before turning professional with Darlington in 1932. After six appearances for the Quakers he returned to his home-town club, York, the following season, for whom he made a similar number of appearances.

Jackie Carr was responsible for bringing Albert Bonass to the Victoria Ground in the summer of 1934, despite his ordinary playing record with his two previous clubs, which did not suggest the potential for the success he was to achieve with Hartlepools.

His debut season, 1934–35, saw him make the left-wing berth his own, missing only four League games, and contributing fully to a forward line including Tommy Hird, Duncan Lindsay and Johnny Wigham to produce a commendable League tally of 80 goals. By contributing 20 goals, Albert Bonass became the first winger to achieve that landmark for the club. The following season, 1935–36, saw 'Pools make further progress in the League to a final position of eighth due to a tighter defensive record. Despite this, Bonass still managed 11 goals in his 39 League

appearances and was a key member of the FA Cup run which saw First Division Grimsby Town taken to a replay.

Albert Bonass left the Victoria Ground at the end of the season to join Chesterfield, where he enjoyed further success and made 97 appearances over the next three seasons, scoring 26 goals. His final move to Queen's Park Rangers, for whom he made three appearances, saw the curtain come down on his career with the outbreak of World War Two, although he continued to make 'guest' appearances for several London clubs throughout the conflict.

An RAF wireless operator with the rank of sergeant, who once had to parachute to safety, he survived the war only to die in a training accident at Tockwith, Yorkshire, on 9 October 1945 at the tragically young age of 33 years.

## BOWRON, Stephen

**(1929–34)**

Full-back, 5ft 9in, 11st 8lb
Born: Chilton, 5 May 1903
Died: West Hartlepool, 22 March 1963
Signed from: Ferryhill Athletic, August 1929, free transfer
Transferred: Aldershot, August 1934, free transfer
Career: Ferryhill Athletic, Swindon Town, Ferryhill Athletic, Preston North End (trial), Hartlepools United, Aldershot, Gainsborough Trinity, Dinnington Athletic

Debut: Darlington, 31 August 1929
Appearances: League: 194 apps, 0 gls; FA Cup: 8 apps, 0 gls; Other: 1 app, 0 gls. Total: 203 apps, 0 gls

Bill Norman made one of his best signings when he brought Steve Bowron, a specialist full-back, from Ferryhill Athletic in the summer of 1929. Bowron had previously had unsuccessful trials with Swindon Town and Preston North End before returning to his local club.

He experienced a traumatic professional debut on the opening day of the season when local rivals Darlington inflicted a heavy home defeat. Despite 'Pools failing to win any of their first seven games, Norman kept faith with the player and he went on to establish himself in the side, missing only two games in his first League season, as 'Pools enjoyed a top-10 finish.

Despite the team's decline the following season to 20th position, his consistency remained unaffected and the appointment of Jackie Carr as manager following Norman's demise saw him ever-present throughout the 1932–33 campaign when 'Pools finished a respectable 14th, despite conceding a record 116 League goals.

Maintaining his form throughout the following season, his last in Hartlepools colours, Steve Bowron accepted an offer from Angus Seed, manager of newly elected Aldershot, to join them for the 1934–35 season. At the time of his departure from the Victoria Ground he had played the highest number of games without scoring a goal!

Steve Bowron's move to Aldershot was not a success and after only six appearances for his new club he joined Gainsborough Trinity of the Midland League, and he later played for Dinnington Athletic. He returned to the town after his professional days were over and continued to participate in local amateur sports. He died in March 1963 in his 60th year.

## BOYD, Adam Mark

**(1999–2006 and 2009–12)**

Centre/Inside-forward, 5ft 9in, 10st 12lb
Born: Hartlepool, 25 May 1982
Signed from: Youth trainee, 20 September 1999
Transferred: Luton Town, 28 July 2006, £500,000
Re-signed: Leyton Orient, 2 May 2009, free transfer
Career: Hartlepool United, Boston United (loan), Luton Town, Leyton Orient, Hartlepool United
Debut: v Barnet, 2 November 1999
Appearances: League: 136+98 apps, 69 gls; Play-off: 6 apps, 2 gls; FA Cup: 7+2 apps, 3 gls; FL Cup: 8+1 apps, 4 gls; Other: 6+5 apps, 1 gl. Total: 163+106 apps, 79 gls

Locally-born Adam Boyd joined 'Pools as a 17-year-old youth trainee in September 1999 and made his debut the following month while still attending the Manor School of Technology. He made four appearances in his debut season, all as substitute, scoring one goal before being given his full debut the following season. Initially the form of Kevin Henderson restricted his appearances, but in the 2001–02 season he started to make his mark.

A natural goalscorer with an eye for the half-chance, Boyd's progress stalled during the 2002–03 season following the departure of manager Chris Turner to Sheffield Wednesday. The arrival of Mike Newell resulted in his appearances being limited to the substitute's bench with a corresponding decline in goals.

Following the surprising release of Newell and the appointment of Neale Cooper at the start of the 2003–04 season, Boyd was loaned to Boston United for a three-month spell, during which time he made 14 full League appearances, scoring four goals. Recalled by Cooper, he rewarded his manager by playing in the final 11 games of the campaign, scoring 12 goals. After that he never looked back.

The momentous 2004–05 season saw him become the first 'Pools player to score over 20 goals in the third level of English football since the creation of a fourth division, when he reached 22 in 45 League appearances. His tally included a memorable hat-trick in the home game against arch rivals Sheffield Wednesday, and in all games he totalled 29 goals for the season. It was now apparent that such goalscoring form would eventually attract attention from so-called bigger clubs. Boyd's career stalled the following season, however, when he received an injury in the 0–1 home defeat by Yeovil Town, resulting in a 22-game lay-off. He returned for the final phase of an unsuccessful relegation battle following manager Martin Scott's departure.

Having proved himself at a higher level it came as no surprise when Adam Boyd was transferred to Championship side Luton Town in the summer of 2006 for a reported £500,000 transfer fee. What was a surprise was that Luton's manager was Mike Newell, who had seemed reluctant to include the player in his Hartlepool sides. The transfer was to prove unsuccessful, however, with Boyd only making five starts, plus 14 substitute appearances, in a season which saw Luton relegated. Following Newell's acrimonious departure in March, new

manager Kevin Blackwell left Boyd out of his team, and in the close season he departed Kenilworth Road by 'mutual consent' to join League One side Leyton Orient on a two-year contract. At the Brisbane Road club he enjoyed a successful first season, finishing as leading scorer with 14 goals in 44 League appearances. His second term was hampered by injuries, and despite missing the last three months of the season he still managed a further nine League goals in 33 appearances. With his Orient contract about to end, Chris Turner offered the popular player a fresh start at Victoria Park and he re-signed for 'Pools in May 2009.

Adam Boyd's return to the Victoria Park fell some way short of expectations after a promising start which saw the striker score a superb winner against Championship team Coventry City in the League Cup. It took him until the seventh game to open his League account and despite contributing the odd goal the arrival of Roy O'Donovan saw the popular player relegated to the substitutes bench for most of the final third of the season.

The start of the 2010–11 campaign saw Adam Boyd as Chris Turner's first choice number nine and he rewarded the manager's faith with sterling displays against Swindon and Sheffield United. The departure of Turner and the appointment of Mick Wadsworth resulted in a downgrading of his role in the team in favour of James Brown resulting in a lengthy absence and infrequent substitute appearances. In common with several other senior players Adam Boyd's season was a frustrating one evidenced by a mere nine League starts and three goals.

Determined to improve for the 2011–12 season, the final one of his contract, Boyd initiated a rigorous fitness regime during the close season which even encompassed boxing. The benefits of this were apparent when, in partnership with new signing Colin Nish, Adam Boyd once again proved his value as a goalscorer in 'Pools nine game record start to the season. The arrival of Neale Cooper coincided with a downturn in form and he was thereafter consigned to a substitutes' role which saw his 'Pools career finally wind down and he was released at the end of the season.

## BROWN, Phillip

**(1980–85)**

Defender, 5ft 11in, 11st 6lb

Born: South Shields, 30 May 1959

Signed from: St Hilda's Juniors, 1 July 1978

Transferred: Halifax Town, 25 July 1985, £1,000

Career: St Hilda's Juniors, Hartlepool United, Halifax Town, Bolton Wanderers, Blackpool

Debut: v Peterborough United, 1 March 1980

Appearances: League: 210+7 apps, 8 gls; FA Cup: 11 apps, 0 gls; FL Cup: 12 apps, 0 gls; Other: 9 apps, 1 gl. Total: 242+7 apps, 9 gls

Tyneside-born Phil Brown joined 'Pools from amateur side St Hilda's Juniors while still a teenager, making his debut shortly before his 21st birthday at the Vic against Peterborough United in a 2–1 defeat. He went on to play over 200 League games for the club during

one of its most difficult periods, missing only four League games in the three seasons following his debut. The turmoil in the club under chairman Vince Barker during the Horner/Duncan/Docherty/Horner cycle of managers saw him fulfilling roles in every part of the pitch, thereby demonstrating his versatility and commitment. Like everyone else associated with the club during this period he fell out with the chairman in his role as the players' PFA representative, even acting as mediator to avoid strike action on one occasion!

It was a surprise when he was released at the end of the 1984–85 season having missed only four League games. He joined Halifax Town, for whom he played 135 League games over the next three seasons, before moving to Bolton Wanderers, recently promoted from Division Four.

It was with Bolton that Phil Brown enhanced his reputation as a model professional, and he was a key member of the side which secured a further promotion and saw him captain his side to victory in the 1989 Sherpa Van Trophy Final at Wembley. After six seasons and 256 League appearances with the Trotters, he joined Blackpool for the 1994–95 season, his final campaign as a player.

Following his retirement from playing Phil Brown returned to Bolton to become a key member of Sam Allardyce's backroom staff, which established the Lancashire side as a force in the FA Premier League. His role as assistant manager to 'Big Sam' attracted attention from other clubs and in 2005 the chance to manage Derby County proved too good to resist and he severed his Bolton ties. After narrowly avoiding relegation in his first season as manager he was replaced by Billy Davies.

Despite his relative failure at Derby he still retained his good reputation in the game and was subsequently appointed manager of Championship side Hull City in January 2007. The following season he led them to the Premiership with a 1–0 win over Bristol City in the Play-off Final at Wembley, the first time the Humberside club had reached the top tier of English football.

Brown's team was initially the sensation of the 2008–09 Premiership season when, after wins at Newcastle, Arsenal and Tottenham, they occupied a Champions League spot. Inevitably Hull's form declined as the season wore on and their place among the footballing elite was only confirmed on the final day of the campaign. Even so, the Hull City fans and the football public at large paid generous tribute to Phil's achievement. Perhaps inevitably Phil Brown and his team suffered from the Premiership's 'second season' syndrome, and after only five wins in 29 games and relegation looking increasingly inevitable he was relieved of his managerial duties and placed on 'gardening leave'. With relegation confirmed, Brown entered into protracted contract negotiations with Hull's Chairman Adam Pearson, which ultimately led to his departure in June 2010.

In January 2011 Phil Brown took over as manager of struggling Championship club Preston North End following the dismissal of Darren Ferguson, so o Sir Alec. After initial success he was unable to prevent Preston's relegation to League One and despite topping the League the following season a run of nine games without a win saw him sacked in December 2011. Since leaving football management Phil Brown has pursued a career in the media as a radio and television pundit.

## BROWN, Robert Beresford

**(1951–56)**

Goalkeeper, 6ft 0in, 12st 4lb
Born: West Hartlepool, 6 September 1927
Died: Hartlepool, 29 June 2001
Signed from: Stockton, 1 August 1951
Transferred: Retired
Career: Blackhall Colliery Welfare, Manchester United, Doncaster Rovers, Stockton, Hartlepools United
Debut: v Crewe Alexandra, 20 August 1951
Appearances: League: 126 apps, 0 gls; FA Cup: 13 apps, 0 gls; Total: 139 apps, 0 gls

West Hartlepool-born Berry Brown started his football career with Manchester United, signing for the Old Trafford giants in August 1946 on completion of his National Service having played for local side Blackhall Colliery Welfare. He made his League debut in January 1948 in the most auspicious circumstances by saving a penalty against Sheffield United, and he

made a further three appearances for the Red Devils before joining Doncaster Rovers in January 1949. He stayed with the Yorkshire club until the end of the campaign, when he returned to the North East to play for non-League Stockton.

The wily Fred Westgarth recognised a good thing when he saw it and he was responsible for reviving Brown's League career when he signed him in August 1951. He made his Hartlepools United debut in the second game of the season, replacing Wally Briggs and keeping a clean sheet in an emphatic 3–0 victory in front of over 11,000 spectators. He went on to make 31 League appearances as well as star in the FA Cup run which ended in a narrow loss to First Division Burnley in front of a 38,000-strong crowd. Brown drew plaudits from all quarters for his display in this game, and his Manchester United experience undoubtedly helped him cope with the 'big match' atmosphere.

Brown missed only four games the following season, 1952–53, which served to provide further evidence of his value to the team. Thereafter he was in competition with Alex Corbett, George Taylor and latterly Jim Dyson for the goalkeeper's jersey. He played 32 League and Cup games in 1954–55 when 'Pools finished fifth and reached the fourth round of the FA Cup, before losing his place to Dyson the following season. He only made four appearances in 1955–56, including the final two games in which he kept clean sheets, and he left the club shortly afterwards.

Brown continued to play in local football for several years following his departure from the professional game. His son David was also a goalkeeper with, among others, Bury and Preston North End, and is now an award-winning head groundsman with Hartlepool United.

Berry Brown died at his Hartlepool home on 29 June 2001, aged 73 years.

## BURLISON, Thomas Henry

**Baron Burlison of Rowlands Gill**
**(1957–64)**

Wing half-back, 5ft 8in, 11st 9lb
Born: Edmondsley, 23 May 1936
Died: London, 20 May 2008
Signed from: Lincoln City, 22 August 1957, free transfer
Transferred: Darlington, 1 August 1964, free transfer
Career: Lincoln City, Hartlepools United, Darlington, Horden CW
Debut: v Workington, 12 October 1957
Appearances: League: 148 apps, 5 gls; FA Cup: 6 apps, 1 gl; FL Cup: 3 apps, 0 gls; Total: 157 apps, 6 gls

Tom Burlison was a versatile player capable of fulfilling both wing-half and inside-forward roles. He was signed by Ray Middleton from Lincoln City, with whom he spent three seasons without making his League debut. A key member of Middleton's rebuilding programme, he initially competed with the legendary Jackie Newton for the right half-back berth and made 19 League appearances in his debut season. Following Newton's departure he was initially first choice for the 1958–59 season before National Service interrupted his playing career, and on his return he was played by an increasingly desperate Middleton in a variety of positions including centre-forward.

The arrival in the 'hot seat' of Bill Robinson saw his appearances restricted by National Service, and he played only two League games in the 1959–60 season and 12 the following campaign. Burlison appeared more frequently during the Chilton/Gurney/Williams era, often playing on the left wing. In May 1964 he shared a joint testimonial with Ken Johnson before moving to Darlington in August and making 26 League appearances in his sole season with the Quakers. He ended his football career the following season with non-League Horden Colliery Welfare.

On leaving football Tom Burlison became a prominent trades union official with the General and Municipal Workers Union, becoming regional secretary in 1978, rising to deputy general secretary of the GMB Union. He was also active in the Labour Party, serving on the NEC and as national treasurer. In October 1997 he was created a life peer as Baron Burlison of Rowlands Gill in the County of Tyne and Wear, thereby earning the distinction of being the first professional footballer to sit in the House of Lords. On becoming a peer he remarked 'I don't know how I got here. I appear to be the only one who is not a millionaire!' In 2006 he was given the Freedom of the Borough by Gateshead Council, an honour he described as 'the ultimate accolade'.

Lord Tom Burlison continued to support 'Pools in his capacity as honorary life president and was at the final League game of the season against Nottingham Forest shortly before his death in May 2008 aged 71 years.

## BURNETT, William John

**(1948–53)**

Outside-right, 5ft 9in, 10st 7lb
Born: Pelaw, 1 March 1926
Died: Gateshead, 9 December 1988
Signed from: Grimsby Town, 4 November 1948, £500
Transferred: Retired
Career: Wardley Colliery Welfare, Grimsby Town, Hartlepools United
Debut: v Wrexham, 6 November 1948
Appearances: League: 194 apps, 17 gls; FA Cup: 10 apps, 2 gls; Total: 204 apps, 19 gls

Tyneside-born Billy Burnett started his professional career with Grimsby Town, for whom he signed in July 1946 from local side Wardley Colliery Welfare. He made 10 League appearances for the Mariners before returning to the North East in November 1948 as replacement for the veteran Jimmy Isaac, who continued to live in Huddersfield and only travelled to Hartlepools on match days.

An outside-right in the classic mould, he quickly made the position his own following his debut, along with Watty Moore, against Wrexham a few days after signing. The following season, 1949–50, saw him make 33 League appearances, scoring six goals, in a side which was not yet the finished article, as evidenced by an 18th-place League finish. Burnett missed only one game the following season, which saw the introduction of Tommy McGuigan along with the prodigious scoring of Eric Wildon with 26 goals, many of the 'assists' coming from Burnett.

Billy Burnett maintained his consistency throughout the 1951–52 campaign, again only missing a solitary game. He was a key member of the side which narrowly lost an FA Cup tie to First Division Burnley, and his value to the team was again evidenced by Eric Wildon's goalscoring feats. Despite making 37 appearances the following season he was released by Fred Westgarth while still only 27 years old, probably due to the manager's frustration at another lowly League finish. He was replaced by Billy Linacre, a player with First Division experience, and left the professional game.

Billy Burnett died on 9 December 1988 at Gateshead, aged 62 years.

## CAMERON, Jack

**(1954–60)**
Right-back, 5ft 9in, 10st 12lb
Born: Dalmuir, 7 March 1931
Died: Aberdeen, 22 June 1982
Signed from: Dumbarton, November 1953, £100
Transferred: Retired
Career: Dalmuir, Dumbarton, Hartlepools United
Debut: v Barrow, 26 April 1954
Appearances: League: 175 apps, 0 gls; FA Cup: 18 apps, 0 gls; Total: 193 apps, 0 gls

Jock Cameron was signed by Fred Westgarth while on National Service in the Army, having played in 'Pools' reserves side. He started his career with home-town club Dalmuir before moving to Dumbarton. His spell of military service brought him to the North East, and after several impressive displays in the reserves the thrifty Westgarth was persuaded to part with the princely sum of £100 for his services.

Cameron made his League debut in the final game of the 1953–54 season and was first choice thereafter. Ultra-reliable, he missed only six League games in his first two seasons as well as playing in all the major Cup games of the mid-1950s, more than holding his own against opposition from higher divisions. Able to play in either full-back position, his solid style and versatility became increasingly useful following the signing of Ken Waugh.

Manager Ray Middleton utilised his versatility in the full-back positions on the retirement of Ray Thompson, and he and Waugh regularly swapped positions. An interesting feature of their 'partnership' was that neither player scored a goal despite making a combined 399 appearances for the club.

Cameron was a member of the 'Pools team which gained the record 10–1 victory over Barrow towards the end of the 1958–59 season. He retired from the game at the end of the following campaign while still in his 20s, another victim of Middleton's so-called 'youth policy'.

Jock Cameron later ran a sub post office in the Stranton area of Hartlepool and enjoyed success on the golf course as a member of the Seaton Carew Golf Club, competing in the Durham County Match-Play Championships. He later returned to his native Scotland and died in Aberdeen on 22 June 1982 aged 51 years.

## CLARK, Benjamin

**(2004–2010)**

Centre Back, 6ft 1in, 13st 11lb
Born: Shotley Bridge, 24 January 1983
Signed from: Sunderland, 22 October 2004, undisclosed fee
Transferred: Released, 12 May 2010
Career: Sunderland, Hartlepool United
Debut: v Peterborough United, 23 October 2004
Appearances: League: 144+18 apps, 6 gls, FA Cup: 14+2 apps, 0 gls, FL Cup: 1 app, 0 gls, Other: 5+1 apps, 0 gls; Total: 164+21apps, 6 gls

Ben Clark was signed from Sunderland in October 2004. A former England Under-19 captain who also played at Under-18 and Under-15 levels, he joined Sunderland as a youth trainee and made his debut in January 2003 as a substitute in a 1–0 defeat against Southampton in the FA Premier League.

He made a further five League appearances the following season and after featuring in Sunderland's opening two fixtures of the 2004–05 season he lost his place and was signed by Neale Cooper in October 2004. Clark made an immediate impact at Victoria Park and went on to make 21 League starts, mainly at centre-half, replacing the injured Chris Westwood. The following season, 2005–06, he started at full-back before forming a solid central-defensive partnership with Michael Nelson in what proved to be a difficult relegation season.

Clark's partnership with Michael Nelson flourished during the record-breaking promotion season of 2006–07, with both players fixtures at the heart of the 'Pools defence. The arrival of Godwin Antwi-Birago on loan from Liverpool restricted Clark's appearances during the 2007–08 League One campaign, which saw him used in a defensive midfield role by Danny Wilson. A versatile team player, Clark's dedication and service gained recognition from his manager in the December with the award of an extension to his contract.

Wilson's acquisition of the experienced Sam Collins appeared to place a question mark over Clark's future at the club; however, an early-season injury to Willie Boland allowed him to make 35 League appearances during the 2008–09 season, many of them in midfield and the problem right-back position. He made a major contribution to 'Pools' ultimately successful relegation battle by converting winning penalties against Danny Wilson's Swindon (in the 89th minute) and Tranmere Rovers in the closing stages of the season.

The 2009–10 season turned out to be a frustrating one for Ben Clark and a succession of injuries meant he played no part in the campaign until December and then only as a substitute. The suspension of Gary Liddle saw him finally appear in three successive games before losing his place once again. In total he made only six starts all season and it was no surprise that he was released by Chris Turner with his contract expired.

## CLARK, Harold Maurice

**(1958–61)**

Inside-forward, 5ft 10in, 11st 4lb
Born: Newcastle upon Tyne, 29 December 1932
Signed from: Sheffield Wednesday, 1 August 1958, free transfer
Transferred: Retired
Career: Eastbourne Old Boys, Darlington, Sheffield Wednesday, Hartlepools United, South Shields, Horden CW
Debut: v Bradford Park Avenue, 1 September 1958
Appearances: League: 118 apps, 43 gls; FA Cup: 5 apps, 0 gls; FL Cup 1 app, 0 gls; Total: 124 apps, 43 gls

Harry Clark was signed by Ray Middleton from Sheffield Wednesday at the start of the 1958–59 season to replace Tommy McGuigan. This was 'Pools' first season in the newly-formed Division Four, and Clark, who could play in either inside-forward

position, was to become a key member of the side over the coming seasons.

Harry Clark spent the first half of his career with local rivals Darlington between 1950 and 1956, making 141 League appearances and scoring 20 goals. His skilful inside-forward play brought him to the attention of Sheffield Wednesday, then in the First Division. He joined the South Yorkshire club in October 1957, managing only a single appearance that season. With his opportunities limited at Hillsborough he returned to the North East with Hartlepools the following August.

Clark made his debut in the fourth game of the season, a 1–4 defeat at Bradford Park Avenue, and thereafter he only missed two more games to finish as leading scorer with 12 goals in 41 appearances. The highlight of the campaign was undoubtedly the record 10–1 win against Barrow in which he scored twice.

The following season, 1959–60, saw Harry Clark at his peak despite 'Pools' decline to bottom place in Division Four. In 44 League appearances he was leading goalscorer with 21 goals, a highly creditable achievement playing in a side which finished bottom of the Football League. His consistency can be gauged from his record of scoring in 18 of the League games in which he appeared.

Harry Clark's final season at the Vic, 1960–61, was another struggle which saw a marginal 'improvement' in the final League position to second bottom. He still performed creditably, however, contributing 10 League goals in 33 appearances and appearing in 'Pools' first-ever Football League Cup tie, a 2–1 defeat at Oldham. Towards the end of the season he lost his place to local player Barry Parkes and was released by Bill Robinson at the end of the campaign, later playing for local north-east clubs South Shields and Horden Colliery Welfare.

After leaving football, Harry Clark worked for many years in local government and continues to live in retirement in Darlington.

## CRILLY, Thomas

**(1920–22)**

Left-back, 5ft 8in, 11st 6lb

Born: Stockton-on-Tees, 20 July 1895

Died: Derby, 18 January 1960

Signed from: Stockton, 25 February 1920, Amateur

Transferred: Derby County, 24 August 1922

Career: Stockton (amateur), Hartlepools United, Derby County, Crystal Palace, Northampton Town, Scunthorpe & Lindsay United

Debut: v Shildon (North Eastern League), 31 January 1920

Appearances: League: 37 apps, 0 gls; FA Cup: 11 apps, 0 gls; Total: 48 apps, 0 gls

Tommy Crilly is one of the rare 'Pools players who 'crossed the great divide' between the North Eastern and Football

Leagues. He started his career with Stockton, then a top amateur side, before moving to the Victoria Ground in January 1920 for the penultimate North Eastern League season, playing 77 games in all prior to the introduction of League football. He signed professional terms in January 1921 and in the first season in Division Three North played in 37 League games, the most of any 'Pools player. Such form was bound to attract interest from bigger clubs, and an enquiry from Leeds United was rebuffed with a transfer fee demand of £1,500, a princely sum at the time.

Following the close-season tour of Spain, Crilly initially agreed to play for 'Pools for the 1922–23 season; however, the appointment of Cecil Potter as manager of Derby County resulted in a change of mind and he joined the Rams in the August. He went on to make a total of 211 appearances over the next five seasons, culminating in promotion to the First Division in 1926.

Tom Crilly joined Crystal Palace in May 1928, playing 116 League games for the South London club, often in the same side as Jimmy Hamilton. He left Selhurst Park in June 1933 to join Division Three South side Northampton Town, playing 46 games before ending his career as player-manager of Midland League side Scunthorpe & Lindsay United at the age of 40 years.

Crilly returned to Derby after his playing days to work in the licensed trade, maintaining his footballing contacts with Derby County by coaching reserve and youth sides during World War Two. He died in Derby in January 1960 aged 65 years.

## DALTON, Paul

**(1989–92)**
Outside-left, 5ft 11in, 11st 7lb
Born: Middlesbrough, 25 April 1967
Signed from: Manchester United, 4 March 1989, £20,000
Transferred: Plymouth Argyle, 5 June 1992, £95,000 plus Ryan Cross
Career: Brandon United, Manchester United, Hartlepool United, Plymouth Argyle, Huddersfield Town, Carlisle United (loan), Gateshead, Dunston Federation, Billingham Town
Debut: v Wrexham, 7 March 1989
Appearances: League: 140+11 apps, 37 gls; FA Cup: 7 apps, 1 gl; FL Cup: 10 apps, 2 gls; Other: 9 apps, 3 gls. Total: 166+11 apps, 43 gls

Paul Dalton's football career began in modest surroundings with Northern League side Brandon United, where his performances attracted the attention of Manchester United. He joined the Old Trafford giants for a £5,000 fee in May 1988, and after failing to make a senior appearance was signed just before the transfer deadline by Bob Moncur for a club record £20,000 in March 1989, money which turned out to be well spent! Despite

initially playing in a struggling team, the arrival of Cyril Knowles transformed his career and he never looked back.

Dalton missed only one League game during the 1989–90 season, scoring 11 goals, before really making his mark during the 1990–91 promotion campaign. As a key member of the side with his speed and skilful wing-play, he played in every game, scoring 11 goals, the highlight being a 23-minute hat-trick at Aldershot.

Continuing his impressive form the following season in Division Three, missing only a handful of games and finishing as joint top scorer with 13 goals, he was bound to attract attention from other clubs. It was no surprise, therefore, when Peter Shilton, manager of Plymouth Argyle, paid £95,000 plus Ryan Cross for his services in the summer of 1992. After three seasons and 98 League appearances with the south coast club he joined Huddersfield Town for another substantial fee and was the Terriers' top scorer in the 1996–97 season.

Dalton had a short loan spell at Carlisle United in 1999 and later played for non-League Gateshead, Dunston Federation and Billingham Town before working as a coach in America. On his return to England he joined Middlesbrough as an academy coach. He continued his association with Hartlepool United by playing in the annual Northern Master tournament.

## DAWES, Malcolm

**(1970–76)**

Central-defender, 5ft 9in, 12st 5lb

Born: Trimdon, 3 March 1944

Signed from: Aldershot, 1 July 1970, free transfer

Transferred: Workington, 19 December 1975 (temporary transfer 27 November 1975)

Career: Darlington, Nuneaton Borough, Horden Colliery Welfare, Aldershot, Hartlepool United, New York Cosmos (USA), Denver Dynamos (USA), Workington, Scarborough

Debut: v Stockport County, 11 September 1970

Appearances: League: 193+2 apps, 12 gls; FA Cup: 5+1 apps, 0 gls; FL Cup: 12 apps, 0 gls; Total: 210+3 apps, 12 gls

Trimdon-born Malcolm Dawes had an unpromising start to his football career, being released by Darlington and playing non-League football with Nuneaton Borough and Horden Colliery Welfare. A visit to his brother, who was a soldier stationed in Aldershot, led to a trial with the local club and he was signed by the Fourth Division club for the start of the 1965–66 season. He went on to play 164 League games, scoring two goals over the next five seasons before a disagreement with manager Jimmy Melia resulted in his departure.

John Simpson signed him at the start of the 1970–71 season and he played 35 League games in his debut season for 'Pools, mainly at left-back. The arrival of Len Ashurst saw him moved to a midfield role, where his control and calm influence could best be utilised. Over the next three seasons Malcolm Dawes missed only a handful of games, testimony to his consistency. During this period he played in the North American Soccer League for New York Cosmos and Denver Dynamos in the close season. He was a key member

of the 'Pools side during the epic League Cup run in 1974–75, when by common consent his play lost nothing in comparison with opponents from more illustrious teams, resulting in a Player of the Year award.

Following Ashurst's departure it was a surprise when Ken Hale transferred him to Workington after only one game of the 1975–76 season. Dawes went on to play 51 League games, scoring one goal, over the next two seasons for the Cumbrian club before a knee injury effectively ended his career. Following a period of rehabilitation he made a solitary appearance for Scarborough before finally retiring from playing. He maintained his contact with the game by coaching local players and scouting for Shrewsbury Town, as well as running his own industrial services company.

## DIXON, Kevin Lynton

**(1983–86 and 1988–89)**

Midfielder/forward, 5ft 10in, 10st 6lb
Born: Blackhill, 27 July 1960
Signed from: Carlisle United (loan October 1983), 10 August 1984
Transferred: Scunthorpe United, 11 August 1987, free transfer
Re-signed: Scunthorpe United, 20 June 1988, free transfer
Transferred: York City, 21 November 1988, free transfer
Career: Annfield Plain, Tow Law Town, Carlisle United, Hartlepool United, Scunthorpe United, Hartlepool United, York City, Scarborough (loan), Gateshead
Debut: v Bury, 29 October 1983
Appearances: League: 123+4 apps, 33 gls; FA Cup: 4 apps, 1 gl; FL Cup: 6+2 apps, 1 gl; Other: 4 apps, 0 gls. Total: 137+6 apps, 35 gls

Kevin Dixon made his Football League debut for Carlisle United at the relatively

advanced age of 23 years, having previously played for non-League clubs Annfield Plain and Tow Law Town. He failed to establish himself with the Cumbrian club, making only nine appearances before joining Hartlepool on loan. This led to Billy Horner signing him on a permanent deal in August 1984, and he went on to play 42 League games, scoring 12 goals.

Although not big in stature for a forward, Kevin Dixon had endless energy and enthusiasm, and his non-stop running saw him play in every forward position. His second season, 1985–86, saw 'Pools seriously in contention for promotion for most of the season. Central to such form was the forward trio, of which Dixon was a key element along with Alan Shoulder and John Borthwick. Such form was not maintained the following campaign, however, in which Dixon missed only three games in a struggling side. The appointment of John Bird saw his appearances limited and he was given a free transfer to Scunthorpe United in August 1987, having spent a short period on loan to the Irons in January 1986.

Ironically, Dixon was re-signed by John Bird for the 1988–89 season, bringing the curtain down on his Hartlepool career after a further 14 League appearances by following him to York City in the November. He made 38 League appearances, scoring eight goals, for the Bootham Crescent club before going to Scarborough on loan in February 1990, making his final three League appearances before retiring from the professional game. He later played for Gateshead and Tyneside junior clubs Hebburn and Newcastle Blue Star, as well as managing Langley Park.

## DRYSDALE, Brian

**(1965–69)**

Left-back, 5ft 7in, 10st 10lb
Born: Wingate, 24 February 1943
Signed from: Lincoln City, 1 July 1965, free transfer
Transferred: Bristol City, 31 May 1969, £15,000
Career: Lincoln City, Hartlepool United, Bristol City, Reading (loan), Oxford United, Frome Town, Shepton Mallett
Debut: v Aldershot, 11 September 1965
Appearances: League: 169+1 apps, 2 gls; FA Cup: 7 apps, 0 gls; FL Cup: 5 apps, 0 gls; Total: 181+1 apps, 2 gls

Wingate-born Bryan Drysdale, nicknamed 'Trapper' after the local newspaper's greyhound correspondent due to his fondness for the sport, was discovered in amateur football by Lincoln City, with whom he turned professional in 1960, making the first of his 21 League appearances for the Imps the following year. He was signed for 'Pools in the summer of 1965 by the much-maligned Geoff Twentyman and turned out to be one of the club's best-ever signings.

His debut against Aldershot in September 1965 could not have been in more auspicious circumstances as he became 'Pools' first-ever substitute when he replaced the injured Peter Thompson. Amazingly this was to be his only substitute appearance in 182 games for the club. His full debut came against Barnsley, a 2–1 defeat, the week prior to Brian Clough taking over as manager. Thereafter he was ever-present through to the end of the season, a run of 34 consecutive games. The following season, 1966–67, Clough's first full season as a manager, saw Drysdale missing only one League game as a key member of the team which improved dramatically to finish in ninth position. Following Clough's departure Gus McLean wisely decided to leave well alone with his team's left-back position, and Brian Drysdale rewarded

him by again missing only a single game in the club's first-ever promotion season.

Despite seeing his side relegated the following season, 1968–69, he remained a model of consistency, so much so that he even maintained his record of missing only a single game and was voted the fans' Footballer of the Year. Inevitably this attracted attention from other clubs and in the close season Bristol City had a £15,000 offer accepted.

Drysdale embarked on a seven-year career with the Ashton Gate club which encompassed 282 League games and culminated in promotion to the First Division after a 65-year absence. In recognition of such outstanding service he was awarded a testimonial in April 1976 against Hereford United.

After being released by Bristol City at the end of the 1976–77 season, following a loan spell with Reading, he joined Oxford United in the close season. Unfortunately, after 15 appearances his League career was ended, ironically against Hereford United, due to a broken leg. He later played and managed south-west sides Frome Town and Shepton Mallett before retiring from the game and working as a carpenter while continuing to live in the Bristol area.

The club's supporters paid their own tribute to Brian Drysdale by voting him Hartlepool United's Player of the 1960s as part of the Centenary Celebrations, a richly deserved tribute.

## ENGLISH, Samuel

**(1936–38)**

Centre-forward, 5ft 9in, 11st 10lb

Born: Crivolea, County Antrim, 18 August 1908

Died: Alexandria, Vale of Leven, 12 April 1967

Signed from: Queen of the South, 1 August 1936

Transferred: Duntocher Hibernian

Career: Port Glasgow Juniors, Old Kilpatrick, Yoker Athletic, Glasgow Rangers, Liverpool, Queen of the South, Hartlepools United, Duntocher Hibernian

Debut: v Southport, 29 August 1936

Appearances: League: 69 apps, 27 gls; FA Cup: 3 apps, 3 gls; Other: 3 apps, 1 gl. Total: 75 apps, 31 gls

The signing of Irish international centre-forward Sam English was considered a major coup for Hartlepools United at the time, but the celebrated player, still in his 20s, who to this day holds the Glasgow Rangers record for goals scored in a season (44 in 1931–32), arrived with a major cloud hanging over him.

During his record-breaking season he had the great misfortune to collide with John Thomson, the Celtic goalkeeper, in an 'Old Firm' derby match and in the process inflicted a depressed fracture on Thomson's skull, from which injury he died in hospital later that day. Despite being totally exonerated by the official enquiry, English was traumatised by the accident and was never the same player again. After winning the Scottish League Championship with Rangers in 1933 he joined Liverpool for a reported £8,000 fee, a fortune in those days. Initially he was a success at Anfield, scoring 13 goals in his first 16 games before his form waned and he moved back to Scotland with Queen of the South in July 1935, making 24 appearances and scoring eight goals. Conscious that he would never escape from the 'Thomson tragedy', Sam took the decision to return to English football in the hope of reviving his faltering career. So it came to pass that one of the outstanding forwards of the inter-war years joined Hartlepools United in the summer of 1936 for a knock-down fee of £275.

English's first season, 1936–37, was a relative success, as 'Pools finished a creditable sixth in Division Three North,

thanks in no small part to his 18 goals and the effective partnership he formed with Johnny Wigham. His second, and last, season was not so successful as both he and Wigham found goals harder to come by, resulting in 'Pools slipping down to 20th place, only avoiding re-election on goal difference. English's season was also blighted by allegations of excessive drinking, thought to be the result of continued taunting by football fans, which resulted in the directors imposing a 14-day suspension.

After leaving the Victoria Ground, Sam English retired from professional football and returned to Scotland to coach Duntocher Hibs and later his first club, Yoker Athletic. At the time of his death he was employed as a sheet iron worker in the Govan shipyards. He died in hospital in Alexandria, Vale of Leven, from motor neurone disease, aged 58 years on 12 April 1967.

## FOGARTY, Ambrose Gerald

**(1963–67)**

Inside-forward/wing half-back, 5ft 7in, 10st 12lb

Born: Dublin, 11 September 1933

Signed from: Sunderland, 21 November 1963, £10,000

Transferred: Cork Hibernian, March 1967, contract cancelled by mutual consent

Career: Home Farm, Bohemians, Glentoran, Sunderland, Hartlepools United, Cork Hibernian

Debut: v Stockport County, 23 November 1963

Appearances: League: 127 apps, 22 gls; FA Cup: 7 apps, 3 gls; FL Cup: 4 apps, 0 gls; Total: 138 apps, 25 gls

Chairman Ernest Ord broke the club transfer record when he paid Sunderland £10,000 (about £250,000 at today's values) to secure the services of Ambrose Fogarty in November 1963 when he was still a member of the Republic of Ireland side, for whom he made a total of 11 appearances. An Irish Cup finalist with Glentoran, Fogarty had joined Sunderland in October 1957 for a reported £3,000 fee and went on to make 174 League and Cup appearances, scoring 44 goals over the next six years for the Wearside club.

Fogarty, to this day the club's only full international when he played against Spain in a European Championship quarter-final 4–1 defeat in Seville in March 1964, added much-needed class and balance to a side still in the doldrums following the constant managerial changes since the death of Fred Westgarth. Ironically he was signed during Bobby Gurney's brief, unhappy tenure of office. Gurney was himself a former favourite at Sunderland.

The public euphoria at Fogarty's signing was dampened by a narrow defeat on his debut at Stockport County, only to be restored in a stunning 4–2 win over Bradford

Park Avenue on his first appearance at the Victoria Ground. This was the game in which local player Terry Francis achieved the rare feat of scoring a hat-trick on his League debut. Such optimism quickly evaporated in the coming games as only two of the next 12 were won. Fogarty finished the season with five goals in 22 appearances and the club made yet another re-election application.

The 1964–65 campaign, Fogarty's first full season, started badly with victory only coming in the sixth League game. After that results gradually improved, with Fogarty forming an effective partnership with Peter Thompson, which yielded 28 League and Cup goals. With support coming from wingers Bradley and Bannister, a final League position of 15th was the first time in the 1960s that the club finished above the re-election zone. Another plus was the home record, which saw only two games lost with a corresponding improvement in attendances.

Fogarty continued to be an influence on the pitch following the appointment of Brian Clough, although the 1965–66 season was one of transition following the departure of Geoff Twentyman. The arrival

of Ernie Phythian provided fresh impetus to the forwards and the goals tally improved as a consequence. Results, however, continued to be mixed, and a final position of 18th was viewed as a disappointment given the progress of the previous campaign.

Fogarty's final season, 1966–67, saw a major improvement as the partnership of Phythian and Mulvaney prospered, in no small part due to Fogarty's promptings and service. Playing in a deeper role at wing half-back, he compensated for lack of pace by utilising his experience to such an extent that the two strikers scored 45 League and Cup goals, ensuring a top-10 League finish for the first time since the 1956–57 season.

In the closing stages of the season the club agreed to cancel Fogarty's contract to allow him to return to his native Ireland to join Cork Hibernian in a player-coach role. Prior to leaving the Vic he was given a benefit against a Sunderland XI led by Charlie Hurley, which drew a 7,000 crowd, testimony to his popularity.

On retiring from playing Fogarty entered management with Cork Celtic, Drumcondra, Galway United, Athlone Town, with whom he qualified for the UEFA Cup, and Galway Rovers.

## GILL, John Barry Anthony

**(1966–71)**

Centre-half, 6ft 0in, 12st 2lb
Born: Wednesbury, 3 February 1941
Signed from: Mansfield Town, 10 February 1966, £4,000
Transferred: Nuneaton Borough, May 1971
Career: Nottingham Forest (juniors), Mansfield Town, Hartlepools United, Nuneaton Borough, Atherstone Town
Debut: v Luton Town, 12 February 1966
Appearances: League: 201+3 apps, 1 gl; FA Cup: 7 apps, 0 gls; FL Cup: 6 apps, 0 gls; Total: 214+3 apps, 1 gl

After failing to make the grade with Nottingham Forest, John Gill joined Mansfield Town in July 1961 and went on to make 139 League appearances for the Stags before being signed by Brian Clough in February 1966 for £4,000 as a replacement for Alan Fox, who had left for Bradford City the previous November.

Described by Peter Taylor as 'terrifyingly tough', John Gill cut an imposing figure on a football field. His arrival coincided with an improvement in results, which ultimately resulted in 'Pools climbing clear of the re-election zone. His second season with the club, 1966–67, saw a settled side moulded in Clough's image, with only 21 players used. Gill, however, had a frustrating season with injuries, which caused him to miss 19 League games, a factor which undoubtedly limited his side to a final League position of eighth, their highest since 1956–57.

Following Clough's departure, Gus McLean wisely retained the core of defenders he inherited, with Gill at the heart of his defence, the new manager only adding experience in goal with the signing of George Smith. The success of this approach was reflected in the home record, which saw only 12 goals conceded and 20 clean sheets kept throughout the promotion season, during which Gill missed only three games. He was equally reliable the following season in the Third Division, continuing to be the mainstay of a defence which did not believe in conceding goals easily. In this and the following season he formed an effective central-defensive partnership with Alan Goad before the arrival of Len Ashurst, also coinciding with the emergence of Bill Green, resulted in his release at the end of the 1970–71 season.

An interesting statistic from his Hartlepool career arose in the 1969–70 season when he set one of the club's stranger records by scoring no fewer than five own-goals.

John Gill's sterling service was rightly rewarded with a testimonial in May 1971 when an All Star team featuring Bobby Kerr, Alan Foggon, Keith Dyson and George Herd, among others, played a Hartlepool side at the Victoria Ground. He joined Southern League side Nuneaton Borough managed by David Pleat, along with his former colleague Tony Bircumshaw, and later played for Atherstone Town.

## GOAD, Alan Michael

**(1967–78)**
Central-defender, 5ft 10in, 10st 10lb
Born: Hailsham, 8 August 1948
Signed from: Exeter City, 1 July 1967
Transferred: Retired, May 1978
Career: Exeter City (juniors), Hartlepool United
Debut: v Brentford, 19 August 1967
Appearances: League: 366+9 apps, 11 gls; FA Cup: 20 apps 0 gls; League Cup: 23 apps 0 gls; Total: 409+9 apps, 11 gls

Alan Goad was signed by Gus McLean during the close season. He was brought in to strengthen a settled squad which had finished a creditable eighth the previous season. Given that Goad had failed to make a single appearance for Exeter City, his signing must rank as one of the most inspired in the club's history, as over the next 11 seasons he was to play over 400 games for 'Pools.

After initially being played at right-back by McLean in the early games of the 1967–68 promotion season, he lost his place to the experienced Tony Bircumshaw and made just 11 League appearances during the season. The following season, 1968–69, he played primarily as a central-defender, covering the right-back berth when Bircumshaw was unavailable. Missing only two games in 1969–70, Goad set a pattern of consistency which few have been able to equal during the service of five managers during his time with the club. The ultimate tribute to his versatility came during the 1976–77 campaign when he was selected in every outfield position (2 to 11) in his 30 League starts, as well as making seven substitute appearances.

Following the signing of Billy Ayre from Scarborough in August 1977 his appearances became less frequent, although he did play at centre-forward when required due to injuries. He retired

at the end of the season and was awarded a well-deserved testimonial when Brian Clough brought his Nottingham Forest side to grace the occasion. After a spell as a publican in the local area, he emigrated to Canada and worked as a coach for Vancouver Whitecaps.

## GREEN, William

**(1969–73)**
Central-defender, 6ft 3in, 12st 8lb
Born: Newcastle upon Tyne, 22 December 1950
Signed from: Newcastle United, 1 July 1969
Transferred: Carlisle United, 20 July 1973, £15,000
Career: Newcastle United (juniors), Hartlepool, Carlisle United, West Ham United, Peterborough United, Chesterfield, Doncaster Rovers
Debut: v Newport County, 15 September 1969
Appearances: League: 128+3 apps, 9 gls; FA Cup: 1+1 apps, 0 gls; FL Cup: 4 apps, 0 gls; Total: 133+4 apps, 9 gls

Signed by Angus McLean from Newcastle United while still a junior as a long-term replacement for John Gill, Bill Green developed into a commanding central-defender who quickly established himself as 'Pools' first choice centre-half. He missed only two League games throughout the 1970–71 season and his consistent performances brought him to the attention of a wider audience. Green's development coincided with the appointment of Len Ashurst as manager, and his defensive knowledge and experience undoubtedly contributed to Green's progress. The appointment of Tommy Aird, a local publican, as chairman resulted in Green being transferred to Carlisle United for a relatively meagre £15,000 in order to balance the books. Still only 22 years old, he had already made 131 League appearances for 'Pools, scoring nine goals.

Green spent three seasons with Carlisle, making 119 League appearances and being a key member of the side which won promotion to the First Division in 1974. Despite their instant relegation, Green had the distinction of appearing in every game, and it was no surprise when he was given

the transfer his talent deserved, joining First Division West Ham United for a £75,000 transfer fee.

After two seasons with the Hammers he moved to Peterborough United and later played for Chesterfield and Doncaster Rovers. He had managerial experience with Scunthorpe United between 1991 and 1993, and after spells with Buxton United and Bradford Park Avenue he joined Sheffield Wednesday as chief scout before being appointed caretaker manager for one game in 2002. Latterly he has worked as a scout for Paul Jewell at Wigan Athletic and, most recently, Nigel Clough at Derby County.

## HARDEN, Leo

**(1946–56)**

Outside-left, 5ft 7in, 10st 9lb

Born: West Hartlepool, 7 May 1923

Died: 5 December 1999

Signed from: Railway Athletic, May 1946

Transferred: Thornley Colliery Welfare, May 1955

Career: Railway Athletic, Hartlepools United, Thornley Colliery Welfare, Horden Colliery Welfare

Debut: v Barrow, 31 August 1946

Appearances: League: 169 apps, 47 gls; FA Cup: 11 apps, 5 gls; Total: 180 apps, 52 gls

Leo Harden, an outside-left in the traditional style, was a product of local nursery side Railway Athletic before making his first appearance for Hartlepools United during the 1945–46 season in the wartime League. He made his Football League debut in the first game of the new campaign following the war, scoring against Barrow in a 1–1 draw. He went on to play 17 games in his debut season, scoring a highly creditable nine goals.

A great character (in the best sense) locally and always a part-time professional, he was nicknamed 'The Flying Dustman'

due to his employment with West Hartlepool Council as the driver of a refuse collection vehicle. His work responsibilities restricted his appearances, yet he still managed to top the 30 games mark in both the 1947–48 and 1949–50 seasons, after which the emergence of Billy McClure limited his chances.

Following McClure's departure he competed with Jimmy McLaughlin for the left-wing berth throughout the 1953–54 campaign. His 'finest hour' in a 10-year career with his home-town club came in October 1953 when, in the space of four days, he scored seven goals, four against Rochdale in a Division Three North fixture and a hat-trick against local rivals Gateshead in a Durham Senior Cup tie. The arrival of George Luke from Newcastle United finally brought the curtain down on his 'Pools career, yet he still managed a goal in his final appearance in April 1956, a 3–1 home win over local rivals Gateshead.

On leaving the Vic he signed for Thornley Colliery Welfare and later played for Horden Colliery Welfare. Like many players of his era he played club cricket to a good standard following his retirement from football. His popularity in the Hartlepools area was demonstrated by the large congregation at his funeral in December 1999.

## HARDY, Cecil

**(1920–27)**
Inside-forward, 5ft 5in, 10st 7lb
Born: Kimblesworth, 1 January 1898
Died: Hartlepool, 1 March 1975
Signed from: Blackhall Colliery, December 1920, free transfer
Transferred: Horden Colliery Welfare, June 1928, free transfer
Career: Blackhall Colliery Welfare, Hartlepools United, Blackhall Colliery Welfare, Horden Colliery Welfare
Debut: v Blyth Spartans (North Eastern League), 20 October 1920
Appearances: League: 124 apps, 45 gls; FA Cup: 11 apps, 3 gls; Total: 135 apps, 48 gls

Cecil Hardy initially joined Hartlepools United as an amateur in October 1920 from Blackhall Colliery Welfare, turning professional in the December of that year. He made 19 appearances in the club's final North Eastern League season, scoring eight goals.

The club's inaugural Football League season saw him make 22 appearances, contributing 10 goals, principally in the inside-left position. The following season saw him make a similar playing contribution (24 appearances, 11 goals) which set the pattern to come. Throughout this period he regularly played for the reserve XI and was selected for North Eastern League representative teams in both the 1923–24 and 1924–25 seasons.

His best season was 1925–26, when, in partnership with Harry Wensley, he scored 15 goals in 33 League appearances, a major factor in 'Pools finishing in sixth place in the League. His personal highlight was a

hat-trick in the 9–3 trouncing of Walsall, 'Pools' record victory at the time. Such was Cec Hardy's popularity at this time that he was awarded a testimonial game at the end of the season, which saw a Hartlepools XI play an International Select XI chosen by Stan Seymour of Newcastle United and England fame. 'Pools won 5–3 in front of a crowd of over 3,000 fans, although Hardy was unable to play due to injury.

After this season his appearances became less frequent as he increasingly took on a coaching role, and he left the club in the summer of 1928 to return to Blackhall Colliery Welfare, later playing for near neighbours Horden Colliery Welfare.

Throughout his playing career Cec Hardy continued to work in Blackhall pit with his younger brother Syd, who also played for Hartlepools, continuing to do so throughout World War Two.

Cec Hardy died in Hartlepool General Hospital on 1 March 1975 aged 77 years, having survived the tragic Blackhall Veterans Bowls Club coach crash at Stanhope three years earlier.

## HARDY, Lawrence Richard

**(1931–37)**

Inside/centre-forward, 5ft 10in, 12st 12lb
Born: South Bank, 28 February 1913
Died: South Bank, 25 July 1995
Signed from: South Bank East End, March 1931
Transferred: Bradford City, August 1937
Career: South Bank East End, Hartlepools United, Bradford City, Shrewsbury Town
Debut: v Barrow, 25 March 1931
Appearances: League: 150 apps, 26 gls; FA Cup: 14 apps, 1 gl; Other: 4 apps, 0 gls. Total: 168 apps, 27 gls

Dick Hardy was signed from Middlesbrough club South Bank East End towards the end of the 1931–32 season, following Jackie Carr's retirement from playing. Initially he signed amateur forms, but he turned professional within a few weeks.

Hardy's signing coincided with the arrival of Johnny Wigham, and together they formed the inside-forward pairing to support Joss Hewitt. Hardy was the creator and provider of chances in a forward line which also included winger Albert Bonass, thereby ensuring for the next several seasons that scoring goals was not the major problem. Indeed, right up to his final season, whenever the defence tightened up, 'Pools' League position improved.

Hardy's best season was 1933–34 when he scored 12 goals in 34 League appearances, one of four players to reach double figures in a total of 89 goals scored. Unfortunately, all-

too-familiar defensive frailties resulted in another mid-table finish.

The arrival of Sam English for the start of the 1936–37 season resulted in a change of role for Hardy, and he made most of his 24 League appearances in defensive positions. He left at the end of that season to join Bradford City, for whom he made 12 appearances, and was with Shrewsbury Town, then a non-League club, at the outbreak of the war.

After the war Dick Hardy maintained his contact with football at a local level in the Teesside area and even acted as trainer to the Smiths Dock Ladies team. He died in South Bank in July 1995 aged 82 years.

## HEWITT, John Joseph

**(1930–34)**

Centre-forward, 5ft 11in, 12st 5lb
Born: Evenwood, 15 June 1911
Died: Dundee, 7 August 1984
Signed from: Everton, 20 August 1930, free transfer
Transferred: Norwich City, 16 May 1934, £1,000 (Hewitt and Harry Proctor)
Career: Rugby Town, Evenwood Town, Everton, Hartlepools United, Norwich City, Northampton Town, Southport
Debut: v Halifax Town, 30 August 1930
Appearances: League: 110 apps, 53 gls; FA Cup: 6 apps, 2 gls; Other: 1 app, 0 gls. Total: 117 apps, 55 gls

Joss Hewitt was signed by Bill Norman from Merseyside giants Everton in the summer of 1930 in what was to prove one of 'Pools' best-ever signings. Tall and of imposing build, Hewitt was to prove the perfect partner for Johnny Wigham in the early 1930s.

After a quiet start, Hewitt made only 28 League appearances in his first two seasons, but he more than compensated with 23 goals in 41 League games in the 1932–33 campaign, inspiring Wigham and Pedwell to contribute 15 goals apiece. Unfortunately, the team's defensive frailties resulted in a record 116 League goals against, limiting 'Pools to a 14th-place League finish.

The pattern was continued the following season, 1933–34, when Hewitt again reached the 20 goal mark, the first 'Pools player to achieve this milestone in

successive seasons, with strong support again coming from Pedwell (18 goals) and Wigham (15 goals). He also became only the second Hartlepools player, after Pedwell, to reach 50 League goals; although he reached the landmark in fewer games, 101.

Following two successful seasons at the Vic, Joss Hewitt joined Second Division Norwich City along with Harry Proctor for a joint £1,000 transfer fee. Hewitt went on to make 13 appearances for the Canaries, scoring two goals, but was released after only one season as an 'economy measure'. He later spent nearly four years with Northampton Town and was with Southport at the outbreak of war which, as with so many professionals, effectively finished his career.

After the war Joss Hewitt continued to play football for Hall's Works FC, his employer's team for whom he made pumps for the Admiralty and Merchant Navy. He died in Dundee in 1984 shortly after his 73rd birthday.

## HOGAN, Roy David

**(1978–82 and 1983–87)**

Midfielder, 5ft 8in, 10st 6lb
Born: West Hartlepool, 24 September 1960
Signed from: Apprentice, 25 September 1978
Transferred: Crook Town, May 1983, free transfer
Re-signed: Crook Town, 22 December 1983, free transfer
Career: Hartlepool United, Crook Town, Hartlepool United, Seaham Red Star
Debut: v Doncaster Rovers, 15 April 1978
Appearances: League: 271+13 apps, 32 gls; FA Cup: 10+1 apps, 2 gls; FL Cup: 11+1 apps, 2 gls; Other: 12 apps, 0 gls. Total: 304+15 apps, 36 gls

Locally born, Roy Hogan joined Hartlepool as an apprentice and went on to make his debut while still only 17 years old, eventually making over 300 appearances for his only League club. He was another from the Billy Horner production line of young players who either moved on, bringing much needed cash to the club, or, as in Roy Hogan's case, gave several seasons of loyal service.

A talented midfield player who was a byword for consistency, Hogan quickly established himself in the team and played 23 games, scoring one goal, during the 1978–79 campaign. He missed only a handful of games in the following two seasons before the arrival of John Duncan saw him surprisingly released at the end of the 1982–83 season. He briefly played for Crook Town before being re-signed by the reinstated Billy Horner, following Duncan's departure in December 1983.

Thereafter Roy Hogan was a key member of Horner's team, playing a major part in the ultimately unsuccessful 1985–86 promotion challenge, scoring eight goals in his 38 League games. He was released by new manager John Bird at the end of the 1986–87 season, despite having once again proved his value to the team by

playing 38 League games, the third season in succession he reached that mark. After a short spell with Seaham Red Star he emigrated to Australia and became involved with football in the Perth area.

## HONOUR, Brian

**(1985–95)**
Midfielder, 5ft 7in, 12st 5lb
Born: Horden, 16 February 1964
Signed from: Peterlee Newtown, 7 February 1985
Transferred: Spennymoor United, 1 August 1994
Career: Darlington, Peterlee Newtown, Hartlepool United, Spennymoor United
Debut: v Peterborough United, 9 February 1985
Appearances: League: 301+18 apps, 26 gls; FA Cup: 21+1 apps, 2 gls; FL Cup: 21+3 apps, 3 gls; Other: 19 apps, 6 gls. Total: 362+22 apps, 37 gls

Billy Horner rescued Brian Honour's professional career when he signed him from non-League football in February 1985. Honour had begun as an apprentice at Darlington, making 74 League appearances before being released by, of all people, Cyril Knowles. Horner effectively rescued him from the dole queue as he struggled to come to terms with life outside the professional game.

His second season, 1985–86, saw him ever-present in all 'Pools' games, and he remained a key figure in the side throughout the various managerial changes. The arrival of Cyril Knowles at a time when he was recovering from injury could have spelt the end of his Hartlepool career; however, the new manager admitted his earlier mistake and Honour went on to become a key member of the promotion side, winning the supporters' Player of the Year award ahead of the favourite Joe Allon.

Honour had an outstanding season in Division Three, only missing two League games, after which his appearances became less frequent due to a legacy of injuries. He retired from playing shortly after the start of the 1994–95 season having made 384 appearances for 'Pools in all competitions, placing him fifth in the all-time list of players.

On his retirement his service to the club was rewarded in August 1995 with a testimonial game against Kevin Keegan's star spangled Newcastle United side in front of a capacity all-ticket crowd. He was briefly joint caretaker manager with Paul Baker in early 1999, following the departure of Mick Tait, and was later assistant to Chris Turner.

After leaving Victoria Park he managed north-east sides Durham City, Horden Colliery Welfare and Bishop Auckland (twice) prior to being appointed manager of West Auckland Town for the 2009–10 season, a post he held for a mere two months before resigning and returning to Horden in December 2009 initially as assistant to Simon Corbett and latterly as manager following the former's departure.

Brian Honour continues to maintain his links with Hartlepool United and has featured in the annual Northern Master Tournament team. His popularity with 'Pools fans was amply demonstrated when they voted him Player of the Decade – 1990s in a poll for the club's Player of the Century awards.

## HOUCHEN, Keith Morton

**(1978–81 and 1993–97)**

Centre-forward, 6ft 2in, 12st 8lb
Born: Middlesbrough, 25 July 1960
Signed from: Chesterfield, 23 February 1978, free transfer
Transferred: Orient, 25 March 1982, £25,000
Re-signed: Port Vale, 1 August 1993, free transfer
Career: Chesterfield (juniors), Hartlepool United, Orient, York City, Scunthorpe United, Coventry City, Hibernian, Port Vale, Hartlepool United
Debut: v Crewe Alexandra, 25 February 1978
Appearances: League: 264+15 apps, 92 gls; FA Cup: 6+1 apps, 0 gls; FL Cup: 17+1 apps, 2 gls; Other: 6 apps, 0 gls. Total: 293+17 apps, 94 gls

Middlesbrough-born Keith Houchen was signed by Billy Horner after a week's trial having been released by Chesterfield as a 17-year-old junior. He initially caught Horner's eye when he scored the winning goal for Nunthorpe Athletic in an FA Youth Cup tie against Hartlepool Juniors at the Vic.

Keith Houchen made his Football League debut within two days of signing, a 1–1 draw against Crewe Alexandra. It was obvious from an early stage that he was a real talent and destined to achieve greater things in the game, which he ultimately did. His record for Hartlepool United stands comparison with the best in the club's history.

Houchen joined 'Pools following the sale of Malcolm Poskett to Brighton, thereby partnering him with another strong, physical forward, Bob Newton. For the next four seasons, from 1978 to 1982 he dominated the club scoring lists, finishing as leading marksman in four successive seasons, a feat equalled only by Eric Wildon. A particular highlight was a 25-minute hat-trick in a 4–4 draw at Peterborough, the fastest League treble for over 50 years. His goals and presence were a major factor in the club achieving 'mid-table respectability' in this period, and it was inevitable that such a player, still only 22 years old, would attract attention from other clubs.

In March 1982, following yet another 'final demand' from the Inland Revenue, Houchen was sold to Orient for the bargain sum of £25,000. He made 76 appearances for the London club, scoring 20 goals, before returning north with York

City for a £15,000 fee. It was during his spell at Bootham Crescent that he attracted national attention by scoring the winning penalty against Arsenal in a fourth-round FA Cup tie which was featured on the BBC's *Match of the Day* programme. Following a spell on the substitute's bench he moved to Scunthorpe United for £40,000 in March 1986, playing a mere nine games for the Lincolnshire side.

In July 1986 Keith Houchen made the move which was to define his career when he joined another club that plays in blue and white, Coventry City, then in the First Division, in a £60,000 transfer deal. Prior to the 1986–87 season Coventry had never won a major trophy, and in an FA Cup campaign which included a surprise win at Old Trafford over Manchester United courtesy of a Houchen goal, the Light Blues reached a Wembley Final for the first time in their history. Their opponents in the Final, Tottenham Hotspur, were hot favourites and led 2–1 when Keith Houchen made his move, scoring with a spectacular diving header to equalise the scores and write his name forever in the annals of FA Cup history. Such a goal turned the game in Coventry's favour and they went on to win in extra-time, 3–2. This goal won him the BBC's Goal of the Season award and was instrumental in his selection for the 'Walk of Fame' as part of the pre-match celebrations for the opening of the new Wembley Stadium prior to the 2007 FA Cup Final.

Houchen then moved on to Scottish club Hibernian in 1989, for whom he played in the UEFA Cup, before returning to English football with Port Vale. After two seasons with the Potteries side he returned to Victoria Park in October 1993 to resume his 'Pools career.

Following the promotion to Division Two, 'Pools had struggled to score goals in the higher division. Manager Viv Busby turned to the former favourite to add presence and firepower to a lightweight forward line. Unfortunately, the damage was already done and, despite scoring eight goals in 34 games, Houchen was unable to prevent an embarrassing relegation. The following season, 1994–95, saw him regain the leading goalscorer spot with 13 goals, the fifth time he achieved such a feat, a club record. Despite this, 'Pools struggled and eventually finished in 18th position.

It was towards the end of this season that Keith Houchen was appointed to the role of player-manager following the departure of David McCreery. He played 36 games the following campaign before finally hanging up his boots in September 1996 to concentrate on his managerial duties. Hampered by a lack of funds to improve the team and a poor run in the second half of the season, which eventually resulted in a 20th-place League finish, meant that he left the club he had served so well overall. In recognition of his services he was awarded a benefit match against Middlesbrough which raised £23,000, and he later joined the Teesside club to work in their highly praised youth development programme.

## HOWARD, Steven John

**(1995–98)**

Centre-forward, 6ft 3in, 14st 6lb
Born: Durham, 10 May 1976
Signed from: Tow Law Town, 8 August 1995, free transfer
Transferred: Northampton Town, 22 February 1999, £120,000
Career: Tow Law Town, Hartlepool United, Northampton Town, Luton Town, Derby County, Leicester City
Debut: v Chester City, 12 August 1995
Appearances: League: 117+25 apps, 26 gls; FA Cup: 3 apps, 0 gls; FL Cup: 6 apps, 1 gl; Other: 5 apps, 2 gls. Total: 131+25 apps, 29 gls

Steve Howard was signed by Keith Houchen from non-League Tow Law Town in August 1995 on a reported £100 per week and was immediately given his debut while still a teenager. With an impressive physique, the manager must have seen something of himself in the young player as Howard was to develop into a centre-forward very much in Keith Houchen's image.

Howard made an impressive 39 League appearances (scoring seven goals) in his debut season, partnering his manager in the forward line on several occasions. Following Houchen's retirement from playing and subsequent departure, Steve Howard established himself at centre-forward throughout the 1996–97 campaign while still only 20 years of age. Although he was not a prolific goalscorer in the Joe Allon mould, his value to the team lay in his ability to act as a 'target man' and cause havoc in opposing defences with his aerial power, particularly from corners.

After a successful 1997–98 season, missing only three League games, he was transferred to Northampton Town in February 1999 for £120,000, going on to play 86 League games for the Cobblers and scoring 18 goals. He joined Luton Town in March 2000 for a bargain fee of £50,000,

going on to make 212 League appearances for the Hatters and scoring an impressive 95 goals over the next five seasons. Such consistency attracts attention and it was no surprise when Derby County signed him for a £1 million transfer fee to be a key member of the squad which ultimately gained promotion through the Play-offs to the FA Premier League.

After making his Premiership debut with Derby County, Steve Howard won his first representative honour when he played for Scotland B against the Republic of Ireland, scoring the equaliser in a 1–1 draw. In January, with Derby bottom of the Premiership, he moved to Championship side Leicester City on a three-and-a-half year deal, and despite scoring a hat-trick against the eventual champions West Bromwich Albion he was unable to prevent the Foxes' first-ever relegation to the third tier of English football.

The following season, 2008–09, was to mark an upturn in Leicester's fortunes when, after numerous managerial changes, they won the League One title having dominated the League throughout the season. Steve Howard played a major role in this revival, scoring 13 goals in 41 appearances, including two at Victoria Park, taking his career total of goals against Hartlepool United to 10.

In common with his manager and teammates at Leicester, Steve Howard believed his club could win promotion to the Premiership in a highly competitive League. His sterling performances in his 37 appearances were a major factor in Leicester reaching the Play-off semi-final only to lose in a penalty shoot-out to Cardiff City despite Howard converting his spot-kick. The following season, 2011–12, was a disappointing one for the 'Foxes' as the anticipated promotion challenge failed to materialise and Steve Howard saw his appearances limited before being released at the end of his contract.

## HOWE, John Robert

**(1934–36)**

Left-back, 5ft 11in, 12st 6lb
Born: West Hartlepool, 7 October 1915
Died: Hartlepool, 5 April 1987
Signed from: Wingate United, 22 December 1933, free transfer
Transferred: Derby County, March 1936, free transfer
Career: Wingate United, Hartlepools United, Derby County, Huddersfield Town, Kings Lynn, Long Sutton, Wisbech Town
Debut: v Chester, 5 September 1934
Appearances: League: 24 apps, 0 gls; Other: 2 apps, 0 gls. Total: 26 apps, 0 gls

Jack Howe, although only playing League football for Hartlepools for a couple of seasons, became celebrated within the town as the only locally-born footballer to play for England in a full international. On top of this he won an FA Cup-winners' medal with Derby County, the club with whom he played the major part of his career.

Howe joined 'Pools as a teenager having represented West Hartlepool schools and played for local junior sides before being signed by Jacky Carr and making his professional debut at left-back against Chester in September 1934 in a 4–1 defeat. He went on to make 16 appearances in his debut season, including one at centre-forward. The following term he played on eight occasions through to the New Year before George Jobey signed him in March for Derby County. He quickly established himself in the Derby side and was a regular before his career was interrupted by the war.

A return to his home-town at the start of the conflict afforded Howe the opportunity to guest for his local club before being called-up for active service with the Cameron Highlanders. As was the case with most professional players they made guest appearances for any club convenient to their circumstances, so Jack Howe played

for a number of Scottish clubs and made a handful of appearances for Hartlepools towards the end of the war.

The 1945–46 season was notable for the resumption of the FA Cup competition on a totally professional basis without the addition of 'guest' players. Returning to the Baseball Ground, Jack Howe found himself in a side bristling with confidence as it despatched Luton, West Bromwich Albion, Brighton and Aston Villa before being taken to a replay by Birmingham City. He had only returned from India three weeks before the semi-final and was required to play at centre-half due to an injury to Leon Leuty. He was restored to the left-back position for the Final, which turned out to be a classic, with Bert Turner of Charlton scoring for both sides to take the game into extra-time, during which the class of the Derby forwards shone through as they scored three times to ensure a famous victory.

Such exploits did not go unnoticed by the England selectors and Jack Howe earned his first full international cap in 1948 against Italy in Turin, a famous 4–0 victory. Further appearances followed the following year against Scotland at Wembley, a disappointing 3–1 defeat, and finally a resounding 9–2 demolition of Northern Ireland at Maine Road, Manchester.

Howe left Derby County in October 1949 for Huddersfield Town, making 29 League appearances for the Leeds Road club and scoring one goal. He left the Terriers in

July 1951 to become player-manager of Kings Lynn, staying four years before joining Long Sutton in a similar role and ending his playing career with Wisbech Town.

On retiring from the professional game Jack Howe returned to Hartlepool to work in the licensed trade. He played in the joint testimonial game for Ken Johnson and Tommy Burlison in May 1964 at the age of 48 years. The grandfather of Steve Fletcher, who played for Hartlepool in the 1990s, he became ill and was admitted to Hartlepool General hospital, where he was able to receive a visit from his former Derby teammates Jackie Stamps and Jim Bullions a few days before he died on 5 April 1987, aged 71 years.

## HUMPHREYS, Richard John

**(2001–Present)**

Midfielder, 5ft 11in, 12st 7lb
Born: Sheffield, 30 November 1977
Signed from: Cambridge United, 18 July 2001, free transfer
Career: Sheffield Wednesday, Scunthorpe United (loan), Cardiff City (loan), Cambridge United, Hartlepool United, Port Vale (loan), Hartlepool United
Debut: v Mansfield Town, 11 August 2001
Appearances: League: 412+38 apps, 33 gls; Play-off: 7 apps, 0 gls; FA Cup: 28+1 apps, 2 gls; FL Cup: 12 apps, 0 gls; Other: 10+3 apps, 1 gl. Total: 469+42 apps, 36 gls

It is highly unlikely that anyone, including Chris Turner who signed him, could have anticipated the service Ritchie Humphreys was to give Hartlepool United when he made his debut against Cambridge United on 18 July 2001. It was to be over five years before he missed his first League game, against Hereford United on 26 August 2006, a total of 234 consecutive League appearances during one of the most exciting periods of 'Pools' history. As if to punish Humphreys for this aberration, Danny Wilson sent him to Port Vale on a month's loan, and quickly recalled him!

Ritchie Humphreys started his career as a youth trainee with Sheffield Wednesday and made his Premiership debut during the 1995–96 season. An immensely talented England Youth and Under-21 international, he played in 29 games the following season when Wednesday finished a creditable seventh in the top division having been top in the opening games. However, his career faltered at Hillsborough during the constant managerial changes and he had loan spells at Scunthorpe and Cardiff before signing for Cambridge United in February 2001.

It was a red letter day for Hartlepool United when Chris Turner brought him to Victoria Park and made him a fixture in the

team. Needless to say, he featured in all the major games of the next six seasons, starting in a more forward role to begin with before reverting to his best position in midfield. He will always be remembered for scoring the vital penalty in the shoot-out against Tranmere Rovers which clinched 'Pools' place in the Play-off Final against Sheffield Wednesday.

The departure of Chris Turner did not affect his form, and in terms of goals he was at his best during the 2002–03 promotion season, scoring 11 times in the League and being voted by his fellow professionals into the PFA Division Three team as well as being named the supporters' Player of the Year. Neale Cooper retained him in the playmaker role for the next two seasons, and he won another Player of the Year award before Martin Scott recognised his defensive values and played him in a deeper, more defensive role, which Danny Wilson continued. Despite his brief loan spell at Port Vale, Ritchie Humphreys still played 38 games during the record-breaking 2006–07 promotion season. His efforts were rewarded by his fellow professionals when he was named in the PFA League Two Team of the Year.

Ritchie Humphreys's major contribution to the club was recognised at an awards evening celebrating Hartlepool United's centenary when he won his third Player of the Year award, and also the Player of the Decade – and to top that he won the Player of the Century accolade too. He wore the burden of such honours lightly during a difficult 2009–10 campaign, making 40 League and Cup appearances and being a major influence on the team. By the end of the season he was second in the club's all-time appearances list and was rewarded by Chris Turner with a one year extension to his contract.

The 2010–11 season was a personal triumph for Ritchie Humphreys with the club announcing in September that he had been awarded a testimonial in recognition of his exemplary 10-year service to 'Pools cause. He topped this accolade when he passed the legendary Watty Moore's longstanding appearances record against Exeter City coming on as a substitute for Joe Gamble. He went on to make 29 League and Cup appearances scoring three goals in the season and was rewarded with a further extension to his contract by Mick Wadsworth.

Premier League Sunderland were the opposition for Humphreys' testimonial on a glorious August evening in front of nearly 6,000 enthusiastic supporters. This was the prelude to another season which saw the 'Peter Pan' of the Victoria Park make a full contribution to his team's season despite being played in a variety of positions and even assisting Mickey Barron during his three games as caretaker boss.

At the end of the 2011–12 season Ritchie Humphreys was at the summit of Hartlepool United's appearances list with 511 in all competitions, scoring 36 goals. It was no surprise when Neale Cooper offered him a contract for another season, his 12th, thereby ensuring that his record would be extended.

## HUTCHISON, Donald

**(1989–90)**

Midfielder, 6ft 1in, 11st 8lb
Born: Gateshead, 9 May 1971
Signed from: Youth trainee, 20 March 1990
Transferred: Liverpool, 27 November 1990, £175,000
Career: Hartlepool United, Liverpool, West Ham United, Sheffield United, Everton, Sunderland, West Ham United, Millwall, Coventry City, Luton Town
Debut: Scunthorpe United, 7 October 1989
Appearances: League: 19+5 apps, 2 gls; FA Cup: 2 apps, 0 gls; FL Cup: 1+1 apps, 0 gls; Other: 1 app, 0 gls. Total: 23+6 apps, 2 gls

Don Hutchison was signed by Bobby Moncur from Redheugh Boys Club as an

18-year-old intermediate player and quickly made his League debut in October 1989. He played 10 consecutive League games before the arrival of Cyril Knowles saw him return to junior football. Initially Knowles was no fan of the talented yet temperamental player, and an incident in an intermediate game in April resulting in a sending off for 'foul and abusive language' towards the referee saw his contract cancelled. This incident followed a club suspension in January for failing to report for a trip to Colchester on New Year's Day. Knowles described the player's attitude as 'very poor'.

It is to Hutchison's credit that he learnt his lesson from his manager's unwavering professional standards and, after pleading to be given another chance, he returned to the team and showed his undoubted prowess. He made 11 League appearances at the start of the 1990–91 promotion season, as well as starring in the League Cup games against Tottenham Hotspur.

Such form brought him to the notice of several major clubs including Liverpool, the top club in the country at the time. He was signed by Kenny Dalglish after only 24 League games, for an initial fee of £175,000 plus bonus payments based on appearances. Such a fee was nearly treble the existing record of £60,000 paid earlier for both Malcolm Poskett and Andrew Linighan. Chairman Garry Gibson, who had facilitated the transfer by circulating a video of Hutchison's performances to several top clubs, immediately put a sizeable part of the transfer fee to good use by settling an outstanding tax bill with the Inland Revenue. On leaving the Vic Hutchison paid tribute to Cyril Knowles for having 'put me on the right lines'.

His three-year stay at Anfield was interrupted by the departure of Kenny Dalglish, and after a spell in the reserves he was transferred to West Ham United with whom he spent two seasons. Thereafter he played for Sheffield United, Everton, Sunderland, West Ham again, Millwall, Coventry City and Luton Town in a career which totalled over 400 games and involved transfer fees in excess of £11 million.

Don Hutchison also played 26 times for Scotland, scoring six goals including the winner in the last England versus Scotland game at Wembley in November 1999, before the stadium was rebuilt. On retiring at the end of the 2007–08 season he donated his final pay cheque at financially stricken Luton to sponsor two youth team players, Scott Sinclair and Jake Howells, for a season.

## INGRAM, Stuart Denevan

**(1993–2000)**

Right-back, 5ft 10in, 12st 1lb
Born: Sunderland, 27 June 1976
Signed from: Youth trainee, 1 July 1994
Transferred: Scarborough, March 2000, free transfer
Career: Hartlepool United, Scarborough, Northwich Victoria, Forest Green Rovers, Halifax Town, Scarborough, Harrogate Town, Whitby Town, Scarborough Athletic

Debut: v Wrexham, 20 November 1993
Appearances: League: 192+7 apps, 10 gls; FA Cup: 7 apps, 0 gls; FL Cup: 13+2 apps, 2 gls; Other: 8 apps, 0 gls. Total: 220+9 apps, 10 gls

Viv Busby gave Denny Ingram his Hartlepool debut against Wrexham in November 1993 in his last game in charge. Ingram was still a youth trainee at the time and only signed professional forms the following July, shortly after his 18th birthday.

A specialist full-back, he went on to make 229 appearances, scoring 10 goals, over the next seven seasons during which he was the model of consistency. This record made him the youngest player in the club's history to reach the 200 games mark. Ingram played for seven managers through to the start of the Chris Turner era and was ever present throughout the 1997–98 and 1998–99 League campaigns. The latter was another relegation battle, which ultimately proved successful, allowing Turner to mould the side in his playing style the following season. A poor start resulted in Ingram losing his place and he never played for 'Pools again, despite having made over 200 appearances while still only 23 years old.

After leaving Hartlepool, Denny Ingram pursued a playing career outside the Football League, joining Scarborough in March 2000 before moving to Northwich Victoria, Forest Green Rovers and Halifax Town. He rejoined Scarborough as player-coach in January 2006, playing through to their dissolution at the end of the season, and later had a spell with Harrogate Town before joining Whitby Town in July 2009. In 2010 he joined newly formed Scarborough Athletic.

## JOHNSON, Kenneth

**(1949–64)**

Centre-forward/wing half-back, 6ft 0in, 12st 8lb
Born: West Hartlepool, 15 February 1931
Died: Hartlepool, 29 December 2011
Signed from: Seaton Holy Trinity
Transferred: Retired May 1964
Career: Seaton Holy Trinity, Hartlepools United
Debut: v Bradford City, 31 December 1949
Appearances: League: 384 apps, 98 gls; FA Cup: 26 apps, 6 gls; FL Cup: 3 apps, 2 gls; Total: 413 apps, 106 gls

Ken Johnson was another product of local league football, playing for Seaton Holy Trinity before being signed by Fred Westgarth for Hartlepools United in 1949 and making his League debut on New Year's Eve, scoring against Bradford City. This game also featured, for the first time, the legendary half-back line of Newton, Moore and Stamper.

National Service in the Army meant he made only six appearances in the next three seasons, but his football development was further enhanced by playing with future England centre-forward Tommy Taylor, then a Barnsley player, in both Regimental and North Wales Leagues before a posting to Hong Kong afforded the opportunity to play in Army representative teams against local opposition.

Resuming his professional playing career, he quickly established himself as a goalscoring centre or inside-forward, making 49 League and Cup appearances in the 1954–55 season when 'Pools finished

fifth and reached the fourth round of the FA Cup. He really hit his stride the following season when Hartlepools went one better and finished fourth, scoring 21 times in 30 League games, which included four against Crewe Alexandra.

He was at his peak during the momentous 1956–57 season, scoring 26 goals in 45 League and Cup appearances, which resulted in his selection for the Football League's North versus South representative game at Coventry. The arrival of Ray Middleton saw him moved to a midfield role in the latter stage of his career, although he played most of the 1960–61 season for Bill Robinson as a forward in support of Bobby Folland. He managed 13 goals in 45 appearances, including Hartlepool's first-ever score in the inaugural Football League Cup competition against Oldham Athletic.

Johnson served a further two Hartlepool managers, Allenby Chilton and Bobby Gurney, before retiring at the end of the 1963–64 campaign. His career record shows he not only scored the most League goals for the club – 98, but also the most hat-tricks (or better) – five, and was only the second Hartlepool player to score 20 or more League goals in successive seasons. He also played in the club's record 10–1 victory against Barrow, yet surprisingly he did not feature among the goalscorers.

He was awarded a joint benefit game with Tommy Burlison on his retirement in May 1964, which attracted an 11,000 crowd, a club record for such an event and testimony to his popularity. Ken Johnson continued to live in Hartlepool, regularly attending the games at the Vic and acting as an ambassador for the club on match days until shortly before his death in December 2011.

The respect with which Ken Johnson was held in the local community was evidenced at his Thanksgiving Service at the Parish Church of Holy Trinity, Seaton Carew attended by the local MP, Ian Wright; Russ Green and Neale Cooper representing the management and staff of Hartlepool United; Mickey Barron, Ritchie Humphreys, Adam Boyd and Anthony Sweeney representing the playing and coaching staff of the club in a packed congregation of family and friends.

## JOHNSON, Kevin Peter

**(1975–76 and 1981–84)**

Midfielder, 5ft 9in, 10st 12lb
Born: Doncaster, 29 August 1952
Signed from: Workington, 5 March 1975 (loan 14 February 1975), £3,000
Transferred: Huddersfield Town, 24 September 1976, £12,000
Re-signed: Halifax Town, 8 January 1981, free transfer
Career: Sheffield Wednesday (apprentice), Southend United, Gillingham (loan), Workington, Hartlepool, Huddersfield Town, Halifax Town, Hartlepool United
Debut: v Bradford City, 15 February 1975
Appearances: League: 134+14 apps, 11 gls; FA Cup: 6+1 apps, 1 gl; FL Cup: 11+1 apps, 2 gls; Other: 4+1 apps, 0 gls. Total: 155+17 apps, 14 gls

Kevin Johnson was signed by Ken Hale from Workington in March 1975 for a £3,000 fee following a successful loan spell. A diminutive ball-playing midfield player, he went on to give sterling service to Hartlepool in two spells over a nearly 10-year period.

Johnson started his career as an apprentice with Sheffield Wednesday, making a single appearance as a substitute before moving to Southend United in September 1972. After a season with Southend, and a brief loan period with Gillingham, he joined Workington in July 1974, going on to make 15 appearances for the Cumbrian club, scoring one goal.

Johnson's signing had been made possible by two Cup runs which saw 'Pools play 12 ties before Christmas. The player joined the team in the middle of a nine-game winless run in the New Year, undoubtedly caused by fatigue. His arrival restored their form sufficiently to finish in a respectable 13th place. The 1975–76 season, his first full term at the Victoria Ground, saw him miss only a handful of games, including the FA Cup defeat against Manchester City, in which his constructive midfield play was badly

missed. At the start of the following season chairman Vince Barker, anxious to stave off yet another financial crisis, accepted Huddersfield Town's £12,000 offer for the player.

Kevin Johnson spent two seasons with Huddersfield, playing 81 League games and scoring 23 goals, before moving to Halifax Town for a club record £25,000, spending three terms at the Shay. Billy Horner brought him back to Hartlepool in January 1981 on a free transfer with 'Pools riding high in the Fourth Division. Despite the promotion challenge fading, Johnson played 32 League games the following season and continued to be a key member of the side through to the end of the 1983–84 season, when he was released by Horner and later played for Gateshead in the Conference.

## KNOWLES, Darren Thomas

**(1997–2001)**

Right-back, 5ft 6in, 11st 2lb
Born: Sheffield, 8 October 1970
Signed from: Scarborough, 27 March 1997, free transfer
Transferred: Northwich Victoria, 19 August 2001, free transfer
Career: Sheffield United, Stockport County, Scarborough, Hartlepool United, Northwich Victoria, Gainsborough Trinity, Ilkeston Town
Debut: v Colchester United, 29 March 1997
Appearances: League: 164+4 apps, 2 gls; Play-off: 2 apps, 0 gls; FA Cup: 5 apps, 0 gls; FL Cup: 7+1 apps, 0 gls; Other: 8 apps, 0 gls. Total: 186+5 apps, 2 gls

Darren Knowles joined his home-town club Sheffield United as a youth trainee before being released and signing for Stockport County in September 1989 while still a teenager. He made 63 appearances for the Edgeley Park club over the next four seasons, establishing himself during the

1991–92 campaign, in which he played 31 times. Knowles then joined Scarborough in August 1993 and played 42 League games during the 1993–94 campaign. His consistent form with the Yorkshire club, missing only 11 games in three seasons, brought him to the attention of Mick Tait, who signed him for 'Pools in March 1997, shortly before the transfer deadline.

To describe Darren Knowles as a 'consistent performer' does not do the player justice. A specialist right full-back, he made 103 consecutive League appearances following his debut against Colchester in March 1997, and over the next three seasons he missed only three League games. He was at the heart of 'Pools' revival under Chris Turner, although ironically he missed the club's first-ever Play-off games, against Darlington, due to injury.

The arrival of Paul Arnison from Newcastle United saw him share the right-back berth throughout the 2000–01 campaign, in which 'Pools finished fourth, and he was released at the end of the season despite playing in both Play-off games against Blackpool. Knowles signed for Northwich Victoria on a free transfer in August 2001 and later played for Gainsborough Trinity and Ilkeston Town.

## KONSTANTOPOULOS, Dimitrios

**(2004–07)**

Goalkeeper, 6ft 4in, 14st 2lb
Born: Kalamata, Greece, 29 November 1978
Signed from: Sporting Farense (Portugal), 22 January 2004, free transfer
Transferred: Coventry City, 25 May 2007, free transfer
Career: Kalamata (Greece), Egaleo (Greece), Sporting Farense (Portugal), Hartlepool United, Coventry City, Swansea City (loan), Cardiff City (loan), AO Kerkyra (Greece), AEK Athens (Greece)
Debut: v Colchester United, 30 August 2004
Appearances: League: 117 apps, 0 gls; FA Cup: 10 apps, 0 gls; FL Cup: 5 apps, 0 gls; Other: 7 apps, 0 gls. Total: 139 apps, 0 gls

Dimitrios Konstantopoulos (Dimi), a Greece Under-21 international, was signed on an 18-month contract by Neale Cooper from Portuguese side Sporting Farense, initially as cover for Jim Provett following the departure of Anthony Williams. He had to wait until the following August to make his League debut, due to Provett's consistent form, and only established himself as Hartlepool's first-choice custodian towards the end of the season, playing in the League Two Play-off Final against Sheffield Wednesday.

Tall and commanding, in the style of his hero Peter Schmeichel, Dimi established himself the following season, 2005–06, with his outstanding performances despite his team's problems both on and off the pitch, which ultimately resulted in relegation. His consistency can be gauged by the fact that despite 'Pools losing their League One status he never conceded more than three goals in any League game during a campaign in which he was ever present.

He set new standards throughout the record-breaking 2006–07 campaign as

Hartlepool United stormed back to League One. Again he was ever present, keeping 22 clean sheets in League games, which included eight in consecutive games to equal the Football League record. It was apparent long before the season ended with promotion that he would attract attention from other clubs, and it was no surprise when he signed for Championship side Coventry City in the close season despite being offered a new, improved contract by Hartlepool.

Dimi made 20 League appearances for Coventry during a difficult season in which relegation was narrowly avoided and also spent a brief spell on loan at Nottingham Forest. The arrival of Chris Coleman as manager saw him loaned out to Swansea City and Cardiff City during the 2008–09 season, and despite impressing at the latter no offer was forthcoming and he found himself back at the Ricoh Arena.

He suffered a frustrating time the following season, making only a handful of appearances due to the outstanding form of Kieran Westwood and was released in June 2010 by new manager Aidy Boothroyd on the expiry of his contract.

On his return to his native Greece Dimi signed for Super League side AO Kerkyra for who he was to display outstanding form in his 30 appearances. Such displays attracted the attention of leading club AEK Athens who he joined at the end of the season, and also the national selectors who gave him his full international debut against Ecuador in 2011 thereby fulfilling his lifetime ambition to represent his country.

## LAWRENCE, Mark

**(1978–84)**

Midfielder, 6ft 0in, 11st 2lb
Born: Stockton-on-Tees, 4 December 1958
Signed from: Nunthorpe Athletic, 1 August 1977
Transferred: Port Vale (loan), March 1983, contract cancelled, November 1983
Career: Nunthorpe Athletic, Hartlepool United, Port Vale (loan), Whitby Town, Bishop Auckland
Debut: v Newport County, 22 April 1978
Appearances: League: 155+13 apps, 24 gls; FA Cup: 8 apps, 0 gls; FL Cup: 7+1 apps, 1 gl; Other: 3 apps, 1 gl. Total: 173+14 apps, 26 gls

Stockton-born Mark Lawrence was another of Billy Horner's prodigies when he signed from non-League Nunthorpe Athletic in August 1977. A gifted midfield player with an eye for goal, he made his League debut towards the end of the 1977–78 season and went on to establish himself the following campaign. Making 38 League appearances, scoring nine goals, he established his goalscoring credentials by scoring all four in the 4–2 victory away to Halifax Town. By doing so, he became only the second Hartlepool player after Ken Johnson in 1956 to score four goals in an away League game.

Mark Lawrence maintained his form the following two seasons, playing 45 games in all competitions during the 1980–81 season. After a spell on the sidelines he recovered his form and consistency during the 1982–83 season following a loan spell at Port Vale, only to be left out of the side by Horner's short-lived successor, Johnny Duncan. He fared even worse with Mick Docherty, who followed Duncan, and after seven

appearances at the start of the 1983–84 campaign had his contract cancelled. Ironically, Docherty left the club the following month to be replaced by Billy Horner, Lawrence's mentor.

After leaving Hartlepool Mark Lawrence played for Northern League side Whitby Town before moving to Bishop Auckland in July 1985. He later had a spell managing Northern League club Guisborough Town.

## LEE, Graeme Barry

**(1996–2003 and 2008)**

Central-defender, 6ft 2in, 13st 7lb
Born: Middlesbrough, 31 May 1978
Signed from: Youth trainee, 2 July 1996
Transferred: Sheffield Wednesday, 2 July 2003, free transfer
Career: Hartlepool United, Sheffield Wednesday, Doncaster Rovers, Hartlepool United (loan), Shrewsbury Town (loan), Bradford City, Notts County, Darlington
Debut: v Bury, 1 January 1996
Appearances: League: 211+11 apps, 19 gls; Play-off: 5+1 apps, 0 gls; FA Cup: 8+1 apps, 0 gls; FL Cup: 7+2 apps, 1 gl; Other: 8+1 apps, 2 gls. Total: 239+16 apps, 22 gls

Graeme Lee joined Hartlepools as a youth trainee and was given his League debut by Keith Houchen while still only 17 years of age. He signed professional terms in the summer of 1996 and went on to establish himself as a reliable and consistent central-defender for the next seven seasons.

After an inevitable settling-in period Lee established himself in Mick Tait's side during the 1997–98 season, making 37 League appearances and scoring three goals. Although 'Pools' results during Tait's spell in charge were not impressive, Graeme Lee was one of a number of players who enhanced their reputations during this time.

The arrival of Chris Turner, Tait's successor, resulted in the signing of Chris Westwood and the forming of a defensive partnership with Lee that compared with the best in the club's history. Lee played 38 League games in 1999–2000, scoring a creditable seven goals, which helped 'Pools to their first Play-offs, against Darlington. The following season his appearances were drastically curtailed due to injury, before he recovered both fitness and form to be a key member of the side which again reached the Play-offs in 2001–02.

Graeme Lee's final season at Victoria Park, 2002–03, saw him miss only a single League game as 'Pools took Division Three by storm, leading the League by 12 points at one stage. The departure of Chris Turner to Sheffield Wednesday and the arrival of Mike Newell caused a slight decline in results, which ultimately cost the Championship.

However, a final position of second still resulted in the long-awaited promotion. Lee's part in the promotion season was recognised by his fellow professionals when he was voted into the 2003 PFA Division Three team.

During the close season Chris Turner returned to sign Graeme Lee for Sheffield Wednesday on a free transfer, the player being out of contract. After three turbulent seasons at Hillsborough and 67 League appearances, he joined Doncaster Rovers in January 2006 in a £50,000 transfer deal. The highlight of his time at the Keepmoat

Stadium was the 2007 Johnstone Paints Trophy success over Bristol Rovers at Wembley in which he scored the winning goal in extra-time to clinch a 3–2 victory.

In February 2008 Lee returned to Victoria Park on a one-month loan deal, during which time he played a further three League games for the club. Released by Doncaster in the close season, he moved to Bradford City on a two-year contract where as captain he made 44 appearances during the 2008–09 season. Financial pressures at Valley Parade saw him leave during the close season to join ambitious League Two side Notts County on a free transfer.

Lee's move to Meadow Lane turned out to be a triumph as County stormed to the League Two title with him contributing 35 appearances and four goals as a key member of the successful team.

In December 2010 Graeme Lee fell victim to the managerial merry-go-round at Meadow Lane when Craig Short, the incumbent at the time, informed him he was no longer part of County's plans. Lee signed for struggling Darlington as a free agent in July 2011 on a one-year deal which was cancelled the following January due to financial difficulties which eventually resulted in the club being relegated four divisions. Despite the financial constraints Graeme Lee continued to play on making a total of 24 appearances, scoring one goal, before a knee injury ended his season.

## LIDDLE, Gary Daniel

**(2006–12)**

Defender, 6ft 1in, 12st 6lb
Born: Middlesbrough, 15 June 1986
Signed from: Middlesbrough, 18 August 2006
Debut: v Burnley, 22 August 2006
Appearances: League: 240+8 apps, 18 gls; FA Cup: 13+2 apps, 2 gls; FL Cup: 12 apps, 0 gls; Other: 9 apps, 1 gls. Total: 274+10 apps, 21 gls

Gary Liddle joined his home-town club as a youngster and went on to win both England Youth honours and an FA Youth Cup-winners' medal when Middlesbrough defeated Aston Villa in both legs of the 2004 Final by a 4–0 aggregate score. A string of injuries prevented this talented player making his Premiership debut, however, and despite being offered a contract extension he chose to join Hartlepool United in the summer of 2006 with the assurance of first-team football.

Liddle made his debut in the Football League Cup at Burnley and his League debut the following weekend, quickly settling into a 'Pools side which was at the start of a record promotion-winning 23-game unbeaten run. Indeed, of the 42 consecutive League games in his debut season, only eight were lost, testimony to his influence in the team and with the wider public, which earned him the Player of the Season award.

The following season, 2007–08, saw Liddle take the challenges of the higher division in his stride, and he missed only five League games in a campaign which tailed off after a promising start. Such consistency attracts attention from scouts for

Championship clubs, of course, and Hartlepool had already turned down offers for the player. A difficult 2008–09 campaign, in which relegation was narrowly avoided, saw a change of manager and continued uncertainty with the goalkeeping position. Apart from missing a handful of games, Liddle was also confined to the substitutes' bench on six occasions before recovering his form and becoming a key member in an ultimately successful relegation battle.

The difficult 2009–10 season saw Gary Liddle form a solid defensive partnership with Stan Collins, which, in tandem with goalkeeper Scott Flinders, was a major factor in preserving 'Pools Leaguer One Status. A personl blight on his overall performance was the three point deduction suffered by the club when he played in the win against Brighton while suspended. This reslulted in a three point deduction which happily for both the player and his club did not prove decisive in the final analysis.

Liddle continued his consistent form throughout 2010–11 missing a mere four League games and scoring six useful goals. At the end of the season the player indicated his desire to move on to another club only for the 'Pools to exercise a clause in his contract tying him to another season. The player did not allow his ambitions away from Victoria Park to affect his performances in his final season, missing only seven League games and despite the team's inconsistent form his value can be measured by a single win in his absence. Despite efforts by Neale Cooper and the offer of a new contract Gary Liddle chose to leave Hartlepool United after six seasons and 284 appearances.

## LINACRE, John Edward

**(1977–81 and 1983–84)**

Midfielder, 5ft 9in, 11st 10lb
Born: Middlesbrough, 13 December 1955
Signed from: Whitby Town, 1 July 1977
Transferred: Released
Re-signed: Hamrun Spartans (Malta), 22 December 1983
Career: Whitby Town, Hartlepool United, Hamrun Spartans, Hartlepool United, Billingham Town
Debut: v Grimsby Town, 13 September 1977
Appearances: League: 207+4 apps, 12 gls; FA Cup: 11+1 apps, 1 gl; FL Cup: 7 apps, 0 gls; Other: 1 app, 0 gls. Total: 226+5 apps, 13 gls

John Linacre, the son of Billy who played for the club in the mid-1950s, joined Hartlepool United in July 1977 from non-League Whitby Town. He made his debut in Billy Horner's side shortly after signing and went on to play a commendable 33 League games in his debut season. He became a fixture in 'Pools' midfield the following season, 1978–79, missing only one League game, and was a key influence on the improvement in results. Horner continued with him in his team's 'engine room' over the next two campaigns in partnership with Roy Hogan and Bobby Kerr, which brought a top-10 finish in the 1980–81 campaign, the first such finish for 10 years.

Linacre missed only four games the following season, which saw the return of Kevin Johnson to add balance to 'Pools' midfield. Despite consistent performances and a willingness to adapt to the team's needs, even playing at right-back on occasions, he found himself increasingly at odds with the management over money caused by an unrealistic transfer valuation. The brief spells which saw both Johnny Duncan and Mick Docherty occupy the hot seat undoubtedly hindered his cause and he left the club in the summer of 1982 with 'Pools in both financial and managerial turmoil.

Linacre went abroad to play for Maltese side Hamrun Spartans before the reinstatement of Billy Horner as manager saw him return to the Victoria Ground in December 1983 along with a number of former players. He played a further 15 League games in the second half of the 1983–84 season (10 alongside his brother Phil), which saw 'Pools finish in a lowly 23rd position, before he left the club for good at the end of the campaign. He joined Billingham Town the following season but was forced to finally retire from the game due to the accumulated impact of injuries sustained throughout his career.

## LINIGHAN, Andrew

**(1981–84)**

Central-defender, 6ft 4in, 13st 0lb
Born: West Hartlepool, 18 June 1962
Signed from: Henry Smith's Boys Club, 19 September 1980
Transferred: Leeds United, 15 May 1984, £60,000
Career: Henry Smith's Boys Club, Hartlepool United, Leeds United, Oldham Athletic, Norwich City, Arsenal, Crystal Palace, Queen's Park Rangers (loan), Oxford United, St Albans City
Debut: v Stockport County, 28 March 1981
Appearances: League: 110 apps, 4 gls; FA Cup: 8 apps, 0 gls; FL Cup: 7+1 apps, 1 gl; Other: 5 apps, 4 gls. Total: 130+1 apps, 9 gls

Andy Linighan was destined to make his mark as a professional footballer from an early age, having been born into a footballing family. Three of his brothers, Brian, John and David, played professionally, and the latter also started his career with Hartlepool United.

Billy Horner gave the 18-year-old Andy his debut towards the end of the 1980–81 season having signed him from the local

Henry Smith's Boys club. Anxious not to rush his protègé, Horner gave him a mere 17 games in 1981–82, and the young player impressed as a central-defender with his towering physique and footballing ability, despite playing in a struggling team in front of record low attendances. The next two seasons saw him make 45 and 42 League appearances respectively before going on to complete a total of 131 games, scoring nine goals, for his home-town club. With interest in the player high among many leading clubs, it was no surprise when Leeds United paid a reported £60,000 for his services in May 1984, shortly before his 22nd birthday.

After two seasons at Elland Road he moved to Oldham Athletic for a similar spell before his true potential was realised at Norwich City, who at the time were a major force in the First Division. Linighan's consistent displays for the Canaries attracted the attention of George Graham, Arsenal's manager, who paid £1.25 million for his services in the summer of 1990.

Andrew Linighan's move to Highbury brought him every major honour in the domestic game, with a Championship medal in 1990 and a double Cup success in 1993, both against Sheffield Wednesday. After winning the Football League Cup in April he returned to Wembley the following month in the FA Cup Final, which went to a replay after a 1–1 draw. With the scores again level after 90 minutes and extra-time almost over he headed home the winner from a corner to complete a much-vaunted treble of medals.

After nearly seven years at Highbury, Andy Linighan joined Crystal Palace, for whom he made over 100 appearances before spending a short spell on loan at Queen's Park Rangers and finishing his League career with Oxford United. He retired after a brief spell with St Albans to start his own plumbing business in Hertfordshire.

## LUKE, George Thomas

**(1953–60)**

Outside-left, 5ft 8in, 11st 2lb

Born: Newcastle upon Tyne, 17 December 1933

Died: Forest Hall, North Tyneside, 23 March 2010

Signed from: Newcastle United, 15 October 1953, free transfer

Transferred: Newcastle United, 14 October 1959, £4,000

Career: Newcastle United (juniors), Hartlepools United, Newcastle United, Darlington, South Shields

Debut: v Grimsby Town, 17 October 1953

Appearances: League: 186 apps, 60 gls; FA Cup: 19 apps, 8 gls; Total: 205 apps, 68 gls

Fred Westgarth signed George Luke, an England schoolboy international, to succeed local favourite Leo Harden in October 1953 from Newcastle United.

Despite his obvious talent and potential, the Tyneside club had Scottish international Bobby Mitchell at the height of his powers and no doubt felt they could afford to release the youngster.

An outside-left in the classic mould, Luke could score goals as well as create them. Hugely popular with supporters, his overall record is impressive and he was the club's leading scorer in the 1955–56 season with 23 League and Cup goals. In this and the following season, 1956–57, in partnership with Ken Johnson, they contributed a total of 90 goals, testimony to Luke's ability as a provider as well as a goalscorer.

Luke played in the 1957–58 Football League North versus South fixture at Crystal Palace, scoring in a 2–2 draw. He had been selected for the representative fixture twice before but was unable to play on both occasions due to injuries. He was also a member of the Hartlepools side which recorded the club's record victory, 10–1 against Barrow, scoring twice in the process.

His sterling service was recognised in April 1959 when he was awarded a benefit game which saw Charlie Hurley bring a full-strength Sunderland side to the Victoria Ground. Fate decreed that George Luke was unable to play due to injury and he watched his benefit game from the stand with Tom Burlison deputising on the left wing.

It was a major blow to 'Pools when Newcastle re-signed him in October 1959 to replace the ageing Mitchell and it is testimony to his footballing abilities that he lost nothing in comparison to Len White, Ivor Allchurch and George Eastham, who were his teammates in the Newcastle side which defeated Everton 8–2 and Manchester United 7–3.

George Luke joined local rivals Darlington in January 1961 for a small fee and went on to make 68 League appearances for the Quakers, scoring 11 goals. A knee injury ended his professional career and he later played for South Shields in the North Regional League. On retiring he established a successful soft furnishing business on North Tyneside where he continued to live until his death in March 2010 after a period of illness.

## LUMLEY, Robert

**(1955–57 and 1960–61)**

Inside-forward, 5ft 10in, 11st 8lb
Born: Leadgate, 6 January 1933
Signed from: Charlton Athletic, 10 February 1955, £1,000
Transferred: Chesterfield, 19 December 1957, £1,250
Re-signed: Gateshead, 1 July 1960
Career: Charlton Athletic, Hartlepools United, Chesterfield, Gateshead, Hartlepools United
Debut: v Rochdale, 12 February 1955
Appearances: League: 145 apps, 25 gls; FA Cup: 7 apps, 1 gl; FL Cup: 1 app, 0 gls; Total: 153 apps, 26 gls

Bobby Lumley was one of Hartlepools United's most popular players during the halcyon days of the 1950s. He started his

career as a junior with First Division Charlton Athletic, going on to make six appearances for the East London club, who were then in the top tier of English football.

A skilful inside-forward, he was signed by Fred Westgarth in February 1955 with 'Pools having their best season in years, primarily to allow Ken Johnson to take over the centre-forward position from Eric Wildon. He was an ever present the following season when the club achieved only the second top-four finish in its history. Lumley started the momentous 1956–57 season as a key member of the side before losing his place due to a freak injury incurred in a head tennis exhibition with Ken Johnson at the Empire Theatre. An injury to Tommy McGuigan allowed him to return to the team, however, and he made 31 League appearances during the campaign. As with several other stalwarts Lumley fell victim to Ray Middleton's 'youth policy', and he joined Chesterfield in December 1957 for £1,250.

After two seasons with the Saltergate club he returned to his native North East with struggling Gateshead, playing through to the end of the Tyneside club's League tenure, including their final game against Hartlepools United. Released by Gateshead following their unsuccessful application for re-election, Bobby Lumley returned to the Victoria Ground for the 1960–61 season, missing only a handful of games and appearing in 'Pools' first Football League Cup tie against Oldham Athletic. This brought the curtain down on his professional League career, although he later played for Kings Lynn. Thereafter he worked as a publican and assisted Billy Horner during his first spell as Hartlepool manager as reserve-team coach.

Bobby Lumley continues to live in Hartlepool and is a regular visitor to Victoria Park on match days.

## McGOVERN, John Prescott

**(1966–68)**

Midfielder, 5ft 10in, 11st 0lb

Born: Montrose, 28 October 1949

Signed from: Apprentice, May 1965

Transferred: Derby County, 12 September 1968, £7,000

Career: Hartlepool United, Derby County, Leeds United, Nottingham Forest, Bolton Wanderers, Horwich RMI

Debut: v Bradford City, 5 May 1966

Appearances: League: 69+3 apps, 5 gls; FA Cup: 2 apps, 0 gls; FL Cup: 2 apps, 2 gls; Total: 73+3 apps, 7 gls

John McGovern became 'Pools' youngest player (at that time) when he was given his debut by Brian Clough against Bradford City in the final game of the 1965–66

season, aged 16 years, 6 months and 23 days. Little did the 4,776 spectators who turned up at the Vic that afternoon realise that they were witnessing the beginning of one of the most successful manager/captain relationships in the history of the game, which would ultimately bring both men the highest honours in club football.

Montrose-born McGovern came to England with his family as a youngster and attended Henry Smith's school, where he was captain of the school rugby team. It was while on holiday in Edinburgh that he caught the 'football bug', and his conversion to the Association code was met with stern disapproval by his headmaster.

McGovern made rapid progress in the season following his debut, 1966–67, making 33 League appearances in a side which was transformed from the struggling outfit of previous campaigns into a team capable of challenging for promotion. He later recalled that the discipline Clough imposed on the team was similar to his family life and greatly assisted him in his early days in professional football.

Having established himself, McGovern had an unhappy relationship with Gus McLean, Clough's successor, who referred to him disparagingly as 'Cloughie's blue-eyed boy'. Despite making 33 appearances in the 1967–68 promotion side, McGovern was anxious to move on and further his career. It was no surprise when, in September 1968, Brian Clough took him to Derby County, then a Second Division side, for a £7,000 fee. Within a season Derby had won promotion to the top tier, whereas 'Pools were relegated to the Fourth Division.

John McGovern was to win First Division Championships with both Derby County and Nottingham Forest under Clough's management, and he reached the pinnacle of club football by captaining the latter to European Champions' Cup triumphs in 1979 and 1980. To this should be added Football League Cup and European Super Cup wins before his transfer to Bolton Wanderers in June 1982 as player-manager. After 16 League appearances for the Trotters he retired from playing to concentrate on management. However, he was unable to stop the club's decline and the arrival of a new chairman, with the club losing £10,000 a week, resulted in his inevitable departure. He later had assistant manager roles at Plymouth Argyle and Hull City before working abroad. On his return to England McGovern worked in the aircraft services business and scouted for Nottingham Forest.

At the start of the 1994–95 season he was persuaded, in partnership with his old teammate Archie Gemmill, to manage Rotherham United in the then Division Two. After two largely unsuccessful seasons resulting in finishes of 17th and 16th respectively, the former Derby and Forest colleagues decided to retire from League management, although McGovern later had spells at Woking, Hull City (as assistant manager) and Ilkeston Town.

John McGovern continues to live in the Derby area and is a football pundit on BBC Radio Nottingham.

## McGUCKIN, Thomas Ian

**(1992–1996 and 1998–1999)**
Central-defender, 6ft 2in, 14st 0lb
Born: Middlesbrough, 24 April 1973
Signed from: Youth trainee, June 1991
Transferred: Fulham, 16 June 1997, undisclosed fee
Re-signed: Fulham (loan), 18 December 1998
Career: Hartlepool United, Fulham, Hartlepool United (loan), Oxford United
Debut: v Darlington, 14 March 1992
Appearances: League: 155+5 apps, 8 gls; FA Cup: 6 apps, 0 gls; FL Cup: 13+1 apps, 1 gl; Other: 6 apps, 0 gls. Total: 180+6 apps, 9 gls

Middlesbrough-born Ian McGuckin joined Hartlepool as a youth trainee in

June 1991 and made his League debut while still a teenager in the derby game against Darlington the following March. He played seven consecutive League games following his debut and gained further experience the following season playing several games in the full-back positions.

Strong and athletic, Ian McGuckin was a natural central-defender who established his position in the side alongside the experienced John MacPhail during the difficult 1993–94 relegation season. He took over the pivotal centre-half role following MacPhail's retirement and played 40 League games during the 1995–96 season, scoring two goals. Such consistency was recognised by Fulham, then in Division Two, and he joined the Cottagers in June 1997 for an undisclosed transfer fee.

He spent an unhappy time at Craven Cottage, failing to make a single appearance, and Chris Turner brought him back to Victoria Park in December 1998 on a loan deal, which saw him play a further eight games. In July 2000 McGuckin joined Division Three side Oxford United, ironically losing his place after seven appearances to former 'Pools star Andrew Linighan.

After a brief spell with Barrow he returned to his native North East in 2002 to play for Durham City, Bishop Auckland and Guisborough. After fulfilling a number of coaching roles McGuckin joined West Auckland Town as assistant manager to his former Hartlepool teammate Brian Honour. On the latter's appointment in March 2010 as manager at Horden CW he rejoined his former teammate as his assistant.

## McGUIGAN, Thomas

**(1950–58)**

Inside-forward, 5ft 8in, 10st 8lb
Born: Whiterigg, 22 November 1922
Died: Hartlepool, 14 December 1997
Signed from: Ayr United, August 1950, free transfer
Transferred: Spennymoor United, May 1958
Career: Burnbank Athletic, Ayr United, Hartlepools United, Spennymoor United, South Shields
Debut: v Crewe Alexandra, 19 August 1950
Appearances: League: 325 apps, 75 gls; FA Cup: 25 apps, 4 gls; Total: 350 apps, 79 gls

One of 'Pools' most popular players of the 1950s, Tommy McGuigan was in his late 20s when Fred Westgarth persuaded him to sign from Ayr United at the start of the 1950–51 season.

McGuigan began his football career with local side Burnbank Athletic before Ayr United manager Bob Ferrier signed him following a trial in a B Division fixture against Airdrie on 17 November 1945. He went on to make 86 League appearances for Ayr as an inside or wing-forward, scoring 24 goals. He also played in 25 Scottish FA and League Cup ties in his time with the Somerset Park club.

Tommy McGuigan proved an instant success as a crafty ball-playing schemer for those alongside him, with Eric Wildon the principal beneficiary, scoring 26 League goals. He also contributed goals himself, as 20 in 51 League and Cup games in the

1954–55 season testified. A measure of his consistency is shown by the fact that he missed just 11 League and Cup games in his first five seasons with the club. He also featured prominently in all 'Pools' major FA Cup games in the 1950s, including the Nottingham Forest and Manchester United ties which attracted record attendances to the Victoria Ground.

The perfect foil to the more direct style of Ken Johnson, he played well into his 30s and eventually became a victim of Ray Middleton's 'youth policy'. Ironically, his last game was also 'Pools' final Division Three North fixture against champions-elect Scunthorpe United, which decided the formation of the new Third and Fourth Divisions. Needing a win to gain a place in the upper division, McGuigan had the misfortune to miss a penalty late in the game, which ultimately consigned his team to defeat.

He was awarded a joint benefit with Frank Stamper in April 1956 in recognition of his outstanding service to the club. Newcastle United provided the opposition with Jimmy Scoular, Bob Stokoe, Len White, Vic Keeble and Bobby Mitchell in their side. Despite the perceived quality of the opposition, 'Pools ran riot in a 6–3 victory which saw Ken Johnson score four times to the obvious delight of the 7,206 crowd.

Tommy McGuigan later played for Spennymoor United and South Shields after his retirement from the professional game and continued his contact with 'Pools in scouting and trainer capacities. He worked and lived in Hartlepool until his death in December 1997, shortly after his 75th birthday.

## McKINNON, Robert

**(1986–91 and 1998–99)**

Left-back, 5ft 11in, 11st 1lb
Born: Glasgow, 31 July 1966
Signed from: Newcastle United, 5 August 1986, free transfer
Transferred: Motherwell, 8 January 1992, £150,000
Re-signed: Heart of Midlothian, 11 February 1999, loan
Career: Rutherglen Glencairn, Newcastle United, Hartlepool United, Manchester United (loan), Motherwell, Twente Enschede, Heart of Midlothian, Hartlepool United (loan), Carlisle United (loan), Clydebank
Debut: v Cardiff City, 23 August 1986
Appearances: League: 253+1 apps, 7 gls; FA Cup: 15 apps, 0 gls; FL Cup: 15 apps, 0 gls; Other: 15 apps, 0 gls. Total: 298+1 apps, 7 gls

Rob McKinnon became a full-back destined for international honours by accident. As an attacking winger with Glasgow non-League club Rutherglen Glencairn, he was thrust into the left-back berth due to an injury crisis and, after an impressive display, was signed by Newcastle United on a scout's recommendation. He spent two years with the Tyneside club, making a solitary First Division appearance against Tottenham Hotspur which pitted him directly against the mercurial England international Chris Waddle.

Released by Newcastle at the end of the 1986 season, McKinnon was signed by Billy Horner, and despite some misgivings he soon settled into life at the Victoria Ground. His debut against Cardiff City, the first game of the 1986–87 season, was the prelude to a run of 27 consecutive League appearances before an injury forced him to miss the only game of the campaign. 'Pools' new manager John Bird even experimented with him on the left wing, his original position, towards the end of the season, but he quickly switched him back to his best position in defence.

The arrival of Bird, also from Newcastle, brought stability to a team which included McKinnon's full-back partner Keith Nobbs, and the ultra-reliable Tony Smith at the heart of the defence. Only a poor run in the closing games prevented real progress and brought a final League position of 16th.

Bird's departure to York City at the start of the 1988–89 campaign saw the arrival of Bobby Moncur, who had even stronger qualifications than his predecessor in terms of defensive experience, as a former Scotland and Newcastle United captain. McKinnon was ever present during the season, which saw 'Pools slip back to 19th position, primarily due to a lack of goals. The following season saw the arrival of yet another manager in the form of the Cyril Knowles, the fifth in less than four seasons during McKinnon's time with the club. Once again the full-back was ever present as the new manager shaped the team in his image with the arrival of solid central-defenders Mick Smith and Ian Bennyworth.

Such signings provided the basis for the fondly remembered 1990–91 promotion season, with McKinnon now a fixture in the side, combining defensive duties with attacking left-wing forays in support of Paul Dalton. After a quiet start, which saw only one win in the first six League games,

'Pools came alight, storming to a promotion which, while obviously relying on the Baker–Allon partnership in attack, nevertheless strongly featured Rob McKinnon in a campaign which saw him miss only a single game.

Such performances and their attendant success inevitably attracts attention from bigger clubs, as was the case with Joe Allon and Paul Dalton. After a summer trial with Manchester United which required a loan registration, McKinnon returned to his homeland with Motherwell for £150,000, a record fee for the Fir Park club at the time, having made 23 appearances in Division Three, the last eight of which were unbeaten, 'Pools' best run that season.

McKinnon spent seven seasons with Motherwell, making 152 appearances in the Scottish Premier League (SPL) and scoring seven goals. He achieved his lifetime ambition in 1994 when he made his Scotland debut against Malta, going on to make a further two international appearances against Japan and the Faroe Isles.

In 1998, after a brief spell with Dutch side Twente Enschede, he joined Heart of Midlothian and made a further 19 SPL appearances. McKinnon returned on loan to Victoria Park in February 1999 to play a further seven games for 'Pools before joining Carlisle United. Released by Hearts at the end of the season, he joined Clydebank of the Scottish Second Division and made 51 League appearances over the next two seasons by playing in every defensive position apart from right-back. Despite finishing fourth in the 2001–02 season, Clydebank were unable to continue due to financial problems and Rob McKinnon's professional career came to an end. He was later involved with junior club Bellshill Athletic in coaching and managerial roles and has appeared for 'Pools in the popular Northern Masters tournament for ex-professionals, as well as being a football pundit for Talk Radio in Edinburgh.

## MacPHAIL, John

**(1990–95)**

Centre-half, 6ft 0in, 12st 3lb

Born: Dundee, 7 December 1955

Signed from: Sunderland, 13 December 1990, free transfer (loan 16 September 1990)

Transferred: Brinkburn CA, August 1995, free transfer

Career: Dundee, Sheffield United, York City, Bristol City, Sunderland, Hartlepool United

Debut: v Rochdale, 18 September 1990

Appearances: League: 159+4 apps, 4 gls; FA Cup: 11 apps, 0 gls; FL Cup: 11 apps, 1 gl; Other: 11 apps, 0 gls. Total: 192+4 apps, 5 gls

John MacPhail, nicknamed 'Monty', was originally signed by Cyril Knowles from Sunderland on a loan deal at the start of the 1990–91 promotion campaign, a transfer that was made permanent in December 1990 following the player's outstanding form in the first half of the season.

Knowles could not have chosen a better player to be at the heart of the 'Pools defence, as the vastly experienced MacPhail went on to prove. He began his career with his home-town club Dundee before moving south in January 1979 to join Sheffield United, playing 135 League games for the Blades over the next four seasons before moving to York City in February 1983. He played a major role in their 1983–84 Division Four promotion-winning season, during which he was ever present. After a further two seasons with the Minstermen he left after a dispute over his contract and was signed by Denis Smith at Bristol City in a £14,000 deal. Following Smith's appointment as Sunderland manager, MacPhail quickly joined him at Roker Park and was a key figure in the Third Division Championship side. A consistent performer, MacPhail played 130 League games for Sunderland and scored a highly creditable 22 goals.

Following the euphoria of the 1991 promotion, Hartlepool United surprised the football world by more than holding their own in the higher division. Their success was based on a solid defence in which MacPhail was a key figure. He played 41 League games, scoring once, for a side which never conceded more than four goals in any game and their total of 57 against was only two more than Champions Brentford. The following campaign, 1992–93, saw both MacPhail and 'Pools continue to rise to the challenge of what was now Division Two

football in a side that could be relied on defensively, but which struggled to score goals.

The enforced sale of Andy Saville due to poor attendances meant the 1993–94 season was always going to be a struggle, and so it turned out. 'Pools were relegated in embarrassing fashion, with MacPhail taking over from Viv Busby as manager in November 1993. His decision to cease playing in order to concentrate on his management duties cost the team dear and they conceded 21 goals in their last five League games as relegation became inevitable.

A poor start to the 1994–95 season saw MacPhail replaced as manager by David McCreery. He returned to playing duties and made a handful of League appearances before retiring nine months short of his 40th birthday. On leaving the Victoria Ground he was highly critical of chairman Gary Gibson for demoralising the players by delaying their wage payments during his spell as manager.

After leaving Hartlepool, John MacPhail played and managed in non-League football on South Tyneside and worked in the motor trade as a luxury car salesman.

## MILLER, Thomas William

**(1997–2001)**

Midfielder, 6ft 0in, 11st 7lb
Born: Easington, 8 January 1979
Signed from: Youth trainee, 8 July 1997
Transferred: Ipswich Town, 16 July 2001, £750,000
Career: Hartlepool United, SK Brann (trialist), Ipswich Town, Sunderland, Preston North End (loan), Ipswich Town, Sheffield Wednesday
Debut: v Chester City, 4 October 1997
Appearances: League: 130+7 apps, 35 gls; Play-off: 4 apps, 0 gls; FA Cup: 5 apps, 2 gls; FL Cup: 6 apps, 3 gls; Other: 8 apps, 5 gls. Total: 153+7 apps, 45 gls

Tommy Miller joined Hartlepool United as a youth trainee in July 1997, having previously been registered with Ipswich Town as an associated schoolboy. Mick Tait brought the young player to the Victoria Ground and immediately confirmed his faith in the teenager by giving him his League debut in October 1997. The next season, 1998–99, saw him make 34 League appearances and score four goals despite the team finishing a lowly 22nd.

The arrival of Chris Turner saw Miller's career take off over the next two seasons when he missed only two League games and scored his first hat-trick, against Barnet. His enthusiastic midfield play was a key feature in 'Pools reaching two successive Play-offs and finally shaking off the 'cinderella club' image. He was outstanding throughout the 2000–01 season playing in every League and Cup game, 54 in total, and scoring 16 goals from midfield.

Such consistent form was obviously going to attract attention, and it was no surprise when Ipswich Town, Miller's first

club, paid £750,000 for his services in July 2001, more than double the previous Hartlepool record paid by Chelsea for Joe Allon 10 years earlier. He spent four years at Ipswich, helping them to an ultimately failed Championship Play-off before signing a two-year contract with Premiership Sunderland in June 2005.

His first season with the Black Cats was ruined by an embarrassing relegation, and after a handful of appearances the following campaign he was loaned out to Preston by new manager Roy Keane. After being released by Sunderland, and attracting interest from a number of Championship clubs, Miller rejoined Ipswich Town in July 2007 on a two-year deal, making 69 League appearances and scoring 10 goals in his second spell for the Tractormen. On becoming a free agent he was quickly signed by Championship side Sheffield Wednesday in May 2009 on a two-year contract.

His move to Hillsborough turned out to be less than a success as his contribution in making 20 League appearances, scoring one goal was not enough to stop his side being relegated to League One on the final day of the season.

Released by Wednesday at the end of his contract Tommy Miller signed a one year deal with Huddersfield Town in July 2011 and enjoyed a successful season culminating in promotion to the Championship with a Play-off Final victory over Sheffield United in a penalty shoot-out after a goalless draw.

## MOORE, Malcolm

(1973–76)

Centre-forward, 5ft 10in, 12st 0lb
Born: Silksworth, 18 December 1948
Signed from: Tranmere Rovers, 1 August 1973, free transfer
Transferred: Workington, 28 August 1976, free transfer
Career: Sunderland (apprentice), Crewe Alexandra (loan), Tranmere Rovers, Hartlepool, Workington, Gateshead, North Shields
Debut: v Brentford, 25 August 1973
Appearances: League: 127+2 apps, 34 gls; FA Cup: 7+1 apps, 3 gls; FL Cup: 12 apps, 5 gls; Total: 146+3 apps, 42 gls

Malcolm Moore began his football career with Sunderland, scoring on his First Division debut in March 1968 against Coventry City. He went on to play 12 games for his local club, scoring three goals before joining Tranmere Rovers, following a brief loan spell with Crewe Alexandra. It

was with the Merseyside club that he established his reputation as a hardworking striker who could contribute important goals. After three seasons with Tranmere he joined Hartlepool to cure what had become a chronic goal shortage under manager Len Ashurst.

The season prior to Moore signing, 1972–73, had seen 'Pools score a meagre 34 goals throughout the League campaign, and despite finishing above the re-election zone Ashurst recognised more power was needed in his forwards. To solve the goal famine he signed not only Moore, but also the powerful Geordie Kevin MacMahon.

Malcolm Moore, in partnership with MacMahon, and supported by winger Alan Gauden, added a new dimension to 'Pools' play, which was reflected in a top-half finish in 1973–74. The arrival of Ken Hale in succession to Ashurst added further attacking impetus and Moore was ever present throughout the 1974–75 campaign, playing 58 League and Cup games and contributing 19 goals. His personal highlight was the equaliser against Aston Villa in the League Cup in front of a record attendance for a floodlight game at the Victoria Ground.

He was equally effective the following season, missing only three games and scoring 16 times. It was a major surprise when Hale released the player at the end of the season and he joined struggling Workington on a free transfer. After the Cumbrians' League relegation the following season, Moore joined Gateshead and helped them to promotion to the Conference, and he finished his playing career with North Shields.

After hanging up his boots Malcolm Moore managed Chester-le-Street, then a Wearside League side for several seasons before becoming a successful businessman.

## MOORE, Watson Evans

**(1948–60)**

Centre-half, 5ft 8in, 10st 8lb
Born: West Hartlepool, 30 August 1925
Died: Hartlepool, 24 April 1967
Signed from: Oxford Street Old Boys
Transferred: Horden Colliery Welfare, August 1960, free transfer
Career: Oxford Street Old Boys, Hartlepools United, Horden Colliery Welfare
Debut: v Wrexham, 6 November 1948
Appearances: League: 447 apps, 3 gls; FA Cup 25 apps; Total: 472 apps, 3 gls

'Watty' (christened Watson) Moore was the epitome of the 'one club' professional, having been discovered by Fred Westgarth

playing for local Church League side Oxford Street Old Boys.

Originally a centre-forward, he made his League debut in 1948, scoring against Wrexham. After two more appearances in that position he was switched to centre-half, where he became a fixture until his retirement in 1960. An ever present in the 1951–52 season, he went on to make 175 consecutive appearances in League and Cup games between April 1954 and November 1957, setting the club record for total appearances of 472.

Standing just under 5ft 9in, relatively small for a centre-half, he was remarkably strong in the air as well as a tenacious tackler, which drew favourable comparisons with England captain Billy Wright. His reading of the game was far in advance of what was normally expected from players in Third Division football, and many experienced observers were at a loss as to understand why a club from a higher division never signed him. His talent was officially noticed when he was selected to play in the Football League North versus South representative fixture at Coventry in 1956–57.

His service to Hartlepools United was recognised as early as September 1955 when the club awarded him a joint benefit with Joe Willetts. Newcastle United, the FA Cup-holders, sent a strong side including Jackie Milburn and Bobby Mitchell, who between them scored all the goals in a 5–0 victory. The result was immaterial as the 5,435 spectators enjoyed the occasion and had the opportunity to pay their respects to Hartlepools' greatest servant.

Watty Moore was one of the few stalwarts of the Westgarth era to continue following the appointment of Ray Middleton. The new manager obviously recognised his value to Hartlepools United and he missed only one League game during the 1957–58 season. A particular highlight in the latter stages of his career was to be a member of the 'Pools side which recorded a club record 10–1 win against Barrow in April 1959.

The appointment of Bill Robinson as manager in succession to Ray Middleton signalled the end of Watty Moore's career, with the player by then at the veteran stage. He played 31 League games in his final season and was given a benefit by the club, with his chosen XI consisting predominately of players from the 'Pools 'golden era' of the mid-1950s.

After his retirement as a professional he continued to live in Hartlepool and played for local side Horden Colliery Welfare as well as appearing in charity games. His last appearance on a football field was in a game to commemorate the amalgamation of the two towns in April 1967, which saw him in direct opposition to Brian Clough, 'Pools' manager at the time. A few weeks later Watty Moore died suddenly at home at the tragically young age of 42 years.

The Professional Footballers' Association, to mark their centenary in 2007, conducted a poll at each League club to find the player supporters rated as the greatest ever. Watty Moore won the Hartlepool United accolade to general public acclaim, polling a third of all votes cast.

## NELSON, Michael John

**(2003–08)**
Centre-half, 6ft 2in, 13st 3lb
Born: Gateshead, 28 March 1980
Signed from: Bury, 10 July 2003, £70,000
Transferred: Norwich City, 1 July 2009, free transfer
Career: Leek Town, Spennymoor United, Bishop Auckland, Bury, Hartlepool United, Norwich City, Scunthorpe United, Kilmarnock
Debut: v Peterborough United, 9 August 2003
Appearances: League: 255+4 apps, 14 gls; Play-off: 5 apps, 0 gls; FA Cup: 20 apps, 2 gls; FL Cup: 13 apps, 0 gls; Other: 9 apps, 0 gls. Total: 302+4 apps, 16 gls

Michael Nelson started his football career at the grass roots with non-League sides Leek Town, Spennymoor United and Bishop Auckland before being offered a trial by Hartlepool on a scout's recommendation. Chris Turner, 'Pools' manager at the time, decided against offering the player a contract, thereby allowing Bury to sign the imposing defender in March 2001.

Nelson took a little while to adapt to League football at Gigg Lane, making 31 appearances in his first full season. After recovering from a serious injury he missed only seven League games during the 2002–03 campaign, scoring five goals and being voted Bury's Player of the Season. He was hailed by manager Andy Preece as 'the best centre-half in Division Three'.

In July 2003 Mickey Nelson became new manager Neale Cooper's first signing when he paid Bury £70,000 for his signature, making an immediate impact by scoring the winner against Peterborough on the opening day of the season. He quickly became a favourite with the supporters with his wholehearted 'they shall not pass' displays, and went on to play 48 League and Cup games, forming a highly effective defensive partnership with Chris Westwood.

His form suffered somewhat during the 2004–05 campaign due to a contractual dispute with the club, which eventually resulted in him requesting a transfer. After missing several games the player withdrew the transfer demand and was reinstated in the team, much to the relief of the supporters. His resulting performances eventually earned him an improved contract and he regained his form during 'Pools' record-breaking 2006–07 season, when in partnership with Ben Clark he played a major part in an 18-game unbeaten run. During the season Nelson deputised as captain for the injured Mickey Barron and was named in the 2006–07 PFA League Two Team of the Year.

The return to League One saw Nelson maintain his consistent form throughout the 2007–08 campaign, missing only a single game. Danny Wilson saw fit to introduce 19-year-old Godwin Antwi-Birago on loan from Liverpool as Nelson's central partner. Despite an impressive start the youngster's form dipped in the New Year and Wilson signed the experienced Sam Collins from Hull City to provide stability to his struggling team. Many fans felt that the break-up of the Nelson-Clark defensive pairing was a major factor in the disappointing 15th-place finish.

It speaks volumes that Michael Nelson, in the final year of his contract, was ever-present throughout the 2008–09 season. With Godwin Antwi-Birago returning to Liverpool, Nelson was paired with Collins throughout the season, with Ben Clark deputising when the latter was injured. Matters were not helped by the goalkeeping situation, with Lee-Barratt and Budtz alternating due to their inconsistent form. At one stage relegation looked a distinct possibility, with survival only confirmed on the last day by goal difference. Nelson's personal highlight was his trademark headed goal against Stoke City in the third round of the FA Cup, which laid the foundation for a famous victory.

At the end of a difficult season the player made it clear he was leaving Victoria Park on the expiry of his contract, and after weeks of speculation he finally signed for newly demoted Norwich City, a Premiership club only four seasons ago, interrupting his honeymoon to do so.

His career at Carrow Road could not have got off to a worse start with an amazing 7–1 home defeat to rivals Colchester United. A rapid change of manager with Paul Lambert replacing Brian Gunn brought about a reversal of fortunes and the Canaries stormed to the League One Championship with Michael Nelson playing a key role making 31 League appearances, scoring three goals, the first of which was against his old club at the Victoria Park.

Michael Nelson's second season with the Canaries was blighted by injury, restricting his appearances, and in January 2011 he joined struggling League One Scunthorpe United for an undisclosed fee. After a difficult 12 months at Glandford Park he moved again, this time north of the border to join Scottish Premier League side Kilmarnock on a 30 month deal.

## NEWTON, John Lochinvar

**(1946–58)**

Wing half-back, 5ft 8in, 10st 7lb
Born: Bishop Auckland, 25 May 1925
Died: Willington, 30 January 2010
Signed from: Newcastle United, May 1946, free transfer
Transferred: Ashington, August 1958, free transfer
Career: Newcastle United, Hartlepools United, Ashington
Debut: v Halifax Town, 2 November 1946
Appearances: League: 332 apps, 15gls; FA Cup: 29 apps, 4 gls. Total: 361 apps, 19 gls

Fred Westgarth made one of his finest captures when he signed Jackie Newton from Newcastle United on a free transfer shortly before the resumption of the Football League programme following World War Two, the player having 'guested' for 'Pools in 1945.

Jackie Newton made his League debut in his first season, 1946–47, but due to his National Service in the Army he only played 23 League games in three seasons. Once back in 'Civvy Street', however, he went on to become the epitome of the one-club professional, making a major contribution in re-establishing the club as a force in League and Cup football. A

constructive wing half-back who could score important goals, he also featured at inside-forward when required.

It was not until the 1949–50 season that he established himself in the side, playing 36 games including the home game against Bradford City which featured, for the first time, the half-back line of Newton, Moore and Stamper. After that he became a fixture in the side, missing only a single game during the 1954–55 season, which included a seven-game FA Cup run that only ended with a fourth-round replay defeat to Nottingham Forest, in which he had the misfortune to miss a penalty. Newton continued to be a key member of the 'Pools side for the next two seasons, playing in the Chelsea and Manchester United Cup games, scoring a memorable goal in the latter. He was awarded a joint benefit with Ray Thompson in April 1954 against a full-strength Newcastle United side, which attracted a near 10,000 crowd, proof of his popularity.

Newton lost his place in the second half of the 1957–58 campaign to Tommy Burlison and was released by Ray Middleton at the end of the season. His total of 361 appearances includes a club record 29 games for 'Pools in FA Cup ties and is testimony to his service and place in the club's history.

Jackie Newton joined Ashington for the 1958–59 season in the newly formed Midland League and made his debut in the opening game at Peterborough in front of 10,000 spectators. On retiring from playing he later managed his local club Willington, where he lived until his death in January 2010, aged 84 years.

## NEWTON, Robert

**(1977–82 and 1985–86)**

Centre-forward, 6ft 0in, 13st 2lb

Born: Chesterfield, 23 November 1956

Signed from: Huddersfield Town, 12 August 1977, £6,000

Transferred: Port Vale, 16 September 1982, £20,000

Re-signed: Chesterfield, 24 July 1985, £17,500

Transferred: Stockport County, 27 March 1986, free transfer

Career: Huddersfield Town, Hartlepool, Port Vale, Chesterfield, Hartlepool United,

New England Tea Men (USA), Jacksonville Tea Men (USA), Stockport County, Bristol Rovers, Chesterfield (non-contract), Lei Sun (Hong Kong)
Debut: v Grimsby Town, 13 August 1977
Appearances: League: 158+3 apps, 50 gls; FA Cup: 11 apps, 10 gls; FL Cup: 8 apps, 2 gls; Other: 4 apps, 0 gls. Total: 181+3 apps, 62 gls

Few players have caused more controversy among 'Pools fans than Bob Newton, a big, bustling centre-forward who scored goals and unsettled defences with his physical style. Billy Horner signed Newton for £6,000 from Huddersfield Town in August 1977 to partner Malcolm Poskett in what he hoped would be a winning combination.

Despite the much-vaunted partnership failing to fire in League games, 'Pools enjoyed an exciting FA Cup run with Newton scoring both goals in the victory over Second Division Crystal Palace. The player then ran into serious trouble off the field when he served a nine-month prison sentence for drink-driving resulting in a crash which killed his friend and teammate, Dave Wiggett.

Newton recovered from this tragedy to form an effective partnership with Keith Houchen, scoring 12 goals in 33 League games during the 1979–80 season. He reached double figures again the following campaign before scoring 15 times in 34 games, following Houchen's departure. It was inevitable such goalscoring exploits would attract attention and, after reputedly turning down an earlier offer of £80,000, cash-strapped Hartlepool accepted £20,000 from Port Vale in September 1982. Ironically, this was further reduced following the transfer deal with Huddersfield, resulting in 'Pools receiving a meagre £12,500 for their star striker. During his first spell with the club

Bob Newton had two summer seasons in the North American Soccer League with New England Tea Men (1980) and Jacksonville Tea Men (1981).

After two seasons with Port Vale, scoring 22 goals in 48 League appearances, Bob Newton moved to his hometown club, Chesterfield, where he continued his goalscoring exploits. It was something of a surprise when Billy Horner paid a club record £17,500 for the burly striker to form a strike partnership with Alan Shoulder at the start of the 1985–86 season. Newton's second spell with the club was, to put it mildly, not a success. Overweight and injury-prone, he played only 11 League games, scoring twice, before being released on loan to Stockport County, for whom he later signed, with Malcolm Poskett returning to the Vic on loan to the end of the season. He also received a second driving ban of five years, in 1986 when found guilty of reckless driving by Derby Crown Court.

After a brief spell at Edgeley Park he returned to Chesterfield as a non-contract player before joining Bristol Rovers, making the final eight League appearances of his much-travelled career. Determined to carry on terrorising defences for as long as possible, Bob Newton had spells with various Midlands clubs including Goole Town and Boston United, a brief sojourn in Cyprus with Evagoras Paphos and a return to Goole followed by a stint in Hong Kong with the Eastern and Lei Sun clubs. He finally hung up his boots after playing for a junior club side in Chesterfield to work in local radio and the media.

To describe Bob Newton's life as 'colourful' is an understatement and he added to his notoriety in 2007 with another driving ban, his third, for an alcohol-related incident. Despite all his trials and tribulations, his popularity with the Victoria Park faithful remained undiminished and he was voted Player of the Decade – 1980s as part of the club's Centenary celebrations.

## NOBBS, Alan Keith

**(1985–93)**

Full-back, 5ft 10in, 11st 10lb

Born: Bishop Auckland, 18 September 1961

Signed from: Bishop Auckland, 15 August 1985, free transfer

Transferred: Gateshead, 1 August 1993, free transfer

Career: Middlesbrough, Halifax Town, Bishop Auckland, Hartlepool United, Bishop Auckland

Debut: v Cambridge United, 17 August 1985

Appearances: League: 274+6 apps, 1 gl; FA Cup: 12+1 apps, 0 gls; FL Cup: 16+1 apps, 0 gls; Other: 16 apps, 0 gls. Total: 318+8 apps, 1 gl

Keith Nobbs joined Middlesbrough as an apprentice in September 1979, making a single League appearance in the First Division against Coventry City while still a teenager. He was transferred to Halifax Town in August 1982 and played 87 League games over the next two seasons before leaving League football to sign for his home-town team, Bishop Auckland. The ever-resourceful Billy Horner initiated Nobbs' return to the professional game by signing him shortly before the start of the 1985–86 season.

Over the next eight seasons Keith Nobbs gave sterling service to Hartlepool United playing mainly at full-back, and he also had spells in a midfield role. He served six managers during his time as a player and it is testimony to his consistency that they all found his services invaluable to the team effort. His first season saw 'Pools in the ascendancy, making a serious promotion challenge before a poor run in March resulted in a final position of seventh. A failure to mount another

promotion challenge the following term, 1986–87, saw Horner replaced by John Bird, and over the next two seasons Nobbs missed only nine League games. Injuries and the arrival of Bobby Moncur restricted his appearances during the difficult 1988–89 campaign, before the arrival of Cyril Knowles saw him restored to the side, often in a midfield role.

Keith Nobbs played a key role in the 1990–91 promotion season, initially starting in midfield before being restored to right-back, effectively swapping places with Paul Olsson. He missed only six League games, even suffering a suspected broken jaw in the derby game at Feethams, and was one of the unsung heroes of the promotion side. He continued such form in the first season in Division Three, playing 41 games in a campaign which exceeded everyone's expectations. The departure of key players and manager Alan Murray saw Nobbs make a creditable 29 appearances in his final season in the newly formed Division Two when 'Pools finished in 16th position despite a chronic lack of goals.

Nobbs left the Victoria Ground in the summer of 1993 to join Vauxhall Conference side Gateshead before rejoining Hartlepool as a coach. He continues his association with the club as Football in the Community officer and makes appearances in the Northern Masters tournament for retired professionals.

## OAKLEY, Norman

**(1958–64)**

Goalkeeper, 5ft 11in, 11st 4lb
Born: Norton-On-Tees, 4 June 1939
Signed from: Doncaster Rovers, 6 September 1958, free transfer
Transferred: Swindon Town, 3 March 1964, £5,000
Career: Wingate Welfare, Doncaster Rovers (juniors), Hartlepools United, Swindon Town, Grimsby Town, Boston United
Debut: v Port Vale, 8 September 1958
Appearances: League: 182 apps, 0 gls; FA Cup: 8 apps, 0 gls; FL Cup: 3 apps, 0 gls; Total: 193 apps, 0 gls

Teesside-born Norman Oakley began his football career as a junior with Darlington club Firth Road Juniors before moving to senior side Wingate Welfare in the Wearside League. His first Football League club was Doncaster Rovers, where he understudied the great Harry Gregg, later of Manchester United and Northern Ireland fame.

Oakley turned professional on signing for Ray Middleton as part of his rebuilding process following the break-up of Fred Westgarth's side. He immediately made his League debut in a 1–5 home defeat by Port Vale, which was to set the pattern for his time with the club.

The following season, 1959–60, saw 'Pools finish bottom of the Fourth Division for the first time and concede 109 goals. Despite this record Oakley, who played 37 consecutive games, was by common consent one of the best custodians in the League. The arrival of Bill Robinson as manager did not affect Oakley's position,

although he conceded over 100 goals in each of the next three seasons.

Norman Oakley gave 'Pools sterling service for five difficult seasons, making 193 appearances in all competitions, a record for a 'Pools goalkeeper. Probably his 'easiest' game between the posts was the record 10–1 victory against Barrow in April 1959.

Oakley's consistency, which regularly drew favourable plaudits from football journalists in a period of turmoil both on and off the field of play, was finally rewarded with a transfer to Second Division Swindon Town in March 1964 for a fee which was described by chairman Ernest Ord as 'less than what he is worth'. After two seasons with the Wiltshire club he moved to Grimsby Town in September 1966 before finishing his playing career on a high note by winning the West Midlands League title with Boston United.

## OLSSON, Paul

**(1989–94)**

Midfielder, 5ft 8in, 10st 11lb
Born: Hull, 24 December 1965
Signed from: Scarborough, 22 December 1989, free transfer
Transferred: Darlington, 1 August 1994, free transfer
Career: Hull City (apprentice), Exeter City, Scarborough, Hartlepool United, Darlington
Debut: Scarborough, 26 December 1989
Appearances: League: 162+9 apps, 13 gls; FA Cup: 10 apps, 0 gls; FL Cup: 11+2 apps, 0 gls; Other: 10+1 apps, 1 gl. Total: 193+12 apps, 14 gls

Paul Olsson began his football career with his local team Hull City when he signed as an apprentice in January 1984. In three seasons with the Tigers he failed to make a single appearance, however, and moved south to join Exeter City in March 1987. He made 43 appearances, scoring two goals for Exeter before returning to his native Yorkshire at the start of the 1988–89 campaign with Scarborough. In 18 months at the McCain Stadium, Olsson spent a great deal of time on the substitutes' bench before Cyril Knowles brought him to the Victoria Ground to help rescue 'Pools from apparently certain relegation.

Knowles had lost his first three League games in charge when Paul Olsson made his debut on Boxing Day against Scarborough, the club he had left literally hours earlier. He was an instant success, having a major influence on the 4–1 victory and another impressive four-goal performance against Grimsby only 48 hours later. After those successes he never looked back.

An energetic, creative midfield player who contributed important goals, Paul Olsson played a key role throughout the 1990–91 season, playing full-back initially, then moving to a defensive midfield role before playing in support of the goalscoring partnership of Paul Baker and Joe Allon. He was in his prime throughout

the 1991–92 season when 'Pools surprised many people with their results and the style of their football. Olsson played in every game, 58 in all, and was substituted only once. He maintained his standards throughout the more difficult 1992–93 campaign when the absence of Joe Allon and Paul Dalton took its toll. He played 39 League games and was a key factor in 'Pools maintaining their Division Two status.

Hartlepool United were not so lucky the following campaign, when the loss of Andy Saville virtually guaranteed relegation. Olsson continued to play his part in his 32 League appearances, but a run of 16 games with only a single win sealed his team's fate.

Paul Olsson left Hartlepool at the end of the relegation season to be reunited with Alan Murray at neighbours Darlington, for whom he played 76 League games, scoring eight goals in a two-season stay which was ended by a knee injury. He later appeared for Gainsborough Trinity, Guiseley and North Ferriby United before working in children's education. Olsson continues to maintain links with Hartlepool United by appearing in the Northern Masters tournaments. In 2010 Olsson joined the newly formed Scarborough Athletic as coach and following the departure of Brian France through illness, was appointed manager in the November.

## PARRY, Anthony John

**(1965–72)**

Central-defender/midfielder, 5ft 8in, 10st 8lb
Born: Burton upon Trent, 8 September 1945
Died: Burton upon Trent, 23 November 2009
Signed from: Burton Albion, 11 November 1965, £2,500
Transferred: Derby County, 19 January 1972, £5,000
Career: Burton Albion, Hartlepools United, Derby County, Mansfield Town (loan), Gresley Rovers
Debut: Colchester United, 18 December 1965
Appearances: League: 181+8 apps, 5 gls; FA Cup: 7 apps, 0 gls; FL Cup: 7+1 apps, 0 gls; Total: 195+9 apps, 5 gls

Tony Parry was signed within weeks of Brian Clough becoming manager, having played for Burton Albion under Peter Taylor. Parry started his career as an inside-forward who was converted by Taylor to a half-back, the position in which he was to excel for 'Pools.

Initially he played mostly in the reserves, making only eight League appearances in the side following his transfer. The next season, 1966–67, saw him take time to settle before making the number-six shirt his own. The departure of Clough did not affect his position and he was in his prime during the promotion season, in which he made 38 appearances. He had the distinction of being voted the fans' first-ever Player of the Year in recognition of his contribution to the triumph. Like most of the experienced players who had taken 'Pools up, Parry struggled in the Third Division, citing the lack of investment in new players as the

primary reason for the team's instant return to the bottom division.

Gus McLean kept faith with the popular midfielder through the difficult season following relegation, and the inevitable managerial changes did not affect his position in the team, testimony to his professionalism. Eventually, in January 1972, Brian Clough returned to the Victoria Ground to sign his former player, thus giving Parry the opportunity to play First Division football. On leaving the Victoria Ground, chairman John Curry remarked that his transfer fee would pay a week's wages!

After two seasons and a handful of appearances at the Baseball Ground, including a brief loan spell at Mansfield Town, Parry brought the curtain down on his playing career with Gresley Rovers. He continued to play in local League football well into his 40s, commenting 'I let the younger lads do the running now'.

Tony Parry returned to Hartlepool to attend a 'Legends Dinner' as part of the club's centenary celebrations in 2008, when on his own admission he was overwhelmed by the reception he received from former players and supporters alike.

It was a great surprise to everyone when Tony Parry died in Burton Queens Hospital in November 2009 after a short illness. His passing was especially poignant given that only two weeks prior to his death he attended the Leyton Orient game and later that day supported a fund-raising event in aid of the Hartlepool Hospice. Several of his former teammates including Bob McLeod, Bill Green, Mick Somers, Les Green, John Sheridan and John McGovern attended his funeral, further testimony to his popularity.

## PEDWELL, Ralph

**(1929–34)**

Outside-left, 5ft 9in, 11st 4lb
Born: Durham 13 April 1908
Died: Durham 19 July 1965
Signed from: Durham West End, 1 August 1929
Transferred: Barnsley, 1 August 1934
Career: Durham West End, South Shields, Hartlepools United, Barnsley, Frickley Colliery, Rotherham United, Doncaster Rovers, Durham City, Spennymoor United
Debut: v Barrow, 16 November 1929
Appearances: League: 156 apps, 66 gls; FA Cup: 7 apps, 2 gls; Other: 1 app, 0 gls. Total: 164 apps, 68 gls

Durham-born Ralph Pedwell was an orthodox outside-left who enjoyed great success with 'Pools in the early 1930s. He started his career with local side Durham West End and had a trial with South Shields, then a Football League side, before his goalscoring exploits brought him to the attention of Bill Norman who signed him in August 1929.

Pedwell made an immediate impact in his first season, 1929–30, scoring 17 goals in 29 League appearances, forming an effective partnership with centre-forward Albert Pape, who top-scored with 21 goals. Pedwell continued to perform consistently for the next four seasons in a free-scoring

forward line which included Josh Hewitt and Johnny Wigham. He was the first Hartlepools player to reach 50 League goals and his overall record of 66 goals in 157 appearances compares favourably with other prominent wingers who later appeared for the club.

His consistent form obviously attracted attention from bigger clubs, and at various times Leicester City, Blackburn Rovers and Barnsley all sent scouts to watch him. Eventually Barnsley signed him for the start of the 1934–35 season, which saw him make a mere 10 League appearances. He left the Oakwell club at the end of the season to join non-League neighbours Frickley Colliery before he regained his goalscoring touch with Rotherham United, scoring 20 goals in 36 League appearances in the 1936–37 season. Pedwell finished his professional career, due to a broken leg, with Doncaster Rovers, for whom he made a single appearance in the 1937–38 campaign, scoring two goals. He later played for local sides Durham City and Spennymoor United.

Ralph Pedwell died in his home city of Durham in July 1965, aged 57 years.

## PHYTHIAN, Ernest Rixon

**(1965–1968)**

Centre-forward, 5ft 9in, 11st 6lb
Born: Farnworth, 16 July 1942
Signed from: Wrexham, 31 May 1965, £5,000
Transferred: Southern Suburbs (South Africa), 18 April 1967, £5,000
Career: Bolton Wanderers, Wrexham, Hartlepools United, Southern Suburbs (SA)
Debut: v Southport, 21 August 1965
Appearances: League: 124 apps, 51 gls; FA Cup: 5 apps, 1 gl; FL Cup: 6 apps, 3 gls; Total: 135 apps, 55 gls

Ernie Phythian played for Lancashire Schoolboys before signing as a junior with

his local club Bolton Wanderers, with whom he made his League debut in 1960 in the First Division while still a teenager. An England Youth international, he was unable to establish himself in the top flight, moving to Wrexham as part of the deal which took Wyn Davies to Burnden Park in March 1962. After 134 League appearances in which he scored 44 goals, helping the Welsh side to promotion to Division Three, he was signed by Geoff Twentyman for a reported £5,000 fee to provide more power to 'Pools' goal-shy attack.

Phythian was an instant success at the Victoria Ground, scoring on his debut in a 3–1 win over Southport and forming a prolific partnership with Jimmy Mulvaney. He was the club's leading goalscorer in both the 1965–66 and 1966–67 campaigns and a key member of the side which won the club's first-ever promotion in 1968.

Following the departure of Brian Clough, Phythian had an unhappy relationship with Gus McLean, who often played him out of position on the right wing. This resulted in him having less of an impact on the promotion campaign than might have been expected, although he still managed 11 goals in 32 appearances. The signing of Bobby Cummings towards the end of the promotion season led to his departure, a premature one in the eyes of many supporters.

Ernie Phythian, despite offers from several English clubs, emigrated to South Africa on the advice of former Ipswich Town goalkeeper Roy Bailey and joined Southern Suburbs, ironically playing against Bobby Cummings as well as Wilson Hepplewhite and Les Green. After retiring from playing he continued to be involved in the game as a manager and was responsible for such stars as Malcolm MacDonald, among others, making guest appearances. He later worked in the motor trade as a sales executive for luxury cars.

## PORTER, Joel William

**(2003–09)**

Forward, 5ft 9in, 11st 13lb

Born: Adelaide, Australia, 25 December 1978

Signed from: Sydney Olympic Sharks, 27 November 2003, free transfer

Transferred: Gold Coast United, Australia, 31 May 2009, free transfer

Career: West Adelaide Sharks (Australia), Melbourne Knights (Australia), Sydney Olympic Sharks (Australia), Hartlepool United, Gold Coast United (Australia).

Debut: v Swindon Town, 29 November 2003

Appearances: League: 135+38 apps, 52 gls, Play-off: 3+2 apps, 1 gl, FA Cup: 11+2 apps, 5 gls, FL Cup: 6+3 apps, 4 gls, Other: 5+4 apps, 4 gls, Total: 160+49 apps, 66 gls

Joel Porter was one of Hartlepool United's most popular players of the modern era. Although short for an attacking forward, his endless drive and spirit so typical of his countrymen allied to a natural goalscoring ability made him one of the most effective players of recent times.

It was Neale Cooper who recognised his potential in November 2003, when Porter came to England following a successful career in his native Australia, which included four full international appearances, scoring five goals, in the 2002 Oceania Cup. After trials with Rayo Vallecano (Spain), Wigan Athletic and Sunderland he was about to return home due to visa problems when Neale Cooper made his approach. Initially the player, by his own admission, was not too keen on the move, and it was due to the persistence of his agent that he finally signed after the visa issues had been resolved.

At first he did not set the world alight, scoring a mere three goals in 27 League appearances in his debut season. He did, however, show glimpses of his potential in scoring the only goal of the televised Burton Albion FA Cup tie, which also saw the legendary Brian Clough make one of his last public appearances.

Joel Porter 'came good' during the 2004–05 season when, in partnership with Adam Boyd, he scored 14 of the 36 League

goals the pair contributed, which resulted in a Play-off place and a Final against Sheffield Wednesday at Cardiff. His efforts were recognised by supporters with a Player of the Year accolade; however, his progress was halted the following campaign when serious injuries saw him make a mere six League starts, scoring three goals, as 'Pools were relegated. He played in the first 16 games of the 2006–07 season before the injury curse struck again and the arrival of the hugely experienced Richie Barker saw him relegated to the substitutes' bench in the final games of a record-breaking promotion campaign.

Joel Porter recovered his form and confidence in the final two seasons of his time at Victoria Park, despite playing in a side that struggled to adapt to the higher demands of League One football. He totally upstaged Richie Barker in a Johnstone Paints Trophy game against Lincoln City when, replacing the veteran forward, he became the first substitute to score a hat-trick for the club.

Ironically, he was at his best in his final season, scoring 23 goals in all competitions despite the loss of his strike partner, the highly promising James Brown, midway through the season. He finished the season on a personal high by winning the local newspaper's Player of the Year award based on performance marks throughout the season. On the completion of his contract Joel Porter returned with his family to his native Australia to join Gold Coast United, a club based in Queensland making, by the end of the 2012 season, 43 appearances and scoring seven goals.

## POSKETT, Malcolm

**(1976–78 and 1985–86)**

Centre-forward, 6ft 0in, 11st 7lb
Born: Middlesbrough, 19 July 1953
Signed from: Whitby Town, 11 November 1976, £100
Transferred: Brighton & Hove Albion, 2 February 1978, £60,000
Re-signed: Stockport County, 28 March 1986, loan
Career: South Bank, Middlesbrough, Whitby Town, Hartlepool, Brighton & Hove Albion, Watford, Carlisle United, Darlington, Stockport County, Hartlepool United (loan), Carlisle United
Debut: v Brentford, 13 November 1976
Appearances: League: 54+2 apps, 20 gls; FA Cup: 3 apps, 1 gl; FL Cup: 2 apps, 0 gls; Total: 59+2 apps, 21 gls

Malcolm Poskett joined his home-town club Middlesbrough in April 1973 from local side South Bank, making one substitute appearance in Boro's 1973–74 promotion-winning side. He was released at the end of the season and joined Hartlepool as a trainee, failing to play a single game for the club. It was with non-League Whitby Town that he established his reputation as a prolific goalscorer and the ever-resourceful Billy Horner brought him back to the Victoria Ground in November 1976 for a fee reputed to be the price of a set of shirts!

Malcolm Poskett made an immediate impact in his second spell with the club,

scoring a hat-trick in only his sixth full appearance and going on to total 10 goals in 30 League appearances. Despite playing in a struggling side he continued his goalscoring form the following campaign, averaging a goal every two games, even scoring after 15 seconds against Barnsley and still finishing on the losing side! Such exploits inevitably brought him to the attention of bigger clubs and his £60,000 transfer to Brighton was easily a record for a Hartlepool player, being four times the fee Carlisle paid for Bill Green.

After leaving Hartlepool in February 1978, Poskett had a successful career over the next 10 years with seven clubs, including a brief second spell with 'Pools. He went on to score over 100 League goals at a rate of one every three games for Brighton, who then sold him to Graham Taylor's Watford for £120,000 in January 1980. He later played for Bob Stokoe's Carlisle, Darlington and Stockport before returning to the Vic in March 1986 in a loan deal which took Bob Newton to Edgeley Park.

Malcolm Poskett finished his League career in a second spell with Carlisle United in 1988 and is a member of the Cumbrians' Hall of Fame. He later played non-League football for Workington and Morecambe, before settling and working in the Carlisle area.

## POTTER, George Ross

**(1971–76)**
Right full-back/midfielder, 5ft 8in, 10st 8lb
Born: Arbroath, 7 October 1946
Signed from: Torquay United, 1 July 1971, free transfer
Transferred: Contract cancelled September 1976
Career: Forfar Athletic, Luton Town, Torquay United, Hartlepool, Gateshead
Debut: v Reading, 14 August 1971
Appearances: League: 212+1 apps, 4 gls; FA Cup: 13 apps, 1 gl; FL Cup: 16 apps, 1 gl; Total: 241+1 apps, 6 gls

Scotsman George Potter began his career with Forfar Athletic before signing for Luton Town in March 1968 and making a mere eight League appearances in a 15-month stay. Potter then moved to Torquay United in July 1969, staying two seasons before Len Ashurst brought him to Hartlepool in the 1971 close season.

Potter quickly established himself in Ashurst's side, initially in a midfield role before taking over the right-back duties from Denis White. After that he never looked back, missing only one League game in his debut season. He was equally consistent in his second season, 1972–73, forming a defensive triangle with Barry Watling and Alan Goad, which conceded a mere 15 goals in home games. The trio continued their partnership throughout the 1973–74 campaign when the manager, confident in his defence, placed more emphasis on attack, resulting in 'Pools finishing in a respectable 11th position.

The arrival of Ken Hale saw Potter return to a midfield role and play a key part in the exciting League Cup run during the 1974–75 season, contributing the vital first goal in the win at Blackburn. He missed only two games during this marathon campaign, testimony to his fitness and professionalism. The following season saw a similar pattern established, with 'Pools relying on a small squad and an FA Cup campaign which ended in dramatic fashion for both Potter and his team at Manchester City.

Hartlepool reached the third round of the Cup following wins against Stockport and Marine before being drawn against Manchester City at Maine Road. Unfortunately, the class of the First Division side shone through from the kick-off and City quickly established an unassailable lead. The match became bad-tempered as 'Pools players' frustration boiled over, when Potter, who had already

been booked, snapped at Denis Tueart's heels once too often, provoking the England international to retaliate with a head butt, breaking Potter's cheekbone. To add insult to injury, as the Hartlepool player was being stretchered away, the referee showed the red card to indicate that he had been sent off along with Tueart. Despite missing the next three League games Potter returned to the side and was ever present through to the end of the season.

Potter was left out of the Hartlepool side by Ken Hale at the start of the 1976–77 season, despite missing only three League games the previous campaign, and following Hale's departure in September in the midst of another financial crisis, he left the club by mutual agreement and later joined Northern Premier League side Gateshead. He later emigrated to Australia to play and coach for clubs in the Brisbane area before becoming a successful businessman with fast-food franchises.

## PROCTOR, John Roxby

**(1934–38)**

Right-back, 5ft 9in, 11st 6lb
Born: North Seaton, Northumberland, 10 August 1910
Died: Blyth, 18 May 1978
Signed from: Bournemouth & Boscombe Athletic, August 1934, free transfer
Transferred: Blyth Spartans, August 1938, free transfer
Career: New Delaval Villa, Huddersfield Town, Bournemouth & Boscombe Athletic, Hartlepools United, Blyth Spartans
Debut: v Walsall, 25 August 1934
Appearances: League: 149 apps, 20 gls; FA Cup: 13 apps, 2 gls; Other: 9 apps, 1 gl. Total: 171 apps, 23 gls

Jack Proctor was signed by Jackie Carr from Bournemouth, for whom he made 53 League appearances, to add much-needed strength and stability to a defence which had conceded 100 goals in all games the previous season.

Proctor began his career with Tyneside club New Delaval Villa before turning professional with Huddersfield Town, then at the height of their fortunes, in May 1931. He failed to make the grade at the Leeds Road club and moved to the south coast with Bournemouth & Boscombe Athletic, with whom he spent two seasons, before returning to his native North East on Jackie Carr's initiative.

Along with centre-half Ossie Park, who came from Newcastle United,

Proctor brought much-needed stability, missing only two games in his debut season. Despite his efforts 'Pools actually finished the season one place lower than before, in 12th. The next two seasons saw Proctor a fixture in the team, which finished eighth and sixth respectively, setting a 'Pools record in 1936–37 by scoring eight times from the penalty spot in League and Cup games.

Proctor's final season, 1937–38, coincided with a decline in 'Pools' League fortunes, in part due to the absence of Ossie Park, who only appeared in six League games. Proctor continued his remarkable penalty success by equalling his own record of eight successful conversions in League and Cup games. He finished his 'Pools career by returning from injury for the last nine games, of which only one was lost.

After leaving the Victoria Ground in the summer of 1938, Proctor played for his local club Blyth Spartans and later worked as a labourer. He died in a nursing home in Blyth in May 1978, shortly before his 68th birthday.

## RICHARDSON, Frederick

**(1947–48 and 1952–56)**

Centre-forward, 5ft 10in, 11st 9lb

Born: Middlestone Moor, Spennymoor, 18 August 1925

Signed from: Chelsea, 16 October 1947, free transfer

Transferred: Barnsley, 14 October 1948, £5,000

Re-signed: Chester, 27 November 1952, £1,000

Career: Spennymoor United, Bishop Auckland, Chelsea, Hartlepools United, Barnsley, West Bromwich Albion, Chester, Hartlepools United, Thornley Colliery Welfare

Debut: v Stockport County, 18 October 1947

Appearances: League: 149 apps, 35 gls; FA Cup: 16 apps, 8 gls; Total: 165 apps, 43 gls

Fred Richardson was one of 'Pools' most celebrated players in the immediate post-war era as he had a genuine pedigree with major clubs. His career began with local side Spennymoor United before he moved to Northern League giants Bishop Auckland, who dominated the amateur game at that time. It was with them that he appeared in the 1946 FA Amateur Cup Final, which Bishops lost 2–3 to Barnet at Stamford Bridge. A Chelsea scout must have watched the Final and been impressed by the 20-year-old Richardson, as he signed professional forms for Chelsea and made two appearances for the Blues in the First Division.

Richardson returned to his north-east roots after a year with Chelsea and was signed for 'Pools in October 1947 by Fred Westgarth, who knew a bargain when he saw one. Over the next 12 months he played 43 League games, scoring 16 goals in a team

which was in transition before second division Barnsley made the club an offer of £5,000 for his services. After a successful season at Oakwell, Richardson returned to the first division with West Bromwich Albion, then a major side. The presence of England internationals Ronnie Allen and Johnny Nichols limited his appearances at the Hawthorns, resulting in a move to Chester before he returned to the Victoria Ground in November 1952 for a fee of £1,000.

His return coincided with the emergence of the celebrated 1950s side which was involved in stirring FA Cup ties, as well as mounting serious challenges for promotion to the Second Division. Although never a prolific goalscorer, Richardson had a 'big game' temperament which was well demonstrated in the 1955 FA Cup saga, which eventually ended after seven games in an extra-time defeat by Nottingham Forest in a fourth-round replay at the City Ground.

The blossoming of Ken Johnson limited his appearances the following season and he suffered the disappointment of being left out for the FA Cup game against his old club Chelsea. He left 'Pools at the end of the season and later played for Thornley Colliery Welfare, retiring the following year due to football related injuries. After his playing days were over Fred Richardson continued to be involved in the game, coaching and managing local teams while working in the building trade.

## SAVILLE, Andrew Victor

**(1992–93)**

Centre-forward, 6ft 0in, 12st 0lb
Born: Hull, 12 December 1964
Signed from: Barnsley, 13 March 1992, £60,000
Transferred: Birmingham City, 22 March 1993, £155,000
Career: Hull City, Walsall, Barnsley, Hartlepool United, Birmingham City, Burnley (loan), Preston North End, Wigan Athletic, Cardiff City, Hull City (loan), Scarborough, Gainsborough Trinity, Goole Town
Debut: v Darlington, 14 March 1992
Appearances: League: 37 apps, 14 gls; FA Cup: 4 apps, 5 gls; FL Cup: 4 apps, 1 gl, Total: 48 apps, 21 gls

Alan Murray broke Hartlepool United's transfer record for the second time in two months when he paid Barnsley £60,000 for Andy Saville in March 1992, having signed Lenny Johnrose from Blackburn for £50,000 the previous month.

Saville was a much-travelled striker who excelled in the Football League over a 16-year career, which ultimately covered 449 games and 121 goals for 10 clubs. His style of play was the perfect foil to the hard running Lenny Johnrose, and together they played a major part in not only keeping 'Pools in a mid-table comfort zone in Division Two, but also providing rich entertainment.

Andy Saville started as a teenager with his local club Hull City in September 1983, making 101 League appearances and scoring 18 goals over a five-year period. He joined Walsall in March 1989, staying a year before returning to his native Yorkshire with Barnsley, for whom he scored 21 goals in 82 League appearances.

Saville had a bittersweet debut for Hartlepool, scoring in the derby win over Darlington and then finding himself sidelined for the rest of the season with a broken arm. He began with a bang the following campaign, 1992–93, scoring four times in the first six League games of an unbeaten start to the season. He was seen at his best during the FA Cup when 'Pools reached the fourth round by defeating Steve Coppell's Crystal Palace, then a Premiership side, courtesy of his coolly taken penalty against England goalkeeper Nigel Martyn.

The ending of the FA Cup run at Sheffield United came during a record 14-game goalless sequence, which was finally ended by Saville at Blackpool. Ironically, he had also scored the previous goal some 1,227 minutes earlier. With the early season promise evaporating and attendances suffering despite the higher standard of football on offer, it became impossible to justify players of the calibre, and subsequent cost, of Andy Saville. Consequently he was transferred to Division One side Birmingham City for £155,000, shortly before the close of the transfer window in March 1993.

After three seasons with Birmingham, including a loan spell at Burnley, Saville continued with his travels and later played for Preston North End, Wigan Athletic and Cardiff City before returning once again to his Yorkshire roots with brief spells at Hull and Scarborough. He spent a couple of seasons in non-League football with Gainsborough Trinity and Goole Town before reviving his association with Hartlepool United by appearing in the 2007 Northern Masters tournament in Newcastle.

## SHERIDAN, John

**(1966–70)**

Wing half-back, 5ft 10in, 11st 9lb
Born: Ramsgate, 25 May 1938
Signed from: Notts County, 25 July 1966, free transfer
Transferred: Retired
Career: Linby Colliery, Notts County, Hartlepools United
Debut: v Aldershot, 20 August 1966
Appearances: League: 117+3 apps, 1 gl; FA Cup: 2 apps, 0 gls; FL Cup: 7 apps, 0 gls, Total: 126+3 apps, 1 gl

John Sheridan spent 11 years with Notts County, making 287 League appearances before being offered a trial by Brian Clough at the Victoria Ground. A badly damaged ankle had cut short his time at Meadow Lane, and he relished the opportunity to revive his career with Hartlepools.

A skilful, stylish player, Sheridan soon made an impression with his new club and went on to make 39 League and Cup appearances in his first season. The following season, 1967–68, saw him captain a Hartlepools United team to their

first-ever promotion in their last season under that name. A measure of Sheridan's influence can be gauged from his side's four defeats at the beginning of the season, which he missed due to a pulled muscle. Results improved on his return to the side against Barnsley and the promotion challenge was back on course.

Following the euphoria of the promotion season, the 1968–69 campaign in Division Three was always going to be difficult without a proven goalscorer in the side. Despite this Sheridan continued to set an example on the pitch and he played 37 League games during a difficult season which ended in the inevitable relegation. The team Gus McLean inherited from Brian Clough was gradually being dismantled and 1969–70 was a struggle even in Division Four, eventually resulting in another re-election application. Sheridan played in the first 13 League games before calling it a day and retiring from playing.

After his departure from Hartlepool, John Sheridan resumed his association with Brian Clough as a coach, firstly with Derby County and later Brighton. In a twist of fate that often happens in football he returned to the Midlands to work for Nottingham Forest in a similar capacity prior to the arrival of Clough and Peter Taylor. Later he coached abroad in Qatar, and after a spell in the licensed trade he joined Nottingham University, where he continues to coach the football team.

## SIMPKINS, Kenneth

**(1964–68)**

Goalkeeper/centre-forward, 5ft 11in, 12st 12lb

Born: Wrexham, 21 December 1943

Signed from: Wrexham, 5 March 1964, free transfer

Transferred: Boston United, August 1968, free transfer

Career: Wrexham, Hartlepools United, Boston United

Debut: v Rochdale, 7 March 1964

Appearances: League: 121 apps, 1 gl; FA Cup: 8 apps, 0 gls; FL Cup: 5 apps, 0 gls; Total: 134 apps, 1 gl

Ken Simpkins made his League debut at 18 years old for Wrexham, his home-town club, and went on to make four League appearances before being signed by Alvan Williams, who had strong connections with the Welsh club, as replacement for Norman Oakley.

Simpkins' career at the Victoria Ground was only interrupted by the appointment of Brian Clough after he had made 70 consecutive League appearances following his debut. His consistency was rewarded by Wales at Under-23 level and he competed with Les Green for the goalkeeper's jersey through to the end of the 1965–66 season, regaining his place the following campaign and making 34 appearances. During his time with the club Simpkins fought a continual battle against his weight and at one point had to train in a rubber suit to sweat off the extra pounds. Such dedication led to manager McLean calling him 'the ideal professional'.

The signing of George Smith for the 1967–68 promotion season limited his chances until McLean, frustrated by the lack of a physical presence in the forwards, selected him to wear the number-nine shirt following a successful trial in the reserves. His burly stature brought added strength in his five appearances as a centre-forward, scoring one goal, the winner in a 3–2 win over Port Vale which he later described as 'my goal of the season'. He managed only a single appearance, in goal, after this and left the Victoria Ground at the end of the promotion season.

Ken Simpkins, along with Peter Thompson, later played for Midlands League club Boston United on a basic salary only £1 less than his Hartlepool pay! He even reprised his centre-forward role with the Lincolnshire club, scoring a hat-trick against Goole Town. His football career ended with the removal of a kneecap, and returning to live in Hartlepool he maintained his sporting links by playing Rugby for Hartlepool Old Boys and regularly attending games at Victoria Park.

## SMITH, Anthony

**(1984–89)**

Centre-half, 5ft 11in, 12st 2lb

Born: Sunderland, 20 February 1957

Signed from: Halifax Town, 1 August 1984, free transfer

Transferred: Retired

Career: Newcastle United, Peterborough United, Halifax Town, Hartlepool United

Debut: v Stockport County, 25 August 1984

Appearances: League: 200 apps, 8 gls; FA Cup: 11 apps, 1 gl; FL Cup: 10 apps, 0 gls; Other: 12 apps, 1 gl. Total: 233 apps, 10 gls

Tony Smith began his career with Newcastle United, graduating from the juniors to make his First Division debut in November 1977 against Wolverhampton Wanderers. His appearances for the Magpies were limited and he moved to Peterborough United in March 1979 in a joint deal with Tony Guy. After three seasons and 68 League games with Peterborough he moved to Halifax Town for two seasons, playing in the same side as Keith Nobbs.

Smith, an England Schoolboy international, was signed by Billy Horner as a replacement for the recently transferred Andy Linighan. Lacking the height and physical presence of his predecessor, Smith compensated through tactical awareness and speed of both thought and movement, which enabled him to give five seasons of consistent service, during which he played 200 League games, scoring eight goals.

His debut season, 1984–85, coincided with the arrival of John Smart as the new chairman and hope of better days. Smith played the most League games, 44, in a side which struggled and could only finish in

19th position. 1985–86 saw a dramatic improvement to seventh thanks to Alan Shoulder's goals and Smith's consistent performances, along with goalkeeper Eddie Blackburn, both players being ever presents. Such improvement was not maintained by 'Pools in the next two seasons, during which Smith missed only a single League game, testimony to his consistency and value to the team.

He retired from the professional game at the end of the 1988–89 season despite being offered a one-year contract by Bob Moncur, joining the north-east based car manufacturer Nissan to train as a computer programmer and maintaining his interest in the game by playing for Newcastle Blue Star.

## SMITH, George Henry

**(1967–70)**
Goalkeeper, 5ft 11in, 12st 8lb
Born: Nottingham, 13 April 1936
Died: Perth, Australia 2008
Signed from: Notts County, 1 July 1967, free transfer
Transferred: Arnold, August 1970
Career: Dale Rovers, Notts County, Hartlepool, Arnold Town
Debut: v Brentford, 19 August 1967
Appearances: League: 112 apps, 0 gls; FA Cup: 5 apps, 0 gls; FL Cup: 5 apps, 0 gls, Total: 122 apps, 0 gls

George Smith joined 'Pools in one of the strangest transfers ever when he was signed by Brian Clough, then manager of Derby County, having previously agreed terms with him on being given a free transfer by Notts County. He actually signed in the Derby boardroom with the knowledge and approval of Clough's successor Gus McLean.

Smith was a vastly experienced goalkeeper who played 323 League games in a 14-year career for the Meadow Lane club, and his confident presence complemented a defence which included

Tony Bircumshaw and Bryan Drysdale in the full-back berths, and the imposing figure of John Gill at the heart. He began his football career with local junior side Dale Rovers, initially as an outside-right, before a playing emergency converted him to a goalkeeper. He signed amateur forms for Notts County in 1953, turning professional four years later.

He made a dream start to his 'Pools career in August 1967 by not conceding a goal until his fifth game. This trend continued throughout the promotion season with only 46 League goals conceded, including 20 clean sheets, testimony to the quality of the man between the posts and his fellow defenders.

After the success of his debut season, 1968–69 in Division Three was always going to be a struggle given the lack of a proven goalscorer at that level. Despite the inevitable relegation George Smith and his defensive colleagues performed admirably throughout the season, managing to keep 12 clean sheets and only conceding more than three goals on five occasions. Their only 'hammering', a 7–0 defeat, came early in the season against Reading.

Smith's final season, 1969–70, saw 'Pools back in Division Four and the break-up of the promotion-winning squad. Despite this he made 32 League appearances and continued to display a professional bearing until his final game. The arrival of Des McPartland from Middlesbrough towards the end of the season brought his 'Pools career to a close. On being released he returned to his Nottinghamshire roots, later playing for Midlands League team Arnold Town.

George Smith finally retired from football in 1975 and emigrated with his family to Australia, settling in the Perth area. He worked for a company manufacturing farming equipment before suffering ill-health due to a heart condition. He died in 2008 aged 71 years.

## SMITH, John

**(1954–60)**

Centre-forward, 5ft 11in, 12st 0lb
Born: West Hartlepool, 24 April 1936
Signed from: Seaton Holy Trinity, May 1953
Transferred: Watford, 21 July 1960, £2,500
Career: Seaton Holy Trinity, Hartlepools United, Watford, Swindon Town, Brighton & Hove Albion, Notts County
Debut: Accrington Stanley, 27 February 1954
Appearances: League: 119 apps, 49 gls; FA Cup: 5 apps, 1 gl; Total: 124 apps, 50 gls

Locally-born Jackie Smith joined Hartlepools United from Seaton Holy Trinity and was given his League debut by Fred Westgarth shortly before his 18th birthday with the team in the middle of a goal drought. Although he was unable to solve the short-term goals problem in his only appearance of the 1953–54 season, he made his mark, averaging a goal a game in his eight appearances during the 1955–56 campaign when his National Service allowed.

Smith could play in either the centre or inside-forward positions, where he utilised his pace and control to contribute goals on a regular basis. He came into his own during the 1957–58 season under Ray Middleton, playing 26 League games and scoring nine goals. Thereafter he was one of the most effective forwards in the Fourth Division, averaging nearly a goal every two games and scoring a hat-trick in 'Pools' record 10–1 win over Barrow.

After 119 League games and 49 goals for 'Pools, Jackie Smith joined Third Division Watford in July 1960 for a meagre £2,500, only staying at Vicarage Road a year and contributing eight goals in 20 League appearances. He signed for Swindon Town in June 1961 for a small fee, going on to be a key member of the side which won promotion in the 1962–63 season to the Second Division by finishing as runners-up to Northampton Town. Smith's contribution of 19 goals in a total of 87 was second only to Ernie Hunt.

After a strong start to their Division Two campaign Swindon's results faltered and, following a heavy defeat to Northampton, Jackie Smith was sold to Brighton for a reported £6,000 in January 1964. In an ironic twist Swindon then used the money to buy Norman Oakley from 'Pools!

With Brighton, Jackie Smith enjoyed another promotion, this time from Division Four, when his team took the League by storm during the 1964–65 season, finishing as champions in style by scoring 102 goals, of which Smith contributed 17. Brighton finished in the lower reaches of Division Three the following season and, despite again reaching double figures for goals scored, Jackie Smith was transferred to Notts County, then a struggling Fourth Division side. He retired at the end of the 1968–69 season having played 78 League games, scoring 12 goals, with the Meadow Lane club.

Jackie Smith later played for non-League Margate and Ramsgate Athletic before joining Southern League Bath City as assistant manager to Bert Head. Following Head's dismissal during the 1975–76 season he managed the team for the remaining games. An interesting footnote to his time with Bath is that their goalkeeper was Kenny Allen, who played for 'Pools in 1969. On leaving Bath following the appointment of Brian Godfrey as player-manager he had a spell as a youth-team coach at Portsmouth.

## SMITH, Robert

(1972–76)

Full-back, 5ft 6in, 10st 2lb
Born: Hull, 25 April 1950
Signed from: Grimsby Town, 1 July 1972, free transfer
Transferred: Scarborough, 1 August 1976, free transfer
Career: Hull City, Grimsby Town, Hartlepool United, Scarborough
Debut: v Lincoln City, 12 August 1972
Appearances: League: 141+11 apps, 4 gls; FA Cup: 11 apps, 0 gls; FL Cup: 13 apps, 0 gls; Total: 165+11 apps, 4 gls

Rob Smith joined his home-town club Hull City as an apprentice in November 1967. He failed to make his League debut, and signed for neighbours Grimsby Town in September 1971. He made 11 consecutive League appearances for the Mariners during the 1971–72 season before being signed by Len Ashurst on a free transfer in July 1972.

Smith played mainly in midfield during his first season at Hartlepool due to the presence of Alan Goad and George Potter

in the full-back positions. He played 42 League games, scoring one goal in a campaign that was notable for a chronic lack of goals due to the manager's emphasis on defence, as evidenced by Smith's midfield role. The following campaign, after continuing in midfield for the early games, he moved to his natural position of right-back when George Potter had a spell on the sidelines. Ashurst's more adventurous approach, which resulted in a mid-table finish, saw Smith reduced to the substitutes' bench for most of the second half of the season.

The arrival of Ken Hale saw Smith restored to his right-back role, with George Potter now in a defensive midfield position. Smith missed only two games, ironically at the start of the season, playing 56 consecutive League and Cup matches during a campaign which featured the League Cup exploits. He continued to be a fixture in 'Pools' defence throughout the 1975–76 season until the Easter period, when the arrival of Paul Luckett, a former apprentice at Hales' old club Coventry, saw Alan Goad restored to right-back and Smith dropped from the team.

Rob Smith was given a free transfer by Ken Hale at the end of the 1975–76 season and joined Northern Premier League club Scarborough, with whom he won an FA Challenge Trophy winners' medal in the 1977 Final victory over Dagenham at Wembley.

## SOUTHALL, Leslie Nicholas

(1991–95)
Midfielder, 5ft 10in, 12st 12lb
Born: Stockton-on-Tees, 28 January 1972
Signed from: Darlington juniors, 21 February 1991
Transferred: Grimsby Town, 12 July 1995, £40,000
Career: Darlington (juniors), Hartlepool United, Grimsby Town, Gillingham, Bolton Wanderers, Norwich City (loan), Gillingham, Nottingham Forest, Gillingham, Dover Athletic, Gillingham
Debut: v Bournemouth, 12 October 1991
Appearances: League: 118+20 apps, 24 gls; FA Cup: 4+4 apps, 0 gls; FL Cup: 6+1 apps, 3 gls; Other: 7+2 apps, 0 gls. Total: 135+27 apps, 27 gls

Nicky Southall was signed by Cyril Knowles from Darlington shortly before the derby game during 'Pools' promotion season. Alan Murray gave him his debut the following term while still a teenager and he impressed sufficiently to make 22 League appearances in a team that was more than holding its own in the higher division.

A skilful midfield player capable of exciting runs into the opposition's penalty area, he became a key member of the 'Pools side which not only survived a second season in what was now Division Two, but also defeated Crystal Palace of the newly formed Premier League in the FA Cup. The following season, 1993–94, saw Nicky Southall make the most appearances and finish as leading scorer in 'Pools' relegated side. He continued his form in

the next campaign, making over 40 appearances in all competitions and recording his first hat-trick in the League game against Colchester United.

It was no surprise when Nicky Southall left Victoria Park in July 1995 to join Grimsby Town in a £40,000 deal, playing in goal on his debut after the goalkeeper was sent off! After 72 League appearances and six goals he moved, for the first time, to Gillingham, playing over 150 games before joining Premiership Bolton Wanderers for the 2001–02 season. He played 18 games, scoring a single goal in the top flight, before returning to Gillingham on a free transfer for a second time having had a brief loan spell at Norwich.

Towards the end of his second spell at Priestfield his form dipped and he lost the support of the local fans. On his release Southall accepted an offer of a two-year deal from Nottingham Forest in the summer of 2005. Now 33 years old, he again demonstrated his value to his team by making 67 League appearances over the next two seasons before returning once again to Gillingham for a third spell in February 2007.

At the start of the 2008–09 season Mark Stimson, the Gillingham manager, sent Southall on loan to Dover Athletic to gain competitive fitness. On his return he made 38 appearances in an ultimately successful campaign, which culminated in promotion to League Two with a victory over Shrewsbury in the Play-off Final at Wembley, although he did not feature in the match. By the end of the season he had played in over 600 games in his professional career, over half of them with Gillingham, who released him at the end of the season allowing him to join Dover Athletic on a permanent deal going on to make 27 appearances for the Kent club.

Anyone thinking that Nicky Southall's association with Gillingham had ended were to be mistaken when he joined the club for a fourth time in July 2010 in the role of player-coach having been released by Dover. In a remarkable twist of fate he was to make his fourth debut for The Gills in a first round FA Cup tie against Dover Athletic!

## STAMPER, Frank Fielden Thorpe

**(1949–58)**

Wing half-back, 5ft 11in, 12st 0lb
Born: West Hartlepool, 22 February 1926
Died: Hartlepool, 19 July 1999
Signed from: Colchester United, 1 August 1949, free transfer
Transferred: Blyth Spartans, 1 August 1958, free transfer
Career: Colchester United, Hartlepools United, Blyth Spartans
Debut: v Bradford City, 3 September 1949
Appearances: League: 301 apps, 26 gls; FA Cup: 25 apps, 4 gls; Total: 326 apps, 30 gls

It was a red-letter day for both Fred Westgarth and Hartlepools United when locally-born Frank Stamper signed on a free transfer from Colchester United on completion of his military service. Described as an attacking wing half-back who also played at inside-forward, he went on to play over 300 League and Cup games for his home-town club, including all the celebrated FA Cup ties the team was involved in during the 1950s.

Stamper made his League debut within a few weeks of joining Hartlepools United in September 1949 at Bradford City, a 3–1 win, before losing his place following a 3–5 defeat in the next game against local rivals Gateshead in front of over 12,000 spectators.

It took the player a little while to establish himself, making only 16 League appearances in his debut season, including the home game against Bradford City which saw the legendary half-back line of Newton, Moore and Stamper play together for the first time, thereby establishing the axis around which 'Pools' teams would revolve in the coming seasons. He played 35 League games the following season and never looked back, even deputising in three games for the injured Watty Moore. Stamper was a key member of the side which achieved 'Pools' first top-10 finish of the post-war era in 1951–52 and saw off competition from Len Richley for the left-half position in the following seasons.

Frank Stamper missed only one game throughout the 1954–55 campaign as Westgarth's side fulfilled their potential by finishing fifth in the League, thanks to a record-breaking run, and had a seven-game FA Cup run which only ended in a replay at Second Division Nottingham Forest.

Another successful season in 1955–56 was a prelude to the 1956–57 season when 'Pools finished as runners-up to Derby County, with Frank Stamper in his prime, contributing 13 goals from 46 appearances during the campaign. An injury to Bobby Lumley required him to play at inside-forward against Manchester United and he contributed the important first goal of an amazing, if ultimately failed, fightback.

Stamper was awarded a joint benefit with Tommy McGuigan in April 1956 against a Newcastle side which included Jimmy Scoular, Len White, Vic Keeble and Bobby Mitchell. Despite the presence of such distinguished players 'Pools romped to a 6–3 victory, to the delight of a 7,206 crowd, with Ken Johnson scoring four goals.

It was perhaps ironic that his final season, 1957–58, was also the last of the Third Division North, and despite making 41 League and Cup appearances he became a victim of Ray Middleton's 'youth policy' and was released. He joined Blyth Spartans for the Midland League's inaugural 1958–59 season and scored in the 2–1 Northumberland Senior Cup Final victory over Ashington at St James' Park.

Frank Stamper finished his playing career at Croft Park and later worked as a pipe fitter with various local companies. He died in a nursing home in Hartlepool on 19 July 1999, aged 73 years.

## STEPHENSON, Paul

**(1998–2002)**
Outside-right/midfielder, 5ft 10in, 12st 6lb
Born: Wallsend, 2 January 1968
Signed from: York City, 20 March 1998, free transfer
Transferred: Retired
Career: Newcastle United, Millwall, Gillingham (loan), Brentford, York City, Hartlepool United
Debut: v Mansfield Town, 18 April 1998
Appearances: League: 136+9 apps, 9 gls; Play-off: 5+1 apps, 0 gls; FA Cup: 4+1 apps, 0 gls; FL Cup: 5+1 apps, 2 gls; Other: 8 apps, 0 gls. Total: 158+12 apps, 11 gls

Wallsend-born Paul Stephenson joined Newcastle United as an apprentice and was a member of the 1985 FA Youth Cup-winning side which included Paul Gascoigne and Joe Allon. An England Youth international, he made his First Division debut at 17 years old and quickly established a reputation as a fast and skilful winger. After 61 League games for the Magpies he joined Millwall in November 1988 for £300,000, quickly establishing himself in a side which included Teddy Sheringham and Tony Cascarino.

After gaining promotion to the First Division for the only time in the club's history, Stephenson found his appearances restricted with the arrival of Mick McCarthy as manager. After a loan spell with Gillingham he joined Brentford in March 1993 for £30,000, spending two seasons at Griffin Park before returning north to sign for York City for £35,000, a fee manager Alan Little described as a 'bargain'. Stephenson made 97 League appearances for the Minstermen before being released for financial reasons following a failed Play-off campaign.

Paul Stephenson joined Hartlepool in March 1998 on a free transfer for the final three games of the season. His signing turned out to be a shrewd piece of business by Mick Tait and, despite struggling initially due to managerial upheavals, his form was galvanised with the arrival of Chris Turner. His transformation from orthodox winger to midfield playmaker in harness with Tommy Miller and Mark Tinkler made him a favourite with 'Pools fans. He was in his prime throughout the 1999–2000 season, playing in every League, Cup and Play-off game – 54 appearances in all – and was a worthy winner of the supporters' Player of the Year award. He was hardly less consistent the following season, missing only six League games as 'Pools again reached the Play-offs; however, the arrival of Paul Smith from Burnley restricted his appearances throughout the 2001–02 season. He made his final appearance against Cheltenham in the Play-off semi-final and had the disappointment of missing a penalty in the deciding shoot-out.

After failing to make a single appearance throughout the 2002–03 season, Stephenson announced his retirement and joined the Hartlepool coaching staff. He was appointed youth-team coach and guided his side to victory in the Under-19 Dallas Cup before being appointed caretaker manager in February 2006 following Martin Scott's dismissal. Unable to prevent the inevitable relegation, Stephenson made clear his intentions to return to coaching pending a permanent appointment, and following Danny Wilson's engagement he resumed his duties as youth-team coach. In November 2007, after nearly 10 years' service with the club, he accepted an offer from former Newcastle United player and manager Glenn Roeder to become coach of Norwich City. Following Glenn Roeder's departure from Carrow Road in January 2009, Stephenson left Norwich to join former Newcastle teammate Lee Clark at Huddersfield Town as development coach.

## SWEENEY, Antony Thomas

**(2001–Present)**

Midfielder, 6ft 0in, 11st 9lb
Born: Stockton-on-Tees, 5 September 1983
Signed from: Youth trainee, 10 January 2002
Transferred: Current player
Career: Hartlepool United
Debut: v York City, 13 October 2001
Appearances: League: 298+34 apps, 51 gls; Play-off: 5 apps, 1 gls, FA Cup: 22 apps, 4 gls; FL Cup: 15 apps, 2 gls; Other: 9+2 apps, 2 gls. Total: 349+36 apps, 60 gls

Antony Sweeney joined 'Pools as a teenager, making two substitute appearances in October 2001 before Chris Turner signed him as youth trainee the following January. He played only a handful of games over the next two seasons before establishing himself throughout the 2004–05 campaign, when he missed only two League games and played 57 matches in all competitions.

An energetic midfield player capable of scoring spectacular and vital goals, he first attracted attention during the 2003–04 Play-off games against Bristol City, scoring a memorable goal at Ashton Gate which nearly won the contest. He was a fixture in Neale Cooper's side the following season, which culminated in the memorable League One Play-off Final against Sheffield Wednesday. Antony Sweeney's value to his team during that momentous 60-game season can be gauged by him only missing three games overall and contributing 13 League goals, only one less than Joel Porter.

Like every other member of the Hartlepool squad, Sweeney was unsettled by the managerial upheavals which led to the sacking of Martin Scott, despite playing in 37 League games during the relegation campaign. The arrival of Danny Wilson saw him return to his best form throughout

the record-breaking 2006–07 season, which culminated in a well-deserved promotion. He missed only two games throughout the unbeaten run which finally came to an end at Barnet, a game Sweeney missed through injury.

The emergence of James Brown and consistency of Willie Boland saw Sweeney often relegated to the substitutes' bench for the first half of the 2007–08 campaign, at one point operating at right-back, the position he was to occupy for much of the following season, when once again his consistency was shown as he missed only two of the 53 games 'Pools played in all competitions.

The 2009–10 campaign saw this popular player operate primarily in his familiar right-sided midfield role until the latter stages when he was relegated to the substitutes' bench to make way for Irishman Joe Gamble. Sweeney started the following season in a more defensive midfield role before the arrival of Mick Wadsworth saw him returned to his familiar attacking position at the expense of Gamble. He made 40 League appearances scoring nine goals, excelling in the FA Cup with four goals which included a hat-trick against Yeovil Town. Tony Sweeney's efforts over the season were officially recognised when he was voted both the fans and players Player of the Year attracting over half the votes polled.

He had a frustrating start to the 2011–12 campaign when he sustained a groin injury in the second game, a Football League Cup tie against Sheffield United, in the process of scoring the equaliser. The result of the injury saw him miss four League games and on his return Wadsworth employed the player in unfamiliar roles. The arrival of Neale Cooper returned Tony Sweeney to his natural role on the right of midfield and he finished the season with 42 League and Cup appearances to his name to bring his total to 385, sixth in the club's all-time list.

## TAIT, Michael Paul

**(1992–97)**

Midfielder, 5ft 11in, 12st 13lb
Born: Wallsend, 30 September 1956
Signed from: Darlington, 1 July 1992, free transfer
Transferred: July 1994, Gretna Green, free transfer
Re-signed: Gretna Green, 9 September 1994, free transfer
Career: Oxford United, Carlisle United, Hull City, Portsmouth, Reading, Darlington, Hartlepool United, Bishop Auckland, Gretna Green (Scotland), Hartlepool United
Debut: v Reading, 15 August 1992
Appearances: League: 134+5 apps, 3 gls; FA Cup: 4 apps, 0 gls; FL Cup: 11 apps, 1 gl; Other: 1 app, 0 gls. Total: 150+5 apps, 4 gls

Mick Tait began his lengthy career with Oxford United, having joined as an apprentice from Wallsend Boys Club in 1972. After turning professional in October 1974 he later joined Carlisle United for £60,000 in February 1977. A series of impressive displays persuaded Hull City to break their transfer record in September 1979 with a £150,000 transfer deal. His stay at Boothferry Park was a short one and he moved to Portsmouth in May 1980 for £100,000, winning a Division Three Championship medal with them in 1983. Over the next seven seasons he went on to play 240 League games for the south-coast club before his £50,000 transfer to Reading at the start of the 1987–88 season. Released by Reading after 99 League appearances over three seasons, Tait joined Darlington in August 1990, spending two seasons at Feethams before making the short journey in July 1992 to the Victoria Ground to join Hartlepool United on a free transfer.

Alan Murray signed Mick Tait to replace John Tinkler, who had moved to Preston North End in the first season of

the newly-named Division Two, the third tier of English football following the creation of the Premier League. Tait, in his 36th year, was signed to add experience and mettle to a team which was to struggle following the departure of key players. He played 35 games, almost all in midfield, scoring once during the 1992–93 season, before becoming increasingly used in defensive roles by John MacPhail, Murray's successor, in a vain attempt to avoid the inevitable relegation.

Tait was released by John MacPhail in the summer of 1994, having a brief spell with Scottish side Gretna before being recalled to the Vic by David McCreery, to continue his Hartlepool career. He made a further 78 League appearances, most notably during the 1995–96 season under Keith Houchen's managership, when he missed only seven League games despite approaching his 40th birthday. One final landmark remained when he became Hartlepool United's oldest player in the game against Fulham on 22 March 1997, aged 40 years, five months and 22 days.

Following his appointment as manager of Hartlepool United, Mick Tait retired from playing having appeared in 760 Football League games, ranking him 15th in the all-time list of professional players, a truly magnificent achievement. He left the club in January 1999 after a difficult couple of years in the hot seat and later managed Blyth Spartans before returning to Darlington in 2002, initially as caretaker manager, then later confirmed as manager. On the return of David Hodgson he became youth development officer before finally severing his ties with the Quakers in February 2008. In May 2009, after a brief spell as manager of Newcastle Blue Star, Mick Tait was appointed manager of Blyth Spartans of the Blue Square North League, thereby continuing his long and distinguished association with the game.

## THOMPSON, Peter

**(1957–58 and 1963–66)**

Centre/inside-forward, 5ft 9in, 12st 0lb
Born: Blackhall, 16 February 1936
Signed from: Wrexham, 1 July 1957, Amateur
Transferred: Derby County, 8 November 1958, £5,000
Re-signed: Bournemouth, 28 September 1963, free transfer
Career: Blackhall Colliery Welfare, Wrexham (amateur), Hartlepools United, Derby County, Bournemouth, Hartlepools United, Boston United
Debut: v Chester, 31 August 1957
Appearances: League: 138 apps, 56 gls; FA Cup: 6 apps, 5 gls; FL Cup: 1 app, 0 gls; Total: 145 apps, 61 gls

Peter Thompson's football career, which began with local club Blackhall Colliery Welfare, could not have had a more auspicious start than his first season, 1956–57. While still a physical instructor in the RAF he was capped on four occasions by England in amateur internationals, before he joined Wrexham and scored 18 goals in 37 League games, played and scored in the victorious Welsh Cup team which defeated Second Division Swansea in the Final and played in the fourth-round FA Cup tie against

Manchester United in front of an all-time record 34,445 crowd at the Racecourse Ground.

On his return to the North East Thompson signed as a professional for Hartlepools United in July 1957 and quickly made his mark in Ray Middleton's new-look side by becoming the club's leading scorer with 20 goals in League and Cup games, including four in the FA Cup tie against Prescot Cables.

Such consistency brought him to the notice of bigger clubs and he moved to Derby County, Middleton's old club, in November 1958 for a modest fee, but he only managed 19 goals in 52 League appearances before moving to Bournemouth. After 18 months and 37 games with the south-coast side he returned to 'Pools and was once again leading goalscorer in both the 1963–64 and 1964–65 campaigns. In all he played 91 games in his second spell with the club, gaining one of Hartlepools' more unusual records when he became the first player to be substituted, by Brian Drysdale, in the League game at Aldershot.

Peter Thompson left the Victoria Ground at the end of the 1965–66 season to become player-manager of Boston United in the United Counties League, signing his former 'Pools colleague Ken Simpkins. After a season with the Lincolnshire club he retired from football and later took a degree in Education Studies, which involved work in projects with a number of local schools and educational establishments.

## THOMPSON, Raymond

**(1947–58)**

Left-back, 6ft 0in, 12st 7lb
Born: Leeholme, 21 October 1925
Died: Sedgefield, 2 January 1997
Signed from: Sunderland, 23 January 1947, free transfer
Transferred: Blyth Spartans, 1 August 1958, free transfer.
Career: Cockerton Hill Juniors, Sunderland, Hartlepools United, Blyth Spartans
Debut: v Southport, 25 January 1947
Appearances: League 396 apps, 2 gls: FA Cup 27 apps. Total: 423 apps, 2 gls

Ray Thompson was signed by Fred Westgarth from his home-town club Sunderland, for whom he made four wartime appearances, having begun his career with Cockerton Hill Juniors alongside Jackie Newton. A left-back in the classical mould, he was noted for attacking forays down the wing in support of his forwards, even making the odd appearance at outside-left.

Thompson made his League debut within days of signing, replacing Fred Gregory and retaining his place through to the end of the season. His first full season, 1947–48, saw him compete with Harry Hooper for the left-back berth, before establishing himself as first choice the following campaign.

His service to Hartlepools United was recognised by the directors as early as April 1954 when he was awarded a joint benefit with Jackie Newton against a star-studded Newcastle United side which attracted a crowd of nearly 10,000, testimony to his popularity.

Thereafter he was a fixture in the team, forming effective full-back partnerships, firstly with Joe Willetts and, from 1954–55, Jock Cameron. Testimony to Ray Thompson's consistency can be gauged from his record of being ever present in the 1953–54 (along with Willetts), 1955–56 and 1956–57 seasons, three of the most memorable in the club's history.

The arrival of Ray Middleton signalled the end of his Hartlepools career and he was released following the 1957–58 campaign in which 'Pools failed to qualify for the newly-formed Third Division. He made 22 League appearances throughout the season, during which he was in competition with Jock Cameron for the left-back berth.

This great servant left the Victoria Ground with his head held high and a playing record that saw only Watty Moore, in the Football League, and Jackie Newton, in the FA Cup, play more games for Hartlepools United. He later played for Blyth Spartans in the newly formed Midland League alongside Frank Stamper.

Ray Thompson died in hospital at Sedgefield in January 1997, aged 71 years.

## TINKLER, John

**(1987–92)**

Midfielder, 5ft 8in, 11st 7lb

Born: Trimdon, 24 August 1968

Signed from: Juniors, 1 December 1986, non-contract

Transferred: Preston North End, 1 July 1992, free transfer

Career: Hartlepool United, Preston North End, Walsall

Debut: v Cambridge United, 24 January 1987

Appearances: League: 153+17 apps, 7 gls; FA Cup: 10+1 apps, 1 gl; FL Cup: 8+2 apps, 1 gl; Other: 12 apps, 2 gls. Total: 183+20 apps, 11 gls

John Tinkler joined Hartlepool in December 1986 while still a teenager and was given his League debut by John Bird the following month. He made only two appearances in his debut season before establishing himself in the side in the second half of the 1987–88 campaign as a hardworking midfield player.

The arrival of Bobby Moncur saw Tinkler become a fixture in 'Pools' team for the 1988–89 season, making 38 League appearances and scoring three goals. Such was his impact that 'Pools received an offer of £80,000 from Scottish side Dundee for his services. Following Moncur's departure Cyril Knowles continued with Tinkler in midfield and further strengthened the side's 'engine room' by signing Paul Olsson and Steve Tupling. This trio, together with Brian Honour, formed the foundation around which Knowles built his promotion-winning side.

John Tinkler missed only a single game during the 1989–90 season, playing 50 matches in all competitions, which was ideal preparation for the momentous campaign to follow. After hardly missing a game the previous two seasons, Tinkler had the misfortune to damage ankle ligaments in September against Blackpool. He returned to the side at the end of November, only to sustain a knee injury against Wrexham in the promotion run-in. In all he featured in 28 League games, scoring twice, and the absence of his aggressive midfield qualities were noticed during the periods he was sidelined.

The retention of the promotion-winning midfield players for 'Pools' first season back in Division Three was a major factor in the team's commendable performances and top half finish. John Tinkler was a key part in this success and constantly caught the eye with his wholehearted displays. He missed only seven League games in his final season and moved to Preston North End in July 1972 on a free transfer.

Tinkler started the 1992–93 season as a first choice, playing 24 League games before losing his place to Neil Whalley. He left Deepdale at the end of the season and signed for Walsall in August 1993, playing in the first six games of the season before being released and retiring from the professional game. He later played for senior north-east non-League clubs Gateshead, Spennymoor United, Bishop Auckland and Blyth Spartans, as well as playing in Hartlepool United teams in the Northern Masters competitions along with Middlesbrough, Newcastle United and Sunderland.

## TINKLER, Mark Roland

**(2000–07)**

Midfielder, 5ft 11in, 12st 3lb

Born: Bishop Auckland, 24 October 1974

Signed from: Southend United, 2 November 2000, free transfer

Transferred: Livingston, 3 July 2007, free transfer

Career: Leeds United, York City, Southend United, Hartlepool United, Livingston

Debut: v Scunthorpe United, 4 November 2000

Appearances: League: 200+11 apps, 34 gls; Play-off: 4+2 apps, 0 gls; FA Cup: 12 apps, 2 gls; FL Cup: 7 apps, 0 gls; Other: 8 apps, 1 gl. Total: 231+13 apps, 37 gls

Mark Tinkler started his career with Leeds United and was a member of the side which won the 1993 FA Youth Cup by beating Manchester United in the Final. An England

Schoolboy and Youth international, Tinkler made his Premiership debut while still a teenager and made 25 appearances as a midfield player in the top tier of English football. In March 1997 he joined York City for a £75,000 transfer fee, making 90 League appearances over the next two seasons. The appointment of Alan Little, Tinkler's former manager at York, to the same role at Southend prompted the player to follow him for what was to be a highly successful spell with the Essex club.

Chris Turner brought Tinkler to Victoria Park in November 2000 and the player became an integral part of the side which was to enjoy unprecedented success over the next seven seasons. Ironically, his Hartlepool career began with a 0–3 defeat at Scunthorpe, which turned out to be the heaviest of the season.

The next two seasons saw Mark Tinkler establish himself in a side which firstly reached the Play-offs, and then gained promotion in 2002–03, with him missing only a single League game and scoring 13 goals in the process, including a hat-trick against Wrexham. His part in the promotion campaign was recognised when his fellow professionals voted for him in the 2003 PFA Division Three team.

He was in his prime during the 2003–04 season when 'Pools surprised the football world by reaching the Division Two Play-offs. Tinkler played 52 games in all competitions, including the memorable games against Bristol City. A regular for most of the 2004–05 campaign, playing 33 League games, injuries resulted in him missing the Play-off Final against Sheffield Wednesday, a blow for a player who had contributed so much to 'Pools' successes in previous seasons.

The appointment of Martin Scott as manager resulted in his appearances becoming less frequent, and after 15 League games in the 2005–06 season he was left out of the side by Danny Wilson for most of the 2006–07 promotion season. Mark Tinkler was released at the end of the season having made 211 League appearances, scoring 34 goals in a seven-year career with the club. He joined Scottish First Division side Livingston in July 2007 on a one-year deal, making 19 appearances and scoring two goals. On being released he returned south of the border to join Whitby Town of the Unibond Premier League for the 2008–09 season, and later played for Shildon of the Northern League.

## WATLING, Barry John

**(1972–76)**

Goalkeeper, 5ft 9in, 11st 12lb

Born: Walthamstow, 16 July 1946

Signed from: Notts County, 1 July 1972, free transfer

Transferred: Sheffield Wednesday, January 1976, free transfer

Career: Leyton Orient (apprentice), Bristol City, Notts County, Hartlepool, Seattle Sounders (USA), Chester (loan), Crewe Alexandra (loan), Rotherham United (loan), Sheffield Wednesday

Debut: v Lincoln City, 12 August 1972

Appearances: League: 139 apps, 0 gls; FA Cup: 7 apps, 0 gls; FL Cup: 12 apps, 0 gls; Total: 158 apps, 0 gls

Len Ashurst pulled off one his shrewdest deals when he signed Barry Watling on a free transfer from Notts County, for whom he made 65 League appearances. Walthamstow-born Watling started with his local club Leyton Orient as an apprentice before spending three years with Bristol City, making his League debut before moving to the Meadow Lane club in July 1969. He was a key member of the side which stormed to the Division Four Championship in the 1970–71 season, missing a mere three games.

Watling's first season at the Victoria Ground, 1972–73, was the stuff of a goalkeeper's dreams. In a side built around defence he was ever present, conceding only 49 goals in the League campaign, including a miserly 15 in home games. This included a run of five games without conceding a goal in the New Year period. Not surprisingly he was voted the fans' Player of the Year. The following season Watling was again ever present and even improved on the previous term by conceding a mere 47 goals, only 16 of them at home. Along with his performances the team improved overall to finish a creditable 11th.

During the 1974 and 1975 summer seasons Barry Watling was a founder member of the Seattle Sounders team in the North American Soccer League, making 43 appearances in a side which included Geoff Hurst, Mike England and Harry Redknapp. He also had the distinction of being named goalkeeper in the 1974 NASL All Star Team.

The arrival of Ken Hale saw him maintain his place through to the final game of the season, a total of 137 consecutive League appearances for the club. The advent of the burly John Hope restricted his appearances the following season and after loan spells with Chester, Crewe and Rotherham United, he joined Sheffield Wednesday in January 1976, making one appearance before being released at the end of the season. The following year he joined Maidstone United as manager, a post he held until 1981.

Barry Watling later managed junior clubs in the south of England before having a successful career in the financial services industry.

## WAUGH, Kenneth

**(1956–62)**

Left-back, 5ft 8in, 10st 6lb
Born: Newcastle upon Tyne, 6 August 1933
Died: Australia, June 2001
Signed from: Newcastle United, 23 December 1956, £680
Transferred: Retired
Career: Film Renters, Newcastle United, Hartlepools United
Debut: v York City, 25 December 1956
Appearances: League: 195 apps, 0 gls; FA Cup: 9 apps, 0 gls; FL Cup: 2 apps, 0 gls; Total: 206 apps, 0 gls

Ken Waugh was Fred Westgarth's last signing when he joined 'Pools in December 1956, making his debut on Christmas Day against York City. A

Geordie born and bred, he joined Newcastle United in August 1952 while still a teenager, from local side Film Renters, going on to make seven League appearances in the 1955–56 season in competition with Dick Keith and Alf McMichael, both full internationals, as well as the experienced Ron Batty, who played in the 1955 FA Cup Final.

Following his debut he retained his place at the expense of Jock Cameron for the remainder of the League campaign, although he was left out for the famous Manchester United Cup tie despite being eligible. A model of consistency, Waugh played every game of the hugely disappointing 1957–58 season, which saw 'Pools effectively relegated to the new Fourth Division.

The following campaign saw him partner Jock Cameron on a regular basis, only missing a single game as 'Pools adapted to life in the bottom tier. An undoubted highlight was the record 10–1 victory over a hapless Barrow side, which unsurprisingly conceded over 100 goals that season.

Ken Waugh continued to be a model of consistency throughout the dreadful 1959–60 season when a new low was reached by an ageing team and Watty Moore played his last game. As the constant changes, of both management and players, took their toll Waugh's appearances became less frequent. The signing of the veteran Ray Bilcliff by Bill Robinson from Middlesbrough was a warning sign, although ironically he was recalled to the team following the disastrous 1–10 defeat at Wrexham to replace his former Newcastle colleague, George Lackenby.

Thereafter he made only a handful of appearances before being released by Bill Robinson at the end of the season and retiring from the professional game. An interesting feature of the player's career with Hartlepools United is that he made the most senior appearances for the club – 206 – without scoring a goal.

Ken Waugh later emigrated to Australia, where he lived until his death in 2001, aged 67 years.

## WESTWOOD, Christopher, John

**(1999–2005)**

Central-defender, 5ft 11in, 12st 10lb
Born: Dudley, 13 February 1977
Signed from: Telford United, 24 March 1999, free transfer
Transferred: Walsall, 1 July 2005, free transfer
Career: Wolverhampton Wanderers, Telford United, Hartlepool United, Walsall, Peterborough United, Wycombe Wanderers, Wrexham
Debut: v Torquay United, 27 March 1999
Appearances: League: 244+6 apps, 7 gls; Play-off: 11 apps, 0 gls, FA Cup: 15 apps, 2 gls; FL Cup: 8 apps, 0 gls; Other: 9 apps, 0 gls. Total: 287+6 apps, 9 gls

Chris Westwood's early career began as a youth trainee with Wolverhampton Wanderers, for whom he made his League debut in September 1997 in Division One. He was released on a free transfer at the end of the season having made four League appearances and joined Nationwide Conference side Telford United. Westwood was not out of the Football League for long when he accepted the offer from Chris Turner, a coach at Wolverhampton during his time with the club, to sign for Hartlepool United in March 1999. He was to prove on countless occasions over the coming seasons that his manager's faith had not been misplaced.

After four appearances towards the end of the 1998–99 season Westwood established himself in Turner's side the following season, forming a central-defensive partnership with Graeme Lee and making 33 League appearances in the first Hartlepool side to reach the Play-offs. For the next five seasons Westwood, who combined strength with mobility, was a

model of consistency, missing only 21 League games during this period as 'Pools enjoyed a promotion, two Play-offs and the momentous Play-off Final at Cardiff. He formed central-defensive partnerships with both Graeme Lee and Michael Nelson, which were at the heart of the club's success during this period. Following the 2003 promotion season he was voted into the PFA Division Three Team of the Year by his fellow professionals.

His final game with the club, the 2004–05 League One Play-off Final against Sheffield Wednesday, is the one for which he will be remembered. With Hartlepool only seven minutes away from the Championship and deservedly leading 2–1, Westwood was adjudged to have committed a professional foul and conceded a penalty from which Wednesday equalised. To make matters worse, he was sent off and Hartlepool lost in extra-time. It was a sad way to end seven seasons of otherwise distinguished service.

Chris Westwood returned to the Midlands area for family reasons during the close season, joining Walsall, with whom he spent two years, and being named in the PFA League Two Team of the Year for the 2006–07 season, when they pipped 'Pools by a point to the Championship.

Westwood moved to League Two side Peterborough United for the 2007–08 season, making 37 League appearances and playing a key role in the promotion-winning side. He continued to share in the success at London Road, making 18 appearances as the Posh, with Darren Ferguson (Sir Alex's son) in the managerial chair, achieved a promotion double to the Championship as runners-up. In July 2009 he signed a two-year deal with Wycombe Wanderers, having had his Peterborough contract cancelled by mutual consent. This was to prove a mixed blessing as the Chairboys suffered relegation from League One with Westwood making 28 League appearances, scoring two goals.

The following season he made a further 27 appearances before being released at the end of his contract and moving in June 2011 to Blue Square Premier Wrexham who narrowly missed promotion back to the Football League, losing in the Play-offs to Luton Town.

## WIGHAM, John

**(1931–39)**
Inside-left, 5ft 9in, 11st 3lb
Born: Hebburn, 9 July 1909
Died: Hebburn, 8 February 1959
Signed from: Hebburn Colliery, 27 June 1931
Transferred: Retired, May 1939
Career: Isabella Colliery, New Delaval Villa, Hebburn Colliery, Hartlepools United
Debut: v Chester, 9 September 1931
Appearances: League: 264 apps, 95 gls; FA Cup: 23 apps, 7 gls; Other: 4 apps, 4 gls. Total: 291 apps, 106 gls

Johnny Wigham, the epitome of the one-club player, was employed as a schoolmaster in the Jarrow area when his exploits as an amateur with Hebburn Colliery brought him to the notice of Frank Perryman in the summer of 1931. He soon became United's regular inside-left, and despite offers from Aston Villa, Stoke City and Huddersfield Town he stayed at the Vic until the outbreak of war in 1939, playing 263 League games and scoring 95 goals, a record at the time.

His debut season, 1931–32, saw him make 24 League appearances, scoring 13 goals and forming a partnership with Joss Hewitt which blossomed to such an extent that the pair scored 73 League goals in the next two seasons. Ironically his finest game, according to contemporary reports, came in the third-round FA Cup tie against Grimsby Town, then in the First Division. In front of a then record attendance for the Vic of 15,064, and having to reorganise following an injury to goalkeeper Mittel, 'Pools matched their opponents, with Johnny Wigham playing the game of his life. The 0–0 scoreline in no way reflected either his, or the team's, efforts, and the First Division side were lucky to escape with the draw. An interesting footnote to the tie was demonstrated in the replay the following Wednesday. Johnny Wigham had initially announced he would be unavailable due to his teaching duties, but his headmaster granted a special dispensation to enable him to play. This clearly demonstrated that Johnny Wigham placed the interests of his pupils above his football commitments.

The signing of Sam English, an international, provided Wigham with another effective partner and their goals helped 'Pools to a top-six finish in the 1936–37 season. He continued to score goals in the final two seasons prior to the war despite the departure of English, and the cessation of the League programme brought his fine career with the club to a close.

Johnny Wigham died at the tragically young age of 49 years old in February 1959 at his home near to Hebburn School, where he taught English. Such was his impact in the seasons preceding World War Two that Arthur Appleton, the highly respected football writer, dubbed him 'The Shack of the Third Division' after the great Sunderland and England player, Len Shackleton.

## WILDON, Leslie Eric

**(1948–55)**

Centre-forward, 5ft 10in, 11st 5lb
Born: Middlesbrough, 5 April 1924
Died: Middlesbrough, 6 September 1998
Signed from: Price's Taylors (Middlesbrough), 1 December 1947, amateur
Transferred: Stockton, 1 August 1955, free transfer
Career: Price's Taylors, Hartlepools United, Stockton
Debut: v Wrexham, 27 March 1948
Appearances: League: 200 apps, 87 gls; FA Cup: 15 apps, 2 gls; Total: 215 apps, 89 gls

Middlesbrough-born Eric Wildon turned out to be another of Fred Westgarth's shrewd signings when he joined 'Pools from local amateur side Price's Taylors in December 1947, having declined to join his home-town club. After a single appearance in the 1947–48 season he started to make his mark towards the end of the following campaign, playing in the final six games at the expense of Jimmy Sloan. He partnered Les Owens throughout the 1949–50 season when 'Pools found goals difficult to come by, as was evidenced by an 18th-place finish.

Wildon came into his own during the 1950–51 season, scoring 26 goals in 44 League games, the first 'Pools player to top the 20-goal mark since Duncan Lindsay in 1934–35. His total included all four goals against Wrexham and hat-tricks against Barrow and Bradford Park Avenue in successive home games. Indeed, 20 of his League goals came before the New Year, a unique feat in 'Pools' history.

For the next three seasons Eric Wildon was a model of consistency as the club's leading goalscorer, the first player to achieve that feat in four consecutive campaigns, and only equalled since by Keith Houchen. The re-signing of Fred Richardson and the emergence of Ken Johnson restricted his appearances in the 1954–55 campaign, although he still managed five goals in 12 games in what turned out to be his final season.

Given his record of consistency it is perhaps surprising that he was not given the opportunity to play at a higher level. It was to 'Pools' benefit that he remained a 'one club man' and, after playing 200 League games, scoring 87 goals, he returned to amateur football with North Eastern League side Stockton.

Eric Wildon, a time-served electrician who practised his trade after retiring, died at his home in Middlesbrough in September 1998, aged 74 years.

## WILLETTS, Joseph

**(1946–56)**

Right-back, 5ft 7in, 10st 7lb
Born: Shotton, 12 July 1924
Died: Durham, 17 July 1980
Signed from: Newcastle United, 1 September 1943, Amateur
Transferred: Horden Colliery Welfare, 1 August 1956, free transfer
Career: Newcastle United (amateur), Hartlepools United, Horden Colliery Welfare
Debut: v Carlisle United, 26 October 1946
Appearances: League: 239 apps, 20 gls; FA Cup: 19 apps, 2 gls; Total: 258 apps, 22 gls

Joe Willetts became one of Fred Westgarth's first signings in September 1943, joining 'Pools as an amateur from Newcastle United, for whom he played a single wartime game. He made 20 appearances in wartime games before his full debut in October 1946 following the resumption of the Football League programme. After making three appearances in his debut season he played only a single game in the next two campaigns due to the demands of National Service, before establishing himself during the 1949–50 season.

Joe Willetts made the right-back position his own the following season, missing only two games and then setting new standards for consistency by being ever-present in each of the next three seasons. This period included a record run of 184 consecutive League appearances. As well as being an ultra-reliable defender, Willetts was also an expert penalty taker, scoring a hat-trick of spot-kicks in a 6–1 defeat of Darlington in March 1951 and equalling Jack Proctor's record in 1951–52 of scoring seven times from the penalty spot in a League season.

The signing of Jock Cameron provided stiff competition for the right-back berth throughout the exciting 1954–55 season, with Willetts deputising for the injured Ray Thompson when required. He appeared in only three League games in his final season, 1955–56, having made 258 appearances for his only club, scoring 22 goals, all penalties. He later played for Horden Colliery Welfare in the North Eastern League and worked in the licensed trade.

Joe Willetts died on 17 July 1980 in Durham, aged 56 years.

## WILLIAMS, Anthony Simon

**(2000–04)**

Goalkeeper, 6ft 1in, 12st 3lb
Born: Maesteg, 20 September 1977
Signed from: Blackburn Rovers, 7 July 2000, free transfer
Transferred: Grimsby Town, 21 July 2004, free transfer
Career: Blackburn Rovers, Queen's Park Rangers (loan), Macclesfield Town (loan), Huddersfield Town (loan), Bristol Rovers (loan), Gillingham (loan), Macclesfield Town (loan), Hartlepool United, Swansea City (loan), Stockport County (loan), Grimsby Town, Carlisle United, Bury (loan), Wrexham, Neath

Debut: v Blackpool, 9 September 2000
Appearances: League: 131 apps, 0 gls; Play-off: 4 apps, 0 gls; FA Cup: 4 apps, 0 gls; FL Cup: 1 app, 0 gls; Other: 5 apps, 0 gls. Total: 145 apps, 0 gls

Chris Turner, a former goalkeeper, obviously saw talents in Anthony Williams that others could not when he signed him from Blackburn Rovers in July 2000. Williams, a Welsh Youth and Under-21 international, had spent six loan spells with five different League clubs since signing for Blackburn Rovers as a youth trainee in July 1996. The fact that he had played a mere 26 League games in that period did not deter Turner from signing him.

He made his debut in the sixth League game of the 2000–01 season, replacing Martin Hollund, and kept his place for the remainder of the campaign, playing 44 consecutive games including the Play-off semi-final against Blackpool. A similar pattern was set the following season, 2001–02, when after Hollund played the early League and Cup games, Williams reclaimed the goalkeeper's jersey to complete 46 consecutive appearances including another Play-off semi-final, this time against Cheltenham Town.

He was at his peak during the 2002–03 promotion campaign, playing in every League game and keeping 16 clean sheets as 'Pools put their Play-off disappointments behind them to finish runners-up to Rushden & Diamonds. The arrival of Neale Cooper saw him dropped after the opening game of the 2003–04 season in favour of Jim Provett and he played only one more game for 'Pools before spending a spell on loan at Stockport County, for whom he made 15 League appearances.

Williams was released by Hartlepool United at the end of the season and joined League Two Grimsby Town, playing in every League game during the 2004–05 season. He then moved to Carlisle United, making 11 appearances before a brief loan spell with Bury preceded a return to the Principality with struggling Wrexham. This signalled the end of his League career, with 14 clubs and a total of 241 appearances, of which over half were with Hartlepool United.

In July 2009 Anthony Williams signed for Welsh Premier League club Neath, managed by former Liverpool and Wales legend Dean Saunders.

## WILLIAMS, Eifion Wyn

**(2002–07)**

Centre/wing-forward, 5ft 11in, 11st 2lb
Born: Bangor, 15 November 1975
Signed from: Torquay United, 6 March 2002, £25,000
Transferred: Wrexham, 10 July 2007, free transfer
Career: Wolverhampton Wanderers (trainee), Caernarfon Town, Barry Town, Torquay United, Hartlepool United, Wrexham

Debut: v Bristol Rovers, 9 March 2002
Appearances: League: 175+33 apps, 50 gls; Play-off: 6+1 apps, 2 gls; FA Cup: 10+3 apps, 1 gl; FL Cup: 4+2 apps, 2 gls; Other: 4+1 apps, 1 gl. Total: 199+40 apps, 56 gls

Eifion Williams joined Wolverhampton Wanderers as an apprentice, returning to his North Wales home without making an appearance and joining Caernarfon Town while still a teenager. After two seasons, making 75 appearances and scoring 63 goals, he joined Barry Town for a £25,000 transfer fee, playing in the Champions League and scoring against Dynamo Kiev. He averaged better than a goal a game for Barry (68 in 59 games) and finally earned the move he coveted to the Football League when Torquay United broke their transfer record with a £70,000 fee in March 1999. At the time this move appeared a stepping stone to greater things, but a record of 24 goals in 107 League games stalled his career.

In March 2002 Chris Turner stepped in to pay Torquay United £25,000 for his services, a move which turned out to be one of the best signings in Hartlepool United's recent history. Williams, a Wales B and Under-21 international, who scored a hat-trick for Torquay on his debut against 'Pools in 1999, was an instant success at Victoria Park, scoring a brace of goals on his first full appearance against Oxford United.

Life at the Vic was never dull during his time with the club. In his first full season, 2002–03, he was a key member of the team which gained promotion, top-scoring with 15 goals in 45 League appearances. The following season saw him leading the attack with equal consistency before the emergence of Adam Boyd resulted in him playing a more supportive role. He continued to be a key member of the side despite a decline

in his goals output, scoring a memorable goal in the Play-off Final against Sheffield Wednesday. He was on the verge of becoming only 'Pools' second full international when he withdrew from the Welsh squad due to an injury sustained in the Play-off Final.

Following the surprise relegation in 2005–06, Eifion Williams made a major contribution to the promotion of the following season. The highlight of his 'Pools career was a truly memorable goal in the 3–0 demolition of Darlington which won him the Prince's Trust North East Football Award for the goal of the season, chosen by Alan Shearer.

Despite these successes he was released, surprisingly in the eyes of many fans, by Danny Wilson at the end of the season and he returned to his homeland with Wrexham on a two-year deal. He made a mere seven starts for the struggling Welshmen, scoring a single goal before retiring due to injuries in March 2008 as Wrexham finished bottom of League Two and were relegated to the Blue Square Premier League.

## WRIGHT, George Clifford

**(1964–70)**

Inside-forward, 5ft 8in, 10st 12lb
Born: Lingdale, 18 October 1944
Signed from: Middlesbrough, 1 June 1964, free transfer
Transferred: Darlington, 26 February 1970, free transfer
Career: Middlesbrough (apprentice), Hartlepools United, Darlington, Boston United
Debut: v Lincoln City, 22 August 1964
Appearances: League: 178+6 apps, 31 gls; FA Cup: 8 apps, 2 gls; FL Cup: 8+1 apps, 1 gl; Total: 194+7 apps, 34 gls

Cliff Wright was signed by Alvan Williams in the summer of 1964 from Middlesbrough, with whom he began his career. He joined the Teesside club as an apprentice in October 1962 and was released less than two years later without playing a first-team game.

Williams immediately recognised Cliff Wright's potential by handing him his League debut in the opening game of the

1964–65 season while still a teenager. A skilful, ball playing inside-forward, he played 27 League games in his debut season, scoring four goals. The following season saw Geoff Twentyman initially leave him out of the team before the arrival of Brian Clough restored Wright to the starting 11. The player rewarded his new manager by scoring during Clough's first game in charge of Hartlepools. After that he was ever present for the remainder of the League campaign, scoring 11 goals in 39 League appearances. The 1966–67 season saw Clough mould together a squad which was capable of challenging for promotion, with Cliff Wright an integral part, playing in both the inside and wing forward positions. A consistent performer, he missed only eight League games, mainly towards the end of the season.

The arrival of Gus McLean for what turned out to be a promotion season saw Wright initially played on the right wing before losing his place to John McGovern. The departure of Albert Broadbent saw him restored to inside-forward and he was a key member of the team which had a 16-game unbeaten run to the end of the season.

Cliff Wright, along with other members of the promotion squad, found life difficult in the Third Division the following season due to a chronic lack of investment by the directors. The side struggled all season to score goals, as can be seen from Wright's solitary League goal in 30 games. After the inevitable relegation he played a further 21 League games before joining neighbours Darlington in February 1970, playing a mere 16 games for the Quakers.

He finished his playing career in the Northern Premier League with Boston United managed by Jim 'Bald Eagle' Smith of Oxford and Newcastle fame. After playing 89 games, scoring 10 goals, Cliff Wright was forced to retire at the end of the 1973–74 season due to hamstring injuries.

## YOUNG, Ronald

**(1968–73)**
Wing forward, 5ft 8in, 10st 10lb
Born: Dunston-on-Tyne, 31 August 1945
Signed from: Hull City, 1 September 1968, £4,000
Transferred: South Shields, 1 August 1973, free transfer
Career: Hull City, Hartlepool, South Shields, Bishop Auckland, Blyth Spartans, North Shields
Debut: v Watford, 16 September 1968
Appearances: League: 177+9 apps, 40 gls; FA Cup: 7+1 apps, 3 gls; FL Cup: 5 apps, 3 gls; Total: 189+10 apps, 46 gls

Gus McLean signed Ron Young from his former club Hull City in September 1968 for a £4,000 fee to add craft and guile to an attack which was already struggling in the Third Division following promotion the previous season.

Young began his professional career with Hull City in August 1963 and went on to make 26 League appearances over the next five seasons, scoring five goals. He made an immediate impact by scoring in 'Pools' first win of the season, 2–1 against Watford, also scoring in their next win, which unfortunately only came at the 14th attempt. In all he played in 39 League games, scoring seven times in this most difficult of seasons. Only Bell and Blowman scored more League goals and neither reached double figures as 'Pools made a swift return to the Fourth Division.

Young's second season, 1969–70, saw a continuation of the previous season's form with 37 appearances and nine goals, predominately from wing positions. Only Terry Bell scored more in what ultimately

proved to be another re-election campaign. The arrival of Len Ashurst following the departures of McLean and Simpson saw even greater emphasis on defence, with Young now required, more than ever, to contribute goals. He was in his prime throughout the 1971–72 campaign, playing in every League game and scoring 18 times. This achievement can be put into perspective when compared to Willie Waddle, who managed a mere seven goals. The following campaign saw Young's appearances restricted due to the emergence of Bobby Veart and Mike Spelman and he was given a free transfer at the end of the season.

After being released by Len Ashurst, Ron Young joined Northern Premier League side South Shields and later played for Bishop Auckland, Blyth Spartans and North Shields before finally finishing his football career at Chester-Le-Street Town in his 50th year.

# The Managers

## Alfred Ernest Priest

*Born: South Bank, 24 July 1875. Died: West Hartlepool, 5 May 1922*

**1 August 1908 to 31 May 1912**

Fred Priest was an ideal choice as Hartlepools United's first manager as he had a genuine pedigree as a footballer and hailed from the local area, so he had an affiliation with the North East and its rapidly expanding football scene.

Born in South Bank, Priest played for his local club in the Northern League before signing for Sheffield United in 1896, where he was to make his name. He initially played outside-left for the Blades, before moving to inside-forward on the arrival of Herbert Lipsham. Together they formed a formidable partnership and won both Championship and FA Cup honours with the Sheffield club. Priest won an England cap in 1900 against Ireland and in 1901–02 finished joint top scorer in the Football League. His sterling service was rewarded with a benefit match in 1903 and he left Sheffield in 1906 having played over 200 games, scoring 71 goals. After a brief spell back at South Bank, Priest joined Middlesbrough to resume his Football League career as well as fulfilling the role of assistant trainer.

Fred Priest was appointed player-manager of newly-formed Hartlepools United in August 1908 on a weekly wage of £2 10s and was responsible for signing the club's first squad of players. He included himself in the early games, ironically at right-back, the opposite to the position in which he excelled. Priest managed the club for the first four seasons of its existence, during which he established 'Pools as a force to be reckoned with in the North Eastern League, finishing in the top four positions on three occasions. The club also twice won the Durham Senior Cup during his stewardship.

On retiring from the game he became licensee of the Market Hotel on the Hartlepool Headland, and it was on these premises that he died after a short illness on 5 May 1922 at the relatively early age of 46 years old. Sheffield United, Middlesbrough and South Bank football clubs, among others, sent representatives to his funeral service in the New Cemetery, Hartlepool, along with floral tributes from the clubs and organisations he had been associated with throughout his life. In October 1922 Sheffield United sent a full-strength side to play a benefit match to raise funds for his widow and family.

## Percy Humphreys

*Born: Cambridge, 3 December 1880. Died: London, 13 April 1959*
**1 August 1912 to 31 May 1913**

Percy Humphreys succeeded Fred Priest in June 1912 as player-manager, having had a highly successful playing career which began with local side Cambridge St Mary's before signing for Queen's Park Rangers of the Southern League. His first Football League club was Notts County, for whom he played 189 League games and scored 66 goals, form which saw him win an England cap against Scotland at Bramall Lane in 1903. He also played for the Football League against the Scottish League. Humphreys went on to play for Leicester Fosse (twice), Chelsea and Tottenham Hotspur, for whom he made a major contribution during their relegation-threatened season of 1909–10, scoring 13 goals in 20 games.

Prior to joining Hartlepools he was in a second spell with Leicester Fosse, and although primarily a centre-forward, he was able to fulfil defensive duties when required. Humphreys was in the veteran stage when he arrived at the Victoria Ground on a one-year contract for the 1912–13 season, and the legacy of knee injuries sustained throughout his career limited his appearances. Despite such handicaps he still managed 15 goals in 32 League and Cup appearances, of which the majority were at centre-forward in a season which saw his team finish a modest 12th in the North Eastern League.

Humphreys was offered another one-year contract but was unable to agree financial terms and left Hartlepools to become one of the first English coaches to work in Europe when employed in that role by FC Basel, their first such appointment. Despite signing a three-year contract with the Swiss side he was forced to return to

England at the outbreak of World War One. On his return to England he signed for Norwich City, then a Southern League side, to play a handful of games. With the ending of the war he returned to Europe to coach in Italy and Switzerland during the 1920s, and when his football days were over he returned to England and worked in the motor industry.

Percy Humphreys died in London from injuries sustained in a fall in April 1959 aged 78 years.

## John (Jack) Manners

*Born: Morpeth, 4 May 1880. Died: West Hartlepool, 2 May 1946*
**3 June 1913 to 1 May 1920 and 25 October 1925 to 31 July 1927**

Jack Manners began his long football career with Morpeth YMCA, whom he captained to the East Northumberland League title in 1898, and he later played for Morpeth Harriers, with whom he demonstrated his versatility by once playing in goal and saving a penalty. His footballing prowess

attracted the attention of a number of clubs, including Bury, a major force during this period, but he turned them down to join West Bromwich Albion for a £50 fee in May 1904 and so began his long association with the Baggies.

Manners made his League debut the following September at centre-half and spent all his professional career with the Midland club, playing 208 games and scoring seven goals, and he was a member of the team which won the Second Division title in the 1910–11 season, retiring as a player at the end of the following season. A very popular character, he had total faith in his own abilities, even laying bets with his teammates that he could score in a Boxing Day game against Barnsley. He did indeed score in the game – an own goal – and no record exists to confirm if he won the bet!

Jack Manners joined Hartlepools United in succession to Percy Humphreys as player-manager for the 1913–14 season and gave quality displays throughout the season in the dual role, making 31 appearances in League and Cup games. His tenure of office was interrupted by World War One, and although he was 42 years old he managed one appearance during the 1919–20 season following the resumption of League football. He 'retired' at the end of that season in order to scout for Midlands clubs, only to return to manage Hartlepools, now a Football League side, for a second time in June 1924.

Succeeding David Gordon, who left after a poor start to the 1925–26 season, Manners' second spell was an initial success with a top-six League position. However, the economic realities of the times were reflected in support for the club, and after another season of declining attendances he left the club as an 'economy measure'.

Jack Manners stayed in the Hartlepools area after his departure from football management, continuing to scout for his old club West Bromwich Albion, for whom he was instrumental in their signing of Billy 'Ginger' Richardson in 1929. A prominent crown green bowler locally, Manners represented the Town Bowls Club on numerous occasions. He died in May 1946 in Camerons Hospital after failing to recover from injuries sustained falling from a ladder two days before his 66th birthday. Wreaths from both Hartlepools United and West Bromwich Albion were sent to his funeral.

## Cecil Bertram Potter

*Born: West Hoathly, 14 November 1888.*
*Died: Sutton, Surrey, 17 October 1975*
**1 May 1920 to 1 July 1922**

Sussex-born Cecil (Cec) Potter began his footballing career in East Anglia with local team Melton before signing for Ipswich Town, then in the Southern Amateur League. Anxious to pursue a career in professional football, Potter requested a trial with Norwich City, then in the

Southern League, and impressed sufficiently to be signed for the 1911–12 season. In all competitions he played 133 games for the Canaries, scoring 33 goals.

The advent of World War One interrupted his career and he played for the 17th Footballers' Battalion Middlesex Regiment and Tottenham Hotspur while a sergeant in the Royal Flying Corps. At the cessation of the conflict he finally achieved his ambition of playing in the Football League when he signed for Hull City, then in Division Two, for the 1919–20 season. He only managed 10 games for the Humberside club before successfully applying to become the player-manager at the Victoria Ground, in succession to Jack Manners, at the youthful age of 31 years old.

Potter's appointment in May 1920 meant he would be in charge of the club's final season in the North Eastern League. As well as playing on several occasions himself, usually at half-back, he used a further 39 players in finishing in eighth position. His playing career effectively ended at West Stanley in January 1921 when he sustained a bad ankle injury. Despite attendances regularly exceeding 5,000 and a record 10-game FA Cup run, the result of which was a very healthy financial position, the directors took the perverse decision in March to effectively 'demote' Potter to secretary-manager on a greatly reduced salary.

Cecil Potter's retained list for Hartlepools United's debut season in the Football League contained few surprises and there was general approval that he had managed to persuade the talented Scottish amateur Lauchlan Henderson to join the professional ranks. Apart from winning their first game at Wrexham, the early part of the season produced mixed results. 'Pools then hit a purple patch over the Christmas and New Year period with nine wins in 12 games before further inconsistency in the closing stages of the season resulted in a highly creditable final position of fourth. Potter used 34 players during the campaign and even played in a solitary game himself, an FA Cup qualifying tie against Stalybridge Celtic. In the close season he took virtually a full-strength squad on a five-match tour of Spain, playing RC Santander (three games) and Oviedo (two games), of which four were won. Potter even played for Santander in one of the games.

Still smarting over the disgraceful treatment of his salary during the most important season in Hartlepools United's history to date, he became actively engaged in securing another managerial position which carried more attractive financial rewards.

Potter found the financial security he craved with Derby County, then in Division Two, when he won the directors' vote to succeed the long-serving Jimmy Methven, from a lengthy list of candidates.

Potter's inability to secure promotion to the top tier of English football led to him being replaced by George Jobey, and after a sojourn as a dairy farmer in Sussex he surprisingly reached the pinnacle of his managerial career when he was appointed manager of Huddersfield Town. He succeeded the legendary Herbert Chapman, who had joined Arsenal, for the 1925–26 season on a reported salary of £600, which took into account his secretarial duties.

Cec Potter inherited a team of immense talent which had won the First Division Championship in the previous two campaigns in fine style and had been strengthened by Chapman during the close season. Huddersfield duly completed a hat-trick of League Championships by adapting to the new offside law quicker than most and finishing five points (two for a win) clear of Chapman's Arsenal. It was a major surprise to the football world when Potter resigned his position in August 1926 citing 'his failing health and that of his family'.

He was tempted back into management by his former club Norwich City in November 1926. Then a Division Three South club, Potter was unable to lift them from the lower reaches of that League, his best finish being a modest 16th place. He left the Canaries in January 1929 following a humiliating 5–0 home defeat in an FA Cup third-round tie by the renowned amateur side, Corinthians.

Cecil Potter died at Sutton in Surrey on 17 October 1975 in his 87th year.

## David (Davy) Smith Gordon

*Born: Leith, Edinburgh, 29 December 1882.*
*Died: Leith, Edinburgh 1958*
**31 July 1922 to 25 October 1925**

Davy Gordon was appointed manager a month after the departure of Cecil Potter.

His was a low-profile appointment based on expediency as Gordon had never managed a Football League club, having previously been secretary-manager of Scottish side Hibernian for three years.

Gordon, a half-back, had a distinguished playing career with Hull City, for whom he made 275 League appearances, scoring 17 goals before World War One. This made him Hull's premier player in terms of appearances at the time. He returned to his home-town club, Leith Athletic, in 1914 and was appointed to his dual role at Hibernian in 1919.

The new manager's first task was to arrange the transfer of the popular Harry Thoms to Derby County, Potter's new club, and he was to be quickly followed by Tom Crilly. Despite such high-profile departures Gordon relied in the main on the players who had led the club into the Football League. The 1922–23 season was notable for two things: a chronic shortage of goals and an away campaign that failed to bring a single victory, yet on their day Norman's side was a match for anyone, as a 5–1 defeat of the eventual Champions Nelson showed. In all Gordon used 31 players in his first season, with only

Tommy Yews playing over 30 games. A lowly finish of 15th meant the manager had much work to do for the following season.

At the start of the 1923–24 season Gordon released several players and recruited, among others, George Keenlyside from South Shields and an Egyptian, Tewfik Abdullah, from Derby County, thereby maintaining the links with Cecil Potter. Despite winning their opening two games, 'Pools struggled in the League, and a five-match run in the autumn failed to produce a single goal. Some relief was provided by the FA Cup with St Peter's Albion being dispatched 10–1, Billy Smith scoring seven times. League results got worse in the New Year and an eight-game run without a win either side of the Easter period consigned 'Pools to 21st place, only goal difference keeping them off the bottom above Barrow. This required the club to apply for re-election, which was a formality in the early years of the expanded Football League.

All the early optimism engendered by election to the Football League had evaporated by the start of Gordon's third season in charge and he was left to ring the changes in the hope his team would find some form. Bobby Best arrived from Sunderland, Cowell replaced Summerfield in goal, and Wensley ousted Billy Smith at centre-forward. Another disappointing League campaign, 'Pools eventually finishing 20th, was relieved by a run in the FA Cup, which saw the team play in the first round proper for the first time, against the holders Newcastle United at St James' Park. In front of over 36,000 spectators Gordon's team reportedly gave a good account of themselves, despite the 4–1 scoreline.

A disastrous six-goal defeat at Rochdale on the opening day of the 1925–26 season signalled the end for David Gordon and, after another hammering, this time at Nelson, he was relieved of his duties with Jack Manners taking over for a second time. Gordon later returned to his Scottish roots and became secretary-manager of local club Edinburgh St Bernard's into the 1930s.

David Gordon died at his home in Leith, Edinburgh, in 1958 aged 75 years.

## William (Bill) Lewis Norman

*Born: Gazeley, Suffolk, 1 June 1873. Died: West Hartlepool, 16 September 1931*

**1 August 1927 to 16 September 1931**

Born into a single-parent family, Bill Norman joined the Border Regiment as a youth and spent seven years in the Army as a reservist. During this time he excelled as an athlete, winning the Army mile and three-mile championships, and later served for three years in the Boer War, leaving with the rank of sergeant-major. Such experiences were to stand him in good stead in his future career in football.

Bill Norman, despite not having any experience as a professional player, seemed the ideal candidate to succeed Jack Manners in the summer of 1927 after gaining the vote of the Hartlepools board over George Fraser, who had managerial experience with Grimsby Town and Lincoln City. Prior to World War One Norman was trainer at Birmingham City and Barnsley and it was with the latter that he enjoyed an FA Cup triumph in 1912, the only occasion on which the Oakwell club has lifted the famous trophy.

The new manager joined Hartlepools from Leeds United, where he had spent four years as trainer to Arthur Fairclough, during which time the Elland Road club won promotion to the First Division. Prior to his spell with Leeds, Norman became the first full-time manager of Blackpool, whom he joined on the resumption of League football following World War One.

The Lancashire club were in the process of major ground improvements and the directors hoped the new manager would quickly achieve promotion to the top tier of English football. Norman's first two seasons at Bloomfield Road saw his side finish in the top four twice, along with a Central League Championship success for the reserve side. He also established a reputation for discovering goalscoring centre-forwards with the signing of Harry Bedford from Nottingham Forest. Bedford went on to score 118 goals in 180 games for the Tangerines and became the club's first player to be capped by England. However, after a decline in 1921–22 to 19th position, followed by the disappointment of another failed promotion campaign, Bill Norman left Blackpool to be succeeded by Major Frank Buckley, who later enjoyed success with Wolverhampton Wanderers.

A local reporter, on meeting the new manager, described Norman, who had a reputation as a disciplinarian and was nicknamed 'sergeant-major', as a 'cheerful personality'. He arrived at the Victoria Ground impeccably dressed with a managerial style based on training and fitness, in which he was assisted by his stepson, Alan Ure. His approach could be best summed up by a story about the players complaining about it being too cold to train. Their manager's characteristic response was to strip naked and roll in the snow! Passers-by claimed they could often hear his barrack-room style commands echoing around the Victoria Ground during training sessions.

His first season, 1927–28, saw Billy Robinson, who had previously failed to impress, set a new club record with 28 goals in 33 League games. Following Robinson's transfer to Bradford Park Avenue, Norman then discovered another legendary centre-forward in W.G. 'Ginger' Richardson, who contributed 19 goals in his 29 appearances for the club before being transferred to West Bromwich Albion. At the Hawthorns Richardson enjoyed great success, setting a club record, which still stands, of 39 goals in the 1935–36 season and also winning an FA Cup-winners' medal and an England cap.

Richardson's transfer paved the way for Albert Pape, who scored 21 goals in his debut season, 1929–30, and the manager later gave debuts to Josh Hewitt and Johnny Wigham, the latter going on to set a club career record through to World War Two. In total his success in the transfer market benefited the club by over £7,000 during his tenure as manager.

The onset of a serious illness during the 1931 close season resulted in Bill Norman being unable to perform his usual managerial duties, a development which was recognised by the club's directors. The board, conscious of the need to prepare for the coming campaign, took the sensible step of signing Jackie Carr from Blackpool as player-coach. Despite his health problems the manager continued to maintain a keen interest in team affairs right up to the week of his demise.

On 16 September 1931 Bill Norman passed away in Howbeck Hospital, West Hartlepool, aged 58 years, leaving a wife and three sons. His funeral was attended by representatives from the Football League and North Eastern League with floral tributes from every club he had been associated with. Arthur Fairclough, his manager at Barnsley and Leeds United, also attended along with the Hartlepools United directors and players, six of whom (Mason, Thornton, Bowron, Buller, Thayne and Thompson) acted as his bearers.

## John (Jacky) Carr

*Born: South Bank, 26 November 1892. Died: 10 May 1942*

**21 April 1932 to 1 April 1935**

Jacky Carr was born into a footballing family of four brothers, in which he became by far the most famous. A teetotaller and non-smoker throughout his life, he began his distinguished career, initially as an amateur, with his local club South Bank, for whom he appeared in the 1910 FA Amateur Cup Final. He signed professional forms with Middlesbrough the following January and it was with the Ayresome Park club that he made his name as a skilled provider of goals from either outside or inside-right positions, playing a key role in the 1927 and 1929 Second Division Championship-winning sides. This form brought him England recognition in both positions, along with Football League honours, and after three decades with the Ayresome Park club he was released. After spending a season with Blackpool he joined Hartlepools as player-coach in August 1931.

In his role as player-coach the 39-year-old Jacky Carr made 10 appearances, scoring one goal, before being appointed acting manager following Bill Norman's death. He was confirmed as manager towards the end of the 1931–32 season following a string of impressive results which saw the emergence of several talented young players. The directors, conscious of past problems with managers' contracts, set Carr's on a fixed salary basis with no provision for a bonus as a percentage of transfer fees, as was increasingly becoming the norm throughout the game.

As part of Carr's team rebuilding for the following season he signed former Everton and Darlington defender Jack O'Donnell to shore up 'Pools' leaky defence. Despite O'Donnell's presence a club record 116 League goals were conceded, with 87 coming in away games. Given the goals against total, a 14th-place League finish could be considered something of an achievement and was primarily due to the scoring feats of Hewitt, Wigham and Pedwell, who contributed 53 League goals.

The next two seasons also resulted in mid-table finishes as Carr tried to solve the defensive problems with the signings of Ossie Park from Newcastle United and Jack Proctor from New Delavel, both experienced players. Such results would normally have satisfied the directors had the club's finances not been in such a dire state, with an accumulated deficit of £6,562 and gate receipts nearly £1,000 down on the previous season.

These financial circumstances forced the board to make hard economic decisions and Jacky Carr left the Victoria Ground as 'an economy measure' in the close season of 1935 to manage Tranmere Rovers. After 18 months with the Merseyside club he returned to his native North East with local rivals Darlington, whom he continued to manage with limited success until his untimely death at the age of 49 years in May 1942.

## James (Jimmy) Hamilton

*Born: Hetton-le-Hole c.1904.*
*Died: Thornaby on Tees*
**1 July 1935 to 30 July 1940**

Jimmy Hamilton joined Hartlepools as a player at the start of the 1931–32 season from Crystal Palace, with whom he spent eight seasons, making 180 League appearances and scoring four goals.

Hamilton signed for Palace on being demobbed from the Army, having been based at Caterham Barracks. He began his career as an attacking centre-half, as was the norm before the change in the offside law. The introduction of three players (rather than two) between the goal and forward player required him to adapt to a more defensive role, which he did with great effect. His value to his team was demonstrated during the 1924–25 season when he sustained a serious eye injury which resulted in him missing the second half of the season, leading to Palace's relegation to the Third Division South. He subsequently made a complete recovery and continued to give Palace sterling service over the next five seasons before being released and joining Hartlepools United in May 1931.

Hamilton made 49 appearances, primarily at centre-half, over the next two seasons, which culminated in heavy defeats in his final games. He moved to Gateshead, officially as player-coach at the end of the 1932–33 season although he made only four League appearances for the Tyneside club. Following the departure of Jacky Carr, Hamilton returned to the Victoria Ground as manager for the start of the 1935–36 campaign.

A former soldier in the Coldstream Guards and Brigade heavyweight boxing champion, Hamilton valued fitness and discipline, which he instilled into his players. This initially brought success with top-10 finishes in his first two seasons and the added bonus in the 1935–36 season of a welcome run in the FA Cup when, after victories against Mansfield and Halifax, 'Pools were drawn at home against Grimsby Town of the First Division. This was the first occasion opponents from the top tier of English football played a competitive game at the Victoria Ground and intense local interest was evidenced by a crowd of over 15,000. They witnessed a hard-fought goalless draw with 'Pools matching their illustrious opponents before losing in the replay at Blundell Park.

The following close season Hamilton achieved one of Hartlepools' greatest-ever signings when he persuaded Sam English, an Irish international of Glasgow Rangers and Liverpool fame, to join the club. These seasons proved to be the highpoint of Hamilton's reign, as re-election was required in 1937–38, despite the signing of new players including Welsh international winger Ernest Curtis, and again in 1938–39, a season which saw the introduction of 21 new faces.

The cancellation, after only three games, of the Football League programme for the 1939–40 season saw 'Pools play in the Regional League North-East Division, finishing in 10th place out of 11 clubs. Once the decision was taken by the directors not to continue with football at the Victoria Ground the next season, Hamilton was effectively out of a job and he left the club. Although never actively involved in professional football after this he continued to take an interest in the fortunes of his former club while running his sub post office and tobacconist business in Thornaby, Teesside.

## Frederick (Fred) Westgarth

*Born: Tow Law, Co. Durham, 1 July 1887.*
*Died: West Hartlepool, 4 February 1957*
**1 August 1943 to 1 February 1957**

Fred Westgarth's football career began as a centre-half with Kingston Villa, an amateur team that preceded the formation of South Shields Adelaide. A leg injury ended his playing days and he subsequently trained as a qualified masseur at South Shields FC, his first job in football.

From South Shields he moved to Stockport County in 1926 in a training role before joining Ebbw Vale as a coach. His nomadic footballing career then progressed to Workington, Luton Town and back to Stockport County in May 1934 for his first managerial post. At Edgeley Park he duly achieved promotion and took Stockport to the fifth round of the FA Cup for the first time in their history.

Westgarth left Stockport in September 1936, and after briefly working as a scout for Manchester United he joined Carlisle

United, a move that was not a success, and he resigned amid reports that he had problems motivating his players. Shortly after his departure from Carlisle in March 1938 Westgarth took over the hot seat at Bradford City, and it was with the Valley Parade club that he achieved his only success in football by winning the Division Three North Cup in 1939. Despite being unanimously offered a new contract by the directors he decided to join Hartlepools United and take on 'the hardest job in football'.

Fred Westgarth's tenure of office at the Victoria Ground was the longest by any manager before or since. He brought stability to the club in the immediate post-war era both on and off the field, and 'Pools were to enjoy a sustained period of relative success in both the Football League and the FA Cup. His policy, enforced by economic reality, of signing players on free transfers, often from lowly Scottish clubs, and introducing talented local players eventually yielded results far in excess of what reasonably could be expected.

After three seasons of wartime football in regional leagues, the 1946–47 season heralded the resumption of competitive football. It speaks volumes for the amount of team rebuilding that Fred Westgarth undertook for the start of the new season that only centre-forward Jack Price played for 'Pools before the war. Of the other 25 players who appeared that season, all were making their Football League debuts. This was a major factor as 'Pools struggled in the early games of the season and attendances were also affected by the dreadful winter. The season finished with 'Pools in 13th place, having averaged 7,556 at home games, a creditable figure given the harsh winter weather.

Following the initial post-war season, the next four campaigns saw relatively modest League finishes as the playing staff evolved. Despite this, attendances remained relatively healthy, with near 10,000 gates a feature. Westgarth's strategy of bringing on local talent supplemented by shrewd free transfer signings to form a settled side finally came to fruition during the 1954–55 season. Of the 19 players used, Moore was an ever present, and McGuigan top-scored with 18 goals, resulting in a final fifth position. The manager continued to build on the progress achieved the previous season by adding Billy Anderson, Joe Rayment and Billy Robinson to his staff for the 1955–56 campaign. The final position of fourth owed much to Johnson and Luke, who shared 40 League goals, as well as a settled team which saw 21 players used.

A feature of the seasons in the early to mid-1950s was the FA Cup, with 'Pools regularly playing teams from higher divisions, such as Burnley, Nottingham Forest and Chelsea. The fact that they consistently gave a good account of themselves encouraged supporters to look forward to the draw for the third round of the Cup with eager anticipation.

So to the 1956–57 season, during which 'Pools were to rewrite their record books. The season began with 10 wins in the first 12 games, with 38 goals scored by eight different players, which resulted in attendances regularly topping the 10,000 mark. A poor spell during October and November saw a run of eight games without a win in the League before the rot was stopped in the FA Cup with wins over non-League sides Selby Town and Blyth Spartans.

These wins put Westgarth's team into the draw for the third round once again. For the second successive season 'Pools drew the reigning League champions at home, this time Manchester United. It was one of life's cruel twists of fate that serious illness was to prevent Fred Westgarth from attending the biggest football match of his life. On being told the third-round draw was against Manchester United, his ironic comment was 'it's just what the doctor ordered!'

On the afternoon of the Manchester United game Fred Westgarth was at home ill confined to his bed. He had earlier received a visit from Tom Curry, the Manchester United trainer who had played for him at Stockport County. The club arranged for the score to be telephoned to his home every 15 minutes, and his feelings after 30 minutes' play with 'Pools three goals down can only be imagined. A stirring second-half fightback saw the scores level at 3–3 before Bill Whelan won the game for the visitors in the closing stages. At the end of the game Matt Busby telephoned to congratulate him on his team's performance, stating that 'I've never known such shocks, your boys had me really worried.'

Fred Westgarth died the following month with his team top of the Third Division North and crowds averaging over 9,000. He had been in charge for 510 games, winning 207, thereby maintaining his career record of more wins than losses at every club he managed. Not only Hartlepools United, but the whole of football lost a great character and his funeral saw virtually every major organisation in the town represented, as well as the football clubs with which he had been associated in his long career.

In the games following his death the loss at Derby County, the ultimate champions, was followed by only two wins in the next six fixtures, consigning 'Pools to the runners'-up position. Westgarth's legacy was the club's highest-ever League position and a record 90 goals scored. His son Ned continued to supervise team affairs through to the end of the season, pending the appointment of a new manager.

## Raymond (Ray) Middleton

*Born: Boldon Colliery, 6 September 1919.*
*Died: Boston, 12 April 1977*
**17 May 1957 to 20 November 1959**

Ray Middleton was appointed manager on 17 May 1957 at the age of 37 years in succession to Fred Westgarth. Born in Boldon Colliery, he played goalkeeper in the Sunderland Boys team which won the English Schools' Football Shield in 1933. After leaving school at the age of 14 years old he played in the Wearside League for Washington Colliery Welfare and North Shields before signing as a professional shortly after his 18th birthday for Chesterfield for a £50 fee, making his debut a year later.

Middleton went on to become a legend with the Saltergate club, appearing in over 500 games, half of which were wartime fixtures. During the conflict he also worked as a miner and reputedly insured his hands for £2,000! He continued with Chesterfield on the resumption of League football after the war, also looking to his future by investing in a grocer's shop in nearby New Whittingdon.

Following the Spireites' relegation in 1951, he was transferred to Derby County, then a First Division club, for a £10,000 transfer fee. Middleton experienced relegation again in his second season at the Baseball Ground and at the end of the 1953–54 campaign he was released. During his career his goalkeeping prowess was officially recognised with England B and FA representative honours, which included a tour of Italy in 1950.

Conscious that footballers, like everyone else, do not get any younger, Middleton, who as a Justice of the Peace had considered a career in politics, accepted the post of player-manager for Boston United. Here he made a reputation for talent spotting and his team, liberally sprinkled with players from his former club, enjoyed Cup success by reaching the third round of the FA Cup, thrashing, ironically, Derby County 6–1 at the Baseball Ground. Although they lost to Tottenham Hotspur in the next round, Middleton had enhanced his reputation and, despite interest from the former Newcastle United Cup-winning captain Joe Harvey, he was appointed manager in succession to Fred Westgarth. In his first interview with the *Hartlepool Mail* he made the ominous statement 'soccer is a young man's game'. From the outset the new manager made clear his intention to be actively involved in fitness and training sessions, a totally different approach to his predecessor.

Initially Middleton relied on the squad of players he inherited, which appeared a sound policy when five of the first six games were won. By December 'Pools were third in the League, before a poor run of results produced only three wins in the next 20 games. By Easter 'Pools fate looked consigned to the new Fourth Division; however, five points over the holiday period gave renewed hope of a top-half finish. The crunch came in the last match at home to the new champions, Scunthorpe United. A crowd of over 8,000 saw Scunthorpe win a narrow 2–1 victory. Hartlepools finished a lowly 17th in their final Division Three North season with 44 points, with much criticism aimed at Middleton for not qualifying for the new Third Division.

The following season, 1958–59, saw the absence of familiar names such as Jackie Newton, Tommy McGuigan and Frank Stamper as the manager reshaped the side in his image. Results continued to decline to 19th in the new Fourth Division, a mere two points above the re-election zone. It was a far cry from the narrow miss for promotion to the Second Division only two seasons before. The one highlight was the record 10–1 victory over Barrow in the spring of 1959, which went some way to ensuring 'safety' for another season.

Ray Middleton's unhappy reign as manager ended early the following season, 1959–60, when a poor start descended into disaster at the beginning of October with a 2–7 defeat by Watford, the forerunner to an 11-game run without a win. Middleton left shortly after the Watford debacle to be replaced by Bill Robinson, who was ultimately unable to prevent the inevitable re-election application, which only proved successful due to Gateshead's surprise rejection.

Ray Middleton later returned to Boston United for a second spell as manager in 1960 and remained with the club as secretary until his death in 1977 aged 56.

## William (Bill) Robinson

*Born: Whitburn, 4 April 1919. Died: Hartlepool, 7 October 1992*

**20 November 1959 to 30 June 1962**

Bill Robinson started his professional career with Sunderland in 1934 as a centre-forward at a period when the Wearside club were a major force, winning both the

League Championship and FA Cup. His opportunities were limited due to the brilliance of Bobby Gurney, himself later to manage Hartlepools, and after guesting for Fred Westgarth's side during the war years, he moved to Charlton Athletic in 1946 for a fee of £1,000.

Robinson was a member of the Charlton side which defeated Burnley to win the FA Cup in 1947 on the very day he became a father with the birth of his only child. He moved to West Ham United two years later for a sizeable £6,000 transfer fee, making 101 League appearances and scoring a highly creditable 60 goals. He later became assistant manager to Ted Fenton at Upton Park and left to join Hartlepools United with his East London side top of the First Division.

It is reasonable to assume that Bill Robinson, an experienced football man both as a player and manager, understood the situation at the Victoria Ground in terms of playing staff and finances. The fact he was inheriting a team in serious decline from their 1950s heyday with no money or resources to improve matters in the short term and declining attendances does not seem to have dissuaded him from accepting the 'hardest job in football'.

Nevertheless, the only thing that could be said about Robinson's tenure as 'Pools manager was his consistency, however dire. In each of his three seasons in charge the team conceded over 100 goals and never rose above second bottom of the Fourth Division. In his second season, 1960–61, 'Pools went 12 League games without a win, only to better that sequence the following season with 13. They only survived as a Football League club due to the demise of Accrington Stanley and even endured their record defeat, 10–1 to Wrexham, despite a public statement by the manager only days before the game that re-election could be avoided!

Robinson relied on veteran players such as George Lackenby, Derek Wilkie and Ray Bilcliff while ignoring the young talent in the club, with the inevitable result that several promising players failed to establish themselves during his period in office. This situation led predictably to the manager being relieved of his duties by the directors at the end of the season. Subsequent revelations in the national press regarding match fixing had a devastating effect on Robinson and he was never involved in football management again, working as a personnel officer for Richardsons & Westgarth until the firm's closure in 1981.

Bill Robinson's parting shot on leaving the Vic was 'things cannot get any worse'! He died suddenly of a heart attack at his Hartlepool home in 1992 aged 73.

## Allenby Chilton

*Born: South Hylton, 16 September 1918.*
*Died: Southwick, 15 June 1996*
**1 July 1962 to 1 April 1963**

Allenby Chilton was a talented schoolboy footballer who played in the Sunderland side which won the England Schools'

Shield in 1933. On leaving school he played for Seaham Colliery before joining Liverpool as an amateur in the summer of 1938, later transferring to Manchester United in November that year. He made his League debut the following season the day before the outbreak of World War Two, against Charlton Athletic on 2 September 1939.

During the war years he served in the Durham Light Infantry and sustained wounds during the D-Day landings in Normandy. As was the practice at the time Chilton 'guested' for several clubs during the war years, including making 13 appearances for Hartlepools United and also playing for Charlton Athletic in their 1944 League South Cup Final triumph at Wembley.

His professional career with Manchester United resumed in 1946 and he went on to play 390 games, 166 of them consecutive, for the Old Trafford side, winning both Championship and FA Cup-winners' medals as well as two England caps and a place in the 1954 World Cup squad in Switzerland.

Matt Busby appointed Chilton to succeed Johnny Carey as captain of Manchester United and he was ever present in his penultimate season before losing his place to Mark Jones, a key member of the Busby Babes side. On leaving Old Trafford on a free transfer he became player-manager of Grimsby Town, leading them to the Division Three North title in 1956, and he later managed Wigan Athletic, then a non-League side.

Chilton seemed perfectly qualified when he was appointed as 'Pools manager in July 1962, having scouted for the club the previous season. The task of lifting the team away from the bottom of the League was to prove beyond even a man with his impeccable credentials. The club was stuck in a rut, without the players or means to

rise above it, and his tenure was to last a mere 34 games, during which only five games were won. From the beginning of December through to mid-April, 'Pools failed to win in 18 consecutive games, although Chilton had already left the club by the end of this depressing sequence.

Allenby Chilton worked in the steel industry in his later years and died in 1996 aged 77.

## Robert (Bobby) Gurney

*Born: Silksworth, 13 October 1907. Died: Sunderland, 21 April 1994*

**6 April 1963 to 6 January 1964**

Bobby Gurney joined Hartlepools United as manager in the spring of 1963 after a five-year absence from Football League management, having previously had a two-year spell at Peterborough United before returning to the North East to occupy the hot seat at neighbours Darlington from 1952 to 1957. For the three years prior to joining 'Pools he managed North Eastern League side Horden Colliery Welfare, while also working as a salesman for a local confectionery firm.

Gurney was a legend in north-east football, having played a prominent part in Sunderland's League and Cup triumphs in the 1930s, becoming the Wearside club's all-time leading goalscorer with an impressive career tally of 228 goals. He was capped by England against Scotland in 1935, then the biggest international game in the football calendar. His playing career officially ended in May 1946, although World War Two severely curtailed his first-class appearances, and he entered management with Peterborough United, then a non-League side.

His tenure at the Victoria Ground lasted only 44 games in a nine-month spell which produced a mere nine wins, although he was involved in the signing of Ambrose Fogarty from his former club. Gurney joined 'Pools in the middle of a run of 18 games without a win, which resulted in the inevitable bottom finish and another re-election application.

A poor start to the following campaign saw 'Pools win only once in their first 11 League games, conceding 34 goals, which

included 6–0 and 7–1 defeats by Carlisle United. Such dismal form, coupled with highly critical comments in the local press, ultimately brought about his dismissal in the New Year following a home defeat by Darlington. A rare high spot was the 4–2 home win over Jimmy Scoular's Bradford Park Avenue, which saw locally born player Terry Francis score a hat-trick on his League debut.

Bobby Gurney later scouted for Leeds United and worked as a travelling salesman for a wine and spirits company. He died in his home town, Sunderland, in April 1994 aged 86.

## Alvan Williams

*Born: Penmon, Anglesey, 21 November 1932. Died: Llandderfel, near Bala, 22 December 2003*

**6 January 1964 to 31 May 1965**

Alvan Williams was initially appointed caretaker manager by chairman Ernest Ord following the departure of Bobby Gurney before being given the full-time job a month later, at the age of 31. Williams had a modest playing career as a forward, starting with Bury at the age of 22 years before going on to Wrexham, Bradford Park Avenue and Exeter City, making a total of 126 League appearances and scoring 30 goals. He had joined Hartlepools as trainer in 1963 from Bangor City, with whom he had finished his playing career.

Williams took over a side second from bottom of the Fourth Division and it was no surprise when he was unable to turn the 1963–64 season around and, once again, Hartlepools United had to apply for re-election. The lack of a serious alternative – Wigan Athletic only polled five votes – made the result a foregone conclusion and 'Pools were re-elected with 36 votes. Results improved the following season,

although it took until the sixth game to record a win, as the team benefited from the influence of record signing Ambrose Fogarty to finish in 15th position. Williams brought stability to the team by only using 19 players throughout the campaign, with goalkeeper Ken Simpkins and full-back Stan Storton ever presents. Crowds returned to the Vic, with over 10,000 present to witness a 1–0 win over high-flying Millwall thanks to a goal from leading scorer Peter Thompson.

Inevitably the emergence of a successful Hartlepools United manager, however relative, was bound to attract attention from other clubs, and so it was with Alvan Williams. In May 1965 the Third Division club Southend United persuaded the manager to join them, taking trainer Peter Gordon with him. He became the first 'Pools manager since Jacky Carr in 1935 to move on to another club at a time of his own choosing.

Williams's two seasons with Southend were not a success, culminating in a first-ever relegation to the Fourth Division. He returned to his native Wales to take charge of Wrexham on a three-year contract and was instrumental, along with coach John Neal, in setting up a youth policy which produced a wealth of talent in the early 1970s. After failing to win promotion at the Racecourse club he resigned following a conviction for drink-driving and left the professional game.

Williams's later life was blighted with a murder charge while a publican in North London. Although acquitted, he received a custodial sentence for affray following the death of a student during an altercation. Ironically he was presented with a lifetime achievement award for services to youth football by the North Wales Football Association shortly before his death in December 2003.

## Geoffrey (Geoff) Twentyman

*Born: Brampton, Cumberland, 19 January 1930. Died: Southport, 16 February 2004*

**1 June 1965 to 29 October 1965**

Following the amicable departure of Alvan Williams, the Hartlepools board appointed the 35-year-old former Liverpool and Carlisle centre-half Geoff Twentyman as his successor in June 1965.

Twentyman made his debut for Carlisle United aged 18 and went on to make nearly 150 appearances for the Cumbrian club before signing for Liverpool in December 1953. His Anfield career coincided with a rare slump in the club's fortunes and he was a member of the side which was relegated from the First Division in 1954. Despite this setback he went on to make 184 appearances for the Merseyside giants before joining Irish League side Ballymena United as player-manager in 1959. He later had a second,

brief spell at Carlisle before becoming the 16th manager at the Victoria Ground.

Geoff Twentyman's reign at Hartlepools was to be one of the shortest for a manager officially appointed on a full-time basis. He was *in situ* for barely five months, during which period his side played 13 League games, winning only three, although he did introduce the striking partnership of Ernie Phythian and Jimmy Mulvaney, which was to serve the club well in the future. His appointment, however, was clearly a mistake, initially resulting in the resignation of chairman Ernest Ord, only for Twentyman to be 'relieved of his duties' by the directors the following day, thereby paving the way for the immediate return of the autocratic Ord.

Twentyman later managed non-League sides Penrith and Morecambe before returning to Anfield as chief scout in 1967, a position he held for over 20 years, during which time Liverpool achieved pre-eminent status in English and European football.

He died in Southport shortly after his 74th birthday in 2004.

## Brian Howard Clough

*Born: Middlesbrough, 21 March 1935. Died: Derby, 20 September 2004*

**29 October 1965 to 5 June 1967**

Following the relative success of Alvan Williams the Hartlepools board, led by Ernest Ord, decided to revert to appointing a young, enthusiastic former player as their next manager, following the short-lived spell of Geoff Twentyman and the many veteran predecessors of Williams. If they thought they had established a 'blueprint' for the model young manager they were mistaken, as what they got was Brian Clough.

Clough had a dynamic playing career with Middlesbrough and Sunderland as a goalscoring centre-forward who amassed a staggering 251 goals in only 274 League appearances, effectively averaging a goal a game. Despite not playing in the top division, his exploits earned him two England caps in 1959 as well as Football League honours. His playing career was cut short by a serious injury sustained in a collision with Bury goalkeeper Chris Harker and, after a season-long layoff and a short attempted comeback, he decided to retire and concentrate on coaching. He lost his position as youth-team coach at Sunderland as an 'economy measure', so on the advice of Len Shackleton he applied for the vacant manager's post at Hartlepools and was appointed on a two-year contract at a reported annual salary of £2,500.

On taking up his appointment the new manager persuaded Ernest Ord to sanction the appointment of his former Middlesbrough colleague Peter Taylor as his assistant. At the time Taylor was manager of Burton Albion and apparently none too keen to live and work in the North East for the impoverished club. Not for the last time Brian Clough's powers of

persuasion won the day, despite the chairman's reservations about another 'high earner' on the payroll.

The new manager made an instant impact by winning his first three games, 3–1 at Bradford City and 4–1 at home to Crewe in the League, plus a convincing 3–1 victory over Workington in the FA Cup. These victories followed a winless six-game run, and understandably expectations soared with over 7,000 attending the Cup game. However, reality quickly bit when none of the next seven League games produced a victory.

During this period Clough signed Tony Parry and Les Green from Burton Albion and established Bryan Drysdale at left-back. He then spent a considerable portion of his meagre transfer budget on acquiring John Gill from Mansfield Town. Results remained mixed for the remainder of the season with a win at home, lose away pattern established. A highlight was the debut of 16-year-old John McGovern, the club's youngest player at the time, in the final game of the season, a 1–1 draw at home to Bradford City. 'Pools finished in 18th position, a couple of places down on the previous campaign.

Brian Clough quickly recognised that being manager of a club like Hartlepools United required more than the traditional coaching and management of the players. He understood that the club had to reach out to both supporters and the wider community, and he spent countless hours visiting social clubs and public places promoting the team and the game in general. Although he was not unique in this respect, his efforts made a lasting impact on supporters conditioned to the 'elder statesman' approach to management. The youthful manager was literally like a breath of fresh air, and everybody recognised his potential, a true 'special one' in the making.

The 1966–67 season opened with a new chairman, John Curry, at the helm and, for the first time for many seasons, a settled squad of players, of whom nine were to make 30 or more League appearances. Interestingly, Brian Clough appeared to be no great fan of the use of substitutes, utilising the option on only nine occasions throughout the League campaign.

In a settled side Ernie Phythian and Jimmy Mulvaney contributed 42 League goals, with Fogarty, Somers and the youthful McGovern providing the service. Simpkins and Green contested the goalkeeper's jersey, while Bircumshaw, Drysdale, Sheridan and Gill formed a solid defence. Parry, McLeod and Wright shared the midfield duties. 'Pools finished the season in eighth position, winning 22 games, their best finish since the 1956–57 season, with Ernie Phythian contributing 23 League goals.

It was apparent that the manager had worked wonders stabilising the club and establishing a settled squad of players capable of further progress. It was no surprise, therefore, when Derby County, on the recommendation of Len Shackleton, offered Brian Clough the vacant manager's post at the Baseball Ground during the close season. The promise of a £70,000 transfer fund from Sam Longson, the Derby chairman, was a critical factor in Clough accepting the post. Despite John Curry immediately offering Peter Taylor the job at the Victoria Ground, he followed his manager to Derby a few weeks later. On leaving the club Brian Clough commented 'the job is unique, there isn't another one like it in the whole of football'.

Whole volumes of books have been written about Brian Clough's managerial career after Hartlepools United. Briefly, he took Derby County into the First Division and won the Championship in the 1971–72 season. After brief spells at Brighton and Leeds he found his spiritual home at the City Ground, home of Nottingham Forest, in 1975. In an 18-year career he took them to their first-ever Championship, won two European Cups, a European Super Cup and four Football League Cups, as well as Anglo-Scottish, Simod and Zenith Data Systems Cup victories.

Clough retired from football management in 1993 and increasing ill-health restricted his public appearances. One of his last visits to a football match was to support his son Nigel as manager of Burton Albion in the televised second-round FA Cup tie against Hartlepool United in December 2003. 'Pools won courtesy of a Joel Porter goal. He died in Derby City Hospital from stomach cancer within a year, aged 69, on 20 September 2004.

## Angus McLean

*Born: Queensferry, 20 September 1925. Died: 1 July 1979*

**5 June 1967 to 24 April 1970**

Chairman John Curry acted quickly to replace Brian Clough with 41-year-old Angus McLean, the trainer-coach of Hull City. He inherited a settled team, which, while not yet the finished product, had shown much promise the previous season.

McLean's playing career started in 1939 with Aberystwyth Town, moving on to Hilton Main before joining Wolverhampton Wanderers as an amateur. He turned professional in 1942 and as a solid defender helped the Molineux club to three consecutive top-six finishes after World War Two. McLean lost his place in a strong Wolves side during the 1948–49 season and with it the chance of an FA Cup-winners' medal. After 144 appearances he rejoined Aberystwyth as player-manager while still only 26, subsequently moving to Bromsgrove Rovers in a playing capacity. In May 1953 he joined Bury as player-coach, and after a short stay with the Lancashire club he finished his playing days with Crewe Alexandra in 1955.

The new manager's first signing was George Smith, a vastly experienced goalkeeper, who had made 323 appearances for Notts County. He promised a more attacking approach than the one adopted by his predecessor, although doubts quickly emerged when, after winning his first two games, a run of six games without a win produced only two goals. He solved the goal drought in the most unconventional manner by playing reserve-team goalkeeper Ken Simpkins at centre-forward for five games before the signing of Bobby Cummings from Darlington.

Cummings's arrival coincided with the emergence of local players John McGovern and Peter Blowman, who together with a team nucleus provided by Clough went on an unbeaten 16-game run which ended in a third-place finish and promotion. This was Gus McLean's

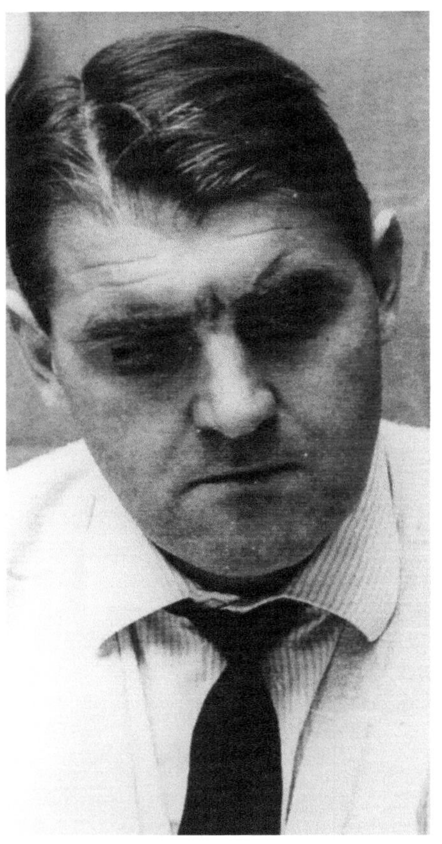

finest hour as he developed the side he inherited and by adding shrewd signings he turned an average team into a good one and gave 'Pools' long-suffering supporters something to finally cheer about.

McLean's second season, 1968–69, in Division Three was destined to be one of continuous struggle. The problem was lack of goals, with 19 games scoreless and a mere 41 goals scored all season, making relegation inevitable. Despite this record 'Pools were only two points from the safety zone in the final analysis. Inevitably supporters were left to wonder what the final outcome would have been had the directors made funds available to strengthen the attacking options. The following season saw the break-up of the promotion side for various reasons. Smith, Sheridan and Wright played their final games, while leading scorer Terry Bell was sold to Reading for a reported £8,000 to ease the financial situation. As usual, little money was made available to the manager to strengthen his team and the arrival of Lance Robson from Darlington proved no substitute for the departing Bell. The team struggled all season and a bottom finish was inevitable in a campaign which saw the team goalless in 22 League games.

McLean resigned after the final game of the season despite having two more years left on his contract, citing a major disagreement with the board as his reason. His departure paved the way for trainer John Simpson to take over following 'Pools' re-election. Bradford Park Avenue lost out in the ballot, to be replaced by Cambridge United.

Gus McLean and his family remained in Hartlepool until August 1970 when he was appointed assistant manager to Dick Conner at Rochdale. Following Conner's departure in 1973 he became secretary to the Spotland club, a post he held until 1975 before making his final move a year later to struggling Southport. McLean left the Haig Avenue club following their relegation from the Football League and at the time of his death in 1979 he was living in the village of Shaw, Lancashire.

## John Simpson

*Born: Hedon, near Hull, 27 October 1918.*
*Died: Market Weighton, 21 June 2000*
**24 April 1970 to 6 March 1971**

John Simpson was appointed manager by chairman John Curry following McLean's departure, having been trainer throughout his predecessor's term of office.

Simpson's playing career as a full-back had been primarily with York City, for whom he made 207 appearances between

1947 and 1954, having previously played for Huddersfield Town, with whom he signed as a professional in March 1939. World War Two delayed his League debut until 1946 and in the meantime he was a physical training instructor in the Army and captained the Southern Command team. As was the practice with players during the conflict, Simpson guested for Plymouth Argyle, Bournemouth, Portsmouth, Aldershot and Leeds United. After five League appearances for Huddersfield he was transferred to York City in March 1948 for £1,000, a record for the Bootham Crescent club at the time. It was with York that he spent the remainder of his playing career, making a total of 220 appearances before retiring in 1954.

Initially Simpson ran a fruit and vegetable shop in Hull before Gus McLean persuaded him back into football as his physiotherapist at Hull City, a partnership which lasted 11 years before the pair moved to the Victoria Ground in June 1967.

Within a week of taking charge Simpson released seven players, among them George Smith and Peter Blowman. To replace them an equal number joined, including former Roker Park favourites George Herd and Nick Sharkey. Defeat at Colchester on the opening day of the 1970–71 season was followed by three successive draws before Simpson recorded his first victory, against Barrow, at the Vic. This proved to be a rare success, as only one of the next 10 games was won, resulting once again with the team being in the re-election zone. The final humiliation came in the FA Cup against Cheshire League side Rhyl, who were worthy winners despite the closeness of the 1–0 scoreline. Simpson struggled on into the New Year, failing to win any of his last nine games, and he resigned at the beginning of March after a five-goal rout at Southport.

After a short period out of the game he became coach/physiotherapist for Cambridge United, as well as preparing the Cambridge University side for their annual game against Oxford University at Wembley. Simpson returned to his roots as physiotherapist at York City in 1977 and remained with the club until 1983 when his service was rewarded with a testimonial match against Leeds United. He lived in retirement with his wife in Market Weighton until his death in 2000.

## Leonard (Len) Ashurst

*Born: Liverpool, 10 March 1939*

**8 March 1971 to 1 June 1974**

Len Ashurst arrived at the Victoria Ground shortly before his 32nd birthday on a free transfer from Sunderland, with whom he had a long and successful career, making over 400 appearances and winning England Youth and Under-23 honours. As a wholehearted full-back who never shirked a tackle he had a reputation as a respected professional who immediately threw himself into the role of player-manager.

The team he inherited was already consigned to the re-election zone and he had little time to effect improvements, as a 23rd-place finish showed. The re-election voting paired Hartlepool joint bottom with Newport County on 33 votes, enough for survival in the absence of a serious contender. The new manager was acutely aware that another application the following season would probably spell the end of his club's League status.

The 1971–72 season saw the inevitable changes in playing personnel as Ashurst sought to improve on the previous season. Neil Warnock arrived from Rotherham United, along with goalkeeper Mick Gadsby and defender George Potter, who was to give sterling service in the coming seasons. Despite the influx of new faces 'Pools again struggled in the early games and only four League wins preceded another embarrassing exit in the FA Cup to a non-League side, this time Boston United. By the New Year the club were bottom of the League and in severe financial difficulties, which resulted in the versatile and popular Tony Parry being sold to Derby County for £5,000.

To further ease the financial burden George Herd agreed to vacate his position as trainer, leaving Ashurst to fill the roles of manager, player, coach and trainer. Incredible though this may seem, it actually worked. 'Pools finally won an away game, at Newport County, and followed this with seven successive home wins before travelling to Darlington, of all places, to save their League status. Nearly 9,000 fans, many supporting the visitors, witnessed a hard-fought game in which 'Pools eventually prevailed 2–1. This win guaranteed the safety of an 18th-place League finish, one place above Darlington.

Ashurst's second season, 1972–73, turned out to be a major disappointment as the manager moulded the team in his image with the emphasis on defence. Prominent in this was goalkeeper Barry Watling, acquired on a free transfer from Notts County. Evidence of the goalscoring problem can be seen from the tally of only 17 goals in home games, which understandably affected attendances. Despite a final League position of 20th, five points above the re-election places, Ashurst realised improvements were needed the following season.

During the close season Bill Green was transferred to Carlisle United for a fee of £15,000 to ease the financial worries and provide the manager with some modest bargaining power in the transfer market. Other departures included Warnock, Waddell and Young. To replace them came Malcolm Moore, Kevin McMahon and Alan Gauden, who were all to make their mark in the coming seasons. Despite the influx of new talent the 1973–74 season began ominously, with only three wins in the first 20 League games. Results improved dramatically in the New Year and a run of five successive wins saw Ashurst win a

Manager of the Month award. A final position of 11th could have been even better except for a poor finish, which failed to produce a win in the final seven games. The progress which Len Ashurst, along with his assistant Tony Toms, had made was recognised by Gillingham, newly promoted to Division Three, and the pair left the Victoria Ground in June to be succeeded by Ken Hale.

Len Ashurst later managed Sheffield Wednesday, Newport County and Cardiff City before returning to Roker Park in March 1984, leading the Wearside club to a Football League Final at Wembley the following season, before being dismissed after a relegation campaign. He later managed in Kuwait and Qatar before returning to Cardiff as manager for a second time. After brief periods in non-League management he worked abroad in Malaysia before working for the FA Premier League, overseeing the development of national academy systems. He now lives in retirement in Whitburn, having celebrated 50 years' service to the professional game.

## Kenneth (Ken) Oliver Hale

*Born: Blyth, 18 September 1939*

**1 June 1974 to 1 October 1976**

Ken Hale began his football career with Newcastle United in October 1956 and made 35 appearances, scoring 16 goals over the next six seasons. His opportunities were limited at St James' Park due to the presence of George Eastham and Ken Leek and he joined Coventry City for a £10,000 fee in December 1962. It was with the Sky Blues that he enjoyed success, winning the Football League Division Three title in 1964 and playing a key role in the rise of the club, which ultimately ended in promotion to the First Division. Hale joined Oxford United in February 1966 and again won Third Division Championship honours before moving to Darlington, whom he was later to manage, in May 1968. Prior to joining Hartlepool he had a spell as player-coach with Halifax Town.

Appointed by new chairman Tommy Aird, Hale's first season as 'Pools manager, 1974–75, was illuminated by a stirring run in the Football League Cup, a competition in which previously 'Pools had little history. After a win at Workington the second round produced a four-game saga against Bournemouth in the days before away goals and penalty shoot-outs. A narrow 1–0 win in a third replay in front of nearly 7,000 fans led to a draw against Blackburn Rovers, who went on to win the Third Division title that season. Following a draw at home 'Pools played above themselves in the replay and went through to the fourth round, winning 2–1 at Ewood Park.

This success brought Aston Villa to the Vic and a record crowd of 12,305 for a floodlight fixture. After conceding a first-half goal 'Pools dominated the second period, with Malcolm Moore's strike scant reward for all their pressure. No further scoring ensured a replay at Villa Park and the heavy fixture burden on a small squad took its toll as the home side ran out 6–1 winners. League form thrived during the Cup run and at one stage 10 wins in 16 games saw the side in the top half of the

League. Results dipped in the New Year and a final position of 13th could be considered satisfactory given the added excitement of the Cup exploits.

Ken Hale's second season in charge bore similarities to his first, inconsistent League results, with spates of wins followed by losses in equal measure and another Cup run which brought temporary respite to the lack of League progress. After wins over Stockport County and non-League Marine in the FA Cup, 'Pools were rewarded with a glamourous third-round tie against Manchester City at Maine Road. City, at the time, were a top side and went on that season to win the Football League Cup and finish runners-up to Liverpool in the First Division. Nearly 27,000 fans, including many supporting the underdogs, saw a one-sided contest result in a six-goal win for the Manchester side. Another mid-table finish, this time one place lower at 14th, was achieved by a strong rally with six wins in the final 10 games after form slumped dramatically following the Cup exit.

The 1976–77 campaign, which now saw local farmer Vince Barker installed as chairman, began in ominous style when only 1,599 diehards turned up for the opening game, a draw against Exeter City. The departure of Malcolm Moore to Workington proved to be a key factor as none of the next six League games were won and only three goals scored, one an own-goal! With gates struggling to reach the 2,000 mark and the new chairman looking for someone to blame, the manager's fate was sealed. Ken Hale took the decision philosophically, commenting 'I'm disappointed but that's football'. After leaving the game he settled in Seaburn, opening a newsagent's shop in the Sunderland area.

## William (Billy) Horner

*Born: Cassop, 7 September 1942*

**1 October 1976 to 31 March 1983 and 15 December 1983 to 1 November 1986**

Chairman Vince Barker appointed first-team coach Billy Horner as manager in succession to Ken Hale following a disastrous start to the 1976–77 season, in which none of the first 10 League games were won.

Horner's football career began with Middlesbrough as a junior and he went on to make 187 League appearances following his debut in the 1960–61 season. After nine years with the Teesside club he joined neighbours Darlington, for whom he gave sterling service, making 218 League appearances before finishing his playing career in 1974 and going on to manage the Quakers.

His tenure in the 'hardest job in football' was to last over 10 years, apart from a nine-month break, during one of the most difficult periods in the club's history, which says something about the character of the man. Under the chairmanship of Vince Barker, a local farmer and businessman, who was constantly at odds with Hartlepool Council over the Victoria Ground, he managed to keep the club afloat by a series of shrewd transfer deals which saw players of the calibre of Malcolm Poskett, Keith Houchen and Andrew Linighan sold to be replaced by bargain buys including Billy Ayre, Bob Newton, Alan Harding and Nigel Walker, among others.

Hartlepool United applied for re-election in both of his first two seasons before reaching a respectable 13th-place League position in 1978–79 despite drawing 12 home games. A highlight was locally born Mark Lawrence's four goals in a 4–2 win at Halifax Town, evidence of a strong youth system which the manager nurtured and encouraged. A dip to 19th position the following season was followed by 'Pools' strongest League challenge since the 1967–68 promotion, when in 1980–81 the dizzy height of ninth place was achieved despite the chairman threatening at one point to move the club to Scarborough! Further evidence of the strength of Hartlepool's youth policy under Billy Horner was the winning of the Northern Intermediate League, which featured clubs such as Newcastle United and Middlesbrough.

The progress was not maintained the following season, 1981–82, and a year later re-election again reared its ugly head in a season in which 'Pools failed to score in 17 League games, resulting in an alarming decline in attendances, which dropped below the 1,000 mark. In such circumstances chairman Barker again looked for the nearest scapegoat and Horner was sacked to be replaced briefly by John Duncan.

Billy Horner remained in a coaching role throughout the brief spells in office of both John Duncan and Mick Docherty. During this period the club came very close to extinction due to a considerable sum owed to the Inland Revenue, the settlement of which was quickly followed by a dispute over the non-payment of players' wages and the threat of strike action. Duncan resigned after a mere nine weeks as manager to be replaced by Mick Docherty, who failed to last until Christmas when he too was sacked and Horner found himself re-instated, albeit on a caretaker basis.

The 1983–84 season was one of the most dismal in the history of Hartlepool United. Apart from the managerial changes the club finished in 23rd position and, despite a brief rally following Horner's return as manager, they won only one of their last 11 League games. By this time attendances had reached a record low and emergency editions of the club programme, consisting of a single folded sheet, were being produced due to the lack of sales.

Billy Horner finally found relief before the start of the 1984–85 season, having initially been told by Barker that the club could run with only 13 full-time professionals, when Tyneside businessman John Smart took over the club. The transfer of Andy Linighan to Leeds for £60,000 brought financial stability, which was reinforced by a successful re-election application. Smart's first instruction to his manager was to 'go out and improve the squad'. This Horner did, with the signings of Alan Shoulder, Les Mutrie, John Brownlie and Alan Stevenson, among others. These recruits, along with the blossoming talents of local players Brian Honour and David Linighan, brought about an immediate improvement. In a campaign which saw 'Pools rise to second by November, only to be deprived of top spot on goal difference, it took a run of nine games without a win either side of the Easter period to end the season in a disappointing seventh position.

The new chairman understandably expected the progress to be maintained the following season, 1986–87, even being photographed with Horner toasting the anticipated promotion campaign. It was a major disappointment for all concerned when none of the first eight League games were won, the run culminating in a heavy home defeat to Crewe in front of only 1,512 spectators. John Smart, having allowed Horner to strengthen the team in order to challenge for promotion, now asked the manager to step down in favour of his assistant John Bird. Ironically, Horner had signed Bird as a player from Newcastle United seven years earlier.

Billy Horner later coached Gateshead, then a Vauxhall Conference side, and returned to the Victoria Ground to assist John MacPhail in a coaching capacity. He was briefly appointed caretaker manager in September 1994 by the well-respected chairman Harold Hornsey following MacPhail's dismissal, taking charge of five League games prior to the appointment of David McCreery.

## John Pearson Duncan

*Born: Dundee, 22 February 1949*

**1 April 1983 to 1 June 1983**

John Duncan joined 'Pools as manager from Scunthorpe United, for whom he briefly played, having previously appeared for Dundee, Tottenham Hotspur and Derby County. He made his reputation as a goalscoring forward at Tottenham following his transfer from Dundee in October 1974 for a £125,000 fee, scoring 53 goals in 103 League appearances between 1974 and 1978.

Duncan was destined to have the shortest reign at the Victoria Ground of any officially appointed manager. Even by the standards of his predecessors his tenure was blighted by financial problems, this time involving not only the Inland Revenue but also the players themselves in the case of unpaid wages. This matter was only resolved on the intervention of the Professional Footballers' Association through their secretary, Gordon Taylor, who persuaded the players to fulfil an away fixture at Halifax Town. Chairman Vince Barker's response to the crisis was to accuse the players of letting the club down. The following home game, against Colchester United, attracted a meagre crowd of 804 and 'Pools finished the 1982–83 season 22nd in Division Four. Perhaps understandably the manager felt his task was hopeless and resigned a mere nine weeks after his appointment, despite the club being yet again re-elected.

Duncan later managed Chesterfield (two spells) and Ipswich Town. It was in his second spell at Saltergate that he achieved a Division Three Play-off success in 1995 and followed this success two years later with a stirring run in the FA Cup which finally ended in a semi-final defeat by Middlesbrough in controversial circumstances. He was sacked in 2000 following Chesterfield's relegation back to Division Three and finally left the professional game to pursue a career in

teaching. He continues to be involved in football through his association with Loughborough University's team in the Midland Football Combination Premier Division.

## Michael (Mick) Docherty

*Born: Preston, 29 October 1950*

**14 June 1983 to 15 December 1983**

Mick Docherty began his football career as an apprentice at Chelsea during his father Tommy's reign as manager. A move to Burnley saw him captain the FA Youth Cup-winning side in 1968, establishing himself as a regular full-back and making 153 appearances between 1969 and 1975. After a brief spell at Manchester City he joined Sunderland in 1976, making 73 appearances in midfield for the Wearside club before retiring from playing due to a chronic knee injury in 1979. With his playing days over Docherty joined the Roker Park coaching staff and managed the team for four matches following the sacking of Ken Knighton.

With no money available to reinforce the team Docherty's reign at the Victoria Ground was doomed to failure from the start. The 1983–84 season was the first year of Football League sponsorship, by Canon, yet despite this the all-too-familiar mood of despondency hung over the club. The new manager only recorded a single victory in his 23 League and Cup games in charge before the inevitable sacking in mid-December. In this he was not helped by the antics of chairman Vince Barker, who terminated the contract of team captain John Bird, saying the player's business interests conflicted with his playing responsibilities. Bird appealed to the Football League, who upheld his objection with the result that Barker had to reinstate him. The effect this must have had on Docherty and his players can only be imagined.

Docherty later had spells at Wolves as coach, and then Blackpool, Burnley and Hull as assistant manager, before fulfilling coaching, caretaker manager and finally permanent manager roles at Rochdale in succession to Dave Sutton. He was dismissed at the end of the following season due to disagreements over his retained list. Thereafter he worked with Ronnie Jepson, firstly as a coach at Burnley, and latterly as his assistant at Gillingham. Following Jepson's departure he assumed the role of caretaker manager in partnership with Iffy Onuora pending the appointment of a permanent manager, an arrangement which lasted until October 2007. He renewed his association with Jepson in May 2008 at Huddersfield Town, when manager Stan Ternent appointed both men to his coaching staff, an arrangement that was terminated following Ternent's sacking later in the year.

## John Charles Bird

*Born: Rossington, near Doncaster, 9 June 1948*

**1 October 1986 to 3 October 1988**

John Bird succeeded Billy Horner on a seven-match trial basis following a dismal start to the 1986–87 season which failed to produce a single victory in the first 10 League and Cup games.

Bird began his career with Doncaster Rovers before moving to Preston North End where he made his name as a strong, determined centre-half. His £60,000 transfer to Newcastle United in September 1975 prompted the resignation of Preston manager Bobby Charlton, and after playing 87 League games for the Magpies he joined 'Pools on a free transfer in May 1980. In a five-year spell at the Victoria Ground he made 138 League appearances, scoring 15 goals, before becoming Horner's assistant.

Bird's first game in charge produced a stunning win at Lincoln City, and despite mixed results in the next six games and rumours concerning the signing of former Nottingham Forest player Ian Bowyer as player-manager, his appointment was confirmed. An improvement in results in the New Year, which saw a rise out of the bottom four, was not reflected in attendances. Barely 1,000 turned up to witness a draw with Aldershot at the beginning of March, with attendances remaining stubbornly below 2,000 through to the end of the season. Given the resources at his disposal and the lack of support, a final League position of 18th could be considered something of an achievement.

The start of the 1987–88 season was marked by a public outburst from chairman John Smart in which he made it clear the club needed a new manager. He considered the previous season to have been abysmal and accused Bird of lacking ambition. Fellow director Alan Bamford publicly supported Bird and after much boardroom wrangling both Smart and Bird remained with the club.

The close season had seen numerous changes in playing personnel, the most notable being the signings of Rob McKinnon and Paul Baker. After a shaky

start 'Pools embarked on a five-game winning streak which saw the team climb the table. An added bonus was a strong run in the Associate Members' Cup, sponsored by Sherpa Vans. After wins over Mansfield, Doncaster and Carlisle the quarter-final saw 'Pools travel to Roker Park to face Sunderland and win through in dreadful conditions with a Brian Honour goal. 'Pools' form in both the League and Cup competitions saw Bird rewarded with two Manager of the Month awards for September and February. However, this was to be the high point, as Preston secured a comfortable win at the Vic in the Sherpa Vans semi-final and League form slumped dramatically in the final 10 games with only a single win, resulting in a disappointing 16th-place League finish.

Bird was confident promotion could be gained in the 1988–89 season after an impressive pre-season, which saw Alex Ferguson's Manchester United despatched

6–0, and the manager backed this up with five wins in the first six games, which saw 'Pools climb to second in the table. Such performances at the Victoria Ground do not pass unnoticed in the wider football world and when York City approached the club following the departure of Bobby Saxton, Bird was quickly installed as the new manager at Bootham Crescent, taking Alan Little with him in the role of coach.

The new manager initially had some success, rescuing the Minstermen from a disastrous start to finish in a respectable mid-table position. His first full season, 1989–90, saw York well placed in the promotion race up to Christmas before a run of 10 games without a win in the New Year resulted in another mid-table finish in 13th place. The following season, in which 'Pools won promotion, ironically saw Bird's club struggle and eventually finish a lowly 21st, resulting in his dismissal. As a postscript Alan Little was also to manage York City from 1993 to 1999 after John Ward, Bird's successor.

He later coached at Doncaster Rovers and in February 1994 became manager of struggling Halifax Town. After two years of continual struggle at the Shay he decided to retire from football to concentrate on his passion, painting.

John Bird is now an accomplished artist with his own studio at Bawtry, near Doncaster. His paintings have sold worldwide to prominent individuals and corporations and in 2006 his representation of a Turner sketch was part of an exhibition of the master's work.

## Robert (Bobby) Moncur

*Born: Perth, 19 January 1945*

**2 November 1988 to 27 November 1989**

Bobby Moncur became manager of Hartlepool United at the behest of his friend John Smart following the departure of John Bird. Initially his appointment was on a temporary basis, but the chairman quickly persuaded Moncur to take charge permanently, with Bryan 'Pop' Robson joining as his assistant.

Moncur was a legend in north-east football circles, having captained Scotland and Newcastle United, for whom he played nearly 300 games and lifted the Inter-Cities Fairs Cup in 1969. After leaving Newcastle to join neighbours Sunderland, with whom he won the Division Two Championship, he finished his playing days with Carlisle United in 1976, later becoming manager. His management experience also embraced Scottish club Hearts, and Plymouth Argyle. Outside of football he was an accomplished yachtsman who competed in the 1985 Around Britain Race, and it was these interests he initially put to one side to manage Hartlepool United.

Immediately on taking charge the new manager found himself embarked on an FA Cup run, once a feature of a Hartlepool season. The first three rounds saw convincing home wins against Third Division sides Wigan, Notts County and Bristol City before another home tie in the fourth round against Second Division

Bournemouth. Despite indifferent League form 'Pools again rose to the challenge of higher League opposition and gained a creditable draw. The replay at Dean Court took on added significance when the fifth-round draw paired the winners with Manchester United. Early mistakes cost 'Pools dear and they never recovered from a Baker own-goal. Goals from Joe Allon and Andy Toman reduced the arrears in the second half, but the home side finished the stronger to run out 5–2 winners.

This proved to be the highlight of Moncur's reign as League results declined and a finish of 19th was meagre reward for a season which promised so much. A postscript to the 1988–89 season was the introduction of automatic relegation to the Football Conference for the bottom side. The days of the old re-election format were now over and Hartlepool United could no longer rely on the munificence of other clubs. If it was any consolation to 'Pools' long-suffering fans, Darlington became the first club to be 'automatically' relegated.

At the start of the 1989–90 season Moncur lost the services of two key players, centre-half Tony Smith and play-maker Andy Toman. On top of this Brian Honour suffered a serious knee injury, which resulted in him missing the first half of the season. To make matters worse the manager embarked on a pre-arranged sailing trip, which resulted in him missing the preparations for the new season. Predictably the opening game away to Halifax resulted in a heavy defeat, with the travelling supporters understandably making their views known to chairman John Smart in plain terms.

A protracted power struggle now took place, with chairman Smart clinging to control before stepping down at the end of October, with board member Gary Gibson taking over. The boardroom upheaval impacted the management and players alike, and after a run of eight League games with only a single win and attendances below the 2,000 mark Moncur voluntarily relinquished his position despite overtures from chairman Gibson to stay.

Although it did not seem like it at the time, Moncur left the team in good order having recruited Joe Allon, Paul Dalton and Mick Smith, given a debut to Don Hutchison and encouraged Rob McKinnon's attacking full-back style. All these players were to make a major impact on future seasons. Moncur left football management to continue developing his sailing interests and act as a media pundit and commentator on programmes such as Sky Sports and local Tyneside radio stations.

## Cyril Barry Knowles

*Born: Fitzwilliam, 13 July 1944. Died: Middlesbrough, 31 August 1991*

**9 December 1989 to 4 March 1991**

Chairman Gary Gibson set his sights high in the search for a successor to Moncur, even considering Malcolm Allison, the flamboyant former Manchester City and Middlesbrough manager. Eventually the chairman wisely appointed Cyril Knowles, the former Tottenham and England full-back, who had previously managed Darlington and Torquay United. Knowles came with a sound reputation for managing lower League sides and making the most of limited resources.

Cyril Knowles began his career on the ground staff at Manchester United and had a trial at Blackpool before signing amateur forms with Middlesbrough, turning professional in April 1963 and making 37 appearances for Boro before moving south to join Tottenham Hotspur. A footballing

full-back in the best traditions of the great North London club, he made his debut in the same game as Pat Jennings on the opening day of the 1964–65 season, going on to play over 400 games for Spurs, including UEFA and Football League Cup-winning sides. He also played in four full England internationals as well as making Under-21 and Football League appearances.

After retiring from playing in 1976, Knowles had a short spell as manager of Hertford Town before joining Doncaster Rovers' coaching staff. In 1981 he moved to Middlesbrough as reserve-team coach, earning promotion to the first-team role the following year. Darlington appointed him as manager in May 1983, a post he held until March 1987, having won promotion to Division Three with the Quakers, before managing Torquay United for two years.

Given the parlous League position Knowles inherited, with the chairman's support he was immediately busy in the transfer market, adding Tupling, MacDonald, Bennyworth and Olsson to his playing staff. The impact was instant with impressive wins against Scarborough and Grimsby over the Christmas period acting as the catalyst for a successful second half to the season. Although the final League position of 19th may not seem overly impressive, the new manager had transformed the club and the campaign ended on a positive note with real optimism for the coming season.

The 1990–91 season began with an impressive win at Chesterfield, only to be followed by a five-game run without a win, which saw 'Pools slump to 23rd position. A possible explanation for the poor early season League form was the Football League Cup run, which culminated in a two-legged second-round tie against Knowles's old club, Tottenham Hotspur. The first leg at White Hart Lane saw a four-goal masterclass from Paul Gascoigne which no team could have resisted, and the 5–0 scoreline hardly seemed to matter. The second leg at the Vic attracted nearly 10,000 fans, despite there being no hope of reversing the deficit – all just turned up to watch 'Gazza', as he was affectionately known. Despite the hype 'Pools gave a good account of themselves, with Paul Dalton scoring a fine individual goal in a 2–1 defeat, after which it was back to the more serious matter of the League.

Results improved in the League with Joe Allon and Paul Baker forming a potent goalscoring partnership, ably supported by Paul Dalton and Brian Honour. By Christmas 'Pools were in eighth position with 30 points from 19 games, five behind leaders Northampton, followed by a strong run in the New Year, which saw the team enter the top six for the first time.

While his team's results continued to improve, Cyril Knowles was suffering from headaches and double vision which eventually required hospital treatment. On the morning of 2 March, prior to the visit of his former club, Torquay United, Knowles was admitted to Middlesbrough General Hospital where tests revealed he had a brain tumour. He never took charge of a game again, his last being at Scunthorpe at the end of February. Despite expert clinical treatment and the support of his family and the public at large, he died on 31 August 1991 shortly after his 47th birthday.

His team finished the season with an unbeaten 14-game run to claim automatic promotion in third position, a single point behind champions Darlington and Stockport County. Despite winning the most games (24), the relatively poor start probably cost 'Pools their first-ever Championship, as by common consent they were the best team in the division after Christmas.

Following the long-awaited ground re-development, chairman Harold Hornsey in July 1995 named the new Clarence Road stand in memory of Cyril Knowles to widespread public acclaim.

## Alan Murray

*Born: Newcastle, 5 November 1949*

**5 March 1991 to 15 February 1993**

Alan Murray was a surprise choice by chairman Gary Gibson as caretaker manager following the untimely death of Cyril Knowles in that he was the club's chief executive at the time. His playing career had taken him to Middlesbrough, York City, Brentford and primarily Doncaster, for whom he made 146 League appearances and scored 21 goals. With his playing days over, Murray had a spell in management with Willington of the Northern League, and prior to joining Hartlepool he was commercial manager at Middlesbrough.

'Pools were 11th in Division Four when Murray took over in March of the 1990–91 season, and his first game in charge, a defeat at Lincoln City, set alarm bells ringing. This proved to be unfounded, as the team embarked on a 16-game run, which included only one further loss and a storming third-place finish, ensuring automatic promotion.

Murray's first full season in charge, 1991–92, saw 'Pools play in Division Three of the Football League and finish a highly creditable 11th, with Murray winning the divisional Manager of the Month award for December. His task was greatly facilitated by the support of chairman Garry Gibson, who brought players of the calibre of Andy Saville and Martin Hodge to the club, as well as the blossoming of young talent such as Rob McKinnon, Joe Allon and Paul Dalton. Despite such success and the higher quality of football on display the Hartlepool public failed to respond in sufficient numbers. Only 2,858 turned up for the opening home game against Reading, and despite sterling performances against opposition, which included Birmingham City, Fulham and

Bolton Wanderers, among others, gates hardly rose above the 4,000 figure.

The departures of McKinnon, Allon and Dalton at the start of the 1992–93 season in what, following the creation of the FA Premier League, was now Division Two, heralded a difficult campaign in which the class of Andy Saville shone through. A final position of 16th was commendable in the circumstances, along with the historic FA Cup win against Premiership Crystal Palace in the third round.

The club's League form suffered in the second half of the season with an 18-game sequence without a win, which included 11 successive games without a goal, and attendances declined dramatically with only 1,791 turning out for the home game against Wigan Athletic. These factors, along with the departure of popular players such as Rob McKinnon and Joe Allon, contributed to Murray's departure in February 1993.

After leaving 'Pools, Alan Murray became manager of local rivals Darlington for two difficult seasons which saw the Quakers narrowly avoid relegation to the Conference. He left Feethams in March 1995 and later had spells at Southampton and Newcastle United as assistant manager to Graeme Souness.

## Vivian (Viv) Dennis Busby

*Born: High Wycombe, 19 June 1949*

**15 February 1993 to 24 November 1993**

Viv Busby enjoyed a varied playing career as a skilful forward with an eye for goal at eight clubs, initially Luton Town, for whom he made 77 appearances and scored 17 goals, and then Fulham, for whom he scored 29 goals in 118 games between 1973 and 1976, as well as playing in the 1975 FA Cup Final defeat against West Ham United. His other clubs included a loan spell at Newcastle United, Norwich, Stoke, Sheffield

United, Blackburn and York. Busby also had two spells in America with Tulsa.

Busby's managerial experience had been primarily as assistant to Denis Smith at York City, for whom he played, and Sunderland, who achieved promotions from both the old Third and Second Divisions resulting in a single season, 1990–91, in the top flight. Following Smith's sacking he joined 'Pools as assistant to Alan Murray, taking over with the team in the middle of a goal drought which saw 11 League games without a single score. Even so, 'Pools rallied towards the end of the season to finish in 16th place in what was now Division Two following the introduction of the FA Premier League.

Despite financial support from chairman Gary Gibson, with the signing of quality players such as Andy Saville, the Hartlepool public never responded in sufficient numbers to the improved standards of play in the higher division. Hence, with the inevitable departures of Saville and Lenny Johnrose, among others, the task for the new manager was almost impossible, and so it proved.

Despite an encouraging start to the 1993–94 campaign, with only two defeats in the first seven League games, a meagre 2,214 turned up to witness the home win against

Blackpool. The next five League games, all goalless, were lost, coupled with an embarrassing FA Cup exit to Macclesfield Town, then a Conference side. Busby's brief reign ended following a home defeat by Wrexham in front of a meagre crowd of 1,530, with attendances set to sink even lower before the season's end.

Viv Busby later held coaching and scouting positions with a number of clubs as well as working for Radio Metro as a match commentator and scouted for West Bromwich Albion and Southampton. He returned to his former club York City in September 2004 as assistant manager to Chris Brass. Two months later he was appointed caretaker manager following the departure of Brass and continued in this position until the following February when he left the club by mutual consent, having won only four of his 14 games in charge. After a spell with Scottish club Gretna as youth academy coach, Busby was appointed assistant manager of Workington in September 2007.

## John MacPhail

*Born: Dundee, 7 December 1955*

**25 November 1993 to 9 September 1994**

John MacPhail began his football career with his home-town club of Dundee before moving into the Football League in 1982 with Sheffield United at the relatively late age of 27. A tough, uncompromising central-defender, MacPhail went on to make 135 appearances for the Blades, scoring seven goals, before moving to York City, where he contributed a healthy 24 goals in 142 appearances and was a key member of the 1983–84 Division Four Championship-winning side. A dispute over his contract resulted in his transfer to Bristol City where, after a brief spell, he returned to the North East with Sunderland, forming a strong partnership

with Gary Bennett in the 1989–90 promotion-winning side. After making 130 League appearances for the Wearside club he joined Hartlepool in September 1990 and was a kingpin in the team that won promotion that season.

MacPhail initially took over from Viv Busby in a player-manager capacity, winning only one of his first 19 League games and combining the dual roles through to the end of the 1993–94 season and the inevitable relegation. He had the dubious distinction of managing a Hartlepools side to their record home defeat, 8–1 to Plymouth Argyle, in the final game of the season. A poor start to the following campaign, in which only one of the first seven League games was won and attendances below the 2,000 mark sealed his managerial fate, along with that of his assistant, Alan Hay.

John MacPhail continued with the club as a player following his dismissal as manager. However, at 39 years old it was obvious his playing days were numbered after his managerial successor David McCreery relegated him to the reserves. He left Hartlepool, complaining that chairman Gary Gibson had demoralised his players with the late payment of wages on more than one occasion.

After leaving the club, John MacPhail played and managed in non-League football on South Tyneside and worked in the motor trade as a luxury car salesman.

## David McCreery

*Born: Belfast, 16 September 1957*

**3 October 1994 to 20 April 1995**

Described by a contemporary as an 'action man' footballer, David McCreery began his career as an apprentice with Manchester United, for whom he went on to make 87 League appearances and enjoy FA Cup success in 1977. He left Old Trafford to join Queen's Park Rangers in August 1979 for £200,000, playing two seasons at Loftus Road before moving to Newcastle United in October 1982 for £75,000. At the Tyneside club he was a key member of the 1984 promotion-winning side, which also included Peter Beardsley and Chris Waddle, and he went on to play 243 League games for the Magpies. His later playing career took him to America with Tulsa Roughnecks, Scottish side Hearts, and Carlisle United. He also had two spells with 'Pools in the early 1990s, making 34 League appearances. McCreery was a stalwart of the Northern Ireland side for many seasons, having been capped as a 17-year-old, and went on to appear in 67 full internationals including the 1982 and 1986 World Cups.

David McCreery was signed by Alan Murray in August 1991 as part of chairman Gary Gibson's ultimately abortive campaign to improve the quality of the playing squad in the vain hope that the Hartlepool public would respond in sufficient numbers to maintain a team in the higher division. He made 30

appearances during the 1991–92 season in which 'Pools finished a creditable 11th in the Third Division.

McCreery left to join Carlisle United in a managerial capacity before returning in October 1994 in the role of player-manager following the dismissal of John MacPhail. He initially made a handful of appearances in his traditional role as a ball-winning midfielder before ironically dropping himself and restoring his predecessor MacPhail to the side following a poor run of results. This move allowed him to focus on his managerial role full-time, which brought three successive wins, only to be followed by a 12-game run without a single victory.

'Pools' results through to the end of the season left him marginally in credit and his team finished in 18th position in the Third Division, the bottom tier of English football. He was replaced by Keith Houchen following a victory over his old club, Carlisle United, with only two matches remaining, having been told that his contract would not be renewed for the coming season.

Following his departure from the Victoria Ground, David McCreery was involved with Blyth Spartans before returning to the United States in 1996 to become involved in the formation of Major League Soccer. On his return he became chairman of Weldmore Ltd, based in Consett, County Durham, a company involved in the supply and hire of welding equipment and associated services.

## Keith Morton Houchen

*Born: Middlesbrough, 25 July 1960*
**20 April 1995 to 4 November 1996**

Keith Houchen took over from David McCreery at the end of the 1994–95 season with 'Pools safely above the relegation zone. The new manager had a prolonged playing career as a goalscoring forward, beginning with Hartlepools and embracing five other League clubs, including Coventry City, with whom he won an FA Cup-winners' medal in 1987, scoring a memorable goal in the final at Wembley which earned him the BBC's *Match of the Day's* Goal of the Season award.

Houchen's first spell at the Vic saw him make 170 League appearances, scoring 65 goals. He had spells with Orient, York, Scunthorpe, Coventry and Port Vale, as well as Scottish side Hibernian, for whom he appeared in the UEFA Cup, before returning to 'Pools in August 1993 at the age of 33, where he continued to contribute vital goals in his second spell.

Chairman Harold Hornsey appointed Keith Houchen as player-manager in succession to David McCreery with the stark warning that, like his predecessor, he would have no money available to strengthen the playing squad. The new manager quickly appointed Mick Tait as his assistant with former boss Billy Horner and long-serving player Brian Honour as coaching staff, enabling him to play a creditable 38 League games, scoring six goals, in the 1995–96 season. Despite having forwards such as Joe Allon, Steven Halliday and Steve Howard at his disposal, his side struggled for goals and declined to 20th position, with the player-manager continually at odds with match officials, resulting in a string of bookings.

Houchen continued playing the following season, appearing in five of the first seven League games, which included three wins, before he ended his playing days at the age of 36. Thereafter, 'Pools' results declined with only a single victory in the next 10 fixtures, with Houchen continually involved in embarrassing altercations with referees following a series of disappointing defeats. After a home defeat to Brighton, their seventh loss in eight games, the manager accepted the inevitable and tendered his resignation to chairman Hornsey, which was duly accepted. His parting shot on leaving the club was to comment 'he felt very, very let down by the supporters'.

In July 1997 Keith Houchen's home-town team Middlesbrough provided the opposition in a benefit match at Victoria Park which attracted a crowd of 2,500 and raised £23,000 for the former player and manager. He later coached at Middlesbrough and assisted schools in the development of young players.

## Michael (Mick) Paul Tait

*Born: Wallsend, 30 September 1956*

**4 November 1996 to 18 January 1999**

Mick Tait had a playing career that spanned over 20 years and embraced seven League clubs for whom he made 760 appearances, placing him 15th in the all-time Football League list. He began as an apprentice with Oxford United before moving to Carlisle for a £60,000 fee. This sum was exceeded when Hull City broke their transfer record by paying £150,000 for his services in 1979. Another move, this time to Portsmouth, quickly followed and he spent six seasons with the Fratton Park club before moving to Reading. He returned to his native North East in 1990 with Darlington before arriving at Victoria Park in July 1992, a close season signing by Alan Murray.

Tait played 139 League games for 'Pools in two spells before becoming manager following Keith Houchen's departure. Towards the end of his playing career he became 'Pools' oldest player, when at the age of 40 years and five months he played against Fulham in March 1997. He took over with 'Pools on an eight-match winless run and crowds once again below the 2,000 mark. An initial improvement in playing results quickly dissipated to be followed by a nine-game run without success, during which time he resumed his playing career.

The following season, 1997–98, saw the club under the ownership of IOR Ltd and with it some improvement on the pitch, with only one defeat in the first nine League games. The promising start was followed by a slump in form in the New Year, which eventually resulted in a 17th-place League finish. This was still considered satisfactory given that several young players such as Mickey Barron, Darren Knowles, Steven Howard and Graeme Lee, among others, continued to make good progress and show promise for the future.

A strong start to the 1998–99 campaign, in which only one of the first five League games was lost, proved to be a false dawn. Only one of the next nine games was won and a similar run over the important Christmas and New Year period signalled the end of Mick Tait's reign. He left the club by mutual consent with IOR spokesman Ian MacRae emphasising that he had not been under pressure to resign. One of his last acts was to sign the former Newcastle United and England star Peter Beardsley on a contract to the end of the season.

Tait was replaced on a caretaker basis by Brian Honour and Paul Baker acting in a joint managerial capacity. He returned to his former club, Darlington, in October 2002 as caretaker manager, being confirmed in the role the following June. The return of David Hodgson in October 2003 resulted in his contract as manager being terminated, only for him to return to the club within the month as youth development officer.

In May 2009, after a brief spell as manager of Newcastle Blue Star, Mick Tait was appointed manager of Blue Square North side Blyth Spartans, continuing his association with the game, which now stretches back 35 years.

## David Paul Baker & Brian Honour (joint caretakers)

*Born: Paul Baker at Newcastle, 5 January 1963. Brian Honour at Horden, 16 February 1964*

**18 January 1999 to 24 February 1999**

The two great Hartlepool United stalwarts were employed in coaching capacities at the time of Mick Tait's departure and were given managerial responsibilities by chairman Ken Hodcroft on a joint caretaker basis pending a permanent appointment. Of their five games in charge two were won and three lost. Following an impressive 2–0 win over Halifax with a brace from the highly promising Steven Howard, the local press strongly favoured Brian Honour for the vacant manager's job.

It was obvious, however, that IOR were intent on appointing a well-known football figure from outside the club, and an impressive list of candidates including Chris Turner, Derek Fazackerley and Chris McMenemy were reported as having interviews. After what seemed an eternity Chris Turner was finally confirmed as manager on a two-and-a-half-year contract, with Brian Honour appointed his assistant. Paul Baker was immediately recalled to playing duties and, not for the first time, played a vital role in preserving Hartlepool United's League status.

David Baker.

Brian Honour.

## Christopher (Chris) Robert Turner

*Born: Sheffield, 15 September 1958*

**24 February 1999 to 7 November 2002 and 15 December 2008 to 19 August 2010**

Chris Turner began his football career with the club he supported as a boy, Sheffield Wednesday, for whom he made his League debut while still a teenager. After 91 appearances for the Owls he spent a brief spell on loan to Lincoln City before joining Sunderland in July 1979 for a £100,000 fee. It was with the Wearside club that he established his reputation as a top-class goalkeeper, resulting in his transfer to Manchester United in July 1985 for £275,000 following Sunderland's relegation from the top flight. He went on to make 64 League appearances for the Red Devils before returning to Sheffield Wednesday in September 1988. A brief loan spell at Leeds followed before he ended his playing days with Leyton Orient, whom he later managed.

It proved to be a red-letter day for Hartlepool United when Chris Turner was appointed manager in February 1999 in preference to several more experienced candidates. He joined from Wolverhampton Wanderers, for whom he held a coaching position, and entered Victoria Park with the now prophetic words, 'I look forward to the day when the club has average attendances of 5,000'! Given that the home game prior to his appointment against local rivals Darlington had failed to attract a 4,000 crowd, this appeared to be nothing more than the usual optimism from a new manager.

Chris Turner's first four games in charge were all drawn, three goalless, and this was followed by two defeats which seemed to consign 'Pools to the Conference. A Peter Beardsley-inspired team then won three of the next four games, with Paul Baker contributing vital goals in two of them. Despite losing at Mansfield, a win and two draws in the final games of the season were sufficient to ensure League survival, the manner of which offered genuine hope for the future.

The 1999–2000 season began with all the optimism of the new millennium which was on the horizon. The mood at Victoria Park quickly changed when only one of the opening seven League games was won and another struggle looked inevitable. The manager's response was to install Martin Hollund in goal, give

Graeme Lee an extended run at centre-half and introduce Chris Westwood as Lee's defensive partner. Results improved dramatically with seven of the next 10 games won and all thoughts of the Conference banished. For the rest of the season 'Pools won more than they lost, with Tommy Miller outstanding, the only disappointment being attendances, which averaged just below 3,000. The reward for a seventh-place finish was a first-ever appearance in the Play-offs against, of all teams, Darlington. The Quakers proved too strong, winning both games with the away second leg notable for a live television transmission back to Victoria Park, which attracted several thousand spectators.

Another slow start in 2000–01, with only two wins in the first nine League games, initially put 'Pools on the back foot. This prompted Turner to introduce Anthony Williams between the posts, Paul Arnison at full-back and Mark Tinkler in midfield. These changes, along with the outstanding form of Tommy Miller and Kevin Henderson, transformed the side. A 21-match unbeaten run took 'Pools to the heady heights of fourth position, just outside the automatic promotion places.

Their opponents in the Play-offs, Blackpool, had only achieved seventh place on the final Saturday and were considered the underdogs. Despite being favourites 'Pools were well beaten in both games which, given their form in the second half of the season, was a major disappointment for the Victoria Park faithful, who were now averaging 3,400, the highest for nearly 20 years.

Hopes were high at the start of the 2001–02 season as Turner relied on the same squad of players to mount a promotion challenge. Such hopes were not unfounded, as 'Pools lost only one of their first 10 games, taking the League by storm. It became apparent that Chris Turner's good work at Victoria Park would not go unnoticed in the wider football world, and so it turned out.

In early November Sheffield Wednesday, Turner's first club, requested permission to speak to him about the vacant manager's position at Hillsborough. Understandably, such an approach from one of English football's 'sleeping giants' met with a positive response, and he duly signed a two-and-a-half-year contract. 'Pools appointed Turner's assistant, Colin West, as caretaker manager pending a permanent appointment. Mike Newell, reserve-team coach at Tranmere Rovers, was subsequently engaged as manager and West moved to Hillsborough to continue his association with Chris Turner.

Chris Turner's tenure as manager of Sheffield Wednesday did not turn out a success and after two years he was replaced by Paul Sturrock. He then moved to struggling Stockport County before returning to Victoria Park at the request of chairman Ken Hodcroft as director of sport in 2006.

Turner's new role did not involve any direct responsibilities for the day-to-day management of players and staff, thereby allowing Danny Wilson to continue as manager with all the responsibilities that such a role entails. The departure of Wilson in December 2008 resulted in Turner taking over such responsibilities for team affairs, including signings of new players, although he retained the title director of sport.

Chris Turner started his second spell as manager of 'Pools with an emphatic win over Southend, thereby ending a six-game winless streak. Defeats by three-goal margins over the Christmas period by Scunthorpe and Crewe gave little clue as to the outcome of the FA Cup third-round tie against Premiership Stoke City. In the event every Hartlepool player excelled themselves in a stunning 2–0 victory, the main feature of which was a 30-yard thunderbolt by David Foley to seal the win.

The reward for Chris Turner's side was another home draw against Premiership opposition in the guise of West Ham United, which also brought live television coverage. In the event the Hammers carried too much class, despite 'Pools' best efforts, and two goals in the closing stages of the opening period, the second a highly dubious penalty, carried the Londoners through.

The remaining 21 League games proved a struggle for Turner and his team as the manager attempted to improve the squad with short-term loan signings. Only four games were won in this period, including a surprise 1–0 victory against Danny Wilson's Swindon, and key goals by Danny Nardiello, on loan from Blackpool, and Joel Porter were just enough to avoid relegation by a single point.

For the 2009–10 season Chris Turner brought in an influx of new players, 14 in all, in every position throughout the team. Perhaps understandably this resulted in an indifferent start with only three wins in the opening 12 League games. Cup defeats to

Grimsby Town (Associate Members) and non-League Kettering (FA Cup) saw attendances sink to a nine year low with virulent criticism aimed at the manager both from the terraces and the local press. An improvement in home form and the loan signing of Roy O'Donovan from Sunderland resulted in a position of relative safety which was threatened by a three point deduction for fielding an ineligible player (Gary Liddle) in the win over Brighton. In the final analysis Chris Turner's team avoided relegation on the final day of the season due to a superior goal differnece over Gillingham. When asked by a local reporter to rate the season overall the manager described it as 'satisfactory'.

Chris Turner further strengthened his playing squad with the signings of Evan Horwood, Fabian Yantorno and Paul Murray who had impressed the manager in preseason friendlies. His one surprise was the sacking of Colin West as reserve team manager for the past three years. In West's place came Mick Wadsworth a highly experienced coach with an in depth knowledge of clubs and players in the third and fourth tiers of the Football League.

The new season began with a point at Rochdale in a goalless draw before 'Pools upset the form book by convincingly beating Sheffield United of the Championship in the first round of the Football League Cup followed by a draw against Danny Wilson's Swindon Town only for Turner to abruptly terminate his second spell with the club by resigning. No reason was given by the club for his departure in a brief statement posted on the club's website although it later transpired that he was a member of a consortium bidding to buy Sheffield Wednesday, his former club. Turner's consortium bid failed and the Hillsborough club was eventually bought by Milan Mandaric, previously owner of Portsmouth and Leicester City.

After several months out of football Chris Turner was appointed chief executive of Chesterfield FC in December 2011, a position he continues to hold.

## Colin West (caretaker)

*Born: Wallsend, 13 November 1962*

**7 November 2002 to 21 November 2002**

Tyneside-born Colin West had a lengthy career as a professional footballer, making his League debut for Sunderland, whom he joined as a teenager. He went on to appear for nine other clubs including Watford, Sheffield Wednesday, West Bromwich Albion and Glasgow Rangers, totalling over 400 appearances. It was at Sunderland that he first played with Chris Turner, thereby establishing a football relationship that was to embrace other clubs later in their careers.

Colin West initially joined Hartlepool United as a player in November 1999, making one appearance as a substitute

before becoming Chris Turner's assistant, a post he held at the time of the latter's appointment by Sheffield Wednesday. His elevation was a short-term solution pending the arrival of a new manager.

West was in charge of the team for two games, Exeter City in the League, which was won 2–1, and a 1–1 draw against Southend United in the first round of the FA Cup, results that led the local press to lobby for his position to be made permanent. However, following the appointment of Mike Newell he rejoined Turner at Sheffield Wednesday as assistant manager, the pair later moving to Stockport County in similar roles.

Colin West then had spells at Millwall, initially as reserve-team coach and later assistant caretaker manager before moving to Southend United in a reserve-team coaching position. In February 2009 he accepted an offer from Chris Turner to reprise his role as assistant manager at Victoria Park which ended in June 2010 following a disappointing campaign which saw relegation avoided only by goal difference on the final day of the season.

In February 2012 another chapter in West's career opened when he was appointed coach to Notts County by manager Keith Curle.

## Michael (Mike) Colin Newell

*Born: Liverpool, 27 January 1965*

**21 November 2002 to 31 May 2003**

Mike Newell was appointed to his first managerial post in November 2002 in succession to Chris Turner, having previously been reserve-team coach at Tranmere Rovers. He was appointed by chairman Ken Hodcroft until the end of the season from a list of 35 candidates, many of them household names.

Newell had a distinguished playing career that embraced 13 League clubs and

saw him make a total of 505 League appearances, scoring 116 goals. He also won England Under-21 and B international honours. His personal highlight was to be a member of the outstanding Blackburn Rovers squad that won the Premiership title in 1994–95.

With Hartlepool flying high in the League, most fans expected a 'steady as she goes' approach from the new manager. In fact, Newell initially strengthened the League position and a six-game unbeaten run in January resulted in a divisional Manager of the Month award. This was followed by an unbeaten run in February, by which time 'Pools were a staggering 12 points clear at the top of the League, prompting many commentators and supporters to assume the long-awaited Championship trophy was a foregone conclusion.

The cracks started to appear at the beginning of March with a resounding defeat at Lincoln. Four of the next five games were goalless with a welcome home win against Leyton Orient immediately followed by a heavy reverse at Scunthorpe. The title chase went to the final game against Rushden and Diamonds, who only needed a draw to clinch their first Championship after only two seasons in the Football League. Despite 'Pools' best efforts Rushden earned the point they needed and, although promotion was secured, the season ended in massive disappointment for most supporters.

At the end of May the club issued a press statement saying that Mike Newell's contract, having expired, was not being renewed. No reason was given for the shock decision and despite persistent pressure from the local media, chairman Ken Hodcroft was not forthcoming as to the reasons. On departing the club Newell admitted that he was not 'a people person' and preferred the coaching and training environment with his players, with whom it was widely accepted he had an excellent rapport.

He later managed Luton Town from 2003 to 2007, winning the Football League One Championship in style before departing the following season after a dispute with the chairman over transfer policy. During his time at Kenilworth Road he caused controversy by, firstly, making sexist comments about a female assistant referee, Amy Ryner, and later making claims that corruption was ripe in transfer deals throughout the professional game. The Football Association took these claims so seriously that they appointed Lord Stevens, a former Metropolitan Police Commissioner, to investigate. He concluded that although the level of corruption was not as high as anticipated, there was cause for concern. Seventeen transfers involving major clubs were investigated with little action forthcoming and it still remains to be seen whether Newell's allegations were well-founded.

Mike Newell was appointed manager of struggling Grimsby Town in October 2008 on a three-and-a-half-year contract. At the time the Mariners were only two places above the League Two relegation zone and still without a victory. He finally recorded his first win after nine games in charge and, backed by his board, made some shrewd signings which eventually paid off with a final position of 22nd, four points above the relegation places. A poor start to the 2009–10 season, in which only 10 points were gained from 13 games, resulted in his contract being terminated a mere 12 months after his appointment.

## Neale James Cooper

*Born: Darjeeling, India, 24 November 1963*
**28 June 2003 to 4 May 2005 and 28 December 2011 to present**

Neale Cooper had a footballing pedigree second to none, having been a member of the successful Aberdeen side managed by Alex Ferguson that won the 1983 European Cup-Winners' Cup, beating Real Madrid in the Final. Cooper left Aberdeen having made 132 appearances and won two Championship medals before joining Aston Villa in July 1986. He made only infrequent appearances in five seasons at Villa Park before moving to Reading in July 1991, playing only a handful of games for the Royals before returning to Scotland with Glasgow Rangers.

Cooper accepted the post of Hartlepool United manager on a six-month rolling contract in June 2003, having previously managed Scottish clubs Forfar Athletic and Ross County. His appointment came as a shock as he had no experience of management in the Football League and was little known as a player outside his native Scotland. However, he turned out to be an inspired choice.

The sudden departure of Mike Newell raised understandable concerns about 'Pools' prospects for the 2003–04 season in Division Two, given that previous promotions had been quickly followed by a return to the lower division. Such doubts were swiftly dispelled when Cooper's side scored a stunning and unexpected victory at Peterborough United on the opening day. Things got even better when, after a steady run of results, Grimsby Town were dispatched 8–1. This victory convinced the normally sceptical Hartlepool public that the side could compete at the higher level and attendances quickly improved, with over 7,000 attending the Sheffield Wednesday game.

The season got better as League form was carried into the FA Cup, and after wins against non-League sides Whitby Town and Burton Albion 'Pools earned the draw of their dreams against Sunderland. A record attendance for any game involving Hartlepool United of 40,816 saw the visitors give the Division One side a terrific struggle before narrowly losing to a quality finish by Julio Arca. The team put any disappointment felt by the Cup exit quickly behind them with a five-match winning run to finish the season confirmed in a Play-off place against Bristol City. Both Play-off games were fiercely contested with United only managing a draw at home. The second game, in front of 18,434 partisan fans, saw both sides play themselves to a standstill before Bristol City prevailed with two late goals, Tony Sweeney having given the visitors the lead.

Cooper's second season, 2004–05, began with impressive victories over Bradford City, Huddersfield Town and Colchester United, confirming the hopes that another promotion push was on the cards. By Christmas 'Pools were in the top six and in the middle of another run in the FA Cup, which this time ended in controversial fashion in a fourth-round replay defeat against Brentford at the Vic. A win would have put 'Pools in the fifth-round draw for the first time in their history. Despite the Cup setback the team performed consistently in the League and only a four-game losing run in March, which included an amazing 6–4 home defeat to Wrexham, prevented them from claiming an automatic promotion spot.

With his team confirmed in the Play-offs and only one League game remaining, the club announced that Neil Cooper had left by 'mutual consent', although speculation in the local press suggested he had been sacked. Despite being linked with a return to Scottish football he joined relegated Championship side Gillingham two weeks later. Cooper's tenure as manager of the Gills lasted only a matter of months following a dreadful start to the 2005–06 season.

Neil Cooper returned to Scotland as coach to Aberdeen's Under-19 side before joining Peterhead as assistant to manager Steve Paterson. Following Paterson's dismissal in January 2008, Cooper was appointed manager of the Scottish Second Division side and immediately saw his side demolish Berwick Rangers 9–2, finishing the season in fifth position. Cooper's team improved the following season, 2008–09, to make the Play-offs for Division One, losing both legs of their semi-final to Airdrie United.

The following season, 2009–10, saw Cooper's team finish fifth in the Scottish Second Division a win away from a Play-off place.

The following season was not so successful and after a run of poor results which left Peterhead in the relegation zone Neale Cooper was dismissed in March 2011. It was therefore a major surprise to the football community of Hartlepool when chairman Ken Hodcroft announced that he would succeed Mick Wadsworth as manager for a second spell.

Neale Cooper had a hugely successful first spell with Hartlepool United which not only saw the club reach a Play-off Final but also play a style which provided entertainment and above all, goals. His return was warmly welcomed by fans who saw the first priority as being an end to the record home losing streak. However, it was quickly recognised after an away loss to Sheffield United and his first home game against a lowly Scunthorpe side which resulted in a 2–1 defeat, that much work needed to be done to motivate a lack lustre squad of players.

The new manager's response was to give youth a chance while roundly criticising the performances of some senior players. The changes resulted in the cycle of home defeats ending with a 2–0 victory over Rochdale with 17-year-old Luke James becoming the club's youngest goalscorer. James quickly followed this up with a brace of goals in the convincing 4–0 win over Play-off challengers Carlisle. Other teenagers were handed their debuts in the closing weeks of the season, Lewis Hawkins and Jordan Richards among others, and Ryan Noble was recruited on loan from Sunderland. Despite inheriting a settled and largely sound defence, goals remained the major problem with a mere five scored in 11 consecutive games in the closing weeks of the campaign.

A final League One position of 13th was not sufficient to persuade the manager to offer new contracts to several senior players, Adam Boyd, James Brown and Steve Haslem among them, and he commented on their departures that 'I need to bring in better players' for next season.

## Martin Scott

*Born: Sheffield, 7 January 1968*

**4 May 2005 to 8 February 2006**

Martin Scott took over initially as caretaker manager following the sudden and unexpected departure of Neale Cooper in the final days of the 2004–05 season, having been his assistant.

Scott began his footballing career with Rotherham United in 1984 as an apprentice. He made his League debut in January 1986 and went on to make 94 League appearances for the Millmoor side at full-back. He then joined Bristol City in December 1990 and played 171 games for the Ashton Gate side, helping them to promotions to Division Two (1990) and Division One (1992). After four years with Bristol City Scott joined Sunderland in December 1994, going on to make 106 League appearances and being a member of the record-breaking side which returned to the Premiership in 1999.

Martin Scott's priority on taking over as manager was to prepare the side for the 2004–05 Play-off semi-final against Tranmere Rovers. 'Pools won the first leg thanks to two Adam Boyd goals before losing the advantage in the return and surviving extra-time. They won through to the final 6–5 on penalties, with Richie Humphreys scoring the decisive goal.

Scott prepared his side well for the League One Play-off Final at Cardiff against Sheffield Wednesday in front of nearly 60,000 spectators. After Wednesday had taken the lead on the stroke of half-time, second-half goals from Williams and Daly gave 'Pools a 2–1 lead before the game swung on a marginal decision, which not only gave Wednesday a penalty, but also resulted in the dismissal of Chris Westwood. With the game going to extra-time, two late goals gave Wednesday a flattering victory.

Despite the disappointment of missing out so narrowly on promotion to the Championship, Martin Scott was confirmed as manager for the 2005–06 season with confidence high that another promotion campaign would soon be underway. Alas, this was most emphatically not the case. The transfer of star striker Adam Boyd, ironically to Mike Newell's Luton Town, and an influx of new players from Scott's former club Sunderland resulted in a disastrous start, which saw only three League wins in the first 12 games. The season took an even worse turn when non-League Tamworth won a second-round FA Cup tie at the Vic, followed by a 10-game run without a win over the Christmas and New Year period.

Clearly, with events both on and off the pitch deteriorating to such an extent, Scott was suspended by the club following a dressing room fracas after the home defeat to Blackpool at the end of January. After an internal investigation the manager was relieved of his duties and youth-team coach Paul Stephenson, a former Hartlepool player, took over on a temporary basis.

Martin Scott later joined Bury on a one-year contract as assistant manager to Chris Casper for the 2006–07 season. On being released at the end of a campaign, which saw the Gigg Lane club finish in 21st position, he accepted a role as coach to the Under-18 team at Middlesbrough, later transferring his coaching duties to the reserve side.

The arrival of Gordon Strachan in October 2009 in succession to Gareth Southgate resulted in the inevitable reorganisation of coaching staff and Martin Scott was released in May 2010.

## Paul Stephenson (caretaker)

*Born: Wallsend, 2 January 1968*

**2 February 2006 to 13 June 2006**

Paul Stephenson was handed the unenviable task of taking over as caretaker manager following the public falling-out and subsequent dismissal of Martin Scott. He inherited a team in disarray following a run of nine games without a win and relegation was almost inevitable.

Stephenson joined Newcastle United as an apprentice and established himself as a key member of the 1985 FA Youth Cup-winning side which included Joe Allon. After 61 League appearances for the Magpies he moved south to play for Millwall, Gillingham and Brentford before returning north with York City. He was signed for 'Pools by Mick Tait in March 1998 and went on to play 145 League games before retiring at the end of the 2001–02 season.

Stephenson was in charge of the team for 15 League games, only three of which were won, and relegation followed,

although a number of drawn games kept the issue open until the final day of the season. He stood down as caretaker manager on the appointment of Danny Wilson and resumed his duties as youth-team coach.

In November 2007 Stephenson left Victoria Park after nearly 10 years' service to join Norwich City as a coach. After the departure of manager Glenn Roeder in January 2009 he joined Huddersfield Town the following month to work for his former Newcastle United teammate, Lee Clark, as director of football development before being promoted to first-team coach in November 2010.

## Daniel (Danny) Joseph Wilson

*Born: Wigan, 1 January 1960*

**14 June 2006 to 15 December 2008**

Danny Wilson had an extended playing career with eight League clubs, which saw him make over 600 appearances in the Football League and win 24 international caps for Northern Ireland. His playing career began with Bury, for whom he made 90 appearances, scoring nine goals before moving to Chesterfield and reaching a century of games before brief spells at Nottingham Forest and Scunthorpe. A four-year spell and 135 games with Brighton was followed by three seasons with Luton Town. The final phase of his playing career was with Sheffield Wednesday and Barnsley, the latter being his first managerial appointment.

Danny Wilson's career in management could not have had a more auspicious start, as he took Barnsley to the dizzy heights of the Premiership. Unsurprisingly, the South Yorkshire side was unable to compete at the top level of club football and the inevitable relegation resulted in his dismissal. Spells at Sheffield Wednesday and Bristol City followed before he joined

Milton Keynes Dons in 2004. Ironically, his last game in charge at the end of the 2005–06 season saw his side relegated along with Hartlepool United, the club he was to join in the close season.

The new manager's first task was to restore confidence to a team which had been badly shaken by relegation only a season after reaching the Play-off Final. Initially he kept to the core squad he inherited, despite early-season results being disappointing. By the end of October the side was firmly rooted in mid-table with 20 points from 16 games before a somewhat fortuitous victory over lowly Barnet set the side on a record-breaking run. Of the next 24 League games only four were drawn and the rest won as 'Pools stormed to the summit of the League. The run finally ended at Barnet in April, by which time an automatic promotion spot was assured. Perhaps understandably for a side which relied on a small number of key players, the playing schedule took its toll and defeats in the final two games robbed Wilson's team of their first-ever Championship trophy.

The 2007–08 season began with seven players making their debuts in a narrow defeat at Luton. It soon became apparent that the side was missing the influence of Dimi Konstantopolous in goal as Wilson tried both his new signings, Arran Lee-Barratt and Jan Budtz in the early stages of the campaign. A poor run in November saw a slide down the table, only for footballing matters to be put in true perspective with the tragic death of Michael Maidens. This affected the whole club both on and off the pitch, and only two wins in 13 League games saw a real prospect of a quick return to League Two. The departure of Ian Moore saw the return to the side of Joel Porter, used mainly as a substitute up to this point, and with it an improvement in results. A final position of 15th was not what the manager, players or fans hoped for at the start of the season, but given everything that had happened they were more than happy to accept it, with the promise of better things next time around.

During the close season there was much speculation locally that Danny Wilson might leave the club. Having signed an influx of players the previous summer on two-year contracts he had little money available to improve his squad for the coming 2008–09 season, and this was reflected in his signings. Matters took a turn for the worse in only the third game of the new season when Willie Boland suffered an injury which ultimately ended his career. Furthermore, the veteran striker Richie Barker, used as a substitute in the opening games, asked to be allowed to return to his South Yorkshire roots, a request the club granted. The one bright spot in all of this was the form of Joel Porter, himself in the final year of his contract.

It was really no surprise when chairman Ken Hodcroft announced that Danny Wilson was leaving, to be replaced by Chris Turner, following a draw with second from-bottom Hereford United courtesy of an own-goal. 'Pools were in 13th position in League One, having gone six games without a win, and home attendances were barely above the 3,000 mark. Despite a stunning win over Premiership side West Bromwich Albion in the Carling Cup, the chairman had referred at length to the financial position at the club's Annual General Meeting and the appointment of Turner, titled director of sport, effectively removed a highly-paid position from the payroll.

Within days of his departure from Victoria Park Danny Wilson was installed as manager of Swindon Town in succession to Maurice Malpas. His first priority was to steady a struggling club in danger of being relegated to the bottom tier of the Football League. After an initial mixed set of results, including a home defeat to 'Pools, his organisational skills impacted the team and a relatively safe finish of 15th resulted. During the close season Wilson completely reshaped the playing squad and achieved a major coup by selling Simon Cox to West Bromwich Albion for a reported fee of nearly £2 million.

The 2009–10 season turned out to be a near triumph for Danny Wilson and his team when after an indifferent start, seven of the opening 12 games were drawn, results including a 3–0 win over Leeads United improved in the New Year. An automatic promotion place was denied when a modest finale resulted in only one win in the final six games to secure a Play-off semi-final against Charlton Athletic which was eventually settled in Swindon's favour 5–4 on penalties after both teams had won their home legs 2–1. The Final at Wembley against Millwall ultimately proved a disappointment as the East London side narrowly won by the only goal of the game to leave Wilson and his players to contemplate another season in League One.

The sale of star striker Billy Paynter had a major impact on Swindon's 2010–11 campaign and the anticipated promotion challenge never materialised to such an extent that by March Swindon was occupying a relegation place. Inevitably such results affected his position and Wilson bowed to the inevitable and resigned.

It was a surprise to many in the football world when ambitious League One Sheffield United appointed Danny Wilson manager in May for the forthcoming 2011–12 season. The campaign proved a fascinating struggle between the two Sheffield clubs for the second automatic promotion place, with Charlton Athletic occupying top place all season. The odds appeared in United's favour only for Wilson's plans to be seriously impacted by the jailing for rape of leading goalscorer Ched Evans in the closing weeks of the regular season. Wednesday clinched automatic promotion on the final day to leave Wilson's team to contest the third place in the Play-offs. Following victory over Stevenage the Final was contested against Yorkshire rivals Huddersfield Town at Wembley. After a goalless two hours during which United were second best the penalty shoot-out totalled 22 kicks before Huddersfield won 8–7. Once again Danny Wilson had seen his team fail to win promotion at the final hurdle.

## Michael (Mick) Wadsworth

*Born: Barnsley, 3 November 1950*

**19 August 2010 to 6 December 2011**

Mick Wadsworth was initially appointed temporary manager in August 2010 following the sudden departure of Chris Turner, having joined the club only weeks earlier as first-team coach. After a short professional playing career with Scunthorpe United he decided to concentrate on the coaching side of the game and steadily progressed to become assistant to Sir Bobby Robson at Newcastle United. His most successful managerial post was with Carlisle United during the 1990s taking the Cumbrians to the old Third Division Championship and the Auto Windscreens Shield Final against Birmingham City at Wembley only losing to a 'golden' goal. He later managed Norwich City before returning to the North Eeast with Newcastle and latterly held posts with Southampton, Oldham Athletic and Huddersfield Town.

The new manager began with a comfortable victory at Yeovil before a run of only one win in six games saw Boyd and Behan dropped in favour of Brown and Larkin. These changes had the desired effect as only two games were lost in a 14-match run through to the New Year which saw 'Pools rise to within three points of a Pay-off place with two games in hand. This spell of relative success was enough to earn Mick Wadsworth the December League One Manager of the Month award with the consistent Sam Collins named Player of the Month.

Wadsworth, like many others before him, must have rued such an accolade as 'Pools form fell away in the New Year and after an FA Cup exit at Watford was followed by a six match winless run in League One all hopes of a Play-off place vanished. The remaining games of the season produced a mixed bag of results with 'Pools final League One position of 16th a fair reflection of a season of variable results and performances. In the close season Wadsworth took the opportunity to release several underperforming players including Armann Bjornsson, Denis Behan, Joe

Gamble and Fabian Yantorno before springing a major surprise in signing Nobby Solano the former Newcastle United and Peru player. The pair had an association during their time on Tyneside and this was reportedly a key factor in persuading the player to sign.

Mick Wadsworth saw his 'Pools side start the League One season with a bang. After a creditable draw on the opening day against promotion favourites Milton Keynes Dons, three further draws followed before a winning streak of five games took 'Pools up to third place in League One and established a new club record start to a season of nine games without defeat. Such a start exceeded all expectations and with home attendances averaging over 5,000 thanks to the £100 season ticket offer the manager had every reason to be optimistic for the remainder of the season.

The record start was ended in early October by Sheffield Wednesday who won more comfortably than the single goal scoreline suggested. A week later 'Pools lost to Notts County in front of the Sky Sports cameras before another home defeat, to Wycombe Wanderers, was balanced by victory at Chesterfield only for the next two games at 'The Vic' to be lost, making four consecutive home defeats. Four points from the next two away games (Leyton Orient draw, Scunthorpe win) were a prelude to further home losses to Yeovil and Preston which resulted in Mick Wadsworth's departure.

Opinions were divided on the merits of Wadsworth's sacking. On the one hand he had seen his team set a new record for an unbeaten start to a season while on the other he was in a run of six consecutive home League defeats. Hartlepool United in a statement on the club website stressed that a factor in the decision was the record run of home defeats and the style of the performances. The statement went on to announce that Mickey Barron would take temporary charge of the first team pending the appointment of a new 'manager'.

## Michael (Mickey) Barron

*Born: Chester le Street, 22 December 1974*

**6 December 2011 to 27 December 2011**

Since retiring from playing in January 2008 Mickey Barron had fulfilled a number of coaching roles, initially with the youth team. At the time of Mick Wadsworth's departure he was reserve team coach.

A hugely popular player with the fans, Barron initially joined 'Pools from Middlesbrough on loan before making the move permanent in 1997. He went on to make 374 League and Cup appearances for the club gaining successive Player of the Year awards in 1998 and 1999 before being rewarded with a testimonial for 10 years sterling service.

He was in charge of the team for three games – a win (1–0 at Oldham); and two defeats (1–2 at Brentford and 0–1 home to Colchester). He did, however, give debuts to two young players, Jack Baldwin and Luke James, both of whom were to demonstrate in later games their rich potential. Following Neale Cooper's appointment Mickey Barron reverted back to his role as reserve team coach.

# SEASON STATISTICS

# 1908-09

## North Eastern League

Manager: Fred Priest

### Did you know that?

Fred Priest was appointed player-manager on a three-year contract at the princely wage of £3 per week. Spectators were charged 6d (21/2p) admission.

The average (estimated) home attendance for Hartlepools United's first season was 4,833.

In the close season the club undertook a tour of Germany, playing friendly matches against Hamburg and (Werder) Bremen and winning both games.

| Match No. | Date | Round | Venue | Opponents | Result | | Scorers | Attendance |
|---|---|---|---|---|---|---|---|---|
| 1 | Sep 5 | | (a) | Hebburn Argyle | D | 2 - 2 | Fletcher 2 | 3,000 |
| 2 | 12 | | (h) | Seaham White Star | D | 0 - 0 | | 5,000 |
| 3 | 19 | | (a) | Darlington | D | 2 - 2 | Brown 2 | 2,000 |
| 4 | 26 | | (h) | North Shields Athletic | W | 2 - 0 | Edgley, Fletcher | 4,000 |
| 6 | Oct 10 | | (h) | Wallsend Park Villa | W | 3 - 1 | Fletcher 2, Hand | 6,000 |
| 9 | 24 | | (h) | Spennymoor United | W | 2 - 1 | Fletcher 2 | 4,000 |
| 10 | 31 | | (h) | Bradford Park Avenue 'A' | D | 1 - 1 | Leneghan | 3,000 |
| 11 | Nov 7 | | (h) | Carlisle United | W | 4 - 1 | Edgley 3, Fletcher | 6,000 |
| 12 | 21 | | (a) | North Shields Athletic | L | 1 - 3 | F.Tweddle | |
| 13 | Dec 19 | | (a) | West Stanley | L | 1 - 3 | F.Tweddle | |
| 14 | 25 | | (h) | West Stanley | W | 2 - 0 | Fletcher, T.Hegarty | 5,000 |
| 15 | 28 | | (h) | Darlington | W | 8 - 1 | Hand (pen), Swift, Fletcher 2, Roberts, Edgley 3 | |
| 16 | Jan 1 | | (h) | Huddersfield Town | W | 4 - 1 | Fletcher, T.Hegarty 2 (2 pens), Roberts | 5,000 |
| 17 | 2 | | (h) | Sunderland 'A' | W | 4 - 1 | Edgley, F.Tweddle, Fletcher, Roberts | 10,000 |
| 18 | 9 | | (a) | Bradford Park Avenue 'A' | L | 0 - 4 | | 2,000 |
| 19 | 30 | | (a) | Spennymoor United | L | 3 - 4 | Fletcher 2, Edgley | |
| 20 | Feb 13 | | (h) | South Shields Adelaide | D | 2 - 2 | Wilson (o.g.), Roberts | 6,000 |
| 21 | 20 | | (a) | Sunderland 'A' | W | 4 - 2 | Brown, R.Hegarty, Smith, Fletcher | 3,000 |
| 22 | 27 | | (h) | Middlesbrough 'A' | W | 1 - 0 | T.Hegarty (pen) | 5,300 |
| 23 | Mar 6 | | (a) | Middlesbrough 'A' | L | 0 - 1 | | 3,000 |
| 24 | 13 | | (a) | Shildon Athletic | D | 2 - 2 | Brown 2 | |
| 25 | 20 | | (h) | Newcastle United 'A' | L | 2 - 4 | Fletcher (pen), F.Tweddle | 6,684 |
| 26 | 31 | | (h) | Shildon Athletic | W | 4 - 1 | Fletcher 2, Brown, F.Tweddle | 2,000 |
| 27 | Apr 3 | | (a) | Sunderland Royal Rovers | W | 1 - 0 | F.Tweddle | |
| 28 | 5 | | (a) | Newcastle United 'A' | L | 1 - 3 | Edgley | 800 |
| 29 | 10 | | (a) | South Shields Adelaide | D | 1 - 1 | Hand | |
| 30 | 12 | | (h) | Workington | W | 5 - 0 | F.Tweddle 2, Edgley, Fletcher, Smith (pen) | 3,000 |
| 31 | 13 | | (h) | Hebburn Argyle | W | 5 - 1 | Stevenson (o.g.), Fletcher, T.Hegarty (pen), Ledger, Ridsdale | |
| 32 | 17 | | (a) | Seaham White Star | W | 5 - 2 | Seal, Edgley, Fletcher 3 | |
| 33 | 21 | | (a) | Huddersfield Town | D | 0 - 0 | | |
| 34 | 22 | | (a) | Carlisle United | L | 0 - 3 | | |
| 35 | 24 | | (a) | Wallsend Park Villa | D | 2 - 2 | Brown, Fletcher | |
| 36 | 28 | | (h) | Sunderland Royal Rovers | W | 5 - 1 | Edgley 2, Fletcher 2, Ledger | 1,500 |
| 37 | 29 | | (a) | Workington | L | 0 - 1 | | |

Final Position : 4th in North Eastern League — Apps.

2 own goals — Goals

**FA Cup**

| Match No. | Date | Round | Venue | Opponents | Result | | Scorers | Attendance |
|---|---|---|---|---|---|---|---|---|
| 5 | Oct 3 | QR1 | (h) | West Hartlepool | W | 2 - 1 | Brown, Smith | 7,000 |
| 7 | 17 | QR2 | (a) | South Bank | D | 2 - 2 | Edgley 2 | |
| 8 | 21 | QR2r | (h) | South Bank | L | 0 - 2 | | 2,000 |

Apps.

Goals

| Mearns | Priest | Hegarty, R. | Tweddle, S. | Hand | Smith | Hewston | Fletcher | Edgley | Lenaghan | Seal | Reed | Brown | Tweddle, F. | Ledger | Wilson | Harvey | Roberts | Maddison | Higgins | Hegarty, T. | Swift | Prosser | Ridsdale | Kelly | Parkinson |
|---|---|---|---|---|---|---|---|---|---|---|---|---|---|---|---|---|---|---|---|---|---|---|---|---|---|
| 1 | 2 | 3 | 4 | 5 | 6 | 7 | 8 | 9 | 10 | 11 | | | | | | | | | | | | | | | |
| 1 | | 3 | 4 | 5 | | | 8 | 9 | 10 | 11 | 2 | 6 | 7 | | | | | | | | | | | | |
| 1 | 2 | 3 | 4 | 5 | | | 7 | 9 | | | | 10 | 8 | 6 | 11 | | | | | | | | | | |
| 1 | 2 | | 4 | 5 | 3 | | 8 | 9 | | | | 10 | 7 | 6 | | | 11 | | | | | | | | |
| 1 | | | 4 | 5 | 3 | | 7 | 9 | | | | 10 | 8 | 6 | | 2 | 11 | | | | | | | | |
| 1 | | 3 | | 5 | | | 7 | 4 | 9 | | | | 8 | 6 | | | 11 | 2 | 10 | | | | | | |
| 1 | | 2 | | 5 | 3 | | 7 | 9 | 4 | | | | 8 | 6 | | | 11 | | 10 | | | | | | |
| 1 | 2 | 3 | | 4 | 5 | | 7 | 9 | | | | 10 | 8 | 6 | | | 11 | | | | | | | | |
| 1 | | | 4 | 5 | 3 | | 7 | 9 | | | | 10 | 8 | 6 | | | 11 | | | 2 | | | | | |
| 1 | | | 4 | 5 | 3 | | 8 | 9 | | | | 10 | 7 | 6 | | | 11 | | | 2 | | | | | |
| 1 | | 3 | | 4 | 5 | | 7 | 9 | | | | 10 | 8 | 6 | | | 11 | | | 2 | | | | | |
| 1 | | 3 | 6 | 4 | 5 | | 7 | 9 | | | | 10 | | | | | 11 | | | 2 | 8 | | | | |
| 1 | | 3 | | 4 | 5 | | 8 | 9 | | | | 10 | 7 | 6 | | | 11 | | | 2 | | | | | |
| 1 | | 3 | | 4 | 5 | | 8 | 9 | | | | 10 | 7 | 6 | | | 11 | | | 2 | | | | | |
| 1 | | 3 | 4 | 5 | | | 8 | 9 | | | | 10 | 7 | 6 | | | 11 | | | 2 | | | | | |
| 1 | | 3 | | 4 | 5 | | 8 | 9 | | | | 10 | 7 | 6 | | | 11 | | | 2 | | | | | |
| 1 | | 3 | 4 | 6 | 5 | | 8 | 9 | | | | 10 | 7 | | | | 11 | | | 2 | | | | | |
| 1 | | 3 | | 6 | 5 | | 8 | 9 | | | | 10 | 7 | | | | 11 | | | 2 | | 4 | | | |
| 1 | | 3 | | 6 | 5 | | 8 | 9 | | | | 10 | 7 | | | | 11 | | | 2 | | 4 | | | |
| 1 | | 3 | | 4 | 5 | | 8 | 9 | | | | 10 | 7 | 6 | | | 11 | | | 2 | | | | | |
| 1 | | 3 | | 4 | 5 | | 8 | 9 | | | | 10 | 7 | 6 | | | 11 | | | 2 | | | | | |
| 1 | | 3 | | 4 | 5 | | 8 | 9 | | | | 10 | 7 | 6 | | | 11 | | | 2 | | | | | |
| | | 2 | 4 | 5 | 3 | | 8 | 9 | | | | 10 | 7 | 6 | | | | | | | | | 11 | 1 | |
| 1 | | 3 | 4 | 5 | | | 8 | 9 | | | | 10 | 7 | 6 | | | | | | 2 | | | 11 | | |
| 1 | | 3 | 4 | 5 | | | 8 | 9 | | | | 10 | 7 | 6 | | | | | | 2 | | | 11 | | |
| | | 2 | 4 | 5 | 3 | | 8 | 9 | | | | 10 | 7 | 6 | | | | | | | | | 11 | 1 | |
| | | 2 | 4 | 5 | 3 | | 8 | 9 | | | | 10 | 7 | 6 | | | 11 | | | | | | | 1 | |
| 1 | | | 4 | 5 | 3 | | 8 | 9 | | | | 10 | 7 | 6 | | | | | | 2 | | | 11 | | |
| 1 | | | 4 | 5 | 3 | | 8 | 9 | | 10 | | | 7 | 6 | | | 11 | | | 2 | | | | | |
| 1 | | | 4 | 5 | 3 | | 8 | 9 | | 10 | | | 7 | 6 | | | 11 | | | 2 | | | | | |
| 1 | | | 4 | 5 | 3 | | 8 | 9 | | | | 10 | 7 | 6 | | | 11 | | | 2 | | | | | |
| | | 3 | 4 | 5 | | | 8 | 9 | | | | 10 | 7 | 6 | | | 11 | | | 2 | | | | 1 | |
| 1 | | 3 | 4 | 5 | | | 8 | 9 | | | | 10 | 7 | 6 | | | 11 | | | 2 | | | | | |
| 1 | | 3 | | 5 | | | 8 | 9 | | | | 10 | 7 | 6 | | | 11 | | | 2 | | | | | 4 |
| 30 | 4 | 26 | 21 | 34 | 25 | 1 | 34 | 34 | 4 | 4 | 1 | 29 | 32 | 28 | 1 | 1 | 26 | 1 | 2 | 23 | 1 | 2 | 5 | 4 | 1 |
| | | 1 | | 3 | 2 | | 27 | 14 | 1 | 1 | | 7 | 8 | 2 | | | 4 | | | 5 | 1 | | 1 | | |

| Mearns | Priest | Hegarty, R. | Tweddle, S. | Hand | Smith | Hewston | Fletcher | Edgley | Lenaghan | Seal | Reed | Brown | Tweddle, F. | Ledger | Wilson | Harvey | Roberts |
|---|---|---|---|---|---|---|---|---|---|---|---|---|---|---|---|---|---|
| 1 | 2 | | 4 | 5 | 3 | | 7 | 9 | | | | 10 | 8 | 6 | | | 11 |
| 1 | 2 | | 4 | 5 | | | 7 | 9 | | | | 10 | 8 | 6 | | 3 | 11 |
| 1 | 3 | | 4 | 5 | | | 8 | 9 | | 11 | | 10 | 7 | 6 | | 2 | |
| 3 | 3 | | 3 | 3 | 1 | | 3 | 3 | | 1 | | 3 | 3 | 3 | | 2 | 2 |
| | | | | | 1 | | | 2 | | | | 1 | | | | | |

## League Table

| | P | W | D | L | F | A | Pts |
|---|---|---|---|---|---|---|---|
| Newcastle United 'A' | 34 | 26 | 4 | 4 | 106 | 48 | 56 |
| South Shields Adelaide | 34 | 22 | 4 | 8 | 80 | 41 | 48 |
| Bradford Park Avenue 'A' | 34 | 19 | 5 | 10 | 84 | 49 | 43 |
| Hartlepools United | 34 | 16 | 9 | 9 | 79 | 51 | 41 |
| Middlesbrough 'A' | 34 | 17 | 6 | 11 | 82 | 45 | 40 |
| Sunderland 'A' | 34 | 18 | 3 | 13 | 81 | 54 | 39 |
| West Stanley | 34 | 18 | 3 | 13 | 73 | 56 | 39 |
| Darlington | 34 | 15 | 8 | 11 | 76 | 73 | 38 |
| North Shields Athletic | 34 | 14 | 6 | 14 | 63 | 48 | 34 |
| Spennymoor United | 34 | 13 | 7 | 14 | 55 | 63 | 33 |
| Wallsend Park Villa | 34 | 13 | 6 | 15 | 55 | 66 | 32 |
| Workington | 34 | 12 | 5 | 17 | 50 | 80 | 29 |
| Seaham White Star | 34 | 10 | 7 | 17 | 55 | 64 | 27 |
| Hebburn Argyle | 34 | 10 | 6 | 18 | 55 | 91 | 26 |
| Carlisle United | 34 | 10 | 4 | 20 | 61 | 84 | 24 |
| Huddersfield Town | 34 | 10 | 4 | 20 | 47 | 78 | 24 |
| Shildon Athletic | 34 | 7 | 6 | 21 | 51 | 101 | 20 |
| Sunderland Royal Rovers | 34 | 7 | 5 | 22 | 39 | 100 | 19 |

# 1909-10

## North Eastern League

Manager: Fred Priest

### Did you know that?

In December Hebburn Argyle were beaten 10–0 to start a run of four consecutive home wins which saw 26 goals scored, including eight by Tommy Brown and six by Joshie Fletcher.

In the club's application for admission to the Football League, the directors stated that the Victoria Ground was three minutes walk from West Hartlepool station! In the event, 'Pools only managed a single vote with Huddersfield Town elected to Division Two.

| Match No. | Date | Round | Venue | Opponents | Result | | Scorers | Attendance |
|---|---|---|---|---|---|---|---|---|
| 1 | Sep 4 | | (a) | Hebburn Argyle | L | 0 - 1 | | 1,000 |
| 2 | 11 | | (a) | Workington | W | 1 - 0 | Brown | |
| 3 | 25 | | (a) | Sunderland 'A' | W | 1 - 0 | T.Hegarty (pen) | |
| 6 | Oct 23 | | (a) | South Shields Adelaide | L | 0 - 1 | | |
| 7 | 30 | | (h) | Darlington | W | 2 - 1 | Hand, Brown | 4,200 |
| 8 | Nov 6 | | (a) | West Stanley | D | 2 - 2 | T.Hegarty (pen), Brown | |
| 9 | 13 | | (h) | Carlisle United | W | 2 - 0 | Brown, Fletcher | 2,500 |
| 10 | 20 | | (a) | Sunderland Royal Rovers | D | 0 - 0 | | |
| 11 | 27 | | (h) | West Stanley | W | 2 - 1 | Smith 2 | 2,000 |
| 12 | Dec 4 | | (a) | Darlington | D | 0 - 0 | | |
| 13 | 18 | | (a) | Shildon Athletic | W | 3 - 0 | Fletcher, F.Tweddle 2 | 800 |
| 14 | 25 | | (a) | Seaham Harbour | D | 1 - 1 | Edgley | |
| 15 | 27 | | (h) | Hebburn Argyle | W | 10 - 0 | Edgley 4, Fletcher 3, Ledger, Brown, T.Hegarty (pen) | 4,600 |
| 16 | 28 | | (h) | Newcastle United 'A' | W | 2 - 0 | F.Tweddle, Brown | 4,200 |
| 17 | Jan 1 | | (h) | Seaham Harbour | W | 6 - 2 | Edgley, Brown 2, Fletcher 2, Bennett | 3,750 |
| 18 | 4 | | (h) | Wallsend Park Villa | W | 8 - 0 | Brown 4, Ledger, Bennett 2, Fletcher | |
| 19 | 8 | | (a) | Wingate Albion | D | 0 - 0 | | |
| 20 | 22 | | (h) | Sunderland Royal Rovers | W | 5 - 1 | Ledger, T.Hegarty (pen), Fletcher 3 | 1,500 |
| 21 | Mar 3 | | (a) | Carlisle United | W | 3 - 1 | Fletcher 2, Thompson | |
| 22 | 5 | | (h) | South Shields Adelaide | W | 3 - 1 | Bennett, Ledger, Fletcher | 7,000 |
| 23 | 12 | | (h) | Wingate Albion | W | 2 - 0 | Hogg, Fletcher | 3,000 |
| 24 | 19 | | (h) | Sunderland 'A' | D | 0 - 0 | | 7,000 |
| 25 | 25 | | (a) | Middlesbrough 'A' | L | 1 - 3 | Hand | 6,000 |
| 26 | 28 | | (h) | Middlesbrough 'A' | D | 2 - 2 | Thompson, Fletcher | |
| 27 | 29 | | (a) | Wallsend Park Villa | W | 3 - 0 | Swift, Fletcher 2 | |
| 28 | Apr 2 | | (a) | Spennymoor United | D | 1 - 1 | Swift | 4,000 |
| 29 | 4 | | (h) | Spennymoor United | D | 1 - 1 | Thompson | |
| 30 | 9 | | (a) | North Shields Athletic | W | 3 - 1 | Fletcher, Hogg, Hedley (o.g.) | 2,000 |
| 31 | 16 | | (h) | North Shields Athletic | W | 4 - 1 | Hogg, Fletcher 2, F.Tweddle | 2,000 |
| 32 | 20 | | (h) | Workington | W | 12 - 0 | Hogg 9, Fletcher 3 | 6,000 |
| 33 | 23 | | (h) | Shildon Athletic | D | 0 - 0 | | 1,000 |
| 34 | 27 | | (a) | Newcastle United 'A' | W | 2 - 0 | Fletcher, Swift | |

Final Position : 4th in North Eastern League — Apps.

1 own goal — Goals

**FA Cup**

| Match No. | Date | Round | Venue | Opponents | Result | | Scorers | Attendance |
|---|---|---|---|---|---|---|---|---|
| 4 | Oct 2 | QR1 | (h) | Wingate Athletic | W | 6 - 3 | Edgley, Brown 2, Fletcher 2, Thompson | 6,000 |
| 5 | 16 | QR2 | (h) | Darlington | L | 0 - 1 | | 8,000 |

Apps.

Goals

| Kelly | Hegarty, T. | Billam | Hand | Smith | Ledger | Tweddle, F. | Fletcher | Edgley | Brown | Thompson | Tweddle, S. | McIver | Black | Bennett | Hogg | Hegarty, R. | Swift |
|---|---|---|---|---|---|---|---|---|---|---|---|---|---|---|---|---|---|
| 1 | 2 | 3 | 4 | 5 | 6 | 7 | 8 | 9 | 10 | 11 | | | | | | | |
| 1 | 2 | 3 | 5 | 6 | | 7 | 8 | 9 | 10 | 11 | 4 | | | | | | |
| 1 | 2 | 3 | 4 | 5 | 6 | 7 | 8 | 9 | 10 | 11 | | | | | | | |
| | 2 | | 6 | 3 | | 7 | 8 | 5 | 10 | 11 | | 1 | 4 | 9 | | | |
| | 2 | 3 | 6 | 5 | | 7 | 8 | 9 | 10 | 11 | | 1 | 4 | | | | |
| | 2 | 3 | 4 | 5 | | 7 | 8 | 9 | 10 | 11 | 6 | 1 | | | | | |
| | 2 | 3 | 6 | 5 | | 7 | 8 | 9 | 10 | 11 | 4 | 1 | | | | | |
| | 2 | 3 | 6 | 5 | | 7 | 8 | 9 | 10 | | 4 | 1 | | 11 | | | |
| | 2 | 3 | | 5 | 6 | 7 | 8 | 9 | 10 | 11 | | 1 | | | 4 | | |
| | 2 | 3 | 4 | 9 | 6 | 7 | 8 | 10 | 11 | | | 1 | | | 5 | | |
| | 2 | 3 | 4 | 5 | 6 | 8 | 7 | 9 | 10 | 11 | | 1 | | | | | |
| | 2 | 3 | 4 | 5 | 6 | 8 | 7 | 9 | 10 | 11 | | 1 | | | | | |
| | 2 | 3 | 4 | 5 | 6 | 7 | 8 | 9 | 10 | 11 | | 1 | | | | | |
| | 2 | 3 | 4 | 5 | 6 | 7 | 8 | 9 | 10 | | | 1 | | 11 | | | |
| | 2 | 3 | 4 | 5 | 6 | 8 | 7 | 9 | 10 | | | 1 | | 11 | | | |
| | | 3 | 4 | 5 | 6 | 8 | 7 | 9 | 10 | | | 1 | | 11 | 2 | | |
| | | 3 | 4 | 5 | 6 | 7 | 8 | 9 | 10 | 11 | | 1 | | | 2 | | |
| | 2 | 3 | 4 | 5 | 6 | 7 | 8 | 9 | | 11 | | 1 | | 10 | | | |
| | 2 | 3 | 4 | 5 | 6 | 7 | 8 | | | 10 | | 1 | | 11 | 9 | | |
| | 2 | 3 | 4 | 5 | 6 | 7 | 8 | | | 10 | | 1 | | 11 | 9 | | |
| | | 3 | 4 | 5 | 6 | 7 | 8 | | | 10 | | 1 | | 11 | 9 | 2 | |
| | 2 | 3 | 4 | 5 | 6 | 7 | 8 | | | 10 | | 1 | | 11 | 9 | | |
| | 2 | 3 | 5 | | 6 | 7 | 8 | | | 10 | 4 | 1 | | 11 | 9 | | |
| | 2 | 3 | 4 | 5 | 6 | 7 | 8 | | | 10 | | 1 | | 11 | 9 | | |
| | 2 | 3 | 4 | | | 7 | 8 | | | 10 | 6 | 1 | | 11 | | 5 | 9 |
| | 2 | 3 | 4 | | | 7 | 8 | | | 10 | 6 | 1 | | 11 | | 5 | 9 |
| | 2 | 3 | 4 | 5 | | 7 | 8 | | | 10 | 6 | 1 | | 11 | | | 9 |
| | 2 | 3 | 4 | 5 | | 7 | 8 | | | 10 | 6 | 1 | | 11 | 9 | | |
| | 2 | 3 | 4 | 5 | | 7 | 8 | | 11 | 10 | 6 | 1 | | | 9 | | |
| | 2 | 3 | 4 | 5 | 6 | 7 | 8 | | 11 | 10 | | 1 | | | 9 | | |
| | 2 | 3 | 5 | | 6 | 8 | 7 | | | 10 | 4 | 1 | | 11 | 9 | | |
| | 2 | 3 | 5 | | 6 | 7 | 8 | | | 10 | 4 | 1 | | 11 | | | 9 |
| 3 | 29 | 31 | 31 | 27 | 21 | 32 | 32 | 18 | 19 | 27 | 12 | 29 | 2 | 18 | 14 | 3 | 4 |
| | 4 | | 2 | 2 | 4 | 4 | 25 | 6 | 12 | 3 | | | | 4 | 12 | | 3 |

| Kelly | Hegarty, T. | Billam | Hand | Smith | Ledger | Tweddle, F. | Fletcher | Edgley | Brown | Thompson | Tweddle, S. | McIver | Black | Bennett | Hogg | Hegarty, R. | Swift |
|---|---|---|---|---|---|---|---|---|---|---|---|---|---|---|---|---|---|
| 1 | 2 | 3 | 4 | 5 | 6 | 7 | 8 | 9 | 10 | 11 | | | | | | | |
| | 2 | | 5 | 6 | | 7 | 8 | 9 | 10 | 11 | 4 | 1 | | | | 3 | |
| 1 | 2 | 1 | 2 | 2 | 1 | 2 | 2 | 2 | 2 | 2 | 1 | 1 | | | | 1 | |
| | | | | | | | 2 | 1 | 2 | 1 | | | | | | | |

## League Table

| | P | W | D | L | F | A | Pts |
|---|---|---|---|---|---|---|---|
| Spennymoor United | 32 | 24 | 3 | 5 | 75 | 39 | 51 |
| Newcastle United 'A' | 32 | 21 | 6 | 5 | 134 | 31 | 48 |
| Middlesbrough 'A' | 32 | 21 | 5 | 6 | 90 | 51 | 47 |
| Hartlepools United | 32 | 18 | 10 | 4 | 82 | 23 | 46 |
| Darlington | 32 | 16 | 5 | 11 | 60 | 55 | 37 |
| Sunderland 'A' | 32 | 15 | 6 | 11 | 65 | 43 | 36 |
| Shildon Athletic | 32 | 13 | 8 | 11 | 61 | 61 | 34 |
| South Shields Athletic | 32 | 14 | 5 | 13 | 77 | 63 | 33 |
| North Shields Athletic | 32 | 12 | 8 | 12 | 60 | 61 | 32 |
| Seaham Harbour | 32 | 14 | 3 | 15 | 56 | 57 | 31 |
| Wallsend Park Villa | 32 | 12 | 6 | 14 | 56 | 67 | 30 |
| Carlisle United | 32 | 11 | 4 | 17 | 52 | 62 | 26 |
| Wingate Albion | 32 | 8 | 8 | 16 | 43 | 80 | 24 |
| West Stanley | 32 | 9 | 5 | 18 | 56 | 85 | 23 |
| Hebburn Argyle | 32 | 8 | 4 | 20 | 33 | 107 | 20 |
| Workington | 32 | 7 | 4 | 21 | 41 | 98 | 18 |
| Sunderland Royal Rovers | 32 | 2 | 5 | 25 | 25 | 83 | 9 |

# 1910-11

## North Eastern League

Manager: Fred Priest

### Did you know that?

After successive Durham Senior Cup wins, 'Pools were prevented from making it a hat-trick by losing to ambitious South Shields, 2–1 in the Final at Sunderland.

The Hartlepools board made a second application to join the Football League hoping to replace relegated Lincoln City. In the event, it was Grimsby Town, demoted the previous season, who won the vote.

| Match No. | Date | Round | Venue | Opponents | Result | | Scorers | Attendance |
|---|---|---|---|---|---|---|---|---|
| 1 | Sep 3 | | (h) | Jarrow | L | 0 - 3 | | 4,000 |
| 2 | 10 | | (h) | Wingate Albion | W | 1 - 0 | Stokoe | 5,000 |
| 4 | 24 | | (h) | Shildon Athletic | W | 4 - 0 | Stokoe, Morgan 2, Larkin | 2,000 |
| 7 | Oct 8 | | (h) | Wallsend Park Villa | W | 3 - 1 | Featherstone 2, Fletcher | 2,000 |
| 8 | 15 | | (a) | Newcastle United 'A' | L | 0 - 4 | | 4,000 |
| 9 | 22 | | (a) | Sunderland 'A' | D | 2 - 2 | Bainbridge, Hedley (pen) | 4,000 |
| 10 | 29 | | (h) | Carlisle United | W | 4 - 1 | Featherstone, Bainbridge 2, Stokoe | 1,500 |
| 11 | Nov 5 | | (a) | West Stanley | W | 3 - 0 | Fletcher, Stokoe, Tomlinson (o.g.) | |
| 12 | 12 | | (h) | Workington | W | 2 - 1 | Featherstone, Fletcher | 1,000 |
| 13 | Dec 3 | | (a) | North Shields Athletic | D | 2 - 2 | Fletcher, Bainbridge | |
| 14 | 10 | | (h) | Spennymoor United | W | 3 - 1 | Ledger, Featherstone, Hedley (pen) | 1,000 |
| 15 | 24 | | (h) | South Shields | D | 1 - 1 | Featherstone | 1,000 |
| 16 | 26 | | (a) | Darlington | D | 0 - 0 | | 3,000 |
| 17 | 31 | | (h) | Sunderland 'A' | D | 2 - 2 | Bainbridge, Featherstone | 3,500 |
| 18 | Jan 2 | | (h) | Sunderland Rovers | W | 5 - 0 | Featherstone 2, Reed (o.g.), Bainbridge, Fletcher | 1,000 |
| 19 | 7 | | (a) | Seaham Harbour | W | 4 - 1 | Fletcher 2, Featherstone, Bainbridge | |
| 20 | 21 | | (a) | Carlisle United | D | 1 - 1 | Blanthorne | |
| 21 | 28 | | (h) | West Stanley | W | 2 - 0 | Bainbridge, Stokoe | 3,091 |
| 22 | Feb 11 | | (h) | Hebburn Argyle | W | 2 - 0 | Bainbridge, Hedley (pen) | 3,194 |
| 23 | 18 | | (a) | Wallsend Park Villa | W | 3 - 0 | Blanthorne 2, MacIntyre | |
| 24 | 25 | | (a) | Shildon Athletic | W | 1 - 0 | MacIntyre | |
| 25 | Mar 4 | | (h) | Newcastle United 'A' | W | 2 - 1 | Stokoe, MacIntyre | 6,197 |
| 26 | 11 | | (a) | Spennymoor United | L | 1 - 2 | MacIntyre | |
| 27 | 18 | | (h) | Middlesbrough 'A' | W | 7 - 4 | Fletcher 4, MacIntyre 2, Bainbridge | |
| 28 | 25 | | (h) | Seaham Harbour | W | 5 - 0 | Fletcher, Griffin, Featherstone, Stokoe 2 | |
| 29 | 27 | | (a) | Wingate Albion | D | 1 - 1 | Hedley (pen) | |
| 30 | Apr 5 | | (a) | Jarrow | L | 0 - 1 | | |
| 31 | 8 | | (a) | Hebburn Argyle | L | 2 - 4 | Griffin, Fletcher | |
| 32 | 14 | | (h) | Darlington | L | 0 - 1 | | 6,000 |
| 33 | 15 | | (h) | North Shields Athletic | W | 4 - 2 | MacIntyre 3, Fletcher | 6,000 |
| 34 | 17 | | (a) | South Shields | L | 0 - 1 | | |
| 35 | 18 | | (a) | Sunderland Rovers | L | 0 - 1 | | |
| 36 | 22 | | (a) | Middlesbrough 'A' | D | 2 - 2 | MacIntyre 2 | 3,000 |
| 37 | 29 | | (a) | Workington | W | 2 - 0 | Fletcher, MacIntyre | |

Final Position : 3rd in North Eastern League

Apps.

2 own goals — Goals

**FA Cup**

| Match No. | Date | Round | Venue | Opponents | Result | | Scorers | Attendance |
|---|---|---|---|---|---|---|---|---|
| 3 | Sep 17 | PR | (h) | Horden Athletic | W | 5 - 0 | Featherstone, Stokoe, Fletcher 3 (1 pen) | 2,000 |
| 5 | Oct 1 | QR1 | (a) | Darlington | D | 1 - 1 | Fletcher | 3,000 |
| 6 | 6 | QR1r | (h) | Darlington | L | 0 - 1 | | 2,500 |

Apps.

Goals

| McIver | Hogg | Hedley | Hand | Gorman | Ledger | Stokoe | Fletcher | Featherstone | Griffin | Bennett | Tweddle | Bainbridge | Larkin | Morgan | Harvey | Tiplady | Billam | Kelly | Blanthorne | McIntyre |
|---|---|---|---|---|---|---|---|---|---|---|---|---|---|---|---|---|---|---|---|---|
| 1 | 2 | 3 | 4 | 5 | 6 | 7 | 8 | 9 | 10 | 11 | | | | | | | | | | |
| 1 | 2 | 3 | 5 | | 6 | 11 | 8 | 9 | 10 | | 4 | 7 | | | | | | | | |
| 1 | 2 | 3 | | | 6 | 10 | 8 | | 11 | | 4 | 7 | 5 | 9 | | | | | | |
| 1 | 2 | | | | 6 | 10 | 8 | 9 | 11 | | 4 | 7 | 5 | | 3 | | | | | |
| 1 | | 2 | 5 | | | 10 | 8 | 9 | 11 | | 4 | 7 | | | 3 | 6 | | | | |
| 1 | 5 | 2 | | | 6 | 10 | 8 | 9 | 11 | | 4 | 7 | | | 3 | | | | | |
| 1 | 5 | 2 | | | 6 | 10 | 8 | 9 | 11 | | 4 | 7 | | | | | 3 | | | |
| 1 | | 2 | | 5 | 6 | 10 | 8 | 9 | 11 | | 4 | 7 | | | | | 3 | | | |
| 1 | 5 | 2 | | | 6 | 10 | 8 | 9 | 11 | 7 | 4 | | | | | | 3 | | | |
| 1 | 5 | 2 | | | 6 | 10 | 8 | 9 | 11 | | 4 | 7 | | | | | 3 | | | |
| | 5 | 3 | | | 6 | 10 | 8 | 9 | 11 | 7 | 4 | | | | 2 | | | 1 | | |
| 1 | 5 | 2 | | | 6 | 10 | 8 | 9 | 11 | | 4 | 7 | | | | | 3 | | | |
| 1 | 5 | 2 | | | 6 | 10 | 8 | 9 | 11 | | 4 | 7 | | | | | 3 | | | |
| 1 | 5 | 2 | 4 | | 6 | 10 | 8 | 9 | 11 | | | 7 | | | | | 3 | | | |
| 1 | 5 | 2 | 4 | | 6 | 10 | 8 | 9 | 11 | | | 7 | | | | | 3 | | | |
| 1 | 5 | 2 | 4 | | 6 | 10 | 8 | 9 | 11 | | | 7 | | | | | 3 | | | |
| 1 | 5 | 2 | 4 | | 6 | 10 | 8 | | 11 | | | 7 | | | | | 3 | | 9 | |
| 1 | 5 | 2 | 4 | | 6 | 10 | 8 | | 11 | | | 7 | | | | | 3 | | 9 | |
| 1 | 5 | 2 | 4 | | | 10 | 8 | | 11 | | | 7 | | | 3 | | | | 9 | 6 |
| 1 | 5 | 2 | 4 | | 6 | | 8 | | 11 | | | 7 | | | | | 3 | | 9 | 10 |
| 1 | 5 | 2 | 4 | | 6 | | 8 | | 11 | | | 7 | | | | | 3 | | 9 | 10 |
| 1 | 5 | 2 | 4 | | 6 | 10 | 8 | | 11 | | | 7 | | | | | 3 | | | 9 |
| 1 | 3 | 2 | 4 | | 6 | 11 | 8 | | | | | 7 | | | | | 10 | | 9 | 5 |
| 1 | 5 | 2 | 4 | | 6 | 10 | 8 | | 11 | | | 7 | | | | | 3 | | | 9 |
| 1 | 5 | 2 | 4 | | 6 | 10 | 8 | 9 | 11 | | | 7 | | | | | 3 | | | |
| 1 | 5 | 2 | 4 | | 6 | 10 | 8 | 9 | 11 | | | 7 | | | | | 3 | | | |
| 1 | 5 | 2 | 4 | | 6 | 10 | 8 | 9 | 11 | | | 7 | | | 3 | | | | | |
| 1 | | 2 | 5 | | 6 | 10 | 8 | | 11 | | 4 | 7 | | | 3 | | | | | 9 |
| 1 | 5 | 2 | | | 6 | 10 | 8 | 9 | 11 | 7 | 4 | | | | 3 | | | | | |
| 1 | 2 | | | 5 | 6 | 10 | 8 | 7 | | 11 | 4 | | | | 3 | | | | | 9 |
| 1 | 3 | 2 | | 5 | 6 | 10 | 8 | 7 | 11 | | 4 | | | | | | | | | 9 |
| 1 | 3 | 2 | | 5 | 6 | 10 | 8 | 7 | 11 | | 4 | | | | | | | | | 9 |
| 1 | 3 | 2 | 6 | 5 | | | 8 | 10 | 11 | | 4 | 7 | | | | | | | | 9 |
| 1 | 3 | 2 | | 5 | 4 | 10 | 8 | | 11 | | 6 | 7 | | | | | | | | 9 |
| 33 | 31 | 32 | 19 | 7 | 31 | 31 | 34 | 23 | 32 | 5 | 19 | 27 | 2 | 1 | 9 | 1 | 18 | 1 | 6 | 12 |
| | | 4 | | | 1 | 8 | 15 | 11 | 2 | | | 10 | 1 | 2 | | | | | 3 | 12 |

| McIver | Hogg | Hedley | Hand | Gorman | Ledger | Stokoe | Fletcher | Featherstone | Griffin | Bennett | Tweddle | Bainbridge | Larkin | Morgan | Harvey | Tiplady | Billam | Kelly | Blanthorne | McIntyre |
|---|---|---|---|---|---|---|---|---|---|---|---|---|---|---|---|---|---|---|---|---|
| 1 | 2 | 3 | 5 | | 6 | 10 | 8 | 9 | 11 | | 4 | 7 | | | | | | | | |
| 1 | 2 | 3 | | | 6 | 10 | 8 | | 11 | | 4 | 7 | 5 | 9 | | | | | | |
| 1 | 2 | 3 | | | 6 | 10 | 8 | | 11 | | 4 | 7 | 5 | 9 | | | | | | |
| 3 | 3 | 3 | 1 | | 3 | 3 | 3 | 1 | 3 | | 3 | 3 | 2 | 2 | | | | | | |
| | | | | | | 1 | 4 | 1 | | | | | | | | | | | | |

## League Table

| | P | W | D | L | F | A | Pts |
|---|---|---|---|---|---|---|---|
| Newcastle United 'A' | 34 | 25 | 4 | 5 | 88 | 25 | 54 |
| Sunderland 'A' | 34 | 20 | 6 | 8 | 81 | 38 | 46 |
| Hartlepools United | 34 | 18 | 8 | 8 | 71 | 40 | 44 |
| Darlington | 34 | 19 | 5 | 10 | 79 | 39 | 43 |
| South Shields | 34 | 18 | 5 | 11 | 56 | 33 | 41 |
| North Shields Athletic | 34 | 19 | 3 | 12 | 57 | 56 | 41 |
| Middlesbrough 'A' | 34 | 16 | 6 | 12 | 83 | 54 | 38 |
| Wingate Albion | 34 | 14 | 7 | 13 | 48 | 39 | 35 |
| Wallsend Park Villa | 34 | 15 | 3 | 16 | 49 | 59 | 33 |
| Hebburn Argyle | 34 | 13 | 6 | 15 | 38 | 62 | 32 |
| Seaham Harbour | 34 | 13 | 5 | 16 | 44 | 63 | 31 |
| Spennymoor United | 33 | 12 | 5 | 16 | 52 | 54 | 29 |
| Workington | 34 | 12 | 3 | 19 | 47 | 72 | 27 |
| Shildon Athletic | 34 | 11 | 3 | 20 | 50 | 64 | 25 |
| Carlisle United | 34 | 8 | 8 | 18 | 45 | 52 | 24 |
| Jarrow | 34 | 11 | 2 | 21 | 34 | 70 | 24 |
| West Stanley | 33 | 10 | 3 | 20 | 39 | 84 | 23 |
| Sunderland Rovers | 34 | 8 | 2 | 24 | 33 | 94 | 18 |

# 1911-12

## North Eastern League

Manager: Fred Priest

### Did you know that?

The Tweddle Brothers, Freddie and Steve, played their final games for the club having made a total of 174 North Eastern league and FA Cup appearances. Freddie Tweddle had returned to 'Pools after spending the previous season with Sheffield United.

| Match No. | Date | Round | Venue | Opponents | | Result | Scorers | Attendance |
|---|---|---|---|---|---|---|---|---|
| 1 | Sep 1 | | (a) | Wallsend Park Villa | L | 0 - 2 | | |
| 2 | 2 | | (h) | Newcastle City | D | 1 - 1 | Fletcher | 4,000 |
| 3 | 6 | | (h) | Hebburn Argyle | W | 3 - 0 | Fletcher 2, Mitchell | |
| 4 | 9 | | (a) | Seaham Harbour | L | 1 - 2 | Fletcher (pen) | |
| 5 | 13 | | (a) | Hebburn Argyle | D | 2 - 2 | Fletcher 2 | |
| 6 | 16 | | (h) | Sunderland 'A' | L | 1 - 2 | Martin | 4,200 |
| 7 | 23 | | (a) | Wingate Albion | D | 1 - 1 | Stokoe | |
| 8 | 30 | | (h) | Middlesbrough 'A' | D | 2 - 2 | Martin, Hogg | |
| 9 | Oct 7 | | (h) | Newcastle United 'A' | L | 0 - 1 | | 4,400 |
| 10 | 21 | | (a) | Sunderland 'A' | D | 1 - 1 | F.Tweddle | |
| 11 | 28 | | (h) | Sunderland Rovers | W | 4 - 1 | Grierson, Martin 2, Fletcher | |
| 12 | Nov 4 | | (a) | Carlisle United | L | 1 - 2 | Grierson | |
| 13 | 11 | | (h) | Gateshead Town | W | 2 - 1 | Stokoe 2 | |
| 15 | 25 | | (a) | Jarrow | W | 4 - 2 | Grierson, Stokoe, Hedley, F.Tweddle | |
| 16 | Dec 2 | | (a) | West Stanley | D | 2 - 2 | Fletcher 2 | 2,000 |
| 17 | 9 | | (h) | South Shields | L | 0 - 1 | | 1,000 |
| 18 | 23 | | (h) | North Shields Athletic | W | 3 - 2 | Fletcher, Hedley (pen), Stokoe | |
| 19 | 25 | | (h) | Wallsend Park Villa | W | 5 - 0 | Grierson, Carr, Griffin, Fletcher, Bennett | 2,500 |
| 20 | 26 | | (h) | Darlington | D | 0 - 0 | | 4,000 |
| 21 | 30 | | (a) | Spennymoor United | L | 0 - 1 | | |
| 22 | Jan 1 | | (h) | Seaham Harbour | W | 5 - 0 | Grierson, Fletcher 2, Prosser, Griffin | 4,000 |
| 23 | 6 | | (a) | Shildon Athletic | W | 3 - 2 | Grierson 2, Martin | |
| 24 | 13 | | (a) | Sunderland Rovers | W | 3 - 0 | Fletcher 2, Grierson | |
| 25 | Feb 10 | | (a) | South Shields | L | 0 - 1 | | 2,000 |
| 26 | 17 | | (h) | Shildon Athletic | W | 5 - 2 | Fletcher, Martin 3, Grierson | |
| 27 | 24 | | (a) | Newcastle City | L | 0 - 4 | | |
| 28 | Mar 2 | | (h) | Jarrow | W | 4 - 2 | Grierson 2, Fletcher, Bennett | |
| 29 | 9 | | (a) | North Shields Athletic | W | 1 - 0 | Fletcher | 1,500 |
| 30 | 23 | | (a) | Gateshead Town | L | 2 - 3 | Hogg 2 | 3,000 |
| 31 | 30 | | (h) | Carlisle United | D | 0 - 0 | | |
| 32 | Apr 5 | | (h) | West Stanley | L | 0 - 1 | | 1,000 |
| 33 | 6 | | (h) | Wingate Albion | L | 0 - 1 | | |
| 34 | 8 | | (a) | Darlington | W | 2 - 0 | Stokoe, Griffin | |
| 35 | 20 | | (a) | Newcastle United 'A' | L | 2 - 3 | Fletcher 2 | 3,000 |
| 36 | 24 | | (h) | Spennymoor United | W | 2 - 0 | Grierson, Fletcher | 500 |
| 37 | 29 | | (a) | Middlesbrough 'A' | L | 0 - 5 | | |

Final Position : 9th in North Eastern League

Apps.
Goals

**FA Cup**

| | | | | | | | | |
|---|---|---|---|---|---|---|---|---|
| 14 | Nov 18 | QR4 | (a) | North Shields Athletic | L | 1 - 2 | Stokoe | 2,000 |

Apps.
Goals

| Carmichael | Hedley | Gatenby | Hogg | Gorman | Ledger | Tweddle, F. | Fletcher | Martin | Grierson | Stokoe | McDonald | Swift | Tweddle, S. | Mitchell | Penman | Griffin | Prosser | Kelly | Little | Bennett | Carr | Herdman | Murphy |
|---|---|---|---|---|---|---|---|---|---|---|---|---|---|---|---|---|---|---|---|---|---|---|---|
| 1 | 2 | 3 | 4 | 5 | 6 | 7 | 8 | 9 | 10 | 11 | | | | | | | | | | | | | |
| 1 | | 3 | 4 | 5 | 6 | 7 | 8 | 9 | 10 | | 2 | 11 | | | | | | | | | | | |
| 1 | | 3 | | 5 | 6 | 7 | 8 | 9 | 10 | | 2 | | 4 | 11 | | | | | | | | | |
| 1 | | 3 | 5 | | 6 | 7 | 8 | 9 | 10 | | 2 | | 4 | 11 | | | | | | | | | |
| 1 | 3 | | | | 6 | 7 | 8 | 9 | 10 | | 2 | | 4 | | 5 | 11 | | | | | | | |
| 1 | 3 | | | | 6 | 7 | 8 | 9 | 10 | 11 | 2 | | 4 | | 5 | | | | | | | | |
| 1 | 3 | | | | 6 | 7 | 8 | 10 | 9 | 11 | 2 | | 4 | | 5 | | | | | | | | |
| 1 | | | 3 | | 6 | 7 | | 9 | 8 | 10 | 2 | | 4 | | 5 | 11 | | | | | | | |
| 1 | 3 | | 6 | | | 7 | 8 | 9 | 10 | | 2 | | 4 | | 5 | 11 | | | | | | | |
| 1 | 3 | | 6 | | | 7 | 8 | | 9 | 10 | 2 | | | | 5 | 11 | 4 | | | | | | |
| 1 | 2 | 3 | | | 6 | 7 | 8 | 9 | 10 | | | | | | 5 | 11 | 4 | | | | | | |
| 1 | 3 | | | | 6 | 7 | 8 | 9 | 10 | | 2 | | 4 | | 5 | 11 | | | | | | | |
| 1 | | | 3 | | 6 | 7 | 8 | 9 | | 10 | 2 | | | | 5 | 11 | 4 | | | | | | |
| 1 | 3 | | | 6 | | 7 | 8 | | 9 | 10 | 2 | | | | 5 | 11 | 4 | | | | | | |
| | 3 | | | 6 | | 7 | 8 | | 9 | 10 | 2 | | | | 5 | 11 | 4 | 1 | | | | | |
| | 3 | | | | 6 | 7 | 8 | | 9 | 10 | 2 | | | | 5 | 11 | 4 | 1 | | | | | |
| | 3 | | 9 | | | 7 | 8 | | | 10 | 2 | | | | 5 | 11 | 4 | 1 | 6 | | | | |
| | 3 | | | | | | 8 | | 10 | | 2 | | | | 5 | 11 | 4 | 1 | 6 | 7 | 9 | | |
| | 3 | | | | | 7 | 8 | | 10 | | 2 | | | | 5 | 11 | 4 | 1 | 6 | | 9 | | |
| | 3 | | 6 | | | 7 | 8 | 9 | 10 | | 2 | | | | 5 | 11 | 4 | 1 | | | | | |
| | 3 | | 6 | | | 7 | 8 | | 10 | | 2 | | | | 5 | 11 | 4 | 1 | | 9 | | | |
| | 3 | | 6 | | | 7 | 8 | 9 | 10 | | 2 | | | | 5 | 11 | 4 | 1 | | | | | |
| | 3 | | 6 | | | 7 | 8 | | 10 | | 2 | | | | 5 | 11 | 4 | 1 | | | 9 | | |
| | 2 | | 11 | | 6 | 7 | 8 | | 10 | | | | 4 | | | | 5 | 1 | | 9 | | 3 | |
| | 3 | | | 5 | 6 | 7 | 8 | 9 | 10 | | 2 | | | | | | 4 | 1 | | 11 | | | |
| | 3 | | | | 6 | | 8 | 9 | 10 | | 2 | | | | 5 | 11 | 4 | 1 | | 7 | | | |
| | 3 | 2 | | | 6 | 7 | 8 | | 10 | | | | | | | 11 | 4 | 1 | | 9 | | | 5 |
| | | 3 | | 5 | 6 | 7 | 8 | | 10 | | 2 | | | | | 11 | 4 | 1 | | 9 | | | |
| | | 3 | 9 | | 6 | 7 | 8 | | 10 | | 2 | | | | 5 | 11 | 4 | 1 | | | | | |
| | | 3 | 9 | | 6 | 7 | 8 | | 10 | | 2 | | 4 | | 5 | 11 | | 1 | | | | | |
| | | 3 | | | | 7 | 8 | | 10 | | 2 | | | | 5 | 11 | 4 | 1 | 6 | 9 | | | |
| | | 3 | 9 | | 6 | 7 | 8 | | | 10 | 2 | | | | | 11 | 4 | 1 | 5 | | | | |
| | | 3 | | | 6 | 7 | 9 | | 10 | 8 | 2 | | | | | 11 | 4 | 1 | 5 | | | | |
| | | 3 | | | 6 | 7 | 9 | | 10 | 8 | 2 | | | | | 11 | 4 | 1 | 5 | | | | |
| | | 3 | | | 6 | 7 | 9 | | 10 | 8 | 2 | | 4 | | | 11 | | 1 | 5 | | | | |
| | | 3 | | | 6 | 7 | | 9 | 10 | 8 | 2 | | 4 | | | 11 | | 1 | 5 | | | | |
| 14 | 22 | 15 | 16 | 7 | 24 | 34 | 34 | 17 | 33 | 15 | 32 | 1 | 12 | 2 | 23 | 28 | 23 | 22 | 9 | 8 | 3 | 1 | 1 |
| | 2 | | 3 | | | 2 | 21 | 8 | 12 | 6 | | | | 1 | | 3 | 1 | | | 2 | 1 | | |

| Carmichael | Hedley | Gatenby | Hogg | Gorman | Ledger | Tweddle, F. | Fletcher | Martin | Grierson | Stokoe | McDonald | Swift | Tweddle, S. | Mitchell | Penman | Griffin | Prosser | Kelly | Little | Bennett | Carr | Herdman | Murphy |
|---|---|---|---|---|---|---|---|---|---|---|---|---|---|---|---|---|---|---|---|---|---|---|---|
| 1 | 3 | | | 4 | | 7 | 8 | | 10 | 9 | 2 | | | | 5 | 11 | 6 | | | | | | |
| 1 | 1 | | | 1 | | 1 | 1 | | 1 | 1 | 1 | | | | 1 | 1 | 1 | | | | | | |
| | | | | | | | | | | 1 | | | | | | | | | | | | | |

## League Table

| | P | W | D | L | F | A | Pts |
|---|---|---|---|---|---|---|---|
| Middlesbrough 'A' | 36 | 28 | 5 | 3 | 122 | 23 | 61 |
| Newcastle United 'A' | 36 | 28 | 2 | 6 | 113 | 33 | 58 |
| Darlington | 36 | 23 | 8 | 5 | 84 | 34 | 54 |
| Sunderland 'A' | 36 | 21 | 5 | 10 | 99 | 52 | 47 |
| South Shields | 36 | 21 | 4 | 11 | 73 | 43 | 46 |
| Spennymoor United | 36 | 18 | 6 | 12 | 62 | 57 | 42 |
| Newcastle City | 36 | 16 | 9 | 11 | 62 | 43 | 41 |
| Gateshead Town | 36 | 16 | 6 | 14 | 64 | 66 | 38 |
| Hartlepools United | 36 | 14 | 8 | 14 | 62 | 50 | 36 |
| West Stanley | 36 | 13 | 10 | 13 | 61 | 58 | 36 |
| North Shields Athletic | 36 | 13 | 9 | 14 | 59 | 72 | 35 |
| Seaham Harbour | 36 | 15 | 2 | 19 | 52 | 67 | 32 |
| Hebburn Argyle | 36 | 11 | 9 | 16 | 56 | 54 | 31 |
| Wingate Albion | 36 | 9 | 11 | 16 | 41 | 84 | 29 |
| Jarrow | 36 | 10 | 7 | 19 | 52 | 87 | 27 |
| Shildon Athletic | 36 | 9 | 6 | 21 | 62 | 97 | 24 |
| Carlisle United | 36 | 7 | 6 | 23 | 27 | 98 | 20 |
| Wallsend Park Villa | 36 | 8 | 3 | 25 | 43 | 93 | 19 |
| Sunderland Rovers | 36 | 2 | 4 | 30 | 42 | 125 | 8 |

# 1912-13

## North Eastern League

Manager: Percy Humphreys

### Did you know that?

John Gatenby made 41 League and Cup appearances at left-back and later served in the King's Royal Rifles during the Great War. He died of his wounds in France in October 1915.

| Match No. | Date | Round | Venue | Opponents | Result | | Scorers | Attendance |
|---|---|---|---|---|---|---|---|---|
| 1 | Sep 2 | | (a) | Gateshead Town | D | 2 - 2 | Hibbert, Stokoe | 2,000 |
| 2 | 7 | | (h) | North Shields Athletic | W | 4 - 2 | Stokoe 2, Fletcher, Baker | 3,500 |
| 3 | 14 | | (h) | Houghton Rovers | W | 3 - 2 | Mayo, Humphreys, Outhwaite | 4,000 |
| 4 | 21 | | (h) | Shildon | W | 3 - 1 | Humphreys 2, Stokoe | 4,000 |
| 5 | 25 | | (a) | Newcastle City | L | 0 - 1 | | |
| 6 | 28 | | (a) | Newcastle United Reserves | D | 1 - 1 | Humphreys | 3,000 |
| 7 | Oct 5 | | (a) | Hebburn Argyle | L | 1 - 4 | Humphreys | |
| 9 | 19 | | (h) | Gateshead Town | W | 5 - 0 | Humphreys 2, Outhwaite, Mayo, Fletcher | 2,000 |
| 10 | 26 | | (h) | Spennymoor United | D | 1 - 1 | Fletcher | 3,500 |
| 12 | Nov 9 | | (h) | South Shields | L | 0 - 4 | | 5,500 |
| 14 | 23 | | (a) | Carlisle United | W | 2 - 1 | Fletcher, Humphreys | |
| 17 | Dec 25 | | (a) | Middlesbrough Reserves | L | 1 - 3 | Humphreys | 8,000 |
| 18 | 26 | | (h) | Darlington | L | 0 - 1 | | 5,600 |
| 19 | 28 | | (h) | Hebburn Argyle | W | 6 - 0 | Butler, Bennett, Fletcher 3, Baker (pen) | 1,000 |
| 20 | Jan 1 | | (h) | Middlesbrough Reserves | L | 0 - 2 | | 5,000 |
| 21 | 2 | | (a) | Seaham Harbour | L | 0 - 2 | | |
| 22 | 4 | | (a) | Sunderland Rovers | W | 5 - 3 | Baker 2, Marsh 2, Fletcher | |
| 23 | 11 | | (a) | Darlington | L | 2 - 5 | Fletcher, Stokoe | |
| 24 | 18 | | (a) | Wingate Albion | L | 0 - 1 | | |
| 25 | Feb 1 | | (h) | Sunderland Reserves | D | 3 - 3 | Brewis, Stokoe 2 | 1,000 |
| 26 | 8 | | (a) | North Shields Athletic | L | 2 - 3 | Baker (pen), Rumney | 1,000 |
| 27 | 15 | | (h) | Sunderland Rovers | W | 3 - 1 | Fletcher, Baker (pen), Brewis | 1,500 |
| 28 | 22 | | (a) | Houghton Rovers | L | 1 - 3 | Mayo | |
| 29 | Mar 1 | | (h) | Jarrow | W | 5 - 1 | Marsh, Brewis 3, Baker (pen) | 1,000 |
| 30 | 8 | | (a) | South Shields | L | 0 - 4 | | 7,000 |
| 31 | 15 | | (a) | Shildon | W | 4 - 0 | Stokoe, Brewis, Fletcher 2 | |
| 32 | 24 | | (h) | Seaham Harbour | D | 1 - 1 | Humphreys | 1,000 |
| 33 | 25 | | (h) | West Stanley | W | 4 - 0 | Marsh, Bennett, Stokoe 2 | |
| 34 | 29 | | (a) | Sunderland Reserves | L | 0 - 1 | | 4,000 |
| 35 | Apr 2 | | (h) | Carlisle United | L | 1 - 2 | Humphreys | |
| 36 | 5 | | (h) | Wallsend | D | 2 - 2 | Fletcher, Marsh | 1,000 |
| 37 | 9 | | (a) | West Stanley | W | 1 - 0 | Mayo | |
| 38 | 12 | | (h) | Newcastle United Reserves | W | 1 - 0 | Bennett | 3,000 |
| 39 | 16 | | (h) | Wingate Albion | W | 2 - 0 | Baker (pen), Mayo | |
| 40 | 19 | | (a) | Spennymoor United | L | 1 - 5 | Fletcher | |
| 41 | 23 | | (a) | Jarrow | W | 2 - 1 | Stokoe, Mayo | |
| 42 | 26 | | (h) | Newcastle City | L | 0 - 1 | | |
| 43 | 30 | | (a) | Wallsend | L | 0 - 2 | | |

Final Position : 12th in North Eastern League

Apps.
Goals

**FA Cup**

| Match No. | Date | Round | Venue | Opponents | Result | | Scorers | Attendance |
|---|---|---|---|---|---|---|---|---|
| 8 | Oct 12 | QR1 | (h) | Houghton Rovers | W | 3 - 1 | Humphreys (pen), Fletcher 2 | 4,000 |
| 11 | Nov 2 | QR2 | (h) | Wingate Albion | W | 4 - 1 | Stokoe, Humphreys 3 | 3,800 |
| 13 | 16 | QR3 | (h) | Sunderland Rovers | W | 2 - 1 | Fletcher, Henderson | 3,000 |
| 15 | 30 | QR4 | (h) | Castleford Town | W | 1 - 0 | Mayo | 4,700 |
| 16 | Dec 14 | QR5 | (a) | Gainsborough Trinity | L | 0 - 4 | | |

Apps.
Goals

| Scott | Ellis | Gatenby | Hauxby | Hibbert | Baker | Barnes | Fletcher | Humphreys | Stokoe | Mayo | Outhwaite | Pearson | McGaven | Little | Pickering | Carr | Marsh | Henderson | Parkinson | Butler | Mason | Bennett | Rumney | Frankland | McCulloch | Noddings | Stokes | Brewis | Birch |
|---|---|---|---|---|---|---|---|---|---|---|---|---|---|---|---|---|---|---|---|---|---|---|---|---|---|---|---|---|---|
| 1 | 2 | 3 | 4 | 5 | 6 | 7 | 8 | 9 | 10 | 11 | | | | | | | | | | | | | | | | | | | |
| 1 | 2 | 3 | 4 | 5 | 6 | | 8 | 9 | 10 | 11 | 7 | | | | | | | | | | | | | | | | | | |
| | 2 | 3 | | 5 | 6 | | 8 | 9 | 10 | 11 | 7 | 1 | 4 | | | | | | | | | | | | | | | | |
| | 2 | 3 | | 5 | 4 | | 8 | 9 | 10 | 11 | 7 | 1 | | 6 | | | | | | | | | | | | | | | |
| | 2 | 3 | | 5 | 4 | | 8 | 9 | 10 | 11 | 7 | 1 | | 6 | | | | | | | | | | | | | | | |
| | 2 | 3 | | 5 | 4 | | 8 | 9 | 10 | 11 | 7 | 1 | | 6 | | | | | | | | | | | | | | | |
| 1 | 2 | 3 | | 5 | 4 | | 8 | 9 | 10 | 11 | 7 | | | 6 | | | | | | | | | | | | | | | |
| | 2 | 3 | | 5 | 4 | | 8 | 9 | 10 | 7 | 11 | 1 | | 6 | | | | | | | | | | | | | | | |
| | 2 | 3 | | 5 | 4 | | 8 | 9 | 10 | 7 | 11 | 1 | | 6 | | | | | | | | | | | | | | | |
| | 2 | 3 | | | 4 | | 8 | | 10 | 7 | | 1 | | 6 | 5 | 9 | 11 | | | | | | | | | | | | |
| | 2 | 3 | | 5 | 4 | | 8 | 9 | 10 | 7 | 11 | 1 | | | | | | | 6 | | | | | | | | | | |
| | 2 | 3 | | | 4 | | 8 | 9 | | 7 | | 1 | | | 6 | | | | | 5 | 10 | 11 | | | | | | | |
| | 2 | 3 | | | 4 | | 8 | 9 | 10 | 7 | | 1 | | | 6 | | | | | 5 | | 11 | | | | | | | |
| | 2 | 3 | | | 4 | | 8 | 9 | 10 | 7 | | 1 | | | 6 | | | | | 5 | | 11 | | | | | | | |
| | 2 | 3 | | | 4 | | 10 | | | 8 | 11 | 1 | | | 6 | | | | | 5 | 9 | 7 | | | | | | | |
| | 2 | 3 | | | 4 | | 10 | | 11 | 8 | | 1 | | | 6 | | | | | 5 | 9 | 7 | | | | | | | |
| | 2 | 3 | | 4 | 9 | | 8 | | | | | 1 | | | 6 | | 11 | | | 5 | | 7 | 10 | | | | | | |
| | | 3 | | | | | 8 | 5 | 10 | | | 1 | | | 6 | | 11 | | | 4 | | 7 | | 2 | 9 | | | | |
| | 2 | 3 | | | 6 | | 8 | 5 | | 11 | | 1 | | | | | | | 10 | 4 | | 7 | | | | 9 | | | |
| | 2 | 3 | | | 4 | | 8 | 5 | 10 | 11 | | | | | | | | | | 6 | | 7 | | | | | 1 | 9 | |
| | 2 | 3 | | | 4 | | 8 | | | 7 | | 1 | | 6 | | | 11 | | | 5 | | | 10 | | | | | 9 | |
| 1 | 2 | 3 | | | 4 | | 8 | | 10 | 7 | | | | 6 | | | | | | 5 | | 11 | | | | | | 9 | |
| 1 | 2 | 3 | | | 4 | | 8 | 5 | | 7 | | | | 6 | | | 11 | | | | | | 10 | | | | | 9 | |
| 1 | 2 | | | | 4 | | 8 | | | 7 | | | | 6 | | | 11 | | | 5 | | | 10 | | | | | 9 | 3 |
| 1 | 2 | 3 | | | 4 | | 8 | | 10 | | | | | | 6 | | 11 | | | 5 | | 7 | | | | | | 9 | |
| 1 | 2 | 3 | | | | | 8 | | 10 | | 7 | | | 6 | 4 | | 11 | | | 5 | | | | | | | | 9 | |
| 1 | 2 | 3 | | 4 | 9 | | 8 | 5 | | 7 | 11 | | | | | | | | | | | 10 | | | | 6 | | | |
| 1 | 2 | | | | 4 | | 8 | 5 | 10 | 7 | | | | | | | 9 | | | 6 | | 11 | | | | | | | 3 |
| 1 | 2 | 3 | | | 4 | | 8 | 5 | 10 | 7 | | | | | | | 9 | | | 6 | | 11 | | | | | | | |
| 1 | 2 | 3 | | | 4 | | | 5 | 10 | 7 | | | | | | | 11 | | | 6 | | | 9 | | | | | 8 | |
| | 2 | 3 | | | 4 | | 8 | 5 | | 7 | | 1 | | | | | 9 | | | 6 | | 11 | | | | 10 | | | |
| | 2 | 3 | | | 4 | | 8 | 9 | | 7 | | 1 | | 6 | | | 10 | | | 5 | | 11 | | | | | | | |
| | 2 | 3 | | | 4 | | 8 | 9 | | 7 | | 1 | | 6 | | | 10 | | | 5 | | 11 | | | | | | | |
| | 2 | 3 | | | 4 | | 8 | | | 7 | 11 | 1 | | 6 | | | 9 | | | 5 | | | 10 | | | | | | |
| | 2 | 3 | | | 4 | | 8 | 9 | | 7 | | 1 | | 6 | | | 10 | | | 5 | | 11 | | | | | | | |
| | 2 | 3 | | | 4 | | 8 | 9 | 10 | 7 | | 1 | | 6 | | | | | | 5 | | 11 | | | | | | | |
| | 2 | 3 | | | 4 | | 8 | 9 | | 7 | | 1 | | 6 | | | 10 | | | 5 | | 11 | | | | | | | |
| 1 | 2 | 3 | | | 4 | | 8 | 9 | 10 | 7 | | | | 6 | | | 11 | | | 5 | | | | | | | | | |
| 13 | 37 | 36 | 2 | 12 | 36 | 1 | 37 | 28 | 24 | 34 | 13 | 24 | 1 | 19 | 10 | 1 | 18 | | 2 | 25 | 3 | 20 | 6 | 1 | 1 | 3 | 1 | 8 | 2 |
| | | | | 1 | 8 | | 14 | 11 | 11 | 6 | 2 | | | | | | 5 | | | 1 | | 3 | 2 | | | | | 5 | |

| Scott | Ellis | Gatenby | Hauxby | Hibbert | Baker | Barnes | Fletcher | Humphreys | Stokoe | Mayo | Outhwaite | Pearson | McGaven | Little | Pickering | Carr | Marsh | Henderson | Parkinson | Butler | Mason | Bennett | Rumney | Frankland | McCulloch | Noddings | Stokes | Brewis | Birch |
|---|---|---|---|---|---|---|---|---|---|---|---|---|---|---|---|---|---|---|---|---|---|---|---|---|---|---|---|---|---|
| | 2 | 3 | | 5 | 4 | | 8 | 9 | 10 | 7 | | 1 | | 6 | | | 11 | | | | | | | | | | | | |
| | 2 | 3 | | 5 | 4 | | 8 | 9 | 10 | 7 | | 1 | | 6 | | | 11 | | | | | | | | | | | | |
| | 2 | 3 | | 5 | 4 | | 8 | | 10 | 7 | | 1 | | | 6 | | 11 | 9 | | | | | | | | | | | |
| | 2 | 3 | | 5 | 4 | | 8 | 9 | 10 | 7 | 11 | 1 | | | 6 | | | | | | | | | | | | | | |
| | 2 | 3 | | | 4 | | 8 | 9 | | 7 | | 1 | | | 6 | | | | | 5 | 10 | 11 | | | | | | | |
| | 5 | 5 | | 4 | 5 | | 5 | 4 | 4 | 5 | 1 | 5 | | 2 | 3 | | 3 | 1 | | 1 | 1 | 1 | | | | | | | |
| | | | | | | | 3 | 4 | 1 | 1 | | | | | | | | 1 | | | | | | | | | | | |

## League Table

| | P | W | D | L | F | A | Pts |
|---|---|---|---|---|---|---|---|
| Darlington | 38 | 31 | 4 | 3 | 116 | 23 | 66 |
| South Shields | 38 | 27 | 7 | 4 | 103 | 30 | 61 |
| Middlesbrough Reserves | 38 | 26 | 6 | 6 | 102 | 40 | 58 |
| Sunderland Reserves | 38 | 26 | 5 | 7 | 100 | 48 | 57 |
| Newcastle United Reserves | 38 | 24 | 5 | 9 | 109 | 47 | 53 |
| Spennymoor United | 38 | 19 | 6 | 13 | 80 | 61 | 44 |
| Shildon | 38 | 17 | 9 | 12 | 79 | 69 | 43 |
| Houghton Rovers | 38 | 15 | 9 | 14 | 53 | 64 | 39 |
| Wallsend | 38 | 14 | 10 | 14 | 83 | 71 | 38 |
| North Shields Athletic | 38 | 15 | 7 | 16 | 72 | 78 | 37 |
| Newcastle City | 38 | 15 | 7 | 16 | 48 | 62 | 37 |
| Hartlepools United | 38 | 15 | 6 | 17 | 69 | 66 | 36 |
| Hebburn Argyle | 38 | 12 | 6 | 20 | 49 | 75 | 30 |
| Carlisle United | 38 | 12 | 5 | 21 | 61 | 98 | 29 |
| Seaham Harbour | 38 | 10 | 7 | 21 | 48 | 77 | 27 |
| Jarrow | 38 | 10 | 5 | 23 | 52 | 86 | 25 |
| West Stanley | 38 | 7 | 10 | 21 | 54 | 94 | 24 |
| Sunderland Rovers | 38 | 7 | 8 | 23 | 39 | 79 | 22 |
| Gateshead Town | 38 | 8 | 6 | 24 | 49 | 112 | 22 |
| Wingate Albion | 38 | 5 | 2 | 31 | 28 | 114 | 12 |

# 1913-14

## North Eastern League

Manager: Jack Manners

### Did you know that?

Ernest Ellis, who made 42 League and Cup appearances at right-back, later played for Heart of Midlothian and served in the Royal Scots during World War One. He was killed in the Battle of the Somme in June 1917.

| Match No. | Date | Round | Venue | Opponents | Result | | Scorers | Attendance |
|---|---|---|---|---|---|---|---|---|
| 1 | Sep 6 | | (h) | South Shields | D | 1 - 1 | Smith | |
| 2 | 10 | | (a) | Jarrow | W | 2 - 0 | Smith 2 | |
| 3 | 13 | | (h) | Middlesbrough Reserves | W | 2 - 1 | Smith, Hibbert (pen) | 6,200 |
| 4 | 20 | | (h) | Houghton Rovers | W | 6 - 0 | Smith, Walker 3, Lowe 2 | 4,500 |
| 7 | Oct 4 | | (a) | Middlesbrough Reserves | L | 1 - 2 | Bennett | 6,000 |
| 9 | 18 | | (h) | Shildon | W | 2 - 0 | Hibbert 2 | 4,500 |
| 10 | 25 | | (a) | Wallsend | W | 3 - 0 | Hibbert (pen), Smith 2 | |
| 12 | Nov 8 | | (h) | West Stanley | W | 3 - 0 | Hibbert 2 (2 pens), Smith | 2,164 |
| 14 | 22 | | (a) | Newcastle United Reserves | W | 1 - 0 | Smith | |
| 16 | Dec 13 | | (a) | Seaham Harbour | D | 0 - 0 | | |
| 17 | 25 | | (a) | Darlington | D | 1 - 1 | Hibbert | |
| 18 | 26 | | (h) | Sunderland Reserves | W | 4 - 0 | Bennett, Lowe, Manners, Smith | 5,371 |
| 19 | Jan 1 | | (h) | Darlington | W | 1 - 0 | Smith | 6,807 |
| 20 | 2 | | (h) | Hebburn Argyle | D | 0 - 0 | | 3,807 |
| 21 | 3 | | (a) | South Shields | L | 2 - 3 | Smith, Young | |
| 22 | 10 | | (a) | Spennymoor United | D | 1 - 1 | Lowe | |
| 23 | 14 | | (a) | Newcastle City | W | 2 - 1 | Bryden, Smith | |
| 24 | 17 | | (h) | Seaham Harbour | D | 1 - 1 | Flanagan | 1,920 |
| 25 | 31 | | (a) | West Stanley | W | 1 - 0 | Bryden | 2,440 |
| 26 | Feb 14 | | (h) | Spennymoor United | W | 2 - 0 | Smith 2 (1 pen) | |
| 27 | 18 | | (a) | Blyth Spartans | L | 0 - 2 | | |
| 28 | 21 | | (h) | Sunderland Rovers | W | 2 - 0 | Young, Mitchell | 2,200 |
| 29 | 28 | | (h) | Carlisle United | W | 4 - 0 | Young, Mitchell 2, Hibbert (pen) | 3,654 |
| 30 | Mar 7 | | (h) | Wallsend | W | 8 - 0 | Walker, Smith 4, Graham, Baker, Hibbert (pen) | 1,300 |
| 31 | 11 | | (a) | North Shields Athletic | W | 2 - 0 | Smith, Baker | |
| 32 | 14 | | (a) | Sunderland Rovers | D | 1 - 1 | Mitchell | |
| 33 | 18 | | (h) | Jarrow | L | 1 - 2 | Young | |
| 34 | 21 | | (a) | Shildon | L | 0 - 2 | | |
| 35 | 28 | | (h) | Newcastle United Reserves | L | 0 - 3 | | |
| 36 | Apr 4 | | (a) | Hebburn Argyle | D | 1 - 1 | Manners | |
| 37 | 10 | | (a) | Gateshead Town | L | 1 - 2 | Hibbert (pen) | |
| 38 | 11 | | (h) | North Shields Athletic | W | 6 - 2 | McGill 2, Wigham, Hibbert (pen), Lowe 2 | |
| 39 | 13 | | (a) | Sunderland Reserves | L | 1 - 2 | Lowe | 2,000 |
| 40 | 14 | | (h) | Newcastle City | L | 0 - 1 | | 1,879 |
| 41 | 18 | | (h) | Gateshead Town | D | 1 - 1 | McGill | |
| 42 | 22 | | (h) | Blyth Spartans | D | 1 - 1 | McGill | 1,000 |
| 43 | 25 | | (a) | Houghton Rovers | L | 2 - 4 | Brown, Manners | |
| 44 | 30 | | (a) | Carlisle United | L | 1 - 2 | Young | |

Final Position : 7th in North Eastern League

Apps.
Goals

**FA Cup**

| Match No. | Date | Round | Venue | Opponents | Result | | Scorers | Attendance |
|---|---|---|---|---|---|---|---|---|
| 5 | Sep 27 | PR | (h) | Sunderland Rovers | D | 0 - 0 | | 5,243 |
| 6 | Oct 1 | PRr | (a) | Sunderland Rovers | W | 2 - 1 | Smith, Hibbert 2 (1 pen) | 2,000 |
| 8 | 11 | QR1 | (h) | Annfield Plain | W | 6 - 1 | Lowe 2, Walker 2, Smith 2 | 4,327 |
| 11 | Nov 1 | QR2 | (h) | Birtley | W | 4 - 0 | Lowe, Smith 2, Bryden | 5,143 |
| 13 | 15 | QR3 | (h) | Horden Athletic | W | 4 - 0 | Smith 3, Manners | 5,300 |
| 15 | 29 | QR4 | (h) | South Shields | L | 0 - 1 | | 12,000 |

Apps.
Goals

| Gill | Ellis | Graham | Baker | Hibbert | Manners | Jobling | Walker | Smith | Lowe | Bennett | Varty | Young | Bryden | Flanagan | Gatenby | Mitchell | McGill | Cuff | Wigham | Miller | Brown |
|---|---|---|---|---|---|---|---|---|---|---|---|---|---|---|---|---|---|---|---|---|---|
| 1 | 2 | 3 | 4 | 5 | 6 | 7 | 8 | 9 | 10 | 11 | | | | | | | | | | | |
| 1 | 2 | 3 | | 5 | 6 | 7 | 8 | 9 | 10 | | 4 | 11 | | | | | | | | | |
| 1 | 2 | 3 | 4 | 5 | 6 | | 8 | 9 | 10 | 7 | | 11 | | | | | | | | | |
| 1 | 2 | 3 | 4 | 5 | 6 | | 8 | 9 | 10 | 7 | | 11 | | | | | | | | | |
| 1 | 2 | 3 | 4 | 5 | 6 | | 8 | 9 | | 7 | 10 | 11 | | | | | | | | | |
| 1 | 2 | 3 | 4 | 5 | | | 8 | 9 | 10 | 7 | 6 | 11 | | | | | | | | | |
| 1 | 2 | 3 | | 4 | 5 | 7 | | 9 | 10 | | 6 | 8 | 11 | | | | | | | | |
| 1 | 2 | 3 | 4 | 5 | 6 | | | 9 | 10 | 7 | | 8 | 11 | | | | | | | | |
| 1 | 2 | 3 | 4 | 5 | 6 | | | 9 | 10 | 7 | | 8 | 11 | | | | | | | | |
| 1 | 2 | 3 | 4 | 5 | 6 | | 8 | 9 | 10 | 7 | | | 11 | | | | | | | | |
| 1 | 2 | 3 | 4 | 5 | 6 | | | 9 | | 7 | | 8 | 11 | 10 | | | | | | | |
| 1 | 2 | 3 | 4 | 5 | 6 | | 8 | 9 | 10 | 7 | | | 11 | | | | | | | | |
| 1 | 2 | 3 | 4 | 5 | 6 | | | 9 | 10 | 7 | | 8 | 11 | | | | | | | | |
| 1 | | 3 | 4 | 5 | | | | 9 | 10 | 7 | 6 | | 11 | 8 | 2 | | | | | | |
| 1 | 2 | 3 | 4 | 5 | 6 | | | 9 | 10 | 7 | | 8 | 11 | | | | | | | | |
| 1 | 2 | 3 | 4 | 5 | 6 | | 8 | 9 | 10 | | | 7 | 11 | | | | | | | | |
| 1 | 2 | | 4 | 5 | 6 | | 8 | 9 | 10 | | | 7 | 11 | | 3 | | | | | | |
| 1 | 2 | | 4 | 5 | 6 | | | 9 | 10 | 7 | | | 11 | 8 | 3 | | | | | | |
| 1 | 2 | 3 | 4 | 5 | 6 | | | 9 | 10 | | | 7 | 11 | | | 8 | | | | | |
| 1 | 2 | 3 | 4 | | | | 10 | 9 | | 7 | 6 | 5 | 11 | | | 8 | | | | | |
| 1 | 2 | 3 | 4 | 5 | | 7 | | 9 | | | 6 | 10 | 11 | | | 8 | | | | | |
| 1 | 2 | 3 | 4 | 5 | | | | 9 | | 7 | 6 | 10 | 11 | | | 8 | | | | | |
| 1 | 2 | 3 | 4 | 5 | | | | | 10 | 7 | 6 | 8 | 11 | | | 9 | | | | | |
| 1 | 2 | 3 | 4 | 5 | | | 10 | 9 | | | 6 | 7 | 11 | | | 8 | | | | | |
| 1 | 2 | 3 | 4 | 5 | 6 | | | 9 | | | | 7 | 11 | | | 8 | 10 | | | | |
| 1 | 2 | 3 | 4 | 5 | | | | | | 7 | 6 | | 11 | | | 8 | 9 | 10 | | | |
| 1 | 2 | 3 | 4 | 5 | 10 | | | | | | 6 | 7 | 11 | | | 8 | 9 | | | | |
| 1 | 2 | 3 | 4 | 5 | 11 | | | | 10 | 7 | 6 | 8 | | | | 9 | | | | | |
| 1 | 2 | 3 | 4 | 5 | 6 | | | | 10 | 7 | | 8 | 11 | | | | | | 9 | | |
| 1 | 2 | | 4 | 5 | 6 | | | | 10 | 7 | | 8 | 11 | | 3 | | | | 9 | | |
| 1 | 2 | | 4 | 5 | | | | | 10 | 7 | 6 | 8 | 11 | | 3 | | 9 | | | | |
| 1 | 2 | 3 | 4 | 5 | | | | | 10 | | 6 | | 11 | | | | 9 | | 8 | 7 | |
| 1 | | 3 | 4 | 5 | | 7 | | | 10 | | 6 | | 11 | | 2 | | | | | 8 | 9 |
| 1 | 2 | 3 | 4 | 5 | | | 9 | | 10 | | 6 | 8 | 11 | | | | | | | 7 | |
| 1 | 2 | 3 | | 5 | | | | | 10 | 7 | 6 | 4 | 11 | | | | 9 | | | 8 | |
| 1 | 2 | 3 | | 5 | 6 | 11 | 10 | | | | 4 | 7 | | | | | 9 | | | 8 | |
| 1 | 2 | 3 | | | 6 | 7 | 4 | | | | 5 | 11 | | | | | | | 9 | 10 | 8 |
| 1 | 2 | 3 | 4 | | 6 | 7 | | | | | 5 | 11 | | | | | | | 8 | 10 | 9 |
| 38 | 36 | 34 | 33 | 35 | 25 | 8 | 15 | 24 | 26 | 23 | 21 | 30 | 28 | 3 | 6 | 10 | 7 | 1 | 5 | 7 | 3 |
| | | 1 | 2 | 11 | 3 | | 4 | 20 | 7 | 2 | | 5 | 2 | 1 | | 4 | 4 | | 1 | | 1 |

| Gill | Ellis | Graham | Baker | Hibbert | Manners | Jobling | Walker | Smith | Lowe | Bennett | Varty | Young | Bryden | Flanagan | Gatenby | Mitchell | McGill | Cuff | Wigham | Miller | Brown |
|---|---|---|---|---|---|---|---|---|---|---|---|---|---|---|---|---|---|---|---|---|---|
| 1 | 2 | 3 | 4 | 5 | 6 | | 8 | 9 | 10 | 7 | | 11 | | | | | | | | | |
| 1 | 2 | 3 | 4 | 5 | 6 | 7 | 8 | 9 | 10 | | | 11 | | | | | | | | | |
| 1 | 2 | 3 | | 5 | 6 | | 8 | 9 | 10 | 7 | 4 | 11 | | | | | | | | | |
| 1 | 2 | | 4 | 5 | 6 | | | 9 | 10 | 7 | | 8 | 11 | | 3 | | | | | | |
| 1 | 2 | 3 | 4 | 5 | 6 | | | 9 | 10 | 7 | | 8 | 11 | | | | | | | | |
| 1 | 2 | 3 | 4 | 5 | 6 | | | 9 | 10 | 7 | | 8 | 11 | | | | | | | | |
| 6 | 6 | 5 | 5 | 6 | 6 | 1 | 3 | 6 | 6 | 5 | 1 | 6 | 3 | | 1 | | | | | | |
| | | | | 2 | 1 | | 2 | 8 | 3 | | | | 1 | | | | | | | | |

## League Table

| | P | W | D | L | F | A | Pts |
|---|---|---|---|---|---|---|---|
| South Shields | 38 | 32 | 5 | 1 | 133 | 29 | 69 |
| Middlesbrough Reserves | 38 | 23 | 8 | 7 | 99 | 37 | 54 |
| Newcastle United Reserves | 38 | 24 | 5 | 9 | 91 | 40 | 53 |
| Darlington | 38 | 20 | 10 | 8 | 72 | 43 | 50 |
| Sunderland Reserves | 38 | 20 | 8 | 10 | 83 | 55 | 48 |
| Blyth Spartans | 38 | 19 | 7 | 12 | 71 | 51 | 45 |
| Hartlepools United | 38 | 17 | 10 | 11 | 68 | 37 | 44 |
| Shildon | 38 | 18 | 3 | 17 | 54 | 60 | 39 |
| Gateshead Town | 38 | 17 | 5 | 16 | 58 | 76 | 39 |
| Hebburn Argyle | 38 | 14 | 11 | 13 | 55 | 50 | 39 |
| Jarrow | 38 | 12 | 10 | 16 | 55 | 63 | 34 |
| North Shields Athletic | 38 | 11 | 10 | 17 | 57 | 81 | 32 |
| Carlisle United | 38 | 11 | 10 | 17 | 48 | 84 | 32 |
| Spennymoor United | 38 | 10 | 11 | 17 | 60 | 63 | 31 |
| Newcastle City | 38 | 7 | 16 | 15 | 34 | 57 | 30 |
| Sunderland Rovers | 38 | 10 | 10 | 18 | 46 | 67 | 30 |
| West Stanley | 38 | 13 | 3 | 22 | 54 | 87 | 29 |
| Houghton Rovers | 38 | 11 | 2 | 25 | 38 | 81 | 24 |
| Seaham Harbour | 38 | 7 | 8 | 23 | 30 | 73 | 22 |
| Wallsend | 38 | 5 | 6 | 27 | 44 | 116 | 16 |

# 1914-15

## North Eastern League

Manager: Jack Manners

### Did you know that?

Rueben Butler joined Hartlepools from Middlesbrough, where he had been a prolific goalscorer in the reserves. He scored 22 goals in 26 games before joining the Army as a dispatch rider, which severely curtailed his appearances in the final weeks of his only season with the club.

| Match No. | Date | Round | Venue | Opponents | Result | | Scorers | Attendance |
|---|---|---|---|---|---|---|---|---|
| 1 | Sep 2 | | (a) | West Stanley | L | 1 - 2 | Smith | |
| 2 | 5 | | (h) | Spennymoor United | L | 1 - 3 | Young | 2,000 |
| 3 | 9 | | (h) | Jarrow | W | 4 - 1 | McGill, Butler 2, Hibbert (pen) | |
| 4 | 12 | | (a) | Spennymoor United | W | 4 - 1 | McGill, Hibbert, Butler 2 | |
| 5 | 19 | | (h) | Blyth Spartans | L | 1 - 2 | Hibbert | |
| 6 | 26 | | (a) | Hebburn Argyle | W | 2 - 1 | Butler, Hibbert (pen) | |
| 7 | Oct 3 | | (h) | Newcastle United Reserves | L | 1 - 2 | Hibbert | |
| 8 | 10 | | (a) | Middlesbrough Reserves | D | 2 - 2 | McGill 2 | 2,000 |
| 9 | 24 | | (h) | Hebburn Argyle | W | 2 - 1 | Bell, Strugnell | 1,683 |
| 10 | 31 | | (h) | West Stanley | W | 3 - 0 | Strugnell, Butler, Luke | 1,073 |
| 11 | Nov 7 | | (a) | Sunderland Reserves | D | 2 - 2 | Butler, McGill | 1,300 |
| 12 | 14 | | (h) | Sunderland Reserves | D | 2 - 2 | Butler, Luke | 2,191 |
| 14 | 28 | | (a) | Blyth Spartans | D | 1 - 1 | Hibbert | 2,793 |
| 16 | Dec 25 | | (a) | South Shields | L | 2 - 6 | Strugnell 2 | |
| 17 | 26 | | (h) | Darlington | W | 3 - 0 | Mahon, Butler 2 | 3,500 |
| 18 | 28 | | (h) | Newcastle City | W | 5 - 1 | Butler 2, Young, Luke, Hibbert | |
| 19 | Jan 1 | | (h) | Gateshead Town | W | 9 - 0 | Luke 4, McGill, Butler 3, Hibbert (pen) | |
| 20 | 2 | | (a) | Darlington | L | 0 - 5 | | |
| 21 | 9 | | (a) | Shildon | D | 0 - 0 | | |
| 22 | 16 | | (h) | Middlesbrough Reserves | W | 1 - 0 | Luke | |
| 23 | 23 | | (h) | Shildon | D | 1 - 1 | Strugnell | 1,000 |
| 24 | Feb 6 | | (a) | Newcastle City | L | 0 - 2 | | 3,538 |
| 25 | 13 | | (h) | Carlisle United | W | 10 - 0 | Butler 3, McGill 3, Strugnell 3, McDougall | 987 |
| 26 | Mar 6 | | (a) | Sunderland Rovers | W | 2 - 1 | Butler 2 | |
| 27 | 10 | | (a) | Wallsend | W | 1 - 0 | Hibbert | |
| 28 | 13 | | (h) | South Shields | L | 0 - 3 | | |
| 29 | 20 | | (h) | Ashington | D | 0 - 0 | | |
| 30 | 24 | | (a) | Ashington | D | 2 - 2 | Mahon, Opponent (o.g.) | |
| 31 | 27 | | (a) | Houghton Rovers | D | 1 - 1 | Young | |
| 32 | Apr 2 | | (a) | Gateshead Town | D | 1 - 1 | Butler | |
| 33 | 3 | | (a) | North Shields Athletic | L | 0 - 1 | | |
| 34 | 5 | | (h) | Sunderland Rovers | W | 3 - 1 | Strugnell 2, Johnson | |
| 35 | 10 | | (a) | Newcastle United Reserves | L | 0 - 4 | | 1,000 |
| 36 | 17 | | (h) | North Shields Athletic | W | 2 - 1 | McDougall, Johnson | 1,050 |
| 37 | 21 | | (a) | Jarrow | L | 0 - 5 | | |
| 38 | 24 | | (a) | Carlisle United | D | 0 - 0 | | |
| 39 | 28 | | (h) | Wallsend | W | 3 - 2 | McDougall, Young 2 | |
| 40 | 30 | | (h) | Houghton Rovers | W | 2 - 0 | Luke, Strugnell | |

Final Position : 7th in North Eastern League

Apps.

1 own goal Goals

**FA Cup**

| Match No. | Date | Round | Venue | Opponents | Result | | Scorers | Attendance |
|---|---|---|---|---|---|---|---|---|
| 13 | Nov 21 | QR4 | (h) | Bishop Auckland | W | 6 - 2 | Strugnell, Butler 3, Hibbert, Luke | |
| 15 | Dec 5 | QR5 | (a) | Rochdale | L | 0 - 2 | | 2,000 |

Apps.

Goals

| Gill | Graham | Taylor | McDougall | Hibbert | Manners | Luke | Vivian | Butler | Strugnell | Ridley | Jameson | Mahon | Young | Bennett | McGill | Stewart | Smith | Hall | Bell | Franks | Boyle | Boyne | Johnson |
|---|---|---|---|---|---|---|---|---|---|---|---|---|---|---|---|---|---|---|---|---|---|---|---|
| 1 | 2 | 3 | 4 | 5 | 6 | 7 | 8 | 9 | 10 | 11 | | | | | | | | | | | | | |
| 1 | 3 | | 5 | | 6 | 7 | 8 | 9 | | | 2 | 4 | 10 | 11 | | | | | | | | | |
| 1 | 3 | 2 | 4 | 5 | 6 | 7 | 10 | 9 | | | | | 11 | | 8 | | | | | | | | |
| 1 | 3 | 2 | 4 | 5 | 6 | | | 9 | 10 | | | | | 7 | 8 | 11 | | | | | | | |
| 1 | 3 | 2 | 4 | 5 | | 7 | | 9 | 10 | | | 6 | | 11 | | | 8 | | | | | | |
| 1 | 3 | | 4 | 5 | 6 | 7 | | 9 | 10 | | | | | | | | 8 | 2 | 11 | | | | |
| 1 | 3 | 2 | 4 | 5 | 6 | 7 | 8 | 9 | 10 | | | | | | | | | | 11 | | | | |
| 1 | 3 | 2 | 4 | 5 | 6 | 7 | | 9 | 10 | | | | | | 8 | | | | 11 | | | | |
| 1 | 3 | 2 | 4 | 5 | 6 | 7 | | 9 | 10 | | | | | | 8 | | | | 11 | | | | |
| 1 | 3 | 2 | 4 | 5 | 6 | 7 | | 9 | 10 | | | | | | 8 | | | | 11 | | | | |
| 1 | 3 | 2 | 4 | 5 | 6 | 7 | | 9 | 10 | | | | | | 8 | | | | 11 | | | | |
| 1 | 3 | 2 | 4 | 5 | 6 | 7 | | 9 | 10 | | | | | | 8 | | | | 11 | | | | |
| 1 | 3 | 2 | 4 | 5 | 6 | 7 | | 9 | 10 | | | | | | 8 | | | | 11 | | | | |
| 1 | 3 | | 4 | 5 | | 7 | | 9 | 10 | | 2 | 6 | 11 | | 8 | | | | | | | | |
| 1 | 3 | 2 | 4 | 5 | 6 | 7 | | 9 | 10 | | | 11 | 8 | | | | | | | | | | |
| 1 | 3 | 2 | 4 | 5 | 6 | 7 | | 9 | 10 | | | 11 | 8 | | | | | | | | | | |
| 1 | | 2 | 4 | 5 | | 7 | | 9 | 10 | | 3 | 6 | | 11 | 8 | | | | | | | | |
| 1 | | 2 | 4 | 5 | 6 | 7 | | 9 | 10 | | | | | 11 | 8 | | | | | 3 | | | |
| 1 | 3 | 2 | 5 | | | 7 | | 9 | 10 | | 4 | 6 | | | 8 | | | | | | 11 | | |
| 1 | 3 | 2 | 4 | | | 7 | | 9 | 10 | | 6 | 5 | | | 8 | | | | 11 | | | | |
| 1 | 3 | 2 | 4 | 5 | | 7 | | 9 | 10 | | 6 | 11 | | | 8 | | | | | | | | |
| 1 | 3 | 2 | 4 | 5 | 6 | 7 | | | 10 | | | 11 | 8 | | 9 | | | | | | | | |
| 1 | 3 | 2 | 4 | 5 | 6 | | | 9 | 10 | | | 11 | 7 | | 8 | | | | | | | | |
| 1 | 3 | 2 | 4 | 5 | | 7 | | 9 | 10 | | | 6 | | 11 | 8 | | | | | | | | |
| 1 | 3 | 2 | 4 | 5 | 6 | 7 | | 9 | 10 | | | | 11 | | 8 | | | | | | | | |
| 1 | 3 | 2 | 4 | 5 | 6 | 7 | | 9 | 10 | | | 11 | | 8 | | | | | | | | | |
| 1 | | 3 | 4 | 5 | | 7 | | | 10 | | 2 | 6 | 8 | 11 | | | | | | | | 9 | |
| 1 | | 3 | 4 | 5 | | 7 | | | 10 | | 2 | 6 | 8 | 11 | | | | | | | | 9 | |
| 1 | 3 | | 4 | 5 | | 7 | | | 10 | | 2 | 6 | 8 | 11 | | | | | | | | 9 | |
| 1 | 3 | | 4 | 5 | 6 | 7 | | 9 | 10 | | 2 | 11 | 8 | | | | | | | | | | |
| 1 | 3 | 2 | 6 | 5 | | | | | 10 | | 4 | 11 | 8 | | | | | | | | 7 | | 9 |
| 1 | 3 | 2 | 5 | | 6 | | | | 10 | | 4 | 9 | | 7 | | | | | 11 | | | | 8 |
| 1 | 3 | | 4 | 5 | 6 | | | | 10 | | 2 | 11 | 8 | 7 | | | | | | | | | 9 |
| 1 | 3 | 2 | 9 | 5 | | | | | 10 | | 4 | 6 | 7 | | | | | | 11 | | | | 8 |
| 1 | 3 | 2 | 9 | 5 | | | | | 10 | | 4 | 6 | 7 | | 8 | | | | 11 | | | | |
| 1 | 3 | 2 | 9 | 5 | 6 | 7 | | | 10 | | 4 | 11 | | | 8 | | | | | | | | |
| 1 | 3 | 2 | 5 | | 6 | | | | 10 | | 4 | 11 | 8 | | 9 | | | | | | 7 | | |
| 1 | 3 | 2 | 5 | | 6 | 7 | | | 10 | | 4 | 11 | | | 9 | | | | | | | | 8 |
| 38 | 34 | 32 | 38 | 32 | 25 | 30 | 4 | 26 | 36 | 1 | 18 | 25 | 17 | 12 | 22 | 1 | 2 | 1 | 12 | 1 | 3 | 3 | 5 |
| | | | 3 | 9 | | 9 | | 22 | 11 | | | 2 | 5 | | 9 | | | | 1 | | | | 2 |

| Gill | Graham | Taylor | McDougall | Hibbert | Manners | Luke | Vivian | Butler | Strugnell | Ridley | Jameson | Mahon | Young | Bennett | McGill | Stewart | Smith | Hall | Bell | Franks | Boyle | Boyne | Johnson |
|---|---|---|---|---|---|---|---|---|---|---|---|---|---|---|---|---|---|---|---|---|---|---|---|
| 1 | 3 | 2 | 4 | 5 | 6 | 7 | | 9 | 10 | | | | | | 8 | | | | 11 | | | | |
| 1 | 3 | 2 | 4 | 5 | 6 | 7 | | 9 | 10 | | | | | | 8 | | | | 11 | | | | |
| 2 | 2 | 2 | 2 | 2 | 2 | 2 | | 2 | 2 | | | | | | 2 | | | | 2 | | | | |
| | | | | 1 | | 1 | | 3 | 1 | | | | | | | | | | | | | | |

## League Table

| | P | W | D | L | F | A | Pts |
|---|---|---|---|---|---|---|---|
| South Shields | 38 | 31 | 4 | 3 | 160 | 34 | 66 |
| Middlesbrough Reserves | 38 | 28 | 5 | 5 | 151 | 35 | 61 |
| Newcastle United Reserves | 38 | 26 | 6 | 6 | 138 | 43 | 58 |
| Darlington | 38 | 25 | 4 | 9 | 109 | 38 | 54 |
| West Stanley | 38 | 24 | 4 | 10 | 79 | 44 | 52 |
| Sunderland Reserves | 38 | 18 | 9 | 11 | 86 | 50 | 45 |
| Hartlepools United | 38 | 16 | 11 | 11 | 74 | 57 | 43 |
| North Shields Athletic | 38 | 19 | 5 | 14 | 67 | 63 | 43 |
| Ashington | 38 | 15 | 11 | 12 | 60 | 65 | 41 |
| Sunderland Rovers | 38 | 17 | 4 | 17 | 74 | 79 | 38 |
| Spennymoor United | 38 | 12 | 9 | 17 | 40 | 82 | 33 |
| Shildon | 38 | 11 | 9 | 18 | 40 | 58 | 31 |
| Hebburn Argyle | 38 | 12 | 6 | 20 | 50 | 73 | 30 |
| Jarrow | 38 | 10 | 10 | 18 | 46 | 85 | 30 |
| Blyth Spartans | 38 | 10 | 9 | 19 | 49 | 75 | 29 |
| Houghton Rovers | 38 | 11 | 4 | 23 | 43 | 123 | 26 |
| Carlisle United | 38 | 8 | 7 | 23 | 50 | 108 | 23 |
| Newcastle City | 38 | 8 | 5 | 25 | 43 | 87 | 21 |
| Gateshead Town | 38 | 8 | 3 | 27 | 52 | 121 | 19 |
| Wallsend | 38 | 6 | 3 | 29 | 44 | 135 | 15 |

# 1919-20

## North Eastern League

Manager: Jack Manners

### Did you know that?

The opening North Eastern league fixture against Ashington saw George Gill as the only survivor of the pre-war side. All the other players were making their Hartlepools debuts.

| Match No. | Date | Round | Venue | Opponents | Result | | Scorers | Attendance |
|---|---|---|---|---|---|---|---|---|
| 1 | Aug 30 | | (h) | Ashington | D | 1 - 1 | Toward (pen) | 2,000 |
| 2 | Sep 6 | | (a) | Ashington | D | 0 - 0 | | |
| 3 | 13 | | (a) | Darlington | L | 0 - 1 | | |
| 4 | 20 | | (h) | Darlington | L | 0 - 2 | | 1,500 |
| 5 | 27 | | (h) | West Stanley | D | 1 - 1 | Hewitt (pen) | |
| 6 | Oct 4 | | (a) | West Stanley | L | 0 - 2 | | |
| 7 | 11 | | (a) | South Shields Reserves | L | 0 - 3 | | 8,000 |
| 8 | 18 | | (a) | Durham City | D | 1 - 1 | Hibbert | |
| 9 | 25 | | (h) | Sunderland Reserves | D | 1 - 1 | Scott (pen) | 4,000 |
| 10 | Nov 1 | | (a) | Sunderland Reserves | L | 0 - 1 | | 4,000 |
| 11 | 15 | | (a) | Houghton Rovers | W | 4 - 2 | Hewitt 4 | |
| 13 | Dec 6 | | (a) | Scotswood | L | 0 - 2 | | |
| 14 | 13 | | (h) | Scotswood | W | 4 - 2 | Bratt 2, Hewitt 2 | |
| 15 | 20 | | (a) | Newcastle United Reserves | L | 1 - 2 | Hewitt | 2,000 |
| 16 | 25 | | (a) | Middlesbrough Reserves | D | 0 - 0 | | 4,000 |
| 17 | 26 | | (h) | Blyth Spartans | L | 2 - 3 | Hewitt 2 (1 pen) | 5,000 |
| 18 | 27 | | (h) | Newcastle United Reserves | L | 0 - 2 | | 3,500 |
| 19 | Jan 1 | | (h) | Middlesbrough Reserves | L | 2 - 3 | Hafekost, Toward | 5,000 |
| 20 | 3 | | (h) | Palmers Jarrow | W | 2 - 0 | Gray, Hafekost (pen) | 1,000 |
| 21 | 17 | | (a) | Wallsend | W | 3 - 0 | Short 2, Dickinson | |
| 22 | 24 | | (h) | Wallsend | D | 0 - 0 | | |
| 23 | 31 | | (h) | Shildon | W | 3 - 0 | Bratt 2, Toward | |
| 24 | Feb 14 | | (h) | Carlisle United | W | 2 - 0 | Bratt 2 | |
| 25 | 21 | | (a) | Carlisle United | L | 0 - 1 | | |
| 26 | 28 | | (h) | Leadgate Park | W | 4 - 0 | Short 3, Bratt | |
| 27 | Mar 6 | | (a) | Leadgate Park | W | 2 - 0 | Bratt 2 | |
| 28 | 13 | | (a) | Palmers Jarrow | L | 0 - 1 | | |
| 29 | Apr 2 | | (a) | Blyth Spartans | D | 2 - 2 | Bratt, Toward | |
| 30 | 3 | | (a) | Spennymoor United | D | 1 - 1 | Toward | |
| 31 | 5 | | (h) | Houghton Rovers | W | 1 - 0 | Hewitt | 3,000 |
| 32 | 17 | | (h) | South Shields Reserves | W | 4 - 2 | Hewitt 2, Short, Crilly (pen) | 4,000 |
| 33 | 24 | | (h) | Spennymoor United | W | 2 - 0 | Hewitt, Short | |
| 34 | 28 | | (a) | Shildon | D | 0 - 0 | | |
| 35 | May 1 | | (h) | Durham City | W | 2 - 0 | Short, Bratt | |

Final Position : 9th in North Eastern League

Apps.
Goals

**FA Cup**

| Match No. | Date | Round | Venue | Opponents | Result | | Scorers | Attendance |
|---|---|---|---|---|---|---|---|---|
| 12 | Nov 22 | QR4 | (a) | Bishop Auckland | L | 0 - 1 | | |

Apps.
Goals

| Gill | Scott | Shields | Spink | Knowles | Topping | Toward | Hewitt | Reed | Jobey | Bryden | McCarron | Franks | Hibbert | Burgon | Burton | Wood | Adams | Gray | Hafekost | Orr | Mordue | Bratt | Oliver | Summerfield | Langley | Thoms | Manners | Corbett | Hepburn | Short | Dickinson | Crilly | Snaith | Maughan | Burrell | Taylor | Gilhespy |
|---|---|---|---|---|---|---|---|---|---|---|---|---|---|---|---|---|---|---|---|---|---|---|---|---|---|---|---|---|---|---|---|---|---|---|---|---|---|
| 1 | 2 | 3 | 4 | 5 | 6 | 7 | 8 | 9 | 10 | 11 | | | | | | | | | | | | | | | | | | | | | | | | | | | |
| 1 | 2 | 3 | 4 | 5 | 6 | 7 | 8 | 9 | | 11 | 10 | | | | | | | | | | | | | | | | | | | | | | | | | | |
| 1 | 3 | | | 5 | 6 | 7 | 8 | 9 | | 11 | 10 | 2 | 4 | | | | | | | | | | | | | | | | | | | | | | | | |
| 1 | 4 | 3 | | | 6 | 7 | 8 | | | | 11 | 2 | 5 | 9 | 10 | | | | | | | | | | | | | | | | | | | | | | |
| 1 | 5 | 3 | 4 | | 6 | 7 | 8 | | | | 11 | 2 | 10 | | | 9 | | | | | | | | | | | | | | | | | | | | | |
| 1 | 5 | 3 | 4 | | 6 | 7 | 8 | | | | 11 | 2 | | 10 | | 9 | | | | | | | | | | | | | | | | | | | | | |
| 1 | 5 | 3 | 4 | | 6 | 7 | 8 | | | | | 2 | | 10 | | 9 | 11 | | | | | | | | | | | | | | | | | | | | |
| 1 | 6 | 3 | | | 5 | 7 | 10 | | | | | 2 | 9 | | | | 11 | 4 | 8 | | | | | | | | | | | | | | | | | | |
| 1 | 5 | 3 | 9 | | 6 | 7 | 10 | | | | | 2 | | | | | | 4 | 8 | 11 | | | | | | | | | | | | | | | | | |
| 1 | 5 | | | | 6 | 7 | 10 | 9 | | | | 2 | | | | | | 4 | 8 | 11 | 3 | | | | | | | | | | | | | | | | |
| 1 | 5 | | | | 6 | 7 | 10 | | | | | 2 | | | | | | 4 | 8 | | 3 | 9 | 11 | | | | | | | | | | | | | | |
| | 5 | | 7 | | | | 8 | | | | | 2 | 6 | | 10 | | | 4 | | | 3 | 9 | | 1 | 11 | | | | | | | | | | | | |
| | 4 | | | | | 7 | 10 | | | | | 2 | | | | | | 6 | 8 | | 3 | 9 | | 1 | 11 | 5 | | | | | | | | | | | |
| 1 | 4 | | | | | 7 | 10 | | | | | 2 | | | | | | 6 | 8 | | 3 | 9 | | | 11 | 5 | | | | | | | | | | | |
| 1 | 2 | | | | 6 | 7 | 10 | | | | | 3 | | | | | | 4 | 8 | | | 9 | | | 11 | 5 | | | | | | | | | | | |
| 1 | 2 | | | | | 7 | 10 | | | | | 3 | | | | | | 4 | 8 | | | 9 | | | 11 | 6 | 5 | | | | | | | | | | |
| | 2 | | | | | 7 | 10 | | | | | | 6 | | | | | 4 | 8 | | 3 | 9 | | 1 | 11 | 5 | | | | | | | | | | | |
| 1 | 2 | | 6 | | | 7 | 10 | | | | | 3 | | | | | | 4 | 8 | | | 9 | | | 11 | 5 | | | | | | | | | | | |
| | 6 | | | | | 7 | 10 | | | | | 3 | | | | | | 4 | 8 | | | | | 1 | 11 | 5 | | 2 | 9 | | | | | | | | |
| | 4 | | | | | 7 | 8 | | | | | 3 | | | | | | 6 | | | | 10 | | 1 | | 5 | | 2 | | 9 | 11 | | | | | | |
| | 4 | | | | | 7 | | | | | | 3 | | | | | | 6 | 8 | | | 9 | | 1 | | 5 | | 2 | | 10 | 11 | | | | | | |
| | 4 | | | | | 7 | 11 | | | | | 2 | | | | | | 6 | 8 | | | 9 | | 1 | | 5 | | | | 10 | | 3 | | | | | |
| | 4 | | | | | 7 | 11 | | | | | 2 | | | | | | 6 | 8 | | | 9 | | 1 | | 5 | | | | 10 | | 3 | | | | | |
| 1 | 4 | | | | | 7 | 8 | | | | | 2 | | | | | | 6 | | | | 9 | | | | 5 | | | | 10 | | 3 | 11 | | | | |
| | | | | | 6 | 7 | 8 | | | | | 2 | | | | | | 4 | | | | 9 | | 1 | | 5 | | | | 10 | | 3 | | 11 | | | |
| 1 | | | | | 6 | 7 | 8 | | | | | 2 | | | | | | 4 | | | | 9 | | | | 5 | | | | 10 | | 3 | | 11 | | | |
| | | | | | 6 | 7 | 8 | | | | | 2 | | | | | | | | | | 9 | | 1 | | 5 | | | | 10 | | 3 | | 11 | 4 | | |
| 1 | 4 | | | | 6 | 7 | 8 | | | | | 2 | | | | | | | | | | 9 | | | | 5 | | | | 10 | | 3 | | 11 | | | |
| 1 | | | | | 6 | 7 | 8 | | | | | 2 | | | | | | 4 | | | | 9 | | | | 5 | | | | 10 | | 3 | | 11 | | | |
| | | | | | 6 | 7 | 8 | | | | | 2 | | | | | | 4 | | | | 9 | | 1 | 10 | 5 | | | | | | 3 | | 11 | | | |
| 1 | | | | | 6 | 7 | 8 | | | | | 2 | | | | | | 4 | | | | 9 | | | | 5 | | | | 10 | | 3 | | 11 | | | |
| | | | | | 6 | 7 | 11 | | | | | 2 | 5 | | | | | 4 | | | | | | 1 | | | | | | 10 | | 3 | | | | 8 | 9 |
| | | | | | 6 | 7 | 9 | | | | | 2 | 5 | | | | | 4 | | | | 8 | | 1 | | | | | | 10 | | 3 | | 11 | | | |
| | | | | | 6 | 7 | 9 | | | | | 2 | | | | | | 4 | | | | 8 | | 1 | | 5 | | | | 10 | | 3 | | 11 | | | |
| 20 | 25 | 8 | 8 | 3 | 22 | 33 | 33 | 4 | 1 | 3 | 5 | 31 | 8 | 3 | 2 | 3 | 2 | 25 | 14 | 2 | 6 | 22 | 1 | 14 | 9 | 20 | 1 | 3 | 1 | 14 | 2 | 13 | 1 | 9 | 1 | 1 | 1 |
| | 1 | | | | | 5 | 14 | | | | | | 1 | | | | | 1 | 2 | | | 11 | | | | | | | | 8 | 1 | 1 | | | | | |

| Gill | Scott | Shields | Spink | Knowles | Topping | Toward | Hewitt | Reed | Jobey | Bryden | McCarron | Franks | Hibbert | Burgon | Burton | Wood | Adams | Gray | Hafekost | Orr | Mordue |
|---|---|---|---|---|---|---|---|---|---|---|---|---|---|---|---|---|---|---|---|---|---|
| 1 | 5 | | | | 6 | 7 | 10 | 9 | | 11 | | 2 | | | | | | 4 | 8 | | 3 |
| 1 | 1 | | | | 1 | 1 | 1 | 1 | | 1 | | 1 | | | | | | 1 | 1 | | 1 |

## League Table

| | P | W | D | L | F | A | Pts |
|---|---|---|---|---|---|---|---|
| Middlesbrough Reserves | 34 | 22 | 7 | 5 | 86 | 30 | 51 |
| Darlington | 34 | 24 | 1 | 9 | 91 | 44 | 49 |
| Newcastle United Reserves | 34 | 22 | 5 | 7 | 82 | 41 | 49 |
| Blyth Spartans | 34 | 18 | 8 | 8 | 62 | 42 | 44 |
| Durham City | 34 | 17 | 6 | 11 | 52 | 41 | 40 |
| Palmers Jarrow | 34 | 16 | 6 | 12 | 55 | 52 | 38 |
| Ashington | 34 | 14 | 8 | 12 | 51 | 51 | 36 |
| South Shields Reserves | 34 | 14 | 7 | 13 | 67 | 57 | 35 |
| Hartlepools United | 34 | 12 | 10 | 12 | 45 | 36 | 34 |
| Sunderland Reserves | 34 | 15 | 4 | 15 | 67 | 49 | 34 |
| Scotswood | 34 | 13 | 6 | 15 | 47 | 55 | 32 |
| West Stanley | 34 | 12 | 7 | 15 | 45 | 63 | 31 |
| Carlisle United | 34 | 12 | 3 | 19 | 47 | 76 | 27 |
| Shildon | 34 | 10 | 6 | 18 | 50 | 75 | 26 |
| Houghton Rovers | 34 | 8 | 8 | 18 | 28 | 60 | 24 |
| Spennymoor United | 34 | 10 | 2 | 22 | 52 | 78 | 22 |
| Leadgate Park | 34 | 8 | 6 | 20 | 51 | 83 | 22 |
| Wallsend | 34 | 6 | 6 | 22 | 26 | 71 | 18 |

# 1920-21

## North Eastern League

Manager: Cecil Potter

### Did you know that?

Admission prices for first-team games were set at one shilling (5p) for adults and sixpence (21/2p) for boys, with a supplement of one shilling for entry to the grandstand.

Billy Short became the first Hartlepools player to be sent off when he was dismissed for fighting a Haverton Hill defender, Boswell, during the FA Cup qualifying replay in October.

'Pools played 10 FA Cup qualifying games, including replays, yet still failed to reach the First Round proper. They eventually lost 3–0 at Swansea in the sixth qualifying round!

| Match No. | Date | Round | Venue | Opponents | Result | | Scorers | Attendance |
|---|---|---|---|---|---|---|---|---|
| 1 | Aug 28 | | (a) | Durham City | L | 0 - 1 | | 2,000 |
| 2 | Sep 1 | | (h) | Middlesbrough Reserves | D | 0 - 0 | | 6,021 |
| 3 | 4 | | (h) | Durham City | W | 1 - 0 | Hewitt | 5,792 |
| 4 | 8 | | (a) | Middlesbrough Reserves | L | 0 - 1 | | 7,000 |
| 5 | 11 | | (a) | Houghton Rovers | D | 1 - 1 | Thoms | |
| 6 | 18 | | (h) | Houghton Rovers | D | 1 - 1 | Thoms | 5,000 |
| 8 | 29 | | (a) | Spennymoor United | L | 0 - 1 | | 3,000 |
| 9 | Oct 2 | | (h) | Leadgate Park | D | 1 - 1 | Hewitt | 4,019 |
| 12 | 16 | | (a) | Blyth Spartans | L | 1 - 3 | Short | |
| 15 | 30 | | (a) | Ashington | D | 2 - 2 | Lister, Thoms | |
| 17 | Nov 13 | | (h) | Sunderland Reserves | W | 2 - 1 | Mulholland, Lister | 6,000 |
| 19 | 27 | | (a) | Carlisle United | L | 1 - 4 | Crawford (o.g.) | |
| 23 | Dec 25 | | (a) | Darlington | W | 4 - 3 | Mulholland 2, Lister, Short | 5,000 |
| 24 | 27 | | (h) | Darlington | L | 0 - 1 | | 4,000 |
| 25 | Jan 1 | | (h) | Scotswood | W | 4 - 1 | Bratt 2, Topping, Mulholland | 7,374 |
| 26 | 3 | | (h) | Spennymoor United | W | 5 - 0 | Mulholland, Hardy 3, Bratt | 7,390 |
| 27 | 8 | | (a) | Scotswood | W | 1 - 0 | Kessler | |
| 28 | 15 | | (a) | Leadgate Park | L | 0 - 1 | | |
| 29 | 29 | | (a) | West Stanley | L | 1 - 3 | Hardy | 5,000 |
| 30 | Feb 12 | | (h) | Shildon | W | 3 - 2 | Thoms, Mulholland 2 | 5,000 |
| 31 | 19 | | (a) | Wallsend | L | 0 - 1 | | |
| 32 | 26 | | (h) | Blyth Spartans | W | 2 - 0 | Lister 2 | 6,000 |
| 33 | Mar 9 | | (a) | South Shields Reserves | W | 3 - 0 | Hardy, Harris, Lister | |
| 34 | 12 | | (h) | South Shields Reserves | W | 5 - 0 | Kessler, Mulholland 2, Lister, Short | 7,000 |
| 35 | 16 | | (a) | Sunderland Reserves | L | 1 - 2 | Bratt | |
| 36 | 19 | | (a) | Newcastle United Reserves | W | 4 - 1 | Hardy 2, Lister 2 | 7,000 |
| 37 | 25 | | (h) | Chester-Le-Street | W | 1 - 0 | Mulholland | 7,000 |
| 38 | 26 | | (a) | Jarrow | L | 1 - 3 | Mulholland | |
| 39 | 29 | | (h) | Jarrow | W | 2 - 1 | Mulholland, Hardy | |
| 40 | Apr 9 | | (a) | Chester-Le-Street | L | 0 - 2 | | |
| 41 | 13 | | (h) | Carlisle United | L | 0 - 5 | | 800 |
| 42 | 16 | | (a) | Bedlington United | W | 3 - 1 | Kessler, Bratt, Robertson | |
| 43 | 20 | | (h) | West Stanley | D | 1 - 1 | Parkinson | 2,500 |
| 44 | 23 | | (h) | Bedlington United | W | 3 - 1 | Lister 3 | |
| 45 | 27 | | (a) | Shildon | L | 0 - 2 | | |
| 46 | 30 | | (h) | Newcastle United Reserves | W | 1 - 0 | Harris | 8,000 |
| 47 | May 4 | | (h) | Ashington | W | 4 - 2 | Lister 3, Mulholland | 3,000 |
| 48 | 7 | | (h) | Wallsend | W | 5 - 1 | Lister 3, Short, Harris | 5,000 |

Final Position : 8th in North Eastern League — Apps.

1 own goal — Goals

**FA Cup**

| Match No. | Date | Round | Venue | Opponents | Result | | Scorers | Attendance |
|---|---|---|---|---|---|---|---|---|
| 7 | Sep 25 | PR | (h) | South Bank East End | W | 7 - 0 | Kessler, Short 3, Hewitt, Ramsey 2 | 5,000 |
| 10 | Oct 6 | QR1 | (h) | Haverton Hill | D | 3 - 3 | Short, Sutheran, Topping | 4,000 |
| 11 | 13 | QR1r | (h) | Haverton Hill | D | 0 - 0* | | 3,000 |
| 13 | 18 | QR1r2# | (a) | Haverton Hill | W | 1 - 0 | Potter | 4,000 |
| 14 | 23 | QR2 | (a) | Scarborough | W | 4 - 1 | Mulholland 2, Hewitt 2 (1 pen) | |
| 16 | Nov 6 | QR3 | (h) | Loftus Albion | W | 2 - 1 | Kessler, Lister | 5,815 |
| 18 | 20 | QR4 | (h) | Houghton Rovers | W | 3 - 0 | Lister 2, Thoms | 7,743 |
| 20 | Dec 11 | QR5 | (h) | Bishop Auckland | D | 1 - 1 | Thoms | 8,000 |
| 21 | 15 | QR5r | (a) | Bishop Auckland | W | 5 - 0 | Lister 3, Hardy, Kessler | 5,000 |
| 22 | 18 | QR6 | (a) | Swansea Town | L | 0 - 3 | | |

# Played at Ayresome Park, Middlesbrough * After extra time — Apps.

Goals

| Gill | Stephenson | Crilly | Potter | Thoms | Topping | Toward | Bratt | Bolton | Short | Kessler | Hewitt | Franks | Ashton | Yews | Ramsey | Sotheran | Lupton | Young | Chapman | Summerfield | Hardy | Mulholland | Lister | Rumney | Lawson | Bassindale | Miller | Boswell | Harris | Lawrence | Aldridge | Hubery | Dougherty | Robertson | Strickland | Parkinson | Cockburn | Boyce | Henderson |
|---|---|---|---|---|---|---|---|---|---|---|---|---|---|---|---|---|---|---|---|---|---|---|---|---|---|---|---|---|---|---|---|---|---|---|---|---|---|---|---|
| 1 | 2 | 3 | 4 | 5 | 6 | 7 | 8 | 9 | 10 | 11 | | | | | | | | | | | | | | | | | | | | | | | | | | | | | |
| 1 | 2 | 3 | 4 | 5 | 6 | 7 | 9 | | 10 | 11 | 8 | | | | | | | | | | | | | | | | | | | | | | | | | | | | |
| 1 | 2 | 3 | 4 | 5 | 6 | 7 | 9 | | 10 | 11 | 8 | | | | | | | | | | | | | | | | | | | | | | | | | | | | |
| 1 | | 3 | 10 | 5 | 6 | 7 | 9 | | | 11 | 8 | 2 | 4 | | | | | | | | | | | | | | | | | | | | | | | | | | |
| 1 | | 3 | 4 | 5 | 6 | 7 | 9 | | 10 | 11 | 8 | 2 | | | | | | | | | | | | | | | | | | | | | | | | | | | |
| 1 | | 3 | 4 | 5 | 6 | | 9 | | 10 | 11 | 8 | 2 | | 7 | | | | | | | | | | | | | | | | | | | | | | | | | |
| 1 | | 3 | 4 | 5 | 6 | 7 | | | 10 | 11 | 8 | 2 | | | 9 | | | | | | | | | | | | | | | | | | | | | | | | |
| 1 | 2 | 3 | 9 | 5 | | | | | | 11 | 10 | | | 7 | | | 4 | 6 | 8 | | | | | | | | | | | | | | | | | | | | |
| | | 3 | | 5 | 6 | | | | 10 | 11 | | 2 | 4 | | | | | | | 1 | 7 | 8 | 9 | | | | | | | | | | | | | | | | |
| 1 | 2 | 3 | 4 | 5 | | | | | | 11 | 10 | | 6 | 7 | | | | | | | | 8 | 9 | | | | | | | | | | | | | | | | |
| 1 | 2 | 3 | 4 | | 5 | | | | | 11 | 10 | | 6 | 7 | | | | | | | | 8 | 9 | | | | | | | | | | | | | | | | |
| 1 | 2 | 3 | | | 6 | | | | 10 | 11 | 8 | | 4 | 7 | | | | | | | | | 9 | 5 | | | | | | | | | | | | | | | |
| 1 | | 3 | 4 | 5 | | | | | 6 | 11 | 7 | | | | | | | | | | 10 | 8 | 9 | | 2 | | | | | | | | | | | | | | |
| 1 | | 3 | 4 | 5 | | | | | 6 | 11 | 7 | | | | | | | | | | 10 | 8 | | | 2 | 9 | | | | | | | | | | | | | |
| | | | 4 | | 5 | | 9 | | 6 | 11 | 7 | 3 | | | | | | | | 1 | 10 | 8 | | | 2 | | | | | | | | | | | | | | |
| 1 | | 3 | | 5 | | | 9 | | 6 | 11 | 7 | 2 | 4 | | | | | | | | 10 | 8 | | | | | | | | | | | | | | | | | |
| 1 | | 3 | 4 | 5 | | | | | 6 | 11 | 7 | 2 | | | | | | | | | 10 | 8 | | | | | 9 | | | | | | | | | | | | |
| 1 | | 3 | | 5 | | | | | 6 | 11 | 7 | 2 | 4 | | | | | | | | 10 | 8 | | | | | 9 | | | | | | | | | | | | |
| 1 | | 3 | 4 | 5 | | | | | 6 | 11 | 7 | 2 | | | | | | | | | 10 | 8 | 9 | | | | | | | | | | | | | | | | |
| 1 | 4 | 3 | | 5 | | | | | 6 | 11 | 7 | | | | | | | | | | 10 | 8 | 9 | | | | | 2 | | | | | | | | | | | |
| 1 | 4 | 3 | | 5 | | | 9 | | 6 | 11 | 7 | 2 | | | | | | | | | 10 | 8 | | | | | | | | | | | | | | | | | |
| 1 | 4 | 3 | | 5 | | | | | 6 | 11 | 7 | 2 | | | | | | | | | 10 | 8 | 9 | | | | | | | | | | | | | | | | |
| 1 | 2 | 3 | | | 4 | | | | 6 | 11 | 7 | | | | | | | | | | 10 | 8 | 9 | | | | | | 5 | | | | | | | | | | |
| 1 | 2 | 3 | | 5 | 4 | | | | 6 | 11 | 7 | | | | | | | | | | 10 | 8 | 9 | | | | | | | | | | | | | | | | |
| 1 | 2 | 3 | | 5 | 4 | | 7 | | 6 | 11 | | | | | | | | | | | 10 | 8 | 9 | | | | | | | | | | | | | | | | |
| 1 | | 3 | | 5 | | | | | 6 | 11 | 7 | 2 | | | | | | | | | 10 | 8 | 9 | | | | | | | 4 | | | | | | | | | |
| 1 | | 3 | | 5 | | | | | 6 | 11 | 7 | 2 | | | | | | | | | 10 | 8 | 9 | | | | | | | 4 | | | | | | | | | |
| 1 | 4 | 3 | | 5 | | | | | | 11 | 7 | 2 | | | | | | | | | 10 | 8 | 9 | | | | | | | 6 | | | | | | | | | |
| | | 3 | | 5 | | | 9 | | 6 | 11 | | | | 7 | | | | | | | 10 | 8 | | | | | | | | 4 | 1 | 2 | | | | | | | |
| 1 | | | | | 6 | | 9 | | | | | 3 | | 7 | | | | | | | 10 | | | | | | | | 8 | 4 | | 2 | 5 | 11 | | | | | |
| | | 3 | | | | | | | 5 | | 9 | | | 7 | | | | | | | | | | | | | | | 8 | 6 | 1 | 2 | | 11 | 4 | 10 | | | |
| 1 | | 3 | | | | | 9 | | 5 | 11 | | 2 | | | | | | | | | | 8 | | | | | | | | 6 | | | | 7 | 4 | 10 | | | |
| 1 | | 3 | | 5 | | | 9 | | 8 | 11 | | 2 | | | | | | | | | | | 4 | | | | | | | 6 | | | | 7 | | 10 | | | |
| 1 | | 3 | | | 6 | | 8 | | 5 | 11 | | | | | | | | | | | | | 9 | | | | | | | | | | 4 | 7 | | | 2 | 10 | |
| 1 | 4 | | | | | | 8 | | 5 | 11 | | 3 | | | | | | | | | | | 9 | | | | | | | 10 | | | 6 | 7 | | | 2 | | |
| 1 | 6 | 3 | | | | | | | 5 | 11 | 7 | 2 | | | | | | | | | | 8 | 9 | | | | | | 10 | | | | 4 | | | | | | |
| 1 | 2 | 3 | | 5 | 6 | | | | | 11 | | | | 7 | | | | | | | | 8 | 9 | | | | | | 10 | | | | 4 | | | | | | |
| 1 | 2 | 3 | | 5 | | | | | 10 | 7 | | | | | | | | | | | | | 9 | | | | | | 8 | | | | 4 | 11 | | | | | 6 |
| 34 | 18 | 35 | 15 | 28 | 17 | 6 | 16 | 1 | 31 | 36 | 27 | 20 | 7 | 9 | 1 | | 1 | 1 | 1 | 2 | 19 | 23 | 20 | 1 | 3 | 1 | 2 | 1 | 6 | 9 | 2 | 3 | 6 | 7 | 2 | 3 | 2 | 1 | 1 |
| | | | | 4 | 1 | | 5 | | 4 | 3 | 2 | | | | | | | | | | 8 | 13 | 18 | | | | | | 3 | | | | | 1 | | 1 | | | |

| Gill | Stephenson | Crilly | Potter | Thoms | Topping | Toward | Bratt | Bolton | Short | Kessler | Hewitt | Franks | Ashton | Yews | Ramsey | Sotheran | Lupton | Young | Chapman | Summerfield | Hardy | Mulholland | Lister | Rumney | Lawson |
|---|---|---|---|---|---|---|---|---|---|---|---|---|---|---|---|---|---|---|---|---|---|---|---|---|---|
| 1 | | 3 | 4 | 5 | 6 | | | | 10 | 11 | 8 | 2 | | 7 | 9 | | | | | | | | | | |
| 1 | 2 | 3 | 4 | 5 | 6 | | | | 10 | 11 | 8 | | | 7 | | 9 | | | | | | | | | |
| | | 3 | 9 | 5 | 6 | | | | 10 | 11 | 8 | 2 | 4 | 7 | | | | | | 1 | | | | | |
| | 6 | 3 | 9 | 5 | | | | | 10 | 11 | 8 | 2 | 4 | 7 | | | | | | 1 | | | | | |
| 1 | 2 | 3 | 4 | 5 | | | | | | 11 | 10 | | 6 | 7 | | | | | | | | 8 | 9 | | |
| 1 | 2 | 3 | 4 | 5 | | | | | | 11 | 10 | | 6 | 7 | | | | | | | | 8 | 9 | | |
| | 2 | 3 | 4 | 5 | | | | | | 11 | 10 | | 6 | 7 | | | | | | 1 | | 8 | 9 | | |
| 1 | 2 | 3 | 4 | 5 | | | | | | 11 | 10 | | 6 | 7 | | | | | | | | 8 | 9 | | |
| 1 | | 3 | 4 | 5 | | | | | 6 | 11 | 7 | | | | | | | | | 2 | 10 | 8 | 9 | | |
| 1 | | 3 | 4 | 5 | | | | | 6 | 11 | 7 | | | | | | | | | | 10 | 8 | 9 | | 2 |
| 7 | 6 | 10 | 10 | 10 | 3 | | | | 6 | 10 | 10 | 3 | 6 | 8 | 1 | 1 | | | | 4 | 2 | 6 | 6 | | 1 |
| | | | 1 | 2 | 1 | | | | 4 | 3 | 3 | | | | 2 | 1 | | | | | 1 | 2 | 6 | | |

## League Table

| | P | W | D | L | F | A | Pts |
|---|---|---|---|---|---|---|---|
| Darlington | 38 | 28 | 4 | 6 | 76 | 29 | 60 |
| Middlesbrough Reserves | 38 | 27 | 5 | 6 | 93 | 35 | 59 |
| Newcastle United Reserves | 38 | 23 | 7 | 8 | 96 | 39 | 53 |
| Sunderland Reserves | 38 | 21 | 10 | 7 | 73 | 49 | 52 |
| Blyth Spartans | 38 | 19 | 11 | 8 | 69 | 34 | 49 |
| Carlisle United | 38 | 18 | 10 | 10 | 79 | 46 | 46 |
| West Stanley | 38 | 14 | 14 | 10 | 54 | 42 | 42 |
| Hartlepools United | 38 | 18 | 6 | 14 | 64 | 50 | 42 |
| Ashington | 38 | 14 | 13 | 11 | 66 | 52 | 41 |
| Jarrow | 38 | 14 | 11 | 13 | 46 | 44 | 39 |
| Durham City | 38 | 16 | 5 | 17 | 51 | 60 | 37 |
| Chester-le-Street | 38 | 13 | 11 | 14 | 50 | 58 | 37 |
| Leadgate Park | 38 | 13 | 10 | 15 | 57 | 58 | 36 |
| South Shields Reserves | 38 | 12 | 11 | 15 | 51 | 66 | 5 |
| Spennymoor United | 38 | 10 | 10 | 18 | 51 | 79 | 30 |
| Houghton Rovers | 38 | 7 | 10 | 21 | 38 | 69 | 24 |
| Shildon | 38 | 8 | 7 | 23 | 41 | 75 | 23 |
| Scotswood | 38 | 8 | 5 | 25 | 35 | 76 | 21 |
| Wallsend | 38 | 6 | 8 | 24 | 39 | 96 | 20 |
| Bedlington United | 38 | 4 | 6 | 28 | 32 | 104 | 14 |

# 1921-22

## Division Three North

Manager: Cecil Potter

### Did you know that?

Tommy Mulholland scored 'Pools' first goal in the opening Division Three North fixture against Wrexham, which turned to be his only goal in the Football League.

George Crowther scored 'Pools first hat-trick in the record 7–0 victory over Chesterfield. He made 17 consecutive appearances during the season, scoring eight goals.

Cec Potter played in an emergency in the FA Cup defeat at Stalybridge Celtic, his final professional appearance. As well as himself, the manager used 34 players to fulfill the club's first Football League season.

United's fouth-place finish, with 42 points from 38 games, was their highest until the 1956–57 season when they were runners-up to Derby County.

The average home attendance was 7,239.

| Match No. | Date | Round | Venue | Opponents | Result | | Scorers | Attendance |
|---|---|---|---|---|---|---|---|---|
| 1 | Aug 27 | | (a) | Wrexham | W | 2 - 0 | "Mulholland, Lister" | "10,000" |
| 2 | Sep 3 | | (h) | Wrexham | L | 0 - 1 | | "10,000" |
| 3 | 10 | | (a) | Southport | L | 0 - 3 | | "3,570" |
| 4 | 17 | | (h) | Southport | W | 1 - 0 | Lister | "8,500" |
| 5 | 24 | | (h) | Stockport County | D | 0 - 0 | | "9,600" |
| 6 | Oct 1 | | (a) | Stockport County | L | 0 - 1 | | "10,000" |
| 7 | 8 | | (a) | Grimsby Town | L | 0 - 2 | | |
| 8 | 15 | | (h) | Grimsby Town | D | 0 - 0 | | "8,500" |
| 9 | 22 | | (a) | Walsall | L | 1 - 3 | Robertson | "8,000" |
| 10 | 29 | | (h) | Walsall | W | 1 - 0 | Scorgie | "7,000" |
| 11 | Nov 5 | | (a) | Halifax Town | L | 0 - 3 | | "6,500" |
| 12 | 12 | | (h) | Halifax Town | W | 4 - 0 | "Robertson, Lee, Parkinson, Scorgie" | "6,500" |
| 13 | 19 | | (h) | Durham City | L | 0 - 1 | | "6,000" |
| 14 | 26 | | (h) | Tranmere Rovers | D | 0 - 0 | | "7,000" |
| 16 | Dec 17 | | (h) | Wigan Borough | D | 0 - 0 | | "6,000" |
| 17 | 24 | | (a) | Wigan Borough | L | 0 - 1 | | "5,000" |
| 18 | 26 | | (a) | Stalybridge Celtic | W | 3 - 1 | "Hardy 2, Dennis (o.g.)" | "5,000" |
| 19 | 27 | | (a) | Tranmere Rovers | W | 2 - 1 | "Bratt, Hardy" | "4,000" |
| 20 | 31 | | (h) | Rochdale | W | 5 - 3 | "Parkinson 2, Robertson, Hardy 2" | "7,000" |
| 21 | Jan 2 | | (h) | Stalybridge Celtic | L | 0 - 1 | | "8,500" |
| 22 | 14 | | (a) | Rochdale | W | 1 - 0 | Robertson | "6,000" |
| 23 | 21 | | (a) | Nelson | W | 4 - 0 | "Parkinson, Yews, Burn, Crowther" | "4,000" |
| 24 | 28 | | (h) | Nelson | W | 6 - 0 | "Parkinson 2, Robertson 2, Thoms, Crowther" | "5,500" |
| 25 | Feb 4 | | (a) | Chesterfield | L | 1 - 2 | Robertson | "5,000" |
| 26 | 11 | | (h) | Chesterfield | W | 7 - 0 | "Parkinson 2, Crowther 3, Robertson 2" | "6,000" |
| 27 | 18 | | (a) | Crewe Alexandra | L | 0 - 2 | | "6,000" |
| 28 | 25 | | (h) | Crewe Alexandra | W | 1 - 0 | Robertson | "7,500" |
| 29 | Mar 4 | | (h) | Accrington Stanley | W | 2 - 1 | "Crowther, Robertson" | "7,500" |
| 30 | 11 | | (a) | Accrington Stanley | L | 1 - 4 | Parkinson | "8,000" |
| 31 | 18 | | (h) | Darlington | D | 0 - 0 | | "11,700" |
| 32 | 25 | | (a) | Darlington | D | 0 - 0 | | "7,840" |
| 33 | Apr 1 | | (h) | Lincoln City | D | 1 - 1 | Crowther | "6,280" |
| 34 | 8 | | (a) | Lincoln City | D | 1 - 1 | Parkinson | "10,000" |
| 35 | 15 | | (h) | Ashington | W | 2 - 1 | Hardy 2 | "5,456" |
| 36 | 18 | | (a) | Durham City | W | 1 - 0 | Hardy | "3,000" |
| 37 | 22 | | (a) | Ashington | L | 1 - 4 | Crowther | "2,000" |
| 38 | 29 | | (h) | Barrow | W | 3 - 1 | "Hardy 2, Robertson" | "3,000" |
| 39 | May 6 | | (a) | Barrow | W | 1 - 0 | Towse | "7,000" |

Final Position : 4th in Division Three North — Apps.

1 own goal — Goals

**FA Cup**

| Match No. | Date | Round | Venue | Opponents | Result | | Scorers | Attendance |
|---|---|---|---|---|---|---|---|---|
| 15 | Dec 3 | QR5 | (a) | Stalybridge Celtic | L | 0 - 2 | | "5,300" |

Apps.

Goals

| Gill | Summerfield | Crilly | Thoms | Franks | Dougherty | Hopkins | Short | Bratt | Kessler | Yews | Thompson | Mulholland | Lister | Lee | Crowther | Robertson | Hardy | Parkinson | Donald | Scorgie | Burn | Hewitt | Harris | Rowe | Nicholson | Henderson | Butler | Parsons | Gregson | Thompson | Potter | Hick | Hubery | Towse |
|---|---|---|---|---|---|---|---|---|---|---|---|---|---|---|---|---|---|---|---|---|---|---|---|---|---|---|---|---|---|---|---|---|---|---|
| 1 | 2 | 3 | 4 | 5 | 6 | 7 | 8 | 9 | 10 | 11 | | | | | | | | | | | | | | | | | | | | | | | | |
| 1 | 3 | 2 | 4 | 5 | 6 | 7 | 8 | 9 | | 11 | 10 | | | | | | | | | | | | | | | | | | | | | | | |
| | 3 | 2 | 4 | 5 | 6 | 7 | 8 | 9 | 10 | 11 | | 1 | | | | | | | | | | | | | | | | | | | | | | |
| | 3 | | 4 | 5 | 6 | | | 9 | 8 | 11 | | 1 | 2 | 7 | 10 | | | | | | | | | | | | | | | | | | | |
| 1 | 3 | | 4 | 5 | 6 | | | | 8 | 11 | | | 2 | 7 | 10 | 9 | | | | | | | | | | | | | | | | | | |
| 1 | 3 | | 4 | 5 | 9 | | | | 8 | 11 | | | 2 | 7 | 10 | | 6 | | | | | | | | | | | | | | | | | |
| 1 | 3 | | 4 | 5 | 6 | 11 | | | 8 | | | | 2 | 7 | 10 | | | 9 | | | | | | | | | | | | | | | | |
| 1 | 3 | 5 | 4 | | 10 | | | 9 | | 11 | | | 2 | | | 8 | 6 | 7 | | | | | | | | | | | | | | | | |
| 1 | 3 | | 4 | 5 | 6 | | 8 | 9 | 10 | 11 | | | 2 | | | | | | 7 | | | | | | | | | | | | | | | |
| 1 | 3 | 4 | | 5 | 6 | | | 9 | 8 | | | | 2 | | | | | | | 7 | 10 | 11 | | | | | | | | | | | | |
| 1 | 3 | 4 | | 5 | 6 | | | 9 | 8 | | | | 2 | | | | | | | 7 | 10 | 11 | | | | | | | | | | | | |
| 1 | 3 | 4 | | 5 | | | | | 8 | | | | 2 | | | | | | | 7 | 10 | 11 | 9 | 6 | | | | | | | | | | |
| 1 | 3 | 4 | | 5 | | | | | 8 | | | | 2 | | | | | | | 7 | 10 | 11 | 9 | 6 | | | | | | | | | | |
| 1 | 3 | 4 | | 5 | | 11 | 8 | | 10 | | | | 2 | | | | | | | 7 | | | 9 | | 6 | | | | | | | | | |
| 1 | 3 | 4 | 9 | 5 | 6 | | | | | | | | 2 | | 8 | | | | | | | | | | | 7 | 10 | 11 | | | | | | |
| 1 | 3 | 4 | | 5 | 6 | | | | | | | | 2 | | 10 | | | | | | 8 | | | | 9 | 7 | | 11 | | | | | | |
| 1 | 3 | 4 | 6 | 5 | | | | | | | | | 2 | | 10 | | | | | | 8 | | | | 9 | 7 | | 11 | | | | | | |
| 1 | 3 | 4 | 6 | 5 | | | | | 11 | | | | 2 | | 10 | | | | | | 8 | | | | 9 | 7 | | | | | | | | |
| 1 | 3 | 4 | 6 | 5 | | | | | 11 | | | | 2 | | 10 | | | | | | 8 | | | | 9 | 7 | | | | | | | | |
| 1 | | 3 | 6 | 5 | | | | | 11 | | | | 2 | | 10 | | | | | | 8 | | | 4 | 9 | 7 | | | | | | | | |
| 1 | 3 | 4 | 6 | 5 | | | | | 10 | | | | 2 | | | | | | | 7 | 8 | | | | | | | 11 | 9 | | | | | |
| 1 | 3 | 4 | 6 | 5 | | | | | | | | | 2 | | | | | | | 7 | 8 | | | | 10 | | | 11 | 9 | | | | | |
| | 3 | 5 | 6 | | | | | | 10 | | | 1 | 2 | | | | | | | 7 | 8 | | | | | | | 11 | 9 | 4 | | | | |
| | 3 | 5 | 6 | | 4 | | | | 10 | | | 1 | 2 | | | | | | | | 8 | | | | | | | 11 | 9 | 7 | | | | |
| | 3 | 5 | 6 | | 4 | 11 | | | 10 | | | 1 | 2 | | | | | | | | 8 | | | | | 7 | | | 9 | | | | | |
| | 3 | 5 | 6 | | 4 | 11 | | | 10 | | | 1 | 2 | | | | | | | | 8 | | | | | 7 | | | 9 | | | | | |
| 1 | 3 | 4 | 6 | 5 | | 11 | | | 10 | | | | 2 | | 7 | | | | | | 8 | | | | | | | | 9 | | | | | |
| 1 | 3 | 4 | 6 | 5 | | 11 | | | 10 | | | | 2 | | 7 | | | | | | 8 | | | | | | | | 9 | | | | | |
| 1 | 3 | 4 | 6 | 5 | | 11 | | | 10 | | | | 2 | | 7 | | | | | | 8 | | | | | | | | 9 | | | | | |
| 1 | 3 | 4 | 6 | 5 | | 11 | | | 10 | | | | 2 | | 7 | | | | | | 8 | | | | | | | | 9 | | | | | |
| 1 | 3 | 4 | 6 | 5 | 10 | 11 | | | | | | | 2 | | 7 | | | | | | 8 | | | | | | | | 9 | | | | | |
| 1 | 3 | 4 | 6 | 5 | 8 | 11 | | | | | | | 2 | | 10 | | | | | | 7 | | | | | | | | 9 | | | | | |
| 1 | 3 | 4 | 6 | 5 | | | | | | | | | 2 | 11 | 10 | | | | | | 8 | | | | | 7 | | | 9 | | | | | |
| 1 | 3 | 4 | 6 | 5 | | | | | | | | | 2 | | 10 | | | | | | 7 | | | | 8 | | | 11 | 9 | | | | | |
| 1 | 3 | 4 | 6 | 5 | | | | | | | | | 2 | | 10 | | | | | | 7 | | | | 8 | | | 11 | 9 | | | | | |
| 1 | 3 | 4 | 6 | 5 | | | | | | | | | | 11 | 10 | | | | | | 7 | | | | | | | | 9 | 8 | 2 | | | |
| 1 | 3 | 4 | 6 | 5 | | | | | 8 | | | | 2 | | 10 | | | | | | | | | | 7 | | | | 9 | | | 11 | | |
| 1 | 3 | 4 | 6 | 5 | | | | | 8 | | | | 2 | | 10 | | | | | | 7 | | | | | | | | | | | 11 | 9 | |
| 32 | 37 | 33 | 32 | 33 | 18 | 13 | 5 | 8 | 26 | 8 | 1 | 6 | 34 | 6 | 22 | 2 | 2 | 2 | 1 | 8 | 26 | 4 | 3 | 3 | 10 | 9 | 1 | 9 | 17 | 3 | 1 | 2 | 1 | 0 |
| | | 1 | | | | | 1 | 2 | 12 | | | | | | 10 | | | | | 1 | 10 | 2 | 1 | | 1 | | | 1 | 8 | | | | 1 | |

| Gill | Summerfield | Crilly | Thoms | Franks | Dougherty | Hopkins | Short | Bratt | Kessler | Yews | Thompson | Mulholland | Lister | Lee | Crowther | Robertson | Hardy | Parkinson | Donald | Scorgie | Burn | Hewitt | Harris | Rowe | Nicholson | Henderson | Butler | Parsons | Gregson | Thompson | Potter | Hick | Hubery | Towse |
|---|---|---|---|---|---|---|---|---|---|---|---|---|---|---|---|---|---|---|---|---|---|---|---|---|---|---|---|---|---|---|---|---|---|---|
| 1 | 3 | 4 | | 5 | | 7 | | 9 | 8 | 11 | | | 2 | | | | | | | | | | | | 10 | | | | | | | | | 6 |
| 1 | 1 | 1 | | 1 | | 1 | | 1 | 1 | 1 | | | 1 | | | | | | | | | | | | 1 | | | | | | | | | 1 |
| | | | | | | | | | | | | | | | | | | | | | | | | | | | | | | | | | | |

## League Table

| | P | W | D | L | F | A | Pts |
|---|---|---|---|---|---|---|---|
| Stockport County | 38 | 24 | 8 | 6 | 60 | 21 | 56 |
| Darlington | 38 | 22 | 6 | 10 | 81 | 37 | 50 |
| Grimsby Town | 38 | 21 | 8 | 9 | 72 | 47 | 50 |
| Hartlepools United | 38 | 17 | 8 | 13 | 52 | 39 | 42 |
| Accrington Stanley | 38 | 19 | 3 | 16 | 73 | 57 | 41 |
| Crewe Alexandra | 38 | 18 | 5 | 15 | 60 | 56 | 41 |
| Stalybridge Celtic | 38 | 18 | 5 | 15 | 62 | 63 | 41 |
| Walsall | 38 | 18 | 3 | 17 | 66 | 65 | 39 |
| Southport | 38 | 14 | 10 | 14 | 55 | 44 | 38 |
| Ashington | 38 | 17 | 4 | 17 | 59 | 66 | 38 |
| Durham City | 38 | 17 | 3 | 18 | 68 | 67 | 37 |
| Wrexham | 38 | 14 | 9 | 15 | 51 | 56 | 37 |
| Chesterfield | 38 | 16 | 3 | 19 | 48 | 67 | 35 |
| Lincoln City | 38 | 14 | 6 | 18 | 48 | 59 | 34 |
| Barrow | 38 | 14 | 5 | 19 | 42 | 54 | 33 |
| Nelson | 38 | 13 | 7 | 18 | 48 | 66 | 33 |
| Wigan Borough | 38 | 11 | 9 | 18 | 46 | 72 | 31 |
| Tranmere Rovers | 38 | 9 | 11 | 18 | 51 | 61 | 29 |
| Halifax Town | 38 | 10 | 9 | 19 | 56 | 76 | 29 |
| Rochdale | 38 | 11 | 4 | 23 | 52 | 77 | 26 |

# 1922-23

## Division Three North

Manager: David Gordon

### Did you know that?

David Gordon, appointed manager in succession to Cec Potter, held the Hull City appearances record up to World War One.

Cecil Potter, by then manager of Derby County, returned to the Victoria Ground to sign Tom Crilly and Harry Thoms, who went on to play a combined total of 406 games for the Rams.

'Pools home League record was identical to their first season: 10 wins, six draws and three defeats. They did, however, fail to win a single away game.

| Match No. | Date | Round | Venue | Opponents | Result | | Scorers | Attendance |
|---|---|---|---|---|---|---|---|---|
| 1 | Aug 26 | | (a) | Walsall | D | 2 - 2 | Robertson, Yews | 10,000 |
| 2 | Sep 2 | | (h) | Walsall | D | 2 - 2 | Robertson 2 | 5,084 |
| 3 | 9 | | (h) | Southport | D | 1 - 1 | Towse | 5,768 |
| 4 | 16 | | (a) | Southport | L | 0 - 1 | | 5,500 |
| 5 | 23 | | (h) | Ashington | W | 3 - 1 | Yews, Robertson (pen), Crowther | 6,084 |
| 6 | 30 | | (a) | Ashington | L | 2 - 4 | Robertson, Rowe | 6,000 |
| 7 | Oct 7 | | (h) | Barrow | W | 2 - 0 | Towse 2 | 5,480 |
| 8 | 14 | | (a) | Barrow | D | 0 - 0 | | 4,000 |
| 9 | 21 | | (a) | Halifax Town | L | 0 - 3 | | 10,000 |
| 10 | 28 | | (h) | Halifax Town | W | 3 - 2 | Hardy 2, Towse | 4,502 |
| 11 | Nov 4 | | (h) | Rochdale | L | 0 - 2 | | 4,774 |
| 12 | 11 | | (a) | Rochdale | L | 0 - 4 | | 6,000 |
| 13 | 18 | | (h) | Wrexham | D | 1 - 1 | Crowther | 4,050 |
| 14 | 25 | | (a) | Wrexham | L | 0 - 2 | | 4,000 |
| 16 | Dec 9 | | (h) | Accrington Stanley | D | 0 - 0 | | 4,053 |
| 18 | 23 | | (a) | Lincoln City | L | 1 - 2 | Bratt | |
| 19 | 25 | | (a) | Darlington | L | 0 - 4 | | 6,000 |
| 20 | 26 | | (h) | Durham City | W | 2 - 1 | Braidford, Parkinson | 3,878 |
| 21 | 30 | | (a) | Nelson | L | 1 - 4 | Braidford | 5,000 |
| 22 | Jan 1 | | (h) | Darlington | W | 1 - 0 | Braidford | 6,500 |
| 23 | 2 | | (h) | Lincoln City | W | 2 - 0 | Hardy 2 | 2,800 |
| 24 | 6 | | (h) | Nelson | W | 5 - 1 | Braidford, Hampson 2 (1 pen), Parkinson, Hardy | 5,447 |
| 25 | 20 | | (a) | Stalybridge Celtic | D | 1 - 1 | Parkinson | 3,000 |
| 26 | 27 | | (h) | Stalybridge Celtic | W | 4 - 0 | Hardy 2, Hampson (pen), Braidford | 4,632 |
| 27 | Feb 10 | | (h) | Bradford Park Avenue | L | 0 - 1 | | 4,592 |
| 28 | 17 | | (a) | Tranmere Rovers | D | 1 - 1 | Parkinson | 6,000 |
| 29 | 24 | | (h) | Tranmere Rovers | L | 0 - 1 | | 4,417 |
| 30 | Mar 3 | | (a) | Durham City | L | 2 - 3 | Parkinson, Hardy | 3,000 |
| 31 | 10 | | (a) | Accrington Stanley | L | 1 - 2 | Hardy | 5,000 |
| 32 | 14 | | (a) | Bradford Park Avenue | D | 1 - 1 | Braidford | 5,000 |
| 33 | 17 | | (h) | Wigan Borough | D | 0 - 0 | | 4,200 |
| 34 | 24 | | (a) | Wigan Borough | L | 0 - 2 | | 10,000 |
| 35 | 31 | | (h) | Chesterfield | W | 5 - 0 | Braidford 2, Parkinson 2, Hardy | 2,500 |
| 36 | Apr 7 | | (a) | Chesterfield | D | 1 - 1 | Braidford | 6,000 |
| 37 | 14 | | (h) | Crewe Alexandra | D | 1 - 1 | Hampson (pen) | 3,633 |
| 38 | 21 | | (a) | Crewe Alexandra | L | 1 - 2 | Robertson | 5,000 |
| 39 | 28 | | (h) | Grimsby Town | W | 2 - 0 | Hopkins, Hardy | 3,000 |
| 40 | May 5 | | (a) | Grimsby Town | L | 0 - 1 | | 6,000 |

Final Position : 15th in Division Three North

Apps.
Goals

**FA Cup**

| Match No. | Date | Round | Venue | Opponents | Result | | Scorers | Attendance |
|---|---|---|---|---|---|---|---|---|
| 15 | Dec 2 | QR5 | (a) | Durham City | W | 1 - 0 | Dowson (pen) | 3,000 |
| 17 | 16 | QR6 | (a) | Wrexham | L | 0 - 1 | | 7,000 |

Apps.
Goals

| Gill | Borthwick | Flanders | Hampson | Hopkins | Dowson | Yews | Robertson | Towse | Hardy | Rowe | Franks | Nicholson | Braidford | Walker | Spencer | Chesser | Parkinson | Crowther | Bratt | Harris | Connell | Summerfield | Dixon | Mordue | Halstead | Longmore | Anderson | Thompson | Mitchell | Cook |
|---|---|---|---|---|---|---|---|---|---|---|---|---|---|---|---|---|---|---|---|---|---|---|---|---|---|---|---|---|---|---|
| 1 | 2 | 3 | 4 | 5 | 6 | 7 | 8 | 9 | 10 | 11 | | | | | | | | | | | | | | | | | | | | |
| 1 | 2 | | 4 | 5 | 6 | 7 | 8 | 9 | 10 | 11 | 3 | | | | | | | | | | | | | | | | | | | |
| 1 | | | 3 | 5 | 6 | 7 | 8 | 9 | | 11 | 2 | 4 | 10 | | | | | | | | | | | | | | | | | |
| 1 | | | 4 | 5 | 6 | | 8 | 9 | | 11 | 2 | | 10 | 3 | 7 | | | | | | | | | | | | | | | |
| 1 | | 3 | | 5 | 6 | 7 | 10 | | | 11 | | | | 2 | | 4 | 8 | 9 | | | | | | | | | | | | |
| 1 | | 3 | | 5 | 6 | 7 | 10 | | | 11 | | | | 2 | | 4 | 8 | 9 | | | | | | | | | | | | |
| 1 | | | | 5 | 6 | 7 | 10 | 9 | | 11 | 3 | | | 2 | | | 8 | | 4 | | | | | | | | | | | |
| 1 | | | | 5 | 6 | 7 | | 9 | | 11 | 3 | | | 2 | | | 8 | | 4 | 10 | | | | | | | | | | |
| 1 | | | | 5 | 6 | 7 | | 9 | 10 | 11 | 3 | | 8 | 2 | | | | | 4 | | | | | | | | | | | |
| 1 | | | | 5 | 6 | 7 | | 9 | 10 | 11 | 3 | | 8 | 2 | | | | | | | 4 | | | | | | | | | |
| 1 | | | | 5 | 6 | 7 | | 9 | 10 | 11 | 3 | | 8 | 2 | | | | | | | 4 | | | | | | | | | |
| | | | | 5 | 10 | | | | | 11 | 3 | 6 | 8 | 2 | | | 7 | 9 | | | 4 | 1 | | | | | | | | |
| | | | | 5 | 6 | | 10 | | | 11 | | | 8 | 2 | | | | 9 | | | 4 | 1 | 3 | 7 | | | | | | |
| | | | | 5 | | | 10 | | | 11 | | 6 | 8 | 2 | | | | 9 | | | 4 | 1 | 3 | 7 | | | | | | |
| | | | | | 6 | | | 10 | | 11 | | | | 2 | | | | 9 | 8 | | 4 | 1 | 3 | 7 | 5 | | | | | |
| | | | | 5 | | | | 10 | | 11 | 2 | 6 | | | | | | 9 | 8 | | 4 | 1 | 3 | 7 | | | | | | |
| | | | | 5 | 6 | 7 | | 10 | | 11 | 2 | | | | | | 8 | 9 | | | 4 | 1 | 3 | | | | | | | |
| | | | | 5 | 6 | 7 | | | 10 | | | | 9 | | | | 8 | | | | | 1 | 3 | 11 | | 2 | 4 | | | |
| | | | | | 6 | 7 | | | 10 | | | | 9 | | | | 8 | | | | | 1 | 3 | 11 | 5 | 2 | 4 | | | |
| | | | 6 | | | 7 | | | 10 | | | | 9 | | | | 8 | | | | | 1 | 3 | 11 | 5 | 2 | 4 | | | |
| | | | 5 | | 6 | 7 | | | 10 | | | | 9 | 2 | | | 8 | | | | 4 | 1 | 3 | 11 | | | | | | |
| | | | 6 | 5 | | 7 | | | 10 | 11 | | | 9 | 2 | | | 8 | | | | 4 | 1 | 3 | | | | | | | |
| | | | 6 | | | 7 | | | 10 | 11 | | | 9 | 2 | | | 8 | | | | 4 | 1 | 3 | | 5 | | | | | |
| | | | 6 | | | 7 | | | 10 | 11 | | | 9 | 2 | | | 8 | | | | 4 | 1 | 3 | | 5 | | | | | |
| | | | 6 | | | 7 | | | 10 | 11 | | | 9 | 2 | | | 8 | | | | 4 | 1 | 3 | | 5 | | | | | |
| | | | | | | 7 | | | 10 | 11 | | | 9 | 2 | | 6 | 8 | | | | 4 | 1 | 3 | | 5 | | | | | |
| | | | 6 | | | 7 | | | 10 | 11 | | | 9 | 2 | | | 8 | | | | 4 | 1 | 3 | | 5 | | | | | |
| | | | 6 | 5 | | | | | 10 | 11 | | | 9 | 2 | | 4 | 8 | | | | | 1 | 3 | | | | | 7 | | |
| | | | 5 | | | 7 | | | 10 | 11 | | | 9 | | | 6 | 8 | | | | | 1 | 3 | | | 2 | 4 | | | |
| | | | 5 | | | 7 | | | 10 | | | | 9 | | | 6 | 8 | | | | | 1 | 3 | | | 2 | 4 | | 11 | |
| | | | 5 | | | 7 | | | 10 | | | | 9 | | | 6 | 8 | | | | | 1 | 3 | | | 2 | 4 | | 11 | |
| | | | 5 | | | 7 | | | 10 | | | | 9 | | | 6 | 8 | | | | | 1 | 3 | | | 2 | 4 | | 11 | |
| | | | 5 | | | 7 | | | 10 | | | | 9 | | | 6 | 8 | | | | | 1 | 3 | | | 2 | 4 | | 11 | |
| | | | 5 | | | 7 | | | | | | | 9 | | | 6 | 8 | | | | | 1 | 3 | | | 2 | 4 | | 11 | 10 |
| | | | 5 | | | 7 | | | 10 | | | | 9 | | | 6 | 8 | | | | | 1 | 3 | | | 2 | 4 | | 11 | |
| | | | 5 | | | 7 | 8 | | | | | | 10 | | | 6 | | | | | | 1 | 3 | | | 2 | 4 | | 11 | 9 |
| | | | 2 | 5 | | 7 | | | 10 | | | | 9 | | | 6 | 8 | | | | | 1 | 3 | | | | 4 | | 11 | |
| | | | 5 | | | 7 | | | 10 | 11 | | | 9 | | | 6 | 8 | | | | | 1 | 3 | | | 2 | 4 | | | |
| 11 | 2 | 3 | 22 | 20 | 18 | 31 | 10 | 12 | 24 | 26 | 11 | 4 | 29 | 20 | 1 | 14 | 26 | 8 | 5 | 1 | 15 | 27 | 26 | 8 | 8 | 12 | 13 | 1 | 8 | 2 |
| | | | 4 | 1 | | 2 | 6 | 4 | 11 | 1 | | | 9 | | | | 7 | 2 | 1 | | | | | | | | | | | |

| Gill | Borthwick | Flanders | Hampson | Hopkins | Dowson | Yews | Robertson | Towse | Hardy | Rowe | Franks | Nicholson | Braidford | Walker | Spencer | Chesser | Parkinson | Crowther | Bratt | Harris | Connell | Summerfield | Dixon | Mordue | Halstead | Longmore | Anderson | Thompson | Mitchell | Cook |
|---|---|---|---|---|---|---|---|---|---|---|---|---|---|---|---|---|---|---|---|---|---|---|---|---|---|---|---|---|---|---|
| | | | | 5 | 6 | | 10 | | | 11 | | | | 2 | | | 8 | | 9 | | 4 | 1 | 3 | 7 | | | | | | |
| | | | | 5 | 6 | | | 10 | | 11 | | | | 2 | | | | 9 | 8 | | 4 | 1 | 3 | 7 | | | | | | |
| | | | | 2 | 2 | | 1 | 1 | | 2 | | | | 2 | | | 1 | 1 | 2 | | 2 | 2 | 2 | 2 | | | | | | |
| | | | | | 1 | | | | | | | | | | | | | | | | | | | | | | | | | |

## League Table

| | P | W | D | L | F | A | Pts |
|---|---|---|---|---|---|---|---|
| Nelson | 38 | 24 | 3 | 11 | 61 | 41 | 51 |
| Bradford Park Avenue | 38 | 19 | 9 | 10 | 67 | 38 | 47 |
| Walsall | 38 | 19 | 8 | 11 | 51 | 44 | 46 |
| Chesterfield | 38 | 19 | 7 | 12 | 68 | 52 | 45 |
| Wigan Borough | 38 | 18 | 8 | 12 | 64 | 39 | 44 |
| Crewe Alexandra | 38 | 17 | 9 | 12 | 48 | 38 | 43 |
| Halifax Town | 38 | 17 | 7 | 14 | 53 | 46 | 41 |
| Accrington Stanley | 38 | 17 | 7 | 14 | 59 | 65 | 41 |
| Darlington | 38 | 15 | 10 | 13 | 59 | 46 | 40 |
| Wrexham | 38 | 14 | 10 | 14 | 38 | 48 | 38 |
| Stalybridge Celtic | 38 | 15 | 6 | 17 | 42 | 47 | 36 |
| Rochdale | 38 | 13 | 10 | 15 | 42 | 53 | 36 |
| Lincoln City | 38 | 13 | 10 | 15 | 39 | 55 | 36 |
| Grimsby Town | 38 | 14 | 5 | 19 | 55 | 52 | 33 |
| Hartlepools United | 38 | 10 | 12 | 16 | 48 | 54 | 32 |
| Tranmere Rovers | 38 | 12 | 8 | 18 | 49 | 59 | 32 |
| Southport | 38 | 12 | 7 | 19 | 32 | 46 | 31 |
| Barrow | 38 | 13 | 4 | 21 | 50 | 60 | 30 |
| Ashington | 38 | 11 | 8 | 19 | 51 | 77 | 30 |
| Durham City | 38 | 9 | 10 | 19 | 43 | 59 | 28 |

# 1923-24

## Division Three North

Manager: David Gordon

### Did you know that?

Tewfik Abdallah, born in Cairo, Egypt, became the first non-European to play for the club, having previously appeared for Derby County.

Billy Smith became the first Hartlepools player to be sent off in a Football League game when he received his marching orders in the 1–0 home defeat to Walsall.

In making their first successful re-election application, 'Pools' results reflected a failure to score in 20 League games, and a total of seven wins was one less than bottom club Barrow. Such performances were reflected in an average home attendance of 3,808.

| Match No. | Date | Round | Venue | Opponents | | Result | Scorers | Attendance |
|---|---|---|---|---|---|---|---|---|
| 1 | Aug 25 | | (a) | Barrow | W | 2 - 1 | Common, Parkinson | 5,000 |
| 2 | Sep 1 | | (h) | Barrow | W | 1 - 0 | Parkinson | 5,954 |
| 3 | 5 | | (a) | Lincoln City | D | 1 - 1 | Hardy | 4,500 |
| 4 | 8 | | (a) | Darlington | L | 0 - 5 | | 5,000 |
| 5 | 15 | | (h) | Darlington | L | 0 - 1 | | 6,569 |
| 6 | 22 | | (a) | Wigan Borough | L | 1 - 4 | Common | 10,000 |
| 7 | 29 | | (h) | Wigan Borough | D | 0 - 0 | | 4,908 |
| 8 | Oct 6 | | (h) | Grimsby Town | D | 1 - 1 | Common | 4,351 |
| 9 | 13 | | (a) | Grimsby Town | W | 1 - 0 | W.Smith | 10,000 |
| 10 | 20 | | (a) | Durham City | L | 0 - 3 | | 5,000 |
| 11 | 27 | | (h) | Durham City | D | 0 - 0 | | 3,960 |
| 12 | Nov 3 | | (h) | New Brighton | L | 0 - 1 | | 2,855 |
| 13 | 10 | | (a) | New Brighton | D | 0 - 0 | | 8,000 |
| 16 | Dec 8 | | (h) | Wolverhampton Wanderers | L | 0 - 1 | | 5,021 |
| 18 | 22 | | (h) | Accrington Stanley | W | 3 - 0 | W.Smith, Young, Hardy | 3,013 |
| 19 | 25 | | (a) | Halifax Town | L | 0 - 1 | | 10,000 |
| 20 | 26 | | (h) | Halifax Town | L | 1 - 3 | W.Smith | 3,200 |
| 21 | 29 | | (a) | Walsall | L | 0 - 2 | | 5,000 |
| 22 | Jan 1 | | (h) | Lincoln City | D | 1 - 1 | Common (pen) | 3,507 |
| 23 | 5 | | (h) | Walsall | L | 0 - 1 | | 2,959 |
| 24 | 12 | | (a) | Rochdale | L | 0 - 1 | | 4,000 |
| 25 | 19 | | (a) | Tranmere Rovers | L | 0 - 2 | | 5,000 |
| 26 | 26 | | (h) | Tranmere Rovers | W | 2 - 1 | W.Smith, Mitchell | 2,554 |
| 27 | Feb 2 | | (a) | Bradford Park Avenue | L | 0 - 4 | | 6,000 |
| 28 | 9 | | (h) | Bradford Park Avenue | D | 0 - 0 | | 2,485 |
| 29 | 11 | | (a) | Wolverhampton Wanderers | L | 1 - 2 | Hardy | 5,000 |
| 30 | 16 | | (a) | Chesterfield | L | 1 - 5 | Hardy | 5,909 |
| 31 | 23 | | (h) | Chesterfield | L | 2 - 3 | Cook, Young | 2,878 |
| 32 | Mar 1 | | (a) | Rotherham County | L | 0 - 5 | | 6,000 |
| 33 | 8 | | (h) | Rotherham County | L | 2 - 5 | W.Smith 2 | 4,555 |
| 34 | 15 | | (h) | Wrexham | W | 4 - 0 | Bell 2, W.Smith, Abdallah | 5,326 |
| 35 | 17 | | (a) | Accrington Stanley | L | 0 - 2 | | 1,500 |
| 36 | 22 | | (a) | Wrexham | L | 0 - 1 | | 4,000 |
| 37 | 29 | | (h) | Doncaster Rovers | D | 1 - 1 | Morris | 3,970 |
| 38 | Apr 5 | | (a) | Doncaster Rovers | L | 1 - 3 | Bell | 5,000 |
| 39 | 12 | | (h) | Rochdale | L | 1 - 2 | Morris | 4,197 |
| 40 | 18 | | (a) | Ashington | D | 0 - 0 | | 6,000 |
| 41 | 21 | | (h) | Crewe Alexandra | D | 2 - 2 | W.Smith 2 | 3,945 |
| 42 | 22 | | (h) | Ashington | L | 0 - 1 | | 2,000 |
| 43 | 26 | | (h) | Southport | W | 1 - 0 | Bell | 1,766 |
| 44 | 30 | | (a) | Crewe Alexandra | L | 1 - 2 | Young | 3,000 |
| 45 | May 3 | | (a) | Southport | D | 2 - 2 | Keenlyside, Cook | 3,000 |

Final Position : 21st in Division Three North

Apps.
Goals

**FA Cup**

| | | | | | | | | |
|---|---|---|---|---|---|---|---|---|
| 14 | Nov 17 | QR4 | (h) | St. Peters Albion | W | 10 - 1 | W.Smith 7 (1 pen), Cook, Lonie, Duthie | 2,929 |
| 15 | Dec 1 | QR5 | (h) | Shildon | W | 3 - 1 | W.Smith 2 (1 pen), Lonie | 4,112 |
| 17 | 15 | QR6 | (a) | Ashington | L | 1 - 2 | Keenlyside | 5,000 |

Apps.
Goals

| Summerfield | Dixon | Boulton | Shaw | Sutcliffe | Chesser | Young, M.S. | Parkinson | Common | Hardy | Keenlyside | Cook | Storey | Walsh | Walker | Lonie | Birnie | Hunt | Smith, W.E. | Mitchell | Smith, E. | Duthie | Gill | Nicholson | Carswell | Wrightson | Mills | Brown | Bell | Morris | Abdallah | Young, A. |
|---|---|---|---|---|---|---|---|---|---|---|---|---|---|---|---|---|---|---|---|---|---|---|---|---|---|---|---|---|---|---|---|
| 1 | 2 | 3 | 4 | 5 | 6 | 7 | 8 | 9 | 10 | 11 | | | | | | | | | | | | | | | | | | | | | |
| 1 | 2 | 3 | 4 | 5 | 6 | 7 | 8 | 9 | 10 | 11 | | | | | | | | | | | | | | | | | | | | | |
| 1 | 2 | 3 | 4 | 5 | 6 | 7 | 8 | 9 | 10 | 11 | | | | | | | | | | | | | | | | | | | | | |
| 1 | 2 | 3 | 4 | 5 | 6 | 7 | | 9 | 10 | 11 | 8 | | | | | | | | | | | | | | | | | | | | |
| 1 | 2 | | 4 | 5 | 6 | 7 | | 8 | 10 | 11 | | 3 | 9 | | | | | | | | | | | | | | | | | | |
| 1 | 2 | | 4 | 5 | 6 | 7 | | 8 | 10 | 11 | | 3 | 9 | | | | | | | | | | | | | | | | | | |
| 1 | | | | | | | | 8 | 10 | 11 | | 3 | 5 | 2 | 4 | 6 | 7 | 9 | | | | | | | | | | | | | |
| 1 | | | | | 6 | | | 8 | 10 | 11 | | 3 | 5 | 2 | 4 | | 7 | 9 | | | | | | | | | | | | | |
| 1 | | | 10 | 5 | | 7 | | 8 | | | | 3 | | 2 | 4 | 6 | | 9 | 11 | | | | | | | | | | | | |
| 1 | | | 10 | 5 | | 7 | | 8 | | | | 3 | | 2 | 4 | 6 | | 9 | 11 | | | | | | | | | | | | |
| 1 | 2 | | | 5 | | 7 | 8 | 9 | | 11 | | 3 | | | 4 | 6 | | 10 | | | | | | | | | | | | | |
| 1 | 2 | | | 5 | | | | 8 | 10 | 7 | | 3 | | | 4 | 6 | | 9 | 11 | | | | | | | | | | | | |
| 1 | 2 | | | 5 | | | | | | 7 | 10 | | 6 | | 4 | | | 9 | 11 | 3 | 8 | | | | | | | | | | |
| 1 | 2 | | | 5 | | 7 | | | 10 | 8 | 11 | | 6 | | 4 | | | 9 | | 3 | | | | | | | | | | | |
| | 2 | | | 5 | | 7 | | 4 | 10 | 8 | 11 | | 6 | | | | | 9 | | 3 | | 1 | | | | | | | | | |
| | 2 | | | 5 | | 7 | | 4 | 10 | 8 | 11 | | 6 | | | | | 9 | | 3 | | 1 | | | | | | | | | |
| | 2 | | | 5 | | 7 | | 8 | 10 | | 11 | | 6 | | 4 | | | 9 | | 3 | | 1 | | | | | | | | | |
| | 2 | | 9 | 5 | | | | 4 | | | 7 | | 6 | | | | | 8 | 11 | 3 | 10 | 1 | | | | | | | | | |
| | 2 | | | 5 | | | | 9 | | | 7 | | 6 | | 4 | | | 8 | 11 | 3 | 10 | 1 | | | | | | | | | |
| | 2 | | | 5 | | 7 | | 4 | | 8 | 10 | | | | | | | 9 | 11 | 3 | | 1 | 6 | | | | | | | | |
| | 2 | | | | | 7 | | 4 | | 8 | 11 | | 6 | | | | | 10 | | 3 | | 1 | 5 | 9 | | | | | | | |
| | 2 | | | | | 7 | | 4 | | 8 | 11 | | 6 | | | | | 10 | | 3 | | 1 | 5 | 9 | | | | | | | |
| | 2 | | | | 6 | | | 4 | 10 | 8 | 7 | | 5 | | | | | 9 | 11 | 3 | | 1 | | | | | | | | | |
| | 2 | | | | 6 | | | 4 | 10 | 8 | 7 | | 5 | | | | | 9 | 11 | 3 | | 1 | | | | | | | | | |
| | | | 10 | | 6 | 7 | 8 | 4 | | | 9 | 2 | 5 | | | | | | 11 | 3 | | 1 | | | | | | | | | |
| 1 | | | 9 | | 6 | 7 | | 4 | 8 | | | 2 | 5 | | | | | | 11 | 3 | | | | | 10 | | | | | | |
| | | | 10 | | 6 | 7 | | 4 | 8 | | 9 | 2 | 5 | | | | | | 11 | 3 | | 1 | | | | | | | | | |
| 1 | | | | | 6 | 7 | | 4 | 8 | | 10 | 2 | 5 | | | | | | 11 | 3 | | | | | | 9 | | | | | |
| | | | | 5 | 6 | 7 | | | | 8 | 10 | | 4 | | | | | | 11 | 3 | | 1 | | | | 9 | 2 | | | | |
| | 2 | | | | 6 | 7 | | 4 | 10 | | | | 5 | | | | | 9 | 11 | 3 | | 1 | | | | | | 8 | | | |
| | 2 | | | | 6 | 7 | | | | | | | 4 | | | | | 10 | 11 | 3 | | 1 | | | | | | 9 | 5 | 8 | |
| 1 | 2 | | | | 6 | 7 | | | | | | 9 | 4 | | | | | | 10 | 3 | | | | | | | | 11 | | 8 | 5 |
| | 2 | | | | 6 | 7 | | 10 | | | | | | | | | | | 11 | 3 | | 1 | | | | | | 9 | 5 | 8 | 4 |
| | 2 | | | | 11 | 7 | | | | | | | 4 | | | | | | 10 | 3 | | 1 | | | | | | 9 | 5 | 8 | 6 |
| | 2 | | | | 6 | | | | | 7 | | | 4 | | | | | 10 | 11 | 3 | | 1 | | | | | | 9 | 5 | 8 | |
| | 2 | | | | 6 | | | | | 11 | | | 4 | | | | | 10 | 9 | 3 | | 1 | | | | | | 7 | 5 | 8 | |
| | 2 | | | | 6 | 7 | | | | | | | 4 | | | | | 9 | 11 | 3 | | 1 | | | | | | 10 | | 8 | 5 |
| | 2 | | | | 6 | 7 | | 4 | | | | | | | | | | 9 | 11 | 3 | | 1 | | | | | | 10 | | 8 | 5 |
| | 2 | | | | 6 | | | 4 | | | 9 | | | | | | | 7 | 11 | 3 | | 1 | | | | | | 10 | | 8 | 5 |
| 1 | 2 | | | | 6 | | | | | 7 | 9 | | | | | | | | 11 | 3 | | | 4 | | | | | 10 | | 8 | 5 |
| 1 | 2 | | | | 6 | 7 | | 4 | | | 10 | | | | | | | 9 | 11 | 3 | | | | | | | | | 5 | 8 | |
| 1 | 2 | | | | 6 | | | 4 | | 7 | 10 | | | | | | | 9 | 11 | 3 | | | | | | | | 8 | 5 | | |
| 20 | 33 | 4 | 12 | 19 | 27 | 29 | 5 | 32 | 19 | 24 | 21 | 13 | 27 | 4 | 10 | 5 | 2 | 27 | 27 | 33 | 3 | 22 | 4 | 2 | 1 | 2 | 1 | 12 | 7 | 11 | 7 |
| | | | | | | 3 | 2 | 4 | 4 | 1 | 2 | | | | | | | 9 | 1 | | | | | | | | | 4 | 2 | 1 | |

| Summerfield | Dixon | Boulton | Shaw | Sutcliffe | Chesser | Young, M.S. | Parkinson | Common | Hardy | Keenlyside | Cook | Storey | Walsh | Walker | Lonie | Birnie | Hunt | Smith, W.E. | Mitchell | Smith, E. | Duthie | Gill | Nicholson | Carswell | Wrightson | Mills | Brown | Bell | Morris | Abdallah | Young, A. |
|---|---|---|---|---|---|---|---|---|---|---|---|---|---|---|---|---|---|---|---|---|---|---|---|---|---|---|---|---|---|---|---|
| 1 | 2 | | | 5 | | 7 | | | | 8 | 11 | | 6 | | 4 | | | 9 | | 3 | 10 | | | | | | | | | | |
| 1 | 2 | | | 5 | | 7 | | | 10 | 8 | 11 | | 6 | | 4 | | | 9 | | 3 | | | | | | | | | | | |
| 1 | 2 | | | 5 | | 7 | | | 10 | 8 | 11 | | 6 | | 4 | | | 9 | | 3 | | | | | | | | | | | |
| 3 | 3 | | | 3 | | 3 | | | 2 | 3 | 3 | | 3 | | 3 | | | 3 | | 3 | 1 | | | | | | | | | | |
| | | | | | | | | | | 1 | 1 | | | | 2 | | | 9 | | | 1 | | | | | | | | | | |

## League Table

| | P | W | D | L | F | A | Pts |
|---|---|---|---|---|---|---|---|
| Wolverhampton W | 42 | 24 | 15 | 3 | 76 | 27 | 63 |
| Rochdale | 42 | 25 | 12 | 5 | 60 | 26 | 62 |
| Chesterfield | 42 | 22 | 10 | 10 | 70 | 39 | 54 |
| Rotherham County | 42 | 23 | 6 | 13 | 70 | 43 | 52 |
| Bradford Park Avenue | 42 | 21 | 10 | 11 | 69 | 43 | 52 |
| Darlington | 42 | 20 | 8 | 14 | 70 | 53 | 48 |
| Southport | 42 | 16 | 14 | 12 | 44 | 42 | 46 |
| Ashington | 42 | 18 | 8 | 16 | 59 | 61 | 44 |
| Doncaster Rovers | 42 | 15 | 12 | 15 | 59 | 53 | 42 |
| Wigan Borough | 42 | 14 | 14 | 14 | 55 | 53 | 42 |
| Grimsby Town | 42 | 14 | 13 | 15 | 49 | 47 | 41 |
| Tranmere Rovers | 42 | 13 | 15 | 14 | 51 | 60 | 41 |
| Accrington Stanley | 42 | 16 | 8 | 18 | 48 | 61 | 40 |
| Halifax Town | 42 | 15 | 10 | 17 | 42 | 59 | 40 |
| Durham City | 42 | 15 | 9 | 18 | 59 | 60 | 39 |
| Wrexham | 42 | 10 | 18 | 14 | 37 | 44 | 38 |
| Walsall | 42 | 14 | 8 | 20 | 44 | 59 | 36 |
| New Brighton | 42 | 11 | 13 | 18 | 40 | 53 | 35 |
| Lincoln City | 42 | 10 | 12 | 20 | 48 | 59 | 32 |
| Crewe Alexandra | 42 | 7 | 13 | 22 | 32 | 58 | 27 |
| Hartlepools United | 42 | 7 | 11 | 24 | 33 | 70 | 25 |
| Barrow | 42 | 8 | 9 | 25 | 35 | 80 | 25 |

# 1924-25

## Division Three North

Manager: David Gordon

### Did you know that?

Hartlepools United reached the FA Cup proper for the first time, losing to the holders Newcastle United at St. James' Park.

Ernie Butler became the first Hartlepools player to be ever present during a Football League season.

| Match No. | Date | Round | Venue | Opponents | Result | | Scorers | Attendance |
|---|---|---|---|---|---|---|---|---|
| 1 | Aug 30 | | (h) | Rochdale | D | 1 - 1 | T.P.Smith | 7,739 |
| 2 | Sep 1 | | (a) | Grimsby Town | L | 1 - 2 | Richardson | 5,000 |
| 3 | 6 | | (a) | Darlington | L | 0 - 2 | | 5,300 |
| 4 | 10 | | (h) | Grimsby Town | W | 2 - 1 | Jobson, Richardson | 4,200 |
| 5 | 13 | | (h) | Bradford Park Avenue | D | 2 - 2 | Allen 2 (2 pen) | 5,430 |
| 6 | 20 | | (a) | Wrexham | L | 1 - 3 | W.Smith | 7,000 |
| 7 | 27 | | (h) | Rotherham County | D | 0 - 0 | | 5,885 |
| 8 | Oct 1 | | (h) | Southport | L | 1 - 2 | W.Smith | 2,677 |
| 9 | 4 | | (a) | Chesterfield | L | 0 - 4 | | 9,000 |
| 10 | 11 | | (h) | Accrington Stanley | W | 3 - 0 | T.P.Smith, C.Hardy, Livingstone | 4,971 |
| 11 | 18 | | (a) | Halifax Town | L | 0 - 2 | | 7,000 |
| 12 | 25 | | (a) | Tranmere Rovers | L | 3 - 4 | T.P.Smith, Richardson, S.Hardy | 4,000 |
| 13 | Nov 1 | | (h) | Lincoln City | D | 1 - 1 | S.Hardy | 4,233 |
| 14 | 8 | | (a) | Barrow | D | 1 - 1 | S.Hardy | 4,000 |
| 17 | 22 | | (a) | Ashington | W | 3 - 0 | S.Hardy, Butler 2 | 4,000 |
| 19 | Dec 6 | | (a) | Doncaster Rovers | L | 0 - 1 | | 6,000 |
| 21 | 20 | | (a) | Crewe Alexandra | L | 1 - 3 | T.P.Smith | 6,000 |
| 22 | 25 | | (h) | Wigan Borough | W | 1 - 0 | Allen (pen) | 5,000 |
| 23 | 26 | | (a) | Wigan Borough | D | 0 - 0 | | 6,000 |
| 24 | 27 | | (a) | Rochdale | L | 1 - 3 | Cook | 5,000 |
| 25 | Jan 1 | | (h) | Walsall | W | 3 - 1 | W.Smith 3 | 3,554 |
| 26 | 3 | | (h) | Darlington | D | 1 - 1 | T.P.Smith | 7,431 |
| 28 | 17 | | (a) | Bradford Park Avenue | L | 0 - 3 | | 10,000 |
| 29 | 24 | | (h) | Wrexham | D | 1 - 1 | W.Smith | 3,205 |
| 30 | 31 | | (a) | Rotherham County | W | 2 - 1 | W.Smith 2 | 3,000 |
| 31 | Feb 7 | | (h) | Chesterfield | W | 1 - 0 | T.P.Smith | 4,443 |
| 32 | 14 | | (a) | Accrington Stanley | L | 1 - 4 | W.Smith | 2,000 |
| 33 | 21 | | (h) | Halifax Town | D | 1 - 1 | Carr | 4,205 |
| 34 | 28 | | (h) | Tranmere Rovers | W | 2 - 1 | Carr, T.P.Smith | 4,771 |
| 35 | Mar 7 | | (a) | Lincoln City | L | 1 - 2 | Carr | 7,000 |
| 36 | 14 | | (h) | Barrow | W | 1 - 0 | Carr | 3,522 |
| 37 | 21 | | (a) | Nelson | L | 0 - 2 | | 5,000 |
| 38 | 25 | | (h) | Nelson | L | 2 - 4 | S.Hardy, Butler | 1,594 |
| 39 | 28 | | (h) | Ashington | L | 0 - 1 | | 3,219 |
| 40 | Apr 4 | | (a) | Southport | L | 0 - 2 | | 4,000 |
| 41 | 10 | | (a) | New Brighton | L | 0 - 2 | | 6,000 |
| 42 | 11 | | (h) | Doncaster Rovers | D | 2 - 2 | Richardson, Carr | 3,213 |
| 43 | 13 | | (h) | New Brighton | L | 0 - 2 | | 2,465 |
| 44 | 18 | | (a) | Durham City | W | 1 - 0 | W.Smith | 1,000 |
| 45 | 22 | | (h) | Durham City | W | 1 - 0 | W.Smith | 1,975 |
| 46 | 25 | | (h) | Crewe Alexandra | W | 2 - 0 | C.Hardy, W.Smith | 2,857 |
| 47 | May 2 | | (a) | Walsall | D | 1 - 1 | C.Hardy | 1,775 |

Final Position : 20th in Division Three North

Apps.
Goals

**FA Cup**

| Match No. | Date | Round | Venue | Opponents | Result | | Scorers | Attendance |
|---|---|---|---|---|---|---|---|---|
| 15 | Nov 15 | QR4 | (h) | Ashington | D | 0 - 0 | | 5,692 |
| 16 | 19 | QR4r | (a) | Ashington | L | 0 - 2 | | 4,000 |
| 18 | 29 | QR5 | (h) | Bishop Auckland | W | 2 - 0 | T.P.Smith, Butler | 5,835 |
| 20 | Dec 13 | QR6 | (h) | St. Albans City | W | 4 - 0 | Cook 2, C.Hardy, Storer | 5,852 |
| 27 | Jan 10 | R1 | (a) | Newcastle United | L | 1 - 4 | S.Hardy | 36,632 |

QR4 Replay. Ashington disqualified for fielding an ineligible player. Hartlepools United reinstated.

Apps.
Goals

| Summerfield | Allen | Lilley | Chape | Young | Jobson | Best | Smith, T.P. | Wayman | Smith, W.E. | Butler | Richardson | Smith, E. | Cowell | Foster | Storer | Livingstone | Hardy, C. | Nicholson | Cook | Hardy, S. | Osmond | Reilly | Walsh | Carr | Robinson | Parkinson | Gray | Lee | Dixon |
|---|---|---|---|---|---|---|---|---|---|---|---|---|---|---|---|---|---|---|---|---|---|---|---|---|---|---|---|---|---|
| 1 | 2 | 3 | 4 | 5 | 6 | 7 | 8 | 9 | 10 | 11 | | | | | | | | | | | | | | | | | | | |
| 1 | 2 | 3 | 4 | 5 | 6 | 7 | 8 | 10 | | 11 | 9 | | | | | | | | | | | | | | | | | | |
| 1 | 2 | 3 | 4 | 5 | 6 | 7 | 8 | 10 | | 11 | 9 | | | | | | | | | | | | | | | | | | |
| 1 | 2 | 3 | | 5 | 4 | 7 | 8 | 10 | | 11 | 9 | 6 | | | | | | | | | | | | | | | | | |
| 1 | 2 | 3 | | 5 | 4 | 7 | 8 | 10 | | 11 | 9 | 6 | | | | | | | | | | | | | | | | | |
| 1 | 2 | 3 | | 5 | 4 | 7 | 8 | | 10 | 11 | 9 | 6 | | | | | | | | | | | | | | | | | |
| | 2 | 3 | | | 4 | 7 | 8 | | 10 | 11 | 9 | 6 | 1 | 5 | | | | | | | | | | | | | | | |
| | 2 | | | | 6 | 7 | 8 | | 10 | 11 | 9 | 3 | 1 | 4 | 5 | | | | | | | | | | | | | | |
| | 2 | | | | 6 | 7 | 9 | | 10 | 11 | | 3 | 1 | 4 | 5 | 8 | | | | | | | | | | | | | |
| | 2 | | | | 6 | 7 | 9 | | | 11 | | 3 | 1 | 4 | 5 | 10 | 8 | | | | | | | | | | | | |
| | 2 | | | | | 7 | | | | 11 | | 3 | 1 | 4 | 5 | 10 | 8 | 6 | 9 | | | | | | | | | | |
| | 2 | | 3 | | | | 9 | | | 7 | 10 | | 1 | 4 | 5 | | | 6 | 8 | 11 | | | | | | | | | |
| | 2 | | | | | | 9 | | | 7 | 10 | | 1 | 4 | 5 | | | 6 | | 11 | 3 | 8 | | | | | | | |
| | 2 | | | | 8 | | 9 | | | 7 | 10 | 3 | 1 | | 5 | | | 6 | | 11 | | | 4 | | | | | | |
| | 2 | | | 6 | 4 | | 8 | | | 7 | | 3 | 1 | | | | 10 | 5 | | 11 | | | | 9 | | | | | |
| | 2 | | | 6 | 4 | | 8 | | | 7 | | 3 | 1 | | 5 | | 10 | | | 11 | | | | 9 | | | | | |
| | 2 | | | 6 | 4 | | 8 | | | 7 | | 3 | 1 | | 5 | | 10 | | | 11 | | | | 9 | | | | | |
| | 2 | | | 6 | 4 | | 8 | | | 7 | | 3 | 1 | | | | 10 | 5 | | 11 | | | | 9 | | | | | |
| | 2 | 3 | | 6 | 4 | | | | | 7 | | | 1 | | 5 | | 10 | | 8 | 11 | | | | 9 | | | | | |
| | 2 | 3 | | 6 | 4 | | 8 | | | 7 | | | 1 | | 5 | | | | 10 | 11 | | | | 9 | | | | | |
| | 2 | 3 | | 6 | 4 | | 8 | | 9 | 7 | | | 1 | | 5 | | 10 | | | 11 | | | | | | | | | |
| | 2 | 3 | | 6 | 4 | | 8 | | | 7 | | | 1 | | 5 | | | | | 11 | | | | 9 | 10 | | | | |
| | 2 | 3 | | 6 | 4 | | | | | 7 | | | 1 | | 5 | | 10 | | 8 | 11 | | | | 9 | | | | | |
| | 2 | | | 6 | 4 | | 8 | | 9 | 7 | | 3 | 1 | | 5 | | 10 | | | 11 | | | | | | | | | |
| | 2 | | | 6 | 4 | | 10 | | 9 | 7 | | 3 | 1 | | 5 | | | | | 11 | | | | | | 8 | | | |
| | 2 | | | 6 | 4 | | 10 | | 9 | 7 | | 3 | 1 | | 5 | | | | | 11 | | | | | | 8 | | | |
| | 2 | | | 6 | 4 | 7 | | | 9 | 11 | | 3 | 1 | | 5 | | | | | | | | | | 10 | 8 | | | |
| | | | | 6 | 4 | 7 | | | 9 | 11 | | 3 | 1 | | 5 | | | | | | | | | 8 | 10 | | 2 | | |
| | | | | 6 | 4 | 7 | 9 | | | 11 | | 3 | 1 | | 5 | | | | | | | | | 8 | 10 | | 2 | | |
| | | | | 6 | 4 | 7 | 10 | | 9 | 11 | | 3 | 1 | | 5 | | | | | | | | | 8 | | | 2 | | |
| | | | | 6 | 4 | 7 | 8 | | | 11 | | 3 | 1 | | 5 | | 10 | | | | | | | 9 | | | 2 | | |
| | | | | 6 | 4 | 7 | 8 | | | 11 | | 3 | 1 | 5 | | | 10 | | | | | | | 9 | | | 2 | | |
| | | | | 6 | 4 | | 8 | | | 7 | | 3 | 1 | 5 | | | 10 | | | 11 | | | | 9 | | | 2 | | |
| | | | | 6 | 4 | | 8 | | 10 | 7 | | 3 | 1 | | 5 | | | | | 11 | | | | 9 | | | 2 | | |
| | 6 | 2 | | | 4 | | | | | 7 | 10 | 3 | 1 | | 5 | | | | | | | | | 9 | | | 8 | 11 | |
| | 5 | 2 | | 6 | 4 | | | | | 7 | 10 | 3 | 1 | | | | | | | | | | | 9 | | | 8 | 11 | |
| | | | | 6 | 4 | 7 | 8 | | | 11 | 10 | | 1 | | 5 | | | | | | | | | 9 | | | 2 | | 3 |
| | | | | 6 | 4 | 7 | | | | 11 | 9 | | 1 | | 5 | | 10 | | | | | | | 8 | | | 2 | | 3 |
| | | 2 | | 6 | 4 | 7 | | | 9 | 11 | | | 1 | | 5 | | 10 | | | | | | | 8 | | | | | 3 |
| | | 2 | | 6 | 4 | 7 | | | 9 | 11 | | | 1 | | 5 | | 10 | | | | | | | 8 | | | | | 3 |
| | | 2 | | 6 | 4 | 7 | | | 9 | 11 | | | 1 | | 5 | | 10 | | | | | | | 8 | | | | | 3 |
| | | 2 | | 6 | | 7 | | | 9 | 11 | | | 1 | 4 | 5 | | 10 | | | | | | | 8 | | | | | 3 |
| 6 | 29 | 18 | 4 | 33 | 38 | 23 | 30 | 5 | 17 | 42 | 14 | 26 | 36 | 10 | 30 | 3 | 18 | 6 | 5 | 17 | 1 | 1 | 1 | 23 | 4 | 3 | 11 | 2 | 6 |
| | 3 | | | | 1 | | 7 | | 12 | 3 | 4 | | | | | 1 | 3 | | 1 | 5 | | | | 5 | | | | | |
| | 2 | | | | 8 | | 9 | | | 7 | 10 | 3 | 1 | | 5 | | | 6 | | 11 | | | 4 | | | | | | |
| | 2 | | | | 4 | | 9 | | | 7 | 10 | 3 | 1 | | 5 | | | 6 | | 11 | | | 8 | | | | | | |
| | 2 | | | 6 | 4 | | 8 | | | 7 | | 3 | 1 | | 5 | | 10 | | 9 | 11 | | | | | | | | | |
| | 2 | | | 6 | 4 | | 8 | | | 7 | | 3 | 1 | | 5 | | 10 | | 9 | 11 | | | | | | | | | |
| | 2 | 3 | | 6 | 4 | | 8 | | | 7 | | | 1 | | 5 | | 10 | | 9 | 11 | | | | | | | | | |
| | 5 | 1 | | 3 | 5 | | 5 | | | 5 | 2 | 4 | 5 | | 5 | | 3 | 2 | 3 | 5 | | | 2 | | | | | | |
| | | | | | | | 1 | | | 1 | | | | | 1 | | 1 | | 2 | 1 | | | | | | | | | |

## League Table

| | P | W | D | L | F | A | Pts |
|---|---|---|---|---|---|---|---|
| Darlington | 42 | 24 | 10 | 8 | 78 | 33 | 58 |
| Nelson | 42 | 23 | 7 | 12 | 79 | 50 | 53 |
| New Brighton | 42 | 23 | 7 | 12 | 75 | 50 | 53 |
| Southport | 42 | 22 | 7 | 13 | 59 | 37 | 51 |
| Bradford Park Avenue | 42 | 19 | 12 | 11 | 84 | 42 | 50 |
| Rochdale | 42 | 21 | 7 | 14 | 75 | 53 | 49 |
| Chesterfield | 42 | 17 | 11 | 14 | 60 | 44 | 45 |
| Lincoln City | 42 | 18 | 8 | 16 | 53 | 58 | 44 |
| Halifax Town | 42 | 16 | 11 | 15 | 56 | 52 | 43 |
| Ashington | 42 | 16 | 10 | 16 | 68 | 76 | 42 |
| Wigan Borough | 42 | 15 | 11 | 16 | 62 | 65 | 41 |
| Grimsby Town | 42 | 15 | 9 | 18 | 60 | 60 | 39 |
| Durham City | 42 | 13 | 13 | 16 | 50 | 68 | 39 |
| Barrow | 42 | 16 | 7 | 19 | 51 | 74 | 39 |
| Crewe Alexandra | 42 | 13 | 13 | 16 | 53 | 78 | 39 |
| Wrexham | 42 | 15 | 8 | 19 | 53 | 61 | 38 |
| Accrington Stanley | 42 | 15 | 8 | 19 | 60 | 72 | 38 |
| Doncaster Rovers | 42 | 14 | 10 | 18 | 54 | 65 | 38 |
| Walsall | 42 | 13 | 11 | 18 | 44 | 53 | 37 |
| Hartlepools United | 42 | 12 | 11 | 19 | 45 | 63 | 35 |
| Tranmere Rovers | 42 | 14 | 4 | 24 | 59 | 78 | 32 |
| Rotherham County | 42 | 7 | 7 | 28 | 42 | 88 | 21 |

# 1925-26

## Division Three North

Managers: David Gordon and Jack Manners

### Did you know that?

Harry Wensley became the first 'Pools player to score 20 or more League goals in a season when he netted 21 times in 42 appearances.

The home game against Walsall on 23 January resulted in a 9–3 victory, which still remains the highest goals aggregate for a Hartlepools game.

'Pools suffered only a single home defeat, against Bradford Park Avenue, in finishing sixth with 44 points, their best total to date.

The playing improvement was reflected in an average home attendance of 4,500.

| Match No. | Date | Round | Venue | Opponents | Result | | Scorers | Attendance |
|---|---|---|---|---|---|---|---|---|
| 1 | Aug 29 | | (a) | Rochdale | L | 0 - 6 | | 9,321 |
| 2 | Sep 2 | | (a) | Accrington Stanley | W | 2 - 1 | Wensley, C.Hardy | 5,177 |
| 3 | 5 | | (h) | Tranmere Rovers | W | 3 - 2 | S.Hardy, C.Hardy, Wensley (pen) | 4,832 |
| 4 | 7 | | (a) | Halifax Town | L | 1 - 2 | Wensley | 4,169 |
| 5 | 12 | | (a) | Walsall | W | 2 - 1 | Birtles, C.Hardy | 5,054 |
| 6 | 16 | | (h) | Accrington Stanley | W | 5 - 1 | Wensley 3, Birtles, C.Hardy | 3,698 |
| 7 | 19 | | (h) | Chesterfield | W | 2 - 1 | Wensley 2 | 5,708 |
| 8 | 26 | | (a) | Bradford Park Avenue | L | 0 - 4 | | 9,849 |
| 9 | Oct 3 | | (h) | Grimsby Town | D | 1 - 1 | C.Hardy | 6,096 |
| 10 | 10 | | (a) | Rotherham United | L | 0 - 1 | | 6,015 |
| 11 | 17 | | (h) | Barrow | W | 2 - 0 | Wensley, Best | 4,498 |
| 12 | 24 | | (a) | Nelson | L | 2 - 5 | Wensley, S.Hardy | 4,892 |
| 13 | 31 | | (h) | New Brighton | W | 6 - 1 | Birtles 2, Foster, S.Hardy, Wensley, C.Hardy | 4,956 |
| 14 | Nov 7 | | (a) | Wigan Borough | L | 0 - 1 | | 1,829 |
| 15 | 14 | | (h) | Doncaster Rovers | W | 2 - 1 | Wensley, Foster | 4,221 |
| 16 | 21 | | (a) | Southport | D | 1 - 1 | S.Hardy | 3,762 |
| 19 | Dec 5 | | (a) | Crewe Alexandra | L | 1 - 2 | C.Hardy | 3,781 |
| 22 | 12 | | (h) | Coventry City | W | 3 - 2 | Wensley, Richardson, Best | 1,956 |
| 23 | 19 | | (a) | Wrexham | D | 2 - 2 | Carr, C.Hardy | 4,410 |
| 24 | 25 | | (h) | Durham City | D | 1 - 1 | Best | 5,306 |
| 25 | 26 | | (h) | Ashington | W | 2 - 1 | Carr 2 | 5,094 |
| 26 | Jan 1 | | (h) | Halifax Town | D | 1 - 1 | Carr | 5,036 |
| 27 | 2 | | (h) | Rochdale | W | 4 - 2 | Best, C.Hardy 2, Carr | 6,057 |
| 28 | 9 | | (h) | Lincoln City | W | 4 - 2 | S.Hardy 2, C.Hardy, Wensley | 4,291 |
| 29 | 16 | | (a) | Tranmere Rovers | L | 0 - 2 | | 4,658 |
| 30 | 23 | | (h) | Walsall | W | 9 - 3 | C.Hardy 3, Best, Wensley, S.Hardy 2, Carr 2 | 3,358 |
| 31 | 30 | | (a) | Chesterfield | L | 2 - 5 | Wensley, S.Hardy | 4,316 |
| 32 | Feb 6 | | (h) | Bradford Park Avenue | L | 0 - 3 | | 7,491 |
| 33 | 13 | | (a) | Grimsby Town | L | 0 - 2 | | 7,859 |
| 34 | 20 | | (h) | Rotherham United | W | 2 - 1 | Richardson 2 (2 pens) | 4,408 |
| 35 | 27 | | (a) | Barrow | W | 4 - 1 | Boland, Robinson 2, Birtles | 1,187 |
| 36 | Mar 6 | | (h) | Nelson | W | 2 - 0 | Robinson, Wensley | 4,397 |
| 37 | 13 | | (a) | New Brighton | L | 2 - 3 | Boland, Birtles | 4,198 |
| 38 | 20 | | (h) | Wigan Borough | D | 0 - 0 | | 4,256 |
| 39 | 27 | | (a) | Doncaster Rovers | L | 1 - 2 | Best | 4,694 |
| 40 | Apr 2 | | (a) | Ashington | L | 0 - 2 | | 4,596 |
| 41 | 3 | | (h) | Southport | W | 5 - 0 | Wensley, Butler, Robinson, Richardson, C.Hardy | 3,984 |
| 42 | 5 | | (a) | Durham City | D | 0 - 0 | | 3,886 |
| 43 | 10 | | (a) | Lincoln City | L | 1 - 2 | Wensley | 3,627 |
| 44 | 17 | | (h) | Crewe Alexandra | D | 0 - 0 | | 2,696 |
| 45 | 24 | | (a) | Coventry City | L | 2 - 5 | Wensley, Richardson | 4,744 |
| 46 | May 1 | | (h) | Wrexham | W | 5 - 0 | Robinson 3, Wensley, Craig | 2,171 |

Final Position : 6th in Division Three North

Apps.
Goals

**FA Cup**

| Match No. | Date | Round | Venue | Opponents | Result | | Scorers | Attendance |
|---|---|---|---|---|---|---|---|---|
| 17 | Nov 28 | R1 | (a) | Blyth Spartans | D | 2 - 2 | S.Hardy, Best | 1,819 |
| 18 | Dec 2 | R1r | (h) | Blyth Spartans | D | 1 - 1* | C.Hardy | 1,994 |
| 20 | 7 | R1r2# | (a) | Blyth Spartans | D | 1 - 1* | Hunter | 2,000 |
| 21 | 9 | R1r3## | (a) | Blyth Spartans | L | 1 - 2 | Wensley | 3,098 |

# Played at St. James' Park, Newcastle  *After extra-time

## Played at Roker Park, Sunderland

Apps.
Goals

| Cowell | Lilley | Robson | Jobson | Storer | Young | Butler | Birtles | Wensley | Hardy, C. | Hardy, S. | Foster | Best | Carr | Dixon | Kell | Richardson | Hunter | Boland | Robinson | Craig | Henderson |
|---|---|---|---|---|---|---|---|---|---|---|---|---|---|---|---|---|---|---|---|---|---|
| 1 | 2 | 3 | 4 | 5 | 6 | 7 | 8 | 9 | 10 | 11 | | | | | | | | | | | |
| 1 | 2 | 3 | 4 | | 6 | 7 | 8 | 9 | 10 | 11 | 5 | | | | | | | | | | |
| 1 | 2 | 3 | 4 | | 6 | 7 | 8 | 9 | 10 | 11 | 5 | | | | | | | | | | |
| 1 | 2 | 3 | 4 | | 6 | 7 | 8 | 9 | 10 | 11 | 5 | | | | | | | | | | |
| 1 | 2 | 3 | 4 | | 6 | 7 | 8 | 9 | 10 | 11 | 5 | | | | | | | | | | |
| 1 | 2 | 3 | 4 | | 6 | 7 | 8 | 9 | 10 | 11 | 5 | | | | | | | | | | |
| 1 | 2 | 3 | 4 | | 6 | 7 | 8 | 9 | 10 | 11 | 5 | | | | | | | | | | |
| 1 | 2 | 3 | 4 | | 6 | | 8 | 9 | 10 | 11 | 5 | 7 | | | | | | | | | |
| 1 | 2 | 3 | 4 | | 6 | | | 9 | 10 | 11 | 5 | 7 | 8 | | | | | | | | |
| 1 | 2 | 3 | 4 | | 6 | | 8 | 9 | 10 | 11 | 5 | 7 | | | | | | | | | |
| 1 | 2 | 3 | 4 | | 6 | | | 9 | 10 | 11 | 5 | 7 | 8 | | | | | | | | |
| 1 | 2 | | 4 | | 6 | | 8 | 9 | 10 | 11 | 5 | 7 | | 3 | | | | | | | |
| 1 | 2 | | 4 | | | | 8 | 9 | 10 | 11 | 5 | 7 | | | 3 | 6 | | | | | |
| 1 | 2 | | 5 | | 4 | 7 | | 9 | 10 | 11 | | | 8 | | 3 | 6 | | | | | |
| 1 | 2 | | 4 | | 6 | 8 | | 9 | 10 | 11 | 5 | 7 | | | 3 | | | | | | |
| 1 | 2 | | 4 | | 6 | | | 9 | 10 | 11 | 5 | 7 | 8 | | 3 | | | | | | |
| 1 | 2 | | 4 | | | | | 9 | 10 | 11 | 5 | 7 | 8 | | 3 | 6 | | | | | |
| 1 | 2 | 3 | 4 | | 5 | | | 8 | 10 | 11 | | 7 | | | | 6 | 9 | | | | |
| 1 | 2 | | 4 | | | | | 8 | 10 | 11 | 5 | 7 | 9 | | 3 | 6 | | | | | |
| 1 | 2 | | 4 | | | | | 9 | 10 | 11 | 5 | 7 | 8 | | 3 | 6 | | | | | |
| 1 | 2 | | 4 | | 5 | | | 9 | 10 | 11 | | 7 | 8 | | 3 | 6 | | | | | |
| 1 | 2 | | 4 | | 5 | | | 9 | 10 | 11 | | 7 | 8 | | 3 | 6 | | | | | |
| 1 | 2 | | 4 | | | | | 9 | 10 | 11 | 5 | 7 | 8 | | 3 | 6 | | | | | |
| 1 | 2 | | 4 | | | | | 9 | 10 | 11 | 5 | 7 | 8 | | 3 | 6 | | | | | |
| 1 | 2 | | 4 | | | | | 9 | 10 | 11 | 5 | 7 | 8 | | 3 | 6 | | | | | |
| 1 | 2 | | 4 | | | | | 9 | 10 | 11 | 5 | 7 | 8 | | 3 | 6 | | | | | |
| 1 | 2 | | 4 | | | | | 9 | 10 | 11 | 5 | 7 | 8 | | 3 | 6 | | | | | |
| 1 | 2 | | 4 | | | 7 | | 9 | 10 | | 5 | | 8 | | 3 | 6 | | 11 | | | |
| 1 | 2 | | 4 | | | | | 9 | 8 | | 5 | 7 | | | 3 | 6 | | 11 | 10 | | |
| 1 | 2 | | 4 | | | | 8 | 9 | 10 | | 5 | 7 | | | 3 | 6 | | 11 | | | |
| 1 | 2 | | | | 4 | | 8 | 9 | | | 5 | 7 | | | 3 | 6 | | 11 | 10 | | |
| 1 | 2 | | | | 4 | | 8 | 9 | | | 5 | 7 | | | 3 | 6 | | 11 | 10 | | |
| 1 | 2 | | | | 4 | | 8 | 9 | | | 5 | 7 | | | 3 | 6 | | 11 | 10 | | |
| 1 | 2 | | | | 4 | | | 9 | | | 5 | 7 | 8 | | 3 | 6 | | 11 | 10 | | |
| 1 | 2 | | | | 4 | 11 | | 9 | 8 | | 5 | 7 | | | 3 | 6 | | | 10 | | |
| 1 | 2 | | | | 4 | 11 | | 9 | | | 5 | 7 | | | 3 | 6 | | | 10 | 8 | |
| 1 | 2 | | 5 | | 4 | 11 | | 9 | 8 | | | 7 | | | 3 | 6 | | | 10 | | |
| 1 | 2 | | 5 | | 4 | 11 | | 9 | 8 | | 6 | 7 | | | 3 | | | | 10 | | |
| 1 | 2 | | 5 | | 4 | 11 | | 9 | | | | 7 | | | 3 | 6 | | | 10 | 8 | |
| 1 | 2 | | 5 | | 4 | | | 9 | | | | 7 | | | 3 | | | 11 | 10 | 8 | 6 |
| 1 | 2 | | 5 | | 4 | | | 9 | | | | 7 | | | 3 | 6 | | 11 | 10 | 8 | |
| 1 | 2 | | 5 | | 4 | 11 | | 9 | | | | 7 | | | 3 | 6 | | | 10 | 8 | |
| 42 | 42 | 12 | 36 | 1 | 30 | 16 | 15 | 42 | 33 | 27 | 32 | 33 | 16 | 1 | 29 | 26 | 1 | 9 | 13 | 5 | 1 |
| | | | | | | 1 | 6 | 21 | 15 | 9 | 2 | 6 | 7 | | | 5 | | 2 | 7 | 1 | |

| Cowell | Lilley | Robson | Jobson | Storer | Young | Butler | Birtles | Wensley | Hardy, C. | Hardy, S. | Foster | Best | Carr | Dixon | Kell | Richardson | Hunter | Boland | Robinson | Craig | Henderson |
|---|---|---|---|---|---|---|---|---|---|---|---|---|---|---|---|---|---|---|---|---|---|
| 1 | | 2 | 4 | | 6 | | | 9 | 10 | 11 | 5 | 7 | 8 | | 3 | | | | | | |
| 1 | | 2 | 4 | | 6 | | | 9 | 10 | 11 | 5 | 7 | 8 | | 3 | | | | | | |
| 1 | 2 | | 4 | | 5 | | | 8 | 10 | 11 | | 7 | | | 3 | 6 | 9 | | | | |
| 1 | 2 | 3 | 4 | | 5 | | | 8 | 10 | 11 | | 7 | | | | 6 | 9 | | | | |
| 4 | 2 | 3 | 4 | | 4 | | | 4 | 4 | 4 | 2 | 4 | 2 | | 3 | 2 | 2 | | | | |
| | | | | | | | | 1 | 1 | 1 | | 1 | | | | | 1 | | | | |

## League Table

| | P | W | D | L | F | A | Pts |
|---|---|---|---|---|---|---|---|
| Grimsby Town | 42 | 26 | 9 | 7 | 91 | 40 | 61 |
| Bradford Park Avenue | 42 | 26 | 8 | 8 | 101 | 43 | 60 |
| Rochdale | 42 | 27 | 5 | 10 | 104 | 58 | 59 |
| Chesterfield | 42 | 25 | 5 | 12 | 100 | 54 | 55 |
| Halifax Town | 42 | 17 | 11 | 14 | 53 | 50 | 45 |
| Hartlepools United | 42 | 18 | 8 | 16 | 82 | 73 | 44 |
| Tranmere Rovers | 42 | 19 | 6 | 17 | 73 | 83 | 44 |
| Nelson | 42 | 16 | 11 | 15 | 89 | 71 | 43 |
| Ashington | 42 | 16 | 11 | 15 | 70 | 62 | 43 |
| Doncaster Rovers | 42 | 16 | 11 | 15 | 80 | 72 | 43 |
| Crewe Alexandra | 42 | 17 | 9 | 16 | 63 | 61 | 43 |
| New Brighton | 42 | 17 | 8 | 17 | 69 | 67 | 42 |
| Durham City | 42 | 18 | 6 | 18 | 63 | 70 | 42 |
| Rotherham United | 42 | 17 | 7 | 18 | 69 | 92 | 41 |
| Lincoln City | 42 | 17 | 5 | 20 | 66 | 82 | 39 |
| Coventry City | 42 | 16 | 6 | 20 | 73 | 82 | 38 |
| Wigan Borough | 42 | 13 | 11 | 18 | 68 | 74 | 37 |
| Accrington Stanley | 42 | 17 | 3 | 22 | 81 | 105 | 37 |
| Wrexham | 42 | 11 | 10 | 21 | 63 | 92 | 32 |
| Southport | 42 | 11 | 10 | 21 | 62 | 92 | 32 |
| Walsall | 42 | 10 | 6 | 26 | 58 | 107 | 26 |
| Barrow | 42 | 7 | 4 | 31 | 50 | 98 | 18 |

# 1926-27

## Division Three North

Manager: Jack Manners

### Did you know that?

For the first time, no goalless draws were recorded during the season.

'Pools suffered their heaviest losses to date in both the Football League and the FA Cup, losing to Accrington Stanley (7–2) and Carlisle United (6–2) respectively.

Harry Wensley played his final game for 'Pools on 30 April, scoring in the 4–0 defeat of New Brighton.

Home attendances averaged 3,020, down by a third on the previous season, with a new low reached against Bradford Park Avenue of 1,278.

| Match No. | Date | Round | Venue | Opponents | Result | | Scorers | Attendance |
|---|---|---|---|---|---|---|---|---|
| 1 | Aug 28 | | (h) | Barrow | D | 1 - 1 | Myers | 5,221 |
| 2 | 31 | | (a) | Southport | L | 0 - 1 | | 5,758 |
| 3 | Sep 4 | | (h) | Halifax Town | L | 0 - 1 | | 3,671 |
| 4 | 11 | | (a) | Lincoln City | W | 2 - 1 | Waite 2 | 5,475 |
| 5 | 13 | | (a) | Stoke City | L | 1 - 3 | Young | 8,306 |
| 6 | 18 | | (h) | Accrington Stanley | W | 3 - 1 | Wensley 2, Waite | 3,285 |
| 7 | 22 | | (h) | Stoke City | L | 1 - 3 | Robinson | 4,348 |
| 8 | 25 | | (a) | Durham City | L | 1 - 2 | Wensley | 2,195 |
| 9 | Oct 2 | | (h) | Tranmere Rovers | W | 2 - 1 | Myers, Thirkell (o.g.) | 3,242 |
| 10 | 9 | | (a) | Rochdale | L | 0 - 3 | | 2,596 |
| 11 | 16 | | (a) | Wigan Borough | L | 0 - 3 | | 2,928 |
| 12 | 23 | | (h) | Doncaster Rovers | W | 3 - 0 | Myers, Thompson, McClenn | 2,681 |
| 13 | 30 | | (a) | Rotherham United | L | 3 - 5 | McClenn, Wensley (pen), Thompson | 3,013 |
| 14 | Nov 6 | | (h) | Bradford Park Avenue | L | 2 - 4 | Wensley (pen), Thompson | 1,278 |
| 15 | 13 | | (a) | Walsall | D | 2 - 2 | Craig, Robinson | 4,276 |
| 16 | 20 | | (h) | Nelson | W | 3 - 2 | Richardson 2, McClenn | 3,171 |
| 18 | Dec 4 | | (h) | Ashington | L | 0 - 1 | | 2,062 |
| 19 | 11 | | (a) | New Brighton | L | 1 - 2 | Wensley | 4,319 |
| 20 | 18 | | (h) | Wrexham | W | 4 - 0 | Myers 2, Craig, Wensley | 1,625 |
| 21 | 25 | | (h) | Crewe Alexandra | D | 1 - 1 | Wensley | 3,098 |
| 22 | 27 | | (a) | Crewe Alexandra | W | 1 - 0 | Boland | 5,973 |
| 23 | Jan 1 | | (h) | Southport | W | 2 - 0 | Robinson, Wensley | 3,426 |
| 24 | 3 | | (h) | Stockport County | L | 1 - 2 | Boland | 4,244 |
| 25 | 15 | | (a) | Barrow | W | 3 - 1 | Craig, Wensley, Boland | 2,955 |
| 26 | 22 | | (a) | Halifax Town | L | 1 - 2 | Waite | 5,930 |
| 27 | 29 | | (h) | Lincoln City | D | 1 - 1 | Waite | 2,452 |
| 28 | Feb 5 | | (a) | Accrington Stanley | L | 2 - 7 | Boland, Myers | 2,877 |
| 29 | 12 | | (h) | Durham City | W | 4 - 0 | Dobell 2, Craig, Myers | 2,537 |
| 30 | 19 | | (a) | Tranmere Rovers | L | 0 - 2 | | 5,584 |
| 31 | 26 | | (h) | Rochdale | W | 3 - 2 | Waite, Jobson (pen), Craig | 4,000 |
| 32 | Mar 5 | | (h) | Wigan Borough | W | 2 - 1 | Myers, Waite | 2,821 |
| 33 | 12 | | (a) | Doncaster Rovers | L | 0 - 2 | | 5,136 |
| 34 | 19 | | (h) | Rotherham United | W | 3 - 1 | Carr, S.Hardy, Wensley | 2,766 |
| 35 | 26 | | (a) | Bradford Park Avenue | L | 1 - 4 | S.Hardy | 5,796 |
| 36 | Apr 2 | | (h) | Walsall | D | 2 - 2 | Wensley 2 | 2,378 |
| 37 | 9 | | (a) | Nelson | L | 2 - 6 | Kell (pen), C.Hardy | 4,369 |
| 38 | 16 | | (h) | Chesterfield | L | 1 - 2 | Dennis (o.g.) | 3,122 |
| 39 | 18 | | (a) | Stockport County | D | 3 - 3 | Wensley 2 (1 pen), Best | 7,503 |
| 40 | 19 | | (a) | Chesterfield | L | 0 - 1 | | 4,405 |
| 41 | 23 | | (a) | Ashington | L | 0 - 1 | | 1,739 |
| 42 | 30 | | (h) | New Brighton | W | 4 - 0 | Best, Hall, C.Hardy, Wensley | 1,983 |
| 43 | May 7 | | (a) | Wrexham | L | 0 - 4 | | 1,536 |

Final Position : 17th in Division Three North

Apps.

2 own goals

Goals

### FA Cup

| Match No. | Date | Round | Venue | Opponents | Result | | Scorers | Attendance |
|---|---|---|---|---|---|---|---|---|
| 17 | Nov 27 | R1 | (a) | Carlisle United | L | 2 - 6 | Robinson, Craig | 7,000 |

Apps.

Goals

| Harrison | Arch | Kell | Young | Jobson | Richardson | Waite | Craig | Wensley | Myers | McClenn | Best | Telford | Boland | Robinson | Carr | Foster | Little | Errington | Hall | Thompson | Walton | Hardy, S. | Hickman | Dobell | Hardy, C. |
|---|---|---|---|---|---|---|---|---|---|---|---|---|---|---|---|---|---|---|---|---|---|---|---|---|---|
| 1 | 2 | 3 | 4 | 5 | 6 | 7 | 8 | 9 | 10 | 11 | | | | | | | | | | | | | | | |
| 1 | 2 | 3 | 4 | 5 | 6 | 7 | 8 | 9 | 10 | 11 | | | | | | | | | | | | | | | |
| 1 | 2 | 3 | 4 | 5 | 6 | 8 | 10 | 9 | | 11 | 7 | | | | | | | | | | | | | | |
| 1 | 2 | 3 | 4 | 5 | 6 | 9 | | 10 | | | 7 | 8 | 11 | | | | | | | | | | | | |
| 1 | 2 | 3 | 4 | 5 | 6 | 8 | | 9 | | | 7 | | 11 | 10 | | | | | | | | | | | |
| 1 | 2 | 3 | 4 | 5 | 6 | 8 | | 9 | | | 7 | | 11 | 10 | | | | | | | | | | | |
| 1 | 2 | 3 | 4 | 5 | 6 | 8 | | 9 | | | 7 | | 11 | 10 | | | | | | | | | | | |
| 1 | 2 | 3 | 4 | 5 | 6 | 8 | | 9 | | | 7 | 10 | 11 | | | | | | | | | | | | |
| 1 | 3 | | 4 | | 6 | 8 | | 9 | 10 | | 7 | | 11 | | 2 | 5 | | | | | | | | | |
| | 3 | | 4 | | 6 | 8 | | 9 | 10 | | 7 | | 11 | | 2 | 5 | 1 | | | | | | | | |
| 1 | 2 | | 4 | | 6 | 8 | | 11 | 10 | | 7 | 9 | | | | 5 | | 3 | | | | | | | |
| 1 | 2 | 3 | | | 6 | | 8 | 11 | 10 | 7 | | | | | | 5 | | | 4 | 9 | | | | | |
| 1 | 2 | 3 | | | | | | 11 | 10 | 7 | | | | 8 | | 5 | | | 4 | 9 | 6 | | | | |
| | 2 | 3 | | | | | 8 | 11 | | 7 | | | | 10 | | 5 | 1 | | 4 | 9 | 6 | | | | |
| | 2 | 3 | | 6 | | | 8 | 11 | | 7 | | | | 10 | | 5 | 1 | | 4 | 9 | | | | | |
| 1 | 2 | 3 | | 6 | 9 | | 8 | | | 7 | | | | 10 | | 5 | | | 4 | | | 11 | | | |
| 1 | 2 | 3 | | 6 | 9 | | 8 | | | 7 | | | | 10 | | 5 | | | 4 | | | 11 | | | |
| 1 | | 3 | | | 6 | | 8 | 9 | 10 | 7 | | | 11 | | 2 | 5 | | | 4 | | | | | | |
| 1 | | 3 | | | 6 | | 8 | 9 | 10 | 7 | | | 11 | | 2 | 5 | | | 4 | | | | | | |
| 1 | | 3 | | | 6 | | 8 | 9 | 10 | 7 | | | 11 | | 2 | 5 | | | 4 | | | | | | |
| 1 | | 3 | | 5 | 6 | 8 | | 9 | 10 | 7 | | | 11 | | 2 | | | | 4 | | | | | | |
| 1 | 2 | 3 | | 5 | 6 | 8 | | 9 | | 7 | | | 11 | 10 | | | | | 4 | | | | | | |
| 1 | 2 | 3 | | 5 | 6 | | 8 | 9 | | 7 | | | 11 | 10 | | | | | 4 | | | | | | |
| 1 | 2 | 3 | | 5 | 6 | 8 | 10 | 9 | | 7 | | | 11 | | | | | | 4 | | | | | | |
| 1 | 2 | 3 | | 5 | 6 | 8 | | 9 | 10 | 7 | | | 11 | | | | | | 4 | | | | | | |
| 1 | 2 | 3 | | 5 | 6 | 8 | | 9 | 10 | 7 | | | 11 | | | | | | 4 | | | | | | |
| | 2 | 3 | | 5 | 6 | 8 | | 9 | 10 | 7 | | | 11 | | | | 1 | | 4 | | | | | | |
| | | 3 | 6 | 5 | | 7 | 8 | | 10 | | | | 11 | | 2 | | | | 4 | | | | 1 | 9 | |
| | | 3 | 6 | 5 | | 7 | 8 | | 10 | | | | 11 | | 2 | | | | 4 | | | | 1 | 9 | |
| | | 3 | 6 | 5 | | 7 | 8 | | 10 | | | | 11 | | 2 | | | | 4 | | | | 1 | 9 | |
| 1 | | 3 | 6 | 5 | | 7 | 8 | | 10 | 11 | | | | | 2 | | | | 4 | | | | | 9 | |
| 1 | | 3 | 6 | 5 | | 7 | 8 | | 10 | | | | | | 2 | | | | 4 | | | 11 | | 9 | |
| 1 | | 3 | 6 | 5 | | 7 | | 9 | 8 | | | | | | 2 | | | | 4 | | | 11 | | | 10 |
| 1 | | 3 | 5 | | 6 | 7 | 8 | 9 | 10 | | | | | | 2 | | | | 4 | | | 11 | | | |
| 1 | | 3 | 6 | 5 | | | 8 | 9 | 10 | | 7 | | | | 2 | | | | 4 | | | 11 | | | |
| 1 | | 3 | 5 | | 6 | | 8 | 9 | | | 7 | | | | 2 | | | | 4 | | | 11 | | | 10 |
| 1 | | | 5 | | 6 | | 8 | 9 | | | 7 | | | | 2 | | | 3 | 4 | | | 11 | | | 10 |
| 1 | | | 5 | 6 | | | 8 | 9 | | | 7 | | | | 2 | | | 3 | 4 | | | 11 | | | 10 |
| 1 | | | 6 | 5 | | 11 | 8 | 9 | | | 7 | | | | 2 | | | 3 | 4 | | | | | | 10 |
| 1 | | | 5 | | 6 | 8 | 7 | 9 | | | | | 11 | | 2 | | | 3 | 4 | | | | | | 10 |
| 1 | | | 5 | | 6 | | | 9 | | | 7 | | 11 | 8 | 2 | | | 3 | 4 | | | | | | 10 |
| 1 | | | 5 | 6 | 10 | | | | | | 7 | | 11 | 8 | 2 | | | 3 | 4 | | | | | 9 | |
| 35 | 23 | 33 | 26 | 28 | 30 | 26 | 25 | 34 | 22 | 20 | 16 | 3 | 23 | 12 | 21 | 12 | 4 | 7 | 31 | 4 | 2 | 9 | 3 | 6 | 7 |
| | | 1 | 1 | 1 | 2 | 7 | 5 | 16 | 8 | 3 | 2 | | 4 | 3 | 1 | | | | 1 | 3 | | 2 | | 2 | 2 |

| Harrison | Arch | Kell | Young | Jobson | Richardson | Waite | Craig | Wensley | Myers | McClenn | Best | Telford | Boland | Robinson | Carr | Foster | Little | Errington | Hall | Thompson | Walton | Hardy, S. | Hickman | Dobell | Hardy, C. |
|---|---|---|---|---|---|---|---|---|---|---|---|---|---|---|---|---|---|---|---|---|---|---|---|---|---|
| 1 | 2 | 3 | | 6 | 9 | | 8 | | | 7 | | | | 10 | | 5 | | | 4 | | | 11 | | | |
| 1 | 1 | 1 | | 1 | 1 | | 1 | | | 1 | | | | 1 | | 1 | | | 1 | | | 1 | | | |
| | | | | | | | 1 | | | | | | | 1 | | | | | | | | | | | |

## League Table

| | P | W | D | L | F | A | Pts |
|---|---|---|---|---|---|---|---|
| Stoke City | 42 | 27 | 9 | 6 | 92 | 40 | 63 |
| Rochdale | 42 | 26 | 6 | 10 | 105 | 65 | 58 |
| Bradford Park Avenue | 42 | 24 | 7 | 11 | 101 | 59 | 55 |
| Halifax Town | 42 | 21 | 11 | 10 | 70 | 53 | 53 |
| Nelson | 42 | 22 | 7 | 13 | 104 | 75 | 51 |
| Stockport County | 42 | 22 | 7 | 13 | 93 | 69 | 49 |
| Chesterfield | 42 | 21 | 5 | 16 | 92 | 68 | 47 |
| Doncaster Rovers | 42 | 18 | 11 | 13 | 81 | 65 | 47 |
| Tranmere Rovers | 42 | 19 | 8 | 15 | 85 | 67 | 46 |
| New Brighton | 42 | 18 | 10 | 14 | 79 | 67 | 46 |
| Lincoln City | 42 | 15 | 12 | 15 | 90 | 78 | 42 |
| Southport | 42 | 15 | 9 | 18 | 80 | 85 | 39 |
| Wrexham | 42 | 14 | 10 | 18 | 65 | 73 | 38 |
| Walsall | 42 | 14 | 10 | 18 | 68 | 81 | 38 |
| Crewe Alexandra | 42 | 14 | 9 | 19 | 71 | 81 | 37 |
| Ashington | 42 | 12 | 12 | 18 | 60 | 90 | 36 |
| Hartlepools United | 42 | 14 | 6 | 22 | 66 | 81 | 34 |
| Wigan Borough | 42 | 11 | 10 | 21 | 66 | 83 | 32 |
| Rotherham United | 42 | 10 | 12 | 20 | 70 | 92 | 32 |
| Durham City | 42 | 12 | 6 | 24 | 58 | 105 | 30 |
| Accrington Stanley | 42 | 10 | 7 | 25 | 62 | 98 | 27 |
| Barrow | 42 | 7 | 8 | 27 | 34 | 117 | 22 |

# 1927-28

## Division Three North

Manager: Bill Norman

### Did you know that?

For the second successive season no goalless draws were played.

Following the home loss to bottom club Nelson on 17 March, attendances slumped dramatically, with only a total of 7,233 diehards attending the final four home fixtures.

Billy Robinson played his final game for the club on 5 May against Stockport, scoring the last of his record 28 goals in a 2–2 draw.

| Match No. | Date | Round | Venue | Opponents | Result | | Scorers | Attendance |
|---|---|---|---|---|---|---|---|---|
| 1 | Aug 27 | | (a) | Wigan Borough | W | 2 - 0 | Dobell, W.Mordue | 6,385 |
| 2 | Sep 3 | | (h) | Doncaster Rovers | W | 1 - 0 | G.W. Richardson | 5,314 |
| 3 | 10 | | (a) | Darlington | L | 0 - 5 | | 6,719 |
| 4 | 14 | | (a) | Wrexham | L | 2 - 3 | Robinson 2 | 2,927 |
| 5 | 17 | | (h) | Ashington | W | 4 - 1 | S.Hardy 2, Robson, Robinson | 4,294 |
| 6 | 24 | | (a) | Crewe Alexandra | L | 0 - 4 | | 3,016 |
| 7 | 27 | | (a) | Accrington Stanley | D | 2 - 2 | Liddle, W.Mordue | 6,353 |
| 8 | Oct 1 | | (h) | Halifax Town | L | 0 - 1 | | 4,571 |
| 9 | 8 | | (a) | Bradford City | L | 1 - 2 | W.Mordue | 13,762 |
| 10 | 15 | | (h) | New Brighton | D | 3 - 3 | S.Hardy, Richardson, W.Mordue | 4,243 |
| 11 | 22 | | (a) | Rotherham United | L | 0 - 5 | | 2,395 |
| 12 | 29 | | (h) | Rochdale | L | 0 - 2 | | 4,086 |
| 13 | Nov 5 | | (a) | Nelson | L | 2 - 4 | Robinson 2 | 2,001 |
| 14 | 12 | | (h) | Southport | W | 2 - 1 | W.Mordue 2 | 2,429 |
| 15 | 19 | | (a) | Durham City | L | 0 - 1 | | 1,580 |
| 17 | Dec 3 | | (a) | Chesterfield | W | 3 - 1 | Robinson, W.Mordue, Rayment | 2,505 |
| 18 | 10 | | (h) | Durham City | W | 2 - 1 | Robinson 2 | 2,497 |
| 19 | 17 | | (a) | Tranmere Rovers | W | 2 - 1 | Robinson (pen), W.Mordue | 4,878 |
| 20 | 24 | | (h) | Stockport County | W | 2 - 1 | Robinson 2 | 2,033 |
| 21 | 26 | | (h) | Lincoln City | L | 1 - 2 | Liddle | 3,961 |
| 22 | 27 | | (a) | Lincoln City | W | 5 - 1 | Robinson 3, J.Mordue, W.Mordue | 9,277 |
| 23 | 31 | | (h) | Wigan Borough | D | 1 - 1 | W.Mordue | 3,546 |
| 24 | Jan 2 | | (h) | Barrow | W | 6 - 2 | Robson 2, Robinson 2, J.Mordue 2 | 3,377 |
| 25 | 7 | | (a) | Doncaster Rovers | D | 1 - 1 | Boland | 7,641 |
| 26 | 14 | | (h) | Bradford Park Avenue | D | 1 - 1 | Robinson (pen) | 5,023 |
| 27 | 21 | | (h) | Darlington | L | 0 - 1 | | 7,485 |
| 28 | 28 | | (a) | Ashington | L | 1 - 3 | W.Mordue | 1,407 |
| 29 | Feb 4 | | (h) | Crewe Alexandra | W | 4 - 3 | Boland, W.Mordue, J.Young, Robinson | 3,100 |
| 30 | 11 | | (a) | Halifax Town | L | 1 - 4 | W.Mordue | 2,424 |
| 31 | 18 | | (h) | Bradford City | L | 2 - 3 | Rayment, Robinson (pen) | 4,475 |
| 32 | 25 | | (a) | New Brighton | L | 1 - 2 | Robinson | 2,861 |
| 33 | Mar 3 | | (h) | Rotherham United | L | 1 - 3 | W.Mordue | 4,190 |
| 34 | 10 | | (a) | Rochdale | W | 1 - 0 | Robinson | 2,582 |
| 35 | 17 | | (h) | Nelson | L | 4 - 5 | Rigg (o.g.), Robinson 3 | 2,972 |
| 36 | 24 | | (a) | Southport | W | 2 - 0 | Boland, Dobell | 2,518 |
| 37 | Apr 6 | | (a) | Barrow | L | 0 - 2 | | 7,059 |
| 38 | 7 | | (a) | Bradford Park Avenue | L | 0 - 3 | | 12,715 |
| 39 | 9 | | (h) | Accrington Stanley | L | 0 - 2 | | 2,245 |
| 40 | 14 | | (h) | Chesterfield | W | 1 - 0 | Robinson | 1,314 |
| 41 | 21 | | (h) | Wrexham | W | 4 - 2 | Robinson, Robson, J.Young, W.Mordue | 1,542 |
| 42 | 28 | | (h) | Tranmere Rovers | W | 2 - 0 | W.Mordue, Robinson | 2,132 |
| 43 | May 5 | | (a) | Stockport County | D | 2 - 2 | Robinson, Robson | 4,991 |

Final Position : 15th in Division Three North — Apps.

1 own goal — Goals

**FA Cup**

| Match No. | Date | Round | Venue | Opponents | Result | | Scorers | Attendance |
|---|---|---|---|---|---|---|---|---|
| 16 | Nov 26 | R1 | (a) | Halifax Town | L | 0 - 3 | | 10,341 |

Apps.

Goals

| Harrison | Carr | Errington | Hall | Young, A. | Richardson, G.W. | Richardson, G.E. | Poyntz | Dobell | Mordue, W. | Hardy, S. | Robson | Robinson | Boland | Robertson | Williams | Liddle | Kell | Harris | Mordue, J. | Hickman | Rayment | Young, J. | Brown, J. | Hardy, C. |
|---|---|---|---|---|---|---|---|---|---|---|---|---|---|---|---|---|---|---|---|---|---|---|---|---|
| 1 | 2 | 3 | 4 | 5 | 6 | 7 | 8 | 9 | 10 | 11 | | | | | | | | | | | | | | |
| 1 | 2 | 3 | 4 | 5 | 6 | 7 | 8 | 9 | 10 | 11 | | | | | | | | | | | | | | |
| 1 | 2 | 3 | 4 | 5 | 6 | 7 | 8 | 9 | 10 | 11 | | | | | | | | | | | | | | |
| 1 | 2 | 3 | | 4 | 6 | | 5 | 9 | 8 | | 7 | 10 | 11 | | | | | | | | | | | |
| 1 | 2 | 3 | | 5 | 6 | | 4 | 9 | 10 | 11 | 7 | 8 | | | | | | | | | | | | |
| 1 | 2 | 3 | 5 | | 6 | | 4 | 9 | 10 | 11 | 7 | 8 | | | | | | | | | | | | |
| 1 | 2 | | 4 | | 6 | | 9 | | 10 | 11 | 7 | | | 3 | 5 | 8 | | | | | | | | |
| 1 | 2 | 3 | | 4 | 6 | | 9 | | 10 | 11 | 7 | | | | 5 | 8 | | | | | | | | |
| 1 | 2 | | 4 | 5 | 9 | | 6 | | 10 | 11 | 7 | | | | | 8 | 3 | | | | | | | |
| 1 | 2 | | 4 | | 9 | | 6 | | 10 | 11 | 7 | | | | 5 | 8 | 3 | | | | | | | |
| 1 | | | 4 | 5 | 6 | | | 9 | 10 | | 7 | | | 2 | | 8 | 3 | 11 | | | | | | |
| 1 | 9 | | 4 | 5 | 6 | | | | 10 | | 7 | | 11 | 2 | | 8 | 3 | | | | | | | |
| 1 | 2 | | 4 | 5 | | | 6 | | 10 | | 7 | 9 | 11 | | | 8 | 3 | | | | | | | |
| 1 | 2 | | 4 | 5 | | | 6 | | 10 | | 7 | 9 | 11 | | | | 3 | | 8 | | | | | |
| | 2 | | 4 | 5 | 6 | | 8 | | 10 | | 7 | 9 | 11 | 3 | | | | | | 1 | | | | |
| | 2 | | 4 | 5 | 6 | | | | 10 | | | 9 | 11 | 3 | | 8 | | | | 1 | 7 | | | |
| | 2 | | 4 | | 5 | | 6 | | 10 | | | 9 | 11 | 3 | | 8 | | | | 1 | 7 | | | |
| | 2 | | 4 | | 6 | | 5 | | 10 | | | 9 | 11 | 3 | | 8 | | | | 1 | 7 | | | |
| 1 | 2 | | 4 | | 6 | | 5 | | 10 | | | 9 | 11 | 3 | | 8 | | | | | 7 | | | |
| 1 | 2 | | 4 | | 6 | | 5 | | 10 | | | 9 | 11 | 3 | | 8 | | | | | 7 | | | |
| 1 | 2 | | 4 | | 6 | | 5 | | 10 | | | 9 | 11 | 3 | | | | | 8 | | 7 | | | |
| 1 | 2 | | 4 | | 6 | | 5 | | 10 | | | 9 | 11 | 3 | | | | | 8 | | 7 | | | |
| 1 | 2 | | 4 | 6 | | | 5 | | 10 | | 7 | 9 | 11 | 3 | | | | | 8 | | | | | |
| 1 | 2 | | 4 | | 6 | | 5 | | 10 | | | 9 | 11 | 3 | | | | | 8 | | 7 | | | |
| 1 | 2 | | 4 | | 6 | | 5 | | 10 | | | 9 | 11 | 3 | | | | | 8 | | 7 | | | |
| 1 | 2 | | | 4 | 6 | | 5 | | 10 | | | 9 | 11 | 3 | | | | | 8 | | 7 | | | |
| 1 | 2 | | | 4 | 6 | | 5 | | 10 | | 7 | 9 | 11 | 3 | | | | | | | | 8 | | |
| 1 | 2 | | 4 | 6 | | | 5 | | 10 | | 7 | 9 | 11 | 3 | | | | | | | | 8 | | |
| 1 | | | 4 | 6 | | | 5 | | 10 | | 7 | 9 | 11 | 3 | | | 2 | | 8 | | | | | |
| 1 | | 3 | 4 | 6 | | | 5 | | 10 | | | 9 | 11 | | | | 2 | | 8 | | 7 | | | |
| 1 | | | 4 | | 6 | | 5 | | 10 | | | 9 | 11 | 2 | 3 | | | | 8 | | 7 | | | |
| 1 | | | 4 | | 6 | | 5 | | 10 | | | 9 | 11 | | 3 | | 2 | | 8 | | 7 | | | |
| | | | 4 | | 6 | | 5 | | 10 | | | 9 | 11 | 2 | 3 | | | | | | 7 | 8 | 1 | |
| | | | 4 | | 6 | | 5 | | 10 | | | 9 | 11 | 2 | 3 | | | | | | 7 | 8 | 1 | |
| 1 | | | 4 | 5 | 6 | | | 9 | | | | 10 | 11 | 2 | 3 | | | | | | 7 | 8 | | |
| | | | 4 | 5 | 6 | | | | 10 | | | 9 | 11 | 2 | 3 | | | | | | 7 | 8 | 1 | |
| | 2 | | 4 | 6 | 10 | | | | | | | 9 | 11 | 3 | 5 | | | | | | 7 | 8 | 1 | |
| | 2 | | 4 | 6 | 8 | | | | | | | 9 | 11 | 3 | 5 | | | | | | 7 | | 1 | 10 |
| 1 | 2 | | 4 | 5 | 6 | | | | 10 | | 7 | 9 | 11 | | 3 | | | | | | | 8 | | |
| 1 | 2 | | 4 | 5 | 6 | | | | 10 | | 7 | 9 | 11 | | 3 | | | | | | | 8 | | |
| 1 | 2 | | 4 | 5 | 6 | | | | 10 | | 7 | 9 | 11 | | 3 | | | | | | | 8 | | |
| 1 | 2 | | 4 | 5 | 6 | | | | 10 | | 7 | 9 | 11 | | 3 | | | | | | | 8 | | |
| 33 | 33 | 8 | 37 | 27 | 36 | 3 | 31 | 8 | 39 | 9 | 20 | 33 | 32 | 25 | 15 | 12 | 9 | 1 | 11 | 4 | 19 | 11 | 5 | 1 |
| | | | | | 2 | | | 2 | 16 | 3 | 5 | 28 | 3 | | | 2 | | | 3 | | 2 | 2 | | |

| Harrison | Carr | Errington | Hall | Young, A. | Richardson, G.W. | Richardson, G.E. | Poyntz | Dobell | Mordue, W. | Hardy, S. | Robson | Robinson | Boland | Robertson | Williams | Liddle | Kell | Harris | Mordue, J. | Hickman | Rayment | Young, J. | Brown, J. | Hardy, C. |
|---|---|---|---|---|---|---|---|---|---|---|---|---|---|---|---|---|---|---|---|---|---|---|---|---|
| 1 | 2 | | 4 | 5 | 9 | | 8 | | 10 | | | | 11 | 3 | 6 | | | | | | 7 | | | |
| 1 | 1 | | 1 | 1 | 1 | | 1 | | 1 | | | | 1 | 1 | 1 | | | | | | 1 | | | |

## League Table

| | P | W | D | L | F | A | Pts |
|---|---|---|---|---|---|---|---|
| Bradford Park Avenue | 42 | 27 | 9 | 6 | 101 | 45 | 63 |
| Lincoln City | 42 | 24 | 7 | 11 | 91 | 64 | 55 |
| Stockport County | 42 | 23 | 8 | 11 | 89 | 51 | 54 |
| Doncaster Rovers | 42 | 23 | 7 | 12 | 80 | 44 | 53 |
| Tranmere Rovers | 42 | 22 | 9 | 11 | 105 | 72 | 53 |
| Bradford City | 42 | 18 | 12 | 12 | 85 | 60 | 48 |
| Darlington | 42 | 21 | 5 | 16 | 89 | 74 | 47 |
| Southport | 42 | 20 | 5 | 17 | 79 | 70 | 45 |
| Accrington Stanley | 42 | 18 | 8 | 16 | 76 | 67 | 44 |
| New Brighton | 42 | 14 | 14 | 14 | 72 | 62 | 42 |
| Wrexham | 42 | 18 | 6 | 18 | 64 | 67 | 42 |
| Halifax Town | 42 | 13 | 15 | 14 | 73 | 71 | 41 |
| Rochdale | 42 | 17 | 7 | 18 | 74 | 77 | 41 |
| Rotherham United | 42 | 14 | 11 | 17 | 65 | 69 | 39 |
| Hartlepools United | 42 | 16 | 6 | 20 | 69 | 81 | 38 |
| Chesterfield | 42 | 13 | 10 | 19 | 71 | 78 | 36 |
| Crewe Alexandra | 42 | 12 | 10 | 20 | 77 | 86 | 34 |
| Ashington | 42 | 11 | 11 | 20 | 77 | 103 | 33 |
| Barrow | 42 | 10 | 11 | 21 | 54 | 102 | 31 |
| Wigan Borough | 42 | 10 | 10 | 22 | 56 | 97 | 30 |
| Durham City | 42 | 11 | 7 | 24 | 53 | 100 | 29 |
| Nelson | 42 | 10 | 6 | 26 | 76 | 136 | 26 |

# 1928-29

## Division Three North

Manager: Bill Norman

### Did you know that?

'Pools lost 18 of their 21 away games, earning a meagre four points with one win and two draws.

Carlisle United, newly elected to the Third Division North, inflicted 'Pools' heaviest defeat to date (8–0) in only their third-ever League game.

'Pools made their second application for re-election after finishing 21st, three points above Ashington who lost their League status in favour of York City.

| Match No. | Date | Round | Venue | Opponents | Result | | Scorers | Attendance |
|---|---|---|---|---|---|---|---|---|
| 1 | Aug 25 | | (h) | Nelson | D | 2 - 2 | Young, Spry | 5,524 |
| 2 | Sep 1 | | (a) | Carlisle United | L | 0 - 8 | | 7,346 |
| 3 | 5 | | (h) | Darlington | W | 2 - 0 | T.Mordue, J.Mordue | 5,271 |
| 4 | 8 | | (h) | Rotherham United | D | 1 - 1 | T.Mordue | 4,867 |
| 5 | 15 | | (a) | Wigan Borough | L | 0 - 2 | | 7,842 |
| 6 | 22 | | (h) | Crewe Alexandra | W | 2 - 1 | J.Mordue, T.Mordue | 4,015 |
| 7 | 25 | | (a) | Accrington Stanley | D | 2 - 2 | J.Mordue 2 | 4,488 |
| 8 | 29 | | (a) | Tranmere Rovers | L | 0 - 3 | | 5,541 |
| 9 | Oct 6 | | (h) | Stockport County | D | 1 - 1 | J.Mordue | 5,305 |
| 10 | 13 | | (a) | Halifax Town | L | 0 - 2 | | 3,747 |
| 11 | 20 | | (h) | South Shields | L | 0 - 5 | | 5,130 |
| 12 | 27 | | (a) | Ashington | L | 1 - 3 | T.Mordue | 1,419 |
| 13 | Nov 3 | | (h) | Doncaster Rovers | D | 2 - 2 | Dobell, T.Mordue | 3,175 |
| 14 | 10 | | (a) | Barrow | L | 1 - 2 | T.Mordue | 3,988 |
| 15 | 17 | | (h) | Chesterfield | L | 0 - 2 | | 2,264 |
| 17 | Dec 1 | | (h) | New Brighton | W | 5 - 2 | Briggs, MacKay, T.Mordue 2, Dixon | 1,843 |
| 18 | 8 | | (a) | Rochdale | L | 4 - 7 | Mason, Briggs 2, Richardson | 3,017 |
| 19 | 15 | | (h) | Southport | W | 4 - 2 | Hall, Richardson 2, T.Mordue | 1,677 |
| 20 | 22 | | (a) | Darlington | L | 1 - 4 | Dixon | 3,080 |
| 21 | 25 | | (h) | Lincoln City | W | 3 - 2 | Hall, Richardson, T.Mordue | 3,699 |
| 22 | 26 | | (a) | Lincoln City | L | 1 - 7 | Richardson | 9,668 |
| 23 | 29 | | (a) | Nelson | L | 0 - 1 | | 3,507 |
| 24 | Jan 1 | | (h) | Bradford City | L | 1 - 3 | Richardson | 4,364 |
| 25 | 5 | | (h) | Carlisle United | W | 1 - 0 | Richardson | 3,000 |
| 26 | 12 | | (a) | Wrexham | L | 1 - 3 | Richardson | 5,043 |
| 27 | 19 | | (a) | Rotherham United | L | 2 - 3 | J.Mordue 2 | 4,339 |
| 28 | 26 | | (h) | Wigan Borough | L | 1 - 3 | Hodgson | 2,848 |
| 29 | Feb 2 | | (a) | Crewe Alexandra | L | 2 - 4 | T.Mordue, Richardson | 3,159 |
| 30 | 9 | | (h) | Tranmere Rovers | W | 4 - 1 | Dixon 2, Richardson 2 | 2,346 |
| 31 | 16 | | (a) | Stockport County | L | 0 - 3 | | 7,468 |
| 32 | 23 | | (h) | Halifax Town | W | 3 - 1 | Richardson 2 (1 pen), Williams | 2,867 |
| 33 | Mar 2 | | (a) | South Shields | D | 1 - 1 | Richardson | 3,728 |
| 34 | 9 | | (h) | Ashington | L | 1 - 3 | Richardson (pen) | 3,398 |
| 35 | 16 | | (a) | Doncaster Rovers | L | 1 - 4 | T.Mordue | 5,111 |
| 36 | 23 | | (h) | Barrow | W | 1 - 0 | Young | 2,314 |
| 37 | 30 | | (a) | Chesterfield | L | 1 - 4 | Spry | 3,394 |
| 38 | Apr 1 | | (h) | Accrington Stanley | L | 1 - 3 | Richardson | 2,331 |
| 39 | 2 | | (a) | Bradford City | L | 1 - 4 | Dixon | 24,630 |
| 40 | 6 | | (h) | Wrexham | L | 0 - 2 | | 2,492 |
| 41 | 13 | | (a) | New Brighton | W | 3 - 1 | Richardson 2, J.Mordue | 2,802 |
| 42 | 20 | | (h) | Rochdale | L | 0 - 2 | | 1,835 |
| 43 | 27 | | (a) | Southport | L | 2 - 6 | Richardson, J.Mordue | 2,056 |

Final Position : 21st in Division Three North

Apps.
Goals

**FA Cup**

| Match No. | Date | Round | Venue | Opponents | Result | | Scorers | Attendance |
|---|---|---|---|---|---|---|---|---|
| 16 | Nov 24 | R1 | (a) | Spennymoor United | L | 2 - 5 | T.Mordue, Donkin (o.g.) | 1,836 |

Apps.

1 own goal

Goals

| Smith | Carr | Williams | Hall | Mason | Dobell | Spry | Young, J. | Christon | Mordue, W. | Fell | Mordue, J. | Errington | Coates | Mordue, T. | Rivers | Robertson | Mackey | Richardson, W. | Hodgson | Dixon | Briggs | Hickman | Harland |
|---|---|---|---|---|---|---|---|---|---|---|---|---|---|---|---|---|---|---|---|---|---|---|---|
| 1 | 2 | 3 | 4 | 5 | 6 | 7 | 8 | 9 | 10 | 11 | | | | | | | | | | | | | |
| 1 | 2 | 3 | 4 | 5 | 6 | 7 | | 9 | 10 | 11 | 8 | | | | | | | | | | | | |
| 1 | 2 | 5 | 4 | | 6 | | | | 10 | 11 | 8 | 3 | 7 | 9 | | | | | | | | | |
| 1 | 2 | 5 | 4 | | 6 | | | | 10 | 11 | 8 | 3 | 7 | 9 | | | | | | | | | |
| | 2 | 5 | 4 | | 6 | | 8 | | 10 | 11 | 7 | 3 | | 9 | 1 | | | | | | | | |
| | 2 | 5 | | | 6 | | | | 10 | 11 | 8 | | | 9 | 1 | 3 | 4 | 7 | | | | | |
| | 2 | 5 | | | | | | | 10 | 7 | 8 | | | 9 | 1 | 3 | 4 | | 6 | 11 | | | |
| | | 3 | 4 | | 6 | | | | 10 | 7 | 8 | | | 9 | 1 | 2 | 5 | | | 11 | | | |
| | 2 | 5 | 4 | | 6 | | | | 10 | 11 | 8 | | | 9 | 1 | 3 | | 7 | | | | | |
| | 2 | 5 | 4 | | 6 | | | | 10 | 11 | 8 | | | 9 | 1 | 3 | | 7 | | | | | |
| | 2 | 5 | 4 | | 6 | | 8 | | 10 | 11 | | | | 9 | 1 | 3 | | | | | 7 | | |
| | 2 | | | 5 | 6 | | 8 | | 10 | 11 | | | | 9 | 1 | 3 | 4 | | | | 7 | | |
| | | 3 | | 5 | 6 | | 8 | | | 11 | | | | 10 | 1 | 2 | 4 | 9 | | | 7 | | |
| | 2 | 6 | | 5 | 4 | | | | 8 | 11 | | | | 10 | 1 | 3 | | 9 | | | 7 | | |
| | 2 | 5 | 4 | | 6 | | | | 8 | 11 | 9 | | | 10 | 1 | 3 | | | | | 7 | | |
| | 2 | 3 | | 5 | | | | | | | 8 | | | 10 | 1 | | 6 | 9 | 4 | 11 | 7 | | |
| | 2 | 3 | 4 | 5 | | | | | 6 | | 8 | | | 10 | | | | 9 | | 11 | 7 | 1 | |
| | 2 | 3 | 4 | 5 | | | | | 6 | | 8 | | | 10 | | | | 9 | | 11 | 7 | 1 | |
| | 2 | 3 | 4 | 5 | 6 | | | | | | 8 | | | 10 | | | | 9 | | 11 | 7 | 1 | |
| | 2 | | 4 | 5 | 6 | | | | | | 8 | 3 | | 10 | | | | 9 | | 11 | 7 | 1 | |
| | 2 | | 4 | 5 | 6 | | | | | | 8 | 3 | | 10 | | | | 9 | | 11 | 7 | 1 | |
| | 2 | | 4 | 5 | | | | | 6 | | 8 | 3 | | 10 | 1 | | | 9 | | 11 | 7 | | |
| | 2 | | 4 | 5 | 6 | | | | | | 8 | 3 | | 10 | 1 | | | 9 | | 11 | 7 | | |
| | 2 | 5 | | | 6 | | | | 4 | 11 | 8 | 3 | | 10 | 1 | | | 9 | | | 7 | | |
| | 2 | 5 | | | 6 | | | | 4 | 11 | 8 | 3 | | 10 | 1 | | | 9 | | | 7 | | |
| | 2 | 5 | | | 6 | | | | 4 | 11 | 8 | 3 | | 10 | 1 | | | 9 | | | 7 | | |
| | 2 | 5 | | | 6 | | | | 4 | 11 | 8 | 3 | | 10 | 1 | | | | 9 | | 7 | | |
| | 2 | 3 | | | 6 | 7 | | | 4 | | 8 | | | 10 | | | 5 | 9 | | 11 | | 1 | |
| | 2 | 3 | | | 6 | 7 | | | 4 | | 8 | | | 10 | | | 5 | 9 | | 11 | | 1 | |
| | 2 | 5 | | | 6 | 7 | | | 4 | | 8 | 3 | | 10 | | | | 9 | | 11 | | 1 | |
| | 2 | 5 | | | 6 | | | | 4 | | 8 | 3 | | 10 | | | | 9 | | 11 | 7 | 1 | |
| | 2 | | 4 | | 6 | | | | | 7 | 8 | 3 | | 10 | | | 5 | 9 | | 11 | | 1 | |
| | 2 | | | | 6 | 7 | | | 4 | | 8 | 3 | | 10 | | | 5 | 9 | | 11 | | 1 | |
| | 2 | | | | 6 | 7 | 8 | | 4 | | | 3 | | 10 | | | 5 | 9 | | 11 | | 1 | |
| | | 2 | | | 6 | 7 | 8 | | 4 | | 10 | 3 | | 9 | | | 5 | | | 11 | | 1 | |
| | 2 | | | | 6 | 7 | 8 | | 4 | | | 3 | | 10 | | | 5 | | 9 | 11 | | 1 | |
| | 2 | | 3 | | 6 | 7 | | | 4 | | 8 | | | 10 | | | 5 | 9 | | 11 | | 1 | |
| | 2 | | | | 6 | 7 | | | 4 | | 8 | | | 10 | | | 5 | 9 | | 11 | | 1 | 3 |
| | | | | | 6 | 7 | | | 4 | 11 | 8 | 3 | | 10 | | | 5 | 9 | | | | 1 | 2 |
| | 2 | | | | 6 | 7 | | | 4 | | 8 | 3 | | 10 | | | 5 | 9 | | 11 | | 1 | |
| | 2 | | | | 6 | 7 | | | 4 | | 8 | 3 | | 10 | | | 5 | 9 | | 11 | | 1 | |
| | 2 | | | | 6 | 7 | | | 4 | | 8 | 3 | | 10 | | | 5 | 9 | | 11 | | 1 | |
| 4 | 38 | 26 | 20 | 13 | 37 | 15 | 8 | 2 | 35 | 21 | 35 | 22 | 2 | 40 | 18 | 10 | 19 | 29 | 4 | 24 | 18 | 20 | 2 |
| | | 1 | 2 | 1 | 1 | 2 | 2 | | | | 9 | | | 12 | | | 1 | 19 | 1 | 5 | 3 | | |

| Smith | Carr | Williams | Hall | Mason | Dobell | Spry | Young, J. | Christon | Mordue, W. | Fell | Mordue, J. | Errington | Coates | Mordue, T. | Rivers | Robertson | Mackey | Richardson, W. | Hodgson | Dixon | Briggs | Hickman | Harland |
|---|---|---|---|---|---|---|---|---|---|---|---|---|---|---|---|---|---|---|---|---|---|---|---|
| | 2 | 3 | | 5 | | | | | 10 | 11 | 8 | | | 9 | 1 | | 6 | | 4 | | 7 | | |
| | 1 | 1 | | 1 | | | | | 1 | 1 | 1 | | | 1 | 1 | | 1 | | 1 | | 1 | | |
| | | | | | | | | | | | | | | 1 | | | | | | | | | |

## League Table

| | P | W | D | L | F | A | Pts |
|---|---|---|---|---|---|---|---|
| Bradford City | 42 | 27 | 9 | 6 | 128 | 43 | 63 |
| Stockport County | 42 | 28 | 6 | 8 | 111 | 58 | 62 |
| Wrexham | 42 | 21 | 10 | 11 | 91 | 69 | 52 |
| Wigan Borough | 42 | 21 | 9 | 12 | 82 | 49 | 51 |
| Doncaster Rovers | 42 | 20 | 10 | 12 | 76 | 66 | 50 |
| Lincoln City | 42 | 21 | 6 | 15 | 91 | 67 | 48 |
| Tranmere Rovers | 42 | 22 | 3 | 17 | 79 | 77 | 47 |
| Carlisle United | 42 | 19 | 8 | 15 | 86 | 77 | 46 |
| Crewe Alexandra | 42 | 18 | 8 | 16 | 80 | 68 | 44 |
| South Shields | 42 | 18 | 8 | 16 | 83 | 74 | 44 |
| Chesterfield | 42 | 18 | 5 | 19 | 71 | 77 | 41 |
| Southport | 42 | 16 | 8 | 18 | 75 | 85 | 40 |
| Halifax Town | 42 | 13 | 13 | 16 | 63 | 62 | 39 |
| New Brighton | 42 | 15 | 9 | 18 | 64 | 71 | 39 |
| Nelson | 42 | 17 | 5 | 20 | 77 | 90 | 39 |
| Rotherham United | 42 | 15 | 9 | 18 | 60 | 77 | 39 |
| Rochdale | 42 | 13 | 10 | 19 | 79 | 96 | 36 |
| Accrington Stanley | 42 | 13 | 8 | 21 | 68 | 82 | 34 |
| Darlington | 42 | 13 | 7 | 22 | 64 | 88 | 33 |
| Barrow | 42 | 10 | 8 | 24 | 64 | 93 | 28 |
| Hartlepools United | 42 | 10 | 6 | 26 | 59 | 112 | 26 |
| Ashington | 42 | 8 | 7 | 27 | 45 | 115 | 23 |

# 1929-30

## Division Three North

Manager: Bill Norman

### Did you know that?

United suffered a record home defeat, 8–2 against Rochdale, for whom the colourfully named Tommy Tippett scored six goals.

Albert Pape finished as leading goalscorer with 21 in 37 League appearances in his only season with the club.

| Match No. | Date | Round | Venue | Opponents | Result | | Scorers | Attendance |
|---|---|---|---|---|---|---|---|---|
| 1 | Aug 31 | | (h) | Darlington | L | 2 - 5 | Pape 2 | 8,500 |
| 2 | Sep 2 | | (h) | Accrington Stanley | D | 2 - 2 | Pape 2 | 4,953 |
| 3 | 7 | | (a) | Southport | D | 1 - 1 | Pape | 4,107 |
| 4 | 9 | | (a) | Accrington Stanley | L | 0 - 3 | | 4,966 |
| 5 | 14 | | (a) | Doncaster Rovers | D | 0 - 0 | | 5,194 |
| 6 | 21 | | (h) | Chesterfield | D | 0 - 0 | | 4,925 |
| 7 | 28 | | (a) | Lincoln City | D | 2 - 2 | T.Mordue 2 | 5,792 |
| 8 | Oct 5 | | (h) | Tranmere Rovers | W | 2 - 0 | Pape 2 | 5,012 |
| 9 | 12 | | (a) | Halifax Town | D | 0 - 0 | | 4,138 |
| 10 | 19 | | (h) | Nelson | L | 1 - 2 | Barson | 5,695 |
| 11 | 26 | | (a) | Carlisle United | L | 2 - 5 | W.Mordue, Pape | 6,228 |
| 12 | Nov 2 | | (h) | Wigan Borough | W | 4 - 0 | Pape, T.Mordue, J.Mordue, Millar | 4,725 |
| 13 | 9 | | (a) | Wrexham | W | 5 - 3 | Pape, J.Mordue, Dixon, Miller 2 | 3,621 |
| 14 | 16 | | (h) | Barrow | W | 2 - 0 | Pape 2 | 4,253 |
| 15 | 23 | | (a) | Port Vale | L | 1 - 2 | Pape | 7,166 |
| 17 | Dec 21 | | (a) | Crewe Alexandra | L | 2 - 5 | J.Mordue, Jones (o.g.) | 3,898 |
| 18 | 25 | | (h) | South Shields | W | 2 - 1 | Pedwell, T.Mordue | 3,175 |
| 19 | 26 | | (a) | South Shields | W | 5 - 3 | Pape 2, Pedwell, J.Mordue, Millar | 4,118 |
| 20 | 28 | | (a) | Darlington | D | 0 - 0 | | 4,197 |
| 21 | Jan 1 | | (h) | Rotherham United | W | 5 - 1 | Thompson (pen), Pedwell 2, T.Mordue, Millar | 4,758 |
| 22 | 4 | | (h) | Southport | D | 1 - 1 | Thompson | 5,405 |
| 23 | 11 | | (h) | New Brighton | D | 1 - 1 | Pape | 3,472 |
| 24 | 18 | | (h) | Doncaster Rovers | W | 3 - 0 | Race 2, W.Mordue | 5,555 |
| 25 | 25 | | (a) | Chesterfield | L | 0 - 2 | | 5,888 |
| 26 | Feb 1 | | (h) | Lincoln City | W | 4 - 0 | Pape 2, T.Mordue, Harrison | 1,716 |
| 27 | 8 | | (a) | Tranmere Rovers | L | 1 - 7 | Harrison | 3,500 |
| 28 | 15 | | (h) | Halifax Town | W | 3 - 0 | Pedwell 2, Thompson | 3,022 |
| 29 | 22 | | (a) | Nelson | L | 2 - 3 | T.Mordue, Pedwell | 2,862 |
| 30 | Mar 1 | | (h) | Carlisle United | W | 1 - 0 | Thompson | 4,816 |
| 31 | 3 | | (a) | Stockport County | L | 1 - 5 | Pedwell | 4,674 |
| 32 | 8 | | (a) | Wigan Borough | W | 3 - 1 | Thompson 3 | 2,709 |
| 33 | 15 | | (h) | Wrexham | W | 5 - 0 | Pedwell 2, Dixon, Pape 2 | 3,200 |
| 34 | 22 | | (a) | Barrow | L | 0 - 3 | | 4,312 |
| 35 | 29 | | (h) | Port Vale | W | 2 - 0 | Pedwell, Thompson | 7,473 |
| 36 | Apr 2 | | (h) | York City | W | 3 - 1 | Pape, Barson, Thompson | 4,390 |
| 37 | 5 | | (a) | New Brighton | D | 0 - 0 | | 4,415 |
| 38 | 12 | | (h) | Stockport County | L | 0 - 1 | | 8,239 |
| 39 | 18 | | (a) | Rochdale | D | 1 - 1 | Pedwell | 2,441 |
| 40 | 19 | | (a) | York City | L | 1 - 4 | J.Mordue | 2,563 |
| 41 | 21 | | (h) | Rochdale | L | 2 - 8 | Pedwell 2 | 3,655 |
| 42 | 26 | | (h) | Crewe Alexandra | W | 5 - 1 | T.Mordue 2, J.Mordue 2, Pedwell | 1,944 |
| 43 | May 3 | | (a) | Rotherham United | W | 4 - 0 | Pedwell 2, Thompson, J.Mordue | 3,477 |
| Final Position : 8th in Division Three North | | | | | | | | Apps. |
| | | | | | | | 1 own goal | Goals |

**FA Cup**

| Match No. | Date | Round | Venue | Opponents | Result | | Scorers | Attendance |
|---|---|---|---|---|---|---|---|---|
| 16 | Nov 30 | R1 | (a) | Scunthorpe United | L | 0 - 1 | | 5,305 |
| | | | | | | | | Apps. |
| | | | | | | | | Goals |

| Rivers | Mason | Bowron | Mordue, W. | Barson | Dobell | Race | Stephenson | Pape | Mordue, J. | Miller | Dixon | Errington | Mordue, T. | Harland | Mackey | Butler | Bell | Pedwell | Nobbs | Thompson | Thornton | Tither | Harrison |
|---|---|---|---|---|---|---|---|---|---|---|---|---|---|---|---|---|---|---|---|---|---|---|---|
| 1 | 2 | 3 | 4 | 5 | 6 | 7 | 8 | 9 | 10 | 11 | | | | | | | | | | | | | |
| 1 | 2 | 3 | 4 | 5 | 6 | | 8 | 9 | 10 | 7 | 11 | | | | | | | | | | | | |
| 1 | | 2 | 4 | 5 | 6 | | 8 | 9 | | 7 | 11 | 3 | 10 | | | | | | | | | | |
| 1 | | 2 | 4 | 5 | 6 | | 8 | 9 | | 7 | 11 | 3 | 10 | | | | | | | | | | |
| 1 | | | 4 | | 6 | | 8 | 9 | | 7 | 11 | 3 | 10 | 2 | 5 | | | | | | | | |
| 1 | | | 7 | | 6 | | 8 | 9 | | | 11 | 3 | 10 | 2 | 5 | 4 | | | | | | | |
| 1 | | 2 | 4 | | 6 | 7 | 8 | 9 | | | 11 | 3 | 10 | | 5 | | | | | | | | |
| 1 | | 2 | 6 | | | | 8 | 9 | | 7 | 11 | 3 | 10 | | 5 | 4 | | | | | | | |
| 1 | | 2 | 4 | | 6 | | 8 | 9 | | 11 | | 3 | 10 | | 5 | 7 | | | | | | | |
| 1 | | 2 | 4 | 5 | | | 8 | 9 | | | 11 | 3 | 10 | | 6 | 7 | | | | | | | |
| 1 | | 2 | 4 | | 6 | 7 | 8 | 9 | | | 11 | 3 | 10 | | 5 | | | | | | | | |
| 1 | | 2 | | | 4 | | | 9 | 8 | 7 | 11 | 3 | 10 | | 5 | | 6 | | | | | | |
| 1 | | 2 | 4 | | | | | 9 | 8 | 7 | 11 | 3 | 10 | | 5 | | 6 | | | | | | |
| 1 | 3 | 2 | 4 | | | | | 9 | 8 | 7 | | | 10 | | 5 | | 6 | 11 | | | | | |
| 1 | | 2 | 4 | | | | | 9 | 8 | 7 | | 3 | 10 | | 5 | | 6 | 11 | | | | | |
| 1 | | 5 | 4 | | | | | 9 | 8 | 7 | | 3 | 10 | 2 | | 6 | | 11 | | | | | |
| 1 | | 2 | 6 | | | | | 9 | 8 | 7 | | 3 | 10 | | | 4 | | 11 | 5 | | | | |
| 1 | | 2 | 6 | | | | | 9 | 8 | 7 | | 3 | 10 | | | 4 | | 11 | 5 | | | | |
| 1 | | 2 | 6 | | | | | 9 | 8 | 7 | | 3 | 10 | | | 4 | | 11 | 5 | | | | |
| 1 | 3 | 2 | 6 | | | | | | 8 | 7 | | | 10 | | | 4 | | 11 | 5 | 9 | | | |
| 1 | | 2 | 6 | | | | | | 8 | 7 | | 3 | 10 | | | 4 | | 11 | 5 | 9 | | | |
| 1 | 3 | 2 | 6 | | | | | 9 | 8 | 7 | | | 10 | | | 4 | | 11 | 5 | | | | |
| 1 | 3 | 2 | 8 | | 9 | 7 | | | | | | | 10 | | | 4 | | 11 | | | 5 | 6 | |
| 1 | 2 | 3 | 6 | | | 7 | | 9 | | | | | 10 | | | 5 | | 11 | | | 4 | | 8 |
| 1 | 2 | 3 | 6 | | | 7 | | 9 | | | | | 10 | | | 4 | | 11 | | | 5 | | 8 |
| 1 | 2 | 3 | 6 | | | 7 | | 9 | | | | | 10 | | | 4 | | 11 | | | 5 | | 8 |
| 1 | 2 | 3 | 6 | | | 7 | | 9 | | | | | 10 | | | 4 | | 11 | | 8 | 5 | | |
| 1 | | 3 | 6 | | | 7 | | 9 | | | | | 10 | 2 | | 4 | | 11 | | 8 | 5 | | |
| 1 | | 3 | 6 | | | 7 | | 9 | | | | | 10 | 2 | | 4 | | 11 | | 8 | 5 | | |
| 1 | | 3 | 6 | | | 7 | | 9 | | | | | 10 | 2 | | 4 | | 11 | | 8 | 5 | | |
| 1 | | 2 | | | | 7 | | 9 | | | 10 | 3 | | | | 6 | | 11 | 5 | 8 | 4 | | |
| 1 | | 2 | | | | | | 9 | 7 | | 10 | 3 | | | | 6 | | 11 | 5 | 8 | 4 | | |
| 1 | | 2 | | | | | | 9 | 7 | | 10 | 3 | | | | 6 | | 11 | 5 | 8 | 4 | | |
| 1 | | 2 | | 5 | | | | 9 | 7 | | | 3 | 10 | | | 6 | | 11 | | 8 | 4 | | |
| 1 | | 2 | | 5 | | | | 9 | 7 | | | 3 | 10 | | | 6 | | 11 | | 8 | 4 | | |
| 1 | | 2 | | | | | | 9 | 7 | | 11 | 3 | 10 | | | 6 | | | 5 | 8 | | | 4 |
| 1 | | 2 | | 5 | | | | 9 | 7 | | | 3 | 10 | | | 6 | | 11 | | 8 | 4 | | |
| 1 | | 2 | | | | | | 9 | 7 | | | 3 | 10 | | | 6 | | 11 | 5 | 8 | 4 | | |
| 1 | | 2 | | | | | | 9 | 7 | | 11 | 3 | 10 | | | 6 | | | 5 | 8 | 4 | | |
| 1 | | 2 | | 5 | | | | 9 | 7 | | | 3 | 10 | | | 6 | | 11 | | 8 | 4 | | |
| 1 | | 2 | | | | 7 | | | 8 | | | 3 | 10 | | | 6 | | 11 | 5 | 9 | 4 | | |
| 1 | | 2 | | | | 7 | | | 8 | | | 3 | 10 | | | 6 | | 11 | 5 | 9 | 4 | | |
| 42 | 10 | 40 | 29 | 9 | 11 | 14 | 11 | 37 | 24 | 18 | 16 | 29 | 37 | 6 | 11 | 31 | 4 | 27 | 14 | 18 | 19 | 1 | 4 |
| | | | 2 | 2 | | 2 | | 21 | 8 | 5 | 2 | | 9 | | | | | 17 | | 10 | | | 2 |

| Rivers | Mason | Bowron | Mordue, W. | Barson | Dobell | Race | Stephenson | Pape | Mordue, J. | Miller | Dixon | Errington | Mordue, T. | Harland | Mackey | Butler | Bell | Pedwell | Nobbs | Thompson | Thornton | Tither | Harrison |
|---|---|---|---|---|---|---|---|---|---|---|---|---|---|---|---|---|---|---|---|---|---|---|---|
| 1 | | 2 | 4 | | | | | 9 | 8 | 7 | | 3 | 10 | | 5 | | 6 | 11 | | | | | |
| 1 | | 1 | 1 | | | | | 1 | 1 | 1 | | 1 | 1 | | 1 | | 1 | 1 | | | | | |

## League Table

| | P | W | D | L | F | A | Pts |
|---|---|---|---|---|---|---|---|
| Port Vale | 42 | 30 | 7 | 5 | 103 | 37 | 67 |
| Stockport County | 42 | 28 | 7 | 7 | 106 | 44 | 63 |
| Darlington | 42 | 22 | 6 | 14 | 108 | 73 | 50 |
| Chesterfield | 42 | 22 | 6 | 14 | 76 | 56 | 50 |
| Lincoln City | 42 | 17 | 14 | 11 | 83 | 61 | 48 |
| York City | 42 | 15 | 16 | 11 | 77 | 64 | 46 |
| South Shields | 42 | 18 | 10 | 14 | 77 | 74 | 46 |
| Hartlepools United | 42 | 17 | 11 | 14 | 81 | 74 | 45 |
| Southport | 42 | 15 | 13 | 14 | 81 | 74 | 43 |
| Rochdale | 42 | 18 | 7 | 17 | 89 | 91 | 43 |
| Crewe Alexandra | 42 | 17 | 8 | 17 | 82 | 71 | 42 |
| Tranmere Rovers | 42 | 16 | 9 | 17 | 83 | 86 | 41 |
| New Brighton | 42 | 16 | 8 | 18 | 69 | 79 | 40 |
| Doncaster Rovers | 42 | 15 | 9 | 18 | 62 | 69 | 39 |
| Carlisle United | 42 | 16 | 7 | 19 | 90 | 101 | 39 |
| Accrington Stanley | 42 | 14 | 9 | 19 | 84 | 81 | 37 |
| Wrexham | 42 | 13 | 8 | 21 | 67 | 88 | 34 |
| Wigan Borough | 42 | 13 | 7 | 22 | 60 | 88 | 33 |
| Nelson | 42 | 13 | 7 | 22 | 51 | 80 | 33 |
| Rotherham United | 42 | 11 | 8 | 23 | 67 | 113 | 30 |
| Halifax Town | 42 | 10 | 8 | 24 | 44 | 79 | 28 |
| Barrow | 42 | 11 | 5 | 26 | 41 | 98 | 27 |

# 1930-31

## Division Three North

Manager: Bill Norman

### Did you know that?

Harry Simmons scored five goals in the 6–1 New Year's Day triumph over Wigan Borough. Bobby Folland equalled his record in 1961.

The first sub-1,000 home attendance was recorded against Crewe Alexandra, a 2–0 win.

United narrowly avoid a third application for re-election, finishing in 20th position above Rochdale by virtue of a superior goal average.

| Match No. | Date | Round | Venue | Opponents | Result | | Scorers | Attendance |
|---|---|---|---|---|---|---|---|---|
| 1 | Aug 30 | | (a) | Halifax Town | L | 1 - 3 | Thornton | 8,051 |
| 2 | Sep 1 | | (h) | Southport | L | 0 - 2 | | 4,123 |
| 3 | 6 | | (h) | New Brighton | W | 4 - 1 | Thompson, Thornton 2 (1 pen), Robson | 4,224 |
| 4 | 10 | | (a) | Wigan Borough | L | 2 - 3 | Thompson 2 | 7,852 |
| 5 | 13 | | (a) | Stockport County | L | 1 - 3 | Thornton (pen) | 6,372 |
| 6 | 20 | | (h) | Gateshead | L | 2 - 3 | Pedwell, Cowan | 2,100 |
| 7 | 27 | | (a) | Doncaster Rovers | D | 1 - 1 | J.Mordue | 3,927 |
| 8 | Oct 4 | | (h) | Hull City | L | 1 - 3 | Cowan | 6,991 |
| 9 | 11 | | (a) | Lincoln City | L | 0 - 1 | | 7,516 |
| 10 | 18 | | (a) | Accrington Stanley | W | 2 - 0 | J.Mordue, Thornton (pen) | 3,344 |
| 11 | 25 | | (h) | Barrow | W | 3 - 2 | Simmons, Pedwell 2 | 3,892 |
| 12 | Nov 1 | | (a) | Crewe Alexandra | L | 1 - 2 | Simmons | 2,697 |
| 13 | 8 | | (h) | Wrexham | W | 2 - 1 | Pedwell, Thompson | 4,419 |
| 14 | 15 | | (a) | Tranmere Rovers | L | 4 - 5 | Waller 2, Thayne, Pedwell | 5,084 |
| 15 | 22 | | (h) | Carlisle United | L | 3 - 5 | J.Mordue, Simmons, Pedwell | 2,140 |
| 17 | Dec 6 | | (h) | Rotherham United | W | 4 - 2 | Waller 3, T.Mordue | 3,020 |
| 18 | 13 | | (a) | Chesterfield | L | 0 - 3 | | 4,745 |
| 19 | 20 | | (h) | Rochdale | W | 4 - 0 | Simmons, J.Mordue, T.Mordue, Pedwell | 3,083 |
| 20 | 25 | | (h) | Nelson | W | 4 - 0 | Thompson 2, Thornton, Powell | 4,518 |
| 21 | 26 | | (a) | Nelson | D | 1 - 1 | T.Mordue | 2,267 |
| 22 | 27 | | (h) | Halifax Town | W | 2 - 1 | Thompson, Simmons | 3,672 |
| 23 | Jan 1 | | (h) | Wigan Borough | W | 6 - 1 | Simmons 5, J.Mordue | 5,397 |
| 24 | 3 | | (a) | New Brighton | L | 0 - 1 | | 2,892 |
| 25 | 17 | | (h) | Stockport County | L | 1 - 2 | Thayne | 4,624 |
| 26 | 24 | | (a) | Gateshead | D | 0 - 0 | | 5,649 |
| 27 | 31 | | (h) | Doncaster Rovers | L | 0 - 2 | | 2,835 |
| 28 | Feb 4 | | (a) | York City | L | 2 - 4 | J.Mordue, Simmons | 1,793 |
| 29 | 11 | | (h) | Lincoln City | L | 0 - 3 | | 3,706 |
| 30 | 21 | | (h) | Accrington Stanley | D | 3 - 3 | T.Mordue 2, Dickenson (pen) | 2,370 |
| 31 | 28 | | (a) | Barrow | L | 0 - 4 | | 6,206 |
| 32 | Mar 7 | | (h) | Crewe Alexandra | W | 2 - 0 | Simmons 2 | 853 |
| 33 | 14 | | (a) | Wrexham | L | 0 - 2 | | 4,139 |
| 34 | 21 | | (h) | Tranmere Rovers | L | 1 - 2 | Thompson | 2,948 |
| 35 | 28 | | (a) | Carlisle United | L | 0 - 3 | | 3,303 |
| 36 | Apr 3 | | (h) | Darlington | D | 1 - 1 | Simmons | 2,528 |
| 37 | 4 | | (h) | York City | W | 3 - 0 | Pedwell, Simmons, Robinson | 3,329 |
| 38 | 6 | | (a) | Darlington | L | 2 - 4 | Pedwell, Simmons | 4,478 |
| 39 | 11 | | (a) | Rotherham United | D | 1 - 1 | Pedwell | 4,182 |
| 40 | 18 | | (h) | Chesterfield | L | 1 - 3 | Thayne (pen) | 1,434 |
| 41 | 20 | | (a) | Hull City | L | 0 - 5 | | 3,221 |
| 42 | 25 | | (a) | Rochdale | W | 2 - 1 | Simmons, Thompson | 1,586 |
| 43 | May 2 | | (a) | Southport | L | 0 - 2 | | 1,986 |

Final Position : 20th in Division Three North

Apps.
Goals

**FA Cup**

| Match No. | Date | Round | Venue | Opponents | Result | | Scorers | Attendance |
|---|---|---|---|---|---|---|---|---|
| 16 | Nov 29 | R1 | (h) | Stockport County | L | 2 - 3 | Dickenson, Waller | 6,038 |

Apps.
Goals

| Rivers | Mason | Bowron | Thornton | Nobbs | Buller | Race | Thompson | Hewitt | Mordue, T. | Pedwell | Errington | Harrison | Dickenson | Mordue, J. | Robson | Thayne | Cowan | Wilson | Harland | Dixon | Simmons | Waller | Swift | Ferguson | Robinson | Tither |
|---|---|---|---|---|---|---|---|---|---|---|---|---|---|---|---|---|---|---|---|---|---|---|---|---|---|---|
| 1 | 2 | 3 | 4 | 5 | 6 | 7 | 8 | 9 | 10 | 11 | | | | | | | | | | | | | | | | |
| 1 | 2 | 3 | 4 | 5 | 6 | 7 | 8 | 9 | 10 | 11 | | | | | | | | | | | | | | | | |
| 1 | | 2 | 8 | | 6 | | 9 | | | 11 | 3 | 4 | 5 | 7 | 10 | | | | | | | | | | | |
| 1 | | 2 | 4 | | 6 | | 9 | | | 11 | 3 | 8 | | 7 | 10 | 5 | | | | | | | | | | |
| 1 | | 2 | 4 | | 6 | | 9 | | | 11 | 3 | 8 | | 7 | 10 | 5 | | | | | | | | | | |
| 1 | | 2 | 4 | | 6 | 7 | 9 | | | 11 | 3 | | | 8 | | 5 | 10 | | | | | | | | | |
| 1 | | 2 | 4 | | 6 | | 8 | 9 | | 11 | | | | 7 | | 5 | 10 | 3 | | | | | | | | |
| 1 | | 3 | 4 | | 6 | | 8 | 9 | | | | | | 7 | | 5 | 10 | | 2 | 11 | | | | | | |
| 1 | | 3 | | | | | 8 | 9 | 10 | 11 | | 4 | 6 | 7 | | 5 | | | 2 | | | | | | | |
| 1 | | 3 | 4 | | | | 9 | | 10 | 11 | | | 6 | 7 | | 5 | | | 2 | | 8 | | | | | |
| 1 | | 3 | 4 | | | | 9 | | 10 | 11 | | | 6 | 7 | | 5 | | | 2 | | 8 | | | | | |
| 1 | | 3 | 4 | 5 | | | 10 | | | 11 | | | 6 | 7 | | 9 | | | 2 | | 8 | | | | | |
| 1 | | 3 | 4 | | | | 10 | | | 11 | | | 6 | 7 | | 5 | | | 2 | | 8 | 9 | | | | |
| 1 | | 3 | 4 | | | | | | 10 | 11 | | | 6 | 7 | | 5 | | | 2 | | 8 | 9 | | | | |
| 1 | | 3 | 4 | | | | 10 | | | 11 | | | 6 | 7 | | 5 | | | 2 | | 8 | 9 | | | | |
| | 3 | 2 | 4 | 5 | | | | | 10 | 11 | | | 6 | 7 | | | | | | | 8 | 9 | 1 | | | |
| 1 | 3 | 2 | 4 | 5 | 6 | | | | 10 | 11 | | | | 7 | | | | | | | 8 | 9 | | | | |
| 1 | 3 | 2 | 4 | | 6 | | 8 | | 10 | 11 | | | 5 | 7 | | | | | | | 9 | | | | | |
| 1 | | 2 | 4 | 5 | 3 | | 8 | | 10 | 11 | | | 6 | 7 | | | | | | | 9 | | | | | |
| 1 | | 2 | 4 | | 3 | | 8 | | 10 | 11 | | | 6 | 7 | | 5 | | | | | 9 | | | | | |
| 1 | | 2 | | 4 | 3 | | 8 | | 10 | 11 | | | 6 | 7 | | 5 | | | | | 9 | | | | | |
| 1 | | 2 | | 4 | 3 | | 8 | | | 11 | | | 6 | 7 | | 5 | | | | 10 | 9 | | | | | |
| 1 | | 2 | | 4 | 3 | | 8 | | | 11 | | | 6 | 7 | | 5 | | | | 10 | 9 | | | | | |
| 1 | | 2 | | 4 | 3 | | 8 | | 10 | 11 | | | 6 | 7 | | 5 | | | | | 9 | | | | | |
| 1 | | 2 | | 4 | 3 | | 8 | | 10 | 11 | | | 6 | 7 | | 5 | | | | | 9 | | | | | |
| 1 | | 2 | | 4 | 3 | | | | 10 | 11 | | | 6 | 7 | | 5 | | | | | 9 | | | 8 | | |
| 1 | | 2 | | 4 | 3 | | 8 | | 10 | 11 | | | 6 | 7 | | 5 | | | | | 9 | | | | | |
| 1 | | 2 | | | 3 | | 8 | | 10 | 11 | | 4 | 6 | 7 | | 5 | | | | | 9 | | | | | |
| | | 2 | | 5 | 3 | | 8 | | 10 | | | 4 | 6 | 7 | | | | | | | 9 | | 1 | | 11 | |
| | | 2 | 4 | | 3 | | 9 | | 10 | | | | | 7 | | 5 | | | | 11 | 8 | | 1 | | | 6 |
| 1 | | 2 | 4 | | 3 | | 9 | | 10 | | | | | 7 | | 5 | | | | 11 | 8 | | | | | 6 |
| 1 | | 2 | 6 | 4 | | | 9 | | 10 | 11 | 3 | | | 7 | | 5 | | | | | 8 | | | | | |
| 1 | | | 6 | 4 | 2 | 7 | 9 | | 10 | 11 | 3 | | | | | 5 | | | | | 8 | | | | | |
| 1 | | | 6 | 4 | 2 | 7 | 9 | | 10 | 11 | 3 | | | | | 5 | | | | | 8 | | | | | |
| 1 | | 2 | 6 | | 4 | | 9 | | 10 | 11 | 3 | | | | | 5 | | | | | 8 | | | | 7 | |
| 1 | | 2 | | 5 | 4 | | 8 | 9 | | 11 | 3 | | 6 | | | | | | | | 10 | | | | 7 | |
| 1 | | 2 | | 5 | 4 | | 8 | 9 | | 11 | 3 | | 6 | | | | | | | | 10 | | | | 7 | |
| 1 | | | 6 | 4 | 2 | | | 9 | | 11 | 3 | | | 8 | | 5 | | | | | 10 | | | | 7 | |
| 1 | | 2 | | 4 | 6 | | 8 | 9 | | 11 | 3 | | | 7 | | 5 | | | | 10 | | | | | | |
| 1 | | | 6 | 4 | 2 | | 8 | 9 | | 11 | 3 | | | | | 5 | | | | 10 | | | | | 7 | |
| 1 | 2 | | 4 | 5 | 6 | | 8 | | | | 3 | | | 7 | | | | | | 11 | 10 | 9 | | | | |
| 1 | 2 | | 4 | 5 | 6 | | 8 | | | | 3 | | | 7 | | | | | | 11 | 10 | 9 | | | | |
| 39 | 7 | 36 | 29 | 24 | 33 | 5 | 37 | 10 | 24 | 36 | 15 | 6 | 23 | 34 | 3 | 30 | 3 | 1 | 8 | 9 | 31 | 7 | 3 | 1 | 6 | 2 |
| | | | 6 | | | | 9 | | 5 | 11 | | | 1 | 6 | 1 | 3 | 2 | | | | 17 | 5 | | | 1 | |

| Rivers | Mason | Bowron | Thornton | Nobbs | Buller | Race | Thompson | Hewitt | Mordue, T. | Pedwell | Errington | Harrison | Dickenson | Mordue, J. | Robson | Thayne | Cowan | Wilson | Harland | Dixon | Simmons | Waller | Swift | Ferguson | Robinson | Tither |
|---|---|---|---|---|---|---|---|---|---|---|---|---|---|---|---|---|---|---|---|---|---|---|---|---|---|---|
| 1 | 3 | 2 | 4 | | | | | | 10 | 11 | | | 6 | 7 | | 5 | | | | | 8 | 9 | | | | |
| 1 | 1 | 1 | 1 | | | | | | 1 | 1 | | | 1 | 1 | | 1 | | | | | 1 | 1 | | | | |
| | | | | | | | | | | | | | 1 | | | | | | | | | 1 | | | | |

## League Table

| | P | W | D | L | F | A | Pts |
|---|---|---|---|---|---|---|---|
| Chesterfield | 42 | 26 | 6 | 10 | 102 | 57 | 58 |
| Lincoln City | 42 | 25 | 7 | 10 | 102 | 59 | 57 |
| Wrexham | 42 | 21 | 12 | 9 | 94 | 62 | 54 |
| Tranmere Rovers | 42 | 24 | 6 | 12 | 111 | 74 | 54 |
| Southport | 42 | 22 | 9 | 11 | 88 | 56 | 53 |
| Hull City | 42 | 20 | 10 | 12 | 99 | 55 | 50 |
| Stockport County | 42 | 20 | 9 | 13 | 77 | 61 | 49 |
| Carlisle United | 42 | 20 | 5 | 17 | 98 | 81 | 45 |
| Gateshead | 42 | 16 | 13 | 13 | 71 | 73 | 45 |
| Wigan Borough | 42 | 19 | 5 | 18 | 76 | 86 | 43 |
| Darlington | 42 | 16 | 10 | 16 | 71 | 59 | 42 |
| York City | 42 | 18 | 6 | 18 | 85 | 82 | 42 |
| Accrington Stanley | 42 | 15 | 9 | 18 | 84 | 108 | 39 |
| Rotherham United | 42 | 13 | 12 | 17 | 81 | 83 | 38 |
| Doncaster Rovers | 42 | 13 | 11 | 18 | 65 | 65 | 37 |
| Barrow | 42 | 15 | 7 | 20 | 68 | 89 | 37 |
| Halifax Town | 42 | 13 | 9 | 20 | 55 | 89 | 35 |
| Crewe Alexandra | 42 | 14 | 6 | 22 | 66 | 93 | 34 |
| New Brighton | 42 | 13 | 7 | 22 | 49 | 76 | 33 |
| Hartlepools United | 42 | 12 | 6 | 24 | 67 | 86 | 30 |
| Rochdale | 42 | 12 | 6 | 24 | 62 | 107 | 30 |
| Nelson | 42 | 6 | 7 | 29 | 43 | 113 | 19 |

# 1931-32

## Division Three North

Manager: Jackie Carr and Bill Norman

### Did you know that?

Johnny Wigham made his debut on 12 September against Darlington. He went on to score a record 104 goals for the club in all competitions, which was later equalled by Ken Johnson.

'Pools conceded 100 goals in 40 League games, yet still finished a respectable 13th, thanks to winning the last five games and scoring 21 goals in the process.

| Match No. | Date | Round | Venue | Opponents | Result | | Scorers | Attendance |
|---|---|---|---|---|---|---|---|---|
| 1 | Aug 29 | | (h) | Carlisle United | D | 2 - 2 | Lumley 2 | 5,295 |
| 2 | 31 | | (a) | Lincoln City | L | 0 - 6 | | 6,539 |
| 3 | Sep 9 | | (h) | Chester | D | 2 - 2 | Mordue, Thompson | 4,717 |
| 4 | 12 | | (h) | Darlington | D | 3 - 3 | Hamilton, Mordue, Lumley | 5,048 |
| 5 | 16 | | (a) | Chester | W | 3 - 2 | Lumley 3 | 8,417 |
| 6 | 19 | | (a) | Halifax Town | L | 0 - 2 | | 4,396 |
| 7 | 23 | | (h) | Southport | W | 2 - 1 | Thompson, Mordue | 3,719 |
| 8 | 26 | | (h) | Walsall | W | 4 - 3 | Carr, Mordue, Thompson, Lumley | 4,873 |
| 9 | Oct 3 | | (a) | Gateshead | L | 1 - 3 | Dixon | 10,223 |
| 10 | 10 | | (h) | New Brighton | W | 1 - 0 | Dixon | 5,094 |
| 11 | 17 | | (h) | Wrexham | L | 0 - 1 | | 4,600 |
| 12 | 24 | | (a) | Accrington Stanley | L | 0 - 5 | | 2,978 |
| 13 | 31 | | (h) | Stockport County | D | 2 - 2 | Buller, Waller | 3,502 |
| 14 | Nov 7 | | (a) | Rotherham United | W | 2 - 1 | Waller, Thornton | 3,294 |
| 15 | 14 | | (h) | Tranmere Rovers | L | 0 - 5 | | 3,653 |
| 16 | 21 | | (a) | York City | L | 1 - 3 | Dixon | 4,113 |
| 18 | Dec 5 | | (a) | Doncaster Rovers | W | 3 - 1 | Mordue, Lumley, Buller | 3,265 |
| 19 | 12 | | (h) | Rochdale | W | 3 - 0 | Hewitt 2, Dixon | 3,085 |
| 20 | 19 | | (a) | Crewe Alexandra | L | 0 - 6 | | 3,815 |
| 21 | 25 | | (a) | Hull City | L | 1 - 3 | Lumley | 13,060 |
| 22 | 26 | | (h) | Hull City | L | 2 - 3 | Thornton (pen), Lumley | 5,897 |
| 23 | Jan 2 | | (a) | Carlisle United | L | 2 - 3 | Wigham, Lumley | 3,867 |
| 24 | 9 | | (h) | Crewe Alexandra | W | 3 - 1 | Wigham 2, Pedwell | 2,807 |
| 25 | 23 | | (a) | Darlington | L | 3 - 6 | Lumley, Wigham, Brown (pen) | 2,812 |
| 26 | 30 | | (h) | Halifax Town | W | 4 - 1 | Lumley 3, Wigham | 2,961 |
| 27 | Feb 6 | | (a) | Walsall | W | 3 - 2 | Wigham 2, Lumley | 2,570 |
| 28 | 13 | | (h) | Gateshead | L | 1 - 2 | Wigham | 3,382 |
| 29 | 20 | | (a) | New Brighton | D | 1 - 1 | Lumley | 2,524 |
| 30 | 27 | | (a) | Wrexham | L | 3 - 5 | Brown, Lumley, Pedwell | 3,288 |
| 31 | Mar 5 | | (h) | Accrington Stanley | W | 1 - 0 | Hewitt | 3,051 |
| 32 | 12 | | (a) | Stockport County | L | 2 - 3 | Pedwell, Nobbs | 4,400 |
| 33 | 19 | | (h) | Rotherham United | L | 1 - 4 | Brown (pen) | 2,967 |
| 34 | 25 | | (h) | Barrow | L | 0 - 2 | | 4,713 |
| 35 | 26 | | (a) | Tranmere Rovers | L | 0 - 5 | | 4,538 |
| 36 | 28 | | (a) | Barrow | L | 1 - 4 | Wigham | 5,632 |
| 37 | Apr 2 | | (h) | York City | W | 7 - 2 | Hewitt 3, Dixon 3, Wigham | 2,590 |
| 38 | 9 | | (a) | Southport | W | 2 - 1 | Wigham 2 | 2,414 |
| 39 | 16 | | (h) | Doncaster Rovers | W | 5 - 0 | Hewitt, Pedwell 2, Wigham, Tither (pen) | 3,520 |
| 40 | 23 | | (a) | Rochdale | W | 3 - 1 | Thornton, Dixon 2 | 1,379 |
| 41 | May 7 | | (h) | Lincoln City | W | 4 - 3 | Hewitt 3, Hardy | 3,723 |

Final Position : 13th in Division Three North

Apps.
Goals

**FA Cup**

| Match No. | Date | Round | Venue | Opponents | Result | | Scorers | Attendance |
|---|---|---|---|---|---|---|---|---|
| 17 | Nov 28 | R1 | (a) | Chester | L | 1 - 4 | Wigham | 9,000 |

Apps.
Goals

| Rivers | Bowron | Allen | Thornton | Hamilton | Buller | Mordue, J. | Carr | Lumley | Dixon | Pedwell | Shotton | Robinson | Thayne | Thompson | Wigham | Nobbs | Hewitt | Brown | Mason | Waller | Harland | Owbridge | Jarps | Tither | Hardy |
|---|---|---|---|---|---|---|---|---|---|---|---|---|---|---|---|---|---|---|---|---|---|---|---|---|---|
| 1 | 2 | 3 | 4 | 5 | 6 | 7 | 8 | 9 | 10 | 11 | | | | | | | | | | | | | | | |
| 1 | 2 | | 4 | 5 | 6 | 7 | | 9 | 10 | 11 | 3 | 8 | | | | | | | | | | | | | |
| 1 | 2 | | 6 | 4 | | 7 | | 9 | 11 | | 3 | | 5 | 8 | 10 | | | | | | | | | | |
| 1 | 2 | | 6 | 4 | | 7 | | 9 | 11 | | 3 | | | 8 | 10 | 5 | | | | | | | | | |
| 1 | 2 | | 6 | 4 | | 7 | | 9 | 11 | | 3 | | | 10 | | 5 | 8 | | | | | | | | |
| 1 | 2 | | 4 | 5 | 6 | 7 | | 9 | 11 | | 3 | | | 10 | | | 8 | | | | | | | | |
| 1 | 2 | | 6 | 4 | | 7 | | 9 | 11 | | 3 | | | 8 | | 5 | | 10 | | | | | | | |
| 1 | 2 | | 6 | 4 | | 7 | 10 | 9 | 11 | | 3 | | | 8 | | 5 | | | | | | | | | |
| 1 | 2 | | 6 | | 4 | 7 | 10 | 9 | 11 | | 3 | | | 8 | | 5 | | | | | | | | | |
| 1 | 2 | | 6 | | 4 | 7 | 10 | | 11 | | | | | 9 | | 5 | | 8 | 3 | | | | | | |
| 1 | 2 | | 6 | 4 | | 7 | 10 | | 11 | | 3 | | | 8 | | 5 | 9 | | | | | | | | |
| 1 | 2 | | 6 | | 4 | 7 | 8 | 9 | 11 | | 3 | | | 10 | | 5 | | | | | | | | | |
| 1 | 2 | | | 6 | 7 | | 8 | | 11 | | 3 | | 5 | | 10 | 4 | | | | 9 | | | | | |
| 1 | 2 | | 6 | | 7 | | 8 | | 11 | | 3 | | 5 | | 10 | 4 | | | | 9 | | | | | |
| 1 | 2 | | 6 | | 7 | | 8 | | 11 | | 3 | | 5 | | 10 | 4 | | | | 9 | | | | | |
| 1 | | | 4 | | 6 | 7 | 8 | | 11 | | 3 | | | 10 | | 5 | 9 | | | | 2 | | | | |
| | 2 | | 6 | | 4 | 7 | | 9 | 11 | | 3 | | | | 10 | 5 | 8 | | | | | 1 | | | |
| | 2 | | 6 | | 4 | 7 | | 9 | 11 | | 3 | | | | 10 | 5 | 8 | | | | | 1 | | | |
| | 2 | | 6 | | 4 | 7 | | 9 | 11 | | 3 | | | | 10 | 5 | 8 | | | | | 1 | | | |
| | 2 | | 6 | | 4 | 7 | | 9 | 11 | | 3 | | | | 10 | 5 | 8 | | | | | | 1 | | |
| | 2 | | 6 | | 4 | | | 7 | 11 | | 3 | | | 9 | 10 | 5 | 8 | | | | | | 1 | | |
| | 2 | | 6 | | 4 | 7 | | 9 | 11 | | 3 | | | | 10 | 5 | 8 | | | | | 1 | | | |
| 1 | 2 | | | 5 | | | | 9 | 7 | 11 | 3 | | | | 8 | 4 | | 10 | | | | | | 6 | |
| 1 | 2 | | | 5 | | | | 9 | 7 | 11 | 3 | | | | 8 | 4 | | 10 | | | | | | 6 | |
| 1 | 2 | | 6 | 5 | | 7 | | 9 | | 11 | 3 | | | | 8 | 4 | | 10 | | | | | | | |
| 1 | 2 | | | 5 | | | | 9 | 7 | 11 | 3 | | | | 8 | 4 | | 10 | | | | | | 6 | |
| 1 | 2 | | | 5 | | | | 9 | 7 | 11 | 3 | | | | 8 | 4 | | 10 | | | | | | 6 | |
| 1 | 2 | | | 5 | | 8 | | 9 | 7 | 11 | 3 | | | | | 4 | | 10 | | | | | | 6 | |
| 1 | 2 | | | 5 | | 8 | | 9 | 7 | 11 | 3 | | | | | 4 | | 10 | | | | | | 6 | |
| 1 | 2 | | | 5 | | 8 | | | 7 | 11 | 3 | | | | | 4 | 9 | 10 | | | | | | 6 | |
| 1 | 2 | | | 5 | | 8 | | | 7 | 11 | 3 | | | | | 4 | 9 | 10 | | | | | | 6 | |
| 1 | | | 4 | 5 | 3 | 8 | | | 7 | 11 | 2 | | | | | | 9 | 10 | | | | | | 6 | |
| 1 | 2 | | 6 | 5 | | 7 | | | | 11 | 3 | | | | 9 | 4 | | 10 | | | | | | | 8 |
| 1 | 2 | | 6 | | 4 | 7 | | 9 | | 11 | 3 | | | | 10 | 5 | | | | | | | | | 8 |
| 1 | 2 | | 6 | | 4 | 7 | | 9 | | 11 | 3 | | | | 10 | 5 | | | | | | | | | 8 |
| | 3 | | 6 | 5 | 4 | | | | 7 | 11 | | | | | 10 | | 9 | | | | 2 | 1 | | | 8 |
| | 3 | | 6 | 5 | 4 | | | | 7 | 11 | | | | | 10 | | 9 | | | | 2 | 1 | | | 8 |
| | 3 | | | 5 | 4 | | | | 7 | 11 | | | | | 10 | | 9 | | | | 2 | 1 | | 6 | 8 |
| | 3 | | 4 | 5 | | | | | 7 | 11 | | | 6 | | 10 | | 9 | | | | 2 | 1 | | | 8 |
| | 3 | | 4 | 5 | | | | | 7 | 11 | | | 6 | | 10 | | 9 | | | | 2 | 1 | | | 8 |
| 29 | 38 | 1 | 30 | 26 | 22 | 27 | 10 | 25 | 36 | 20 | 33 | 1 | 6 | 12 | 24 | 30 | 18 | 13 | 1 | 3 | 6 | 9 | 2 | 10 | 8 |
| | | | 3 | 1 | 2 | 5 | 1 | 18 | 9 | 5 | | | | 3 | 13 | 1 | 10 | 3 | | 2 | | | | 1 | 1 |

| Rivers | Bowron | Allen | Thornton | Hamilton | Buller | Mordue, J. | Carr | Lumley | Dixon | Pedwell | Shotton | Robinson | Thayne | Thompson | Wigham | Nobbs | Hewitt | Brown | Mason | Waller | Harland | Owbridge | Jarps | Tither | Hardy |
|---|---|---|---|---|---|---|---|---|---|---|---|---|---|---|---|---|---|---|---|---|---|---|---|---|---|
| 1 | 2 | | 6 | 4 | | 7 | | 9 | 11 | | 3 | | | | 10 | 5 | 8 | | | | | | | | |
| 1 | 1 | | 1 | 1 | | 1 | | 1 | 1 | | 1 | | | | 1 | 1 | 1 | | | | | | | | |
| | | | | | | | | | | | | | | | 1 | | | | | | | | | | |

## League Table

| | P | W | D | L | F | A | Pts |
|---|---|---|---|---|---|---|---|
| Lincoln City | 40 | 26 | 5 | 9 | 106 | 47 | 57 |
| Gateshead | 40 | 25 | 7 | 8 | 94 | 48 | 57 |
| Chester | 40 | 21 | 8 | 11 | 78 | 60 | 50 |
| Tranmere Rovers | 40 | 19 | 11 | 10 | 107 | 58 | 49 |
| Barrow | 40 | 24 | 1 | 15 | 86 | 59 | 49 |
| Crewe Alexandra | 40 | 21 | 6 | 13 | 95 | 66 | 48 |
| Southport | 40 | 18 | 10 | 12 | 58 | 53 | 46 |
| Hull City | 40 | 20 | 5 | 15 | 82 | 53 | 45 |
| York City | 40 | 18 | 7 | 15 | 76 | 81 | 43 |
| Wrexham | 40 | 18 | 7 | 15 | 64 | 69 | 43 |
| Darlington | 40 | 17 | 4 | 19 | 66 | 69 | 38 |
| Stockport County | 40 | 13 | 11 | 16 | 55 | 53 | 37 |
| Hartlepools United | 40 | 16 | 5 | 19 | 78 | 100 | 37 |
| Accrington Stanley | 40 | 15 | 6 | 19 | 75 | 80 | 36 |
| Doncaster Rovers | 40 | 16 | 4 | 20 | 59 | 80 | 36 |
| Walsall | 40 | 16 | 3 | 21 | 57 | 85 | 35 |
| Halifax Town | 40 | 13 | 8 | 19 | 61 | 87 | 34 |
| Carlisle United | 40 | 11 | 11 | 18 | 64 | 79 | 33 |
| Rotherham United | 40 | 14 | 4 | 22 | 63 | 72 | 32 |
| New Brighton | 40 | 8 | 8 | 24 | 38 | 76 | 24 |
| Rochdale | 40 | 4 | 3 | 33 | 48 | 135 | 11 |

# 1932-33

## Division Three North

Manager: Jackie Carr

### Did you know that?

'Pools fielded 21 players during the season, the fewest since entering the League, including four goalkeepers: Owbridge, Rivers, Tremain and Wilks.

For the first time, four Hartlepools players scored 10 or more League goals in a season: Joss Hewitt (23), Johnny Wigham (15), Ralph Pedwell (15) and Bobby Dixon (11).

| Match No. | Date | Round | Venue | Opponents | Result | | Scorers | Attendance |
|---|---|---|---|---|---|---|---|---|
| 1 | Aug 27 | | (a) | Tranmere Rovers | D | 3 - 3 | Hewitt, Proctor 2 | 5,392 |
| 2 | 31 | | (a) | HalifaxTown | L | 0 - 4 | | 5,663 |
| 3 | Sep 3 | | (h) | Wrexham | W | 3 - 1 | Dixon, Hewitt 2 | 4,757 |
| 4 | 7 | | (h) | HalifaxTown | D | 1 - 1 | Dixon | 4,587 |
| 5 | 10 | | (a) | Walsall | L | 1 - 4 | Hardy | 6,191 |
| 6 | 17 | | (h) | Gateshead | D | 2 - 2 | Dixon, Hewitt (pen) | 5,735 |
| 7 | 24 | | (a) | Stockport County | L | 2 - 6 | Proctor, Hewitt | 6,725 |
| 8 | Oct 1 | | (h) | Darlington | W | 2 - 1 | Makepeace, Wigham | 3,894 |
| 9 | 8 | | (a) | Doncaster Rovers | L | 1 - 4 | Ridley | 3,237 |
| 10 | 15 | | (h) | Hull City | L | 0 - 1 | | 4,553 |
| 11 | 22 | | (a) | Accrington Stanley | L | 1 - 7 | Dixon | 2,927 |
| 12 | 29 | | (h) | New Brighton | W | 3 - 2 | Makepeace, Wigham, Hewitt | 1,916 |
| 13 | Nov 5 | | (a) | Chester | D | 3 - 3 | Pedwell, Wigham 2 | 6,947 |
| 14 | 12 | | (h) | Barrow | L | 0 - 1 | | 3,603 |
| 15 | 19 | | (a) | Carlisle United | L | 1 - 3 | Pedwell | 4,594 |
| 17 | Dec 3 | | (a) | Crewe Alexandra | L | 2 - 6 | Hewitt, Thornton | 4,641 |
| 19 | 17 | | (a) | Southport | L | 3 - 6 | Pedwell 2, Dixon | 2,439 |
| 20 | 24 | | (h) | Mansfield Town | W | 6 - 3 | Hewitt 2, Dixon 2, Pedwell, Wigham | 3,872 |
| 21 | 26 | | (a) | Barnsley | L | 2 - 3 | Hewitt, Hamilton | 9,138 |
| 22 | 27 | | (h) | Barnsley | W | 6 - 4 | Hewitt 3, Dixon, Hardy, Wigham | 4,996 |
| 23 | 31 | | (h) | Tranmere Rovers | L | 2 - 3 | Pedwell 2 | 3,954 |
| 24 | Jan 2 | | (h) | Rochdale | W | 3 - 0 | Hewitt, Pedwell, Wigham | 3,359 |
| 25 | 7 | | (a) | Wrexham | L | 1 - 8 | Wigham | 4,809 |
| 26 | 14 | | (h) | York City | W | 4 - 2 | Pedwell 2, Proctor, Wigham | 3,105 |
| 27 | 21 | | (h) | Walsall | W | 2 - 0 | Proctor, Wigham | 4,693 |
| 28 | 28 | | (a) | Gateshead | L | 1 - 3 | Proctor | 4,171 |
| 29 | Feb 4 | | (h) | Stockport County | D | 1 - 1 | Thayne | 4,027 |
| 30 | 11 | | (a) | Darlington | W | 2 - 1 | Dixon 2 | 3,160 |
| 31 | 18 | | (h) | Doncaster Rovers | W | 4 - 0 | Dixon, Pedwell, Hewitt, Wigham | 1,341 |
| 32 | 25 | | (a) | Hull City | L | 0 - 3 | | 5,323 |
| 33 | Mar 4 | | (h) | Accrington Stanley | W | 3 - 1 | Pedwell, Hewitt (pen), Wigham | 3,410 |
| 34 | 11 | | (a) | New Brighton | L | 2 - 5 | Hardy Proctor | 3,055 |
| 35 | 18 | | (h) | Chester | W | 3 - 1 | Hewitt 2, Hardy | 5,293 |
| 36 | 25 | | (a) | Barrow | L | 1 - 3 | O'Donnell (pen) | 3,358 |
| 37 | Apr 1 | | (h) | Carlisle United | W | 2 - 1 | Wigham, Proctor | 3,232 |
| 38 | 8 | | (a) | York City | D | 1 - 1 | Hewitt | 3,720 |
| 39 | 14 | | (h) | Rotherham United | W | 2 - 0 | Wigham, Pedwell | 3,682 |
| 40 | 15 | | (h) | Crewe Alexandra | W | 3 - 2 | Hardy, Pedwell, O'Donnell (pen) | 3,391 |
| 41 | 17 | | (a) | Rotherham United | D | 1 - 1 | Thayne | 2,659 |
| 42 | 26 | | (a) | Rochdale | L | 2 - 6 | Hewitt, Hardy | 3,249 |
| 43 | 29 | | (h) | Southport | W | 4 - 2 | Wigham, Pedwell, Hewitt 2 | 1,135 |
| 44 | May 6 | | (a) | Mansfield Town | L | 1 - 7 | Hewitt | 2,381 |

Final Position : 14th in Division Three North

Apps.
Goals

**FA Cup**

| Match No. | Date | Round | Venue | Opponents | Result | | Scorers | Attendance |
|---|---|---|---|---|---|---|---|---|
| 16 | Nov 26 | R1 | (a) | Marine | W | 5 - 2 | Wigham 2, Thornton, Hewitt, Dixon | 2,347 |
| 18 | Dec 10 | R2 | (a) | Walsall | L | 1 - 2 | Thornton | 8,841 |

Apps.
Goals

| Owbridge | Harland | Bowron | Thornton | Hamilton | Thayne | Dixon | Proctor | Hewitt | Wigham | Pedwell | Hardy | Makepeace | Ridley | Rivers | O'Donnell | Wilks | Tither | Hill | Tremain | Burluraux |
|---|---|---|---|---|---|---|---|---|---|---|---|---|---|---|---|---|---|---|---|---|
| 1 | 2 | 3 | 4 | 5 | 6 | 7 | 8 | 9 | 10 | 11 | | | | | | | | | | |
| 1 | 2 | 3 | 4 | 5 | 6 | 7 | 8 | 9 | | 11 | 10 | | | | | | | | | |
| 1 | 2 | 3 | 4 | 5 | | 7 | | 9 | 10 | 11 | 8 | 6 | | | | | | | | |
| 1 | 2 | 3 | | 5 | 4 | 7 | | 9 | 10 | 11 | 8 | 6 | | | | | | | | |
| 1 | 2 | 3 | | 5 | 4 | 7 | | 9 | 10 | 11 | 8 | 6 | | | | | | | | |
| 1 | 2 | 3 | | 5 | 4 | 11 | 8 | 9 | 10 | | | 6 | 7 | | | | | | | |
| | 2 | 3 | | 5 | 4 | 11 | 8 | 9 | 10 | | | 6 | 7 | 1 | | | | | | |
| 1 | 2 | 3 | | 5 | 4 | 11 | 8 | 9 | 10 | | | 6 | 7 | | | | | | | |
| 1 | 2 | 3 | 4 | | 5 | 11 | 8 | 9 | 10 | | | 6 | 7 | | | | | | | |
| 1 | 2 | 3 | | 5 | 4 | 11 | 10 | 9 | 8 | | | 6 | 7 | | | | | | | |
| 1 | | 2 | | 5 | 4 | 11 | 8 | 9 | 10 | | | 6 | 7 | | 3 | | | | | |
| | | 2 | 6 | | 4 | 11 | | 9 | 10 | | 8 | 5 | 7 | | 3 | 1 | | | | |
| | | 2 | 6 | | 4 | | | 9 | 10 | 11 | 8 | 5 | 7 | | 3 | 1 | | | | |
| | | 2 | 6 | | 4 | 7 | | 9 | 10 | 11 | 8 | 5 | | | 3 | 1 | | | | |
| | | 2 | 4 | | 5 | 7 | 9 | | 10 | 11 | 8 | | | | 3 | 1 | 6 | | | |
| | | 2 | 6 | 5 | 4 | 7 | | 9 | 10 | 11 | 8 | | | | 3 | 1 | | | | |
| | | 2 | 10 | 5 | 4 | 7 | | 9 | | 11 | 8 | | | | 3 | 1 | 6 | | | |
| | | 2 | 6 | 5 | 4 | 7 | | 9 | 10 | 11 | 8 | | | | 3 | 1 | | | | |
| | 3 | 2 | 6 | 5 | 4 | 7 | 8 | 9 | 10 | 11 | | | | | | 1 | | | | |
| | | 2 | 6 | 5 | 4 | 7 | | 9 | 10 | 11 | 8 | | | | 3 | 1 | | | | |
| | | 2 | 6 | 5 | 4 | 7 | | 9 | 10 | 11 | 8 | | | | 3 | 1 | | | | |
| | 3 | 2 | 6 | 5 | 4 | 7 | | 9 | 10 | 11 | 8 | | | | | 1 | | | | |
| | 2 | 3 | 6 | 5 | 4 | 7 | | 9 | 10 | 11 | 8 | | | | | 1 | | | | |
| | | 2 | 4 | | | 7 | 8 | 9 | 10 | 11 | | 6 | | | 3 | 1 | | 5 | | |
| | | 2 | 7 | | 4 | | 8 | 9 | 10 | 11 | | 6 | | | 3 | 1 | | 5 | | |
| | | 2 | 7 | | 4 | | 8 | 9 | | 11 | 10 | 6 | | | 3 | 1 | | 5 | | |
| | | 2 | | | 4 | 7 | | 9 | 10 | 11 | 8 | 6 | | | 3 | | | 5 | 1 | |
| | | 2 | | | 4 | 7 | | 9 | 10 | 11 | 8 | 6 | | | 3 | | | 5 | 1 | |
| | | 2 | | | 4 | 7 | | 9 | 10 | 11 | 8 | 6 | | | 3 | | | 5 | 1 | |
| | | 2 | | | 4 | 7 | | 9 | 10 | 11 | 8 | 6 | | | 3 | | | 5 | 1 | |
| | | 2 | | | 4 | | 7 | 9 | 10 | 11 | 8 | 6 | | | 3 | | | 5 | 1 | |
| | | 2 | | | 4 | | 7 | 9 | 10 | 11 | 8 | 6 | | | 3 | | | 5 | 1 | |
| | | 2 | | | 4 | | 8 | 10 | 9 | 11 | 7 | 6 | | | 3 | | | 5 | 1 | |
| | | 2 | | | 4 | | 8 | 9 | 10 | 11 | 7 | 6 | | | 3 | | | 5 | 1 | |
| | | 2 | | | 4 | | 8 | 9 | 10 | 11 | 7 | 6 | | | 3 | | | 5 | 1 | |
| | | 2 | | | 4 | | 8 | 9 | 10 | 11 | 7 | 6 | | | 3 | | | 5 | 1 | |
| | | 2 | | | 4 | 7 | | 9 | 10 | 11 | 8 | 6 | | | 3 | | | 5 | 1 | |
| | | 2 | | 4 | 6 | | 8 | 9 | 10 | 11 | 7 | | | | 3 | | | 5 | 1 | |
| | | 2 | | | 4 | 7 | 8 | 9 | 10 | 11 | 6 | | | | 3 | | | 5 | 1 | |
| | | 2 | | 6 | 4 | | 8 | 9 | 10 | 11 | 7 | | | | 3 | | | 5 | 1 | |
| | | 2 | | 6 | 4 | | 8 | 9 | 10 | 11 | 7 | | | | 3 | | | 5 | 1 | |
| | | 3 | | 6 | 4 | | 8 | 9 | 10 | 11 | 7 | | | | | | | 5 | 1 | 2 |
| 10 | 13 | 42 | 19 | 22 | 40 | 29 | 24 | 41 | 39 | 35 | 32 | 26 | 8 | 1 | 28 | 15 | 2 | 19 | 16 | 1 |
| | | | 1 | 1 | 2 | 11 | 8 | 23 | 15 | 15 | 6 | 2 | 1 | | 2 | | | | | |

| Owbridge | Harland | Bowron | Thornton | Hamilton | Thayne | Dixon | Proctor | Hewitt | Wigham | Pedwell | Hardy | Makepeace | Ridley | Rivers | O'Donnell | Wilks | Tither | Hill | Tremain | Burluraux |
|---|---|---|---|---|---|---|---|---|---|---|---|---|---|---|---|---|---|---|---|---|
| | | 2 | 6 | 5 | 4 | 7 | | 9 | 10 | 11 | 8 | | | | 3 | 1 | | | | |
| | | 2 | 6 | 5 | 4 | 7 | | 9 | 10 | 11 | 8 | | | | 3 | 1 | | | | |
| | | 2 | 2 | 2 | 2 | 2 | | 2 | 2 | 2 | 2 | | | | 2 | 2 | | | | |
| | | | 2 | | | 1 | | 1 | 2 | | | | | | | | | | | |

## League Table

| | P | W | D | L | F | A | Pts |
|---|---|---|---|---|---|---|---|
| Hull City | 42 | 26 | 7 | 9 | 100 | 45 | 59 |
| Wrexham | 42 | 24 | 9 | 9 | 106 | 51 | 57 |
| Stockport County | 42 | 21 | 12 | 9 | 99 | 58 | 54 |
| Chester | 42 | 22 | 8 | 12 | 94 | 66 | 52 |
| Walsall | 42 | 19 | 10 | 13 | 75 | 58 | 48 |
| Doncaster Rovers | 42 | 17 | 14 | 11 | 77 | 79 | 48 |
| Gateshead | 42 | 19 | 9 | 14 | 78 | 67 | 47 |
| Barnsley | 42 | 19 | 8 | 15 | 92 | 80 | 46 |
| Barrow | 42 | 18 | 7 | 17 | 60 | 60 | 43 |
| Crewe Alexandra | 42 | 20 | 3 | 19 | 80 | 84 | 43 |
| Tranmere Rovers | 42 | 17 | 8 | 17 | 70 | 66 | 42 |
| Southport | 42 | 17 | 7 | 18 | 70 | 67 | 41 |
| Accrington Stanley | 42 | 15 | 10 | 17 | 78 | 76 | 40 |
| Hartlepools United | 42 | 16 | 7 | 19 | 87 | 116 | 39 |
| Halifax Town | 42 | 15 | 8 | 19 | 71 | 90 | 38 |
| Mansfield Town | 42 | 14 | 7 | 21 | 84 | 100 | 35 |
| Rotherham United | 42 | 14 | 6 | 22 | 60 | 84 | 34 |
| Rochdale | 42 | 13 | 7 | 22 | 58 | 80 | 33 |
| Carlisle United | 42 | 13 | 7 | 22 | 51 | 75 | 33 |
| York City | 42 | 13 | 6 | 23 | 72 | 92 | 32 |
| New Brighton | 42 | 11 | 10 | 21 | 63 | 88 | 32 |
| Darlington | 42 | 10 | 8 | 24 | 66 | 109 | 28 |

# 1933-34

## Division Three North

Manager: Jackie Carr

### Did you know that?

Joss Hewitt became the first Hartlepools player to score 20 or more League goals in successive seasons, having scored 23 in the previous campaign. He played his final game for 'Pools on 28 April, scoring in a 4–0 defeat of Rotherham.

Ralph Pedwell played his final game for the club on 5 May, a 5–0 loss at Walsall.

| Match No. | Date | Round | Venue | Opponents | Result | | Scorers | Attendance |
|---|---|---|---|---|---|---|---|---|
| 1 | Aug 26 | | (a) | Mansfield Town | D | 1 - 1 | Pedwell | 7,101 |
| 2 | 30 | | (h) | Rochdale | W | 2 - 1 | Wigham, Hardy | 4,580 |
| 3 | Sep 2 | | (h) | York City | W | 2 - 0 | Thayne, Wigham | 5,310 |
| 4 | 5 | | (a) | Rochdale | L | 0 - 3 | | 4,766 |
| 5 | 9 | | (h) | Wrexham | W | 4 - 1 | Hardy, Hewitt, Pedwell 2 | 4,951 |
| 6 | 16 | | (a) | Southport | W | 2 - 0 | Wigham, Hewitt | 2,946 |
| 7 | 23 | | (h) | Darlington | W | 6 - 2 | Thayne, Hewitt, Hird, Pedwell 3 | 5,795 |
| 8 | 30 | | (a) | Gateshead | L | 3 - 6 | Hardy, Hewitt 2 | 4,292 |
| 9 | Oct 7 | | (h) | Accrington Stanley | W | 3 - 0 | Hewitt 2, Hardy | 4,605 |
| 10 | 14 | | (a) | Chesterfield | L | 1 - 3 | Hardy | 12,341 |
| 11 | 21 | | (a) | Chester | D | 3 - 3 | Hewitt, Wigham 2 | 6,368 |
| 12 | 28 | | (h) | Doncaster Rovers | D | 2 - 2 | Hewitt, Hardy | 2,701 |
| 13 | Nov 4 | | (a) | Barrow | D | 2 - 2 | Wigham 2 | 4,676 |
| 14 | 11 | | (h) | Carlisle United | W | 3 - 2 | Hewitt 2, Wigham | 4,706 |
| 15 | 18 | | (a) | Stockport County | L | 2 - 5 | Hewitt 2 | 7,437 |
| 17 | Dec 2 | | (a) | Crewe Alexandra | L | 0 - 1 | | 3,247 |
| 20 | 16 | | (a) | Rotherham United | L | 2 - 4 | Hird, Wigham | 3,148 |
| 21 | 23 | | (h) | Walsall | L | 0 - 1 | | 3,556 |
| 22 | 25 | | (h) | Barnsley | L | 0 - 2 | | 5,461 |
| 23 | 26 | | (a) | Barnsley | L | 4 - 5 | Pedwell, Hewitt (pen), Catton, Proctor | 8,559 |
| 24 | 30 | | (h) | Mansfield Town | W | 3 - 1 | Hird, Wigham, Proctor | 2,759 |
| 25 | Jan 1 | | (h) | Halifax Town | W | 5 - 0 | Hird 2, Hewitt (pen), Pedwell, Catton | 2,408 |
| 26 | 6 | | (a) | York City | W | 3 - 1 | Catton, Hird, Wigham | 4,118 |
| 28 | 20 | | (a) | Wrexham | L | 1 - 3 | Hardy | 5,292 |
| 29 | 27 | | (h) | Southport | L | 1 - 2 | Pedwell | 2,592 |
| 30 | Feb 3 | | (a) | Darlington | L | 3 - 5 | Pedwell 2, Hird | 3,397 |
| 31 | 10 | | (h) | Gateshead | D | 3 - 3 | Wigham 2, Hewitt | 3,755 |
| 32 | 14 | | (h) | New Brighton | W | 2 - 1 | Pedwell, Bower (o.g.) | 1,441 |
| 33 | 17 | | (a) | Accrington Stanley | D | 2 - 2 | Hewitt, Corcoran (o.g.) | 1,977 |
| 34 | 24 | | (h) | Chesterfield | L | 0 - 3 | | 5,739 |
| 35 | Mar 3 | | (h) | Chester | W | 1 - 0 | Proctor | 2,900 |
| 36 | 10 | | (a) | Doncaster Rovers | L | 0 - 3 | | 3,770 |
| 37 | 17 | | (h) | Barrow | W | 7 - 0 | Hird, Proctor 3, Hewitt, Pedwell 2 | 1,836 |
| 38 | 24 | | (a) | Carlisle United | L | 1 - 4 | Wigham | 3,119 |
| 39 | 30 | | (h) | Tranmere Rovers | D | 1 - 1 | Thayne (pen) | 4,147 |
| 40 | 31 | | (h) | Stockport County | W | 3 - 1 | Hird, Hewitt (pen), Hardy | 4,766 |
| 41 | Apr 2 | | (a) | Tranmere Rovers | L | 2 - 3 | Hardy 2 | 3,971 |
| 42 | 7 | | (a) | Halifax Town | L | 2 - 6 | Pedwell, Hird | 4,849 |
| 43 | 14 | | (h) | Crewe Alexandra | W | 2 - 1 | Wigham, Pedwell | 2,332 |
| 44 | 21 | | (a) | New Brighton | L | 1 - 4 | Pedwell | 2,878 |
| 45 | 28 | | (h) | Rotherham United | W | 4 - 0 | Hardy 2, Hewitt, Pedwell | 1,083 |
| 46 | May 5 | | (a) | Walsall | L | 0 - 5 | | 4,616 |
| Final Position : 11th in Division Three North | | | | | | | | Apps. |
| | | | | | | | 2 own goals | Goals |

**FA Cup**

| Match No. | Date | Round | Venue | Opponents | Result | | Scorers | Attendance |
|---|---|---|---|---|---|---|---|---|
| 16 | Nov 25 | R1 | (a) | York City | W | 3 - 2 | Hewitt, Pedwell, Wigham | 6,734 |
| 18 | Dec 9 | R2 | (a) | Halifax Town | D | 1 - 1 | Hardy | 13,400 |
| 19 | 13 | R2r | (h) | Halifax Town | L | 1 - 2 | Pedwell | 9,500 |
| | | | | | | | | Apps. |
| | | | | | | | | Goals |

**Division 3 North Cup**

| Match No. | Date | Round | Venue | Opponents | Result | | Scorers | Attendance |
|---|---|---|---|---|---|---|---|---|
| 27 | Jan 13 | R1 | (a) | York City | L | 1 - 2 | Hird | 300 |
| | | | | | | | | Apps. |
| | | | | | | | | Goals |

| Knox | Bowron | Fairhurst | Thayne | Hill | Reilly | Hird | Hardy | Hewitt | Wigham | Pedwell | Johnson, M. | Proctor | Makepeace | Brown | Catton | Harland | Johnson, J. | Strong | Welsh | Finnigan | Odhams |
|---|---|---|---|---|---|---|---|---|---|---|---|---|---|---|---|---|---|---|---|---|---|
| 1 | 2 | 3 | 4 | 5 | 6 | 7 | 8 | 9 | 10 | 11 | | | | | | | | | | | |
| 1 | 2 | 3 | 4 | 5 | 6 | 7 | 8 | 9 | 10 | 11 | | | | | | | | | | | |
| 1 | 2 | 3 | 4 | 5 | 6 | 7 | 8 | 9 | 10 | 11 | | | | | | | | | | | |
| 1 | 2 | 3 | 4 | 5 | 6 | 7 | 8 | 10 | | 11 | 9 | | | | | | | | | | |
| 1 | 2 | 3 | 4 | 5 | 6 | 7 | 8 | 9 | 10 | 11 | | | | | | | | | | | |
| 1 | 2 | 3 | 4 | 5 | | 7 | 8 | 9 | 10 | 11 | | 6 | | | | | | | | | |
| 1 | 2 | 3 | 4 | 5 | | 7 | 8 | 9 | 10 | 11 | | 6 | | | | | | | | | |
| 1 | 2 | 3 | 4 | 5 | | 7 | 8 | 9 | 10 | 11 | | 6 | | | | | | | | | |
| 1 | 2 | 3 | 5 | | 6 | 7 | 8 | 9 | 10 | 11 | | 4 | | | | | | | | | |
| 1 | 2 | 3 | 5 | | 6 | 7 | 8 | 9 | 10 | 11 | | 4 | | | | | | | | | |
| 1 | 2 | 3 | 4 | | | 7 | 8 | 9 | 10 | 11 | | 6 | 5 | | | | | | | | |
| 1 | 2 | 3 | 4 | | | 7 | 8 | 9 | 10 | 11 | | 6 | 5 | | | | | | | | |
| 1 | 2 | 3 | 4 | | | 7 | 8 | 9 | 10 | | 11 | 6 | 5 | | | | | | | | |
| 1 | 2 | 3 | 4 | | | 7 | 8 | 9 | 10 | | 11 | 6 | 5 | | | | | | | | |
| 1 | 2 | 3 | 4 | | | 7 | 8 | 9 | 10 | | 11 | 6 | 5 | | | | | | | | |
| 1 | 2 | 3 | 4 | | | 7 | 8 | 9 | | 11 | | 10 | 5 | 6 | | | | | | | |
| 1 | 2 | 3 | | 4 | | 7 | | 8 | 10 | 11 | 9 | 6 | 5 | | | | | | | | |
| 1 | 2 | 3 | | 4 | | 7 | | 9 | 10 | 11 | | 6 | 5 | | 8 | | | | | | |
| 1 | 2 | 3 | | | | 7 | 8 | 9 | 10 | 11 | | 6 | 5 | 4 | | | | | | | |
| 1 | 3 | | | | | 7 | 4 | 9 | 10 | 11 | | 6 | 5 | | 8 | 2 | | | | | |
| 1 | 2 | 3 | 4 | | | 7 | | 9 | 10 | 11 | | 6 | 5 | | 8 | | | | | | |
| 1 | 2 | 3 | | | | 7 | 4 | 9 | 10 | 11 | | 6 | 5 | | 8 | | | | | | |
| 1 | 2 | 3 | | | | 7 | 4 | 9 | 10 | 11 | | 6 | 5 | | 8 | | | | | | |
| 1 | 2 | 3 | 4 | | | 7 | 8 | 9 | | 11 | | 6 | 5 | | 10 | | | | | | |
| 1 | 2 | 3 | 4 | | | 7 | 10 | 9 | | 11 | | 6 | 5 | | 8 | | | | | | |
| | 2 | 3 | 4 | | | 7 | 10 | 8 | | 11 | | 6 | 5 | | 9 | | 1 | | | | |
| | | 3 | | 5 | | 7 | | 9 | 10 | 11 | | 4 | 6 | | | 2 | | 1 | 8 | | |
| | 2 | 3 | | 5 | | 7 | 10 | 9 | | 11 | | 6 | | | | | 1 | | 8 | 4 | |
| | | 3 | | 5 | | 7 | 8 | 9 | 10 | 11 | | 6 | | | | 2 | 1 | | | 4 | |
| | | 3 | | 5 | | 7 | | 9 | 10 | 11 | | 6 | | | | 2 | 1 | | 8 | 4 | |
| | 2 | 3 | 4 | 5 | | 7 | 8 | 9 | 10 | 11 | | 6 | | | | | 1 | | | | |
| | 2 | 3 | 4 | 5 | | 7 | 8 | 9 | 10 | | 11 | 6 | | | | | 1 | | | | |
| | 2 | 3 | | 5 | | 7 | | 8 | 10 | 11 | | 9 | 6 | 4 | | | 1 | | | | |
| | | 3 | 2 | 5 | | 7 | | 8 | 10 | 11 | | 9 | 6 | 4 | | | 1 | | | | |
| | 2 | 3 | 6 | 5 | | 7 | | 8 | 10 | 11 | | 9 | | 4 | | | 1 | | | | |
| | 2 | 3 | | 5 | | 7 | 9 | 8 | 10 | 11 | | 6 | | 4 | | | 1 | | | | |
| | 2 | 3 | | 5 | | 7 | 9 | 8 | 10 | 11 | | 6 | | 4 | | | | | | | 1 |
| | 2 | 3 | | 5 | | 7 | 9 | 8 | 10 | 11 | | 6 | | 4 | | | 1 | | | | |
| | 2 | 3 | | 5 | | 7 | 9 | 8 | 10 | 11 | | 6 | | 4 | | | 1 | | | | |
| | 2 | 3 | | 5 | | 7 | 9 | 8 | 10 | 11 | | 6 | | 4 | | | 1 | | | | |
| | 2 | 3 | | 5 | | 7 | 9 | 8 | 10 | 11 | | 6 | | 4 | | | 1 | | | | |
| | 2 | 3 | 6 | 5 | | 7 | 9 | | 10 | 11 | | 8 | | 4 | | | 1 | | | | |
| 25 | 38 | 41 | 25 | 26 | 7 | 42 | 34 | 41 | 36 | 38 | 6 | 37 | 19 | 12 | 8 | 4 | 15 | 1 | 3 | 3 | 1 |
| | | | 3 | 1 | | 9 | 12 | 20 | 15 | 18 | | 6 | | | 3 | | | | | | |

| Knox | Bowron | Fairhurst | Thayne | Hill | Reilly | Hird | Hardy | Hewitt | Wigham | Pedwell | Johnson, M. | Proctor | Makepeace | Brown | Catton | Harland | Johnson, J. | Strong | Welsh | Finnigan | Odhams |
|---|---|---|---|---|---|---|---|---|---|---|---|---|---|---|---|---|---|---|---|---|---|
| 1 | 2 | 3 | 4 | | | 7 | 8 | 9 | 10 | 11 | | 6 | 5 | | | | | | | | |
| 1 | 2 | 3 | 4 | | | 7 | 8 | 9 | 10 | 11 | | 6 | 5 | | | | | | | | |
| 1 | 2 | 3 | 4 | | | 7 | 8 | 9 | 10 | 11 | | 6 | 5 | | | | | | | | |
| 3 | 3 | 3 | 3 | | | 3 | 3 | 3 | 3 | 3 | | 3 | 3 | | | | | | | | |
| | | | | | | | 1 | 1 | 1 | 2 | | | | | | | | | | | |

| Knox | Bowron | Fairhurst | Thayne | Hill | Reilly | Hird | Hardy | Hewitt | Wigham | Pedwell | Johnson, M. | Proctor | Makepeace | Brown | Catton | Harland | Johnson, J. | Strong | Welsh | Finnigan | Odhams |
|---|---|---|---|---|---|---|---|---|---|---|---|---|---|---|---|---|---|---|---|---|---|
| 1 | 2 | 3 | 4 | | | 7 | | 9 | 10 | 11 | | 6 | 5 | | 8 | | | | | | |
| 1 | 1 | 1 | 1 | | | 1 | | 1 | 1 | 1 | | 1 | 1 | | 1 | | | | | | |
| | | | | | | 1 | | | | | | | | | | | | | | | |

## League Table

| | P | W | D | L | F | A | Pts |
|---|---|---|---|---|---|---|---|
| Barnsley | 42 | 27 | 8 | 7 | 118 | 61 | 62 |
| Chesterfield | 42 | 27 | 7 | 8 | 86 | 43 | 61 |
| Stockport County | 42 | 24 | 11 | 7 | 115 | 52 | 59 |
| Walsall | 42 | 23 | 7 | 12 | 97 | 60 | 53 |
| Doncaster Rovers | 42 | 22 | 9 | 11 | 83 | 61 | 53 |
| Wrexham | 42 | 23 | 5 | 14 | 102 | 73 | 51 |
| Tranmere Rovers | 42 | 20 | 7 | 15 | 84 | 63 | 47 |
| Barrow | 42 | 19 | 9 | 14 | 116 | 94 | 47 |
| Halifax Town | 42 | 20 | 4 | 18 | 80 | 91 | 44 |
| Chester | 42 | 17 | 6 | 19 | 89 | 86 | 40 |
| Hartlepools United | 42 | 16 | 7 | 19 | 89 | 93 | 39 |
| York City | 42 | 15 | 8 | 19 | 71 | 74 | 38 |
| Carlisle United | 42 | 15 | 8 | 19 | 66 | 81 | 38 |
| Crewe Alexandra | 42 | 15 | 6 | 21 | 81 | 97 | 36 |
| New Brighton | 42 | 14 | 8 | 20 | 62 | 87 | 36 |
| Darlington | 42 | 13 | 9 | 20 | 70 | 101 | 35 |
| Mansfield Town | 42 | 11 | 12 | 19 | 81 | 88 | 34 |
| Southport | 42 | 8 | 17 | 17 | 63 | 90 | 33 |
| Gateshead | 42 | 12 | 9 | 21 | 76 | 110 | 33 |
| Accrington Stanley | 42 | 13 | 7 | 22 | 65 | 101 | 33 |
| Rotherham United | 42 | 10 | 8 | 24 | 53 | 91 | 28 |
| Rochdale | 42 | 9 | 6 | 27 | 53 | 103 | 24 |

# 1934-35

## Division Three North

Manager: Jackie Carr

### Did you know that?

Average attendances fell by over 15 per cent on the previous season to 3,114, despite a respectable 12th-place finish. The decline meant that the accumulated debt had increased to £6,562 and was a factor in Jacky Carr leaving to manage Tranmere Rovers.

West Hartlepool-born Jack Howe made his League debut against Chester on 5 September, a 4–1 defeat. He later played for Derby County and England.

| Match No. | Date | Round | Venue | Opponents | Result | | Scorers | Attendance |
|---|---|---|---|---|---|---|---|---|
| 1 | Aug 25 | | (a) | Walsall | W | 2 - 1 | Bonass, Lindsay | 9,389 |
| 2 | 29 | | (h) | Chester | L | 0 - 2 | | 5,496 |
| 3 | Sep 1 | | (h) | Crewe Alexandra | W | 4 - 2 | Wigham, Lindsay, Hardy, Hird | 4,206 |
| 4 | 5 | | (a) | Chester | L | 1 - 4 | Hird | 8,979 |
| 5 | 8 | | (a) | Stockport County | L | 2 - 3 | Hardy, Wigham | 9,586 |
| 6 | 15 | | (h) | Gateshead | L | 1 - 2 | Wigham | 4,638 |
| 7 | 22 | | (a) | Accrington Stanley | W | 4 - 0 | Lindsay 2, Bonass 2 | 1,993 |
| 8 | 29 | | (h) | Darlington | L | 0 - 1 | | 3,751 |
| 9 | Oct 6 | | (a) | York City | L | 1 - 3 | Hird | 4,387 |
| 10 | 13 | | (h) | New Brighton | D | 2 - 2 | Hird, Huggins | 3,208 |
| 11 | 20 | | (a) | Chesterfield | L | 0 - 4 | | 4,915 |
| 12 | 27 | | (h) | Mansfield Town | D | 1 - 1 | Lindsay (pen) | 2,206 |
| 13 | Nov 3 | | (a) | Barrow | L | 0 - 2 | | 3,979 |
| 14 | 10 | | (h) | Carlisle United | W | 5 - 2 | Hardy, Hird 2, Huggins, Wigham | 1,586 |
| 15 | 17 | | (a) | Rochdale | L | 2 - 3 | Lindsay, Bonass | 3,782 |
| 18 | Dec 1 | | (a) | Tranmere Rovers | L | 0 - 3 | | 5,238 |
| 20 | 15 | | (a) | Halifax Town | L | 1 - 4 | Lindsay | 8,526 |
| 21 | 25 | | (h) | Doncaster Rovers | W | 2 - 1 | Lindsay, Hird | 3,616 |
| 22 | 26 | | (a) | Doncaster Rovers | L | 1 - 3 | Flowers (o.g.) | 10,904 |
| 23 | 29 | | (h) | Walsall | W | 2 - 1 | Bonass, Proctor (pen) | 2,375 |
| 24 | Jan 1 | | (h) | Wrexham | W | 4 - 3 | Lindsay 2, Lewis (o.g.), Bonass | 2,605 |
| 25 | 5 | | (a) | Crewe Alexandra | D | 1 - 1 | Lindsay | 4,100 |
| 26 | 12 | | (h) | Lincoln City | L | 1 - 5 | Lindsay | 2,694 |
| 27 | 19 | | (h) | Stockport County | W | 4 - 0 | Hird, Bonass, Proctor 2 (2 pens) | 2,626 |
| 29 | 26 | | (a) | Gateshead | L | 1 - 2 | Hird | 1,899 |
| 30 | Feb 2 | | (h) | Accrington Stanley | W | 4 - 2 | Moses, Lindsay, Bonass 2 | 2,259 |
| 31 | 9 | | (a) | Darlington | L | 0 - 3 | | 4,898 |
| 32 | 16 | | (h) | York City | W | 3 - 1 | Lindsay 2, Bonass | 2,014 |
| 34 | 23 | | (a) | New Brighton | W | 4 - 1 | Hird, Milligan (o.g.), Lindsay, Bonass | 2,428 |
| 35 | Mar 2 | | (h) | Chesterfield | D | 1 - 1 | Lindsay (pen) | 3,895 |
| 36 | 6 | | (h) | Rotherham United | W | 3 - 1 | Lindsay, Hardy, Hird | 2,211 |
| 37 | 9 | | (a) | Mansfield Town | L | 1 - 2 | Bonass | 4,006 |
| 38 | 16 | | (h) | Barrow | W | 5 - 2 | Hird (pen), Bonass 3, Wigham | 3,378 |
| 39 | 23 | | (a) | Carlisle United | D | 2 - 2 | Wigham, Bonass | 4,091 |
| 40 | 30 | | (h) | Rochdale | D | 0 - 0 | | 2,955 |
| 41 | Apr 6 | | (a) | Lincoln City | L | 1 - 2 | Hill | 2,847 |
| 43 | 13 | | (h) | Tranmere Rovers | W | 6 - 1 | Wigham 2, Hill, Lindsay, Bonass 2 | 3,960 |
| 44 | 19 | | (a) | Southport | D | 1 - 1 | Hird | 3,472 |
| 45 | 20 | | (a) | Wrexham | W | 2 - 0 | Hill, Hardy | 3,251 |
| 46 | 22 | | (h) | Southport | W | 4 - 1 | Lindsay 2, Bonass 2 | 3,315 |
| 47 | 27 | | (h) | Halifax Town | L | 0 - 3 | | 2,404 |
| 48 | May 4 | | (a) | Rotherham United | W | 1 - 0 | Wigham | 3,231 |

Final Position : 12th in Division Three North

Apps.

3 own goals — Goals

### FA Cup

| Match No. | Date | Round | Venue | Opponents | Result | | Scorers | Attendance |
|---|---|---|---|---|---|---|---|---|
| 16 | Nov 24 | R1 | (a) | Halifax Town | D | 1 - 1 | Bonass | 12,439 |
| 17 | 28 | R1r | (h) | Halifax Town | W | 2 - 0 | Bonass, Lindsay | 8,787 |
| 19 | Dec 8 | R2 | (h) | Coventry City | L | 0 - 4 | | 13,054 |

Apps.

Goals

### Division 3 North Cup

| Match No. | Date | Round | Venue | Opponents | Result | | Scorers | Attendance |
|---|---|---|---|---|---|---|---|---|
| 28 | Jan 23 | R1 | (h) | Darlington | W | 3 - 1 | Hird, Lindsay 2 | 2,509 |
| 33 | Feb 20 | R2 | (h) | York City | W | 4 - 0 | Wigham 2, Lindsay, Colquhoun | 1,700 |
| 42 | Apr 8 | Semi | (a) | Stockport County | L | 2 - 6 | Bonass, Lindsay | 1,318 |

Apps.

Goals

| Johnson | Proctor | Fairhurst | Graham | Park | Warren | Hird | Westmoreland | Lindsay | Wigham | Bonass | Hardy | Howe | Brown | Hill | Huggins | Coulthard | Fairhurst | Dreyer | Moses | Cleugh | Murray | Colquhoun |
|---|---|---|---|---|---|---|---|---|---|---|---|---|---|---|---|---|---|---|---|---|---|---|
| 1 | 2 | 3 | 4 | 5 | 6 | 7 | 8 | 9 | 10 | 11 | | | | | | | | | | | | |
| 1 | 2 | 3 | 4 | 5 | 6 | 7 | 8 | 9 | 10 | 11 | | | | | | | | | | | | |
| 1 | 2 | | 4 | 5 | 6 | 7 | 3 | 9 | 10 | 11 | 8 | | | | | | | | | | | |
| 1 | 2 | | | 5 | 6 | 7 | 10 | 9 | | 11 | 8 | 3 | 4 | | | | | | | | | |
| 1 | 2 | | | 5 | 6 | 7 | | 9 | 10 | 11 | 8 | 3 | 4 | | | | | | | | | |
| 1 | 2 | | | 5 | 6 | 7 | | 9 | 10 | 11 | 8 | 3 | 4 | | | | | | | | | |
| 1 | 2 | 3 | | 5 | 6 | 7 | | 9 | 10 | 11 | 8 | | | 4 | | | | | | | | |
| 1 | 2 | 3 | | 5 | 6 | 7 | | 9 | 10 | 11 | 8 | | | 4 | | | | | | | | |
| 1 | 2 | 3 | | 5 | 6 | 7 | | 9 | | 11 | 8 | | | 4 | 10 | | | | | | | |
| 1 | 2 | 3 | | 5 | 6 | 7 | 8 | 9 | | 11 | | | | 4 | 10 | | | | | | | |
| 1 | 2 | 3 | | 5 | 6 | 7 | 8 | 9 | | | | | | 4 | 10 | 11 | | | | | | |
| 1 | 2 | | | 5 | 6 | 7 | | 9 | 10 | | 8 | 3 | | 4 | | 11 | | | | | | |
| 1 | | | | 2 | 6 | 7 | | 9 | | | 8 | 3 | | 4 | 10 | 11 | 5 | | | | | |
| 1 | | | | 2 | 6 | 7 | | | 10 | | 8 | 3 | | 4 | 9 | 11 | 5 | | | | | |
| 1 | 2 | | | | 6 | 7 | 3 | 9 | 10 | 11 | 8 | | | 4 | | | 5 | | | | | |
| 1 | 2 | 3 | 8 | 5 | | 7 | | | 10 | 11 | 9 | | 6 | 4 | | | | | | | | |
| 1 | 2 | 3 | | 5 | | 7 | | 9 | 10 | 11 | 8 | | 6 | 4 | | | | | | | | |
| 1 | 2 | 3 | | 5 | | 7 | | 9 | 10 | 11 | | | | 6 | | | | 4 | 8 | | | |
| 1 | 2 | 3 | | 5 | | 7 | | | 10 | 11 | | | 6 | 4 | 9 | | | | 8 | | | |
| 1 | 2 | 3 | | 5 | | 7 | | | 10 | 11 | 8 | 9 | 6 | 4 | | | | | | | | |
| 1 | 2 | 3 | | 5 | | 7 | | 9 | 10 | 11 | 8 | | 6 | 4 | | | | | | | | |
| 1 | 2 | 3 | | 5 | | 7 | | 9 | 10 | 11 | 8 | | 6 | 4 | | | | | | | | |
| 1 | 2 | 3 | | 5 | | 7 | | 9 | 10 | 11 | 8 | | 6 | 4 | | | | | | | | |
| 1 | 2 | | | 5 | | 7 | | 9 | | 11 | 8 | 3 | 6 | 4 | | | | | 10 | | | |
| 1 | 2 | | | 5 | | 7 | | 9 | | 11 | 8 | 3 | | 4 | | | | | 10 | 6 | | |
| 1 | 2 | 3 | | 5 | | 7 | | 9 | 8 | 11 | | | 6 | 4 | | | | | 10 | | | |
| 1 | 2 | 3 | | 5 | | 7 | | 9 | 8 | 11 | | | 6 | 4 | | | | | 10 | | | |
| 1 | 2 | | | 5 | | 7 | | 9 | | 11 | 8 | 3 | | 6 | | | | 4 | 10 | | | |
| 1 | 2 | | | 5 | | 7 | | 9 | 8 | 11 | 10 | 3 | | 6 | | | | 4 | | | | |
| 1 | 2 | | | | | 7 | | 9 | 8 | 11 | | 3 | 6 | 5 | | | | 4 | 10 | | | |
| 1 | 2 | | | 5 | | 7 | | 9 | | 11 | 8 | 3 | | 6 | | | | 4 | 10 | | | |
| 1 | 2 | | | 5 | | 7 | | 9 | 8 | 11 | 10 | | | 6 | | | 3 | 4 | | | | |
| 1 | 2 | | | 5 | | 7 | | 9 | 8 | 11 | | | | 6 | | | 3 | 4 | 10 | | | |
| 1 | 2 | | | | | 7 | | 9 | 8 | 11 | 10 | | 5 | 6 | | | 3 | 4 | | | | |
| 1 | 2 | | | | | 7 | | 9 | 8 | 11 | | | 5 | 6 | | | 3 | 4 | 10 | | | |
| 1 | 2 | | | | | 7 | | 9 | 8 | 11 | 10 | | 5 | 6 | | | 3 | 4 | | | | |
| 1 | 2 | | | 5 | | 7 | | 9 | 8 | 11 | 10 | 3 | | 6 | | | | 4 | | | | |
| | 2 | | | 5 | | 7 | | 9 | 8 | 11 | 10 | 3 | | 6 | | | | 4 | | | 1 | |
| | 2 | | | 5 | | 7 | | 9 | 8 | 11 | 10 | 3 | | 6 | | | | 4 | | | 1 | |
| | 2 | | | 5 | | 7 | | 9 | 8 | 11 | 10 | | | 6 | | | 3 | 4 | | | 1 | |
| | 2 | | 10 | 5 | | 7 | | 9 | 8 | 11 | 4 | | | 6 | | | 3 | | | | 1 | |
| | 2 | | | 5 | | 7 | | | 8 | 11 | 10 | | | 6 | 9 | | 3 | 4 | | | 1 | |
| 37 | 40 | 17 | 5 | 37 | 15 | 42 | 7 | 37 | 33 | 38 | 31 | 16 | 17 | 36 | 7 | 4 | 17 | 15 | 11 | 1 | 5 | |
| | 3 | | | | | 13 | | 21 | 9 | 20 | 5 | | | 3 | 2 | | | | 1 | | | |

| Johnson | Proctor | Fairhurst | Graham | Park | Warren | Hird | Westmoreland | Lindsay | Wigham | Bonass | Hardy | Howe | Brown | Hill | Huggins | Coulthard | Fairhurst | Dreyer | Moses | Cleugh | Murray | Colquhoun |
|---|---|---|---|---|---|---|---|---|---|---|---|---|---|---|---|---|---|---|---|---|---|---|
| 1 | 2 | 3 | | 5 | | 7 | | 9 | 10 | 11 | 8 | | 6 | 4 | | | | | | | | |
| 1 | 2 | 3 | | 5 | | 7 | | 9 | 10 | 11 | 8 | | 6 | 4 | | | | | | | | |
| 1 | 2 | 3 | | 5 | | 7 | | 9 | 10 | 11 | 8 | | 6 | 4 | | | | | | | | |
| 3 | 3 | 3 | | 3 | | 3 | | 3 | 3 | 3 | 3 | | 3 | 3 | | | | | | | | |
| | | | | | | | | 1 | | 2 | | | | | | | | | | | | |

| Johnson | Proctor | Fairhurst | Graham | Park | Warren | Hird | Westmoreland | Lindsay | Wigham | Bonass | Hardy | Howe | Brown | Hill | Huggins | Coulthard | Fairhurst | Dreyer | Moses | Cleugh | Murray | Colquhoun |
|---|---|---|---|---|---|---|---|---|---|---|---|---|---|---|---|---|---|---|---|---|---|---|
| 1 | 2 | | | 5 | | 7 | | 9 | | 11 | 8 | 3 | 6 | 4 | | | | | 10 | | | |
| 1 | 2 | | | 5 | | 7 | | 9 | 8 | | | 3 | | 6 | | | | 4 | 10 | | | 11 |
| 1 | 2 | | | | | 7 | | 9 | | 11 | 8 | | 5 | 6 | 10 | | 3 | 4 | | | | |
| 3 | 3 | | | 2 | | 3 | | 3 | 1 | 2 | 2 | 2 | 2 | 3 | 1 | | 1 | 2 | 2 | | | 1 |
| | | | | | | 1 | | 4 | 2 | 1 | | | | | | | | | | | | 1 |

## League Table

| | P | W | D | L | F | A | Pts |
|---|---|---|---|---|---|---|---|
| Doncaster Rovers | 42 | 26 | 5 | 11 | 87 | 44 | 57 |
| Halifax Town | 42 | 25 | 5 | 12 | 76 | 67 | 55 |
| Chester | 42 | 20 | 14 | 8 | 91 | 58 | 54 |
| Lincoln City | 42 | 22 | 7 | 13 | 87 | 58 | 51 |
| Darlington | 42 | 21 | 9 | 12 | 80 | 59 | 51 |
| Tranmere Rovers | 42 | 20 | 11 | 11 | 74 | 55 | 51 |
| Stockport County | 42 | 22 | 3 | 17 | 90 | 72 | 47 |
| Mansfield Town | 42 | 19 | 9 | 14 | 75 | 62 | 47 |
| Rotherham United | 42 | 19 | 7 | 16 | 86 | 73 | 45 |
| Chesterfield | 42 | 17 | 10 | 15 | 71 | 52 | 44 |
| Wrexham | 42 | 16 | 11 | 15 | 76 | 69 | 43 |
| Hartlepools United | 42 | 17 | 7 | 18 | 80 | 78 | 41 |
| Crewe Alexandra | 42 | 14 | 11 | 17 | 66 | 86 | 39 |
| Walsall | 42 | 13 | 10 | 19 | 81 | 72 | 36 |
| York City | 42 | 15 | 6 | 21 | 76 | 82 | 36 |
| New Brighton | 42 | 14 | 8 | 20 | 59 | 76 | 36 |
| Barrow | 42 | 13 | 9 | 20 | 58 | 87 | 35 |
| Accrington Stanley | 42 | 12 | 10 | 20 | 63 | 89 | 34 |
| Gateshead | 42 | 13 | 8 | 21 | 58 | 96 | 34 |
| Rochdale | 42 | 11 | 11 | 20 | 53 | 71 | 33 |
| Southport | 42 | 10 | 12 | 20 | 55 | 85 | 32 |
| Carlisle United | 42 | 8 | 7 | 27 | 51 | 102 | 23 |

# 1935-36

## Division Three North

Manager: Jimmy Hamilton

**Did you know that?**

Reg Hill made his debut on the opening day of the season against Halifax. He went on to make 157 appearances for the club, scoring six goals. His son, also called Reg, is the writer of the Dalziel and Pascoe detective novels, which have been made into a successful television series.

United reached the third round proper of the FA Cup for the first time, losing to First Division Grimsby Town in a replay after a goalless draw at The Vic in front of 15,064 spectators, a record at the time.

| Match No. | Date | Round | Venue | Opponents | | Result | Scorers | Attendance |
|---|---|---|---|---|---|---|---|---|
| 1 | Aug 31 | | (h) | Halifax Town | W | 1 - 0 | Thompson | 5,815 |
| 2 | Sep 4 | | (h) | Oldham Athletic | L | 0 - 1 | | 6,582 |
| 3 | 7 | | (a) | Darlington | L | 2 - 4 | Proctor (pen), Thompson | 5,276 |
| 4 | 9 | | (a) | Oldham Athletic | D | 2 - 2 | Bonass, Hughes | 6,459 |
| 5 | 14 | | (h) | Gateshead | W | 2 - 0 | Bonass, Thompson | 4,487 |
| 6 | 18 | | (a) | Wrexham | L | 0 - 1 | | 3,555 |
| 7 | 21 | | (a) | Tranmere Rovers | L | 1 - 3 | Hughes | 6,902 |
| 9 | 28 | | (h) | Walsall | W | 5 - 0 | Robertson, Hughes, Wigham 2, Thompson | 4,422 |
| 10 | Oct 5 | | (a) | Carlisle United | D | 0 - 0 | | 7,618 |
| 11 | 12 | | (h) | Crewe Alexandra | W | 1 - 0 | Bonass | 4,692 |
| 12 | 19 | | (a) | Accrington Stanley | L | 2 - 3 | Thompson, Graham | 2,677 |
| 13 | 26 | | (h) | Southport | W | 2 - 1 | Pickard, Hill | 3,767 |
| 14 | Nov 2 | | (a) | Chester | L | 0 - 4 | | 5,503 |
| 15 | 9 | | (h) | Lincoln City | D | 1 - 1 | Bonass | 3,560 |
| 16 | 16 | | (a) | Rochdale | W | 1 - 0 | Bonass | 4,878 |
| 17 | 23 | | (h) | York City | W | 4 - 2 | Wigham 2, Bonass, Thompson | 4,247 |
| 19 | Dec 7 | | (h) | New Brighton | W | 4 - 1 | Bonass, Wigham 2, Robertson | 3,249 |
| 22 | 21 | | (h) | Stockport County | D | 1 - 1 | Chatterton | 3,375 |
| 24 | 25 | | (h) | Mansfield Town | W | 4 - 1 | Wigham 2, Bonass, Proctor (pen) | 5,679 |
| 25 | 26 | | (a) | Mansfield Town | L | 0 - 4 | | 2,595 |
| 26 | 28 | | (a) | Halifax Town | W | 1 - 0 | Graham | 4,624 |
| 27 | Jan 1 | | (h) | Wrexham | D | 1 - 1 | Wigham | 5,037 |
| 28 | 4 | | (h) | Darlington | W | 2 - 1 | Wigham 2 | 6,125 |
| 31 | 23 | | (a) | Barrow | D | 1 - 1 | Robertson | 1,568 |
| 32 | 29 | | (h) | Tranmere Rovers | D | 2 - 2 | Bonass, Thompson | 1,820 |
| 33 | Feb 1 | | (a) | Walsall | L | 0 - 6 | | 5,970 |
| 34 | 8 | | (h) | Carlisle United | D | 1 - 1 | Wigham | 4,107 |
| 35 | 12 | | (a) | Gateshead | L | 0 - 1 | | 1,973 |
| 36 | 15 | | (a) | Crewe Alexandra | L | 2 - 3 | Moses, Wigham | 3,808 |
| 37 | 22 | | (h) | Accrington Stanley | W | 2 - 1 | Wigham, Robertson | 4,056 |
| 38 | Mar 7 | | (h) | Chester | L | 0 - 2 | | 4,167 |
| 39 | 14 | | (a) | Southport | D | 1 - 1 | Bonass | 1,850 |
| 40 | 18 | | (a) | Lincoln City | L | 0 - 1 | | 2,598 |
| 41 | 21 | | (h) | Rochdale | W | 1 - 0 | Harris | 4,110 |
| 42 | 28 | | (a) | York City | D | 2 - 2 | Thompson, Wigham | 2,686 |
| 43 | Apr 4 | | (h) | Barrow | D | 0 - 0 | | 2,863 |
| 44 | 10 | | (h) | Rotherham United | W | 5 - 1 | Park, Thompson 2 (1 pen), Wigham, Bonass | 4,051 |
| 45 | 11 | | (a) | New Brighton | D | 0 - 0 | | 2,187 |
| 46 | 13 | | (a) | Rotherham United | L | 0 - 3 | | 4,593 |
| 47 | 18 | | (h) | Chesterfield | W | 2 - 1 | Nobbs, Graham | 4,073 |
| 48 | 25 | | (a) | Stockport County | L | 1 - 2 | Thompson | 3,008 |
| 49 | 27 | | (a) | Chesterfield | L | 0 - 2 | | 7,552 |

Final Position : 8th in Division Three North

Apps.
Goals

**FA Cup**

| Match No. | Date | Round | Venue | Opponents | | Result | Scorers | Attendance |
|---|---|---|---|---|---|---|---|---|
| 18 | Nov 30 | R1 | (a) | Mansfield Town | W | 3 - 2 | Bonass, Robertson, Proctor (pen) | 4,651 |
| 20 | Dec 14 | R2 | (a) | Halifax Town | D | 1 - 1 | Robertson | 7,698 |
| 21 | 18 | R2r | (h) | Halifax Town | D | 0 - 0* | | 7,713 |
| 23 | 23 | R2r2# | (a) | Halifax Town | W | 4 - 1 | Wigham 3, Robertson | 4,900 |
| 29 | Jan 11 | R3 | (h) | Grimsby Town | D | 0 - 0 | | 15,064 |
| 30 | 14 | R3r | (a) | Grimsby Town | L | 1 - 4 | Bonass | 11,500 |

\# Played at St. James' Park, Newcastle   * After extra-time

Apps.
Goals

**Division 3 North Cup**

| Match No. | Date | Round | Venue | Opponents | | Result | Scorers | Attendance |
|---|---|---|---|---|---|---|---|---|
| 8 | Sept 23 | R1 | (a) | Carlisle United | L | 2 - 4 | Thompson, Lloyd (o.g.) | 2,400 |

Apps.

1 own goal   Goals

| Mittell | Proctor | Howe | Hill | Park | Heward | Thompson | Wigham | Huggins | Robertson | Bonass | Hughes | Allison | Brown | Hardy | Moses | Graham | Pickard | Murray | Bradford | Chatterton | Scrimshaw | Owens | Harris | Nobbs | Firman | Aitken |
|---|---|---|---|---|---|---|---|---|---|---|---|---|---|---|---|---|---|---|---|---|---|---|---|---|---|---|
| 1 | 2 | 3 | 4 | 5 | 6 | 7 | 8 | 9 | 10 | 11 | | | | | | | | | | | | | | | | |
| 1 | 2 | 3 | 4 | 5 | 6 | 7 | 8 | 9 | 10 | 11 | | | | | | | | | | | | | | | | |
| 1 | 2 | 3 | 4 | 5 | 6 | 7 | | 8 | 10 | 11 | 9 | | | | | | | | | | | | | | | |
| 1 | 2 | | 8 | 5 | 6 | 7 | | | 10 | 11 | 9 | 3 | 4 | | | | | | | | | | | | | |
| 1 | 2 | | 8 | 5 | 6 | 7 | | | 10 | 11 | 9 | 3 | 4 | | | | | | | | | | | | | |
| 1 | 2 | | 6 | 5 | | 7 | | | 10 | 11 | 9 | 3 | 4 | 8 | | | | | | | | | | | | |
| 1 | 2 | | 6 | 5 | | 7 | 8 | | | 11 | 9 | 3 | 4 | | 10 | | | | | | | | | | | |
| 1 | 2 | | 4 | 5 | 6 | 7 | 8 | | 10 | 11 | 9 | 3 | | | | | | | | | | | | | | |
| 1 | 2 | | 4 | 5 | 6 | 7 | 8 | | 10 | 11 | 9 | 3 | | | | | | | | | | | | | | |
| 1 | 2 | | 4 | 5 | 6 | 7 | 8 | | 10 | 11 | 9 | 3 | | | | | | | | | | | | | | |
| 1 | 2 | | 4 | 5 | 6 | 7 | 8 | | 10 | 11 | | 3 | | | | 9 | | | | | | | | | | |
| 1 | 2 | | 4 | 5 | 6 | | 8 | | | 11 | | 3 | | | 10 | 9 | 7 | | | | | | | | | |
| 1 | | 2 | 4 | 5 | 6 | | 8 | | | 11 | | 3 | | | 10 | 9 | 7 | | | | | | | | | |
| 1 | 2 | | 6 | 5 | | 7 | 8 | | 10 | 11 | | 3 | 4 | | | 9 | | | | | | | | | | |
| 1 | 2 | | 6 | 5 | | 7 | 8 | | 10 | 11 | | 3 | 4 | | | 9 | | | | | | | | | | |
| 1 | 2 | | 6 | 5 | | 7 | 8 | | 10 | 11 | | 3 | 4 | | | 9 | | | | | | | | | | |
| | 2 | | 6 | 5 | | 7 | 8 | | 10 | 11 | | 3 | 4 | | | 9 | | 1 | | | | | | | | |
| 1 | | | 5 | | 6 | 7 | | | | 11 | | 3 | 4 | 8 | 10 | | | | 2 | 9 | | | | | | |
| 1 | 2 | | 8 | 5 | 6 | | 9 | 7 | 10 | 11 | | 3 | 4 | | | | | | | | | | | | | |
| 1 | 2 | | | 5 | 6 | | 9 | | | | | 3 | 4 | 8 | 10 | 11 | 7 | | | | | | | | | |
| 1 | 2 | 3 | 8 | | 6 | | | | 10 | 11 | | | 5 | 7 | | 9 | | | | | 4 | | | | | |
| 1 | 2 | | 8 | 5 | 6 | | 9 | | 10 | 11 | | 3 | 4 | 7 | | | | | | | | | | | | |
| 1 | 2 | 3 | 8 | 5 | 6 | | 9 | | 10 | 11 | | | 4 | 7 | | | | | | | | | | | | |
| | 2 | | 6 | 5 | | 7 | | | 10 | 11 | | 3 | 4 | 8 | | 9 | | 1 | | | | | | | | |
| 1 | 2 | | 6 | | | 7 | | | 10 | 11 | | 3 | 5 | 8 | | 9 | | | | | 4 | | | | | |
| 1 | 2 | | 6 | | | 7 | 9 | | | 11 | | 3 | 4 | 5 | | | | | | | 8 | 10 | | | | |
| 1 | 2 | | 6 | 5 | | 7 | 9 | | 10 | 11 | | 3 | 4 | | | | | | | | 8 | | | | | |
| 1 | 2 | | 6 | 5 | | 7 | | | 10 | 11 | | 3 | 4 | 9 | | | | | | | 8 | | | | | |
| 1 | | | 4 | 5 | 6 | 7 | 9 | | | 11 | | 3 | | 8 | 10 | | | | 2 | | | | | | | |
| 1 | 2 | | | 5 | 6 | 7 | 9 | | 10 | 11 | | 3 | 4 | 8 | | | | | | | | | | | | |
| 1 | 2 | | 8 | 5 | 6 | 7 | 9 | | 10 | 11 | | 3 | 4 | | | | | | | | | | | | | |
| 1 | 2 | 3 | 4 | | 6 | 7 | 8 | | | 11 | | | | 5 | | 9 | | | | | 10 | | | | | |
| 1 | 2 | 3 | 4 | | 6 | 7 | | | 8 | 11 | | | | 5 | | 9 | | | | | 10 | | | | | |
| 1 | 2 | | 4 | | 6 | | 10 | | | 11 | | 3 | | 5 | 7 | | | | | | 8 | | 9 | | | |
| 1 | 2 | | 8 | 5 | 6 | 7 | 9 | | | | | 3 | | | | | | | | | 10 | | | 4 | 11 | |
| 1 | 2 | | | 5 | 6 | 7 | 10 | | | | | 3 | | 8 | | | | | | 9 | | | | 4 | 11 | |
| 1 | 2 | | 8 | 5 | 6 | 7 | 9 | | 10 | 11 | | 3 | | | | | | | | | | | | 4 | | |
| 1 | 2 | | 4 | 5 | | 7 | 8 | | 10 | 11 | | 3 | | 6 | | 9 | | | | | | | | | | |
| 1 | 2 | | 4 | 5 | | 7 | 8 | | 10 | 11 | | 3 | | 6 | | 9 | | | | | | | | | | |
| 1 | 2 | | 6 | | | 7 | 8 | | | 11 | | | 5 | 10 | | 9 | | | 3 | | | | | 4 | | |
| | 2 | | 5 | | 6 | 7 | 8 | | 10 | 11 | | 3 | | 4 | | 9 | | | | | | | | | | 1 |
| 1 | 2 | | 4 | 5 | 6 | 7 | | | 10 | 11 | | 3 | | 8 | | 9 | | | | | | | | | | |
| 39 | 39 | 8 | 39 | 33 | 28 | 34 | 31 | 4 | 30 | 39 | 8 | 34 | 22 | 21 | 7 | 18 | 3 | 2 | 3 | 2 | 9 | 1 | 1 | 4 | 2 | 1 |
| | 2 | | 1 | 1 | | 11 | 16 | | 4 | 11 | 3 | | | | 1 | 3 | 1 | | | 1 | | | 1 | 1 | | |

| Mittell | Proctor | Howe | Hill | Park | Heward | Thompson | Wigham | Huggins | Robertson | Bonass | Hughes | Allison | Brown | Hardy | Moses | Graham |
|---|---|---|---|---|---|---|---|---|---|---|---|---|---|---|---|---|
| 1 | 2 | | 6 | 5 | | 7 | 8 | | 10 | 11 | | 3 | 4 | | | 9 |
| 1 | 2 | | 6 | 5 | | 7 | 8 | | 10 | 11 | | 3 | 4 | 9 | | |
| 1 | 2 | | 6 | 5 | | 7 | 8 | | 10 | 11 | | 3 | 4 | | | 9 |
| 1 | 2 | | 6 | 5 | | 7 | 9 | | 10 | 11 | | 3 | 4 | 8 | | |
| 1 | 2 | | 8 | 5 | 6 | | 9 | | 10 | 11 | | 3 | 4 | 7 | | |
| 1 | 2 | | 8 | 5 | 6 | | 9 | | 10 | 11 | | 3 | 4 | 7 | | |
| 6 | 6 | | 6 | 6 | 2 | 4 | 6 | | 6 | 6 | | 6 | 6 | 4 | | 2 |
| | 1 | | | | | | 3 | | 3 | 2 | | | | | | |

| Mittell | Proctor | Howe | Hill | Park | Heward | Thompson | Wigham | Huggins | Robertson | Bonass | Hughes | Allison | Brown | Hardy | Moses |
|---|---|---|---|---|---|---|---|---|---|---|---|---|---|---|---|
| 1 | 2 | | 6 | 5 | | 7 | | 9 | 8 | 11 | | 3 | | 4 | 10 |
| 1 | 1 | | 1 | 1 | | 1 | | 1 | 1 | 1 | | 1 | | 1 | 1 |
| | | | | | | 1 | | | | | | | | | |

## League Table

| | P | W | D | L | F | A | Pts |
|---|---|---|---|---|---|---|---|
| Chesterfield | 42 | 24 | 12 | 6 | 92 | 39 | 60 |
| Chester | 42 | 22 | 11 | 9 | 100 | 45 | 55 |
| Tranmere Rovers | 42 | 22 | 11 | 9 | 93 | 58 | 55 |
| Lincoln City | 42 | 22 | 9 | 11 | 91 | 51 | 53 |
| Stockport County | 42 | 20 | 8 | 14 | 65 | 49 | 48 |
| Crewe Alexandra | 42 | 19 | 9 | 14 | 80 | 76 | 47 |
| Oldham Athletic | 42 | 18 | 9 | 15 | 86 | 73 | 45 |
| Hartlepools United | 42 | 15 | 12 | 15 | 57 | 61 | 42 |
| Accrington Stanley | 42 | 17 | 8 | 17 | 63 | 72 | 42 |
| Walsall | 42 | 16 | 9 | 17 | 79 | 59 | 41 |
| Rotherham United | 42 | 16 | 9 | 17 | 69 | 66 | 41 |
| Darlington | 42 | 17 | 6 | 19 | 74 | 79 | 40 |
| Carlisle United | 42 | 14 | 12 | 16 | 56 | 62 | 40 |
| Gateshead | 42 | 13 | 14 | 15 | 56 | 76 | 40 |
| Barrow | 42 | 13 | 12 | 17 | 58 | 65 | 38 |
| York City | 42 | 13 | 12 | 17 | 62 | 95 | 38 |
| Halifax Town | 42 | 15 | 7 | 20 | 57 | 61 | 37 |
| Wrexham | 42 | 15 | 7 | 20 | 66 | 75 | 37 |
| Mansfield Town | 42 | 14 | 9 | 19 | 80 | 91 | 37 |
| Rochdale | 42 | 10 | 13 | 19 | 58 | 88 | 33 |
| Southport | 42 | 11 | 9 | 22 | 48 | 90 | 31 |
| New Brighton | 42 | 9 | 6 | 27 | 43 | 102 | 24 |

# 1936-37

## Division Three North

Manager: Jimmy Hamilton

### Did you know that?

The 5–5 draw at Darlington remains the highest score draw in the club's history and featured five goalscorers: Scott, Hill, English, Robertson and Wigham.

'Pools finished sixth in Division Three North, their best since the 1925–26 season, with a playing staff of 21, the same number as the 1932–33 season.

Home League gates averaged 5,740, the highest since the 1921–22 season.

| Match No. | Date | Round | Venue | Opponents | Result | | Scorers | Attendance |
|---|---|---|---|---|---|---|---|---|
| 1 | Aug 29 | | (a) | Southport | D | 1 - 1 | Wigham | 5,364 |
| 2 | Sep 2 | | (h) | Accrington Stanley | W | 1 - 0 | English | 7,342 |
| 3 | 5 | | (h) | Tranmere Rovers | W | 2 - 1 | Robertson, English | 8,729 |
| 4 | 12 | | (a) | Halifax Town | L | 0 - 2 | | 5,798 |
| 5 | 19 | | (h) | Mansfield Town | W | 3 - 0 | Self, English, Proctor (pen) | 7,178 |
| 6 | 26 | | (a) | Crewe Alexandra | D | 1 - 1 | Robertson | 4,016 |
| 7 | 29 | | (a) | Accrington Stanley | W | 2 - 1 | Moses, English | 3,919 |
| 8 | Oct 3 | | (h) | Chester | L | 0 - 1 | | 12,220 |
| 10 | 10 | | (a) | Rochdale | D | 1 - 1 | Scrimshaw | 5,171 |
| 11 | 17 | | (h) | Oldham Athletic | W | 1 - 0 | English | 6,138 |
| 12 | 24 | | (a) | Port Vale | L | 0 - 1 | | 6,659 |
| 13 | 31 | | (h) | Rotherham United | L | 0 - 2 | | 5,892 |
| 14 | Nov 7 | | (a) | Stockport County | D | 1 - 1 | Hardy | 8,092 |
| 15 | 14 | | (h) | Wrexham | W | 2 - 0 | English 2 | 4,683 |
| 16 | 21 | | (a) | Darlington | D | 5 - 5 | J.Scott, Hill, English, Robertson, Wigham | 4,817 |
| 19 | Dec 5 | | (a) | Hull City | L | 0 - 1 | | 5,676 |
| 22 | 19 | | (a) | Lincoln City | L | 0 - 3 | | 4,032 |
| 23 | 25 | | (a) | York City | L | 1 - 4 | J.Scott | 7,170 |
| 24 | 26 | | (h) | Southport | W | 2 - 0 | English, J.Scott | 6,574 |
| 25 | 28 | | (h) | York City | W | 2 - 0 | English (pen), Hardy | 2,744 |
| 26 | Jan 1 | | (h) | Barrow | W | 3 - 1 | Robertson, Wigham, J.Scott | 6,783 |
| 27 | 2 | | (a) | Tranmere Rovers | L | 0 - 1 | | 6,809 |
| 28 | 9 | | (h) | Halifax Town | W | 5 - 3 | McCambridge 3, Robertson, Self | 6,154 |
| 29 | 16 | | (h) | Gateshead | W | 6 - 1 | J.Scott 3, Robertson 2, McCambridge | 7,405 |
| 30 | 23 | | (a) | Mansfield Town | L | 2 - 8 | Proctor (pen), Wigham | 2,696 |
| 31 | 30 | | (h) | Crewe Alexandra | W | 4 - 1 | Wigham, English, Scott (o.g.), Proctor (pen) | 2,058 |
| 32 | Feb 6 | | (a) | Chester | L | 0 - 3 | | 5,444 |
| 33 | 13 | | (h) | Rochdale | W | 4 - 1 | Proctor (pen), J.Scott, English, Self | 4,180 |
| 34 | 20 | | (a) | Oldham Athletic | L | 0 - 2 | | 4,363 |
| 35 | 27 | | (h) | Port Vale | W | 2 - 0 | English 2 | 2,645 |
| 36 | Mar 6 | | (a) | Rotherham United | W | 4 - 2 | J.Scott 3, Self | 2,601 |
| 37 | 13 | | (h) | Stockport County | L | 2 - 4 | Wigham, Self | 7,105 |
| 39 | 20 | | (a) | Wrexham | W | 1 - 0 | Robertson | 3,083 |
| 40 | 26 | | (a) | Carlisle United | L | 0 - 2 | | 8,366 |
| 41 | 27 | | (h) | Darlington | L | 1 - 3 | English | 4,604 |
| 42 | 29 | | (h) | Carlisle United | W | 3 - 0 | Self, Proctor (pen), Robertson | 4,748 |
| 43 | Apr 3 | | (a) | Gateshead | D | 2 - 2 | J.Scott, Robertson | 2,738 |
| 44 | 10 | | (h) | Hull City | D | 2 - 2 | Annables (o.g.), English | 4,936 |
| 45 | 17 | | (a) | New Brighton | L | 0 - 4 | | 1,865 |
| 46 | 24 | | (h) | Lincoln City | W | 3 - 1 | Robertson, Self, Proctor | 5,552 |
| 47 | 28 | | (h) | New Brighton | W | 5 - 0 | English 2, Wigham 2, Proctor (pen) | 2,870 |
| 48 | May 1 | | (a) | Barrow | L | 1 - 3 | Proctor (pen) | 3,395 |

Final Position : 6th in Division Three North — Apps.

2 own goals — Goals

**FA Cup**

| | | | | | | | | |
|---|---|---|---|---|---|---|---|---|
| 17 | Nov 28 | R1 | (a) | Rotherham United | D | 4 - 4 | Proctor (pen), English, Self, Park | 11,552 |
| 18 | Dec 2 | R1r | (h) | Rotherham United | W | 2 - 0 | Self, J.Scott | 8,532 |
| 20 | 12 | R2 | (a) | Crewe Alexandra | D | 1 - 1 | English | 5,104 |
| 21 | 16 | R2r | (h) | Crewe Alexandra | L | 1 - 2 | Self | 7,636 |

Apps.
Goals

**Division 3 North Cup**

| | | | | | | | | |
|---|---|---|---|---|---|---|---|---|
| 9 | Oct 7 | R1 | (a) | Lincoln City | W | 2 - 0 | Robertson, Firman | 1,115 |
| 38 | Mar 17 | R2 | (a) | York City | L | 0 - 5 | | 1,600 |

Apps.
Goals

| Mittell | Proctor | Allison | Nobbs | Park | Dreyer | Scott, J. | Wigham | English | Robertson | Self | Hardy | Middleton | Hill | Moses | Scott, T. | Scrimshaw | Moore | Bradford | Graham | McCambridge | Firman | Oxley |
|---|---|---|---|---|---|---|---|---|---|---|---|---|---|---|---|---|---|---|---|---|---|---|
| 1 | 2 | 3 | 4 | 5 | 6 | 7 | 8 | 9 | 10 | 11 | | | | | | | | | | | | |
| 1 | 2 | 3 | 4 | 5 | 6 | 7 | | 9 | 10 | 11 | 8 | | | | | | | | | | | |
| 1 | 2 | 3 | 6 | 5 | 4 | 7 | 8 | 9 | 10 | 11 | | | | | | | | | | | | |
| 1 | 2 | 3 | 6 | 5 | 4 | 7 | 8 | 9 | | 11 | | 10 | | | | | | | | | | |
| 1 | 2 | 3 | 4 | 5 | | 7 | 8 | 9 | | 11 | | | 6 | 10 | | | | | | | | |
| 1 | 2 | 3 | 4 | 5 | | 7 | 8 | 9 | 10 | 11 | | | 6 | | | | | | | | | |
| 1 | 2 | 3 | 6 | 5 | | | | 9 | | 11 | | | 4 | 10 | 7 | 8 | | | | | | |
| 1 | 2 | 3 | 6 | 5 | | | 8 | 9 | 10 | 11 | | | 4 | | 7 | | | | | | | |
| 1 | 2 | 3 | 6 | 5 | | | 10 | 9 | | 11 | | | 4 | | 7 | 8 | | | | | | |
| 1 | 2 | 3 | 6 | 5 | | | 10 | 9 | | 11 | | | 4 | | 7 | 8 | | | | | | |
| | 2 | 3 | 6 | 5 | | | 11 | 9 | 10 | | | | 4 | | 7 | 8 | 1 | | | | | |
| | 2 | 3 | 6 | 5 | | 7 | 8 | 9 | | | | | 4 | | 11 | 10 | 1 | | | | | |
| | 2 | 3 | | 5 | 4 | | 8 | 9 | 10 | 11 | 7 | | 6 | | | | 1 | | | | | |
| | 2 | 3 | | | 4 | 7 | 8 | 9 | 10 | 11 | 5 | | 6 | | | | 1 | | | | | |
| | 2 | 3 | | | 4 | 7 | 8 | 9 | 10 | 11 | 5 | | 6 | | | | 1 | | | | | |
| | 2 | 3 | | | 4 | 7 | 9 | | 10 | 11 | 5 | | 6 | | | 8 | 1 | | | | | |
| 1 | 2 | 3 | | 5 | 4 | 7 | 9 | | 10 | 11 | | | 6 | | | 8 | | | | | | |
| 1 | | 3 | 9 | | 4 | 7 | 8 | | 10 | 11 | 5 | | 6 | | | | | 2 | | | | |
| | | 3 | | | 4 | 7 | 8 | 9 | 10 | 11 | 5 | | 6 | | | | 1 | 2 | | | | |
| | | 3 | | | 4 | 7 | 8 | 9 | 10 | 11 | 5 | | | | | | 1 | 2 | 6 | | | |
| | | 3 | | | 4 | 7 | 8 | 9 | 10 | 11 | 5 | | | | | | 1 | 2 | 6 | | | |
| | | 3 | | | 4 | 7 | | | 10 | 11 | 5 | | 9 | 8 | | | 1 | 2 | 6 | | | |
| | 2 | 3 | | | 4 | 7 | 8 | | 10 | 11 | 5 | | | | | | 1 | | 6 | 9 | | |
| | 2 | 3 | | | | 7 | 8 | | 10 | 11 | 5 | | 4 | | | | 1 | | 6 | 9 | | |
| | 2 | 3 | | | | 7 | 8 | | 10 | 11 | 5 | | 4 | | | | 1 | | 6 | 9 | | |
| 1 | 2 | 3 | | 5 | 4 | 7 | 8 | 9 | 10 | 11 | | | | | | | | | 6 | | | |
| 1 | 2 | 3 | 6 | 5 | 4 | 7 | 8 | 9 | 10 | 11 | | | | | | | | | | | | |
| 1 | 2 | 3 | | 5 | 4 | 7 | 8 | 9 | 10 | 11 | | | 6 | | | | | | | | | |
| 1 | 2 | 3 | | 5 | 4 | 8 | | | 10 | 11 | 6 | | | | | | | | 7 | 9 | | |
| 1 | 2 | 3 | | 5 | 4 | 7 | 8 | 9 | 10 | 11 | | | | | | | | | | 6 | | |
| 1 | 2 | 3 | | 5 | 4 | 7 | | 9 | 10 | 11 | 8 | | | | | | | | | 6 | | |
| 1 | 2 | 3 | | 5 | 4 | 7 | 8 | 9 | 10 | 11 | | | | | | | | | | 6 | | |
| | 2 | 3 | 4 | 5 | | 7 | | 9 | 10 | 11 | 6 | | | | | | 1 | | | 8 | | |
| | 2 | 3 | 4 | 5 | | 7 | | 9 | 10 | 11 | 6 | | | | | | 1 | | | 8 | | |
| | 2 | 3 | | 5 | 4 | 7 | 11 | 9 | 10 | | | | | | | 8 | 1 | | | 6 | | |
| 1 | 2 | 3 | | 5 | | 7 | | 9 | 10 | 11 | 4 | | | | | | | | 6 | 8 | | |
| 1 | 2 | 3 | | 5 | | 7 | | 9 | 10 | 11 | 4 | | | | | | | | 6 | 8 | | |
| 1 | 2 | 3 | 4 | 5 | | 11 | 8 | 9 | 10 | | 7 | | | | | | | | 6 | | | |
| 1 | 2 | 3 | | 5 | | 7 | 11 | 9 | 10 | | 4 | | | | | | | | 6 | 8 | | |
| 1 | 2 | 3 | | | 4 | 7 | 8 | 9 | 10 | 11 | 5 | | | | | | | | | 6 | | |
| 1 | 2 | 3 | | | 4 | 7 | 8 | 9 | 10 | 11 | 5 | | | | | | | | | 6 | | |
| 1 | 2 | | | | 4 | 7 | | 9 | 10 | 11 | 5 | | | | | 8 | | 3 | | 6 | | |
| 26 | 37 | 41 | 17 | 28 | 26 | 36 | 32 | 34 | 36 | 37 | 24 | 1 | 19 | 3 | 6 | 9 | 16 | 6 | 12 | 16 | | |
| | 8 | | | | | 12 | 8 | 18 | 11 | 7 | 2 | | 1 | 1 | | 1 | | | | 4 | | |

| Mittell | Proctor | Allison | Nobbs | Park | Dreyer | Scott, J. | Wigham | English | Robertson | Self | Hardy | Middleton | Hill | Moses | Scott, T. | Scrimshaw | Moore | Bradford | Graham | McCambridge | Firman | Oxley |
|---|---|---|---|---|---|---|---|---|---|---|---|---|---|---|---|---|---|---|---|---|---|---|
| 1 | 2 | 3 | | 5 | 4 | 7 | 8 | 9 | 10 | 11 | | | 6 | | | | | | | | | |
| 1 | 2 | 3 | | 5 | 4 | 7 | 9 | | 10 | 11 | 8 | | 6 | | | | | | | | | |
| 1 | 2 | 3 | | 5 | 4 | 7 | 8 | 9 | 10 | 11 | | | 6 | | | | | | | | | |
| 1 | 2 | 3 | | 5 | 4 | 7 | 8 | | 10 | 11 | 9 | | 6 | | | | | | | | | |
| 4 | 4 | 4 | | 4 | 4 | 4 | 4 | 2 | 4 | 4 | 2 | | 4 | | | | | | | | | |
| | 1 | | | 1 | | 1 | | 2 | | 3 | | | | | | | | | | | | |

| Mittell | Proctor | Allison | Nobbs | Park | Dreyer | Scott, J. | Wigham | English | Robertson | Self | Hardy | Middleton | Hill | Moses | Scott, T. | Scrimshaw | Moore | Bradford | Graham | McCambridge | Firman | Oxley |
|---|---|---|---|---|---|---|---|---|---|---|---|---|---|---|---|---|---|---|---|---|---|---|
| 1 | 2 | 3 | 6 | 5 | | | | 9 | 10 | | | | 4 | | 7 | 8 | | | | | 11 | |
| 1 | 2 | 3 | | | 4 | 7 | | | 10 | 11 | 5 | | | | | 8 | | | | 6 | | 9 |
| 2 | 2 | 2 | 1 | 1 | 1 | 1 | | 1 | 2 | 1 | 1 | | 1 | | 1 | 2 | | | | 1 | 1 | 1 |
| | | | | | | | | | 1 | | | | | | | | | | | | 1 | |

## League Table

| | P | W | D | L | F | A | Pts |
|---|---|---|---|---|---|---|---|
| Stockport County | 42 | 23 | 14 | 5 | 84 | 39 | 60 |
| Lincoln City | 42 | 25 | 7 | 10 | 103 | 57 | 57 |
| Chester | 42 | 22 | 9 | 11 | 87 | 57 | 53 |
| Oldham Athletic | 42 | 20 | 11 | 11 | 77 | 59 | 51 |
| Hull City | 42 | 17 | 12 | 13 | 68 | 69 | 46 |
| Hartlepools United | 42 | 19 | 7 | 16 | 75 | 69 | 45 |
| Halifax Town | 42 | 18 | 9 | 15 | 68 | 63 | 45 |
| Wrexham | 42 | 16 | 12 | 14 | 71 | 57 | 44 |
| Mansfield Town | 42 | 18 | 8 | 16 | 91 | 76 | 44 |
| Carlisle United | 42 | 18 | 8 | 16 | 65 | 68 | 44 |
| Port Vale | 42 | 17 | 10 | 15 | 58 | 64 | 44 |
| York City | 42 | 16 | 11 | 15 | 79 | 70 | 43 |
| Accrington Stanley | 42 | 16 | 9 | 17 | 76 | 69 | 41 |
| Southport | 42 | 12 | 13 | 17 | 73 | 87 | 37 |
| New Brighton | 42 | 13 | 11 | 18 | 55 | 70 | 37 |
| Barrow | 42 | 13 | 10 | 19 | 70 | 86 | 36 |
| Rotherham United | 42 | 14 | 7 | 21 | 78 | 91 | 35 |
| Rochdale | 42 | 13 | 9 | 20 | 69 | 86 | 35 |
| Tranmere Rovers | 42 | 12 | 9 | 21 | 71 | 88 | 33 |
| Crewe Alexandra | 42 | 10 | 12 | 20 | 55 | 83 | 32 |
| Gateshead | 42 | 11 | 10 | 21 | 63 | 98 | 32 |
| Darlington | 42 | 8 | 14 | 20 | 66 | 96 | 30 |

# 1937-38

## Division Three North

Manager: Jimmy Hamilton

### Did you know that?

Only a late run of seven games without defeat prevented 'Pools from making another re-election application, finishing in 20th position above Barrow by virtue of a superior goal average.

For the second time in their League history United failed to win on their travels, 'amassing' four points from drawn games.

Jack Proctor played his final game for the club on 7 May, a 2–0 win over Wrexham.

| Match No. | Date | Round | Venue | Opponents | Result | | Scorers | Attendance |
|---|---|---|---|---|---|---|---|---|
| 1 | Aug 26 | | (a) | Lincoln City | L | 1 - 2 | Scott | 8,779 |
| 2 | Sep 1 | | (h) | Accrington Stanley | W | 2 - 0 | English, Proctor (pen) | 7,751 |
| 3 | 4 | | (h) | Hull City | D | 2 - 2 | Wigham 2 | 8,173 |
| 4 | 6 | | (a) | Accrington Stanley | L | 1 - 2 | Embleton | 4,812 |
| 5 | 11 | | (a) | New Brighton | L | 1 - 4 | Proctor (pen) | 5,419 |
| 6 | 13 | | (a) | Wrexham | L | 3 - 6 | West, Curtis, English | 2,752 |
| 7 | 18 | | (h) | Gateshead | L | 1 - 3 | Proctor (pen) | 7,503 |
| 8 | 25 | | (a) | Oldham Athletic | L | 1 - 3 | Wigham | 6,861 |
| 9 | Oct 2 | | (h) | Darlington | W | 2 - 1 | English, Wigham | 6,867 |
| 10 | 9 | | (a) | Port Vale | L | 1 - 5 | Scott | 7,951 |
| 11 | 16 | | (h) | Chester | L | 0 - 1 | | 5,955 |
| 13 | 23 | | (a) | Rotherham United | L | 1 - 3 | Robertson | 4,700 |
| 15 | 30 | | (h) | Rochdale | D | 3 - 3 | Wigham 2, Scott | 5,087 |
| 16 | Nov 6 | | (a) | Doncaster Rovers | D | 3 - 3 | Proctor (pen), Scott 2 | 10,538 |
| 17 | 13 | | (h) | Southport | L | 1 - 2 | Wigham | 4,384 |
| 18 | 20 | | (a) | Bradford City | L | 1 - 4 | Self | 5,202 |
| 20 | Dec 4 | | (a) | Tranmere Rovers | L | 0 - 4 | | 5,128 |
| 22 | 18 | | (a) | Carlisle United | L | 1 - 3 | Smith | 3,855 |
| 23 | 25 | | (h) | Crewe Alexandra | D | 2 - 2 | Embleton, Wigham | 6,267 |
| 24 | 27 | | (a) | Crewe Alexandra | L | 0 - 2 | | 5,167 |
| 25 | Jan 1 | | (h) | Lincoln City | W | 2 - 0 | English, Scott | 5,126 |
| 26 | 12 | | (h) | York City | D | 0 - 0 | | 2,665 |
| 27 | 15 | | (a) | Hull City | L | 0 - 4 | | 8,607 |
| 28 | 29 | | (a) | Gateshead | L | 1 - 2 | Self | 7,308 |
| 29 | Feb 2 | | (h) | New Brighton | W | 1 - 0 | Proctor (pen) | 1,911 |
| 30 | 5 | | (h) | Oldham Athletic | W | 2 - 0 | Embleton, English | 5,310 |
| 31 | 12 | | (a) | Darlington | L | 0 - 2 | | 4,610 |
| 33 | 19 | | (h) | Port Vale | W | 2 - 1 | English, Scott | 4,483 |
| 34 | 26 | | (a) | Chester | L | 0 - 6 | | 3,723 |
| 35 | Mar 5 | | (h) | Rotherham United | W | 4 - 0 | Nevin, Mackie 2, English | 5,639 |
| 36 | 12 | | (a) | Rochdale | D | 2 - 2 | Nevin, Self | 5,615 |
| 37 | 19 | | (h) | Doncaster Rovers | D | 0 - 0 | | 5,547 |
| 38 | 26 | | (a) | Southport | L | 0 - 2 | | 3,140 |
| 39 | Apr 2 | | (h) | Bradford City | D | 1 - 1 | Proctor (pen) | 3,801 |
| 40 | 9 | | (a) | York City | L | 0 - 1 | | 3,565 |
| 41 | 15 | | (h) | Barrow | D | 1 - 1 | Wigham | 5,449 |
| 42 | 16 | | (h) | Tranmere Rovers | D | 2 - 2 | Proctor, English | 4,826 |
| 43 | 18 | | (a) | Barrow | D | 0 - 0 | | 3,991 |
| 44 | 23 | | (a) | Halifax Town | D | 0 - 0 | | 2,821 |
| 45 | 30 | | (h) | Carlisle United | W | 4 - 1 | English, Scott, Embleton, Hughes | 2,766 |
| 46 | May 4 | | (h) | Halifax Town | W | 2 - 0 | Embleton, Watt | 4,940 |
| 47 | 7 | | (h) | Wrexham | W | 2 - 0 | West, Embleton | 5,135 |

Final Position : 20th in Division Three North

Apps.
Goals

**FA Cup**

| Match No. | Date | Round | Venue | Opponents | Result | | Scorers | Attendance |
|---|---|---|---|---|---|---|---|---|
| 19 | Nov 27 | R1 | (h) | Southport | W | 3 - 1 | Scott, English, Embleton | 7,415 |
| 21 | Dec 11 | R2 | (a) | Tranmere Rovers | L | 1 - 3 | Self | 7,994 |

Apps.
Goals

**Division 3 North Cup**

| Match No. | Date | Round | Venue | Opponents | Result | | Scorers | Attendance |
|---|---|---|---|---|---|---|---|---|
| 12 | Oct 21 | R1 | (a) | Hull City | D | 1 - 1 | Wigham | 4,000 |
| 14 | 27 | R1r | (h) | Hull City | W | 3 - 0 | English, Embleton, Procter (pen) | 1,900 |
| 32 | Feb 15 | R2 | (a) | Southport | L | 0 - 6 | | 1,000 |

Apps.
Goals

| Taylor | Proctor | Allison | Curtis | Davidson | Hughes | Scott | Wigham | English | Robertson | Self | Thomas | Embleton | Reid | Thompson | Fenton | West | Telling | Brown | Pickering | Smith | Rutherford | Whyte | Park | Mackie | Turner | McLean | Copeman | Rodger | Johnson | Nevin | Oliver | Mathison |
|---|---|---|---|---|---|---|---|---|---|---|---|---|---|---|---|---|---|---|---|---|---|---|---|---|---|---|---|---|---|---|---|---|
|1|2|3|4|5|6|7|8|9|10|11||||||||||||||||||||||
|1|2|3|6|5||7|8|9|10|11|4|||||||||||||||||||||
|1|2|3|6|5||7|8|9||11|4|10||||||||||||||||||||
|1|2|3|10||6|||||11|4|8|5|9|7|||||||||||||||||
|1|2|3|6|||7|8|9||11|4||5|||10||||||||||||||||
|1|2|3|8|||7||9||11|4||5|||10|6|||||||||||||||
||2|3|4|||7|8|9||11|||5|||10|6|1||||||||||||||
|1|2|3|8|5|6||10|9||11|4|7||||||||||||||||||||
|1|2|3|6|5||7|8|9|10|11|4|||||||||||||||||||||
|1|2|3||5|4|7|8|9|10|11|||||||||6||||||||||||||
|1|2|3|||4|7|8|9|10|11|||5|||||||6|||||||||||||
||2||||6|7|9||10|11||8|5|||||||4|1|3|||||||||||
||2||||6|7|8|9|10|11|||5|||||||4|1|3|||||||||||
||2|3|||6|7|9||10|11||8||||||||4|1||5||||||||||
|1|2|3|||6|7|8|9|10|||||||||||4|||5|11|||||||||
|1|2|3|||6|7||9|10|11||8||||||||4|||5||||||||||
|||3|||6|7|9|10||11||8||||||||4|1||5||2||||||||
|1|2|3|||6||8|||11|4|7||||10||||9|||5||||||||||
|1||3|||6|7|8|9||11|5|10||||||||4|||2||||||||||
|1||3|8||6|7|||10|11|5|||||||||4||2||||9|||||||
|1|2|3|8||6|7||9|10|11|5|||||||||4|||||||||||||
|1|2|3|8||6|7||9|10|11|5|||||||||4|||||||||||||
|1||3|||6|7|8|9||11|5|10||||||||4|||||||2||||||
|1|2|3|||6||7|9||11|4|8||||||||10||||||||5|||||
||2|3|8||6|7||9||11||10||||||||4||||||||5|1||||
||2|3|||6|7|8|9||11||10||||||||4||||||||5|1||||
||2|3|||6|7|8|9||11||10||||||||4||||||||5|1||||
|||3|||6|7|8|9||11|5|10||||||||4||||||||2|1||||
|||3|||6|7|8|9||11|4|10||||||||2||||||||5|1||||
|||2|||6||8|10||7|5|||||||||4||3||11|||||1|9|||
|1||2|||6||8|10||7|5|||||||||4||3||11||||||9|||
|1|2||||6||8|10||7|5|||||||||4||||11||||||9|3||
|1|||||6||8|10||7|5|||||||||4||||11||||2||9|3||
|1|2|3|10||6|7||9||11|4|||||||||8|||||||||||5||
|1|2||8||6|7|9|10||11|5|||||||||4|||||||||||3||
|1|2|3|8||6|7|9|10||11|5|||||||||4|||||||||||||
||2|3|||6|7|8|9||11|5|10||||||||4|||||||||1||||
||2||||6|7|8|9||11|5|10||||||||||||||||4|1||3||
||2||||6|7|8|9||11|5|10||||||||||||||||4|1||3||
||2||||6|7|8|9||11|5|10||||||||||||||||4|1||3||
||2||||6|7||||11|5|10||||9||||8||||||||4|1||3||
||2||||6|7|8|||11|5|10||||9||||||||||||4|1||3||
|25|33|32|16|6|36|34|33|35|13|41|29|22|7|1|1|6|2|1|1|28|4|5|6|5|1|1|1|12|12|4|9||
||7||1||1|8|9|9|1|3||6||||3||||1||||2||||||2|||

| Taylor | Proctor | Allison | Curtis | Davidson | Hughes | Scott | Wigham | English | Robertson | Self | Thomas | Embleton | Reid | Thompson | Fenton | West | Telling | Brown | Pickering | Smith | Rutherford | Whyte | Park | Mackie | Turner | McLean | Copeman | Rodger | Johnson | Nevin | Oliver | Mathison |
|---|---|---|---|---|---|---|---|---|---|---|---|---|---|---|---|---|---|---|---|---|---|---|---|---|---|---|---|---|---|---|---|---|
|1||3|||6|7|9|10||11||8||||||||4|||5||2||||||||
|||3|||6|7|9||10|11||8||||||||4|1|2|5||||||||||
|1||2|||2|2|2|1|1|2||2||||||||2|1|1|2||1||||||||
|||||||1||1||1||1|||||||||||||||||||||

| Taylor | Proctor | Allison | Curtis | Davidson | Hughes | Scott | Wigham | English | Robertson | Self | Thomas | Embleton | Reid | Thompson | Fenton | West | Telling | Brown | Pickering | Smith | Rutherford | Whyte | Park | Mackie | Turner | McLean | Copeman | Rodger | Johnson | Nevin | Oliver | Mathison |
|---|---|---|---|---|---|---|---|---|---|---|---|---|---|---|---|---|---|---|---|---|---|---|---|---|---|---|---|---|---|---|---|---|
||2||||6||8||10|11||7|5|||||||4|1|3||||||||9|||
||2||||6|7||9|10|11||8|5|||||||4|1|3|||||||||||
|1|2|||||||9|8|11|4|||||||||7||3||10||||5||||6|
|1|3||||2|1|1|2|3|3|1|2|2|||||||3|2|3||1||||1||1||1|
||1||||||1|1||||1|||||||||||||||||||||

## League Table

| | P | W | D | L | F | A | Pts |
|---|---|---|---|---|---|---|---|
| Tranmere Rovers | 42 | 23 | 10 | 9 | 81 | 41 | 56 |
| Doncaster Rovers | 42 | 21 | 12 | 9 | 74 | 49 | 54 |
| Hull City | 42 | 20 | 13 | 9 | 80 | 43 | 53 |
| Oldham Athletic | 42 | 19 | 13 | 10 | 67 | 46 | 51 |
| Gateshead | 42 | 20 | 11 | 11 | 84 | 59 | 51 |
| Rotherham United | 42 | 20 | 10 | 12 | 68 | 56 | 50 |
| Lincoln City | 42 | 19 | 8 | 15 | 66 | 50 | 46 |
| Crewe Alexandra | 42 | 18 | 9 | 15 | 71 | 53 | 45 |
| Chester | 42 | 16 | 12 | 14 | 77 | 72 | 44 |
| Wrexham | 42 | 16 | 11 | 15 | 58 | 63 | 43 |
| York City | 42 | 16 | 10 | 16 | 70 | 68 | 42 |
| Carlisle United | 42 | 15 | 9 | 18 | 57 | 67 | 39 |
| New Brighton | 42 | 15 | 8 | 19 | 60 | 61 | 38 |
| Bradford City | 42 | 14 | 10 | 18 | 66 | 69 | 38 |
| Port Vale | 42 | 12 | 14 | 16 | 65 | 73 | 38 |
| Southport | 42 | 12 | 14 | 16 | 53 | 82 | 38 |
| Rochdale | 42 | 13 | 11 | 18 | 67 | 78 | 37 |
| Halifax Town | 42 | 12 | 12 | 18 | 44 | 66 | 36 |
| Darlington | 42 | 11 | 10 | 21 | 54 | 79 | 32 |
| Hartlepools United | 42 | 10 | 12 | 20 | 53 | 80 | 32 |
| Barrow | 42 | 11 | 10 | 21 | 41 | 71 | 32 |
| Accrington Stanley | 42 | 11 | 7 | 24 | 45 | 75 | 29 |

# 1938-39

## Division Three North

Manager: Jimmy Hamilton

### Did you know that?

'Pools' 1–0 win at Bradford City on 15 October brought to an end a run of 31 consecutive away games without success, which stretched back to 26 March 1937.

Johnny Wigham played his final game for the club on 6 May, a goalless draw against Wrexham.

United finished in 21st position and made a third successful application for re-election, along with Accrington Stanley. Average home gates were 4,164.

| Match No. | Date | Round | Venue | Opponents | Result | | Scorers | Attendance |
|---|---|---|---|---|---|---|---|---|
| 1 | Aug 27 | | (a) | Carlisle United | L | 0 - 2 | | 7,014 |
| 2 | 29 | | (a) | Wrexham | L | 0 - 3 | | 4,908 |
| 3 | Sep 3 | | (h) | Crewe Alexandra | L | 0 - 1 | | 5,863 |
| 4 | 7 | | (a) | Darlington | L | 0 - 3 | | 3,125 |
| 5 | 10 | | (a) | Southport | L | 0 - 2 | | 5,053 |
| 6 | 14 | | (h) | Darlington | W | 3 - 0 | Wigham, Lealman, McGarry | 3,942 |
| 7 | 17 | | (h) | Doncaster Rovers | L | 1 - 3 | Musgrave | 5,722 |
| 8 | 24 | | (a) | Rotherham United | L | 1 - 5 | West | 7,698 |
| 9 | Oct 1 | | (h) | Rochdale | W | 4 - 2 | Woods, Wigham 2, Self | 4,446 |
| 10 | 8 | | (a) | York City | L | 0 - 2 | | 6,208 |
| 11 | 15 | | (a) | Bradford City | W | 1 - 0 | McGarry | 6,552 |
| 12 | 22 | | (h) | Hull City | D | 3 - 3 | Woods, Wigham, McGarry | 6,189 |
| 13 | 29 | | (a) | Lincoln City | D | 2 - 2 | McGarry, Self | 4,682 |
| 14 | Nov 5 | | (h) | Stockport County | W | 4 - 2 | McGarry 3, Wigham | 6,519 |
| 15 | 12 | | (a) | Accrington Stanley | D | 0 - 0 | | 5,063 |
| 16 | 19 | | (h) | Barnsley | L | 0 - 1 | | 8,582 |
| 18 | Dec 3 | | (h) | Halifax Town | W | 1 - 0 | Love | 4,603 |
| 20 | 17 | | (h) | Barrow | L | 1 - 2 | Woods | 2,926 |
| 21 | 24 | | (h) | Carlisle United | W | 2 - 1 | Price, Musgrave (pen) | 2,435 |
| 22 | 26 | | (h) | Chester | L | 2 - 5 | Musgrave (pen), Robbins | 5,177 |
| 23 | 27 | | (a) | Chester | L | 2 - 8 | Self 2 | 7,748 |
| 24 | 31 | | (a) | Crewe Alexandra | L | 2 - 3 | Self, Lealman | 4,969 |
| 26 | Jan 7 | | (a) | Oldham Athletic | L | 2 - 4 | Price, Robbins | 2,708 |
| 27 | 14 | | (h) | Southport | L | 0 - 2 | | 3,985 |
| 28 | 18 | | (a) | New Brighton | L | 2 - 5 | Woods 2 | 1,453 |
| 29 | 26 | | (a) | Doncaster Rovers | L | 1 - 3 | Price | 2,675 |
| 30 | 28 | | (h) | Rotherham United | D | 1 - 1 | Wigham | 2,604 |
| 31 | Feb 4 | | (a) | Rochdale | W | 4 - 3 | Robbins 2, Wigham, McGarry | 5,557 |
| 32 | 11 | | (h) | York City | W | 3 - 2 | Wigham 2, McGarry | 3,105 |
| 33 | 18 | | (h) | Bradford City | L | 1 - 3 | Wigham | 4,344 |
| 34 | 25 | | (a) | Hull City | L | 1 - 4 | McGarry | 4,565 |
| 35 | Mar 4 | | (h) | Lincoln City | W | 2 - 1 | McGarry, Wigham | 2,393 |
| 37 | 11 | | (a) | Stockport County | L | 0 - 5 | | 5,198 |
| 39 | 18 | | (h) | Accrington Stanley | W | 2 - 1 | Diamond, Love | 2,463 |
| 40 | 25 | | (a) | Barnsley | L | 0 - 2 | | 11,611 |
| 42 | Apr 1 | | (h) | Oldham Athletic | D | 0 - 0 | | 3,147 |
| 43 | 7 | | (h) | Gateshead | W | 3 - 1 | West 2, Robbins | 3,992 |
| 44 | 8 | | (a) | Halifax Town | L | 0 - 2 | | 3,379 |
| 45 | 10 | | (a) | Gateshead | L | 0 - 2 | | 4,593 |
| 46 | 15 | | (h) | New Brighton | W | 3 - 2 | Woffinden, Woods, West | 1,554 |
| 47 | 22 | | (a) | Barrow | D | 1 - 1 | Self | 4,356 |
| 48 | May 6 | | (h) | Wrexham | D | 0 - 0 | | 3,455 |

Final Position: 21st in Division Three North

Apps.
Goals

**FA Cup**

| Match No. | Date | Round | Venue | Opponents | Result | | Scorers | Attendance |
|---|---|---|---|---|---|---|---|---|
| 17 | Nov 26 | R1 | (h) | Accrington Stanley | W | 2 - 1 | Woods, Self | 7,068 |
| 19 | Dec 10 | R2 | (h) | Queen's Park Rangers | L | 0 - 2 | | 11,924 |

Apps.
Goals

**Division 3 North Cup**

| Match No. | Date | Round | Venue | Opponents | Result | | Scorers | Attendance |
|---|---|---|---|---|---|---|---|---|
| 25 | Jan 2 | R1 | (h) | Darlington | W | 4 - 1 | McGarry 2, Wigham, Robbins | 2,000 |
| 36 | Mar 8 | R2 | (a) | Gateshead | D | 0 - 0 | | 290 |
| 38 | 15 | R2r | (h) | Gateshead | W | 5 - 1 | Diamond 4, Price | 700 |
| 41 | 29 | Semi | (a) | Bradford City | L | 2 - 5 | Love, Spencer (pen) | 1,125 |

Apps.
Goals

| Wallace | Wright | Johnson | Don | Thomas | Musgrave | Price | Wigham | Love | Robbins | Self | Race | Woods | Leaman | Robinson | Wilson | Douglas | McGarry | Rose | West | Chapman | Mackie | Calder | Brown | Diamond | Woffinden | Peart | Copeland | Halliday | Spencer |
|---|---|---|---|---|---|---|---|---|---|---|---|---|---|---|---|---|---|---|---|---|---|---|---|---|---|---|---|---|---|
| 1 | 2 | 3 | 4 | 5 | 6 | 7 | 8 | 9 | 10 | 11 | | | | | | | | | | | | | | | | | | | |
| 1 | 2 | 3 | 4 | 5 | 6 | 7 | | | 10 | 11 | 8 | 9 | | | | | | | | | | | | | | | | | |
| 1 | 2 | 3 | 4 | 5 | 6 | | | | 10 | 11 | 8 | 9 | 7 | | | | | | | | | | | | | | | | |
| | 2 | 3 | 4 | 5 | 6 | 7 | 10 | 9 | | 11 | | 8 | | 1 | | | | | | | | | | | | | | | |
| | 2 | | | 4 | 6 | | 10 | | | 11 | 8 | | 7 | 1 | 3 | 5 | 9 | | | | | | | | | | | | |
| 1 | 2 | | | 4 | 6 | | 8 | | 10 | 11 | | | 7 | | 3 | 5 | 9 | | | | | | | | | | | | |
| 1 | 2 | | | 4 | 6 | | 8 | | 10 | 11 | | | 7 | | 3 | 5 | 9 | | | | | | | | | | | | |
| 1 | 2 | 3 | | 5 | 4 | 7 | 8 | | 10 | 11 | | | | | | | | 6 | 9 | | | | | | | | | | |
| 1 | 2 | 3 | | 5 | | 7 | 10 | | | 11 | | 8 | | | | | 9 | 6 | | 4 | | | | | | | | | |
| 1 | | 2 | | 5 | | 7 | 10 | | | 11 | | 8 | | | 3 | | 9 | 6 | | 4 | | | | | | | | | |
| 1 | | 2 | | 5 | | | 10 | | | 11 | | 8 | 7 | | 3 | | 9 | 6 | | 4 | | | | | | | | | |
| 1 | | 2 | | 5 | | | 10 | | | 11 | | 8 | 7 | | 3 | | 9 | 6 | | 4 | | | | | | | | | |
| 1 | | 2 | | 5 | | 7 | 10 | | | 11 | | 8 | | | 3 | | 9 | 6 | | 4 | | | | | | | | | |
| 1 | | 2 | | 5 | | 7 | 10 | | | 11 | | 8 | | | 3 | | 9 | 6 | | 4 | | | | | | | | | |
| 1 | | 2 | | 5 | | 7 | 10 | | | 11 | | 8 | | | 3 | | 9 | 6 | | 4 | | | | | | | | | |
| 1 | | 2 | | 5 | | 7 | 10 | | | | | 8 | | | 3 | | 9 | 6 | | 4 | 11 | | | | | | | | |
| 1 | | 2 | | 5 | 4 | 7 | 10 | 9 | 8 | 11 | | | | | 3 | | | 6 | | | | | | | | | | | |
| 1 | 2 | | | 5 | | 7 | 8 | 10 | | 11 | | 9 | | | 3 | | | 6 | | 4 | | | | | | | | | |
| 1 | 2 | | | 5 | 4 | 7 | 9 | | 8 | 11 | | | | | 3 | | | 6 | 10 | | | | | | | | | | |
| 1 | 2 | | | 5 | 4 | 7 | 10 | | 8 | 11 | | | | | | | 9 | | | | | 3 | 6 | | | | | | |
| 1 | 2 | 3 | | 4 | 8 | 7 | | | 10 | 11 | | | | | | | 9 | | | | | 5 | 6 | | | | | | |
| 1 | 4 | 2 | | 5 | 6 | | 10 | | 8 | 11 | | | 7 | | 3 | | 9 | | | | | | | | | | | | |
| | 4 | 2 | | 5 | 6 | 7 | 10 | | 8 | 11 | | | | 1 | 3 | | 9 | | | | | | | | | | | | |
| 1 | 3 | 2 | | 4 | 6 | 7 | | | 8 | 11 | | | | | | 5 | | | 10 | | | | | 9 | | | | | |
| 1 | 4 | 2 | | 5 | 6 | 7 | | | | 11 | | 8 | | | | | | | 10 | | | 3 | | 9 | | | | | |
| 1 | 4 | 2 | | 5 | 6 | 7 | | | | 11 | | 8 | | | 3 | | | | 10 | | | | | 9 | | | | | |
| 1 | 4 | | | 5 | 6 | 7 | 10 | | | 11 | | 8 | | | 3 | | | | | | | | 2 | 9 | | | | | |
| 1 | 2 | 3 | | 5 | | 4 | 10 | | 11 | 7 | | 8 | | | | | 9 | | | | | | | | 6 | | | | |
| 1 | 2 | 3 | | 5 | | 4 | 10 | | 11 | 7 | | 8 | | | | | 9 | | | | | | | | 6 | | | | |
| 1 | 2 | 3 | | 5 | | 4 | 10 | | 11 | 7 | | 8 | | | | | 9 | | | | | | | | 6 | | | | |
| | 2 | | | 5 | | 4 | 10 | 9 | 11 | | | 8 | | 1 | | | 7 | | | | | 3 | | | 6 | | | | |
| 1 | 2 | | | 5 | | 4 | 8 | 9 | 11 | | | | | | 3 | | 7 | | 10 | | | | | | 6 | | | | |
| 1 | 2 | | | 5 | | 4 | 8 | 9 | 11 | 7 | | | | | 3 | | | | 10 | | | | | | 6 | | | | |
| 1 | 2 | | | | | 4 | 8 | 10 | 11 | | | 7 | | | 3 | | | | | | | | | 9 | 6 | 5 | | | |
| 1 | 2 | | | | | 4 | 8 | 10 | 11 | | | 7 | | | 3 | | | | | | | | | 9 | 6 | 5 | | | |
| | 2 | | | | | 4 | 8 | 10 | 11 | 7 | | | | 1 | 3 | | | | | | | | | 9 | 6 | 5 | | | |
| | 2 | | | | 7 | 4 | 8 | | 11 | | | | | 1 | 3 | | | | 10 | | | | | 9 | 6 | 5 | | | |
| | 2 | | | | 4 | 7 | 8 | | | 11 | | | | 1 | 3 | | | | 10 | | | | | 9 | 6 | 5 | | | |
| | 2 | | | | | 4 | 8 | | 11 | 7 | | 9 | | 1 | 3 | | | | 10 | | | | | | 6 | 5 | | | |
| | 2 | 3 | | | | 4 | 8 | 7 | | 11 | | 9 | | 1 | | | | | 10 | | | | | | 6 | 5 | | | |
| | 2 | | | | | 4 | 7 | 8 | | 11 | | 9 | | 1 | | | | | 10 | | | | 3 | | 6 | 5 | | | |
| | 2 | | | | | 4 | 7 | 8 | | 11 | | 9 | | 1 | | 5 | | | 10 | | | | 3 | | 6 | | | | |
| 31 | 34 | 24 | 4 | 33 | 20 | 35 | 36 | 13 | 24 | 36 | 3 | 25 | 7 | 11 | 25 | 5 | 20 | 12 | 13 | 9 | 1 | 4 | 5 | 9 | 15 | 8 | | | |
| | | | | | 3 | 3 | 10 | 2 | 5 | 6 | | 6 | 2 | | | | 12 | | 4 | | | | | 1 | 1 | | | | |

| Wallace | Wright | Johnson | Don | Thomas | Musgrave | Price | Wigham | Love | Robbins | Self | Race | Woods | Leaman | Robinson | Wilson | Douglas | McGarry | Rose | West | Chapman | Mackie | Calder | Brown | Diamond | Woffinden | Peart | Copeland | Halliday | Spencer |
|---|---|---|---|---|---|---|---|---|---|---|---|---|---|---|---|---|---|---|---|---|---|---|---|---|---|---|---|---|---|
| 1 | | 2 | | 5 | | 7 | 10 | | | 11 | | 8 | | | 3 | | 9 | 6 | | 4 | | | | | | | | | |
| 1 | | 2 | | 5 | | 7 | 10 | | 8 | 11 | | | | | 3 | | 9 | 6 | | 4 | | | | | | | | | |
| 2 | | 2 | | 2 | | 2 | 2 | | 1 | 2 | | 1 | | | 2 | | 2 | 2 | | 2 | | | | | | | | | |
| | | | | | | | | | | 1 | | 1 | | | | | | | | | | | | | | | | | |

| Wallace | Wright | Johnson | Don | Thomas | Musgrave | Price | Wigham | Love | Robbins | Self | Race | Woods | Leaman | Robinson | Wilson | Douglas | McGarry | Rose | West | Chapman | Mackie | Calder | Brown | Diamond | Woffinden | Peart | Copeland | Halliday | Spencer |
|---|---|---|---|---|---|---|---|---|---|---|---|---|---|---|---|---|---|---|---|---|---|---|---|---|---|---|---|---|---|
| 1 | 4 | 2 | | 5 | 6 | | 10 | | 8 | 11 | | | 7 | | 3 | | 9 | | | | | | | | | | | | |
| 1 | 2 | | | | | 4 | | 9 | 11 | | | | | | 3 | | 8 | | 10 | | | | | | | 5 | 7 | | 6 |
| 1 | 2 | | | 4 | | 8 | | | 11 | 7 | | | | | 3 | | | | | | | | | 9 | | 5 | | 10 | 6 |
| 1 | 2 | | | | | 4 | | 9 | 8 | 11 | | | | | 3 | | | | | | | | | | | 5 | 7 | 10 | 6 |
| 4 | 4 | 1 | | 2 | 1 | 3 | 1 | 2 | 4 | 3 | | | 1 | | 4 | | 2 | | 1 | | | | | 1 | | 3 | 2 | 2 | 3 |
| | | | | | | 1 | 1 | 1 | 1 | | | | | | | | 2 | | | | | | | 4 | | | | | 1 |

## League Table

| | P | W | D | L | F | A | Pts |
|---|---|---|---|---|---|---|---|
| Barnsley | 42 | 30 | 7 | 5 | 94 | 34 | 67 |
| Doncaster Rovers | 42 | 21 | 14 | 7 | 87 | 47 | 56 |
| Bradford City | 42 | 22 | 8 | 12 | 89 | 56 | 52 |
| Southport | 42 | 20 | 10 | 12 | 75 | 54 | 50 |
| Oldham Athletic | 42 | 22 | 5 | 15 | 76 | 59 | 49 |
| Chester | 42 | 20 | 9 | 13 | 88 | 70 | 49 |
| Hull City | 42 | 18 | 10 | 14 | 83 | 74 | 46 |
| Crewe Alexandra | 42 | 19 | 6 | 17 | 82 | 70 | 44 |
| Stockport County | 42 | 17 | 9 | 16 | 91 | 77 | 43 |
| Gateshead | 42 | 14 | 14 | 14 | 74 | 67 | 42 |
| Rotherham United | 42 | 17 | 8 | 17 | 64 | 64 | 42 |
| Halifax Town | 42 | 13 | 16 | 13 | 52 | 54 | 42 |
| Barrow | 42 | 16 | 9 | 17 | 66 | 65 | 41 |
| Wrexham | 42 | 17 | 7 | 18 | 66 | 79 | 41 |
| Rochdale | 42 | 15 | 9 | 18 | 92 | 82 | 39 |
| New Brighton | 42 | 15 | 9 | 18 | 68 | 73 | 39 |
| Lincoln City | 42 | 12 | 9 | 21 | 66 | 92 | 33 |
| Darlington | 42 | 13 | 7 | 22 | 62 | 92 | 33 |
| Carlisle United | 42 | 13 | 7 | 22 | 66 | 111 | 33 |
| York City | 42 | 12 | 8 | 22 | 64 | 92 | 32 |
| Hartlepools United | 42 | 12 | 7 | 23 | 55 | 94 | 31 |
| Accrington Stanley | 42 | 7 | 6 | 29 | 49 | 103 | 20 |

# 1939-40

## Division Three North

Manager: Jimmy Hamilton

| Match No. | Date | Round | Venue | Opponents | Result | | Scorers | Attendance |
|---|---|---|---|---|---|---|---|---|
| 1 | Aug 26 | | (h) | Barrow | D | 1 - 1 | Mantle | 6,380 |
| 2 | 30 | | (a) | Gateshead | L | 0 - 3 | | 2,702 |
| 3 | Sep 2 | | (a) | Crewe Alexandra | D | 0 - 0 | | 3,849 |

**Records expunged due to outbreak of war**

Apps.
Goals

# 1939-40

## FL North East Regional Division

Manager : Jimmy Hamilton

### Did you know that?

Guest players in the first season of wartime football included Wilf Copping (Leeds, Arsenal and England), Bill Nicholson (Spurs and England), Gordon Hodgson (Liverpool, Leeds and England) and Raich Carter, Sunderland's Championship and FA Cup-winning captain.

Hartlepools finished 10th of 11 clubs in the wartime Football League North East with 13 points from 20 games. It should be noted that due to the prevailing situation not all clubs played the same number of games.

| Match No. | Date | Round | Venue | Opponents | Result | | Scorers | Attendance |
|---|---|---|---|---|---|---|---|---|
| 1 | Oct 21 | | (h) | Newcastle United | L | 1 - 2 | Wilson | 4,000 |
| 2 | 28 | | (a) | Hull City | W | 3 - 2 | Maguire 2, Stephens | 2,500 |
| 3 | Nov 11 | | (h) | Halifax Town | W | 3 - 2 | Stephens, Morton, West | 2,000 |
| 4 | 18 | | (a) | Leeds United | L | 1 - 2 | Stephens | 4,000 |
| 5 | 25 | | (h) | Bradford City | W | 4 - 1 | Stephens 3, West | 1,100 |
| 6 | Dec 2 | | (a) | Darlington | L | 0 - 4 | | 2,536 |
| 7 | 25 | | (h) | York City | L | 1 - 2 | Scrimshaw | 2,000 |
| 8 | Feb 10 | | (a) | Newcastle United | L | 0 - 3 | | 4,333 |
| 9 | 24 | | (h) | Hull City | W | 3 - 2 | Stephens 3 | 1,500 |
| 10 | Mar 2 | | (a) | Middlesbrough | L | 0 - 2 | | 1,480 |
| 11 | 9 | | (a) | Halifax Town | L | 1 - 3 | Marshall | 2,000 |
| 12 | 16 | | (h) | Leeds United | W | 2 - 1 | Howe (pen), West | 1,500 |
| 13 | 22 | | (h) | Bradford Park Avenue | L | 0 - 4 | | 2,500 |
| 14 | 23 | | (a) | Bradford City | L | 0 - 4 | | 2,500 |
| 15 | 25 | | (a) | Huddersfield Town | L | 1 - 4 | West | 4,326 |
| 16 | 30 | | (h) | Darlington | W | 3 - 1 | Armes, Middleton, Glassey | 1,300 |
| 17 | May 18 | | (a) | York City | L | 1 - 2 | West | |
| 18 | 20 | | (a) | Bradford Park Avenue | L | 0 - 2 | | 469 |
| 19 | 25 | | (h) | Middlesbrough | L | 1 - 2 | Middleton | 1,000 |
| 20 | June 1 | | (h) | Huddersfield Town | D | 2 - 2 | Carr 2 | 1,000 |

**FL North War Cup**

| Match No. | Date | Round | Venue | Opponents | Result | | Scorers | Attendance |
|---|---|---|---|---|---|---|---|---|
| 17 | Apr 13 | PR | (h) | Halifax Town | W | 2 - 1 | Heslop, Gallon | 1,000 |
| 18 | 20 | R1 | (a) | Barnsley | L | 0 - 3 | | 2,000 |
| 19 | 27 | R2 | (h) | Barnsley | D | 1 - 1 | Dawson | 1,000 |

Appearances: Agar 1; Armes* 2; Blenkinsop* 8; Brown 1; Carr* 1; Carter* 6; Copping* 1; Daniels 1; Dawson* 1; Deacon 3; Docking* 6; Dodds 4; Douglas 3; Earl 6; Fairhurst 3; Finlay* 1; Foreman 3; Fowler* 3; Gallon 1; Glassey 6; Gorman* 1; Hall J* 3; Hall JL* 13; Hastings* 1; Hepplewhite* 4; Heslop 1; Heywood* 2; Hodgson* 1; Howe* 13; Isaac* 2; Johnston* 16; Laidler* 6; Laurence* 1; Leadman* 1; Logan* 2; Love 2; Maguire* 3; Mantle 2; Marshall* 5; McDermott* 1; McMahon* 6; McPhillips* 1; Middleton 5; Molloy* 1; Mordue* 8; Morton* 1; Nealle* 1; Neowe* 3; Nicholson* 1; Price 1; Robinson J 2; Robinson J* 1; Scrimshaw* 3; Shanks* 1; Smailes* 1; Smith* 6; Sphuler* 2; Stephens* 6; Thomas 16; Turner 3; Wallace 1; Wardle* 13; West 19; Wilson 4; Wright 3.
* Guest player.

Goals: 30 Stephens 9, West 5, Carr 2, Maguire 2, Middleton 2, Armes 1, Dawson 1, Gallon 1, Glassey 1, Heslop 1, Howe 1, Marshall 1, Morton 1, Scrimshaw 1, Wilson 1.

| Robinson | Wright | Brown | Price | Turner | Deacon | Foreman | Earle | Mantle | West | Dodds | Wilson | Daniels | Wallace | Thomas |
|---|---|---|---|---|---|---|---|---|---|---|---|---|---|---|
| 1 | 2 | 3 | 4 | 5 | 6 | 7 | 8 | 9 | 10 | 11 | | | | |
| 1 | 2 | | | 5 | 6 | 7 | 8 | 9 | 10 | 11 | 3 | 4 | | |
| | 2 | 3 | | 5 | 6 | 7 | 8 | 9 | 10 | 11 | | | 1 | 4 |
| 2 | 3 | 2 | 1 | 3 | 3 | 3 | 3 | 3 | 3 | 3 | 1 | 1 | 1 | 1 |
| | | | | | | | | 1 | | | | | | |

# 1943-44

## FL North First Championship

Manager : Fred Westgarth

### Did you know that?

United finished 10th in the Football League North on 23 points, the same as Sunderland, with Newcastle and Middlesbrough in the lower reaches of the table, each on 14 points.

Albert 'Napper' Heywood made 38 League and Cup appearances as a guest player on Sunderland's books. He signed for Hartlepools after the war and went on to play 41 League and Cup games for the club during the 1946–47 season.

| Match No. | Date | Round | Venue | Opponents | Result | | Scorers | Attendance |
|---|---|---|---|---|---|---|---|---|
| 1 | Aug 28 | | (h) | Middlesbrough | W | 1 - 0 | Scrimshaw | 2,584 |
| 2 | Sep 4 | | (a) | Middlesbrough | L | 2 - 3 | Bamford (pen), Mullen | 4,000 |
| 3 | 11 | | (h) | Sunderland | L | 0 - 3 | | 6,208 |
| 4 | 18 | | (a) | Sunderland | L | 0 - 3 | | 9,840 |
| 5 | 25 | | (a) | Gateshead | D | 3 - 3 | Barrett (pen), Adams, Short | 3,000 |
| 6 | Oct 2 | | (h) | Gateshead | W | 5 - 0 | Johnson 2, Adams 2, Robinson | 4,649 |
| 7 | 9 | | (a) | York City | L | 0 - 2 | | 5,868 |
| 8 | 16 | | (h) | York City | W | 4 - 1 | Robinson, Phillips, Corbett, Johnson | 5,241 |
| 9 | 23 | | (a) | Newcastle United | W | 1 - 0 | Barrett (pen) | 10,065 |
| 10 | 30 | | (h) | Newcastle United | W | 5 - 4 | Short 2, Scott, Mullen, Adams | 7,472 |
| 11 | Nov 6 | | (h) | Darlington | W | 2 - 1 | Short, Bamford (pen) | 7,200 |
| 12 | 13 | | (a) | Darlington | D | 2 - 2 | Robinson, Short | 7,009 |
| 13 | 20 | | (a) | Middlesbrough | W | 3 - 1 | Adams, Robinson, Short | 4,000 |
| 14 | 27 | | (h) | Middlesbrough | L | 3 - 4 | Adams, Short, Mullen | 7,000 |
| 15 | Dec 4 | | (a) | Sunderland | W | 2 - 1 | Short, Johnson | 6,000 |
| 16 | 11 | | (h) | Sunderland | D | 1 - 1 | Skinner | 6,585 |
| 17 | 18 | | (h) | Darlington | W | 5 - 1 | Short 3, Robinson, Adams | 4,492 |
| 18 | 25 | | (a) | Darlington | W | 5 - 1 | Corbett, Robinson 2, Drake, Skinner | 8,890 |

**FL North Second Championship**

| Match No. | Date | Round | Venue | Opponents | Result | | Scorers | Attendance |
|---|---|---|---|---|---|---|---|---|
| 19 | Dec 27 | | (a) | Middlesbrough | D | 1 - 1 | Robinson | 8,500 |
| 20 | Jan 1 | | (h) | Middlesbrough | D | 1 - 1 | Skinner | 9,100 |
| 21 | 8 | | (h) | Newcastle United | L | 1 - 2 | Short | 6,326 |
| 22 | 15 | | (a) | Newcastle United | L | 1 - 5 | Robinson | 13,835 |
| 23 | 22 | | (a) | Sunderland | W | 4 - 3 | Bamford 2, Adams, Ward | 7,500 |
| 24 | 29 | | (h) | Sunderland | W | 4 - 2 | Farrington 2, Wardle, Hamilton | 7,000 |
| 25 | Feb 5 | | (h) | Darlington | W | 2 - 1 | Short, Skinner | 8,000 |
| 26 | 12 | | (a) | Darlington | W | 4 - 2 | Tooze 2 (2 own goals), Robinson, Farrington | 10,000 |
| 27 | 19 | | (h) | Gateshead | L | 5 - 6 | Short 2 (1 pen), Scott, Smallwood 2 | 7,000 |
| 28 | 26 | | (a) | Gateshead | D | 2 - 2 | Short 2 (1 pen) | 2,000 |
| 29 | Mar 4 | | (h) | Newcastle United | W | 3 - 1 | Scott, Short, Bamford | 8,432 |
| 30 | 11 | | (a) | Newcastle United | L | 0 - 3 | | 26,110 |
| 31 | 18 | | (a) | Sunderland | L | 0 - 3 | | 3,000 |
| 32 | 25 | | (h) | Sunderland | W | 2 - 1 | Short, Scott | 4,835 |
| 33 | Apr 1 | | (a) | Gateshead | L | 2 - 3 | Short, Farrington | 2,000 |
| 34 | 8 | | (h) | Gateshead | D | 3 - 3 | Baines 2, Drake | 5,419 |
| 35 | 15 | | (h) | Middlesbrough | L | 2 - 6 | Bamford, Short | 3,670 |
| 36 | 22 | | (a) | Middlesbrough | W | 5 - 0 | Scott, Nettleton 2, Baines, Own Goal | 2,000 |
| 37 | Apr 29 | | (a) | Gateshead | L | 1 - 3 | Baines | 500 |
| 38 | May 6 | | (h) | Gateshead | W | 6 - 2 | Baines 3, Farrington, Scott, Short | 2,000 |

Note: The following games counted towards the various cup competitions as follows -

Games 19 - 28Football League North Cup Qualifying competition.

Games 29 - 34Football League Cup KO competition played on a two-legged basis.

Games 35 - 38The Tyne-Tees Cup played on a two-legged basis.

Appearances : Adams* 12; Atkinson 10; Baines* 7; Bamford* 13; Barrett* 19; Batey* 1; Beresford 1; Corbett 3; Cox* 1; Daniels 4; Dawes* 5; Deacon* 1; Delaney* 1; Drake 5; Farrington* 16; Forde* 9; Frazer* 1; Gledson 1; Hamilton* 4; Harrison* 1; Heal 1; Heywood* 38; Hipkin* 1; Howe* 2; Hyslop* 2; ohnston 3; Levitt 1; Makepeace* 23; Malpass* 4; Martin* 1; Milne 3; Mitchell 3; Mullen 20; Nettleton* 2; Phillips* 20; Robinson* 31; Rookes* 5; Rudkin* 1; Scott* 38; Scrimshaw* 2; Short* 31; Skinner* 21; Slack 3; Smallwood* 8; Tabram* 11; Thomas 1; Toothill* 3; Tracey* 1; Tunney* 16; Ward 1; Wardle* 2; Wilson* 2; Woodgate* 1; Woods* 1. * Guest player.

Goals: 93 Short 22, Robinson 10, Adams 8, Baines 7, Bamford 6, Scott 6, Farrington 5, Johnston 4, Skinner 4, Mullen 3, Barrett 2, Corbett 2, Drake 2, Nettleton 2, Smallwood 2, Hamilton 1, Phillips 1, Scrimshaw 1, Ward 1, Wardle 1, own goals 3.

# 1944-45

## FL North First Championship

Manager : Fred Westgarth

### Did you know that?

'Pools finished a lowly 37th in the Football League North on 15 points, the same as Newcastle and two more than Middlesbrough.

Notable guest players included Harry Catterick (Everton), Allenby Chilton (Manchester United and England), later to manage 'Pools, and Joe Harvey, Newcastle United's double Cup-winning captain.

| Match No. | Date | Round | Venue | Opponents | Result | | Scorers | Attendance |
|---|---|---|---|---|---|---|---|---|
| 1 | Aug 26 | | (a) | York City | L | 1 - 3 | Nettleton | 4,000 |
| 2 | Sept 2 | | (h) | York City | W | 5 - 0 | Horton 3, Copeland, Short | 2,500 |
| 3 | 9 | | (h) | Darlington | W | 4 - 2 | Horton 2, Copeland, Smallwood | 6,240 |
| 4 | 16 | | (a) | Darlington | L | 1 - 2 | Horton | 6,736 |
| 5 | 23 | | (a) | Gateshead | W | 3 - 1 | Horton, Nettleton, Smallwood | 2,000 |
| 6 | 30 | | (h) | Gateshead | L | 2 - 5 | Barrett (pen), Short | 6,000 |
| 7 | Oct 7 | | (h) | Bradford Park Avenue | D | 0 - 0 | | 8,057 |
| 8 | 14 | | (a) | Bradford Park Avenue | L | 1 - 4 | Nettleton | 7,184 |
| 9 | 21 | | (h) | Sunderland | L | 2 - 6 | Catterick, Short | 8,484 |
| 10 | 28 | | (a) | Sunderland | L | 2 - 4 | Scott, West | 10,000 |
| 11 | Nov 4 | | (h) | Middlesbrough | L | 2 - 3 | Harrison 2 | 4,784 |
| 12 | 11 | | (a) | Middlesbrough | W | 3 - 0 | West, Short, Turney | 6,000 |
| 13 | 18 | | (a) | Leeds United | L | 2 - 6 | Cochrane, Copeland | 8,000 |
| 14 | 25 | | (h) | Leeds United | W | 3 - 0 | Nettleton, Scott, Cochrane | 4,940 |
| 15 | Dec 2 | | (h) | Newcastle United | L | 2 - 3 | Nettleton, Cochrane | 7,204 |
| 16 | 9 | | (a) | Newcastle United | L | 0 - 3 | | 12,000 |
| 17 | 16 | | (a) | Bradford City | W | 4 - 2 | Horton, Cochrane (pen), Harrison 2 | 2,000 |
| 18 | 23 | | (h) | Bradford City | W | 4 - 3 | Brown 3, Wardle | 5,500 |

**FL North Second Championship**

| Match No. | Date | Round | Venue | Opponents | Result | | Scorers | Attendance |
|---|---|---|---|---|---|---|---|---|
| 19 | Dec 26 | | (a) | Middlesbrough | D | 0 - 0 | | 10,000 |
| 20 | 30 | | (h) | Middlesbrough | W | 6 - 4 | Short, Cochrane 2, Brown 2, Harrison | 8,000 |
| 21 | Jan 6 | | (a) | Gateshead | W | 2 - 1 | Harrison, Brown | 3,000 |
| 22 | 13 | | (h) | Gateshead | D | 1 - 1 | Brown | 6,756 |
| 23 | 20 | | (a) | Darlington | L | 2 - 3 | Brown, Cochrane | 4,199 |
| 24 | Feb 10 | | (a) | Newcastle United | L | 1 - 4 | Short | 15,467 |
| 25 | 17 | | (a) | Sunderland | L | 2 - 6 | Short, Robinson | 12,200 |
| 26 | 24 | | (h) | Sunderland | W | 3 - 1 | Adams, Brown 2 | 9,817 |
| 27 | Mar 3 | | (h) | Newcastle United | W | 2 - 1 | Douglas, Brown | 9,523 |
| 28 | 10 | | (h) | York City | D | 1 - 1 | Brown | 5,590 |
| 29 | 17 | | (h) | Darlington | L | 0 - 3 | | 11,869 |
| 30 | 24 | | (h) | Middlesbrough | W | 3 - 0 | Short, Brown 2 | 4,132 |
| 31 | 31 | | (a) | Middlesbrough | W | 3 - 1 | Lyons 2, Skinner | 3,000 |
| 32 | Apr 7 | | (h) | Huddersfield Town | L | 1 - 6 | Lyons | 6,046 |
| 33 | 14 | | (a) | Huddersfield Town | L | 3 - 6 | Williams 2, Howe (own goal) | 2,210 |
| 34 | 21 | | (a) | Sunderland | L | 0 - 5 | | 10,000 |
| 35 | 28 | | (h) | Sunderland | L | 0 - 2 | | 3,275 |
| 36 | May 5 | | (h) | Darlington | W | 2 - 0 | Bainbridge, Skinner | 2,000 |
| 37 | 12 | | (a) | Darlington | L | 0 - 3 | | 3,173 |
| 38 | 19 | | (a) | Middlesbrough | W | 2 - 1 | Short, Robertson | 2,500 |
| 39 | 21 | | (h) | Darlington | L | 0 - 5 | | 2,500 |

Note: The following games counted towards the various cup competitions as follows -

Games 19 - 28Football League North Cup Qualifying competition.

Games 29 - 34Football League Cup KO competition played on a two-legged basis.

Games 36 - 37The Tyne-Tees Cup played on a two-legged basis.

Appearances : Adams* 7; Atkinson 25; Bainbridge T 1; Bainbridge W* 3; Barrett* 14; Birse* 1; Brown* 14; Catterick* 1; Forde* 36; Harrison* 22; Harvey* 2; Havlin 6; Hetherington* 1; Horton* 12; Jackson 1; James* 2; Keeys 5; Lilley* 1; Lloyd* 6; Lyon 3; Makepeace* 5; Male 1; Mitchell 1; Morris 3; Mullen 6; Murphy* 1; Nesbit* 1; Nettleton 12; Porter 5; Price 1; Purvis* 1; Robertson 4; Robinson GH* 3; Robinson J 2; Rutherford* 30; Saxton 2; Scott F* 1; Scott WR* 33; Shore* 1; Short* 24; Skinner* 22; Smallwood* 4; Spelman* 10; Tabram* 6; Tomlinson 7; Tootill* 8; Troman 1; Turney 4; Wardle* 2; West 7; Wharton 1; Williams 1. * Guest player.

Goals: 75 Brown 14, Short 9, Horton 8, Cochrane 7, Harrison 6, Nettleton 5, Copeland 3, Lyons 3, Scott W 2, Skinner 2, Smallwood 2, West 2, Williams 2, Adams 1, Bainbridge W 1, Barrett 1, Catterick 1, Douglas 1, Robertson 1, Robinson G 1, Turney 1, Wardle 1, own goal 1.

# 1945-46

## FA Cup

Manager: Fred Westgarth

| Match No. | Date | Round | Venue | Opponents | Result | | Scorers | Attendance |
|---|---|---|---|---|---|---|---|---|
| 1 | Nov 17 | R1/1 | (h) | Gateshead | L | 1 - 2 | McMahon (pen) | 5,148 |
| 2 | 24 | R1/2 | (a) | Gateshead | L | 2 - 6 | Holland, McMahon | 6,152 |
| | | | | | | | | Apps. |
| | | | | | | | | Goals |

# 1945-46

## FL 3 North East Championship

Manager : Fred Westgarth

**Did you know that?**

Leo Harden, Jackie Newton, and Joe Willetts made their Hartlepools debuts in the final season of wartime football. All three went on to be major players for the club in the immediate post-war era.

'Pools had the misfortune of finishing bottom of the re-structured Football League North East with only three wins in their 18 games.

| Match No. | Date | Round | Venue | Opponents | Result | | Scorers | Attendance |
|---|---|---|---|---|---|---|---|---|
| 1 | Aug 25 | | (h) | Doncaster Rovers | D | 1 - 1 | Short | 5,997 |
| 2 | Sept 1 | | (a) | Doncaster Rovers | L | 0 - 2 | | 7,000 |
| 3 | 8 | | (a) | Rotherham United | L | 0 - 3 | | 7,000 |
| 4 | 15 | | (h) | Rotherham United | L | 2 - 4 | Dryden, Robertson | 5,000 |
| 5 | 22 | | (h) | Bradford City | W | 3 - 2 | Baines, Robertson, Short | 3,754 |
| 6 | 29 | | (a) | Bradford City | L | 0 - 2 | | 7,647 |
| 7 | Oct 6 | | (a) | Carlisle United | W | 3 - 1 | Short 2, Robertson | 6,000 |
| 8 | 13 | | (h) | Carlisle United | W | 3 - 2 | Short 2 (1 pen), Robertson | 5,813 |
| 9 | 20 | | (h) | Gateshead | L | 0 - 2 | | 6,000 |
| 10 | 27 | | (a) | Gateshead | L | 1 - 3 | Harrison | 5,613 |
| 11 | Nov 3 | | (h) | York City | L | 0 - 2 | | 4,000 |
| 12 | 10 | | (a) | York City | L | 2 - 5 | Morris 2 | 4,000 |
| 15 | Dec 1 | | (a) | Halifax Town | L | 2 - 3 | Robinson, McMahon | 4,000 |
| 16 | 8 | | (h) | Halifax Town | D | 0 - 0 | | 3,000 |
| 17 | 22 | | (a) | Lincoln City | L | 2 - 4 | McMahon, Johnson | 5,000 |
| 18 | 25 | | (h) | Darlington | D | 0 - 0 | | 5,961 |
| 19 | 26 | | (a) | Darlington | L | 2 - 5 | Johnson, McMahon | 8,518 |
| 20 | Jan 1 | | (a) | Lincoln City | L | 1 - 4 | Price | 4,689 |

**FL 3 North East Cup Qualifying**

| Match No. | Date | Round | Venue | Opponents | Result | | Scorers | Attendance |
|---|---|---|---|---|---|---|---|---|
| 21 | 5 | Q1 | (a) | Halifax Town | W | 5 - 2 | Copeland 2, Johnson, McMahon, Woolletts | 3,000 |
| 22 | 12 | Q2 | (a) | Rotherham United | D | 1 - 1 | McMahon | 8,436 |
| 23 | 19 | Q3 | (h) | Rotherham United | L | 2 - 3 | Short, Johnson | 5,000 |
| 24 | 26 | Q4 | (a) | Darlington | L | 1 - 3 | Johnson | 5,161 |
| 25 | Feb 2 | Q5 | (h) | Darlington | W | 5 - 1 | McMahon 2 (1 pen), Copeland, Short, Johnson | 4,596 |
| 26 | 9 | Q6 | (h) | Carlisle United | W | 5 - 3 | Johnson 4, Short | 5,238 |
| 27 | 16 | Q7 | (a) | Carlisle United | W | 3 - 1 | Johnson 3 | 7,000 |
| 28 | 23 | Q8 | (h) | Bradford City | D | 0 - 0 | | 5,144 |
| 29 | Mar 2 | Q9 | (a) | Bradford City | L | 2 - 6 | Short 2 | 5,000 |
| 30 | 9 | Q10 | (h) | Halifax Town | D | 1 - 1 | Moses | 5,874 |

**FL 3 North East Cup Proper**

| Match No. | Date | Round | Venue | Opponents | Result | | Scorers | Attendance |
|---|---|---|---|---|---|---|---|---|
| 31 | 23 | R1 1leg | (a) | Crewe Alexandra | W | 2 - 1 | Price, Oakes | 5,000 |
| 32 | 30 | R1 2leg | (h) | Crewe Alexandria | D | 3 - 3 | Tabram, McMahon, Price | 6,000 |
| 33 | Apr 6 | R2 1leg | (h) | Southport | L | 1 - 2 | Copeland | 7,122 |
| 34 | 13 | R2 2leg | (a) | Southport | D | 1 - 1 | Price | 5,000 |

**FL North Second Championship**

| Match No. | Date | Round | Venue | Opponents | Result | | Scorers | Attendance |
|---|---|---|---|---|---|---|---|---|
| 35 | 19 | | (h) | Barrow | W | 3 - 1 | Harden, McMahon, Copeland | 5,837 |
| 36 | 20 | | (a) | Darlington | L | 1 - 4 | Tabram | 3,372 |
| 37 | 22 | | (a) | Barrow | L | 1 - 2 | Spelman (pen) | 3,600 |
| 38 | 27 | | (a) | York City | W | 3 - 2 | Price 2, Harden | 2,000 |
| 39 | May 4 | | (h) | York City | W | 6 - 2 | Price 2, McMahon 2, Scott, Spelman (pen) | 4,150 |

Appearances : Baines* 3; Barkas* 1; Beardshaw* 1; Brunskill* 1; Copeland 23; Daniels 3; Dryden 6; Fenton* 1; Flatley* 1; Flinton* 2; Flood 1; Flynn 1; Forde* 8; Foreman 1; Gorman 2; Harden 5; Harrison* 3; Hesford* 6; Heywood 25; Holland 2; Hooper* 2; Howe* 1; Jarrie 2, Johnson 11; Johnstone 1; Jones* 1; Keeys 26; Lloyd* 10; Makepeace 4; Mason 1; McKinley 1; McMahon 27; Morris 13; Moses 3; Mullen 1; Mulroy 1; Nash* 1; Nettleton* 1; Newton* 1; Oakes* 1; Parker* 1; Porter 24; Price 11; Roberts 1; Robertson 14; Robinson* 4; Russell* 3; Scott S 12; Scott WR* 3; Short* 12; Sidlow* 3; Simpson* 1; Skinner* 4; Spelman* 34; Tabram 8; Tootill* 17; Troman 6; Turney 5; Weir* 1; West 4; Wheatman 4; Willetts 20; Woods 9; Woollett* 1. * Guest player.

Goals: 68 Johnson 13, McMahon 11, Short 11, Price 8, Copeland 5, Robertson 4, Harden 2, Morris 2, Spelman 2, Tabram 2, Baines 1, Dryden 1, Harrison 1, Moses 1, Oakes 1, Robinson 1, Scott 1, Woolletts 1.

| Jarrie | Gorman | Porter | Cliff | Keeys | Troman | Morris | Robertson | Lewis | West | McMahon | Brown | Woods | Holland |
|---|---|---|---|---|---|---|---|---|---|---|---|---|---|
| 1 | 2 | 3 | 4 | 5 | 6 | 7 | 8 | 9 | 10 | 11 | | | |
| 1 | 2 | 3 | | | 5 | 7 | 10 | | 9 | 11 | 4 | 6 | 8 |
| 2 | 2 | 2 | 1 | 1 | 2 | 2 | 2 | 1 | 2 | 2 | 1 | 1 | 1 |
| | | | | | | | | | | 2 | | | 1 |

# 1946-47

## Division Three North

Manager: Fred Westgarth

### Did you know that?

Jack Price was the only player to feature in the first game, against Barrow, having played in the final game of the 1938–39 season against Wrexham.

The home game against New Brighton saw their manager, Neil McBain, play in goal due to the absence of the regular custodian. McBain was aged 52 years four months at the time, the oldest player to appear in a Football League game.

The average attendance following the resumption of League football, and the worst winter in living memory, was 7,562.

| Match No. | Date | Round | Venue | Opponents | Result | | Scorers | Attendance |
|---|---|---|---|---|---|---|---|---|
| 1 | Aug 31 | | (h) | Barrow | D | 1 - 1 | Harden | 7,259 |
| 2 | Sep 4 | | (a) | Gateshead | W | 1 - 0 | Price | 3,740 |
| 3 | 7 | | (a) | Crewe Alexandra | D | 1 - 1 | Moses | 7,385 |
| 4 | 11 | | (a) | Darlington | L | 1 - 2 | Copeland | 7,201 |
| 5 | 14 | | (h) | Lincoln City | W | 2 - 0 | Scott, Moses | 8,027 |
| 6 | 16 | | (h) | Darlington | W | 4 - 1 | Copeland, Jones, Scott, Moses | 9,546 |
| 7 | 21 | | (a) | Southport | D | 3 - 3 | Price, McMahon (pen), Copeland | 5,000 |
| 8 | 28 | | (h) | Rotherham United | W | 2 - 1 | Scott, Moses | 12,800 |
| 9 | Oct 5 | | (a) | Chester | L | 1 -2 | Harden | 8,323 |
| 10 | 12 | | (h) | York City | D | 1 - 1 | McMahon (pen) | 9,238 |
| 11 | 19 | | (h) | Accrington Stanley | L | 0 - 2 | | 8,945 |
| 12 | 26 | | (a) | Carlisle United | L | 1 - 5 | Scott | 10,775 |
| 13 | Nov 2 | | (h) | Halifax Town | L | 1 - 4 | Copeland | 6,709 |
| 14 | 9 | | (a) | New Brighton | L | 1 - 2 | Sloan | 4,857 |
| 15 | 16 | | (h) | Rochdale | L | 0 - 3 | | 7,323 |
| 16 | 23 | | (a) | Doncaster Rovers | L | 1 - 5 | Sloan | 13,093 |
| 18 | Dec 7 | | (a) | Stockport County | W | 2 - 1 | Sloan, McMahon (pen) | 6,928 |
| 20 | 21 | | (a) | Bradford City | W | 2 - 1 | Sloan, Copeland | 6,445 |
| 21 | 25 | | (h) | Hull City | D | 0 - 0 | | 8,130 |
| 22 | 26 | | (a) | Hull City | D | 1 - 1 | Sloan | 30,064 |
| 23 | 28 | | (a) | Barrow | L | 0 - 2 | | 7,701 |
| 24 | Jan 1 | | (h) | Wrexham | L | 1 - 3 | Copeland | 8,931 |
| 25 | 4 | | (h) | Crewe Alexandra | W | 5 - 2 | Copeland, Sloan, Scott 2, Price | 6,877 |
| 26 | 11 | | (h) | Oldham Athletic | D | 1 - 1 | Sloan | 4,818 |
| 27 | 18 | | (a) | Lincoln City | L | 2 - 5 | McMahon 2 | 7,414 |
| 28 | 25 | | (h) | Southport | W | 3 - 0 | Copeland, McMahon 2 | 5,869 |
| 29 | Feb 1 | | (a) | Rotherham United | L | 0 - 4 | | 9,354 |
| 30 | 8 | | (h) | Chester | W | 5 - 1 | Mitchell 2, Harden, Price 2 | 4,462 |
| 31 | 22 | | (a) | Accrington Stanley | L | 1 - 2 | Price | 3,560 |
| 32 | Mar 1 | | (h) | Carlisle United | W | 4 - 1 | Harden, Scott, Sloan, Price | 4,372 |
| 33 | 15 | | (h) | New Brighton | W | 3 - 0 | Copeland, Sloan, Harden | 5,874 |
| 34 | 22 | | (a) | Rochdale | L | 0 - 1 | | 7,504 |
| 35 | 29 | | (h) | Doncaster Rovers | L | 0 - 2 | | 8,310 |
| 36 | Apr 4 | | (h) | Tranmere Rovers | W | 1 - 0 | Harden | 9,679 |
| 37 | 5 | | (a) | Wrexham | L | 1 - 4 | Harden | 4,877 |
| 38 | 7 | | (a) | Tranmere Rovers | L | 1 - 4 | Scott | 10,690 |
| 39 | 12 | | (h) | Stockport County | W | 1 - 0 | Russell | 8,002 |
| 40 | 19 | | (a) | Oldham Athletic | D | 0 - 0 | | 8,714 |
| 41 | 26 | | (h) | Bradford City | D | 0 - 0 | | 6,623 |
| 42 | May 10 | | (a) | York City | W | 4 - 1 | Wilkinson, Morris, Scott, Harden | 4,514 |
| 43 | 24 | | (a) | Halifax Town | W | 4 - 1 | Scott 2, Harden, Morris | 3,949 |
| 44 | 26 | | (h) | Gateshead | L | 1 - 3 | Scott | 7,000 |

Final Position : 13th in Division Three North

Apps.
Goals

**FA Cup**

| Match No. | Date | Round | Venue | Opponents | Result | | Scorers | Attendance |
|---|---|---|---|---|---|---|---|---|
| 17 | Nov 30 | R1 | (h) | North Shields | W | 6 - 0 | Sloan 4, Scott 2 | 8,000 |
| 19 | Dec 12 | R2 | (h) | Rochdale | L | 1 - 6 | McMahon | 7,000 |

Apps.
Goals

| Heywood | Brown | Gregory | Spelman | Lambert | Jones | Copeland | Moses | Price | McMahon | Harden | Russell | Scott | Allison | Anderson | Hughes | Porter | Willetts | Morris | Newton | Sloan | Parkes | Thompson | Mitchell | Mason | Wilkinson |
|---|---|---|---|---|---|---|---|---|---|---|---|---|---|---|---|---|---|---|---|---|---|---|---|---|---|
| 1 | 2 | 3 | 4 | 5 | 6 | 7 | 8 | 9 | 10 | 11 | | | | | | | | | | | | | | | |
| 1 | 2 | 3 | 4 | 5 | 6 | 7 | 8 | 9 | 11 | | 10 | | | | | | | | | | | | | | |
| 1 | 2 | 3 | 4 | 5 | 6 | 7 | 10 | 9 | 11 | | 8 | | | | | | | | | | | | | | |
| 1 | 2 | 3 | 4 | 5 | 6 | 7 | 10 | 9 | 11 | | 8 | | | | | | | | | | | | | | |
| 1 | 2 | 3 | 4 | 5 | 6 | 7 | 10 | 9 | 11 | | | 8 | | | | | | | | | | | | | |
| 1 | 2 | 3 | 4 | 5 | 6 | 7 | 10 | 9 | 11 | | | 8 | | | | | | | | | | | | | |
| 1 | 2 | 3 | | 5 | 6 | 7 | 10 | 9 | 11 | | | | 8 | 4 | | | | | | | | | | | |
| 1 | 2 | 3 | 4 | 5 | 6 | 7 | 10 | 9 | 11 | | | 8 | | | | | | | | | | | | | |
| 1 | 2 | 3 | 4 | 5 | 6 | 7 | 10 | 9 | | 11 | | | 8 | | | | | | | | | | | | |
| 1 | 2 | 3 | 4 | 5 | 6 | 7 | 10 | 9 | 11 | | | 8 | | | | | | | | | | | | | |
| 1 | 2 | | 4 | | 6 | 7 | | | 10 | 11 | | 8 | 9 | | 5 | 3 | | | | | | | | | |
| 1 | 2 | | 4 | 5 | 6 | | 10 | 9 | 11 | | | 8 | | | | | 3 | 7 | | | | | | | |
| 1 | 2 | 3 | 4 | 5 | | 7 | 9 | | 11 | | | 8 | 10 | | | | | | 6 | | | | | | |
| 1 | 2 | 3 | | 5 | | 7 | 10 | 4 | 11 | | | 8 | | | | | | | 6 | 9 | | | | | |
| 1 | 2 | 3 | 4 | 5 | | 7 | | 10 | 11 | | 8 | | | | | | | | 6 | 9 | | | | | |
| 1 | 2 | 3 | | 5 | 4 | 7 | | 10 | 11 | | 8 | | | | | | | | 6 | 9 | | | | | |
| 1 | 2 | 3 | 4 | 5 | 6 | | 10 | 8 | 11 | | | 7 | | | | | | | | 9 | | | | | |
| 1 | 2 | | 4 | | 6 | 7 | 3 | 8 | 11 | | 10 | | | | 5 | | | | | 9 | | | | | |
| 1 | 2 | 3 | 4 | | 6 | 7 | | 8 | 11 | | 10 | | | | 5 | | | | | 9 | | | | | |
| 1 | 2 | 3 | 4 | | 6 | 7 | | 8 | 11 | | | 10 | | | 5 | | | | | 9 | | | | | |
| 1 | 2 | 3 | 4 | | 6 | 7 | | 8 | 11 | | | 10 | | | 5 | | | | | 9 | | | | | |
| 1 | 2 | | 4 | | 6 | 7 | | 8 | 11 | | | | 10 | | 5 | 3 | | | | 9 | | | | | |
| | 2 | 3 | 4 | | 6 | 7 | | 8 | 11 | | | 10 | | 5 | | | | | | 9 | 1 | | | | |
| | 2 | 3 | 4 | | 6 | 7 | | 8 | 11 | | | 10 | | | 5 | | | | | 9 | 1 | | | | |
| | 2 | 3 | 4 | | 6 | 7 | | 8 | 11 | | | 10 | | | 5 | | | | | 9 | 1 | | | | |
| 1 | 2 | | 4 | | 6 | 7 | 10 | 9 | 11 | | 8 | | | | 5 | | | | | | | 3 | | | |
| 1 | 2 | | 4 | | 6 | 7 | | 10 | 11 | | 8 | | | | 5 | | | | | 9 | | 3 | | | |
| 1 | 2 | | | | 6 | 7 | | 10 | | 11 | | 8 | | | 5 | | | | 4 | | | 3 | 9 | | |
| 1 | 2 | | | | 6 | 7 | 11 | 10 | | | | 8 | | | 5 | | | | 4 | | | 3 | 9 | | |
| 1 | 2 | | 4 | | 6 | 7 | | 10 | | 11 | | 8 | | | 5 | | | | | 9 | | 3 | | | |
| 1 | 2 | | | | 6 | 7 | 4 | 10 | | 11 | | 8 | | | 5 | | | | | 9 | | 3 | | | |
| 1 | 2 | | | | 6 | 7 | | 10 | | 11 | | 8 | | | 5 | | | | | 9 | | 3 | | 4 | |
| 1 | 2 | | | | 6 | 7 | | 10 | | 11 | | 8 | | | 5 | | | | | | | 3 | 9 | 4 | |
| 1 | 2 | | | | 6 | 7 | | 10 | | 11 | | 8 | | | 5 | | | | | 9 | | 3 | | 4 | |
| 1 | 2 | | | | | 7 | | 10 | | 11 | | 8 | 6 | | 5 | | | | | 9 | | 3 | | 4 | |
| 1 | 2 | | | | | | | 10 | | 11 | 8 | 9 | 6 | | 5 | | | 7 | | | | 3 | | 4 | |
| 1 | 2 | | | | | 7 | | 10 | | 11 | 8 | 9 | 6 | | 5 | | | | | | | 3 | | | 4 |
| 1 | 2 | | | | 6 | 7 | | 10 | | 11 | 8 | 9 | 4 | | 5 | | | | | | | 3 | | | |
| 1 | 2 | | | | 6 | 7 | | 10 | | 11 | | 8 | 4 | | 5 | | | | | | | 3 | | | 9 |
| 1 | 2 | | | | | | 6 | 10 | | 11 | | 8 | 4 | | 5 | | | 7 | | | | 3 | | | 9 |
| 1 | 2 | | | | | | | 10 | | 11 | | 8 | 4 | | 5 | | 6 | 7 | | | | 3 | | | 9 |
| 1 | 2 | | | | | | | 10 | | 11 | | 8 | 4 | | 5 | | 6 | 7 | | | | 3 | | | 9 |
| 39 | 42 | 21 | 25 | 16 | 33 | 36 | 19 | 40 | 26 | 17 | 12 | 29 | 13 | 2 | 25 | 2 | 3 | 5 | 6 | 18 | 3 | 17 | 3 | 5 | 5 |
| | | | | | 1 | 9 | 4 | 7 | 7 | 9 | 1 | 12 | | | | | | 2 | | 9 | | | 2 | | 1 |

| Heywood | Brown | Gregory | Spelman | Lambert | Jones | Copeland | Moses | Price | McMahon | Harden | Russell | Scott | Allison | Anderson | Hughes | Porter | Willetts | Morris | Newton | Sloan | Parkes | Thompson | Mitchell | Mason | Wilkinson |
|---|---|---|---|---|---|---|---|---|---|---|---|---|---|---|---|---|---|---|---|---|---|---|---|---|---|
| 1 | 2 | 3 | 4 | 5 | 6 | | 10 | 8 | 11 | | | 7 | | | | | | | | 9 | | | | | |
| 1 | 2 | 3 | 4 | 5 | 6 | | 10 | 8 | 11 | | | 7 | | | | | | | | 9 | | | | | |
| 2 | 2 | 2 | 2 | 2 | 2 | | 2 | 2 | 2 | | | 2 | | | | | | | | 2 | | | | | |
| | | | | | | | | | 1 | | | 2 | | | | | | | | 4 | | | | | |

## League Table

| | P | W | D | L | F | A | Pts |
|---|---|---|---|---|---|---|---|
| Doncaster Rovers | 42 | 33 | 6 | 3 | 123 | 40 | 72 |
| Rotherham United | 42 | 29 | 6 | 7 | 114 | 53 | 64 |
| Chester | 42 | 25 | 6 | 11 | 95 | 51 | 56 |
| Stockport County | 42 | 24 | 2 | 16 | 78 | 53 | 50 |
| Bradford City | 42 | 20 | 10 | 12 | 62 | 47 | 50 |
| Rochdale | 42 | 19 | 10 | 13 | 80 | 64 | 48 |
| Wrexham | 42 | 17 | 12 | 13 | 65 | 51 | 46 |
| Crewe Alexandra | 42 | 17 | 9 | 16 | 70 | 74 | 43 |
| Barrow | 42 | 17 | 7 | 18 | 54 | 62 | 41 |
| Tranmere Rovers | 42 | 17 | 7 | 18 | 66 | 77 | 41 |
| Hull City | 42 | 16 | 8 | 18 | 49 | 53 | 40 |
| Lincoln City | 42 | 17 | 5 | 20 | 86 | 87 | 39 |
| Hartlepools United | 42 | 15 | 9 | 18 | 64 | 73 | 39 |
| Gateshead | 42 | 16 | 6 | 20 | 62 | 72 | 38 |
| York City | 42 | 14 | 9 | 19 | 67 | 81 | 37 |
| Carlisle United | 42 | 14 | 9 | 19 | 70 | 93 | 37 |
| Darlington | 42 | 15 | 6 | 21 | 68 | 80 | 36 |
| New Brighton | 42 | 14 | 8 | 20 | 57 | 77 | 36 |
| Oldham Athletic | 42 | 12 | 8 | 22 | 55 | 80 | 32 |
| Accrington Stanley | 42 | 14 | 4 | 24 | 56 | 92 | 32 |
| Southport | 42 | 7 | 11 | 24 | 53 | 85 | 25 |
| Halifax Town | 42 | 8 | 6 | 28 | 43 | 92 | 22 |

# 1947-48

## Division Three North

Manager: Fred Westgarth

### Did you know that?

'Pools had three different goalkeepers in their opening three fixtures – Sid Parkes, Fred Jarrie and Cam Theaker. Following a 7–0 hammering at Gateshead on Christmas Day, Norman Rimmington took over as custodian for the rest of the season.

Despite a decline to 19th position for the season, home attendances averaged 7,485.

| Match No. | Date | Round | Venue | Opponents | Result | | Scorers | Attendance |
|---|---|---|---|---|---|---|---|---|
| 1 | Aug 23 | | (a) | Accrington Stanley | L | 2 - 4 | Wilkinson 2 | 6,104 |
| 2 | 27 | | (h) | Tranmere Rovers | D | 1 - 1 | Isaac | 9,133 |
| 3 | 30 | | (h) | Rotherham United | D | 2 - 2 | Price, Wilkinson | 9,798 |
| 4 | Sep 2 | | (a) | Tranmere Rovers | L | 0 - 1 | | 7,985 |
| 5 | 6 | | (a) | Carlisle United | D | 1 - 1 | Simpson | 14,223 |
| 6 | 13 | | (h) | Crewe Alexandra | L | 0 - 1 | | 8,406 |
| 7 | 16 | | (a) | Oldham Athletic | W | 2 - 0 | Baines, Isaac | 7,819 |
| 8 | 20 | | (a) | Chester | L | 0 - 2 | | 7,146 |
| 9 | 27 | | (h) | Mansfield Town | W | 1 - 0 | Isaac | 7,497 |
| 10 | Oct 4 | | (a) | York City | L | 0 - 4 | | 9,219 |
| 11 | 11 | | (a) | Hull City | L | 0 - 5 | | 25,414 |
| 12 | 18 | | (h) | Stockport County | D | 0 - 0 | | 6,903 |
| 13 | 25 | | (a) | Bradford City | L | 1 - 3 | Richardson | 11,544 |
| 14 | Nov 1 | | (h) | Barrow | L | 0 - 3 | | 6,761 |
| 15 | 8 | | (a) | Wrexham | L | 1 - 3 | Harden | 9,223 |
| 16 | 15 | | (h) | Halifax Town | D | 1 - 1 | Harden | 5,461 |
| 17 | 22 | | (a) | Rochdale | W | 2 - 0 | Sloan 2 | 4,502 |
| 21 | Dec 25 | | (a) | Gateshead | L | 0 - 7 | | 6,329 |
| 22 | 27 | | (h) | Gateshead | W | 3 - 2 | Scott 2, Harden | 6,608 |
| 23 | Jan 1 | | (h) | Oldham Athletic | W | 3 - 1 | Hayes (o.g.), Richardson, Harden | 8,097 |
| 24 | 3 | | (a) | Rotherham United | L | 2 - 3 | Hooper (pen), Harden | 13,765 |
| 25 | 10 | | (h) | New Brighton | W | 1 - 0 | Wilkinson | 6,927 |
| 26 | 17 | | (h) | Carlisle United | D | 1 - 1 | Isaac | 7,522 |
| 27 | 24 | | (h) | Lincoln City | L | 1 - 2 | Sloan | 8,090 |
| 28 | 31 | | (a) | Crewe Alexandra | L | 0 - 2 | | 5,343 |
| 29 | Feb 7 | | (h) | Chester | W | 2 - 1 | Scott 2 | 6,353 |
| 30 | 14 | | (a) | Mansfield Town | L | 2 - 3 | Isaac, Scott | 12,326 |
| 31 | 21 | | (h) | York City | D | 2 - 2 | Sloan, Harden | 4,890 |
| 32 | 28 | | (h) | Hull City | W | 3 - 1 | Richardson, Sloan 2 | 8,333 |
| 33 | Mar 6 | | (a) | Stockport County | L | 0 - 2 | | 9,991 |
| 34 | 13 | | (h) | Bradford City | L | 0 - 2 | | 8,330 |
| 35 | 20 | | (a) | Barrow | W | 2 - 1 | Nevins 2 | 7,484 |
| 36 | 26 | | (a) | Darlington | L | 0 - 1 | | 10,294 |
| 37 | 27 | | (h) | Wrexham | L | 0 - 2 | | 9,389 |
| 38 | 29 | | (h) | Darlington | W | 3 - 0 | Hooper (pen), Isaac, Richardson | 8,713 |
| 39 | Apr 3 | | (a) | Halifax Town | D | 0 - 0 | | 5,920 |
| 40 | 10 | | (h) | Rochdale | W | 4 - 1 | Donaldson 2, Richardson 2 | 7,907 |
| 41 | 17 | | (a) | New Brighton | W | 2 - 1 | Richardson, Hooper (pen) | 2,810 |
| 42 | 19 | | (a) | Southport | L | 0 - 2 | | 9,991 |
| 43 | 24 | | (h) | Southport | W | 2 - 0 | Nevins 2 | 5,941 |
| 44 | 28 | | (h) | Accrington Stanley | W | 4 - 0 | Nevins 2, Sloan, Isaac | 6,126 |
| 45 | May 1 | | (a) | Lincoln City | L | 0 - 5 | | 20,024 |

Final Position : 19th in Division Three North — Apps.

1 own goal — Goals

**FA Cup**

| Match No. | Date | Round | Venue | Opponents | Result | | Scorers | Attendance |
|---|---|---|---|---|---|---|---|---|
| 18 | Nov 29 | R1 | (h) | Darlington | W | 1 - 0 | Isaac | 11,290 |
| 19 | Dec 13 | R2 | (h) | Brighton & Hove Albion | D | 1 - 1* | Isaac | 11,000 |
| 20 | 20 | R2r | (a) | Brighton & Hove Albion | L | 1 - 2 | Harden | 15,000 |

* After extra-time — Apps.

Goals

| Parkes | Brown | Thompson | Hughes | Tootill | Jones | Baines | Isaac | Wilkinson | Price | McMahon | Jarrie | Simpson | Harden | Theaker | Scott | Copeland | Hooper | Newton | Morris | Richardson | Sloan | Donaldson | Cairns | Russell | Rimmington | Underwood | Nevins | Hawkins | Wildon |
|---|---|---|---|---|---|---|---|---|---|---|---|---|---|---|---|---|---|---|---|---|---|---|---|---|---|---|---|---|---|
| 1 | 2 | 3 | 4 | 5 | 6 | 7 | 8 | 9 | 10 | 11 |  |  |  |  |  |  |  |  |  |  |  |  |  |  |  |  |  |  |  |
|  | 2 | 3 | 4 | 5 | 6 |  | 8 | 9 | 10 |  | 1 | 7 | 11 |  |  |  |  |  |  |  |  |  |  |  |  |  |  |  |  |
|  | 2 | 3 | 4 | 5 | 6 |  |  | 9 | 10 |  |  | 7 | 11 | 1 | 8 |  |  |  |  |  |  |  |  |  |  |  |  |  |  |
|  | 2 | 3 | 4 | 5 | 6 | 10 |  | 9 |  | 11 |  | 7 |  | 1 | 8 |  |  |  |  |  |  |  |  |  |  |  |  |  |  |
|  | 2 | 3 | 4 | 5 | 6 | 10 | 7 | 9 |  |  |  | 11 |  | 1 | 8 |  |  |  |  |  |  |  |  |  |  |  |  |  |  |
|  | 2 | 3 | 4 | 5 | 6 | 10 |  | 9 |  |  |  | 11 |  | 1 | 8 | 7 |  |  |  |  |  |  |  |  |  |  |  |  |  |
|  | 2 |  | 4 | 5 |  | 10 | 7 | 9 |  |  |  | 11 |  | 1 | 8 |  | 3 | 6 |  |  |  |  |  |  |  |  |  |  |  |
|  | 2 |  | 4 | 5 | 6 | 8 | 7 | 9 | 10 |  |  | 11 |  | 1 |  |  | 3 |  |  |  |  |  |  |  |  |  |  |  |  |
|  | 2 |  | 4 | 5 | 6 | 9 | 8 |  |  |  |  | 7 | 11 | 1 | 10 |  | 3 |  |  |  |  |  |  |  |  |  |  |  |  |
|  | 2 |  | 4 | 5 | 6 | 10 | 8 | 9 |  |  |  | 7 | 11 | 1 |  |  | 3 |  |  |  |  |  |  |  |  |  |  |  |  |
|  | 2 |  | 4 | 5 | 8 | 10 | 7 | 9 |  |  |  | 11 |  | 1 |  |  | 3 | 6 |  |  |  |  |  |  |  |  |  |  |  |
|  | 2 | 3 | 4 | 5 |  |  |  |  |  |  |  | 11 |  | 1 |  |  | 8 | 6 | 7 | 9 | 10 |  |  |  |  |  |  |  |  |
| 1 | 2 | 3 | 4 | 5 | 6 |  |  |  | 10 |  |  |  | 11 |  |  |  |  |  | 7 | 9 | 8 |  |  |  |  |  |  |  |  |
|  | 2 | 3 | 4 |  | 6 |  | 7 |  | 10 |  |  |  | 11 | 1 |  |  | 5 |  |  | 9 | 8 |  |  |  |  |  |  |  |  |
|  | 2 | 3 |  |  |  |  |  | 6 |  |  |  | 7 | 11 | 1 |  |  | 5 |  |  | 9 | 8 | 4 | 10 |  |  |  |  |  |  |
|  | 2 | 3 |  | 5 |  |  | 10 | 6 |  |  |  | 7 | 11 | 1 |  |  |  |  |  | 9 | 8 | 4 |  |  |  |  |  |  |  |
|  | 2 | 3 | 5 |  |  |  | 10 | 6 |  |  |  |  | 11 | 1 |  | 7 |  |  |  | 9 | 8 | 4 |  |  |  |  |  |  |  |
| 1 |  | 3 | 5 | 2 |  |  | 10 | 6 |  |  |  |  | 11 |  |  |  |  |  |  | 9 | 8 | 4 |  | 7 |  |  |  |  |  |
|  | 2 |  | 5 |  |  |  | 10 | 6 |  |  |  |  | 11 |  | 7 |  | 3 |  |  | 9 | 8 | 4 |  |  | 1 |  |  |  |  |
|  | 2 |  | 5 |  |  |  | 10 | 6 |  |  |  |  | 11 |  | 7 |  | 3 |  |  | 9 | 8 | 4 |  |  | 1 |  |  |  |  |
|  |  |  | 5 | 2 |  |  | 10 | 6 |  |  |  |  | 11 |  | 7 |  | 3 |  |  | 9 | 8 | 4 |  |  | 1 |  |  |  |  |
|  |  |  | 5 | 2 |  |  | 10 | 6 |  |  |  |  | 11 |  | 7 |  | 3 |  |  | 9 | 8 | 4 |  |  | 1 |  |  |  |  |
|  |  | 3 | 5 |  |  |  | 10 | 6 |  |  |  |  | 11 |  | 7 |  | 2 |  |  | 9 | 8 | 4 |  |  | 1 |  |  |  |  |
|  | 2 |  | 5 |  |  |  | 10 | 6 |  |  |  |  | 11 |  | 7 |  | 3 |  |  | 9 | 8 | 4 |  |  | 1 |  |  |  |  |
|  | 2 |  | 5 |  |  |  | 10 | 6 |  |  |  |  | 11 |  |  |  | 3 |  |  | 9 | 8 | 4 |  |  | 1 | 7 |  |  |  |
|  | 2 |  | 5 |  |  |  | 10 | 6 |  |  |  |  | 11 |  | 7 |  | 3 |  |  | 9 | 8 | 4 |  |  | 1 |  |  |  |  |
|  | 2 |  | 5 |  |  |  | 10 | 6 |  |  |  |  | 11 |  | 7 |  | 3 |  |  | 9 | 8 | 4 |  |  | 1 |  |  |  |  |
|  | 2 |  |  | 5 |  |  | 10 | 6 |  |  |  |  | 11 |  | 7 |  | 3 |  |  | 9 | 8 | 4 |  |  | 1 |  |  |  |  |
|  | 2 |  | 5 |  | 4 |  | 7 | 6 |  |  |  |  | 11 |  |  |  | 3 |  |  | 9 | 8 | 10 |  |  | 1 |  |  |  |  |
|  | 2 | 3 | 5 |  | 4 |  | 7 | 6 |  |  |  |  |  |  |  |  |  |  |  | 9 | 8 | 10 |  |  | 1 |  | 11 |  |  |
|  | 2 | 3 | 5 |  |  |  | 7 | 6 |  |  |  |  |  |  |  |  |  |  |  | 9 | 8 | 4 |  |  | 1 |  | 11 | 10 |  |
|  | 2 | 3 | 5 |  | 6 |  | 8 |  |  |  |  |  | 7 |  |  |  |  |  |  | 9 |  | 4 | 10 |  | 1 |  | 11 |  |  |
|  | 2 | 3 | 5 |  | 6 |  | 8 |  |  |  |  |  | 11 |  |  |  |  |  | 7 | 9 |  | 4 | 10 |  | 1 |  |  |  |  |
|  | 2 | 3 | 5 |  | 6 |  | 7 |  |  |  |  |  | 11 |  |  |  |  |  |  | 8 |  | 4 | 10 |  | 1 |  |  |  | 9 |
|  | 2 |  | 5 |  | 4 |  | 10 | 6 |  |  |  |  | 11 |  | 7 |  | 3 |  |  | 9 |  | 8 |  |  | 1 |  |  |  |  |
|  | 2 |  | 5 |  | 4 |  | 10 | 6 |  |  |  |  | 11 |  | 7 |  | 3 |  |  | 9 |  | 8 |  |  | 1 |  |  |  |  |
|  | 2 |  | 5 |  | 4 |  | 10 | 6 |  |  |  |  | 11 |  | 7 |  | 3 |  |  | 9 |  | 8 |  |  | 1 |  |  |  |  |
|  | 2 |  | 5 |  | 4 |  | 10 | 6 |  |  |  |  | 11 |  | 7 |  | 3 |  |  | 9 |  | 8 |  |  | 1 |  |  |  |  |
|  | 2 |  | 5 |  | 4 |  | 10 | 6 |  |  |  |  | 11 |  |  |  | 3 |  |  | 9 | 7 | 8 |  |  | 1 |  |  |  |  |
|  | 2 | 3 | 5 |  | 4 |  | 10 | 6 |  |  |  |  |  |  |  |  |  |  |  | 9 | 7 | 8 |  |  | 1 |  | 11 |  |  |
|  | 2 | 3 | 5 |  | 4 |  | 10 | 6 |  |  |  |  |  |  |  |  |  |  |  | 9 | 7 | 8 |  |  | 1 |  | 11 |  |  |
|  | 2 | 3 | 5 |  | 4 |  | 10 | 6 |  |  |  |  |  |  | 7 |  |  |  |  | 9 |  | 8 |  |  | 1 |  | 11 |  |  |
| 3 | 38 | 22 | 39 | 18 | 25 | 9 | 36 | 35 | 6 | 2 | 1 | 13 | 29 | 14 | 20 | 2 | 24 | 3 | 3 | 31 | 23 | 28 | 4 | 1 | 24 | 1 | 6 | 1 | 1 |
|  |  |  |  |  |  | 1 | 7 | 4 | 1 |  |  | 1 | 6 |  | 5 |  | 3 |  |  | 7 | 7 | 2 |  |  |  |  | 6 |  |  |

| Parkes | Brown | Thompson | Hughes | Tootill | Jones | Baines | Isaac | Wilkinson | Price | McMahon | Jarrie | Simpson | Harden | Theaker | Scott | Copeland | Hooper | Newton | Morris | Richardson | Sloan | Donaldson | Cairns | Russell | Rimmington | Underwood | Nevins | Hawkins | Wildon |
|---|---|---|---|---|---|---|---|---|---|---|---|---|---|---|---|---|---|---|---|---|---|---|---|---|---|---|---|---|---|
| 1 | 2 | 3 | 5 |  |  |  | 10 | 6 |  |  |  |  | 11 |  |  | 7 |  |  |  | 9 | 8 | 4 |  |  |  |  |  |  |  |
|  | 2 | 3 | 5 |  |  |  | 10 | 6 |  |  |  |  | 11 | 1 |  | 7 |  |  |  | 9 | 8 | 4 |  |  |  |  |  |  |  |
| 1 | 2 | 3 | 5 |  |  |  | 10 | 6 |  |  |  | 7 | 11 |  |  |  |  |  |  | 9 | 8 | 4 |  |  |  |  |  |  |  |
| 2 | 3 | 3 | 3 |  |  |  | 3 | 3 |  |  |  | 1 | 3 | 1 |  | 2 |  |  |  | 3 | 3 | 3 |  |  |  |  |  |  |  |
|  |  |  |  |  |  |  | 2 |  |  |  |  |  | 1 |  |  |  |  |  |  |  |  |  |  |  |  |  |  |  |  |

## League Table

| | P | W | D | L | F | A | Pts |
|---|---|---|---|---|---|---|---|
| Lincoln City | 42 | 26 | 8 | 8 | 81 | 40 | 60 |
| Rotherham United | 42 | 25 | 9 | 8 | 95 | 49 | 59 |
| Wrexham | 42 | 21 | 8 | 13 | 74 | 54 | 50 |
| Gateshead | 42 | 19 | 11 | 12 | 75 | 57 | 49 |
| Hull City | 42 | 18 | 11 | 13 | 59 | 48 | 47 |
| Accrington Stanley | 42 | 20 | 6 | 16 | 62 | 59 | 46 |
| Barrow | 42 | 16 | 13 | 13 | 49 | 40 | 45 |
| Mansfield Town | 42 | 17 | 11 | 14 | 57 | 51 | 45 |
| Carlisle United | 42 | 18 | 7 | 17 | 88 | 77 | 43 |
| Crewe Alexandra | 42 | 18 | 7 | 17 | 61 | 63 | 43 |
| Oldham Athletic | 42 | 14 | 13 | 15 | 63 | 64 | 41 |
| Rochdale | 42 | 15 | 11 | 16 | 48 | 72 | 41 |
| York City | 42 | 13 | 14 | 15 | 65 | 60 | 40 |
| Bradford City | 42 | 15 | 10 | 17 | 65 | 66 | 40 |
| Southport | 42 | 14 | 11 | 17 | 60 | 63 | 39 |
| Darlington | 42 | 13 | 13 | 16 | 54 | 70 | 39 |
| Stockport County | 42 | 13 | 12 | 17 | 63 | 67 | 38 |
| Tranmere Rovers | 42 | 16 | 4 | 22 | 54 | 72 | 36 |
| Hartlepools United | 42 | 14 | 8 | 20 | 51 | 73 | 36 |
| Chester | 42 | 13 | 9 | 20 | 64 | 67 | 35 |
| Halifax Town | 42 | 7 | 13 | 22 | 43 | 76 | 27 |
| New Brighton | 42 | 8 | 9 | 25 | 38 | 81 | 25 |

# 1948-49

## Division Three North

Manager: Fred Westgarth

### Did you know that?

Harry Hooper made 27 League appearances at right-back, scoring one goal. He captained the Sheffield United side that lost the 1936 FA Cup Final to Arsenal. His son, also called Harry, had a successful career in the 1950s and early 1960s with West Ham United, Birmingham City, Wolverhampton Wanderers, and Sunderland.

The two Division Three North fixtures against Hull City attracted record League attendances for Hartlepools United games, both at home (17,118) and away (35,357). Hull, the eventual champions, won both games 2–0.

| Match No. | Date | Round | Venue | Opponents | Result | | Scorers | Attendance |
|---|---|---|---|---|---|---|---|---|
| 1 | Aug 21 | | (h) | Rochdale | W | 6 - 1 | Price, Hawkins 2, Richardson 2, Watson (o.g.) | 10,383 |
| 2 | 25 | | (a) | Darlington | L | 0 - 2 | | 12,393 |
| 3 | 28 | | (a) | New Brighton | D | 1 - 1 | Richardson | 9,093 |
| 4 | 30 | | (h) | Darlington | L | 0 - 1 | | 14,585 |
| 5 | Sep 4 | | (h) | Chester | W | 2 - 1 | Hooper (pen), Hawkins | 9,181 |
| 6 | 6 | | (a) | Rotherham United | L | 1 - 2 | Richardson | 15,468 |
| 7 | 11 | | (a) | Southport | W | 2 - 1 | Isaac, Richardson | 7,801 |
| 8 | 13 | | (h) | Rotherham United | L | 1 - 4 | Richardson | 12,777 |
| 9 | 18 | | (h) | Crewe Alexandra | W | 4 - 1 | Nevins, Richardson 3 | 9,279 |
| 10 | 25 | | (a) | York City | L | 0 - 4 | | 10,706 |
| 11 | Oct 2 | | (h) | Stockport County | D | 0 - 0 | | 9,298 |
| 12 | 9 | | (h) | Hull City | L | 0 - 2 | | 17,118 |
| 13 | 16 | | (a) | Doncaster Rovers | D | 0 - 0 | | 14,766 |
| 14 | 23 | | (h) | Bradford City | W | 1 - 0 | Wildon | 8,516 |
| 15 | 30 | | (a) | Halifax Town | L | 0 - 2 | | 9,735 |
| 16 | Nov 6 | | (h) | Wrexham | D | 2 - 2 | Moore, Harden | 8,789 |
| 17 | 13 | | (a) | Barrow | L | 0 - 2 | | 5,788 |
| 18 | 20 | | (h) | Mansfield Town | D | 1 - 1 | Isaac | 7,394 |
| 20 | Dec 4 | | (h) | Oldham Athletic | L | 1 - 2 | Harden | 6,892 |
| 21 | 11 | | (a) | Accrington Stanley | W | 2 - 1 | Sherratt 2 | 3,408 |
| 22 | 18 | | (a) | Rochdale | W | 1 - 0 | Sloan | 5,803 |
| 23 | 25 | | (a) | Gateshead | L | 1 - 2 | Sherratt | 7,146 |
| 24 | 27 | | (h) | Gateshead | L | 1 - 3 | Burnett | 9,035 |
| 25 | Jan 1 | | (h) | New Brighton | W | 3 - 1 | Hughes (pen), Sloan 2 | 7,891 |
| 26 | 8 | | (h) | Accrington Stanley | W | 1 - 0 | Hawkins | 5,724 |
| 27 | 15 | | (a) | Chester | D | 0 - 0 | | 3,215 |
| 28 | 22 | | (h) | Southport | D | 2 - 2 | Sloan 2 | 7,192 |
| 29 | 29 | | (a) | Tranmere Rovers | W | 2 - 0 | Sherratt, Burnett | 8,577 |
| 30 | Feb 5 | | (a) | Crewe Alexandra | L | 0 - 3 | | 6,187 |
| 31 | 19 | | (h) | York City | L | 2 - 3 | Donaldson, Douglas | 8,148 |
| 32 | 26 | | (a) | Stockport County | L | 0 - 4 | | 6,954 |
| 33 | Mar 5 | | (a) | Hull City | L | 0 - 2 | | 35,357 |
| 34 | 12 | | (h) | Doncaster Rovers | W | 2 - 1 | Hughes, Sloan | 6,925 |
| 35 | 19 | | (a) | Bradford City | D | 0 - 0 | | 7,452 |
| 36 | 26 | | (h) | Halifax Town | D | 0 - 0 | | 4,756 |
| 37 | Apr 2 | | (a) | Wrexham | L | 0 - 1 | | 4,538 |
| 38 | 9 | | (h) | Barrow | W | 1 - 0 | Summerbee (o.g.) | 5,435 |
| 39 | 15 | | (h) | Carlisle United | W | 1 - 0 | Nevins | 8,874 |
| 40 | 16 | | (a) | Mansfield Town | L | 0 - 1 | | 9,017 |
| 41 | 18 | | (a) | Carlisle United | D | 0 - 0 | | 7,055 |
| 42 | 23 | | (h) | Tranmere Rovers | W | 3 - 0 | Wildon 2, Burnett | 6,527 |
| 43 | 30 | | (a) | Oldham Athletic | L | 1 - 5 | Sloan | 12,898 |

Final Position : 16th in Division Three North — Apps.

2 own goals — Goals

**FA Cup**

| Match No. | Date | Round | Venue | Opponents | Result | | Scorers | Attendance |
|---|---|---|---|---|---|---|---|---|
| 19 | Nov 27 | R1 | (h) | Chester | L | 1 - 3 | Price | 8,583 |

Apps.

Goals

| Rimmington | Wilkinson | Thompson | Donaldson | Hughes | Jones | Isaac | Hawkins | Richardson | Price | Nevins | Hooper | Wildon | Sloan | O'Connor | Harden | Brownlow | Burnett | Moore | Leonard | Douglas | Newton | Sharratt | Cairns | Willetts | Morris |
|---|---|---|---|---|---|---|---|---|---|---|---|---|---|---|---|---|---|---|---|---|---|---|---|---|---|
| 1 | 2 | 3 | 4 | 5 | 6 | 7 | 8 | 9 | 10 | 11 | | | | | | | | | | | | | | | |
| 1 | 2 | 3 | 4 | 5 | 6 | 7 | 8 | 9 | 10 | 11 | | | | | | | | | | | | | | | |
| 1 | 2 | 3 | 4 | 5 | 6 | 7 | 8 | 9 | 10 | 11 | | | | | | | | | | | | | | | |
| 1 | 2 | 3 | 4 | 5 | 6 | 7 | 8 | 9 | 10 | 11 | | | | | | | | | | | | | | | |
| 1 | | 3 | 4 | 5 | 6 | 7 | 10 | 9 | 8 | 11 | 2 | | | | | | | | | | | | | | |
| 1 | 4 | 3 | | 5 | 6 | 7 | 10 | 9 | 8 | 11 | 2 | | | | | | | | | | | | | | |
| 1 | | 3 | 4 | 5 | 6 | 7 | 10 | 9 | | 11 | 2 | 8 | | | | | | | | | | | | | |
| 1 | | 3 | 4 | 5 | 6 | 7 | 10 | 9 | | 11 | 2 | | 8 | | | | | | | | | | | | |
| 1 | | 3 | 4 | 5 | 6 | 7 | 10 | 9 | | 11 | 2 | | 8 | | | | | | | | | | | | |
| 1 | 6 | 3 | 4 | 5 | | | 10 | 9 | | | 2 | | 8 | 7 | 11 | | | | | | | | | | |
| 1 | | 3 | 4 | 5 | 6 | | 10 | 9 | 8 | | 2 | 7 | | | 11 | | | | | | | | | | |
| 1 | | 3 | 4 | 5 | 6 | 8 | 10 | 9 | | | 2 | 7 | | | 11 | | | | | | | | | | |
| 1 | 2 | 3 | 4 | 5 | 6 | 8 | 10 | | | | | 9 | | | 11 | 7 | | | | | | | | | |
| 1 | 2 | 3 | 4 | 5 | 6 | 8 | 10 | | | | | 9 | | | 11 | 7 | | | | | | | | | |
| 1 | 2 | 3 | 4 | 5 | 6 | 8 | 10 | | | | | 9 | | | 11 | 7 | | | | | | | | | |
| 1 | 2 | 3 | 4 | 5 | 6 | 8 | 10 | | | | | | | | 11 | | 7 | 9 | | | | | | | |
| 1 | | 3 | 4 | 5 | 6 | 8 | | | | | | | 10 | | 11 | | 7 | 9 | 2 | | | | | | |
| 1 | | 3 | 4 | 5 | 6 | 8 | 9 | | 10 | 11 | | | | | | | 7 | | 2 | | | | | | |
| 1 | | 3 | 2 | 4 | | 8 | | | | | | 9 | 10 | | 11 | | 7 | | | 5 | 6 | | | | |
| 1 | | 3 | 4 | 5 | | | 10 | | | | 2 | | 8 | | 11 | | 7 | | | | 6 | 9 | | | |
| 1 | | 3 | 4 | 5 | | | 10 | | | | 2 | | 8 | | 11 | | 7 | | | | 6 | 9 | | | |
| 1 | 2 | 3 | 4 | 5 | | | 10 | | | | | | 8 | | 11 | | 7 | | | | 6 | 9 | | | |
| 1 | 4 | 3 | 2 | 5 | | | 10 | | | | | | 8 | 11 | | | 7 | | | 6 | | 9 | | | |
| 1 | | 3 | | 5 | | | 10 | | | | | | 8 | | 11 | | 7 | | | 6 | | 9 | 4 | 2 | |
| 1 | | 3 | 4 | 5 | | | 10 | | | | 2 | | 8 | | 11 | | 7 | | | 6 | | 9 | | | |
| 1 | | 3 | 4 | 5 | | | 10 | | | | 2 | | 8 | | 11 | | 7 | | | 6 | | 9 | | | |
| 1 | | 3 | 4 | 5 | | | 10 | | | | 2 | | 8 | | 11 | | 7 | | | 6 | | 9 | | | |
| 1 | | 3 | 4 | 5 | | | 10 | | | | 2 | | 8 | | 11 | | 7 | | | 6 | | 9 | | | |
| 1 | | 3 | 4 | 5 | | | 10 | | | | 2 | | 8 | | 11 | | 7 | | | 6 | | 9 | | | |
| 1 | | 3 | 4 | 5 | | | 10 | | | | 2 | | 8 | | 11 | | 7 | | | 6 | | 9 | | | |
| 1 | 3 | | 4 | 5 | | | 11 | | | | | | 8 | | | | 7 | | | 2 | 6 | 9 | 10 | | |
| 1 | | 3 | 4 | 5 | | | | | | | 2 | 9 | 8 | | 11 | | 7 | | | 6 | | | 10 | | |
| 1 | | 3 | 10 | 5 | | | | | | | 2 | | 8 | | 11 | | | | | 4 | 6 | 9 | | | 7 |
| 1 | | 3 | 10 | 5 | | | | | | | 2 | | 8 | | 11 | | | | | 4 | 6 | 9 | | | 7 |
| 1 | | 3 | 4 | 5 | | 10 | | | | | 2 | | 8 | | 11 | | | | | | 6 | 9 | | | 7 |
| 1 | | 3 | 4 | 5 | | | | | | | 2 | | 8 | | 11 | | 7 | | | 10 | 6 | 9 | | | |
| 1 | | 3 | 4 | 5 | | 8 | | | | | 2 | 9 | | | 11 | | 7 | | | 10 | 6 | | | | |
| 1 | | 3 | 4 | 5 | | 8 | | | | 11 | 2 | 9 | | | | | 7 | | | 10 | 6 | | | | |
| 1 | | 3 | 4 | 5 | | | | | | 11 | 2 | 9 | | | | | 7 | | | 6 | 10 | 8 | | | |
| 1 | | 3 | 4 | 5 | | | | | | | 2 | 9 | | | 11 | | | 10 | | 6 | | 8 | | | 7 |
| 1 | | 3 | 10 | 5 | | | | | | | 2 | 9 | | | 11 | | 7 | | | 4 | 6 | 8 | | | |
| 1 | | 3 | 4 | 5 | | | | | | | 2 | 9 | 10 | | 11 | | 7 | | | | 6 | 8 | | | |
| 42 | 13 | 41 | 40 | 42 | 17 | 20 | 29 | 12 | 8 | 12 | 27 | 14 | 23 | 2 | 28 | 3 | 23 | 3 | 2 | 19 | 14 | 20 | 3 | 1 | 4 |
| | | | 1 | 2 | | 2 | 4 | 9 | 1 | 2 | 1 | 3 | 7 | | 2 | | 3 | 1 | | 1 | | 4 | | | |

| Rimmington | Wilkinson | Thompson | Donaldson | Hughes | Jones | Isaac | Hawkins | Richardson | Price | Nevins | Hooper | Wildon | Sloan | O'Connor | Harden | Brownlow | Burnett | Moore | Leonard | Douglas | Newton | Sharratt | Cairns | Willetts | Morris |
|---|---|---|---|---|---|---|---|---|---|---|---|---|---|---|---|---|---|---|---|---|---|---|---|---|---|
| 1 | | 3 | 4 | 5 | | 8 | 9 | | 10 | 11 | | | | | | | 7 | | 2 | | 6 | | | | |
| 1 | | 1 | 1 | 1 | | 1 | 1 | | 1 | 1 | | | | | | | 1 | | 1 | | 1 | | | | |
| | | | | | | | | | 1 | | | | | | | | | | | | | | | | |

## League Table

| | P | W | D | L | F | A | Pts |
|---|---|---|---|---|---|---|---|
| Hull City | 42 | 27 | 11 | 4 | 93 | 28 | 65 |
| Rotherham United | 42 | 28 | 6 | 8 | 90 | 46 | 62 |
| Doncaster Rovers | 42 | 20 | 10 | 12 | 53 | 40 | 50 |
| Darlington | 42 | 20 | 6 | 16 | 83 | 74 | 46 |
| Gateshead | 42 | 16 | 13 | 13 | 69 | 58 | 45 |
| Oldham Athletic | 42 | 18 | 9 | 15 | 75 | 67 | 45 |
| Rochdale | 42 | 18 | 9 | 15 | 55 | 53 | 45 |
| Stockport County | 42 | 16 | 11 | 15 | 61 | 56 | 43 |
| Wrexham | 42 | 17 | 9 | 16 | 56 | 62 | 43 |
| Mansfield Town | 42 | 14 | 14 | 14 | 52 | 48 | 42 |
| Tranmere Rovers | 42 | 13 | 15 | 14 | 46 | 57 | 41 |
| Crewe Alexandra | 42 | 16 | 9 | 17 | 52 | 74 | 41 |
| Barrow | 42 | 14 | 12 | 16 | 41 | 48 | 40 |
| York City | 42 | 15 | 9 | 18 | 74 | 74 | 39 |
| Carlisle United | 42 | 14 | 11 | 17 | 60 | 77 | 39 |
| Hartlepools United | 42 | 14 | 10 | 18 | 45 | 58 | 38 |
| New Brighton | 42 | 14 | 8 | 20 | 46 | 58 | 36 |
| Chester | 42 | 11 | 13 | 18 | 57 | 56 | 35 |
| Halifax Town | 42 | 12 | 11 | 19 | 45 | 62 | 35 |
| Accrington Stanley | 42 | 12 | 10 | 20 | 55 | 64 | 34 |
| Southport | 42 | 11 | 9 | 22 | 45 | 64 | 31 |
| Bradford City | 42 | 10 | 9 | 23 | 48 | 77 | 29 |

# 1949-50

## Division Three North

Manager: Fred Westgarth

### Did you know that?

During the second-round FA Cup tie against Norwich City, the local fire brigade were called to extinguish a fire at the rear of the Clarence Road stand. Despite billowing smoke, the game continued uninterrupted and finished a 1–1 draw. Norwich convincingly won the replay 5–1 without any reported dramas.

| Match No. | Date | Round | Venue | Opponents | Result | | Scorers | Attendance |
|---|---|---|---|---|---|---|---|---|
| 1 | Aug 20 | | (a) | Halifax Town | W | 2 - 1 | Burnett, Mycock (o.g.) | 9,002 |
| 2 | 22 | | (h) | New Brighton | W | 2 - 0 | Owens, Dunn | 9,738 |
| 3 | 27 | | (h) | Rochdale | L | 1 - 2 | Owens | 10,519 |
| 4 | 31 | | (a) | New Brighton | L | 0 - 1 | | 6,225 |
| 5 | Sep 3 | | (a) | Bradford City | W | 3 - 1 | Newton, McCready, Owens (pen) | 10,463 |
| 6 | 5 | | (h) | Gateshead | L | 3 - 5 | Harden 2, Burnett | 12,078 |
| 7 | 10 | | (h) | Chester | W | 5 - 1 | Owens 4, Harden | 9,341 |
| 8 | 17 | | (a) | Southport | L | 1 - 2 | Dunn | 7,663 |
| 9 | 24 | | (h) | Stockport County | W | 1 - 0 | Owens | 10,036 |
| 10 | Oct 1 | | (a) | Doncaster Rovers | D | 0 - 0 | | 16,155 |
| 11 | 8 | | (h) | Lincoln City | W | 2 - 1 | Wildon, Harden | 10,871 |
| 12 | 15 | | (a) | Rotherham United | L | 1 - 5 | Wildon | 10,721 |
| 13 | 22 | | (h) | Carlisle United | L | 1 - 5 | Moore | 10,145 |
| 14 | 29 | | (a) | Mansfield Town | L | 1 - 7 | McCready | 13,166 |
| 15 | Nov 5 | | (h) | Accrington Stanley | D | 0 - 0 | | 6,689 |
| 16 | 12 | | (a) | Wrexham | L | 0 - 1 | | 7,836 |
| 17 | 19 | | (h) | Oldham Athletic | L | 0 - 2 | | 6,669 |
| 19 | Dec 3 | | (h) | Tranmere Rovers | W | 2 - 0 | Wildon 2 | 6,423 |
| 22 | 17 | | (h) | Halifax Town | D | 3 - 3 | Burnett, Owens 2 | 3,896 |
| 23 | 24 | | (a) | Rochdale | L | 0 - 4 | | 7,439 |
| 24 | 26 | | (a) | Barrow | D | 0 - 0 | | 8,476 |
| 25 | 27 | | (h) | Barrow | L | 2 - 3 | Sloan, Willetts (pen) | 6,910 |
| 26 | 31 | | (h) | Bradford City | W | 3 - 0 | Owens, Burnett, Johnson | 7,283 |
| 27 | Jan 2 | | (a) | Gateshead | L | 0 - 2 | | 9,813 |
| 28 | 14 | | (a) | Chester | L | 0 - 3 | | 5,138 |
| 29 | 21 | | (h) | Southport | W | 1 - 0 | Harrison (o.g.) | 5,789 |
| 30 | 28 | | (a) | York City | W | 2 - 0 | Clarke, Cairns | 5,913 |
| 31 | Feb 4 | | (a) | Stockport County | L | 0 - 1 | | 20,873 |
| 32 | 11 | | (a) | Crewe Alexandra | L | 0 - 1 | | 6,552 |
| 33 | 18 | | (h) | Doncaster Rovers | D | 1 - 1 | Wildon | 9,523 |
| 34 | 25 | | (a) | Oldham Athletic | L | 1 - 3 | Cairns | 8,041 |
| 35 | Mar 4 | | (h) | York City | W | 2 - 0 | Owens, McCready | 6,134 |
| 36 | 11 | | (a) | Carlisle United | L | 1 - 2 | Wildon | 8,219 |
| 37 | 18 | | (h) | Mansfield Town | L | 1 - 3 | Wildon | 5,555 |
| 38 | 25 | | (a) | Accrington Stanley | W | 2 - 1 | Harden, Webster (o.g.) | 4,771 |
| 39 | Apr 1 | | (h) | Wrexham | W | 3 - 1 | Sloan, Newton, Burnett | 5,200 |
| 40 | 7 | | (h) | Darlington | W | 2 - 0 | Burnett, Sloan | 9,383 |
| 41 | 8 | | (a) | Lincoln City | L | 0 - 6 | | 9,116 |
| 42 | 10 | | (a) | Darlington | L | 0 - 1 | | 4,480 |
| 43 | 15 | | (h) | Rotherham United | L | 1 - 2 | Morris | 5,951 |
| 44 | 22 | | (a) | Tranmere Rovers | L | 1 - 2 | Harden | 6,194 |
| 45 | 29 | | (h) | Crewe Alexandra | L | 1 - 6 | Wildon | 3,662 |

Final Position : 18th in Division Three North — Apps.

3 own goals — Goals

**FA Cup**

| Match No. | Date | Round | Venue | Opponents | Result | | Scorers | Attendance |
|---|---|---|---|---|---|---|---|---|
| 18 | Nov 26 | R1 | (a) | Accrington Stanley | W | 1 - 0 | Owens | 8,000 |
| 20 | Dec 10 | R2 | (h) | Norwich City | D | 1 - 1 | Clarke | 11,144 |
| 21 | 15 | R2r | (a) | Norwich City | L | 1 - 5 | Harden | 18,064 |

Apps.

Goals

| Rimmington | Hooper | Thompson | Donaldson | Hughes | Newton | Burnett | Dunn | Owens | McCready | Harden | Douglas | Vitty | Kerr | Stamper | Briggs | Wildon | Sloan | Morris | Moore | Denham | Willetts | Clarke | Johnson | Holmes | Ramsden | Cairns | Miller | Sykes |
|---|---|---|---|---|---|---|---|---|---|---|---|---|---|---|---|---|---|---|---|---|---|---|---|---|---|---|---|---|
| 1 | 2 | 3 | 4 | 5 | 6 | 7 | 8 | 9 | 10 | 11 | | | | | | | | | | | | | | | | | | |
| 1 | 2 | 3 | 4 | | 6 | 7 | 8 | 9 | 10 | 11 | 5 | | | | | | | | | | | | | | | | | |
| 1 | 2 | 3 | 4 | | 6 | 7 | 8 | 9 | 10 | 11 | 5 | | | | | | | | | | | | | | | | | |
| 1 | | 3 | 8 | | 6 | 7 | | 9 | 10 | 11 | 5 | 2 | 4 | | | | | | | | | | | | | | | |
| 1 | | 3 | 4 | | 6 | 7 | | 9 | 10 | 11 | 5 | 2 | | 8 | | | | | | | | | | | | | | |
| 1 | | 3 | 4 | | 6 | 7 | | 9 | 10 | 11 | 5 | 2 | | 8 | | | | | | | | | | | | | | |
| | | 3 | 4 | 5 | 6 | 7 | 8 | 9 | 10 | 11 | | 2 | | | 1 | | | | | | | | | | | | | |
| | | 3 | 4 | 5 | 6 | 7 | 8 | 9 | 10 | 11 | | 2 | | | 1 | | | | | | | | | | | | | |
| | 2 | 3 | 4 | 5 | 6 | | | 9 | 10 | 11 | | | 7 | | 1 | 8 | | | | | | | | | | | | |
| | 2 | 3 | 4 | 5 | 6 | 7 | | 9 | 10 | 11 | | | | | 1 | 8 | | | | | | | | | | | | |
| | 2 | 3 | 4 | 5 | 6 | 7 | | 9 | 8 | 11 | | | | | 1 | 10 | | | | | | | | | | | | |
| 1 | 2 | 3 | 4 | 5 | 6 | 7 | | | 8 | 11 | | | | | | 10 | 9 | | | | | | | | | | | |
| | 2 | 3 | 4 | 5 | 6 | | | | 8 | 11 | | | | | 1 | 10 | | 7 | 9 | | | | | | | | | |
| | 2 | | 4 | 5 | 6 | 7 | 10 | 9 | 8 | 11 | | | | | 1 | | | | | 3 | | | | | | | | |
| | 2 | 3 | 4 | 5 | 6 | 7 | | 9 | 8 | 11 | | | | | 1 | 10 | | | | | | | | | | | | |
| 1 | | 3 | 4 | 5 | 6 | 7 | | 9 | 8 | 11 | | | | | | 10 | | | | | 2 | | | | | | | |
| 1 | | 3 | 4 | 5 | | 7 | | 9 | 8 | 11 | 6 | | | | | 10 | | | | | 2 | | | | | | | |
| 1 | | 3 | 4 | 5 | 6 | 7 | | 8 | | 11 | | | | | | 10 | | | | | 2 | 9 | | | | | | |
| 1 | | 3 | | 5 | 6 | 7 | | 9 | | 11 | | | | 4 | | 10 | 8 | | | | 2 | | | | | | | |
| | 3 | | 7 | 5 | 6 | | | 9 | 8 | 11 | 4 | | | | 1 | 10 | | | | | 2 | | | | | | | |
| | 3 | | 4 | 5 | 6 | 7 | | 8 | 10 | | | | | | 1 | 11 | | | | | 2 | 9 | | | | | | |
| | 3 | | 4 | 5 | 6 | | | 9 | | 11 | | | | | 1 | 10 | 8 | | | | 2 | 7 | | | | | | |
| | 3 | | | | 6 | 7 | 10 | 9 | | | | | | 4 | 1 | 11 | | | 5 | | 2 | | 8 | | | | | |
| | 3 | | | | 6 | 7 | 10 | 9 | | | | | | 4 | 1 | 11 | 8 | | 5 | | 2 | | | | | | | |
| | | | | | 4 | 7 | 8 | 9 | 10 | 11 | | | | 6 | 1 | | | | 5 | | 3 | | | 2 | | | | |
| | | | | | 4 | | 8 | 9 | 10 | | | | | 6 | 1 | 11 | | 7 | 5 | | 3 | | | | 2 | | | |
| | | | | | 4 | 7 | 8 | | | | | | | 6 | 1 | 11 | | | 5 | | 3 | 9 | | | 2 | 10 | | |
| | | | | | 4 | 7 | 8 | | | | | | | 6 | 1 | 11 | | | 5 | | 3 | 9 | | | 2 | 10 | | |
| | | | | | 4 | | 8 | | | | | | | 6 | 1 | 11 | | 7 | 5 | | 3 | 9 | | | 2 | 10 | | |
| | | | | | 4 | 7 | | 9 | 8 | | | | | 6 | 1 | 11 | | | 5 | | 3 | | | | 2 | 10 | | |
| | | | | | 4 | 7 | | 9 | 10 | | | | | 6 | 1 | 11 | | | 5 | | 3 | | | | 2 | 8 | | |
| | | | | | 6 | 7 | | 9 | 10 | | | | | | 1 | 11 | | | 5 | | 3 | | | | 2 | 8 | 4 | |
| | | | 2 | | 4 | 7 | | 9 | 10 | | | | | 6 | 1 | 11 | | | 5 | | 3 | | | | | 8 | | |
| | | | | | 4 | 7 | | | 10 | | | | | 6 | 1 | 11 | | | 5 | | 3 | 9 | | | 2 | 8 | | |
| 1 | | | 4 | | 6 | 7 | | | 10 | 11 | | | | | | 9 | 8 | | 5 | | 3 | | | | 2 | | | |
| 1 | | | 4 | | 6 | 7 | | | 10 | 11 | | | | | | 9 | 8 | | 5 | | 3 | | | | 2 | | | |
| 1 | | | 4 | | 6 | 7 | | | 10 | 11 | | | | | | 9 | 8 | | 5 | | 3 | | | | 2 | | | |
| 1 | | | 4 | | | 7 | | | 10 | 11 | | | | 6 | | | 9 | | 5 | | 3 | | 8 | | 2 | | | |
| 1 | | | 4 | 6 | | 7 | | | 10 | 11 | | | | | | 9 | 8 | | 5 | | 2 | | | | | | | 3 |
| 1 | | | 4 | | | | | | 10 | 11 | | | | 6 | | 9 | 8 | 7 | 5 | | 3 | | | | 2 | | | |
| 1 | | | 4 | | | | | | 10 | 11 | 6 | 2 | | | | 9 | 8 | 7 | 5 | | 3 | | | | | | | |
| 1 | | | 4 | | | | | | 10 | 11 | | 2 | | | | 9 | 8 | 7 | 5 | | 3 | | | | | 6 | | |
| 19 | 15 | 18 | 30 | 18 | 36 | 33 | 13 | 28 | 34 | 30 | 8 | 7 | 2 | 16 | 23 | 31 | 12 | 6 | 21 | 1 | 27 | 7 | 2 | 1 | 13 | 9 | 1 | 1 |
| | | | | | 2 | 6 | 2 | 12 | 3 | 6 | | | | | | 8 | 3 | 1 | 1 | | 1 | 1 | 1 | | | 2 | | |

| Rimmington | Hooper | Thompson | Donaldson | Hughes | Newton | Burnett | Dunn | Owens | McCready | Harden | Douglas | Vitty | Kerr | Stamper | Briggs | Wildon | Sloan | Morris | Moore | Denham | Willetts | Clarke | Johnson | Holmes | Ramsden | Cairns | Miller | Sykes |
|---|---|---|---|---|---|---|---|---|---|---|---|---|---|---|---|---|---|---|---|---|---|---|---|---|---|---|---|---|
| 1 | | 3 | 4 | 5 | 6 | 7 | | 9 | 8 | 11 | | | | | | 10 | | | | | 2 | | | | | | | |
| 1 | | 3 | 4 | 5 | 6 | | | 8 | 7 | 11 | | | | | | 10 | | | | | 2 | 9 | | | | | | |
| 1 | | 3 | 4 | 5 | 6 | 7 | | 8 | | 11 | | | | | | 10 | | | | | 2 | 9 | | | | | | |
| 3 | | 3 | 3 | 3 | 3 | 2 | | 3 | 2 | 3 | | | | | | 3 | | | | | 3 | 2 | | | | | | |
| | | | | | | | | 1 | | 1 | | | | | | | | | | | | 1 | | | | | | |

## League Table

| | P | W | D | L | F | A | Pts |
|---|---|---|---|---|---|---|---|
| Doncaster Rovers | 42 | 19 | 17 | 6 | 66 | 38 | 55 |
| Gateshead | 42 | 23 | 7 | 12 | 87 | 54 | 53 |
| Rochdale | 42 | 21 | 9 | 12 | 68 | 41 | 51 |
| Lincoln City | 42 | 21 | 9 | 12 | 60 | 39 | 51 |
| Tranmere Rovers | 42 | 19 | 11 | 12 | 51 | 48 | 49 |
| Rotherham United | 42 | 19 | 10 | 13 | 80 | 59 | 48 |
| Crewe Alexandra | 42 | 17 | 14 | 11 | 68 | 55 | 48 |
| Mansfield Town | 42 | 18 | 12 | 12 | 66 | 54 | 48 |
| Carlisle United | 42 | 16 | 15 | 11 | 68 | 51 | 47 |
| Stockport County | 42 | 19 | 7 | 16 | 55 | 52 | 45 |
| Oldham Athletic | 42 | 16 | 11 | 15 | 58 | 63 | 43 |
| Chester | 42 | 17 | 6 | 19 | 70 | 79 | 40 |
| Accrington Stanley | 42 | 16 | 7 | 19 | 57 | 62 | 39 |
| New Brighton | 42 | 14 | 10 | 18 | 45 | 63 | 38 |
| Barrow | 42 | 14 | 9 | 19 | 47 | 53 | 37 |
| Southport | 42 | 12 | 13 | 17 | 51 | 71 | 37 |
| Darlington | 42 | 11 | 13 | 18 | 56 | 69 | 35 |
| Hartlepools United | 42 | 14 | 5 | 23 | 52 | 79 | 33 |
| Bradford City | 42 | 12 | 8 | 22 | 61 | 76 | 32 |
| Wrexham | 42 | 10 | 12 | 20 | 39 | 54 | 32 |
| Halifax Town | 42 | 12 | 8 | 22 | 58 | 85 | 32 |
| York City | 42 | 9 | 13 | 20 | 52 | 70 | 31 |

# 1950-51

## Division Three North

Manager: Fred Westgarth

### Did you know that?

Eric Wildon scored 26 goals in 44 League appearances, 20 before the New Year, making him the only Hartlepools player to reach the landmark by that date.

The second-round FA Cup tie against Oldham Athletic attracted a crowd of 15,360, the highest cup attendance at the time. 'Pools lost the tie 2–1.

| Match No. | Date | Round | Venue | Opponents | Result | | Scorers | Attendance |
|---|---|---|---|---|---|---|---|---|
| 1 | Aug 19 | | (h) | Crewe Alexandra | L | 0 - 2 | | 10,359 |
| 2 | 21 | | (a) | York City | L | 0 - 3 | | 10,522 |
| 3 | 26 | | (a) | New Brighton | L | 0 - 1 | | 6,079 |
| 4 | 28 | | (h) | York City | W | 4 - 1 | McGuigan 2, Wildon, Willetts (pen) | 8,648 |
| 5 | Sep 2 | | (h) | Bradford City | D | 1 - 1 | Wildon | 9,107 |
| 6 | 7 | | (a) | Carlisle United | L | 0 - 1 | | 14,780 |
| 7 | 9 | | (a) | Rochdale | L | 1 - 3 | McGuigan | 9,146 |
| 8 | 11 | | (h) | Carlisle United | D | 3 - 3 | Willetts (pen), McKeown, Wildon | 8,654 |
| 9 | 16 | | (h) | Chester | L | 1 - 2 | McKeown | 8,773 |
| 10 | 23 | | (a) | Shrewsbury Town | L | 0 - 1 | | 9,268 |
| 11 | 30 | | (h) | Lincoln City | D | 2 - 2 | Wildon 2 | 6,729 |
| 12 | Oct 7 | | (h) | Wrexham | W | 4 - 1 | Wildon 4 | 8,386 |
| 13 | 14 | | (a) | Oldham Athletic | L | 1 - 5 | McGuigan | 11,831 |
| 14 | 21 | | (h) | Mansfield Town | D | 1 - 1 | Wildon | 8,524 |
| 15 | 28 | | (a) | Scunthorpe United | D | 0 - 0 | | 10,576 |
| 16 | Nov 4 | | (h) | Barrow | W | 6 - 1 | Wildon 3, McClure 2, McGuigan | 5,783 |
| 17 | 11 | | (a) | Rotherham United | L | 1 - 2 | Noble (o.g.) | 10,440 |
| 18 | 18 | | (h) | Bradford Park Avenue | W | 3 - 1 | Wildon 3 | 7,538 |
| 20 | Dec 2 | | (h) | Southport | W | 3 - 2 | Wildon 2, Burnett | 7,868 |
| 22 | 16 | | (a) | Crewe Alexandra | L | 1 - 3 | Donaldson | 3,741 |
| 23 | 23 | | (h) | New Brighton | L | 0 - 1 | | 4,520 |
| 24 | 25 | | (a) | Gateshead | W | 1 - 0 | Wildon | 8,595 |
| 25 | 26 | | (h) | Gateshead | W | 3 - 0 | Burnett, McGuigan, McKeown | 9,269 |
| 26 | 30 | | (a) | Bradford City | L | 1 - 3 | Wildon | 7,772 |
| 27 | Jan 6 | | (h) | Halifax Town | W | 5 - 2 | McClure 3, Wildon 2 | 2,987 |
| 28 | 13 | | (h) | Rochdale | D | 0 - 0 | | 7,585 |
| 29 | 20 | | (a) | Chester | L | 1 - 2 | McClure | 4,809 |
| 30 | 27 | | (a) | Halifax Town | L | 0 - 1 | | 6,674 |
| 31 | Feb 3 | | (h) | Shrewsbury Town | W | 1 - 0 | Fisher (o.g.) | 7,081 |
| 32 | 10 | | (h) | Stockport County | W | 2 - 0 | McKeown, McClure | 7,162 |
| 33 | 17 | | (a) | Lincoln City | L | 0 - 1 | | 10,336 |
| 34 | 24 | | (a) | Wrexham | L | 0 - 1 | | 7,386 |
| 35 | Mar 3 | | (h) | Oldham Athletic | L | 0 - 1 | | 8,075 |
| 36 | 10 | | (a) | Mansfield Town | L | 0 - 1 | | 7,282 |
| 37 | 17 | | (h) | Scunthorpe United | W | 4 - 2 | McKeown 2, McClure, Wildon | 5,365 |
| 38 | 23 | | (h) | Darlington | W | 6 - 1 | Willetts 3 (3 pens), McKeown, McClure, Wildon | 10,003 |
| 39 | 24 | | (a) | Barrow | L | 0 - 3 | | 6,289 |
| 40 | 26 | | (a) | Darlington | W | 1 - 0 | McClure | 4,498 |
| 41 | 31 | | (h) | Rotherham United | W | 3 - 1 | Wildon, Harden, Noble (o.g.) | 8,706 |
| 42 | Apr 7 | | (a) | Bradford Park Avenue | D | 1 - 1 | Newton | 6,910 |
| 43 | 14 | | (h) | Tranmere Rovers | W | 2 - 1 | Newton, McGuigan | 7,626 |
| 44 | 17 | | (a) | Tranmere Rovers | L | 0 - 1 | | 7,999 |
| 45 | 21 | | (a) | Southport | L | 0 - 3 | | 3,990 |
| 46 | 25 | | (a) | Accrington Stanley | L | 0 - 2 | | 4,091 |
| 47 | 28 | | (h) | Accrington Stanley | W | 1 - 0 | Wildon | 3,568 |
| 48 | May 5 | | (a) | Stockport County | L | 0 - 2 | | 6,005 |

Final Position : 16th in Division Three North | Apps.

3 own goals | Goals

**FA Cup**

| Match No. | Date | Round | Venue | Opponents | Result | | Scorers | Attendance |
|---|---|---|---|---|---|---|---|---|
| 19 | Nov 25 | R1 | (a) | Worcester City | W | 4 - 1 | McGuigan 2, Burnett, Wildon | 10,000 |
| 21 | Dec 9 | R2 | (h) | Oldham Athletic | L | 1 - 2 | Stamper | 15,360 |

Apps.

Goals

| Briggs | Ollerenshaw | Thompson | McKeown | Sales | Newton | Burnett | McGuigan | Bain | Wildon | McClure | Willetts | Donaldson | Moore | Stamper | Rimmington | Sloan | Whitelock | Harden | Ballantyne | Morris | Derbyshire |
|---|---|---|---|---|---|---|---|---|---|---|---|---|---|---|---|---|---|---|---|---|---|
| 1 | 2 | 3 | 4 | 5 | 6 | 7 | 8 | 9 | 10 | 11 | | | | | | | | | | | |
| 1 | 2 | 3 | 4 | 5 | 6 | 7 | 8 | 9 | 10 | 11 | | | | | | | | | | | |
| 1 | | 3 | 8 | | 6 | 7 | 10 | | 9 | 11 | 2 | 4 | 5 | | | | | | | | |
| 1 | | 3 | 8 | | 6 | 7 | 10 | | 9 | 11 | 2 | 4 | 5 | | | | | | | | |
| 1 | | 3 | 8 | | 6 | 7 | 10 | | 9 | 11 | 2 | 4 | 5 | | | | | | | | |
| 1 | | 3 | 8 | | | 7 | 10 | | 9 | 11 | 2 | 4 | 5 | 6 | | | | | | | |
| 1 | | 3 | 8 | | | 7 | 10 | | 9 | 11 | 2 | 4 | 5 | 6 | | | | | | | |
| 1 | | 3 | 8 | | | 7 | 10 | | 9 | 11 | 2 | 4 | 5 | 6 | | | | | | | |
| 1 | | 3 | 8 | | | 7 | 10 | | 9 | 11 | 2 | 4 | 5 | 6 | | | | | | | |
| | | 3 | 8 | | 6 | 7 | 10 | | | 11 | 2 | 4 | 5 | | 1 | 9 | | | | | |
| | | 3 | 8 | | 6 | 7 | 10 | | 9 | 11 | 2 | 4 | 5 | | 1 | | | | | | |
| | | 3 | 8 | | 6 | 7 | 10 | | 9 | 11 | 2 | 4 | 5 | | 1 | | | | | | |
| | | 3 | 8 | | 6 | 7 | 10 | | 9 | 11 | 2 | | 5 | 4 | 1 | | | | | | |
| | | 3 | 8 | | 4 | 7 | 10 | | 9 | 11 | 2 | | 5 | 6 | 1 | | | | | | |
| | | 3 | 8 | | 4 | 7 | 10 | | 9 | 11 | 2 | | 5 | 6 | 1 | | | | | | |
| | | 3 | 8 | | 4 | 7 | 10 | | 9 | 11 | 2 | | 5 | 6 | 1 | | | | | | |
| | | 3 | 8 | | 4 | 7 | 10 | | 9 | 11 | 2 | | 5 | 6 | 1 | | | | | | |
| | | 3 | 8 | | 4 | 7 | 10 | | 9 | 11 | 2 | | 5 | 6 | 1 | | | | | | |
| | | 3 | 8 | | 4 | 7 | 10 | | 9 | 11 | 2 | | 5 | 6 | 1 | | | | | | |
| | | 3 | 8 | | 4 | 7 | 10 | | | 11 | 2 | 9 | 5 | 6 | 1 | | | | | | |
| | | 3 | 8 | | 4 | 7 | 10 | | 9 | 11 | 2 | | 5 | 6 | 1 | | | | | | |
| | | 3 | 6 | | | 7 | 10 | | 9 | 11 | 2 | 4 | 5 | | 1 | 8 | | | | | |
| | | 3 | 8 | | 6 | 7 | 10 | | 9 | 11 | 2 | 4 | 5 | | 1 | | | | | | |
| | | 3 | 8 | | 6 | 7 | 10 | | 9 | 11 | 2 | 4 | 5 | | 1 | | | | | | |
| | | | 8 | | 4 | 7 | 10 | | 9 | 11 | 3 | 2 | 5 | 6 | 1 | | | | | | |
| | | | 8 | 3 | 4 | 7 | 10 | | 9 | 11 | 2 | | 5 | 6 | 1 | | | | | | |
| | | | 8 | | 6 | 7 | 10 | | 9 | 11 | 2 | 4 | 5 | 3 | 1 | | | | | | |
| | | | 8 | | 6 | 7 | 10 | | 9 | 11 | 2 | 4 | 5 | 3 | 1 | | | | | | |
| | | 3 | 8 | | 4 | 7 | 10 | | 9 | 11 | 2 | | 5 | 6 | 1 | | | | | | |
| | | 3 | 8 | | 4 | 7 | 10 | | 9 | 11 | 2 | | 5 | 6 | 1 | | | | | | |
| | | 3 | 8 | | 6 | 7 | 10 | | 9 | 11 | 2 | 4 | | 5 | 1 | | | | | | |
| | | 3 | 8 | | 6 | 7 | | | 10 | 11 | 2 | 4 | 5 | 9 | 1 | | | | | | |
| | | | 3 | | 6 | 7 | 8 | | 9 | 11 | 2 | 4 | 5 | 10 | 1 | | | | | | |
| | | | 8 | | 4 | | 10 | | 9 | 11 | 3 | 7 | 5 | 6 | 1 | | 2 | | | | |
| 1 | | | 8 | | 4 | 7 | 10 | | 9 | 11 | 3 | | 5 | 6 | | | 2 | | | | |
| 1 | | | 8 | | 4 | 7 | 10 | | 9 | 11 | 3 | | 5 | 6 | | | 2 | | | | |
| 1 | | | 8 | | 4 | 7 | 10 | | 9 | 11 | 3 | | 5 | 6 | | | 2 | | | | |
| 1 | | 3 | 8 | | 4 | 7 | 10 | | 9 | 11 | 2 | | 5 | 6 | | | | | | | |
| 1 | | 3 | 8 | | 4 | 7 | 10 | | 9 | | 2 | | 5 | 6 | | | | 11 | | | |
| 1 | | 3 | 8 | | 4 | 7 | 10 | | 9 | | 2 | | 5 | 6 | | | | 11 | | | |
| 1 | | 3 | 8 | | 6 | 7 | 10 | | 9 | 11 | 2 | 4 | | 5 | | | | | | | |
| 1 | | 3 | 8 | | 6 | 7 | 10 | | 9 | 11 | 2 | 4 | | 5 | | | | | | | |
| 1 | | | 8 | | 6 | 7 | 10 | | 9 | 11 | 3 | 4 | | 5 | | | 2 | | | | |
| 1 | | | 4 | | | 8 | | | 10 | 11 | 3 | | 5 | 6 | | 9 | | | 2 | 7 | |
| 1 | | | 8 | | | 7 | | | 10 | 11 | 3 | | 5 | 6 | | 9 | 2 | | 4 | | |
| | | | 8 | | 4 | 7 | | | 10 | 11 | 2 | | 5 | 6 | | 9 | | | 3 | | 1 |
| 20 | 2 | 33 | 46 | 3 | 39 | 45 | 42 | 2 | 44 | 44 | 44 | 24 | 40 | 35 | 25 | 5 | 6 | 2 | 3 | 1 | 1 |
| | | | 7 | | 2 | 2 | 7 | | 26 | 10 | 5 | 1 | | | | | | 1 | | | |

| Briggs | Ollerenshaw | Thompson | McKeown | Sales | Newton | Burnett | McGuigan | Bain | Wildon | McClure | Willetts | Donaldson | Moore | Stamper | Rimmington | Sloan | Whitelock | Harden | Ballantyne | Morris | Derbyshire |
|---|---|---|---|---|---|---|---|---|---|---|---|---|---|---|---|---|---|---|---|---|---|
| | | 3 | 8 | | 4 | 7 | 10 | | 9 | 11 | 2 | | 5 | 6 | 1 | | | | | | |
| | | 3 | 8 | | 4 | 7 | 10 | | 9 | 11 | 2 | | 5 | 6 | 1 | | | | | | |
| | | 2 | 2 | | 2 | 2 | 2 | | 2 | 2 | 2 | | 2 | 2 | 2 | | | | | | |
| | | | | | | 1 | 2 | | 1 | | | | | 1 | | | | | | | |

## League Table

| | P | W | D | L | F | A | Pts |
|---|---|---|---|---|---|---|---|
| Rotherham United | 46 | 31 | 9 | 6 | 103 | 41 | 71 |
| Mansfield Town | 46 | 26 | 12 | 8 | 78 | 48 | 64 |
| Carlisle United | 46 | 25 | 12 | 9 | 79 | 50 | 62 |
| Tranmere Rovers | 46 | 24 | 11 | 11 | 83 | 62 | 59 |
| Lincoln City | 46 | 25 | 8 | 13 | 89 | 58 | 58 |
| Bradford Park Avenue | 46 | 23 | 8 | 15 | 90 | 72 | 54 |
| Bradford City | 46 | 21 | 10 | 15 | 90 | 63 | 52 |
| Gateshead | 46 | 21 | 8 | 17 | 84 | 62 | 50 |
| Crewe Alexandra | 46 | 19 | 10 | 17 | 61 | 60 | 48 |
| Stockport County | 46 | 20 | 8 | 18 | 63 | 63 | 48 |
| Rochdale | 46 | 17 | 11 | 18 | 69 | 62 | 45 |
| Scunthorpe United | 46 | 13 | 18 | 15 | 58 | 57 | 44 |
| Chester | 46 | 17 | 9 | 20 | 62 | 64 | 43 |
| Wrexham | 46 | 15 | 12 | 19 | 55 | 71 | 42 |
| Oldham Athletic | 46 | 16 | 8 | 22 | 73 | 73 | 40 |
| Hartlepools United | 46 | 16 | 7 | 23 | 64 | 66 | 39 |
| York City | 46 | 12 | 15 | 19 | 66 | 77 | 39 |
| Darlington | 46 | 13 | 13 | 20 | 59 | 77 | 39 |
| Barrow | 46 | 16 | 6 | 24 | 51 | 76 | 38 |
| Shrewsbury Town | 46 | 15 | 7 | 24 | 43 | 74 | 37 |
| Southport | 46 | 13 | 10 | 23 | 56 | 72 | 36 |
| Halifax Town | 46 | 11 | 12 | 23 | 50 | 69 | 34 |
| Accrington Stanley | 46 | 11 | 10 | 25 | 42 | 101 | 32 |
| New Brighton | 46 | 11 | 8 | 27 | 40 | 90 | 30 |

# 1951-52

## Division Three North

Manager: Fred Westgarth

### Did you know that?

The FA Cup tie against Cheshire County League side Rhyl attracted a crowd of 13,037 – a record for any game at the Victoria Ground against non-League opposition.

Average home League attendances reached a record high of 9,248.

| Match No. | Date | Round | Venue | Opponents | Result | | Scorers | Attendance |
|---|---|---|---|---|---|---|---|---|
| 1 | Aug 18 | | (a) | Tranmere Rovers | L | 1 - 4 | McGuigan | 10,406 |
| 2 | 20 | | (h) | Crewe Alexandra | W | 3 - 0 | Wildon, McGuigan, McClure | 11,394 |
| 3 | 25 | | (h) | Scunthorpe United | W | 3 - 1 | Wildon, Willetts (pen), Elder | 9,028 |
| 4 | 29 | | (a) | Crewe Alexandra | L | 2 - 4 | Willetts (pen), McClure | 4,804 |
| 5 | Sep 1 | | (a) | Lincoln City | L | 3 - 4 | Wildon, Elder 2 | 11,888 |
| 6 | 3 | | (h) | Gateshead | W | 1 - 0 | Wildon | 12,225 |
| 7 | 8 | | (h) | Chester | W | 2 - 1 | Harden 2 | 11,053 |
| 8 | 10 | | (a) | Gateshead | L | 0 - 2 | | 9,367 |
| 9 | 15 | | (a) | York City | L | 1 - 3 | Wildon | 5,935 |
| 10 | 19 | | (a) | Darlington | L | 1 - 2 | Moore | 5,082 |
| 11 | 22 | | (h) | Bradford City | W | 2 - 1 | Wildon, McClure | 8,483 |
| 12 | 29 | | (h) | Halifax Town | W | 6 - 1 | Sloan 2, McGuigan 3, McClure | 8,979 |
| 13 | Oct 6 | | (a) | Rochdale | L | 0 - 3 | | 5,574 |
| 14 | 13 | | (h) | Accrington Stanley | W | 4 - 2 | Elder 2, McClure, Burnett | 8,617 |
| 15 | 20 | | (a) | Carlisle United | L | 1 - 2 | Wildon | 8,893 |
| 16 | 27 | | (h) | Stockport County | L | 0 - 1 | | 9,280 |
| 17 | Nov 3 | | (a) | Workington | D | 1 - 1 | Elder | 6,152 |
| 18 | 10 | | (h) | Barrow | W | 3 - 1 | Wildon, Elder, Willetts (pen) | 8,372 |
| 19 | 17 | | (a) | Grimsby Town | L | 0 - 2 | | 12,296 |
| 21 | Dec 1 | | (a) | Chesterfield | D | 2 - 2 | Elder, Wildon | 9,552 |
| 22 | 8 | | (h) | Bradford Park Avenue | W | 2 - 1 | Wildon 2 | 5,973 |
| 24 | 22 | | (a) | Scunthorpe United | L | 0 - 2 | | 7,320 |
| 25 | 25 | | (h) | Mansfield Town | W | 2 - 0 | Wildon, Newton | 10,542 |
| 26 | 26 | | (a) | Mansfield Town | W | 1 - 0 | McClure | 9,185 |
| 27 | 29 | | (h) | Lincoln City | D | 1 - 1 | Wildon | 11,420 |
| 28 | Jan 1 | | (h) | Wrexham | W | 1 - 0 | Newton | 8,910 |
| 29 | 5 | | (a) | Chester | D | 3 - 3 | McGuigan, Willetts (pen), Wildon | 4,902 |
| 31 | 16 | | (h) | Southport | W | 3 - 1 | Stamper, Willetts (pen), McGuigan | 5,844 |
| 32 | 19 | | (h) | York City | W | 3 - 2 | Stamper 2, Wildon | 9,168 |
| 33 | 26 | | (a) | Bradford City | W | 2 - 0 | McClure, Stamper | 13,717 |
| 34 | Feb 2 | | (a) | Southport | L | 0 - 2 | | 4,107 |
| 35 | 9 | | (a) | Halifax Town | L | 0 - 2 | | 5,503 |
| 36 | 16 | | (h) | Rochdale | D | 1 - 1 | Elder | 8,403 |
| 37 | 23 | | (h) | Darlington | W | 2 - 0 | Howe (o.g.), Wildon | 9,516 |
| 38 | Mar 1 | | (a) | Accrington Stanley | D | 0 - 0 | | 4,755 |
| 39 | 8 | | (h) | Carlisle United | W | 1 - 0 | Stamper | 9,233 |
| 40 | 15 | | (a) | Stockport County | W | 1 - 0 | Wildon | 11,020 |
| 41 | 22 | | (h) | Workington | L | 0 - 1 | | 8,175 |
| 42 | 29 | | (a) | Barrow | L | 1 - 2 | McGuigan | 2,264 |
| 43 | Apr 5 | | (h) | Grimsby Town | W | 2 - 1 | Stamper, Burnett | 9,063 |
| 44 | 11 | | (a) | Oldham Athletic | L | 2 - 5 | Willetts (pen), McClure | 15,972 |
| 45 | 12 | | (a) | Wrexham | D | 0 - 0 | | 7,788 |
| 46 | 14 | | (h) | Oldham Athletic | D | 1 - 1 | Newton | 12,013 |
| 47 | 19 | | (h) | Chesterfield | W | 4 - 1 | Elder, Burnett, Wildon, Willetts (pen) | 8,665 |
| 48 | 26 | | (a) | Bradford Park Avenue | W | 2 - 1 | Wildon, McClure | 7,415 |
| 49 | 30 | | (h) | Tranmere Rovers | L | 0 - 1 | | 8,342 |

Final Position : 9th in Division Three North — Apps.

1 own goal — Goals

**FA Cup**

| Match No. | Date | Round | Venue | Opponents | Result | | Scorers | Attendance |
|---|---|---|---|---|---|---|---|---|
| 20 | Nov 24 | R1 | (h) | Rhyl | W | 2 - 0 | Elder, Harden | 13,037 |
| 23 | Dec 15 | R2 | (a) | Watford | W | 2 - 1 | McClure, Burnett | 15,108 |
| 30 | Jan 12 | R3 | (a) | Burnley | L | 0 - 1 | | 38,608 |

Apps.

Goals

| Briggs | Willetts | Thompson | Newton | Moore | Stamper | Burnett | Wildon | Willox | McGuigan | McClure | Brown | Elder | Rimmington | Harden | Donaldson | Morrison | Ballantyne | Sloan | Richley |
|---|---|---|---|---|---|---|---|---|---|---|---|---|---|---|---|---|---|---|---|
| 1 | 2 | 3 | 4 | 5 | 6 | 7 | 8 | 9 | 10 | 11 | | | | | | | | | |
| | 2 | 3 | 4 | 5 | 6 | 7 | 9 | | 10 | 11 | 1 | 8 | | | | | | | |
| | 2 | 3 | 4 | 5 | 6 | 7 | 9 | | 10 | 11 | 1 | 8 | | | | | | | |
| | 2 | 3 | 4 | 5 | 6 | 7 | 9 | | 10 | 11 | 1 | 8 | | | | | | | |
| | 2 | 3 | 4 | 5 | 6 | 7 | 9 | | 10 | 11 | 1 | 8 | | | | | | | |
| | 2 | 3 | 4 | 5 | 6 | 7 | 9 | | 10 | 11 | | 8 | 1 | | | | | | |
| | 2 | 3 | 4 | 5 | 6 | 7 | 9 | | 10 | | | 8 | 1 | 11 | | | | | |
| | 2 | 3 | 4 | 5 | 6 | 7 | 9 | | 10 | | | 8 | 1 | 11 | | | | | |
| | 3 | | | 2 | 6 | 7 | 9 | | 10 | | | 8 | 1 | 11 | 4 | 5 | | | |
| | 2 | | | 5 | 6 | 7 | 9 | | 10 | | | 8 | 1 | 11 | 4 | | 3 | | |
| | 2 | | | 5 | 6 | 7 | 9 | | 10 | 11 | | 8 | 1 | | 4 | | 3 | | |
| | 2 | | | 5 | 6 | 7 | | | 10 | 11 | | 8 | 1 | | 4 | | 3 | 9 | |
| | 2 | | | 5 | 6 | 7 | | | 10 | 11 | | 8 | 1 | | 4 | | 3 | 9 | |
| | 2 | | | 5 | 6 | 7 | 9 | | 10 | 11 | | 8 | 1 | | 4 | | 3 | | |
| | 2 | | | 5 | 6 | 7 | 9 | | 10 | 11 | | 8 | 1 | | 4 | | 3 | | |
| | 2 | | | 5 | 6 | 7 | 9 | | 10 | 11 | | 8 | 1 | | 4 | | 3 | | |
| | 2 | | 4 | 5 | 6 | 7 | 9 | | 10 | | | 8 | 1 | 11 | | | 3 | | |
| | 2 | | 4 | 5 | 6 | 7 | 9 | | 10 | 11 | | 8 | 1 | | | | 3 | | |
| | 2 | | 4 | 5 | 6 | 7 | 9 | | 10 | 11 | | 8 | 1 | | | | 3 | | |
| | 2 | 3 | 4 | 5 | | 7 | 11 | | 10 | | 1 | 8 | | | | 9 | | | 6 |
| | 2 | 3 | 4 | 5 | | 7 | 9 | | 10 | 11 | 1 | 8 | | | | | | | 6 |
| | 2 | 3 | 4 | 5 | | 7 | 9 | | 8 | 10 | 1 | | | 11 | | | | | 6 |
| | 2 | 3 | 4 | 5 | | 7 | 9 | | 8 | 10 | 1 | | | 11 | | | | | 6 |
| | 2 | 3 | 4 | 5 | | 7 | 8 | 9 | 10 | 11 | 1 | | | | | | | | 6 |
| | 2 | 3 | 4 | 5 | | 7 | 8 | 9 | 10 | 11 | 1 | | | | | | | | 6 |
| | 2 | 3 | 4 | 5 | | 7 | 9 | | 10 | 11 | 1 | 8 | | | | | | | 6 |
| | 2 | 3 | 4 | 5 | 8 | 7 | 9 | | 10 | 11 | 1 | | | | | | | | 6 |
| | 2 | 3 | 4 | 5 | 8 | 7 | 9 | | 10 | 11 | 1 | | | | | | | | 6 |
| | 2 | 3 | 4 | 5 | 8 | 7 | 9 | | 10 | 11 | 1 | | | | | | | | 6 |
| | 2 | 3 | 4 | 5 | 8 | 7 | 9 | | 10 | 11 | 1 | | | | | | | | 6 |
| | 2 | 3 | 4 | 5 | 8 | 7 | 9 | | 10 | 11 | 1 | | | | | | | | 6 |
| | 2 | 3 | 4 | 5 | 8 | 7 | | 9 | 10 | 11 | 1 | | | | | | | | 6 |
| | 2 | 3 | 4 | 5 | | 7 | 9 | | 10 | 11 | 1 | 8 | | | | | | | 6 |
| | 2 | 3 | 4 | 5 | | | 9 | 7 | 10 | 11 | 1 | 8 | | | | | | | 6 |
| | 2 | 3 | 4 | 5 | | 8 | | 7 | 10 | 11 | 1 | 9 | | | | | | | 6 |
| | 2 | 3 | 4 | 5 | 10 | 7 | 9 | | | 11 | 1 | 8 | | | | | | | 6 |
| | 2 | 3 | 4 | 5 | | 7 | 9 | | 10 | 11 | 1 | 8 | | | | | | | 6 |
| | 2 | 3 | 4 | 5 | | 7 | 9 | | 10 | 11 | 1 | 8 | | | | | | | 6 |
| | 2 | 3 | 4 | 5 | 9 | 7 | | | 10 | 11 | 1 | 8 | | | | | | | 6 |
| | 2 | 3 | 4 | 5 | 9 | 7 | | | 10 | 11 | 1 | 8 | | | | | | | 6 |
| | 2 | 3 | 4 | 5 | 9 | 7 | | | 10 | 11 | 1 | 8 | | | | | | | 6 |
| | 2 | 3 | 4 | 5 | 9 | 7 | 8 | | 10 | 11 | 1 | | | | | | | | 6 |
| | 2 | 3 | 4 | 5 | 9 | 7 | 8 | | 10 | 11 | 1 | | | | | | | | 6 |
| | 2 | 3 | | 5 | 9 | 7 | 10 | | | 11 | 1 | 8 | | | 4 | | | | 6 |
| | 2 | 3 | | 5 | 4 | 7 | 9 | | 10 | 11 | 1 | 8 | | | | | | | 6 |
| | 2 | 3 | | 5 | 4 | 7 | 9 | | 10 | 11 | 1 | 8 | | | | | | | 6 |
| 1 | 46 | 35 | 35 | 46 | 34 | 45 | 39 | 6 | 44 | 40 | 31 | 33 | 14 | 7 | 9 | 2 | 10 | 2 | 27 |
| | 7 | | 3 | 1 | 6 | 3 | 19 | | 8 | 9 | | 10 | | 2 | | | | 2 | |

| Briggs | Willetts | Thompson | Newton | Moore | Stamper | Burnett | Wildon | Willox | McGuigan | McClure | Brown | Elder | Rimmington | Harden | Donaldson | Morrison | Ballantyne | Sloan | Richley |
|---|---|---|---|---|---|---|---|---|---|---|---|---|---|---|---|---|---|---|---|
| | 2 | 3 | 4 | 5 | 6 | 7 | 9 | | 10 | | | 8 | 1 | 11 | | | | | |
| | 2 | 3 | 4 | 5 | | 7 | 9 | | 10 | 11 | 1 | 8 | | | | | | | 6 |
| | 2 | 3 | 4 | 5 | 8 | 7 | 9 | | 10 | 11 | 1 | | | | | | | | 6 |
| | 3 | 3 | 3 | 3 | 2 | 3 | 3 | | 3 | 2 | 2 | 2 | 1 | 1 | | | | | 2 |
| | | | | | | 1 | | | | 1 | | 1 | | 1 | | | | | |

## League Table

| | P | W | D | L | F | A | Pts |
|---|---|---|---|---|---|---|---|
| Lincoln City | 46 | 30 | 9 | 7 | 121 | 52 | 69 |
| Grimsby Town | 46 | 29 | 8 | 9 | 96 | 45 | 66 |
| Stockport County | 46 | 23 | 13 | 10 | 74 | 40 | 59 |
| Oldham Athletic | 46 | 24 | 9 | 13 | 90 | 61 | 57 |
| Gateshead | 46 | 21 | 11 | 14 | 66 | 49 | 53 |
| Mansfield Town | 46 | 22 | 8 | 16 | 73 | 60 | 52 |
| Carlisle United | 46 | 19 | 13 | 14 | 62 | 57 | 51 |
| Bradford Park Avenue | 46 | 19 | 12 | 15 | 74 | 64 | 50 |
| Hartlepools United | 46 | 21 | 8 | 17 | 71 | 65 | 50 |
| York City | 46 | 18 | 13 | 15 | 73 | 52 | 49 |
| Tranmere Rovers | 46 | 21 | 6 | 19 | 76 | 71 | 48 |
| Barrow | 46 | 17 | 12 | 17 | 57 | 61 | 46 |
| Chesterfield | 46 | 17 | 11 | 18 | 65 | 66 | 45 |
| Scunthorpe United | 46 | 14 | 16 | 16 | 65 | 74 | 44 |
| Bradford City | 46 | 16 | 10 | 20 | 61 | 68 | 42 |
| Crewe Alexandra | 46 | 17 | 8 | 21 | 63 | 82 | 42 |
| Southport | 46 | 15 | 11 | 20 | 53 | 71 | 41 |
| Wrexham | 46 | 15 | 9 | 22 | 63 | 73 | 39 |
| Chester | 46 | 15 | 9 | 22 | 72 | 85 | 39 |
| Halifax Town | 46 | 14 | 7 | 25 | 61 | 97 | 35 |
| Rochdale | 46 | 11 | 13 | 22 | 47 | 79 | 35 |
| Accrington Stanley | 46 | 10 | 12 | 24 | 61 | 92 | 32 |
| Darlington | 46 | 11 | 9 | 26 | 64 | 103 | 31 |
| Workington | 46 | 11 | 7 | 28 | 50 | 91 | 29 |

# 1952-53

## Division Three North

Manager: Fred Westgarth

### Did you know that?

'Pools finished 17th, using only 19 players throughout the season, a record. Five players appeared in 40 or more League games: Brown, McGuigan, Moore, Thompson and Willetts, who was ever-present.

| Match No. | Date | Round | Venue | Opponents | Result | | Scorers | Attendance |
|---|---|---|---|---|---|---|---|---|
| 1 | Aug 23 | | (h) | Accrington Stanley | W | 4 - 1 | McGuigan, Elder, Weatherspoon, McClure | 10,765 |
| 2 | 25 | | (a) | Halifax Town | L | 2 - 3 | McGuigan, Willetts (pen) | 9,246 |
| 3 | 30 | | (a) | Carlisle United | L | 1 - 4 | Weatherspoon | 10,876 |
| 4 | Sep 1 | | (h) | Halifax Town | D | 0 - 0 | | 10,826 |
| 5 | 6 | | (h) | Southport | W | 3 - 0 | Willetts (pen), Elder, Wildon | 8,452 |
| 6 | 8 | | (a) | Gateshead | D | 1 - 1 | Elder | 3,147 |
| 7 | 13 | | (a) | Crewe Alexandra | L | 0 - 2 | | 5,581 |
| 8 | 15 | | (h) | Gateshead | D | 0 - 0 | | 8,370 |
| 9 | 20 | | (h) | Port Vale | W | 2 - 0 | McClure, Wildon | 9,945 |
| 10 | 22 | | (h) | York City | W | 2 - 1 | Wildon, Willetts (pen) | 9,626 |
| 11 | 27 | | (a) | Chester | W | 1 - 0 | Elder | 4,110 |
| 12 | Oct 1 | | (a) | Bradford City | D | 1 - 1 | Wildon | 2,265 |
| 13 | 4 | | (h) | Scunthorpe United | D | 1 - 1 | Elder | 9,060 |
| 14 | 11 | | (h) | Mansfield Town | W | 2 - 0 | Wildon, Elder | 8,554 |
| 15 | 18 | | (a) | Oldham Athletic | L | 2 - 4 | Wildon 2 | 17,833 |
| 16 | 25 | | (h) | Bradford Park Avenue | L | 0 - 1 | | 9,554 |
| 17 | Nov 1 | | (a) | Wrexham | L | 2 - 3 | Elder, McClure | 9,243 |
| 18 | 8 | | (h) | Barrow | W | 2 - 0 | Wildon, Stamper | 7,396 |
| 19 | 15 | | (a) | Grimsby Town | L | 0 - 7 | | 13,096 |
| 21 | 29 | | (a) | Tranmere Rovers | W | 2 - 0 | Elder, McGuigan | 5,473 |
| 23 | Dec 13 | | (a) | Workington | D | 1 - 1 | McGuigan | 4,083 |
| 24 | 20 | | (a) | Accrington Stanley | D | 1 - 1 | Elder | 3,195 |
| 25 | 25 | | (a) | Stockport County | D | 1 - 1 | McGuigan | 8,891 |
| 26 | 27 | | (h) | Stockport County | L | 0 - 2 | | 7,387 |
| 27 | Jan 1 | | (h) | Bradford City | D | 0 - 0 | | 5,999 |
| 28 | 3 | | (h) | Carlisle United | W | 1 - 0 | Willetts (pen) | 5,773 |
| 29 | 10 | | (h) | Darlington | W | 1 - 0 | Howe (o.g.) | 7,787 |
| 30 | 17 | | (a) | Southport | D | 0 - 0 | | 4,592 |
| 31 | 24 | | (h) | Crewe Alexandra | W | 2 - 1 | Richardson, McClure | 7,209 |
| 32 | 31 | | (a) | Darlington | L | 0 - 3 | | 4,879 |
| 33 | Feb 7 | | (a) | Port Vale | L | 0 - 3 | | 13,919 |
| 34 | 14 | | (h) | Chester | D | 2 - 2 | Harden, Wildon | 6,499 |
| 35 | 21 | | (a) | Scunthorpe United | D | 0 - 0 | | 7,076 |
| 36 | 28 | | (a) | Mansfield Town | L | 0 - 2 | | 6,720 |
| 37 | Mar 7 | | (h) | Oldham Athletic | W | 4 - 1 | Burnett, Newton, Richardson, McClure | 9,421 |
| 38 | 14 | | (a) | Bradford Park Avenue | D | 1 - 1 | McGuigan | 6,006 |
| 39 | 21 | | (h) | Wrexham | L | 1 - 2 | Richardson | 7,919 |
| 40 | 28 | | (a) | Barrow | L | 1 - 2 | Elder | 4,061 |
| 41 | Apr 3 | | (h) | Rochdale | W | 2 - 1 | Harden, Newton | 8,777 |
| 42 | 4 | | (h) | Grimsby Town | W | 2 - 0 | Harden 2 | 8,714 |
| 43 | 6 | | (a) | Rochdale | L | 1 - 3 | Richardson | 3,378 |
| 44 | 11 | | (a) | York City | L | 0 - 1 | | 7,939 |
| 45 | 18 | | (h) | Tranmere Rovers | W | 4 - 1 | Johnson, McGuigan, Harden, Steele (o.g.) | 6,357 |
| 46 | 20 | | (h) | Chesterfield | W | 2 - 0 | McGuigan, Wildon | 6,996 |
| 47 | 25 | | (a) | Chesterfield | L | 0 - 2 | | 6,511 |
| 48 | 29 | | (h) | Workington | D | 2 - 2 | Wildon, McGuigan | 4,327 |

Final Position : 17th in Division Three North — Apps.

2 own goals — Goals

**FA Cup**

| Match No. | Date | Round | Venue | Opponents | Result | | Scorers | Attendance |
|---|---|---|---|---|---|---|---|---|
| 20 | Nov 22 | R1 | (a) | Chester | W | 1 - 0 | McClure | 6,778 |
| 22 | Dec 6 | R2 | (a) | Tranmere Rovers | L | 1 - 2 | Elder | 11,297 |

Apps.

Goals

| Brown | Willetts | Thompson | Stamper | Moore | Richley | Burnett | Elder | Weatherspoon | McGuigan | McClure | Newton | Johnson | Wildon | Powton | Richardson | Harden | Todd | Pearson |
|---|---|---|---|---|---|---|---|---|---|---|---|---|---|---|---|---|---|---|
| 1 | 2 | 3 | 4 | 5 | 6 | 7 | 8 | 9 | 10 | 11 | | | | | | | | |
| 1 | 2 | 3 | 4 | 5 | 6 | 7 | 8 | 9 | 10 | 11 | | | | | | | | |
| 1 | 2 | 3 | 4 | 5 | 6 | 7 | 8 | 9 | 10 | 11 | | | | | | | | |
| 1 | 2 | 3 | 8 | 5 | 6 | | | | 10 | 11 | 4 | 7 | 9 | | | | | |
| 1 | 2 | 3 | 6 | 5 | | 7 | 8 | | 10 | 11 | 4 | | 9 | | | | | |
| 1 | 2 | 3 | 6 | 5 | | 7 | 8 | | 10 | 11 | 4 | | 9 | | | | | |
| 1 | 2 | 3 | 6 | 5 | | 7 | 8 | | 10 | 11 | 4 | | 9 | | | | | |
| 1 | 2 | 3 | 6 | 5 | | 7 | 8 | | 10 | 11 | 4 | | 9 | | | | | |
| 1 | 2 | 3 | 6 | 5 | | 7 | 8 | | 10 | 11 | 4 | | 9 | | | | | |
| 1 | 2 | 3 | 6 | 5 | | 7 | 8 | | 10 | 11 | 4 | | 9 | | | | | |
| 1 | 2 | 3 | 6 | 5 | 4 | 7 | 8 | | 10 | 11 | | | 9 | | | | | |
| 1 | 2 | 3 | 6 | 5 | | 7 | 8 | | 10 | 11 | 4 | | 9 | | | | | |
| 1 | 2 | 3 | 6 | 5 | | 7 | 8 | | 10 | 11 | 4 | | 9 | | | | | |
| 1 | 2 | 3 | 6 | 5 | 4 | 7 | 8 | | 10 | 11 | | | 9 | | | | | |
| 1 | 2 | 3 | 6 | 5 | 4 | 7 | 8 | | 10 | 11 | | | 9 | | | | | |
| | 2 | 3 | 6 | 5 | 4 | 7 | 8 | | 10 | 11 | | | 9 | 1 | | | | |
| | 2 | | 3 | 5 | 6 | 7 | 8 | | 10 | 11 | 4 | | 9 | 1 | | | | |
| | 2 | 3 | 10 | 5 | 6 | | 8 | | 7 | 11 | 4 | | 9 | 1 | | | | |
| | 2 | 3 | 10 | 5 | 6 | | 8 | | 7 | 11 | 4 | | 9 | 1 | | | | |
| 1 | 2 | 3 | 5 | | 6 | 7 | 8 | | 10 | | 4 | | 11 | | 9 | | | |
| 1 | 2 | | 3 | 5 | 6 | | 8 | | 10 | 11 | 4 | | 7 | | 9 | | | |
| 1 | 2 | | 3 | 5 | 6 | | 8 | | 10 | 11 | 4 | | 7 | | 9 | | | |
| 1 | 2 | | 3 | 5 | 6 | 7 | 8 | | 10 | 11 | 4 | | | | 9 | | | |
| 1 | 2 | | 3 | 5 | 6 | 7 | 8 | | 10 | 11 | 4 | | | | 9 | | | |
| 1 | 2 | 3 | | 5 | 6 | | 8 | | 10 | 11 | 4 | | 7 | | 9 | | | |
| 1 | 2 | 3 | 6 | 5 | | 7 | | | 10 | 11 | 4 | | 8 | | 9 | | | |
| 1 | 2 | 3 | 6 | 5 | | 7 | | | 10 | 11 | 4 | | 8 | | 9 | | | |
| 1 | 2 | 3 | 6 | 5 | | 7 | | | 10 | 11 | 4 | | 8 | | 9 | | | |
| 1 | 2 | 3 | 6 | 5 | | 7 | | | 10 | 11 | 4 | | 8 | | 9 | | | |
| 1 | 2 | 3 | 6 | 5 | | 7 | | | 10 | 11 | 4 | | 8 | | 9 | | | |
| 1 | 2 | 3 | 6 | 5 | | 7 | 8 | | 10 | 11 | 4 | | | | 9 | | | |
| 1 | 2 | 3 | 6 | 5 | | 7 | | | 10 | | 4 | | 8 | | 9 | 11 | | |
| 1 | 2 | 3 | 6 | 5 | | 7 | | | 8 | | 4 | | 10 | | 9 | 11 | | |
| 1 | 2 | 3 | 6 | 5 | | 7 | | | 8 | | 4 | | 10 | | 9 | 11 | | |
| 1 | 2 | 3 | 6 | 5 | | 7 | 8 | | 10 | 11 | 4 | | | | 9 | | | |
| 1 | 2 | 3 | 6 | 5 | | 7 | 8 | | 10 | 11 | 4 | | | | 9 | | | |
| 1 | 2 | 3 | 6 | 5 | | 7 | 8 | | 10 | 11 | 4 | | | | 9 | | | |
| 1 | 2 | 3 | 6 | 5 | | 7 | 8 | | | 11 | 4 | | | | 9 | | 10 | |
| 1 | 2 | 3 | | 5 | 6 | 7 | 8 | | 10 | | 4 | | | | 9 | 11 | | |
| 1 | 2 | 3 | | 5 | 6 | 7 | 8 | | 10 | | 4 | | | | 9 | 11 | | |
| 1 | 2 | 3 | | 5 | 6 | 7 | 8 | | 10 | | 4 | | | | 9 | 11 | | |
| 1 | 3 | | | 5 | 6 | 7 | | | 10 | | 4 | 8 | | | 9 | 11 | | 2 |
| 1 | 2 | 3 | | 5 | 6 | 7 | | | 10 | | 4 | 8 | | | 9 | 11 | | |
| 1 | 2 | 3 | | 5 | 6 | | | | 10 | | 4 | 8 | 7 | | 9 | 11 | | |
| 1 | 2 | 3 | | 5 | 6 | | | | 10 | | 4 | 8 | 7 | | 9 | 11 | | |
| 1 | 2 | 3 | | 5 | 6 | | | | 10 | | 4 | 8 | 7 | | 9 | 11 | | |
| 42 | 46 | 40 | 37 | 45 | 25 | 37 | 32 | 3 | 45 | 34 | 39 | 6 | 31 | 4 | 27 | 11 | 1 | 1 |
| | 4 | | 1 | | | 1 | 10 | 2 | 9 | 5 | 2 | 1 | 11 | | 4 | 5 | | |

| Brown | Willetts | Thompson | Stamper | Moore | Richley | Burnett | Elder | Weatherspoon | McGuigan | McClure | Newton | Johnson | Wildon |
|---|---|---|---|---|---|---|---|---|---|---|---|---|---|
| 1 | 2 | | 3 | 5 | 6 | 7 | 8 | | 10 | 11 | 4 | | 9 |
| 1 | 2 | 3 | 5 | | 6 | 7 | 8 | | 10 | 11 | 4 | | 9 |
| 2 | 2 | 1 | 2 | 1 | 2 | 2 | 2 | | 2 | 2 | 2 | | 2 |
| | | | | | | | 1 | | | 1 | | | |

## League Table

| | P | W | D | L | F | A | Pts |
|---|---|---|---|---|---|---|---|
| Oldham Athletic | 46 | 22 | 15 | 9 | 77 | 45 | 59 |
| Port Vale | 46 | 20 | 18 | 8 | 67 | 35 | 58 |
| Wrexham | 46 | 24 | 8 | 14 | 86 | 66 | 56 |
| York City | 46 | 20 | 13 | 13 | 60 | 45 | 53 |
| Grimsby Town | 46 | 21 | 10 | 15 | 75 | 59 | 52 |
| Southport | 46 | 20 | 11 | 15 | 63 | 60 | 51 |
| Bradford Park Avenue | 46 | 19 | 12 | 15 | 75 | 61 | 50 |
| Gateshead | 46 | 17 | 15 | 14 | 76 | 60 | 49 |
| Carlisle United | 46 | 18 | 13 | 15 | 82 | 68 | 49 |
| Crewe Alexandra | 46 | 20 | 8 | 18 | 70 | 68 | 48 |
| Stockport County | 46 | 17 | 13 | 16 | 82 | 69 | 47 |
| Tranmere Rovers | 46 | 21 | 5 | 20 | 65 | 63 | 47 |
| Chesterfield | 46 | 18 | 11 | 17 | 65 | 63 | 47 |
| Halifax Town | 46 | 16 | 15 | 15 | 68 | 68 | 47 |
| Scunthorpe United | 46 | 16 | 14 | 16 | 62 | 56 | 46 |
| Bradford City | 46 | 14 | 18 | 14 | 75 | 80 | 46 |
| Hartlepools United | 46 | 16 | 14 | 16 | 57 | 61 | 46 |
| Mansfield Town | 46 | 16 | 14 | 16 | 55 | 62 | 46 |
| Barrow | 46 | 16 | 12 | 18 | 66 | 71 | 44 |
| Chester | 46 | 11 | 15 | 20 | 64 | 85 | 37 |
| Darlington | 46 | 14 | 6 | 26 | 58 | 96 | 34 |
| Rochdale | 46 | 14 | 5 | 27 | 62 | 83 | 33 |
| Workington | 46 | 11 | 10 | 25 | 55 | 91 | 32 |
| Accrington Stanley | 46 | 8 | 11 | 27 | 39 | 89 | 27 |

# 1953-54

## Division Three North

Manager: Fred Westgarth

### Did you know that?

Eric Wildon was leading goalscorer for the fourth successive season, a record later equalled by Keith Houchen between 1978 and 1982.

Billy Linacre made his Hartlepools debut on 22 August at Chester, a 1–1 draw. He went on to play 101 games, scoring 12 goals for the club. His sons, John and Phil, also played for the club in the 1970s and 1980s.

| Match No. | Date | Round | Venue | Opponents | Result | | Scorers | Attendance |
|---|---|---|---|---|---|---|---|---|
| 1 | Aug 22 | | (a) | Chester | D | 1 - 1 | Johnson | 6,695 |
| 2 | 24 | | (h) | York City | D | 2 - 2 | McLaughlin, McGuigan | 11,854 |
| 3 | 29 | | (h) | Crewe Alexandra | D | 0 - 0 | | 9,701 |
| 4 | 31 | | (a) | York City | L | 0 - 5 | | 3,645 |
| 5 | Sep 5 | | (a) | Port Vale | L | 1 - 3 | Burnett | 20,052 |
| 6 | 7 | | (h) | Southport | D | 1 - 1 | McGuigan | 8,925 |
| 7 | 12 | | (h) | Bradford Park Avenue | L | 0 - 2 | | 8,409 |
| 8 | 15 | | (a) | Southport | L | 1 - 2 | McGuigan | 4,566 |
| 9 | 19 | | (a) | Barnsley | L | 2 - 3 | McGuigan, Harden | 10,757 |
| 10 | 21 | | (h) | Scunthorpe United | W | 3 - 2 | Harden, Johnson, Wildon | 6,174 |
| 11 | 26 | | (h) | Darlington | W | 1 - 0 | Wildon | 7,865 |
| 12 | Oct 1 | | (a) | Scunthorpe United | D | 0 - 0 | | 9,102 |
| 13 | 3 | | (h) | Halifax Town | W | 2 - 0 | Harden, Wildon | 8,255 |
| 14 | 10 | | (a) | Accrington Stanley | L | 0 - 2 | | 7,729 |
| 15 | 17 | | (h) | Grimsby Town | W | 3 - 0 | Stamper, Wildon 2 | 9,039 |
| 16 | 24 | | (a) | Stockport County | L | 0 - 1 | | 8,867 |
| 17 | 31 | | (h) | Rochdale | W | 6 - 0 | Harden 4, Linacre, Johnson | 6,763 |
| 18 | Nov 7 | | (a) | Wrexham | L | 0 - 2 | | 7,106 |
| 19 | 14 | | (h) | Mansfield Town | W | 3 - 1 | Wildon, Linacre, Johnson | 7,128 |
| 22 | 28 | | (h) | Bradford City | D | 1 - 1 | Wildon | 8,353 |
| 23 | Dec 5 | | (a) | Chesterfield | L | 1 - 2 | Wildon | 7,038 |
| 26 | 19 | | (h) | Chester | W | 2 - 0 | Richardson, Wildon | 5,481 |
| 27 | 25 | | (a) | Workington | D | 0 - 0 | | 9,103 |
| 28 | 26 | | (h) | Workington | D | 2 - 2 | Wildon, Willetts (pen) | 6,731 |
| 29 | Jan 1 | | (a) | Tranmere Rovers | L | 2 - 3 | Willetts (pen), Wildon | 6,973 |
| 30 | 2 | | (a) | Crewe Alexandra | L | 0 - 3 | | 2,938 |
| 32 | 16 | | (h) | Port Vale | W | 2 - 1 | McGuigan 2 | 8,554 |
| 33 | 23 | | (a) | Bradford Park Avenue | L | 0 - 5 | | 5,998 |
| 34 | 30 | | (a) | Carlisle United | W | 3 - 2 | McGuigan, Richardson | 5,024 |
| 35 | Feb 6 | | (h) | Barnsley | L | 0 - 1 | | 7,276 |
| 36 | 20 | | (a) | Halifax Town | L | 0 - 1 | | 4,861 |
| 37 | 27 | | (h) | Accrington Stanley | L | 0 - 1 | | 7,518 |
| 38 | Mar 6 | | (a) | Grimsby Town | L | 0 - 3 | | 5,628 |
| 39 | 13 | | (h) | Stockport County | W | 6 - 0 | McGuigan 3, Willetts (pen), Johnson, Linacre | 5,879 |
| 40 | 20 | | (a) | Rochdale | D | 2 - 2 | Johnson, McLaughlin | 6,583 |
| 41 | 24 | | (a) | Darlington | W | 1 - 0 | Richardson | 3,516 |
| 42 | 27 | | (h) | Wrexham | D | 1 - 1 | Burnett | 6,209 |
| 43 | Apr 3 | | (a) | Mansfield Town | L | 0 - 1 | | 5,948 |
| 44 | 5 | | (h) | Tranmere Rovers | L | 1 - 2 | Richardson | 5,010 |
| 45 | 10 | | (h) | Barrow | D | 2 - 2 | Thompson, Johnson | 5,328 |
| 46 | 12 | | (h) | Carlisle United | D | 1 - 1 | Wildon | 5,398 |
| 47 | 16 | | (h) | Gateshead | W | 1 - 0 | Wildon | 8,701 |
| 48 | 17 | | (a) | Bradford City | D | 1 - 1 | Richardson | 7,150 |
| 49 | 19 | | (a) | Gateshead | W | 3 - 1 | Wildon 2, Harden | 3,962 |
| 50 | 24 | | (h) | Chesterfield | L | 0 - 1 | | 6,238 |
| 51 | 26 | | (a) | Barrow | D | 1 - 1 | Johnson | 3,915 |

Final Position : 18th in Division Three North

Apps.
Goals

**FA Cup**

| Match No. | Date | Round | Venue | Opponents | Result | | Scorers | Attendance |
|---|---|---|---|---|---|---|---|---|
| 20 | Nov 21 | R1 | (h) | Mansfield Town | D | 1 - 1 | Willetts (pen) | 11,779 |
| 21 | 25 | R1r | (a) | Mansfield Town | W | 3 - 0 | Wildon, Linacre, Richardson | 6,237 |
| 24 | Dec 12 | R2 | (a) | Northampton Town | D | 1 - 1 | Harden | 18,772 |
| 25 | 16 | R2r | (h) | Northampton Town | W | 1 - 0 | Linacre | 12,169 |
| 31 | Jan 9 | R3 | (a) | Stoke City | L | 2 - 6 | Richardson 2 | 23,927 |

Apps.
Goals

| Corbett | Willetts | Thompson | Newton | Stamper | Clarke | Linacre | Johnson | Richardson | McGuigan | McLaughlin | Richley | Wildon | Moore | Burnett | Brown | Wilkinson | Harden | Desmond | Luke | Taylor | Todd | Smith | Davison | MacGregor | Cameron |
|---|---|---|---|---|---|---|---|---|---|---|---|---|---|---|---|---|---|---|---|---|---|---|---|---|---|
| 1 | 2 | 3 | 4 | 5 | 6 | 7 | 8 | 9 | 10 | 11 | | | | | | | | | | | | | | | |
| 1 | 2 | 3 | 4 | 5 | 6 | 7 | 8 | 9 | 10 | 11 | | | | | | | | | | | | | | | |
| 1 | 2 | 3 | 4 | 5 | | 7 | | 9 | 10 | 11 | 6 | 8 | | | | | | | | | | | | | |
| 1 | 2 | 3 | 4 | 5 | | 7 | 8 | 9 | 10 | 11 | 6 | | | | | | | | | | | | | | |
| 1 | 2 | 3 | | 4 | | | 8 | 9 | 10 | 11 | 6 | | 5 | 7 | | | | | | | | | | | |
| 1 | 2 | 3 | | 6 | | | 8 | 9 | 10 | 11 | 4 | | 5 | 7 | | | | | | | | | | | |
| 1 | 2 | 3 | | 4 | | 8 | | 9 | 10 | 11 | 6 | | 5 | 7 | | | | | | | | | | | |
| | 2 | 3 | | 6 | | 7 | | 8 | 10 | | | 9 | 5 | | 1 | 4 | 11 | | | | | | | | |
| | 2 | 3 | | 6 | | 7 | | 8 | 10 | | | 9 | 5 | | 1 | 4 | 11 | | | | | | | | |
| | 2 | 3 | | 6 | | 7 | 8 | | | | | 9 | 5 | | 1 | 4 | 11 | 10 | | | | | | | |
| | 2 | 3 | | 6 | | 7 | 8 | | 10 | | | 9 | 5 | | 1 | 4 | 11 | | | | | | | | |
| | 2 | 3 | | 6 | | 7 | 8 | | 10 | | | 9 | 5 | | 1 | 4 | 11 | | | | | | | | |
| | 2 | 3 | | 6 | | 7 | 8 | | 10 | | | 9 | 5 | | 1 | 4 | 11 | | | | | | | | |
| | 2 | 3 | | 6 | | 7 | 8 | | 10 | | | 9 | 5 | | 1 | 4 | 11 | | | | | | | | |
| | 2 | 3 | | 6 | | 7 | 8 | | 10 | | | 9 | 5 | | 1 | 4 | | | 11 | | | | | | |
| | 2 | 3 | | 6 | | 7 | 8 | | 10 | | | 9 | 5 | | 1 | 4 | | | 11 | | | | | | |
| | 2 | 3 | | 6 | | 7 | 8 | | 10 | | | 9 | 5 | | 1 | 4 | 11 | | | | | | | | |
| | 2 | 3 | 4 | 6 | | 7 | 8 | 9 | 10 | | | | 5 | | 1 | | 11 | | | | | | | | |
| | 2 | 3 | | 6 | | 7 | 8 | | 10 | | | 9 | 5 | | 1 | 4 | 11 | | | | | | | | |
| | 2 | 3 | 4 | 6 | | 7 | | 8 | 10 | | | 9 | 5 | | 1 | | 11 | | | | | | | | |
| | 2 | 3 | 4 | 6 | | 7 | | 8 | 10 | 11 | | 9 | 5 | | 1 | | | | | | | | | | |
| | 2 | 3 | 4 | | | 7 | 9 | 8 | 10 | | | 11 | 5 | | 1 | 6 | | | | | | | | | |
| | 2 | 3 | 4 | | | | 7 | 8 | 10 | | | 9 | 5 | | 1 | 6 | 11 | | | | | | | | |
| | 2 | 3 | 4 | | | 7 | | 8 | 10 | | 6 | 9 | 5 | | 1 | | 11 | | | | | | | | |
| | 2 | 3 | 4 | | | | | 8 | 10 | | | 9 | 5 | 7 | 1 | 6 | 11 | | | | | | | | |
| | 2 | 3 | 4 | | | | 8 | 10 | 6 | | | 9 | 5 | 7 | 1 | | 11 | | | | | | | | |
| | 2 | 3 | | | | 7 | | 8 | 10 | | 4 | 9 | 5 | | 1 | 6 | 11 | | | | | | | | |
| | 2 | 3 | | | | 7 | | 8 | 10 | | 6 | 9 | 5 | | 1 | 4 | 11 | | | | | | | | |
| | 2 | 3 | 4 | | | 7 | 8 | 9 | 10 | 11 | | | 5 | | | | | | | 1 | 6 | | | | |
| | 2 | 3 | 4 | | | 7 | 8 | 9 | 10 | 11 | | | 5 | | | | | | | 1 | 6 | | | | |
| | 2 | 3 | 4 | | | 7 | 8 | 9 | 10 | 11 | | | 5 | | | | | | | 1 | 6 | | | | |
| | 2 | 3 | 4 | | | 7 | | 8 | 10 | | 6 | | 5 | | | | 11 | | | 1 | | 9 | | | |
| | 2 | 3 | 4 | | | 7 | 8 | 9 | 10 | | | 11 | 5 | | | 6 | | | | 1 | | | | | |
| | 2 | 3 | 4 | | | 7 | 8 | 9 | 10 | | 6 | | 5 | | | | | | 11 | 1 | | | | | |
| | 2 | 3 | 4 | | | 7 | 8 | 9 | 10 | 11 | 6 | | 5 | | | | | | | 1 | | | | | |
| | 2 | 3 | 4 | | | | 8 | 9 | 10 | | 6 | | 5 | 7 | | | | | 11 | 1 | | | | | |
| | 2 | 3 | 4 | | | | 8 | 9 | 10 | 11 | 6 | | 5 | 7 | | | | | | 1 | | | | | |
| | 2 | 3 | 4 | | | 11 | 8 | 9 | 10 | | 6 | | 5 | 7 | | | | | | 1 | | | | | |
| | 2 | 3 | 4 | | | 11 | 8 | 9 | 10 | | 6 | | | 7 | | | | | | 1 | | | 5 | | |
| | 2 | 3 | 4 | | | | 8 | 9 | 10 | | 6 | | 5 | 7 | | | 11 | | | 1 | | | | | |
| | 2 | 3 | 4 | | | | 8 | | 10 | | 6 | 9 | 5 | 7 | | | 11 | | | 1 | | | | | |
| | 2 | 3 | 4 | | | 7 | | 8 | 10 | | 6 | 9 | 5 | | | | 11 | | | 1 | | | | | |
| | 2 | 3 | 4 | | | 7 | | 8 | 10 | | | 9 | 5 | | | | 11 | | | 1 | | | | 6 | |
| | 2 | 3 | 4 | | | 7 | | 8 | 10 | | 6 | 9 | 5 | | | | 11 | | | 1 | | | | | |
| | 2 | 3 | 4 | | | 7 | | 8 | 10 | | 6 | 9 | 5 | | | | 11 | | | 1 | | | | | |
| | 3 | 11 | 4 | 6 | | 7 | 10 | 8 | | | | 9 | 5 | | | | | | | 1 | | | | | 2 |
| 7 | 46 | 46 | 30 | 22 | 2 | 37 | 31 | 36 | 44 | 13 | 20 | 28 | 41 | 11 | 21 | 17 | 24 | 1 | 4 | 18 | 3 | 1 | 1 | 1 | 1 |
| | 3 | 1 | | 1 | | 3 | 8 | 6 | 10 | 2 | | 15 | | 2 | | | 8 | | | | | | | | |

| Corbett | Willetts | Thompson | Newton | Stamper | Clarke | Linacre | Johnson | Richardson | McGuigan | McLaughlin | Richley | Wildon | Moore | Burnett | Brown | Wilkinson | Harden | Desmond | Luke |
|---|---|---|---|---|---|---|---|---|---|---|---|---|---|---|---|---|---|---|---|
| | 2 | 3 | 4 | 6 | | 7 | 8 | | 10 | | | 9 | 5 | | 1 | | | | 11 |
| | 2 | 3 | 4 | 6 | | 7 | | 8 | 10 | | | 9 | 5 | | 1 | | | | 11 |
| | 2 | 3 | 4 | 6 | | 7 | | 8 | 10 | | | 9 | 5 | | 1 | | 11 | | |
| | 2 | 3 | 4 | 6 | | 7 | 9 | 8 | 10 | | | 11 | 5 | | 1 | | | | |
| | 2 | 3 | 4 | | | 7 | | 8 | 10 | | | 9 | 5 | | 1 | 6 | 11 | | |
| | 5 | 5 | 5 | 4 | | 5 | 2 | 4 | 5 | | | 5 | 5 | | 5 | 1 | 2 | | 2 |
| | 1 | | | | | 2 | | 3 | | | | 1 | | | | | 1 | | |

## League Table

| | P | W | D | L | F | A | Pts |
|---|---|---|---|---|---|---|---|
| Port Vale | 46 | 26 | 17 | 3 | 74 | 21 | 69 |
| Barnsley | 46 | 24 | 10 | 12 | 77 | 57 | 58 |
| Scunthorpe United | 46 | 21 | 15 | 10 | 77 | 56 | 57 |
| Gateshead | 46 | 21 | 13 | 12 | 74 | 55 | 55 |
| Bradford City | 46 | 22 | 9 | 15 | 60 | 55 | 53 |
| Chesterfield | 46 | 19 | 14 | 13 | 76 | 64 | 52 |
| Mansfield Town | 46 | 20 | 11 | 15 | 88 | 67 | 51 |
| Wrexham | 46 | 21 | 9 | 16 | 81 | 68 | 51 |
| Bradford Park Avenue | 46 | 18 | 14 | 14 | 77 | 68 | 50 |
| Stockport County | 46 | 18 | 11 | 17 | 77 | 67 | 47 |
| Southport | 46 | 17 | 12 | 17 | 63 | 60 | 46 |
| Barrow | 46 | 16 | 12 | 18 | 72 | 71 | 44 |
| Carlisle United | 46 | 14 | 15 | 17 | 83 | 71 | 43 |
| Tranmere Rovers | 46 | 18 | 7 | 21 | 59 | 70 | 43 |
| Accrington Stanley | 46 | 16 | 10 | 20 | 66 | 74 | 42 |
| Crewe Alexandra | 46 | 14 | 13 | 19 | 49 | 67 | 41 |
| Grimsby Town | 46 | 16 | 9 | 21 | 51 | 77 | 41 |
| Hartlepools United | 46 | 13 | 14 | 19 | 59 | 65 | 40 |
| Rochdale | 46 | 15 | 10 | 21 | 59 | 77 | 40 |
| Workington | 46 | 13 | 14 | 19 | 59 | 80 | 40 |
| Darlington | 46 | 12 | 14 | 20 | 50 | 71 | 38 |
| York City | 46 | 12 | 13 | 21 | 64 | 86 | 37 |
| Halifax Town | 46 | 12 | 10 | 24 | 44 | 73 | 34 |
| Chester | 46 | 11 | 10 | 25 | 48 | 67 | 32 |

# 1954-55

## Division Three North

Manager: Fred Westgarth

### Did you know that?

'Pools achieved their best finish – fifth – since their inaugural League season of 1921–22. In doing so they equalled their record of only using 19 players, with Watty Moore an ever-present and Cameron, Johnson, Linacre, McGuigan, Newton, and Stamper each playing over 40 League games.

The four home FA Cup ties attracted average attendances of 14,276.

| Match No. | Date | Round | Venue | Opponents | | Result | Scorers | Attendance |
|---|---|---|---|---|---|---|---|---|
| 1 | Aug 21 | | (h) | Crewe Alexandra | W | 2 - 1 | Wildon, McGuigan | 7,390 |
| 2 | 23 | | (a) | York City | L | 0 - 1 | | 10,156 |
| 3 | 28 | | (a) | Carlisle United | L | 2 - 3 | Wildon 2 | 7,425 |
| 4 | 30 | | (h) | York City | W | 1 - 0 | Harden | 8,103 |
| 5 | Sep 4 | | (h) | Chester | W | 3 - 1 | Wildon, McGuigan, Harden | 7,909 |
| 6 | 6 | | (a) | Gateshead | L | 0 - 3 | | 4,577 |
| 7 | 11 | | (a) | Grimsby Town | L | 0 - 1 | | 10,117 |
| 8 | 13 | | (h) | Gateshead | D | 0 - 0 | | 8,628 |
| 9 | 18 | | (h) | Bradford Park Avenue | L | 0 - 1 | | 8,279 |
| 10 | 20 | | (a) | Stockport County | W | 2 - 0 | Richardson, Harden | 5,152 |
| 11 | 25 | | (a) | Rochdale | L | 1 - 2 | Johnson | 6,222 |
| 12 | 27 | | (h) | Stockport County | W | 2 - 1 | Richardson, McGuigan | 6,604 |
| 13 | Oct 2 | | (h) | Tranmere Rovers | W | 4 - 0 | Harden, McGuigan 2, Johnson | 7,610 |
| 14 | 9 | | (h) | Halifax Town | W | 1 - 0 | Harden | 7,422 |
| 15 | 16 | | (a) | Oldham Athletic | W | 1 - 0 | Richardson | 6,925 |
| 16 | 23 | | (h) | Bradford City | D | 0 - 0 | | 7,140 |
| 17 | 30 | | (a) | Barnsley | D | 0 - 0 | | 10,377 |
| 18 | Nov 6 | | (h) | Scunthorpe United | W | 4 - 2 | Richardson, McGuigan 2, Luke | 7,621 |
| 19 | 13 | | (a) | Wrexham | W | 4 - 1 | McGuigan 2, Johnson 2 | 5,362 |
| 21 | 27 | | (a) | Mansfield Town | W | 2 - 0 | Richardson, Linacre | 7,855 |
| 22 | Dec 4 | | (h) | Workington | W | 3 - 2 | Richardson, McGuigan, Luke | 8,290 |
| 24 | 18 | | (a) | Crewe Alexandra | D | 1 - 1 | McGuigan | 3,384 |
| 25 | 25 | | (h) | Darlington | W | 1 - 0 | Harden | 12,430 |
| 26 | 27 | | (a) | Darlington | W | 1 - 0 | Harden | 17,576 |
| 27 | Jan 1 | | (h) | Carlisle United | W | 1 - 0 | Richardson | 12,445 |
| 30 | 15 | | (a) | Chester | L | 0 - 1 | | 1,723 |
| 34 | Feb 5 | | (a) | Bradford Park Avenue | L | 0 - 1 | | 7,373 |
| 35 | 12 | | (h) | Rochdale | W | 3 - 1 | McGuigan, Lumley 2 | 6,611 |
| 36 | 19 | | (a) | Tranmere Rovers | L | 1 - 3 | McGuigan | 4,250 |
| 37 | Mar 5 | | (h) | Oldham Athletic | W | 2 - 0 | Johnson, McGuigan | 7,195 |
| 38 | 12 | | (a) | Bradford City | W | 1 - 0 | Johnson | 6,839 |
| 39 | 19 | | (h) | Barnsley | L | 0 - 3 | | 8,411 |
| 40 | 23 | | (h) | Grimsby Town | W | 3 - 2 | Linacre, McGuigan, Luke | 4,134 |
| 41 | 26 | | (a) | Scunthorpe United | L | 1 - 5 | Linacre | 4,155 |
| 42 | 28 | | (a) | Halifax Town | L | 0 - 1 | | 3,693 |
| 43 | 30 | | (h) | Southport | W | 2 - 1 | Richardson, Thompson | 5,417 |
| 44 | Apr 2 | | (h) | Wrexham | W | 3 - 0 | McGuigan, Linacre, Johnson | 6,373 |
| 45 | 8 | | (a) | Chesterfield | L | 0 - 3 | | 10,886 |
| 46 | 9 | | (a) | Accrington Stanley | W | 5 - 2 | Johnson, Wildon, Stamper 2, Linacre | 11,267 |
| 47 | 11 | | (h) | Chesterfield | W | 2 - 0 | Linacre, Newton (pen) | 9,551 |
| 48 | 16 | | (h) | Mansfield Town | L | 1 - 2 | Johnson | 7,484 |
| 49 | 18 | | (a) | Barrow | W | 2 - 0 | McGuigan, Lumley | 3,378 |
| 50 | 23 | | (a) | Workington | W | 1 - 0 | McGuigan | 5,161 |
| 51 | 25 | | (h) | Accrington Stanley | L | 1 - 3 | Luke | 9,371 |
| 52 | 30 | | (h) | Barrow | D | 0 - 0 | | 5,708 |
| 53 | May 2 | | (a) | Southport | L | 0 - 1 | | 2,200 |

Final Position : 5th in Division Three North — Apps. / Goals

**FA Cup**

| Match No. | Date | Round | Venue | Opponents | | Result | Scorers | Attendance |
|---|---|---|---|---|---|---|---|---|
| 20 | Nov 20 | R1 | (h) | Chesterfield | W | 1 - 0 | Richardson | 12,643 |
| 23 | Dec 11 | R2 | (h) | Aldershot | W | 4 - 0 | McGuigan 2, Richardson, Willetts (pen) | 14,813 |
| 28 | Jan 8 | R3 | (h) | Darlington | D | 1 - 1 | Harden | 12,450 |
| 29 | 12 | R3r | (a) | Darlington | D | 2 - 2* | Richardson 2 | 10,598 |
| 31 | 17 | R3r2# | (a) | Darlington | W | 2 - 0 | Richardson, Newton (pen) | 10,891 |
| 32 | 29 | R4 | (h) | Nottingham Forest | D | 1 - 1 | Newton (pen) | 17,200 |
| 33 | Feb 2 | R4r | (a) | Nottingham Forest | L | 1 - 2* | Stamper | 20,479 |

# Played at Ayresome Park, Middlesbrough  * After extra-time — Apps. / Goals

| Taylor | Cameron | Willetts | Newton | Moore | Stamper | Linacre | Johnson | Wildon | McGuigan | Thompson | Harden | Richardson | Brown | Luke | Willis | MacGregor | Lumley | Dyson |
|---|---|---|---|---|---|---|---|---|---|---|---|---|---|---|---|---|---|---|
| 1 | 2 | 3 | 4 | 5 | 6 | 7 | 8 | 9 | 10 | 11 | | | | | | | | |
| 1 | 2 | 3 | 4 | 5 | 6 | 7 | 8 | 9 | 10 | 11 | | | | | | | | |
| 1 | 2 | | 4 | 5 | 6 | 7 | 8 | 9 | 10 | 3 | 11 | | | | | | | |
| 1 | 2 | | 4 | 5 | 6 | 7 | 8 | 9 | 10 | 3 | 11 | | | | | | | |
| 1 | 2 | | 4 | 5 | 6 | 7 | 8 | 9 | 10 | 3 | 11 | | | | | | | |
| 1 | 2 | | 4 | 5 | 6 | 7 | 8 | 9 | 10 | 3 | 11 | | | | | | | |
| 1 | 2 | | 4 | 5 | 6 | 7 | 8 | 9 | 10 | 3 | 11 | | | | | | | |
| 1 | 2 | | 4 | 5 | 6 | 7 | 8 | 9 | 10 | 3 | | 11 | | | | | | |
| | 2 | | 4 | 5 | 6 | 7 | 8 | 9 | 10 | 3 | 11 | | 1 | | | | | |
| | 2 | | 4 | 5 | 6 | 7 | 8 | | 10 | 3 | 11 | 9 | 1 | | | | | |
| | 2 | 3 | 4 | 5 | 6 | 7 | 8 | | 10 | | 11 | 9 | 1 | | | | | |
| | 2 | 3 | 4 | 5 | 6 | 7 | 8 | | 10 | | 11 | 9 | 1 | | | | | |
| | 2 | 3 | 4 | 5 | 6 | 7 | 8 | | 10 | | 11 | 9 | 1 | | | | | |
| | 2 | 3 | 4 | 5 | 6 | 7 | 8 | | 10 | | 11 | 9 | 1 | | | | | |
| | 2 | 3 | 4 | 5 | | 7 | 8 | 10 | 6 | | 11 | 9 | 1 | | | | | |
| | 2 | 3 | 4 | 5 | 6 | 7 | 8 | | 10 | | 11 | 9 | 1 | | | | | |
| | 2 | 3 | 4 | 5 | 6 | 7 | 8 | | 10 | | | 9 | 1 | 11 | | | | |
| | 2 | 3 | 4 | 5 | 6 | 7 | 8 | | 10 | | | 9 | 1 | 11 | | | | |
| | 2 | 3 | 4 | 5 | 6 | 7 | 8 | | 10 | | | 9 | 1 | 11 | | | | |
| | 2 | 3 | 4 | 5 | 6 | 7 | 8 | | 10 | | | 9 | 1 | 11 | | | | |
| | 2 | 3 | 4 | 5 | 6 | 7 | 8 | | 10 | | | 9 | 1 | 11 | | | | |
| | 2 | 3 | 4 | 5 | 6 | 7 | 8 | | 10 | | | 9 | 1 | 11 | | | | |
| | 2 | 3 | 4 | 5 | 6 | | 8 | | 10 | | 11 | 9 | 1 | 7 | | | | |
| | 2 | 3 | 4 | 5 | 6 | | 8 | | 10 | | 11 | 9 | 1 | | 7 | | | |
| | 2 | 3 | 4 | 5 | 6 | 7 | 8 | | 10 | | 11 | 9 | 1 | | | | | |
| 1 | 2 | 3 | 4 | 5 | 6 | | 8 | | 10 | | 11 | 9 | | 7 | | | | |
| 1 | 2 | 4 | | 5 | 6 | 7 | 8 | | | 3 | | | | 11 | 9 | 10 | | |
| 1 | 2 | | 4 | 5 | 6 | 7 | 9 | | 10 | 3 | | | | 11 | | | 8 | |
| 1 | 2 | | 4 | 5 | 6 | 7 | 9 | | 10 | 3 | | | | 11 | | | 8 | |
| | 2 | | 4 | 5 | 6 | 7 | 9 | | 10 | 3 | | | 1 | 11 | | | 8 | |
| | 2 | | 4 | 5 | 6 | 7 | 9 | | 10 | 3 | | | 1 | 11 | | | 8 | |
| | 2 | | 4 | 5 | 6 | 7 | 9 | | 10 | 3 | | | 1 | 11 | | | 8 | |
| | 2 | | 4 | 5 | 6 | 7 | 8 | | 10 | 3 | | 9 | 1 | 11 | | | | |
| | 2 | | 4 | 5 | 6 | 7 | 8 | | 10 | 3 | | 9 | 1 | 11 | | | | |
| | 2 | | 4 | 5 | 6 | 7 | 8 | | 10 | 3 | | 9 | 1 | 11 | | | | |
| | 2 | | 4 | 5 | 6 | 7 | 8 | | 10 | 3 | 11 | 9 | 1 | | | | | |
| | 2 | | 4 | 5 | 6 | 7 | 8 | | 10 | 3 | 11 | 9 | 1 | | | | | |
| 1 | 2 | | 4 | 5 | 6 | 7 | 8 | | 10 | 3 | 11 | 9 | | | | | | |
| | 2 | | 4 | 5 | 6 | 7 | 9 | 11 | 10 | 3 | | | 1 | | | | 8 | |
| | 2 | | 4 | 5 | 6 | 7 | 9 | | 10 | 3 | | | 1 | 11 | | | 8 | |
| | 2 | | 4 | 5 | 6 | 7 | 9 | 10 | | 3 | | | 1 | 11 | | | 8 | |
| 1 | 2 | | 4 | 5 | 6 | 7 | | | 10 | 3 | | 9 | | 11 | | | 8 | |
| 1 | | 2 | 4 | 5 | 6 | 7 | | | 10 | 3 | | 9 | | 11 | | | 8 | |
| 1 | | 2 | 4 | 5 | 6 | 7 | | | 10 | 3 | | 9 | | 11 | | | 8 | |
| | | 2 | 4 | 5 | 6 | 7 | 9 | | 10 | 3 | | | | 11 | | | 8 | 1 |
| | | 2 | 4 | 5 | 6 | 7 | | | 10 | 3 | | 9 | | 11 | | | 8 | 1 |
| 16 | 42 | 23 | 45 | 46 | 45 | 43 | 42 | 12 | 44 | 30 | 20 | 28 | 28 | 24 | 2 | 1 | 13 | 2 |
| | | | 1 | | 2 | 6 | 9 | 5 | 18 | 1 | 7 | 8 | | 4 | | | 3 | |

| Taylor | Cameron | Willetts | Newton | Moore | Stamper | Linacre | Johnson | Wildon | McGuigan | Thompson | Harden | Richardson | Brown | Luke |
|---|---|---|---|---|---|---|---|---|---|---|---|---|---|---|
| | 2 | 3 | 4 | 5 | 6 | 7 | 8 | | 10 | | | 9 | 1 | 11 |
| | 2 | 3 | 4 | 5 | 6 | 7 | 8 | | 10 | | | 9 | 1 | 11 |
| | 2 | 3 | 4 | 5 | 6 | 7 | 8 | | 10 | | 11 | 9 | 1 | |
| | 2 | 3 | 4 | 5 | 6 | 7 | 8 | | 10 | | 11 | 9 | 1 | |
| 1 | 2 | | 4 | 5 | 6 | 7 | 8 | | 10 | 3 | | 9 | | 11 |
| 1 | 2 | | 4 | 5 | 6 | 7 | 8 | | 10 | 3 | | 9 | | 11 |
| 1 | 2 | | 4 | 5 | 6 | 7 | 8 | | 10 | 3 | | 9 | | 11 |
| 3 | 7 | 4 | 7 | 7 | 7 | 7 | 7 | | 7 | 3 | 2 | 7 | 4 | 5 |
| | | 1 | 2 | | 1 | | | | 2 | | 1 | 5 | | |

## League Table

| | P | W | D | L | F | A | Pts |
|---|---|---|---|---|---|---|---|
| Barnsley | 46 | 30 | 5 | 11 | 86 | 46 | 65 |
| Accrington Stanley | 46 | 25 | 11 | 10 | 96 | 67 | 61 |
| Scunthorpe United | 46 | 23 | 12 | 11 | 81 | 53 | 58 |
| York City | 46 | 24 | 10 | 12 | 92 | 63 | 58 |
| Hartlepools United | 46 | 25 | 5 | 16 | 64 | 49 | 55 |
| Chesterfield | 46 | 24 | 6 | 16 | 81 | 70 | 54 |
| Gateshead | 46 | 20 | 12 | 14 | 65 | 69 | 52 |
| Workington | 46 | 18 | 14 | 14 | 68 | 55 | 50 |
| Stockport County | 46 | 18 | 12 | 16 | 84 | 70 | 48 |
| Oldham Athletic | 46 | 19 | 10 | 17 | 74 | 68 | 48 |
| Southport | 46 | 16 | 16 | 14 | 47 | 44 | 48 |
| Rochdale | 46 | 17 | 14 | 15 | 69 | 66 | 48 |
| Mansfield Town | 46 | 18 | 9 | 19 | 65 | 71 | 45 |
| Halifax Town | 46 | 15 | 13 | 18 | 63 | 67 | 43 |
| Darlington | 46 | 14 | 14 | 18 | 62 | 73 | 42 |
| Bradford Park Avenue | 46 | 15 | 11 | 20 | 56 | 70 | 41 |
| Barrow | 46 | 17 | 6 | 23 | 70 | 89 | 40 |
| Wrexham | 46 | 13 | 12 | 21 | 65 | 77 | 38 |
| Tranmere Rovers | 46 | 13 | 11 | 22 | 55 | 70 | 37 |
| Carlisle United | 46 | 15 | 6 | 25 | 78 | 89 | 36 |
| Bradford City | 46 | 13 | 10 | 23 | 47 | 55 | 36 |
| Crewe Alexandra | 46 | 10 | 14 | 22 | 68 | 91 | 34 |
| Grimsby Town | 46 | 13 | 8 | 25 | 47 | 78 | 34 |
| Chester | 46 | 12 | 9 | 25 | 44 | 77 | 33 |

# 1955-56

## Division Three North

Manager: Fred Westgarth

### Did you know that?

'Pools finished fourth in Division Three North, equalling their highest position since joining the Football League in 1921–22 and setting a new record of 26 wins.

Stalwarts of the early post-war years, Berry Brown, Leo Harden, and Joe Willetts, all made their final appearances during the season.

| Match No. | Date | Round | Venue | Opponents | Result | | Scorers | Attendance |
|---|---|---|---|---|---|---|---|---|
| 1 | Aug 20 | | (h) | Darlington | W | 3 - 0 | Smith, Rayment, Luke | 10,194 |
| 2 | 24 | | (a) | Workington | L | 1 - 5 | Stamper | 5,553 |
| 3 | 27 | | (a) | Stockport County | L | 0 - 4 | | 5,942 |
| 4 | 29 | | (h) | Workington | W | 1 - 0 | Luke | 8,761 |
| 5 | Sep 3 | | (h) | Mansfield Town | W | 4 - 2 | Smith 3, Luke | 7,714 |
| 6 | 5 | | (h) | York City | L | 0 - 1 | | 9,184 |
| 7 | 10 | | (a) | Wrexham | W | 3 - 1 | McGuigan, Lumley, Luke | 13,702 |
| 8 | 12 | | (a) | York City | L | 0 - 3 | | 10,171 |
| 9 | 17 | | (h) | Halifax Town | W | 3 - 2 | Richardson, Lumley, Luke | 7,348 |
| 10 | 19 | | (h) | Derby County | W | 2 - 0 | Linacre, Luke | 9,170 |
| 11 | 24 | | (a) | Bradford City | L | 0 - 2 | | 13,418 |
| 12 | 27 | | (a) | Oldham Athletic | L | 2 - 3 | Luke, Lumley | 3,097 |
| 13 | Oct 1 | | (h) | Scunthorpe United | L | 0 - 2 | | 8,170 |
| 14 | 8 | | (h) | Southport | W | 1 - 0 | Smith | 5,650 |
| 15 | 15 | | (a) | Accrington Stanley | L | 0 - 1 | | 8,824 |
| 16 | 22 | | (h) | Chesterfield | W | 3 - 0 | Robinson, Smith 2 | 5,479 |
| 17 | 29 | | (a) | Rochdale | W | 4 - 1 | Luke 2, Lumley, Robinson | 4,388 |
| 18 | Nov 5 | | (h) | Bradford Park Avenue | W | 3 - 1 | Smith, McGuigan 2 | 6,383 |
| 19 | 12 | | (a) | Grimsby Town | L | 0 - 1 | | 14,481 |
| 21 | 26 | | (a) | Chester | W | 1 - 0 | Johnson | 5,876 |
| 22 | Dec 3 | | (h) | Barrow | W | 1 - 0 | Robinson | 5,853 |
| 24 | 17 | | (a) | Darlington | D | 0 - 0 | | 5,578 |
| 25 | 24 | | (h) | Stockport County | D | 0 - 0 | | 9,299 |
| 26 | 26 | | (h) | Crewe Alexandra | W | 6 - 1 | Johnson 4, Luke, Lumley | 6,959 |
| 27 | 27 | | (a) | Crewe Alexandra | W | 3 - 1 | Stamper, Johnson, Luke | 3,948 |
| 28 | 31 | | (a) | Mansfield Town | L | 1 - 5 | Luke | 7,294 |
| 29 | Jan 2 | | (h) | Oldham Athletic | W | 1 - 0 | Luke | 8,646 |
| 31 | 14 | | (h) | Wrexham | W | 3 - 2 | McGuigan, Robinson, Johnson | 3,851 |
| 32 | 21 | | (a) | Halifax Town | W | 2 - 0 | Johnson 2 | 7,346 |
| 33 | 28 | | (a) | Tranmere Rovers | D | 2 - 2 | Johnson, Lumley | 6,788 |
| 34 | Feb 4 | | (h) | Bradford City | W | 1 - 0 | Rayment | 5,169 |
| 35 | 11 | | (a) | Scunthorpe United | L | 1 - 5 | Johnson | 5,614 |
| 36 | 18 | | (a) | Southport | D | 0 - 0 | | 6,219 |
| 37 | Mar 3 | | (a) | Chesterfield | W | 3 - 2 | Rayment, Johnson 2 | 9,161 |
| 38 | 10 | | (h) | Rochdale | W | 1 - 0 | Luke (pen) | 8,150 |
| 39 | 17 | | (a) | Carlisle United | W | 3 - 0 | Lumley, Johnson 2 | 4,118 |
| 40 | 24 | | (h) | Grimsby Town | L | 1 - 2 | Rayment | 10,360 |
| 41 | 30 | | (a) | Gateshead | L | 1 - 2 | McGuigan | 5,757 |
| 42 | 31 | | (a) | Bradford Park Avenue | W | 3 - 1 | Luke, Johnson 2 | 6,579 |
| 43 | Apr 2 | | (h) | Gateshead | W | 3 - 1 | Harden, McGuigan, March (o.g.) | 8,450 |
| 44 | 7 | | (h) | Chester | W | 3 - 1 | Johnson, McGuigan, Luke | 6,646 |
| 45 | 14 | | (a) | Barrow | L | 2 - 3 | McGuigan, Johnson | 4,734 |
| 46 | 21 | | (h) | Tranmere Rovers | W | 4 - 0 | Lumley, Luke, Johnson 2 | 6,262 |
| 47 | 28 | | (a) | Derby County | L | 2 - 3 | Luke, Rayment | 10,794 |
| 48 | 30 | | (h) | Carlisle United | W | 3 - 0 | Robinson, Waters (o.g.), Luke | 5,445 |
| 49 | May 3 | | (h) | Accrington Stanley | D | 0 - 0 | | 7,331 |

Final Position : 4th in Division Three North — Apps.

2 own goals — Goals

### FA Cup

| Match No. | Date | Round | Venue | Opponents | Result | | Scorers | Attendance |
|---|---|---|---|---|---|---|---|---|
| 20 | Nov 19 | R1 | (h) | Gateshead | W | 3 - 0 | Luke 2, Lumley | 10,890 |
| 23 | Dec 10 | R2 | (a) | Chesterfield | W | 2 - 1 | Luke 2 | 10,280 |
| 30 | Jan 7 | R3 | (h) | Chelsea | L | 0 - 1 | | 16,862 |

Apps.

Goals

| Dyson | Cameron | Thompson | Newton | Moore | Stamper | Rayment | Lumley | Smith | McGuigan | Luke | Linacre | Johnson | Willetts | Healey | Richardson | Brown | Robinson | Anderson | Harden | Wilkinson |
|---|---|---|---|---|---|---|---|---|---|---|---|---|---|---|---|---|---|---|---|---|
| 1 | 2 | 3 | 4 | 5 | 6 | 7 | 8 | 9 | 10 | 11 | | | | | | | | | | |
| 1 | 2 | 3 | 4 | 5 | 6 | | 8 | | 10 | 11 | 7 | 9 | | | | | | | | |
| 1 | | 3 | 4 | 5 | 6 | 7 | 8 | | 10 | 11 | | 9 | 2 | | | | | | | |
| 1 | 2 | 3 | 4 | 5 | 6 | 7 | 8 | 9 | 10 | 11 | | | | | | | | | | |
| 1 | 2 | 3 | 4 | 5 | | 7 | 8 | 9 | 10 | 11 | | | | 6 | | | | | | |
| 1 | 2 | 3 | 4 | 5 | | 7 | 8 | | 10 | 11 | | | | 6 | 9 | | | | | |
| | 2 | 3 | | 5 | 6 | | 8 | | 10 | 11 | 7 | | | 4 | 9 | 1 | | | | |
| | 2 | 3 | | 5 | 6 | | 8 | | 10 | 11 | 7 | | | 4 | 9 | 1 | | | | |
| 1 | 2 | 3 | | 5 | 6 | | 8 | | 10 | 11 | 7 | | | 4 | 9 | | | | | |
| 1 | 2 | 3 | | 5 | 6 | | 8 | | 10 | 11 | 7 | | 4 | | 9 | | | | | |
| 1 | 2 | 3 | 4 | 5 | 6 | | 8 | | 10 | 11 | 7 | | | | 9 | | | | | |
| 1 | 2 | 3 | 4 | 5 | 6 | 7 | 8 | | 10 | 11 | | | | | 9 | | | | | |
| 1 | 2 | 3 | 4 | 5 | 6 | | 8 | | 10 | 11 | 7 | | | | 9 | | | | | |
| 1 | 2 | 3 | 4 | 5 | | | 8 | 9 | 10 | 11 | 7 | | | 6 | | | | | | |
| 1 | 2 | 3 | 4 | 5 | 6 | | 8 | 9 | 10 | 11 | 7 | | | | | | | | | |
| 1 | 2 | 3 | 4 | 5 | 6 | | 8 | 9 | 10 | 11 | | | | | | | 7 | | | |
| 1 | 2 | 3 | 4 | 5 | 6 | | 8 | 9 | 10 | 11 | | | | | | | 7 | | | |
| 1 | 2 | 3 | 4 | 5 | 6 | | 8 | 9 | 10 | 11 | | | | | | | 7 | | | |
| 1 | 2 | 3 | 4 | 5 | 6 | | 8 | | 10 | 11 | | 9 | | | | | 7 | | | |
| 1 | 2 | 3 | 4 | 5 | 6 | | 8 | | | 11 | | 9 | | | 10 | | 7 | | | |
| 1 | 2 | 3 | 4 | 5 | 6 | | 8 | | | 11 | | 9 | | | 10 | | 7 | | | |
| 1 | 2 | 3 | 4 | 5 | 6 | | 8 | | | 11 | | 9 | | | 10 | | 7 | | | |
| 1 | 2 | 3 | 4 | 5 | 6 | | 8 | | | 11 | | 9 | | | 10 | | 7 | | | |
| 1 | 2 | 3 | 4 | 5 | 6 | 7 | 8 | | 10 | 11 | | 9 | | | | | | | | |
| 1 | 2 | 3 | 4 | 5 | 6 | 7 | 8 | | | 11 | | 9 | | | 10 | | | | | |
| 1 | 2 | 3 | 4 | 5 | 6 | | 8 | | | 11 | | 9 | | | 10 | | 7 | | | |
| 1 | 2 | 3 | 4 | 5 | 6 | | 8 | | 10 | 11 | | 9 | | | 7 | | | | | |
| 1 | 2 | 3 | 4 | 5 | 6 | | 8 | | 10 | 11 | | 9 | | | | | 7 | | | |
| 1 | 2 | 3 | 4 | 5 | 6 | 7 | 8 | | 10 | 11 | | 9 | | | | | | | | |
| 1 | 2 | 3 | 4 | 5 | 6 | 7 | 8 | | 10 | 11 | | 9 | | | | | | | | |
| 1 | 2 | 3 | 4 | 5 | 6 | 7 | 8 | | 10 | 11 | | 9 | | | | | | | | |
| 1 | 2 | 3 | 4 | 5 | 6 | 7 | 8 | | 10 | 11 | | 9 | | | | | | | | |
| 1 | 2 | 3 | 4 | 5 | 6 | 7 | 8 | | 10 | 11 | | 9 | | | | | | | | |
| 1 | 2 | 3 | 4 | 5 | | 7 | 8 | | 10 | 11 | | 9 | | | | | | 6 | | |
| 1 | 2 | 3 | 4 | 5 | | 7 | 8 | | 10 | 11 | | 9 | | | | | | 6 | | |
| 1 | 2 | 3 | 4 | 5 | | 7 | 8 | | 10 | 11 | | 9 | | | | | | 6 | | |
| 1 | 2 | 3 | 4 | 5 | | 7 | 8 | | 10 | 11 | | 9 | | | | | | 6 | | |
| 1 | 2 | 3 | 4 | 5 | | 7 | 8 | | 10 | 11 | | 9 | | | | | | 6 | | |
| 1 | 2 | 3 | 4 | 5 | | 7 | 8 | | 10 | 11 | | 9 | | | | | | 6 | | |
| 1 | 2 | 3 | 4 | 5 | | 7 | 8 | | 10 | | | 9 | | | | | | 6 | 11 | |
| 1 | 2 | 3 | 4 | 5 | | 7 | 8 | | 10 | 11 | | 9 | | | | | | 6 | | |
| 1 | | 3 | 4 | 5 | | 7 | 8 | | 10 | 11 | | 9 | 2 | | | | | 6 | | |
| 1 | 2 | 3 | | 5 | | 7 | 8 | | 10 | 11 | | 9 | | | | | | 6 | | 4 |
| 1 | 2 | 3 | | 5 | | 7 | 8 | | 10 | 11 | | 9 | | | | | | 6 | | 4 |
| | 2 | 3 | | 5 | | | 8 | | 10 | 11 | | 9 | | | | 1 | 7 | 6 | | 4 |
| | 2 | 3 | | 5 | | | 8 | | 10 | 11 | | 9 | | | | 1 | 7 | 6 | | 4 |
| 42 | 44 | 46 | 38 | 46 | 30 | 24 | 46 | 8 | 40 | 45 | 9 | 30 | 3 | 6 | 15 | 4 | 12 | 13 | 1 | 4 |
| | | | | | 2 | 5 | 8 | 8 | 8 | 19 | 1 | 21 | | | 1 | | 5 | | 1 | |

| Dyson | Cameron | Thompson | Newton | Moore | Stamper | Rayment | Lumley | Smith | McGuigan | Luke | Linacre | Johnson | Willetts | Healey | Richardson | Brown | Robinson |
|---|---|---|---|---|---|---|---|---|---|---|---|---|---|---|---|---|---|
| 1 | 2 | 3 | 4 | 5 | 6 | | 8 | | | 11 | | 9 | | | 10 | | 7 |
| 1 | 2 | 3 | 4 | 5 | 6 | | 8 | | | 11 | | 9 | | | 10 | | 7 |
| 1 | 2 | 3 | 4 | 5 | 6 | 7 | 8 | | 10 | 11 | | 9 | | | | | |
| 3 | 3 | 3 | 3 | 3 | 3 | 1 | 3 | | 1 | 3 | | 3 | | | 2 | | 2 |
| | | | | | | | 1 | | | 4 | | | | | | | |

## League Table

| | P | W | D | L | F | A | Pts |
|---|---|---|---|---|---|---|---|
| Grimsby Town | 46 | 31 | 6 | 9 | 76 | 29 | 68 |
| Derby County | 46 | 28 | 7 | 11 | 110 | 55 | 63 |
| Accrington Stanley | 46 | 25 | 9 | 12 | 92 | 57 | 59 |
| Hartlepools United | 46 | 26 | 5 | 15 | 81 | 60 | 57 |
| Southport | 46 | 23 | 11 | 12 | 66 | 53 | 57 |
| Chesterfield | 46 | 25 | 4 | 17 | 94 | 66 | 54 |
| Stockport County | 46 | 21 | 9 | 16 | 90 | 61 | 51 |
| Bradford City | 46 | 18 | 13 | 15 | 78 | 64 | 49 |
| Scunthorpe United | 46 | 20 | 8 | 18 | 75 | 63 | 48 |
| Workington | 46 | 19 | 9 | 18 | 75 | 63 | 47 |
| York City | 46 | 19 | 9 | 18 | 85 | 72 | 47 |
| Rochdale | 46 | 17 | 13 | 16 | 66 | 84 | 47 |
| Gateshead | 46 | 17 | 11 | 18 | 77 | 84 | 45 |
| Wrexham | 46 | 16 | 10 | 20 | 66 | 73 | 42 |
| Darlington | 46 | 16 | 9 | 21 | 60 | 73 | 41 |
| Tranmere Rovers | 46 | 16 | 9 | 21 | 59 | 84 | 41 |
| Chester | 46 | 13 | 14 | 19 | 52 | 82 | 40 |
| Mansfield Town | 46 | 14 | 11 | 21 | 84 | 81 | 39 |
| Halifax Town | 46 | 14 | 11 | 21 | 66 | 76 | 39 |
| Oldham Athletic | 46 | 10 | 18 | 18 | 76 | 86 | 38 |
| Carlisle United | 46 | 15 | 8 | 23 | 71 | 95 | 38 |
| Barrow | 46 | 12 | 9 | 25 | 61 | 83 | 33 |
| Bradford Park Avenue | 46 | 13 | 7 | 26 | 61 | 122 | 33 |
| Crewe Alexandra | 46 | 9 | 10 | 27 | 50 | 105 | 28 |

# 1956-57

## Division Three North

Manager: Fred Westgarth

### Did you know that?

'Pools reached their highest-ever League position as runners-up to Derby County, equalling their record of only using 19 players, three of whom were ever-presents (Guthrie, Moore and Thompson), while Johnson, Luke and Stamper each made over 40 appearances.

Home attendances for all games, including cup ties, reach a record average of 9,627.

| Match No. | Date | Round | Venue | Opponents | Result | | Scorers | Attendance |
|---|---|---|---|---|---|---|---|---|
| 1 | Aug 18 | | (h) | Chesterfield | W | 5 - 1 | Lumley, Rayment, Johnson, McGuigan, Stamper | 5,444 |
| 2 | 22 | | (a) | Wrexham | D | 2 - 2 | Newton, Rayment | 9,936 |
| 3 | 25 | | (a) | Chester | W | 1 - 0 | Rayment | 8,374 |
| 4 | 27 | | (h) | Wrexham | W | 2 - 1 | McGuigan, Johnson | 3,974 |
| 5 | Sep 1 | | (a) | Gateshead | L | 3 - 4 | Lumley 2 (2 pens), McGuigan | 7,246 |
| 6 | 4 | | (a) | Southport | W | 6 - 1 | Johnson 4, Robinson 2 | 5,037 |
| 7 | 8 | | (h) | Bradford City | W | 2 - 0 | Johnson, McGuigan | 10,821 |
| 8 | 10 | | (h) | Southport | W | 5 - 2 | Lumley, Rankin (og), Stamper, Johnson, Luke | 10,474 |
| 9 | 15 | | (a) | Stockport County | W | 4 - 2 | Stamper, McGuigan, Johnson, Luke | 13,577 |
| 10 | 18 | | (a) | Tranmere Rovers | W | 1 - 0 | Robinson | 5.763 |
| 11 | 22 | | (h) | Carlisle United | W | 2 - 1 | Robinson, Luke | 12,267 |
| 12 | 24 | | (h) | Tranmere Rovers | W | 5 - 1 | Johnson 4, Luke | 10,219 |
| 13 | 28 | | (a) | Accrington Stanley | L | 1 - 2 | Johnson | 10,969 |
| 14 | Oct 6 | | (h) | Derby County | W | 2 - 1 | Anderson, Johnson | 12,072 |
| 15 | 13 | | (a) | Crewe Alexandra | W | 2 - 1 | Rayment, Stamper | 5,676 |
| 16 | 20 | | (h) | Darlington | W | 2 - 1 | McGuigan, Devlin (o.g.) | 13,202 |
| 17 | 27 | | (a) | Rochdale | L | 0 - 1 | | 12,237 |
| 18 | Nov 3 | | (h) | Halifax Town | L | 0 - 1 | | 10,273 |
| 19 | 10 | | (a) | Workington Town | D | 1 - 1 | Luke | 7,658 |
| 21 | 24 | | (a) | Barrow | L | 1 - 3 | Luke | 6,033 |
| 22 | Dec 1 | | (h) | Scunthorpe United | D | 0 - 0 | | 7,881 |
| 24 | 15 | | (a) | Chesterfield | L | 1 - 5 | Luke | 9,257 |
| 25 | 22 | | (h) | Chester | D | 2 - 2 | Newton (pen), Johnson | 6,515 |
| 26 | 25 | | (a) | York City | D | 3 - 3 | Robinson, Luke, Johnson | 8,663 |
| 27 | 26 | | (h) | York City | W | 2 - 0 | Stamper, Johnson | 6,954 |
| 28 | 29 | | (h) | Gateshead | W | 4 - 1 | Stamper 2, Luke 2 | 9,254 |
| 29 | Jan 1 | | (h) | Hull City | D | 3 - 3 | Stamper, Newton (pen), Johnson | 9,768 |
| 31 | 12 | | (a) | Bradford City | D | 1 - 1 | Smith | 22,126 |
| 32 | 19 | | (h) | Stockport County | W | 4 - 1 | Stamper 2, Luke, Rayment | 8,155 |
| 33 | 26 | | (h) | Oldham Athletic | W | 4 - 1 | Smith 2, Luke, Rayment | 9,127 |
| 34 | Feb 2 | | (a) | Carlisle United | L | 1 - 2 | Stamper | 12,121 |
| 35 | 9 | | (h) | Accrington Stanley | W | 2 - 1 | Johnson, Smith | 12,518 |
| 36 | 16 | | (a) | Derby County | L | 0 - 2 | | 24,644 |
| 37 | 23 | | (h) | Crewe Alexandra | W | 2 - 0 | Johnson, Luke | 8,164 |
| 38 | Mar 2 | | (a) | Darlington | L | 1 - 3 | Smith | 14,051 |
| 39 | 9 | | (h) | Rochdale | D | 0 - 0 | | 9,339 |
| 40 | 16 | | (a) | Halifax Town | L | 0 - 2 | | 5,652 |
| 41 | 23 | | (h) | Workington Town | W | 2 - 1 | Rayment, Johnson | 11,794 |
| 42 | 30 | | (a) | Hull City | L | 0 - 2 | | 13,310 |
| 43 | Apr 6 | | (h) | Barrow | W | 2 - 0 | Luke, Rayment | 6,878 |
| 44 | 13 | | (a) | Scunthorpe United | W | 2 - 1 | Luke, Johnson | 4,599 |
| 45 | 16 | | (a) | Oldham Athletic | D | 0 - 0 | | 4,956 |
| 46 | 19 | | (h) | Mansfield Town | W | 2 - 1 | Rushby (o.g.), Luke | 8,984 |
| 47 | 20 | | (h) | Bradford Park Avenue | W | 2 - 1 | Luke 2 | 8,102 |
| 48 | 23 | | (a) | Mansfield Town | L | 1 - 4 | Johnson | 10,963 |
| 49 | 27 | | (a) | Bradford Park Avenue | W | 2 - 0 | Rayment, Luke | 6,193 |

Final Position : 2nd in Division Three North

Apps.

2 own goals — Goals

**FA Cup**

| Match No. | Date | Round | Venue | Opponents | Result | | Scorers | Attendance |
|---|---|---|---|---|---|---|---|---|
| 20 | Nov 17 | R1 | (h) | Selby Town | W | 3 - 1 | Luke, Stamper, Robinson | 11,227 |
| 23 | Dec 8 | R2 | (a) | Blyth Spartans | W | 1 - 0 | Johnson | 10,168 |
| 30 | Jan 5 | R3 | (h) | Manchester United | L | 3 - 4 | Stamper, Johnson, Newton | 17,264 |

Apps.

Goals

| Guthrie | Cameron | Thompson | Anderson | Moore | Stamper | Rayment | Lumley | Johnson | McGuigan | Luke | Newton | Robinson | Smith | MacCallum | Willis | MacGregor | Waugh | Howells |
|---|---|---|---|---|---|---|---|---|---|---|---|---|---|---|---|---|---|---|
| 1 | 2 | 3 | 4 | 5 | 6 | 7 | 8 | 9 | 10 | 11 | | | | | | | | |
| 1 | 2 | 3 | 4 | 5 | 6 | 7 | 8 | 9 | 10 | | 11 | | | | | | | |
| 1 | 2 | 3 | 4 | 5 | 6 | 7 | 8 | 9 | 10 | | 11 | | | | | | | |
| 1 | 2 | 3 | 4 | 5 | 6 | 7 | 8 | 9 | 10 | 11 | | | | | | | | |
| 1 | 2 | 3 | 4 | 5 | 6 | 7 | 8 | 9 | 10 | 11 | | | | | | | | |
| 1 | 2 | 3 | 4 | 5 | 6 | | 8 | 9 | 10 | 11 | | 7 | | | | | | |
| 1 | 2 | 3 | 4 | 5 | 6 | | 8 | 9 | 10 | 11 | | 7 | | | | | | |
| 1 | 2 | 3 | 4 | 5 | 6 | | 8 | 9 | 10 | 11 | | 7 | | | | | | |
| 1 | 2 | 3 | 4 | 5 | 6 | | 8 | 9 | 10 | 11 | | 7 | | | | | | |
| 1 | 2 | 3 | 4 | 5 | 6 | | 8 | 9 | 10 | 11 | | 7 | | | | | | |
| 1 | 2 | 3 | 4 | 5 | 6 | | 8 | 9 | 10 | 11 | | 7 | | | | | | |
| 1 | 2 | 3 | 4 | 5 | 6 | | 8 | 9 | 10 | 11 | | 7 | | | | | | |
| 1 | 2 | 3 | 4 | 5 | 6 | | 8 | 9 | 10 | 11 | | 7 | | | | | | |
| 1 | 2 | 3 | 4 | 5 | 6 | 7 | 8 | 9 | 10 | | | 11 | | | | | | |
| 1 | | 3 | 4 | 5 | 6 | 7 | 8 | 9 | 10 | | 2 | 11 | | | | | | |
| 1 | 2 | 3 | 4 | 5 | 6 | | | 8 | 10 | 11 | | 7 | 9 | | | | | |
| 1 | 2 | 3 | 8 | 5 | 6 | | | 9 | 10 | 11 | | 7 | | 4 | | | | |
| 1 | 2 | 3 | 4 | 5 | 6 | | | 9 | 10 | 11 | | 7 | | | 8 | | | |
| 1 | 2 | 3 | 4 | 5 | 6 | | 8 | 9 | 10 | 11 | | 7 | | | | | | |
| 1 | 2 | 3 | 4 | 5 | 6 | | 8 | 9 | 10 | 11 | | 7 | | | | | | |
| 1 | 2 | 3 | | 5 | 6 | 7 | 10 | 9 | | 11 | 4 | | | | 8 | | | |
| 1 | 2 | 3 | 6 | 5 | | 7 | | 9 | 10 | 11 | 4 | | | | | 8 | | |
| 1 | 2 | 3 | | 5 | 6 | 7 | | 9 | 10 | 11 | 4 | | | | | 8 | | |
| 1 | | 3 | 6 | 5 | 8 | | | 9 | 10 | 11 | 4 | 7 | | | | | 2 | |
| 1 | | 3 | 6 | 5 | 10 | | | 9 | | 11 | 4 | 7 | | | | 8 | 2 | |
| 1 | | 3 | 6 | 5 | 8 | | | 9 | 10 | 11 | 4 | 7 | | | | | 2 | |
| 1 | | 3 | 6 | 5 | 8 | | | 9 | 10 | | 4 | 7 | | | | | 2 | 11 |
| 1 | | 3 | 6 | 5 | 10 | | | | 8 | 11 | 4 | 7 | 9 | | | | 2 | |
| 1 | | 3 | 6 | 5 | 10 | 7 | | | 8 | 11 | | | 9 | 4 | | | 2 | |
| 1 | | 3 | 6 | 5 | 10 | 7 | | | 8 | 11 | 4 | | 9 | | | | 2 | |
| 1 | | 3 | 6 | 5 | 10 | 7 | | | | 11 | 4 | | 9 | | | 8 | 2 | |
| 1 | | 3 | 6 | 5 | 10 | 7 | | 8 | | 11 | 4 | | 9 | | | | 2 | |
| 1 | | 3 | 6 | 5 | 10 | 7 | | 8 | | 11 | 4 | | 9 | | | | 2 | |
| 1 | | 3 | 6 | 5 | | 7 | 10 | 8 | | 11 | 4 | | 9 | | | | 2 | |
| 1 | | 3 | 6 | 5 | | 7 | 10 | 8 | | 11 | 4 | | 9 | | | | 2 | |
| 1 | | 3 | 6 | 5 | 10 | 7 | 8 | 9 | | 11 | 4 | | | | | | 2 | |
| 1 | | 3 | 6 | 5 | 10 | 7 | 8 | 9 | | 11 | 4 | | | | | | 2 | |
| 1 | | 3 | | 5 | 6 | 7 | 8 | 9 | | 11 | 4 | | 10 | | | | 2 | |
| 1 | | 3 | | 5 | 6 | 7 | 8 | 9 | | 11 | 4 | | 10 | | | | 2 | |
| 1 | | 3 | | 5 | 6 | 7 | 8 | 9 | | 11 | 4 | | 10 | | | | 2 | |
| 1 | | 3 | | 5 | 6 | 7 | 8 | 9 | | 11 | 4 | | 10 | | | | 2 | |
| 1 | | 3 | | 5 | 6 | | 8 | 9 | | 11 | 4 | | 10 | | 7 | | 2 | |
| 1 | | 3 | | 5 | 6 | 7 | 8 | 9 | 10 | 11 | 4 | | | | | | 2 | |
| 1 | | 3 | | 5 | 6 | 7 | 8 | 9 | 10 | 11 | 4 | | | | | | 2 | |
| 1 | | 3 | 4 | 5 | 6 | 7 | 8 | 9 | 10 | 11 | | | | | | | 2 | |
| 1 | | 3 | | 5 | 6 | 7 | 8 | 9 | 10 | 11 | 4 | | | | | | 2 | |
| 46 | 22 | 46 | 36 | 46 | 43 | 27 | 31 | 42 | 32 | 41 | 27 | 20 | 14 | 2 | 3 | 4 | 23 | 1 |
| | | | 1 | | 11 | 9 | 4 | 24 | 6 | 19 | 3 | 5 | 5 | | | | | |

| Guthrie | Cameron | Thompson | Anderson | Moore | Stamper | Rayment | Lumley | Johnson | McGuigan | Luke | Newton | Robinson |
|---|---|---|---|---|---|---|---|---|---|---|---|---|
| 1 | 2 | 3 | 4 | 5 | 6 | | 8 | 9 | 10 | 11 | | 7 |
| 1 | 2 | 3 | | 5 | 6 | 7 | 8 | 9 | 10 | 11 | 4 | |
| 1 | 2 | 3 | 6 | 5 | 10 | | | 9 | 8 | 11 | 4 | 7 |
| 3 | 3 | 3 | 2 | 3 | 3 | 1 | 2 | 3 | 3 | 3 | 2 | 2 |
| | | | | | 2 | | | 2 | | 1 | 1 | 1 |

## League Table

| | P | W | D | L | F | A | Pts |
|---|---|---|---|---|---|---|---|
| Derby County | 46 | 26 | 11 | 9 | 111 | 53 | 63 |
| Hartlepools United | 46 | 25 | 9 | 12 | 90 | 63 | 59 |
| Accrington Stanley | 46 | 25 | 8 | 13 | 95 | 64 | 58 |
| Workington | 46 | 24 | 10 | 12 | 93 | 63 | 58 |
| Stockport County | 46 | 23 | 8 | 15 | 91 | 75 | 54 |
| Chesterfield | 46 | 22 | 9 | 15 | 96 | 79 | 53 |
| York City | 46 | 21 | 10 | 15 | 75 | 61 | 52 |
| Hull City | 46 | 21 | 10 | 15 | 84 | 69 | 52 |
| Bradford City | 46 | 22 | 8 | 16 | 78 | 68 | 52 |
| Barrow | 46 | 21 | 9 | 16 | 76 | 62 | 51 |
| Halifax Town | 46 | 21 | 7 | 18 | 65 | 70 | 49 |
| Wrexham | 46 | 19 | 10 | 17 | 97 | 74 | 48 |
| Rochdale | 46 | 18 | 12 | 16 | 65 | 65 | 48 |
| Scunthorpe United | 46 | 15 | 15 | 16 | 71 | 69 | 45 |
| Carlisle United | 46 | 16 | 13 | 17 | 76 | 85 | 45 |
| Mansfield Town | 46 | 17 | 10 | 19 | 91 | 90 | 44 |
| Gateshead | 46 | 17 | 10 | 19 | 72 | 90 | 44 |
| Darlington | 46 | 17 | 8 | 21 | 82 | 95 | 42 |
| Oldham Athletic | 46 | 12 | 15 | 19 | 66 | 74 | 39 |
| Bradford Park Avenue | 46 | 16 | 3 | 27 | 66 | 93 | 35 |
| Chester | 46 | 10 | 13 | 23 | 55 | 84 | 33 |
| Southport | 46 | 10 | 12 | 24 | 52 | 94 | 32 |
| Tranmere Rovers | 46 | 7 | 13 | 26 | 51 | 91 | 27 |
| Crewe Alexandra | 46 | 6 | 9 | 31 | 43 | 110 | 21 |

# 1957-58

## Division Three North

Manager: Ray Middleton

### Did you know that?

Watty Moore's run of 162 consecutive League games ended following a seven-goal defeat at Rochdale on 2 November.

Tommy McGuigan, Jackie Newton, Frank Stamper and Ray Thompson played their final games for the club during the season. Between them, they made 1,460 appearances for Hartlepools United.

| Match No. | Date | Round | Venue | Opponents | Result | | Scorers | Attendance |
|---|---|---|---|---|---|---|---|---|
| 1 | Aug 24 | | (a) | Accrington Stanley | W | 2 - 1 | McGuigan, Smith | 9,678 |
| 2 | 26 | | (h) | Darlington | W | 5 - 1 | Lumley 2, Willis 2, Smith | 14,876 |
| 3 | 31 | | (h) | Chester | W | 2 - 1 | P.Thompson, Smith | 11,629 |
| 4 | Sep 4 | | (a) | Darlington | W | 3 - 1 | P.Thompson 2, Newton (pen) | 9,509 |
| 5 | 7 | | (a) | Chesterfield | L | 1 - 2 | Willis | 11,511 |
| 6 | 9 | | (h) | Oldham Athletic | W | 4 - 1 | Luke 2, Smith 2 | 11,084 |
| 7 | 14 | | (h) | Tranmere Rovers | D | 1 - 1 | Smith | 10,823 |
| 8 | 17 | | (a) | Oldham Athletic | L | 0 - 4 | | 5,566 |
| 9 | 21 | | (a) | Gateshead | D | 0 - 0 | | 5,976 |
| 10 | 23 | | (h) | Barrow | W | 4 - 1 | K.Johnson 3, Smith | 6,112 |
| 11 | 28 | | (a) | Bradford Park Avenue | W | 3 - 2 | Lumley 2, Stamper | 9,220 |
| 12 | 30 | | (a) | Barrow | D | 3 - 3 | Willis, Luke, K.Johnson | 4,896 |
| 13 | Oct 5 | | (h) | Carlisle United | L | 0 - 1 | | 10,119 |
| 14 | 12 | | (h) | Workington | W | 1 - 0 | Newton (pen) | 8,469 |
| 15 | 19 | | (a) | Wrexham | L | 1 - 3 | Smith | 8,962 |
| 16 | 26 | | (h) | Crewe Alexandra | D | 1 - 1 | P.Thompson | 8,326 |
| 17 | Nov 2 | | (a) | Rochdale | L | 0 - 7 | | 5,508 |
| 18 | 9 | | (h) | HalifaxTown | W | 5 - 0 | Luke 2, McGuigan 2, P.Thompson | 6,195 |
| 20 | 23 | | (h) | Hull City | W | 5 - 1 | K.Johnson 2, P.Thompson 2, McGuigan | 8,754 |
| 21 | 30 | | (a) | Bradford City | W | 1 - 0 | K.Johnson | 11,417 |
| 23 | Dec 14 | | (a) | Mansfield Town | L | 1 - 5 | Hogan | 8,097 |
| 24 | 21 | | (h) | Accrington Stanley | D | 1 - 1 | Stamper | 7,179 |
| 25 | 25 | | (h) | York City | D | 2 - 2 | Wragg (o.g.), McGuigan (pen) | 6,837 |
| 26 | 26 | | (a) | York City | D | 2 - 2 | McGuigan 2, | 10,785 |
| 27 | 28 | | (a) | Chester | L | 1 - 2 | Hartnett | 7,725 |
| 28 | Jan 1 | | (h) | Southport | W | 2 - 1 | K.Johnson, Willis | 7,582 |
| 29 | 4 | | (a) | Southport | D | 0 - 0 | | 2,639 |
| 30 | 11 | | (h) | Chesterfield | L | 0 - 2 | | 8,129 |
| 31 | 18 | | (a) | Tranmere Rovers | L | 2 - 3 | P.Thompson, Rayment | 8,338 |
| 32 | Feb 1 | | (h) | Gateshead | D | 2 - 2 | P.Thompson, McGuigan | 6,183 |
| 33 | 8 | | (h) | Bradford Park Avenue | D | 0 - 0 | | 4,805 |
| 34 | 15 | | (a) | Carlisle United | W | 2 - 1 | K.Johnson, Rayment | 7,670 |
| 35 | 22 | | (a) | Hull City | D | 1 - 1 | Rayment | 11,926 |
| 36 | Mar 1 | | (h) | Wrexham | L | 1 - 2 | P.Thompson | 6,749 |
| 37 | 8 | | (a) | Crewe Alexandra | L | 1 - 2 | Robinson | 3,771 |
| 38 | 15 | | (h) | Rochdale | L | 1 - 3 | P.Thompson | 5,862 |
| 39 | 22 | | (a) | Workington | L | 0 - 1 | | 4,055 |
| 40 | 29 | | (h) | Stockport County | L | 1 - 2 | Mitchell | 3,070 |
| 41 | Apr 4 | | (h) | Bury | W | 2 - 1 | P.Thompson, McGuigan (pen) | 7,824 |
| 42 | 5 | | (a) | Scunthorpe United | L | 0 - 2 | | 8,684 |
| 43 | 7 | | (a) | Bury | D | 3 - 3 | Stamper, P.Thompson, Mitchell | 6,987 |
| 44 | 12 | | (h) | Bradford City | W | 2 - 0 | P.Thompson 2 | 6,628 |
| 45 | 14 | | (a) | Stockport County | L | 1 - 2 | Mitchell | 8,046 |
| 46 | 19 | | (a) | HalifaxTown | L | 0 - 3 | | 7,368 |
| 47 | 26 | | (h) | Mansfield Town | W | 2 - 0 | Smith, Thomas (o.g.) | 4,922 |
| 48 | 28 | | (h) | Scunthorpe United | L | 1 - 2 | Thompson | 8,159 |

Final Position : 17th in Division Three North

Apps.

2 own goals — Goals

### FA Cup

| Match No. | Date | Round | Venue | Opponents | Result | | Scorers | Attendance |
|---|---|---|---|---|---|---|---|---|
| 19 | Nov 16 | R1 | (h) | Prescot Cables | W | 5 - 0 | Newton, P.Thompson 4 | 9,424 |
| 22 | Dec 7 | R2 | (a) | Stockport County | L | 1 - 2 | K.Johnson | 12,500 |

Apps.

Goals

| Guthrie | Waugh | Thompson, R. | Newton | Moore | Stamper | Willis | Lumley | Smith | McGuigan | Luke | Thompson, P. | Robinson | Johnson, K | Burlison | Hogan | Edwards | Anderson | Dyson | Cameron | Johnson, D. | Hartnett | Wilkinson | Rayment | Mitchell |
|---|---|---|---|---|---|---|---|---|---|---|---|---|---|---|---|---|---|---|---|---|---|---|---|---|
| 1 | 2 | 3 | 4 | 5 | 6 | 7 | 8 | 9 | 10 | 11 | | | | | | | | | | | | | | |
| 1 | 2 | 3 | 4 | 5 | 6 | 7 | 8 | 9 | 10 | 11 | | | | | | | | | | | | | | |
| 1 | 2 | 3 | 4 | 5 | 6 | 7 | 8 | 9 | | 11 | 10 | | | | | | | | | | | | | |
| 1 | 2 | 3 | 4 | 5 | 6 | 7 | 8 | 9 | | 11 | 10 | | | | | | | | | | | | | |
| 1 | 2 | 3 | 4 | 5 | 6 | 7 | 8 | 9 | | 11 | 10 | | | | | | | | | | | | | |
| 1 | 2 | 3 | 4 | 5 | 6 | | 8 | 9 | 7 | 11 | 10 | | | | | | | | | | | | | |
| 1 | 2 | 3 | 4 | 5 | 6 | | 8 | 9 | 10 | 11 | | 7 | | | | | | | | | | | | |
| 1 | 2 | 3 | 4 | 5 | 6 | | 8 | 9 | 10 | 11 | | | 7 | | | | | | | | | | | |
| 1 | 2 | 3 | 4 | 5 | 6 | | 10 | 8 | 7 | 11 | | | 9 | | | | | | | | | | | |
| 1 | 2 | 3 | 4 | 5 | 6 | 7 | 10 | 8 | | 11 | | | 9 | | | | | | | | | | | |
| 1 | 2 | 3 | 4 | 5 | 6 | 7 | 10 | 8 | | 11 | | | 9 | | | | | | | | | | | |
| 1 | 2 | 3 | 4 | 5 | 6 | 7 | 10 | 8 | | 11 | | | 9 | | | | | | | | | | | |
| 1 | 2 | 3 | 4 | 5 | 6 | 7 | 10 | 8 | | 11 | | | 9 | | | | | | | | | | | |
| 1 | 2 | 3 | 7 | 5 | 6 | | | | 10 | | 9 | 11 | | 4 | 8 | | | | | | | | | |
| 1 | 2 | | 4 | 5 | | | | 7 | 10 | 11 | 9 | | | | 8 | 3 | 6 | | | | | | | |
| 1 | 2 | 3 | | 5 | 6 | | 8 | 9 | | 11 | 10 | 7 | | 4 | | | | | | | | | | |
| 1 | 2 | 3 | | 5 | 6 | | 10 | 8 | | 11 | 9 | 7 | | 4 | | | | | | | | | | |
| | 2 | | 6 | | 5 | | 7 | 8 | 10 | 11 | 9 | | | 4 | | | | 1 | 3 | | | | | |
| | 2 | | | 5 | 6 | | | 8 | 10 | 11 | 9 | | 7 | 4 | | | | 1 | 3 | | | | | |
| | 2 | | | 5 | 6 | | | 8 | 10 | 11 | 9 | | 7 | 4 | | | | 1 | 3 | | | | | |
| | 2 | | | 5 | 6 | | 7 | 11 | 10 | | | | 9 | 4 | 8 | | | 1 | 3 | | | | | |
| | 2 | | | 5 | 6 | | | 8 | 10 | 11 | | 7 | 9 | 4 | | | | 1 | 3 | | | | | |
| | 2 | | | 5 | 6 | | | | 8 | | | 7 | 9 | | | | 4 | 1 | 3 | 10 | 11 | | | |
| 1 | 2 | | | 5 | 6 | | | | 8 | | | 7 | 9 | | | | 4 | | 3 | 10 | 11 | | | |
| 1 | 2 | | | 5 | 6 | | | 10 | 8 | | | 7 | 9 | | | | 4 | | 3 | | 11 | | | |
| 1 | 2 | | | 5 | 10 | 7 | | | 8 | | | | 9 | | | | 4 | | 3 | | 11 | 6 | | |
| 1 | 2 | | | 5 | 6 | 7 | | | 10 | | | | 9 | 4 | | | 8 | | 3 | | 11 | | | |
| 1 | 2 | | | 5 | 6 | | | 9 | 10 | 11 | | | 8 | | | | 4 | | 3 | | | | 7 | |
| | 2 | | | 5 | 6 | | | | 10 | 11 | 9 | | 8 | | | | 4 | 1 | 3 | | | | 7 | |
| | 2 | | | 5 | 6 | | | | 10 | 11 | 9 | | 8 | | | | 4 | 1 | 3 | | | | 7 | |
| | 2 | 3 | | 5 | 6 | | | 8 | 10 | 11 | 9 | | 4 | | | | | 1 | | | | | 7 | |
| | 2 | 3 | 4 | 5 | 6 | | | | 10 | 11 | 9 | | 8 | | | | | 1 | | | | | 7 | |
| | 2 | 3 | 4 | 5 | 6 | | | | 10 | | 9 | 11 | 8 | | | | | 1 | | | | | 7 | |
| | 2 | 3 | | 5 | 6 | | | | | | 9 | 11 | 8 | | 10 | | 4 | 1 | | | | | 7 | |
| | 2 | 3 | 4 | 5 | 6 | 11 | | | | | 9 | 7 | 8 | | | | 10 | 1 | | | | | | |
| | 2 | 3 | 4 | 5 | 6 | | | | 10 | | 8 | | 9 | | | | | 1 | | | 11 | | | 7 |
| 1 | 2 | | | 5 | 6 | | | | 10 | | 8 | | 9 | 4 | | | | | 3 | | 11 | | | 7 |
| 1 | 2 | | | 5 | 6 | | | | 10 | | 8 | | 9 | 4 | | | | | 3 | | | | 7 | 11 |
| 1 | 2 | | | 5 | | | | | 10 | | 9 | | | 4 | 8 | | 6 | | 3 | | | | 7 | 11 |
| 1 | 2 | | | 5 | | | | | 10 | | 9 | | | 4 | 8 | | 6 | | 3 | | | | 7 | 11 |
| 1 | 3 | | | 5 | 10 | | | | | | 9 | | | 4 | 8 | | 6 | | 2 | | | | 7 | 11 |
| 1 | 2 | | | 5 | | | | | 10 | | 9 | | | 4 | 8 | | 6 | | 3 | | | | 7 | 11 |
| 1 | 2 | | | 5 | | 7 | | | 10 | | 9 | | | 4 | 8 | | 6 | | 3 | | | | | 11 |
| 1 | 2 | | | 5 | 8 | 7 | | | 10 | | 9 | | | 4 | | | 6 | | 3 | | | | | 11 |
| 1 | 2 | | | 5 | | 7 | | 8 | 10 | | 9 | | | 4 | | | 6 | | 3 | | | | | 11 |
| 1 | 2 | | | 5 | | 7 | | 8 | 10 | | 9 | | | 4 | | | 6 | | 3 | | | | | 11 |
| 32 | 46 | 22 | 20 | 45 | 39 | 16 | 17 | 26 | 34 | 25 | 29 | 11 | 26 | 19 | 9 | 1 | 19 | 14 | 23 | 2 | 7 | 1 | 12 | 11 |
| | | | 2 | | 3 | 5 | 4 | 9 | 9 | 5 | 16 | 1 | 9 | | 1 | | | | | | 1 | | 3 | 3 |

| Guthrie | Waugh | Thompson, R. | Newton | Moore | Stamper | Willis | Lumley | Smith | McGuigan | Luke | Thompson, P. | Robinson | Johnson, K | Burlison | Hogan | Edwards | Anderson | Dyson | Cameron |
|---|---|---|---|---|---|---|---|---|---|---|---|---|---|---|---|---|---|---|---|
| | 2 | | 6 | | 5 | | 7 | 8 | 10 | 11 | 9 | | | 4 | | | | 1 | 3 |
| | 2 | | | 5 | 6 | | | 8 | 10 | 11 | 9 | | 7 | 4 | | | | 1 | 3 |
| | 2 | | 1 | 1 | 2 | | 1 | 2 | 2 | 2 | 2 | | 1 | 2 | | | | 2 | 2 |
| | | | 1 | | | | | | | | 4 | | 1 | | | | | | |

## League Table

| | P | W | D | L | F | A | Pts |
|---|---|---|---|---|---|---|---|
| Scunthorpe United | 46 | 29 | 8 | 9 | 88 | 50 | 66 |
| Accrington Stanley | 46 | 25 | 9 | 12 | 83 | 61 | 59 |
| Bradford City | 46 | 21 | 15 | 10 | 73 | 49 | 57 |
| Bury | 46 | 23 | 10 | 13 | 94 | 62 | 56 |
| Hull City | 46 | 19 | 15 | 12 | 78 | 67 | 53 |
| Mansfield Town | 46 | 22 | 8 | 16 | 100 | 92 | 52 |
| Halifax Town | 46 | 20 | 11 | 15 | 83 | 69 | 51 |
| Chesterfield | 46 | 18 | 15 | 13 | 71 | 69 | 51 |
| Stockport County | 46 | 18 | 11 | 17 | 74 | 67 | 47 |
| Rochdale | 46 | 19 | 8 | 19 | 79 | 67 | 46 |
| Tranmere Rovers | 46 | 18 | 10 | 18 | 82 | 76 | 46 |
| Wrexham | 46 | 17 | 12 | 17 | 61 | 63 | 46 |
| York City | 46 | 17 | 12 | 17 | 68 | 76 | 46 |
| Gateshead | 46 | 15 | 15 | 16 | 68 | 76 | 45 |
| Oldham Athletic | 46 | 14 | 17 | 15 | 72 | 84 | 45 |
| Carlisle United | 46 | 19 | 6 | 21 | 80 | 78 | 44 |
| Hartlepools United | 46 | 16 | 12 | 18 | 73 | 76 | 44 |
| Barrow | 46 | 13 | 15 | 18 | 66 | 74 | 41 |
| Workington | 46 | 14 | 13 | 19 | 72 | 81 | 41 |
| Darlington | 46 | 17 | 7 | 22 | 78 | 89 | 41 |
| Chester | 46 | 13 | 13 | 20 | 73 | 81 | 39 |
| Bradford Park Avenue | 46 | 13 | 11 | 22 | 68 | 95 | 37 |
| Southport | 46 | 11 | 6 | 29 | 52 | 88 | 28 |
| Crewe Alexandra | 46 | 8 | 7 | 31 | 47 | 93 | 23 |

# 1958-59

## Division Four

Manager: Ray Middleton

### Did you know that?

Albert Mundy scored for Aldershot within six seconds of the start of the game on 25 October.

The record 10–1 win over Barrow on 4 April saw United score five goals in a 14-minute spell. Ironically, 'Pools all-time record League goalscorer, Ken Johnson, did not feature on the scoresheet!

| Match No. | Date | Round | Venue | Opponents | Result | | Scorers | Attendance |
|---|---|---|---|---|---|---|---|---|
| 1 | Aug 23 | | (h) | Shrewsbury Town | L | 0 - 2 | | 7,344 |
| 2 | 25 | | (h) | Bradford Park Avenue | W | 3 - 0 | Anderson (pen), Willis, Dunn | 6,994 |
| 3 | 30 | | (a) | Southport | D | 1 - 1 | Willis | 3,642 |
| 4 | Sep 1 | | (a) | Bradford Park Avenue | L | 1 - 4 | Smith | 7,688 |
| 5 | 6 | | (h) | Torquay United | L | 2 - 4 | Clark, Nicholson | 6,472 |
| 6 | 8 | | (h) | Port Vale | L | 1 - 5 | Anderson (pen) | 6,158 |
| 7 | 13 | | (a) | Crewe Alexandra | W | 2 - 0 | Langland, Thompson | 7,106 |
| 8 | 15 | | (a) | Port Vale | D | 1 - 1 | Mitchell | 9,313 |
| 9 | 20 | | (h) | Northampton Town | W | 3 - 0 | Thompson 2, Luke | 7,463 |
| 10 | 22 | | (h) | Crystal Palace | W | 4 - 1 | Mitchell 2, Thompson, Luke | 8,368 |
| 11 | 27 | | (a) | Workington | L | 0 - 3 | | 5,085 |
| 12 | Oct 1 | | (a) | Crystal Palace | W | 2 - 1 | Thompson, Luke | 16,596 |
| 13 | 4 | | (h) | York City | L | 1 - 5 | Clark | 9,799 |
| 14 | 8 | | (a) | Chester | D | 1 - 1 | Thompson | 3,220 |
| 15 | 11 | | (h) | Walsall | D | 1 - 1 | Clark | 6,434 |
| 16 | 18 | | (a) | Millwall | L | 2 - 3 | Smith 2 | 14,157 |
| 17 | 25 | | (h) | Aldershot | L | 0 - 3 | | 6,158 |
| 18 | Nov 1 | | (a) | Gateshead | L | 0 - 3 | | 3,927 |
| 19 | 8 | | (h) | Oldham Athletic | W | 4 - 0 | Langland 2, Johnson, Anderson (pen) | 4,329 |
| 22 | 22 | | (h) | Carlisle United | L | 1 - 2 | Clark | 4,064 |
| 24 | 29 | | (a) | Gillingham | L | 1 - 4 | Johnson | 6,121 |
| 26 | Dec 13 | | (a) | Coventry City | L | 1 - 4 | Johnson | 11,118 |
| 27 | 20 | | (a) | Shrewsbury Town | L | 0 - 3 | | 4,783 |
| 28 | 26 | | (h) | Darlington | W | 1 - 0 | Anderson (pen) | 5,689 |
| 29 | 27 | | (a) | Darlington | L | 1 - 3 | Anderson | 6,861 |
| 30 | Jan 1 | | (h) | Chester | L | 1 - 3 | Langland | 3,952 |
| 31 | 3 | | (h) | Southport | D | 1 - 1 | Clark | 4,137 |
| 32 | 17 | | (a) | Torquay United | W | 3 - 1 | Denham 2, Smith | 3,990 |
| 33 | 24 | | (h) | Exeter City | D | 3 - 3 | Luke, Scott, Denham | 4,413 |
| 34 | 31 | | (h) | Crewe Alexandra | W | 2 - 1 | Luke, Smith | 5,118 |
| 35 | Feb 7 | | (a) | Northampton Town | L | 1 - 2 | Clark | 6,055 |
| 36 | 14 | | (h) | Workington | L | 0 - 3 | | 3,641 |
| 37 | 21 | | (a) | York City | D | 1 - 1 | Anderson (pen) | 5,339 |
| 38 | 28 | | (a) | Walsall | D | 0 - 0 | | 7,285 |
| 39 | Mar 7 | | (h) | Millwall | W | 3 - 1 | Clark, Scott, Luke | 3,489 |
| 40 | 14 | | (a) | Aldershot | W | 4 - 2 | Langland 3, Scott | 3,932 |
| 41 | 21 | | (h) | Gateshead | D | 0 - 0 | | 4,156 |
| 42 | 27 | | (h) | Watford | W | 4 - 3 | Luke 2 (1 pen), Smith, Burlison | 6,716 |
| 43 | 28 | | (a) | Oldham Athletic | L | 0 - 1 | | 5,154 |
| 44 | 30 | | (a) | Watford | L | 1 - 4 | Anderson | 6,480 |
| 45 | Apr 4 | | (h) | Barrow | W | 10 - 1 | Smith 3, Luke 2, Clark 2, Scott, Langland, Marsden (o.g.) | 4,126 |
| 46 | 11 | | (a) | Carlisle United | L | 0 - 1 | | 4,828 |
| 47 | 18 | | (h) | Gillingham | W | 3 - 1 | Clark, Langland, Smith | 3,169 |
| 48 | 21 | | (a) | Barrow | D | 1 - 1 | Clark | 3,101 |
| 49 | 25 | | (a) | Exeter City | L | 0 - 3 | | 6,561 |
| 50 | 27 | | (h) | Coventry City | W | 2 - 1 | MacGregor, Clark | 4,288 |

Final Position : 19th in Division Four

Apps.

Goals

### FA Cup

| Match No. | Date | Round | Venue | Opponents | Result | | Scorers | Attendance |
|---|---|---|---|---|---|---|---|---|
| 20 | Nov 15 | R1 | (h) | Rochdale | D | 1 - 1 | Luke | 7,154 |
| 21 | 19 | R1r | (a) | Rochdale | D | 3 - 3* | Luke 2, Johnson | 8,763 |
| 23 | 27 | R1r2# | (a) | Rochdale | W | 2 - 1 | Smith, Johnson | 6,126 |
| 25 | Dec 6 | R2 | (a) | Barrow | L | 0 - 2 | | 5,718 |

# Played at Old Trafford, Manchester * After extra-time

Apps.

Goals

| Dyson | Waugh | Cameron | Burlison | Moore | Anderson | Willis | Smith | Thompson | Nicholson | Dunn | Mitchell | Clark | Oakley | Dixon | Gibbon | Johnson | Herring | Langland | Luke | Welford | Roberts | Scott | Denham | MacGregor |
|---|---|---|---|---|---|---|---|---|---|---|---|---|---|---|---|---|---|---|---|---|---|---|---|---|
| 1 | 2 | 3 | 4 | 5 | 6 | 7 | 8 | 9 | 10 | 11 | | | | | | | | | | | | | | |
| 1 | 2 | 3 | 4 | 5 | 6 | 7 | 8 | 9 | 10 | 11 | | | | | | | | | | | | | | |
| 1 | 2 | 3 | 4 | 5 | 6 | 7 | 8 | 9 | 10 | 11 | | | | | | | | | | | | | | |
| 1 | 2 | 3 | 4 | 5 | 6 | | 8 | 9 | | 11 | 7 | 10 | | | | | | | | | | | | |
| 1 | 2 | 3 | 4 | 5 | 6 | | | 9 | 10 | 11 | 7 | 8 | | | | | | | | | | | | |
| | | | | 5 | 4 | | | 9 | 10 | 11 | | 8 | 1 | 2 | 3 | 6 | 7 | | | | | | | |
| | 2 | | | 5 | 4 | | | 10 | | | | 8 | 1 | | 3 | 6 | 7 | 9 | 11 | | | | | |
| | 2 | | | 5 | 4 | | | 10 | | | 7 | 8 | 1 | | 3 | 6 | | 9 | 11 | | | | | |
| | 2 | | | 5 | 4 | | | 10 | | | 7 | 8 | 1 | | 3 | 6 | | 9 | 11 | | | | | |
| | 2 | | | 5 | 4 | | | 10 | | | 7 | 8 | 1 | | 3 | 6 | | 9 | 11 | | | | | |
| | 2 | | | 5 | 4 | | | 10 | | | 7 | 8 | 1 | | 3 | 6 | | 9 | 11 | | | | | |
| | 2 | | | 5 | 4 | | | 10 | | | 7 | 8 | 1 | | 3 | 6 | | 9 | 11 | | | | | |
| | 2 | | | 5 | 4 | | 7 | 10 | | | | 8 | 1 | | 3 | 6 | | 9 | 11 | | | | | |
| | 2 | | | | 4 | | | 10 | | 11 | 7 | 8 | 1 | 5 | 3 | 6 | | 9 | | | | | | |
| | 2 | | | | 4 | | | 8 | | | 7 | 10 | 1 | 5 | 3 | 6 | | 9 | 11 | | | | | |
| | 2 | | | | 4 | | 9 | 10 | | | 7 | | 1 | 5 | 3 | 6 | | 8 | 11 | | | | | |
| | 2 | | 4 | | | | 9 | 10 | | | | 8 | 1 | 5 | 3 | 6 | | 7 | 11 | | | | | |
| | 2 | | 4 | 5 | | 9 | | 10 | | | 7 | 8 | 1 | | 3 | 6 | | | 11 | | | | | |
| | 3 | 2 | | | 6 | | | | | | | 7 | 1 | 5 | | 8 | | 9 | 11 | 4 | 10 | | | |
| | 3 | 2 | | | 6 | | | | | | | 7 | 1 | 5 | | 8 | | 9 | 11 | 4 | 10 | | | |
| | 3 | 2 | | | 6 | | 9 | | | 11 | 7 | 8 | 1 | 5 | | 10 | | | | 4 | | | | |
| | 3 | 2 | | | 6 | | 9 | | 10 | | | 7 | 1 | 5 | | 8 | | | 11 | 4 | | | | |
| | 3 | 2 | 10 | | 6 | | 9 | | | | | 7 | 1 | 5 | | 8 | | | 11 | 4 | | | | |
| | 3 | 2 | 9 | 5 | 6 | | | | | | | 7 | 1 | | | 8 | | 10 | 11 | 4 | | | | |
| | 3 | 2 | 9 | 5 | 6 | | | | | | | 7 | 1 | | | 8 | | 10 | 11 | 4 | | | | |
| | 3 | 2 | 9 | 5 | 6 | | | | | | | 7 | 1 | | | 8 | | 10 | 11 | 4 | | | | |
| | 3 | 2 | 4 | 5 | 6 | | 9 | | | | | 7 | 1 | | | 8 | | | 11 | | | 10 | | |
| | 3 | 2 | | 5 | 6 | | 9 | | | | | 10 | 1 | | | 4 | | | 11 | | | 8 | 7 | |
| | 3 | 2 | | 5 | 6 | | 9 | | | | | 10 | 1 | | | 4 | | | 11 | | | 8 | 7 | |
| | 3 | 2 | | 5 | 6 | | 9 | | | | | 10 | 1 | | | 4 | | | 11 | | | 8 | 7 | |
| | 3 | 2 | 11 | 5 | 6 | | 9 | | | | | 10 | 1 | | | 4 | | | | | | 8 | 7 | |
| | 3 | 2 | 9 | 5 | 6 | | | | | | | 10 | 1 | | | 4 | | | 11 | | | 8 | 7 | |
| | 3 | 2 | 7 | 5 | 6 | | | | | | | 10 | 1 | | | 4 | | 9 | 11 | | | 8 | | |
| | 3 | 2 | | 5 | 6 | | | | 8 | 11 | | 10 | 1 | | | 4 | | 9 | 7 | | | | | |
| | 3 | 2 | 7 | 5 | 6 | | | | | | | 10 | 1 | | | 4 | | 9 | 11 | | | 8 | | |
| | 3 | 2 | 7 | 5 | 6 | | | | | | | 10 | 1 | | | 4 | | 9 | 11 | | | 8 | | |
| | 3 | 2 | 7 | 5 | 6 | | | | | | | 10 | 1 | | | 4 | | 9 | 11 | | | 8 | | |
| | 3 | 2 | 7 | 5 | 6 | | 9 | | | | | | 1 | | | 4 | | | 11 | | 10 | 8 | | |
| | 3 | 2 | 7 | 5 | 6 | | 9 | | | | | 10 | 1 | | | 4 | | | 11 | | | 8 | | |
| | 3 | 2 | | 5 | 6 | | 9 | | | | | 10 | 1 | | | 4 | | 7 | 11 | | | 8 | | |
| | 3 | 2 | | 5 | 6 | | 9 | | | | | 10 | 1 | | | 4 | | 8 | 11 | | | 7 | | |
| | 3 | 2 | | 5 | 6 | | 9 | | | 11 | | 10 | 1 | | | 4 | | 8 | | | | 7 | | |
| | 3 | 2 | 11 | 5 | 6 | | 9 | | | | | 10 | 1 | | | 4 | | 8 | | | | 7 | | |
| | 3 | 2 | 11 | 5 | 6 | | 9 | | | | | 10 | 1 | | | 4 | | 8 | | | | 7 | | |
| | 3 | 2 | 11 | 5 | 6 | | 9 | | | | | 10 | 1 | | | 4 | | 8 | | | | 7 | | |
| | 3 | 2 | 11 | 5 | 6 | | 9 | | | | | 10 | 1 | | | 4 | | | | | | 7 | | 8 |
| 5 | 45 | 33 | 24 | 37 | 44 | 4 | 24 | 18 | 7 | 10 | 12 | 41 | 41 | 10 | 13 | 41 | 2 | 27 | 32 | 8 | 3 | 19 | 5 | 1 |
| | | | 1 | | 7 | 2 | 10 | 6 | 1 | 1 | 3 | 12 | | | | 3 | | 9 | 10 | | | 4 | 3 | 1 |

| Dyson | Waugh | Cameron | Burlison | Moore | Anderson | Willis | Smith | Thompson | Nicholson | Dunn | Mitchell | Clark | Oakley | Dixon | Gibbon | Johnson | Herring | Langland | Luke | Welford | Roberts | Scott | Denham | MacGregor |
|---|---|---|---|---|---|---|---|---|---|---|---|---|---|---|---|---|---|---|---|---|---|---|---|---|
| | 3 | 2 | | | 6 | | | | | | | 7 | 1 | 5 | | 8 | | 9 | 11 | 4 | 10 | | | |
| | 3 | 2 | | | 6 | | | | | | | 7 | 1 | 5 | | 8 | | 9 | 11 | 4 | 10 | | | |
| | 3 | 2 | | | 6 | | 9 | | | | | 7 | 1 | 5 | | 8 | | | 11 | 4 | 10 | | | |
| | 3 | 2 | | | 6 | | 9 | | 10 | | | 7 | 1 | 5 | | 8 | | | 11 | 4 | | | | |
| | 4 | 4 | | | 4 | | 2 | | 1 | | | 4 | 4 | 4 | | 4 | | 2 | 4 | 4 | 3 | | | |
| | | | | | | | 1 | | | | | | | | | 2 | | | 3 | | | | | |

## League Table

| | P | W | D | L | F | A | Pts |
|---|---|---|---|---|---|---|---|
| Port Vale | 46 | 26 | 12 | 8 | 110 | 58 | 64 |
| Coventry City | 46 | 24 | 12 | 10 | 84 | 47 | 60 |
| York City | 46 | 21 | 18 | 7 | 73 | 52 | 60 |
| Shrewsbury Town | 46 | 24 | 10 | 12 | 101 | 63 | 58 |
| Exeter City | 46 | 23 | 11 | 12 | 87 | 61 | 57 |
| Walsall | 46 | 21 | 10 | 15 | 95 | 64 | 52 |
| Crystal Palace | 46 | 20 | 12 | 14 | 90 | 71 | 52 |
| Northampton Town | 46 | 21 | 9 | 16 | 85 | 78 | 51 |
| Millwall | 46 | 20 | 10 | 16 | 76 | 69 | 50 |
| Carlisle United | 46 | 19 | 12 | 15 | 62 | 65 | 50 |
| Gillingham | 46 | 20 | 9 | 17 | 82 | 77 | 49 |
| Torquay United | 46 | 16 | 12 | 18 | 78 | 77 | 44 |
| Chester | 46 | 16 | 12 | 18 | 72 | 84 | 44 |
| Bradford Park Avenue | 46 | 18 | 7 | 21 | 75 | 77 | 43 |
| Watford | 46 | 16 | 10 | 20 | 81 | 79 | 42 |
| Darlington | 46 | 13 | 16 | 17 | 66 | 68 | 42 |
| Workington | 46 | 12 | 17 | 17 | 63 | 78 | 41 |
| Crewe Alexandra | 46 | 15 | 10 | 21 | 70 | 82 | 40 |
| Hartlepools United | 46 | 15 | 10 | 21 | 74 | 88 | 40 |
| Gateshead | 46 | 16 | 8 | 22 | 56 | 85 | 40 |
| Oldham Athletic | 46 | 16 | 4 | 26 | 59 | 84 | 36 |
| Aldershot | 46 | 14 | 7 | 25 | 63 | 97 | 35 |
| Barrow | 46 | 9 | 10 | 27 | 51 | 104 | 28 |
| Southport | 46 | 7 | 12 | 27 | 41 | 86 | 26 |

# 1959-60

## Division Four

Managers: Ray Middleton and Bill Robinson

### Did you know that?

The season proved to be record breaking for two (dubious) reasons – 29 of the 46 League fixtures were lost and 109 goals conceded, both Fourth Division records at the time.

United made their fourth application for re-election and only survived at the expense of neighbours Gateshead, who were rejected in favour of Peterborough United.

| Match No. | Date | Round | Venue | Opponents | Result | | Scorers | Attendance |
|---|---|---|---|---|---|---|---|---|
| 1 | Aug 22 | | (h) | Aldershot | W | 3 - 0 | Smith 2, Clark | 6,016 |
| 2 | 25 | | (a) | Walsall | D | 2 - 2 | Smith, Luke | 11,244 |
| 3 | 29 | | (a) | Crewe Alexandra | L | 0 - 1 | | 8,005 |
| 4 | 31 | | (h) | Walsall | L | 1 - 2 | Smith | 6,877 |
| 5 | Sep 5 | | (h) | Chester | L | 2 - 3 | Clark, Smith | 5,112 |
| 6 | 7 | | (h) | Oldham Athletic | D | 2 - 2 | Langland, Clark | 4,404 |
| 7 | 12 | | (a) | Crystal Palace | L | 2 - 5 | Smith, Langland | 14,722 |
| 8 | 15 | | (a) | Oldham Athletic | W | 2 - 1 | Smith, McGill (o.g.) | 5,697 |
| 9 | 19 | | (h) | Bradford Park Avenue | W | 3 - 0 | Clark 2, Scott | 4,109 |
| 10 | 21 | | (h) | Notts County | L | 2 - 4 | Smith 2 | 3,926 |
| 11 | 26 | | (a) | Stockport County | L | 1 - 2 | Clark | 5,931 |
| 12 | Oct 1 | | (a) | Notts County | L | 0 - 4 | | 10,732 |
| 13 | 3 | | (h) | Exeter City | W | 4 - 3 | Anderson (pen), Luke, Clark 2 | 3,804 |
| 14 | 10 | | (h) | Gateshead | W | 3 - 0 | Clark, Smith, McKenna | 3,832 |
| 15 | 13 | | (a) | Watford | L | 2 - 7 | McKenna, Luke | 11,183 |
| 16 | 17 | | (a) | Rochdale | L | 0 - 2 | | 4,856 |
| 17 | 24 | | (h) | Workington | L | 1 - 4 | Smith | 2,717 |
| 18 | 31 | | (a) | Doncaster Rovers | L | 1 - 5 | Clark | 4,149 |
| 19 | Nov 7 | | (h) | Northampton Town | L | 1 - 4 | Scott | 1,953 |
| 21 | 21 | | (h) | Millwall | L | 0 - 2 | | 2,677 |
| 22 | 28 | | (a) | Southport | L | 1 - 2 | Smith | 3,208 |
| 23 | Dec 12 | | (a) | Barrow | D | 2 - 2 | Clark, Clark (o.g.) | 4,445 |
| 24 | 19 | | (a) | Aldershot | L | 0 - 3 | | 2,857 |
| 25 | 26 | | (h) | Darlington | L | 1 - 2 | Smith | 5,018 |
| 26 | 28 | | (a) | Darlington | L | 0 - 2 | | 5,109 |
| 27 | Jan 2 | | (h) | Crewe Alexandra | W | 2 - 0 | Smith, Clark | 3,398 |
| 28 | 9 | | (a) | Torquay United | L | 0 - 3 | | 5,082 |
| 29 | 16 | | (a) | Chester | D | 1 - 1 | McKenna | 4,653 |
| 30 | 23 | | (h) | Crystal Palace | L | 0 - 1 | | 3,981 |
| 31 | 30 | | (h) | Gillingham | W | 3 - 1 | Clark 2, Smith | 2,659 |
| 32 | Feb 6 | | (a) | Bradford Park Avenue | L | 2 - 6 | Scott, Johnson | 6,921 |
| 33 | 13 | | (h) | Stockport County | W | 2 - 1 | Smith, Clark | 2,870 |
| 34 | 20 | | (a) | Exeter City | L | 0 - 5 | | 6,996 |
| 35 | 27 | | (a) | Gateshead | D | 1 - 1 | Clark | 2,652 |
| 36 | Mar 5 | | (h) | Rochdale | L | 0 - 1 | | 3,286 |
| 37 | 12 | | (a) | Workington | L | 0 - 3 | | 3,663 |
| 38 | 19 | | (h) | Doncaster Rovers | L | 2 - 6 | Bircham, Clark | 2,893 |
| 39 | 23 | | (h) | Watford | D | 0 - 0 | | 2,189 |
| 40 | 26 | | (a) | Northampton Town | L | 0 - 3 | | 5,954 |
| 41 | Apr 2 | | (h) | Torquay United | W | 4 - 0 | McKenna 2, Smith, Clark | 2,754 |
| 42 | 9 | | (a) | Millwall | L | 0 - 4 | | 11,356 |
| 43 | 15 | | (a) | Carlisle United | D | 1 - 1 | Clark | 3,164 |
| 44 | 16 | | (h) | Southport | W | 3 - 2 | Clark, Scott (pen), Bircham | 3,249 |
| 45 | 18 | | (h) | Carlisle United | L | 1 - 2 | Clark | 3,603 |
| 46 | 23 | | (a) | Gillingham | L | 1 - 3 | Butler | 5,373 |
| 47 | 30 | | (h) | Barrow | L | 0 - 1 | | 2,533 |

Final Position : 24th in Division Four

Apps.

2 own goals — Goals

**FA Cup**

| Match No. | Date | Round | Venue | Opponents | Result | | Scorers | Attendance |
|---|---|---|---|---|---|---|---|---|
| 20 | Nov 14 | R1 | (a) | Bury | L | 0 - 5 | | 9,694 |

Apps.

Goals

| Oakley | Waugh | Cameron | Johnson | Atkinson | Anderson | McKenna | Scott | Smith | Clark | Luke | Oldham | Robinson | Moore | Burlison | Langland | MacGregor | Dixon | Dunn | Butler | Bircham | Peek | Folland | Wilkinson |
|---|---|---|---|---|---|---|---|---|---|---|---|---|---|---|---|---|---|---|---|---|---|---|---|
| 1 | 2 | 3 | 4 | 5 | 6 | 7 | 8 | 9 | 10 | 11 | | | | | | | | | | | | | |
| 1 | | 2 | 4 | 5 | 6 | 7 | 8 | 9 | 10 | 11 | 3 | | | | | | | | | | | | |
| 1 | | 2 | 4 | 5 | 6 | 7 | 8 | 9 | 10 | 11 | 3 | | | | | | | | | | | | |
| 1 | | 2 | 4 | 5 | 6 | 7 | 8 | 9 | 10 | 11 | 3 | | | | | | | | | | | | |
| 1 | 2 | 3 | 4 | 5 | 6 | 7 | | 9 | 10 | 11 | | 8 | | | | | | | | | | | |
| 1 | 2 | 3 | 4 | 6 | | | | 9 | 10 | 11 | | | 5 | 7 | 8 | | | | | | | | |
| 1 | 2 | 3 | 7 | 6 | 4 | | | 9 | 10 | 11 | | | 5 | | 8 | | | | | | | | |
| 1 | 3 | | 4 | 6 | 2 | 7 | 8 | 9 | 10 | 11 | | | 5 | | | | | | | | | | |
| 1 | 3 | | 4 | 6 | 2 | 7 | 8 | 9 | 10 | 11 | | | 5 | | | | | | | | | | |
| 1 | 3 | | 4 | 6 | 2 | | 8 | 9 | 10 | 11 | | | 5 | | | 7 | | | | | | | |
| 1 | 3 | | 4 | 6 | 2 | | 8 | 9 | 10 | 11 | | | 5 | | | 7 | | | | | | | |
| 1 | | | 4 | 5 | 2 | 7 | 8 | 9 | 10 | 11 | | 6 | | | | | 3 | | | | | | |
| 1 | | | 4 | 5 | 2 | 7 | 8 | 9 | 10 | 11 | | 6 | | | | | 3 | | | | | | |
| 1 | | 3 | 4 | 5 | 2 | 7 | 8 | 9 | 10 | 11 | | 6 | | | | | | | | | | | |
| 1 | | | 4 | 5 | 2 | 7 | 8 | 9 | 10 | 11 | | 6 | | | | | 3 | | | | | | |
| 1 | | 3 | 4 | 5 | 2 | 7 | 8 | 9 | 10 | | | 6 | | | | | | 11 | | | | | |
| 1 | | 3 | 4 | 5 | 2 | 7 | 8 | 9 | 10 | | | 6 | | | | | | 11 | | | | | |
| 1 | 2 | | 8 | | 6 | | 7 | 9 | 10 | | | | 5 | | | 4 | 3 | 11 | | | | | |
| 1 | 3 | | 6 | 5 | 2 | 7 | 8 | 9 | 10 | | | | | 4 | | | | 11 | | | | | |
| 1 | 2 | | 4 | 3 | 6 | 7 | 8 | 9 | | | | | 5 | | 11 | 10 | | | | | | | |
| 1 | 2 | | 4 | 3 | 6 | 7 | 8 | 9 | | | | | 5 | | 11 | 10 | | | | | | | |
| 1 | 2 | | 4 | 3 | 6 | 7 | 8 | 9 | 10 | | | | 5 | | 11 | | | | | | | | |
| 1 | 2 | | 4 | | 6 | 7 | 8 | 9 | 10 | | | | 5 | | 11 | | 3 | | | | | | |
| 1 | 2 | | 4 | | 6 | 7 | 8 | 9 | 10 | | | | 5 | | 11 | | 3 | | | | | | |
| 1 | 2 | | 4 | | 6 | 7 | 8 | 9 | 10 | | | | 5 | | | | 3 | 11 | | | | | |
| 1 | 2 | | 4 | | 6 | | 8 | 9 | 7 | | | | 5 | | 10 | | 3 | 11 | | | | | |
| 1 | 2 | | 4 | | 6 | 11 | 8 | 9 | 7 | | 3 | | 5 | | 10 | | | | | | | | |
| 1 | 2 | | 4 | | 6 | 7 | 8 | 9 | 10 | | 3 | | 5 | | | | | | 11 | | | | |
| 1 | 2 | | 4 | | 6 | 7 | 8 | 9 | 10 | | 3 | | 5 | | | | | | 11 | | | | |
| 1 | 2 | | 4 | | 6 | 7 | 8 | 9 | 10 | | 3 | | 5 | | | | | | 11 | | | | |
| 1 | 2 | | 4 | | 6 | | 8 | 9 | 10 | | 3 | | 5 | | | | | | 11 | 7 | | | |
| 1 | 2 | | 4 | | 6 | | 8 | 9 | 10 | | 3 | | 5 | | | | | | 11 | 7 | | | |
| 1 | 2 | | 4 | | 6 | | 8 | 9 | 10 | | 3 | | 5 | | | | | | 11 | 7 | | | |
| 1 | 2 | | 4 | | 6 | | 8 | 9 | 10 | | 3 | | 5 | | | | | | 11 | 7 | | | |
| 1 | 2 | | 4 | | 6 | | 8 | 9 | 10 | | 3 | | 5 | | | | | | 11 | 7 | | | |
| 1 | 3 | | | | 4 | | 8 | 10 | 11 | | | 6 | 5 | | | | | | | 7 | 2 | 9 | |
| 1 | 3 | | | | 4 | 9 | 8 | 10 | 11 | | | 6 | 5 | | | | | | | 7 | 2 | | |
| | 2 | | | | 6 | 9 | 8 | 10 | 11 | | | | 5 | | | 4 | | | | 7 | 3 | | 1 |
| | 2 | | | | 6 | 9 | 8 | 10 | 11 | | | | 5 | | | 4 | | | | 7 | 3 | | 1 |
| | 2 | | | | 6 | 9 | 7 | 10 | 11 | | | | 5 | | 8 | 4 | | | | | 3 | | 1 |
| | 2 | | 4 | | 6 | 9 | 7 | 10 | 11 | | | | 5 | | 8 | | | | | | 3 | | 1 |
| | 3 | | 8 | | 6 | 9 | 7 | 10 | 11 | | | | 5 | | | 4 | | | | | 2 | | 1 |
| | 2 | | 4 | 5 | 3 | | 8 | 9 | 10 | | | | | | | 6 | | | 11 | 7 | | | 1 |
| | 2 | | 4 | | 3 | 7 | 8 | 9 | 10 | | | | 5 | | | 6 | | | 11 | | | | 1 |
| | 2 | | | 5 | 3 | 7 | 8 | 9 | 10 | | | | | | | 4 | 6 | | 11 | | | | 1 |
| | 2 | | | 5 | 3 | | 7 | 8 | 10 | | | | | | | 4 | 6 | | 11 | | | 9 | 1 |
| 37 | 37 | 10 | 39 | 24 | 45 | 32 | 43 | 46 | 44 | 15 | 12 | 9 | 31 | 2 | 11 | 13 | 10 | 6 | 12 | 10 | 7 | 2 | 9 |
| | | | 1 | | 1 | 5 | 4 | 17 | 21 | 3 | | | | | 2 | | | | 1 | 2 | | | |

| Oakley | Waugh | Cameron | Johnson | Atkinson | Anderson | McKenna | Scott | Smith | Clark | Luke | Oldham | Robinson | Moore | Burlison | Langland | MacGregor | Dixon | Dunn | Butler | Bircham | Peek | Folland | Wilkinson |
|---|---|---|---|---|---|---|---|---|---|---|---|---|---|---|---|---|---|---|---|---|---|---|---|
| 1 | 3 | | 6 | 5 | 2 | 7 | 8 | 9 | | | | | | 4 | 10 | | | 11 | | | | | |
| 1 | 1 | | 1 | 1 | 1 | 1 | 1 | 1 | 1 | | | | | 1 | 1 | | | 1 | | | | | |
| | | | | | | | | | | | | | | | | | | | | | | | |

## League Table

| | P | W | D | L | F | A | Pts |
|---|---|---|---|---|---|---|---|
| Walsall | 46 | 28 | 9 | 9 | 102 | 60 | 65 |
| Notts County | 46 | 26 | 8 | 12 | 107 | 69 | 60 |
| Torquay United | 46 | 26 | 8 | 12 | 84 | 58 | 60 |
| Watford | 46 | 24 | 9 | 13 | 92 | 67 | 57 |
| Millwall | 46 | 18 | 17 | 11 | 84 | 61 | 53 |
| Northampton Town | 46 | 22 | 9 | 15 | 85 | 63 | 53 |
| Gillingham | 46 | 21 | 10 | 15 | 74 | 69 | 52 |
| Crystal Palace | 46 | 19 | 12 | 15 | 84 | 64 | 50 |
| Exeter City | 46 | 19 | 11 | 16 | 80 | 70 | 49 |
| Stockport County | 46 | 19 | 11 | 16 | 58 | 54 | 49 |
| Bradford Park Avenue | 46 | 17 | 15 | 14 | 70 | 68 | 49 |
| Rochdale | 46 | 18 | 10 | 18 | 65 | 60 | 46 |
| Aldershot | 46 | 18 | 9 | 19 | 77 | 74 | 45 |
| Crewe Alexandra | 46 | 18 | 9 | 19 | 79 | 88 | 45 |
| Darlington | 46 | 17 | 9 | 20 | 63 | 73 | 43 |
| Workington | 46 | 14 | 14 | 18 | 68 | 60 | 42 |
| Doncaster Rovers | 46 | 16 | 10 | 20 | 69 | 76 | 42 |
| Barrow | 46 | 15 | 11 | 20 | 77 | 87 | 41 |
| Carlisle United | 46 | 15 | 11 | 20 | 51 | 66 | 41 |
| Chester | 46 | 14 | 12 | 20 | 59 | 77 | 40 |
| Southport | 46 | 10 | 14 | 22 | 48 | 92 | 34 |
| Gateshead | 46 | 12 | 9 | 25 | 58 | 86 | 33 |
| Oldham Athletic | 46 | 8 | 12 | 26 | 41 | 83 | 28 |
| Hartlepools United | 46 | 10 | 7 | 29 | 59 | 109 | 27 |

# 1960-61

## Division Four

Manager: Bill Robinson

### Did you know that?

During the season, Hartlepools featured seven players born in the town: Johnny Dixon, Bobby Folland, Ken Johnson, Gordon Lithgo, Terry MacGregor, Alan Melville and Barry Parkes.

Despite making a fifth, and second successive, application for re-election, the absence of any serious contender meant the vote was a formality.

| Match No. | Date | Round | Venue | Opponents | Result | | Scorers | Attendance |
|---|---|---|---|---|---|---|---|---|
| 1 | Aug 20 | | (a) | Southport | L | 0 - 2 | | 4,062 |
| 2 | 22 | | (h) | Peterborough United | L | 0 - 2 | | 10,784 |
| 3 | 27 | | (h) | Darlington | W | 5 - 0 | Clark, Anderson 2 (2 pens), Folland, Johnson | 5,852 |
| 4 | 29 | | (a) | Peterborough United | L | 2 - 3 | Johnson 2 | 15,245 |
| 5 | Sep 3 | | (a) | Crystal Palace | D | 2 - 2 | MacGregor, Folland | 19,099 |
| 6 | 5 | | (h) | Stockport County | L | 0 - 2 | | 7,937 |
| 7 | 10 | | (h) | Doncaster Rovers | W | 2 - 1 | Lumley, Folland | 4,711 |
| 8 | 12 | | (a) | Stockport County | D | 1 - 1 | Clark | 8,958 |
| 9 | 17 | | (a) | Crewe Alexandra | L | 0 - 3 | | 5,535 |
| 10 | 19 | | (h) | Exeter City | D | 0 - 0 | | 3,156 |
| 11 | 24 | | (a) | Wrexham | L | 0 - 1 | | 6,340 |
| 12 | 26 | | (a) | Exeter City | L | 1 - 2 | Patterson | 4,376 |
| 13 | Oct 1 | | (h) | Carlisle United | L | 0 - 1 | | 3,259 |
| 14 | 3 | | (a) | Rochdale | L | 0 - 4 | | 3,852 |
| 15 | 8 | | (h) | Accrington Stanley | W | 4 - 1 | Johnson 3 (1 pen), Clark | 2,525 |
| 17 | 15 | | (a) | Millwall | L | 2 - 5 | Butler, Bircham | 7,855 |
| 18 | 22 | | (h) | Barrow | L | 0 - 2 | | 2,939 |
| 19 | 29 | | (a) | Gillingham | L | 1 - 5 | Bircham | 3,816 |
| 21 | Nov 12 | | (a) | Northampton Town | D | 3 - 3 | Cooper 2, Lumley | 9,484 |
| 22 | 19 | | (h) | Aldershot | W | 3 - 1 | Cooper, Lumley, Clark | 2,767 |
| 23 | Dec 3 | | (h) | Workington | W | 4 - 1 | Johnson, Cooper, Clark, Dixon (pen) | 2,662 |
| 24 | 10 | | (a) | Chester | W | 2 - 1 | Clark, Johnson | 2,644 |
| 25 | 17 | | (h) | Southport | L | 1 - 5 | Johnson | 3,735 |
| 26 | 26 | | (a) | Mansfield Town | L | 1 - 2 | Cooper | 6,283 |
| 27 | 27 | | (h) | Mansfield Town | W | 3 - 2 | Bradley (o.g.), Cooper, Clark | 4,094 |
| 28 | 31 | | (a) | Darlington | L | 0 - 4 | | 7,994 |
| 29 | Jan 2 | | (h) | York City | L | 1 - 3 | Dixon (pen) | 5,337 |
| 30 | 7 | | (a) | Oldham Athletic | L | 1 - 2 | Johnson | 13,551 |
| 31 | 14 | | (h) | Crystal Palace | L | 2 - 4 | Bircham, McNichol (o.g.) | 4,430 |
| 32 | 21 | | (a) | Doncaster Rovers | L | 3 - 5 | Clark, Lumley, Lunn (o.g.) | 2,771 |
| 33 | 28 | | (h) | Bradford Park Avenue | L | 2 - 4 | Lumley, Clark | 3,207 |
| 34 | Feb 4 | | (h) | Crewe Alexandra | L | 1 - 2 | Godbold | 3,317 |
| 35 | 11 | | (h) | Wrexham | D | 0 - 0 | | 2,672 |
| 36 | 18 | | (a) | Carlisle United | D | 2 - 2 | Godbold, Clark | 3,667 |
| 37 | 25 | | (a) | Accrington Stanley | L | 0 - 3 | | 2,059 |
| 38 | Mar 4 | | (h) | Millwall | D | 2 - 2 | Godbold, Lumley | 2,698 |
| 39 | 11 | | (a) | Barrow | L | 1 - 2 | Parkes | 3,083 |
| 40 | 18 | | (h) | Gillingham | W | 1 - 0 | Godbold | 2,332 |
| 41 | 25 | | (a) | Bradford Park Avenue | W | 3 - 1 | Johnson 2, Folland | 8,975 |
| 42 | 31 | | (a) | York City | L | 0 - 4 | | 8,933 |
| 43 | Apr 1 | | (h) | Northampton Town | W | 4 - 2 | Parkes 3 (2 pens), Folland | 3,460 |
| 44 | 8 | | (a) | Aldershot | L | 0 - 4 | | 5,153 |
| 45 | 15 | | (h) | Oldham Athletic | W | 5 - 1 | Folland 5 | 4,078 |
| 46 | 22 | | (a) | Workington | L | 0 - 2 | | 2,246 |
| 47 | 24 | | (h) | Rochdale | W | 2 - 0 | Parkes 2 | 3,771 |
| 48 | 29 | | (h) | Chester | D | 4 - 4 | Folland 2, Lithgo, Parkes (pen) | 4,381 |

Final Position : 23rd in Division Four — Apps.

3 own goals — Goals

**FA Cup**

| | | | | | | | | |
|---|---|---|---|---|---|---|---|---|
| 20 | Nov 5 | R1 | (a) | Halifax Town | L | 1 - 5 | Cooper | 6,402 |

Apps.
Goals

**League Cup**

| | | | | | | | | |
|---|---|---|---|---|---|---|---|---|
| 16 | Oct 11 | R1 | (a) | Oldham Athletic | L | 1 - 2 | Johnson | 3,630 |

Apps.
Goals

| Wilkinson | Waugh | Anderson | Johnson | Lackenby | Patterson | Bircham | Lumley | Cooper | Clark | Butler | Clydesdale | Folland | MacGregor | Dunn | Cain | Dixon | Burlison | Oakley | Atkinson | Lonsdale | Melville | Godbold | Bilcliff | Jones | Parkes | Lithgo |
|---|---|---|---|---|---|---|---|---|---|---|---|---|---|---|---|---|---|---|---|---|---|---|---|---|---|---|
| 1 | 2 | 3 | 4 | 5 | 6 | 7 | 8 | 9 | 10 | 11 | | | | | | | | | | | | | | | | |
| 1 | 2 | 3 | 4 | 5 | 6 | 7 | 8 | 9 | 10 | 11 | | | | | | | | | | | | | | | | |
| 1 | 2 | 6 | 8 | 5 | 4 | | 10 | | 7 | 11 | 3 | 9 | | | | | | | | | | | | | | |
| 1 | 2 | 6 | 8 | 5 | 4 | | 10 | | 7 | 11 | 3 | 9 | | | | | | | | | | | | | | |
| 1 | 2 | 3 | 8 | 5 | 6 | | 10 | | 7 | | | 9 | 4 | 11 | | | | | | | | | | | | |
| 1 | 2 | 3 | 8 | 5 | 6 | | 10 | | 7 | | | 9 | 4 | 11 | | | | | | | | | | | | |
| 1 | 2 | 6 | 8 | 5 | | | 10 | | 7 | | 3 | 9 | | 11 | 4 | | | | | | | | | | | |
| 1 | 2 | 6 | 8 | 5 | | | 10 | | 7 | | 3 | | | 11 | 4 | 9 | | | | | | | | | | |
| 1 | 2 | 6 | 8 | 5 | 4 | | 10 | | 7 | | 3 | 9 | | 11 | | | | | | | | | | | | |
| 1 | 2 | 6 | 8 | 5 | 4 | | 10 | 9 | 7 | | 3 | | | 11 | | | | | | | | | | | | |
| 1 | 2 | 6 | 9 | 5 | 4 | 7 | 8 | | 10 | | 3 | | | 11 | | | | | | | | | | | | |
| 1 | 2 | 6 | 9 | 5 | 8 | 7 | 10 | | | | 3 | | | 11 | 4 | | | | | | | | | | | |
| 1 | 2 | 6 | 9 | 5 | 8 | 7 | 10 | | | | 3 | | | 11 | 4 | | | | | | | | | | | |
| 1 | 2 | | 9 | 5 | 6 | 7 | 8 | | 10 | 11 | 3 | | | | 4 | | | | | | | | | | | |
| 1 | 2 | | 9 | 5 | 4 | 7 | 8 | | 10 | 11 | 3 | | | | 6 | | | | | | | | | | | |
| 1 | 2 | 6 | 9 | 5 | | 7 | 8 | | 10 | 11 | 3 | | 4 | | | | | | | | | | | | | |
| 1 | 2 | | 9 | 5 | | 7 | 8 | | 10 | 11 | 3 | | 4 | | | | 6 | | | | | | | | | |
| 1 | 2 | 3 | 9 | 5 | | 7 | 10 | 8 | 11 | | | | 4 | | | 6 | | | | | | | | | | |
| | | 6 | 9 | 2 | | 7 | 10 | 8 | 11 | | | | 4 | | | 5 | | 1 | 3 | | | | | | | |
| | | 6 | | 5 | | 7 | 8 | 9 | 10 | | | | 4 | 11 | | 2 | | 1 | | 3 | | | | | | |
| | | 6 | 8 | 5 | | 7 | 10 | 9 | 11 | | | | 4 | | | 2 | | 1 | | 3 | | | | | | |
| | | 6 | 11 | 5 | | 7 | 8 | 9 | 10 | | | | 4 | | | 2 | | 1 | | 3 | | | | | | |
| | | 6 | 11 | 5 | | 7 | 8 | 9 | 10 | | | | 4 | | | 2 | | 1 | | 3 | | | | | | |
| | | 6 | 11 | 5 | | 7 | 8 | 9 | 10 | | | | 4 | | | 2 | | 1 | | 3 | | | | | | |
| | | 3 | 11 | | 6 | 7 | 8 | 9 | 10 | | | | 4 | | | 2 | | 1 | | | 5 | | | | | |
| | | | 11 | 5 | 6 | 7 | 8 | 9 | 10 | | | | 4 | | | 2 | | 1 | | 3 | | | | | | |
| | | | 4 | 5 | | 7 | 8 | 9 | 10 | | | | 6 | 11 | | 2 | | 1 | 3 | | | | | | | |
| | 2 | | 11 | 5 | 6 | 7 | 8 | 9 | 10 | | | | 4 | | | 3 | | 1 | | | | | | | | |
| | 2 | | 10 | 5 | 6 | 7 | 8 | 9 | | | | | 4 | | | 3 | | 1 | | | | 11 | | | | |
| | | | 9 | 5 | 6 | 7 | 8 | | 10 | | | | 4 | | | 2 | | 1 | | 3 | | 11 | | | | |
| | | | 6 | 5 | | 7 | 8 | | 10 | | | 9 | 4 | | | | | 1 | | | | 11 | 2 | 3 | | |
| 1 | | | 8 | 4 | | 7 | | 9 | | | | | | | | 6 | | | | | 5 | 11 | 2 | 3 | 10 | |
| 1 | | | 9 | 5 | | 7 | 8 | | 10 | | | | 4 | | | | 6 | | | | | 11 | 2 | 3 | | |
| 1 | | | 9 | 5 | | 7 | 8 | | 10 | | | | 4 | | | | 6 | | | | | 11 | 2 | 3 | | |
| 1 | | | 9 | 5 | | 7 | 8 | | 10 | | | | 4 | | | | 6 | | | | | 11 | 2 | 3 | | |
| 1 | | | 9 | 5 | | | 8 | | 10 | | | | 4 | | | | 6 | | | 7 | | 11 | 2 | 3 | | |
| 1 | | | | 5 | | | 8 | | 9 | | | | | | 4 | | 6 | | | 7 | | 11 | 2 | 3 | 10 | |
| 1 | | | | 5 | | 7 | 8 | | | | | 9 | | | 4 | | 6 | | | | | 11 | 2 | 3 | 10 | |
| 1 | 2 | | 8 | 5 | | 7 | | | | | | 9 | | | 4 | | 6 | | | | | 11 | | 3 | 10 | |
| 1 | 2 | | 8 | 5 | | 7 | 11 | | | | 3 | 9 | | | 4 | | 6 | | | | | | | | 10 | |
| 1 | | | 8 | 5 | | 7 | | | | | | 9 | | | 4 | | 6 | | | | | 11 | 2 | 3 | 10 | |
| 1 | | | 8 | 5 | | 7 | | | | | | 9 | | | 4 | | 6 | | | | | 11 | 2 | 3 | 10 | |
| 1 | 2 | | 8 | 5 | | 7 | | | | | | 9 | | | 4 | | 6 | | | | | 11 | | 3 | 10 | |
| 1 | 2 | | 8 | 5 | | 7 | | | | | | 9 | | | 6 | | | | | | | 11 | 4 | 3 | 10 | |
| 1 | | | 6 | 5 | | 7 | | | | | | 9 | | | 4 | | | | | | | 11 | 2 | 3 | 10 | 8 |
| 1 | | | 6 | 5 | | 7 | | | | | | 9 | | | 4 | | | | | | | 11 | 2 | 3 | 10 | 8 |
| 33 | 24 | 22 | 43 | 45 | 18 | 36 | 38 | 16 | 33 | 8 | 14 | 16 | 22 | 11 | 16 | 15 | 12 | 13 | 2 | 9 | 2 | 17 | 13 | 15 | 11 | 2 |
| | | 2 | 12 | | 1 | 3 | 6 | 6 | 10 | 1 | | 12 | 1 | | | 2 | | | | | | 4 | | | 7 | 1 |

| Wilkinson | Waugh | Anderson | Johnson | Lackenby | Patterson | Bircham | Lumley | Cooper | Clark | Butler | Clydesdale | Folland | MacGregor | Dunn | Cain | Dixon | Burlison | Oakley | Atkinson | Lonsdale | Melville | Godbold | Bilcliff | Jones | Parkes | Lithgo |
|---|---|---|---|---|---|---|---|---|---|---|---|---|---|---|---|---|---|---|---|---|---|---|---|---|---|---|
| | 2 | 3 | 9 | 5 | | 7 | 10 | 8 | 11 | | | | 4 | | | 6 | | 1 | | | | | | | | |
| | 1 | 1 | 1 | 1 | | 1 | 1 | 1 | 1 | | | | 1 | | | 1 | | 1 | | | | | | | | |
| | | | | | | | | 1 | | | | | | | | | | | | | | | | | | |

| Wilkinson | Waugh | Anderson | Johnson | Lackenby | Patterson | Bircham | Lumley | Cooper | Clark | Butler | Clydesdale | Folland | MacGregor | Dunn | Cain | Dixon | Burlison | Oakley | Atkinson | Lonsdale | Melville | Godbold | Bilcliff | Jones | Parkes | Lithgo |
|---|---|---|---|---|---|---|---|---|---|---|---|---|---|---|---|---|---|---|---|---|---|---|---|---|---|---|
| 1 | 2 | | 9 | 5 | 4 | 7 | 8 | | 10 | 11 | 3 | | | | 6 | | | | | | | | | | | |
| 1 | 1 | | 1 | 1 | 1 | 1 | 1 | | 1 | 1 | 1 | | | | 1 | | | | | | | | | | | |
| | | | 1 | | | | | | | | | | | | | | | | | | | | | | | |

## League Table

| | P | W | D | L | F | A | Pts |
|---|---|---|---|---|---|---|---|
| Peterborough United | 46 | 28 | 10 | 8 | 134 | 65 | 66 |
| Crystal Palace | 46 | 29 | 6 | 11 | 110 | 69 | 64 |
| Northampton Town | 46 | 25 | 10 | 11 | 90 | 62 | 60 |
| Bradford Park Avenue | 46 | 26 | 8 | 12 | 84 | 74 | 60 |
| York City | 46 | 21 | 9 | 16 | 80 | 60 | 51 |
| Millwall | 46 | 21 | 8 | 17 | 97 | 86 | 50 |
| Darlington | 46 | 18 | 13 | 15 | 78 | 70 | 49 |
| Workington | 46 | 21 | 7 | 18 | 74 | 76 | 49 |
| Crewe Alexandra | 46 | 20 | 9 | 17 | 61 | 67 | 49 |
| Aldershot | 46 | 18 | 9 | 19 | 79 | 69 | 45 |
| Doncaster Rovers | 46 | 19 | 7 | 20 | 76 | 78 | 45 |
| Oldham Athletic | 46 | 19 | 7 | 20 | 79 | 88 | 45 |
| Stockport County | 46 | 18 | 9 | 19 | 57 | 66 | 45 |
| Southport | 46 | 19 | 6 | 21 | 69 | 67 | 44 |
| Gillingham | 46 | 15 | 13 | 18 | 64 | 66 | 43 |
| Wrexham | 46 | 17 | 8 | 21 | 62 | 56 | 42 |
| Rochdale | 46 | 17 | 8 | 21 | 60 | 66 | 42 |
| Accrington Stanley | 46 | 16 | 8 | 22 | 74 | 88 | 40 |
| Carlisle United | 46 | 13 | 13 | 20 | 61 | 79 | 39 |
| Mansfield Town | 46 | 16 | 6 | 24 | 71 | 78 | 38 |
| Exeter City | 46 | 14 | 10 | 22 | 66 | 94 | 38 |
| Barrow | 46 | 13 | 11 | 22 | 52 | 79 | 37 |
| Hartlepools United | 46 | 12 | 8 | 26 | 71 | 103 | 32 |
| Chester | 46 | 11 | 9 | 26 | 61 | 104 | 31 |

# 1961-62

## Division Four

Manager: Bill Robinson

### Did you know that?

Hartlepools United's record 10–1 defeat at Wrexham on 3 March is still the only instance when three players, Wyn Davies, Roy Ambler and Ron Barnes, each scored a hat-trick in the same League game.

The record defeat at Wrexham coincided with Accrington Stanley's resignation from the Football League due to unsustainable debts of £60,000. This made 'Pools' third successive re-election application a formality as Oxford United were voted in to replace hapless Accrington.

| Match No. | Date | Round | Venue | Opponents | Result | | Scorers | Attendance |
|---|---|---|---|---|---|---|---|---|
| 1 | Aug 19 | | (a) | Rochdale | L | 1 - 3 | Milburn (o.g.) | 2,400 |
| 2 | 21 | | (h) | Oldham Athletic | D | 1 - 1 | Folland | 6,167 |
| 3 | 26 | | (h) | Southport | W | 4 - 2 | Folland 2, Edgar, Price | 4,804 |
| 4 | 30 | | (a) | Oldham Athletic | L | 2 - 5 | Godbold, Edgar | 12,777 |
| 5 | Sep 1 | | (a) | Tranmere Rovers | L | 2 - 3 | Edgar, Folland | 9,728 |
| 6 | 4 | | (h) | Stockport County | D | 2 - 2 | Folland, Godbold | 6,313 |
| 7 | 9 | | (h) | Chester | L | 1 - 3 | Folland | 4,838 |
| 9 | 16 | | (a) | Colchester United | L | 1 - 6 | Edgar | 5,036 |
| 10 | 20 | | (a) | Crewe Alexandra | L | 0 - 3 | | 5,948 |
| 11 | 23 | | (h) | Carlisle United | L | 0 - 3 | | 3,831 |
| 12 | 25 | | (h) | Crewe Alexandra | W | 2 - 1 | Edgar, Folland | 2,904 |
| 13 | 30 | | (a) | Bradford City | L | 1 - 5 | Lithgo | 4,347 |
| 14 | Oct 2 | | (h) | Aldershot | L | 0 - 2 | | 3,374 |
| 15 | 7 | | (a) | Exeter City | D | 1 - 1 | Edgar | 4,173 |
| 16 | 9 | | (a) | Aldershot | D | 1 - 1 | Edgar | 7,671 |
| 17 | 14 | | (h) | Wrexham | L | 1 - 4 | Edgar | 6,798 |
| 18 | 21 | | (h) | Doncaster Rovers | W | 3 - 0 | Malloy (o.g.), Folland 2 | 4,621 |
| 19 | 28 | | (h) | Workington | L | 0 - 1 | | 5,076 |
| 21 | Nov 11 | | (h) | Chesterfield | L | 1 - 2 | Johnson | 4,116 |
| 22 | 18 | | (a) | Gillingham | L | 0 - 4 | | 6,562 |
| 24 | Dec 2 | | (a) | Mansfield Town | L | 1 - 3 | Hinchcliffe | 6,619 |
| 25 | 9 | | (h) | Barrow | L | 2 - 3 | Johnson, McLean | 3,206 |
| 26 | 16 | | (h) | Rochdale | W | 3 - 1 | Edgar 2, Folland | 2,387 |
| 27 | 23 | | (a) | Southport | W | 1 - 0 | Bircham | 3,850 |
| 29 | Jan 13 | | (h) | Tranmere Rovers | D | 0 - 0 | | 4,121 |
| 30 | 20 | | (a) | Chester | D | 4 - 4 | Bircham, Edgar 3 | 2,602 |
| 31 | 27 | | (h) | Millwall | W | 2 - 0 | Bircham, Johnson | 5,008 |
| 32 | Feb 3 | | (h) | Colchester United | D | 1 - 1 | Bircham | 6,918 |
| 33 | 10 | | (a) | Carlisle United | L | 0 - 1 | | 4,208 |
| 34 | 17 | | (h) | Bradford City | L | 1 - 3 | Edgar | 4,757 |
| 35 | 24 | | (h) | Exeter City | D | 0 - 0 | | 3,113 |
| 36 | Mar 3 | | (a) | Wrexham | L | 1 - 10 | Folland | 6,546 |
| 37 | 10 | | (a) | Doncaster Rovers | D | 2 - 2 | Price 2 | 2,291 |
| 38 | 17 | | (a) | Workington | D | 1 - 1 | McLean | 2,355 |
| 39 | 19 | | (a) | York City | L | 0 - 2 | | 6,613 |
| 40 | 24 | | (h) | York City | L | 0 - 2 | | 3,130 |
| 41 | 31 | | (a) | Chesterfield | L | 0 - 2 | | 2,701 |
| 42 | Apr 7 | | (h) | Gillingham | L | 1 - 3 | Edgar | 2,434 |
| 43 | 9 | | (a) | Stockport County | D | 1 - 1 | Johnson | 4,024 |
| 44 | 14 | | (a) | Millwall | L | 2 - 3 | Burlison, Edgar | 10,709 |
| 45 | 20 | | (h) | Darlington | W | 2 - 0 | Edgar 2 | 4,899 |
| 46 | 21 | | (h) | Mansfield Town | L | 0 - 1 | | 2,239 |
| 47 | 23 | | (a) | Darlington | W | 2 - 1 | Edgar 2 | 3,380 |
| 48 | 28 | | (a) | Barrow | L | 1 - 5 | Johnson | 3,811 |

Final Position : 22nd in Division Four

Apps.

2 own goals — Goals

**FA Cup**

| Match No. | Date | Round | Venue | Opponents | Result | | Scorers | Attendance |
|---|---|---|---|---|---|---|---|---|
| 20 | Nov 4 | R1 | (h) | Blyth Spartans | W | 5 - 1 | Folland 3, Johnson, Parkes | 5,416 |
| 23 | 25 | R2 | (h) | Accrington Stanley | W | 2 - 1 | Folland, McLean | 5,227 |
| 28 | Jan 6 | R3 | (a) | Fulham | L | 1 - 3 | Burlison | 18,044 |

Apps.

Goals

**League Cup**

| Match No. | Date | Round | Venue | Opponents | Result | | Scorers | Attendance |
|---|---|---|---|---|---|---|---|---|
| 8 | Sep 11 | R1 | (a) | Bristol Rovers | L | 1 - 2 | Lithgo | 8,469 |

Apps.

Goals

| Wilkinson | Bilcliff | Jones | Johnson | Lackenby | Burlison | Bircham | Edgar | Price | Parkes | Godbold | Waugh | Folland | Hawkes | Melville | Lithgo | Cain | Oakley | Wilkie | Hinchcliffe | McLean | Fraser | MacGregor |
|---|---|---|---|---|---|---|---|---|---|---|---|---|---|---|---|---|---|---|---|---|---|---|
| 1 | 2 | 3 | 4 | 5 | 6 | 7 | 8 | 9 | 10 | 11 | | | | | | | | | | | | |
| 1 | | 3 | 4 | 5 | 6 | | 8 | 7 | 10 | 11 | 2 | 9 | | | | | | | | | | |
| 1 | | 3 | 4 | 5 | 6 | | 8 | 7 | 10 | 11 | 2 | 9 | | | | | | | | | | |
| 1 | | 3 | 4 | 5 | 6 | | 8 | 7 | | 11 | 2 | 9 | 10 | | | | | | | | | |
| 1 | | 3 | 4 | 5 | 6 | 7 | 8 | | 10 | 11 | 2 | 9 | | | | | | | | | | |
| 1 | | 3 | 4 | 5 | 6 | 7 | 8 | | 10 | 11 | 2 | 9 | | | | | | | | | | |
| 1 | | 3 | 4 | | 6 | 7 | 8 | | | 11 | 2 | 9 | | 5 | 10 | | | | | | | |
| 1 | | 3 | 4 | | | 7 | 8 | | | 11 | 2 | 9 | | 5 | 10 | 6 | | | | | | |
| | 3 | | 4 | | | | 8 | 7 | | 11 | 2 | 9 | | 5 | 10 | 6 | 1 | | | | | |
| | 3 | | 4 | | | 7 | 8 | | | | 2 | 9 | 11 | | 10 | 6 | 1 | 5 | | | | |
| 1 | 3 | | 4 | | | | 8 | | 10 | | 2 | 9 | 11 | | 7 | 6 | | 5 | | | | |
| 1 | 3 | | 4 | | | | 8 | | 10 | | 2 | 9 | 11 | | 7 | 6 | | 5 | | | | |
| 1 | 3 | | 10 | 4 | | | 8 | | | | 2 | 9 | 11 | | 7 | 6 | | 5 | | | | |
| 1 | 3 | | 7 | 4 | | | 8 | | 10 | 11 | 2 | 9 | | | | 6 | | 5 | | | | |
| 1 | 3 | | 7 | 4 | | | 8 | | 10 | 11 | 2 | 9 | | | | 6 | | 5 | | | | |
| 1 | 3 | | 11 | 6 | | | 8 | | 10 | | 2 | 9 | | | | | | 5 | 4 | 7 | | |
| 1 | 3 | | | 2 | | | 8 | | 10 | 11 | | 9 | | | | 6 | | 5 | 4 | 7 | | |
| 1 | 3 | | | 2 | | | 8 | | 10 | 11 | | 9 | | | | 6 | | 5 | 4 | 7 | | |
| 1 | 3 | | 8 | 2 | | | | | | 11 | | 9 | 10 | | | 6 | | 5 | 4 | 7 | | |
| 1 | 3 | | 7 | 2 | | | 8 | | | 11 | | 9 | 10 | | | 6 | | 5 | 4 | | | |
| 1 | 3 | | 8 | 2 | | | | | 10 | 11 | | 9 | | | | 6 | | 5 | 4 | 7 | | |
| 1 | 3 | | 8 | 2 | | 11 | | | | | | 9 | | | | 6 | | 5 | 10 | 7 | 4 | |
| 1 | 2 | 3 | | | 6 | 7 | 10 | | | 11 | | 9 | | | | | | 5 | 4 | 8 | | |
| 1 | 2 | 3 | | | 6 | 7 | 10 | | | 11 | | 9 | | | | | | 5 | 4 | 8 | | |
| 1 | 2 | 3 | | | 6 | 7 | 10 | | | 11 | | 9 | | | | | | 5 | 4 | 8 | | |
| 1 | 2 | 3 | | | 6 | 7 | 10 | | | 11 | | 9 | | | | | | 5 | 4 | 8 | | |
| 1 | | 3 | 9 | 2 | 6 | 7 | 10 | | | | | | 11 | | | | | 5 | 4 | 8 | | |
| 1 | | 3 | 9 | 2 | 6 | 7 | 10 | | | 11 | | | | | | | | 5 | 4 | 8 | | |
| 1 | 2 | 3 | 9 | | 6 | 7 | 10 | | | 11 | | | | | | | | 5 | 4 | 8 | | |
| 1 | 2 | 3 | 9 | | 6 | 7 | 10 | | | | | | 11 | | | | | | 4 | 8 | 5 | |
| 1 | 2 | 3 | | 4 | 6 | 7 | 10 | | | 11 | | 9 | | | | | | 5 | | 8 | | |
| 1 | 2 | 3 | | 5 | 6 | 7 | 10 | | | 11 | | 9 | | | | | | | 4 | 8 | | |
| 1 | 2 | | 11 | | 6 | 7 | 10 | 9 | | | 3 | | | | | | | 5 | 4 | 8 | | |
| 1 | 2 | | 11 | 3 | 6 | 7 | 10 | 9 | | | | | | | | | | 5 | 4 | 8 | | |
| | 2 | | 11 | 3 | | 7 | 10 | 9 | | | | | | | | | 1 | 5 | 4 | 8 | 6 | |
| | 2 | | 8 | 3 | 6 | 7 | | | 10 | 11 | | 9 | | | | | 1 | 5 | | | 4 | |
| | 2 | | 8 | 3 | 6 | 7 | 9 | | | 11 | | | | | 10 | | 1 | 5 | | | 4 | |
| | 2 | | | 3 | 6 | 7 | 9 | | | 11 | | | | | 10 | | 1 | 5 | | 8 | 4 | |
| | 2 | | 10 | 3 | 11 | 7 | 9 | | | | | | | | | | 1 | 5 | | 8 | 4 | 6 |
| | 2 | | 10 | 3 | 11 | 7 | 9 | | | | | | | | | | 1 | 5 | | 8 | 4 | 6 |
| | | | 10 | 3 | 11 | 7 | 9 | | | | 2 | | | | | | 1 | 5 | | 8 | 4 | 6 |
| | | | 10 | 3 | 11 | 7 | 9 | | | | 2 | | | | | | 1 | 5 | | 8 | 4 | 6 |
| | | | 10 | 3 | 11 | 7 | 9 | | | | 2 | | | | | | 1 | 5 | | 8 | 4 | 6 |
| | | | 10 | 3 | 11 | 7 | 9 | | | | 2 | | | | | | 1 | 5 | | 8 | 4 | 6 |
| 32 | 31 | 18 | 35 | 31 | 28 | 29 | 40 | 8 | 14 | 27 | 20 | 28 | 9 | 3 | 9 | 14 | 12 | 33 | 19 | 26 | 12 | 6 |
| | | | 5 | | 1 | 4 | 20 | 3 | | 2 | | 11 | | | 1 | | | | 1 | 2 | | |

| Wilkinson | Bilcliff | Jones | Johnson | Lackenby | Burlison | Bircham | Edgar | Price | Parkes | Godbold | Waugh | Folland | Hawkes | Melville | Lithgo | Cain | Oakley | Wilkie | Hinchcliffe | McLean | Fraser | MacGregor |
|---|---|---|---|---|---|---|---|---|---|---|---|---|---|---|---|---|---|---|---|---|---|---|
| 1 | 3 | | 8 | 2 | | | | | 10 | 11 | | 9 | | | | 6 | | 5 | 4 | 7 | | |
| 1 | 3 | | 8 | 2 | | | | | 10 | 11 | | 9 | | | | 6 | | 5 | 4 | 7 | | |
| 1 | 2 | 3 | | | 6 | 7 | 10 | | | 11 | | 9 | | | | | | 5 | 4 | 8 | | |
| 3 | 3 | 1 | 2 | 2 | 1 | 1 | 1 | | 2 | 3 | | 3 | | | | 2 | | 3 | 3 | 3 | | |
| | | | 1 | | 1 | | | | 1 | | | 4 | | | | | | | | 1 | | |

| Wilkinson | Bilcliff | Jones | Johnson | Lackenby | Burlison | Bircham | Edgar | Price | Parkes | Godbold | Waugh | Folland | Hawkes | Melville | Lithgo | Cain | Oakley | Wilkie | Hinchcliffe | McLean | Fraser | MacGregor |
|---|---|---|---|---|---|---|---|---|---|---|---|---|---|---|---|---|---|---|---|---|---|---|
| 1 | | 3 | 4 | | | 7 | 8 | | | 11 | 2 | 9 | | 5 | 10 | 6 | | | | | | |
| 1 | | 1 | 1 | | | 1 | 1 | | | 1 | 1 | 1 | | 1 | 1 | 1 | | | | | | |
| | | | | | | | | | | | | | | | 1 | | | | | | | |

## League Table

| | P | W | D | L | F | A | Pts |
|---|---|---|---|---|---|---|---|
| Millwall | 44 | 23 | 10 | 11 | 87 | 62 | 56 |
| Colchester United | 44 | 23 | 9 | 12 | 104 | 71 | 55 |
| Wrexham | 44 | 22 | 9 | 13 | 96 | 56 | 53 |
| Carlisle United | 44 | 22 | 8 | 14 | 64 | 63 | 52 |
| Bradford City | 44 | 21 | 9 | 14 | 94 | 86 | 51 |
| York City | 44 | 20 | 10 | 14 | 84 | 53 | 50 |
| Aldershot | 44 | 22 | 5 | 17 | 81 | 60 | 49 |
| Workington | 44 | 19 | 11 | 14 | 69 | 70 | 49 |
| Barrow | 44 | 17 | 14 | 13 | 74 | 58 | 48 |
| Crewe Alexandra | 44 | 20 | 6 | 18 | 79 | 70 | 46 |
| Oldham Athletic | 44 | 17 | 12 | 15 | 77 | 70 | 46 |
| Rochdale | 44 | 19 | 7 | 18 | 71 | 71 | 45 |
| Darlington | 44 | 18 | 9 | 17 | 61 | 73 | 45 |
| Mansfield Town | 44 | 19 | 6 | 19 | 77 | 66 | 44 |
| Tranmere Rovers | 44 | 20 | 4 | 20 | 70 | 81 | 44 |
| Stockport County | 44 | 17 | 9 | 18 | 70 | 69 | 43 |
| Southport | 44 | 17 | 9 | 18 | 61 | 71 | 43 |
| Exeter City | 44 | 13 | 11 | 20 | 62 | 77 | 37 |
| Chesterfield | 44 | 14 | 9 | 21 | 70 | 87 | 37 |
| Gillingham | 44 | 13 | 11 | 20 | 73 | 94 | 37 |
| Doncaster Rovers | 44 | 11 | 7 | 26 | 60 | 85 | 29 |
| Hartlepools United | 44 | 8 | 11 | 25 | 52 | 101 | 27 |
| Chester | 44 | 7 | 12 | 25 | 54 | 96 | 26 |

# 1962-63

## Division Four

Managers: Allenby Chilton and Bobby Gurney

### Did you know that?

Jock Brown was ever present throughout the season. A left-back he played the last five games of the season as an emergency centre-forward and scored five goals.

A meagre total of 25 points condemned 'Pools to a bottom finish and a fourth successive season of conceding over 100 goals, resulting in another re-election application. Once again, the lack of a serious alternative candidate resulted in the club being successful for a seventh time.

| Match No. | Date | Round | Venue | Opponents | Result | | Scorers | Attendance |
|---|---|---|---|---|---|---|---|---|
| 1 | Aug 18 | | (h) | Newport County | L | 2 - 3 | Edgar (pen), Bircham | 5,391 |
| 2 | 20 | | (a) | Southport | D | 1 - 1 | Edgar | 4,520 |
| 3 | 25 | | (a) | Oxford United | L | 2 - 6 | McLean, Edgar (pen) | 9,099 |
| 4 | 27 | | (h) | Southport | W | 4 - 0 | Bircham 2, McLean 2 | 5,172 |
| 5 | Sep 1 | | (h) | Bradford City | D | 2 - 2 | McLean, Edgar | 6,450 |
| 6 | 3 | | (h) | Darlington | L | 0 - 2 | | 8,690 |
| 8 | 8 | | (a) | Tranmere Rovers | L | 1 - 6 | Manning (o.g.) | 6,143 |
| 9 | 10 | | (a) | Darlington | W | 2 - 0 | McLean, Younger | 6,888 |
| 11 | 15 | | (h) | Torquay United | L | 0 - 3 | | 5,248 |
| 12 | 19 | | (a) | Aldershot | L | 2 - 3 | Bircham 2 | 5,849 |
| 13 | 22 | | (a) | Lincoln City | L | 1 - 4 | Edgar | 5,014 |
| 14 | 24 | | (h) | Aldershot | L | 1 - 2 | Younger | 3,250 |
| 15 | 29 | | (h) | Oldham Athletic | L | 0 - 1 | | 4,129 |
| 16 | Oct 2 | | (a) | Brentford | L | 0 - 4 | | 10,729 |
| 17 | 6 | | (h) | Rochdale | W | 4 - 0 | McLean 2, Edgar 2 | 3,850 |
| 18 | 13 | | (a) | Chesterfield | D | 2 - 2 | Burlison, McLean | 6,540 |
| 19 | 20 | | (h) | Exeter City | L | 0 - 2 | | 5,143 |
| 20 | 27 | | (a) | Workington | D | 0 - 0 | | 2,442 |
| 22 | Nov 10 | | (a) | Doncaster Rovers | W | 3 - 2 | Douglas, Burlison, McLean | 7,640 |
| 23 | 17 | | (h) | Stockport County | W | 3 - 0 | McLean 2, Miller | 3,856 |
| 24 | Dec 1 | | (h) | Crewe Alexandra | L | 1 - 5 | Thomson | 5,180 |
| 25 | 7 | | (a) | Chester | L | 0 - 1 | | 4,441 |
| 26 | 15 | | (a) | Newport County | L | 1 - 2 | Younger | 2,388 |
| 27 | 22 | | (h) | Oxford United | L | 1 - 2 | Edgar | 3,308 |
| 28 | Feb 2 | | (a) | Torquay United | L | 0 - 2 | | 2,736 |
| 29 | Mar 9 | | (a) | Exeter City | L | 1 - 3 | Edgar | 2,815 |
| 30 | 12 | | (a) | Rochdale | L | 1 - 2 | Godbold | 2,857 |
| 31 | 16 | | (h) | Workington | D | 2 - 2 | Johnson, Folland | 2,602 |
| 32 | 23 | | (a) | Mansfield Town | L | 1 - 3 | Douglas | 7,554 |
| 33 | 25 | | (a) | York City | L | 0 - 2 | | 4,558 |
| 34 | 30 | | (a) | Gillingham | L | 1 - 5 | Miller | 5,330 |
| 35 | Apr 1 | | (h) | Gillingham | D | 1 - 1 | Douglas | 2,629 |
| 36 | 6 | | (a) | Stockport County | L | 1 - 4 | Hinchcliffe (pen) | 2,619 |
| 37 | 8 | | (h) | Chesterfield | D | 1 - 1 | Hinchcliffe (pen) | 2,565 |
| 38 | 12 | | (h) | Barrow | D | 1 - 1 | Godbold | 3,494 |
| 39 | 13 | | (h) | Doncaster Rovers | D | 1 - 1 | Douglas | 2,686 |
| 40 | 15 | | (a) | Barrow | L | 0 - 2 | | 4,010 |
| 41 | 20 | | (a) | Crewe Alexandra | L | 1 - 4 | Edgar | 5,002 |
| 42 | 22 | | (h) | Brentford | W | 2 - 1 | Edgar, Lackenby | 3,465 |
| 43 | 27 | | (h) | Chester | L | 0 - 3 | | 2,728 |
| 44 | 29 | | (h) | York City | D | 1 - 1 | Thomson | 2,659 |
| 45 | May 4 | | (h) | Lincoln City | W | 3 - 0 | Jones (o.g.), Brown, Bircham | 2,683 |
| 46 | 8 | | (a) | Oldham Athletic | L | 1 - 6 | Brown | 12,283 |
| 47 | 11 | | (a) | Bradford City | D | 1 - 1 | Brown | 2,095 |
| 48 | 13 | | (h) | Mansfield Town | L | 3 - 4 | Brown 2, Younger | 2,735 |
| 49 | 18 | | (h) | Tranmere Rovers | L | 0 - 2 | | 2,028 |

Final Position : 24th in Division Four

Apps.

2 own goals — Goals

**FA Cup**

| | | | | | | | | |
|---|---|---|---|---|---|---|---|---|
| 21 | Nov 3 | R1 | (a) | Carlisle United | L | 1 - 2 | O'Connell (o.g.) | 6,627 |

Apps.

1 own goal — Goals

**League Cup**

| | | | | | | | | |
|---|---|---|---|---|---|---|---|---|
| 7 | Sep 6 | R1 | (h) | Barnsley | D | 1 - 1 | Younger | 2,393 |
| 10 | 13 | R1r | (a) | Barnsley | L | 1 - 2 | Bircham | 5,130 |

Apps.

Goals

| Oakley | Bilcliff | Brown | Hinchcliffe | Wilkie | Fraser | Bircham | McLean | Edgar | Parkes | Younger | Burlison | Folland | Godbold | Atkinson | Johnson | Lithgo | Thomson | Lackenby | MacGregor | Miller | Douglas |
|---|---|---|---|---|---|---|---|---|---|---|---|---|---|---|---|---|---|---|---|---|---|
| 1 | 2 | 3 | 4 | 5 | 6 | 7 | 8 | 9 | 10 | 11 | | | | | | | | | | | |
| 1 | 2 | 3 | 4 | 5 | 6 | 7 | 8 | 9 | 10 | 11 | | | | | | | | | | | |
| 1 | 2 | 3 | 4 | 5 | 6 | 7 | 8 | 9 | 10 | 11 | | | | | | | | | | | |
| 1 | 2 | 3 | 4 | 5 | | 7 | 8 | | | 10 | 6 | 9 | 11 | | | | | | | | |
| 1 | 2 | 3 | 4 | 5 | | 7 | 8 | 9 | | 10 | 6 | | 11 | | | | | | | | |
| 1 | 2 | 3 | 4 | 5 | | 7 | 8 | 9 | | 10 | 6 | | 11 | | | | | | | | |
| 1 | 2 | 3 | 4 | | | 7 | 8 | 10 | | 11 | 6 | 9 | | 5 | | | | | | | |
| 1 | 2 | 3 | 4 | 5 | | 7 | 8 | 9 | | 10 | 6 | | 11 | | | | | | | | |
| 1 | 2 | 3 | 4 | 5 | | 7 | 8 | 9 | | 10 | 6 | | 11 | | | | | | | | |
| 1 | 2 | 3 | | 5 | | 7 | | 9 | | 10 | 6 | | 11 | | 4 | 8 | | | | | |
| 1 | 2 | 3 | | 5 | | 7 | | 9 | | 10 | 6 | | 11 | | 4 | 8 | | | | | |
| 1 | 2 | 3 | 4 | 5 | | 7 | 8 | 9 | | 10 | 11 | | | | 6 | | | | | | |
| 1 | 2 | 3 | 4 | 5 | | 7 | 8 | 9 | | 10 | 11 | | | | 6 | | | | | | |
| 1 | 2 | 3 | 4 | 5 | | 7 | 8 | 9 | | 10 | 11 | | | | 6 | | | | | | |
| 1 | 2 | 3 | 4 | 5 | | 7 | 8 | 9 | | 10 | 11 | | | | 6 | | | | | | |
| 1 | 2 | 3 | 4 | | | 7 | 8 | 9 | | 10 | 11 | | | | 6 | | 5 | | | | |
| 1 | | 3 | | | | 7 | 8 | 9 | | 10 | 11 | | | | 6 | | 5 | 2 | 4 | | |
| 1 | 2 | 3 | | | 4 | 7 | 8 | | | 10 | 11 | 9 | | | 6 | | 5 | | | | |
| 1 | 2 | 3 | | | 4 | | 7 | | | 10 | 11 | | | | 6 | | 5 | | | 8 | 9 |
| 1 | 2 | 3 | | | 4 | | 7 | | | 10 | 11 | | | | 6 | | 5 | | | 8 | 9 |
| 1 | 2 | 3 | | | 4 | | 7 | | | 10 | 11 | | | | 6 | | 5 | | | 8 | 9 |
| 1 | | 3 | | | 4 | | 7 | 8 | | 10 | 11 | | | | 6 | | 5 | 2 | | 9 | |
| 1 | | 3 | | | 4 | | 7 | 8 | | 10 | 11 | | | | 6 | | 5 | 2 | | | 9 |
| 1 | | 3 | | | 4 | 7 | | 8 | | 10 | 11 | | | | 6 | | 5 | 2 | | | 9 |
| 1 | 2 | 3 | | | 4 | | 7 | 8 | | 10 | | | | | 9 | | 5 | 6 | | 11 | |
| 1 | 2 | 3 | | | 4 | | 7 | 8 | | 10 | 11 | | | | 6 | 9 | 5 | | | | |
| 1 | 2 | 3 | | | 4 | | 7 | 8 | | 10 | | | 11 | | 6 | | 5 | 9 | | | |
| 1 | 2 | 3 | | | 4 | | 7 | 8 | | 10 | | 9 | 11 | | 6 | | 5 | | | | |
| 1 | 2 | 3 | | | 4 | | 7 | | | 10 | 6 | 9 | 11 | | | | 5 | | | | 8 |
| 1 | | 3 | | | 4 | | 7 | | | 10 | 6 | 9 | 11 | | | | 5 | 2 | | | 8 |
| 1 | 2 | 3 | | | 4 | | 8 | | 10 | | 6 | 9 | 11 | | | | 5 | | | 7 | |
| 1 | | 3 | | 2 | 4 | | | | | 10 | 6 | 9 | 11 | | | | 5 | | | 7 | 8 |
| 1 | | 3 | 6 | 2 | 4 | | | | | | | 9 | 11 | | 10 | | 5 | | | 7 | 8 |
| 1 | | 3 | 6 | 2 | 4 | | | | | | | 9 | 11 | | 10 | | 5 | | | 7 | 8 |
| 1 | | 3 | 6 | 2 | 4 | | 7 | | | | | 9 | 11 | 5 | 10 | | | | | | 8 |
| 1 | | 3 | 6 | 2 | 4 | 7 | 8 | | | | | 10 | 11 | 5 | | | | | | | 9 |
| 1 | | 3 | 6 | 2 | 4 | 7 | 8 | 10 | | | | | 11 | | | | 5 | | | | 9 |
| 1 | | 3 | 6 | 2 | 4 | 7 | 8 | 10 | | | | | 11 | | | | 5 | 9 | | | |
| 1 | | 3 | 6 | 2 | 4 | 7 | 8 | 10 | | | | | 11 | | | | 5 | 9 | | | |
| 1 | | 3 | 6 | 2 | 4 | 7 | 8 | 10 | | | | | 11 | | | | 5 | 9 | | | |
| 1 | 2 | 3 | 4 | | | 7 | 8 | 10 | | 11 | 6 | | | | 9 | | 5 | | | | |
| 1 | 2 | 9 | 4 | 3 | | 7 | 8 | 10 | | 11 | 6 | | | | | | 5 | | | | |
| 1 | 2 | 9 | 4 | 3 | | 7 | 8 | 10 | | 11 | 6 | | | | | | 5 | | | | |
| 1 | 2 | 9 | 4 | 3 | | 7 | 8 | 10 | | 11 | 6 | | | | | | 5 | | | | |
| 1 | 2 | 9 | 4 | 3 | | 7 | 8 | 10 | | 11 | 6 | | | 5 | | | | | | | |
| 1 | 2 | 9 | 4 | 3 | | 7 | 8 | | | 11 | 6 | | | | 10 | | 5 | | | | |
| 46 | 32 | 46 | 28 | 28 | 26 | 30 | 40 | 32 | 4 | 37 | 32 | 12 | 21 | 4 | 24 | 3 | 28 | 10 | 1 | 9 | 13 |
| | | 5 | 2 | 1 | | 6 | 11 | 11 | | 4 | 2 | 1 | 2 | | 1 | | 2 | 1 | | 2 | 4 |

| Oakley | Bilcliff | Brown | Hinchcliffe | Wilkie | Fraser | Bircham | McLean | Edgar | Parkes | Younger | Burlison | Folland | Godbold | Atkinson | Johnson | Lithgo | Thomson | Lackenby | MacGregor | Miller | Douglas |
|---|---|---|---|---|---|---|---|---|---|---|---|---|---|---|---|---|---|---|---|---|---|
| 1 | 2 | 3 | | | 4 | 7 | 8 | | | 10 | 11 | 9 | | | 6 | | 5 | | | | |
| 1 | 1 | 1 | | | 1 | 1 | 1 | | | 1 | 1 | 1 | | | 1 | | 1 | | | | |

| Oakley | Bilcliff | Brown | Hinchcliffe | Wilkie | Fraser | Bircham | McLean | Edgar | Parkes | Younger | Burlison | Folland | Godbold | Atkinson | Johnson | Lithgo | Thomson | Lackenby | MacGregor | Miller | Douglas |
|---|---|---|---|---|---|---|---|---|---|---|---|---|---|---|---|---|---|---|---|---|---|
| 1 | 2 | 3 | 4 | | | 7 | 8 | 10 | | 11 | 6 | 9 | | 5 | | | | | | | |
| 1 | 2 | 3 | 4 | 5 | | 7 | 8 | 9 | | 10 | 6 | | 11 | | | | | | | | |
| 2 | 2 | 2 | 2 | 1 | | 2 | 2 | 2 | | 2 | 2 | 1 | 1 | 1 | | | | | | | |

## League Table

| | P | W | D | L | F | A | Pts |
|---|---|---|---|---|---|---|---|
| Brentford | 46 | 27 | 8 | 11 | 98 | 64 | 62 |
| Oldham Athletic | 46 | 24 | 11 | 11 | 95 | 60 | 59 |
| Crewe Alexandra | 46 | 24 | 11 | 11 | 86 | 58 | 59 |
| Mansfield Town | 46 | 24 | 9 | 13 | 108 | 69 | 57 |
| Gillingham | 46 | 22 | 13 | 11 | 71 | 49 | 57 |
| Torquay United | 46 | 20 | 16 | 10 | 75 | 56 | 56 |
| Rochdale | 46 | 20 | 11 | 15 | 67 | 59 | 51 |
| Tranmere Rovers | 46 | 20 | 10 | 16 | 81 | 67 | 50 |
| Barrow | 46 | 19 | 12 | 15 | 82 | 80 | 50 |
| Workington | 46 | 17 | 13 | 16 | 76 | 68 | 47 |
| Aldershot | 46 | 15 | 17 | 14 | 73 | 69 | 47 |
| Darlington | 46 | 19 | 6 | 21 | 72 | 87 | 44 |
| Southport | 46 | 15 | 14 | 17 | 72 | 106 | 44 |
| York City | 46 | 16 | 11 | 19 | 67 | 62 | 43 |
| Chesterfield | 46 | 13 | 16 | 17 | 70 | 64 | 42 |
| Doncaster Rovers | 46 | 14 | 14 | 18 | 64 | 77 | 42 |
| Exeter City | 46 | 16 | 10 | 20 | 57 | 77 | 42 |
| Oxford United | 46 | 13 | 15 | 18 | 70 | 71 | 41 |
| Stockport County | 46 | 15 | 11 | 20 | 56 | 70 | 41 |
| Newport County | 46 | 14 | 11 | 21 | 76 | 90 | 39 |
| Chester | 46 | 15 | 9 | 22 | 51 | 66 | 39 |
| Lincoln City | 46 | 13 | 9 | 24 | 68 | 89 | 35 |
| Bradford City | 46 | 11 | 10 | 25 | 64 | 93 | 32 |
| Hartlepools United | 46 | 7 | 11 | 28 | 56 | 104 | 25 |

# 1963-64

## Division Four

Managers: Bobby Gurney and Alvan Williams

### Did you know that?

Norman Oakley made the last of his 193 appearances, a record for a Hartlepools goalkeeper, against Barrow on 28 February.

Ken Johnson played his final game on 6 April against Newport County, a 1–1 draw. His joint testimonial with Tom Burlison drew a crowd of over 11,000 to see their All-Star side lose to a full-strength Sunderland, captained by Charlie Hurley.

| Match No. | Date | Round | Venue | Opponents | Result | | Scorers | Attendance |
|---|---|---|---|---|---|---|---|---|
| 1 | Aug 24 | | (a) | Aldershot | L | 1 - 4 | Devereux (o.g.) | 5,666 |
| 2 | 26 | | (h) | Torquay United | L | 1 - 4 | Hinshelwood | 5,415 |
| 3 | 31 | | (h) | Bradford City | W | 1 - 0 | Hinchcliffe | 3,749 |
| 5 | Sep 7 | | (a) | Lincoln City | L | 2 - 4 | Hinchcliffe, Hinshelwood | 6,110 |
| 6 | 11 | | (a) | Torquay United | L | 2 - 4 | Lithgo 2 | 4,942 |
| 7 | 14 | | (h) | Gillingham | D | 0 - 0 | | 3,022 |
| 8 | 16 | | (h) | Carlisle United | L | 0 - 6 | | 3,815 |
| 9 | 21 | | (a) | Southport | L | 1 - 2 | Hinshelwood | 3,242 |
| 10 | 28 | | (h) | Exeter City | D | 1 - 1 | Brown | 2,821 |
| 11 | Oct 1 | | (a) | Carlisle United | L | 1 - 7 | Lithgo | 7,075 |
| 12 | 5 | | (h) | Brighton & Hove Albion | D | 2 - 2 | Hinchcliffe (pen), Lithgo | 3,552 |
| 13 | 7 | | (a) | Tranmere Rovers | W | 3 - 2 | Johnson, Thompson, Brown | 6,008 |
| 14 | 12 | | (a) | York City | W | 1 - 0 | Thompson | 5,460 |
| 15 | 19 | | (h) | Barrow | D | 0 - 0 | | 5,267 |
| 16 | 21 | | (a) | Darlington | D | 0 - 0 | | 6,376 |
| 17 | 26 | | (a) | Rochdale | L | 0 - 2 | | 2,764 |
| 18 | Nov 2 | | (h) | Oxford United | W | 2 - 1 | McLean, Brown | 4,096 |
| 19 | 9 | | (a) | Workington | L | 0 - 2 | | 4,117 |
| 21 | 23 | | (a) | Stockport County | L | 0 - 1 | | 3,216 |
| 22 | 30 | | (h) | Bradford Park Avenue | W | 4 - 2 | Burlison, Francis 3 | 5,632 |
| 23 | Dec 14 | | (h) | Aldershot | L | 1 - 4 | Fogarty | 5,116 |
| 24 | 21 | | (a) | Bradford City | L | 0 - 2 | | 3,534 |
| 25 | 26 | | (h) | Chester | W | 2 - 0 | Thompson, Hinchcliffe (pen) | 5,531 |
| 26 | 28 | | (a) | Chester | L | 1 - 2 | Hamilton | 6,317 |
| 27 | Jan 1 | | (h) | Darlington | L | 0 - 2 | | 8,642 |
| 28 | 11 | | (h) | Lincoln City | L | 1 - 2 | Bradley | 4,330 |
| 29 | 18 | | (a) | Gillingham | L | 0 - 2 | | 7,536 |
| 30 | 25 | | (a) | Chesterfield | W | 2 - 0 | Fogarty 2 | 3,689 |
| 31 | Feb 1 | | (h) | Southport | L | 2 - 3 | Thompson 2 | 3,869 |
| 32 | 8 | | (a) | Exeter City | L | 1 - 2 | Thompson | 6,077 |
| 33 | 15 | | (a) | Brighton & Hove Albion | L | 1 - 4 | Fogarty | 8,664 |
| 34 | 22 | | (h) | York City | L | 0 - 1 | | 3,278 |
| 35 | 28 | | (a) | Barrow | W | 2 - 1 | Fraser, Thompson | 2,834 |
| 36 | Mar 7 | | (h) | Rochdale | D | 1 - 1 | Fraser | 2,836 |
| 37 | 14 | | (a) | Oxford United | L | 1 - 5 | McLean | 4,300 |
| 38 | 21 | | (h) | Workington | L | 1 - 2 | Bradley | 1,805 |
| 39 | 23 | | (h) | Tranmere Rovers | W | 3 - 2 | Bradley, Brown 2 | 2,587 |
| 40 | 27 | | (h) | Halifax Town | D | 1 - 1 | Bradley | 4,841 |
| 41 | 28 | | (a) | Doncaster Rovers | D | 2 - 2 | Lithgo (pen), Johnson | 5,816 |
| 42 | 30 | | (a) | Halifax Town | L | 1 - 4 | Hamilton | 4,860 |
| 43 | Apr 4 | | (h) | Stockport County | W | 3 - 0 | Johnson, Lithgo, Hamilton | 2,641 |
| 44 | 6 | | (h) | Newport County | D | 1 - 1 | Thompson | 4,266 |
| 45 | 11 | | (a) | Bradford Park Avenue | L | 1 - 3 | McLean | 5,104 |
| 46 | 17 | | (h) | Chesterfield | W | 1 - 0 | Hamilton | 4,401 |
| 47 | 20 | | (h) | Doncaster Rovers | W | 2 - 1 | Hinchcliffe (pen), Fogarty | 4,385 |
| 48 | 25 | | (a) | Newport County | L | 1 - 2 | Bradley | 2,521 |

Final Position : 23rd in Division Four — Apps.

1 own goal — Goals

**FA Cup**

| | | | | | | | | |
|---|---|---|---|---|---|---|---|---|
| 20 | Nov 18 | R1 | (h) | Lincoln City | L | 0 - 1 | | 5,698 |

Apps.
Goals

**League Cup**

| | | | | | | | | |
|---|---|---|---|---|---|---|---|---|
| 4 | Sep 4 | R1 | (a) | Lincoln City | L | 2 - 3 | Johnson, Hinchcliffe | 4,748 |

Apps.
Goals

| Oakley | Wilkie | Hinshelwood | Hinchcliffe | Atkinson | Fraser | Hamilton | McLean | Brown | Bradley | Lithgo | Cunningham | Bilcliff | Burlison | Johnson | Wallis | McCubbin | Stonehouse | Thompson | Fogarty | Francis | Simpkins | Morrell |
|---|---|---|---|---|---|---|---|---|---|---|---|---|---|---|---|---|---|---|---|---|---|---|
| 1 | 2 | 3 | 4 | 5 | 6 | 7 | 8 | 9 | 10 | 11 | | | | | | | | | | | | |
| 1 | 2 | 6 | 4 | 5 | | 7 | 8 | 3 | 10 | 11 | 9 | | | | | | | | | | | |
| 1 | | 6 | 4 | 5 | | 7 | 8 | 3 | 10 | 11 | 9 | 2 | | | | | | | | | | |
| 1 | | 6 | 8 | | 5 | 7 | | 3 | 10 | 11 | | 2 | 4 | 9 | | | | | | | | |
| 1 | | 6 | 8 | 5 | 4 | 7 | | 3 | 10 | 11 | | 2 | | 9 | | | | | | | | |
| 1 | | 6 | | 5 | 4 | 7 | | 3 | 10 | 11 | | 2 | 8 | | 9 | | | | | | | |
| 1 | | 6 | 10 | 5 | 4 | 7 | | 3 | | 11 | | 2 | 8 | | 9 | | | | | | | |
| 1 | | 6 | 4 | 5 | 8 | 9 | | 3 | | 11 | | 2 | 10 | | | 7 | | | | | | |
| 1 | 3 | | 4 | 5 | 8 | | | 9 | 10 | 11 | | 2 | 6 | | | 7 | | | | | | |
| 1 | | | 4 | 5 | 8 | 7 | | | 10 | 11 | | 2 | 6 | | | | 3 | 9 | | | | |
| 1 | | | 4 | | 5 | | | 10 | 7 | 11 | | 2 | 6 | 8 | | | 3 | 9 | | | | |
| 1 | 3 | | 4 | | 5 | | | 10 | 7 | 11 | | 2 | 6 | 8 | | | | 9 | | | | |
| 1 | 3 | | 4 | | 5 | | | 10 | 7 | 11 | | 2 | 6 | 8 | | | | 9 | | | | |
| 1 | 3 | | 4 | | 5 | | | 10 | 7 | 11 | | 2 | 6 | 8 | | | | 9 | | | | |
| 1 | | | 4 | | 5 | | 10 | 9 | 7 | 11 | | 2 | 6 | 8 | | | 3 | | | | | |
| 1 | | | 4 | | 5 | | 10 | 9 | 7 | 11 | | 2 | 6 | 8 | | | 3 | | | | | |
| 1 | | | 4 | | 5 | | 7 | 10 | 11 | | | 2 | 6 | 8 | | | 3 | 9 | | | | |
| 1 | | | 4 | | 5 | | 7 | 10 | 11 | | | 2 | 6 | 8 | | | 3 | 9 | | | | |
| 1 | | 10 | 4 | | 5 | | 7 | 9 | 11 | | | 2 | 6 | | | | 3 | | 8 | | | |
| 1 | | | 4 | | 5 | | 7 | | 11 | | | 2 | 6 | | | | 3 | 9 | 8 | 10 | | |
| 1 | | | 4 | | 5 | | 7 | | 11 | | | 2 | 6 | | | | 3 | 9 | 8 | 10 | | |
| 1 | | | 4 | | 5 | | 7 | | 11 | | | 2 | 6 | | | | 3 | 9 | 8 | 10 | | |
| 1 | | | 4 | | 5 | | 7 | | 11 | | | 2 | 6 | | | | 3 | 9 | 8 | 10 | | |
| 1 | | 10 | 4 | | 5 | 7 | | | 11 | | | 2 | 6 | | | | 3 | | 8 | 9 | | |
| 1 | 2 | | 4 | | 5 | | | | 7 | 11 | | | 6 | | | | 3 | 9 | 8 | 10 | | |
| 1 | 3 | 6 | 7 | | 5 | | | 9 | 11 | | | 4 | | | | | 2 | | 8 | 10 | | |
| 1 | | 6 | 7 | | 5 | | 10 | | 9 | | | 2 | 11 | 4 | | | 3 | | 8 | | | |
| 1 | | 6 | 7 | | 5 | | 10 | | 9 | | | 2 | 11 | 4 | | | 3 | | 8 | | | |
| 1 | | 6 | 7 | | 5 | | 10 | | 11 | | | 2 | | 4 | | | 3 | 9 | 8 | | | |
| 1 | | 6 | 7 | | 5 | | | | 10 | | | 2 | 11 | 4 | | | 3 | 9 | 8 | | | |
| 1 | | 6 | 7 | | 5 | | | | 10 | | | 2 | 11 | 4 | | | 3 | 9 | 8 | | | |
| 1 | | 6 | 4 | | 5 | | 7 | | 10 | | | 2 | | | | | 3 | 9 | 8 | 11 | | |
| 1 | | | 4 | 5 | 10 | | 7 | | 11 | | | 2 | | 6 | | | 3 | 9 | 8 | | | |
| | | | 4 | 5 | 9 | | 7 | | 10 | | | 2 | 11 | 6 | | | 3 | | 8 | | 1 | |
| | 3 | | 4 | 5 | 10 | | 7 | | 11 | | | 2 | 6 | 9 | | | | | 8 | | 1 | |
| | | | 10 | 5 | 9 | | 7 | | 11 | | | 2 | | 6 | | | 3 | | 8 | | 1 | 4 |
| | 3 | | | 5 | 6 | | | 9 | 7 | | | 2 | 11 | | | | | | 8 | 10 | 1 | 4 |
| | 3 | | | 5 | 6 | | | 9 | 7 | | | 2 | 11 | | | | | | 8 | 10 | 1 | 4 |
| | 3 | | | 2 | 5 | 7 | | | | 11 | | | 6 | 9 | | | | | 8 | 10 | 1 | 4 |
| | 3 | | | 2 | 5 | 7 | | | | 11 | | | 6 | 9 | | | | | 8 | 10 | 1 | 4 |
| | | | 6 | | 5 | 7 | | | | 11 | | 2 | | 9 | | | 3 | | 8 | 10 | 1 | 4 |
| | | | 6 | | 5 | 7 | | | | 11 | | 2 | | 9 | | | 3 | 10 | 8 | | 1 | 4 |
| | | | 6 | | 5 | | 7 | | | 11 | | 2 | | | | | 3 | 9 | 8 | 10 | 1 | 4 |
| | | | 6 | | 5 | 7 | | 9 | | 11 | | 2 | | | | | 3 | 10 | 8 | | 1 | 4 |
| | | | 6 | | 5 | 7 | 10 | | 11 | | | 2 | | | | | 3 | 9 | 8 | | 1 | 4 |
| | | | 6 | | 5 | 7 | 10 | | 11 | | | 2 | | | | | 3 | 9 | 8 | | 1 | 4 |
| 33 | 13 | 17 | 41 | 17 | 44 | 17 | 23 | 22 | 38 | 23 | 2 | 41 | 31 | 23 | 2 | 2 | 29 | 22 | 28 | 14 | 13 | 11 |
| | | 3 | 5 | | 2 | 4 | 3 | 5 | 5 | 6 | | | 1 | 3 | | | | 8 | 5 | 3 | | |
| | | | | | | | | | | | | | | | | | | | | | | |
| 1 | | 10 | 4 | | 5 | | 7 | 9 | 11 | | | 2 | 6 | 8 | | | 3 | | | | | |
| 1 | | 1 | 1 | | 1 | | 1 | 1 | 1 | | | 1 | 1 | 1 | | | 1 | | | | | |
| | | | | | | | | | | | | | | | | | | | | | | |
| | | | | | | | | | | | | | | | | | | | | | | |
| 1 | | 6 | 4 | | 5 | 7 | | 3 | | 11 | 9 | 2 | 10 | 8 | | | | | | | | |
| 1 | | 1 | 1 | | 1 | 1 | | 1 | | 1 | 1 | 1 | 1 | 1 | | | | | | | | |
| | | | 1 | | | | | | | | | | | 1 | | | | | | | | |

## League Table

| | P | W | D | L | F | A | Pts |
|---|---|---|---|---|---|---|---|
| Gillingham | 46 | 23 | 14 | 9 | 59 | 30 | 60 |
| Carlisle United | 46 | 25 | 10 | 11 | 113 | 58 | 60 |
| Workington | 46 | 24 | 11 | 11 | 76 | 52 | 59 |
| Exeter City | 46 | 20 | 18 | 8 | 62 | 37 | 58 |
| Bradford City | 46 | 25 | 6 | 15 | 76 | 62 | 56 |
| Torquay United | 46 | 20 | 11 | 15 | 80 | 54 | 51 |
| Tranmere Rovers | 46 | 20 | 11 | 15 | 85 | 73 | 51 |
| Brighton & Hove Albion | 46 | 19 | 12 | 15 | 71 | 52 | 50 |
| Aldershot | 46 | 19 | 10 | 17 | 83 | 78 | 48 |
| Halifax Town | 46 | 17 | 14 | 15 | 77 | 77 | 48 |
| Lincoln City | 46 | 19 | 9 | 18 | 67 | 75 | 47 |
| Chester | 46 | 19 | 8 | 19 | 65 | 60 | 46 |
| Bradford Park Avenue | 46 | 18 | 9 | 19 | 75 | 81 | 45 |
| Doncaster Rovers | 46 | 15 | 12 | 19 | 70 | 75 | 42 |
| Newport County | 46 | 17 | 8 | 21 | 64 | 73 | 42 |
| Chesterfield | 46 | 15 | 12 | 19 | 57 | 71 | 42 |
| Stockport County | 46 | 15 | 12 | 19 | 50 | 68 | 42 |
| Oxford United | 46 | 14 | 13 | 19 | 59 | 63 | 41 |
| Darlington | 46 | 14 | 12 | 20 | 66 | 93 | 40 |
| Rochdale | 46 | 12 | 15 | 19 | 56 | 59 | 39 |
| Southport | 46 | 15 | 9 | 22 | 63 | 88 | 39 |
| York City | 46 | 14 | 7 | 25 | 52 | 66 | 35 |
| Hartlepools United | 46 | 12 | 9 | 25 | 54 | 93 | 33 |
| Barrow | 46 | 6 | 18 | 22 | 51 | 93 | 30 |

# 1964-65

## Division Four

Manager: Alvan Williams

### Did you know that?

The home League game against Millwall on 3 October attracted a crowd of 10,734, the first five-figure crowd since the visit of Peterborough United at the start of the 1960–61 season.

Alvan Williams used only 19 players during the season to equal the club record. Simpkins and Storton were ever-presents, with five other players, Bannister, Bradley, Fox, Harrison and Marshall, playing 40 or more League games.

| Match No. | Date | Round | Venue | Opponents | Result | | Scorers | Attendance |
|---|---|---|---|---|---|---|---|---|
| 1 | Aug 22 | | (a) | Lincoln City | L | 2 - 4 | Bradley, Harrison | 5,222 |
| 2 | 24 | | (h) | York City | D | 2 - 2 | Francis, Bradley | 6,473 |
| 3 | 29 | | (h) | Brighton & Hove Albion | D | 1 - 1 | Thompson | 6,708 |
| 4 | 31 | | (a) | York City | D | 0 - 0 | | 5,601 |
| 6 | Sep 5 | | (a) | Oxford United | L | 0 - 3 | | 7,990 |
| 7 | 7 | | (h) | Stockport County | W | 4 - 3 | Thompson 2, Bradley, Bannister | 6,619 |
| 8 | 12 | | (h) | Barrow | W | 3 - 0 | Thompson, Fogarty 2 | 7,128 |
| 9 | 14 | | (a) | Stockport County | W | 1 - 0 | Fogarty | 5,259 |
| 10 | 18 | | (a) | Tranmere Rovers | L | 1 - 5 | Wright | 11,861 |
| 11 | 21 | | (h) | Torquay United | W | 1 - 0 | Thompson | 8,563 |
| 12 | 26 | | (a) | Rochdale | L | 0 - 3 | | 3,736 |
| 13 | 28 | | (h) | Chester | D | 1 - 1 | Fogarty (pen) | 8,822 |
| 14 | Oct 3 | | (h) | Millwall | W | 1 - 0 | Thompson | 10,734 |
| 15 | 7 | | (a) | Chester | L | 0 - 4 | | 7,796 |
| 16 | 10 | | (h) | Crewe Alexandra | L | 2 - 4 | Bradley, Fogarty | 7,276 |
| 17 | 17 | | (a) | Newport County | L | 0 - 2 | | 3,587 |
| 18 | 19 | | (a) | Torquay United | L | 1 - 2 | Entwhistle | 4,409 |
| 19 | 24 | | (h) | Halifax Town | W | 4 - 0 | Entwhistle, Wright, Bradley, Bannister | 4,525 |
| 20 | 28 | | (a) | Wrexham | L | 0 - 3 | | 7,766 |
| 21 | 31 | | (a) | Notts County | L | 0 - 1 | | 4,924 |
| 22 | Nov 7 | | (h) | Chesterfield | D | 1 - 1 | Entwhistle | 4,433 |
| 24 | 21 | | (h) | Aldershot | D | 1 - 1 | Harrison | 5,165 |
| 25 | 28 | | (a) | Bradford Park Avenue | L | 0 - 4 | | 5,721 |
| 28 | Dec 12 | | (h) | Lincoln City | W | 3 - 0 | Bannister 2, Fogarty | 3,102 |
| 29 | 19 | | (a) | Brighton & Hove Albion | L | 0 - 5 | | 12,267 |
| 30 | 26 | | (h) | Darlington | W | 4 - 3 | Fogarty, Hamilton, Bradley, Harrison | 3,166 |
| 31 | Jan 2 | | (h) | Oxford United | D | 1 - 1 | Bannister | 4,955 |
| 32 | 16 | | (a) | Barrow | L | 2 - 4 | Thompson, Hamilton | 1,781 |
| 33 | 23 | | (h) | Tranmere Rovers | W | 2 - 0 | Fogarty, Thompson | 4,578 |
| 34 | 30 | | (a) | Doncaster Rovers | W | 1 - 0 | Hamilton | 6,383 |
| 35 | Feb 6 | | (h) | Rochdale | D | 1 - 1 | Bradley | 5,049 |
| 36 | 13 | | (a) | Millwall | D | 0 - 0 | | 7,142 |
| 37 | 20 | | (a) | Crewe Alexandra | W | 3 - 2 | Thompson 2, Bannister | 5,625 |
| 38 | 22 | | (a) | Darlington | W | 3 - 2 | Bradley, Atkinson (o.g.), Fogarty (pen) | 4,869 |
| 39 | 27 | | (h) | Newport County | L | 2 - 4 | Thompson, Fogarty | 6,461 |
| 40 | Mar 13 | | (h) | Notts County | D | 2 - 2 | Bradley, Thompson | 5,031 |
| 41 | 16 | | (a) | Halifax Town | L | 1 - 2 | Thompson | 1,916 |
| 42 | 20 | | (a) | Chesterfield | L | 1 - 3 | Ashworth | 3,806 |
| 43 | 29 | | (h) | Doncaster Rovers | D | 1 - 1 | Thompson | 5,935 |
| 44 | Apr 3 | | (a) | Aldershot | L | 0 - 3 | | 3,234 |
| 45 | 5 | | (h) | Southport | W | 2 - 1 | Bannister 2 | 5,192 |
| 46 | 10 | | (h) | Bradford Park Avenue | W | 2 - 0 | Wright, Bradley | 4,697 |
| 47 | 16 | | (h) | Bradford City | D | 2 - 2 | Wright, Ingle (o.g.) | 6,791 |
| 48 | 17 | | (a) | Southport | D | 1 - 1 | Thompson | 1,872 |
| 49 | 19 | | (a) | Bradford City | L | 0 - 4 | | 2,888 |
| 50 | 24 | | (h) | Wrexham | W | 1 - 0 | Thompson | 3,923 |

Final Position : 15th in Division Four — Apps.

2 own goals — Goals

**FA Cup**

| Match No. | Date | Round | Venue | Opponents | Result | | Scorers | Attendance |
|---|---|---|---|---|---|---|---|---|
| 23 | Nov 14 | R1 | (a) | Corby Town | W | 3 - 1 | Entwhistle 2, Fogarty (pen) | 4,511 |
| 26 | Dec 5 | R2 | (h) | Darlington | D | 0 - 0 | | 9,027 |
| 27 | 9 | R2r | (a) | Darlington | L | 1 - 4 | Fogarty | 14,566 |

Apps.
Goals

**League Cup**

| Match No. | Date | Round | Venue | Opponents | Result | | Scorers | Attendance |
|---|---|---|---|---|---|---|---|---|
| 5 | Sep 2 | R1 | (a) | Chesterfield | L | 0 - 3 | | 4,513 |

Apps.
Goals

| Simpkins | Storton | Marshall | Morrell | Fox | Harrison | Bannister | Fogarty | Thompson | Wright | Bradley | Hamilton | Francis | Scott | Entwhistle | Stonehouse | Brass | Hodgson | Ashworth |
|---|---|---|---|---|---|---|---|---|---|---|---|---|---|---|---|---|---|---|
| 1 | 2 | 3 | 4 | 5 | 6 | 7 | 8 | 9 | 10 | 11 | | | | | | | | |
| 1 | 2 | 3 | 4 | 5 | 6 | | | 9 | 8 | 11 | 7 | 10 | | | | | | |
| 1 | 2 | 3 | 4 | 5 | 6 | | | 9 | 8 | 11 | 7 | 10 | | | | | | |
| 1 | 2 | 3 | 4 | 5 | 6 | | | 9 | 8 | 11 | 7 | 10 | | | | | | |
| 1 | 2 | 3 | 4 | 5 | 6 | 7 | | 9 | 8 | 10 | | | 11 | | | | | |
| 1 | 2 | 3 | 4 | 5 | 6 | 7 | 8 | 9 | 10 | 11 | | | | | | | | |
| 1 | 2 | 3 | 4 | 5 | 6 | 7 | 8 | 9 | 10 | 11 | | | | | | | | |
| 1 | 2 | 3 | 4 | 5 | 6 | | 8 | 9 | 10 | 11 | 7 | | | | | | | |
| 1 | 2 | 3 | 4 | 5 | 6 | 7 | 8 | 9 | 10 | 11 | | | | | | | | |
| 1 | 2 | 3 | 4 | 5 | 6 | 7 | 8 | 9 | 10 | 11 | | | | | | | | |
| 1 | 2 | 3 | 4 | 5 | 6 | 7 | 8 | 9 | 10 | 11 | | | | | | | | |
| 1 | 2 | 3 | 4 | 5 | 6 | 7 | 8 | 9 | 10 | 11 | | | | | | | | |
| 1 | 2 | 3 | 4 | 5 | 6 | 7 | 8 | 9 | 10 | 11 | | | | | | | | |
| 1 | 2 | 3 | 4 | 5 | 6 | 7 | 8 | 9 | 10 | 11 | | | | | | | | |
| 1 | 2 | 3 | 4 | 5 | 6 | 9 | 8 | | 10 | 11 | 7 | | | | | | | |
| 1 | 2 | 3 | 4 | 5 | 6 | 9 | 8 | | | 10 | 7 | | 11 | | | | | |
| 1 | 2 | 3 | 4 | 5 | 6 | 11 | 8 | | | 10 | 7 | | | 9 | | | | |
| 1 | 2 | 3 | 4 | 5 | 6 | 7 | 10 | | 8 | 11 | | | | 9 | | | | |
| 1 | 2 | 3 | 4 | 5 | 6 | 7 | 10 | | 8 | 11 | | | | 9 | | | | |
| 1 | 5 | 3 | 4 | | 6 | 11 | | | 8 | | 7 | 10 | | 9 | 2 | | | |
| 1 | 2 | 3 | 4 | 5 | 6 | 7 | 10 | | 8 | 11 | | | | 9 | | | | |
| 1 | 2 | | 4 | 5 | 6 | 7 | 10 | 9 | | 11 | | | | 8 | 3 | | | |
| 1 | 2 | | 4 | 5 | 6 | 7 | 10 | 8 | | 11 | | | | 9 | 3 | | | |
| 1 | 2 | | | 5 | 6 | 11 | 8 | 9 | 10 | | | | | | 3 | 4 | 7 | |
| 1 | 9 | 2 | | 5 | 6 | 11 | 8 | | 10 | | 7 | | | | 3 | 4 | | |
| 1 | 2 | 3 | | 5 | 6 | 11 | 8 | 9 | | 10 | 7 | | | | | 4 | | |
| 1 | 2 | 3 | | 5 | 6 | 11 | 8 | 9 | | 10 | 7 | | | | | 4 | | |
| 1 | 2 | 3 | | 5 | 6 | 11 | 8 | 9 | | 10 | 7 | | | | | 4 | | |
| 1 | 2 | 3 | | 5 | 6 | 11 | 8 | 9 | | 10 | 7 | | | | | 4 | | |
| 1 | 2 | 3 | | 5 | 6 | 11 | 8 | 9 | | 10 | 7 | | | | | 4 | | |
| 1 | 2 | 3 | | 5 | 6 | 11 | 8 | 9 | | 10 | 7 | | | | | 4 | | |
| 1 | 2 | 3 | | 5 | 6 | 11 | 8 | 9 | | 10 | 7 | | | | | 4 | | |
| 1 | 2 | 3 | | 5 | 6 | 11 | 8 | 9 | | 10 | 7 | | | | | 4 | | |
| 1 | 2 | 3 | | 5 | 6 | 7 | 8 | 9 | | 11 | | | | 10 | | 4 | | |
| 1 | 2 | 3 | | 5 | 6 | 7 | 8 | 9 | | 11 | | | | 10 | | 4 | | |
| 1 | 2 | 3 | | 5 | 6 | 7 | 8 | 9 | | 11 | | | | | | 4 | | 10 |
| 1 | 2 | 3 | | 5 | 6 | | 8 | 9 | | 11 | 7 | | | 10 | | | | 4 |
| 1 | 2 | 3 | | 5 | 6 | 7 | | 9 | 8 | 11 | | | | 10 | | | | 4 |
| 1 | 2 | 3 | | 5 | | 7 | 8 | 9 | | 11 | | | | 10 | | 6 | | 4 |
| 1 | 2 | 3 | | 5 | | 7 | 8 | 10 | | 11 | | | | 9 | | 6 | | 4 |
| 1 | 2 | 3 | | 5 | | 7 | 8 | 10 | | 11 | | | | 9 | | 6 | | 4 |
| 1 | 2 | 3 | | 5 | 6 | 7 | 8 | 9 | 10 | 11 | | | | | | | | 4 |
| 1 | 2 | 3 | | 5 | 6 | 7 | 8 | 9 | 10 | 11 | | | | | | | | 4 |
| 1 | 2 | 3 | | 5 | 6 | 7 | 8 | 9 | 10 | 11 | | | | | | | | 4 |
| 1 | 2 | 3 | | 5 | 6 | 7 | 8 | 9 | 10 | 11 | | | | | | | | 4 |
| 1 | 2 | 3 | | 5 | 6 | 7 | | 9 | 10 | 11 | | | | | | 4 | | 8 |
| 46 | 46 | 43 | 23 | 45 | 43 | 41 | 39 | 38 | 27 | 43 | 18 | 4 | 2 | 14 | 5 | 17 | 1 | 11 |
| | | | | | 3 | 8 | 10 | 16 | 4 | 10 | 3 | 1 | | 3 | | | | 1 |

| Simpkins | Storton | Marshall | Morrell | Fox | Harrison | Bannister | Fogarty | Thompson | Wright | Bradley | Hamilton | Francis | Scott | Entwhistle | Stonehouse | Brass | Hodgson | Ashworth |
|---|---|---|---|---|---|---|---|---|---|---|---|---|---|---|---|---|---|---|
| 1 | 2 | | 4 | 5 | 6 | 7 | 10 | 9 | | 11 | | | | 8 | 3 | | | |
| 1 | 2 | | 4 | 5 | 6 | 7 | 10 | 9 | 8 | 11 | | | | | 3 | | | |
| 1 | 2 | | 4 | 5 | 6 | | 7 | 8 | 10 | 11 | | | | 9 | 3 | | | |
| 3 | 3 | | 3 | 3 | 3 | 2 | 3 | 3 | 2 | 3 | | | | 2 | 3 | | | |
| | | | | | | | 2 | | | | | | | 2 | | | | |

| Simpkins | Storton | Marshall | Morrell | Fox | Harrison | Bannister | Fogarty | Thompson | Wright | Bradley | Hamilton | Francis | Scott | Entwhistle | Stonehouse | Brass | Hodgson | Ashworth |
|---|---|---|---|---|---|---|---|---|---|---|---|---|---|---|---|---|---|---|
| 1 | 2 | 3 | 4 | 5 | 6 | | | | 8 | 10 | 7 | 9 | 11 | | | | | |
| 1 | 1 | 1 | 1 | 1 | 1 | | | | 1 | 1 | 1 | 1 | 1 | | | | | |

## League Table

| | P | W | D | L | F | A | Pts |
|---|---|---|---|---|---|---|---|
| Brighton & Hove Albion | 46 | 26 | 11 | 9 | 102 | 57 | 63 |
| Millwall | 46 | 23 | 16 | 7 | 78 | 45 | 62 |
| York City | 46 | 28 | 6 | 12 | 91 | 56 | 62 |
| Oxford United | 46 | 23 | 15 | 8 | 87 | 44 | 61 |
| Tranmere Rovers | 46 | 27 | 6 | 13 | 99 | 56 | 60 |
| Rochdale | 46 | 22 | 14 | 10 | 74 | 53 | 58 |
| Bradford Park Avenue | 46 | 20 | 17 | 9 | 86 | 62 | 57 |
| Chester | 46 | 25 | 6 | 15 | 119 | 81 | 56 |
| Doncaster Rovers | 46 | 20 | 11 | 15 | 84 | 72 | 51 |
| Crewe Alexandra | 46 | 18 | 13 | 15 | 90 | 81 | 49 |
| Torquay United | 46 | 21 | 7 | 18 | 70 | 70 | 49 |
| Chesterfield | 46 | 20 | 8 | 18 | 58 | 70 | 48 |
| Notts County | 46 | 15 | 14 | 17 | 61 | 73 | 44 |
| Wrexham | 46 | 17 | 9 | 20 | 84 | 92 | 43 |
| Hartlepools United | 46 | 15 | 13 | 18 | 61 | 85 | 43 |
| Newport County | 46 | 17 | 8 | 21 | 85 | 81 | 42 |
| Darlington | 46 | 18 | 6 | 22 | 84 | 87 | 42 |
| Aldershot | 46 | 15 | 7 | 24 | 64 | 84 | 37 |
| Bradford City | 46 | 12 | 8 | 26 | 70 | 88 | 32 |
| Southport | 46 | 8 | 16 | 22 | 58 | 89 | 32 |
| Barrow | 46 | 12 | 6 | 28 | 59 | 105 | 30 |
| Lincoln City | 46 | 11 | 6 | 29 | 58 | 99 | 28 |
| Halifax Town | 46 | 11 | 6 | 29 | 54 | 103 | 28 |
| Stockport County | 46 | 10 | 7 | 29 | 44 | 87 | 27 |

# 1965-66

## Division Four

Managers: Geoff Twentyman and Brian Clough

### Did you know that?

From 25 September to 1 January 'Pools played 15 League games, losing 10 and winning a mere two. The wins, against Bradford City and Crewe, coincided with the arrival of Brian Clough as manager.

John McGovern made his debut against Bradford City in the final game of the season at the age of 16 years 6 months and 23 days. This made him the youngest Hartlepools player at the time.

| Match No. | Date | Round | Venue | Opponents | Result | | Scorers | Attendance |
|---|---|---|---|---|---|---|---|---|
| 1 | Sep 5 | | (a) | Hebburn Argyle | D | 2 - 2 | Fletcher 2 | 3,000 |
| | | | | | | | | |
| 1 | Aug 21 | | (h) | Southport | W | 3 - 1 | Mulvaney, Ashworth, Phythian | 5,758 |
| 2 | 24 | | (a) | Doncaster Rovers | L | 0 - 4 | | 10,851 |
| 3 | 28 | | (a) | Wrexham | D | 1 - 1 | Mulvaney | 6,437 |
| 5 | Sep 4 | | (h) | Bradford Park Avenue | L | 2 - 3 | Thompson, Phythian | 4,205 |
| 6 | 11 | | (a) | Aldershot | L | 0 - 5 | | 5,001 |
| 7 | 13 | | (h) | Doncaster Rovers | W | 2 - 0 | Cooper, Wright | 5,324 |
| 8 | 18 | | (h) | Newport County | W | 5 - 2 | Phythian 3, Ashworth, Wright | 4,949 |
| 10 | 25 | | (a) | Torquay United | L | 0 - 2 | | 4,423 |
| 11 | Oct 2 | | (h) | Chesterfield | L | 1 - 2 | Phythian | 5,184 |
| 12 | 4 | | (a) | Barrow | L | 0 - 2 | | 4,581 |
| 13 | 9 | | (h) | Tranmere Rovers | D | 0 - 0 | | 4,245 |
| 14 | 16 | | (a) | Colchester United | L | 0 - 2 | | 4,421 |
| 15 | 23 | | (h) | Barnsley | L | 1 - 2 | Harrison | 4,194 |
| 16 | 30 | | (a) | Bradford City | W | 3 - 1 | Wright, Mulvaney 2 | 2,373 |
| 17 | Nov 6 | | (h) | Crewe Alexandra | W | 4 - 1 | Phythian 2, Wright 2 | 4,302 |
| 19 | 20 | | (h) | Halifax Town | L | 1 - 2 | Wright | 4,282 |
| 20 | 27 | | (a) | Chester | L | 0 - 2 | | 6,547 |
| 22 | Dec 11 | | (a) | Lincoln City | L | 1 - 2 | McPheat | 3,332 |
| 23 | 18 | | (h) | Colchester United | L | 0 - 1 | | 4,067 |
| 24 | 27 | | (h) | Darlington | D | 1 - 1 | Thompson | 9,290 |
| 25 | 28 | | (a) | Darlington | D | 1 - 1 | Phythian | 8,316 |
| 26 | Jan 1 | | (a) | Tranmere Rovers | L | 1 - 6 | Wright | 5,479 |
| 27 | 8 | | (h) | Port Vale | W | 2 - 0 | Thompson, Phythian | 4,284 |
| 28 | 15 | | (a) | Barnsley | D | 2 - 2 | Thompson 2 | 3,471 |
| 30 | 29 | | (a) | Southport | L | 1 - 4 | Wright | 4,983 |
| 31 | Feb 5 | | (h) | Wrexham | W | 4 - 2 | Phythian 2, Fogarty, Thompson | 3,959 |
| 32 | 12 | | (a) | Luton Town | L | 1 - 2 | Thompson | 6,131 |
| 33 | 26 | | (h) | Aldershot | W | 3 - 0 | Phythian, Fogarty (pen), Thompson | 4,410 |
| 34 | Mar 5 | | (h) | Luton Town | W | 2 - 0 | Phythian, Wright | 4,896 |
| 35 | 12 | | (a) | Newport County | L | 0 - 3 | | 2,285 |
| 36 | 19 | | (h) | Torquay United | L | 0 - 2 | | 4,789 |
| 37 | 21 | | (a) | Port Vale | D | 0 - 0 | | 4,908 |
| 38 | 25 | | (a) | Chesterfield | W | 3 - 1 | Mulvaney, Phythian, Parry | 2,653 |
| 39 | Apr 1 | | (a) | Crewe Alexandra | L | 1 - 3 | Wright | 3,148 |
| 40 | 8 | | (h) | Stockport County | W | 2 - 1 | Phythian, Mulvaney | 4,393 |
| 41 | 9 | | (h) | Notts County | W | 2 - 0 | Fogarty, Thompson | 4,001 |
| 42 | 11 | | (a) | Stockport County | W | 2 - 1 | Thompson, Mulvaney | 5,453 |
| 43 | 15 | | (a) | Halifax Town | L | 0 - 1 | | 1,533 |
| 44 | 19 | | (a) | Bradford Park Avenue | L | 1 - 4 | Gill | 3,755 |
| 45 | 23 | | (h) | Chester | W | 2 - 0 | Phythian, Fogarty | 4,138 |
| 46 | 26 | | (a) | Rochdale | L | 1 - 3 | McPheat | 1,964 |
| 47 | 30 | | (a) | Notts County | L | 0 - 1 | | 4,448 |
| 48 | May 7 | | (h) | Lincoln City | W | 3 - 1 | Mulvaney 2, Fogarty | 4,904 |
| 49 | 9 | | (h) | Barrow | W | 3 - 0 | Ashworth, Wright, Mulvaney | 5,236 |
| 50 | 16 | | (h) | Rochdale | D | 0 - 0 | | 5,779 |
| 51 | 21 | | (h) | Bradford City | D | 1 - 1 | Livingstone | 4,776 |

Final Position : 18th in Division Four

Apps.
Sub.Apps.
Goals

**FA Cup**

| | | | | | | | | |
|---|---|---|---|---|---|---|---|---|
| 18 | Nov 13 | R1 | (h) | Workington | W | 3 - 1 | McPheat 2, Brass | 7,466 |
| 21 | Dec 4 | R2 | (h) | Wrexham | W | 2 - 0 | Wright, Mulvaney | 6,897 |
| 29 | Jan 25 | R3 | (a) | Huddersfield Town | L | 1 - 3 | Thompson | 24,505 |

Apps.
Sub.Apps.
Goals

**League Cup**

| | | | | | | | | |
|---|---|---|---|---|---|---|---|---|
| 4 | Sep 1 | R1 | (h) | Bradford City | W | 1 - 0 | Mulvaney | 3,515 |
| 21 | 22 | R2 | (a) | Leeds United | L | 2 - 4 | Cooper, Wright | 11,081 |

Apps.
Sub.Apps.
Goals

| Simpkins | Storton | Marshall | Ashworth | Fox | Harrison | Cooper | Fogarty | Thompson | Phythian | Mulvaney | Wright | Drysdale | McPheat | Bradley | Small | Brass | Hamilton | Green | Parry | Grant | McLeod | Gill | Bates | McGovern | Livingstone |
|---|---|---|---|---|---|---|---|---|---|---|---|---|---|---|---|---|---|---|---|---|---|---|---|---|---|
| 1 | 2 | 3 | 4 | 5 | 6 | 7 | 8 | 9 | 10 | 11 | | | | | | | | | | | | | | | |
| | | | | | | | | | | | | | | | | | | | | | | | | | |
| 1 | 2 | 3 | 4 | 5 | 6 | 7 | 8 | 9 | 10 | 11 | | | | | | | | | | | | | | | |
| 1 | 2 | 3 | 4 | 5 | 6 | 7 | 8 | 9 | 10 | 11 | | | | | | | | | | | | | | | |
| 1 | 2 | 3 | 4 | 5 | 6 | 7 | 8 | 9 | 10 | 11 | | | | | | | | | | | | | | | |
| 1 | 2 | 3 | 4 | 5 | 6 | 7 | 8 | 9 | 10 | 11 | | | | | | | | | | | | | | | |
| 1 | 2 | 3 | 4 | 5 | 6 | 7 | | *9* | 10 | 11 | 8 | *12* | | | | | | | | | | | | | |
| 1 | 2 | 3 | 4 | 5 | | 7 | 6 | | 9 | | 8 | | 10 | 11 | | | | | | | | | | | |
| 1 | 2 | 3 | 4 | 5 | | 7 | 6 | | 9 | | 8 | | 10 | 11 | | | | | | | | | | | |
| 1 | 2 | 3 | 4 | 5 | | 7 | 6 | | 9 | 11 | 8 | | 10 | | | | | | | | | | | | |
| 1 | 2 | 3 | 4 | 5 | 6 | 7 | 8 | | 9 | | | | 10 | 11 | | | | | | | | | | | |
| 1 | 2 | 3 | 4 | 5 | 6 | 7 | 10 | | 9 | | 8 | | | 11 | | | | | | | | | | | |
| 1 | 2 | 3 | 4 | 5 | 6 | 7 | 10 | 9 | 8 | | | | | 11 | | | | | | | | | | | |
| | 2 | 3 | 4 | 5 | 6 | 7 | 10 | *9* | 8 | | *12* | | | 11 | 1 | | | | | | | | | | |
| | 2 | | | 5 | 6 | *7* | 4 | | 9 | 11 | 8 | 3 | | 10 | 1 | *12* | | | | | | | | | |
| 1 | | 2 | 6 | | 5 | 7 | 4 | | 9 | 11 | 8 | 3 | 10 | | | | | | | | | | | | |
| 1 | | 2 | | | 5 | 7 | 4 | | 9 | 11 | 8 | 3 | 10 | | | 6 | | | | | | | | | |
| 1 | 2 | | | | 5 | | 4 | | 9 | 11 | 8 | 3 | 10 | | | 6 | 7 | | | | | | | | |
| | 2 | | 4 | | 5 | | | | 9 | | 8 | 3 | 10 | 11 | | 6 | 7 | 1 | | | | | | | |
| | 2 | | 4 | | 5 | 7 | 11 | | 9 | | 8 | 3 | 10 | | | 6 | | 1 | | | | | | | |
| | 2 | | | | 5 | | 4 | | 9 | 11 | 8 | 3 | 10 | | | 6 | | 1 | 7 | | | | | | |
| | *2* | | | | 5 | 7 | 4 | 10 | 9 | *12* | 11 | 3 | | | | 6 | | 1 | 8 | | | | | | |
| | | | 4 | | 5 | 7 | 2 | 10 | 9 | | 11 | 3 | | | | 6 | | 1 | 8 | | | | | | |
| | | | 4 | | 5 | | 2 | 10 | 9 | | 11 | 3 | | 7 | | 6 | | 1 | 8 | | | | | | |
| | | | 4 | | 5 | | 10 | 8 | 9 | | 11 | 3 | | 7 | | 6 | | 1 | | 2 | | | | | |
| | 6 | | 4 | | 5 | 11 | 10 | 8 | 9 | | | 3 | | 7 | | | | 1 | | 2 | | | | | |
| | 6 | | 4 | | 5 | | 10 | 8 | 9 | | 11 | 3 | *12* | 7 | | | | 1 | | *2* | | | | | |
| | 2 | | 4 | | | | 10 | 8 | 9 | | 7 | 3 | | 11 | | 6 | | 1 | | | 5 | | | | |
| | 6 | | 4 | | | | 10 | 8 | 9 | | 7 | 3 | | 11 | | | | 1 | | 2 | | 5 | | | |
| | 6 | | 4 | | | | 10 | 8 | 9 | | 7 | 3 | | 11 | | | | 1 | | 2 | | 5 | | | |
| | 6 | | 4 | | | | 10 | 8 | 9 | | 7 | 3 | | 11 | | | | 1 | | 2 | | 5 | | | |
| | 6 | | 4 | | | | | 8 | 9 | | 7 | 3 | 10 | 11 | | | | 1 | | 2 | | 5 | | | |
| 1 | 2 | | 4 | | 6 | | | 10 | 9 | | 11 | 3 | | | | | | | 8 | | | 5 | 7 | | |
| 1 | | | | | 6 | | *4* | 8 | 9 | 11 | 10 | 3 | | | | | | | *12* | 2 | | 5 | 7 | | |
| 1 | | | | | 6 | | | 4 | 9 | 11 | 10 | 3 | | | | | | | 8 | 2 | | 5 | 7 | | |
| 1 | | | | | 6 | | | 4 | 9 | 11 | 10 | 3 | | | | | | | 8 | 2 | | 5 | 7 | | |
| 1 | | | | | 6 | | 4 | 8 | 9 | 11 | 10 | 3 | | | | | | | | 2 | | 5 | 7 | | |
| 1 | | | 4 | | 6 | | 10 | 8 | 9 | 11 | 7 | 3 | | | | | | | | 2 | | 5 | | | |
| 1 | | | | | 6 | | 4 | 8 | 9 | 11 | 10 | 3 | | | | | | | | 2 | | 5 | 7 | | |
| 1 | | | | | 6 | | 4 | 8 | 9 | 11 | 10 | 3 | | | | | | | | 2 | | 5 | 7 | | |
| 1 | | | | | 6 | | 4 | 8 | 9 | 11 | 10 | 3 | | | | | | | | 2 | | 5 | 7 | | |
| 1 | | | 4 | | 6 | | 10 | 8 | 9 | | 11 | 3 | | | | | | | | 2 | | 5 | 7 | | |
| 1 | | | 4 | | 6 | | 10 | 8 | 9 | | 11 | 3 | 7 | | | | | | | 2 | | 5 | | | |
| | | | 4 | | 6 | | | 8 | 9 | | 11 | 3 | 10 | | | | | 1 | | 2 | | 5 | 7 | | |
| | | | 4 | | 6 | | 10 | *8* | 9 | 11 | 7 | 3 | | | | | *12* | 1 | | 2 | | 5 | | | |
| | | | 4 | | *6* | | 10 | | 9 | 8 | 11 | 3 | *12* | | | | 7 | 1 | | 2 | | 5 | | | |
| | | | 4 | | 6 | | 10 | | 9 | 8 | 11 | 3 | | | | | | 1 | | 2 | | 5 | 7 | | |
| | | | 4 | | 6 | | 10 | | 9 | | 11 | 3 | | | | | | 1 | | 2 | | 5 | | 7 | 8 |
| 25 | 26 | 14 | 34 | 13 | 38 | 19 | 39 | 31 | 46 | 22 | 38 | 34 | 13 | 17 | 2 | 10 | 3 | 19 | 7 | 22 | 1 | 20 | 11 | 1 | 1 |
| | | | | | | | | | | 1 | 1 | 1 | 2 | | | 1 | 1 | | 1 | | | | | | |
| | | | 3 | | 1 | 1 | 5 | 10 | 17 | 10 | 11 | | 2 | | | | | | 1 | | | 1 | | | 1 |
| | | | | | | | | | | | | | | | | | | | | | | | | | |
| 1 | 2 | | | | 5 | 7 | 4 | | 9 | 11 | 8 | 3 | 10 | | | 6 | | | | | | | | | |
| 1 | 2 | | 4 | | 5 | | 7 | | 9 | 11 | 8 | 3 | 10 | | | 6 | | | | | | | | | |
| 1 | 6 | | 4 | | 5 | | 10 | 8 | 9 | | 11 | 3 | | 7 | | | | | | 2 | | | | | |
| 3 | 3 | | 2 | | 3 | 1 | 3 | 1 | 3 | 2 | 3 | 3 | 2 | 1 | | 2 | | | | 1 | | | | | |
| | | | | | | | | | | | | | | | | | | | | | | | | | |
| | | | | | | | | 1 | | 1 | 1 | | 2 | | | 1 | | | | | | | | | |
| | | | | | | | | | | | | | | | | | | | | | | | | | |
| 1 | 2 | 3 | 4 | 5 | 6 | 7 | 8 | 9 | 10 | 11 | | | | | | | | | | | | | | | |
| 1 | 2 | 3 | 4 | 5 | 6 | 7 | 10 | | 9 | | 8 | | | 11 | | | | | | | | | | | |
| 2 | 2 | 2 | 2 | 2 | 2 | 2 | 2 | 1 | 2 | 1 | 1 | | | 1 | | | | | | | | | | | |
| | | | | | | | | | | | | | | | | | | | | | | | | | |
| | | | | | | 1 | | | | 1 | 1 | | | | | | | | | | | | | | |

**Substitutions**

*Italic* player replaced by No 12.

## League Table

| | P | W | D | L | F | A | Pts |
|---|---|---|---|---|---|---|---|
| Doncaster Rovers | 46 | 24 | 11 | 11 | 85 | 54 | 59 |
| Darlington | 46 | 25 | 9 | 12 | 72 | 53 | 59 |
| Torquay United | 46 | 24 | 10 | 12 | 72 | 49 | 58 |
| Colchester United | 46 | 23 | 10 | 13 | 70 | 47 | 56 |
| Tranmere Rovers | 46 | 24 | 8 | 14 | 93 | 66 | 56 |
| Luton Town | 46 | 24 | 8 | 14 | 90 | 70 | 56 |
| Chester | 46 | 20 | 12 | 14 | 79 | 70 | 52 |
| Notts County | 46 | 19 | 12 | 15 | 61 | 53 | 50 |
| Newport County | 46 | 18 | 12 | 16 | 75 | 75 | 48 |
| Southport | 46 | 18 | 12 | 16 | 68 | 69 | 48 |
| Bradford Park Avenue | 46 | 21 | 5 | 20 | 102 | 92 | 47 |
| Barrow | 46 | 16 | 15 | 15 | 72 | 76 | 47 |
| Stockport County | 46 | 18 | 6 | 22 | 71 | 70 | 42 |
| Crewe Alexandra | 46 | 16 | 9 | 21 | 61 | 63 | 41 |
| Halifax Town | 46 | 15 | 11 | 20 | 67 | 75 | 41 |
| Barnsley | 46 | 15 | 10 | 21 | 74 | 78 | 40 |
| Aldershot | 46 | 15 | 10 | 21 | 75 | 84 | 40 |
| Hartlepools United | 46 | 16 | 8 | 22 | 63 | 75 | 40 |
| Port Vale | 46 | 15 | 9 | 22 | 48 | 59 | 39 |
| Chesterfield | 46 | 13 | 13 | 20 | 62 | 78 | 39 |
| Rochdale | 46 | 16 | 5 | 25 | 71 | 87 | 37 |
| Lincoln City | 46 | 13 | 11 | 22 | 57 | 82 | 37 |
| Bradford City | 46 | 12 | 13 | 21 | 63 | 94 | 37 |
| Wrexham | 46 | 13 | 9 | 24 | 72 | 104 | 35 |

# 1966-67

## Division Four

Manager: Brian Clough

### Did you know that?

In his only full season as manager Brian Clough took 'Pools to their highest League position since the 1956–57 season. This included a run of seven games unbeaten, which had also not been achieved for 10 years.

At this early stage of his managerial career, Brian Clough was clearly reluctant to make use of a substitute, as only eight of the 46 League games saw the introduction of the one allowed.

| Match No. | Date | Round | Venue | Opponents | Result | | Scorers | Attendance |
|---|---|---|---|---|---|---|---|---|
| 1 | Aug 20 | | (a) | Aldershot | D | 1 - 1 | Livingstone | 3,590 |
| 3 | 27 | | (h) | Wrexham | W | 2 - 1 | Livingstone, Phythian | 5,664 |
| 5 | Sep 2 | | (a) | Southend United | L | 0 - 2 | | 6,689 |
| 6 | 5 | | (h) | Barrow | W | 2 - 1 | Fogarty (pen), Livingstone | 5,463 |
| 7 | 10 | | (h) | Tranmere Rovers | L | 0 - 2 | | 5,903 |
| 8 | 17 | | (a) | Bradford City | L | 0 - 3 | | 3,727 |
| 9 | 19 | | (h) | Newport County | L | 0 - 1 | | 4,096 |
| 10 | 24 | | (h) | Exeter City | W | 3 - 1 | Phythian 2, Mulvaney | 4,227 |
| 11 | 26 | | (a) | Barrow | W | 3 - 2 | Mulvaney, Phythian 2 | 5,662 |
| 12 | Oct 1 | | (h) | Crewe Alexandra | L | 1 - 2 | Phythian | 4,394 |
| 13 | 7 | | (a) | York City | D | 1 - 1 | Mulvaney | 5,203 |
| 14 | 15 | | (h) | Lincoln City | W | 5 - 0 | Phythian, Mulvaney 2, Fogarty (pen), Wright (pen) | 3,987 |
| 15 | 17 | | (a) | Newport County | W | 2 - 0 | Phythian, Sheridan | 5,463 |
| 16 | 22 | | (a) | Chesterfield | L | 0 - 1 | | 5,275 |
| 17 | 29 | | (h) | Stockport County | W | 1 - 0 | Phythian | 5,976 |
| 18 | Nov 5 | | (a) | Rochdale | L | 2 - 3 | Mulvaney, Phythian | 2,005 |
| 19 | 12 | | (h) | Southport | D | 1 - 1 | Mulvaney | 5,516 |
| 20 | 19 | | (a) | Notts County | D | 0 - 0 | | 3,922 |
| 22 | Dec 3 | | (a) | Bradford Park Avenue | W | 2 - 1 | Wright, Taylor (o.g.) | 4,309 |
| 23 | 10 | | (h) | Port Vale | W | 2 - 1 | Wright, Phythian | 5,342 |
| 24 | 17 | | (h) | Aldershot | W | 3 - 2 | Mulvaney 2, Wright | 5,159 |
| 25 | 26 | | (h) | Brentford | D | 2 - 2 | Phythian (pen), Livingstone | 8,420 |
| 26 | 27 | | (a) | Brentford | W | 2 - 1 | Phythian 2 | 5,775 |
| 27 | 31 | | (a) | Wrexham | L | 1 - 4 | Mulvaney | 12,005 |
| 28 | Jan 6 | | (h) | Southend United | L | 1 - 2 | Phythian | 9,586 |
| 29 | 13 | | (a) | Tranmere Rovers | L | 0 - 2 | | 6,149 |
| 30 | 21 | | (h) | Bradford City | W | 1 - 0 | Phythian | 6,109 |
| 31 | 30 | | (h) | Chester | W | 3 - 2 | Phythian, Wright, Mulvaney | 7,988 |
| 32 | Feb 4 | | (a) | Exeter City | L | 0 - 1 | | 3,702 |
| 33 | 11 | | (a) | Crewe Alexandra | W | 2 - 1 | Mulvaney, Wright | 6,331 |
| 34 | 18 | | (h) | Barnsley | D | 1 - 1 | Bell | 6,715 |
| 35 | 25 | | (h) | York City | W | 4 - 2 | Mulvaney 3, Wright | 6,638 |
| 36 | Mar 4 | | (a) | Lincoln City | L | 0 - 3 | | 4,667 |
| 37 | 11 | | (a) | Barnsley | W | 2 - 1 | Phythian 2 | 6,479 |
| 38 | 18 | | (h) | Chesterfield | W | 3 - 2 | Mulvaney, Phythian 2 | 5,604 |
| 39 | 24 | | (h) | Luton Town | W | 2 - 1 | Phythian, Mulvaney | 8,442 |
| 40 | 25 | | (a) | Chester | L | 0 - 1 | | 3,126 |
| 41 | 27 | | (a) | Luton Town | W | 2 - 1 | Parry, McGovern | 7,370 |
| 42 | Apr 1 | | (h) | Rochdale | W | 2 - 1 | Somers, Broadbent | 5,952 |
| 43 | 8 | | (a) | Southport | L | 1 - 3 | Broadbent | 4,277 |
| 44 | 11 | | (a) | Halifax Town | L | 1 - 2 | Broadbent | 3,252 |
| 45 | 15 | | (h) | Notts County | W | 2 - 1 | Mulvaney 2 | 4,674 |
| 46 | 21 | | (a) | Stockport County | L | 0 - 2 | | 8,865 |
| 47 | 24 | | (h) | Halifax Town | L | 1 - 3 | Parry | 3,479 |
| 48 | 29 | | (h) | Bradford Park Avenue | W | 2 - 0 | Somers, Phythian | 3,567 |
| 49 | May 6 | | (a) | Port Vale | D | 0 - 0 | | 3,178 |

Final Position : 8th in Division Four

Apps.
Sub.Apps.
Goals

**FA Cup**

| | | | | | | | | |
|---|---|---|---|---|---|---|---|---|
| 21 | Nov 26 | R1 | (a) | Shrewsbury Town | L | 2 - 5 | Phythian, Fogarty | 6,515 |

Apps.
Sub.Apps.
Goals

**League Cup**

| | | | | | | | | |
|---|---|---|---|---|---|---|---|---|
| 2 | Aug 23 | R1 | (a) | Bradford Park Avenue | D | 2 - 2 | Phythian, Livingstone | 4,128 |
| 4 | 31 | R1r | (h) | Bradford Park Avenue | L | 1 - 2 | Phythian | 4,835 |

Apps.
Sub.Apps.
Goals

| Green | Grant | Drysdale | Sheridan | Gill | Parry | Wright | Fogarty | Phythian | Livingstone | Somers | Simpkins | McGovern | Bircumshaw | Bell | Mulvaney | Beresford | McLeod | Aston | Broadbent | Joyce |
|---|---|---|---|---|---|---|---|---|---|---|---|---|---|---|---|---|---|---|---|---|
| 1 | 2 | 3 | 4 | 5 | 6 | 7 | 8 | 9 | 10 | 11 | | | | | | | | | | |
| | 2 | 3 | 4 | 5 | 6 | 7 | 8 | 9 | 10 | 11 | 1 | | | | | | | | | |
| | 2 | 3 | 4 | 5 | 6 | 7 | 8 | 9 | 10 | 11 | 1 | | | | | | | | | |
| | 2 | 3 | 4 | 5 | 6 | *12* | 8 | *9* | 10 | 11 | 1 | 7 | | | | | | | | |
| | 2 | 3 | 4 | 5 | 6 | | 8 | 9 | 10 | 11 | 1 | 7 | | | | | | | | |
| | | 3 | 4 | 5 | | 8 | 6 | 9 | *10* | 11 | 1 | 7 | 2 | *12* | | | | | | |
| | | 3 | 4 | 5 | | 8 | | 6 | 9 | 11 | 1 | 7 | 2 | 10 | | | | | | |
| | | 3 | 4 | 5 | | 8 | 6 | 9 | | 11 | 1 | 7 | 2 | | 10 | | | | | |
| | | 3 | 4 | 5 | | 8 | 6 | 9 | | 11 | 1 | 7 | 2 | | 10 | | | | | |
| | | 3 | 4 | 5 | | 8 | 6 | 9 | | 11 | 1 | 7 | 2 | | 10 | | | | | |
| | | 3 | 4 | 5 | | 8 | 6 | 9 | | 11 | 1 | 7 | 2 | | 10 | | | | | |
| | | 3 | 4 | 5 | | 8 | 6 | 9 | | 11 | 1 | 7 | 2 | | 10 | | | | | |
| | | 3 | 4 | 5 | | 8 | | 9 | | 11 | 1 | | 2 | 7 | 10 | 6 | | | | |
| | | 3 | 4 | 5 | | 8 | | 9 | | 11 | 1 | | 2 | 7 | 10 | 6 | | | | |
| | | 3 | 4 | 5 | | 11 | | 9 | | 6 | 1 | 7 | 2 | 8 | 10 | | | | | |
| | | 3 | 4 | 5 | | | 7 | 9 | | 11 | 1 | | 2 | 8 | 10 | 6 | | | | |
| | | 3 | 4 | 5 | | 7 | 6 | 9 | | 11 | 1 | | 2 | 8 | 10 | | | | | |
| | | 3 | 4 | 5 | | 7 | 6 | 9 | | 11 | 1 | | 2 | 8 | 10 | | | | | |
| 1 | | 3 | 4 | | 8 | 11 | 6 | 9 | | | | 7 | 2 | | 10 | | 5 | | | |
| 1 | | 3 | 4 | 5 | *12* | 8 | 6 | 9 | | *11* | | 7 | 2 | | 10 | | | | | |
| 1 | | 3 | 4 | 5 | | 11 | 6 | 9 | | | | 7 | 2 | 8 | 10 | | | | | |
| 1 | | 3 | 4 | 5 | | 11 | | 6 | 9 | | | 7 | 2 | 8 | 10 | | | | | |
| 1 | | 3 | 4 | | 6 | 11 | | 9 | 8 | | | 7 | 2 | | 10 | | | 5 | | |
| 1 | | 3 | 4 | | 6 | 11 | | 9 | 8 | | | 7 | 2 | | 10 | | | 5 | | |
| 1 | | 3 | 4 | | | 11 | | 9 | *8* | 6 | | 7 | 2 | *12* | 10 | | | 5 | | |
| 1 | | 3 | 4 | | 6 | 8 | | 9 | | 11 | | 7 | 2 | | 10 | | | 5 | | |
| | | 3 | 4 | | | 7 | | 9 | 8 | *11* | 1 | *12* | 2 | 6 | 10 | | | 5 | | |
| | | 3 | 4 | | | 11 | 6 | 9 | | | 1 | 7 | 2 | 8 | 10 | | | 5 | | |
| | | 3 | 4 | 6 | | 11 | *8* | 9 | | | 1 | 7 | 2 | *12* | 10 | | | 5 | | |
| | 2 | 3 | 4 | | 7 | 11 | | 9 | | | 1 | | | 8 | 10 | | 6 | 5 | | |
| | 2 | 3 | 4 | | | 11 | | 9 | | | 1 | 7 | | 8 | 10 | | 6 | 5 | | |
| | 2 | 3 | 4 | | | 11 | 6 | 9 | | | 1 | 7 | | | 10 | | | 5 | 8 | |
| 1 | 2 | | *4* | | 7 | 11 | 6 | 9 | | | | *12* | 3 | | 10 | | | 5 | 8 | |
| 1 | 2 | 3 | | | 6 | 11 | | 9 | | | | 7 | | | 10 | | 4 | 5 | 8 | |
| 1 | 2 | 3 | | | 6 | 11 | | 9 | | | | 7 | | | 10 | | 4 | 5 | 8 | |
| 1 | 2 | 3 | | | 6 | *11* | | 9 | | | | 7 | | *12* | 10 | | 4 | 5 | 8 | |
| 1 | 2 | 3 | | | 6 | | | 9 | | | | 7 | | 11 | 10 | | 4 | 5 | 8 | |
| 1 | | 3 | | | 6 | | | 9 | | 11 | | 7 | 2 | | 10 | | 4 | 5 | 8 | |
| | | 3 | | | 6 | | | 9 | | 11 | 1 | 7 | 2 | | 10 | | 4 | 5 | 8 | |
| | | 3 | | 5 | 6 | 7 | | 9 | 10 | 11 | 1 | | 2 | | | | 4 | | 8 | |
| | | 3 | | 5 | 6 | 7 | | 9 | 10 | 11 | 1 | | 2 | | | | 4 | | 8 | |
| | | 3 | 4 | 5 | | | | 9 | | 11 | 1 | 7 | 2 | | 10 | | 6 | | 8 | |
| | | 3 | | | 6 | | | 9 | | 11 | 1 | 7 | 2 | | 10 | | 4 | 5 | 8 | |
| | | 3 | | | 6 | 11 | | 9 | | *12* | 1 | *7* | 2 | | 10 | | 4 | 5 | 8 | |
| | | 3 | 4 | 5 | 6 | | | 9 | | 11 | 1 | | 2 | | 10 | | | | 8 | 7 |
| | | 3 | 4 | 5 | 6 | 7 | | 9 | | 11 | 1 | | 2 | | 10 | | | | 8 | |
| 15 | 13 | 45 | 36 | 27 | 23 | 37 | 21 | 46 | 14 | 30 | 31 | 31 | 34 | 14 | 37 | 3 | 14 | 19 | 15 | 1 |
| | | | | | 1 | 1 | | | | 1 | | 2 | | 4 | | | | | | |
| | | | 1 | | 2 | 7 | 2 | 23 | 4 | 2 | | 1 | | 1 | 19 | | | | 3 | |

| Green | Grant | Drysdale | Sheridan | Gill | Parry | Wright | Fogarty | Phythian | Livingstone | Somers | Simpkins | McGovern | Bircumshaw | Bell | Mulvaney | Beresford | McLeod | Aston | Broadbent | Joyce |
|---|---|---|---|---|---|---|---|---|---|---|---|---|---|---|---|---|---|---|---|---|
| | | 3 | 4 | 5 | | 11 | 6 | 9 | | | 1 | 7 | 2 | 8 | 10 | | | | | |
| | | 1 | 1 | 1 | | 1 | 1 | 1 | | | 1 | 1 | 1 | 1 | 1 | | | | | |
| | | | | | | | | | | | | | | | | | | | | |
| | | | | | | | 1 | 1 | | | | | | | | | | | | |

| Green | Grant | Drysdale | Sheridan | Gill | Parry | Wright | Fogarty | Phythian | Livingstone | Somers | Simpkins | McGovern | Bircumshaw | Bell | Mulvaney | Beresford | McLeod | Aston | Broadbent | Joyce |
|---|---|---|---|---|---|---|---|---|---|---|---|---|---|---|---|---|---|---|---|---|
| | 2 | 3 | 4 | 5 | 6 | 7 | 8 | 9 | 10 | 11 | 1 | | | | | | | | | |
| | 2 | 3 | 4 | 5 | 6 | 7 | 8 | 9 | 10 | 11 | 1 | | | | | | | | | |
| | 2 | 2 | 2 | 2 | 2 | 2 | 2 | 2 | 2 | 2 | 2 | | | | | | | | | |
| | | | | | | | | | | | | | | | | | | | | |
| | | | | | | | | 2 | 1 | | | | | | | | | | | |

## League Table

| | P | W | D | L | F | A | Pts |
|---|---|---|---|---|---|---|---|
| Stockport County | 46 | 26 | 12 | 8 | 69 | 42 | 64 |
| Southport | 46 | 23 | 13 | 10 | 69 | 42 | 59 |
| Barrow | 46 | 24 | 11 | 11 | 76 | 54 | 59 |
| Tranmere Rovers | 46 | 22 | 14 | 10 | 66 | 43 | 58 |
| Crewe Alexandra | 46 | 21 | 12 | 13 | 70 | 55 | 54 |
| Southend United | 46 | 22 | 9 | 15 | 70 | 49 | 53 |
| Wrexham | 46 | 16 | 20 | 10 | 76 | 62 | 52 |
| Hartlepools United | 46 | 22 | 7 | 17 | 66 | 64 | 51 |
| Brentford | 46 | 18 | 13 | 15 | 58 | 56 | 49 |
| Aldershot | 46 | 18 | 12 | 16 | 72 | 57 | 48 |
| Bradford City | 46 | 19 | 10 | 17 | 74 | 62 | 48 |
| Halifax Town | 46 | 15 | 14 | 17 | 59 | 68 | 44 |
| Port Vale | 46 | 14 | 15 | 17 | 55 | 58 | 43 |
| Exeter City | 46 | 14 | 15 | 17 | 50 | 60 | 43 |
| Chesterfield | 46 | 17 | 8 | 21 | 60 | 63 | 42 |
| Barnsley | 46 | 13 | 15 | 18 | 60 | 64 | 41 |
| Luton Town | 46 | 16 | 9 | 21 | 59 | 73 | 41 |
| Newport County | 46 | 12 | 16 | 18 | 56 | 63 | 40 |
| Chester | 46 | 15 | 10 | 21 | 54 | 78 | 40 |
| Notts County | 46 | 13 | 11 | 22 | 53 | 72 | 37 |
| Rochdale | 46 | 13 | 11 | 22 | 53 | 75 | 37 |
| York City | 46 | 12 | 11 | 23 | 65 | 79 | 35 |
| Bradford Park Avenue | 46 | 11 | 13 | 22 | 52 | 79 | 35 |
| Lincoln City | 46 | 9 | 13 | 24 | 58 | 82 | 31 |

# 1967-68

## Division Four

Manager: Angus McLean

### Did you know that?

'Pools gained their first-ever promotion by finishing third in Division Four. Their success was based on remaining undefeated in the final 16 games of the season and losing only once at home (to Southend United).

The signing of Bobby Cummings from Darlington proved to be the catalyst for a successful promotion campaign. After making his debut against Wrexham on 3 February, he tasted defeat only once in 18 games scoring nine goals.

| Match No. | Date | Round | Venue | Opponents | Result | | Scorers | Attendance |
|---|---|---|---|---|---|---|---|---|
| 1 | Aug 19 | | (h) | Brentford | W | 2 - 0 | Phythian, Mulvaney | 5,372 |
| 3 | 26 | | (a) | Bradford Park Avenue | W | 1 - 0 | Wright | 3,780 |
| 4 | Sep 1 | | (h) | Doncaster Rovers | D | 0 - 0 | | 7,669 |
| 5 | 4 | | (h) | Rochdale | D | 1 - 1 | McGovern | 8,361 |
| 6 | 9 | | (a) | Luton Town | L | 0 - 1 | | 8,347 |
| 8 | 16 | | (h) | Southend United | L | 0 - 1 | | 5,946 |
| 9 | 23 | | (a) | Wrexham | L | 0 - 6 | | 7,381 |
| 10 | 25 | | (a) | Rochdale | D | 1 - 1 | Bell | 2,041 |
| 11 | 29 | | (h) | Barnsley | W | 2 - 1 | Phythian 2 | 5,002 |
| 12 | Oct 3 | | (a) | Newport County | L | 0 - 2 | | 2,781 |
| 13 | 7 | | (a) | Workington | L | 1 - 2 | Phythian (pen) | 2,500 |
| 14 | 13 | | (h) | Lincoln City | D | 1 - 1 | A.Smith | 5,031 |
| 15 | 21 | | (a) | Halifax Town | L | 0 - 3 | | 4,865 |
| 16 | 23 | | (h) | Newport County | W | 2 - 0 | Mulvaney, Phythian | 4,942 |
| 17 | 27 | | (h) | Bradford City | W | 1 - 0 | Bell | 5,476 |
| 18 | Nov 4 | | (a) | Crewe Alexandra | L | 1 - 2 | Bradshaw (o.g.) | 5,604 |
| 19 | 10 | | (h) | Notts County | W | 3 - 1 | Blowman 2, Wright | 4,141 |
| 20 | 14 | | (a) | Doncaster Rovers | W | 1 - 0 | Bell | 7,818 |
| 21 | 18 | | (a) | Port Vale | W | 3 - 2 | Bell, Blowman, Simpkins | 3,875 |
| 22 | 24 | | (h) | Chester | D | 0 - 0 | | 4,638 |
| 23 | Dec 2 | | (a) | Chesterfield | L | 1 - 3 | Bircumshaw | 10,800 |
| 25 | 16 | | (a) | Brentford | W | 1 - 0 | Phythian | 6,210 |
| 26 | 22 | | (h) | Bradford Park Avenue | W | 2 - 0 | Blowman, Phythian | 4,268 |
| 27 | 26 | | (h) | Darlington | W | 1 - 0 | Bell | 9,488 |
| 28 | 30 | | (a) | Darlington | W | 3 - 2 | Bell, Phythian 2 | 5,715 |
| 29 | Jan 13 | | (h) | Luton Town | W | 2 - 1 | Phythian, Bell | 4,766 |
| 30 | 20 | | (a) | Southend United | L | 1 - 2 | Blowman | 8,452 |
| 31 | 27 | | (a) | Aldershot | L | 0 - 2 | | 4,425 |
| 32 | Feb 2 | | (h) | Wrexham | W | 3 - 0 | Blowman 2, Phythian (pen) | 4,726 |
| 33 | 10 | | (a) | Barnsley | L | 0 - 4 | | 12,896 |
| 34 | 24 | | (h) | Port Vale | D | 2 - 2 | Cummings, McGovern | 4,388 |
| 35 | Mar 2 | | (a) | Lincoln City | W | 2 - 1 | Somers, Bell | 4,363 |
| 36 | 9 | | (h) | Aldershot | W | 1 - 0 | Bell | 4,943 |
| 37 | 15 | | (h) | Halifax Town | D | 0 - 0 | | 5,158 |
| 38 | 23 | | (a) | Bradford City | D | 1 - 1 | Cummings | 6,196 |
| 39 | 30 | | (h) | Crewe Alexandra | D | 1 - 1 | Wright | 5,944 |
| 40 | Apr 1 | | (h) | Exeter City | W | 3 - 1 | McGovern, Bell, Cummings | 4,502 |
| 41 | 6 | | (a) | Notts County | W | 3 - 0 | Bell, Cummings (pen), Wright | 4,976 |
| 42 | 12 | | (h) | York City | W | 1 - 0 | Cummings | 9,128 |
| 43 | 13 | | (h) | Workington | W | 2 - 1 | Cummings 2 (1 pen) | 6,063 |
| 44 | 15 | | (a) | York City | W | 2 - 0 | Bell 2 | 5,916 |
| 45 | 20 | | (a) | Chester | W | 2 - 0 | Bell, Wright | 3,990 |
| 46 | 26 | | (h) | Chesterfield | W | 2 - 1 | Hepplewhite, Cummings | 11,399 |
| 47 | May 4 | | (a) | Exeter City | D | 0 - 0 | | 3,693 |
| 48 | 6 | | (a) | Swansea Town | W | 2 - 0 | Cummings, Hepplewhite | 3,491 |
| 49 | 11 | | (h) | Swansea Town | W | 2 - 0 | Wright, McGovern | 11,011 |

Final Position : 3rd in Division Four - Promoted

Apps.
Sub.Apps.
1 own goal Goals

**FA Cup**

| Match No. | Date | Round | Venue | Opponents | Result | | Scorers | Attendance |
|---|---|---|---|---|---|---|---|---|
| 24 | Dec 9 | R1 | (h) | Bury | L | 2 - 3 | Bell, Wright | 4,830 |

Apps.
Sub.Apps.
Goals

**League Cup**

| Match No. | Date | Round | Venue | Opponents | Result | | Scorers | Attendance |
|---|---|---|---|---|---|---|---|---|
| 2 | Aug 23 | R1 | (h) | Bradford City | W | 2 - 0 | Broadbent, Phythian | 4,946 |
| 7 | Sep 13 | R2 | (a) | Derby County | L | 0 - 4 | | 17,810 |

Apps.
Sub.Apps.
Goals

| Smith, G. | Goad | Drysdale | Sheridan | Gill | Hepplewhite | Wright | Mulvaney | Phythian | Broadbent | Somers | McGovern | Bell | Aston | Parry | Bircumshaw | McLeod | Adamson | King | White | Smith, A. | Simpkins | Blowman | Cummings |
|---|---|---|---|---|---|---|---|---|---|---|---|---|---|---|---|---|---|---|---|---|---|---|---|
| 1 | 2 | 3 | 4 | 5 | 6 | 7 | 8 | 9 | 10 | 11 | | | | | | | | | | | | | |
| 1 | 2 | 3 | 4 | 5 | 6 | 7 | 8 | 9 | 10 | 11 | | | | | | | | | | | | | |
| 1 | 2 | 3 | 4 | 5 | 6 | 7 | 8 | 9 | 10 | 11 | | | | | | | | | | | | | |
| 1 | 2 | 3 | 4 | 5 | 6 | | | 9 | 10 | 11 | 7 | *8* | *12* | | | | | | | | | | |
| 1 | 2 | 3 | 4 | 5 | 6 | | 8 | 9 | 10 | 11 | 7 | | | | | | | | | | | | |
| 1 | 2 | 3 | | 5 | 10 | 8 | *12* | 9 | | 11 | 7 | | *4* | 6 | | | | | | | | | |
| 1 | | 3 | | 5 | 6 | *12* | 8 | 9 | 10 | *11* | 7 | | | | 2 | 4 | | | | | | | |
| 1 | 2 | 3 | | 5 | 6 | 11 | | *9* | 10 | | 7 | 8 | | *12* | | | 4 | | | | | | |
| 1 | | 3 | 4 | 5 | 6 | 11 | | 9 | 10 | | 7 | 8 | | | 2 | | | | | | | | |
| 1 | | 3 | 4 | 5 | 6 | | | 9 | | 11 | 7 | 8 | | 10 | 2 | | | | | | | | |
| 1 | 2 | 3 | 4 | *5* | 6 | | 7 | 9 | | 11 | | 8 | | 10 | | | | *12* | | | | | |
| 1 | | | 4 | 5 | 6 | | | 9 | 10 | 11 | 7 | | | | 2 | | | | 3 | 8 | | | |
| 1 | | 3 | 4 | 5 | 6 | | | 9 | 10 | 11 | 7 | | | *12* | 2 | | | | | *8* | | | |
| 1 | | 11 | 4 | 5 | 3 | 8 | 10 | 7 | | | | | | 6 | 2 | | | | | | 9 | | |
| 1 | | 11 | 4 | 5 | 3 | 8 | 10 | 7 | | | | 9 | | 6 | 2 | | | | | | | | |
| 1 | | 3 | 4 | 5 | 6 | 8 | | 7 | | | 11 | 9 | | 10 | 2 | | | | | | | | |
| 1 | | 3 | 4 | 5 | | 11 | | 7 | | | | 10 | | 6 | 2 | | | | | | 9 | 8 | |
| 1 | | 3 | | 5 | 6 | 11 | | 7 | | *12* | | *10* | | 4 | 2 | | | | | | 9 | 8 | |
| 1 | | 3 | | 5 | 6 | 11 | | 7 | | *12* | | 10 | | 4 | 2 | | | | | | *9* | 8 | |
| 1 | | 3 | | 5 | 6 | 11 | | 7 | | | | 10 | | 4 | 2 | | | | | | 9 | 8 | |
| 1 | | 3 | 10 | 5 | 6 | | | 7 | | 11 | | 9 | | 4 | 2 | | | | *12* | | | *8* | |
| 1 | 2 | 3 | | 5 | 6 | | | 9 | | 11 | 7 | 10 | | 4 | | | | | | | | 8 | |
| 1 | | 3 | | 5 | 6 | | | 9 | | 11 | 7 | 10 | | 4 | 2 | | | | | | | 8 | |
| 1 | | 3 | 4 | | 6 | | | 9 | | 11 | 7 | 10 | | 5 | 2 | | | | | | | 8 | |
| 1 | | 3 | 4 | | 6 | | | 9 | | 11 | 7 | 10 | | 5 | 2 | | | | | | | 8 | |
| 1 | | 3 | | 5 | 6 | | | 9 | | 11 | 7 | 10 | | 4 | 2 | | | | | | | 8 | |
| 1 | | 3 | *12* | 5 | 6 | | | 9 | | 11 | 7 | 10 | | 4 | *2* | | | | | | | 8 | |
| 1 | *2* | 3 | *12* | 5 | 6 | | | 9 | | 11 | 7 | 10 | | 4 | | | | | | | | 8 | |
| 1 | | 3 | 4 | 5 | 6 | | | 7 | | 11 | | 10 | | 2 | | | | | | | | 8 | 9 |
| 1 | | 3 | 4 | 5 | 6 | | | 7 | | 11 | *12* | 10 | | 2 | | | | | | | | *8* | 9 |
| 1 | | 3 | *12* | 5 | *6* | | | 10 | | 11 | 7 | | | 4 | 2 | | | | | | | 8 | 9 |
| 1 | | 3 | 4 | 5 | | 10 | | | | 11 | 7 | 8 | | 6 | 2 | | | | | | | | 9 |
| 1 | | 3 | 4 | | 6 | 10 | | | | 11 | 7 | 8 | | 5 | 2 | | | | | | | | 9 |
| 1 | | 3 | 4 | 5 | | 11 | | | | | 7 | 10 | | 6 | 2 | | | | | | | 8 | 9 |
| 1 | | 3 | 4 | 5 | | 10 | | | | 11 | 7 | 8 | | 6 | 2 | | | | | | | | 9 |
| 1 | | 3 | 4 | 5 | | 10 | | 7 | | 11 | | 8 | | 6 | 2 | | | | | | | | 9 |
| | | 3 | 4 | 5 | | 10 | | | | 11 | 7 | 8 | | 6 | 2 | | | | | | 1 | | 9 |
| 1 | | 3 | 4 | 5 | | 10 | | | | 11 | 7 | 8 | | 6 | 2 | | | | | | | | 9 |
| 1 | | 3 | 4 | 5 | | 10 | | | | 11 | 7 | 8 | | 6 | 2 | | | | | | | | 9 |
| 1 | | 3 | 4 | 5 | | 10 | | | | 11 | 7 | 8 | | 6 | 2 | | | | | | | | 9 |
| 1 | | 3 | | 5 | 4 | 10 | | | | 11 | 7 | 8 | | 6 | 2 | | | | | | | | 9 |
| 1 | 4 | 3 | | 5 | 11 | 10 | | | | | 7 | 8 | | 6 | 2 | | | | | | | | 9 |
| 1 | | 3 | 4 | 5 | 11 | 10 | | | | | 7 | 8 | | 6 | 2 | | | | | | | | 9 |
| 1 | | 3 | | 5 | 4 | 10 | | | | 11 | 7 | *8* | | 6 | 2 | | | | | | | *12* | 9 |
| 1 | | 3 | 4 | 5 | 11 | 10 | | | | | 7 | 8 | | 6 | 2 | | | | | | | | 9 |
| 1 | | 3 | 4 | 5 | 11 | 10 | | | | | 7 | 8 | | 6 | 2 | | | | | | | | 9 |
| 45 | 11 | 45 | 31 | 43 | 37 | 28 | 8 | 32 | 10 | 32 | 32 | 36 | 1 | 36 | 34 | 1 | 1 | | 1 | 2 | 6 | 16 | 18 |
| | | | 3 | | | 1 | 1 | | | 2 | 1 | | 1 | 2 | | | | 1 | 1 | | | 1 | |
| | | | | | 2 | 6 | 2 | 11 | | 1 | 4 | 14 | | | 1 | | | | | 1 | 1 | 7 | 9 |
| | | | | | | | | | | | | | | | | | | | | | | | |
| 1 | | 3 | | 5 | 6 | 11 | | 8 | | | 7 | 10 | | 4 | 2 | | | | | | 9 | | |
| 1 | | 1 | | 1 | 1 | 1 | | 1 | | | 1 | 1 | | 1 | 1 | | | | | | 1 | | |
| | | | | | | | | | | | | | | | | | | | | | | | |
| | | | | | | 1 | | | | | | 1 | | | | | | | | | | | |
| | | | | | | | | | | | | | | | | | | | | | | | |
| 1 | 2 | 3 | 4 | 5 | 6 | 7 | 8 | 9 | 10 | 11 | | | | | | | | | | | | | |
| 1 | 2 | 3 | *4* | 5 | 8 | *12* | | 9 | 10 | 11 | 7 | | | 6 | | | | | | | | | |
| 2 | 2 | 2 | 2 | 2 | 2 | 1 | 1 | 2 | 2 | 2 | 1 | | | 1 | | | | | | | | | |
| | | | | | | 1 | | | | | | | | | | | | | | | | | |
| | | | | | | | | 1 | 1 | | | | | | | | | | | | | | |

## League Table

| | P | W | D | L | F | A | Pts |
|---|---|---|---|---|---|---|---|
| Luton Town | 46 | 27 | 12 | 7 | 87 | 44 | 66 |
| Barnsley | 46 | 24 | 13 | 9 | 68 | 46 | 61 |
| Hartlepools United | 46 | 25 | 10 | 11 | 60 | 46 | 60 |
| Crewe Alexandra | 46 | 20 | 18 | 8 | 74 | 49 | 58 |
| Bradford City | 46 | 23 | 11 | 12 | 72 | 51 | 57 |
| Southend United | 46 | 20 | 14 | 12 | 77 | 58 | 54 |
| Chesterfield | 46 | 21 | 11 | 14 | 71 | 50 | 53 |
| Wrexham | 46 | 20 | 13 | 13 | 72 | 53 | 53 |
| Aldershot | 46 | 18 | 17 | 11 | 70 | 55 | 53 |
| Doncaster Rovers | 46 | 18 | 15 | 13 | 66 | 56 | 51 |
| Halifax Town | 46 | 15 | 16 | 15 | 52 | 49 | 46 |
| Newport County | 46 | 16 | 13 | 17 | 58 | 63 | 45 |
| Lincoln City | 46 | 17 | 9 | 20 | 71 | 68 | 43 |
| Brentford | 46 | 18 | 7 | 21 | 61 | 64 | 43 |
| Swansea Town | 46 | 16 | 10 | 20 | 63 | 77 | 42 |
| Darlington | 46 | 12 | 17 | 17 | 47 | 53 | 41 |
| Notts County | 46 | 15 | 11 | 20 | 53 | 79 | 41 |
| Port Vale | 46 | 12 | 15 | 19 | 61 | 72 | 39 |
| Rochdale | 46 | 12 | 14 | 20 | 51 | 72 | 38 |
| Exeter City | 46 | 11 | 16 | 19 | 45 | 65 | 38 |
| York City | 46 | 11 | 14 | 21 | 65 | 68 | 36 |
| Chester | 46 | 9 | 14 | 23 | 57 | 78 | 32 |
| Workington | 46 | 10 | 11 | 25 | 54 | 87 | 31 |
| Bradford Park Avenue | 46 | 4 | 15 | 27 | 30 | 82 | 23 |

# 1968-69

## Division Three

Manager: Angus McLean

### Did you know that?

When 'Pools lost 4–1 at home to Barrow on 1 November it ended a run of 27 consecutive home League games without defeat, which began on 29 September 1967 with a 2–1 win over Barnsley.

John McGovern played his final game for the club on 13 September against Shrewsbury Town before rejoining Brian Clough at Derby County.

| Match No. | Date | Round | Venue | Opponents | | Result | Scorers | Attendance |
|---|---|---|---|---|---|---|---|---|
| 1 | Aug 10 | | (h) | Bournemouth | D | 1 - 1 | Bell | 6,791 |
| 3 | 17 | | (a) | Crewe Alexandra | L | 0 - 1 | | 5,564 |
| 4 | 24 | | (h) | Swindon Town | D | 0 - 0 | | 5,732 |
| 5 | 30 | | (a) | Reading | L | 0 - 7 | | 8,969 |
| 6 | Sep 6 | | (a) | Bristol Rovers | L | 1 - 2 | Wright | 7,284 |
| 7 | 13 | | (h) | Shrewsbury Town | D | 0 - 0 | | 5,348 |
| 8 | 16 | | (h) | Watford | W | 2 - 1 | R.Young, Cummings (pen) | 5,140 |
| 9 | 21 | | (a) | Northampton Town | D | 0 - 0 | | 6,749 |
| 10 | 28 | | (h) | Stockport County | D | 0 - 0 | | 5,336 |
| 11 | Oct 4 | | (h) | Mansfield Town | D | 1 - 1 | R.Young | 5,776 |
| 12 | 9 | | (a) | Plymouth Argyle | L | 0 - 3 | | 7,565 |
| 13 | 12 | | (a) | Luton Town | L | 0 - 3 | | 13,145 |
| 14 | 14 | | (h) | Plymouth Argyle | D | 1 - 1 | Bircumshaw | 4,748 |
| 15 | 18 | | (h) | Barnsley | W | 2 - 1 | R.Young, Blowman | 4,658 |
| 16 | 26 | | (a) | Orient | W | 1 - 0 | Solan | 6,134 |
| 17 | Nov 1 | | (h) | Barrow | L | 1 - 4 | Blowman | 3,086 |
| 18 | 6 | | (h) | Southport | D | 2 - 2 | Blowman 2 | 3,625 |
| 19 | 9 | | (a) | Rotherham United | D | 1 - 1 | Hague (o.g.) | 8,970 |
| 22 | 23 | | (a) | Oldham Athletic | W | 2 - 1 | Blowman 2 | 2,849 |
| 23 | 29 | | (h) | Tranmere Rovers | L | 2 - 4 | R.Young, Cummings | 4,355 |
| 24 | Dec 14 | | (h) | Luton Town | W | 1 - 0 | Blowman | 3,887 |
| 25 | 21 | | (a) | Barnsley | L | 1 - 2 | R.Young | 7,701 |
| 26 | 26 | | (a) | Mansfield Town | L | 0 - 2 | | 6,683 |
| 27 | Jan 4 | | (h) | Torquay United | D | 2 - 2 | Thompson, Atkinson | 3,695 |
| 28 | 11 | | (a) | Barrow | W | 2 - 1 | Bircumshaw, Drysdale | 4,622 |
| 29 | 18 | | (h) | Rotherham United | L | 0 - 3 | | 3,677 |
| 30 | 24 | | (a) | Southport | L | 0 - 3 | | 4,150 |
| 31 | Feb 1 | | (a) | Gillingham | D | 2 - 2 | Thompson, Cummings | 4,885 |
| 32 | 4 | | (a) | Swindon Town | D | 1 - 1 | Thompson | 19,124 |
| 33 | 22 | | (h) | Brighton & Hove Albion | L | 2 - 5 | Thompson, Bell | 2,924 |
| 34 | 25 | | (h) | Oldham Athletic | L | 0 - 2 | | 2,535 |
| 35 | Mar 1 | | (a) | Bournemouth | L | 0 - 4 | | 6,246 |
| 36 | 3 | | (a) | Torquay United | L | 0 - 3 | | 5,903 |
| 37 | 10 | | (h) | Gillingham | D | 1 - 1 | Bell | 2,401 |
| 38 | 19 | | (a) | Brighton & Hove Albion | D | 1 - 1 | Bell | 11,334 |
| 39 | 22 | | (h) | Reading | W | 2 - 0 | Bell 2 | 2,754 |
| 40 | 28 | | (h) | Bristol Rovers | W | 1 - 0 | Parry | 3,447 |
| 41 | Apr 4 | | (h) | Walsall | D | 1 - 1 | R.Young | 6,695 |
| 42 | 5 | | (a) | Stockport County | L | 0 - 1 | | 4,375 |
| 43 | 7 | | (a) | Watford | D | 0 - 0 | | 20,771 |
| 44 | 11 | | (h) | Northampton Town | W | 3 - 0 | Thompson, Bell, Drysdale | 3,729 |
| 45 | 15 | | (a) | Walsall | W | 2 - 1 | Thompson, Blowman | 5,003 |
| 46 | 19 | | (a) | Shrewsbury Town | D | 1 - 1 | Thompson | 7,793 |
| 47 | 21 | | (h) | Orient | D | 0 - 0 | | 4,237 |
| 48 | 24 | | (a) | Tranmere Rovers | L | 0 - 1 | | 2,861 |
| 49 | May 5 | | (h) | Crewe Alexandra | D | 0 - 0 | | 2,035 |

Final Position : 22nd in Division Three - Relegated

Apps.
Sub.Apps.
1 own goal Goals

**FA Cup**

| Match No. | Date | Round | Venue | Opponents | | Result | Scorers | Attendance |
|---|---|---|---|---|---|---|---|---|
| 20 | Nov 16 | R1 | (h) | Rotherham United | D | 1 - 1 | R.Young | 6,579 |
| 21 | 19 | R1r | (a) | Rotherham United | L | 0 - 3 | | 11,518 |

Apps.
Sub.Apps.
Goals

**League Cup**

| Match No. | Date | Round | Venue | Opponents | | Result | Scorers | Attendance |
|---|---|---|---|---|---|---|---|---|
| 2 | Aug 14 | R1 | (a) | Bradford City | L | 2 - 3 | McGovern 2 | 4,183 |

Apps.
Sub.Apps.
Goals

| Smith | Bircumshaw | Drysdale | Sheridan | Gill, J.B.A. | Parry | McGovern | Bell | Cummings | Blowman | Hepplewhite | Goad | Wright | Somers | Atkinson | McLeod | Joyce | Young, R. | Oliver | Solan | Thompson | Tunstall | Allen | Gill, J. | Young, J.D. | Pearson | Gale | Hold |
|---|---|---|---|---|---|---|---|---|---|---|---|---|---|---|---|---|---|---|---|---|---|---|---|---|---|---|---|
| 1 | 2 | 3 | 4 | 5 | 6 | 7 | 8 | 9 | 10 | 11 | | | | | | | | | | | | | | | | | |
| 1 | | 3 | 4 | 5 | 6 | 7 | 8 | 9 | | | 2 | 10 | 11 | | | | | | | | | | | | | | |
| 1 | | 3 | 4 | 5 | 6 | 7 | 8 | 9 | | 11 | 2 | 10 | | | | | | | | | | | | | | | |
| 1 | *2* | 3 | 4 | 5 | | 7 | 8 | 9 | *12* | 11 | 6 | 10 | | | | | | | | | | | | | | | |
| 1 | | 3 | 4 | 5 | | 11 | 8 | 9 | *12* | 6 | 2 | *10* | | 7 | | | | | | | | | | | | | |
| 1 | 2 | 3 | 4 | 5 | | | 8 | 9 | | 11 | | 10 | | | 6 | 7 | | | | | | | | | | | |
| 1 | 2 | 3 | 4 | 5 | | | | 9 | 8 | 6 | | 10 | | | | 7 | 11 | | | | | | | | | | |
| 1 | 2 | 3 | 4 | 5 | | | | 9 | 8 | 6 | | 10 | | | *12* | *7* | 11 | | | | | | | | | | |
| 1 | 2 | 3 | 4 | 5 | | | | 9 | 8 | 6 | | 10 | | 7 | | | 11 | | | | | | | | | | |
| 1 | 2 | 3 | 4 | 5 | | | | 9 | 8 | 6 | | 10 | | 7 | | | 11 | | | | | | | | | | |
| 1 | 2 | 3 | 4 | 5 | 11 | | | 9 | | 6 | | 8 | | *7* | | | 10 | *12* | | | | | | | | | |
| 1 | 2 | 3 | 4 | 5 | | | 10 | 9 | | 11 | 6 | 8 | | | | | 7 | | | | | | | | | | |
| 1 | 2 | 3 | 4 | 5 | | | 10 | 9 | | | 6 | *8* | | 7 | *12* | | 11 | | | | | | | | | | |
| 1 | 2 | 3 | 4 | 5 | | | 10 | *9* | 8 | | 6 | | | 7 | *12* | | 11 | | | | | | | | | | |
| 1 | 2 | 3 | 4 | 5 | | | 9 | *12* | 8 | | 6 | | | *7* | | | 11 | | 10 | | | | | | | | |
| 1 | 2 | 3 | 4 | 5 | | | 8 | 9 | 7 | | 6 | | | | | | 11 | | 10 | | | | | | | | |
| 1 | 2 | 3 | 4 | 5 | | | 9 | | 8 | 11 | 6 | | | | | | 7 | | 10 | | | | | | | | |
| 1 | 2 | 3 | 4 | 9 | | | | | 8 | 11 | 6 | | | | 5 | | 7 | | 10 | | | | | | | | |
| 1 | 2 | 3 | 4 | 5 | 6 | | | 9 | 8 | *12* | | *11* | | | | | 7 | | 10 | | | | | | | | |
| 1 | | 3 | 4 | 5 | 6 | | | 9 | 8 | | 2 | 11 | | | | | 7 | | 10 | | | | | | | | |
| 1 | 2 | | 4 | 5 | 6 | | | 8 | 7 | | 3 | 10 | | | | | 11 | | | 9 | | | | | | | |
| 1 | 2 | 3 | *4* | 5 | 6 | | | 8 | 7 | | | 10 | | | | | 11 | | | 9 | *12* | | | | | | |
| 1 | 2 | 3 | | 5 | 4 | | 8 | | 7 | | 6 | 10 | | | | | 11 | | | 9 | | | | | | | |
| | 2 | 3 | 4 | | 6 | | 8 | | | | | 10 | | 7 | 5 | | 11 | | | 9 | | 1 | | | | | |
| | 2 | 3 | | 5 | 4 | | 8 | | | *12* | 6 | 10 | | | | | 11 | | | 9 | | | 1 | *7* | | | |
| | 2 | 3 | | 5 | 4 | | 8 | | | | 6 | 10 | | | | | 11 | | | 9 | | | 1 | 7 | | | |
| | 2 | 3 | | | 4 | | *12* | | 7 | | 6 | 10 | | | 5 | | 11 | | | 9 | | | 1 | | *8* | | |
| | 2 | 3 | 4 | 5 | 7 | | | 10 | 8 | | 6 | | | | | | 11 | | | 9 | | | 1 | | | | |
| | 2 | 3 | 4 | 5 | 7 | | | 10 | 8 | | 6 | | | | | | 11 | | | 9 | | 1 | | | | | |
| | | 3 | | 5 | 6 | | 8 | | *7* | | 4 | *10* | | | *12* | | 11 | | | 9 | | 1 | | | | 2 | |
| | 2 | 3 | | 5 | 6 | | *8* | | 7 | | 4 | 10 | | | *12* | | 11 | | | 9 | | 1 | | | | | |
| | | 3 | | 5 | 6 | | *12* | 8 | *7* | | 2 | 10 | | | | | 11 | | | 9 | | 1 | | 4 | | | |
| | | 3 | | 5 | 4 | | 7 | 8 | | | 2 | 10 | | | 6 | | 11 | | | 9 | | 1 | | | | | |
| | | 3 | | 5 | 4 | | 7 | 8 | | | 2 | 10 | | | 6 | | 11 | | | 9 | | 1 | | | | | |
| 1 | 2 | 3 | 4 | 5 | 7 | | 8 | 10 | | | 6 | | | | | | 11 | | | 9 | | | | | | | |
| 1 | 2 | 3 | 4 | 5 | 7 | | 8 | 10 | | | 6 | | | | | | 11 | | | 9 | | | | | | | |
| 1 | 2 | 3 | 4 | 5 | 7 | | 8 | 10 | | | 6 | | | | | | 11 | | | 9 | | | | | | | |
| 1 | 2 | 3 | 4 | 5 | 7 | | 8 | 10 | | | 6 | *12* | | | | | *11* | | | 9 | | | | | | | |
| 1 | 2 | 3 | 4 | | 7 | | *8* | 10 | *12* | | 6 | 11 | | | 5 | | | | | 9 | | | | | | | |
| 1 | 2 | 3 | 4 | 5 | 7 | | | 10 | 8 | | 6 | | | | | | 11 | | | 9 | | | | | | | |
| 1 | 2 | 3 | 4 | 5 | 7 | | 8 | | 10 | | 6 | | | | | | 11 | | | 9 | | | | | | | |
| 1 | 2 | 3 | 4 | 5 | 7 | | 8 | | 10 | | 6 | | | | | | 11 | | | 9 | | | | | | | |
| 1 | 2 | 3 | 4 | 5 | 7 | | 8 | *12* | *10* | | 6 | | | | | | 11 | | | 9 | | | | | | | |
| 1 | 2 | 3 | 4 | 5 | 7 | | 8 | *12* | *10* | | 6 | | | | | | 11 | | | 9 | | | | | | | |
| 1 | 2 | 3 | 4 | 5 | 7 | | *8* | *12* | | | 6 | 10 | | | | | 11 | | | 9 | | | | | | | |
| 1 | 2 | 3 | 4 | 5 | 7 | | 8 | | | | 6 | 10 | | | | | 11 | | | 9 | | | | | | | |
| 35 | 38 | 45 | 37 | 43 | 32 | 5 | 31 | 30 | 26 | 13 | 36 | 29 | 1 | 8 | 7 | 3 | 39 | | 6 | 26 | | 7 | 4 | 3 | 1 | 1 | |
| | | | | | | | 2 | 4 | 3 | | | 1 | | | 5 | | | 1 | | | 1 | | | | | | |
| | 2 | 2 | | | 1 | | 7 | 3 | 8 | 2 | | 1 | | 1 | | | 6 | | 1 | 7 | | | | | | | |

| Smith | Bircumshaw | Drysdale | Sheridan | Gill, J.B.A. | Parry | McGovern | Bell | Cummings | Blowman | Hepplewhite | Goad | Wright | Somers | Atkinson | McLeod | Joyce | Young, R. | Oliver | Solan | Thompson | Tunstall | Allen | Gill, J. | Young, J.D. | Pearson | Gale | Hold |
|---|---|---|---|---|---|---|---|---|---|---|---|---|---|---|---|---|---|---|---|---|---|---|---|---|---|---|---|
| 1 | 2 | 3 | 4 | 5 | | | | | 8 | 11 | 6 | | | | | | 7 | | 10 | | | | | | | | 9 |
| 1 | 2 | 3 | | 5 | 6 | | | 9 | 8 | 11 | | | | | 4 | | 7 | | 10 | | | | | | | | |
| 2 | 2 | 2 | 1 | 2 | 1 | | | 1 | 2 | 2 | 1 | | | | 1 | | 2 | | 2 | | | | | | | | 1 |
| | | | | | | | | | | | | | | | | | | | | | | | | | | | |
| | | | | | | | | | | | | | | | | | 1 | | | | | | | | | | |

| Smith | Bircumshaw | Drysdale | Sheridan | Gill, J.B.A. | Parry | McGovern | Bell | Cummings | Blowman | Hepplewhite | Goad | Wright | Somers | Atkinson | McLeod | Joyce | Young, R. | Oliver | Solan | Thompson | Tunstall | Allen | Gill, J. | Young, J.D. | Pearson | Gale | Hold |
|---|---|---|---|---|---|---|---|---|---|---|---|---|---|---|---|---|---|---|---|---|---|---|---|---|---|---|---|
| 1 | 2 | 3 | 4 | 5 | 6 | 7 | 8 | 9 | | | | 10 | 11 | | | | | | | | | | | | | | |
| 1 | 1 | 1 | 1 | 1 | 1 | 1 | 1 | 1 | | | | 1 | 1 | | | | | | | | | | | | | | |
| | | | | | | | | | | | | | | | | | | | | | | | | | | | |
| | | | | | | 2 | | | | | | | | | | | | | | | | | | | | | |

## League Table

| | P | W | D | L | F | A | Pts |
|---|---|---|---|---|---|---|---|
| Watford | 46 | 27 | 10 | 9 | 74 | 34 | 64 |
| Swindon Town | 46 | 27 | 10 | 9 | 71 | 35 | 64 |
| Luton Town | 46 | 25 | 11 | 10 | 74 | 38 | 61 |
| Bournemouth | 46 | 21 | 9 | 16 | 60 | 45 | 51 |
| Plymouth Argyle | 46 | 17 | 15 | 14 | 53 | 49 | 49 |
| Torquay United | 46 | 18 | 12 | 16 | 54 | 46 | 48 |
| Tranmere Rovers | 46 | 19 | 10 | 17 | 70 | 68 | 48 |
| Southport | 46 | 17 | 13 | 16 | 71 | 64 | 47 |
| Stockport County | 46 | 16 | 14 | 16 | 67 | 68 | 46 |
| Barnsley | 46 | 16 | 14 | 16 | 58 | 63 | 46 |
| Rotherham United | 46 | 16 | 13 | 17 | 56 | 50 | 45 |
| Brighton & Hove Albion | 46 | 16 | 13 | 17 | 72 | 65 | 45 |
| Walsall | 46 | 14 | 16 | 16 | 50 | 49 | 44 |
| Reading | 46 | 15 | 13 | 18 | 67 | 66 | 43 |
| Mansfield Town | 46 | 16 | 11 | 19 | 58 | 62 | 43 |
| Bristol Rovers | 46 | 16 | 11 | 19 | 63 | 71 | 43 |
| Shrewsbury Town | 46 | 16 | 11 | 19 | 51 | 67 | 43 |
| Orient | 46 | 14 | 14 | 18 | 51 | 58 | 42 |
| Barrow | 46 | 17 | 8 | 21 | 56 | 75 | 42 |
| Gillingham | 46 | 13 | 15 | 18 | 54 | 63 | 41 |
| Northampton Town | 46 | 14 | 12 | 20 | 54 | 61 | 40 |
| Hartlepool | 46 | 10 | 19 | 17 | 40 | 70 | 39 |
| Crewe Alexandra | 46 | 13 | 9 | 24 | 52 | 76 | 35 |
| Oldham Athletic | 46 | 13 | 9 | 24 | 50 | 83 | 35 |

# 1969-70

## Division Four

Manager: Angus McLean

### Did you know that?

'Pools finished 23rd, losing their last seven games without scoring a single goal. During the season they failed to score in 22 League games. Bottom club Barrow were voted out and replaced by Cambridge United.

Given the dismal results and final League position, seven players were given free transfers: George Smith, Bob Dobbing, Tommy Lee, Andy McCluskey, Derek Tail, Peter Blowman and Malcolm Thompson.

| Match No. | Date | Round | Venue | Opponents | Result | | Scorers | Attendance |
|---|---|---|---|---|---|---|---|---|
| 1 | Aug 9 | | (h) | Brentford | D | 0 - 0 | | 3,020 |
| 3 | 16 | | (a) | Grimsby Town | L | 0 - 2 | | 3,507 |
| 4 | 23 | | (h) | York City | D | 2 - 2 | Bell, Dobbing | 2,990 |
| 5 | 25 | | (h) | Swansea City | W | 3 - 0 | Bell 2, Young | 3,540 |
| 6 | 30 | | (a) | Chesterfield | L | 0 - 3 | | 3,997 |
| 8 | Sep 6 | | (h) | Northampton Town | D | 1 - 1 | Bell | 3,090 |
| 9 | 13 | | (a) | Southend United | W | 2 - 0 | Young, Thompson | 8,271 |
| 10 | 15 | | (a) | Newport County | D | 1 - 1 | Bell | 2,950 |
| 11 | 20 | | (h) | Colchester United | D | 0 - 0 | | 3,627 |
| 12 | 27 | | (a) | Peterborough United | L | 0 - 4 | | 6,872 |
| 13 | Oct 1 | | (a) | Aldershot | L | 1 - 4 | Wright | 5,172 |
| 14 | 4 | | (h) | Oldham Athletic | D | 1 - 1 | Goad | 2,744 |
| 15 | 6 | | (h) | Grimsby Town | L | 0 - 1 | | 2,758 |
| 16 | 11 | | (a) | Chester | L | 1 - 2 | Bell | 4,175 |
| 17 | 18 | | (h) | Bradford Park Avenue | W | 5 - 2 | Kirk 2, Bell 3 | 2,816 |
| 18 | 25 | | (a) | Scunthorpe United | L | 1 - 3 | Kirk | 3,600 |
| 19 | Nov 1 | | (h) | Wrexham | L | 1 - 3 | Thompson | 3,024 |
| 20 | 8 | | (a) | Workington | W | 3 - 1 | Trail, Young, Parry | 1,351 |
| 22 | 22 | | (h) | Crewe Alexandra | D | 1 - 1 | Young | 2,613 |
| 23 | 24 | | (h) | Darlington | L | 1 - 3 | Young | 2,353 |
| 25 | Dec 13 | | (h) | Southend United | W | 2 - 1 | Bell, Bircumshaw (pen) | 1,824 |
| 26 | 20 | | (a) | Northampton Town | W | 1 - 0 | Bell | 2,979 |
| 27 | 26 | | (a) | York City | D | 0 - 0 | | 4,581 |
| 28 | 27 | | (h) | Chesterfield | D | 0 - 0 | | 3,248 |
| 29 | Jan 10 | | (a) | Colchester United | D | 1 - 1 | Kirk | 3,200 |
| 30 | 17 | | (h) | Peterborough United | W | 4 - 2 | Trail, Bell, Young, Goad | 2,382 |
| 31 | 24 | | (a) | Exeter City | L | 0 - 6 | | 4,241 |
| 32 | 31 | | (a) | Oldham Athletic | L | 0 - 1 | | 3,026 |
| 33 | Feb 2 | | (h) | Aldershot | L | 1 - 3 | Bircumshaw (pen) | 2,245 |
| 34 | 7 | | (h) | Chester | L | 1 - 2 | Young | 2,233 |
| 35 | 20 | | (h) | Scunthorpe United | L | 1 - 2 | Wright | 1,555 |
| 36 | 23 | | (a) | Brentford | L | 0 - 3 | | 7,352 |
| 37 | 28 | | (a) | Wrexham | L | 0 - 1 | | 7,071 |
| 38 | Mar 2 | | (h) | Notts County | W | 4 - 0 | Young, Goad 2, Needham (o.g.) | 1,797 |
| 39 | 9 | | (a) | Port Vale | L | 0 - 3 | | 5,456 |
| 40 | 14 | | (h) | Lincoln City | L | 0 - 3 | | 2,555 |
| 41 | 16 | | (h) | Exeter City | W | 2 - 0 | Robson 2 | 1,980 |
| 42 | 21 | | (a) | Notts County | L | 0 - 1 | | 5,313 |
| 43 | 27 | | (h) | Workington | W | 1 - 0 | Young | 2,852 |
| 44 | 28 | | (h) | Port Vale | L | 0 - 2 | | 2,227 |
| 45 | 31 | | (a) | Bradford Park Avenue | L | 0 - 3 | | 2,294 |
| 46 | Apr 4 | | (a) | Swansea City | L | 0 - 3 | | 7,691 |
| 47 | 10 | | (a) | Crewe Alexandra | L | 0 - 3 | | 2,477 |
| 48 | 13 | | (h) | Newport County | L | 0 - 1 | | 1,473 |
| 49 | 18 | | (a) | Lincoln City | L | 0 - 3 | | 3,772 |
| 50 | 22 | | (a) | Darlington | L | 0 - 4 | | 2,259 |

Final Position : 23rd in Division Four

Apps.
Sub.Apps.
1 own goal — Goals

**FA Cup**

| Match No. | Date | Round | Venue | Opponents | Result | | Scorers | Attendance |
|---|---|---|---|---|---|---|---|---|
| 21 | Nov 15 | R1 | (h) | North Shields | W | 3 - 0 | Bell 2, Kirk | 2,713 |
| 24 | Dec 6 | R2 | (h) | Wrexham | L | 0 - 1 | | 2,989 |

Apps.
Sub.Apps.
Goals

**League Cup**

| Match No. | Date | Round | Venue | Opponents | Result | | Scorers | Attendance |
|---|---|---|---|---|---|---|---|---|
| 2 | Aug 12 | R1 | (a) | Scunthorpe United | W | 2 - 0 | R.Young 2 | 2,800 |
| 7 | Sep 7 | R2 | (h) | Derby County | L | 1 - 3 | Bell | 7,700 |

Apps.
Sub.Apps.
Goals

| Smith | White | Dobbing | Sheridan | Parry | Goad | Young, Ron | Lee | Thompson, M. | Wright | Trail | Blowman | Forrest | Gill | Bell | Bircumshaw | Green | Humphreys | Hunter | Kirk | Thompson, K. | McCluskey | Blythe | Boylan | Robson | Walker | McPartland | Young, Roy |
|---|---|---|---|---|---|---|---|---|---|---|---|---|---|---|---|---|---|---|---|---|---|---|---|---|---|---|---|
| 1 | 2 | 3 | 4 | 5 | 6 | 7 | *8* | 9 | 10 | 11 | *12* | | | | | | | | | | | | | | | | |
| 1 | 2 | 3 | 4 | 5 | 6 | 7 | 9 | | 10 | 11 | *8* | *12* | | | | | | | | | | | | | | | |
| 1 | 2 | 3 | 4 | | 6 | 7 | | 9 | 10 | 11 | | | 5 | 8 | | | | | | | | | | | | | |
| 1 | | 3 | 4 | *12* | 6 | 7 | *8* | | 10 | 11 | | | 5 | 9 | 2 | | | | | | | | | | | | |
| 1 | | 3 | 4 | *12* | 6 | 7 | *8* | | 10 | 11 | | | 5 | 9 | 2 | | | | | | | | | | | | |
| 1 | | 3 | 4 | 7 | 6 | 11 | | *12* | 10 | | *8* | | 5 | 9 | 2 | | | | | | | | | | | | |
| 1 | | 3 | 4 | | 6 | 7 | | 8 | 10 | 11 | | | 5 | 9 | 2 | | | | | | | | | | | | |
| 1 | | 3 | 4 | | 6 | 7 | | 8 | 10 | 11 | | | *5* | 9 | 2 | *12* | | | | | | | | | | | |
| 1 | | *3* | 4 | | 6 | 7 | | 8 | 10 | 11 | | | 5 | 9 | 2 | *12* | | | | | | | | | | | |
| 1 | | 3 | 4 | 7 | 6 | | | 8 | 10 | *11* | *12* | | 5 | 9 | 2 | | | | | | | | | | | | |
| 1 | | | 4 | 6 | 3 | | | 8 | 10 | 11 | *7* | | 5 | 9 | 2 | *12* | | | | | | | | | | | |
| 1 | *12* | 3 | 4 | 7 | 6 | | | *8* | 10 | 11 | | | 5 | 9 | 2 | | | | | | | | | | | | |
| 1 | *12* | 3 | 4 | 7 | 6 | | | | 10 | 11 | | 8 | 5 | 9 | *2* | | | | | | | | | | | | |
| | 2 | 3 | | 6 | 4 | | | | 10 | 11 | | 8 | 5 | 9 | | | 1 | 7 | | | | | | | | | |
| | 2 | 3 | | 6 | 4 | | | | 10 | 7 | | 8 | 5 | 9 | | | 1 | | 11 | | | | | | | | |
| | 3 | | | 6 | | | | | 10 | 7 | | 8 | 5 | 9 | 2 | | 1 | | 11 | 4 | | | | | | | |
| | | 3 | | 4 | 6 | 10 | | 8 | | 7 | | | *12* | 9 | 2 | *5* | 1 | | 11 | | | | | | | | |
| 1 | | 3 | | 4 | 6 | 10 | | | | 7 | 8 | | | 9 | 2 | 5 | | | 11 | | | | | | | | |
| 1 | | 3 | | 4 | 6 | 8 | | | *10* | 7 | *12* | | 5 | 9 | 2 | | | | 11 | | | | | | | | |
| 1 | | 3 | | | 6 | 7 | | *12* | | 10 | *8* | | 5 | 9 | 2 | 4 | | | 11 | | | | | | | | |
| 1 | 3 | | | | 6 | 7 | | | | 10 | 8 | | 5 | 9 | 2 | | | | 11 | | 4 | | | | | | |
| 1 | *4* | 3 | | | 6 | 7 | | | | 10 | 8 | | 5 | 9 | 2 | | | | 11 | | *12* | | | | | | |
| 1 | 4 | 3 | | | 6 | 7 | | | | 10 | 8 | | 5 | 9 | 2 | | | | 11 | | | | | | | | |
| 1 | 4 | 3 | | | 6 | 7 | | | | 10 | 8 | | 5 | 9 | 2 | | | | 11 | | | | | | | | |
| 1 | *4* | 3 | | | 6 | 7 | | | | 10 | 8 | | 5 | 9 | 2 | | | | 11 | | *12* | | | | | | |
| 1 | 4 | 3 | | | 6 | 7 | | | | 10 | 8 | | 5 | 9 | 2 | | | | 11 | | | | | | | | |
| 1 | 4 | 3 | | | 6 | 7 | | | | 10 | 8 | | 5 | 9 | 2 | | | | 11 | | | | | | | | |
| 1 | 3 | | | | 6 | 7 | | | | 10 | 8 | | 5 | 9 | 2 | | | | 11 | | 4 | | | | | | |
| 1 | 3 | | | 4 | 6 | 7 | | | 10 | *12* | | | 5 | 9 | 2 | | | | 11 | | | *8* | | | | | |
| 1 | *4* | | | 6 | 3 | 7 | | | *12* | 10 | 8 | | 5 | 9 | 2 | | | | 11 | | | | | | | | |
| 1 | *4* | | | 6 | 3 | 8 | | | 10 | 7 | | | 5 | 9 | 2 | | | | 11 | | | | *12* | | | | |
| 1 | | | | 6 | 3 | 8 | | *12* | 10 | *7* | | | 5 | 9 | 2 | | | | 11 | | | | 4 | | | | |
| 1 | | 3 | | 4 | 8 | 7 | | | | 10 | | | 5 | | 2 | | | | 11 | | | | 6 | 9 | | | |
| 1 | | 3 | | 4 | 8 | 7 | | | | 10 | | | 5 | | 2 | | | | 11 | | | | 6 | 9 | | | |
| 1 | | 3 | | 4 | 8 | 7 | | | | | | | 5 | | 2 | | | | 11 | | | | 6 | 9 | 10 | | |
| 1 | | 3 | | 6 | 8 | 7 | | | | *12* | | | 5 | | 2 | | | | 11 | | | | *4* | 9 | 10 | | |
| | | 3 | | 4 | 6 | 11 | | 8 | | 7 | | | 5 | | 2 | | | | | | | | | 9 | 10 | 1 | |
| | | 3 | | 4 | 6 | 11 | | 8 | | *7* | | | 5 | | 2 | | | | *12* | | | | | 9 | 10 | 1 | |
| | | 3 | | *4* | 6 | 7 | | 9 | | | *12* | | 5 | | 2 | | | | 11 | | | | | 8 | 10 | 1 | |
| | | 3 | | | 6 | 7 | | 9 | | 10 | | | 5 | | 2 | | | | 11 | | | | | 8 | 4 | 1 | |
| | | 3 | | | 8 | 7 | | 9 | | *12* | | | 5 | | 2 | 6 | | | 11 | | | | 4 | | *10* | 1 | |
| | 2 | 3 | | | | 7 | | 9 | | | | | 5 | | | 6 | | | 11 | | 10 | | 4 | | 8 | 1 | |
| | 3 | | | 6 | 4 | | | 9 | | | | | 5 | | 2 | | | | 11 | | 10 | | 8 | | 7 | 1 | |
| | 3 | | | 6 | 8 | | | | | 7 | | | 5 | | 2 | 4 | | | 11 | | | | 9 | | 10 | 1 | |
| | 3 | | | 10 | 6 | 7 | 9 | | | | 8 | | 5 | | 2 | 4 | | | 11 | | | | | | | 1 | |
| | 3 | | | 10 | 6 | 7 | 8 | 9 | | | *12* | | 5 | | 2 | 4 | | | *11* | | | | | | | 1 | |
| 32 | 22 | 34 | 13 | 28 | 44 | 37 | 6 | 17 | 20 | 36 | 15 | 4 | 42 | 30 | 40 | 8 | 4 | 1 | 30 | 1 | 4 | 1 | 9 | 8 | 10 | 10 | |
| | 2 | | | 2 | | | | 3 | 1 | 3 | 5 | 1 | 1 | | | 3 | | | 1 | | 2 | | 1 | | | | |
| | | 1 | | 1 | 4 | 9 | | 2 | 2 | 2 | | | | 12 | 2 | | | | 4 | | | | | 2 | | | |

| Smith | White | Dobbing | Sheridan | Parry | Goad | Young, Ron | Lee | Thompson, M. | Wright | Trail | Blowman | Forrest | Gill | Bell | Bircumshaw | Green | Humphreys | Hunter | Kirk | Thompson, K. | McCluskey | Blythe | Boylan | Robson | Walker | McPartland | Young, Roy |
|---|---|---|---|---|---|---|---|---|---|---|---|---|---|---|---|---|---|---|---|---|---|---|---|---|---|---|---|
| 1 | | 3 | | 4 | 6 | 8 | | | 10 | 7 | | | 5 | 9 | 2 | *12* | | | 11 | | | | | | | | |
| 1 | | 3 | | 4 | 6 | 7 | | *12* | | 10 | 8 | | 5 | 9 | 2 | | | | 11 | | | | | | | | |
| 2 | | 2 | | 2 | 2 | 2 | | | 1 | 2 | 1 | | 2 | 2 | 2 | | | | 2 | | | | | | | | |
| | | | | | | | | 1 | | | | | | | | 1 | | | | | | | | | | | |
| | | | | | | | | | | | | | | 2 | | | | | 1 | | | | | | | | |

| Smith | White | Dobbing | Sheridan | Parry | Goad | Young, Ron | Lee | Thompson, M. | Wright | Trail | Blowman | Forrest | Gill | Bell | Bircumshaw | Green | Humphreys | Hunter | Kirk | Thompson, K. | McCluskey | Blythe | Boylan | Robson | Walker | McPartland | Young, Roy |
|---|---|---|---|---|---|---|---|---|---|---|---|---|---|---|---|---|---|---|---|---|---|---|---|---|---|---|---|
| 1 | 2 | 3 | 4 | 5 | 6 | 7 | 8 | 9 | 10 | | | | | | | | | | | | | | | | | | 11 |
| 1 | | 3 | 4 | 7 | 6 | 11 | | 8 | 10 | | | | 5 | 9 | 2 | | | | | | | | | | | | |
| 2 | 1 | 2 | 2 | 2 | 2 | 2 | 1 | 2 | 2 | | | | 1 | 1 | 1 | | | | | | | | | | | | 1 |
| | | | | | | | | | | | | | | | | | | | | | | | | | | | |
| | | | | | | | | | | | | | | 1 | | | | | | | | | | | | | 2 |

## League Table

| | P | W | D | L | F | A | Pts |
|---|---|---|---|---|---|---|---|
| Chesterfield | 46 | 27 | 10 | 9 | 77 | 32 | 64 |
| Wrexham | 46 | 26 | 9 | 11 | 84 | 49 | 61 |
| Swansea Town | 46 | 21 | 18 | 7 | 66 | 45 | 60 |
| Port Vale | 46 | 20 | 19 | 7 | 61 | 33 | 59 |
| Brentford | 46 | 20 | 16 | 10 | 58 | 39 | 56 |
| Aldershot | 46 | 20 | 13 | 13 | 78 | 65 | 53 |
| Notts County | 46 | 22 | 8 | 16 | 73 | 62 | 52 |
| Lincoln City | 46 | 17 | 16 | 13 | 66 | 52 | 50 |
| Peterborough United | 46 | 17 | 14 | 15 | 77 | 69 | 48 |
| Colchester United | 46 | 17 | 14 | 15 | 64 | 63 | 48 |
| Chester | 46 | 21 | 6 | 19 | 58 | 66 | 48 |
| Scunthorpe United | 46 | 18 | 10 | 18 | 67 | 65 | 46 |
| York City | 46 | 16 | 14 | 16 | 55 | 62 | 46 |
| Northampton Town | 46 | 16 | 12 | 18 | 64 | 55 | 44 |
| Crewe Alexandra | 46 | 16 | 12 | 18 | 51 | 51 | 44 |
| Grimsby Town | 46 | 14 | 15 | 17 | 54 | 58 | 43 |
| Southend United | 46 | 15 | 10 | 21 | 59 | 85 | 40 |
| Exeter City | 46 | 14 | 11 | 21 | 57 | 59 | 39 |
| Oldham Athletic | 46 | 13 | 13 | 20 | 60 | 65 | 39 |
| Workington | 46 | 12 | 14 | 20 | 46 | 64 | 38 |
| Newport County | 46 | 13 | 11 | 22 | 53 | 74 | 37 |
| Darlington | 46 | 13 | 10 | 23 | 53 | 73 | 36 |
| Hartlepool | 46 | 10 | 10 | 26 | 42 | 82 | 30 |
| Bradford Park Avenue | 46 | 6 | 11 | 29 | 41 | 96 | 23 |

# 1970-71

## Division Four

Managers: John Simpson and Len Ashurst

### Did you know that?

'Pools only manage to score six goals in away games all season, the last being at Scunthorpe on 23 January. This resulted in United drawing a blank in the remaining 11 away games to the end of the campaign.

Harry Kirk became the first substitute to score for the club when, on replacing Ron Young, he netted in the 2–1 defeat at Stockport County.

Average home League attendances reached a low of 2,459.

| Match No. | Date | Round | Venue | Opponents | Result | | Scorers | Attendance |
|---|---|---|---|---|---|---|---|---|
| 1 | Aug 15 | | (a) | Colchester United | L | 0 - 1 | | 4,866 |
| 3 | 22 | | (h) | Workington | D | 1 - 1 | Wilson (o.g.) | 2,945 |
| 4 | 29 | | (a) | Grimsby Town | D | 1 - 1 | Sharkey | 4,456 |
| 5 | 31 | | (h) | Darlington | D | 2 - 2 | Wright, Crook | 5,032 |
| 6 | Sep 5 | | (h) | Barrow | W | 2 - 1 | Sharkey, Bircumshaw (pen) | 3,667 |
| 7 | 11 | | (a) | Stockport County | L | 1 - 2 | Kirk | 4,146 |
| 8 | 19 | | (h) | Aldershot | D | 1 - 1 | Bircumshaw (pen) | 3,262 |
| 9 | 21 | | (h) | Southend United | L | 0 - 1 | | 3,755 |
| 10 | 26 | | (a) | Cambridge United | L | 0 - 2 | | 5,225 |
| 11 | 30 | | (h) | Notts County | W | 2 - 1 | Young, Crook | 2,772 |
| 12 | Oct 3 | | (h) | Newport County | D | 2 - 2 | Crook, Bircumshaw (pen) | 3,247 |
| 13 | 10 | | (a) | Exeter City | D | 1 - 1 | Bircumshaw | 4,857 |
| 14 | 17 | | (h) | Colchester United | L | 1 - 2 | Sharkey | 2,930 |
| 15 | 21 | | (a) | Crewe Alexandra | L | 0 - 1 | | 2,031 |
| 16 | 24 | | (h) | Southport | L | 1 - 2 | Sharkey | 2,174 |
| 17 | 31 | | (a) | Northampton Town | L | 0 - 2 | | 6,049 |
| 18 | Nov 7 | | (h) | Peterborough United | L | 1 - 2 | Sharkey | 2,038 |
| 19 | 9 | | (h) | Oldham Athletic | L | 0 - 1 | | 1,762 |
| 20 | 14 | | (a) | Bournemouth | L | 0 - 3 | | 5,801 |
| 22 | 28 | | (a) | Chester | W | 1 - 0 | Sharkey | 4,471 |
| 23 | Dec 5 | | (h) | Lincoln City | D | 0 - 0 | | 1,965 |
| 24 | 19 | | (a) | Workington | W | 1 - 0 | Sharkey | 2,316 |
| 25 | 25 | | (h) | York City | W | 2 - 1 | Lees, Young | 2,368 |
| 26 | Jan 9 | | (a) | Notts County | L | 0 - 3 | | 11,540 |
| 27 | 16 | | (h) | Crewe Alexandra | L | 0 - 2 | | 1,989 |
| 28 | 23 | | (a) | Scunthorpe United | L | 1 - 2 | Sharkey | 3,867 |
| 29 | 30 | | (h) | Chester | L | 0 - 2 | | 1,332 |
| 30 | Feb 6 | | (a) | Lincoln City | L | 0 - 2 | | 3,993 |
| 31 | 13 | | (h) | Scunthorpe United | D | 1 - 1 | Bircumshaw | 1,267 |
| 32 | 24 | | (a) | Brentford | L | 0 - 1 | | 9,246 |
| 33 | 27 | | (h) | Northampton Town | D | 2 - 2 | Thompson, Dawes | 1,288 |
| 34 | Mar 5 | | (a) | Southport | L | 0 - 5 | | 1,436 |
| 35 | 10 | | (a) | Southend United | L | 0 - 2 | | 3,839 |
| 36 | 13 | | (h) | Bournemouth | W | 2 - 1 | Bircumshaw, Young | 2,111 |
| 37 | 15 | | (h) | Brentford | D | 0 - 0 | | 2,936 |
| 38 | 20 | | (a) | Peterborough United | L | 0 - 5 | | 3,881 |
| 39 | 27 | | (a) | Barrow | L | 0 - 3 | | 1,776 |
| 40 | 30 | | (a) | Oldham Athletic | L | 0 - 2 | | 9,116 |
| 41 | Apr 3 | | (h) | Grimsby Town | D | 2 - 2 | Young, Green | 1,734 |
| 42 | 9 | | (h) | Stockport County | W | 3 - 0 | Veart 2, Young | 2,702 |
| 43 | 10 | | (a) | York City | L | 0 - 4 | | 7,734 |
| 44 | 13 | | (a) | Newport County | L | 0 - 2 | | 3,173 |
| 45 | 17 | | (h) | Exeter City | W | 3 - 0 | Wright 2, Veart | 1,525 |
| 46 | 24 | | (a) | Aldershot | L | 0 - 1 | | 3,687 |
| 47 | 26 | | (a) | Darlington | L | 0 - 2 | | 2,234 |
| 48 | May 1 | | (h) | Cambridge United | D | 0 - 0 | | 1,767 |

Final Position : 23rd in Division Four

Apps.
Sub.Apps.
1 own goal — Goals

**FA Cup**

| | | | | | | | | |
|---|---|---|---|---|---|---|---|---|
| 21 | Nov 21 | R1 | (a) | Rhyl | L | 0 - 1 | | 3,000 |

Apps.
Sub.Apps.
Goals

**League Cup**

| | | | | | | | | |
|---|---|---|---|---|---|---|---|---|
| 2 | Aug 19 | R1 | (h) | York City | L | 2 - 3 | Young, Sharkey | 3,734 |

Apps.
Sub.Apps.
Goals

| McPartland | Goad | White | Clarke | Parry | Crook | Young | Herd | Sharkey | Wright | Kirk | Green | Barlow | Bircumshaw | Forrest | Dawes | Gill | Ellison | Veart | Lees | Bradbury | Thompson | Hunter | Ashurst | Henderson | Harvey |
|---|---|---|---|---|---|---|---|---|---|---|---|---|---|---|---|---|---|---|---|---|---|---|---|---|---|
| 1 | 2 | 3 | 4 | 5 | 6 | 7 | 8 | 9 | 10 | 11 | | | | | | | | | | | | | | | |
| 1 | 2 | 3 | 6 | 4 | 10 | | 8 | 11 | 9 | | 5 | *7* | *12* | | | | | | | | | | | | |
| 1 | 3 | 11 | 7 | 4 | 6 | | 8 | 10 | | | 5 | *9* | 2 | *12* | | | | | | | | | | | |
| 1 | *3* | 11 | 8 | 4 | 6 | | 7 | 9 | 10 | | 5 | *12* | 2 | | | | | | | | | | | | |
| 1 | | 3 | 10 | 4 | 6 | *7* | 8 | 11 | 9 | *12* | 5 | | 2 | | | | | | | | | | | | |
| 1 | | | 11 | 4 | 6 | *7* | 8 | 9 | 10 | *12* | 5 | | 2 | | 3 | | | | | | | | | | |
| *1* | | | 10 | 4 | 6 | *12* | 8 | 7 | 9 | 11 | 5 | | 2 | | 3 | | | | | | | | | | |
| 1 | | | 10 | 4 | 6 | *12* | 8 | 7 | *9* | 11 | 5 | | 2 | | 3 | | | | | | | | | | |
| 1 | | | 6 | 4 | *12* | 7 | *8* | 10 | | 11 | 5 | 9 | 2 | | 3 | | | | | | | | | | |
| 1 | | | 10 | *8* | 6 | 7 | *12* | 9 | | 11 | 5 | | 2 | | 3 | 4 | | | | | | | | | |
| 1 | | | 10 | *8* | 6 | 7 | *12* | 9 | | 11 | 5 | | 2 | | 3 | 4 | | | | | | | | | |
| 1 | | | 10 | 8 | 6 | 7 | | 9 | | 11 | 5 | | 2 | | 3 | 4 | | | | | | | | | |
| 1 | | | 10 | 8 | 6 | 7 | *12* | 9 | | 11 | 5 | | *2* | | 3 | 4 | | | | | | | | | |
| 1 | | 2 | 10 | 8 | 6 | 7 | | 9 | | 11 | 5 | | | | 3 | 4 | | | | | | | | | |
| 1 | | 2 | 4 | 8 | 6 | 7 | | 9 | | 11 | | | | | 3 | 5 | 10 | | | | | | | | |
| 1 | 3 | *2* | 10 | 8 | 6 | 7 | *12* | 9 | | | 5 | | | | | 4 | 11 | | | | | | | | |
| 1 | 3 | | *12* | *8* | | 11 | 7 | 9 | | | 5 | | 2 | | 6 | 4 | 10 | | | | | | | | |
| 1 | 6 | 3 | | *12* | | | | 9 | | 11 | 5 | | 2 | | 10 | 4 | 8 | *7* | | | | | | | |
| 1 | 3 | | *12* | 7 | 6 | | | 9 | | 11 | 5 | | 2 | | *10* | 4 | 8 | | | | | | | | |
| 1 | 10 | | | 8 | 6 | 11 | | 7 | 9 | | 5 | | 2 | | 3 | 4 | | | | | | | | | |
| 1 | 10 | | | 8 | 6 | 11 | | 7 | 9 | | 5 | | 2 | | 3 | 4 | | | | | | | | | |
| 1 | 10 | | | 8 | 6 | 11 | | 7 | 9 | | 5 | | 2 | | 3 | 4 | | | | | | | | | |
| 1 | 10 | | | 8 | | 11 | | 7 | 9 | | 5 | | 2 | | 3 | 4 | | | 6 | | | | | | |
| 1 | 6 | | 7 | | | 11 | | 9 | 10 | | 5 | | 2 | | 3 | 4 | | | 8 | | | | | | |
| 1 | | | | 8 | 6 | 11 | | 7 | 9 | | 5 | | 2 | | 3 | 4 | | | 10 | | | | | | |
| 1 | 6 | | | 8 | *12* | 11 | | 7 | *10* | | 5 | | 2 | | 3 | 4 | | | 9 | | | | | | |
| 1 | 7 | | *12* | 8 | | 11 | | 10 | | | 5 | | 2 | | 3 | 4 | | | 9 | *6* | | | | | |
| 1 | 4 | 3 | | | 6 | 11 | | *10* | | | 5 | | 7 | | 2 | *12* | | | 8 | | 9 | | | | |
| 1 | 4 | 3 | | 8 | 6 | 11 | | | | | 5 | | 7 | | 2 | 9 | | | | | 10 | | | | |
| 1 | 4 | *6* | | | | 11 | | | | | 5 | *12* | 2 | | 3 | 9 | | | 7 | 10 | | 8 | | | |
| 1 | 4 | | | | | 11 | | 7 | | | 5 | *10* | 2 | | 3 | *12* | | | 8 | 6 | 9 | | | | |
| 1 | 4 | | | | | 11 | | 7 | | | 5 | | 2 | | 3 | 9 | | | 8 | 6 | 10 | | | | |
| 1 | 4 | | | | | 11 | | 7 | 9 | | 5 | | 2 | | *12* | *10* | | | 8 | 6 | | | 3 | | |
| 1 | 4 | | | 10 | | 11 | | 7 | 9 | | 5 | | 2 | | 8 | | | | | 6 | | | 3 | | |
| 1 | 4 | | | 10 | | 11 | | 7 | 9 | | 5 | | 2 | | 8 | | | *12* | | *6* | | | 3 | | |
| 1 | 4 | | | 10 | | | | 8 | 9 | | 5 | | 2 | | 6 | | | 7 | 11 | | | | 3 | | |
| 1 | 4 | | | 10 | | | | 8 | 9 | | 5 | | 2 | | 6 | | | 7 | 11 | | | | 3 | | |
| 1 | 4 | | 11 | *10* | | *12* | | 8 | | | 5 | | 2 | | 3 | | | 7 | 6 | | | | | 9 | |
| 1 | 4 | | *11* | | | *12* | | 8 | 9 | | 5 | | 2 | | 10 | | | 7 | 6 | | | | 3 | | |
| 1 | 4 | | 11 | 10 | | 7 | | *8* | *12* | | 5 | | 2 | | | | | 9 | 6 | | | | 3 | | |
| 1 | 4 | 2 | 11 | 8 | | *7* | | | | | 5 | | *12* | | | | | 10 | 6 | | 9 | | 3 | | |
| 1 | | | | 10 | 8 | 11 | | | | | 5 | *7* | 2 | | | 4 | | 9 | 6 | | | | 3 | | *12* |
| 1 | | 2 | | 10 | | 11 | | | 8 | | 5 | | *12* | | | 4 | | 9 | 6 | | | | 3 | | *7* |
| 1 | | | | 4 | | 10 | | | 8 | | 5 | 11 | | | | 2 | | 9 | 6 | | | | 3 | | 7 |
| 1 | | 2 | | 4 | | 11 | | | | | 5 | 8 | | | 10 | | | 9 | 6 | | | | 3 | | 7 |
| 1 | | 2 | 11 | | | 10 | | | 7 | | 5 | 8 | | | 6 | *4* | | 9 | | | | | 3 | | *12* |
| 46 | 29 | 16 | 22 | 37 | 23 | 35 | 10 | 38 | 23 | 12 | 44 | 8 | 36 | | 34 | 26 | 5 | 12 | 20 | 7 | 5 | 1 | 13 | 1 | 3 |
| | | | 3 | 1 | 2 | 4 | 4 | | 1 | 2 | | 2 | 3 | 1 | 1 | 2 | | 1 | | | | | | | 2 |
| | | | | | 3 | 5 | | 9 | 3 | 1 | 1 | | 6 | | 1 | | | 3 | 1 | | 1 | | | | |

| McPartland | Goad | White | Clarke | Parry | Crook | Young | Herd | Sharkey | Wright | Kirk | Green | Barlow | Bircumshaw | Forrest | Dawes | Gill | Ellison | Veart | Lees | Bradbury | Thompson | Hunter | Ashurst | Henderson | Harvey |
|---|---|---|---|---|---|---|---|---|---|---|---|---|---|---|---|---|---|---|---|---|---|---|---|---|---|
| 1 | 3 | *12* | 10 | 8 | 6 | 7 | | 9 | | | 5 | | 2 | | *11* | 4 | | | | | | | | | |
| 1 | 1 | | 1 | 1 | 1 | 1 | | 1 | | | 1 | | 1 | | 1 | 1 | | | | | | | | | |
| | | 1 | | | | | | | | | | | | | | | | | | | | | | | |
| | | | | | | | | | | | | | | | | | | | | | | | | | |

| McPartland | Goad | White | Clarke | Parry | Crook | Young | Herd | Sharkey | Wright | Kirk | Green | Barlow | Bircumshaw | Forrest | Dawes | Gill | Ellison | Veart | Lees | Bradbury | Thompson | Hunter | Ashurst | Henderson | Harvey |
|---|---|---|---|---|---|---|---|---|---|---|---|---|---|---|---|---|---|---|---|---|---|---|---|---|---|
| 1 | 2 | 3 | 4 | 5 | 6 | 11 | 8 | 7 | 9 | | | | | | 10 | | | | | | | | | | |
| 1 | 1 | 1 | 1 | 1 | 1 | 1 | 1 | 1 | 1 | | | | | | 1 | | | | | | | | | | |
| | | | | | | | | | | | | | | | | | | | | | | | | | |
| | | | | | | 1 | | 1 | | | | | | | | | | | | | | | | | |

## League Table

| | P | W | D | L | F | A | Pts |
|---|---|---|---|---|---|---|---|
| Notts County | 46 | 30 | 9 | 7 | 89 | 36 | 69 |
| Bournemouth | 46 | 24 | 12 | 10 | 81 | 46 | 60 |
| Oldham Athletic | 46 | 24 | 11 | 11 | 88 | 63 | 59 |
| York City | 46 | 23 | 10 | 13 | 78 | 54 | 56 |
| Chester | 46 | 24 | 7 | 15 | 69 | 55 | 55 |
| Colchester United | 46 | 21 | 12 | 13 | 70 | 54 | 54 |
| Northampton Town | 46 | 19 | 13 | 14 | 63 | 59 | 51 |
| Southport | 46 | 21 | 6 | 19 | 63 | 57 | 48 |
| Exeter City | 46 | 17 | 14 | 15 | 67 | 68 | 48 |
| Workington | 46 | 18 | 12 | 16 | 48 | 49 | 48 |
| Stockport County | 46 | 16 | 14 | 16 | 49 | 65 | 46 |
| Darlington | 46 | 17 | 11 | 18 | 58 | 57 | 45 |
| Aldershot | 46 | 14 | 17 | 15 | 66 | 71 | 45 |
| Brentford | 46 | 18 | 8 | 20 | 66 | 62 | 44 |
| Crewe Alexandra | 46 | 18 | 8 | 20 | 75 | 76 | 44 |
| Peterborough United | 46 | 18 | 7 | 21 | 70 | 71 | 43 |
| Scunthorpe United | 46 | 15 | 13 | 18 | 56 | 61 | 43 |
| Southend United | 46 | 14 | 15 | 17 | 53 | 66 | 43 |
| Grimsby Town | 46 | 18 | 7 | 21 | 57 | 71 | 43 |
| Cambridge United | 46 | 15 | 13 | 18 | 51 | 66 | 43 |
| Lincoln City | 46 | 13 | 13 | 20 | 70 | 71 | 39 |
| Newport County | 46 | 10 | 8 | 28 | 55 | 85 | 28 |
| Hartlepool | 46 | 8 | 12 | 26 | 34 | 74 | 28 |
| Barrow | 46 | 7 | 8 | 31 | 51 | 90 | 22 |

# 1971-72

## Division Four

Manager: Len Ashurst

### Did you know that?

When player-manager Len Ashurst scored at Stockport on 1 October, he ended a run of 14 consecutive away League games without a goal.

Following the departure of George Herd as an 'economy measure', Len Ashurst fulfilled the roles of manager, player, coach and trainer!

In February 'Pools players recorded a song Never Say Die, written by Ed Welch and Richard Ogden. It was hoped the record sales would raise some urgently needed cash for the club. In the event, it sold well locally but was largely ignored by the national radio stations.

| Match No. | Date | Round | Venue | Opponents | Result | | Scorers | Attendance |
|---|---|---|---|---|---|---|---|---|
| 1 | Aug 14 | | (h) | Reading | W | 3 - 1 | Ellis 2 (2 pens), Young | 2,470 |
| 3 | 20 | | (a) | Colchester United | L | 0 - 1 | | 5,672 |
| 5 | 28 | | (h) | Southend United | D | 2 - 2 | Young 2 | 5,479 |
| 6 | 30 | | (h) | Darlington | L | 2 - 3 | Veart 2 | 7,158 |
| 7 | Sep 4 | | (a) | Brentford | L | 0 - 6 | | 8,712 |
| 8 | 11 | | (h) | Workington | L | 1 - 3 | Wood (o.g.) | 3,182 |
| 9 | 18 | | (a) | Gillingham | L | 0 - 1 | | 5,477 |
| 10 | 25 | | (h) | Barrow | W | 4 - 3 | Ellis, Welsh, Green, Warnock | 2,641 |
| 11 | 27 | | (h) | Peterborough United | W | 1 - 0 | Warnock | 3,487 |
| 12 | Oct 1 | | (a) | Stockport County | L | 1 - 2 | Ashurst | 2,573 |
| 13 | 9 | | (h) | Newport County | L | 0 - 1 | | 3,010 |
| 14 | 16 | | (a) | Reading | L | 0 - 3 | | 3,176 |
| 15 | 19 | | (a) | Bury | D | 1 - 1 | Warnock | 2,849 |
| 16 | 23 | | (a) | Chester | L | 0 - 4 | | 3,466 |
| 17 | 30 | | (h) | Aldershot | L | 0 - 1 | | 2,197 |
| 18 | Nov 6 | | (a) | Grimsby Town | L | 2 - 3 | Ellis, Sharkey | 8,709 |
| 19 | 13 | | (h) | Doncaster Rovers | D | 0 - 0 | | 2,129 |
| 21 | 27 | | (h) | Crewe Alexandra | W | 1 - 0 | Veart | 2,599 |
| 22 | Dec 4 | | (a) | Northampton Town | L | 1 - 2 | Welsh | 4,507 |
| 24 | 18 | | (h) | Brentford | L | 1 - 2 | Sharkey | 2,199 |
| 25 | 27 | | (a) | Scunthorpe United | D | 2 - 2 | Sharkey, Young | 7,270 |
| 26 | Jan 1 | | (h) | Gillingham | W | 3 - 1 | Young 2, Spelman | 2,932 |
| 27 | 7 | | (a) | Southend United | L | 1 - 3 | Young | 6,505 |
| 28 | 15 | | (h) | Cambridge United | L | 1 - 2 | Green | 2,396 |
| 29 | 22 | | (a) | Peterborough United | D | 2 - 2 | Young, Ward | 4,525 |
| 30 | 29 | | (h) | Bury | W | 3 - 1 | Warnock, Veart 2 | 2,128 |
| 31 | Feb 5 | | (a) | Lincoln City | L | 1 - 2 | Young | 7,261 |
| 32 | 12 | | (h) | Chester | W | 2 - 1 | Young 2 | 2,718 |
| 33 | 19 | | (a) | Aldershot | L | 0 - 2 | | 2,760 |
| 34 | 26 | | (h) | Grimsby Town | L | 0 - 1 | | 3,194 |
| 35 | Mar 4 | | (a) | Doncaster Rovers | L | 1 - 2 | Young | 2,571 |
| 36 | 10 | | (a) | Newport County | W | 2 - 0 | Ashurst, Sharkey | 3,170 |
| 37 | 15 | | (a) | Cambridge United | L | 1 - 2 | Waddell | 3,619 |
| 38 | 18 | | (h) | Colchester United | W | 3 - 2 | Waddell, Smith (pen), Young | 2,729 |
| 39 | 25 | | (a) | Workington | D | 0 - 0 | | 2,147 |
| 40 | 27 | | (h) | Exeter City | W | 1 - 0 | Veart | 3,501 |
| 41 | 31 | | (h) | Stockport County | W | 5 - 0 | Green, Young 2, Waddell, Smith | 5,537 |
| 42 | Apr 1 | | (h) | Scunthorpe United | W | 1 - 0 | Young | 6,197 |
| 43 | 3 | | (a) | Barrow | L | 0 - 2 | | 2,717 |
| 44 | 8 | | (h) | Lincoln City | W | 2 - 1 | Potter, Young | 5,975 |
| 45 | 10 | | (h) | Southport | W | 1 - 0 | Young | 6,472 |
| 46 | 15 | | (a) | Crewe Alexandra | W | 2 - 1 | Waddell 2 | 1,686 |
| 47 | 19 | | (a) | Exeter City | L | 0 - 1 | | 3,791 |
| 48 | 22 | | (h) | Northampton Town | W | 2 - 0 | Waddell, Potter | 6,907 |
| 49 | 24 | | (a) | Darlington | W | 2 - 1 | Green, Waddell | 8,809 |
| 50 | 28 | | (a) | Southport | L | 0 - 1 | | 1,550 |

Final Position : 18th in Division Four

Apps.
Sub.Apps.
Goals

**FA Cup**

| Match No. | Date | Round | Venue | Opponents | Result | | Scorers | Attendance |
|---|---|---|---|---|---|---|---|---|
| 20 | Nov 20 | R1 | (h) | Scarborough | W | 6 - 1 | Ellis,Young 2, Warnock, Veart 2 | 3,374 |
| 23 | Dec 11 | R2 | (a) | Boston United | L | 1 - 2 | Veart | 4,400 |

Apps.
Sub.Apps.
1 own goal Goals

**League Cup**

| Match No. | Date | Round | Venue | Opponents | Result | | Scorers | Attendance |
|---|---|---|---|---|---|---|---|---|
| 2 | Aug 18 | R1 | (a) | Barnsley | D | 0 - 0 | | 5,985 |
| 4 | 23 | R1r | (h) | Barnsley | L | 0 - 1 | | 9,577 |

Apps.
Sub.Apps.
Goals

| Gadsby | White | Ashurst | Goad | Green | Potter | Welsh | Young | Ellis | Clarke | Warnock | Veart | Parry | Dawes | Parkinson | Sharkey | Kelly | Spelman | Smith | Boylan | Ross | Noble | Nesbitt | Hillyard | Ward | Waddell |
|---|---|---|---|---|---|---|---|---|---|---|---|---|---|---|---|---|---|---|---|---|---|---|---|---|---|
|1|2|3|4|5|6|7|8|9|10|11|||||||||||||||
|1|2|3|4|5|6|7|8|9|10|11|||||||||||||||
|1|2|3|4|5|6|7|*8*|9|10|11|*12*||||||||||||||
|1|2|3|4|5|6|7|*12*|9|*10*|11|8||||||||||||||
|1|2|3|4|5|6|7|8|10||11|9||||||||||||||
|1|2|3|*4*|5|6|7|8|10||11|9|*12*|||||||||||||
|1|2||3|5|6|7|8|10||*11*|9|4|*12*||||||||||||
|1|2||3|5|6|7|8|9||11|*12*|4|*10*||||||||||||
|1|2|3|4||6|7|8|9||11|*12*|5|*10*||||||||||||
|1|2|*3*|4||6|7|8|9|*12*|11||5|10||||||||||||
|1|2|3|4||10|7|*12*|8||11|9|5||*6*|||||||||||
|1|*2*|3|4||6|*12*|8|7|10|11||5|||9||||||||||
|1||6|4||2||8|7|10|11||5|||9|3|||||||||
|1||6|4||2|*12*|*8*|7|10|11||5|||9|3|||||||||
|1||4|2||||10|7||11||5|||9|3|6|8|||||||
|1|||4||2||10|7||11||5|||9|3|6|8|||||||
|1||4|3||2||10|9||11|*12*|5|||||6|7|*8*||||||
|1||4|3||2|7|10|*9*||11|*12*|5||||||8||6|||||
|1||4|3||2|7|10|||11|9|5|||||6|8|||||||
|||4|3||2||*12*|||11|9|5|*10*||7|||8||6|1||||
|1|||3||2||10|||11|9|5|4||7||6|8|||||||
||||3|*9*|2||10|||11|*12*|5|4||7||6|8||||1|||
||||3|*9*|2||10|||11|*12*|5|4||7||6|8|||||1||
||||3|9|2||*10*|*12*||11||5|4||7||6|8|||||1||
||||3|5|2||10|||11|9||4||*12*||*6*|8|||||1|7||
||||3|5|2||10|*12*||11|*9*||4||8|||6|||||1|7||
|1|*2*||3|5|6||10|||11|9||4||*12*|||8||||||7||
|||*12*|3|5|*2*||10|8||11|9||4|||||6|||||1|7||
||||3|5|2||10|8||11|9||4|||||6|||||1|7||
|||4|3|5|2||10|8||11|||||9|||6|||||1|7||
||||3|5|2||10|||11|9||4||8|||6|||||1|7||
|||4|3|5|2||10|||11|9||6||7|||8|||||1|||
|||4|3|5|2||10|||11|*9*||6||7|||8|||||1||*12*|
|||4|3|5|2||10|||11|9||6|||||8|||||1||7|
|||4|3|5|2||10|||11|9||6|||||8|||||1||7|
||||3|5|2||10|6||11|9||4|||||8|||||1||7|
|||*12*|3|5|2||10|6||11|*9*||4|||||8|||||1||7|
||||3|5|2||10|6||11|9||4|||||8|||||1||7|
|||4|3|5|2||*10*|9||11|||6||*12*|||8|||||1||7|
||||3|5|2||10|6||11|9||4||*12*|||8|||||1||*7*|
||||3|5|2||10|6||11|9||4|||||8|||||1||7|
||||3|5|2||10|6||11|9||4|||||8|||||1||7|
||||3|5|2||10|*6*||11|9||4||*12*|||8|||||1||7|
||||3|5|2||10|6||11|9||4|||||8|||||1||7|
|||*12*|3|5|2||*10*|6||11|||4||9|||8|||||1||7|
|||||5|2||10|6|||11||4||9|3||8|||||1||7|
|21|13|23|45|33|45|13|44|32|7|45|27|18|29|1|17|5|9|32|1|2|1|1|23|7|13|
|||3||||2|2|2|1||7|1|1||5||||||||||1|
|||2||4|2|2|18|4||4|6||||4||1|2||||||1|7|

| Gadsby | White | Ashurst | Goad | Green | Potter | Welsh | Young | Ellis | Clarke | Warnock | Veart | Parry | Dawes | Parkinson | Sharkey | Kelly | Spelman | Smith | Boylan | Ross | Noble | Nesbitt | Hillyard | Ward | Waddell |
|---|---|---|---|---|---|---|---|---|---|---|---|---|---|---|---|---|---|---|---|---|---|---|---|---|---|
|1||4|3||2|7|10|9||11|*12*|5|||||*6*|8||||||||
|1||4|3||2|*7*|10|||11|9|5|||*12*||6|8||||||||
|2||2|2||2|2|2|1||2|1|2|||||2|2||||||||
||||||||||||1||||1||||||||||||
||||||||2|1||1|3|||||||||||||||

| Gadsby | White | Ashurst | Goad | Green | Potter | Welsh | Young | Ellis | Clarke | Warnock | Veart | Parry | Dawes | Parkinson | Sharkey | Kelly | Spelman | Smith | Boylan | Ross | Noble | Nesbitt | Hillyard | Ward | Waddell |
|---|---|---|---|---|---|---|---|---|---|---|---|---|---|---|---|---|---|---|---|---|---|---|---|---|---|
|1|2|*3*|4|5|6|7|8|9|10|11||*12*||||||||||||||
|1|2|3|4|5|6|7|*8*|9|10|11|*12*||||||||||||||
|2|2|2|2|2|2|2|2|2|2|2|||||||||||||||
||||||||||||1|1||||||||||||||
|||||||||||||||||||||||||||

## League Table

| | P | W | D | L | F | A | Pts |
|---|---|---|---|---|---|---|---|
| Grimsby Town | 46 | 28 | 7 | 11 | 88 | 56 | 63 |
| Southend United | 46 | 24 | 12 | 10 | 81 | 55 | 60 |
| Brentford | 46 | 24 | 11 | 11 | 76 | 44 | 59 |
| Scunthorpe United | 46 | 22 | 13 | 11 | 56 | 37 | 57 |
| Lincoln City | 46 | 21 | 14 | 11 | 77 | 59 | 56 |
| Workington | 46 | 16 | 19 | 11 | 50 | 34 | 51 |
| Southport | 46 | 18 | 14 | 14 | 66 | 46 | 50 |
| Peterborough United | 46 | 17 | 16 | 13 | 82 | 64 | 50 |
| Bury | 46 | 19 | 12 | 15 | 73 | 59 | 50 |
| Cambridge United | 46 | 17 | 14 | 15 | 62 | 60 | 48 |
| Colchester United | 46 | 19 | 10 | 17 | 70 | 69 | 48 |
| Doncaster Rovers | 46 | 16 | 14 | 16 | 56 | 63 | 46 |
| Gillingham | 46 | 16 | 13 | 17 | 61 | 67 | 45 |
| Newport County | 46 | 18 | 8 | 20 | 60 | 72 | 44 |
| Exeter City | 46 | 16 | 11 | 19 | 61 | 68 | 43 |
| Reading | 46 | 17 | 8 | 21 | 56 | 76 | 42 |
| Aldershot | 46 | 9 | 22 | 15 | 48 | 54 | 40 |
| Hartlepool | 46 | 17 | 6 | 23 | 58 | 69 | 40 |
| Darlington | 46 | 14 | 11 | 21 | 64 | 82 | 39 |
| Chester | 46 | 10 | 18 | 18 | 47 | 56 | 38 |
| Northampton Town | 46 | 12 | 13 | 21 | 66 | 79 | 37 |
| Barrow | 46 | 13 | 11 | 22 | 40 | 71 | 37 |
| Stockport County | 46 | 9 | 14 | 23 | 55 | 87 | 32 |
| Crewe Alexandra | 46 | 10 | 9 | 27 | 43 | 69 | 29 |

# 1972-73

## Division Four

Manager: Len Ashurst

### Did you know that?

'Pools scored a mere 17 goals in their home League games, a record low, which included six goalless draws. The meagre total included five penalties and one own-goal, resulting in United's forwards managing only 11 goals in 23 League games from open play.

Len Ashurst played the last game of his career, which spanned 454 League games, against Northampton Town on 21 April in a 3–1 defeat.

| Match No. | Date | Round | Venue | Opponents | Result | | Scorers | Attendance |
|---|---|---|---|---|---|---|---|---|
| 1 | Aug 12 | | (a) | Lincoln City | W | 2 - 1 | Coyne, Green | 5,789 |
| 3 | 19 | | (h) | Colchester United | W | 2 - 1 | Coyne, R.W. Smith (pen) | 5,672 |
| 4 | 26 | | (a) | Torquay United | L | 0 - 1 | | 4,726 |
| 5 | 28 | | (a) | Exeter City | D | 1 - 1 | Warnock | 4,304 |
| 6 | Sep 2 | | (h) | Reading | L | 1 - 2 | R.W. Smith (pen) | 5,195 |
| 8 | 9 | | (a) | Cambridge United | D | 1 - 1 | Waddell | 2,627 |
| 9 | 16 | | (h) | Workington | W | 1 - 0 | R.W. Smith (pen) | 4,608 |
| 10 | 18 | | (h) | Darlington | D | 0 - 0 | | 7,193 |
| 11 | 23 | | (a) | Bradford City | W | 2 - 0 | Coyne, Conlon | 3,387 |
| 12 | 27 | | (a) | Aldershot | L | 1 - 2 | Young | 3,825 |
| 13 | 30 | | (h) | Southport | L | 0 - 2 | | 4,982 |
| 14 | Oct 7 | | (a) | Hereford United | D | 0 - 0 | | 7,521 |
| 15 | 11 | | (a) | Chester | L | 0 - 2 | | 3,426 |
| 16 | 14 | | (h) | Crewe Alexandra | D | 1 - 1 | R. Smith | 2,528 |
| 17 | 21 | | (a) | Newport County | L | 1 - 5 | Coyne | 3,392 |
| 18 | 23 | | (h) | Gillingham | W | 2 - 0 | Veart, R.W. Smith (pen) | 3,462 |
| 19 | 28 | | (h) | Bury | D | 1 - 1 | Green | 3,942 |
| 20 | Nov 4 | | (h) | Aldershot | D | 1 - 1 | Waddell | 3,181 |
| 21 | 11 | | (a) | Darlington | W | 2 - 1 | Coyne 2 | 3,724 |
| 24 | 25 | | (a) | Peterborough United | L | 0 - 3 | | 4,378 |
| 26 | Dec 2 | | (h) | Doncaster Rovers | D | 0 - 0 | | 2,964 |
| 27 | 8 | | (a) | Barnsley | L | 1 - 2 | Young | 1,897 |
| 28 | 16 | | (h) | Stockport County | D | 0 - 0 | | 2,448 |
| 29 | 23 | | (a) | Mansfield Town | L | 0 - 2 | | 4,208 |
| 30 | 26 | | (h) | Bradford City | W | 1 - 0 | Veart | 4,139 |
| 31 | 29 | | (a) | Colchester United | D | 1 - 1 | Veart | 3,172 |
| 32 | Jan 6 | | (h) | Torquay United | W | 1 - 0 | Green | 2,951 |
| 33 | 13 | | (a) | Gillingham | L | 0 - 2 | | 2,772 |
| 34 | 20 | | (a) | Reading | L | 0 - 1 | | 5,360 |
| 35 | 27 | | (h) | Cambridge United | D | 0 - 0 | | 3,036 |
| 36 | Feb 3 | | (h) | Chester | D | 0 - 0 | | 2,845 |
| 37 | 10 | | (a) | Workington | D | 0 - 0 | | 1,413 |
| 38 | 17 | | (h) | Lincoln City | W | 1 - 0 | Conlon | 2,892 |
| 39 | 23 | | (a) | Stockport County | W | 1 - 0 | Coyne | 3,324 |
| 40 | Mar 3 | | (h) | Hereford United | L | 0 - 1 | | 5,253 |
| 41 | 5 | | (h) | Northampton Town | W | 2 - 0 | Coyne, Green | 3,822 |
| 42 | 10 | | (a) | Crewe Alexandra | L | 0 - 2 | | 1,760 |
| 43 | 16 | | (h) | Newport County | W | 1 - 0 | R.W. Smith (pen) | 3,696 |
| 44 | 24 | | (a) | Bury | D | 1 - 1 | Coyne | 2,358 |
| 45 | 31 | | (h) | Peterborough United | L | 0 - 1 | | 2,888 |
| 46 | Apr 7 | | (a) | Doncaster Rovers | L | 1 - 2 | Conlon | 1,488 |
| 47 | 14 | | (h) | Barnsley | L | 1 - 4 | Honour | 2,448 |
| 48 | 20 | | (h) | Mansfield Town | D | 1 - 1 | Pate (o.g.) | 2,855 |
| 49 | 21 | | (a) | Northampton Town | L | 1 - 3 | Roberts (o.g.) | 1,478 |
| 50 | 23 | | (a) | Southport | D | 1 - 1 | Honour | 6,525 |
| 51 | 28 | | (h) | Exeter City | D | 0 - 0 | | 1,887 |

Final Position : 20th in Division Four

Apps.
Sub.Apps.
2 own goals Goals

**FA Cup**

| Match No. | Date | Round | Venue | Opponents | Result | | Scorers | Attendance |
|---|---|---|---|---|---|---|---|---|
| 22 | Nov 18 | R1 | (h) | Scunthorpe United | D | 0 - 0 | | 4,586 |
| 23 | 21 | R1r | (a) | Scunthorpe United | D | 0 - 0* | | 4,478 |
| 25 | 27 | R1r2# | (a) | Scunthorpe United | L | 1 - 2 | Veart | 7,917 |

# Played at Roker Park, Sunderland * After extra-time

Apps.
Sub.Apps.
Goals

**League Cup**

| Match No. | Date | Round | Venue | Opponents | Result | | Scorers | Attendance |
|---|---|---|---|---|---|---|---|---|
| 2 | Aug 16 | R1 | (h) | Doncaster Rovers | W | 1 - 0 | R.W. Smith (pen) | 6,752 |
| 7 | Sep 5 | R2 | (a) | Coventry City | L | 0 - 1 | | 8,687 |

Apps.
Sub.Apps.
Goals

| Watling | Potter | Goad | Dawes | Green | Smith, R. | Waddell | Smith, R.W. | Coyne | Spelman | Warnock | Veart | Ward | Young | Conton | Ashurst | Honour | Gadston | McGeough | White | Gribbin | Pringle |
|---|---|---|---|---|---|---|---|---|---|---|---|---|---|---|---|---|---|---|---|---|---|
| 1 | 2 | 3 | 4 | 5 | 6 | 7 | 8 | 9 | 10 | 11 | | | | | | | | | | | |
| 1 | 2 | 3 | 4 | 5 | 6 | | 8 | 9 | 10 | | 7 | 11 | | | | | | | | | |
| 1 | 2 | 3 | 4 | 5 | *6* | 7 | 8 | 9 | 10 | 11 | | | *12* | | | | | | | | |
| 1 | 2 | 3 | 4 | 5 | 6 | 7 | 8 | 9 | 10 | 11 | | | | | | | | | | | |
| 1 | *2* | 3 | 4 | 5 | 6 | 7 | 8 | 9 | 10 | 11 | | | *12* | | | | | | | | |
| 1 | 2 | 3 | 4 | 5 | 6 | 7 | 8 | 9 | 10 | 11 | | | | | | | | | | | |
| 1 | 2 | 3 | 4 | 5 | 6 | 7 | 8 | *12* | 10 | *11* | | | | 9 | | | | | | | |
| 1 | 2 | 3 | 4 | 5 | 6 | *7* | 8 | *12* | 10 | 11 | | | | 9 | | | | | | | |
| 1 | 2 | 3 | 4 | 5 | 6 | | | 7 | 10 | 11 | | | 8 | 9 | | | | | | | |
| 1 | 2 | 3 | 4 | 5 | 6 | | *12* | 7 | *10* | 11 | | | 8 | 9 | | | | | | | |
| 1 | 2 | 3 | 4 | 5 | *12* | | *6* | 7 | 10 | 11 | | | 8 | 9 | | | | | | | |
| 1 | 2 | 3 | 4 | 5 | 6 | 7 | | | 10 | 11 | | | 8 | 9 | | | | | | | |
| 1 | 2 | 3 | 4 | 5 | 6 | 7 | | *12* | 10 | 11 | | | *8* | 9 | | | | | | | |
| 1 | 2 | 3 | 4 | | 6 | | *12* | 8 | 10 | 11 | 7 | | | 9 | *5* | | | | | | |
| 1 | 2 | 3 | 4 | *5* | 6 | | 8 | 7 | | *12* | 11 | | 10 | 9 | | | | | | | |
| 1 | 2 | 3 | 4 | 5 | 6 | | 8 | 7 | | | 11 | | | 9 | | 10 | | | | | |
| 1 | 2 | *3* | 4 | 5 | 6 | *12* | 8 | 7 | | | 11 | | 10 | 9 | | | | | | | |
| 1 | 2 | 3 | 4 | | *6* | 7 | 8 | | | *12* | 11 | | 10 | 9 | 5 | | | | | | |
| 1 | 2 | 3 | 4 | | 6 | 7 | 8 | *12* | | | 11 | | | *9* | 5 | 10 | | | | | |
| 1 | *2* | 3 | 4 | 5 | 6 | 7 | | 9 | 8 | | 11 | | *12* | | | 10 | | | | | |
| 1 | 2 | 3 | 4 | 5 | 6 | 7 | 8 | 9 | | | 11 | | 10 | | | | | | | | |
| 1 | 2 | 3 | | 5 | 6 | 7 | 8 | 9 | | | 11 | | 10 | | 4 | | | | | | |
| 1 | 2 | 3 | | 5 | 6 | 7 | 8 | 9 | | | 11 | | *10* | | 4 | *12* | | | | | |
| 1 | 2 | 3 | 4 | 5 | 6 | *12* | *8* | 9 | | | 7 | | 10 | | | 11 | | | | | |
| 1 | 2 | 3 | 4 | 5 | 6 | 7 | | 9 | | | 11 | | *8* | *12* | | 10 | | | | | |
| 1 | 2 | 3 | 4 | 5 | 6 | 7 | | 9 | | | 11 | | 8 | | | 10 | | | | | |
| 1 | 2 | 3 | 4 | 5 | 6 | 7 | | *9* | | | 11 | | 8 | *12* | | 10 | | | | | |
| 1 | 2 | 3 | 4 | 5 | 6 | 7 | | 9 | | | 11 | | 8 | *12* | | *10* | | | | | |
| 1 | 2 | *3* | 4 | 5 | 6 | | 8 | | *12* | | 11 | | 10 | 9 | | 7 | | | | | |
| 1 | 2 | 3 | 4 | 5 | 6 | *12* | 8 | | | | *11* | | 10 | 9 | | 7 | | | | | |
| 1 | 2 | 3 | 4 | 5 | 6 | | 8 | | | | | 7 | 10 | 11 | | *12* | *9* | | | | |
| 1 | 2 | 3 | 4 | 5 | 6 | | 8 | 9 | 10 | | | 7 | | 11 | | | | | | | |
| 1 | 2 | | 4 | 5 | 3 | | 8 | 9 | 6 | | *12* | *7* | 10 | 11 | | | | | | | |
| 1 | 2 | | 4 | 5 | 3 | | 8 | 9 | 6 | | | 7 | 10 | 11 | | | | | | | |
| 1 | 2 | | 4 | 5 | *3* | | 8 | 9 | 6 | | *12* | 7 | 10 | 11 | | | | | | | |
| 1 | 2 | 3 | 4 | *5* | | | 8 | 9 | 6 | | *12* | 7 | | 11 | | 10 | | | | | |
| 1 | 2 | *3* | 4 | 5 | | | 8 | 9 | 6 | | | 7 | | 11 | | 10 | | *12* | | | |
| 1 | 2 | 3 | 4 | 5 | | *12* | 8 | 9 | 6 | | | 7 | | *11* | | | | 10 | | | |
| 1 | 2 | | 4 | 5 | | 7 | 8 | 9 | 6 | | | | | 11 | | 10 | | | 3 | | |
| 1 | | | 4 | 5 | 3 | 7 | 8 | 9 | 6 | | 11 | *12* | | | | 10 | | | *2* | | |
| 1 | | | 4 | 5 | 3 | 7 | 8 | 9 | 6 | | *12* | | | 11 | | 10 | | | *2* | | |
| 1 | | 2 | 4 | 5 | 8 | 7 | | *12* | 6 | | *9* | 11 | | | | 10 | | | | 3 | |
| 1 | | 3 | 4 | 5 | 2 | 7 | 8 | 9 | 6 | | | *11* | | | *12* | 10 | | | | | |
| 1 | | 3 | 4 | 5 | 2 | 11 | 8 | 9 | 7 | | | *12* | | | *6* | 10 | | | | | |
| 1 | 2 | 3 | 4 | 5 | 10 | | 8 | 9 | 6 | | | 7 | | | | 11 | | | | | |
| 1 | 2 | *12* | 4 | 5 | 3 | | 8 | 9 | 6 | | | 11 | | | | 10 | | | | | 7 |
| 46 | 41 | 39 | 44 | 43 | 41 | 25 | 35 | 36 | 30 | 13 | 20 | 13 | 22 | 25 | 6 | 20 | 1 | 1 | 3 | 1 | 1 |
| | | 1 | | | 1 | 4 | 2 | 5 | 1 | 2 | 4 | 2 | 3 | 3 | 1 | 2 | | 1 | | | |
| | | | | 4 | 1 | 2 | 5 | 9 | | 1 | 3 | | 2 | 3 | | 2 | | | | | |

| Watling | Potter | Goad | Dawes | Green | Smith, R. | Waddell | Smith, R.W. | Coyne | Spelman | Warnock | Veart | Ward | Young | Conton | Ashurst | Honour | Gadston | McGeough | White | Gribbin | Pringle |
|---|---|---|---|---|---|---|---|---|---|---|---|---|---|---|---|---|---|---|---|---|---|
| 1 | 2 | 3 | 4 | | 6 | 7 | 8 | 9 | | | 11 | | *12* | | 5 | *10* | | | | | |
| 1 | 2 | 3 | 4 | | 6 | 7 | 8 | 9 | | | 11 | | | | 5 | 10 | | | | | |
| 1 | 2 | 3 | 4 | | 6 | 7 | 8 | 9 | | | 11 | | | | 5 | 10 | | | | | |
| 3 | 3 | 3 | 3 | | 3 | 3 | 3 | 3 | | | 3 | | | | 3 | 3 | | | | | |
| | | | | | | | | | | | | | 1 | | | | | | | | |
| | | | | | | | | | | | 1 | | | | | | | | | | |

| Watling | Potter | Goad | Dawes | Green | Smith, R. | Waddell | Smith, R.W. | Coyne | Spelman | Warnock | Veart | Ward | Young | Conton | Ashurst | Honour | Gadston | McGeough | White | Gribbin | Pringle |
|---|---|---|---|---|---|---|---|---|---|---|---|---|---|---|---|---|---|---|---|---|---|
| 1 | 2 | 3 | 4 | 5 | 6 | 7 | 8 | 9 | 10 | 11 | *12* | | | | | | | | | | |
| 1 | 2 | 3 | 4 | 5 | 6 | 7 | 8 | 9 | 10 | 11 | | | | | | | | | | | |
| 2 | 2 | 2 | 2 | 2 | 2 | 2 | 2 | 2 | 2 | 2 | | | | | | | | | | | |
| | | | | | | | | | | | 1 | | | | | | | | | | |
| | | | | | | | 1 | | | | | | | | | | | | | | |

## League Table

| | P | W | D | L | F | A | Pts |
|---|---|---|---|---|---|---|---|
| Southport | 46 | 26 | 10 | 10 | 71 | 48 | 62 |
| Hereford United | 46 | 23 | 12 | 11 | 56 | 38 | 58 |
| Cambridge United | 46 | 20 | 17 | 9 | 67 | 57 | 57 |
| Aldershot | 46 | 22 | 12 | 12 | 60 | 38 | 56 |
| Newport County | 46 | 22 | 12 | 12 | 64 | 44 | 56 |
| Mansfield Town | 46 | 20 | 14 | 12 | 78 | 51 | 54 |
| Reading | 46 | 17 | 18 | 11 | 51 | 38 | 52 |
| Exeter City | 46 | 18 | 14 | 14 | 57 | 51 | 50 |
| Gillingham | 46 | 19 | 11 | 16 | 63 | 58 | 49 |
| Lincoln City | 46 | 16 | 16 | 14 | 64 | 57 | 48 |
| Stockport County | 46 | 18 | 12 | 16 | 53 | 53 | 48 |
| Bury | 46 | 14 | 18 | 14 | 58 | 51 | 46 |
| Workington | 46 | 17 | 12 | 17 | 59 | 61 | 46 |
| Barnsley | 46 | 14 | 16 | 16 | 58 | 60 | 44 |
| Chester | 46 | 14 | 15 | 17 | 61 | 52 | 43 |
| Bradford City | 46 | 16 | 11 | 19 | 61 | 65 | 43 |
| Doncaster Rovers | 46 | 15 | 12 | 19 | 49 | 58 | 42 |
| Torquay United | 46 | 12 | 17 | 17 | 44 | 47 | 41 |
| Peterborough United | 46 | 14 | 13 | 19 | 71 | 76 | 41 |
| Hartlepool | 46 | 12 | 17 | 17 | 34 | 49 | 41 |
| Crewe Alexandra | 46 | 9 | 18 | 19 | 38 | 61 | 36 |
| Colchester United | 46 | 10 | 11 | 25 | 48 | 76 | 31 |
| Northampton Town | 46 | 10 | 11 | 25 | 40 | 73 | 31 |
| Darlington | 46 | 7 | 15 | 24 | 42 | 85 | 29 |

# 1973-74

## Division Four

Manager: Len Ashurst

### Did you know that?

From 26 January to 12 April, a total of 14 consecutive games, 'Pools started with the same team: Watling; Potter, Shoulder; Dawes, Goad, Honour; Heath, Gauden, Moore, McMahon, Ward.

When Malcolm Moore scored 'Pools' third goal against Scunthorpe on 22 December, it was the first time since the 5–0 defeat of Stockport on 31 March 1972, a run of 75 League games, that United had scored more than twice.

The Scunthorpe League game attracted a 'crowd' of 844, the lowest post-war attendance at the time for a home Hartlepool fixture.

| Match No. | Date | Round | Venue | Opponents | Result | | Scorers | Attendance |
|---|---|---|---|---|---|---|---|---|
| 1 | Aug 25 | | (h) | Brentford | W | 1 - 0 | Gauden | 3,447 |
| 3 | 31 | | (a) | Chester | L | 1 - 3 | Smith | 2,369 |
| 4 | Sep 8 | | (h) | Reading | L | 1 - 2 | K.McMahon | 2,736 |
| 5 | 11 | | (a) | Bury | L | 0 - 1 | | 4,436 |
| 6 | 15 | | (a) | Rotherham United | D | 2 - 2 | Gauden (pen), K.McMahon | 3,764 |
| 7 | 17 | | (h) | Exeter City | L | 1 - 3 | Gauden (pen) | 2,625 |
| 8 | 22 | | (h) | Gillingham | W | 2 - 1 | Dawes, Moore | 1,399 |
| 9 | 29 | | (a) | Scunthorpe United | D | 1 - 1 | Gauden | 2,626 |
| 10 | Oct 3 | | (a) | Exeter City | L | 0 - 2 | | 4,461 |
| 11 | 6 | | (h) | Colchester United | D | 0 - 0 | | 1,926 |
| 12 | 13 | | (a) | Mansfield Town | L | 0 - 2 | | 3,086 |
| 13 | 20 | | (a) | Doncaster Rovers | D | 2 - 2 | Dawes, Coyne | 1,676 |
| 14 | 22 | | (h) | Bury | D | 1 - 1 | Gauden | 1,939 |
| 15 | 27 | | (h) | Lincoln City | L | 0 - 2 | | 1,898 |
| 16 | Nov 3 | | (a) | Northampton Town | L | 0 - 1 | | 3,715 |
| 17 | 10 | | (h) | Crewe Alexandra | W | 1 - 0 | Ward | 1,221 |
| 18 | 12 | | (h) | Newport County | L | 0 - 1 | | 1,656 |
| 19 | 17 | | (a) | Swansea City | D | 0 - 0 | | 2,358 |
| 21 | Dec 1 | | (a) | Peterborough United | L | 0 - 2 | | 7,537 |
| 22 | 8 | | (h) | Barnsley | L | 1 - 2 | Gauden | 1,101 |
| 23 | 22 | | (h) | Scunthorpe United | W | 3 - 0 | Goad, Moore 2 | 844 |
| 24 | 26 | | (a) | Workington | W | 2 - 0 | Moore, Gauden (pen) | 1,312 |
| 25 | 29 | | (a) | Reading | D | 1 - 1 | Gauden | 4,663 |
| 26 | Jan 1 | | (h) | Chester | D | 0 - 0 | | 3,104 |
| 27 | 5 | | (h) | Northampton Town | W | 1 - 0 | Potter | 2,078 |
| 28 | 12 | | (h) | Rotherham United | W | 2 - 0 | K.McMahon, Ward | 2,016 |
| 29 | 19 | | (a) | Brentford | W | 2 - 1 | Nelmes (o.g.), K.McMahon | 4,646 |
| 30 | 26 | | (h) | Torquay United | D | 0 - 0 | | 2,960 |
| 31 | Feb 3 | | (h) | Stockport County | W | 3 - 0 | K.McMahon, Gauden (pen), Dawes | 5,747 |
| 32 | 10 | | (a) | Gillingham | L | 0 - 3 | | 8,724 |
| 33 | 17 | | (h) | Mansfield Town | W | 4 - 0 | K.McMahon 2, Heath, Moore | 4,067 |
| 34 | 22 | | (a) | Colchester United | L | 0 - 3 | | 5,608 |
| 35 | Mar 3 | | (h) | Workington | W | 3 - 0 | Dawes 2, Heath | 2,827 |
| 36 | 6 | | (a) | Bradford City | L | 0 - 2 | | 2,098 |
| 37 | 9 | | (a) | Lincoln City | W | 1 - 0 | Gauden | 1,800 |
| 38 | 17 | | (h) | Doncaster Rovers | W | 3 - 0 | Shoulder, Ward, Gauden | 3,502 |
| 39 | 23 | | (a) | Crewe Alexandra | W | 3 - 1 | Ward 2, K.McMahon | 1,370 |
| 40 | 27 | | (h) | Bradford City | W | 1 - 0 | Dawes | 3,798 |
| 41 | Apr 3 | | (a) | Torquay United | W | 2 - 0 | Moore 2 | 2,014 |
| 42 | 6 | | (a) | Newport County | D | 0 - 0 | | 1,685 |
| 43 | 12 | | (h) | Darlington | L | 1 - 2 | Cattrell (o.g.) | 6,739 |
| 44 | 13 | | (h) | Swansea City | L | 0 - 1 | | 2,665 |
| 45 | 16 | | (a) | Darlington | D | 1 - 1 | Ward | 6,723 |
| 46 | 20 | | (a) | Barnsley | L | 0 - 2 | | 3,555 |
| 47 | 22 | | (a) | Stockport County | D | 1 - 1 | Gauden | 1,311 |
| 48 | 27 | | (h) | Peterborough United | L | 0 - 1 | | 2,283 |

Final Position : 11th in Division Four

Apps.
Sub.Apps.
2 own goals Goals

**FA Cup**

| Match No. | Date | Round | Venue | Opponents | Result | | Scorers | Attendance |
|---|---|---|---|---|---|---|---|---|
| 20 | Nov 24 | R1 | (a) | Altrincham | L | 0 - 2 | | 2,923 |

Apps.
Sub.Apps.
Goals

**League Cup**

| Match No. | Date | Round | Venue | Opponents | Result | | Scorers | Attendance |
|---|---|---|---|---|---|---|---|---|
| 2 | Aug 29 | R1 | (a) | Rochdale | L | 3 - 5 | Gauden 2, K.McMahon | 1,836 |

Apps.
Sub.Apps.
Goals

| Watling | Potter | Goad | Embleton | Conlon | Smith | Moore | Heath | McMahon, K. | Spelman | Gauden | Ward | Dawes | Coyne | Honour | Shoulder | McMahon, F.G. | Waddell | McNamee | Maddison |
|---|---|---|---|---|---|---|---|---|---|---|---|---|---|---|---|---|---|---|---|
| 1 | 2 | 3 | 4 | 5 | 6 | 7 | 8 | *9* | 10 | 11 | *12* | | | | | | | | |
| 1 | 2 | 3 | | 5 | 6 | *7* | 8 | 9 | 10 | 11 | | 4 | *12* | | | | | | |
| 1 | 2 | 3 | | 5 | 6 | | 8 | 9 | 10 | *11* | *12* | 4 | 7 | | | | | | |
| 1 | 2 | 3 | 5 | | 8 | 7 | | 9 | | 11 | | 4 | 10 | 6 | | | | | |
| 1 | 2 | 3 | 5 | | 8 | 7 | | 9 | | 11 | | 4 | 10 | 6 | | | | | |
| 1 | | 3 | *5* | | 2 | 7 | *12* | 9 | 8 | 11 | | 4 | 10 | 6 | | | | | |
| 1 | 2 | 3 | | 5 | 8 | 7 | | | | 11 | | 4 | 9 | 6 | 10 | | | | |
| 1 | 2 | 3 | | 5 | 8 | 7 | | 9 | | 11 | | 4 | | 6 | 10 | | | | |
| 1 | 2 | 3 | | 5 | 8 | 7 | | 9 | | *11* | | 4 | *12* | 6 | 10 | | | | |
| 1 | 2 | 3 | | 5 | 8 | 7 | | 9 | | *11* | | 4 | *12* | 6 | 10 | | | | |
| 1 | *12* | 3 | | 5 | 2 | | | 9 | 6 | | 11 | 4 | 10 | *7* | 8 | | | | |
| 1 | | 3 | | 5 | 2 | | | 9 | 8 | 11 | *12* | 4 | 10 | | 7 | *6* | | | |
| 1 | | 3 | | 5 | 2 | | | *9* | 8 | 11 | *12* | 4 | 10 | | 7 | 6 | | | |
| 1 | | 3 | | 5 | 2 | | | *12* | 8 | 11 | 7 | 4 | 9 | | *10* | 6 | | | |
| 1 | | | | 5 | 2 | *10* | | *12* | 8 | | 11 | 4 | 9 | 7 | 3 | 6 | | | |
| 1 | | 3 | | *5* | 2 | 7 | | | 8 | 11 | 9 | 4 | | | *12* | 6 | 10 | | |
| 1 | | 5 | | | 2 | | | | 8 | 11 | 7 | 4 | 9 | | 3 | 6 | 10 | | |
| 1 | 4 | 5 | | | 2 | | | | 8 | 11 | 9 | | | 7 | 3 | 6 | 10 | | |
| 1 | 2 | 4 | | | 7 | *12* | | | 8 | 11 | *9* | | | 6 | 3 | | 10 | 5 | |
| 1 | 2 | 3 | | | 7 | 9 | | | *12* | 8 | 11 | 4 | | 6 | | | *10* | 5 | |
| 1 | 2 | 5 | | | | 9 | 7 | 10 | | 8 | 11 | 4 | | 6 | 3 | | | | |
| 1 | 2 | 5 | | | | 9 | 7 | 10 | | 8 | 11 | 4 | | 6 | 3 | | | | |
| 1 | 2 | 5 | | | *12* | 9 | 7 | 10 | | 8 | 11 | 4 | | *6* | 3 | | | | |
| 1 | 2 | 5 | | | | 9 | 7 | 10 | | 8 | 11 | 4 | | 6 | 3 | | | | |
| 1 | 2 | 5 | | | *12* | 9 | 7 | *10* | | 8 | 11 | 4 | | 6 | 3 | | | | |
| 1 | 2 | 5 | | | *12* | 9 | 7 | *10* | | 8 | 11 | 4 | | 6 | 3 | | | | |
| 1 | 5 | | | | 2 | 9 | 7 | 10 | | 8 | 11 | 4 | | 6 | 3 | | | | |
| 1 | 2 | 5 | | | | 9 | 7 | 10 | | 8 | 11 | 4 | | 6 | 3 | | | | |
| 1 | 2 | 5 | | | *12* | 9 | 7 | 10 | | 8 | 11 | 4 | | 6 | 3 | | | | |
| 1 | 2 | 5 | | | | 9 | 7 | 10 | | 8 | 11 | 4 | | 6 | 3 | | | | |
| 1 | 2 | 5 | | | | 9 | 7 | 10 | | 8 | 11 | 4 | | 6 | 3 | | | | |
| 1 | 2 | 5 | | | *12* | 9 | 7 | 10 | | 8 | *11* | 4 | | 6 | 3 | | | | |
| 1 | 2 | 5 | | | | 9 | 7 | 10 | | 8 | 11 | 4 | | 6 | 3 | | | | |
| 1 | 2 | 5 | | | | 9 | 7 | 10 | *12* | 8 | 11 | 4 | | 6 | *3* | | | | |
| 1 | 2 | 5 | | | *12* | 9 | 7 | 10 | | 8 | 11 | 4 | | 6 | 3 | | | | |
| 1 | 2 | 5 | | | | 9 | 7 | 10 | | 8 | 11 | 4 | | 6 | 3 | | | | |
| 1 | 2 | 5 | | | | 9 | 7 | 10 | | 8 | 11 | 4 | | 6 | 3 | | | | |
| 1 | 2 | 5 | | | | 9 | 7 | 10 | | 8 | 11 | 4 | | 6 | 3 | | | | |
| 1 | 2 | 5 | | | | 9 | 7 | 10 | | 8 | 11 | 4 | | 6 | 3 | | | | |
| 1 | 2 | 5 | | | | 9 | 7 | 10 | | 8 | 11 | 4 | | 6 | 3 | | | | |
| 1 | 2 | 5 | | | *12* | 9 | 7 | 10 | | 8 | 11 | 4 | | *6* | 3 | | | | |
| 1 | 2 | 5 | | | | 9 | 7 | 10 | 6 | 8 | 11 | 4 | | | 3 | | | | |
| 1 | 2 | 5 | | | *12* | 9 | 7 | *10* | | 8 | 11 | 4 | | 6 | 3 | | | | |
| 1 | 2 | 5 | | | | 9 | 7 | *10* | *12* | 8 | 11 | 4 | | 6 | 3 | | | | |
| 1 | 2 | 5 | | | 8 | 9 | 7 | | *12* | 10 | *11* | 4 | | 6 | 3 | | | | |
| 1 | 2 | 5 | | | 8 | *9* | 7 | | | 10 | 11 | 4 | | 6 | 3 | | | | *12* |
| 46 | 38 | 44 | 4 | 13 | 23 | 38 | 29 | 36 | 14 | 44 | 34 | 43 | 11 | 37 | 38 | 7 | 5 | 2 | |
| | 1 | | | | 8 | 1 | 1 | 2 | 4 | | 4 | | 3 | | 1 | | | | 1 |
| | 1 | 1 | | | 1 | 7 | 2 | 8 | | 12 | 6 | 6 | 1 | | 1 | | | | |

| Watling | Potter | Goad | Embleton | Conlon | Smith | Moore | Heath | McMahon, K. | Spelman | Gauden | Ward | Dawes | Coyne | Honour | Shoulder | McMahon, F.G. | Waddell | McNamee | Maddison |
|---|---|---|---|---|---|---|---|---|---|---|---|---|---|---|---|---|---|---|---|
| 1 | 4 | 5 | | | 2 | *12* | *7* | | 8 | 11 | 9 | | | 6 | 3 | | 10 | | |
| 1 | 1 | 1 | | | 1 | | 1 | | 1 | 1 | 1 | | | 1 | 1 | | 1 | | |
| | | | | | | 1 | | | | | | | | | | | | | |
| | | | | | | | | | | | | | | | | | | | |

| Watling | Potter | Goad | Embleton | Conlon | Smith | Moore | Heath | McMahon, K. | Spelman | Gauden | Ward | Dawes | Coyne | Honour | Shoulder | McMahon, F.G. | Waddell | McNamee | Maddison |
|---|---|---|---|---|---|---|---|---|---|---|---|---|---|---|---|---|---|---|---|
| 1 | 2 | 3 | 4 | 5 | 6 | 7 | *8* | 9 | 10 | 11 | *12* | | | | | | | | |
| 1 | 1 | 1 | 1 | 1 | 1 | 1 | 1 | 1 | 1 | 1 | | | | | | | | | |
| | | | | | | | | | | | 1 | | | | | | | | |
| | | | | | | | | 1 | | 2 | | | | | | | | | |

## League Table

| | P | W | D | L | F | A | Pts |
|---|---|---|---|---|---|---|---|
| Peterborough United | 46 | 27 | 11 | 8 | 75 | 38 | 65 |
| Gillingham | 46 | 25 | 12 | 9 | 90 | 49 | 62 |
| Colchester United | 46 | 24 | 12 | 10 | 73 | 36 | 60 |
| Bury | 46 | 24 | 11 | 11 | 81 | 49 | 59 |
| Northampton Town | 46 | 20 | 13 | 13 | 63 | 48 | 53 |
| Reading | 46 | 16 | 19 | 11 | 58 | 37 | 51 |
| Chester | 46 | 17 | 15 | 14 | 54 | 55 | 49 |
| Bradford City | 46 | 17 | 14 | 15 | 58 | 52 | 48 |
| Newport County | 46 | 16 | 14 | 16 | 56 | 65 | 45 |
| Exeter City | 45 | 18 | 8 | 19 | 58 | 55 | 44 |
| Hartlepool | 46 | 16 | 12 | 18 | 48 | 47 | 44 |
| Lincoln City | 46 | 16 | 12 | 18 | 63 | 67 | 44 |
| Barnsley | 46 | 17 | 10 | 19 | 58 | 64 | 44 |
| Swansea City | 46 | 16 | 11 | 19 | 45 | 46 | 43 |
| Rotherham United | 46 | 15 | 13 | 18 | 56 | 58 | 43 |
| Torquay United | 46 | 13 | 17 | 16 | 52 | 57 | 43 |
| Mansfield Town | 46 | 13 | 17 | 16 | 62 | 69 | 43 |
| Scunthorpe United | 45 | 14 | 12 | 19 | 47 | 64 | 42 |
| Brentford | 46 | 12 | 16 | 18 | 48 | 50 | 40 |
| Darlington | 46 | 13 | 13 | 20 | 40 | 62 | 39 |
| Crewe Alexandra | 46 | 14 | 10 | 22 | 43 | 71 | 38 |
| Doncaster Rovers | 46 | 12 | 11 | 23 | 47 | 80 | 35 |
| Workington | 46 | 11 | 13 | 22 | 43 | 74 | 35 |
| Stockport County | 46 | 7 | 20 | 19 | 44 | 69 | 34 |

# 1974-75

## Division Four

Manager: Ken Hale

### Did you know that?

The Football League Cup, a competition in which United previously had a lean record, provided nine absorbing ties, finally ending at Aston Villa in a replay. The games attracted aggregate attendances of 70,741, nearly 10,000 more than watched the 23 home League games, clear evidence of the importance of a Cup run to a club like Hartlepool.

| Match No. | Date | Round | Venue | Opponents | Result | | Scorers | Attendance |
|---|---|---|---|---|---|---|---|---|
| 1 | Aug 17 | | (h) | Newport County | W | 2 - 0 | Moore, Gauden | 2,557 |
| 3 | 24 | | (a) | Chester | L | 0 - 3 | | 2,942 |
| 4 | 31 | | (h) | Southport | D | 1 - 1 | Dawes | 1,914 |
| 5 | Sep 7 | | (a) | Crewe Alexandra | L | 0 - 2 | | 2,211 |
| 7 | 14 | | (h) | Rotherham United | W | 3 - 2 | Moore, Goodfellow (o.g.), Shoulder | 2,401 |
| 9 | 21 | | (a) | Scunthorpe United | D | 1 - 1 | McMahon | 2,069 |
| 12 | 28 | | (h) | Swansea City | L | 0 - 2 | | 2,850 |
| 13 | Oct 1 | | (a) | Cambridge United | L | 2 - 3 | Shoulder, Smith | 2,774 |
| 14 | 5 | | (a) | Shrewsbury Town | W | 1 - 0 | Moore | 4,222 |
| 16 | 12 | | (h) | Torquay United | D | 0 - 0 | | 2,177 |
| 18 | 19 | | (a) | Barnsley | L | 1 - 2 | McMahon | 3,135 |
| 19 | 26 | | (h) | Mansfield Town | W | 2 - 1 | Dawes, Potter | 2,632 |
| 20 | 28 | | (a) | Stockport County | D | 1 - 1 | Moore | 2,047 |
| 21 | Nov 2 | | (h) | Workington | W | 3 - 0 | Gauden 2, Dawes | 2,632 |
| 22 | 6 | | (h) | Reading | L | 2 - 3 | Dawes, Honour | 3,204 |
| 23 | 9 | | (a) | Darlington | W | 2 - 1 | Spelman, McMahon | 3,974 |
| 25 | 16 | | (h) | Brentford | W | 3 - 2 | McMahon, Spelman, Honour | 2,864 |
| 28 | Dec 7 | | (a) | Doncaster Rovers | L | 0 - 3 | | 1,357 |
| 31 | 21 | | (h) | Rochdale | W | 5 - 0 | Honour, McMahon 2, Moore 2 | 1,991 |
| 32 | 26 | | (a) | Rotherham United | W | 2 - 1 | McBurney, McMahon | 5,784 |
| 33 | Jan 1 | | (h) | Northampton Town | W | 2 - 0 | McMahon, Moore | 5,178 |
| 34 | 4 | | (a) | Exeter City | L | 0 - 1 | | 3,424 |
| 35 | 11 | | (h) | Doncaster Rovers | W | 2 - 1 | Moore, McMahon | 2,950 |
| 36 | 17 | | (a) | Lincoln City | L | 0 - 2 | | 5,459 |
| 37 | 29 | | (a) | Bradford City | L | 0 - 3 | | 2,225 |
| 38 | Feb 1 | | (h) | Darlington | W | 2 - 0 | McMahon, Goad | 4,138 |
| 39 | 12 | | (h) | Lincoln City | W | 2 - 0 | Moore 2 | 2,632 |
| 40 | 15 | | (h) | Bradford City | L | 1 - 2 | Moore | 3,278 |
| 41 | 22 | | (a) | Brentford | L | 0 - 1 | | 5,516 |
| 42 | 24 | | (a) | Reading | D | 0 - 0 | | 5,980 |
| 43 | 28 | | (a) | Southport | D | 0 - 0 | | 1,451 |
| 44 | Mar 8 | | (h) | Stockport County | D | 1 - 1 | Johnson | 2,593 |
| 45 | 10 | | (h) | Exeter City | L | 0 - 3 | | 2,178 |
| 46 | 15 | | (a) | Swansea City | L | 0 - 1 | | 2,303 |
| 47 | 17 | | (a) | Newport County | L | 0 - 2 | | 1,535 |
| 48 | 22 | | (h) | Crewe Alexandra | D | 1 - 1 | Johnson | 1,923 |
| 49 | 28 | | (h) | Scunthorpe United | W | 1 - 0 | McMahon | 2,471 |
| 50 | 29 | | (a) | Rochdale | L | 0 - 3 | | 1,297 |
| 51 | Apr 1 | | (a) | Northampton Town | L | 0 - 3 | | 2,758 |
| 52 | 5 | | (a) | Mansfield Town | L | 0 - 2 | | 8,860 |
| 53 | 7 | | (h) | Cambridge United | D | 1 - 1 | Ward | 1,627 |
| 54 | 12 | | (h) | Shrewsbury Town | D | 1 - 1 | McMahon | 2,182 |
| 55 | 15 | | (a) | Workington | D | 1 - 1 | Moore | 1,319 |
| 56 | 19 | | (a) | Torquay United | L | 1 - 2 | McMahon | 2,444 |
| 57 | 21 | | (h) | Chester | W | 1 - 0 | Moore | 2,047 |
| 58 | 26 | | (h) | Barnsley | W | 4 - 3 | Ward 2, Moore, Dawes | 2,159 |

Final Position : 13th in Division Four

Apps.
Sub.Apps.
1 own goal — Goals

**FA Cup**

| Match No. | Date | Round | Venue | Opponents | Result | | Scorers | Attendance |
|---|---|---|---|---|---|---|---|---|
| 26 | Nov 23 | R1 | (h) | Bradford City | W | 1 - 0 | Honour | 3,677 |
| 29 | Dec 14 | R2 | (h) | Lincoln City | D | 0 - 0 | | 2,838 |
| 30 | 17 | R2r | (a) | Lincoln City | L | 0 - 1 | | 4,985 |

Apps.
Sub.Apps.
Goals

**League Cup**

| Match No. | Date | Round | Venue | Opponents | Result | | Scorers | Attendance |
|---|---|---|---|---|---|---|---|---|
| 2 | Aug 21 | R1 | (a) | Workington | W | 2 - 1 | McMahon, Gauden | 2,011 |
| 6 | Sep 11 | R2 | (a) | Bournemouth | D | 1 - 1 | Gauden | 4,971 |
| 8 | 18 | R2r | (h) | Bournemouth | D | 2 - 2* | Moore 2 | 5,160 |
| 10 | 23 | R2r2 | (a) | Bournemouth | D | 1 - 1* | Moore | 4,496 |
| 11 | 26 | R2r3 | (h) | Bournemouth | W | 1 - 0 | Ward | 6,970 |
| 15 | Oct 9 | R3 | (h) | Blackburn Rovers | D | 1 - 1 | Moore | 5,995 |
| 17 | 16 | R3r | (a) | Blackburn Rovers | W | 2 - 1 | Potter, McMahon | 11,145 |
| 24 | Nov 12 | R4 | (h) | Aston Villa | D | 1 - 1 | Moore | 12,305 |
| 27 | 25 | R4r | (a) | Aston Villa | L | 1 - 6 | Gauden | 17,686 |

* After extra-time

Apps.
Sub.Apps.
Goals

| Watling | Potter | Shoulder | Dawes | Goad | Honour | Park | Gauden | Moore | McMahon | Ward | Smith, R.M.S. | Heath | Spelman | McBurney | Embleton | Johnson, K.P. | Smith, D.B. | Johnson, D. | Worthington | Maddison | Guy | Griffiths |
|---|---|---|---|---|---|---|---|---|---|---|---|---|---|---|---|---|---|---|---|---|---|---|
| 1 | 2 | 3 | 4 | 5 | 6 | 7 | 8 | 9 | 10 | 11 | | | | | | | | | | | | |
| 1 | 2 | 3 | 4 | 5 | 7 | 6 | 8 | 9 | 10 | *11* | *12* | | | | | | | | | | | |
| 1 | 2 | 3 | 4 | 5 | 7 | 6 | *8* | 9 | 10 | 11 | *12* | | | | | | | | | | | |
| 1 | 6 | 3 | 4 | 5 | | | 8 | 9 | 10 | | 2 | 7 | 11 | | | | | | | | | |
| 1 | 6 | 3 | 4 | 5 | | | 8 | 9 | 10 | | 2 | 7 | 11 | | | | | | | | | |
| 1 | 6 | 3 | 4 | 5 | | | 8 | 9 | 10 | | 2 | 7 | 11 | | | | | | | | | |
| 1 | 6 | 3 | 4 | 5 | *12* | | 8 | 9 | *10* | 11 | 2 | 7 | | | | | | | | | | |
| 1 | 6 | 3 | 4 | 5 | 11 | | 8 | 9 | 10 | | 2 | 7 | | | | | | | | | | |
| 1 | 6 | 3 | 4 | 5 | 11 | | 8 | 9 | 10 | | 2 | 7 | | | | | | | | | | |
| 1 | 6 | 3 | 4 | 5 | 11 | | 8 | 9 | 10 | | 2 | 7 | | | | | | | | | | |
| 1 | 6 | 3 | 4 | 5 | 7 | *11* | 8 | 9 | 10 | *12* | 2 | | | | | | | | | | | |
| 1 | 6 | 3 | 4 | 5 | 7 | | 8 | 9 | 10 | 11 | 2 | | | | | | | | | | | |
| 1 | 6 | 3 | 4 | 5 | 7 | | 8 | 9 | 10 | 11 | 2 | | | | | | | | | | | |
| 1 | 6 | 3 | 4 | 5 | 7 | | 8 | 9 | 10 | 11 | 2 | | | | | | | | | | | |
| 1 | 6 | 3 | 4 | 5 | 7 | | 8 | 9 | 10 | *11* | 2 | | *12* | | | | | | | | | |
| 1 | 6 | 3 | 4 | 5 | 7 | | 8 | 9 | 10 | | 2 | | 11 | | | | | | | | | |
| 1 | 6 | 3 | 4 | 5 | 7 | | 8 | 9 | 10 | | 2 | | 11 | | | | | | | | | |
| 1 | 6 | 3 | 4 | 5 | 7 | | 8 | 9 | 10 | | 2 | | 11 | *12* | | | | | | | | |
| 1 | 6 | 3 | 4 | 5 | 7 | | 8 | 9 | 10 | 11 | 2 | | | | | | | | | | | |
| 1 | 6 | *3* | 4 | 5 | *12* | | | 9 | 10 | 7 | 2 | | 11 | 8 | | | | | | | | |
| 1 | 2 | | 4 | 5 | | 6 | | 9 | 10 | 7 | 3 | | 11 | 8 | | | | | | | | |
| 1 | 2 | | 4 | | | 6 | | 9 | 10 | 7 | 3 | | 11 | 8 | 5 | | | | | | | |
| 1 | 6 | 3 | 4 | 5 | | | | 9 | 10 | 7 | 2 | | 11 | 8 | | | | | | | | |
| 1 | 6 | 3 | 4 | 5 | | | | 9 | 10 | 7 | 2 | | 11 | 8 | | | | | | | | |
| 1 | 6 | 3 | 4 | 5 | 8 | | | 9 | 10 | 7 | 2 | | *11* | | *12* | | | | | | | |
| 1 | 6 | *3* | 4 | 5 | 8 | 11 | | 9 | 10 | 7 | 2 | | | | *12* | | | | | | | |
| 1 | 6 | | 4 | 5 | 8 | 11 | | 9 | 10 | 7 | 2 | | | | 3 | | | | | | | |
| 1 | 6 | | *4* | 5 | 8 | 11 | | 9 | 10 | 7 | 2 | | | | 3 | *12* | | | | | | |
| 1 | 3 | | 4 | 5 | 6 | | | 9 | 10 | 7 | 2 | | | | | 11 | 8 | | | | | |
| 1 | 6 | | 4 | 5 | 10 | | | 9 | | 7 | 2 | | | | 3 | 11 | 8 | | | | | |
| 1 | 6 | | 4 | 5 | | 10 | | 9 | | 7 | 2 | | | | 3 | 11 | 8 | | | | | |
| 1 | | | 4 | 5 | 10 | 6 | | 9 | | 7 | 2 | | | | 3 | 11 | 8 | | | | | |
| 1 | | | 4 | 5 | 6 | 3 | | 9 | | 7 | 2 | | | | | 11 | 8 | 10 | | | | |
| 1 | 6 | | 4 | 5 | 10 | | | 9 | | | 2 | | | | | 11 | 8 | | 3 | 7 | | |
| 1 | 6 | | 4 | 5 | 10 | | | 9 | | *12* | 2 | | | | | 11 | *8* | | 3 | 7 | | |
| 1 | 6 | | *4* | 5 | 8 | *12* | | 9 | | 11 | 2 | | | | | 10 | | | 3 | 7 | | |
| 1 | 2 | | | 5 | 8 | | | 9 | 10 | 7 | 4 | | | | 6 | 11 | | | 3 | | | |
| 1 | 2 | | | 5 | 8 | *12* | | 9 | 10 | 7 | 4 | | | | *6* | 11 | | | 3 | | | |
| 1 | 6 | | 4 | 5 | 7 | 8 | | 9 | 10 | | 2 | | | | | 11 | | | 3 | | | |
| 1 | 4 | | 3 | 5 | | | | 9 | 10 | 7 | 2 | | 11 | | 6 | 8 | | | | | | |
| 1 | 4 | | 3 | 5 | | | | 9 | 10 | 7 | 2 | | 11 | | 6 | 8 | | | | | | |
| 1 | 4 | | 3 | 5 | *12* | | | 9 | 10 | 7 | 2 | | *11* | | 6 | 8 | | | | | | |
| 1 | 3 | | | 5 | *8* | *12* | | 9 | 10 | 7 | 2 | | 4 | | 6 | 11 | | | | | | |
| 1 | 3 | | | 5 | | 8 | | 9 | 10 | 7 | 2 | | 4 | | 6 | 11 | | | | | | |
| 1 | 3 | | 4 | 5 | | | | 9 | 10 | 7 | 2 | | 8 | | 6 | 11 | | | | | | |
| | 3 | | 4 | 5 | | | | 9 | 10 | 7 | 2 | | *8* | | 6 | 11 | | | | | 1 | *12* |
| 45 | 44 | 24 | 42 | 45 | 30 | 14 | 19 | 46 | 39 | 33 | 43 | 7 | 19 | 5 | 15 | 18 | 7 | 1 | 6 | 3 | 1 | |
| | | | | | 3 | 3 | | | | 2 | 2 | | 1 | 1 | 2 | 1 | | | | | | 1 |
| | 1 | 2 | 5 | 1 | 3 | | 3 | 14 | 13 | 3 | 1 | | 2 | 1 | | 2 | | | | | | |
| | | | | | | | | | | | | | | | | | | | | | | |
| 1 | 6 | 3 | 4 | 5 | 7 | | 8 | 9 | 10 | | 2 | | 11 | | | | | | | | | |
| 1 | 6 | 3 | | 5 | 7 | | 8 | 9 | 10 | 4 | 2 | | 11 | | | | | | | | | |
| 1 | 6 | 3 | *12* | 5 | 7 | | *8* | 9 | 10 | 4 | 2 | | 11 | | | | | | | | | |
| 3 | 3 | 3 | 1 | 3 | 3 | | 3 | 3 | 3 | 2 | 3 | | 3 | | | | | | | | | |
| | | | 1 | | | | | | | | | | | | | | | | | | | |
| | | | | | 1 | | | | | | | | | | | | | | | | | |
| | | | | | | | | | | | | | | | | | | | | | | |
| 1 | 2 | 3 | 4 | 5 | 7 | 6 | 8 | 9 | 10 | 11 | | | | | | | | | | | | |
| 1 | 6 | 3 | 4 | 5 | | | 8 | 9 | 10 | | 2 | 7 | 11 | | | | | | | | | |
| 1 | 6 | 3 | 4 | 5 | | | 8 | 9 | 10 | | 2 | 7 | 11 | | | | | | | | | |
| 1 | 6 | 3 | 4 | 5 | | | 8 | 9 | 10 | | 2 | 7 | 11 | | | | | | | | | |
| 1 | 6 | 3 | 4 | 5 | | | 8 | 9 | 10 | *12* | 2 | 7 | *11* | | | | | | | | | |
| 1 | 6 | 3 | 4 | 5 | 11 | | 8 | 9 | 10 | | 2 | 7 | | | | | | | | | | |
| 1 | 6 | 3 | 4 | 5 | 7 | *12* | 8 | 9 | 10 | | 2 | | *11* | | | | | | | | | |
| 1 | 6 | 3 | 4 | 5 | 7 | | 8 | 9 | 10 | | 2 | | 11 | | | | | | | | | |
| 1 | 6 | 3 | 4 | 5 | 7 | | 8 | 9 | 10 | | 2 | | 11 | | | | | | | | | |
| 9 | 9 | 9 | 9 | 9 | 5 | 1 | 9 | 9 | 9 | 1 | 8 | 5 | 7 | | | | | | | | | |
| | | | | | | 1 | | | | 1 | | | | | | | | | | | | |
| | 1 | | | | | | 3 | 5 | 2 | 1 | | | | | | | | | | | | |

## League Table

| | P | W | D | L | F | A | Pts |
|---|---|---|---|---|---|---|---|
| Mansfield Town | 46 | 28 | 12 | 6 | 90 | 40 | 68 |
| Shrewsbury Town | 46 | 26 | 10 | 10 | 80 | 43 | 62 |
| Rotherham United | 46 | 22 | 15 | 9 | 71 | 41 | 59 |
| Chester | 46 | 23 | 11 | 12 | 64 | 38 | 57 |
| Lincoln City | 46 | 21 | 15 | 10 | 79 | 48 | 57 |
| Cambridge United | 46 | 20 | 14 | 12 | 62 | 44 | 54 |
| Reading | 46 | 21 | 10 | 15 | 63 | 47 | 52 |
| Brentford | 46 | 18 | 13 | 15 | 53 | 45 | 49 |
| Exeter City | 46 | 19 | 11 | 16 | 60 | 63 | 49 |
| Bradford City | 46 | 17 | 13 | 16 | 56 | 51 | 47 |
| Southport | 46 | 15 | 17 | 14 | 56 | 56 | 47 |
| Newport County | 46 | 19 | 9 | 18 | 68 | 75 | 47 |
| Hartlepool | 46 | 16 | 11 | 19 | 52 | 62 | 43 |
| Torquay United | 46 | 14 | 14 | 18 | 46 | 61 | 42 |
| Barnsley | 46 | 15 | 11 | 20 | 62 | 65 | 41 |
| Northampton Town | 46 | 15 | 11 | 20 | 67 | 73 | 41 |
| Doncaster Rovers | 46 | 14 | 12 | 20 | 65 | 79 | 40 |
| Crewe Alexandra | 46 | 11 | 18 | 17 | 34 | 47 | 40 |
| Rochdale | 46 | 13 | 13 | 20 | 59 | 75 | 39 |
| Stockport County | 46 | 12 | 14 | 20 | 43 | 70 | 38 |
| Darlington | 46 | 13 | 10 | 23 | 54 | 67 | 36 |
| Swansea City | 46 | 15 | 6 | 25 | 46 | 73 | 36 |
| Workington | 46 | 10 | 11 | 25 | 36 | 66 | 31 |
| Scunthorpe United | 46 | 7 | 15 | 24 | 41 | 78 | 29 |

# 1975-76

## Division Four

Manager: Ken Hale

### Did you know that?

The six-goal FA Cup defeat by Manchester City was the prelude to a run of 13 League games without a win. The signing of Barry Endean was the catalyst for a late run of five wins in six games, which resulted in a respectable mid-table 14th-place finish.

Malcolm Moore's hat-trick in the 6–3 victory over non-League Marine was the first for the club in the FA Cup since the 1961–62 season when Bobby Folland recorded a treble in the 5–1 win over Blyth Spartans, another non-League side.

| Match No. | Date | Round | Venue | Opponents | Result | | Scorers | Attendance |
|---|---|---|---|---|---|---|---|---|
| 1 | Aug 16 | | (h) | Bournemouth | D | 1 - 1 | D.Smith | 2,228 |
| 3 | 23 | | (a) | Brentford | D | 1 - 1 | Goad | 4,948 |
| 5 | 30 | | (h) | Lincoln City | D | 2 - 2 | D.Smith 2 | 1,908 |
| 6 | Sep 6 | | (a) | Watford | L | 1 - 2 | Skillen | 3,598 |
| 7 | 13 | | (h) | Scunthorpe United | L | 1 - 2 | Johnson | 1,972 |
| 8 | 19 | | (a) | Southport | W | 4 - 2 | Johnson, McMahon, Moore, D.Smith | 1,012 |
| 9 | 22 | | (h) | Reading | L | 2 - 4 | Rowlands, R.Smith | 2,269 |
| 10 | 27 | | (h) | Tranmere Rovers | L | 1 - 2 | Rowlands | 1,559 |
| 11 | Oct 4 | | (a) | Crewe Alexandra | D | 0 - 0 | | 2,326 |
| 12 | 11 | | (h) | Torquay United | L | 0 - 1 | | 1,695 |
| 13 | 13 | | (h) | Exeter City | W | 2 - 1 | Moore, D.Smith | 1,323 |
| 14 | 18 | | (a) | Exeter City | L | 1 - 3 | Goad | 2,406 |
| 15 | 22 | | (h) | Stockport County | W | 3 - 0 | Moore, D.Smith, McMahon | 1,683 |
| 16 | 25 | | (h) | Barnsley | W | 1 - 0 | D.Smith | 2,350 |
| 17 | Nov 1 | | (a) | Huddersfield Town | L | 0 - 2 | | 4,183 |
| 18 | 3 | | (a) | Darlington | W | 2 - 1 | McMahon, Scaife | 4,275 |
| 19 | 8 | | (h) | Doncaster Rovers | W | 2 - 1 | Rowlands, McMahon | 3,592 |
| 20 | 15 | | (a) | Bradford City | W | 2 - 1 | Johnson, Honour | 2,009 |
| 22 | 29 | | (h) | Newport County | W | 4 - 1 | Moore, Screen (o.g.), Johnson, McMahon | 2,661 |
| 23 | Dec 6 | | (a) | Swansea City | L | 1 - 3 | McMahon | 2,354 |
| 26 | 20 | | (a) | Rochdale | D | 1 - 1 | Scaife | 1,156 |
| 27 | 26 | | (h) | Northampton Town | W | 3 - 0 | D.Smith 2, McMahon | 5,077 |
| 28 | 27 | | (a) | Workington | W | 2 - 1 | McMahon, Moore | 2,553 |
| 30 | Jan 10 | | (a) | Lincoln City | L | 0 - 3 | | 7,581 |
| 31 | 17 | | (h) | Southport | D | 0 - 0 | | 2,953 |
| 32 | 30 | | (a) | Stockport County | L | 0 - 2 | | 1,565 |
| 33 | Feb 7 | | (h) | Darlington | L | 2 - 3 | Rowlands, D.Smith | 3,689 |
| 34 | 14 | | (a) | Doncaster Rovers | L | 0 - 3 | | 5,035 |
| 35 | 18 | | (h) | Cambridge United | D | 2 - 2 | Goad, Moore | 1,434 |
| 36 | 21 | | (h) | Bradford City | D | 2 - 2 | D.Smith 2 | 1,899 |
| 37 | 25 | | (a) | Reading | L | 0 - 1 | | 6,473 |
| 38 | 28 | | (a) | Barnsley | L | 1 - 3 | Scaife | 2,772 |
| 39 | Mar 2 | | (a) | Scunthorpe United | L | 1 - 5 | D.Smith | 3,098 |
| 40 | 6 | | (h) | Huddersfield Town | D | 1 - 1 | Rowlands | 2,058 |
| 41 | 10 | | (h) | Crewe Alexandra | L | 1 - 3 | Moore | 1,506 |
| 42 | 13 | | (a) | Torquay United | D | 1 - 1 | Moore | 2,826 |
| 43 | 20 | | (a) | Newport County | W | 1 - 0 | Moore | 1,230 |
| 44 | 27 | | (h) | Swansea City | W | 1 - 0 | Rowlands | 1,708 |
| 45 | 31 | | (h) | Rochdale | W | 3 - 0 | Spelman, Moore 2 | 1,561 |
| 46 | Apr 3 | | (a) | Bournemouth | L | 2 - 4 | Endean, Johnson | 3,102 |
| 47 | 6 | | (a) | Tranmere Rovers | W | 2 - 1 | Endean, Griffiths (o.g.) | 3,450 |
| 48 | 10 | | (h) | Watford | W | 2 - 1 | Endean, Moore | 2,028 |
| 49 | 16 | | (a) | Cambridge United | L | 0 - 4 | | 2,136 |
| 50 | 17 | | (a) | Northampton Town | L | 2 - 5 | Moore, Johnson (pen) | 7,555 |
| 51 | 20 | | (h) | Workington | L | 0 - 2 | | 1,765 |
| 52 | 24 | | (h) | Brentford | W | 1 - 0 | Scaife | 1,276 |

Final Position : 14th in Division Four

Apps.
Sub.Apps.
2 own goals Goals

**FA Cup**

| Match No. | Date | Round | Venue | Opponents | Result | | Scorers | Attendance |
|---|---|---|---|---|---|---|---|---|
| 21 | Nov 22 | R1 | (h) | Stockport County | W | 3 - 0 | D.Smith, McMahon, Potter | 3,348 |
| 24 | Dec 13 | R2 | (a) | Marine | D | 1 - 1 | Scaife | 2,300 |
| 25 | 15 | R2r | (h) | Marine | W | 6 - 3 | Moore 3, Johnson (pen), Rowlands, Scaife | 5,673 |
| 29 | Jan 3 | R3 | (a) | Manchester City | L | 0 - 6 | | 26,863 |

Apps.
Sub.Apps.
Goals

**League Cup**

| Match No. | Date | Round | Venue | Opponents | Result | | Scorers | Attendance |
|---|---|---|---|---|---|---|---|---|
| 2 | Aug 19 | R1/1 | (a) | Halifax Town | L | 1 - 4 | Johnson | 1,476 |
| 4 | 25 | R1/2 | (h) | Halifax Town | W | 2 - 1 | McMahon, Skillen | 1,725 |

Apps.
Sub.Apps.
Goals

| Hope | Smith, R.M.S. | Crowther | Potter | Goad | Dawes | Honour | Smith, D.B. | Moore | McMahon | Johnson | Skillen | Richardson | Embleton | Watling | Spelman | Scaife | Rowlands | Bielby | Maggiore | Charlton | Elliott | Wann | Jacques | Luckett | Rylands | Endean | Ableson |
|---|---|---|---|---|---|---|---|---|---|---|---|---|---|---|---|---|---|---|---|---|---|---|---|---|---|---|---|
| 1 | 2 | 3 | *4* | 5 | 6 | 7 | 8 | 9 | 10 | 11 | *12* | | | | | | | | | | | | | | | | |
| | 3 | 2 | 4 | 5 | | 7 | 8 | *12* | 10 | 11 | 9 | 1 | *6* | | | | | | | | | | | | | | |
| | 2 | 3 | 6 | 5 | | 4 | 8 | 9 | 10 | 11 | 7 | | | 1 | | | | | | | | | | | | | |
| | 2 | | 6 | 5 | | | *8* | 9 | 10 | 11 | 7 | | | 1 | 3 | 4 | *12* | | | | | | | | | | |
| | 2 | | 6 | 5 | | | *8* | 9 | 10 | 11 | 7 | 1 | | | 3 | 4 | *12* | | | | | | | | | | |
| | 3 | | 2 | | | | 8 | 9 | 10 | 11 | | 1 | 6 | | 7 | 4 | 5 | | | | | | | | | | |
| | 3 | | 2 | | | | 8 | 9 | 10 | 11 | | 1 | 6 | | 7 | 4 | 5 | | | | | | | | | | |
| 1 | 3 | | 2 | 6 | | | 8 | 9 | 10 | 11 | *12* | | | | 7 | *4* | 5 | | | | | | | | | | |
| 1 | | | 4 | 2 | | 7 | 8 | 9 | | 6 | | | 3 | | 10 | 11 | 5 | | | | | | | | | | |
| 1 | | | 4 | 2 | | 7 | 8 | *9* | *12* | 6 | | | 3 | | 10 | 11 | 5 | | | | | | | | | | |
| 1 | 2 | | 4 | 3 | | 7 | 8 | 9 | 10 | 6 | | | | | 11 | | 5 | | | | | | | | | | |
| 1 | 2 | | 4 | 3 | | 7 | 8 | 9 | 10 | 6 | | | | | 11 | | 5 | | | | | | | | | | |
| 1 | 2 | | 4 | 3 | | 7 | 8 | 9 | 10 | 6 | | | | | 11 | | 5 | | | | | | | | | | |
| 1 | 2 | | 4 | 3 | | 7 | 8 | 9 | 10 | 6 | | | | | 11 | | 5 | | | | | | | | | | |
| 1 | 2 | | 4 | 3 | | 7 | 8 | 9 | 10 | 6 | | | | | 11 | *12* | 5 | | | | | | | | | | |
| 1 | 2 | | 4 | 3 | | 7 | 8 | 9 | 10 | 6 | | | | | | 11 | 5 | | | | | | | | | | |
| 1 | 2 | | 4 | 3 | | 7 | 8 | 9 | 10 | 6 | | | | | | 11 | 5 | | | | | | | | | | |
| 1 | 2 | | 4 | 3 | | 7 | 8 | 9 | 10 | 6 | | | | | | 11 | 5 | *12* | | | | | | | | | |
| 1 | 2 | | *4* | 3 | | | 8 | 9 | 10 | 6 | | | | | | 11 | 5 | 7 | *12* | | | | | | | | |
| 1 | 2 | | 4 | 3 | | | 8 | 9 | 10 | 6 | | | | | | 11 | 5 | 7 | | | | | | | | | |
| 1 | 2 | | 4 | 3 | | | 8 | 9 | 10 | *6* | | | | | 7 | 11 | 5 | *12* | | | | | | | | | |
| 1 | 2 | | 4 | 3 | | 7 | 8 | 9 | 10 | | | | | | 6 | 11 | 5 | | | | | | | | | | |
| 1 | 2 | | 4 | 3 | | 7 | 8 | 9 | *10* | | | | | | 6 | 11 | 5 | *12* | | | | | | | | | |
| 1 | 2 | | | 3 | | | 8 | | 10 | | | | | | | 11 | 5 | 6 | 4 | 7 | 9 | | | | | | |
| 1 | 2 | | | 3 | | | 8 | | 10 | | | | | | | 11 | 5 | 6 | 4 | 7 | | 9 | | | | | |
| 1 | 2 | | | | | 7 | 8 | 9 | 10 | 6 | | | | | | 11 | 5 | | 3 | | | | 4 | | | | |
| 1 | 2 | | 4 | | | 7 | 8 | 9 | *10* | 6 | | | | | | 11 | 5 | | 3 | *12* | | | | | | | |
| | | | 4 | 3 | | | | 9 | 10 | 6 | | 1 | | | 7 | 11 | 5 | *12* | 2 | | | *8* | | | | | |
| | 2 | | 4 | 3 | | | 8 | 9 | 10 | 6 | | 1 | | | 7 | 11 | 5 | *12* | | | | | | | | | |
| | 2 | | 4 | 3 | | 7 | 8 | 9 | | | | 1 | | | 10 | 11 | 5 | | | | | | 6 | | | | |
| | 2 | | 4 | 3 | | 7 | 8 | 9 | | | | 1 | | | 10 | 11 | 5 | | | | | | 6 | | | | |
| | 2 | | 4 | 3 | | 7 | 8 | 9 | | | | 1 | | | *10* | 11 | 5 | *12* | | | | | 6 | | | | |
| 1 | | | 4 | 3 | | | 8 | 9 | | 6 | | | | | 10 | 11 | | | 2 | | 7 | | 5 | | | | |
| | 2 | | 4 | 3 | | | 8 | 9 | 10 | 6 | | 1 | | | 7 | 11 | 5 | | | | | | | | | | |
| | 2 | | 4 | 3 | | | *8* | 9 | 10 | 6 | | 1 | | | 7 | 11 | 5 | *12* | | | | | | | | | |
| | 2 | | 4 | | | | | 9 | | 6 | | 1 | | | 7 | 11 | 10 | | *12* | | | | | *3* | 5 | 8 | |
| | 2 | | 4 | | | | | 9 | | 6 | | 1 | | | 7 | 11 | 10 | | | | | | | 3 | 5 | 8 | |
| | 2 | | 4 | | | | | 9 | | 6 | | 1 | | | 7 | 11 | 10 | | | | | | | 3 | 5 | 8 | |
| | | | 4 | 2 | | | | 9 | | 6 | | 1 | | | 7 | 11 | 10 | | | | | | | 3 | 5 | 8 | |
| | | | 4 | 2 | | | 10 | 9 | | 6 | | 1 | | | 7 | 11 | | | | | | | | 3 | 5 | 8 | |
| | | | 4 | 2 | | | | 9 | | 10 | | 1 | | | 7 | 11 | | | 6 | | | | | 3 | 5 | 8 | |
| | | | 4 | 2 | | | | 9 | | 10 | | 1 | | | 7 | *11* | | *12* | 6 | | | | | 3 | 5 | 8 | |
| | | | 4 | 2 | | | | 9 | | 10 | | *1* | | | 7 | *12* | | 11 | 6 | | | | | 3 | 5 | 8 | |
| 1 | | | 4 | | | | | 9 | | 10 | | | | | 2 | 7 | | 11 | 6 | | | | | 3 | 5 | 8 | |
| | | | 4 | | | | | 9 | | 6 | | 1 | | | 2 | 10 | | 11 | *12* | | 7 | | | 3 | *5* | 8 | |
| | | | 4 | 2 | | | | *9* | | | | 1 | | | 7 | 10 | | 11 | *12* | | 6 | | | 3 | 5 | 8 | |
| 23 | 34 | 3 | 43 | 37 | 1 | 20 | 35 | 43 | 29 | 38 | 4 | 21 | 5 | 2 | 34 | 37 | 33 | 8 | 10 | 2 | 4 | 2 | 5 | 11 | 11 | 11 | |
| | | | | | | | | 1 | 1 | | 2 | | | | | 2 | 2 | 8 | 4 | 1 | | | | | | | |
| | 1 | | | 3 | | 1 | 13 | 13 | 8 | 6 | 1 | | | | 1 | 4 | 6 | | | | | | | | | 3 | |

| Hope | Smith, R.M.S. | Crowther | Potter | Goad | Dawes | Honour | Smith, D.B. | Moore | McMahon | Johnson | Skillen | Richardson | Embleton | Watling | Spelman | Scaife | Rowlands | Bielby | Maggiore | Charlton | Elliott | Wann | Jacques | Luckett | Rylands | Endean | Ableson |
|---|---|---|---|---|---|---|---|---|---|---|---|---|---|---|---|---|---|---|---|---|---|---|---|---|---|---|---|
| 1 | 2 | | 4 | 3 | | | 8 | 9 | 10 | 6 | | | | | | 11 | 5 | 7 | | | | | | | | | |
| 1 | 2 | | 4 | 3 | | | 8 | 9 | 10 | 6 | | | | | 7 | 11 | 5 | | | | | | | | | | |
| 1 | 2 | | 4 | 3 | | | 8 | 9 | 10 | 6 | | | | | 7 | 11 | 5 | | | | | | | | | | |
| 1 | 2 | | 4 | 3 | | 7 | 8 | 9 | 10 | | | | | | | 11 | 5 | 6 | | | | | | | | | |
| 4 | 4 | | 4 | 4 | | 1 | 4 | 4 | 4 | 3 | | | | | 2 | 4 | 4 | 2 | | | | | | | | | |
| | | | | | | | | | | | | | | | | | | | | | | | | | | | |
| | | | 1 | | | | 1 | 3 | 1 | 1 | | | | | | 2 | 1 | | | | | | | | | | |

| Hope | Smith, R.M.S. | Crowther | Potter | Goad | Dawes | Honour | Smith, D.B. | Moore | McMahon | Johnson | Skillen | Richardson | Embleton | Watling | Spelman | Scaife | Rowlands | Bielby | Maggiore | Charlton | Elliott | Wann | Jacques | Luckett | Rylands | Endean | Ableson |
|---|---|---|---|---|---|---|---|---|---|---|---|---|---|---|---|---|---|---|---|---|---|---|---|---|---|---|---|
| 1 | 3 | 2 | 4 | 5 | | 7 | 8 | 9 | 10 | 11 | | | | | | | | | | | | | | | | | 6 |
| | 2 | 3 | 6 | 5 | | 4 | 8 | 9 | 10 | 11 | 7 | 1 | | | | | | | | | | | | | | | |
| 1 | 2 | 2 | 2 | 2 | | 2 | 2 | 2 | 2 | 2 | 1 | 1 | | | | | | | | | | | | | | | |
| | | | | | | | | | | | | | | | | | | | | | | | | | | | |
| | | | | | | | | | 1 | 1 | 1 | | | | | | | | | | | | | | | | |

## League Table

| | P | W | D | L | F | A | Pts |
|---|---|---|---|---|---|---|---|
| Lincoln City | 46 | 32 | 10 | 4 | 111 | 39 | 74 |
| Northampton Town | 46 | 29 | 10 | 7 | 87 | 40 | 68 |
| Reading | 46 | 24 | 12 | 10 | 70 | 51 | 60 |
| Tranmere Rovers | 46 | 24 | 10 | 12 | 89 | 55 | 58 |
| Huddersfield Town | 46 | 21 | 14 | 11 | 56 | 41 | 56 |
| Bournemouth | 46 | 20 | 12 | 14 | 57 | 48 | 52 |
| Exeter City | 46 | 18 | 14 | 14 | 56 | 47 | 50 |
| Watford | 46 | 22 | 6 | 18 | 62 | 62 | 50 |
| Torquay United | 46 | 18 | 14 | 14 | 55 | 63 | 50 |
| Doncaster Rovers | 46 | 19 | 11 | 16 | 75 | 69 | 49 |
| Swansea City | 46 | 16 | 15 | 15 | 66 | 57 | 47 |
| Barnsley | 46 | 14 | 16 | 16 | 52 | 48 | 44 |
| Cambridge United | 46 | 14 | 15 | 17 | 58 | 62 | 43 |
| Hartlepool | 46 | 16 | 10 | 20 | 62 | 78 | 42 |
| Rochdale | 46 | 12 | 18 | 16 | 40 | 54 | 42 |
| Crewe Alexandra | 46 | 13 | 15 | 18 | 58 | 57 | 41 |
| Bradford City | 46 | 12 | 17 | 17 | 63 | 65 | 41 |
| Brentford | 46 | 14 | 13 | 19 | 56 | 60 | 41 |
| Scunthorpe United | 46 | 14 | 10 | 22 | 50 | 59 | 38 |
| Darlington | 46 | 14 | 10 | 22 | 48 | 57 | 38 |
| Stockport County | 46 | 13 | 12 | 21 | 43 | 76 | 38 |
| Newport County | 46 | 13 | 9 | 24 | 57 | 90 | 35 |
| Southport | 46 | 8 | 10 | 28 | 41 | 77 | 26 |
| Workington | 46 | 7 | 7 | 32 | 30 | 87 | 21 |

# 1976-77

## Division Four

Managers: Ken Hale and Billy Horner

### Did you know that?

'Pools made their 11th application for re-election, having finished in 22nd place. In the event, they successfully polled 43 votes, with Workington (21 votes) losing their League status in favour of Wimbledon (26 votes).

Billy Horner made locally born Peter Creamer, an England schoolboy international, his first signing from Doncaster Rovers for a reported £5,000 transfer fee.

Average League attendances of 1,911 were the lowest to this point.

| Match No. | Date | Round | Venue | Opponents | Result | | Scorers | Attendance |
|---|---|---|---|---|---|---|---|---|
| 3 | Aug 21 | | (h) | Exeter City | D | 2 - 2 | Endean, Elliott | 1,599 |
| 4 | 24 | | (a) | Watford | L | 0 - 4 | | 4,667 |
| 5 | 26 | | (a) | Crewe Alexandra | L | 1 - 3 | Lugg (o.g.) | 2,012 |
| 6 | Sep 4 | | (h) | Bournemouth | L | 0 - 1 | | 1,548 |
| 7 | 11 | | (a) | Workington | D | 1 - 1 | Harley | 1,505 |
| 8 | 18 | | (h) | Southend United | D | 1 - 1 | Rowlands | 1,612 |
| 9 | 24 | | (a) | Halifax Town | L | 0 - 1 | | 1,393 |
| 10 | Oct 2 | | (a) | Scunthorpe United | L | 0 - 2 | | 3,514 |
| 11 | 9 | | (h) | Cambridge United | D | 2 - 2 | Scaife, Rowlands | 1,452 |
| 12 | 16 | | (a) | Colchester United | L | 2 - 6 | Bielby 2 | 3,180 |
| 13 | 23 | | (h) | Rochdale | W | 2 - 0 | Scaife, Reed (pen) | 1,492 |
| 14 | 26 | | (a) | Newport County | D | 1 - 1 | Scaife | 2,334 |
| 15 | 30 | | (h) | Huddersfield Town | L | 0 - 1 | | 2,628 |
| 16 | Nov 1 | | (h) | Stockport County | D | 1 - 1 | Rowlands | 1,685 |
| 17 | 5 | | (a) | Doncaster Rovers | L | 1 - 2 | Scaife | 2,631 |
| 18 | 13 | | (h) | Brentford | W | 2 - 0 | Davies (pen), Rowlands | 1,888 |
| 20 | 27 | | (a) | Aldershot | L | 0 - 3 | | 3,494 |
| 21 | Dec 18 | | (a) | Barnsley | L | 0 - 3 | | 3,667 |
| 22 | 22 | | (a) | Bradford City | D | 2 - 2 | Poskett, Bielby | 3,552 |
| 23 | 27 | | (h) | Darlington | D | 1 - 1 | O'Donnell | 4,885 |
| 24 | Jan 1 | | (h) | Doncaster Rovers | D | 0 - 0 | | 2,206 |
| 25 | 8 | | (h) | Torquay United | W | 4 - 0 | Poskett 3, Bielby | 2,128 |
| 26 | 15 | | (h) | Watford | W | 1 - 0 | Wiggett (pen) | 2,411 |
| 27 | 22 | | (a) | Exeter City | L | 1 - 3 | Goldthorpe | 3,285 |
| 28 | 29 | | (a) | Swansea City | L | 2 - 4 | Bartley (o.g.), Creamer | 5,034 |
| 29 | Feb 5 | | (h) | Crewe Alexandra | W | 3 - 0 | Poskett 2, Scaife | 1,972 |
| 30 | 12 | | (a) | Bournemouth | L | 0 - 2 | | 4,409 |
| 31 | 15 | | (a) | Huddersfield Town | L | 1 - 4 | Creamer | 5,493 |
| 32 | 19 | | (h) | Workington | W | 2 - 0 | Endean, Johnston (o.g.) | 1,774 |
| 33 | 25 | | (a) | Southend United | L | 0 - 1 | | 6,619 |
| 34 | Mar 5 | | (h) | Halifax Town | W | 1 - 0 | Bielby | 1,673 |
| 35 | 7 | | (a) | Stockport County | L | 0 - 1 | | 2,649 |
| 36 | 12 | | (h) | Scunthorpe United | W | 3 - 0 | Poskett, Creamer, Scaife | 1,698 |
| 37 | 19 | | (a) | Cambridge United | L | 0 - 2 | | 3,853 |
| 38 | 26 | | (h) | Colchester United | D | 2 - 2 | Poskett 2 (1pen) | 1,831 |
| 39 | 28 | | (h) | Southport | D | 1 - 1 | Turnbull | 1,539 |
| 40 | Apr 2 | | (a) | Rochdale | W | 1 - 0 | Cunningham | 858 |
| 41 | 8 | | (a) | Darlington | L | 1 - 3 | Poskett | 4,419 |
| 42 | 9 | | (h) | Bradford City | L | 0 - 1 | | 2,765 |
| 43 | 16 | | (h) | Newport County | L | 0 - 1 | | 1,522 |
| 44 | 18 | | (h) | Swansea City | D | 2 - 2 | Goad, McMordie | 1,169 |
| 45 | 23 | | (a) | Brentford | L | 1 - 3 | Turnbull | 5,978 |
| 46 | 30 | | (h) | Aldershot | L | 0 - 2 | | 1,202 |
| 47 | May 4 | | (a) | Torquay United | L | 0 - 1 | | 1,831 |
| 48 | 7 | | (a) | Southport | W | 2 - 1 | Turnbull, Bielby | 880 |
| 49 | 14 | | (h) | Barnsley | L | 0 - 2 | | 1,274 |
| Final Position : 22nd in Division Four | | | | | | | | Apps. |
| | | | | | | | | Sub.Apps. |
| | | | | | | | 3 own goals | Goals |

**FA Cup**

| Match No. | Date | Round | Venue | Opponents | Result | | Scorers | Attendance |
|---|---|---|---|---|---|---|---|---|
| 19 | Nov 20 | R1 | (a) | Chester | L | 0 - 1 | | 3,724 |
| | | | | | | | | Apps. |
| | | | | | | | | Sub.Apps. |
| | | | | | | | | Goals |

**League Cup**

| Match No. | Date | Round | Venue | Opponents | Result | | Scorers | Attendance |
|---|---|---|---|---|---|---|---|---|
| 1 | Aug 14 | R1/1 | (a) | Huddersfield Town | L | 0 - 2 | | 3,603 |
| 2 | 18 | R1/2 | (h) | Huddersfield Town | L | 1 - 2 | Turnbull | 2,000 |
| | | | | | | | | Apps. |
| | | | | | | | | Sub.Apps. |
| | | | | | | | | Goals |

| Richardson | O'Donnell | Goad | Veitch | Scott | Maggiore | Spelman | Elliott | Endean | Scaife | Bielby | Potter | Edgar | Luckett | Johnson | Rowlands | Harley | Prudham | Reed | Wiggett | Creamer | McMaster | Davies | Poskett | Spraggon | Simpkin | McMordie | Goldthorpe | Turnbull | Cunningham | Smith |
|---|---|---|---|---|---|---|---|---|---|---|---|---|---|---|---|---|---|---|---|---|---|---|---|---|---|---|---|---|---|---|
| 1 | 2 | 3 | 4 | 5 | 6 | 7 | 8 | 9 | 10 | 11 | | | | | | | | | | | | | | | | | | | | |
| 1 | 2 | 3 | 4 | 5 | 6 | 7 | 8 | 9 | 10 | *11* | *12* | | | | | | | | | | | | | | | | | | | |
| | 2 | *9* | 4 | 5 | 6 | 10 | 8 | | 7 | *12* | | 1 | 3 | 11 | | | | | | | | | | | | | | | | |
| | | 2 | 4 | 5 | | 7 | *12* | 8 | | *11* | | 1 | 3 | 9 | 6 | 10 | | | | | | | | | | | | | | |
| | | 2 | 4 | 5 | | 8 | *7* | | *12* | | | 1 | 3 | 11 | 6 | 9 | 10 | | | | | | | | | | | | | |
| | | 2 | 4 | 5 | | *8* | *12* | | 7 | | | 1 | 3 | 11 | 6 | 9 | 10 | | | | | | | | | | | | | |
| | | 2 | 4 | 5 | 11 | | 8 | 9 | 7 | | | 1 | 3 | | 6 | | 10 | | | | | | | | | | | | | |
| | | 2 | 10 | 5 | 4 | 7 | *12* | 8 | 11 | | | 1 | 3 | | 6 | *9* | | | | | | | | | | | | | | |
| | | 2 | 10 | 5 | | 7 | 4 | 8 | 11 | *12* | | 1 | *3* | | 6 | | | 9 | | | | | | | | | | | | |
| | | 2 | 4 | 5 | | 7 | | | 10 | 11 | | 1 | 3 | | 8 | | | 9 | 6 | | | | | | | | | | | |
| | | 6 | | 5 | 4 | | 10 | | 7 | 11 | | 1 | | | 8 | | | 9 | 3 | 2 | | | | | | | | | | |
| | | 6 | | 5 | 4 | | *10* | *12* | 7 | 11 | | 1 | | | 8 | | | 9 | 3 | 2 | | | | | | | | | | |
| | | *6* | | 5 | 4 | | 10 | | 7 | 11 | | 1 | | | 8 | | | 9 | 3 | 2 | *12* | | | | | | | | | |
| | | 6 | | 5 | | | 10 | | 7 | 11 | | 1 | | | 8 | | | 4 | 3 | 2 | 9 | | | | | | | | | |
| | 4 | 8 | | 5 | | | 10 | | 7 | 11 | | 1 | | | 6 | | | | 3 | 2 | | 9 | | | | | | | | |
| | 4 | 8 | | 5 | | | *10* | | 7 | 11 | | 1 | | | 6 | | | | 3 | 2 | | 9 | *12* | | | | | | | |
| | 4 | 8 | | | | | 10 | | 7 | 11 | | 1 | | | 6 | | | | 3 | 2 | | | 9 | 5 | | | | | | |
| | 4 | *12* | | 5 | | | | | 7 | *11* | | 1 | | | | | | | 3 | 2 | | 9 | 10 | | 6 | 8 | | | | |
| | *4* | *12* | | 5 | | | | | 7 | 11 | | 1 | | | | | | | 3 | 2 | | 9 | 10 | | 6 | 8 | | | | |
| | 4 | *12* | | 5 | | | | | 7 | 11 | | 1 | | | | | | | 3 | 2 | | 9 | *10* | | 6 | 8 | | | | |
| 1 | 4 | | | 5 | | | | *9* | 7 | 11 | | | | | | | | | 3 | 2 | | | 10 | | 6 | 8 | *12* | | | |
| 1 | 4 | | | 5 | | | | | 7 | 11 | | | | | | | | | 3 | 2 | | | 10 | | 6 | 8 | 9 | | | |
| 1 | 4 | *12* | | 5 | | | | | 7 | 11 | | | | | | | | | 3 | 2 | | | 10 | | 6 | 8 | 9 | | | |
| 1 | 4 | *11* | | 5 | | | | | 7 | *12* | | | | | | | | | 3 | 2 | | | 10 | | 6 | 8 | 9 | | | |
| 1 | 4 | | | 5 | | | | | 7 | 11 | | | | | | | | | 3 | 2 | | | 10 | | 6 | 8 | 9 | | | |
| 1 | 4 | | | 5 | | | | | 7 | 11 | | | | | | | | | 3 | 2 | | | 10 | | 6 | 8 | 9 | | | |
| 1 | *4* | *12* | | 5 | | | | | 7 | 11 | | | | | | | | | 3 | 2 | | | 10 | | 6 | 8 | 9 | | | |
| 1 | | *12* | | 5 | | | 4 | 9 | 7 | 11 | | | | | | | | | 3 | 2 | | | 10 | | *6* | 8 | | | | |
| | | | | 5 | | | 4 | 9 | 7 | 11 | | 1 | | | | | | | 3 | 2 | | | 10 | | 6 | 8 | | | | |
| | 11 | | | 5 | | | 4 | 9 | 7 | | | 1 | | | | | | | 3 | 2 | | | 10 | | 6 | 8 | | | | |
| | 11 | 5 | | | | | *4* | 9 | 7 | *12* | | 1 | | | | | | | 3 | 2 | | | 10 | | 6 | 8 | | | | |
| | 11 | 5 | | | | | 4 | *9* | 7 | *12* | | 1 | | | | | | | 3 | 2 | | | 10 | | 6 | 8 | | | | |
| | *4* | 5 | | | | | | | 7 | 11 | | 1 | | | | | | | 3 | 2 | | | 10 | | 6 | 8 | | 9 | *12* | |
| | 4 | 5 | | | | | | | 7 | *11* | | 1 | | | | | | | 3 | 2 | | | 10 | | 6 | 8 | | 9 | *12* | |
| | | 4 | | 5 | | | | | 7 | | | 1 | | | | | | | 3 | 2 | | | 10 | | 6 | 8 | | 9 | 11 | |
| | *12* | 6 | | | 2 | | | | 7 | 4 | | 1 | | | | | | | 3 | 5 | | | 10 | | | 8 | | 9 | 11 | |
| | 4 | 8 | | 5 | 2 | | | | 7 | | | 1 | | | | | | | 3 | | | | 10 | | 6 | | | 9 | 11 | |
| | 4 | 7 | | 5 | 2 | | 8 | | | *12* | | 1 | | | | | | | 3 | | | | 10 | | 6 | | | 9 | *11* | |
| | 4 | | | 5 | 2 | | | | | *12* | | 1 | | | | | | | 3 | 7 | | | 10 | | 6 | 8 | | *9* | 11 | |
| | 4 | | | 5 | 2 | | | 9 | | *12* | | 1 | | | | | | | 3 | 7 | | | *10* | | 6 | 8 | | | 11 | |
| | 4 | 10 | | 5 | 3 | | | | | 11 | | 1 | | | | | | | | 2 | | | | | 6 | 8 | | 9 | 7 | |
| | 4 | 7 | | 5 | | | | | | 11 | | 1 | | | | | | | 3 | 2 | | | 10 | | 6 | 8 | | 9 | | |
| | *4* | *12* | | 5 | | | 8 | | 7 | 11 | | 1 | | | | | | | 3 | 2 | | | 10 | | 6 | | | 9 | | |
| | 4 | 5 | | | | | | | 7 | 11 | | 1 | | | | | | | 3 | 2 | | | 10 | | 6 | | | 9 | 8 | |
| | 4 | | | | | | | | 7 | 11 | | 1 | | | | | | | 3 | 2 | | | 10 | | 6 | | | 9 | 8 | 5 |
| | | 4 | | | | | | | | 11 | | 1 | | | | | | | 3 | 2 | 7 | | 10 | | 6 | | | 9 | 8 | 5 |
| 10 | 30 | 30 | 10 | 37 | 14 | 9 | 20 | 13 | 38 | 31 | | 36 | 8 | 4 | 14 | 4 | 3 | 6 | 36 | 34 | 2 | 5 | 29 | 1 | 28 | 23 | 6 | 13 | 10 | 2 |
| | 1 | 7 | | | | | 3 | 1 | 1 | 8 | 1 | | | | | | | | | | 1 | | 1 | | | | 1 | | 2 | |
| | 1 | 1 | | | | | 1 | 2 | 6 | 6 | | | | | 4 | 1 | | 1 | 1 | 3 | | 1 | 10 | | | 1 | 1 | 3 | 1 | |

| Richardson | O'Donnell | Goad | Veitch | Scott | Maggiore | Spelman | Elliott | Endean | Scaife | Bielby | Potter | Edgar | Luckett | Johnson | Rowlands | Harley | Prudham | Reed | Wiggett | Creamer | McMaster | Davies | Poskett | Spraggon | Simpkin | McMordie | Goldthorpe | Turnbull | Cunningham | Smith |
|---|---|---|---|---|---|---|---|---|---|---|---|---|---|---|---|---|---|---|---|---|---|---|---|---|---|---|---|---|---|---|
| | 4 | 8 | | 5 | 9 | | 10 | | 7 | 11 | | 1 | | | 6 | | | | 3 | 2 | | | | | | | | | | |
| | 1 | 1 | | 1 | 1 | | 1 | | 1 | 1 | | 1 | | | 1 | | | | 1 | 1 | | | | | | | | | | |
| | | | | | | | | | | | | | | | | | | | | | | | | | | | | | | |
| | | | | | | | | | | | | | | | | | | | | | | | | | | | | | | |

| Richardson | O'Donnell | Goad | Veitch | Scott | Maggiore | Spelman | Elliott | Endean | Scaife | Bielby | Potter | Edgar | Luckett | Johnson | Rowlands | Harley | Prudham | Reed | Wiggett | Creamer | McMaster | Davies | Poskett | Spraggon | Simpkin | McMordie | Goldthorpe | Turnbull | Cunningham | Smith |
|---|---|---|---|---|---|---|---|---|---|---|---|---|---|---|---|---|---|---|---|---|---|---|---|---|---|---|---|---|---|---|
| 1 | 2 | 3 | | 5 | 6 | 4 | 7 | 10 | 8 | 11 | | | | 9 | | | | | | | | | | | | | | | | |
| 1 | 2 | 3 | | 5 | 6 | 4 | *12* | *8* | 7 | 11 | | | | 9 | | | | | | | | | | | | | | 10 | | |
| 2 | 2 | 2 | | 2 | 2 | 2 | 1 | 2 | 2 | 2 | | | | 2 | | | | | | | | | | | | | | 1 | | |
| | | | | | | | 1 | | | | | | | | | | | | | | | | | | | | | | | |
| | | | | | | | | | | | | | | | | | | | | | | | | | | | | 1 | | |

## League Table

| | P | W | D | L | F | A | Pts |
|---|---|---|---|---|---|---|---|
| Cambridge United | 46 | 26 | 13 | 7 | 87 | 40 | 65 |
| Exeter City | 46 | 25 | 12 | 9 | 70 | 46 | 62 |
| Colchester United | 46 | 25 | 9 | 12 | 77 | 43 | 59 |
| Bradford City | 46 | 23 | 13 | 10 | 78 | 51 | 59 |
| Swansea City | 46 | 25 | 8 | 13 | 92 | 68 | 58 |
| Barnsley | 46 | 23 | 9 | 14 | 62 | 39 | 55 |
| Watford | 46 | 18 | 15 | 13 | 67 | 50 | 51 |
| Doncaster Rovers | 46 | 21 | 9 | 16 | 71 | 65 | 51 |
| Huddersfield Town | 46 | 19 | 12 | 15 | 60 | 49 | 50 |
| Southend United | 46 | 15 | 19 | 12 | 52 | 45 | 49 |
| Darlington | 46 | 18 | 13 | 15 | 59 | 64 | 49 |
| Crewe Alexandra | 46 | 19 | 11 | 16 | 47 | 60 | 49 |
| Bournemouth | 46 | 15 | 18 | 13 | 54 | 44 | 48 |
| Stockport County | 46 | 13 | 19 | 14 | 53 | 57 | 45 |
| Brentford | 46 | 18 | 7 | 21 | 77 | 76 | 43 |
| Torquay United | 46 | 17 | 9 | 20 | 59 | 67 | 43 |
| Aldershot | 46 | 16 | 11 | 19 | 49 | 59 | 43 |
| Rochdale | 46 | 13 | 12 | 21 | 50 | 59 | 38 |
| Newport County | 46 | 14 | 10 | 22 | 42 | 58 | 38 |
| Scunthorpe United | 46 | 13 | 11 | 22 | 49 | 73 | 37 |
| Halifax Town | 46 | 11 | 14 | 21 | 47 | 58 | 36 |
| Hartlepool | 46 | 10 | 12 | 24 | 47 | 73 | 32 |
| Southport | 46 | 3 | 19 | 24 | 33 | 77 | 25 |
| Workington | 46 | 4 | 11 | 31 | 41 | 102 | 19 |

# 1977-78

## Division Four

Manager: Billy Horner

### Did you know that?

A 21st League finish required Hartlepool to make a 12th application for re-election in competition with ambitious Wigan Athletic. United received 33 votes, 10 less than the previous season, and after a tie with Southport on 26 votes Wigan were duly elected on a second ballot.

Billy Horner was able to pit his managerial talents against the game's finest in the FA Cup, when after a third-round victory over Crystal Palace managed by Terry Venables he lost in the fourth round to Bobby Robson's Ipswich Town.

| Match No. | Date | Round | Venue | Opponents | Result | | Scorers | Attendance |
|---|---|---|---|---|---|---|---|---|
| 3 | Aug 20 | | (h) | Torquay United | L | 1 - 2 | Malone | 2,351 |
| 4 | 23 | | (a) | Halifax Town | L | 0 - 3 | | 1,714 |
| 5 | 27 | | (a) | Southport | D | 1 - 1 | Goad | 1,628 |
| 6 | Sep 3 | | (h) | Scunthorpe United | W | 1 - 0 | Malone | 1,960 |
| 7 | 10 | | (h) | Wimbledon | W | 2 - 0 | McMordie, Poskett | 2,731 |
| 8 | 13 | | (a) | Grimsby Town | L | 1 - 2 | Downing | 4,021 |
| 9 | 17 | | (a) | Northampton Town | L | 3 - 5 | Poskett 2, Newton | 3,499 |
| 10 | 24 | | (h) | Reading | W | 2 - 1 | Ayre, Downing | 2,402 |
| 11 | 27 | | (h) | Rochdale | W | 1 - 0 | Ayre | 3,389 |
| 12 | Oct 1 | | (a) | Crewe Alexandra | L | 0 - 1 | | 2,051 |
| 13 | 4 | | (a) | Huddersfield Town | L | 1 - 3 | Ayre | 3,966 |
| 14 | 8 | | (h) | Bournemouth | L | 0 - 1 | | 2,601 |
| 15 | 14 | | (a) | Southend United | D | 1 - 1 | Poskett | 5,686 |
| 16 | 22 | | (h) | Brentford | W | 3 - 1 | Poskett 2, Ayre | 2,470 |
| 17 | 29 | | (a) | Barnsley | L | 2 - 3 | Poskett 2 | 4,287 |
| 18 | Nov 5 | | (h) | Watford | L | 1 - 2 | Poskett | 3,143 |
| 19 | 11 | | (a) | Stockport County | L | 0 - 6 | | 4,179 |
| 20 | 19 | | (h) | Doncaster Rovers | L | 0 - 2 | | 2,309 |
| 23 | Dec 3 | | (a) | Newport County | L | 2 - 4 | Ayre, Newton | 3,323 |
| 24 | 10 | | (h) | Aldershot | D | 2 - 2 | Gaffney, Ayre | 2,082 |
| 26 | 26 | | (a) | York City | L | 0 - 1 | | 3,603 |
| 27 | 27 | | (h) | Darlington | W | 2 - 1 | Downing, Poskett | 5,299 |
| 28 | 31 | | (h) | Swansea City | L | 0 - 4 | | 3,211 |
| 29 | Jan 2 | | (a) | Watford | L | 0 - 1 | | 16,866 |
| 31 | 14 | | (a) | Torquay United | D | 0 - 0 | | 2,421 |
| 33 | Feb 7 | | (h) | Halifax Town | D | 1 - 1 | Downing | 3,537 |
| 34 | 18 | | (a) | Reading | W | 3 - 2 | Gibb, Ayre, White (o.g.) | 4,322 |
| 35 | 20 | | (a) | Wimbledon | L | 0 - 3 | | 1,440 |
| 36 | 25 | | (h) | Crewe Alexandra | D | 1 - 1 | Roberts (o.g.) | 2,506 |
| 37 | 28 | | (h) | Southport | W | 2 - 1 | Gibb, Ayre | 2,432 |
| 38 | Mar 4 | | (a) | Bournemouth | L | 0 - 1 | | 2,992 |
| 39 | 7 | | (h) | Grimsby Town | W | 3 - 1 | Bielby (pen), Foggon, G.Smith | 2,595 |
| 40 | 11 | | (h) | Southend United | W | 1 - 0 | Bielby (pen) | 3,115 |
| 41 | 14 | | (h) | York City | W | 4 - 2 | G.Smith, Newton, Ayre, Gibb | 3,496 |
| 42 | 18 | | (a) | Brentford | L | 0 - 2 | | 7,499 |
| 43 | 24 | | (h) | Barnsley | L | 1 - 2 | Houchen | 4,315 |
| 44 | 25 | | (a) | Darlington | W | 2 - 1 | Foggon, Hocuen | 3,372 |
| 45 | Apr 1 | | (a) | Swansea City | L | 0 - 8 | | 7,149 |
| 46 | 4 | | (a) | Rochdale | W | 1 - 0 | Houchen | 972 |
| 47 | 8 | | (h) | Stockport County | W | 2 - 0 | Gibb, Ayre | 2,416 |
| 48 | 11 | | (h) | Northampton Town | L | 0 - 2 | | 2,844 |
| 49 | 15 | | (a) | Doncaster Rovers | L | 0 - 2 | | 2,040 |
| 50 | 18 | | (a) | Scunthorpe United | L | 0 - 2 | | 2,317 |
| 51 | 22 | | (h) | Newport County | D | 1 - 1 | Houchen | 2,027 |
| 52 | 25 | | (h) | Huddersfield Town | W | 3 - 2 | Ayre 2, Larkin | 1,926 |
| 53 | 29 | | (a) | Aldershot | L | 0 - 3 | | 3,624 |

Final Position : 21st in Division Four

| | | | | | | | | Apps. |
|---|---|---|---|---|---|---|---|---|
| | | | | | | | | Sub.Apps. |
| | | | | | | | 2 own goals | Goals |

**FA Cup**

| Match No. | Date | Round | Venue | Opponents | Result | | Scorers | Attendance |
|---|---|---|---|---|---|---|---|---|
| 21 | Nov 26 | R1 | (a) | Tranmere Rovers | D | 1 - 1 | T.Smith | 3,564 |
| 22 | 29 | R1r | (h) | Tranmere Rovers | W | 3 - 1 | Newton, Ayre, Bielby | 4,827 |
| 25 | Dec 17 | R2 | (h) | Runcorn | W | 4 - 2 | Bielby, Newton 2, Poskett (pen) | 6,112 |
| 30 | Jan 7 | R3 | (h) | Crystal Palace | W | 2 - 1 | Newton 2 | 4,502 |
| 32 | 28 | R4 | (a) | Ipswich Town | L | 1 - 4 | Downing | 24,207 |

Apps.
Sub.Apps.
Goals

**League Cup**

| Match No. | Date | Round | Venue | Opponents | Result | | Scorers | Attendance |
|---|---|---|---|---|---|---|---|---|
| 1 | Aug 13 | R1/1 | (a) | Grimsby Town | L | 0 - 3 | | 2,318 |
| 2 | 16 | R1/2 | (h) | Grimsby Town | L | 1 - 2 | Bielby | 2,733 |

Apps.
Sub.Apps.
Goals

| Edgar | Malone | Wiggett | Gibb | Ayre | Creamer | McMordie | Downing | Newton | Poskett | Bielby | Gaffney | Simpkin | Goad | Scarfe | Linacre | Darling | Richardson | Smith, G. | Smith, T. | Livsey | Harris | Foggon | Houchen | Hogan | Lawrence | Larkin | McMaster |
|---|---|---|---|---|---|---|---|---|---|---|---|---|---|---|---|---|---|---|---|---|---|---|---|---|---|---|---|
| 1 | 2 | 3 | 4 | 5 | 6 | 7 | 8 | 9 | 10 | *11* | *12* | | | | | | | | | | | | | | | | |
| 1 | 2 | 3 | 4 | 5 | | 7 | 8 | | 10 | | | 6 | 9 | 11 | | | | | | | | | | | | | |
| 1 | 2 | 3 | 4 | 5 | | 7 | 8 | | 10 | 11 | | 6 | 9 | | | | | | | | | | | | | | |
| 1 | 2 | 3 | 4 | 5 | | 7 | 8 | | 10 | 11 | | 6 | 9 | | | | | | | | | | | | | | |
| 1 | 2 | 3 | 4 | 5 | | 7 | 8 | 9 | 10 | 11 | | 6 | | | | | | | | | | | | | | | |
| 1 | *2* | 3 | 4 | 5 | | 7 | 8 | 9 | 10 | 11 | | 6 | | | *12* | | | | | | | | | | | | |
| 1 | | 3 | | 5 | 2 | 7 | 8 | 9 | 10 | 11 | | 6 | | | 4 | | | | | | | | | | | | |
| 1 | | 3 | | 5 | 2 | | 8 | 9 | 10 | 11 | | 6 | | 7 | *4* | *12* | | | | | | | | | | | |
| 1 | | 3 | 4 | 5 | 2 | | 8 | 9 | 10 | 11 | | 6 | | | 7 | | | | | | | | | | | | |
| 1 | | 3 | 4 | 5 | 2 | | 8 | 9 | 10 | 11 | | 6 | | | *7* | *12* | | | | | | | | | | | |
| | | 3 | 4 | 5 | 2 | | 8 | 9 | 10 | *12* | | 6 | | | *7* | 11 | 1 | | | | | | | | | | |
| 1 | | 3 | 4 | 5 | 2 | 7 | 8 | 9 | 10 | 11 | | 6 | | | | | | | | | | | | | | | |
| 1 | 2 | | 4 | 5 | | 7 | 3 | 9 | 10 | | | 6 | | | 8 | 11 | | | | | | | | | | | |
| 1 | 2 | | 4 | 5 | | 7 | 3 | 9 | 10 | 11 | | 6 | | | 8 | | | | | | | | | | | | |
| 1 | 2 | | 4 | 5 | | *7* | 3 | 9 | 10 | 11 | | 6 | | | *12* | | | 8 | | | | | | | | | |
| 1 | | | 4 | 5 | | | 3 | 9 | 10 | 11 | 7 | 6 | | | 8 | | | 2 | | | | | | | | | |
| 1 | | | 4 | 5 | | | 3 | 9 | | | 7 | 6 | 11 | | 8 | | | 2 | 10 | | | | | | | | |
| 1 | | 3 | 4 | 5 | | | 2 | 9 | | 11 | *10* | | *12* | | 7 | | | 8 | 6 | | | | | | | | |
| 1 | | 3 | 4 | 5 | | | 8 | 9 | | 11 | 10 | | | | 7 | | | 2 | 6 | | | | | | | | |
| | | 3 | 4 | 5 | *2* | | 8 | 9 | | 11 | *12* | | 10 | | 7 | | 1 | | 6 | | | | | | | | |
| | 2 | 3 | 4 | 5 | | | 8 | 9 | 10 | 11 | | 6 | | | | | | 7 | | 1 | | | | | | | |
| | 2 | *3* | 4 | 5 | | | 8 | 9 | 10 | *12* | | 6 | | | 7 | | | | 11 | 1 | | | | | | | |
| | 2 | | 4 | 5 | | | *3* | 9 | 10 | 11 | | 6 | | | 7 | | | | 8 | 1 | *12* | | | | | | |
| | 2 | | 4 | 5 | 11 | | 3 | 9 | 10 | | | | | | 7 | | | 6 | 8 | 1 | | | | | | | |
| 1 | *2* | | 4 | 5 | 7 | 8 | 3 | 9 | 10 | 11 | | | | | | | | 6 | *12* | | | | | | | | |
| 1 | 2 | | 4 | 5 | 7 | 8 | 3 | 9 | | 11 | | | | | | | | 6 | | | | 10 | | | | | |
| 1 | 2 | | 4 | 5 | 7 | 8 | 3 | 9 | | 11 | | | | | | | | 6 | | | | 10 | | | | | |
| 1 | 2 | | 4 | 5 | 7 | 8 | 3 | 9 | | *11* | | | | | | | | 6 | *12* | | | 10 | | | | | |
| 1 | 2 | | 4 | 5 | | 8 | 3 | | | 11 | | | | | 7 | | | 6 | | | | 10 | 9 | | | | |
| 1 | 2 | | 4 | 5 | | 8 | 3 | | | 11 | | | | | 7 | | | 6 | | | | 10 | 9 | | | | |
| 1 | 2 | | 4 | 5 | 11 | 8 | 3 | 9 | | | | | | | 7 | | | 6 | | | | 10 | | | | | |
| 1 | 2 | | 4 | 5 | 7 | 8 | 3 | 9 | | 11 | | | | | *12* | | | 6 | | | | *10* | | | | | |
| 1 | 2 | | 4 | 5 | 7 | 8 | 3 | 9 | | 11 | | | | | | | | 6 | | | | 10 | | | | | |
| 1 | 2 | | 4 | 5 | 7 | 8 | 3 | 9 | | 11 | | | | | | | | 6 | | | | 10 | | | | | |
| *1* | 2 | 3 | 4 | 5 | 7 | 8 | | 9 | | 11 | | | | | 10 | | | 6 | *12* | | | | | | | | |
| 1 | *2* | | 4 | 5 | 7 | 8 | | | | 11 | | | | | *12* | | | 6 | 3 | | | 10 | 9 | | | | |
| | | | 2 | 5 | 7 | | 3 | | | 11 | 8 | | | | 4 | | 1 | 6 | | | | 10 | 9 | | | | |
| | *2* | | 4 | 5 | 7 | | | | | 3 | 11 | | | | 8 | | 1 | 6 | *12* | | | 10 | 9 | | | | |
| 1 | | | 4 | 5 | 2 | | 3 | | | 11 | *12* | | | | 8 | | | 6 | 7 | | | 10 | *9* | | | | |
| 1 | 2 | | 4 | 5 | 7 | | 3 | | | 11 | | | | | 8 | | | 6 | | | | 10 | 9 | | | | |
| 1 | 2 | | 4 | 5 | 7 | *12* | 3 | | | 11 | | | | | *8* | | | 6 | | | | 10 | 9 | | | | |
| 1 | 2 | | | 5 | 6 | | 3 | | | 11 | 7 | | 10 | | 8 | | | | | | | | 9 | 4 | | | |
| 1 | 2 | | *4* | 5 | 7 | | 3 | | | *12* | 11 | | | | 8 | | | 6 | | | | 10 | 9 | | | | |
| 1 | 2 | | | 5 | 3 | | | | | *12* | 7 | | | | 8 | | | | 6 | | | 10 | 9 | | 4 | *11* | |
| | 2 | | | 5 | 3 | | | | | | 7 | | | | 8 | | | 6 | | 1 | | *10* | 9 | 4 | *12* | 11 | |
| | 2 | | | 5 | 3 | | | | | *12* | | | | | 7 | | | 6 | | 1 | | | 9 | 4 | 8 | 11 | *10* |
| 36 | 33 | 18 | 40 | 46 | 29 | 23 | 40 | 30 | 21 | 35 | 10 | 19 | 6 | 2 | 29 | 2 | 4 | 27 | 10 | 6 | | 18 | 13 | 3 | 2 | 3 | 1 |
| | | | | | | 1 | | | | 5 | 3 | | 1 | | 4 | 2 | | | 4 | | 1 | | | | 1 | | |
| | 2 | | 4 | 12 | | 1 | 4 | 3 | 10 | 2 | 1 | | 1 | | | | | 2 | | | | 2 | 4 | | | 1 | |

| Edgar | Malone | Wiggett | Gibb | Ayre | Creamer | McMordie | Downing | Newton | Poskett | Bielby | Gaffney | Simpkin | Goad | Scarfe | Linacre | Darling | Richardson | Smith, G. | Smith, T. |
|---|---|---|---|---|---|---|---|---|---|---|---|---|---|---|---|---|---|---|---|
| 1 | | 3 | 4 | 5 | | | 8 | 9 | | 11 | | | 10 | | 7 | | | 2 | 6 |
| 1 | | 3 | 4 | 5 | | | 8 | 9 | | 11 | | | 2 | | 7 | | | 10 | 6 |
| 1 | | 3 | 4 | 5 | | | 8 | 9 | 10 | 11 | | | | | 7 | | | 2 | 6 |
| 1 | 2 | | 4 | 5 | 7 | 8 | 3 | 9 | 10 | 11 | | | | | | | | 6 | |
| 1 | 2 | | 4 | 5 | 7 | *8* | 3 | 9 | 10 | 11 | | | | | *12* | | | 6 | |
| 5 | 2 | 3 | 5 | 5 | 2 | 2 | 5 | 5 | 3 | 5 | | | 2 | | 3 | | | 5 | 3 |
| | | | | | | | | | | | | | | | 1 | | | | |
| | | | | 1 | | | 1 | 5 | 1 | 2 | | | | | | | | | 1 |

| Edgar | Malone | Wiggett | Gibb | Ayre | Creamer | McMordie | Downing | Newton | Poskett | Bielby | Gaffney | Simpkin |
|---|---|---|---|---|---|---|---|---|---|---|---|---|
| 1 | 2 | 3 | 4 | 5 | | 7 | 8 | 9 | 10 | 11 | *12* | 6 |
| 1 | 2 | 3 | 4 | 5 | | 7 | 8 | 9 | 10 | 11 | *12* | *6* |
| 2 | 2 | 2 | 2 | 2 | | 2 | 2 | 2 | 2 | 2 | | 2 |
| | | | | | | | | | | | 2 | |
| | | | | | | | | | | 1 | | |

## League Table

| | P | W | D | L | F | A | Pts |
|---|---|---|---|---|---|---|---|
| Watford | 46 | 30 | 11 | 5 | 85 | 38 | 71 |
| Southend United | 46 | 25 | 10 | 11 | 66 | 39 | 60 |
| Swansea City | 46 | 23 | 10 | 13 | 87 | 47 | 56 |
| Brentford | 46 | 21 | 14 | 11 | 86 | 54 | 56 |
| Aldershot | 46 | 19 | 16 | 11 | 67 | 47 | 54 |
| Grimsby Town | 46 | 21 | 11 | 14 | 57 | 51 | 53 |
| Barnsley | 46 | 18 | 14 | 14 | 61 | 49 | 50 |
| Reading | 46 | 18 | 14 | 14 | 55 | 52 | 50 |
| Torquay United | 46 | 16 | 15 | 15 | 57 | 56 | 47 |
| Northampton Town | 46 | 17 | 13 | 16 | 63 | 68 | 47 |
| Huddersfield Town | 46 | 15 | 15 | 16 | 63 | 55 | 45 |
| Doncaster Rovers | 46 | 14 | 17 | 15 | 52 | 65 | 45 |
| Wimbledon | 46 | 14 | 16 | 16 | 66 | 67 | 44 |
| Scunthorpe United | 46 | 14 | 16 | 16 | 50 | 55 | 44 |
| Crewe Alexandra | 46 | 15 | 14 | 17 | 50 | 69 | 44 |
| Newport County | 46 | 16 | 11 | 19 | 65 | 73 | 43 |
| Bournemouth | 46 | 14 | 15 | 17 | 41 | 51 | 43 |
| Stockport County | 46 | 16 | 10 | 20 | 56 | 56 | 42 |
| Darlington | 46 | 14 | 13 | 19 | 52 | 59 | 41 |
| Halifax Town | 46 | 10 | 21 | 15 | 52 | 62 | 41 |
| Hartlepool United | 46 | 15 | 7 | 24 | 51 | 84 | 37 |
| York City | 46 | 12 | 12 | 22 | 50 | 69 | 36 |
| Southport | 46 | 6 | 19 | 21 | 52 | 76 | 31 |
| Rochdale | 46 | 8 | 8 | 30 | 43 | 85 | 24 |

# 1978-79

## Division Four

Manager: Billy Horner

### Did you know that?

Jim Platt, a Northern Ireland international, played 13 games for 'Pools in a loan spell, during which only three games were lost. In a 12-year career with Middlesbrough, Platt made 401 League appearances in goal.

A mid-table finish of 13th saw average attendances rise to 2,997, up by 1,000 on two seasons earlier.

| Match No. | Date | Round | Venue | Opponents | Result | | Scorers | Attendance |
|---|---|---|---|---|---|---|---|---|
| 3 | Aug 19 | | (h) | Doncaster Rovers | L | 3 - 4 | Linacre, Newton, Crumplin | 2,634 |
| 4 | 23 | | (a) | Northampton Town | D | 1 - 1 | Newton | 4,288 |
| 5 | 25 | | (h) | Portsmouth | D | 1 - 1 | Crumplin | 3,136 |
| 6 | Sep 2 | | (a) | Bournemouth | W | 1 - 0 | Newton (pen) | 2,658 |
| 7 | 9 | | (h) | Hereford United | W | 2 - 1 | Linacre, Hogan | 2,995 |
| 8 | 11 | | (a) | Stockport County | L | 0 - 4 | | 4,259 |
| 9 | 16 | | (a) | Grimsby Town | W | 1 - 0 | Goldthorpe | 4,958 |
| 10 | 23 | | (h) | Halifax Town | W | 3 - 1 | Houchen, Newton (pen), Goldthorpe | 3,760 |
| 11 | 25 | | (h) | Newport County | D | 0 - 0 | | 5,495 |
| 12 | 30 | | (a) | Torquay United | L | 1 - 4 | Houchen | 3,033 |
| 13 | Oct 7 | | (h) | Darlington | L | 0 - 2 | | 4,854 |
| 14 | 14 | | (a) | Aldershot | D | 1 - 1 | Brooks | 2,968 |
| 15 | 17 | | (h) | Scunthorpe United | D | 1 - 1 | Lawrence | 2,981 |
| 16 | 21 | | (a) | Crewe Alexandra | W | 1 - 0 | T.Smith | 2,023 |
| 17 | 28 | | (h) | Rochdale | W | 5 - 1 | Ayre, Goldthorpe 2, Lawrence, Houchen | 3,084 |
| 18 | Nov 4 | | (a) | Port Vale | L | 0 - 2 | | 3,195 |
| 19 | 11 | | (h) | Bournemouth | D | 0 - 0 | | 3,239 |
| 20 | 18 | | (a) | Portsmouth | L | 0 - 3 | | 10,957 |
| 22 | Dec 9 | | (h) | Wimbledon | D | 1 - 1 | Ayre | 3,098 |
| 24 | 23 | | (h) | Barnsley | D | 1 - 1 | Goldthorpe | 5,956 |
| 25 | 26 | | (a) | York City | D | 1 - 1 | Crumplin | 3,825 |
| 27 | Jan 20 | | (h) | Grimsby Town | W | 1 - 0 | Newton (pen) | 2,222 |
| 28 | Feb 2 | | (a) | Newport County | L | 2 - 3 | Newton (pen), Linacre | 3,659 |
| 29 | 10 | | (h) | Torquay United | W | 3 - 2 | Newton 2, Houchen | 2,419 |
| 30 | 24 | | (h) | Aldershot | D | 2 - 2 | Ayre, Houchen | 2,908 |
| 31 | 26 | | (a) | Reading | L | 1 - 3 | Houchen | 7,052 |
| 32 | Mar 3 | | (h) | Crewe Alexandra | D | 2 - 2 | Houchen, Crumplin | 2,470 |
| 33 | 7 | | (a) | Hereford United | L | 0 - 1 | | 2,439 |
| 34 | 10 | | (a) | Rochdale | D | 1 - 1 | Crumplin | 1,931 |
| 35 | 13 | | (h) | Stockport County | L | 1 - 3 | Linacre | 2,449 |
| 36 | 23 | | (a) | Doncaster Rovers | D | 0 - 0 | | 2,552 |
| 37 | 31 | | (a) | Huddersfield Town | L | 0 - 2 | | 2,420 |
| 38 | Apr 3 | | (h) | Wigan Athletic | D | 1 - 1 | Houchen | 2,128 |
| 39 | 7 | | (h) | Bradford City | D | 2 - 2 | Lawrence, Houchen | 2,183 |
| 40 | 12 | | (a) | Barnsley | L | 0 - 1 | | 11,398 |
| 41 | 14 | | (h) | York City | D | 1 - 1 | Houchen | 2,357 |
| 42 | 16 | | (a) | Wigan Athletic | D | 2 - 2 | Goldthorpe (pen), Linacre | 8,217 |
| 43 | 21 | | (h) | Reading | D | 0 - 0 | | 2,526 |
| 44 | 24 | | (a) | Scunthorpe United | L | 1 - 3 | Houchen | 1,339 |
| 45 | 28 | | (a) | Wimbledon | L | 1 - 3 | Houchen | 3,546 |
| 46 | May 2 | | (a) | Bradford City | W | 2 - 1 | Ayre, Harding | 1,950 |
| 47 | 5 | | (h) | Huddersfield Town | W | 2 - 0 | Norton 2 | 2,251 |
| 48 | 7 | | (a) | Darlington | W | 1 - 0 | Lawrence | 3,513 |
| 49 | 10 | | (h) | Port Vale | L | 1 - 2 | Houchen | 2,007 |
| 50 | 14 | | (a) | Halifax Town | W | 4 - 2 | Lawrence 4 | 1,012 |
| 51 | 17 | | (h) | Northampton Town | W | 2 - 0 | Lawrence, Ayre | 1,769 |

Final Position : 13th in Division Four

Apps.
Sub.Apps.
Goals

**FA Cup**

| Match No. | Date | Round | Venue | Opponents | Result | | Scorers | Attendance |
|---|---|---|---|---|---|---|---|---|
| 21 | Nov 25 | R1 | (h) | Grimsby Town | W | 1 - 0 | Goldthorpe | 3,584 |
| 23 | Dec 16 | R2 | (a) | Crewe Alexandra | W | 1 - 0 | Crumplin | 2,626 |
| 26 | Jan 18 | R3 | (h) | Leeds United | L | 2 - 6 | Newton 2 (2 pens) | 16,000 |

Apps.
Sub.Apps.
Goals

**League Cup**

| Match No. | Date | Round | Venue | Opponents | Result | | Scorers | Attendance |
|---|---|---|---|---|---|---|---|---|
| 1 | Aug 12 | R1/1 | (a) | Rotherham United | L | 0 - 5 | | 2,431 |
| 2 | 15 | R1/2 | (h) | Rotherham United | D | 1 - 1 | Newton | 1,746 |

Apps.
Sub.Apps.
Goals

| Richardson | Malone | Gorry | Smith, G. | Brooks | Ayre | Linacre | Houchen | Newton | Crumplin | Guy | Larkin | Platt | Smith, T. | Lawrence | Goldthorpe | Hogan | Loadwick | Edgar | Norton | Harding | Watson | Evans |
|---|---|---|---|---|---|---|---|---|---|---|---|---|---|---|---|---|---|---|---|---|---|---|
| 1 | *2* | 3 | 4 | 5 | 6 | 7 | 8 | 9 | 10 | 11 | *12* | | | | | | | | | | | |
| | | 3 | 4 | 5 | 6 | 7 | | 9 | *10* | 11 | | 1 | 2 | 8 | *12* | | | | | | | |
| | | 3 | *4* | 5 | 6 | 7 | 8 | 9 | 10 | 11 | | 1 | 2 | | *12* | | | | | | | |
| | | 3 | 2 | 5 | 6 | 7 | | 9 | 10 | *11* | | 1 | | 8 | *12* | 4 | | | | | | |
| | 2 | | 3 | 5 | 6 | 7 | | 9 | 10 | 11 | | 1 | | | 8 | 4 | | | | | | |
| | 2 | 3 | 4 | 5 | 6 | 7 | | 9 | 10 | *11* | | 1 | | | *12* | 8 | | | | | | |
| | | 3 | 2 | 5 | 6 | 7 | 10 | 9 | | *12* | | 1 | | 11 | 8 | *4* | | | | | | |
| | | 3 | 2 | 5 | 6 | 7 | *10* | 9 | *12* | | | 1 | | 11 | 8 | 4 | | | | | | |
| | | 3 | 2 | 5 | 6 | 7 | *10* | 9 | *12* | | | 1 | | 11 | 8 | 4 | | | | | | |
| | | 3 | 2 | 5 | 6 | 7 | 10 | 9 | | *12* | | 1 | | 11 | 8 | *4* | | | | | | |
| | | 3 | 2 | 5 | 6 | 7 | 9 | | 10 | 11 | | 1 | | 4 | 8 | | | | | | | |
| | | 3 | 2 | 5 | 6 | 7 | 9 | | 10 | | | 1 | | 4 | 8 | | 11 | | | | | |
| | | | 2 | 5 | 6 | 7 | 11 | 9 | 10 | *12* | | 1 | 3 | 4 | *8* | | | | | | | |
| | | | 2 | 5 | 6 | 7 | *10* | 9 | *12* | | | 1 | 3 | 4 | 8 | | 11 | | | | | |
| | | | 2 | 5 | 6 | 7 | 10 | 9 | | | | | 3 | 4 | 8 | 11 | | 1 | | | | |
| | | | 2 | 5 | 6 | 7 | 10 | 9 | | | | | 3 | 4 | 8 | | 11 | 1 | | | | |
| 1 | | 3 | 2 | 5 | 6 | 7 | 10 | 9 | | | | | | 4 | 8 | | 11 | | | | | |
| 1 | | 3 | 2 | 5 | 6 | 7 | 10 | 9 | | | | | | 4 | 8 | | 11 | | | | | |
| 1 | | 3 | 2 | 5 | 6 | *7* | 10 | | 9 | | | | | 4 | 8 | | 11 | | *12* | | | |
| 1 | | 3 | 2 | 5 | 6 | 7 | | 10 | 9 | | | | | 4 | 8 | | 11 | | | | | |
| 1 | | 3 | 2 | 5 | 6 | 7 | | 10 | 9 | | | | | 4 | 8 | | 11 | | | | | |
| 1 | | 3 | 2 | | | 7 | *12* | 10 | 9 | | | | 5 | | *8* | 4 | 11 | | 6 | | | |
| 1 | | 3 | 2 | 5 | | 7 | | 10 | 9 | | | | 6 | | 8 | *4* | 11 | | *12* | | | |
| 1 | | 3 | 2 | 5 | | 7 | 8 | 10 | 9 | | | | 6 | | | 4 | 11 | | | | | |
| 1 | | 3 | 2 | 5 | 6 | 7 | 8 | 10 | 9 | | | | | | | 4 | 11 | | | | | |
| 1 | | 3 | 2 | 5 | 6 | 7 | 8 | 10 | *9* | | | | | *12* | | 4 | 11 | | | | | |
| | | 3 | | 5 | 6 | 7 | 8 | | 9 | | | | 2 | 4 | 10 | | 11 | 1 | | | | |
| 1 | | 3 | 2 | 5 | 6 | 7 | 10 | | 9 | | | | | 4 | 8 | | 11 | | | | | |
| 1 | | 3 | 2 | *5* | 6 | 7 | 10 | | 9 | | | | *12* | 4 | 8 | | 11 | | | | | |
| 1 | | 3 | 2 | | 6 | 7 | 10 | | 9 | | | | 5 | 4 | *8* | *12* | 11 | | | | | |
| 1 | | 3 | 2 | | 6 | 7 | 8 | | 9 | | | | 5 | 4 | | | 11 | | | 10 | | |
| 1 | | 3 | 2 | | | 7 | 8 | | 9 | | | | | 4 | 5 | 11 | | | 6 | 10 | | |
| 1 | | 3 | 2 | | 6 | 7 | 8 | | 9 | | *10* | | | *12* | 5 | | 11 | | | 4 | | |
| 1 | | 3 | *2* | | 6 | 7 | 8 | | 9 | | | | *12* | 10 | 5 | | 11 | | | 4 | | |
| | | 3 | 2 | | 6 | 7 | 8 | | | | | | | 9 | 5 | 4 | *12* | | *11* | 10 | 1 | |
| | | 3 | | | 6 | 7 | 8 | | *12* | | | | 2 | 9 | 5 | | 11 | | *4* | 10 | 1 | |
| | | 3 | 2 | | 6 | 7 | 8 | | | | | | | *9* | 5 | 11 | | | 4 | 10 | 1 | *12* |
| | | 3 | 2 | | 6 | *7* | 8 | | | | | | | 9 | 5 | 11 | | | 4 | 10 | 1 | *12* |
| | | 3 | 2 | | 6 | | 8 | | | | *12* | | | 7 | 5 | 11 | | | *4* | 10 | 1 | 9 |
| | | 3 | *4* | | 6 | 7 | 8 | | | | | | 2 | *12* | 5 | 11 | 9 | | | 10 | 1 | |
| | | 3 | 8 | 5 | 6 | 7 | 9 | | | | | | 2 | *12* | 4 | | 11 | | | *10* | 1 | |
| | | 3 | *4* | 5 | 6 | 7 | 9 | | | | | | | 8 | 2 | *12* | 11 | | 10 | | 1 | |
| | | 3 | 4 | 5 | 6 | 7 | 9 | | | | | | | 8 | 2 | | 11 | | | 10 | 1 | |
| | | 3 | 4 | 5 | 6 | 7 | 9 | | | | | | | 8 | 2 | *12* | *11* | | | 10 | 1 | |
| | | 3 | 4 | 5 | 6 | 7 | 9 | | | | | | | 8 | 2 | | 11 | | | 10 | 1 | |
| | | 3 | | 5 | 6 | 7 | 9 | | | | | | | 8 | 2 | 4 | 11 | | *12* | *10* | 1 | |
| 18 | 3 | 41 | 43 | 34 | 42 | 45 | 38 | 23 | 25 | 7 | 1 | 13 | 15 | 34 | 37 | 20 | 28 | 3 | 8 | 15 | 12 | 1 |
| | | | | | | | 1 | | 4 | 3 | 2 | | 2 | 4 | 4 | 3 | 1 | | 3 | | | 2 |
| | | | | 1 | 5 | 5 | 13 | 8 | 5 | | | | 1 | 9 | 6 | 1 | | | 2 | 1 | | |

| Richardson | Malone | Gorry | Smith, G. | Brooks | Ayre | Linacre | Houchen | Newton | Crumplin | Guy | Larkin | Platt | Smith, T. | Lawrence | Goldthorpe | Hogan | Loadwick | Edgar | Norton | Harding | Watson | Evans |
|---|---|---|---|---|---|---|---|---|---|---|---|---|---|---|---|---|---|---|---|---|---|---|
| 1 | | 3 | 2 | 5 | 6 | *7* | 10 | | 9 | | | | | 4 | 8 | *12* | 11 | | | | | |
| 1 | | 3 | | 5 | 6 | 7 | | 10 | 9 | | | | 2 | 4 | 8 | | 11 | | | | | |
| 1 | | 3 | 2 | | | 7 | | 10 | 9 | | | | 5 | 4 | 8 | | 11 | | 6 | | | |
| 3 | | 3 | 2 | 2 | 2 | 3 | 1 | 2 | 3 | | | | 2 | 3 | 3 | | 3 | | 1 | | | |
| | | | | | | | | | | | | | | | | 1 | | | | | | |
| | | | | | | | | 2 | 1 | | | | | | 1 | | | | | | | |

| Richardson | Malone | Gorry | Smith, G. | Brooks | Ayre | Linacre | Houchen | Newton | Crumplin | Guy | Larkin | Platt | Smith, T. | Lawrence | Goldthorpe | Hogan | Loadwick | Edgar | Norton | Harding | Watson | Evans |
|---|---|---|---|---|---|---|---|---|---|---|---|---|---|---|---|---|---|---|---|---|---|---|
| 1 | 2 | 3 | 4 | 5 | 6 | 7 | *8* | 9 | 10 | 11 | *12* | | | | | | | | | | | |
| 1 | 2 | 3 | 4 | 5 | 6 | 7 | 8 | 9 | 10 | 11 | | | | | | | | | | | | |
| 2 | 2 | 2 | 2 | 2 | 2 | 2 | 2 | 2 | 2 | 2 | | | | | | | | | | | | |
| | | | | | | | | | | | 1 | | | | | | | | | | | |
| | | | | | | | | 1 | | | | | | | | | | | | | | |

## League Table

| | P | W | D | L | F | A | Pts |
|---|---|---|---|---|---|---|---|
| Reading | 46 | 26 | 13 | 7 | 76 | 35 | 65 |
| Grimsby Town | 46 | 26 | 9 | 11 | 82 | 49 | 61 |
| Wimbledon | 46 | 25 | 11 | 10 | 78 | 46 | 61 |
| Barnsley | 46 | 24 | 13 | 9 | 73 | 42 | 61 |
| Aldershot | 46 | 20 | 17 | 9 | 63 | 47 | 57 |
| Wigan Athletic | 46 | 21 | 13 | 12 | 63 | 48 | 55 |
| Portsmouth | 46 | 20 | 12 | 14 | 62 | 48 | 52 |
| Newport County | 46 | 21 | 10 | 15 | 66 | 55 | 52 |
| Huddersfield Town | 46 | 18 | 11 | 17 | 57 | 53 | 47 |
| York City | 46 | 18 | 11 | 17 | 51 | 55 | 47 |
| Torquay United | 46 | 19 | 8 | 19 | 58 | 65 | 46 |
| Scunthorpe United | 46 | 17 | 11 | 18 | 54 | 60 | 45 |
| Hartlepool United | 46 | 13 | 18 | 15 | 57 | 66 | 44 |
| Hereford United | 46 | 15 | 13 | 18 | 53 | 53 | 43 |
| Bradford City | 46 | 17 | 9 | 20 | 62 | 68 | 43 |
| Port Vale | 46 | 14 | 14 | 18 | 57 | 70 | 42 |
| Stockport County | 46 | 14 | 12 | 20 | 58 | 60 | 40 |
| Bournemouth | 46 | 14 | 11 | 21 | 47 | 48 | 39 |
| Northampton Town | 46 | 15 | 9 | 22 | 64 | 76 | 39 |
| Rochdale | 46 | 15 | 9 | 22 | 47 | 64 | 39 |
| Darlington | 46 | 11 | 15 | 20 | 49 | 66 | 37 |
| Doncaster Rovers | 46 | 13 | 11 | 22 | 50 | 73 | 37 |
| Halifax Town | 46 | 9 | 8 | 29 | 39 | 72 | 26 |
| Crewe Alexandra | 46 | 6 | 14 | 26 | 43 | 90 | 26 |

# 1979-80

## Division Four

Manager: Billy Horner

### Did you know that?

Billy Horner won the divisional 'Manager of the Month' award for January following 'Pools' seven-match unbeaten run. This was followed by a nine-game winless run to the end of the season resulting in a 19th-place finish.

Horner used 30 players during the season, including 13 who each made fewer than 10 League appearances.

| Match No. | Date | Round | Venue | Opponents | Result | | Scorers | Attendance |
|---|---|---|---|---|---|---|---|---|
| 3 | Aug 18 | | (h) | Portsmouth | L | 0 - 3 | | 3,110 |
| 4 | 21 | | (a) | Scunthorpe United | W | 3 - 1 | Brooks, Lawrence, Linacre | 1,822 |
| 5 | 24 | | (a) | Rochdale | L | 0 - 1 | | 2,180 |
| 6 | Sep 1 | | (h) | Aldershot | W | 1 - 0 | Houchen | 3,084 |
| 7 | 8 | | (h) | Darlington | W | 3 - 1 | Goldthorpe 2 (1 pen), Ayre | 3,697 |
| 8 | 15 | | (a) | Walsall | L | 1 - 3 | Ayre | 4,205 |
| 9 | 19 | | (a) | Wigan Athletic | L | 1 - 2 | Houchen | 4,877 |
| 10 | 22 | | (h) | Torquay United | D | 2 - 2 | Houchen, Ayre | 2,520 |
| 11 | 29 | | (a) | Halifax Town | L | 1 - 2 | Newton | 2,293 |
| 12 | Oct 6 | | (a) | Bournemouth | L | 1 - 2 | Harding | 3,180 |
| 13 | 9 | | (h) | Scunthorpe United | W | 3 - 2 | Lawrence, Newton 2 | 2,803 |
| 14 | 13 | | (h) | Port Vale | W | 2 - 1 | Newton, Ayre | 2,441 |
| 15 | 20 | | (a) | Peterborough United | L | 0 - 2 | | 3,412 |
| 16 | 22 | | (a) | Stockport County | D | 0 - 0 | | 1,983 |
| 17 | 27 | | (h) | Crewe Alexandra | W | 3 - 1 | Harding, Lawrence, Newton | 2,619 |
| 18 | Nov 3 | | (a) | Portsmouth | L | 1 - 2 | Newton | 14,295 |
| 19 | 6 | | (h) | Stockport County | L | 1 - 2 | Ayre | 2,639 |
| 20 | 10 | | (h) | Hereford United | W | 3 - 0 | Loadwick, Newton 2 | 2,282 |
| 21 | 17 | | (a) | Northampton Town | L | 1 - 2 | Newton | 2,251 |
| 23 | 30 | | (a) | Lincoln City | D | 3 - 3 | Lawrence 2, Hampton | 3,526 |
| 24 | Dec 8 | | (h) | Newport County | D | 0 - 0 | | 2,565 |
| 25 | 21 | | (a) | Bradford City | L | 0 - 2 | | 3,789 |
| 26 | 26 | | (h) | York City | W | 3 - 1 | Ayre, Houchen, Hampton | 2,947 |
| 27 | 29 | | (h) | Rochdale | D | 1 - 1 | Houchen | 3,151 |
| 28 | Jan 5 | | (h) | Tranmere Rovers | W | 2 - 1 | Houchen 2 | 2,517 |
| 29 | 12 | | (a) | Aldershot | W | 2 - 0 | Houchen, Newton | 3,516 |
| 30 | 19 | | (a) | Darlington | W | 1 - 0 | Lawrence | 4,045 |
| 31 | 26 | | (h) | Huddersfield Town | D | 1 - 1 | Ayre (pen) | 5,959 |
| 32 | Feb 2 | | (h) | Walsall | D | 2 - 2 | Newton, Houchen | 4,598 |
| 33 | 16 | | (h) | Halifax Town | L | 1 - 2 | Newton | 3,410 |
| 34 | 23 | | (a) | Port Vale | D | 1 - 1 | Houchen | 3,702 |
| 35 | Mar 1 | | (h) | Peterborough United | L | 1 - 2 | Hampton | 2,887 |
| 36 | 8 | | (a) | Crewe Alexandra | L | 1 - 2 | Houchen | 2,425 |
| 37 | 11 | | (a) | Doncaster Rovers | W | 2 - 0 | Houchen, Hampton | 2,453 |
| 38 | 15 | | (h) | Bournemouth | W | 3 - 1 | Cunningham (o.g.), Ayre (pen), Hampton | 2,201 |
| 39 | 22 | | (a) | Hereford United | L | 1 - 2 | Hampton | 2,782 |
| 40 | 29 | | (h) | Northampton Town | W | 2 - 1 | Hampton, Houchen | 1,995 |
| 41 | Apr 4 | | (h) | Bradford City | L | 0 - 1 | | 3,860 |
| 42 | 5 | | (a) | York City | L | 1 - 2 | McNamee | 2,711 |
| 43 | 8 | | (h) | Doncaster Rovers | L | 1 - 2 | Houchen | 2,228 |
| 44 | 11 | | (a) | Tranmere Rovers | L | 0 - 1 | | 1,590 |
| 45 | 15 | | (h) | Wigan Athletic | D | 1 - 1 | Ayre (pen) | 1,836 |
| 46 | 19 | | (h) | Lincoln City | D | 0 - 0 | | 1,706 |
| 47 | 23 | | (a) | Torquay United | L | 1 - 3 | Harding | 1,581 |
| 48 | 26 | | (a) | Newport County | L | 0 - 1 | | 8,383 |
| 49 | May 3 | | (a) | Huddersfield Town | L | 1 - 2 | Linacre | 16,807 |

Final Position : 19th in Division Four

Apps.
Sub.Apps.
1 own goal — Goals

**FA Cup**

| | | | | | | | | |
|---|---|---|---|---|---|---|---|---|
| 22 | Nov 24 | R1 | (a) | Barnsley | L | 2 - 5 | Linacre, Newton | 12,548 |

Apps.
Sub.Apps.
Goals

**League Cup**

| | | | | | | | | |
|---|---|---|---|---|---|---|---|---|
| 1 | Aug 11 | R1/1 | (a) | Chesterfield | L | 1 - 5 | Harding | 3,493 |
| 2 | 14 | R1/2 | (h) | Chesterfield | W | 2 - 1 | Goldthorpe (pen), Lawrence | 1,763 |

Apps.
Sub.Apps.
Goals

| Watson | Norton | Gorry | Goldthorpe | Brooks | Ayre | Linacre | Smith | Houchen | Harding | Lawrence | Crumplin | Loadwick | Newton | Staff | Normanton | Larkin | Richardson | Sweeney | Carr | Burleigh | Hogan | Higgins | Hampton | McNamee | Fagan | Brown | Vass | Fowler | Evans | Pimblett |
|---|---|---|---|---|---|---|---|---|---|---|---|---|---|---|---|---|---|---|---|---|---|---|---|---|---|---|---|---|---|---|
|1|2|3|4|5|6|7|8|9|10|11||||||||||||||||||||
|1|2|3|4|5|6|7|8|9|10|11||||||||||||||||||||
|1|2|3|4|5|6|7|*8*|9|10|11||*12*||||||||||||||||||
|1||3|4|5|6|7|2|*8*|10|11|||9|*12*||||||||||||||||
|1||3|*4*|5|6|7||8|10|2||11|9|*12*||||||||||||||||
|1||3|*4*|5|6|7|*12*|8|10|2||11|9||||||||||||||||||
|1||||5|6|7|4|8|*10*|3||11|9||2|*12*||||||||||||||
|||||5|6|7|4|8|10|2||11|9||3||1||||||||||||||
|1||||5|6||4|8|*10*|7||11|9||3|*12*||2||||||||||||
||||||6||*7*|8|10|4||11|9||3|*12*|1|2|5|||||||||||
||||||6|*7*||8|10|4||11|9||3|||2|5|1|*12*||||||||||
|||||5|6||*12*|8|10|7||11|9||*3*|||2|4|1||||||||||
||||||6|||8|10|4||11|9||3|*12*||2|5|1|*7*||||||||||
||||||6|7||8|10|4||11|9||3|||2|5|1||||||||||
||||||6|7||8|10|4||11|9||3|||2|5|1||||||||||
||||||6|7||8|10|4||11|9||3|||2|5|1||||||||||
|||||*12*|6|7||8|10|4||11|9||3|||*2*|5|1||||||||||
|||7|||6|||8|10|4||11|9||3|||2|5|1||||||||||
|||7|||6|||8|10|4||11|9|||||2|3|1||5||||||||
|||*7*|||6|||*12*|10|4||8|9|||||2|3|1||5|11|||||||
|||||5|6|||8||4||7|9|*10*||*12*||2|3|1|||11|||||||
|||||5|6|7||*12*|10|4||8|*9*|||||2|3|1|||11|||||||
|||||5|6|7||*12*|10|4||8|9|||||2|*3*|1|||11|||||||
|||||5|6|*7*||*12*|10|4||8|9|||||2|3|1|||11|||||||
|||3||5|6|7||10||4||8|9|||||2||1|||11|||||||
|||||5|6|7||8||4|||9||10|||2|3|1|||11|||||||
|||10||5|6|7||8|*9*|4||||*12*||||2|3|1|||11|||||||
|||10||5|6|||8|9|4||||||||2|3|1|||11|7||||||
|||10|||*6*|7||*12*|8|4|||9|||||2|3|1|||11||5|||||
|||10|||6|7||*12*|*8*|4|||9|||||2|3|1|||11||5|||||
|||10||||7||8||4|||9||6|||2|3|1|||11||5|||||
|||||||7||8||4|||9|||||2|3|1|||11||5|6|10|||
|||||||7||8|10|4|||9|||||2||1|||11||5|6|3|||
||||||6|7||8|10|4|||9|||||2||1|*12*||11||*5*||3|||
||3||||6|7||8|10|4|||9|||||2||1|||11|||||5|||
||3||||6|7||8|*10*|9||||||||2||1|*12*||11|||5||4|||
|||||5|6|7||8|10|3|||9|||||2||1|||11|||||4|||
|||||5|6|7||8|10|3|||9|||||2||1|||11|||||4|||
|||||5|6|7||*8*|10|3|||9|||||2||1|||11|*12*||||4|||
|||||5|6|7|*12*|8||4||||9||||*2*||1|||11|||3||10|||
||2|||5|6|7|8||10|4||||||*12*||||1||||||3|||*9*|11|
|||||5|6|7|*2*||10|4||||8||*12*||||1|||9|||3||||11|
|||3||5|6|7|||10|||||||8|1||||4||9|||2||||11|
|||3||5|6|7|*12*||10||||||9||1||||4||11|*8*||2|||||
|||3||5|6|7|8||*10*|11|||||*12*||1||||4||9|||2|||||
|||||5|6|7||9|10||||||||1||||8||11||3|4|2||||
|8|6|18|6|28|43|37|11|35|40|43||21|33|3|15|1|6|32|22|32|5|2|26|2|7|10|4|6|1|3|
|||||1|||4|6||||1||3|1|7|||||3|||1|||||||
||||2|1|9|2||14|3|6||1|12||||||||||7|1|||||||

| Watson | Norton | Gorry | Goldthorpe | Brooks | Ayre | Linacre | Smith | Houchen | Harding | Lawrence | Crumplin | Loadwick | Newton | Staff | Normanton | Larkin | Richardson | Sweeney | Carr | Burleigh | Hogan | Higgins | Hampton | McNamee | Fagan | Brown | Vass | Fowler | Evans | Pimblett |
|---|---|---|---|---|---|---|---|---|---|---|---|---|---|---|---|---|---|---|---|---|---|---|---|---|---|---|---|---|---|---|
|||2|||6|7||8|10|4||11|9||||||3|1||5|||||||||
|||1|||1|1||1|1|1||1|1||||||1|1||1|||||||||
||||||||||||||||||||||||||||||||
|||||||1|||||||1||||||||||||||||||

| Watson | Norton | Gorry | Goldthorpe | Brooks | Ayre | Linacre | Smith | Houchen | Harding | Lawrence | Crumplin | Loadwick | Newton | Staff | Normanton | Larkin | Richardson | Sweeney | Carr | Burleigh | Hogan | Higgins | Hampton | McNamee | Fagan | Brown | Vass | Fowler | Evans | Pimblett |
|---|---|---|---|---|---|---|---|---|---|---|---|---|---|---|---|---|---|---|---|---|---|---|---|---|---|---|---|---|---|---|
|1||3||5|6|7|2|9|10|4|*8*|11|||||||||*12*||||||||||
|1|2|3|4|5|6|7|8|9|10|*12*||*11*|||||||||||||||||||
|2|1|2|1|2|2|2|2|2|2|1|1|2|||||||||||||||||||
|||||||||||1||||||||||1||||||||||
||||1||||||1|1||||||||||||||||||||

## League Table

| | P | W | D | L | F | A | Pts |
|---|---|---|---|---|---|---|---|
| Huddersfield Town | 46 | 27 | 12 | 7 | 101 | 48 | 66 |
| Walsall | 46 | 23 | 18 | 5 | 75 | 47 | 64 |
| Newport County | 46 | 27 | 7 | 12 | 83 | 50 | 61 |
| Portsmouth | 46 | 24 | 12 | 10 | 91 | 49 | 60 |
| Bradford City | 46 | 24 | 12 | 10 | 77 | 50 | 60 |
| Wigan Athletic | 46 | 21 | 13 | 12 | 76 | 61 | 55 |
| Lincoln City | 46 | 18 | 17 | 11 | 64 | 42 | 53 |
| Peterborough United | 46 | 21 | 10 | 15 | 58 | 47 | 52 |
| Torquay United | 46 | 15 | 17 | 14 | 70 | 69 | 47 |
| Aldershot | 46 | 16 | 13 | 17 | 62 | 53 | 45 |
| Bournemouth | 46 | 13 | 18 | 15 | 52 | 51 | 44 |
| Doncaster Rovers | 46 | 15 | 14 | 17 | 62 | 63 | 44 |
| Northampton Town | 46 | 16 | 12 | 18 | 51 | 66 | 44 |
| Scunthorpe United | 46 | 14 | 15 | 17 | 58 | 75 | 43 |
| Tranmere Rovers | 46 | 14 | 13 | 19 | 50 | 56 | 41 |
| Stockport County | 46 | 14 | 12 | 20 | 48 | 72 | 40 |
| York City | 46 | 14 | 11 | 21 | 65 | 82 | 39 |
| Halifax Town | 46 | 13 | 13 | 20 | 46 | 72 | 39 |
| Hartlepool United | 46 | 14 | 10 | 22 | 59 | 64 | 38 |
| Port Vale | 46 | 12 | 12 | 22 | 56 | 70 | 36 |
| Hereford United | 46 | 11 | 14 | 21 | 38 | 52 | 36 |
| Darlington | 46 | 9 | 17 | 20 | 50 | 74 | 35 |
| Crewe Alexandra | 46 | 11 | 13 | 22 | 35 | 68 | 35 |
| Rochdale | 46 | 7 | 13 | 26 | 33 | 79 | 27 |

# 1980-81

## League One

Manager: Fred Priest

### Did you know that?

'Pools won 20 League games in finishing ninth, with only the promoted teams winning more. At the beginning of February they were in a fourth promotion place, only for a run of five successive defeats to ruin their chances.

Average League attendances of 3,115 were the highest since the 1972–73 season.

| Match No. | Date | Round | Venue | Opponents | Result | | Scorers | Attendance |
|---|---|---|---|---|---|---|---|---|
| 3 | Aug 16 | | (a) | Wigan Athletic | W | 3 - 0 | Forster 2, Houchen | 5,233 |
| 4 | 19 | | (h) | Bury | L | 1 - 2 | Forster | 3,656 |
| 5 | 23 | | (a) | Rochdale | D | 1 - 1 | Brown | 5,230 |
| 6 | 30 | | (h) | Doncaster Rovers | W | 1 - 0 | Bird | 2,112 |
| 7 | Sep 6 | | (h) | Northampton Town | L | 2 - 3 | Hogan, Forster | 2,435 |
| 8 | 13 | | (a) | York City | W | 1 - 0 | Houchen | 2,504 |
| 9 | 16 | | (a) | Bournemouth | L | 0 - 1 | | 2,413 |
| 10 | 20 | | (h) | Hereford United | W | 2 - 0 | Houchen, Ayre | 2,345 |
| 11 | 26 | | (a) | Southend United | L | 0 - 4 | | 4,971 |
| 12 | 30 | | (h) | Bournemouth | W | 1 - 0 | Lawrence | 2,419 |
| 13 | Oct 4 | | (h) | Aldershot | W | 1 - 0 | Linacre | 2,872 |
| 14 | 7 | | (a) | Scunthorpe United | D | 3 - 3 | Newton 2, Houchen | 2,900 |
| 15 | 11 | | (a) | Wimbledon | L | 0 - 5 | | 1,971 |
| 16 | 18 | | (h) | Lincoln City | W | 2 - 0 | Bird, Newton | 2,712 |
| 17 | 21 | | (h) | Mansfield Town | L | 0 - 1 | | 3,419 |
| 18 | 25 | | (a) | Port Vale | D | 1 - 1 | Kerr | 3,072 |
| 19 | 27 | | (a) | Stockport County | W | 2 - 0 | Newton, Houchen | 2,066 |
| 20 | Nov 1 | | (h) | Crewe Alexandra | W | 6 - 2 | Kerr, Houchen 2, Newton 2, Hampton | 3,098 |
| 21 | 4 | | (h) | Scunthorpe United | W | 2 - 0 | Sweeney, Hampton | 4,400 |
| 22 | 8 | | (a) | Halifax Town | W | 2 - 1 | Hampton, Hogan | 1,692 |
| 23 | 11 | | (a) | Bury | D | 0 - 0 | | 2,301 |
| 24 | 15 | | (h) | Wigan Athletic | W | 3 - 1 | Hogan, Houchen 2 | 5,035 |
| 26 | 29 | | (h) | Torquay United | L | 0 - 2 | | 3,419 |
| 27 | Dec 5 | | (a) | Tranmere Rovers | D | 2 - 2 | Houchen, Hamilton (o.g.) | 1,523 |
| 28 | 20 | | (h) | Peterborough United | D | 1 - 1 | Hampton | 3,121 |
| 29 | 26 | | (a) | Darlington | L | 0 - 3 | | 7,155 |
| 30 | 27 | | (h) | Bradford City | D | 2 - 2 | Hampton, Hogan | 3,695 |
| 31 | Jan 10 | | (h) | Port Vale | W | 3 - 0 | Newton 2 (1 pen), Hogan | 3,116 |
| 32 | 17 | | (a) | Torquay United | L | 1 - 2 | Newton | 1,647 |
| 33 | 24 | | (a) | Doncaster Rovers | W | 2 - 1 | Hogan, Hampton | 6,814 |
| 34 | 31 | | (h) | Rochdale | D | 2 - 2 | Houchen 2 (1 pen) | 3,867 |
| 35 | Feb 7 | | (h) | York City | W | 1 - 0 | Bird | 3,119 |
| 36 | 14 | | (a) | Northampton Town | L | 1 - 3 | Hampton | 2,032 |
| 37 | 21 | | (h) | Southend United | L | 1 - 3 | Bird | 3,748 |
| 38 | 28 | | (a) | Hereford United | L | 0 - 3 | | 2,313 |
| 39 | Mar 7 | | (a) | Aldershot | L | 1 - 2 | Houchen | 2,252 |
| 40 | 14 | | (h) | Wimbledon | L | 2 - 3 | Houchen, Newton | 2,138 |
| 41 | 16 | | (a) | Mansfield Town | W | 1 - 0 | Harding | 3,737 |
| 42 | 21 | | (a) | Lincoln City | L | 0 - 2 | | 3,969 |
| 43 | 28 | | (h) | Stockport County | W | 1 - 0 | Harding | 1,928 |
| 44 | Apr 3 | | (a) | Crewe Alexandra | L | 0 - 2 | | 2,419 |
| 45 | 11 | | (h) | Halifax Town | W | 3 - 0 | Hogan, Houchen, Lawrence | 1,579 |
| 46 | 17 | | (h) | Darlington | W | 2 - 0 | Howard, Linacre | 5,578 |
| 47 | 19 | | (a) | Bradford City | L | 0 - 2 | | 1,614 |
| 48 | 25 | | (a) | Peterborough United | D | 1 - 1 | Lawrence | 3,560 |
| 49 | May 2 | | (h) | Tranmere Rovers | W | 3 - 0 | Houchen 2 (1 pen), Sweeney | 1,826 |

Final Position : 9th in Division Four

Apps.
Sub.Apps.
1 own goal — Goals

**FA Cup**

| | | | | | | | | |
|---|---|---|---|---|---|---|---|---|
| 25 | Nov 22 | R1 | (a) | Scunthorpe United | L | 1 - 3 | Hampton | 5,162 |

Apps.
Sub.Apps.
Goals

**League Cup**

| | | | | | | | | |
|---|---|---|---|---|---|---|---|---|
| 1 | Aug 9 | R1/1 | (a) | York City | L | 1 - 2 | Forster | 2,444 |
| 2 | 12 | R1/2 | (h) | York City | D | 0 - 0 | | 3,496 |

Apps.
Sub.Apps.
Goals

| Burleigh | Brown | Vaas | Sweeney | Hogan | Bird | Fagan | Linacre, J. | Kerr | Houchen | Forster | Hampton | Ayre | Lawrence | Richardson | Harding | Newton | Linacre, P. | Johnson | Normanton | Graycome | Stimpson | Linighan | Howard | Staff |
|---|---|---|---|---|---|---|---|---|---|---|---|---|---|---|---|---|---|---|---|---|---|---|---|---|
| 1 | 2 | | 3 | 4 | 5 | 6 | 7 | 8 | 9 | 10 | 11 | | | | | | | | | | | | | |
| 1 | 2 | | 3 | 4 | 5 | | 7 | 8 | 9 | *10* | 11 | 6 | *12* | | | | | | | | | | | |
| | 3 | | | 4 | 5 | 2 | 7 | 8 | | 10 | *11* | 6 | *12* | 1 | 9 | | | | | | | | | |
| | 3 | | | 4 | 5 | 2 | 7 | 8 | *12* | 10 | | 6 | *9* | 1 | 11 | | | | | | | | | |
| | 3 | | | 4 | 5 | 2 | 7 | 8 | *12* | 10 | | 6 | 9 | 1 | *11* | | | | | | | | | |
| | 3 | | 2 | 4 | 5 | *6* | | 8 | 9 | 10 | *12* | | 7 | 1 | 11 | | | | | | | | | |
| | 3 | | 2 | 4 | 5 | | | 8 | 10 | *12* | | 6 | *7* | 1 | 11 | 9 | | | | | | | | |
| | 3 | | 2 | 4 | 5 | | | 8 | 10 | *12* | | 6 | 7 | 1 | 11 | *9* | | | | | | | | |
| | 3 | | 2 | 4 | 5 | | | 7 | 10 | *12* | | 6 | 8 | 1 | *11* | 9 | | | | | | | | |
| | 3 | | 2 | 4 | 5 | | | 7 | 10 | 11 | | 6 | 8 | 1 | | 9 | | | | | | | | |
| | 3 | | 2 | 4 | 5 | | 6 | 7 | 10 | 11 | | | 8 | 1 | | 9 | | | | | | | | |
| | 3 | | 2 | 4 | 5 | | 6 | 7 | 10 | *11* | *12* | | 8 | 1 | | 9 | | | | | | | | |
| | 3 | | 2 | 4 | 5 | | 6 | 7 | 10 | 11 | | | 8 | 1 | | 9 | | | | | | | | |
| 1 | 3 | | 2 | 4 | 5 | | 6 | 7 | 10 | | 11 | | 8 | | | 9 | | | | | | | | |
| 1 | 3 | | 2 | *4* | 5 | | 6 | 7 | 10 | *12* | 11 | | 8 | | | 9 | | | | | | | | |
| 1 | 3 | | 2 | 4 | 5 | | 6 | 7 | 10 | | 11 | | 8 | | | 9 | | | | | | | | |
| 1 | 3 | | 2 | 4 | 5 | | 6 | 7 | 10 | | 11 | | 8 | | | 9 | | | | | | | | |
| 1 | 3 | | 2 | 4 | 5 | | 6 | 7 | 10 | | 11 | | 8 | | | 9 | | | | | | | | |
| 1 | 3 | | 2 | 4 | 5 | | 6 | 7 | 10 | | 11 | | 8 | | | 9 | | | | | | | | |
| 1 | 3 | | 2 | 4 | 5 | | 6 | 7 | 10 | | 11 | | 8 | | | 9 | | | | | | | | |
| 1 | 3 | | 2 | 4 | 5 | | 6 | 7 | 10 | | 11 | | 8 | | | 9 | | | | | | | | |
| 1 | 3 | | 2 | 4 | 5 | | 6 | 7 | 10 | | 11 | | 8 | | | 9 | | | | | | | | |
| 1 | 3 | | 2 | 4 | 5 | | 6 | 7 | 10 | | 11 | | 8 | | *12* | *9* | | | | | | | | |
| 1 | 3 | | 2 | 4 | 5 | | 6 | 7 | 10 | | 11 | | 8 | | | 9 | | | | | | | | |
| 1 | 3 | | 2 | 4 | | 5 | 6 | 7 | 10 | | 11 | | 8 | | | | 9 | | | | | | | |
| 1 | 3 | | | 4 | 5 | | 6 | 7 | 10 | | 11 | 2 | 8 | | 9 | | | | | | | | | |
| 1 | 3 | | | 4 | 5 | *12* | *6* | 7 | 10 | | 11 | 2 | 8 | | | 9 | | | | | | | | |
| | 3 | | | 4 | 5 | 2 | 6 | 7 | 10 | | *11* | | 8 | 1 | | 9 | | *12* | | | | | | |
| | 3 | | | 4 | 5 | 2 | 6 | *7* | 10 | | 11 | | 8 | 1 | | 9 | | *12* | | | | | | |
| | 3 | | 8 | 4 | 5 | 6 | 2 | 7 | *12* | | 11 | | | 1 | | 9 | | *10* | | | | | | |
| | 3 | | 8 | 4 | 5 | 6 | 2 | 7 | 9 | | 11 | | *12* | 1 | | | | *10* | | | | | | |
| | 3 | | 8 | 4 | 5 | 6 | 2 | 7 | 9 | | 11 | | *12* | 1 | | | | *10* | | | | | | |
| | 3 | | 8 | *4* | 5 | 6 | 2 | 7 | 9 | | 11 | | 10 | 1 | | | | *12* | | | | | | |
| | 3 | | 2 | 4 | 5 | | | 7 | 9 | | 11 | | 8 | 1 | | | | *12* | 6 | *10* | | | | |
| | 2 | | 3 | 4 | 5 | | | 7 | 10 | | *12* | | *8* | 1 | | 9 | | 11 | 6 | | | | | |
| | 6 | | 3 | | 5 | 8 | 2 | 7 | 10 | | | | | 1 | 4 | 9 | | 11 | | | | | | |
| | 6 | | 3 | *12* | 5 | 8 | 2 | 7 | 10 | | | | | 1 | *4* | 9 | | 11 | | | | | | |
| | 6 | | | 11 | 5 | 8 | 2 | 7 | 10 | | | | 3 | 1 | *4* | 9 | | *12* | | | | | | |
| | 6 | | | 11 | 5 | 8 | 2 | 7 | 10 | | | | 3 | 1 | 4 | 9 | | | | | | | | |
| | 6 | | | | 5 | | 2 | 7 | 10 | | *12* | | 4 | 1 | 11 | | | *9* | | | 3 | 8 | | |
| | 6 | | | | 5 | | 2 | 7 | 10 | | *12* | | 4 | 1 | 11 | | | *9* | | | 3 | 8 | | |
| | 6 | | | 11 | 5 | | 2 | 7 | 10 | | | | 4 | 1 | | | | | | | 3 | 8 | *9* | *12* |
| | 6 | | | 11 | 5 | | 2 | 7 | 10 | | | | 4 | 1 | | | | | | | 3 | 8 | 9 | |
| | 6 | | 3 | 11 | 5 | 8 | 2 | 7 | 10 | | *9* | | 4 | 1 | | | | *12* | | | | | | |
| | 6 | | 3 | *11* | 5 | | 2 | 7 | 10 | | *12* | | 4 | 1 | | | | | | | | 8 | | 9 |
| | 6 | | 3 | 11 | 5 | | 2 | 7 | 10 | | | | 4 | 1 | | | | | | | | 8 | *12* | *9* |
| 16 | 46 | | 33 | 42 | 45 | 17 | 39 | 46 | 42 | 10 | 25 | 10 | 38 | 30 | 14 | 27 | 1 | 8 | 2 | 1 | 4 | 6 | 2 | 2 |
| | | | | 1 | | 1 | | | 3 | 4 | 6 | | 4 | | 1 | | | 6 | | | | | 1 | 1 |
| | 1 | | 2 | 7 | 4 | | 2 | 2 | 17 | 4 | 7 | 1 | 3 | | 2 | 10 | | | | | | | 1 | |

| Burleigh | Brown | Vaas | Sweeney | Hogan | Bird | Fagan | Linacre, J. | Kerr | Houchen | Forster | Hampton | Ayre | Lawrence | Richardson | Harding | Newton | Linacre, P. | Johnson | Normanton | Graycome | Stimpson | Linighan | Howard | Staff |
|---|---|---|---|---|---|---|---|---|---|---|---|---|---|---|---|---|---|---|---|---|---|---|---|---|
| 1 | 3 | | 2 | 4 | 5 | | 6 | 7 | 10 | | 11 | | 8 | | | 9 | | | | | | | | |
| 1 | 1 | | 1 | 1 | 1 | | 1 | 1 | 1 | | 1 | | 1 | | | 1 | | | | | | | | |
| | | | | | | | | | | | | | | | | | | | | | | | | |
| | | | | | | | | | | | 1 | | | | | | | | | | | | | |

| Burleigh | Brown | Vaas | Sweeney | Hogan | Bird | Fagan | Linacre, J. | Kerr | Houchen | Forster | Hampton | Ayre | Lawrence | Richardson | Harding | Newton | Linacre, P. | Johnson | Normanton | Graycome | Stimpson | Linighan | Howard | Staff |
|---|---|---|---|---|---|---|---|---|---|---|---|---|---|---|---|---|---|---|---|---|---|---|---|---|
| 1 | 2 | 3 | | | 5 | 6 | 7 | 8 | 9 | 10 | 11 | | 4 | | | | | | | | | | | |
| 1 | 2 | | 3 | | 5 | 6 | 7 | 8 | 9 | 10 | 11 | | 4 | | | | | | | | | | | |
| 2 | 2 | 1 | 1 | | 2 | 2 | 2 | 2 | 2 | 2 | 2 | | 2 | | | | | | | | | | | |
| | | | | | | | | | | | | | | | | | | | | | | | | |
| | | | | | | | | | | 1 | | | | | | | | | | | | | | |

## League Table

| | P | W | D | L | F | A | Pts |
|---|---|---|---|---|---|---|---|
| Southend United | 46 | 30 | 7 | 9 | 79 | 31 | 67 |
| Lincoln City | 46 | 25 | 15 | 6 | 66 | 25 | 65 |
| Doncaster Rovers | 46 | 22 | 12 | 12 | 59 | 49 | 56 |
| Wimbledon | 46 | 23 | 9 | 14 | 64 | 46 | 55 |
| Peterborough United | 46 | 17 | 18 | 11 | 68 | 54 | 52 |
| Aldershot | 46 | 18 | 14 | 14 | 43 | 41 | 50 |
| Mansfield Town | 46 | 20 | 9 | 17 | 58 | 44 | 49 |
| Darlington | 46 | 19 | 11 | 16 | 65 | 59 | 49 |
| Hartlepool United | 46 | 20 | 9 | 17 | 64 | 61 | 49 |
| Northampton Town | 46 | 18 | 13 | 15 | 65 | 67 | 49 |
| Wigan Athletic | 46 | 18 | 11 | 17 | 51 | 55 | 47 |
| Bury | 46 | 17 | 11 | 18 | 70 | 62 | 45 |
| Bournemouth | 46 | 16 | 13 | 17 | 47 | 48 | 45 |
| Bradford City | 46 | 14 | 16 | 16 | 53 | 60 | 44 |
| Rochdale | 46 | 14 | 15 | 17 | 60 | 70 | 43 |
| Scunthorpe United | 46 | 11 | 20 | 15 | 60 | 69 | 42 |
| Torquay United | 46 | 18 | 5 | 23 | 55 | 63 | 41 |
| Crewe Alexandra | 46 | 13 | 14 | 19 | 48 | 61 | 40 |
| Port Vale | 46 | 12 | 15 | 19 | 57 | 70 | 39 |
| Stockport County | 46 | 16 | 7 | 23 | 44 | 57 | 39 |
| Tranmere Rovers | 46 | 13 | 10 | 23 | 59 | 73 | 36 |
| Hereford United | 46 | 11 | 13 | 22 | 38 | 62 | 35 |
| Halifax Town | 46 | 11 | 12 | 23 | 44 | 71 | 34 |
| York City | 46 | 12 | 9 | 25 | 47 | 66 | 33 |

# 1981-82

## Division Four

Manager: Billy Horner

### Did you know that?

Horden Colliery elected to play their first-round FA Cup tie against Blackpool at the Victoria Ground for financial reasons. A crowd of 4,465 saw Wayne Harrison score the only goal to give the Seasiders a narrow victory.

This season saw the introduction of the 'three points for a win' rule. 'Pools' first three-pointer was against Wigan Athletic, a 2–1 win in their third game of the season.

| Match No. | Date | Round | Venue | Opponents | Result | | Scorers | Attendance |
|---|---|---|---|---|---|---|---|---|
| 4 | Aug 29 | | (h) | Colchester United | L | 1 - 3 | Harding | 2,006 |
| 6 | Sep 5 | | (a) | Rochdale | L | 1 - 2 | Houchen | 1,481 |
| 7 | 12 | | (h) | Wigan Athletic | W | 2 - 1 | J.Linacre, Hampton | 1,712 |
| 9 | 18 | | (a) | York City | W | 2 - 1 | Houchen, Newton | 2,241 |
| 10 | 22 | | (a) | Scunthorpe United | L | 1 - 2 | Newton | 2,060 |
| 11 | 26 | | (h) | Halifax Town | W | 3 - 2 | Hampton 2, Houchen | 1,800 |
| 12 | 30 | | (h) | Hull City | W | 3 - 2 | Houchen (pen), Hampton, Newton | 2,654 |
| 13 | Oct 3 | | (a) | Hereford United | D | 1 - 1 | Bird | 2,247 |
| 14 | 10 | | (h) | Peterborough United | L | 0 - 1 | | 2,450 |
| 15 | 17 | | (a) | Sheffield United | D | 1 - 1 | Bird | 12,752 |
| 16 | 20 | | (a) | Tranmere Rovers | L | 0 - 1 | | 1,456 |
| 17 | 24 | | (h) | Torquay United | D | 0 - 0 | | 2,099 |
| 18 | 31 | | (a) | Aldershot | W | 2 - 1 | Newton, J.Linacre | 2,658 |
| 19 | Nov 4 | | (h) | Crewe Alexandra | L | 1 - 2 | Houchen | 2,328 |
| 20 | 8 | | (a) | Bradford City | L | 0 - 1 | | 5,753 |
| 21 | 14 | | (h) | Northampton Town | W | 3 - 1 | Newton 2, Hogan | 1,641 |
| 24 | 28 | | (a) | Port Vale | L | 2 - 5 | Howard, Hogan | 2,477 |
| 25 | Dec 5 | | (h) | Bournemouth | D | 1 - 1 | Newton | 1,763 |
| 27 | Jan 16 | | (a) | Mansfield Town | L | 2 - 3 | Brown, Houchen | 2,011 |
| 28 | 19 | | (a) | Bury | D | 1 - 1 | Houchen (pen) | 2,997 |
| 29 | 23 | | (a) | Colchester United | D | 3 - 3 | Houchen 2 (1 pen), Bird | 2,862 |
| 30 | 25 | | (a) | Stockport County | W | 2 - 0 | Bird, Brown | 1,924 |
| 31 | 30 | | (h) | York City | W | 3 - 2 | Houchen, Fagan, Newton | 2,291 |
| 32 | Feb 3 | | (h) | Darlington | L | 1 - 2 | Bird | 4,548 |
| 33 | 6 | | (a) | Wigan Athletic | D | 1 - 1 | Newton | 6,315 |
| 34 | 10 | | (h) | Scunthorpe United | D | 3 - 3 | Houchen (pen), Johnson 2 | 2,001 |
| 35 | 13 | | (h) | Hereford United | W | 2 - 1 | Howard 2 | 1,811 |
| 36 | 20 | | (a) | Hull City | L | 2 - 5 | Houchen 2 (1 pen) | 3,040 |
| 37 | 27 | | (a) | Peterborough United | D | 4 - 4 | Houchen 3 (1 pen), Staff | 4,610 |
| 38 | Mar 6 | | (h) | Sheffield United | L | 2 - 3 | P.Linacre, Staff | 4,145 |
| 39 | 10 | | (h) | Tranmere Rovers | D | 0 - 0 | | 1,633 |
| 40 | 13 | | (a) | Torquay United | D | 1 - 1 | Staff | 1,532 |
| 41 | 16 | | (a) | Crewe Alexandra | W | 2 - 1 | Houchen, Hogan | 1,116 |
| 42 | 20 | | (h) | Aldershot | D | 2 - 2 | Newton, Bainbridge | 1,702 |
| 43 | 27 | | (h) | Bradford City | L | 0 - 2 | | 2,512 |
| 44 | 31 | | (h) | Rochdale | D | 1 - 1 | Brown | 1,259 |
| 45 | Apr 3 | | (a) | Northampton Town | L | 1 - 2 | Bird | 1,890 |
| 46 | 10 | | (h) | Stockport County | D | 2 - 2 | Stimpson, Brown | 1,506 |
| 47 | 12 | | (a) | Darlington | L | 2 - 5 | Harding, Clarke | 4,575 |
| 48 | 17 | | (a) | Bournemouth | L | 1 - 5 | Hogan | 6,567 |
| 49 | 24 | | (h) | Port Vale | W | 3 - 1 | P.Linacre, Newton (pen), Staff | 1,439 |
| 50 | 28 | | (h) | Blackpool | D | 2 - 2 | Newton 2 | 1,387 |
| 51 | May 1 | | (a) | Halifax Town | L | 0 - 2 | | 1,305 |
| 52 | 5 | | (h) | Mansfield Town | W | 3 - 0 | Newton, Staff, Linacre | 1,202 |
| 53 | 8 | | (h) | Bury | W | 1 - 0 | P.Linacre | 1,370 |
| 54 | 15 | | (a) | Blackpool | D | 2 - 2 | P.Linacre, Newton | 1,824 |

Final Position : 14th in Division Four

Apps.
Sub.Apps.
Goals

**FA Cup**

| Match No. | Date | Round | Venue | Opponents | Result | | Scorers | Attendance |
|---|---|---|---|---|---|---|---|---|
| 22 | Nov 21 | R1 | (a) | Wigan Athletic | D | 2 - 2 | P.Linacre, Newton | 5,303 |
| 23 | 25 | R1r | (h) | Wigan Athletic | W | 1 - 0 | Newton | 3,739 |
| 26 | Jan 4 | R2 | (a) | Hull City | L | 0 - 2 | | 4,975 |

Apps.
Sub.Apps.
Goals

**League Cup**

| Match No. | Date | Round | Venue | Opponents | Result | | Scorers | Attendance |
|---|---|---|---|---|---|---|---|---|
| 5 | Sep 1 | R1/1 | (a) | Northampton Town | L | 0 - 2 | | 1,480 |
| 8 | 16 | R1/2 | (h) | Northampton Town | W | 2 - 1 | Newton, Houchen | 1,975 |

Apps.
Sub.Apps.
Goals

| Burleigh | Brown | Stimpson | Hogan | Bird | Linighan, A. | Kerr | Sweeney | Staff | Houchen | Harding | Hampton | Fagan | Johnson | Linacre, J. | Newton | Linacre, P. | Howard | Dobson | Bainbridge | Lowe | Watson | Linighan, D. | Clarke | Lawrence |
|---|---|---|---|---|---|---|---|---|---|---|---|---|---|---|---|---|---|---|---|---|---|---|---|---|
| 1 | 2 | 3 | 4 | 5 | 6 | *7* | 8 | 9 | 10 | 11 | *12* | | | | | | | | | | | | | |
| 1 | 2 | 3 | 4 | | 6 | 7 | 8 | *9* | 10 | 11 | | 5 | *12* | | | | | | | | | | | |
| 1 | 7 | 3 | 4 | 5 | | | 2 | | 10 | | 9 | 6 | 11 | 8 | | | | | | | | | | |
| 1 | 6 | 3 | 4 | | 5 | | 2 | | 10 | | 9 | | 11 | 7 | 8 | | | | | | | | | |
| 1 | 6 | 3 | 4 | | 5 | | 2 | | 10 | | 9 | | 11 | 7 | 8 | | | | | | | | | |
| 1 | *12* | 3 | *4* | 5 | 6 | | 2 | | 10 | | 9 | | 11 | 7 | 8 | | | | | | | | | |
| 1 | *12* | 3 | *4* | 5 | 6 | | 2 | | 10 | | 9 | | 11 | 7 | 8 | | | | | | | | | |
| 1 | 3 | | 4 | 5 | 6 | | 2 | | 10 | | 9 | | 11 | 7 | 8 | | | | | | | | | |
| 1 | 3 | | 4 | 5 | 6 | | 2 | *12* | 10 | | 9 | | *11* | 7 | 8 | | | | | | | | | |
| 1 | | 3 | *4* | 5 | 6 | | 2 | | 10 | *12* | 9 | | 11 | 7 | 8 | | | | | | | | | |
| 1 | | 3 | 4 | 5 | 6 | | 2 | | 10 | *12* | 9 | | *11* | 7 | 8 | | | | | | | | | |
| 1 | 2 | 3 | *12* | 5 | 6 | | | | 10 | 4 | 9 | | | 7 | 8 | *11* | | | | | | | | |
| 1 | 2 | 3 | | 5 | 6 | | | | 10 | 4 | 9 | | | 7 | 8 | 11 | | | | | | | | |
| 1 | 2 | 3 | *12* | 5 | *6* | | | | 10 | 4 | 9 | | | 7 | 8 | 11 | | | | | | | | |
| 1 | 2 | 3 | *12* | 5 | 6 | | 9 | 10 | | *4* | | | | 7 | 8 | 11 | | | | | | | | |
| 1 | 2 | 3 | 4 | 5 | 6 | | 10 | | | | | | 11 | 7 | 8 | 9 | | | | | | | | |
| 1 | 2 | 3 | 4 | 5 | 6 | *12* | | | 10 | | | | *11* | | 8 | 9 | 7 | | | | | | | |
| 1 | 2 | | 4 | 5 | 6 | | 9 | | 10 | | | | 11 | 7 | 8 | 3 | | | | | | | | |
| 1 | 4 | 3 | | 5 | | | *2* | 9 | 10 | | | 6 | 11 | 7 | | 8 | *12* | | | | | | | |
| 1 | 4 | | | 5 | | | 2 | *8* | 10 | | | 6 | 11 | 7 | 9 | 3 | *12* | | | | | | | |
| 1 | 4 | | 8 | 5 | | | 2 | 11 | 10 | | | 6 | | 7 | 9 | 3 | | | | | | | | |
| 1 | 4 | | 8 | 5 | | | 2 | 11 | 10 | | | 6 | | 7 | 9 | 3 | | | | | | | | |
| 1 | 4 | | 8 | 5 | | | 2 | 11 | 10 | | | 6 | | 7 | 9 | 3 | | | | | | | | |
| 1 | 4 | | 8 | 5 | | | 2 | 11 | 10 | | | 6 | *12* | 7 | *9* | 3 | | | | | | | | |
| 1 | 4 | | 8 | 5 | | | 2 | 11 | *10* | | | 6 | *12* | 7 | 9 | 3 | | | | | | | | |
| 1 | 4 | | 8 | 5 | | | *2* | | 10 | | | 6 | 11 | 7 | 9 | 3 | | *12* | | | | | | |
| 1 | 2 | | 4 | 5 | | | | 8 | 10 | | | | 11 | 7 | | 3 | 9 | | 6 | | | | | |
| 1 | 2 | | 4 | *5* | | | | | 10 | | *12* | | 11 | 7 | | 3 | 9 | | 6 | 8 | | | | |
| 1 | 2 | 3 | 4 | 5 | | | | 8 | 10 | | | 6 | | 7 | 9 | 11 | | | | | | | | |
| 1 | 2 | 3 | | 5 | | | | 8 | 10 | | | | 4 | 7 | 9 | 11 | | | 6 | | | | | |
| 1 | 6 | 3 | | 5 | | | 2 | 8 | 10 | | | | 4 | 7 | 9 | 11 | | | | | | | | |
| 1 | 6 | 3 | 4 | 5 | | | | 8 | 10 | *7* | | | 11 | 2 | 9 | *12* | | | | | | | | |
| 1 | 6 | *12* | 4 | | | | | 8 | 10 | 7 | | | *11* | 2 | 9 | 3 | | | 5 | | | | | |
| 1 | 6 | | 4 | 5 | | | | 8 | 10 | | | | 11 | 2 | 9 | 3 | | | 7 | | | | | |
| | 6 | | 4 | 5 | | | | 8 | | | | | 11 | 2 | | 3 | *9* | *12* | 7 | | 1 | 10 | | |
| | 10 | | 4 | 5 | | | | 8 | | | | | 11 | 2 | | 3 | | *9* | 6 | *12* | 1 | 7 | | |
| | 10 | | 4 | 5 | | | | 8 | | *12* | | | 11 | 2 | | 3 | | *9* | 6 | | 1 | 7 | | |
| | 9 | *3* | 4 | 5 | | | 8 | *12* | | | 10 | | 11 | 2 | | | | | 6 | | 1 | 7 | | |
| 1 | 9 | 3 | 4 | 5 | | | 10 | *12* | | 7 | | | 11 | 2 | | | | | | | | 6 | *8* | |
| 1 | 9 | 3 | 4 | 5 | | | 2 | 11 | | 7 | | | 10 | | | | | | *12* | | | 6 | *8* | |
| | 6 | 3 | 4 | 5 | | | 2 | 8 | | | | | *11* | 7 | 9 | 10 | | | | | 1 | | | *12* |
| | 6 | 3 | | 5 | | | 2 | | | | 11 | | | 7 | 9 | 10 | | | | *4* | 1 | | 8 | *12* |
| | 6 | 3 | | 5 | | | 2 | | | | 11 | | | 7 | 9 | 10 | | | | *8* | 1 | | *12* | 4 |
| | 6 | 3 | 4 | 5 | | | 2 | 8 | | | | | | 7 | 9 | 10 | | | | | 1 | | *12* | *11* |
| | 6 | 3 | 4 | 5 | | | 2 | | | | | | | 7 | 9 | 10 | | *12* | | | 1 | | 8 | *11* |
| | 6 | 3 | 4 | 5 | | | *2* | 11 | | | | | | 7 | 9 | 10 | | | | | 1 | | 8 | *12* |
| 36 | 42 | 29 | 36 | 42 | 17 | 2 | 32 | 24 | 32 | 10 | 15 | 11 | 29 | 42 | 34 | 31 | 4 | 2 | 9 | 3 | 10 | 6 | 5 | 3 |
| | 2 | 1 | 3 | | | 1 | | 3 | | 3 | 2 | | 3 | | | 1 | 2 | 3 | 1 | 1 | | | 2 | 3 |
| | 4 | 1 | 4 | 6 | | | | 5 | 17 | 2 | 4 | 1 | 2 | 3 | 15 | 4 | 3 | | 1 | | | | 1 | |

| Burleigh | Brown | Stimpson | Hogan | Bird | Linighan, A. | Kerr | Sweeney | Staff | Houchen | Harding | Hampton | Fagan | Johnson | Linacre, J. | Newton | Linacre, P. | Howard | Dobson | Bainbridge | Lowe | Watson | Linighan, D. | Clarke | Lawrence |
|---|---|---|---|---|---|---|---|---|---|---|---|---|---|---|---|---|---|---|---|---|---|---|---|---|
| 1 | 2 | 3 | *4* | 5 | 6 | | 10 | | | | | | 11 | 7 | 8 | 9 | | | | | | | *12* | |
| 1 | 2 | 3 | 4 | 5 | 6 | | 10 | | *12* | | | | 11 | 7 | 8 | *9* | | | | | | | | |
| 1 | 4 | | | | 6 | 8 | 2 | | 10 | | 9 | | 11 | 7 | | 3 | | | 5 | | | | | |
| 3 | 3 | 2 | 2 | 2 | 3 | 1 | 3 | | 1 | | 1 | | 3 | 3 | 2 | 3 | | | 1 | | | | | |
| | | | | | | | | | 1 | | | | | | | | | | | | | | 1 | |
| | | | | | | | | | | | | | | | 2 | 1 | | | | | | | | |

| Burleigh | Brown | Stimpson | Hogan | Bird | Linighan, A. | Kerr | Sweeney | Staff | Houchen | Harding | Hampton | Fagan | Johnson | Linacre, J. | Newton | Linacre, P. | Howard | Dobson | Bainbridge | Lowe | Watson | Linighan, D. | Clarke | Lawrence |
|---|---|---|---|---|---|---|---|---|---|---|---|---|---|---|---|---|---|---|---|---|---|---|---|---|
| 1 | 2 | 3 | 4 | | 6 | 7 | 8 | 9 | 10 | *11* | | 5 | *12* | | | | | | | | | | | |
| 1 | 6 | *3* | 4 | | *12* | | 2 | | 10 | | 9 | 5 | 11 | 7 | 8 | | | | | | | | | |
| 2 | 2 | 2 | 2 | | 1 | 1 | 2 | 1 | 2 | 1 | 1 | 2 | 1 | 1 | 1 | | | | | | | | | |
| | | | | | 1 | | | | | | | | 1 | | | | | | | | | | | |
| | | | | | | | | | 1 | | | | | | 1 | | | | | | | | | |

## League Table

| | P | W | D | L | F | A | Pts |
|---|---|---|---|---|---|---|---|
| Sheffield United | 46 | 27 | 15 | 4 | 94 | 41 | 96 |
| Bradford City | 46 | 26 | 13 | 7 | 88 | 45 | 91 |
| Wigan Athletic | 46 | 26 | 13 | 7 | 80 | 46 | 91 |
| Bournemouth | 46 | 23 | 19 | 4 | 62 | 30 | 88 |
| Peterborough United | 46 | 24 | 10 | 12 | 71 | 57 | 82 |
| Colchester United | 46 | 20 | 12 | 14 | 82 | 57 | 72 |
| Port Vale | 46 | 18 | 16 | 12 | 56 | 49 | 70 |
| Hull City | 46 | 19 | 12 | 15 | 70 | 61 | 69 |
| Bury | 46 | 17 | 17 | 12 | 80 | 59 | 68 |
| Hereford United | 46 | 16 | 19 | 11 | 64 | 58 | 67 |
| Tranmere Rovers | 46 | 14 | 18 | 14 | 51 | 56 | 60 |
| Blackpool | 46 | 15 | 13 | 18 | 66 | 60 | 58 |
| Darlington | 46 | 15 | 13 | 18 | 61 | 62 | 58 |
| Hartlepool United | 46 | 13 | 16 | 17 | 73 | 84 | 55 |
| Torquay United | 46 | 14 | 13 | 19 | 47 | 59 | 55 |
| Aldershot | 46 | 13 | 15 | 18 | 57 | 68 | 54 |
| York City | 46 | 14 | 8 | 24 | 69 | 91 | 50 |
| Stockport County | 46 | 12 | 13 | 21 | 48 | 67 | 49 |
| Halifax Town | 46 | 9 | 22 | 15 | 51 | 72 | 49 |
| Mansfield Town | 46 | 13 | 10 | 23 | 63 | 81 | 47 |
| Rochdale | 46 | 10 | 16 | 20 | 50 | 62 | 46 |
| Northampton Town | 46 | 11 | 9 | 26 | 57 | 84 | 42 |
| Scunthorpe United | 46 | 9 | 15 | 22 | 43 | 79 | 42 |
| Crewe Alexandra | 46 | 6 | 9 | 31 | 29 | 84 | 27 |

# 1982-83

## Division Four

Managers: Billy Horner and John Duncan

### Did you know that?

In the game at Torquay on 2 October 'Pools had three players sent off: Roy Hogan for persistent fouling and Kevin Johnson along with Trevor Smith for 'a heated exchange of words'!

'Pools failed to score in 17 League games as average home attendances reach an all-time low of 1,368.

Hartlepool's 13th application for re-election saw them muster 36 votes, 10 more than Maidstone United, who many felt were unlucky not to be elected on this occasion.

| Match No. | Date | Round | Venue | Opponents | Result | | Scorers | Attendance |
|---|---|---|---|---|---|---|---|---|
| 4 | Aug 28 | | (h) | Scunthorpe United | D | 0 - 0 | | 1,009 |
| 6 | Sep 4 | | (a) | Peterborough United | L | 1 - 2 | Stimpson | 3,499 |
| 7 | 7 | | (a) | Rochdale | L | 0 - 2 | | 987 |
| 8 | 11 | | (h) | Northampton Town | W | 2 - 1 | Bird, Hogan | 947 |
| 10 | 18 | | (a) | Hull City | D | 1 - 1 | Smith | 3,913 |
| 11 | 25 | | (h) | Tranmere Rovers | W | 4 - 0 | Linacre, A.Lininghan 2, Lawrence (pen) | 1,233 |
| 12 | 29 | | (h) | Crewe Alexandra | W | 1 - 0 | Higgins | 1,654 |
| 13 | Oct 2 | | (a) | Torquay United | L | 2 - 3 | Brown, Hogan | 2,164 |
| 15 | 8 | | (a) | Stockport County | D | 1 - 1 | Johnson | 1,915 |
| 16 | 16 | | (h) | Bristol City | W | 3 - 1 | Bird, Lawrence (pen), Dobson | 1,449 |
| 17 | 18 | | (a) | Port Vale | L | 0 - 3 | | 3,664 |
| 18 | 23 | | (h) | Aldershot | D | 1 - 1 | Bird | 1,412 |
| 20 | 30 | | (a) | York City | L | 1 - 5 | Smith | 1,971 |
| 21 | Nov 3 | | (h) | Mansfield Town | L | 0 - 4 | | 1,325 |
| 22 | 6 | | (h) | Wimbledon | W | 1 - 0 | Linacre | 1,081 |
| 23 | 13 | | (a) | Hereford United | L | 0 - 1 | | 2,298 |
| 25 | 27 | | (h) | Halifax Town | L | 1 - 2 | A.Linighan | 1,367 |
| 26 | Dec 4 | | (a) | Chester | L | 1 - 2 | Lane (o.g.) | 1,243 |
| 29 | 18 | | (a) | Swindon Town | L | 0 - 3 | | 4,291 |
| 30 | 27 | | (h) | Darlington | W | 2 - 0 | Lawrence 2 (1 pen) | 3,337 |
| 31 | 28 | | (a) | Bury | L | 0 - 4 | | 3,275 |
| 32 | Jan 1 | | (h) | Blackpool | W | 2 - 1 | Linacre, Smith | 1,569 |
| 33 | 3 | | (a) | Colchester United | L | 1 - 4 | Brown | 2,239 |
| 34 | 12 | | (h) | Peterborough United | D | 0 - 0 | | 1,161 |
| 35 | 16 | | (a) | Scunthorpe United | L | 0 - 3 | | 4,261 |
| 36 | 22 | | (h) | Hull City | D | 0 - 0 | | 2,295 |
| 37 | 29 | | (a) | Northampton Town | L | 1 - 3 | Lowe | 2,181 |
| 38 | Feb 5 | | (a) | Tranmere Rovers | D | 1 - 1 | Dobson | 1,545 |
| 39 | 12 | | (h) | Torquay United | L | 0 - 2 | | 1,159 |
| 40 | 19 | | (h) | Stockport County | W | 3 - 2 | Lawrence 2 (1 pen), Dobson | 1,029 |
| 41 | 26 | | (a) | Bristol City | L | 0 - 2 | | 4,207 |
| 42 | Mar 2 | | (h) | Port Vale | D | 2 - 2 | Staff, Linacre | 1,398 |
| 43 | 5 | | (a) | Aldershot | W | 2 - 0 | Staff, Robinson | 1,439 |
| 44 | 12 | | (h) | York City | W | 2 - 0 | Staff, Linacre | 1,606 |
| 45 | 14 | | (a) | Mansfield Town | L | 0 - 3 | | 1,991 |
| 46 | 19 | | (a) | Wimbledon | L | 0 - 2 | | 2,324 |
| 47 | 26 | | (h) | Hereford United | L | 0 - 1 | | 1,151 |
| 48 | Apr 2 | | (h) | Bury | L | 0 - 1 | | 1,288 |
| 49 | 4 | | (a) | Darlington | L | 1 - 2 | Robinson | 3,131 |
| 50 | 9 | | (h) | Chester | W | 1 - 0 | Dobson | 1,039 |
| 51 | 15 | | (a) | Crewe Alexandra | L | 0 - 3 | | 2,042 |
| 52 | 23 | | (h) | Swindon Town | L | 1 - 2 | Dobson | 1,126 |
| 53 | 29 | | (a) | Halifax Town | D | 1 - 1 | Dobson | 1,245 |
| 54 | May 2 | | (h) | Colchester United | L | 1 - 4 | Linacre | 804 |
| 55 | 7 | | (h) | Rochdale | W | 3 - 0 | Hogan (pen), Staff, Dobson | 1,015 |
| 56 | 14 | | (a) | Blackpool | W | 2 - 1 | D.Linighan, Dobson | 2,184 |

Final Position : 22nd in Division Four

Apps.

Sub.Apps.

1 own goal — Goals

**FA Cup**

| Match No. | Date | Round | Venue | Opponents | Result | | Scorers | Attendance |
|---|---|---|---|---|---|---|---|---|
| 24 | Nov 20 | R1 | (h) | Lincoln City | W | 3 - 0 | Linacre 2, Hogan | 2,204 |
| 27 | Dec 11 | R2 | (h) | York City | D | 1 - 1 | Dobson | 3,344 |
| 28 | 14 | R2r | (a) | York City | L | 0 - 4 | | 4,206 |

Apps.

Sub.Apps.

Goals

**League Cup**

| Match No. | Date | Round | Venue | Opponents | Result | | Scorers | Attendance |
|---|---|---|---|---|---|---|---|---|
| 5 | Aug 31 | R1/1 | (a) | Chesterfield | L | 1 - 2 | A.Linighan | 1,690 |
| 9 | Sep 15 | R1/2 | (h) | Chesterfield | W | 2 - 0* | Barker, Bainbridge | 1,122 |
| 14 | Oct 6 | R2/1 | (a) | Derby County | L | 0 - 2 | | 7,656 |
| 19 | 25 | R2/2 | (h) | Derby County | W | 4 - 2* | Barker, Smith, Staff, Johnson | 3,596 |

* After extra-time. Derby County won on Away goals.

Apps.

Sub.Apps.

Goals

| Watson | Brown | Stimpson | Hogan | Bird | Linighan, A. | Bainbridge | Lawrence | Smith | Staff | Johnson | Dobson | Newton | Barker | Linacre | Higgins | Lowe | Taylor | Hamilton | Wright | Smithies | Borthwick | Blackburn | Stalker | Robinson | Harding | Langridge | Linighan, D. | McNamee | Boam | Stewart | Winn | Fagan |
|---|---|---|---|---|---|---|---|---|---|---|---|---|---|---|---|---|---|---|---|---|---|---|---|---|---|---|---|---|---|---|---|---|
| 1 | 2 | 3 | 4 | 5 | 6 | 7 | 8 | 9 | *10* | 11 | *12* | | | | | | | | | | | | | | | | | | | | | |
| 1 | 2 | 3 | 4 | 5 | 6 | 7 | 10 | 8 | | 11 | | 9 | | | | | | | | | | | | | | | | | | | | |
| 1 | 2 | 3 | 4 | 5 | 6 | 7 | 10 | 8 | | 11 | | 9 | | | | | | | | | | | | | | | | | | | | |
| 1 | 2 | 3 | 4 | 5 | 6 | 7 | 10 | 8 | | 11 | | *9* | *12* | | | | | | | | | | | | | | | | | | | |
| 1 | 2 | *3* | 4 | *12* | 6 | 7 | 10 | 8 | | 11 | | | 5 | 9 | | | | | | | | | | | | | | | | | | |
| 1 | 2 | 3 | 4 | | 6 | 7 | 10 | 8 | | 11 | | | 5 | 9 | | | | | | | | | | | | | | | | | | |
| 1 | 2 | 3 | 4 | 5 | 6 | 7 | 10 | 8 | | 11 | | | | | 9 | | | | | | | | | | | | | | | | | |
| 1 | 2 | 3 | 4 | 5 | 6 | 7 | 10 | 8 | | 11 | | | | | 9 | | | | | | | | | | | | | | | | | |
| 1 | 2 | 3 | 4 | 5 | 6 | 7 | *10* | | 8 | 11 | *12* | | | 9 | | | | | | | | | | | | | | | | | | |
| 1 | 2 | 3 | | 5 | 6 | 7 | 10 | | | | 8 | | 11 | 9 | | 4 | | | | | | | | | | | | | | | | |
| 1 | 2 | 3 | 4 | 5 | | 6 | 10 | | | | *8* | | 11 | 9 | *12* | 7 | | | | | | | | | | | | | | | | |
| 1 | | 3 | 4 | 5 | 6 | *12* | | *8* | 10 | 11 | | | 7 | | 9 | | 2 | | | | | | | | | | | | | | | |
| 1 | 2 | 3 | 4 | 5 | 6 | | 9 | 8 | *7* | 10 | | | 11 | | | *12* | | | | | | | | | | | | | | | | |
| 1 | 2 | 3 | 4 | 5 | 6 | | 9 | *8* | 7 | 10 | | | 11 | | | | | *12* | | | | | | | | | | | | | | |
| | 2 | 3 | 4 | 5 | 6 | | *9* | | 7 | | *12* | | 11 | 10 | | 8 | | | 1 | | | | | | | | | | | | | |
| | 2 | 3 | 4 | 5 | 6 | | 9 | | *12* | | | | 11 | 10 | | *8* | | 7 | 1 | | | | | | | | | | | | | |
| | 2 | 3 | 4 | | 6 | | *10* | | 7 | *12* | 8 | | 5 | 9 | | | | 11 | 1 | | | | | | | | | | | | | |
| | 10 | 3 | 4 | | 6 | *11* | *12* | 2 | 7 | | 8 | | 5 | 9 | | | | | 1 | | | | | | | | | | | | | |
| | 2 | | 4 | 5 | 6 | | 11 | 10 | *12* | 3 | *8* | | 7 | 9 | | | | | 1 | | | | | | | | | | | | | |
| | 2 | | 4 | | 6 | 11 | 10 | 8 | 7 | 3 | | | 5 | 9 | | | | | 1 | | | | | | | | | | | | | |
| | 2 | | 4 | | 6 | 11 | *10* | 8 | 7 | 3 | | | 5 | 9 | | | | | 1 | *12* | | | | | | | | | | | | |
| | 4 | 3 | | | 6 | | 10 | 8 | 7 | 11 | | | 5 | 9 | | | | | 1 | 2 | | | | | | | | | | | | |
| | 4 | 3 | | | 6 | | 10 | *8* | 7 | 11 | | | 5 | 9 | | | | | 1 | 2 | *12* | | | | | | | | | | | |
| | 10 | | 4 | 5 | 6 | | 8 | | 7 | 11 | | | 3 | | | | | | | 2 | | 1 | 9 | | | | | | | | | |
| | 10 | | 4 | 5 | 6 | | 8 | | 7 | 11 | *12* | | 3 | | | | | | | 2 | | 1 | *9* | | | | | | | | | |
| | 10 | | 4 | 5 | 6 | | 8 | | | 11 | | | 3 | | | 7 | | | | 2 | | 1 | 9 | | | | | | | | | |
| | 2 | | | 5 | 6 | | 8 | | | *11* | 10 | | 3 | 9 | | 7 | | | | | | 1 | *12* | 4 | | | | | | | | |
| | 2 | | | 5 | 6 | | | | 8 | | 9 | | 3 | *11* | | 7 | | | | | 10 | 1 | | 4 | *12* | | | | | | | |
| | 2 | | | *5* | 6 | | 10 | *12* | 8 | | 9 | | 3 | 11 | | 7 | | | | | | 1 | | 4 | | | | | | | | |
| | 2 | 3 | | | 6 | | 10 | *12* | *8* | | 9 | | 5 | 11 | | 7 | | | | | | 1 | | 4 | | | | | | | | |
| | 2 | 3 | | | 6 | | 10 | 8 | | | 9 | | 5 | *11* | | 7 | | | | | | 1 | | 4 | | *12* | | | | | | |
| | 2 | | | 5 | 6 | | | 8 | 11 | | *9* | | 3 | *12* | | 7 | | | | | | 1 | | 4 | | 10 | | | | | | |
| | 2 | 3 | | 5 | 6 | | | 8 | 11 | | 9 | | | 10 | | 7 | | | | | | 1 | | 4 | | | | | | | | |
| | 2 | 3 | | 5 | 6 | | | 8 | 11 | | 10 | | | 9 | | 7 | | | | | | 1 | | 4 | | | | | | | | |
| | 2 | 3 | | 5 | 6 | | | 8 | 11 | | *12* | | | 9 | | 7 | | | 1 | | | | | 4 | | *10* | | | | | | |
| | 2 | | | | 6 | | | 8 | 11 | | *10* | | 3 | 9 | | 7 | | | | | | 1 | | 4 | | | 5 | *12* | | | | |
| | 2 | | | 5 | 6 | | | | | 11 | | | 3 | 9 | | *7* | | | | | | 1 | | 4 | | 10 | | | 8 | *12* | | |
| | | 3 | | 5 | 6 | | | 8 | | *12* | | | | *9* | | 7 | | | | 2 | | 1 | | 4 | | 10 | | | | 11 | | |
| | *12* | | | 5 | 6 | | | 8 | | | | | 11 | 9 | | 7 | | | | *2* | | 1 | | 4 | | | 3 | | | | 10 | |
| | 7 | | | 5 | 6 | | | *4* | | | 10 | | 11 | 9 | | | | | | 2 | | 1 | | *12* | | | 3 | | | 8 | | |
| | 7 | | | 5 | 6 | | | 4 | | | 10 | | 11 | | | *12* | | | | 2 | | 1 | | | | 9 | *3* | | | 8 | | |
| | 7 | 3 | | 5 | 6 | | | 4 | 9 | | 10 | | | *12* | | | | | | 2 | | 1 | | 11 | | | | | | *8* | | |
| | 7 | 3 | 4 | 5 | 6 | | | | 9 | | 10 | | | | | | | | | 2 | | 1 | | 11 | | | | | | 8 | | |
| | *7* | 3 | 4 | 5 | 6 | | | | 9 | | 10 | | | *12* | | | | | | 2 | | 1 | | 11 | | | | | | 8 | | |
| | *12* | 3 | 4 | | 7 | | | 2 | 9 | | 10 | | 11 | | | 8 | | | 1 | | | | | | | | 6 | | | | | *5* |
| | 5 | 3 | 4 | | 7 | | | 2 | 9 | | 10 | | 11 | | | 8 | | | 1 | | | | | | | | *6* | | | *12* | | |
| 14 | 43 | 31 | 27 | 33 | 45 | 14 | 28 | 30 | 27 | 22 | 22 | 3 | 32 | 27 | 3 | 20 | 1 | 2 | 12 | 12 | 1 | 20 | 3 | 16 | | 5 | 6 | | 1 | 6 | 1 | 1 |
| | 1 | | | 1 | | 1 | 1 | 2 | 2 | 2 | 4 | | 1 | 3 | 1 | 2 | | 1 | | 1 | 1 | | 1 | 1 | 1 | 1 | | 1 | | 2 | | |
| | 2 | 1 | 3 | 3 | 3 | | 6 | 3 | 4 | 1 | 8 | | | 6 | 1 | 1 | | | | | | | | 2 | | | 1 | | | | | |

| Watson | Brown | Stimpson | Hogan | Bird | Linighan, A. | Bainbridge | Lawrence | Smith | Staff | Johnson | Dobson | Newton | Barker | Linacre | Higgins | Lowe | Taylor | Hamilton |
|---|---|---|---|---|---|---|---|---|---|---|---|---|---|---|---|---|---|---|
| 1 | 2 | 3 | 4 | | 6 | | 10 | | 7 | | 9 | | 11 | 5 | | | | 8 |
| 1 | 10 | 3 | 4 | | 6 | | 11 | 2 | 7 | | 8 | | 5 | 9 | | | | |
| 1 | 10 | *3* | 4 | 5 | 6 | | 11 | 2 | | *12* | 8 | | 7 | 9 | | | | |
| 3 | 3 | 3 | 3 | 1 | 3 | | 3 | 2 | 2 | | 3 | | 3 | 3 | | | | 1 |
| | | | | | | | | | | 1 | | | | | | | | |
| | | | 1 | | | | | | | | 1 | | | 2 | | | | |

| Watson | Brown | Stimpson | Hogan | Bird | Linighan, A. | Bainbridge | Lawrence | Smith | Staff | Johnson | Dobson | Newton | Barker | Linacre | Higgins |
|---|---|---|---|---|---|---|---|---|---|---|---|---|---|---|---|
| 1 | 2 | 3 | 4 | 5 | 6 | 7 | 8 | 10 | | 11 | | 9 | | | |
| 1 | 2 | 3 | 4 | | 6 | 7 | 8 | 10 | | 11 | | | 5 | 9 | |
| 1 | 2 | 3 | 4 | 5 | 6 | 7 | 10 | 8 | | 11 | | | | *12* | *9* |
| 1 | 2 | 3 | 4 | 5 | 6 | | 9 | 8 | 7 | 10 | | | 11 | | |
| 4 | 4 | 4 | 4 | 3 | 4 | 3 | 4 | 4 | 1 | 4 | | 1 | 2 | 1 | 1 |
| | | | | | | | | | | | | | | 1 | |
| | | | | | 1 | 1 | | 1 | 1 | 1 | | | 2 | | |

## League Table

| | P | W | D | L | F | A | Pts |
|---|---|---|---|---|---|---|---|
| Wimbledon | 46 | 29 | 11 | 6 | 96 | 45 | 98 |
| Hull City | 46 | 25 | 15 | 6 | 75 | 34 | 90 |
| Port Vale | 46 | 26 | 10 | 10 | 67 | 34 | 88 |
| Scunthorpe United | 46 | 23 | 14 | 9 | 71 | 42 | 83 |
| Bury | 46 | 23 | 12 | 11 | 74 | 46 | 81 |
| Colchester United | 46 | 24 | 9 | 13 | 75 | 55 | 81 |
| York City | 46 | 22 | 13 | 11 | 88 | 58 | 79 |
| Swindon Town | 46 | 19 | 11 | 16 | 61 | 54 | 68 |
| Peterborough United | 46 | 17 | 13 | 16 | 58 | 52 | 64 |
| Mansfield Town | 46 | 16 | 13 | 17 | 61 | 70 | 61 |
| Halifax Town | 46 | 16 | 12 | 18 | 59 | 66 | 60 |
| Torquay United | 46 | 17 | 7 | 22 | 56 | 65 | 58 |
| Chester | 46 | 15 | 11 | 20 | 55 | 60 | 56 |
| Bristol City | 46 | 13 | 17 | 16 | 59 | 70 | 56 |
| Northampton Town | 46 | 14 | 12 | 20 | 65 | 75 | 54 |
| Stockport County | 46 | 14 | 12 | 20 | 60 | 79 | 54 |
| Darlington | 46 | 13 | 13 | 20 | 61 | 71 | 52 |
| Aldershot | 46 | 12 | 15 | 19 | 61 | 82 | 51 |
| Tranmere Rovers | 46 | 13 | 11 | 22 | 49 | 71 | 50 |
| Rochdale | 46 | 11 | 16 | 19 | 55 | 73 | 49 |
| Blackpool | 46 | 13 | 12 | 21 | 55 | 74 | 49 |
| Hartlepool United | 46 | 13 | 9 | 24 | 46 | 76 | 48 |
| Crewe Alexandra | 46 | 11 | 8 | 27 | 53 | 71 | 41 |
| Hereford United | 46 | 11 | 8 | 27 | 42 | 79 | 41 |

# 1983-84

## Division Four

Managers: Mick Docherty and Billy Horner

### Did you know that?

The game at Mansfield on 22 October featured 22 players who were all 'free transfers'. The home side obviously chose more wisely than the visitors as the 5–0 scoreline confirms.

Ray Kennedy, one of English football's biggest names in the 1970s, joined 'Pools from Swansea City. A multi-medal winner with Arsenal and Liverpool, he made his debut at Reading on 17 December, scoring in a 5–1 defeat. In total he made 24 appearances, scoring two goals, before retiring due to the onset of Parkinson's disease.

'Pools finished second bottom and made a record 14th (and final) re-election application along with Chester City, Rochdale and Halifax Town. For the second successive season they are successful at the expense of unlucky Maidstone United.

| Match No. | Date | Round | Venue | Opponents | Result | | Scorers | Attendance |
|---|---|---|---|---|---|---|---|---|
| 1 | Aug 27 | | (a) | Peterborough United | L | 1 - 3 | M.Robinson | 3,213 |
| 3 | Sep 3 | | (h) | Aldershot | L | 0 - 1 | | 1,831 |
| 4 | 7 | | (h) | Chesterfield | D | 2 - 2 | Waddle, A.Linighan | 1,661 |
| 5 | 10 | | (a) | Bristol City | L | 0 - 2 | | 5,310 |
| 7 | 17 | | (h) | Doncaster Rovers | W | 1 - 0 | Staff | 1,611 |
| 8 | 23 | | (a) | Halifax Town | L | 2 - 3 | Waddle, Lowe | 1,416 |
| 9 | 27 | | (a) | Rochdale | L | 0 - 2 | | 1,380 |
| 10 | Oct 1 | | (h) | Tranmere Rovers | L | 0 - 1 | | 1,226 |
| 11 | 8 | | (a) | Torquay United | D | 0 - 0 | | 1,850 |
| 12 | 15 | | (h) | Wrexham | D | 1 - 1 | Bird | 982 |
| 13 | 19 | | (h) | Chester City | D | 1 - 1 | Bird | 1,150 |
| 14 | 22 | | (a) | Mansfield Town | L | 0 - 5 | | 1,906 |
| 15 | 29 | | (h) | Bury | L | 1 - 3 | Dixon | 1,125 |
| 16 | Nov 1 | | (a) | Crewe Alexandra | L | 0 - 2 | | 2,117 |
| 17 | 5 | | (h) | Hereford United | D | 0 - 0 | | 1,021 |
| 18 | 12 | | (a) | Swindon Town | L | 2 - 3 | Gibson (o.g.), Ray | 3,257 |
| 21 | 26 | | (h) | York City | L | 2 - 3 | Dixon 2 | 2,012 |
| 22 | Dec 3 | | (a) | Colchester United | L | 0 - 6 | | 1,935 |
| 23 | 17 | | (a) | Reading | L | 1 - 5 | Kennedy | 2,955 |
| 24 | 26 | | (h) | Darlington | W | 2 - 1 | Dobson 2 | 2,968 |
| 25 | 27 | | (a) | Blackpool | L | 0 - 1 | | 4,562 |
| 26 | 31 | | (h) | Northampton Town | W | 2 - 0 | Burrows (o.g.), Hogan (pen) | 1,706 |
| 27 | Jan 2 | | (a) | Stockport County | L | 0 - 1 | | 1,799 |
| 28 | 7 | | (a) | Aldershot | L | 1 - 2 | Staff | 1,637 |
| 29 | 28 | | (h) | Bristol City | D | 2 - 2 | Dobson, Staff | 1,881 |
| 30 | Feb 3 | | (a) | Tranmere Rovers | W | 1 - 0 | P.Linacre | 1,770 |
| 31 | 11 | | (h) | Halifax Town | W | 3 - 0 | P.Linacre, Kennedy, Hogan | 1,658 |
| 32 | 15 | | (h) | Crewe Alexandra | W | 2 - 1 | Lowe, Dobson | 2,059 |
| 33 | 18 | | (a) | Bury | L | 0 - 3 | | 1,565 |
| 35 | 25 | | (h) | Mansfield Town | W | 4 - 1 | Kennedy, P.Linacre (pen), Dobson 2 | 1,730 |
| 36 | Mar 3 | | (a) | Chester City | L | 1 - 4 | Staff (pen) | 1,402 |
| 37 | 7 | | (a) | Hereford United | L | 0 - 5 | | 2,071 |
| 38 | 10 | | (h) | Swindon Town | L | 0 - 1 | | 1,274 |
| 39 | 17 | | (h) | Torquay United | W | 2 - 1 | Bird, Dobson | 969 |
| 40 | 24 | | (a) | Wrexham | W | 4 - 1 | Dobson 3, Barker | 1,181 |
| 41 | 27 | | (h) | Peterborough United | D | 1 - 1 | Robinson | 1,689 |
| 42 | 31 | | (h) | Rochdale | L | 1 - 2 | P.Linacre (pen) | 1,245 |
| 43 | Apr 7 | | (a) | Chesterfield | L | 1 - 4 | P.Linacre | 2,263 |
| 44 | 10 | | (a) | Northampton Town | D | 1 - 1 | Staff | 1,109 |
| 45 | 14 | | (h) | Colchester United | D | 0 - 0 | | 1,001 |
| 46 | 20 | | (h) | Blackpool | L | 0 - 1 | | 1,817 |
| 47 | 21 | | (a) | Darlington | L | 0 - 2 | | 2,574 |
| 48 | 26 | | (a) | York City | L | 0 - 2 | | 6,063 |
| 49 | May 5 | | (h) | Stockport County | L | 1 - 2 | P.Linacre | 790 |
| 50 | 12 | | (h) | Reading | D | 3 - 3 | D.Linighan, P.Linacre, Dobson | 1,214 |
| 51 | 15 | | (a) | Doncaster Rovers | W | 1 - 0 | Dobson | 3,770 |

Final Position : 23rd in Division Four

Apps.
Sub.Apps.
2 own goals — Goals

**FA Cup**

| Match No. | Date | Round | Venue | Opponents | Result | | Scorers | Attendance |
|---|---|---|---|---|---|---|---|---|
| 19 | Nov 19 | R1 | (a) | Rotherham United | D | 0 - 0 | | 3,325 |
| 20 | 23 | R1r | (h) | Rotherham United | L | 0 - 1* | | 2,635 |

* After extra time

Apps.
Sub.Apps.
Goals

**League Cup**

| Match No. | Date | Round | Venue | Opponents | Result | | Scorers | Attendance |
|---|---|---|---|---|---|---|---|---|
| 2 | Aug 30 | R1/1 | (a) | Rotherham United | D | 0 - 0 | | 4,384 |
| 6 | Sep 14 | R1/2 | (h) | Rotherham United | L | 0 - 1 | | 2,321 |

Apps.
Sub.Apps.
Goals

| Blackburn | Brown | Wilson | Buckley | Linighan, A. | Bainbridge | Staff | Whitfield | Waddle | Johnson | Robinson, M. | Stimpson | Lowe | Weir | Linighan, D. | Lawrence | Bird | Bassett | Dixon, K. | Campbell | Ray | Prudhoe | Barker | Borthwick | Malley | Dixon, C. | Kennedy | Hogan | Linacre, J. | Dobson | Smithies | Linacre, P. | Roberts | Robinson, D. | Taylor | Harrington | Finch | Woof |
|---|---|---|---|---|---|---|---|---|---|---|---|---|---|---|---|---|---|---|---|---|---|---|---|---|---|---|---|---|---|---|---|---|---|---|---|---|---|
| 1 | 2 | 3 | 4 | 5 | 6 | 7 | 8 | 9 | *10* | 11 | *12* | | | | | | | | | | | | | | | | | | | | | | | | | | |
| 1 | 2 | 3 | 4 | 5 | 6 | 7 | 8 | 9 | 10 | 11 | | | | | | | | | | | | | | | | | | | | | | | | | | | |
| 1 | 2 | 3 | 4 | 5 | *6* | | 8 | 9 | 10 | 11 | | 7 | *12* | | | | | | | | | | | | | | | | | | | | | | | | |
| 1 | 2 | 3 | 4 | 5 | | *12* | 8 | *9* | 10 | 11 | | 7 | 6 | | | | | | | | | | | | | | | | | | | | | | | | |
| 1 | 2 | 3 | 4 | 5 | | 7 | 8 | 9 | | 11 | | 10 | 6 | | | | | | | | | | | | | | | | | | | | | | | | |
| 1 | 2 | 3 | 4 | 5 | | *10* | 8 | 9 | | 11 | | 7 | 6 | *12* | | | | | | | | | | | | | | | | | | | | | | | |
| 1 | 2 | 3 | | 5 | | 10 | 8 | 9 | | | | 7 | 6 | 11 | 4 | | | | | | | | | | | | | | | | | | | | | | |
| 1 | 2 | 3 | | 5 | | 7 | 8 | 9 | | 11 | | *10* | 6 | *12* | 4 | | | | | | | | | | | | | | | | | | | | | | |
| 1 | 2 | 3 | | 10 | | | | 9 | 11 | | | 7 | 4 | 6 | 8 | 5 | | | | | | | | | | | | | | | | | | | | | |
| 1 | 2 | 3 | | 5 | | | | 9 | *11* | | | 7 | 6 | 10 | 8 | 4 | *12* | | | | | | | | | | | | | | | | | | | | |
| 1 | 2 | | | 5 | | 10 | *8* | 9 | 6 | 7 | 3 | | | | 11 | 4 | *12* | | | | | | | | | | | | | | | | | | | | |
| 1 | *2* | | | 5 | | 10 | 8 | 9 | | 7 | 3 | | | 6 | 11 | 4 | *12* | | | | | | | | | | | | | | | | | | | | |
| 1 | 2 | 3 | | 5 | | *7* | 6 | | | 8 | | | | | 11 | 4 | 10 | 9 | *12* | | | | | | | | | | | | | | | | | | |
| *1* | | 3 | | 5 | *12* | | 8 | | | 7 | | | 6 | | | 4 | 11 | 9 | 10 | 2 | | | | | | | | | | | | | | | | | |
| | *12* | 3 | | 5 | | | 6 | | | *8* | | 11 | 2 | | | 4 | 10 | 9 | | 7 | 1 | | | | | | | | | | | | | | | | |
| | 7 | 3 | | 5 | | 10 | 6 | | | 8 | | 11 | | 4 | | | | 9 | | 2 | 1 | | | | | | | | | | | | | | | | |
| | 7 | 3 | | 5 | | | *12* | | 11 | 8 | | | | 4 | | | | 9 | | 2 | 1 | 6 | *10* | | | | | | | | | | | | | | |
| 1 | 7 | 3 | | 5 | | 10 | | | 11 | *8* | | | | 4 | | | | 9 | | 2 | | 6 | | *12* | | | | | | | | | | | | | |
| 1 | 4 | | | | 5 | 10 | *2* | | | | | 11 | | 3 | | | 9 | | *12* | | | 8 | | | 6 | 7 | | | | | | | | | | | |
| 1 | 2 | | | 5 | | 11 | | | *12* | | | | | *6* | | | | | | | | 3 | 9 | | | 7 | 4 | 8 | 10 | | | | | | | | |
| 1 | 2 | | | 5 | 6 | 11 | | | | | | | | | | | | | | | | 3 | 9 | | | 7 | 4 | 8 | 10 | | | | | | | | |
| 1 | 2 | | | 5 | 6 | 11 | | | | | | | | | | | | | | | | 3 | 10 | | | 7 | 4 | 8 | 9 | | | | | | | | |
| 1 | 2 | | | 5 | 6 | 11 | | | 7 | | | *12* | | | | | | | | | | 3 | 10 | | | | 4 | *8* | 9 | | | | | | | | |
| 1 | *2* | | | 5 | 6 | 11 | | | | | | | | | | | | | | | | 3 | 10 | | | 7 | 4 | 8 | 9 | *12* | | | | | | | |
| 1 | | | | 5 | | 11 | | | | | | | | 6 | | | | | | | | 3 | | | | 7 | 4 | 8 | 10 | 2 | 9 | | | | | | |
| 1 | | | | 5 | | 11 | | | | | | | | 6 | | | | | | | | 3 | | | | 7 | 4 | 8 | 10 | 2 | 9 | | | | | | |
| 1 | | | | 5 | | 11 | | | | | | 8 | | 6 | | | | | | | | 3 | | | | 7 | 4 | | 10 | 2 | 9 | | | | | | |
| 1 | | | | 5 | 6 | 11 | | | | | | 8 | | | | | | | | | | 3 | | | | 7 | 4 | | 10 | 2 | 9 | | | | | | |
| 1 | *12* | | | 5 | *6* | | | | | | | 8 | | | | | | | | | | 3 | | | | 7 | 4 | 11 | 10 | 2 | 9 | | | | | | |
| 1 | 6 | | | 5 | | 11 | | | | | | 8 | | | | | | | | | | 3 | | | | 7 | 4 | | 10 | 2 | 9 | | | | | | |
| 1 | 6 | | | 5 | | 11 | | | *12* | | | 8 | | | | | | | | | | 3 | 9 | | | 7 | 4 | | *10* | 2 | | | | | | | |
| 1 | | | | 5 | | 11 | | | 8 | | | | | 6 | | | | | | | | 3 | | | | 7 | 4 | | 10 | 2 | 9 | | | | | | |
| 1 | *2* | | | 5 | | 11 | | | | | | 7 | | | | 6 | | | | | | 3 | | | | *12* | 4 | 8 | 10 | | 9 | | | | | | |
| 1 | | | | 5 | | 11 | | | | *8* | | *7* | | 3 | | 6 | | | | | | | | | | *12* | 4 | 2 | 10 | | 9 | | | | | | |
| 1 | | | | 5 | | 11 | | | 8 | | | *7* | | | | 6 | | | | | | 3 | | | | *12* | 4 | 2 | 10 | | 9 | | | | | | |
| 1 | | | | 5 | | *11* | | | 8 | 7 | | | | 6 | | | | | | | | 3 | | | | *12* | 4 | 2 | 10 | | 9 | | | | | | |
| 1 | | | | 5 | | | | | 8 | 7 | | 11 | | *6* | | | | | | | | 3 | | | | *12* | 4 | 2 | 10 | | 9 | | | | | | |
| | | | | 5 | | 11 | | | *8* | | | | | *12* | | | | | | | | 3 | | | | 7 | 4 | 2 | 10 | 6 | 9 | 1 | | | | | |
| 1 | | | | 5 | | 11 | | | | | | 8 | | | | | | | | | | 3 | | | | 7 | 4 | | 10 | 6 | 9 | | 2 | | | | |
| 1 | | | | 5 | | | | | | | | 8 | | | | | | | | | | 3 | | | | 7 | 4 | | 10 | 6 | 9 | | 2 | 11 | | | |
| 1 | | | | 5 | | | | | | | | 8 | | | | 6 | | | | | | | *12* | | | 7 | 4 | | 10 | 3 | *9* | | 2 | 11 | | | |
| 1 | | | | 5 | | | | | | | | 8 | | *12* | | 6 | | | | | | | 9 | | | 7 | 4 | | 10 | 3 | | | 2 | 11 | | | |
| 1 | 7 | | | 5 | | | | | | | | 8 | | | | 6 | | | | | | 3 | *12* | | | | 4 | | 10 | 2 | *9* | | | 11 | | | |
| 1 | 7 | | | | | | | | | | | 8 | | 5 | | 6 | | | | | | 3 | | | | | 4 | 11 | 10 | *2* | 9 | | *12* | | | | |
| 1 | *8* | | | | | 7 | | | | | | | | 6 | | 5 | | | | | | 3 | | | | | 4 | | 10 | | 9 | | 2 | 11 | *12* | | |
| | *8* | | | | 5 | 7 | | | | | | 9 | | 6 | | | | | | | | 3 | | | | | 4 | | 10 | | | | 2 | 11 | *12* | 1 | |
| 41 | 29 | 16 | 6 | 42 | 11 | 32 | 15 | 12 | 15 | 18 | 2 | 27 | 9 | 19 | 7 | 15 | 4 | 6 | 1 | 5 | 3 | 27 | 8 | | 1 | 18 | 27 | 15 | 27 | 15 | 19 | 1 | 6 | 6 | | 1 | |
| | 2 | | | | 1 | 1 | 1 | | 2 | | 1 | 1 | 1 | 4 | | | 3 | | 2 | | | | 2 | 1 | | 5 | | | | 1 | | | 1 | | 2 | | |
| | | | | 1 | | 5 | | 2 | | 2 | | 2 | | 1 | | 3 | | 3 | | 1 | | 1 | | | | 3 | 2 | | 12 | | 7 | | | | | | |

| Blackburn | Brown | Wilson | Buckley | Linighan, A. | Bainbridge | Staff | Whitfield | Waddle | Johnson | Robinson, M. | Stimpson | Lowe | Weir | Linighan, D. | Lawrence | Bird | Bassett | Dixon, K. | Campbell | Ray | Prudhoe | Barker | Borthwick | Malley | Dixon, C. | Kennedy | Hogan | Linacre, J. | Dobson | Smithies | Linacre, P. | Roberts | Robinson, D. | Taylor | Harrington | Finch | Woof |
|---|---|---|---|---|---|---|---|---|---|---|---|---|---|---|---|---|---|---|---|---|---|---|---|---|---|---|---|---|---|---|---|---|---|---|---|---|---|
| | 7 | 3 | | 5 | | 10 | 6 | | | 8 | | 11 | | 4 | | | *9* | | | 2 | | | | | | | | | | | | 1 | | | | | *12* |
| | 7 | 3 | | 5 | | 10 | 6 | | | 8 | | *11* | | 4 | | | 9 | | | 2 | | | | | | | | | | | | 1 | | | | | *12* |
| | 2 | 2 | | 2 | | 2 | 2 | | | 2 | | 2 | | 2 | | | 2 | | | 2 | | | | | | | | | | | | 2 | | | | | |
| | | | | | | | | | | | | | | | | | | | | | | | | | | | | | | | | | | | | | |
| | | | | | | | | | | | | | | | | | | | | | | | | | | | | | | | | | | | | | |

| Blackburn | Brown | Wilson | Buckley | Linighan, A. | Bainbridge | Staff | Whitfield | Waddle | Johnson | Robinson, M. | Stimpson | Lowe | Weir | Linighan, D. | Lawrence | Bird | Bassett | Dixon, K. | Campbell | Ray | Prudhoe | Barker | Borthwick | Malley | Dixon, C. | Kennedy | Hogan | Linacre, J. | Dobson | Smithies | Linacre, P. | Roberts | Robinson, D. | Taylor | Harrington | Finch | Woof |
|---|---|---|---|---|---|---|---|---|---|---|---|---|---|---|---|---|---|---|---|---|---|---|---|---|---|---|---|---|---|---|---|---|---|---|---|---|---|
| 1 | 2 | 3 | 4 | 5 | 6 | *7* | 8 | 9 | 10 | 11 | | *12* | | | | | | | | | | | | | | | | | | | | | | | | | |
| 1 | 2 | 3 | 4 | 5 | | 9 | 8 | | *10* | 11 | | 7 | 6 | *12* | | | | | | | | | | | | | | | | | | | | | | | |
| 2 | 2 | 2 | 2 | 2 | 1 | 2 | 2 | 1 | 2 | 2 | | 1 | 1 | | | | | | | | | | | | | | | | | | | | | | | | |
| | | | | | | | | | | | | 1 | | 1 | | | | | | | | | | | | | | | | | | | | | | | |
| | | | | | | | | | | | | | | | | | | | | | | | | | | | | | | | | | | | | | |

## League Table

| | P | W | D | L | F | A | Pts |
|---|---|---|---|---|---|---|---|
| York City | 46 | 31 | 8 | 7 | 96 | 39 | 101 |
| Doncaster Rovers | 46 | 24 | 13 | 9 | 82 | 54 | 85 |
| Reading | 46 | 22 | 16 | 8 | 84 | 56 | 82 |
| Bristol City | 46 | 24 | 10 | 12 | 70 | 44 | 82 |
| Aldershot | 46 | 22 | 9 | 15 | 76 | 69 | 75 |
| Blackpool | 46 | 21 | 9 | 16 | 70 | 52 | 72 |
| Peterborough United | 46 | 18 | 14 | 14 | 72 | 48 | 68 |
| Colchester United | 46 | 17 | 16 | 13 | 69 | 53 | 67 |
| Torquay United | 46 | 18 | 13 | 15 | 59 | 64 | 67 |
| Tranmere Rovers | 46 | 17 | 15 | 14 | 53 | 53 | 66 |
| Hereford United | 46 | 16 | 15 | 15 | 54 | 53 | 63 |
| Stockport County | 46 | 17 | 11 | 18 | 60 | 64 | 62 |
| Chesterfield | 46 | 15 | 15 | 16 | 59 | 61 | 60 |
| Darlington | 46 | 17 | 8 | 21 | 49 | 50 | 59 |
| Bury | 46 | 15 | 14 | 17 | 61 | 64 | 59 |
| Crewe Alexandra | 46 | 16 | 11 | 19 | 56 | 67 | 59 |
| Swindon Town | 46 | 15 | 13 | 18 | 58 | 56 | 58 |
| Northampton Town | 46 | 13 | 14 | 19 | 53 | 78 | 53 |
| Mansfield Town | 46 | 13 | 13 | 20 | 66 | 70 | 52 |
| Wrexham | 46 | 11 | 15 | 20 | 59 | 74 | 48 |
| Halifax Town | 46 | 12 | 12 | 22 | 55 | 89 | 48 |
| Rochdale | 46 | 11 | 13 | 22 | 52 | 80 | 46 |
| Hartlepool United | 46 | 10 | 10 | 26 | 47 | 85 | 40 |
| Chester City | 46 | 7 | 13 | 26 | 45 | 82 | 34 |

# 1984-85

## Division Four

Manager: Billy Horner

### Did you know that?

For the first time Hartlepool United players had a sponsor's name on their shirts – 'New County', the title of Chairman John Smart's company.

At the end of the season, the by now infamous wooden Clarence Road stand was finally demolished. Chairman John Smart personally assisted by taking a pickaxe to the decrepit structure.

| Match No. | Date | Round | Venue | Opponents | Result | | Scorers | Attendance |
|---|---|---|---|---|---|---|---|---|
| 1 | Aug 25 | | (a) | Stockport County | L | 1 - 4 | Dixon | 1,619 |
| 3 | Sep 1 | | (h) | Swindon Town | D | 2 - 2 | Hogan, Brownlie | 1,703 |
| 5 | 8 | | (a) | Port Vale | D | 1 - 1 | Linighan | 3,232 |
| 6 | 15 | | (h) | Rochdale | L | 0 - 2 | | 1,574 |
| 7 | 19 | | (h) | Chesterfield | W | 1 - 0 | Hedley | 1,686 |
| 8 | 22 | | (a) | Peterborough United | L | 1 - 3 | Hogan | 3,491 |
| 9 | 29 | | (h) | Crewe Alexandra | W | 3 - 0 | Hogan, Mutrie, Wardrobe | 1,502 |
| 10 | Oct 2 | | (a) | Darlington | W | 1 - 0 | Mutrie | 5,221 |
| 11 | 6 | | (a) | Tranmere Rovers | W | 2 - 1 | Mutrie, Wardrobe | 1,619 |
| 12 | 13 | | (h) | Hereford United | D | 2 - 2 | Smith, Dixon | 3,138 |
| 13 | 20 | | (a) | Torquay United | W | 1 - 0 | Mooney (o.g.) | 1,285 |
| 14 | 24 | | (h) | Southend United | W | 2 - 1 | Hedley (pen), Dobson | 4,297 |
| 15 | 27 | | (h) | Mansfield Town | D | 0 - 0 | | 4,349 |
| 16 | Nov 3 | | (a) | Wrexham | D | 1 - 1 | Taylor | 1,368 |
| 17 | 5 | | (h) | Exeter City | D | 1 - 1 | Hedley | 3,657 |
| 18 | 9 | | (a) | Colchester United | L | 0 - 1 | | 2,136 |
| 20 | 24 | | (h) | Scunthorpe United | W | 3 - 2 | Mutrie (pen), Dobson, Taylor | 3,292 |
| 21 | Dec 1 | | (a) | Aldershot | L | 0 - 1 | | 2,069 |
| 23 | 15 | | (h) | Northampton Town | D | 0 - 0 | | 2,207 |
| 24 | 22 | | (h) | Chester City | W | 2 - 1 | Dixon, Dobson | 1,949 |
| 25 | 26 | | (a) | Halifax Town | W | 3 - 2 | Dixon 2, Linighan | 1,409 |
| 26 | 29 | | (a) | Blackpool | L | 1 - 2 | Smith | 4,778 |
| 27 | Jan 2 | | (h) | Bury | L | 0 - 1 | | 3,199 |
| 28 | 19 | | (h) | Port Vale | D | 2 - 2 | Dixon 2 | 2,285 |
| 30 | Feb 1 | | (a) | Crewe Alexandra | L | 0 - 2 | | 1,547 |
| 32 | 9 | | (h) | Peterborough United | L | 0 - 3 | | 1,353 |
| 33 | 12 | | (a) | Chesterfield | D | 0 - 0 | | 2,617 |
| 34 | 17 | | (h) | Darlington | L | 1 - 2 | Taylor | 5,947 |
| 35 | 23 | | (h) | Wrexham | W | 2 - 0 | Hedley (pen), Dobson | 1,432 |
| 36 | Mar 2 | | (a) | Mansfield Town | L | 0 - 2 | | 1,940 |
| 37 | 4 | | (a) | Southend United | D | 1 - 1 | Hedley (pen) | 1,644 |
| 38 | 9 | | (h) | Torquay United | W | 3 - 1 | Dixon, Hedley 2 (1 pen) | 1,364 |
| 39 | 16 | | (a) | Hereford United | L | 1 - 2 | Hedley (pen) | 3,279 |
| 40 | 23 | | (h) | Tranmere Rovers | L | 2 - 4 | Hedley (pen), Dixon | 1,326 |
| 41 | 30 | | (a) | Exeter City | L | 2 - 3 | Gollogly, Dobson | 1,578 |
| 42 | 31 | | (a) | Swindon Town | L | 1 - 2 | Dixon | 2,414 |
| 43 | Apr 3 | | (h) | Stockport County | W | 5 - 1 | Borthwick, Dixon (pen), Dobson 2, Brown | 1,148 |
| 44 | 6 | | (h) | Halifax Town | L | 0 - 1 | | 1,577 |
| 45 | 8 | | (a) | Bury | L | 0 - 1 | | 3,726 |
| 46 | 13 | | (h) | Colchester United | W | 2 - 1 | Dobson 2 | 1,329 |
| 47 | 15 | | (a) | Northampton Town | L | 0 - 2 | | 1,181 |
| 48 | 19 | | (a) | Scunthorpe United | L | 0 - 2 | | 2,037 |
| 49 | 27 | | (h) | Aldershot | W | 1 - 0 | Taylor | 1,201 |
| 50 | 30 | | (a) | Rochdale | L | 3 - 4 | Dixon (pen), Dobson, Gavin | 910 |
| 51 | May 6 | | (h) | Blackpool | L | 0 - 2 | | 2,496 |
| 52 | 11 | | (a) | Chester City | L | 0 - 1 | | 1,626 |

Final Position : 19th in Division Four

Apps.
Sub.Apps.
1 own goal — Goals

**FA Cup**

| Match No. | Date | Round | Venue | Opponents | Result | | Scorers | Attendance |
|---|---|---|---|---|---|---|---|---|
| 19 | Nov 17 | R1 | (h) | Derby County | W | 2 - 1 | Taylor, Dixon | 7,431 |
| 22 | Dec 8 | R2 | (h) | York City | L | 0 - 2 | | 8,554 |

Apps.
Sub.Apps.
Goals

**League Cup**

| Match No. | Date | Round | Venue | Opponents | Result | | Scorers | Attendance |
|---|---|---|---|---|---|---|---|---|
| 2 | Aug 29 | R1/1 | (a) | Derby County | L | 1 - 5 | Hedley | 9,281 |
| 4 | Sep 5 | R1/2 | (h) | Derby County | L | 0 - 1 | | 1,862 |

Apps.
Sub.Apps.
Goals

| Finch | Brownlie | Liddle | Hedley | Smith | Bird | Brown | Taylor | Wardrobe | Dixon | Dobson | Linighan | Robinson | Hogan | Mutrie | Stevenson | Farnaby | Proudlock | Stimpson | Pollard | Waddle | Blackburn | Honour | Borthwick | Gollogly | Gavin | Venus |
|---|---|---|---|---|---|---|---|---|---|---|---|---|---|---|---|---|---|---|---|---|---|---|---|---|---|---|
| 1 | 2 | 3 | 4 | *5* | 6 | 7 | 8 | 9 | 10 | 11 | *12* | | | | | | | | | | | | | | | |
| 1 | 2 | *12* | 4 | 5 | 6 | 7 | | | *9* | 10 | | 3 | 11 | 8 | | | | | | | | | | | | |
| | | 3 | 4 | 5 | 2 | 7 | *12* | | 9 | *10* | 6 | | 11 | 8 | 1 | | | | | | | | | | | |
| | *2* | 3 | 4 | 5 | | 7 | | *12* | 9 | 10 | 6 | | 11 | 8 | 1 | | | | | | | | | | | |
| | | 3 | 4 | 5 | | 6 | 11 | 9 | *7* | *12* | | 2 | 10 | 8 | 1 | | | | | | | | | | | |
| | | 3 | 4 | 5 | | 6 | 11 | 9 | | 7 | | 2 | 10 | 8 | 1 | | | | | | | | | | | |
| | | 3 | 4 | 5 | | 6 | 11 | 9 | 7 | | | 2 | 10 | 8 | 1 | | | | | | | | | | | |
| | | 3 | 4 | 5 | | 6 | 11 | 9 | 7 | | | 2 | 10 | 8 | 1 | | | | | | | | | | | |
| | | 3 | | 5 | *12* | 6 | 11 | 9 | 7 | | | 2 | 10 | 8 | 1 | *4* | | | | | | | | | | |
| | | 3 | 4 | 5 | | 6 | *11* | 9 | 7 | *12* | | 2 | 10 | 8 | 1 | | | | | | | | | | | |
| | | 3 | 4 | | | 6 | 11 | *9* | 7 | *12* | 5 | 2 | 10 | 8 | 1 | | | | | | | | | | | |
| | | 3 | 4 | | | 6 | 11 | 9 | 7 | *12* | 5 | 2 | 10 | *8* | 1 | | | | | | | | | | | |
| | | 3 | 4 | 5 | | 6 | 11 | *9* | 7 | *12* | | 2 | 10 | 8 | 1 | | | | | | | | | | | |
| | 3 | | 4 | 5 | | 6 | 11 | *9* | 7 | *12* | | 2 | 10 | 8 | 1 | | | | | | | | | | | |
| | 3 | | 4 | 5 | | 6 | 11 | *9* | 7 | *12* | | 2 | 10 | 8 | 1 | | | | | | | | | | | |
| | 3 | | 4 | 5 | | 6 | *11* | 9 | 7 | 8 | | 2 | 10 | | 1 | | *12* | | | | | | | | | |
| | 3 | | 4 | 5 | | 6 | 11 | | 7 | 9 | | 2 | 10 | 8 | 1 | | | | | | | | | | | |
| | 3 | | 4 | 5 | | 6 | 11 | | 7 | 9 | | 2 | 10 | 8 | 1 | | | | | | | | | | | |
| | 3 | | 4 | 5 | | | 11 | *12* | 7 | *9* | 6 | 2 | 10 | 8 | 1 | | | | | | | | | | | |
| | 3 | | 4 | 5 | | | 11 | *9* | 8 | *12* | 6 | 2 | 10 | | 1 | | | 7 | | | | | | | | |
| | 2 | | 4 | 5 | | 7 | 11 | 9 | 8 | | 6 | | 10 | | 1 | | | 3 | | | | | | | | |
| | 2 | | 4 | 5 | | 7 | *11* | 9 | 8 | *12* | 6 | | 10 | | 1 | | | 3 | | | | | | | | |
| | 2 | | | 5 | | 7 | | 4 | *8* | 9 | 6 | | 10 | 11 | 1 | | *12* | 3 | | | | | | | | |
| | 2 | | *4* | 5 | | *12* | | 9 | 8 | | 6 | | 10 | | 1 | | 11 | 3 | 7 | | | | | | | |
| | | | 4 | 5 | | 6 | 11 | | 9 | | | 2 | 10 | | 1 | | | 3 | 7 | 8 | | | | | | |
| | | | | 5 | | 6 | 11 | | 7 | 9 | 3 | 2 | | | | *10* | *12* | | | 8 | 1 | 4 | | | | |
| | | | | 5 | | 6 | *11* | | 7 | 9 | 10 | 2 | | | 1 | | *12* | 3 | | 8 | | 4 | | | | |
| | | | | 5 | | 6 | 11 | *12* | 7 | 9 | *10* | 2 | | | 1 | | | 3 | | 8 | | 4 | | | | |
| | | | 11 | 5 | | 6 | | | 7 | 9 | 10 | 2 | | | 1 | | 8 | 3 | | | | 4 | | | | |
| | | | 8 | 5 | | | 7 | | | *9* | 6 | 2 | | | 1 | 11 | 10 | 3 | | | | 4 | *12* | | | |
| | | | 11 | 5 | 6 | | | 7 | | 9 | | 2 | 8 | | 1 | | 10 | 3 | | | | 4 | | | | |
| | | | 8 | 5 | | 6 | | 9 | 10 | | | 2 | 7 | | 1 | | 11 | 3 | | | | 4 | | | | |
| | | | 8 | 5 | | 6 | | | 10 | 9 | | 2 | 7 | | 1 | | 11 | 3 | | | | 4 | | | | |
| | | | 8 | 5 | | 6 | 11 | | 10 | 9 | *12* | *2* | 7 | | 1 | | | 3 | | | | 4 | | | | |
| | | | 8 | 5 | | 6 | *11* | | 10 | 9 | | 2 | 7 | | 1 | | *12* | 3 | | | | | | 4 | | |
| | | | 8 | 5 | | 6 | 11 | | 10 | *9* | | 2 | 7 | | 1 | | *12* | 3 | | | | | | 4 | | |
| | | | *8* | 5 | | 6 | 11 | | 10 | 9 | | 2 | 7 | | 1 | | | 3 | | | | | *12* | 4 | | |
| | | | | 5 | | 6 | 7 | | | 9 | | 2 | | | 1 | *10* | *12* | 3 | | | | | 8 | 4 | 11 | |
| | | | | 5 | | 6 | 7 | | 10 | 9 | | 2 | | | | | | | | | 1 | 8 | *12* | 4 | 11 | *3* |
| | | | | 5 | | 6 | *12* | | 8 | 9 | | 2 | 4 | | | | | | | | 1 | 7 | | *10* | 11 | 3 |
| | | | | 5 | | 6 | | | 10 | 9 | | 2 | 4 | | | | *8* | | | | 1 | 7 | *12* | | 11 | 3 |
| | 3 | | | 5 | | 6 | | 8 | 10 | 9 | | 2 | 4 | | | | | | | | 1 | 7 | | | 11 | |
| | 3 | | | 5 | | 6 | 7 | 9 | 10 | | | 2 | 4 | | | | | | | | 1 | 8 | | | 11 | |
| | 3 | | | 5 | | 6 | 7 | *9* | 10 | *12* | | 2 | 4 | | | | | | | | 1 | 8 | | | 11 | |
| | 3 | | | 5 | | 6 | 11 | | 10 | 9 | | 2 | 4 | | | | | | | | 1 | 7 | *12* | *8* | | |
| | 2 | | | 5 | | 6 | *11* | *12* | 9 | 10 | | | 4 | | | 8 | | | | | 1 | 7 | | | | 3 |
| 2 | 19 | 12 | 32 | 44 | 4 | 41 | 34 | 23 | 42 | 28 | 15 | 38 | 38 | 18 | 35 | 5 | 7 | 18 | 2 | 4 | 9 | 17 | 1 | 7 | 7 | 4 |
| | | 1 | | | 1 | 1 | 2 | 4 | | 10 | 2 | | | | | | 7 | | | | | | 5 | | | |
| | 1 | | 9 | 2 | | 1 | 4 | 2 | 12 | 10 | 2 | | 3 | 4 | | | | | | | | | 1 | 1 | 1 | |

| Finch | Brownlie | Liddle | Hedley | Smith | Bird | Brown | Taylor | Wardrobe | Dixon | Dobson | Linighan | Robinson | Hogan | Mutrie | Stevenson |
|---|---|---|---|---|---|---|---|---|---|---|---|---|---|---|---|
| | 3 | | 4 | 5 | | 6 | 11 | | 7 | 9 | | 2 | 10 | 8 | 1 |
| | 3 | | 4 | 5 | | 6 | 11 | | 7 | 9 | | 2 | 10 | 8 | 1 |
| | 2 | | 2 | 2 | | 2 | 2 | | 2 | 2 | | 2 | 2 | 2 | 2 |
| | | | | | | | | | | | | | | | |
| | | | | | | | 1 | | 1 | | | | | | |

| Finch | Brownlie | Liddle | Hedley | Smith | Bird | Brown | Taylor | Wardrobe | Dixon | Dobson | Linighan | Robinson | Hogan | Mutrie | Stevenson |
|---|---|---|---|---|---|---|---|---|---|---|---|---|---|---|---|
| 1 | 3 | | 4 | 5 | 6 | 8 | | | 10 | 11 | | 2 | 7 | 9 | |
| | 2 | | 4 | 5 | | 7 | *12* | | 9 | 10 | 6 | *3* | 11 | 8 | 1 |
| 1 | 2 | | 2 | 2 | 1 | 2 | | | 2 | 2 | 1 | 2 | 2 | 2 | 1 |
| | | | | | | | 1 | | | | | | | | |
| | | | 1 | | | | | | | | | | | | |

## League Table

| | P | W | D | L | F | A | Pts |
|---|---|---|---|---|---|---|---|
| Chesterfield | 46 | 26 | 13 | 7 | 64 | 35 | 91 |
| Blackpool | 46 | 24 | 14 | 8 | 73 | 39 | 86 |
| Darlington | 46 | 24 | 13 | 9 | 66 | 49 | 85 |
| Bury | 46 | 24 | 12 | 10 | 76 | 50 | 84 |
| Hereford United | 46 | 22 | 11 | 13 | 65 | 47 | 77 |
| Tranmere Rovers | 46 | 24 | 3 | 19 | 83 | 66 | 75 |
| Colchester United | 46 | 20 | 14 | 12 | 87 | 65 | 74 |
| Swindon Town | 46 | 21 | 9 | 16 | 62 | 58 | 72 |
| Scunthorpe United | 46 | 19 | 14 | 13 | 83 | 62 | 71 |
| Crewe Alexandra | 46 | 18 | 12 | 16 | 65 | 69 | 66 |
| Peterborough United | 46 | 16 | 14 | 16 | 54 | 53 | 62 |
| Port Vale | 46 | 14 | 18 | 14 | 61 | 59 | 60 |
| Aldershot | 46 | 17 | 8 | 21 | 56 | 63 | 59 |
| Mansfield Town | 46 | 13 | 18 | 15 | 41 | 38 | 57 |
| Wrexham | 46 | 15 | 9 | 22 | 67 | 70 | 54 |
| Chester City | 46 | 15 | 9 | 22 | 60 | 72 | 54 |
| Rochdale | 46 | 13 | 14 | 19 | 55 | 69 | 53 |
| Exeter City | 46 | 13 | 14 | 19 | 57 | 79 | 53 |
| Hartlepool United | 46 | 14 | 10 | 22 | 54 | 67 | 52 |
| Southend United | 46 | 13 | 11 | 22 | 58 | 83 | 50 |
| Halifax Town | 46 | 15 | 5 | 26 | 42 | 69 | 50 |
| Stockport County | 46 | 13 | 8 | 25 | 58 | 79 | 47 |
| Northampton Town | 46 | 14 | 5 | 27 | 53 | 74 | 47 |
| Torquay United | 46 | 9 | 14 | 23 | 38 | 63 | 41 |

# 1985-86

## Division Four

Manager: Billy Horner

### Did you know that?

Following their 1–0 victory over Preston on 5 February, 'Pools were in third place in Division Four, five points clear of Port Vale with a game in hand. This was followed by nine games without a win, which resulted in a final position of seventh, nine points adrift of fourth-place Port Vale.

After a spell of bad weather in February, a safety inspection revealed that the roofs of the Rink and Town end stands were unsafe and had to be demolished. This had the effect of reducing the capacity of the Victoria Ground to 2,100 for the rest of the season.

| Match No. | Date | Round | Venue | Opponents | Result | | Scorers | Attendance |
|---|---|---|---|---|---|---|---|---|
| 1 | Aug 17 | | (a) | Cambridge United | L | 2 - 4 | Shoulder, Newton (pen) | 1,821 |
| 3 | 24 | | (h) | Crewe Alexandra | W | 4 - 1 | Davis (o.g.), Dixon, Newton, Shoulder | 2,160 |
| 4 | 26 | | (a) | Chester City | D | 1 - 1 | Smith | 1,473 |
| 5 | 31 | | (h) | Orient | L | 1 - 2 | Shoulder | 2,206 |
| 7 | Sep 7 | | (a) | Burnley | L | 0 - 2 | | 3,175 |
| 8 | 13 | | (h) | Rochdale | W | 2 - 0 | Dixon, Borthwick | 2,148 |
| 9 | 18 | | (h) | Northampton Town | W | 2 - 1 | Honour, Walker | 2,200 |
| 10 | 21 | | (a) | Torquay United | W | 3 - 1 | Borthwick, Honour 2 | 946 |
| 11 | 28 | | (h) | Swindon Town | W | 1 - 0 | Dobson | 2,411 |
| 12 | 30 | | (a) | Port Vale | L | 0 - 4 | | 3,015 |
| 13 | Oct 5 | | (h) | Peterborough United | W | 2 - 1 | Borthwick, Hogan (pen) | 2,138 |
| 14 | 11 | | (a) | Stockport County | W | 3 - 1 | Gollogly, Honour, Shoulder | 1,827 |
| 15 | 19 | | (h) | Hereford United | W | 2 - 1 | Smith, Shoulder | 2,974 |
| 16 | 22 | | (a) | Preston North End | L | 1 - 2 | Hogan (pen) | 3,608 |
| 17 | 26 | | (a) | Exeter City | W | 2 - 1 | Hogan, Shoulder | 1,934 |
| 18 | Nov 2 | | (h) | Mansfield Town | D | 1 - 1 | Hogan (pen) | 4,195 |
| 19 | 6 | | (h) | Aldershot | W | 2 - 1 | Nobbs, Dobson | 3,324 |
| 20 | 8 | | (a) | Southend United | L | 2 - 3 | Walker, Borthwick | 2,748 |
| 22 | 23 | | (h) | Tranmere Rovers | W | 1 - 0 | Walker | 2,707 |
| 24 | Dec 14 | | (h) | Colchester United | W | 4 - 1 | Shoulder 2 (1 pen), Dixon, Robinson | 2,161 |
| 25 | 20 | | (a) | Crewe Alexandra | D | 0 - 0 | | 1,070 |
| 26 | 26 | | (a) | Scunthorpe United | L | 0 - 1 | | 2,495 |
| 27 | Jan 1 | | (h) | Halifax Town | W | 3 - 0 | Shoulder 2, Dixon | 3,391 |
| 28 | 8 | | (h) | Chester City | D | 1 - 1 | Holden (o.g.) | 3,675 |
| 29 | 11 | | (a) | Orient | D | 1 - 1 | Honour | 3,667 |
| 30 | 18 | | (h) | Cambridge United | W | 2 - 1 | Honour 2 | 3,045 |
| 32 | 25 | | (a) | Rochdale | W | 2 - 0 | Borthwick, Shoulder (pen) | 2,301 |
| 34 | Feb 1 | | (h) | Burnley | W | 3 - 1 | Shoulder 2 (2 pens), Linighan | 3,359 |
| 35 | 5 | | (h) | Preston North End | W | 1 - 0 | Shoulder | 2,986 |
| 36 | 25 | | (a) | Wrexham | L | 0 - 1 | | 957 |
| 37 | Mar 5 | | (h) | Port Vale | D | 1 - 1 | Sproson (o.g.) | 2,550 |
| 38 | 8 | | (a) | Peterborough United | L | 1 - 3 | Borthwick | 2,324 |
| 39 | 11 | | (a) | Northampton Town | L | 0 - 3 | | 1,815 |
| 40 | 14 | | (h) | Stockport County | D | 1 - 1 | Lester | 2,675 |
| 41 | 22 | | (h) | Exeter City | D | 0 - 0 | | 2,204 |
| 42 | 25 | | (a) | Swindon Town | L | 1 - 3 | Smith | 6,172 |
| 43 | 28 | | (a) | Halifax Town | L | 2 - 3 | Shoulder 2 (1 pen) | 2,064 |
| 44 | Apr 1 | | (h) | Scunthorpe United | L | 0 - 1 | | 2,575 |
| 45 | 5 | | (a) | Aldershot | W | 1 - 0 | Walker | 1,277 |
| 46 | 9 | | (a) | Hereford United | D | 2 - 2 | Hogan (pen), Honour | 2,023 |
| 47 | 12 | | (h) | Southend United | W | 3 - 2 | Little, Honour, Walker | 1,927 |
| 48 | 15 | | (h) | Torquay United | W | 1 - 0 | Compton (o.g.) | 1,348 |
| 49 | 18 | | (a) | Tranmere Rovers | L | 2 - 4 | Shoulder (pen), Hogan | 1,161 |
| 50 | 22 | | (a) | Mansfield Town | L | 0 - 4 | | 5,545 |
| 51 | 26 | | (h) | Wrexham | D | 3 - 3 | Borthwick, Dixon, Hogan (pen) | 1,282 |
| 52 | May 2 | | (a) | Colchester United | L | 1 - 3 | Hogan (pen) | 2,410 |

Final Position : 7th in Division Four

Apps.
Sub.Apps.
4 own goals — Goals

**FA Cup**

| Match No. | Date | Round | Venue | Opponents | Result | | Scorers | Attendance |
|---|---|---|---|---|---|---|---|---|
| 21 | Nov 16 | R1 | (a) | Macclesfield Town | W | 2 - 1 | Shoulder 2 | 3,217 |
| 23 | Dec 7 | R2 | (h) | Frickley Athletic | L | 0 - 1 | | 4,100 |

Apps.
Sub.Apps.
Goals

**League Cup**

| Match No. | Date | Round | Venue | Opponents | Result | | Scorers | Attendance |
|---|---|---|---|---|---|---|---|---|
| 2 | Aug 21 | R1/1 | (a) | Derby County | L | 0 - 3 | | 8,419 |
| 6 | Sep 4 | R1/2 | (h) | Derby County | W | 2 - 0 | Linighan, Hogan | 1,611 |

Apps.
Sub.Apps.
Goals

| Blackburn | Nobbs | Kelly | Little | Smith | Linighan | Shoulder | Honour | Newton | Walker | Dixon | Gollogly | Hogan | Borthwick | Dobson | Robinson | Taylor | Chilton | Chambers | Lester | Carney | Poskett | Hewitt | Proudlock |
|---|---|---|---|---|---|---|---|---|---|---|---|---|---|---|---|---|---|---|---|---|---|---|---|
| 1 | 2 | 3 | 4 | 5 | 6 | 7 | 8 | 9 | 10 | *11* | *12* | | | | | | | | | | | | |
| 1 | 2 | 3 | 4 | 5 | 6 | 7 | 8 | 9 | 10 | 11 | | | | | | | | | | | | | |
| 1 | 2 | 3 | 4 | 5 | 6 | 7 | 8 | 9 | 10 | *11* | | *12* | | | | | | | | | | | |
| 1 | 2 | 3 | *4* | 5 | 6 | 7 | 8 | 9 | 10 | 11 | | | *12* | | | | | | | | | | |
| 1 | 2 | 3 | | 5 | *6* | | 8 | 9 | 10 | 11 | *12* | 4 | | 7 | | | | | | | | | |
| 1 | 2 | 3 | | 5 | 6 | | 7 | | 10 | 11 | 8 | 4 | 9 | | | | | | | | | | |
| 1 | | 3 | | 5 | 6 | | 7 | | 10 | 11 | 8 | 4 | *9* | *12* | 2 | | | | | | | | |
| 1 | 2 | 3 | | 5 | 6 | | 7 | | 10 | 11 | 8 | 4 | 9 | | | | | | | | | | |
| 1 | 2 | 3 | | 5 | 6 | | 7 | | 10 | 11 | 8 | 4 | *9* | *12* | | | | | | | | | |
| 1 | 2 | *3* | | 5 | 6 | | 7 | | 10 | 11 | 8 | 4 | | 9 | | *12* | | | | | | | |
| 1 | 2 | 3 | | 5 | 6 | *11* | 7 | | 10 | | 8 | 4 | 9 | *12* | | | | | | | | | |
| 1 | 2 | 3 | | 5 | 6 | 11 | 7 | | 10 | | 8 | 4 | 9 | | | | | | | | | | |
| 1 | 2 | *3* | | 5 | 6 | 11 | 7 | | 10 | 8 | | 4 | 9 | | | *12* | | | | | | | |
| 1 | 2 | | | 5 | 6 | 11 | 7 | | 10 | *8* | | 4 | 9 | | | *12* | 3 | | | | | | |
| 1 | 11 | | | 5 | 6 | 8 | 7 | | 10 | *12* | | 4 | *9* | | 2 | | 3 | | | | | | |
| 1 | 11 | | | 5 | 6 | 8 | 7 | | 10 | | | 4 | *9* | *12* | 2 | | 3 | | | | | | |
| 1 | 11 | | | 5 | 6 | 8 | 7 | | 10 | | | 4 | *9* | *12* | 2 | | | 3 | | | | | |
| 1 | 2 | | | 5 | 6 | 8 | 7 | | 10 | 11 | | 4 | *9* | *12* | | | | 3 | | | | | |
| 1 | 2 | | | 5 | 6 | 8 | 7 | | 10 | | 11 | | *9* | *12* | 4 | | | 3 | | | | | |
| 1 | 2 | | | 5 | 6 | 8 | 7 | | 10 | 9 | 11 | | | | 4 | | | 3 | | | | | |
| 1 | 2 | | | 5 | 6 | 8 | 7 | | 10 | 9 | 11 | *12* | | | *4* | | | 3 | | | | | |
| 1 | 2 | | | 5 | 6 | 8 | 7 | | 10 | 9 | | 4 | | | 11 | | | 3 | | | | | |
| 1 | 2 | | | 5 | 6 | 8 | 7 | | 10 | 9 | | 4 | | | 11 | | | 3 | | | | | |
| 1 | 2 | | | 5 | *6* | 8 | 7 | *12* | 10 | 9 | | 4 | | | 11 | | | 3 | | | | | |
| 1 | 2 | | | 5 | | | 7 | *12* | *10* | 9 | 6 | 4 | | 8 | 11 | | | 3 | | | | | |
| 1 | 2 | | | 5 | | 8 | 7 | 9 | 10 | | | 4 | | | 6 | | | 3 | 11 | | | | |
| 1 | 2 | | | 5 | 6 | 8 | 7 | | 10 | | | 4 | 9 | | | | | 3 | 11 | | | | |
| 1 | 2 | | | 5 | 6 | 8 | 7 | | 10 | | | 4 | 9 | | | | | 3 | 11 | | | | |
| 1 | 2 | | | 5 | 6 | 8 | 7 | | 10 | | | 4 | 9 | | | | | 3 | 11 | | | | |
| 1 | 2 | | | 5 | 6 | 8 | 7 | | 10 | | | 4 | 9 | | | | | 3 | 11 | | | | |
| 1 | 2 | | | 5 | 6 | 8 | 7 | | 10 | | | 4 | *9* | *12* | | | | 3 | 11 | | | | |
| 1 | 2 | | | 5 | 6 | 8 | 7 | | 10 | | | *4* | 9 | | *12* | | | 3 | 11 | | | | |
| 1 | 2 | | | 5 | 6 | 8 | 7 | | | | | | *9* | *12* | 4 | 10 | | 3 | 11 | | | | |
| 1 | 2 | | *4* | 5 | 6 | 8 | 7 | *12* | 10 | | | | 9 | | | | | 3 | 11 | | | | |
| 1 | 2 | | 4 | 5 | 6 | 8 | 7 | 9 | *10* | | | | *12* | | | | | 3 | 11 | | | | |
| 1 | | | | 5 | 6 | 8 | 7 | 9 | *12* | | | 4 | | *10* | 2 | | | 3 | 11 | | | | |
| 1 | 2 | | | 5 | 6 | 8 | 7 | | 10 | | | 4 | 9 | | | | | 3 | | 11 | | | |
| 1 | 2 | | | 5 | 6 | 11 | 7 | | 10 | | | 4 | 9 | *12* | | | | 3 | | | *8* | | |
| 1 | | | 9 | 5 | *12* | *11* | 7 | | 10 | | | 4 | | | 2 | | | 3 | | 6 | 8 | | |
| 1 | | | 11 | 5 | | 8 | 7 | | 10 | | | 4 | *12* | | 2 | | | 3 | | 6 | *9* | | |
| 1 | | | 11 | 5 | | 8 | 7 | | 10 | | | 4 | *12* | | 2 | | | 3 | | 6 | *9* | | |
| 1 | | | 11 | 5 | | 8 | 7 | | 10 | | | 4 | 9 | | 2 | | | 3 | | 6 | | | |
| 1 | 2 | | *11* | 5 | | 8 | 7 | | 10 | | | 4 | 9 | | | | | 3 | | 6 | *12* | | |
| 1 | *12* | 3 | | 5 | 6 | | 7 | | *10* | | | 4 | 9 | 8 | | | | | | 2 | | | 11 |
| 1 | 2 | | | 5 | 6 | | 7 | | 10 | 8 | | 4 | 9 | | *11* | | | 3 | | | | *12* | |
| 1 | | *12* | 11 | 5 | | | 7 | | 10 | 8 | | 4 | *9* | | 6 | 2 | | 3 | | | | | |
| 46 | 38 | 14 | 12 | 46 | 38 | 36 | 46 | 8 | 44 | 21 | 11 | 36 | 28 | 5 | 20 | 2 | 3 | 29 | 11 | 7 | 4 | | 1 |
| | 1 | 1 | | | 1 | | | 3 | 1 | 1 | 1 | 2 | 4 | 10 | 1 | 3 | | | | | 1 | 1 | |
| | 1 | | 1 | 3 | 1 | 17 | 9 | 2 | 5 | 5 | 1 | 8 | 7 | 2 | 1 | | | | 1 | | | | |

| Blackburn | Nobbs | Kelly | Little | Smith | Linighan | Shoulder | Honour | Newton | Walker | Dixon | Gollogly | Hogan | Borthwick | Dobson | Robinson | Taylor | Chilton | Chambers | Lester | Carney | Poskett | Hewitt | Proudlock |
|---|---|---|---|---|---|---|---|---|---|---|---|---|---|---|---|---|---|---|---|---|---|---|---|
| 1 | 2 | | | 5 | 6 | 11 | 7 | | 10 | | | 4 | 9 | | | | | 3 | | | | | 8 |
| 1 | 2 | | | 5 | 6 | 8 | 7 | | 10 | | 11 | | *9* | *12* | 4 | | | 3 | | | | | |
| 2 | 2 | | | 2 | 2 | 2 | 2 | | 2 | | 1 | 1 | 2 | | 1 | | | 2 | | | | | 1 |
| | | | | | | | | | | | | | | 1 | | | | | | | | | |
| | | | | | | 2 | | | | | | | | | | | | | | | | | |

| Blackburn | Nobbs | Kelly | Little | Smith | Linighan | Shoulder | Honour | Newton | Walker | Dixon | Gollogly | Hogan | Borthwick | Dobson | Robinson | Taylor | Chilton | Chambers | Lester | Carney | Poskett | Hewitt | Proudlock |
|---|---|---|---|---|---|---|---|---|---|---|---|---|---|---|---|---|---|---|---|---|---|---|---|
| 1 | 2 | 3 | 4 | 5 | 6 | 7 | 8 | 9 | 10 | 11 | | | | | | | | | | | | | |
| 1 | 2 | 3 | | 6 | 5 | | 8 | 9 | 10 | 11 | | 4 | | 7 | | | | | | | | | |
| 2 | 2 | 2 | 1 | 2 | 2 | 1 | 2 | 2 | 2 | 2 | | 1 | | 1 | | | | | | | | | |
| | | | | | | | | | | | | | | | | | | | | | | | |
| | | | | | 1 | | | | | | | 1 | | | | | | | | | | | |

## League Table

| | P | W | D | L | F | A | Pts |
|---|---|---|---|---|---|---|---|
| Swindon Town | 46 | 32 | 6 | 8 | 82 | 43 | 102 |
| Chester City | 46 | 23 | 15 | 8 | 83 | 50 | 84 |
| Mansfield Town | 46 | 23 | 12 | 11 | 74 | 47 | 81 |
| Port Vale | 46 | 21 | 16 | 9 | 67 | 37 | 79 |
| Orient | 46 | 20 | 12 | 14 | 79 | 64 | 72 |
| Colchester United | 46 | 19 | 13 | 14 | 88 | 63 | 70 |
| Hartlepool United | 46 | 20 | 10 | 16 | 68 | 67 | 70 |
| Northampton Town | 46 | 18 | 10 | 18 | 79 | 58 | 64 |
| Southend United | 46 | 18 | 10 | 18 | 69 | 67 | 64 |
| Hereford United | 46 | 18 | 10 | 18 | 74 | 73 | 64 |
| Stockport County | 46 | 17 | 13 | 16 | 63 | 71 | 64 |
| Crewe Alexandra | 46 | 18 | 9 | 19 | 54 | 61 | 63 |
| Wrexham | 46 | 17 | 9 | 20 | 68 | 80 | 60 |
| Burnley | 46 | 16 | 11 | 19 | 60 | 65 | 59 |
| Scunthorpe United | 46 | 15 | 14 | 17 | 50 | 55 | 59 |
| Aldershot | 46 | 17 | 7 | 22 | 66 | 74 | 58 |
| Peterborough United | 46 | 13 | 17 | 16 | 52 | 64 | 56 |
| Rochdale | 46 | 14 | 13 | 19 | 57 | 77 | 55 |
| Tranmere Rovers | 46 | 15 | 9 | 22 | 74 | 73 | 54 |
| Halifax Town | 46 | 14 | 12 | 20 | 60 | 71 | 54 |
| Exeter City | 46 | 13 | 15 | 18 | 47 | 59 | 54 |
| Cambridge United | 46 | 15 | 9 | 22 | 65 | 80 | 54 |
| Preston North End | 46 | 11 | 10 | 25 | 54 | 89 | 43 |
| Torquay United | 46 | 9 | 10 | 27 | 43 | 88 | 37 |

# 1986-87

## Division Four

Managers: Billy Horner and John Bird

### Did you know that?

The opening day of the season saw two Football League games played at the Victoria Ground on the same day. Firstly 'Pools played a 1–1 draw with Cardiff, followed by Middlesbrough's home Third Division fixture against Port Vale.

Within three days of their 'home' League fixture against Port Vale, Middlesbrough returned to the Victoria Ground to fulfil an away first-round, first-leg Football League Cup tie against United, which ended 1–1. Hence, they played their opening home and away fixtures on the same ground against different clubs!

| Match No. | Date | Round | Venue | Opponents | Result | | Scorers | Attendance |
|---|---|---|---|---|---|---|---|---|
| 1 | Aug 23 | | (h) | Cardiff City | D | 1 - 1 | Smith | 2,804 |
| 3 | 29 | | (a) | Southend United | D | 1 - 1 | Shoulder | 2,216 |
| 5 | Sep 6 | | (h) | Cambridge United | D | 2 - 2 | Gibb, Dixon | 1,956 |
| 6 | 13 | | (a) | Burnley | D | 1 - 1 | Lowe | 2,465 |
| 7 | 16 | | (a) | Colchester United | L | 1 - 2 | Hogan (pen) | 2,326 |
| 8 | 21 | | (h) | Wrexham | L | 0 - 1 | | 2,437 |
| 9 | 27 | | (a) | Orient | L | 0 - 2 | | 2,610 |
| 10 | Oct 1 | | (h) | Crewe Alexandra | L | 0 - 5 | | 1,512 |
| 11 | 5 | | (a) | Lincoln City | W | 4 - 1 | Strodder (o.g.), Gollogly 2, Walker | 2,101 |
| 12 | 10 | | (h) | Hereford United | D | 0 - 0 | | 1,939 |
| 13 | 18 | | (h) | Peterborough United | L | 1 - 2 | Gollogly | 1,482 |
| 14 | 22 | | (a) | Exeter City | L | 0 - 2 | | 2,660 |
| 15 | 25 | | (a) | Aldershot | D | 1 - 1 | Turner | 1,902 |
| 16 | Nov 1 | | (h) | Northampton Town | D | 3 - 3 | Hogan (pen), Dixon, Wilcox (o.g.) | 1,657 |
| 17 | 4 | | (h) | Torquay United | W | 2 - 1 | Dixon, Honour | 1,623 |
| 18 | 8 | | (a) | Rochdale | W | 2 - 0 | Honour, Dixon | 1,467 |
| 20 | 22 | | (a) | Swansea City | L | 0 - 1 | | 4,420 |
| 21 | 28 | | (h) | Stockport County | W | 1 - 0 | Hogan (pen) | 1,586 |
| 24 | Dec 13 | | (h) | Wolverhampton Wanderers | L | 0 - 1 | | 1,785 |
| 25 | 26 | | (h) | Halifax Town | D | 0 - 0 | | 1,676 |
| 26 | 27 | | (a) | Preston North End | D | 0 - 0 | | 7,782 |
| 27 | Jan 1 | | (a) | Scunthorpe United | W | 2 - 1 | Hewitt, Dixon | 2,726 |
| 28 | 3 | | (h) | Swansea City | D | 1 - 1 | Dixon | 1,784 |
| 29 | 10 | | (a) | Tranmere Rovers | D | 1 - 1 | Walker | 2,395 |
| 30 | 24 | | (a) | Cambridge United | L | 0 - 3 | | 1,749 |
| 31 | 31 | | (h) | Burnley | D | 2 - 2 | Hewitt, Dixon | 1,506 |
| 32 | Feb 6 | | (h) | Colchester United | W | 1 - 0 | Walker | 1,245 |
| 33 | 14 | | (a) | Wrexham | D | 1 - 1 | Toman | 1,824 |
| 34 | 21 | | (h) | Orient | L | 1 - 3 | Dixon | 1,439 |
| 35 | 28 | | (a) | Crewe Alexandra | L | 0 - 1 | | 1,314 |
| 36 | Mar 4 | | (a) | Northampton Town | D | 1 - 1 | Hogan | 5,470 |
| 37 | 7 | | (h) | Aldershot | D | 1 - 1 | Toman | 1,018 |
| 38 | 14 | | (a) | Peterborough United | L | 1 - 3 | McCaffery | 4,116 |
| 39 | 18 | | (h) | Exeter City | W | 1 - 0 | Shoulder | 1,092 |
| 40 | 21 | | (a) | Hereford United | L | 0 - 4 | | 1,832 |
| 41 | 29 | | (h) | Lincoln City | W | 2 - 1 | Shoulder 2 (1 pen) | 1,483 |
| 42 | Apr 4 | | (h) | Rochdale | D | 1 - 1 | Shoulder (pen) | 1,168 |
| 43 | 11 | | (a) | Torquay United | W | 1 - 0 | Shoulder (pen) | 1,773 |
| 44 | 14 | | (h) | Southend United | W | 1 - 0 | Shoulder (pen) | 1,323 |
| 45 | 17 | | (h) | Scunthorpe United | L | 0 - 2 | | 1,805 |
| 46 | 20 | | (a) | Halifax Town | L | 0 - 1 | | 1,115 |
| 47 | 24 | | (h) | Tranmere Rovers | D | 1 - 1 | Toman | 1,195 |
| 48 | May 1 | | (a) | Stockport County | W | 2 - 0 | Gibb, Toman | 2,228 |
| 49 | 4 | | (h) | Preston North End | D | 2 - 2 | Gibb, Toman | 2,449 |
| 50 | 7 | | (a) | Cardiff City | L | 0 - 4 | | 1,334 |
| 51 | 9 | | (a) | Wolverhampton Wanderers | L | 1 - 4 | Dixon | 8,610 |

Final Position : 18th in Division Four

Apps.
Sub.Apps.
2 own goals Goals

**FA Cup**

| Match No. | Date | Round | Venue | Opponents | Result | | Scorers | Attendance |
|---|---|---|---|---|---|---|---|---|
| 19 | Nov 15 | R1 | (a) | Wrexham | L | 1 - 2 | Hogan | 4,420 |

Apps.
Sub.Apps.
Goals

**League Cup**

| Match No. | Date | Round | Venue | Opponents | Result | | Scorers | Attendance |
|---|---|---|---|---|---|---|---|---|
| 2 | Aug 26 | R1/1 | (h) | Middlesbrough | D | 1 - 1 | Hogan | 2,356 |
| 4 | Sep 2 | R1/2 | (a) | Middlesbrough | L | 0 - 2 | | 7,735 |

Apps.
Sub.Apps.
Goals

| Blackburn | Gollogly | McKinnon | Hogan | Smith | Sword | Honour | Shoulder | Borthwick | Walker | Lowe | Dixon, K. | Gibb | Nobbs | Byron | Robinson | Turner | Hewitt | Robson | Edwards | Smithies | Lockhart | Barratt | McGinley | Toman | Tinkler | Cochrane | McCaffrey | Stokle | McLean | Dixon, A. |
|---|---|---|---|---|---|---|---|---|---|---|---|---|---|---|---|---|---|---|---|---|---|---|---|---|---|---|---|---|---|---|
| 1 | 2 | 3 | 4 | 5 | 6 | 7 | *8* | 9 | 10 | 11 | *12* | | | | | | | | | | | | | | | | | | | |
| 1 | 2 | 3 | 4 | 5 | 6 | 7 | 8 | *9* | 10 | *12* | | 11 | | | | | | | | | | | | | | | | | | |
| 1 | 2 | 3 | 4 | 5 | 6 | 7 | 8 | | | 9 | 11 | 10 | | | | | | | | | | | | | | | | | | |
| 1 | 2 | 3 | 4 | 5 | 6 | | 8 | | *10* | 9 | 11 | 7 | *12* | | | | | | | | | | | | | | | | | |
| 1 | 2 | 3 | 4 | 5 | 6 | | 8 | | 10 | 9 | 11 | 7 | | | | | | | | | | | | | | | | | | |
| 1 | 2 | 3 | 4 | 5 | 6 | 7 | *8* | | *12* | 9 | 11 | 10 | | | | | | | | | | | | | | | | | | |
| 1 | | 3 | 4 | 5 | 6 | 7 | *8* | | *12* | 9 | 11 | 10 | 2 | | | | | | | | | | | | | | | | | |
| 1 | | 3 | *4* | 5 | | 7 | 8 | | *12* | | 9 | 10 | 2 | 6 | 11 | | | | | | | | | | | | | | | |
| 1 | 4 | 3 | 8 | 5 | 6 | 7 | | | 10 | 11 | 9 | | 2 | | | | | | | | | | | | | | | | | |
| 1 | 4 | 3 | 8 | *5* | 6 | 7 | | | 10 | 11 | 9 | *12* | 2 | | | | | | | | | | | | | | | | | |
| 1 | 4 | 3 | 8 | | | 7 | | | 10 | *11* | 9 | 2 | 6 | | *12* | 5 | | | | | | | | | | | | | | |
| 1 | *4* | 3 | 8 | 5 | | 7 | | | 10 | 11 | 9 | *12* | 2 | | | 6 | | | | | | | | | | | | | | |
| 1 | | 3 | 4 | 5 | 6 | 7 | | | 10 | *12* | 11 | *8* | 2 | | | 9 | | | | | | | | | | | | | | |
| 1 | | 3 | 4 | 5 | 6 | 7 | | | 10 | 8 | 11 | | 2 | | | 9 | | | | | | | | | | | | | | |
| 1 | 8 | 3 | 4 | 5 | 6 | 7 | | | 10 | *11* | 9 | | 2 | | | | *12* | | | | | | | | | | | | | |
| 1 | | *3* | 4 | 5 | 6 | 7 | | | 10 | | 8 | | 2 | | | 9 | *12* | 11 | | | | | | | | | | | | |
| | | 3 | 4 | 5 | 6 | 7 | *11* | | 10 | | 8 | | 2 | | | 9 | | | 1 | *12* | | | | | | | | | | |
| 1 | | 3 | 4 | 5 | 6 | 7 | 11 | | 10 | | 8 | | 2 | | | 9 | | | | | | | | | | | | | | |
| 1 | | 3 | 4 | 5 | 6 | | 8 | 9 | 10 | | 7 | *12* | 2 | | | | | | | | *11* | | | | | | | | | |
| 1 | | 3 | 4 | 5 | | *12* | 8 | 9 | 10 | | 7 | 2 | 6 | | | | | | | | *11* | | | | | | | | | |
| 1 | | 3 | 4 | 5 | | 7 | | | 10 | | 11 | 9 | 6 | | | | 8 | | | 2 | | | | | | | | | | |
| 1 | | 3 | 6 | 5 | | 7 | | | | | 11 | 9 | 4 | | | | 8 | | | 2 | | 10 | | | | | | | | |
| 1 | | 3 | 6 | 5 | | *12* | | | | | *10* | 9 | 4 | | | | 8 | | | 2 | | 7 | 11 | | | | | | | |
| 1 | | 3 | 6 | 5 | | | | 9 | 7 | | 10 | | 4 | | | | 8 | | | 2 | | | 11 | | | | | | | |
| 1 | | 3 | | 5 | | 11 | | *9* | 7 | | 10 | | 4 | | | | 8 | | | 2 | | | | 6 | *12* | | | | | |
| 1 | | 3 | | 5 | 6 | *12* | | | 7 | | 9 | | 4 | | | | 8 | | | | | 2 | | 10 | | *11* | | | | |
| 1 | | *3* | 4 | 5 | 6 | *12* | | | 11 | | 9 | | 2 | | | | 8 | | | | | 7 | | 10 | | | | | | |
| 1 | | | 4 | 5 | | 10 | | | 11 | | 9 | *12* | 3 | | | | *8* | | | | | 2 | | 7 | | | 6 | | | |
| 1 | | 11 | 4 | 5 | | *12* | | | 10 | | 9 | | 3 | | | | *8* | | | | | 2 | | 7 | | | 6 | | | |
| 1 | | 11 | 4 | 5 | | *12* | | 8 | 10 | | 9 | | 3 | | | | | | | | | 2 | | | | *7* | 6 | | | |
| 1 | | 11 | 4 | 5 | | | | 8 | 10 | | 9 | | 3 | | | | | | | | | 2 | | 7 | | | | 6 | | |
| 1 | | 11 | 4 | 5 | | | | *8* | 10 | | 9 | *12* | 3 | | | | | | | | | 2 | | 7 | | | | 6 | | |
| 1 | | 11 | 4 | 5 | | | | 9 | 10 | | | | 3 | | | | 8 | | | | | 2 | | 7 | | | 6 | | | |
| 1 | | 3 | 4 | 5 | | 11 | 8 | | 10 | | 9 | | 6 | | | | | | | | | 2 | | 7 | | | | | | |
| 1 | | 3 | | 5 | | | 8 | | 10 | | 9 | 11 | 6 | | | | *7* | | | | | 2 | | 4 | *12* | | | | | |
| 1 | | 3 | | 5 | | | 8 | | 10 | | 9 | *12* | | | | | | | | | | 2 | | 7 | | | *4* | 6 | 11 | |
| 1 | | 3 | | 5 | | | 8 | | 10 | | *9* | *12* | 2 | | | | | | | | | 11 | | 7 | | | | 6 | 4 | |
| 1 | | 3 | | 5 | | | 8 | | | | 9 | 10 | 2 | | | | | | | | | 11 | | 7 | | | | 6 | 4 | |
| 1 | | 3 | *12* | 5 | | | 8 | | 11 | | 10 | *9* | 6 | | | | | | | | | 2 | | 7 | | | | | 4 | |
| 1 | | 3 | 4 | 5 | | *12* | 8 | | 11 | | 10 | *9* | 6 | | | | | | | | | 2 | | 7 | | | | | | |
| 1 | | 3 | 4 | 5 | | | 8 | | *12* | | 10 | *9* | 2 | | | | | | | | | 11 | | 7 | | | 6 | | | |
| 1 | | 3 | 4 | 5 | | | 8 | 9 | | | 10 | 11 | 6 | | | | | | | | | 2 | | 7 | | | | | | |
| 1 | | 3 | 4 | 5 | | 10 | 8 | 9 | | | | 11 | 6 | | | | | | | | | 2 | | 7 | | | | | | |
| 1 | | 3 | 4 | 5 | | 10 | 8 | *9* | | | *12* | 11 | 6 | | | | | | | | | 2 | | 7 | | | | | | |
| 1 | | 3 | | 5 | | 10 | 8 | *9* | | | *12* | 11 | 6 | | | | | | | | | 2 | | 7 | | | | | 4 | |
| 1 | | 3 | | 5 | | 10 | 8 | | | | 9 | *11* | 6 | | | | | | | | | 2 | | 7 | | | | | 4 | *2* |
| 45 | 11 | 45 | 37 | 45 | 18 | 25 | 25 | 14 | 33 | 12 | 40 | 23 | 39 | 1 | 1 | 7 | 11 | 1 | 1 | 5 | 2 | 23 | 2 | 21 | | 2 | 6 | 5 | 6 | |
| | | | 1 | | | 7 | | | 4 | 2 | 3 | 7 | 1 | | 1 | | 2 | | | 1 | | | | | 2 | | | | | 1 |
| | 3 | | 4 | 1 | | 2 | 7 | | 3 | 1 | 9 | 3 | | | | 1 | 2 | | | | | | | 5 | | | | | | |

| Blackburn | Gollogly | McKinnon | Hogan | Smith | Sword | Honour | Shoulder | Borthwick | Walker | Lowe | Dixon, K. | Gibb | Nobbs | Byron | Robinson | Turner | Hewitt | Robson | Edwards | Smithies |
|---|---|---|---|---|---|---|---|---|---|---|---|---|---|---|---|---|---|---|---|---|
| 1 | | | 4 | 5 | 6 | 7 | 8 | | 10 | | 9 | | 2 | | | | 11 | | | 3 |
| 1 | | | 1 | 1 | 1 | 1 | 1 | | 1 | | 1 | | 1 | | | | 1 | | | 1 |
| | | | | | | | | | | | | | | | | | | | | |
| | | | 1 | | | | | | | | | | | | | | | | | |

| Blackburn | Gollogly | McKinnon | Hogan | Smith | Sword | Honour | Shoulder | Borthwick | Walker | Lowe | Dixon, K. | Gibb |
|---|---|---|---|---|---|---|---|---|---|---|---|---|
| 1 | 2 | 3 | 4 | 5 | 6 | 7 | 8 | **9** | *11* | **13** | *12* | 10 |
| 1 | 2 | 3 | 4 | 5 | 6 | 7 | 8 | | 10 | 9 | *12* | 11 |
| 2 | 2 | 2 | 2 | 2 | 2 | 2 | 2 | 1 | 2 | 1 | | 2 |
| | | | | | | | | | | 1 | 2 | |
| | | | 1 | | | | | | | | | |

## League Table

| | P | W | D | L | F | A | Pts |
|---|---|---|---|---|---|---|---|
| Northampton Town | 46 | 30 | 9 | 7 | 103 | 53 | 99 |
| Preston North End | 46 | 26 | 12 | 8 | 72 | 47 | 90 |
| Southend United | 46 | 25 | 5 | 16 | 68 | 55 | 80 |
| Wolverhampton W. | 46 | 24 | 7 | 15 | 69 | 50 | 79 |
| Colchester United | 46 | 21 | 7 | 18 | 64 | 56 | 70 |
| Aldershot | 46 | 20 | 10 | 16 | 64 | 57 | 70 |
| Orient | 46 | 20 | 9 | 17 | 64 | 61 | 69 |
| Scunthorpe United | 46 | 18 | 12 | 16 | 73 | 57 | 66 |
| Wrexham | 46 | 15 | 20 | 11 | 70 | 51 | 65 |
| Peterborough United | 46 | 17 | 14 | 15 | 57 | 50 | 65 |
| Cambridge United | 46 | 17 | 11 | 18 | 60 | 62 | 62 |
| Swansea City | 46 | 17 | 11 | 18 | 56 | 61 | 62 |
| Cardiff City | 46 | 15 | 16 | 15 | 48 | 50 | 61 |
| Exeter City | 46 | 11 | 23 | 12 | 53 | 49 | 56 |
| Halifax Town | 46 | 15 | 10 | 21 | 59 | 74 | 55 |
| Hereford United | 46 | 14 | 11 | 21 | 60 | 61 | 53 |
| Crewe Alexandra | 46 | 13 | 14 | 19 | 70 | 72 | 53 |
| Hartlepool United | 46 | 11 | 18 | 17 | 44 | 65 | 51 |
| Stockport County | 46 | 13 | 12 | 21 | 40 | 69 | 51 |
| Tranmere Rovers | 46 | 11 | 17 | 18 | 54 | 72 | 50 |
| Rochdale | 46 | 11 | 17 | 18 | 54 | 73 | 50 |
| Burnley | 46 | 12 | 13 | 21 | 53 | 74 | 49 |
| Torquay United | 46 | 10 | 18 | 18 | 56 | 72 | 48 |
| Lincoln City | 46 | 12 | 12 | 22 | 45 | 65 | 48 |

# 1987-88

## Division Four

Manager: John Bird

### Did you know that?

In a seven-game spell starting on 5 September against Leyton Orient, Paul Baker scored 13 goals, including two hat-tricks.

Tony Smith was ever present in 57 League and Cup games. In four seasons he had missed only three League games, amassing a total of 209 appearances.

| Match No. | Date | Round | Venue | Opponents | Result | | Scorers | Attendance |
|---|---|---|---|---|---|---|---|---|
| 1 | Aug 15 | | (h) | Newport County | D | 0 - 0 | | 1,846 |
| 3 | 22 | | (a) | Wrexham | L | 1 - 2 | McKinnon | 1,816 |
| 5 | 29 | | (h) | Darlington | L | 2 - 5 | Dixon, Baker | 1,808 |
| 6 | 31 | | (a) | Swansea City | L | 1 - 2 | Toman | 3,569 |
| 7 | Sep 5 | | (h) | Leyton Orient | D | 2 - 2 | Toman, Baker | 1,110 |
| 8 | 12 | | (a) | Carlisle United | W | 3 - 1 | Baker 2, Toman | 2,463 |
| 9 | 16 | | (h) | Cambridge United | W | 2 - 1 | Baker 2 | 1,454 |
| 10 | 19 | | (h) | Colchester United | W | 3 - 1 | Baker 3 (2 pens) | 1,619 |
| 11 | 26 | | (a) | Bolton Wanderers | W | 2 - 1 | McKinnon, Baker (pen) | 4,398 |
| 12 | 30 | | (h) | Exeter City | W | 3 - 1 | Baker 3 | 2,971 |
| 13 | Oct 3 | | (a) | Crewe Alexandra | D | 1 - 1 | Baker (pen) | 2,128 |
| 14 | 10 | | (a) | Burnley | L | 0 - 1 | | 5,216 |
| 15 | 17 | | (h) | Torquay United | D | 0 - 0 | | 2,462 |
| 16 | 21 | | (h) | Halifax Town | W | 2 - 1 | Toman, Barratt | 2,472 |
| 17 | 24 | | (a) | Scarborough | D | 1 - 1 | Toman (pen) | 3,909 |
| 19 | 31 | | (h) | Scunthorpe United | W | 1 - 0 | Toman | 2,532 |
| 20 | Nov 3 | | (a) | Stockport County | L | 0 - 1 | | 1,408 |
| 21 | 7 | | (a) | Peterborough United | W | 1 - 0 | Toman | 3,232 |
| 23 | 21 | | (h) | Tranmere Rovers | L | 1 - 2 | Toman | 2,443 |
| 24 | 28 | | (a) | Cardiff City | D | 1 - 1 | Barratt | 3,232 |
| 27 | Dec 12 | | (h) | Wolverhampton Wanderers | D | 0 - 0 | | 2,631 |
| 28 | 19 | | (a) | Hereford United | L | 2 - 4 | Toman 2 (1 pen) | 1,676 |
| 29 | 26 | | (h) | Bolton Wanderers | D | 0 - 0 | | 4,304 |
| 30 | 28 | | (a) | Rochdale | W | 2 - 0 | Baker, Whellans | 1,851 |
| 31 | Jan 1 | | (a) | Darlington | D | 1 - 1 | Baker | 4,735 |
| 32 | 2 | | (h) | Carlisle United | D | 0 - 0 | | 3,139 |
| 34 | 15 | | (a) | Colchester United | D | 0 - 0 | | 1,768 |
| 35 | 26 | | (h) | Wrexham | W | 1 - 0 | Borthwick | 1,524 |
| 36 | 30 | | (h) | Swansea City | L | 0 - 2 | | 2,050 |
| 38 | Feb 6 | | (a) | Leyton Orient | W | 2 - 0 | Baker, Toman | 4,188 |
| 40 | 13 | | (h) | Rochdale | D | 1 - 1 | Toman | 2,120 |
| 41 | 19 | | (a) | Newport County | W | 3 - 2 | Toman (pen), Borthwick 2 | 1,880 |
| 42 | 27 | | (h) | Crewe Alexandra | W | 2 - 1 | Toman (pen), Baker | 1,624 |
| 43 | Mar 2 | | (a) | Exeter City | L | 0 - 1 | | 1,573 |
| 44 | 5 | | (a) | Torquay United | D | 1 - 1 | Barratt | 2,857 |
| 46 | 12 | | (h) | Burnley | W | 2 - 1 | Baker, Borthwick | 2,893 |
| 47 | 19 | | (a) | Scunthorpe United | L | 0 - 3 | | 3,783 |
| 48 | 26 | | (h) | Scarborough | W | 1 - 0 | Borthwick | 2,453 |
| 49 | Apr 2 | | (h) | Peterborough United | L | 0 - 1 | | 2,315 |
| 50 | 4 | | (a) | Tranmere Rovers | L | 1 - 3 | Toman | 3,921 |
| 51 | 9 | | (h) | Stockport County | L | 1 - 3 | Toman | 1,269 |
| 52 | 19 | | (a) | Cambridge United | D | 1 - 1 | Crowe (o.g.) | 1,492 |
| 53 | 23 | | (a) | Halifax Town | L | 1 - 3 | Baker | 876 |
| 54 | 30 | | (h) | Cardiff City | L | 0 - 1 | | 1,101 |
| 55 | May 2 | | (a) | Wolverhampton Wanderers | L | 0 - 2 | | 17,895 |
| 56 | 7 | | (h) | Hereford United | L | 1 - 2 | Toman | 823 |

Final Position : 16th in Division Four

Apps.
Sub.Apps.
1 own goal Goals

**FA Cup**

| Match No. | Date | Round | Venue | Opponents | Result | | Scorers | Attendance |
|---|---|---|---|---|---|---|---|---|
| 22 | Nov 14 | R1 | (a) | Chorley | W | 2 - 0 | Gibb, Baker | 2,462 |
| 25 | Dec 5 | R2 | (a) | York City | D | 1 - 1 | Baker | 3,394 |
| 26 | 9 | R2r | (h) | York City | W | 3 - 1 | Baker, Toman 2 | 4,057 |
| 33 | Jan 9 | R3 | (h) | Luton Town | L | 1 - 2 | Toman | 6,056 |

Apps.
Sub.Apps.
Goals

**League Cup**

| Match No. | Date | Round | Venue | Opponents | Result | | Scorers | Attendance |
|---|---|---|---|---|---|---|---|---|
| 2 | Aug 18 | R1/1 | (a) | Scunthorpe United | L | 1 - 3 | Baker | 1,613 |
| 4 | 26 | R1/2 | (h) | Scunthorpe United | L | 0 - 1 | | 972 |

Apps.
Sub.Apps.
Goals

| Owers | Barratt | Nobbs | Haigh | Smith | Stokes | Honour | Toman | Baker | Shoulder | Butler | Gibb | McKinnon | Borthwick | Prudhoe | Thomson | Dixon | Kennedy | Carr | Tinkler | Hall | Whellans | Danskin | Stokle | Doig | Grayson | McCarthy |
|---|---|---|---|---|---|---|---|---|---|---|---|---|---|---|---|---|---|---|---|---|---|---|---|---|---|---|
| 1 | 2 | 3 | 4 | 5 | 6 | 7 | 8 | 9 | 10 | *11* | *12* | | | | | | | | | | | | | | | |
| 1 | 2 | | 4 | 5 | 6 | 7 | 8 | 9 | *10* | 11 | | 3 | *12* | | | | | | | | | | | | | |
| | 11 | 2 | 4 | 5 | 6 | 7 | **8** | 9 | | *12* | | *3* | | 1 | 10 | **14** | | | | | | | | | | |
| | *12* | 2 | | 5 | 6 | 7 | 8 | 9 | | *11* | | 3 | | 1 | 4 | 10 | | | | | | | | | | |
| | **14** | 2 | 4 | 5 | 6 | 7 | 8 | 9 | 11 | *12* | | **3** | | 1 | | *10* | | | | | | | | | | |
| | *12* | 2 | 4 | 5 | 6 | 7 | 8 | 9 | 11 | | | *3* | | 1 | **14** | **10** | | | | | | | | | | |
| | | 2 | 4 | 5 | 6 | 7 | 8 | 9 | *11* | *12* | | 3 | 10 | 1 | | | | | | | | | | | | |
| | 11 | 2 | 4 | 5 | 6 | 7 | 8 | 9 | | | | 3 | 10 | 1 | | | | | | | | | | | | |
| | 11 | 2 | 4 | 5 | 6 | 7 | 8 | 9 | | | | 3 | 10 | 1 | | | | | | | | | | | | |
| | 11 | 2 | 4 | 5 | 6 | 7 | 8 | 9 | | | | 3 | 10 | 1 | | | | | | | | | | | | |
| | 11 | 2 | 4 | 5 | 6 | 7 | 8 | 9 | | | | 3 | 10 | 1 | | | | | | | | | | | | |
| | **11** | 2 | 4 | 5 | 6 | 7 | 8 | 9 | | | *12* | 3 | *10* | 1 | | | **14** | | | | | | | | | |
| | 2 | 4 | | 5 | 6 | 7 | 8 | 9 | | | | 11 | 10 | 1 | | | 3 | | | | | | | | | |
| | 2 | 4 | | 5 | 6 | 7 | 8 | 9 | | | | 11 | | 1 | | 10 | 3 | | | | | | | | | |
| | 2 | 4 | 11 | 5 | 6 | 7 | 8 | *9* | | | 10 | 3 | *12* | 1 | | | | | | | | | | | | |
| | | 4 | 2 | 5 | 6 | 7 | 8 | 9 | | 11 | 10 | | | | | | 3 | 1 | | | | | | | | |
| | *11* | 4 | 2 | 5 | 6 | 7 | 8 | 9 | | | 10 | *12* | | | | | 3 | 1 | | | | | | | | |
| | | 4 | 2 | 5 | 6 | 7 | 8 | 9 | | 11 | 10 | 3 | | | | | | 1 | | | | | | | | |
| | **14** | 4 | 2 | 5 | 6 | 7 | 8 | *9* | | **11** | 10 | 3 | *12* | | | | | 1 | | | | | | | | |
| | 11 | 4 | 2 | 5 | 6 | 7 | 8 | 9 | | | *12* | 3 | *10* | | | | | 1 | | | | | | | | |
| | 11 | | 2 | 5 | 6 | 7 | 8 | 9 | | | | 3 | 10 | | | | | 1 | 4 | | | | | | | |
| | 11 | | 2 | 5 | 6 | 7 | 8 | | | | *12* | 3 | 10 | | | *9* | | 1 | **4** | **14** | | | | | | |
| | 11 | 4 | 2 | 5 | 6 | 7 | 8 | | | | 9 | 3 | 10 | | | | | 1 | | | | | | | | |
| | 11 | 4 | 2 | 5 | 6 | 7 | 8 | 9 | | | | 3 | | | | | | 1 | | | 10 | | | | | |
| | 11 | 4 | 2 | 5 | | 7 | 8 | 9 | | | *12* | 3 | | | | | | 1 | 6 | | *10* | | | | | |
| | 11 | 4 | 2 | 5 | | 7 | 8 | 9 | | | *12* | 3 | | | | | | 1 | *6* | | 10 | | | | | |
| | 2 | 4 | 6 | 5 | | | 8 | 9 | | | | 3 | 11 | | | | | 1 | *12* | | 10 | *7* | | | | |
| | 2 | 4 | 6 | 5 | | | 8 | 9 | | | | 3 | 11 | | | | | 1 | *12* | | 10 | *7* | | | | |
| | 2 | 4 | 6 | 5 | | 14 | 8 | 9 | | | 10 | 3 | 11 | | | | | 1 | *12* | | | *7* | | | | |
| | 2 | 4 | 6 | 5 | | 7 | 8 | 9 | | | | 3 | 11 | | | | | 1 | 10 | | | | | | | |
| | 2 | 4 | 6 | 5 | | 7 | 8 | 9 | | | | 3 | 11 | | | | | 1 | 10 | | | | | | | |
| | 2 | 4 | 6 | 5 | | 7 | 8 | | | | *9* | 3 | 11 | | | *12* | | 1 | 10 | | | | | | | |
| | 2 | 4 | *6* | 5 | | 7 | 8 | 9 | | | | 3 | 11 | | | | | 1 | 10 | | *12* | | | | | |
| | 2 | 4 | | 5 | | 7 | 8 | 9 | | | *12* | 3 | 11 | | | | | 1 | 6 | | *10* | | | | | |
| | 2 | 4 | | 5 | | 7 | 8 | 9 | | | | 3 | 11 | | | | | 1 | 10 | | | | 6 | | | |
| | 2 | 4 | | 5 | | 7 | 8 | 9 | | | | 3 | 11 | | | | | 1 | 10 | | | | 6 | | | |
| | 2 | 4 | | 5 | | *7* | 8 | | | | *12* | 3 | 11 | | | **14** | | 1 | **10** | | 9 | | 6 | | | |
| | 2 | 4 | 6 | 5 | | 7 | 8 | | | | *9* | 3 | 11 | | | | | 1 | | | *12* | | | 10 | | |
| | 2 | **4** | 6 | 5 | | 7 | 8 | *9* | | | | 3 | 11 | | | | | 1 | **14** | | *12* | | | 10 | | |
| | 2 | 4 | 6 | 5 | | *12* | 8 | 9 | | | | 3 | 11 | | | | | 1 | *7* | | | | | 10 | | |
| | 2 | 4 | 6 | 5 | | 7 | 8 | *9* | | | | 3 | 11 | | | *12* | | 1 | | | | | | 10 | | |
| | 2 | 4 | 6 | 5 | | 7 | 8 | *12* | | | | 3 | 11 | | | | | 1 | | | 9 | | | *10* | | |
| | 2 | **14** | 6 | 5 | | 7 | 8 | 9 | | | | 3 | *11* | | | *12* | | 1 | **4** | | | | | 10 | | |
| | 2 | 4 | 6 | 5 | | 7 | 8 | 9 | | | | 3 | *12* | | | 10 | | 1 | | | | | | *11* | | |
| | 2 | 4 | 3 | 5 | | 7 | 8 | | | | *12* | | 9 | | | 10 | | 1 | 6 | | | | | *11* | | |
| | 2 | 4 | 3 | 5 | | 7 | 8 | | | | | | **10** | | | *12* | | 1 | 6 | | | | | *11* | 9 | **14** |
| 2 | 40 | 42 | 39 | 46 | 24 | 42 | 46 | 38 | 5 | 6 | 10 | 41 | 30 | 13 | 2 | 7 | 4 | 31 | 16 | | 8 | 3 | 3 | 9 | 1 | |
| | 3 | 1 | | | | 2 | | 1 | | 3 | 8 | 1 | 4 | | 1 | 6 | 1 | | 4 | 1 | 3 | | | | | 1 |
| | 3 | | | | | | 17 | 20 | | | | 2 | 5 | | | 1 | | | | | 1 | | | | | |

| Owers | Barratt | Nobbs | Haigh | Smith | Stokes | Honour | Toman | Baker | Shoulder | Butler | Gibb | McKinnon | Borthwick | Prudhoe | Thomson | Dixon | Kennedy | Carr | Tinkler | Hall | Whellans | Danskin | Stokle | Doig | Grayson | McCarthy |
|---|---|---|---|---|---|---|---|---|---|---|---|---|---|---|---|---|---|---|---|---|---|---|---|---|---|---|
| | | 4 | 2 | 5 | 6 | 7 | 8 | 9 | | 11 | 10 | 3 | | | | | | 1 | | | | | | | | |
| | 11 | *4* | 2 | 5 | 6 | 7 | 8 | 9 | | | | 3 | 10 | | | | | 1 | | *12* | | | | | | |
| | 11 | | 2 | 5 | 6 | 7 | 8 | 9 | | | | 3 | 10 | | | | | 1 | 4 | | | | | | | |
| | 2 | 4 | 6 | 5 | | 7 | 8 | 9 | | | *11* | 3 | | | | | | 1 | *12* | | 10 | | | | | |
| | 3 | 3 | 4 | 4 | 3 | 4 | 4 | 4 | | 1 | 2 | 4 | 2 | | | | | 4 | 1 | | 1 | | | | | |
| | | | | | | | | | | | | | | | | | | | 1 | 1 | | | | | | |
| | | | | | | | 3 | 3 | | | 1 | | | | | | | | | | | | | | | |

| Owers | Barratt | Nobbs | Haigh | Smith | Stokes | Honour | Toman | Baker | Shoulder | Butler | Gibb | McKinnon | Borthwick | Prudhoe | Thomson | Dixon | Kennedy | Carr | Tinkler | Hall | Whellans | Danskin | Stokle | Doig | Grayson | McCarthy |
|---|---|---|---|---|---|---|---|---|---|---|---|---|---|---|---|---|---|---|---|---|---|---|---|---|---|---|
| 1 | 2 | 3 | 4 | 5 | 6 | 7 | *8* | 9 | 10 | 11 | | | | | | *12* | | | | | | | | | | |
| 1 | 2 | | 4 | 5 | 6 | 7 | 8 | 9 | | *11* | | 3 | | | 10 | *12* | | | | | | | | | | |
| 2 | 2 | 1 | 2 | 2 | 2 | 2 | 2 | 2 | 1 | 2 | | 1 | | | 1 | | | | | | | | | | | |
| | | | | | | | | | | | | | | | | 2 | | | | | | | | | | |
| | | | | | | | | 1 | | | | | | | | | | | | | | | | | | |

**Substitutions**

*Italic* player replaced by No 12.

**Bold** player replaced by No 14.

## League Table

| | P | W | D | L | F | A | Pts |
|---|---|---|---|---|---|---|---|
| Wolverhampton W. | 46 | 27 | 9 | 10 | 82 | 43 | 90 |
| Cardiff City | 46 | 24 | 13 | 9 | 66 | 41 | 85 |
| Bolton Wanderers | 46 | 22 | 12 | 12 | 66 | 42 | 78 |
| Scunthorpe United | 46 | 20 | 17 | 9 | 76 | 51 | 77 |
| Torquay United | 46 | 21 | 14 | 11 | 66 | 41 | 77 |
| Swansea City | 46 | 20 | 10 | 16 | 62 | 56 | 70 |
| Peterborough United | 46 | 20 | 10 | 16 | 52 | 53 | 70 |
| Leyton Orient | 46 | 19 | 12 | 15 | 85 | 63 | 69 |
| Colchester United | 46 | 19 | 10 | 17 | 47 | 51 | 67 |
| Burnley | 46 | 20 | 7 | 19 | 57 | 62 | 67 |
| Wrexham | 46 | 20 | 6 | 20 | 69 | 58 | 66 |
| Scarborough | 46 | 17 | 14 | 15 | 56 | 48 | 65 |
| Darlington | 46 | 18 | 11 | 17 | 71 | 69 | 65 |
| Tranmere Rovers | 46 | 19 | 9 | 18 | 61 | 53 | 64 |
| Cambridge United | 46 | 16 | 13 | 17 | 50 | 52 | 61 |
| Hartlepool United | 46 | 15 | 14 | 17 | 50 | 57 | 59 |
| Crewe Alexandra | 46 | 13 | 19 | 14 | 57 | 53 | 58 |
| Halifax Town | 46 | 14 | 14 | 18 | 54 | 59 | 55 |
| Hereford United | 46 | 14 | 12 | 20 | 41 | 59 | 54 |
| Stockport County | 46 | 12 | 15 | 19 | 44 | 58 | 51 |
| Rochdale | 46 | 11 | 15 | 20 | 47 | 76 | 48 |
| Exeter City | 46 | 11 | 13 | 22 | 53 | 68 | 46 |
| Carlisle United | 46 | 12 | 8 | 26 | 57 | 86 | 44 |
| Newport County | 46 | 6 | 7 | 33 | 35 | 105 | 25 |

# 1988-89

## Division Four

Managers: John Bird and Bobby Moncur

### Did you know that?

Following their victory over Bristol City in the FA Cup, Hartlepool United were the only north-east club to participate in the fourth round, losing in a replay to Bournemouth.

After five wins from the opening six League games, John Bird had the rare experience for a Hartlepool manager of being 'head hunted' by York City. He left the Victoria Park saying York had made the proverbial 'offer you cannot refuse'.

| Match No. | Date | Round | Venue | Opponents | Result | | Scorers | Attendance |
|---|---|---|---|---|---|---|---|---|
| 1 | Aug 27 | | (a) | Lincoln City | W | 1 - 0 | Toman | 3,547 |
| 3 | Sep 3 | | (h) | Darlington | W | 2 - 1 | Toman, Smith | 2,477 |
| 5 | 10 | | (a) | Torquay United | L | 0 - 2 | | 2,027 |
| 6 | 17 | | (h) | Leyton Orient | W | 1 - 0 | Tinkler | 1,873 |
| 7 | 20 | | (a) | York City | W | 3 - 2 | Honour, Doig, Dixon | 2,611 |
| 8 | 24 | | (h) | Cambridge United | W | 3 - 2 | Dixon 2 (2 pens), Toman | 2,357 |
| 9 | 30 | | (a) | Tranmere Rovers | L | 1 - 2 | Dixon | 3,624 |
| 10 | Oct 4 | | (h) | Rochdale | L | 0 - 1 | | 2,363 |
| 11 | 8 | | (a) | Doncaster Rovers | L | 0 - 1 | | 2,091 |
| 12 | 15 | | (h) | Wrexham | L | 1 - 3 | Baker | 2,194 |
| 13 | 22 | | (h) | Crewe Alexandra | L | 0 - 3 | | 1,794 |
| 14 | 24 | | (a) | Stockport County | L | 0 - 3 | | 2,098 |
| 15 | 29 | | (h) | Hereford United | D | 1 - 1 | Barratt | 1,585 |
| 16 | Nov 4 | | (a) | Halifax Town | L | 0 - 1 | | 2,182 |
| 17 | 9 | | (a) | Peterborough United | W | 1 - 0 | Grayson | 3,148 |
| 18 | 12 | | (h) | Grimsby Town | W | 2 - 1 | Grayson, Toman | 1,787 |
| 20 | 26 | | (h) | Exeter City | D | 2 - 2 | Grayson, Smith | 2,107 |
| 22 | Dec 3 | | (a) | Burnley | D | 0 - 0 | | 6,289 |
| 25 | 17 | | (h) | Carlisle United | L | 0 - 2 | | 1,863 |
| 26 | 26 | | (a) | Scunthorpe United | D | 1 - 1 | Allon | 4,595 |
| 27 | 30 | | (a) | Colchester United | W | 2 - 1 | Borthwick, Stokes | 2,359 |
| 28 | Jan 2 | | (h) | Rotherham United | D | 1 - 1 | Grayson | 3,471 |
| 30 | 14 | | (a) | Darlington | D | 0 - 0 | | 3,521 |
| 31 | 21 | | (h) | Lincoln City | W | 3 - 2 | Atkinson 2, Grayson | 2,808 |
| 34 | Feb 4 | | (h) | York City | L | 0 - 1 | | 2,794 |
| 35 | 11 | | (a) | Cambridge United | L | 0 - 6 | | 2,273 |
| 36 | 18 | | (h) | Doncaster Rovers | W | 2 - 1 | Tinkler, Grayson | 1,919 |
| 37 | 28 | | (h) | Stockport County | D | 2 - 2 | Toman, Grayson | 1,598 |
| 38 | Mar 4 | | (a) | Crewe Alexandra | L | 0 - 3 | | 3,981 |
| 39 | 7 | | (a) | Wrexham | L | 3 - 4 | Grayson 2, Baker | 2,438 |
| 40 | 11 | | (h) | Halifax Town | W | 2 - 0 | Grayson, Toman | 1,706 |
| 41 | 15 | | (a) | Hereford United | L | 0 - 2 | | 2,157 |
| 42 | 18 | | (h) | Torquay United | L | 0 - 1 | | 1,351 |
| 43 | 21 | | (a) | Leyton Orient | L | 3 - 4 | Baker 2 (1 pen), Atkinson | 3,408 |
| 44 | 25 | | (a) | Rotherham United | L | 0 - 4 | | 4,889 |
| 45 | 27 | | (h) | Scunthorpe United | L | 0 - 2 | | 1,895 |
| 46 | Apr 1 | | (a) | Carlisle United | L | 1 - 2 | Grayson | 3,158 |
| 47 | 5 | | (a) | Scarborough | L | 0 - 2 | | 2,155 |
| 48 | 8 | | (h) | Colchester United | W | 2 - 1 | Tinkler, Baker | 1,371 |
| 49 | 11 | | (h) | Scarborough | W | 3 - 1 | Allon, Baker (pen), Dalton | 1,845 |
| 50 | 15 | | (h) | Tranmere Rovers | D | 2 - 2 | Baker (pen), McKinnon | 2,355 |
| 51 | 22 | | (a) | Rochdale | D | 0 - 0 | | 1,406 |
| 52 | 29 | | (a) | Exeter City | L | 1 - 2 | Allon | 2,380 |
| 53 | May 1 | | (h) | Peterborough United | W | 2 - 1 | Grayson, Dalton | 1,553 |
| 54 | 6 | | (h) | Burnley | D | 2 - 2 | Grayson, McKinnon | 2,038 |
| 55 | 13 | | (a) | Grimsby Town | L | 0 - 3 | | 3,801 |

Final Position : 19th in Division Four

Apps.
Sub.Apps.
Goals

**FA Cup**

| Match No. | Date | Round | Venue | Opponents | Result | | Scorers | Attendance |
|---|---|---|---|---|---|---|---|---|
| 19 | Nov 19 | R1 | (h) | Wigan Athletic | W | 2 - 0 | Smith, Borthwick | 2,476 |
| 23 | Dec 10 | R2 | (h) | Notts County | W | 1 - 0 | Allon | 3,182 |
| 29 | Jan 7 | R3 | (h) | Bristol City | W | 1 - 0 | Baker (pen) | 4,033 |
| 32 | 28 | R4 | (h) | Bournemouth | D | 1 - 1 | Honour | 6,240 |
| 33 | 31 | R4r | (a) | Bournemouth | L | 2 - 5 | Allon, Toman | 10,142 |

Apps.
Sub.Apps.
Goals

**League Cup**

| Match No. | Date | Round | Venue | Opponents | Result | | Scorers | Attendance |
|---|---|---|---|---|---|---|---|---|
| 2 | Aug 30 | R1/1 | (h) | Sheffield United | D | 2 - 2 | Powell (o.g.), Dixon (pen) | 2,480 |
| 4 | Sep 6 | R1/2 | (a) | Sheffield United | L | 0 - 2* | | 6,577 |

* After extra-time

Apps.
Sub.Apps.
1 own goal Goals

| McKellar | Haigh | McKinnon | Tinkler | Smith | Stokes | Honour | Toman | Borthwick | Dixon | Barratt | Grayson | Doig | Atkinson | Tunks | Baker | Ogden | Norton | Muggleton | Allon | Nobbs | Moverley | Dalton | Barras | Plaskett | McAndrew | Hepple | Locker |
|---|---|---|---|---|---|---|---|---|---|---|---|---|---|---|---|---|---|---|---|---|---|---|---|---|---|---|---|
| 1 | 2 | 3 | 4 | 5 | 6 | 7 | 8 | *9* | 10 | 11 | *12* |  |  |  |  |  |  |  |  |  |  |  |  |  |  |  |  |
| 1 | 2 | 3 | 4 | 5 | 6 | 7 | 8 | *10* | 9 | 11 | *12* |  |  |  |  |  |  |  |  |  |  |  |  |  |  |  |  |
| 1 | 2 | **3** | 4 | 5 | 6 | 7 | 8 | 10 | *9* | 11 | *12* | **14** |  |  |  |  |  |  |  |  |  |  |  |  |  |  |  |
| 1 |  | 3 | 4 | 5 | 6 | 7 | 8 |  | 9 | 2 | 10 | 11 |  |  |  |  |  |  |  |  |  |  |  |  |  |  |  |
| 1 |  | 3 | 4 | 5 | 6 | 7 | 8 | **12** | 9 | 2 | *10* | 11 | **14** |  |  |  |  |  |  |  |  |  |  |  |  |  |  |
|  |  | 3 | 4 | 5 | 6 | 7 | 8 |  | 9 | 2 | 10 | 11 |  | 1 |  |  |  |  |  |  |  |  |  |  |  |  |  |
|  |  | 3 | *4* | 5 | 6 | 7 | 8 |  | 9 | 2 | 10 | 11 |  | 1 | *12* |  |  |  |  |  |  |  |  |  |  |  |  |
|  |  | 3 | 4 |  | 6 | 7 | 8 |  | 9 | 2 | 10 | 11 |  | 1 | 5 |  |  |  |  |  |  |  |  |  |  |  |  |
|  | *12* | 3 | 4 |  | 6 | 7 | 8 |  | 9 | 2 | *10* | **11** |  | 1 | 5 | **14** |  |  |  |  |  |  |  |  |  |  |  |
|  | 5 | 3 | 4 |  | 6 | 7 | 8 |  | 9 | 2 | *12* | *11* |  | 1 | 10 |  |  |  |  |  |  |  |  |  |  |  |  |
|  | *2* | 3 | 4 | 5 | 6 | 7 | 8 |  | 9 | *12* |  | 11 |  |  | 10 |  | 1 |  |  |  |  |  |  |  |  |  |  |
|  | 11 | 3 | 4 | 5 | 6 | 7 | 8 |  | 9 | 2 |  |  |  |  | 10 |  | 1 |  |  |  |  |  |  |  |  |  |  |
|  | 11 | 3 | 4 | 5 | 6 | 7 | 8 |  |  | 2 |  |  |  |  | 10 |  |  | 1 | 9 |  |  |  |  |  |  |  |  |
|  | 11 | 3 | *4* | 5 | 6 | 7 | 8 |  |  | 2 | **12** | **14** |  |  | 10 |  |  | 1 | 9 |  |  |  |  |  |  |  |  |
|  | 2 | 3 |  | 5 |  | 7 | 8 |  | *4* | 11 | 10 | *12* |  |  | 6 |  |  | 1 | 9 |  |  |  |  |  |  |  |  |
|  | 2 | 3 |  | 5 |  | 7 | 8 |  | 4 | 11 | 10 |  |  |  | 6 |  |  | 1 | 9 |  |  |  |  |  |  |  |  |
|  |  | 3 |  | 5 |  | 7 | 8 | 9 |  | *11* | 10 | 4 | *12* |  | 6 |  |  | 1 |  | 2 |  |  |  |  |  |  |  |
|  |  | 3 |  | 5 |  | 7 | 8 |  |  |  | 10 | 4 |  |  | 6 | 11 |  | 1 | 9 | 2 |  |  |  |  |  |  |  |
|  |  | 3 |  |  | 5 | 7 | 8 | *12* |  | 4 | 10 |  | **14** |  | 6 | **11** |  | 1 | *9* | 2 |  |  |  |  |  |  |  |
|  |  | 3 | 4 |  | 5 | 7 | *8* | *12* |  | 11 | 10 |  |  |  | 6 |  |  | 1 | 9 | 2 |  |  |  |  |  |  |  |
|  |  | 3 | 4 |  | 5 | 7 | 8 | 9 |  | 11 | 10 |  |  |  | 6 |  |  |  |  | 2 | 1 |  |  |  |  |  |  |
|  |  | 3 | 4 |  | 5 | 7 | 8 | 9 |  | 11 | 10 |  |  |  | 6 |  |  |  |  | 2 | 1 |  |  |  |  |  |  |
|  |  | 3 | 4 |  | 5 | 7 | 8 |  |  | 11 | 10 |  |  |  | 6 |  |  |  | 9 | 2 | 1 |  |  |  |  |  |  |
|  |  | 3 | 4 |  | 5 | 7 |  |  |  | 2 | 10 |  | 11 |  | 6 | 8 |  |  | 9 |  | 1 |  |  |  |  |  |  |
|  |  | 3 | 4 |  | 5 | 7 | 8 |  |  | 2 | 10 |  | 11 |  | 6 |  |  |  | 9 |  | 1 |  |  |  |  |  |  |
|  |  | 3 | 4 |  | 5 | 7 | 8 |  |  | 11 | *10* | *12* |  |  | 6 |  |  |  | 9 | 2 | 1 |  |  |  |  |  |  |
|  |  | 3 | 4 |  | 5 | 7 | 8 | *12* |  | 11 | 10 | **14** |  |  | 6 |  |  |  | *9* | **2** | 1 |  |  |  |  |  |  |
|  |  | 3 | 4 |  | 5 | 7 | 8 | 9 |  | 2 | 10 | *12* | *11* |  | 6 |  |  |  |  |  | 1 |  |  |  |  |  |  |
|  |  | 3 | 4 |  | 5 | 7 | 8 | *9* |  | 2 | 10 | *12* | **11** |  | 6 |  |  |  |  | **14** | 1 |  |  |  |  |  |  |
|  |  | 3 | 4 |  | 5 | 7 | 8 | 9 |  | 2 | 10 |  |  |  | 6 |  |  |  |  |  | 1 | 11 |  |  |  |  |  |
|  |  | 3 | 4 |  |  | 7 | 8 | 9 |  | 2 | 10 |  |  |  | 6 |  |  |  |  | *5* | 1 | 11 | *12* |  |  |  |  |
|  |  | 3 | 4 |  | 5 | 7 | 8 | *9* |  | 2 | 10 | *12* |  |  | 6 |  |  |  |  |  | 1 | 11 |  |  |  |  |  |
|  |  | 3 | 4 |  | 5 | 7 | 8 | 9 |  | 2 |  | *10* |  |  | 6 |  |  |  |  |  | 1 | 11 | *12* |  |  |  |  |
|  |  | 3 | 4 |  | 5 | *7* | 8 | 9 |  |  |  |  | *12* |  | 6 |  |  |  |  |  | 1 | 11 | 10 | 2 |  |  |  |
|  |  | 3 | **4** |  | 5 |  | 8 |  |  |  | *10* |  | 7 |  | 9 | **14** |  |  |  |  | 1 | 11 |  | 2 | 6 | *12* |  |
|  |  | 3 | 4 |  | 5 |  | 8 |  |  |  | 10 |  |  |  | 9 | 7 | 1 |  |  |  |  | 11 |  | 2 | 6 |  |  |
|  |  | 3 | 4 |  | 5 |  | 8 |  |  |  | 10 |  |  |  | 9 |  | 1 |  | 7 |  |  | 11 |  | 2 | 6 |  |  |
|  |  | 3 | 4 |  | 5 |  | 8 |  |  |  | 10 |  |  |  | 9 |  | 1 |  | 7 |  |  | 11 |  | 2 | 6 |  |  |
|  |  | 3 | 4 |  | 5 |  | 8 |  |  |  | *10* |  | *12* |  | 9 |  |  |  | 7 | 6 | 1 | 11 |  | 2 |  |  |  |
|  |  | 3 | 4 |  | 5 |  | 8 |  |  |  | 10 |  |  |  | 9 |  |  |  | 7 | 6 | 1 | 11 |  | 2 |  |  |  |
|  |  | 3 | 4 |  | 5 |  | 8 |  |  |  | 10 |  |  |  | 9 |  |  |  | 7 | 6 | 1 | 11 |  | 2 |  |  |  |
|  |  | 3 | 4 |  | *5* |  | 8 |  |  |  | 10 |  | *12* |  | 9 |  |  |  | 7 | 6 | 1 | 11 |  | 2 |  |  |  |
|  |  | 3 | *4* | 5 |  |  | 8 |  |  |  | 10 |  |  |  | 9 | *12* |  |  | 7 | 6 | 1 | 11 |  | 2 |  |  |  |
|  |  | 3 |  | 5 |  |  | 8 |  |  |  | 10 |  |  |  | 9 | 4 |  |  | 7 | 6 | 1 | 11 |  | 2 |  |  |  |
|  |  | 3 |  | *5* |  |  | 8 | *12* |  |  | 10 |  | **14** |  | 9 | **4** |  |  | 7 | 6 | 1 | 11 |  | 2 |  |  |  |
|  |  | *3* |  | 5 |  |  | 8 | 6 |  |  | 10 |  | 7 |  | 9 | 4 |  |  |  |  | 1 | 11 |  |  |  | 2 | *12* |
| 5 | 10 | 46 | 38 | 19 | 37 | 34 | 45 | 14 | 14 | 31 | 36 | 11 | 6 | 5 | 39 | 7 | 5 | 8 | 21 | 17 | 23 | 17 | 1 | 12 | 4 | 1 |  |
|  | 1 |  |  |  |  |  |  | 5 |  | 1 | 5 | 8 | 7 |  | 1 | 3 |  |  |  | 1 |  |  | 2 |  |  | 1 | 1 |
|  |  | 2 | 3 | 2 | 1 | 1 | 6 | 1 | 4 | 1 | 13 | 1 | 3 |  | 7 |  |  |  | 3 |  |  | 2 |  |  |  |  |  |

| McKellar | Haigh | McKinnon | Tinkler | Smith | Stokes | Honour | Toman | Borthwick | Dixon | Barratt | Grayson | Doig | Atkinson | Tunks | Baker | Ogden | Norton | Muggleton | Allon | Nobbs | Moverley | Dalton | Barras | Plaskett | McAndrew | Hepple | Locker |
|---|---|---|---|---|---|---|---|---|---|---|---|---|---|---|---|---|---|---|---|---|---|---|---|---|---|---|---|
|  | 2 | 3 |  | 5 |  | 7 | 8 | 9 | 4 | 11 | 10 |  |  |  | 6 |  | 1 |  |  |  |  |  |  |  |  |  |  |
|  |  | 3 |  | 5 |  | 7 | 8 |  |  | 4 | 10 |  |  |  | 6 | 11 |  |  | 9 | 2 | 1 |  |  |  |  |  |  |
|  |  | 3 | 4 |  | 5 | 7 | 8 | *9* |  | 11 | 10 |  |  |  | 6 |  |  |  | *12* | 2 | 1 |  |  |  |  |  |  |
|  |  | 3 | 4 |  | 5 | 7 | 8 |  |  | 2 | 10 | *12* | *11* |  | 6 |  |  |  | 9 |  | 1 |  |  |  |  |  |  |
|  |  | 3 | 4 |  | 5 | 7 | 8 |  |  | 2 | 10 |  | 11 |  | 6 |  |  |  | 9 |  | 1 |  |  |  |  |  |  |
|  | 1 | 5 | 3 | 2 | 3 | 5 | 5 | 2 | 1 | 5 | 5 |  | 2 |  | 5 | 1 | 1 |  | 3 | 2 | 4 |  |  |  |  |  |  |
|  |  |  |  |  |  |  |  |  |  |  |  | 1 |  |  |  |  |  |  | 1 |  |  |  |  |  |  |  |  |
|  |  |  |  | 1 |  | 1 | 1 | 1 |  |  |  |  |  |  | 1 |  |  |  | 2 |  |  |  |  |  |  |  |  |

| McKellar | Haigh | McKinnon | Tinkler | Smith | Stokes | Honour | Toman | Borthwick | Dixon | Barratt | Grayson | Doig | Atkinson | Tunks | Baker | Ogden | Norton | Muggleton | Allon | Nobbs | Moverley | Dalton | Barras | Plaskett | McAndrew | Hepple | Locker |
|---|---|---|---|---|---|---|---|---|---|---|---|---|---|---|---|---|---|---|---|---|---|---|---|---|---|---|---|
| 1 | 2 | 3 | **4** | 5 | 6 | 7 | 8 | 10 | 9 | *11* | *12* |  |  |  |  |  |  |  |  | **14** |  |  |  |  |  |  |  |
| 1 | 2 | 3 |  | 5 | 6 | 7 | 8 | *10* | 4 | **11** | 9 |  | *12* |  |  | **14** |  |  |  |  |  |  |  |  |  |  |  |
| 2 | 2 | 2 | 1 | 2 | 2 | 2 | 2 | 2 | 2 | 2 | 1 |  |  |  |  |  |  |  |  |  |  |  |  |  |  |  |  |
|  |  |  |  |  |  |  |  |  |  |  | 1 |  | 1 |  |  | 1 |  |  |  | 1 |  |  |  |  |  |  |  |
|  |  |  |  |  |  |  |  |  | 1 |  |  |  |  |  |  |  |  |  |  |  |  |  |  |  |  |  |  |

## League Table

|  | P | W | D | L | F | A | Pts |
|---|---|---|---|---|---|---|---|
| Rotherham United | 46 | 22 | 16 | 8 | 76 | 35 | 82 |
| Tranmere Rovers | 46 | 21 | 17 | 8 | 62 | 43 | 80 |
| Crewe Alexandra | 46 | 21 | 15 | 10 | 67 | 48 | 78 |
| Scunthorpe United | 46 | 21 | 14 | 11 | 77 | 57 | 77 |
| Scarborough | 46 | 21 | 14 | 11 | 67 | 52 | 77 |
| Leyton Orient | 46 | 21 | 12 | 13 | 86 | 50 | 75 |
| Wrexham | 46 | 19 | 14 | 13 | 77 | 63 | 71 |
| Cambridge United | 46 | 18 | 14 | 14 | 71 | 62 | 68 |
| Grimsby Town | 46 | 17 | 15 | 14 | 65 | 59 | 66 |
| Lincoln City | 46 | 18 | 10 | 18 | 64 | 60 | 64 |
| York City | 46 | 17 | 13 | 16 | 62 | 63 | 64 |
| Carlisle United | 46 | 15 | 15 | 16 | 53 | 52 | 60 |
| Exeter City | 46 | 18 | 6 | 22 | 65 | 68 | 60 |
| Torquay United | 46 | 17 | 8 | 21 | 45 | 60 | 59 |
| Hereford United | 46 | 14 | 16 | 16 | 66 | 72 | 58 |
| Burnley | 46 | 14 | 13 | 19 | 52 | 61 | 55 |
| Peterborough United | 46 | 14 | 12 | 20 | 52 | 74 | 54 |
| Rochdale | 46 | 13 | 14 | 19 | 56 | 82 | 53 |
| Hartlepool United | 46 | 14 | 10 | 22 | 50 | 78 | 52 |
| Stockport County | 46 | 10 | 21 | 15 | 54 | 52 | 51 |
| Halifax Town | 46 | 13 | 11 | 22 | 69 | 75 | 50 |
| Colchester United | 46 | 12 | 14 | 20 | 60 | 78 | 50 |
| Doncaster Rovers | 46 | 13 | 10 | 23 | 49 | 78 | 49 |
| Darlington | 46 | 8 | 18 | 20 | 53 | 76 | 42 |

# 1989-90

## Division Four

Managers: Bobby Moncur and Cyril Knowles

### Did you know that?

Throughout the season, 'Pools used a record 41 players, including seven goalkeepers: Berryman, Bowling, Carr, Dearden, Moverley, Priestley and Siddall.

Although his time as manager was not a success, Bob Moncur signed Joe Allon and Paul Dalton as well as giving a League debut to Don Hutchison. These three players were later sold for transfer fees totalling several hundred thousand pounds.

| Match No. | Date | Round | Venue | Opponents | Result | | Scorers | Attendance |
|---|---|---|---|---|---|---|---|---|
| 1 | Aug 19 | | (a) | Halifax Town | L | 0 - 4 | | 1,686 |
| 3 | 26 | | (h) | Exeter City | L | 0 - 3 | | 1,618 |
| 5 | Sep 1 | | (a) | Southend United | L | 0 - 3 | | 3,236 |
| 6 | 9 | | (h) | Gillingham | L | 1 - 2 | Dalton | 1,379 |
| 7 | 15 | | (a) | Stockport County | L | 0 - 6 | | 3,884 |
| 8 | 23 | | (h) | Peterborough United | D | 2 - 2 | Allon, Baker | 1,760 |
| 9 | 26 | | (a) | Rochdale | D | 0 - 0 | | 1,511 |
| 10 | 30 | | (h) | Doncaster Rovers | L | 0 - 6 | | 1,757 |
| 11 | Oct 7 | | (h) | Scunthorpe United | W | 3 - 2 | Baker, McEwan (pen), Tinkler | 1,815 |
| 12 | 14 | | (a) | Burnley | D | 0 - 0 | | 7,450 |
| 13 | 17 | | (a) | Torquay United | L | 3 - 4 | Allon 2, Hutchison | 2,108 |
| 14 | 21 | | (h) | York City | L | 1 - 2 | Dalton | 2,252 |
| 15 | 28 | | (a) | Carlisle United | L | 0 - 1 | | 3,699 |
| 16 | 31 | | (h) | Cambridge United | L | 1 - 2 | Hutchison | 1,695 |
| 17 | Nov 4 | | (h) | Wrexham | W | 3 - 0 | McEwan (pen), Allon, Dalton | 1,724 |
| 19 | 11 | | (a) | Aldershot | L | 1 - 6 | Smith | 2,137 |
| 21 | 25 | | (a) | Chesterfield | L | 1 - 3 | Baker | 3,488 |
| 23 | Dec 2 | | (h) | Hereford United | L | 1 - 2 | Dalton | 1,491 |
| 24 | 16 | | (a) | Maidstone United | L | 2 - 4 | Baker, Doig | 1,501 |
| 25 | 26 | | (h) | Scarborough | W | 4 - 1 | Smith, Baker, Bennyworth, Kamara (o.g.) | 3,698 |
| 26 | 30 | | (h) | Grimsby Town | W | 4 - 2 | Dalton 2, Bennyworth, Allon | 3,418 |
| 27 | Jan 1 | | (a) | Colchester United | L | 1 - 3 | Dalton | 3,826 |
| 28 | 6 | | (h) | Lincoln City | D | 1 - 1 | McKinnon | 2,499 |
| 29 | 13 | | (a) | Exeter City | L | 1 - 3 | Allon | 4,959 |
| 30 | 20 | | (h) | Halifax Town | W | 2 - 0 | Allon, Smith | 2,409 |
| 31 | 27 | | (a) | Gillingham | D | 0 - 0 | | 3,690 |
| 32 | Feb 7 | | (a) | Peterborough United | W | 2 - 0 | Allon, Tinkler | 2,813 |
| 33 | 10 | | (h) | Stockport County | W | 5 - 0 | Baker 4, Macdonald | 2,938 |
| 34 | 13 | | (h) | Southend United | D | 1 - 1 | Allon | 3,578 |
| 35 | 17 | | (a) | Hereford United | L | 1 - 4 | Baker | 2,049 |
| 36 | 24 | | (h) | Chesterfield | W | 3 - 1 | Baker, Dalton, Allon | 2,907 |
| 37 | Mar 3 | | (a) | Lincoln City | L | 1 - 4 | Allon | 3,503 |
| 38 | 6 | | (a) | Doncaster Rovers | D | 2 - 2 | Smith, Allon | 2,518 |
| 39 | 10 | | (h) | Rochdale | W | 2 - 1 | Brown (o.g.), Tupling | 2,771 |
| 40 | 17 | | (a) | Scunthorpe United | W | 1 - 0 | Dalton | 3,868 |
| 41 | 20 | | (h) | Burnley | W | 3 - 0 | Baker, Olsson, Dalton | 3,187 |
| 42 | 24 | | (h) | Torquay United | D | 1 - 1 | Allon | 2,723 |
| 43 | 31 | | (a) | York City | D | 1 - 1 | P.Atkinson | 2,891 |
| 44 | Apr 7 | | (h) | Carlisle United | W | 1 - 0 | Allon | 3,724 |
| 45 | 10 | | (a) | Cambridge United | L | 1 - 2 | Smith | 3,254 |
| 46 | 14 | | (h) | Colchester United | L | 0 - 2 | | 3,407 |
| 47 | 16 | | (a) | Scarborough | L | 1 - 4 | Baker | 2,762 |
| 48 | 21 | | (h) | Maidstone United | W | 4 - 2 | Berry (o.g.), Allon 2, Baker | 2,177 |
| 49 | 24 | | (a) | Grimsby Town | D | 0 - 0 | | 8,687 |
| 50 | 28 | | (h) | Aldershot | W | 2 - 0 | Dalton, Baker | 2,638 |
| 51 | May 5 | | (a) | Wrexham | W | 2 - 1 | Allon, Olsson | 2,759 |
| Final Position : 19th in Division Four | | | | | | | | Apps. |
| | | | | | | | | Sub.Apps. |
| | | | | | | | 3 own goals | Goals |

**FA Cup**

| Match No. | Date | Round | Venue | Opponents | Result | | Scorers | Attendance |
|---|---|---|---|---|---|---|---|---|
| 20 | Nov 18 | R1 | (h) | Huddersfield Town | L | 0 - 2 | | 3,160 |
| | | | | | | | | Apps. |
| | | | | | | | | Sub.Apps. |
| | | | | | | | | Goals |

**League Cup**

| Match No. | Date | Round | Venue | Opponents | Result | | Scorers | Attendance |
|---|---|---|---|---|---|---|---|---|
| 2 | Aug 23 | R1/1 | (h) | York City | D | 3 - 3 | Grayson 2, Baker | 1,507 |
| 4 | 29 | R1/2 | (a) | York City | L | 1 - 4 | Dalton | 2,236 |
| | | | | | | | | Apps. |
| | | | | | | | | Sub.Apps. |
| | | | | | | | | Goals |

| Bowling | Barras | McKinnon | Tinkler | Stokes | Stokle | Atkinson, P.D. | Ogden | Baker | Grayson | Dalton | Curry | Carr | Nobbs | Doig | Davies | Allon | Spiers | Dearden | McEwan | Dunbar | Plaskett | Entwhistle | Lamb | Smith | Trewick | Hutchison | Williams | Moverley | Sinclair | McStay | Priestley | Olsson | Bennyworth | Tupling | MacDonald | Honour | Siddall | Atkinson, P. | Berryman | Wilson |
|---|---|---|---|---|---|---|---|---|---|---|---|---|---|---|---|---|---|---|---|---|---|---|---|---|---|---|---|---|---|---|---|---|---|---|---|---|---|---|---|---|
| 1 | 2 | 3 | 4 | 5 | 6 | 7 | 8 | 9 | 10 | 11 | 12 | | | | | | | | | | | | | | | | | | | | | | | | | | | | | |
| | 6 | 3 | 4 | | | 13 | | 5 | 10 | 11 | | 1 | 2 | 7 | 8 | 9 | 12 | | | | | | | | | | | | | | | | | | | | | | | |
| | 6 | 3 | 4 | | | | | 9 | | 11 | | | 2 | | 8 | 7 | | 1 | 5 | 10 | | | | | | | | | | | | | | | | | | | | |
| | 6 | 3 | 4 | | | 12 | | 9 | | 11 | | | 8 | | | 7 | | 1 | 5 | | 2 | 10 | | | | | | | | | | | | | | | | | | |
| | 6 | 3 | 4 | | | | 8 | 9 | | 11 | | | | | | 7 | | 1 | 5 | | 2 | 10 | | | | | | | | | | | | | | | | | | |
| | 6 | 3 | 4 | | | 12 | | 9 | | 11 | | | 5 | | | 7 | | 1 | 8 | | 2 | | 10 | | | | | | | | | | | | | | | | | |
| | 6 | 3 | 4 | | | | | 9 | | 11 | | | 5 | | | 7 | | 1 | 8 | | 2 | | 10 | | | | | | | | | | | | | | | | | |
| | 6 | 3 | 4 | | | | | 9 | | 11 | | | 5 | | | 7 | | 1 | 8 | | 2 | | 10 | | | | | | | | | | | | | | | | | |
| | | 3 | 4 | | | | | 9 | | 11 | | | 2 | | | 7 | | 1 | 6 | | | | | 5 | 8 | 10 | | | | | | | | | | | | | | |
| | | 3 | 4 | | | 12 | | 9 | | 11 | | | | | | 7 | | 1 | 2 | | | | | 5 | 8 | 10 | 6 | | | | | | | | | | | | | |
| | | 3 | 4 | | | 12 | | 9 | | 11 | | | | | | 7 | | 1 | 2 | | | | | 5 | 8 | 10 | 6 | | | | | | | | | | | | | |
| | | 3 | 4 | | | 9 | | | | 11 | | | | | | 7 | | 1 | 2 | | | | | 5 | 8 | 10 | 6 | | | | | | | | | | | | | |
| | | 3 | 4 | | | | | | | 11 | | | | | | 7 | | | 2 | | 9 | | 12 | 5 | 8 | 10 | 6 | 1 | | | | | | | | | | | | |
| | | 3 | 4 | | | 9 | | | | 11 | | | | | | 7 | | | 5 | | 2 | | 12 | | 8 | 10 | 6 | 1 | | | | | | | | | | | | |
| | | 3 | 4 | | | | | 2 | | 11 | | | | | | 7 | | | 6 | | | | 12 | 5 | 8 | 10 | 9 | 1 | | | | | | | | | | | | |
| | 13 | 3 | | | | | | 2 | | 11 | | | | | | 7 | | | 6 | | 12 | | 9 | 5 | 8 | 10 | | 1 | 4 | | | | | | | | | | | |
| | | 3 | 4 | | | | | 9 | | 11 | | | | | | 7 | | | | | | | | 5 | | 10 | 6 | 1 | 8 | 2 | | | | | | | | | | |
| | | 3 | 4 | | | | | 9 | | 11 | | | 6 | | | 7 | | | | | | | | 5 | | 10 | 12 | 1 | 8 | 2 | | | | | | | | | | |
| | | 3 | 4 | | | | | 9 | | 11 | | | 6 | 8 | | 7 | | | | | | | 12 | 5 | | | | | 10 | 2 | 1 | | | | | | | | | |
| | | 3 | 4 | | | | | 9 | | 11 | | | 10 | 13 | | 7 | | | | | | | | 5 | | 12 | | | | | 1 | 2 | 6 | 8 | | | | | | |
| | | 3 | 4 | | | | | 9 | | 11 | | | 10 | | | 7 | | | | | | | | 5 | | | | | | | 1 | 2 | 6 | 8 | 12 | | | | | |
| | | 3 | 4 | | | | | 9 | | 11 | | | 10 | | | 7 | | | | | | | | 5 | | | | | | | 1 | 2 | 6 | 8 | 12 | | | | | |
| | | 3 | 4 | | | | | 9 | | 11 | | | 10 | | | 7 | | | | | | | | 5 | | | | | | | 1 | 2 | 6 | 8 | 12 | | | | | |
| | | 3 | 4 | | | | | 9 | | 11 | | | 10 | | | 7 | | | | | | | 12 | 5 | | | | | | | 1 | 2 | 6 | 8 | | 13 | | | | |
| | | 3 | 4 | | | | | 9 | | 11 | | | 10 | | | 7 | | | | | | | | 5 | | | | | | | 1 | | 6 | 8 | 2 | 12 | | | | |
| | | 3 | 4 | | | | | 9 | | 12 | | | 10 | | | 7 | | | | | | | | 5 | | | | | | | 1 | 11 | 6 | 8 | 2 | 13 | | | | |
| | | 3 | 4 | | | | | 9 | | 12 | | | 10 | | | 7 | | | | | | | | 5 | | | | | | | 1 | 13 | 6 | 8 | 2 | 11 | | | | |
| | | 3 | 4 | | | | | 9 | | 11 | | | 10 | | | 7 | | | | | | | | 5 | | | | | | | 1 | 13 | 6 | 8 | 2 | 12 | | | | |
| | | 3 | 4 | | | | | 9 | | 11 | | | 10 | | | 7 | | | | | | | | 5 | | | | | | | 1 | 8 | 6 | | 2 | 12 | | | | |
| | | 3 | 4 | | | | | 9 | | 12 | | | 10 | | | 7 | | | | | | | | 5 | | | | | | | 1 | 13 | 6 | 8 | 2 | 11 | | | | |
| | | 3 | 4 | | | | | 9 | | 10 | | | 2 | | | 7 | | | | | | | | 5 | | | | | | | 1 | | 6 | 8 | | 11 | | | | |
| | | 3 | 4 | | | | | 9 | | 10 | | | | 12 | | 7 | | | | | | | | 5 | | | | | | | 1 | 2 | 6 | 8 | | 11 | | | | |
| | | 3 | 4 | | | | | 9 | | 10 | | | 2 | | | 7 | | | | | | | | 5 | | | | | | | 1 | 11 | 6 | 8 | | | | | | |
| | | 3 | 4 | | | | | 9 | | 10 | | | 2 | 12 | | 7 | | | | | | | | 5 | | | | | | | 1 | | 6 | 8 | 11 | | | | | |
| | | 3 | 4 | | | | | 9 | | 10 | | | 2 | | | 7 | | | | | | | | 5 | | | | | | | | 11 | 6 | 8 | | | 1 | | | |
| | | 3 | 4 | | | | | 9 | | 10 | | | 2 | | | 7 | | | | | | | 12 | 5 | | | | | | | | 11 | 6 | 8 | | | 1 | 13 | | |
| | | 3 | 4 | | | | | 9 | | 10 | | | 2 | | | 7 | | | | | | | | 5 | | | | | | | | 11 | 6 | 8 | | | 1 | 12 | | |
| | | 3 | 4 | | | | | 9 | | 10 | | | 2 | | | 7 | | | | | | | | 5 | | | | | | | | 11 | 6 | 8 | | | 1 | 12 | | |
| | | 3 | 4 | | | | | 9 | | 10 | | | 2 | | | 7 | | | | | | | | 5 | | | | | | | | | 6 | 8 | | | 1 | 11 | | |
| | | 3 | 4 | | | | | 9 | | 13 | | | | | | 7 | | | | | | | | 5 | | 10 | | | | | | 11 | 6 | 8 | 2 | | | 12 | 1 | |
| | | 3 | 4 | | | | | 9 | | 10 | | | | | | 7 | | | | | | | | | | | | | | | | 2 | 6 | 8 | 5 | | 1 | 11 | | 12 |
| | | 3 | 4 | | | | | 9 | | 10 | | | | | 5 | 7 | | | | | | | | | | 11 | | | | | | 2 | 6 | 8 | 13 | | 1 | 12 | | |
| | | 3 | 4 | | | | | 9 | | 12 | | | 2 | | | 7 | | | | | | | | 5 | | | | | | | | 10 | 6 | 8 | 13 | | 1 | 11 | | |
| | | 3 | 4 | | | | | 9 | | | | | 2 | | | 7 | | | | | | | | 5 | | | | | | | | 10 | 6 | 8 | | | 1 | 11 | | |
| | | 3 | 4 | | | | | 9 | | 11 | | | 2 | | | 7 | | | | | | | | 5 | | | | | | | | 10 | 6 | 8 | 13 | | 1 | 12 | | |
| | | 3 | 4 | | | | | 9 | | 11 | | | 2 | | | 7 | | | | | | | | 5 | | | | | | | | 12 | 6 | 8 | 13 | | 1 | 10 | | |
| 1 | 8 | 46 | 45 | 1 | 1 | 3 | 2 | 43 | 2 | 40 | | 1 | 32 | 2 | 3 | 45 | | 10 | 14 | 1 | 7 | 2 | 4 | 35 | 8 | 12 | 7 | 6 | 4 | 3 | 16 | 19 | 27 | 26 | 6 | 4 | 11 | 5 | 1 | |
| | 1 | | | | | 5 | | | | 5 | 1 | | | 3 | | | 1 | | | | 1 | | 6 | | | 1 | 1 | | | | | 4 | | | 7 | 5 | | 6 | | 1 |
| | | 1 | 2 | | | | | 15 | | 11 | | | | 1 | | 17 | | | 2 | | | | | 5 | | 2 | | | | | | 2 | 2 | 1 | 1 | | | 1 | | |
| | | | | | | | | | | | | | | | | | | | | | | | | | | | | | | | | | | | | | | | | |
| | 6 | 3 | 4 | | | 13 | | 9 | | 11 | | | | | | 7 | | | 2 | | | | 12 | | | 10 | 5 | 1 | 8 | | | | | | | | | | | |
| | 1 | 1 | 1 | | | | | 1 | | 1 | | | | | | 1 | | | 1 | | | | | | | 1 | 1 | 1 | 1 | | | | | | | | | | | |
| | | | | | | 1 | | | | | | | | | | | | | | | | | 1 | | | | | | | | | | | | | | | | | |
| | | | | | | | | | | | | | | | | | | | | | | | | | | | | | | | | | | | | | | | | |
| | | | | | | | | | | | | | | | | | | | | | | | | | | | | | | | | | | | | | | | | |
| | 5 | 3 | 4 | | 6 | | | 9 | 10 | 11 | | 1 | 2 | 7 | 8 | | | | | | | | | | | | | | | | | | | | | | | | | |
| | 6 | 3 | 4 | | | | | 9 | | 11 | | 1 | 2 | 12 | 8 | 7 | 10 | | 5 | | | | | | | | | | | | | | | | | | | | | |
| | 2 | 2 | 2 | | 1 | | | 2 | 1 | 2 | | 2 | 2 | 1 | 2 | 1 | 1 | | 1 | | | | | | | | | | | | | | | | | | | | | |
| | | | | | | | | | | | | | | 1 | | | | | | | | | | | | | | | | | | | | | | | | | | |
| | | | | | | | | 1 | 2 | 1 | | | | | | | | | | | | | | | | | | | | | | | | | | | | | | |

## League Table

| | P | W | D | L | F | A | Pts |
|---|---|---|---|---|---|---|---|
| Exeter City | 46 | 28 | 5 | 13 | 83 | 48 | 89 |
| Grimsby Town | 46 | 22 | 13 | 11 | 70 | 47 | 79 |
| Southend United | 46 | 22 | 9 | 15 | 61 | 48 | 75 |
| Stockport County | 46 | 21 | 11 | 14 | 68 | 62 | 74 |
| Maidstone United | 46 | 22 | 7 | 17 | 77 | 61 | 73 |
| Cambridge United | 46 | 21 | 10 | 15 | 76 | 66 | 73 |
| Chesterfield | 46 | 19 | 14 | 13 | 63 | 50 | 71 |
| Carlisle United | 46 | 21 | 8 | 17 | 61 | 60 | 71 |
| Peterborough United | 46 | 17 | 17 | 12 | 59 | 46 | 68 |
| Lincoln City | 46 | 18 | 14 | 14 | 48 | 48 | 68 |
| Scunthorpe United | 46 | 17 | 15 | 14 | 69 | 54 | 66 |
| Rochdale | 46 | 20 | 6 | 20 | 52 | 55 | 66 |
| York City | 46 | 16 | 16 | 14 | 55 | 53 | 64 |
| Gillingham | 46 | 17 | 11 | 18 | 46 | 48 | 62 |
| Torquay United | 46 | 15 | 12 | 19 | 53 | 66 | 57 |
| Burnley | 46 | 14 | 14 | 18 | 45 | 55 | 56 |
| Hereford United | 46 | 15 | 10 | 21 | 56 | 62 | 55 |
| Scarborough | 46 | 15 | 10 | 21 | 60 | 73 | 55 |
| Hartlepool United | 46 | 15 | 10 | 21 | 66 | 88 | 55 |
| Doncaster Rovers | 46 | 14 | 9 | 23 | 53 | 60 | 51 |
| Wrexham | 46 | 13 | 12 | 21 | 51 | 67 | 51 |
| Aldershot | 46 | 12 | 14 | 20 | 49 | 69 | 50 |
| Halifax Town | 46 | 12 | 13 | 21 | 57 | 65 | 49 |
| Colchester United | 46 | 11 | 10 | 25 | 48 | 75 | 43 |

# 1990-91

## Division Four

Managers: Cyril Knowles and Alan Murray

### Did you know that?

'Pools gained only their second-ever promotion by finishing in third place with 82 points. At the beginning of October they were in 23rd position, having won only one of their opening six League games.

Joe Allon, Paul Baker and Paul Dalton were magnificent, playing in every game, 55 in total. Allon scored 28 League goals, equalling Billy Robinson's record, and 35 in total, a new record for a Hartlepool player.

| Match No. | Date | Round | Venue | Opponents | | Result | Scorers | Attendance |
|---|---|---|---|---|---|---|---|---|
| 1 | Aug 25 | | (a) | Chesterfield | W | 3 - 2 | Tupling, Baker, Fletcher | 3,821 |
| 3 | Sep 1 | | (h) | Cardiff City | L | 0 - 2 | | 2,897 |
| 4 | 8 | | (a) | Gillingham | L | 0 - 3 | | 3,180 |
| 6 | 18 | | (h) | Rochdale | D | 2 - 2 | Dalton, O'Shaughnessy (o.g.) | 5,725 |
| 7 | 22 | | (a) | Carlisle United | L | 0 - 1 | | 3,303 |
| 9 | 29 | | (a) | Blackpool | L | 0 - 2 | | 4,092 |
| 10 | Oct 2 | | (h) | Aldershot | W | 1 - 0 | Allon | 1,916 |
| 11 | 6 | | (h) | Maidstone United | W | 1 - 0 | Dalton | 2,069 |
| 13 | 13 | | (a) | Doncaster Rovers | D | 2 - 2 | Place (o.g.), Allon | 2,801 |
| 14 | 16 | | (h) | York City | L | 0 - 1 | | 2,746 |
| 15 | 20 | | (a) | Wrexham | D | 2 - 2 | Smith, Hutchison | 1,733 |
| 16 | 23 | | (h) | Peterborough United | W | 2 - 0 | Allon, Baker | 2,190 |
| 17 | 27 | | (h) | Hereford United | W | 2 - 1 | Allon (pen), Olsson | 2,139 |
| 18 | Nov 3 | | (a) | Northampton Town | L | 2 - 3 | Fletcher, Baker | 3,342 |
| 19 | 10 | | (a) | Darlington | W | 1 - 0 | Allon | 5,113 |
| 21 | 24 | | (h) | Scarborough | W | 2 - 0 | Baker, Tinkler | 2,122 |
| 23 | Dec 1 | | (a) | Torquay United | W | 1 - 0 | Allon | 2,835 |
| 25 | 15 | | (h) | Lincoln City | W | 2 - 0 | Allon 2 | 2,055 |
| 27 | 22 | | (a) | Burnley | L | 0 - 4 | | 8,514 |
| 28 | Jan 1 | | (a) | Halifax Town | W | 2 - 1 | Allon 2 | 1,707 |
| 29 | 12 | | (a) | Cardiff City | L | 0 - 1 | | 2,619 |
| 30 | 19 | | (h) | Chesterfield | W | 2 - 0 | Allon, Tupling | 2,134 |
| 32 | 26 | | (a) | York City | D | 0 - 0 | | 3,089 |
| 33 | 29 | | (h) | Stockport County | W | 3 - 1 | Baker, Allon 2 | 2,384 |
| 34 | Feb 5 | | (h) | Carlisle United | W | 4 - 1 | Allon 2 (1 pen), Honour, Dalton | 2,670 |
| 35 | 16 | | (a) | Scarborough | L | 0 - 2 | | 1,804 |
| 36 | 23 | | (h) | Darlington | D | 0 - 0 | | 6,100 |
| 37 | 26 | | (a) | Scunthorpe United | L | 1 - 2 | Allon (pen) | 2,220 |
| 38 | Mar 2 | | (h) | Torquay United | D | 0 - 0 | | 2,209 |
| 39 | 9 | | (a) | Lincoln City | L | 1 - 3 | Allon | 2,575 |
| 40 | 12 | | (a) | Aldershot | W | 5 - 1 | Dalton 3, Allon, Tinkler | 1,579 |
| 41 | 16 | | (h) | Blackpool | L | 1 - 2 | McKinnon | 2,840 |
| 42 | 23 | | (a) | Maidstone United | W | 4 - 1 | Honour 2, Dalton, Baker | 1,704 |
| 43 | 26 | | (h) | Walsall | W | 2 - 1 | Allon 2 | 2,556 |
| 44 | 29 | | (a) | Stockport County | W | 3 - 1 | Baker, Allon 2 | 5,217 |
| 45 | Apr 1 | | (h) | Burnley | D | 0 - 0 | | 4,967 |
| 46 | 6 | | (a) | Walsall | W | 1 - 0 | Allon | 2,758 |
| 47 | 9 | | (h) | Scunthorpe United | W | 2 - 0 | Dalton, Baker | 3,040 |
| 48 | 13 | | (h) | Halifax Town | W | 2 - 1 | Baker, Allon | 3,195 |
| 49 | 16 | | (h) | Doncaster Rovers | D | 1 - 1 | MacPhail | 3,363 |
| 50 | 20 | | (h) | Wrexham | W | 2 - 1 | Allon, Baker | 3,077 |
| 51 | 23 | | (a) | Rochdale | D | 0 - 0 | | 1,686 |
| 52 | 27 | | (a) | Peterborough United | D | 1 - 1 | Allon | 7,636 |
| 53 | 30 | | (h) | Gillingham | W | 1 - 0 | Allon | 3,782 |
| 54 | May 4 | | (a) | Hereford United | W | 3 - 1 | Baker, Dalton 2 | 2,387 |
| 55 | 11 | | (h) | Northampton Town | W | 3 - 1 | Dalton, Allon, Baker | 6,957 |

Final Position: 3rd in Division Four - Promoted

Apps.
Sub.Apps.
2 own goals Goals

**FA Cup**

| Match No. | Date | Round | Venue | Opponents | | Result | Scorers | Attendance |
|---|---|---|---|---|---|---|---|---|
| 20 | Nov 17 | R1 | (a) | Runcorn | W | 3 - 0 | Allon 3 | 1,695 |
| 24 | Dec 8 | R2 | (a) | Wigan Athletic | L | 0 - 2 | | 2,492 |

Apps.
Sub.Apps.
Goals

**League Cup**

| Match No. | Date | Round | Venue | Opponents | | Result | Scorers | Attendance |
|---|---|---|---|---|---|---|---|---|
| 2 | Aug 28 | R1/1 | (a) | Chesterfield | W | 2 - 1 | Allon, Honour | 2,934 |
| 5 | Sep 11 | R1/2 | (h) | Chesterfield | D | 2 - 2 | Allon, Baker | 2,911 |
| 8 | 26 | R2/1 | (a) | Tottenham Hotspur | L | 0 - 5 | | 19,760 |
| 12 | Oct 9 | R2/2 | (h) | Tottenham Hotspur | L | 1 - 2 | Dalton | 9,631 |

Apps.
Sub.Apps.
Goals

| Cox | Olsson | McKinnon | Tinkler | Smith | Bennyworth | Allon | Tupling | Baker | Fletcher | Dalton | Honour | Nobbs | Duggan | Hutchison | Harbron | MacPhail | Shotton | MacDonald | Dunbar | Davies, K. | Davies, A. | Lamb | Heaney | Poole | Gabbiadini | Nesbitt |
|---|---|---|---|---|---|---|---|---|---|---|---|---|---|---|---|---|---|---|---|---|---|---|---|---|---|---|
| 1 | 2 | 3 | 4 | *5* | 6 | 7 | 8 | 9 | 10 | 11 | *12* | | | | | | | | | | | | | | | |
| 1 | **2** | 3 | 4 | | 6 | 7 | 8 | 9 | **13** | *11* | *12* | 5 | 10 | | | | | | | | | | | | | |
| 1 | 2 | 3 | **4** | | 6 | 7 | 8 | *12* | *9* | 11 | 10 | | 5 | **13** | | | | | | | | | | | | |
| 1 | 2 | 3 | 4 | | 6 | 7 | 8 | 9 | | *11* | 10 | *12* | | | | 5 | | | | | | | | | | |
| 1 | 2 | 3 | 4 | | 6 | 7 | 8 | 9 | | *11* | | 10 | | | | 5 | *12* | | | | | | | | | |
| 1 | 2 | 3 | 4 | | **6** | 7 | *8* | 9 | | 11 | *12* | 10 | | **13** | | 5 | | | | | | | | | | |
| 1 | | 3 | | | 6 | 7 | 8 | 9 | | 11 | 2 | 10 | | 4 | | 5 | | | | | | | | | | |
| 1 | | 3 | | 9 | 6 | 7 | 8 | *12* | | 11 | 2 | 10 | | 4 | | 5 | | | | | | | | | | |
| 1 | **13** | 3 | | *5* | 6 | 7 | 8 | 9 | | 11 | | 10 | | **4** | | 2 | | *12* | | | | | | | | |
| 1 | 4 | 3 | | 5 | *6* | 7 | 8 | 9 | | *12* | | 10 | | **13** | | 2 | | **11** | | | | | | | | |
| 1 | 4 | 3 | | **5** | | 7 | 8 | 9 | **13** | *11* | 10 | 2 | | *12* | | 6 | | | | | | | | | | |
| 1 | 4 | 3 | | | 6 | 7 | **13** | *9* | *12* | 11 | 10 | **2** | | 8 | | 5 | | | | | | | | | | |
| 1 | 4 | 3 | | | 6 | 7 | | 9 | | *11* | 10 | 2 | | 8 | | 5 | | | *12* | | | | | | | |
| 1 | 4 | 3 | | | 6 | 7 | | 9 | *11* | *12* | 10 | 2 | | 8 | | 5 | | | | | | | | | | |
| 1 | 4 | 3 | **13** | | 6 | 7 | 8 | 9 | *11* | *12* | 10 | **2** | | | | 5 | | | | | | | | | | |
| 1 | 2 | 3 | 4 | | | 7 | | 9 | **13** | **11** | 10 | | | 8 | | 5 | | | *12* | *6* | | | | | | |
| 1 | 2 | 3 | 4 | | 6 | 7 | | 9 | | 11 | 10 | | | | | 5 | | | | | 8 | | | | | |
| 1 | 2 | 3 | | | 6 | 7 | 8 | 9 | *12* | *11* | 10 | 4 | | | | 5 | | | | | | | | | | |
| 1 | 4 | 3 | | | *12* | 7 | 8 | **9** | | 11 | *10* | 2 | | | | 5 | | | | | 6 | **13** | | | | |
| 1 | 4 | 3 | | | 6 | 7 | 8 | *9* | | 11 | 10 | 2 | | | | 5 | | | | | | *12* | | | | |
| 1 | 4 | 3 | *12* | | 6 | 7 | **8** | 9 | | *11* | 10 | 2 | | | | 5 | | | | | | **13** | | | | |
| 1 | *4* | 3 | *12* | | 6 | 7 | 8 | 9 | | **11** | 10 | 2 | | | | 5 | | | | | | | **13** | | | |
| 1 | 4 | 3 | | | 6 | 7 | 8 | 9 | | *12* | 10 | 2 | | | | 5 | | | | | | | *11* | | | |
| 1 | 4 | 3 | | | 6 | 7 | 8 | 9 | | *12* | 10 | *2* | | | | 5 | | | | | **13** | | **11** | | | |
| 1 | **4** | 3 | | | *6* | 7 | 8 | 9 | | 11 | 10 | 2 | | | | 5 | | | | | *12* | **13** | | | | |
| 1 | 4 | 3 | | *12* | 6 | 7 | 8 | 9 | | *11* | 10 | 2 | | | | 5 | | | | | | | | | | |
| 1 | | 3 | 4 | | 6 | 7 | 8 | 9 | | 11 | 10 | 2 | | | | 5 | | | | | | | | | | |
| 1 | | 3 | 4 | 11 | 6 | 7 | 8 | *9* | | *12* | 10 | **2** | | | | 5 | | | | **13** | | | | | | |
| 1 | | 3 | 4 | | 6 | 7 | 8 | *12* | 9 | *11* | 10 | 2 | | | | 5 | | | | | | | | | | |
| 1 | | 3 | 4 | 5 | 6 | 7 | 8 | 9 | *12* | *11* | 10 | 2 | | | | | | | | | | | | | | |
| 1 | | | 4 | 5 | 6 | 7 | 8 | **9** | *12* | *11* | 10 | 2 | | | | 3 | | | | **13** | | | | | | |
| 1 | | 3 | 4 | 5 | 6 | 7 | 8 | 9 | *12* | *11* | 10 | | | | | 2 | | | | | | | | | | |
| 1 | | 3 | 4 | 5 | 6 | 7 | 8 | 9 | | 11 | 10 | | | | | 2 | | | | | | | | | | |
| 1 | | 3 | 4 | *5* | 6 | 7 | 8 | 9 | | 11 | 10 | *12* | | | | 2 | | | | | | | | | | |
| | | 3 | 4 | | 6 | 7 | 8 | 9 | *12* | *11* | 10 | 2 | | | | 5 | | | | | | | | 1 | | |
| | | 3 | 4 | | 6 | 7 | 8 | 9 | | 11 | 10 | 2 | | | | 5 | | | | | | | | 1 | | |
| | | 3 | 4 | | 6 | 7 | 8 | 9 | | *11* | 10 | 2 | | | | 5 | | | | | | | | 1 | *12* | |
| | | 3 | 4 | | 6 | 7 | 8 | 9 | | 11 | 10 | 2 | | | | 5 | | | | | | | | 1 | | |
| | **13** | 3 | 4 | | 6 | 7 | **8** | 9 | | *11* | 10 | 2 | | | | 5 | | | | | | | | 1 | *12* | |
| | | 3 | 4 | | 6 | 7 | 8 | 9 | | *11* | 10 | 2 | | | | 5 | | | | | | | | 1 | *12* | |
| | 8 | 3 | **4** | | *6* | 7 | *12* | 9 | | 11 | 10 | 2 | | | | 5 | | | | | | | | 1 | **13** | |
| | 4 | 3 | | | | 7 | 8 | 9 | | 11 | | 6 | | | | 5 | | | | | | | | 1 | 10 | 2 |
| | 8 | 3 | | | 6 | 7 | 4 | 9 | | 11 | 10 | 2 | | | | 5 | | | | | | | | 1 | | |
| | 8 | 3 | | | 6 | 7 | 4 | 9 | | 11 | 10 | 2 | | | | 5 | | | | | | | | 1 | | |
| | 8 | 3 | | | 6 | 7 | 4 | 9 | | 11 | 10 | 2 | | | | 5 | | | | | | | | 1 | | |
| | 8 | 3 | | | 6 | 7 | 4 | 9 | | 11 | 10 | 2 | | | | 5 | | | | | | | | 1 | | |
| 34 | 29 | 45 | 23 | 10 | 42 | 46 | 40 | 43 | 5 | 40 | 39 | 38 | 2 | 7 | | 42 | | 1 | | 1 | 2 | | | 12 | 1 | 1 |
| | 2 | | 3 | 2 | 1 | | 2 | 3 | 9 | 6 | 3 | 2 | | 4 | | | 1 | 1 | 2 | 2 | 2 | 4 | 3 | | 4 | |
| | 1 | 1 | 2 | 1 | | 28 | 2 | 12 | 2 | 11 | 3 | | | 1 | | 1 | | | | | | | | | | |

| Cox | Olsson | McKinnon | Tinkler | Smith | Bennyworth | Allon | Tupling | Baker | Fletcher | Dalton | Honour | Nobbs | Duggan | Hutchison | Harbron | MacPhail | Shotton | MacDonald | Dunbar | Davies, K. | Davies, A. | Lamb | Heaney | Poole | Gabbiadini | Nesbitt |
|---|---|---|---|---|---|---|---|---|---|---|---|---|---|---|---|---|---|---|---|---|---|---|---|---|---|---|
| 1 | 4 | 3 | | | 6 | 7 | 2 | 9 | *12* | *11* | 10 | | | 8 | | 5 | | | | | | | | | | |
| 1 | 2 | 3 | | | *6* | 7 | 4 | 9 | | 11 | 10 | *12* | | | | 5 | | | | | 8 | | | | | |
| 2 | 2 | 2 | | | 2 | 2 | 2 | 2 | | 2 | 2 | | | 1 | | 2 | | | | | 1 | | | | | |
| | | | | | | | | | 1 | | | 1 | | | | | | | | | | | | | | |
| | | | | | | 3 | | | | | | | | | | | | | | | | | | | | |

| Cox | Olsson | McKinnon | Tinkler | Smith | Bennyworth | Allon | Tupling | Baker | Fletcher | Dalton | Honour | Nobbs | Duggan | Hutchison | Harbron | MacPhail | Shotton | MacDonald | Dunbar | Davies, K. | Davies, A. | Lamb | Heaney | Poole | Gabbiadini | Nesbitt |
|---|---|---|---|---|---|---|---|---|---|---|---|---|---|---|---|---|---|---|---|---|---|---|---|---|---|---|
| 1 | 2 | 3 | 4 | | 6 | **7** | 8 | 9 | | 11 | *12* | 5 | | | | | | | | *10* | | | | | | |
| 1 | 2 | 3 | **4** | | 6 | 7 | 8 | 9 | | 11 | **13** | 10 | *12* | | *5* | | | | | | | | | | | |
| 1 | **2** | 3 | 4 | *5* | 6 | 7 | 8 | 9 | | 11 | **13** | 10 | | *12* | | | | | | | | | | | | |
| 1 | *12* | 3 | | 5 | 6 | 7 | *8* | 9 | | 11 | **2** | 10 | | 4 | | | | **13** | | | | | | | | |
| 4 | 3 | 4 | 3 | 2 | 4 | 4 | 4 | 4 | | 4 | 1 | 4 | | 1 | 1 | | | | | 1 | | | | | | |
| | 1 | | | | | | | | | | 3 | | 1 | 1 | | | | 1 | | | | | | | | |
| | | | | | | 2 | | 1 | | 1 | 1 | | | | | | | | | | | | | | | |

## League Table

| | P | W | D | L | F | A | Pts |
|---|---|---|---|---|---|---|---|
| Darlington | 46 | 22 | 17 | 7 | 68 | 38 | 83 |
| Stockport County | 46 | 23 | 13 | 10 | 84 | 47 | 82 |
| Hartlepool United | 46 | 24 | 10 | 12 | 67 | 48 | 82 |
| Peterborough United | 46 | 21 | 17 | 8 | 67 | 45 | 80 |
| Blackpool | 46 | 23 | 10 | 13 | 78 | 47 | 79 |
| Burnley | 46 | 23 | 10 | 13 | 70 | 51 | 79 |
| Torquay United | 46 | 18 | 18 | 10 | 64 | 47 | 72 |
| Scunthorpe United | 46 | 20 | 11 | 15 | 71 | 62 | 71 |
| Scarborough | 46 | 19 | 12 | 15 | 59 | 56 | 69 |
| Northampton Town | 46 | 18 | 13 | 15 | 57 | 58 | 67 |
| Doncaster Rovers | 46 | 17 | 14 | 15 | 56 | 46 | 65 |
| Rochdale | 46 | 15 | 17 | 14 | 50 | 53 | 62 |
| Cardiff City | 46 | 15 | 15 | 16 | 43 | 54 | 60 |
| Lincoln City | 46 | 14 | 17 | 15 | 50 | 61 | 59 |
| Gillingham | 46 | 12 | 18 | 16 | 57 | 60 | 54 |
| Walsall | 46 | 12 | 17 | 17 | 48 | 51 | 53 |
| Hereford United | 46 | 13 | 14 | 19 | 53 | 58 | 53 |
| Chesterfield | 46 | 13 | 14 | 19 | 47 | 62 | 53 |
| Maidstone United | 46 | 13 | 12 | 21 | 66 | 71 | 51 |
| Carlisle United | 46 | 13 | 9 | 24 | 47 | 89 | 48 |
| York City | 46 | 11 | 13 | 22 | 45 | 57 | 46 |
| Halifax Town | 46 | 12 | 10 | 24 | 59 | 79 | 46 |
| Aldershot | 46 | 10 | 11 | 25 | 61 | 101 | 41 |
| Wrexham | 46 | 10 | 10 | 26 | 48 | 74 | 40 |

# 1991-92

## Division Three

Manager: Alan Murray

### Did you know that?

'Pools finished a creditable 11th in Division Three, with victories over Reading, Birmingham City, Wigan Athletic, Hull City, Fulham, and West Bromwich Albion, all teams that were to later play in the FA Premiership.

Nicky Southall made his debut on 12 October at Bournemouth, a 2–0 defeat. In a playing career spanning 18 seasons with six different clubs, he made 634 League appearances, scoring 66 goals.

| Match No. | Date | Round | Venue | Opponents | Result | | Scorers | Attendance |
|---|---|---|---|---|---|---|---|---|
| 1 | Aug 17 | | (a) | Torquay United | L | 1 - 3 | Baker | 4,163 |
| 3 | 24 | | (h) | Reading | W | 2 - 0 | Baker, Olsson | 2,858 |
| 5 | 31 | | (a) | Bradford City | D | 1 - 1 | Rush | 5,872 |
| 6 | Sep 3 | | (h) | Brentford | W | 1 - 0 | Gabbiadini | 3,660 |
| 7 | 7 | | (h) | Leyton Orient | L | 2 - 3 | Dalton, Rush | 3,581 |
| 8 | 14 | | (a) | Exeter City | D | 1 - 1 | Baker (pen) | 2,906 |
| 9 | 17 | | (a) | Stoke City | L | 2 - 3 | Baker, Olsson | 9,419 |
| 10 | 21 | | (h) | Birmingham City | W | 1 - 0 | Baker | 4,643 |
| 12 | 28 | | (a) | Bury | D | 1 - 1 | Gabbiadini | 2,600 |
| 13 | Oct 5 | | (h) | Wigan Athletic | W | 4 - 3 | Honour, Dalton 2, McKinnon | 3,047 |
| 15 | 12 | | (a) | Bournemouth | L | 0 - 2 | | 4,817 |
| 16 | 19 | | (h) | Hull City | L | 2 - 3 | Southall 2 | 2,868 |
| 17 | 26 | | (a) | Peterborough United | L | 2 - 3 | Bennyworth, Honour | 3,385 |
| 18 | Nov 2 | | (a) | Darlington | L | 0 - 4 | | 5,041 |
| 19 | 5 | | (h) | West Bromwich Albion | D | 0 - 0 | | 2,970 |
| 20 | 9 | | (h) | Fulham | W | 2 - 0 | Honour, Morgan (o.g.) | 2,999 |
| 23 | 23 | | (a) | Shrewsbury Town | W | 4 - 1 | Olsson 2, Dalton, Baker | 2,368 |
| 24 | 30 | | (h) | Huddersfield Town | D | 0 - 0 | | 4,017 |
| 26 | Dec 14 | | (a) | Preston North End | W | 4 - 1 | Baker 2, Dalton, Johnson | 5,034 |
| 27 | 20 | | (a) | Reading | W | 1 - 0 | Baker | 2,535 |
| 28 | 26 | | (h) | Bradford City | W | 1 - 0 | Baker | 5,413 |
| 29 | 28 | | (h) | Torquay United | D | 1 - 1 | Johnson | 3,812 |
| 30 | Jan 1 | | (a) | Brentford | L | 0 - 1 | | 7,102 |
| 33 | 11 | | (h) | Chester City | W | 1 - 0 | Honour | 3,088 |
| 35 | 18 | | (a) | Bolton Wanderers | D | 2 - 2 | Olsson, Kelly (o.g.) | 6,129 |
| 37 | Feb 1 | | (a) | Hull City | W | 2 - 0 | Dalton, Baker | 3,483 |
| 39 | 8 | | (h) | Peterborough United | L | 0 - 1 | | 2,479 |
| 40 | 11 | | (a) | Huddersfield Town | L | 0 - 1 | | 5,559 |
| 41 | 15 | | (h) | Preston North End | W | 2 - 0 | Peake, Baker | 2,140 |
| 42 | 18 | | (h) | Stockport County | L | 0 - 1 | | 2,473 |
| 43 | 22 | | (a) | Chester City | L | 0 - 2 | | 1,072 |
| 44 | 29 | | (h) | Swansea City | L | 0 - 1 | | 2,669 |
| 45 | Mar 3 | | (h) | Bolton Wanderers | L | 0 - 4 | | 2,254 |
| 46 | 6 | | (a) | Stockport County | W | 1 - 0 | Baker | 4,473 |
| 47 | 11 | | (a) | West Bromwich Albion | W | 2 - 1 | Dalton 2 (1 pen) | 10,307 |
| 48 | 14 | | (h) | Darlington | W | 2 - 0 | Saville, Dalton | 4,442 |
| 49 | 20 | | (a) | Fulham | L | 0 - 1 | | 4,359 |
| 50 | 28 | | (h) | Shrewsbury Town | W | 4 - 2 | Thomas, Dalton, Fletcher, Johnrose (pen) | 2,515 |
| 51 | 31 | | (h) | Exeter City | W | 3 - 1 | Dalton 2, Southall | 2,222 |
| 52 | Apr 4 | | (a) | Leyton Orient | L | 0 - 4 | | 4,245 |
| 53 | 11 | | (h) | Stoke City | D | 1 - 1 | Olsson | 4,362 |
| 54 | 18 | | (a) | Birmingham City | L | 1 - 2 | Fletcher | 13,698 |
| 55 | 20 | | (h) | Bury | D | 0 - 0 | | 2,503 |
| 56 | 24 | | (a) | Wigan Athletic | D | 1 - 1 | MacPhail | 2,002 |
| 57 | 28 | | (a) | Swansea City | D | 1 - 1 | Dalton | 2,167 |
| 58 | May 2 | | (h) | Bournemouth | W | 1 - 0 | Johnrose | 2,612 |

Final Position : 11th in Division Three

Apps.
Sub.Apps.
2 own goals — Goals

**FA Cup**

| Match No. | Date | Round | Venue | Opponents | Result | | Scorers | Attendance |
|---|---|---|---|---|---|---|---|---|
| 21 | Nov 16 | R1 | (h) | Shrewsbury Town | W | 3 - 2 | Tinkler, Johnson, Baker (pen) | 2,864 |
| 25 | Dec 7 | R2 | (a) | Darlington | W | 2 - 1 | Dalton, Honour | 5,509 |
| 31 | Jan 4 | R3 | (a) | Ipswich Town | D | 1 - 1 | Baker | 12,507 |
| 34 | 15 | R3r | (h) | Ipswich Town | L | 0 - 2 | | 6,700 |

Apps.
Sub.Apps.
Goals

**League Cup**

| Match No. | Date | Round | Venue | Opponents | Result | | Scorers | Attendance |
|---|---|---|---|---|---|---|---|---|
| 2 | Aug 20 | R1/1 | (h) | Bury | W | 1 - 0 | Baker | 2,833 |
| 4 | 27 | R1/2 | (a) | Bury | D | 2 - 2 | Gabbiadini, Fletcher | 1,917 |
| 11 | Sep 25 | R2/1 | (h) | Crystal Palace | D | 1 - 1 | Honour | 6,697 |
| 14 | Oct 8 | R2/2 | (a) | Crystal Palace | L | 1 - 6 | Tinkler | 9,153 |

Apps.
Sub.Apps.
Goals

| Hodge | Nesbitt | McKinnon | McCreery | Nobbs | Bennyworth | Rush | Olsson | Baker | Honour | Dalton | McPhail | Tinkler | Fletcher | Gabbiadini | Tupling | Smith, M. | Southall | Johnson | Smith, A. | Cross | Peake | Johnrose | Davies | McGuckin | Saville | Thomas | Jones |
|---|---|---|---|---|---|---|---|---|---|---|---|---|---|---|---|---|---|---|---|---|---|---|---|---|---|---|---|
| 1 | *2* | 3 | 4 | 5 | 6 | 7 | 8 | 9 | 10 | 11 | *12* | | | | | | | | | | | | | | | | |
| 1 | | 3 | *4* | 2 | 6 | 7 | 8 | 9 | 10 | 11 | 5 | *12* | | | | | | | | | | | | | | | |
| 1 | | 3 | *4* | 2 | 6 | 7 | 8 | 9 | 10 | 11 | 5 | *12* | | | | | | | | | | | | | | | |
| 1 | | 3 | | 2 | 6 | 7 | 8 | | 10 | 11 | 5 | 4 | *9* | *12* | | | | | | | | | | | | | |
| 1 | | 3 | | 2 | 6 | 7 | 8 | | 10 | 11 | 5 | 4 | *9* | *12* | | | | | | | | | | | | | |
| 1 | | 3 | | 2 | 6 | 7 | 8 | 9 | 10 | 11 | 5 | 4 | | | | | | | | | | | | | | | |
| 1 | | 3 | *12* | 2 | 6 | **7** | 8 | 9 | *10* | 11 | 5 | 4 | | | **13** | | | | | | | | | | | | |
| 1 | | 3 | | 2 | 6 | 7 | 8 | 9 | 10 | 11 | 5 | 4 | | | | | | | | | | | | | | | |
| 1 | | 3 | *7* | 2 | 6 | | 8 | 9 | 10 | 11 | 5 | 4 | | *12* | | | | | | | | | | | | | |
| 1 | | 3 | | 2 | 6 | | 8 | 9 | 10 | 11 | 5 | *4* | **13** | **7** | *12* | | | | | | | | | | | | |
| 1 | | 3 | | 2 | | | *8* | 9 | 10 | 11 | 5 | 4 | | *12* | | 6 | 7 | | | | | | | | | | |
| 1 | | 3 | | 2 | | | 8 | 9 | 10 | 11 | 5 | 4 | | | | 6 | 7 | | | | | | | | | | |
| 1 | | 3 | 4 | 2 | 6 | | 8 | 9 | 10 | 11 | 5 | | | *12* | | | *7* | | | | | | | | | | |
| 1 | | 3 | **13** | 2 | **6** | | 8 | | 10 | 11 | 5 | 4 | | *12* | | | *7* | 9 | | | | | | | | | |
| 1 | | 3 | *4* | 2 | | | 8 | | 10 | 11 | 5 | 7 | 9 | | 6 | | *12* | | | | | | | | | | |
| 1 | | 3 | *4* | 2 | | | 8 | | 10 | 11 | 5 | 7 | 9 | | 6 | | *12* | | | | | | | | | | |
| 1 | | 3 | | 2 | | | 8 | 9 | 10 | 11 | 5 | 4 | | | 6 | | *12* | *7* | | | | | | | | | |
| 1 | | 3 | | **2** | | | 8 | 9 | 10 | 11 | 5 | 4 | | | 6 | **13** | *12* | *7* | | | | | | | | | |
| 1 | | 3 | 4 | | | | 8 | 9 | 10 | 11 | 5 | | | | 6 | 2 | | 7 | | | | | | | | | |
| 1 | | 3 | *4* | 2 | | | 8 | 9 | 10 | 11 | 5 | *12* | | | 6 | | | 7 | | | | | | | | | |
| 1 | | 3 | 4 | 2 | | | 8 | 9 | 10 | | 5 | | | | 6 | 11 | | 7 | | | | | | | | | |
| 1 | | 3 | *4* | 2 | | | 8 | 9 | 10 | 11 | 5 | *12* | | | 6 | | | 7 | | | | | | | | | |
| 1 | | 3 | 4 | 2 | | | 8 | 9 | 10 | 11 | 5 | *12* | | | 6 | | *7* | | | | | | | | | | |
| 1 | | | *4* | 2 | | | 8 | 9 | 10 | 11 | 5 | *12* | 7 | | 6 | | | | 3 | | | | | | | | |
| 1 | | | | 2 | | | 8 | 9 | 10 | *11* | 5 | 4 | 7 | | 6 | | *12* | | 3 | | | | | | | | |
| 1 | | | | 2 | | | 8 | 9 | 10 | 11 | 5 | 4 | | | 6 | | *12* | | *7* | 3 | | | | | | | |
| 1 | | | *4* | 2 | | | 8 | 9 | 10 | 11 | 5 | *12* | | **13** | 6 | | **7** | | | 3 | | | | | | | |
| 1 | | | | 2 | | | 8 | 9 | 10 | 11 | 5 | 4 | | *12* | 6 | | *7* | | | 3 | | | | | | | |
| 1 | | | | 2 | | | 8 | 9 | 10 | 11 | 5 | 4 | | | 6 | | | | | 3 | 7 | | | | | | |
| 1 | | | | 2 | | | 8 | 9 | 10 | 11 | 5 | 4 | | | 6 | | | | *12* | 3 | *7* | | | | | | |
| 1 | | | | 2 | | | 8 | 9 | 10 | 11 | 5 | 4 | | | **13** | | *12* | | *6* | 3 | **7** | | | | | | |
| 1 | | | | 2 | | | 8 | 9 | 10 | | 5 | 4 | *12* | | | 6 | | | | 3 | *11* | 7 | | | | | |
| 1 | | | *12* | | | | 8 | 9 | 10 | | 5 | 4 | | | 2 | 6 | | | | *3* | 11 | 7 | | | | | |
| 1 | | | 2 | | | | 8 | 9 | 10 | 11 | 5 | 4 | | | | *6* | *12* | | | **3** | **13** | 7 | | | | | |
| 1 | | | 2 | | | | 8 | | 10 | 11 | 5 | 4 | 9 | | | | | | | 3 | | 7 | 6 | | | | |
| 1 | | | 2 | | | | 8 | | 10 | 11 | | 4 | | | | | | | | 3 | | 9 | 6 | 5 | 7 | | |
| 1 | | | 2 | 6 | | | 8 | | 10 | 11 | | 4 | 7 | | | | | | | 3 | | 9 | *12* | *5* | | | |
| 1 | | | 2 | 6 | | | 8 | | 10 | 11 | | 4 | *12* | | | | | | | 3 | | 9 | | 5 | | *7* | |
| 1 | | | *2* | 6 | | | 8 | | 10 | 11 | | 4 | | | | | *12* | | | 3 | | 9 | | 5 | | 7 | |
| 1 | | | 2 | 6 | | | 8 | | 10 | 11 | | 4 | *12* | | | | | | | 3 | | 9 | | 5 | | *7* | |
| | | | 2 | 6 | | | 8 | | | 11 | 4 | | 10 | | | | *7* | | | 3 | | 9 | | 5 | | *12* | 1 |
| | | | 2 | 6 | | | 8 | | | 11 | 4 | | 10 | | | | *7* | | | 3 | | 9 | | 5 | | *12* | 1 |
| | | | 2 | 6 | | | 8 | | | 11 | 5 | | 10 | | | | 4 | | | 3 | | 9 | | | | 7 | 1 |
| | | | 2 | 6 | | | 8 | | | 11 | 5 | *12* | 10 | | | | 4 | | | 3 | | 9 | | | | *7* | 1 |
| | | | 2 | 6 | | | 8 | | | 11 | 5 | 4 | 10 | | | | 7 | | | 3 | | 9 | | | | | 1 |
| | | | *2* | 6 | | | 8 | | | 11 | 5 | 4 | 10 | | *12* | | 7 | | | 3 | | 9 | | | | | 1 |
| 40 | 1 | 23 | 27 | 41 | 12 | 8 | 46 | 29 | 40 | 43 | 40 | 31 | 14 | 1 | 17 | 7 | 13 | 7 | 4 | 21 | 5 | 15 | 2 | 7 | 1 | 5 | 6 |
| | | | 3 | | | | | | | | 1 | 8 | 4 | 8 | 4 | 1 | 9 | | 1 | | 1 | | 1 | | | 1 | |
| | | 1 | | | 1 | 2 | 6 | 13 | 4 | 13 | 1 | | 2 | 2 | | | 3 | 2 | | | 1 | 2 | | | 1 | 1 | |

| Hodge | Nesbitt | McKinnon | McCreery | Nobbs | Bennyworth | Rush | Olsson | Baker | Honour | Dalton | McPhail | Tinkler | Fletcher | Gabbiadini | Tupling | Smith, M. | Southall | Johnson |
|---|---|---|---|---|---|---|---|---|---|---|---|---|---|---|---|---|---|---|
| 1 | | 3 | | 2 | | | 8 | 9 | 10 | 11 | *5* | 4 | | | 6 | | *12* | 7 |
| 1 | | 3 | 4 | 2 | | | 8 | 9 | 10 | 11 | 5 | | | | 6 | | | 7 |
| 1 | | 3 | 4 | 2 | | | 8 | 9 | | 11 | 5 | *10* | *12* | | 6 | | 7 | |
| 1 | | | *4* | 2 | | | 8 | 9 | 10 | 11 | 5 | 3 | 7 | | 6 | | *12* | |
| 4 | | 3 | 3 | 4 | | | 4 | 4 | 3 | 4 | 4 | 3 | 1 | | 4 | | 1 | 2 |
| | | | | | | | | | | | | | 1 | | | | 2 | |
| | | | | | | | | 2 | 1 | 1 | | 1 | | | | | | 1 |

| Hodge | Nesbitt | McKinnon | McCreery | Nobbs | Bennyworth | Rush | Olsson | Baker | Honour | Dalton | McPhail | Tinkler | Fletcher | Gabbiadini | Tupling |
|---|---|---|---|---|---|---|---|---|---|---|---|---|---|---|---|
| 1 | | 3 | *4* | 2 | 6 | | 8 | 9 | 10 | 11 | 5 | *12* | | 7 | |
| 1 | | 3 | **4** | 2 | 6 | | 8 | 9 | 10 | 11 | | **13** | *12* | *7* | 5 |
| 1 | | 3 | *12* | 2 | 6 | | 8 | 9 | 10 | 11 | 5 | 4 | | *7* | |
| 1 | | 3 | | 2 | *6* | | 8 | 9 | 10 | 11 | 5 | 4 | *12* | **7** | **13** |
| 4 | | 4 | 2 | 4 | 4 | | 4 | 4 | 4 | 4 | 3 | 2 | | 4 | 1 |
| | | | 1 | | | | | | | | | 2 | 2 | | 1 |
| | | | | | | | | 1 | 1 | | | 1 | 1 | 1 | |

## League Table

| | P | W | D | L | F | A | Pts |
|---|---|---|---|---|---|---|---|
| Brentford | 46 | 25 | 7 | 14 | 81 | 55 | 82 |
| Birmingham City | 46 | 23 | 12 | 11 | 69 | 52 | 81 |
| Huddersfield Town | 46 | 22 | 12 | 12 | 59 | 38 | 78 |
| Stoke City | 46 | 21 | 14 | 11 | 69 | 49 | 77 |
| Stockport County | 46 | 22 | 10 | 14 | 75 | 51 | 76 |
| Peterborough United | 46 | 20 | 14 | 12 | 65 | 58 | 74 |
| West Bromwich Albion | 46 | 19 | 14 | 13 | 64 | 49 | 71 |
| Bournemouth | 46 | 20 | 11 | 15 | 52 | 48 | 71 |
| Fulham | 46 | 19 | 13 | 14 | 57 | 53 | 70 |
| Leyton Orient | 46 | 18 | 11 | 17 | 62 | 52 | 65 |
| Hartlepool United | 46 | 18 | 11 | 17 | 57 | 57 | 65 |
| Reading | 46 | 16 | 13 | 17 | 59 | 62 | 61 |
| Bolton Wanderers | 46 | 14 | 17 | 15 | 57 | 56 | 59 |
| Hull City | 46 | 16 | 11 | 19 | 54 | 54 | 59 |
| Wigan Athletic | 46 | 15 | 14 | 17 | 58 | 64 | 59 |
| Bradford City | 46 | 13 | 19 | 14 | 62 | 61 | 58 |
| Preston North End | 46 | 15 | 12 | 19 | 61 | 72 | 57 |
| Chester City | 46 | 14 | 14 | 18 | 56 | 59 | 56 |
| Swansea City | 46 | 14 | 14 | 18 | 55 | 65 | 56 |
| Exeter City | 46 | 14 | 11 | 21 | 57 | 80 | 53 |
| Bury | 46 | 13 | 12 | 21 | 55 | 74 | 51 |
| Shrewsbury Town | 46 | 12 | 11 | 23 | 53 | 68 | 47 |
| Torquay United | 46 | 13 | 8 | 25 | 42 | 68 | 47 |
| Darlington | 46 | 10 | 7 | 29 | 56 | 90 | 37 |

# 1992-93

## Division Two

Managers: Alan Murray and Viv Busby

**Did you know that?**

'Pools went a record 11 League games without scoring, from 9 January to 2 March. Andy Saville finally broke the sequence in the 1–1 draw at Blackpool.

The BBC's Match of the Day cameras covered the third-round FA Cup tie against Premiership Crystal Palace at the Victoria Ground. 'Pools pulled off the shock of the round, winning 1–0 courtesy of an Andy Saville penalty.

| Match No. | Date | Round | Venue | Opponents | Result | | Scorers | Attendance |
|---|---|---|---|---|---|---|---|---|
| 1 | Aug 15 | | (h) | Reading | D | 1 - 1 | Saville (pen) | 4,129 |
| 3 | 22 | | (a) | Rotherham United | D | 0 - 0 | | 4,427 |
| 5 | 29 | | (h) | Huddersfield Town | W | 1 - 0 | Olsson | 4,120 |
| 6 | Sep 1 | | (h) | Chester City | W | 2 - 0 | R.Cross, Emerson | 2,983 |
| 7 | 5 | | (a) | Bournemouth | W | 2 - 0 | R.Cross, Saville | 4,446 |
| 8 | 11 | | (a) | Wigan Athletic | D | 2 - 2 | Saville 2 | 2,073 |
| 9 | 15 | | (h) | Leyton Orient | L | 0 - 2 | | 3,286 |
| 10 | 19 | | (h) | Port Vale | D | 1 - 1 | Olsson | 2,815 |
| 12 | 26 | | (a) | Preston North End | W | 2 - 0 | Gallacher, Johnrose | 4,347 |
| 13 | Oct 2 | | (h) | Blackpool | W | 1 - 0 | Saville (pen) | 2,675 |
| 15 | 10 | | (a) | Bolton Wanderers | W | 2 - 1 | Johnrose, Saville | 5,097 |
| 16 | 17 | | (h) | Swansea City | L | 0 - 1 | | 4,396 |
| 17 | 24 | | (a) | Brighton & Hove Albion | D | 1 - 1 | Honour | 5,918 |
| 18 | 31 | | (h) | Bradford City | W | 2 - 0 | Southall, Wratten | 4,349 |
| 19 | Nov 3 | | (a) | West Bromwich Albion | L | 1 - 3 | Southall | 13,046 |
| 20 | 7 | | (h) | Exeter City | L | 1 - 3 | P.Cross | 2,893 |
| 22 | 28 | | (h) | Stockport County | W | 3 - 2 | Johnrose, McGuckin, Saville | 2,949 |
| 25 | Dec 12 | | (a) | Plymouth Argyle | D | 2 - 2 | Johnrose, Saville | 5,996 |
| 27 | 19 | | (h) | Stoke City | L | 1 - 2 | Honour | 4,136 |
| 28 | 26 | | (h) | Hull City | W | 1 - 0 | Johnrose | 4,232 |
| 29 | 28 | | (a) | Fulham | W | 3 - 1 | Saville 2 (1 pen), Southall | 4,403 |
| 31 | Jan 9 | | (a) | Leyton Orient | D | 0 - 0 | | 5,531 |
| 33 | 16 | | (h) | Preston North End | D | 0 - 0 | | 2,748 |
| 35 | 27 | | (a) | Huddersfield Town | L | 0 - 3 | | 4,153 |
| 36 | 30 | | (h) | Rotherham United | L | 0 - 2 | | 3,869 |
| 37 | Feb 6 | | (a) | Reading | L | 0 - 2 | | 3,431 |
| 38 | 9 | | (a) | Port Vale | L | 0 - 2 | | 6,629 |
| 39 | 13 | | (h) | Bournemouth | L | 0 - 1 | | 2,197 |
| 40 | 16 | | (a) | Mansfield Town | L | 0 - 2 | | 2,655 |
| 41 | 20 | | (a) | Chester City | L | 0 - 1 | | 1,912 |
| 42 | 27 | | (h) | Bolton Wanderers | L | 0 - 2 | | 2,717 |
| 43 | Mar 2 | | (h) | Wigan Athletic | D | 0 - 0 | | 1,791 |
| 44 | 6 | | (a) | Blackpool | D | 1 - 1 | Saville | 4,926 |
| 45 | 9 | | (h) | Burnley | D | 0 - 0 | | 3,021 |
| 46 | 13 | | (a) | Exeter City | L | 1 - 3 | Tait | 2,636 |
| 47 | 20 | | (h) | West Bromwich Albion | D | 2 - 2 | Saville 2 (1 pen) | 3,697 |
| 48 | 23 | | (a) | Stockport County | L | 1 - 3 | Southall | 4,154 |
| 49 | 27 | | (h) | Mansfield Town | L | 0 - 1 | | 2,316 |
| 50 | Apr 3 | | (a) | Burnley | L | 0 - 3 | | 8,226 |
| 51 | 5 | | (h) | Plymouth Argyle | W | 1 - 0 | Honour | 1,822 |
| 52 | 10 | | (a) | Hull City | L | 2 - 3 | Ellison, Southall | 3,562 |
| 53 | 12 | | (h) | Fulham | L | 0 - 3 | | 2,361 |
| 54 | 17 | | (a) | Stoke City | W | 1 - 0 | Johnrose | 17,331 |
| 55 | 24 | | (a) | Swansea City | L | 0 - 3 | | 5,301 |
| 56 | May 1 | | (h) | Brighton & Hove Albion | W | 2 - 0 | Southall, Peverell | 2,693 |
| 57 | 8 | | (a) | Bradford City | W | 2 - 0 | MacPhail, Thompson | 5,612 |

Final Position : 16th in the New Division Two

Apps.
Sub.Apps.
Goals

**FA Cup**

| Match No. | Date | Round | Venue | Opponents | Result | | Scorers | Attendance |
|---|---|---|---|---|---|---|---|---|
| 21 | Nov 14 | R1 | (a) | Doncaster Rovers | W | 2 - 1 | Johnrose, Saville (pen) | 4,513 |
| 23 | Dec 6 | R2 | (h) | Southport | W | 4 - 0 | Peverell, Saville 3 | 4,171 |
| 30 | Jan 2 | R3 | (h) | Crystal Palace | W | 1 - 0 | Saville (pen) | 6,721 |
| 34 | 23 | R4 | (a) | Sheffield United | L | 0 - 1 | | 20,074 |

Apps.
Sub.Apps.
Goals

**League Cup**

| Match No. | Date | Round | Venue | Opponents | Result | | Scorers | Attendance |
|---|---|---|---|---|---|---|---|---|
| 2 | Aug 18 | R1/1 | (a) | Halifax Town | W | 2 - 1 | MacPhail, Johnrose | 1,370 |
| 4 | 25 | R1/2 | (h) | Halifax Town | W | 3 - 2 | Johnrose 2, Southall | 2,191 |
| 11 | Sep 23 | R2/1 | (a) | Sheffield Wednesday | L | 0 - 3 | | 10,112 |
| 14 | Oct 6 | R2/2 | (h) | Sheffield Wednesday | D | 2 - 2 | Saville (pen), Johnrose | 4,667 |

Apps.
Sub.Apps.
Goals

| Hodge | Cross, R. | Cross, P. | Tait | McPhail | Emerson | Johnrose | Olsson | Saville | Honour | Gallacher | Southall | Nobbs | Proudlock | Wratten | Jones | McGuckin | Johnson | Gilchrist | Peverell | Talia | Thompson | Ellison | Skedd | Lynch |
|---|---|---|---|---|---|---|---|---|---|---|---|---|---|---|---|---|---|---|---|---|---|---|---|---|
| 1 | 2 | 3 | 4 | 5 | 6 | 7 | 8 | 9 | 10 | 11 | | | | | | | | | | | | | | |
| 1 | 2 | 3 | 4 | 5 | 6 | 7 | 8 | 9 | 10 | *11* | *12* | | | | | | | | | | | | | |
| 1 | 2 | 3 | 4 | 5 | 6 | 7 | 8 | 9 | 10 | | 11 | | | | | | | | | | | | | |
| 1 | 2 | 3 | 4 | 5 | 6 | 7 | 8 | 9 | | | 11 | 10 | | | | | | | | | | | | |
| 1 | 2 | 3 | 4 | 5 | 6 | 7 | 8 | 9 | | | 11 | 10 | | | | | | | | | | | | |
| 1 | 2 | 3 | 4 | 5 | 6 | 7 | 8 | 9 | | | *11* | 10 | *12* | | | | | | | | | | | |
| 1 | **2** | 3 | 4 | 5 | 6 | 7 | 8 | 9 | | *12* | *11* | 10 | **13** | | | | | | | | | | | |
| 1 | **13** | 3 | 4 | 5 | 6 | 7 | 8 | 9 | | 11 | **12** | 10 | *2* | | | | | | | | | | | |
| 1 | 2 | 3 | 4 | 5 | 6 | 7 | 8 | 9 | | 11 | | 10 | | | | | | | | | | | | |
| 1 | *2* | 3 | 4 | 5 | 6 | 7 | 8 | 9 | *12* | **11** | | 10 | **13** | | | | | | | | | | | |
| 1 | 2 | 3 | 4 | | 6 | 7 | 8 | 9 | 11 | | *12* | 10 | *5* | | | | | | | | | | | |
| 1 | 2 | 3 | 4 | | | 7 | 8 | 9 | 11 | | *12* | 10 | 5 | *6* | | | | | | | | | | |
| 1 | 2 | 3 | 4 | 5 | 6 | *7* | 8 | 9 | 11 | | *12* | 10 | | | | | | | | | | | | |
| 1 | 2 | 3 | 4 | 5 | 6 | | 8 | 9 | 10 | | 7 | | | 11 | | | | | | | | | | |
| 1 | 2 | 3 | 4 | *5* | 6 | **13** | 8 | 9 | 10 | *12* | **7** | | | 11 | | | | | | | | | | |
| | 2 | 3 | 4 | | 6 | *12* | 8 | 9 | 10 | | *7* | | | 11 | 1 | 5 | | | | | | | | |
| 1 | 2 | 3 | | 5 | 6 | 7 | 8 | 9 | 10 | | | | | | | 4 | 11 | | | | | | | |
| 1 | 2 | 3 | | 5 | 6 | 7 | 8 | 9 | 10 | | | | | | | 4 | 11 | | | | | | | |
| *1* | 2 | 3 | | 5 | 6 | 7 | 8 | 9 | 10 | | *12* | | | | | | **11** | 4 | **13** | | | | | |
| | 2 | 3 | | 5 | 6 | 7 | 8 | 9 | 10 | | 11 | | | | 1 | | | 4 | | | | | | |
| | 2 | *3* | | 5 | 6 | 7 | 8 | 9 | 10 | *12* | 11 | | | | 1 | | | 4 | | | | | | |
| | 2 | 3 | | 5 | 6 | 7 | 8 | 9 | 10 | | 11 | | | | | | | 4 | | 1 | | | | |
| | 2 | 3 | | 5 | *6* | 7 | **8** | 9 | 10 | | **13** | | | *12* | | | | 4 | 11 | 1 | | | | |
| | 2 | 3 | 6 | 5 | | *7* | | 9 | 10 | 11 | **8** | | | *12* | | | | 4 | **13** | 1 | | | | |
| | | 3 | 6 | 5 | | 7 | | 9 | 10 | 11 | | | | 4 | | 2 | | | *8* | 1 | *12* | | | |
| | | 3 | | 5 | | 7 | | 9 | 10 | 11 | *12* | 8 | | 4 | | *2* | | 6 | | 1 | | | | |
| | 2 | 3 | | 5 | | 7 | | 9 | 10 | 11 | *6* | | | 8 | | *12* | | 4 | | 1 | | | | |
| | **2** | 3 | 6 | 5 | | 7 | | 9 | 10 | *11* | *12* | | | 8 | | | | 4 | **13** | 1 | | | | |
| | 2 | 3 | 6 | 5 | | 7 | | 9 | 10 | 11 | 8 | | | | | | | 4 | | 1 | | | | |
| | | **3** | 6 | 5 | | 7 | | 9 | 10 | 11 | 2 | | | *8* | | **13** | | 4 | *12* | 1 | | | | |
| | | | 6 | 5 | | 7 | 8 | 9 | 10 | 11 | 3 | 2 | | | | | | 4 | | 1 | | | | |
| | | | 6 | 5 | | 7 | 8 | 9 | 10 | | 11 | 2 | | | | 3 | | 4 | | 1 | | | | |
| | | | 6 | 5 | | *7* | 8 | 9 | 10 | | 11 | 2 | | | | 3 | | 4 | *12* | 1 | | | | |
| | | | 6 | 5 | | *7* | 8 | 9 | 10 | | 11 | 2 | | | | 3 | | 4 | *12* | 1 | | | | |
| | | | 6 | 5 | | | 8 | 9 | 10 | | 11 | 2 | | *12* | | 3 | | 4 | *7* | 1 | | | | |
| 1 | | | 11 | 5 | 6 | | 8 | 9 | 10 | | | 2 | | *12* | | 3 | | 4 | *7* | | | | | |
| 1 | | | 11 | 5 | 6 | | 8 | | 10 | | 9 | 2 | | *12* | | 3 | | 4 | *7* | | | | | |
| 1 | 2 | | 11 | 5 | 6 | | 8 | | 10 | *12* | 7 | *3* | | | | | | 4 | **13** | | | **9** | | |
| 1 | 2 | **13** | 11 | 5 | 6 | | 8 | | | *12* | 7 | 3 | | **10** | | | | 4 | | | | *9* | | |
| 1 | 2 | | 11 | 5 | *6* | | 8 | | 10 | 9 | 7 | 3 | | | | | | 4 | *12* | | | | | |
| 1 | 2 | **3** | 11 | | 6 | *12* | 8 | | | 10 | 7 | 5 | | | | | | 4 | **13** | | | *9* | | |
| 1 | | 3 | 11 | 5 | 6 | | 8 | | 10 | 9 | 7 | 2 | | | | | | *4* | *12* | | | | | |
| 1 | 2 | 3 | 11 | 5 | | *9* | 8 | | 10 | | 7 | 6 | | | | | | 4 | *12* | | | | | |
| 1 | | 3 | | 5 | 6 | *9* | 8 | | 10 | | 2 | 11 | | | | 4 | | | 7 | | | *12* | | |
| 1 | | 3 | 4 | 5 | 6 | 9 | 8 | | 10 | | 11 | 2 | | | | | | | 7 | | | | | |
| 1 | 2 | 3 | | 5 | 6 | 9 | 8 | | | | 7 | 4 | | | | | | | *10* | | *12* | | **11** | **14** |
| 29 | 32 | 36 | 35 | 42 | 32 | 35 | 39 | 36 | 36 | 16 | 30 | 27 | 3 | 10 | 3 | 12 | 3 | 24 | 7 | 14 | | 3 | 1 | |
| | 1 | 1 | | | | 3 | | | 1 | 5 | 9 | | 3 | 5 | | 2 | | | 12 | | 2 | 1 | | 1 |
| | 2 | 1 | 1 | 1 | 1 | 6 | 2 | 13 | 3 | 1 | 6 | | | 1 | | 1 | | | 1 | | 1 | 1 | | |

| Hodge | Cross, R. | Cross, P. | Tait | McPhail | Emerson | Johnrose | Olsson | Saville | Honour | Gallacher | Southall | Nobbs | Proudlock | Wratten | Jones | McGuckin | Johnson | Gilchrist | Peverell |
|---|---|---|---|---|---|---|---|---|---|---|---|---|---|---|---|---|---|---|---|
| 1 | 2 | 3 | 4 | 5 | 6 | 7 | 8 | 9 | 10 | | | | | 11 | | | | | |
| 1 | 2 | 3 | | 5 | **6** | 7 | 8 | 9 | 10 | | *12* | | | **13** | | 4 | | | *11* |
| | 2 | 3 | | 5 | 6 | 7 | 8 | 9 | 10 | | 11 | | | | 1 | | | 4 | |
| | 2 | 3 | 6 | 5 | | 7 | | 9 | 10 | *8* | 11 | | | | 1 | | | 4 | *12* |
| 2 | 4 | 4 | 2 | 4 | 3 | 4 | 3 | 4 | 4 | 1 | 2 | | | 1 | 2 | 1 | | 2 | 1 |
| | | | | | | | | | | | 1 | | | 1 | | | | | 1 |
| | | | | | | 1 | | 5 | | | | | | | | | | | 1 |

| Hodge | Cross, R. | Cross, P. | Tait | McPhail | Emerson | Johnrose | Olsson | Saville | Honour | Gallacher | Southall | Nobbs | Proudlock | Wratten |
|---|---|---|---|---|---|---|---|---|---|---|---|---|---|---|
| 1 | 2 | 3 | 4 | 5 | 6 | 7 | 8 | 9 | 10 | *11* | *12* | | | |
| 1 | 2 | 3 | 4 | 5 | 6 | 7 | 8 | 9 | 10 | | 11 | | | |
| 1 | 2 | 3 | 4 | 5 | 6 | 7 | 8 | 9 | | *11* | | 10 | | *12* |
| 1 | 2 | 3 | 4 | 5 | 6 | 7 | 8 | 9 | 11 | | | 10 | | |
| 4 | 4 | 4 | 4 | 4 | 4 | 4 | 4 | 4 | 3 | 2 | 1 | 2 | | |
| | | | | | | | | | | | 1 | | | 1 |
| | | | | 1 | | 4 | | 1 | | | 1 | | | |

## League Table

| | P | W | D | L | F | A | Pts |
|---|---|---|---|---|---|---|---|
| Stoke City | 46 | 27 | 12 | 7 | 73 | 34 | 93 |
| Bolton Wanderers | 46 | 27 | 9 | 10 | 80 | 41 | 90 |
| Port Vale | 46 | 26 | 11 | 9 | 79 | 44 | 89 |
| West Bromwich Albion | 46 | 25 | 10 | 11 | 88 | 54 | 85 |
| Swansea City | 46 | 20 | 13 | 13 | 65 | 47 | 73 |
| Stockport County | 46 | 19 | 15 | 12 | 81 | 57 | 72 |
| Leyton Orient | 46 | 21 | 9 | 16 | 69 | 53 | 72 |
| Reading | 46 | 18 | 15 | 13 | 66 | 51 | 69 |
| Brighton & Hove Albion | 46 | 20 | 9 | 17 | 63 | 59 | 69 |
| Bradford City | 46 | 18 | 14 | 14 | 69 | 67 | 68 |
| Rotherham United | 46 | 17 | 14 | 15 | 60 | 60 | 65 |
| Fulham | 46 | 16 | 17 | 13 | 57 | 55 | 65 |
| Burnley | 46 | 15 | 16 | 15 | 57 | 59 | 61 |
| Plymouth Argyle | 46 | 16 | 12 | 18 | 59 | 64 | 60 |
| Huddersfield Town | 46 | 17 | 9 | 20 | 54 | 61 | 60 |
| Hartlepool United | 46 | 14 | 12 | 20 | 42 | 60 | 54 |
| Bournemouth | 46 | 12 | 17 | 17 | 45 | 52 | 53 |
| Blackpool | 46 | 12 | 15 | 19 | 63 | 75 | 51 |
| Exeter City | 46 | 11 | 17 | 18 | 54 | 69 | 50 |
| Hull City | 46 | 13 | 11 | 22 | 46 | 69 | 50 |
| Preston North End | 46 | 13 | 8 | 25 | 65 | 94 | 47 |
| Mansfield Town | 46 | 11 | 11 | 24 | 52 | 80 | 44 |
| Wigan Athletic | 46 | 10 | 11 | 25 | 43 | 72 | 41 |
| Chester City | 46 | 8 | 5 | 33 | 49 | 102 | 29 |

# 1993-94

## Division Two

Managers: Viv Busby and John MacPhail

### Did you know that?

'Pools earned a meagre nine points from 23 away games, with one win and six draws, their lowest total since the introduction of three points for a win.

An interesting event for the visit of Burnley on 26 March was the presence of the future Prime Minister Tony Blair, accompanied by his press secretary Alistair Campbell and Peter Mandelson, MP for Hartlepool. Campbell, a lifelong Burnley supporter, had to endure a rare sparkling performance from 'Pools, who ran out convincing 4–1 winners.

| Match No. | Date | Round | Venue | Opponents | Result | | Scorers | Attendance |
|---|---|---|---|---|---|---|---|---|
| 1 | Aug 14 | | (h) | Fulham | L | 0 - 1 | | 2,542 |
| 3 | 21 | | (a) | Brighton & Hove Albion | D | 1 - 1 | Gallacher | 5,230 |
| 5 | 28 | | (h) | Bournemouth | D | 1 - 1 | Honour | 2,482 |
| 6 | 31 | | (a) | Leyton Orient | W | 2 - 1 | West, Southall | 3,399 |
| 7 | Sep 4 | | (a) | Exeter City | L | 1 - 2 | Southall | 2,644 |
| 8 | 11 | | (h) | Stockport County | W | 1 - 0 | Thompson | 2,473 |
| 9 | 14 | | (h) | Blackpool | W | 2 - 0 | West, Honour | 2,214 |
| 10 | 18 | | (a) | Port Vale | L | 0 - 1 | | 7,279 |
| 12 | 25 | | (h) | York City | L | 0 - 2 | | 3,050 |
| 14 | Oct 2 | | (a) | Burnley | L | 0 - 2 | | 9,528 |
| 16 | 9 | | (h) | Brentford | L | 0 - 1 | | 1,802 |
| 17 | 16 | | (a) | Cambridge United | L | 0 - 1 | | 3,318 |
| 18 | 23 | | (h) | Bradford City | L | 1 - 2 | Johnrose | 2,536 |
| 19 | 30 | | (a) | Cardiff City | D | 2 - 2 | Johnrose, West | 3,710 |
| 20 | Nov 2 | | (h) | Barnet | W | 2 - 1 | Houchen, Johnrose | 1,960 |
| 21 | 6 | | (a) | Bristol Rovers | D | 1 - 1 | West | 5,205 |
| 24 | 20 | | (h) | Wrexham | L | 1 - 2 | Southall | 1,530 |
| 25 | 27 | | (a) | Plymouth Argyle | L | 0 - 2 | | 5,881 |
| 26 | Dec 4 | | (a) | Blackpool | L | 1 - 2 | Stoneman (o.g.) | 3,121 |
| 27 | 11 | | (h) | Brighton & Hove Albion | D | 2 - 2 | Southall, Honour (pen) | 1,558 |
| 28 | 17 | | (a) | Fulham | L | 0 - 2 | | 2,998 |
| 29 | 27 | | (h) | Huddersfield Town | L | 1 - 4 | Southall (pen) | 3,286 |
| 30 | 28 | | (a) | Hull City | L | 0 - 1 | | 4,607 |
| 31 | Jan 1 | | (h) | Rotherham United | W | 2 - 0 | Houchen 2 | 2,101 |
| 32 | 8 | | (a) | Reading | L | 0 - 4 | | 6,217 |
| 33 | 15 | | (h) | Cambridge United | L | 0 - 2 | | 1,690 |
| 34 | 22 | | (a) | Brentford | L | 0 - 1 | | 6,334 |
| 35 | 28 | | (a) | Swansea City | D | 1 - 1 | Thompson | 2,573 |
| 36 | Feb 5 | | (a) | Bradford City | L | 1 - 2 | Thompson | 7,907 |
| 37 | 12 | | (h) | Reading | L | 1 - 4 | McGuckin | 2,218 |
| 38 | 19 | | (a) | Bournemouth | D | 0 - 0 | | 3,201 |
| 39 | 26 | | (h) | Exeter City | L | 1 - 2 | McGuckin | 1,695 |
| 40 | Mar 5 | | (a) | Stockport County | L | 0 - 5 | | 4,076 |
| 41 | 8 | | (h) | Leyton Orient | D | 1 - 1 | Southall | 1,251 |
| 42 | 12 | | (h) | Port Vale | L | 1 - 4 | MacPhail | 1,798 |
| 43 | 19 | | (a) | York City | L | 0 - 3 | | 3,191 |
| 44 | 22 | | (h) | Cardiff City | W | 3 - 0 | Olsson, Southall (pen), Houchen | 1,077 |
| 45 | 26 | | (h) | Burnley | W | 4 - 1 | Houchen 2, Southall, Thompson | 2,879 |
| 46 | 29 | | (h) | Swansea City | W | 1 - 0 | Houchen | 1,354 |
| 47 | Apr 2 | | (a) | Huddersfield Town | D | 1 - 1 | West | 5,717 |
| 48 | 4 | | (h) | Hull City | L | 0 - 1 | | 2,448 |
| 49 | 9 | | (a) | Rotherham United | L | 0 - 7 | | 2,792 |
| 50 | 23 | | (h) | Bristol Rovers | W | 2 - 1 | Houchen, Peverell | 1,409 |
| 51 | 26 | | (a) | Barnet | L | 2 - 3 | Southall, Olsson | 1,352 |
| 52 | 30 | | (a) | Wrexham | L | 0 - 2 | | 2,090 |
| 53 | May 7 | | (h) | Plymouth Argyle | L | 1 - 8 | Peverell | 2,389 |

Final Position: 23rd in Division Two - Relegated

Apps.
Sub.Apps.
1 own goal — Goals

**FA Cup**

| Match No. | Date | Round | Venue | Opponents | Result | | Scorers | Attendance |
|---|---|---|---|---|---|---|---|---|
| 23 | Nov 13 | R1 | (a) | Macclesfield Town | L | 0 - 2 | | 2,747 |

Apps.
Sub.Apps.
Goals

**League Cup**

| Match No. | Date | Round | Venue | Opponents | Result | | Scorers | Attendance |
|---|---|---|---|---|---|---|---|---|
| 2 | Aug 17 | R1/1 | (a) | Stockport County | D | 1 - 1 | West | 2,915 |
| 4 | 24 | R1/2 | (h) | Stockport County | W | 2 - 1 | Tait, Honour | 2,273 |
| 11 | Sep 21 | R2/1 | (a) | Grimsby Town | L | 0 - 3 | | 2,353 |
| 15 | Oct 5 | R2/2 | (h) | Grimsby Town | L | 0 - 2 | | 1,385 |

Apps.
Sub.Apps.
Goals

| Carter | Cross, R. | Cross, P. | McGuckin | MacPhail | Emerson | Gallacher | Wratten | West | Honour | Peverell | Southall | Gilchrist | Nobbs | Tait | Thompson | Johnrose | Houchen | Olsson | Ingram | Halliday | Skedd | Jones | Lynch | Garrett | Oliver |
|---|---|---|---|---|---|---|---|---|---|---|---|---|---|---|---|---|---|---|---|---|---|---|---|---|---|
| 1 | 2 | 3 | 4 | 5 | *6* | 7 | 8 | 9 | 10 | **11** | *12* | **13** | | | | | | | | | | | | | |
| 1 | 2 | 3 | 4 | 5 | *12* | 7 | 8 | 9 | 10 | | *11* | | | 6 | | | | | | | | | | | |
| 1 | 2 | 3 | | 5 | 6 | | 8 | 9 | 10 | **13** | 11 | **4** | | *7* | *12* | | | | | | | | | | |
| 1 | 2 | 3 | 4 | 5 | 6 | | 8 | 9 | 10 | *12* | 11 | | | | *7* | | | | | | | | | | |
| 1 | 2 | 3 | 4 | 5 | 6 | | 8 | *9* | 10 | *12* | 11 | | | | 7 | | | | | | | | | | |
| 1 | 2 | 3 | 4 | 5 | 6 | | 8 | 9 | 10 | | 11 | | | | *7* | *12* | | | | | | | | | |
| 1 | 2 | 3 | 4 | 5 | 6 | | 8 | 9 | 10 | | 11 | | | | *7* | *12* | | | | | | | | | |
| 1 | 2 | 3 | 4 | 5 | 6 | | 8 | 9 | 10 | | *11* | | | | 7 | *12* | | | | | | | | | |
| 1 | 2 | 3 | 4 | 5 | 6 | | 8 | 9 | 10 | | 11 | | | | *7* | *12* | | | | | | | | | |
| 1 | 2 | *3* | 4 | 5 | 6 | | 8 | *7* | 10 | | | *12* | | | | 11 | 9 | | | | | | | | |
| 1 | 2 | 3 | 4 | 5 | 6 | | **8** | *7* | 10 | | | **13** | | | | 11 | 9 | *12* | | | | | | | |
| 1 | 2 | 3 | | 5 | 6 | | 8 | | | **13** | *12* | *4* | | 7 | | **10** | 9 | 11 | | | | | | | |
| 1 | 2 | 3 | 4 | 5 | *6* | | 8 | | | *12* | | | | 7 | | 10 | 9 | 11 | | | | | | | |
| 1 | 2 | 3 | 4 | 5 | | | 8 | 11 | | *12* | | | | 7 | | 10 | *9* | 6 | | | | | | | |
| 1 | 2 | *3* | 4 | 5 | | | 8 | 11 | | | | *12* | | 7 | | 10 | 9 | 6 | | | | | | | |
| 1 | 2 | 3 | 4 | 5 | | | 8 | 11 | | | | *7* | | | | 10 | 9 | 6 | | | | | | | |
| 1 | | | 4 | 5 | | | | | | | *7* | 3 | | 6 | | 8 | 9 | *12* | 2 | 10 | 11 | | | | |
| 1 | 2 | | | 5 | | | 11 | *12* | 10 | | 7 | 6 | | 4 | | 8 | 9 | | | | *3* | | | | |
| | | | *12* | *5* | | | 8 | **11** | 10 | | 7 | 6 | | 4 | | | 9 | **13** | 2 | | 3 | 1 | | | |
| | | | 5 | | | | 8 | 11 | 10 | | 7 | 6 | | 4 | | | 9 | | 2 | | 3 | 1 | | | |
| | | | | 5 | | | **8** | 11 | 10 | | 7 | 6 | | 4 | **13** | | 9 | | *2* | | 3 | 1 | *12* | | |
| | | | | 5 | | | **8** | 11 | *10* | | 7 | | | 4 | **13** | | 9 | 6 | 2 | | *12* | 1 | 3 | | |
| | | | | 5 | | | 8 | 11 | | | 7 | 6 | | 2 | | | 9 | 4 | | | 10 | 1 | 3 | | |
| | | | | 5 | | | 8 | 11 | | | 7 | 6 | | 2 | | | 9 | 4 | | | 10 | 1 | 3 | | |
| | | | | 5 | | | 8 | 11 | | | 7 | 6 | | 2 | | | 9 | 4 | | | 10 | 1 | 3 | | |
| | | | | 5 | | | *8* | **11** | | **13** | 7 | 6 | | 2 | 9 | | | 4 | | *12* | 10 | 1 | 3 | | |
| | | | 5 | *12* | | | 8 | | | | 7 | *6* | | 11 | **9** | | | 4 | 2 | **13** | 10 | 1 | 3 | | |
| | | | 5 | *12* | | | 8 | | | | 7 | | | 6 | **13** | | 9 | 4 | 2 | **11** | 10 | 1 | *3* | | |
| | | | 5 | | | | *8* | | | | 7 | 11 | | 6 | *12* | | 9 | 4 | 2 | **13** | 10 | 1 | **3** | | |
| | | | 5 | | | | *8* | | | | 7 | 11 | | 6 | *12* | | 9 | 4 | 2 | **13** | 10 | 1 | **3** | | |
| | | | 5 | | | | 8 | | | | 2 | 11 | | 6 | 7 | | 9 | 4 | | | 10 | 1 | 3 | | |
| | | | 5 | *12* | | | 8 | **13** | 10 | | 2 | 6 | | | 7 | | 9 | 4 | | **11** | | 1 | *3* | | |
| | | | 5 | 6 | | | *8* | 10 | | *12* | **11** | 3 | | | 7 | | 9 | 4 | | | | 1 | | 2 | **13** |
| | | | 5 | 4 | | | 8 | 10 | | | 11 | 3 | | | 7 | | 9 | | | | 6 | 1 | | 2 | |
| | | | 5 | 4 | | | | 10 | | *12* | 11 | 3 | | | *7* | | 9 | 8 | | | 6 | 1 | | 2 | |
| | | | 5 | 4 | | | | 10 | | | 11 | 3 | | | 7 | | 9 | 8 | | | 6 | 1 | | 2 | |
| | | | 5 | | | | 10 | | | | 11 | 4 | | | 7 | | 9 | 8 | | | 6 | 1 | 3 | 2 | |
| | | | 5 | | | | 10 | *12* | | | 11 | 4 | | | 7 | | *9* | 8 | | | 6 | 1 | 3 | 2 | |
| | | | 5 | | | | 10 | *12* | | **13** | 11 | 4 | | | 7 | | *9* | 8 | | | 6 | 1 | **3** | 2 | |
| | | | 5 | | | | 10 | 6 | | | 11 | 4 | | | 7 | | 9 | 8 | | | | 1 | 3 | 2 | |
| | | | 5 | | | | 10 | 6 | | | 11 | 4 | | | 7 | | 9 | 8 | | | | 1 | 3 | 2 | |
| | | | 5 | | | | *10* | 6 | | 9 | 11 | 4 | | *12* | 7 | | | 8 | | | | 1 | 3 | 2 | |
| | | | | | | | 6 | | | 8 | 11 | 4 | | 5 | | | 9 | 7 | 3 | 10 | | 1 | | 2 | |
| | | | **13** | | | | **6** | *12* | | *8* | 11 | 4 | | 5 | | | 9 | 7 | 3 | 10 | | 1 | | 2 | |
| | | | *5* | | | | **6** | **13** | | 8 | 11 | *12* | | 4 | | | 9 | 7 | 3 | 10 | | 1 | | 2 | |
| | | | | | | | | *12* | | 8 | 11 | 5 | | 4 | | | *9* | 7 | 3 | 10 | **6** | 1 | **13** | 2 | |
| 18 | 17 | 16 | 33 | 29 | 12 | 2 | 42 | 29 | 17 | 6 | 38 | 30 | | 25 | 20 | 9 | 34 | 29 | 13 | 7 | 21 | 28 | 17 | 14 | |
| | | | 2 | 3 | 1 | | | 7 | | 10 | 2 | 5 | | 1 | 6 | 4 | | 3 | | 4 | 1 | | 2 | | 1 |
| | | | 2 | 1 | | 1 | | 5 | 3 | 2 | 9 | | | | 4 | 3 | 8 | 2 | | | | | | | |

| Carter | Cross, R. | Cross, P. | McGuckin | MacPhail | Emerson | Gallacher | Wratten | West | Honour | Peverell | Southall | Gilchrist | Nobbs | Tait | Thompson | Johnrose | Houchen | Olsson | Ingram | Halliday | Skedd | Jones | Lynch | Garrett | Oliver |
|---|---|---|---|---|---|---|---|---|---|---|---|---|---|---|---|---|---|---|---|---|---|---|---|---|---|
| 1 | 2 | | 4 | 5 | | | *8* | **11** | *12* | | **13** | 7 | | | | 10 | 9 | 6 | | | 3 | | | | |
| 1 | 1 | | 1 | 1 | | | 1 | 1 | | | | 1 | | | | 1 | 1 | 1 | | | 1 | | | | |
| | | | | | | | | | 1 | | 1 | | | | | | | | | | | | | | |
| | | | | | | | | | | | | | | | | | | | | | | | | | |

| Carter | Cross, R. | Cross, P. | McGuckin | MacPhail | Emerson | Gallacher | Wratten | West | Honour | Peverell | Southall | Gilchrist | Nobbs | Tait | Thompson | Johnrose | Houchen | Olsson | Ingram | Halliday | Skedd | Jones | Lynch | Garrett | Oliver |
|---|---|---|---|---|---|---|---|---|---|---|---|---|---|---|---|---|---|---|---|---|---|---|---|---|---|
| 1 | 2 | 3 | 4 | 5 | | 7 | 8 | 9 | 10 | | 11 | | 6 | | | | | | | | | | | | |
| 1 | 2 | 3 | 4 | 5 | 6 | | **8** | 9 | 10 | *12* | *11* | **13** | | 7 | | | | | | | | | | | |
| 1 | 2 | 3 | 4 | 5 | 6 | | 8 | 9 | 10 | | 11 | | | | *7* | *12* | | | | | | | | | |
| 1 | 2 | 3 | 4 | 5 | 6 | | 8 | *7* | 10 | | | | | | | 11 | 9 | *12* | | | | | | | |
| 4 | 4 | 4 | 4 | 4 | 3 | 1 | 4 | 4 | 4 | | 3 | | 1 | 1 | 1 | 1 | 1 | | | | | | | | |
| | | | | | | | | | | 1 | | 1 | | | | 1 | | 1 | | | | | | | |
| | | | | | | | | 1 | 1 | | | | 1 | | | | | | | | | | | | |

## League Table

| | P | W | D | L | F | A | Pts |
|---|---|---|---|---|---|---|---|
| Reading | 46 | 26 | 11 | 9 | 81 | 44 | 89 |
| Port Vale | 46 | 26 | 10 | 10 | 79 | 46 | 88 |
| Plymouth Argyle | 46 | 25 | 10 | 11 | 88 | 56 | 85 |
| Stockport County | 46 | 24 | 13 | 9 | 74 | 44 | 85 |
| York City | 46 | 21 | 12 | 13 | 64 | 40 | 75 |
| Burnley | 46 | 21 | 10 | 15 | 79 | 58 | 73 |
| Bradford City | 46 | 19 | 13 | 14 | 61 | 53 | 70 |
| Bristol Rovers | 46 | 20 | 10 | 16 | 60 | 59 | 70 |
| Hull City | 46 | 18 | 14 | 14 | 62 | 54 | 68 |
| Cambridge United | 46 | 19 | 9 | 18 | 79 | 73 | 66 |
| Huddersfield Town | 46 | 17 | 14 | 15 | 58 | 61 | 65 |
| Wrexham | 46 | 17 | 11 | 18 | 66 | 77 | 62 |
| Swansea City | 46 | 16 | 12 | 18 | 56 | 58 | 60 |
| Brighton & Hove Albion | 46 | 15 | 14 | 17 | 60 | 67 | 59 |
| Rotherham United | 46 | 15 | 13 | 18 | 63 | 60 | 58 |
| Brentford | 46 | 13 | 19 | 14 | 57 | 55 | 58 |
| Bournemouth | 46 | 14 | 15 | 17 | 51 | 59 | 57 |
| Leyton Orient | 46 | 14 | 14 | 18 | 57 | 71 | 56 |
| Cardiff City | 46 | 13 | 15 | 18 | 66 | 79 | 54 |
| Blackpool | 46 | 16 | 5 | 25 | 63 | 75 | 53 |
| Fulham | 46 | 14 | 10 | 22 | 50 | 63 | 52 |
| Exeter City | 46 | 11 | 12 | 23 | 52 | 83 | 45 |
| Hartlepool United | 46 | 9 | 9 | 28 | 41 | 87 | 36 |
| Barnet | 46 | 5 | 13 | 28 | 41 | 86 | 28 |

# 1994-95

## Division Three

Managers: John MacPhail, David McCreery, and Keith Houchen

### Did you know that?

Keith Houchen was leading goalscorer, with 13 goals in 32 League appearances, the fifth time he achieved the feat, a club record.

Brian Honour played the last of his 384 games for the club on 16 August against Bury in the Football League Cup. He was awarded a benefit against Newcastle United in August 1995, which attracted a sell-out crowd.

| Match No. | Date | Round | Venue | Opponents | Result | | Scorers | Attendance |
|---|---|---|---|---|---|---|---|---|
| 1 | Aug 13 | | (a) | Gillingham | D | 0 - 0 | | 2,959 |
| 3 | 20 | | (h) | Darlington | W | 1 - 0 | Lynch | 3,053 |
| 5 | 27 | | (a) | Bury | L | 0 - 2 | | 2,145 |
| 6 | 30 | | (h) | Barnet | L | 0 - 1 | | 2,096 |
| 7 | Sep 3 | | (h) | Chesterfield | L | 0 - 2 | | 2,173 |
| 8 | 10 | | (a) | Colchester United | L | 0 - 1 | | 2,428 |
| 9 | 13 | | (a) | Northampton Town | D | 1 - 1 | Halliday | 2,466 |
| 10 | 17 | | (h) | Gillingham | W | 2 - 0 | Houchen, Walsh (pen) | 1,756 |
| 12 | 24 | | (h) | Lincoln City | L | 0 - 3 | | 1,537 |
| 13 | Oct 1 | | (a) | Exeter City | L | 1 - 2 | Halliday | 2,390 |
| 15 | 8 | | (a) | Mansfield Town | L | 0 - 2 | | 2,545 |
| 16 | 15 | | (h) | Preston North End | W | 3 - 1 | Houchen, Ainsley, Foster | 2,003 |
| 18 | 22 | | (h) | Walsall | D | 1 - 1 | Houchen | 1,862 |
| 19 | 29 | | (a) | Scunthorpe United | D | 0 - 0 | | 2,624 |
| 20 | Nov 5 | | (h) | Wigan Athletic | L | 0 - 1 | | 1,683 |
| 23 | 19 | | (a) | Doncaster Rovers | L | 0 - 3 | | 2,507 |
| 24 | 26 | | (h) | Rochdale | W | 1 - 0 | Sloan | 1,387 |
| 25 | Dec 10 | | (a) | Darlington | W | 2 - 1 | Southall, Houchen | 3,193 |
| 26 | 17 | | (h) | Bury | W | 3 - 1 | Houchen 3 | 1,746 |
| 27 | 26 | | (h) | Carlisle United | L | 1 - 5 | Skedd | 3,854 |
| 28 | 27 | | (a) | Torquay United | D | 2 - 2 | Southall (pen), Thompson | 3,172 |
| 29 | 31 | | (h) | Fulham | L | 1 - 2 | Southall (pen) | 1,698 |
| 30 | Jan 14 | | (h) | Scarborough | D | 3 - 3 | Thompson 2, Sloan | 1,784 |
| 31 | 28 | | (h) | Scunthorpe United | L | 1 - 4 | Thompson | 1,660 |
| 32 | Feb 4 | | (a) | Rochdale | L | 0 - 1 | | 1,848 |
| 33 | 18 | | (a) | Scarborough | D | 2 - 2 | McGuckin, Houchen | 1,517 |
| 34 | 21 | | (a) | Hereford United | L | 0 - 1 | | 1,741 |
| 35 | 25 | | (h) | Exeter City | D | 2 - 2 | Houchen, McGuckin | 1,452 |
| 36 | 28 | | (a) | Wigan Athletic | L | 0 - 2 | | 1,452 |
| 37 | Mar 4 | | (a) | Lincoln City | L | 0 - 3 | | 6,477 |
| 38 | 7 | | (a) | Walsall | L | 1 - 4 | McGuckin | 3,314 |
| 39 | 11 | | (h) | Colchester United | W | 3 - 1 | Southall 3 (2 pens) | 1,371 |
| 40 | 18 | | (a) | Barnet | L | 0 - 4 | | 1,557 |
| 41 | 21 | | (h) | Doncaster Rovers | W | 2 - 1 | Houchen 2 | 1,354 |
| 42 | 25 | | (a) | Chesterfield | L | 0 - 2 | | 4,125 |
| 43 | Apr 1 | | (h) | Northampton Town | D | 1 - 1 | Houchen | 2,113 |
| 44 | 8 | | (a) | Fulham | L | 0 - 1 | | 3,465 |
| 45 | 15 | | (h) | Torquay United | D | 1 - 1 | Henderson | 1,596 |
| 46 | 17 | | (a) | Carlisle United | W | 1 - 0 | Houchen | 10,242 |
| 47 | 22 | | (h) | Hereford United | W | 4 - 0 | Holmes 2, Henderson 2 | 1,784 |
| 48 | 29 | | (a) | Preston North End | L | 0 - 3 | | 9,129 |
| 49 | May 6 | | (h) | Mansfield Town | W | 3 - 2 | Halliday 3 | 3,049 |

Final Position : 18th in Division Three

Apps.
Sub.Apps.
Goals

**FA Cup**

| | | | | | | | | |
|---|---|---|---|---|---|---|---|---|
| 22 | Nov 12 | R1 | (a) | Port Vale | L | 0 - 6 | | 6,199 |

Apps.
Sub.Apps.
Goals

**League Cup**

| | | | | | | | | |
|---|---|---|---|---|---|---|---|---|
| 2 | Aug 16 | R1/1 | (a) | Bury | L | 0 - 2 | | 1,515 |
| 4 | 23 | R1/2 | (h) | Bury | W | 5 - 1 | Houchen, Southall 2, Jackson (o.g.), Thompson | 1,505 |
| 11 | Sep 21 | R2/1 | (h) | Arsenal | L | 0 - 5 | | 4,421 |
| 14 | Oct 5 | R2/2 | (a) | Arsenal | L | 0 - 2 | | 20,250 |

Apps.
Sub.Apps.
1 own goal
Goals

| Horne | Ingram | Sweeney | Gilchrist | McGuckin | Oliver | Ainsley | Sloan | Houchen | Honour | Southall | Skedd | Thompson | Lynch | Halliday | Hyson | Tait | Garrett | Gourlay | Burgess | Walsh | McCreery | Foster | Cook | Reddish | MacPhail | Daughtry | Peverell | Jones | Sunley | Henderson | Holmes | Homer |
|---|---|---|---|---|---|---|---|---|---|---|---|---|---|---|---|---|---|---|---|---|---|---|---|---|---|---|---|---|---|---|---|---|
| 1 | 2 | 3 | 4 | 5 | 6 | 7 | 8 | 9 | 10 | 11 | | | | | | | | | | | | | | | | | | | | | | |
| 1 | 2 | | 4 | 5 | 6 | | 8 | 9 | | 11 | 3 | 7 | 10 | *12* | | | | | | | | | | | | | | | | | | |
| 1 | 2 | | 4 | 5 | | *6* | | 9 | | 11 | 3 | 7 | 10 | 8 | *12* | | | | | | | | | | | | | | | | | |
| 1 | 2 | | 4 | 5 | 6 | | | 9 | | 11 | 3 | 7 | 10 | *8* | *12* | | | | | | | | | | | | | | | | | |
| 1 | 2 | | 4 | **5** | 6 | 8 | | 9 | | *11* | 3 | 7 | 10 | *12* | **13** | | | | | | | | | | | | | | | | | |
| 1 | 2 | | 4 | | 6 | 8 | 11 | 9 | | | **3** | 7 | *10* | | *12* | 5 | **13** | | | | | | | | | | | | | | | |
| 1 | 2 | | 4 | | 6 | *8* | 11 | 9 | | | | 7 | 3 | 10 | | 5 | | *12* | | | | | | | | | | | | | | |
| 1 | | | 4 | 5 | *6* | | 11 | 9 | | | | 7 | *12* | 10 | | 8 | | | 2 | 3 | | | | | | | | | | | | |
| 1 | | | 4 | 5 | *6* | | | 9 | | | *12* | 7 | **13** | 10 | *11* | 8 | | | 2 | 3 | | | | | | | | | | | | |
| 1 | 8 | | 4 | 5 | 6 | 11 | *12* | 9 | | | | *7* | | 10 | | | | | 2 | 3 | | | | | | | | | | | | |
| 1 | 8 | | 4 | 5 | **6** | 11 | *12* | 9 | | 7 | | **13** | | 10 | | | | | 2 | *3* | | | | | | | | | | | | |
| 1 | 3 | | 4 | 5 | | 6 | 7 | 9 | | 11 | | | | | | | | | 2 | | 8 | 10 | | | | | | | | | | |
| 1 | 3 | | 4 | 5 | | 6 | 7 | *9* | | 11 | | *12* | | | | | | | 2 | | 8 | 10 | | | | | | | | | | |
| 1 | 3 | | 4 | 5 | | 6 | 7 | 9 | | 11 | | | | | | | | | 2 | | 8 | 10 | | | | | | | | | | |
| 1 | 3 | | 4 | 5 | | 6 | **7** | 9 | | 11 | **13** | *12* | | | | | | | 2 | | 8 | *10* | | | | | | | | | | |
| 1 | 10 | | 4 | 5 | | **6** | *9* | | | 11 | | 7 | | *12* | | | | | 2 | | **13** | | 3 | 8 | | | | | | | | |
| 1 | | | 4 | | | | 10 | | | 11 | 6 | 9 | | *12* | | | | | 2 | | | | 3 | 8 | 5 | 7 | | | | | | |
| 1 | | | 4 | 5 | | | 10 | 9 | | 11 | 6 | | | | | 8 | | | 2 | | | | 3 | | | 7 | | | | | | |
| 1 | 2 | | 4 | 5 | | | 10 | 9 | | 11 | 6 | | | | | 8 | | | | | | | 3 | | | 7 | | | | | | |
| 1 | 2 | | 4 | | | | *10* | | | 11 | 6 | 9 | | *12* | | 5 | | | | | | | 3 | 8 | | 7 | | | | | | |
| 1 | 2 | | 4 | | | 8 | 10 | | | 11 | | 9 | | | | 6 | | | | | | | 3 | | 5 | 7 | | | | | | |
| 1 | 2 | | 4 | 5 | | 8 | 10 | | | 11 | 3 | *9* | | | | 6 | | | | | | | | | | 7 | *12* | | | | | |
| **1** | 2 | | | 5 | | | 10 | | | 11 | | 9 | | *12* | | 6 | | | | | | | 3 | 8 | 4 | 7 | | **13** | | | | |
| | 2 | | | 5 | | | 10 | | | 11 | | 9 | | *12* | | 6 | | | | | | | 3 | 8 | 4 | 7 | | 1 | | | | |
| 1 | 2 | | 4 | 5 | | **13** | 10 | | | 11 | | 9 | | *12* | | 6 | | | | | | | 3 | **8** | | 7 | | | | | | |
| 1 | 2 | | | 5 | | | 10 | **9** | | 11 | *12* | 4 | | | | 6 | | | | | **13** | | 3 | 8 | | *7* | | | | | | |
| 1 | 2 | | | 5 | | | 10 | 9 | | 11 | | 4 | | | | 6 | | | | | | | 3 | 8 | | 7 | | | | | | |
| 1 | 2 | | | 5 | | | 10 | 9 | | 11 | **13** | **4** | | *12* | | 6 | | | | | | | 3 | 8 | | *7* | | | | | | |
| 1 | **2** | | | 5 | | | 10 | 9 | | 11 | *12* | | | 7 | | 6 | | | | | | | 3 | *8* | 4 | | | | **13** | | | |
| 1 | | | | | 4 | | 10 | 9 | | 11 | | | | 7 | | 6 | | | | | | | 3 | 8 | 5 | | | | 2 | | | |
| 1 | | | | 5 | 4 | | 10 | | | 11 | *12* | | | 7 | | 6 | | | | | *8* | | 3 | 2 | | | | | | 9 | | |
| 1 | | | | 5 | 8 | | | 9 | | 11 | | | | 7 | | 6 | | | | | | | 3 | 2 | | | | | | 10 | 4 | |
| 1 | 2 | | | 5 | | | | 9 | | 11 | | | | 7 | | | | | | | | | 3 | 6 | | 8 | | | | 10 | 4 | |
| 1 | 8 | | | 5 | | | *12* | 9 | | 11 | 3 | | | 7 | | **6** | | | | | | | | 2 | | **13** | | | | 10 | *4* | |
| 1 | 6 | | | 5 | | | | 9 | | 11 | 3 | 4 | | 7 | | | | | | | | | | 2 | | 8 | | | | 10 | | |
| 1 | 6 | | | 5 | | | | 9 | | 11 | 3 | 4 | | 7 | | | | | | | *8* | | *12* | 2 | | | | | | 10 | | |
| 1 | 9 | | | | | | | | | 11 | 10 | 4 | *12* | 7 | | | | | | | *8* | | 3 | 2 | | | | | | 5 | | 6 |
| 1 | 6 | | | | 4 | | *10* | 9 | | 11 | 3 | 8 | | 7 | | | | | | | | | *12* | 2 | | | | | | 5 | | |
| 1 | 2 | | | 5 | 4 | | | 9 | | 11 | 3 | | | | | | | | | | | | 7 | 8 | | | | | | 10 | 6 | |
| 1 | 2 | | | 5 | 4 | | | 9 | | 11 | | | 3 | | | | | | | | | | 7 | 8 | | | | | | 10 | 6 | |
| 1 | 2 | | | 5 | 4 | | | 9 | | 11 | 3 | *12* | | *10* | | | | | | | | | 7 | 8 | | | | | | 6 | | |
| 1 | 6 | | | 5 | 4 | | | 9 | | 11 | | | 3 | 8 | | | | | | | | | 7 | 2 | | | | | | 10 | | |
| 41 | 35 | 1 | 23 | 34 | 18 | 14 | 26 | 32 | 1 | 37 | 17 | 24 | 8 | 19 | 1 | 20 | | | 11 | 4 | 7 | 4 | 22 | 23 | 6 | 14 | | 1 | 1 | 12 | 5 | 1 |
| | | | | | | 1 | 3 | | | | 6 | 4 | 3 | 9 | 4 | | 1 | 1 | | | 2 | | 2 | | | 1 | 1 | 1 | 1 | | | |
| | | | | 3 | | 1 | 2 | 13 | | 6 | 1 | 4 | 1 | 5 | | | | | | 1 | | 1 | | | | | | | | 3 | 2 | |

| Horne | Ingram | Sweeney | Gilchrist | McGuckin | Oliver | Ainsley | Sloan | Houchen | Honour | Southall | Skedd | Thompson | Lynch | Halliday | Hyson | Tait | Garrett | Gourlay | Burgess | Walsh | McCreery | Foster | Cook | Reddish | MacPhail | Daughtry | Peverell | Jones | Sunley | Henderson | Holmes | Homer |
|---|---|---|---|---|---|---|---|---|---|---|---|---|---|---|---|---|---|---|---|---|---|---|---|---|---|---|---|---|---|---|---|---|
| 1 | 2 | | 4 | 5 | | **6** | *12* | 9 | | 11 | **13** | 7 | | 10 | | | | | | 3 | *8* | | | | | | | | | | | |
| 1 | 1 | | 1 | 1 | | 1 | | 1 | | 1 | | 1 | | 1 | | | | | | 1 | 1 | | | | | | | | | | | |
| | | | | | | | 1 | | | | 1 | | | | | | | | | | | | | | | | | | | | | |
| | | | | | | | | | | | | | | | | | | | | | | | | | | | | | | | | |

| Horne | Ingram | Sweeney | Gilchrist | McGuckin | Oliver | Ainsley | Sloan | Houchen | Honour | Southall | Skedd | Thompson | Lynch | Halliday | Hyson | Tait | Garrett | Gourlay | Burgess | Walsh | McCreery | Foster | Cook | Reddish | MacPhail | Daughtry | Peverell | Jones | Sunley | Henderson | Holmes | Homer |
|---|---|---|---|---|---|---|---|---|---|---|---|---|---|---|---|---|---|---|---|---|---|---|---|---|---|---|---|---|---|---|---|---|
| | 2 | *3* | 4 | 5 | 6 | 7 | 8 | 9 | **10** | 11 | | **13** | *12* | | | | | | | | | | | | | | | 1 | | | | |
| | 2 | | 4 | 5 | 6 | | *8* | 9 | | 11 | 3 | 7 | 10 | *12* | | | | | | | | | | | | | | 1 | | | | |
| 1 | **13** | | 4 | 5 | **6** | | | 9 | | | | 7 | *11* | 10 | *12* | 8 | | | 2 | 3 | | | | | | | | | | | | |
| 1 | 8 | | 4 | 5 | 6 | 11 | **13** | 9 | | | *12* | *7* | | **10** | | | | | 2 | 3 | | | | | | | | | | | | |
| 2 | 3 | 1 | 4 | 4 | 4 | 2 | 2 | 4 | 1 | 2 | 1 | 3 | 2 | 2 | | 1 | | | 2 | 2 | | | | | | | | 2 | | | | |
| | 1 | | | | | | 1 | | | | 1 | 1 | 1 | 1 | 1 | | | | | | | | | | | | | | | | | |
| | | | | | | | | 1 | | 2 | | 1 | | | | | | | | | | | | | | | | | | | | |

## League Table

| | P | W | D | L | F | A | Pts |
|---|---|---|---|---|---|---|---|
| Carlisle United | 42 | 27 | 10 | 5 | 67 | 31 | 91 |
| Walsall | 42 | 24 | 11 | 7 | 75 | 40 | 83 |
| Chesterfield | 42 | 23 | 12 | 7 | 62 | 37 | 81 |
| Bury | 42 | 23 | 11 | 8 | 73 | 36 | 80 |
| Preston North End | 42 | 19 | 10 | 13 | 58 | 41 | 67 |
| Mansfield Town | 42 | 18 | 11 | 13 | 84 | 59 | 65 |
| Scunthorpe United | 42 | 18 | 8 | 16 | 68 | 63 | 62 |
| Fulham | 42 | 16 | 14 | 12 | 60 | 54 | 62 |
| Doncaster Rovers | 42 | 17 | 10 | 15 | 58 | 43 | 61 |
| Colchester United | 42 | 16 | 10 | 16 | 56 | 64 | 58 |
| Barnet | 42 | 15 | 11 | 16 | 56 | 63 | 56 |
| Lincoln City | 42 | 15 | 11 | 16 | 54 | 55 | 56 |
| Torquay United | 42 | 14 | 13 | 15 | 54 | 57 | 55 |
| Wigan Athletic | 42 | 14 | 10 | 18 | 53 | 60 | 52 |
| Rochdale | 42 | 12 | 14 | 16 | 44 | 67 | 50 |
| Hereford United | 42 | 12 | 13 | 17 | 45 | 62 | 49 |
| Northampton Town | 42 | 10 | 14 | 18 | 45 | 67 | 44 |
| Hartlepool United | 42 | 11 | 10 | 21 | 43 | 69 | 43 |
| Gillingham | 42 | 10 | 11 | 21 | 46 | 64 | 41 |
| Darlington | 42 | 11 | 8 | 23 | 43 | 57 | 41 |
| Scarborough | 42 | 8 | 10 | 24 | 49 | 70 | 34 |
| Exeter City | 42 | 8 | 10 | 24 | 36 | 70 | 34 |

# 1995-96

## Division Three

Manager: Keith Houchen

### Did you know that?

'Pools won their first-ever penalty shoot-out, 7–6 against Scarborough in the second leg of their first round Coca Cola Cup tie.

Average home League attendances of 2,072 included 14 games below the 2,000 mark. The lowest of 1,198 was surprisingly against Fulham, who became a Premiership side within five seasons.

| Match No. | Date | Round | Venue | Opponents | Result | | Scorers | Attendance |
|---|---|---|---|---|---|---|---|---|
| 1 | Aug 12 | | (a) | Chester City | L | 0 - 2 | | 2,286 |
| 3 | 19 | | (h) | Exeter City | D | 0 - 0 | | 2,346 |
| 5 | 26 | | (a) | Rochdale | L | 0 - 4 | | 1,794 |
| 6 | 29 | | (h) | Northampton Town | W | 2 - 1 | Hughes (o.g.), Henderson | 2,391 |
| 7 | Sep 2 | | (a) | Doncaster Rovers | L | 0 - 1 | | 2,304 |
| 8 | 9 | | (h) | Darlington | D | 1 - 1 | Houchen | 2,706 |
| 9 | 12 | | (h) | Torquay United | D | 2 - 2 | Houchen, Lowe | 1,945 |
| 10 | 16 | | (a) | Leyton Orient | L | 1 - 4 | Houchen | 4,520 |
| 12 | 23 | | (h) | Cardiff City | W | 2 - 1 | Lowe 2 | 2,172 |
| 13 | 30 | | (a) | Cambridge United | W | 1 - 0 | Howard | 2,849 |
| 15 | Oct 7 | | (a) | Colchester United | L | 1 - 4 | Howard | 2,618 |
| 16 | 14 | | (h) | Scunthorpe United | W | 2 - 0 | Howard, Henderson | 2,603 |
| 18 | 21 | | (a) | Wigan Athletic | L | 0 - 1 | | 2,104 |
| 19 | 28 | | (h) | Gillingham | D | 1 - 1 | Halliday | 2,355 |
| 20 | 31 | | (h) | Barnet | D | 0 - 0 | | 1,713 |
| 21 | Nov 4 | | (a) | Lincoln City | D | 1 - 1 | Allon | 2,939 |
| 24 | 18 | | (h) | Plymouth Argyle | D | 2 - 2 | Ingram, Howard | 1,830 |
| 25 | 25 | | (a) | Preston North End | L | 0 - 3 | | 9,466 |
| 26 | Dec 9 | | (a) | Cardiff City | L | 0 - 2 | | 2,934 |
| 27 | 16 | | (h) | Cambridge United | L | 1 - 2 | Allon | 1,612 |
| 28 | 23 | | (a) | Mansfield Town | W | 3 - 0 | Houchen 2, Halliday | 1,982 |
| 29 | Jan 1 | | (a) | Bury | W | 3 - 0 | Houchen, Halliday, McGuckin | 2,927 |
| 30 | 6 | | (h) | Scarborough | D | 1 - 1 | Allon | 2,252 |
| 31 | 20 | | (h) | Chester City | W | 2 - 1 | Halliday, Tait | 1,864 |
| 32 | 30 | | (a) | Exeter City | L | 0 - 1 | | 2,468 |
| 33 | Feb 3 | | (h) | Rochdale | D | 1 - 1 | Tait | 1,929 |
| 34 | 10 | | (a) | Fulham | D | 2 - 2 | Allon 2 | 3,700 |
| 35 | 17 | | (a) | Torquay United | D | 0 - 0 | | 2,580 |
| 36 | 20 | | (h) | Doncaster Rovers | L | 0 - 1 | | 1,367 |
| 37 | 24 | | (h) | Leyton Orient | W | 4 - 1 | Conlon, Allon, McGuckin, Lynch | 1,915 |
| 38 | 27 | | (a) | Darlington | L | 0 - 1 | | 4,332 |
| 39 | Mar 2 | | (a) | Scarborough | W | 2 - 1 | Conlon 2 | 2,420 |
| 40 | 5 | | (h) | Hereford United | L | 0 - 1 | | 1,473 |
| 41 | 9 | | (h) | Mansfield Town | D | 1 - 1 | Howard | 1,758 |
| 42 | 12 | | (h) | Fulham | W | 1 - 0 | Conlon | 1,198 |
| 43 | 19 | | (a) | Northampton Town | D | 0 - 0 | | 3,537 |
| 44 | 23 | | (h) | Bury | L | 1 - 2 | Ingram | 1,802 |
| 45 | 30 | | (h) | Colchester United | W | 2 - 1 | Halliday, Howard | 1,364 |
| 46 | Apr 2 | | (a) | Scunthorpe United | L | 1 - 2 | Halliday | 2,100 |
| 47 | 6 | | (a) | Gillingham | L | 0 - 2 | | 6,263 |
| 48 | 8 | | (h) | Wigan Athletic | L | 1 - 2 | Canham | 1,877 |
| 49 | 13 | | (a) | Barnet | L | 1 - 5 | Halliday | 2,530 |
| 50 | 20 | | (h) | Lincoln City | W | 3 - 0 | Henderson, Allon 2 | 2,112 |
| 51 | 27 | | (h) | Preston North End | L | 0 - 2 | | 5,076 |
| 52 | 30 | | (a) | Hereford United | L | 1 - 4 | Howard | 4,045 |
| 53 | May 4 | | (a) | Plymouth Argyle | L | 0 - 3 | | 11,526 |

Final Position : 20th in Division Three

Apps.
Sub.Apps.
1 own goal — Goals

### FA Cup

| Match No. | Date | Round | Venue | Opponents | Result | | Scorers | Attendance |
|---|---|---|---|---|---|---|---|---|
| 23 | Nov 11 | R1 | (h) | Darlington | L | 2 - 4 | Sloan, Halliday | 3,834 |

Apps.
Sub.Apps.
Goals

### League Cup

| Match No. | Date | Round | Venue | Opponents | Result | | Scorers | Attendance |
|---|---|---|---|---|---|---|---|---|
| 2 | Aug 15 | R1/1 | (a) | Scarborough | L | 0 - 1 | | 1,555 |
| 4 | 22 | R1/2 | (h) | Scarborough | W | 1 - 0* | McGuckin | 2,134 |
| 11 | Sep 19 | R2/1 | (h) | Arsenal | L | 0 - 3 | | 4,945 |
| 14 | Oct 3 | R2/2 | (a) | Arsenal | L | 0 - 5 | | 27,194 |

* Won 7 - 6 on penalties

Apps.
Sub.Apps.
Goals

| Jones | Ingram | McAuley | Billing | McGuckin | Howard | Halliday | Tait | Houchen | Henderson | Canham | Horne | Lynch | Oliver | Sloan | Foster | Reddish | Homer | Lowe | Ford | Allon | Debont | Roberts | Dixon | Key | Lee | Conlon | Stokoe | Walton | Allinson | Slater | O'Connor | Gallagher | Hutt |
|---|---|---|---|---|---|---|---|---|---|---|---|---|---|---|---|---|---|---|---|---|---|---|---|---|---|---|---|---|---|---|---|---|---|
|1|2|3|4|5|6|7|8|9|10|11| | | | | | | | | | | | | | | | | | | | | | | |
| |2|3|4|5|6|10|8|*12*|9|11|1|*7*| | | | | | | | | | | | | | | | | | | | | |
| | |3|4| |**7**|10|8|*9*|5|2|1|11|6|*12*|**13**| | | | | | | | | | | | | | | | | | |
| | |**3**|4|5|*6*|10|8| |9|11|1|7|*12*| | |2|**13**| | | | | | | | | | | | | | | | |
| | |3|4|5| |*7*|8|9|10|11|1|*12*| | | |2| |6| | | | | | | | | | | | | | | |
| | |3|4|5| |7|8|9|*10*|11|1| | | | |2| |6|*12*| | | | | | | | | | | | | | |
| | |3|4|5| |10|8|9| |11|1|*12*|**13**| | |2| |**6**|*7*| | | | | | | | | | | | | | |
| | |3|4|5| |10|8|9|*12*|11|1| | | | |2| |6|*7*| | | | | | | | | | | | | | |
| | |11|4|5| |10|8|**9**|**13**|7|1|3|*12*| | |*2*| |6| | | | | | | | | | | | | | | |
|*12*|**13**|3| |5|11|10|8|9|4|**2**|*1*| |7| | | | |6| | | | | | | | | | | | | | | |
|1|2|3|4|5|11|10|8| |9| | | |*7*| | | |*12*|6| | | | | | | | | | | | | | | |
| |2|3|4|5|11|10|8| |9| | | | | | | |*12*|6| |*7*|1| | | | | | | | | | | | |
| |2|3|4|5|11| |8|*9*|*12*| | | | | | | |10|6| |7| |1| | | | | | | | | | | |
| |2|3|4|5|11|*12*|8|9|10| | | | | | |13| |6| |**7**| |1| | | | | | | | | | | |
| |2|3|4|5|*12*|11| |*9*|6| | |**13**| | | |**8**| |10| |7| |1| | | | | | | | | | | |
| |2|3|4|5|*12*|**13**|8|**9**|6| | | | | | |*11*| |10| |7| |1| | | | | | | | | | | |
| |2|3|4|5|*12*|10|***14***|**13**|6|*11*|1| | |**7**| | | |***8***| | | | |9| | | | | | | | | | |
| |2|3|4|5|11|***10***|8|9|6|**12**|1| | |***14***| |**13**| | | | | | |*7*| | | | | | | | | | |
| |2|6|4| |11|10|8|9|5| |1|3| |*12*| | | | | | | | |*7*| | | | | | | | | | |
| |2|3|4|5|*11*|10|8|9| | | |*12*| | | |6| | | |7| | | |1| | | | | | | | | |
| |2|3|4|5| |10|*8*|9|6| |1|11|*12*| | |7| | | | | | | | | | | | | | | | | |
| | |3|4|5|**7**|10| |*9*| | |1|11|8|*12*| |2|**13**| | | | | | | |6| | | | | | | | |
| | |3|4|5|9|10| | | | |1|11|8|*12*| |2| | | |7| | | | |*6*| | | | | | | | |
| |2|11|4|5|*12*|10|*8*|9| | |1|3| | | |6| | | |7| | | | | | | | | | | | | |
| |2|11|4|5|*12*|10|8|9| | |1|*3*| | | |6| | | |7| | | | | | | | | | | | | |
| |2|3|4|5|11|10|8|9| | |1| |*12*| | |6| | | |*7*| | | | | | | | | | | | | |
| |2|3|4|5|11|*10*|8|9| | |1| |*12*| | |6| | | |7| | | | | | | | | | | | | |
| | |3| |*5*|6| | |9|4|11|1|10|8| | |2| | | |**7**| | | | |*12*|**13**| | | | | | | |
| |4|3| | |6| |8|*9*|5|*12*|1|11|**10**| | |2| | | |7| | | | | |**13**| | | | | | | |
| |2|3| |5|*12*| |8|*9*|4|**11**|1|**13**| | | | | | | |7| | | | | |10|6| | | | | | |
| |2|3| |5|*12*| |8|9|4|11|1|**13**| | | | | | | |*7*| | | | | |**10**|6| | | | | | |
| |2|3|4|5| | |8|9|7|11|1| | | | | | | | | | | | | | |10|6| | | | | | |
| |2|3|4|5|9| |8| | |11|1| | | | | | | | |7| | | | | |10|6| | | | | | |
| |2|3|4|5|9|*12*|8| | | |1|11| | | | | | | |7| | | | | |*10*|6| | | | | | |
| |2|3| |5|11|10|8|9|4| |1| | | | | | | | | | | | | | |7|6| | | | | | |
| |2|3| |5|11|10|8|9|4|*12*|1| | | | | | | | | | | | | | |*7*|6| | | | | | |
| |2|3| |5|11|10|8|9|4|*12*|1| | | | | | | | | | | | | | |*7*|6| | | | | | |
| |*2*|3|*12*|**5**|6|10|8|9|4|11|1| | | | | | | | | | | | | | |***7***| |**13**|***14***| | | | |
| | |3|2| |6|10|8|9|4|11|1| | | | | | | | | | | | | |**13**|**7**| |*12*|*5*| | | | |
|*12*|**2**|3|7| |6|10|8|9|4|11|*1*| | | | | | | | | | | | | | | | |**13**|5| | | | |
|1| |3|2| |6|10|8|9|4|11| | | | | | | | | | | | | | | |*7*| |*12*|**5**|**13**| | | |
|1| |3|2|5|6|10|8|9|4|11| | | | | | | | | |7| | | | | | | | | | | | | |
| |2|3|8|5|6|10| |**9**|*4*|11| | | | | | | | | |7| | | | |*12*|**13**| | | | |1| | |
|1|2|3| |5|6|10|8|9|4|11| | | | | | | | | |7| | | | | | | | | | | | | |
|1|8|3|2|5|6|10| | |4|*11*| | | | | | | | | |7| | | | | |*12*| |9| | | | | |
|1|**2**|3| |5|9|10| | |4|11| | | | | | | | | |7| | | | |6| | |*12*| | | |*8*|**13**|
|7|32|46|35|40|32|36|38|36|33|25|32|13|7|1| |18|1|13|2|22|1|4|3|1|3|11|8|1|3| |1|1| |
|2|1| |1| |7|3|1|2|3|4| |6|6|5|1|2|4| |1| | | | | |3|4| |5|1|1| | |1|
| |2| | |2|7|7|2|6|3|1| |1| | | | | | | |8| | | | | |4| | | | | | | |

| Jones | Ingram | McAuley | Billing | McGuckin | Howard | Halliday | Tait | Houchen | Henderson | Canham | Horne | Lynch | Oliver | Sloan | Foster | Reddish | Homer | Lowe | Ford | Allon | Debont | Roberts | Dixon | Key | Lee | Conlon | Stokoe | Walton | Allinson | Slater | O'Connor | Gallagher | Hutt |
|---|---|---|---|---|---|---|---|---|---|---|---|---|---|---|---|---|---|---|---|---|---|---|---|---|---|---|---|---|---|---|---|---|---|
| |2|11|4|5|9|10|*8*| |6| |1|**13**|*12*|7| | | | | | | | | | | | | | |**3**| | | | |
| |1|1|1|1|1|1|1| |1| |1| | |1| | | | | | | | | | | | | | |1| | | | |
| | | | | | | | | | | | |1|1| | | | | | | | | | | | | | | | | | | | |
| | | | | | |1| | | | | | | |1| | | | | | | | | | | | | | | | | | | |

| Jones | Ingram | McAuley | Billing | McGuckin | Howard | Halliday | Tait | Houchen | Henderson | Canham | Horne | Lynch | Oliver | Sloan | Foster | Reddish | Homer | Lowe | Ford | Allon | Debont | Roberts | Dixon | Key | Lee | Conlon | Stokoe | Walton | Allinson | Slater | O'Connor | Gallagher | Hutt |
|---|---|---|---|---|---|---|---|---|---|---|---|---|---|---|---|---|---|---|---|---|---|---|---|---|---|---|---|---|---|---|---|---|---|
|1|*2*|3|4|5|6|7|8|9|**10**|11| |*12*|**13**| | | | | | | | | | | | | | | | | | | | |
| |*2*|3|4|5|**6**|7|8|9|10|11|1|*12*|**13**| | | | | | | | | | | | | | | | | | | | |
| | |11|4|5| |10|8|**9**|**13**|7|1|*3*|*12*| | |2| |***6***|***14***| | | | | | | | | | | | | | |
|1|**2**|3|4|5|*11*|10|***8***| |9| | |**13**|7| | | |*12*|6| | | | | | |***14***| | | | | | | | |
|2|3|4|4|4|3|4|4|3|3|3|2|1|1| | |1| |2| | | | | | | | | | | | | | | |
| | | | | | | | | |1| | |3|3| | | |1| |1| | | | | |1| | | | | | | | |
| | | | |1| | | | | | | | | | | | | | | | | | | | | | | | | | | | | |

**Substitutions**
*Italic* player replaced by No 12.
**Bold** player replaced by No 13.
***Bold Italic*** player replaced by No 14.

## League Table

| | P | W | D | L | F | A | Pts |
|---|---|---|---|---|---|---|---|
| Preston North End | 46 | 23 | 17 | 6 | 78 | 38 | 86 |
| Gillingham | 46 | 22 | 17 | 7 | 49 | 20 | 83 |
| Bury | 46 | 22 | 13 | 11 | 66 | 48 | 79 |
| Plymouth Argyle | 46 | 22 | 12 | 12 | 68 | 49 | 78 |
| Darlington | 46 | 20 | 18 | 8 | 60 | 42 | 78 |
| Hereford United | 46 | 20 | 14 | 12 | 65 | 47 | 74 |
| Colchester United | 46 | 18 | 18 | 10 | 61 | 51 | 72 |
| Chester City | 46 | 18 | 16 | 12 | 72 | 53 | 70 |
| Barnet | 46 | 18 | 16 | 12 | 65 | 45 | 70 |
| Wigan Athletic | 46 | 20 | 10 | 16 | 62 | 56 | 70 |
| Northampton Town | 46 | 18 | 13 | 15 | 51 | 44 | 67 |
| Scunthorpe United | 46 | 15 | 15 | 16 | 67 | 61 | 60 |
| Doncaster Rovers | 46 | 16 | 11 | 19 | 49 | 60 | 59 |
| Exeter City | 46 | 13 | 18 | 15 | 46 | 53 | 57 |
| Rochdale | 46 | 14 | 13 | 19 | 57 | 61 | 55 |
| Cambridge United | 46 | 14 | 12 | 20 | 61 | 71 | 54 |
| Fulham | 46 | 12 | 17 | 17 | 57 | 63 | 53 |
| Lincoln City | 46 | 13 | 14 | 19 | 57 | 73 | 53 |
| Mansfield Town | 46 | 11 | 20 | 15 | 54 | 64 | 53 |
| Hartlepool United | 46 | 12 | 13 | 21 | 47 | 67 | 49 |
| Leyton Orient | 46 | 12 | 11 | 23 | 44 | 63 | 47 |
| Cardiff City | 46 | 11 | 12 | 23 | 41 | 64 | 45 |
| Scarborough | 46 | 8 | 16 | 22 | 39 | 69 | 40 |
| Torquay United | 46 | 5 | 14 | 27 | 30 | 84 | 29 |

# 1996-97

## Division Three

Managers: Keith Houchen and Mick Tait

### Did you know that?

United failed to score in 15 League games and were dragged into a relegation battle until the return of Paul Baker alongside Joe Allon acted as a catalyst for a late revival which resulted in a final 20th position.

Player-manager Mick Tait made the last League appearance of his career on 15 March against Rochdale, a 2–1 defeat. In total he played a staggering 760 League games for seven different clubs, including Hartlepool United.

| Match No. | Date | Round | Venue | Opponents | Result | | Scorers | Attendance |
|---|---|---|---|---|---|---|---|---|
| 1 | Sep 5 | | (a) | Hebburn Argyle | D | 2 - 2 | Fletcher 2 | 3,000 |
| | | | | | | | | |
| 1 | Aug 17 | | (a) | Colchester United | W | 2 - 0 | Allon, McAuley | 2,942 |
| 3 | 24 | | (h) | Fulham | W | 2 - 1 | Cooper, Davies | 2,457 |
| 4 | 27 | | (h) | Mansfield Town | D | 2 - 2 | Cooper, Ingram | 2,750 |
| 5 | 31 | | (a) | Leyton Orient | L | 0 - 2 | | 4,344 |
| 7 | Sep 7 | | (a) | Hereford United | W | 1 - 0 | Halliday | 2,729 |
| 8 | 10 | | (h) | Carlisle United | L | 1 - 2 | Cooper | 3,077 |
| 9 | 14 | | (h) | Wigan Athletic | D | 1 - 1 | Cooper | 2,433 |
| 10 | 21 | | (a) | Hull City | L | 0 - 1 | | 3,886 |
| 11 | 28 | | (h) | Chester City | W | 2 - 0 | Allon, Cooper (pen) | 2,042 |
| 12 | Oct 1 | | (a) | Doncaster Rovers | L | 1 - 2 | Beech | 1,471 |
| 13 | 5 | | (a) | Cambridge United | L | 0 - 1 | | 3,406 |
| 14 | 12 | | (h) | Darlington | L | 1 - 2 | Halliday | 3,799 |
| 15 | 15 | | (h) | Swansea City | D | 1 - 1 | Halliday | 1,810 |
| 16 | 19 | | (a) | Barnet | L | 0 - 1 | | 2,265 |
| 17 | 26 | | (a) | Exeter City | L | 0 - 2 | | 3,043 |
| 18 | 29 | | (h) | Northampton Town | L | 0 - 2 | | 1,254 |
| 19 | Nov 2 | | (h) | Brighton & Hove Albion | L | 2 - 3 | Mike, Cooper | 1,683 |
| 20 | 9 | | (a) | Scarborough | W | 4 - 2 | Howard, Clegg, Halliday 2 | 3,157 |
| 22 | 23 | | (a) | Torquay United | W | 1 - 0 | Allon | 1,856 |
| 24 | 30 | | (h) | Exeter City | D | 1 - 1 | Irvine | 1,419 |
| 25 | Dec 3 | | (a) | Scunthorpe United | L | 1 - 2 | Clegg | 1,778 |
| 27 | 14 | | (a) | Rochdale | W | 3 - 1 | Beech, Howard, Allon | 1,618 |
| 28 | 21 | | (h) | Lincoln City | W | 2 - 1 | Cooper (pen), Sunderland | 1,344 |
| 29 | 26 | | (a) | Carlisle United | L | 0 - 1 | | 6,947 |
| 30 | 28 | | (h) | Hereford United | W | 2 - 1 | Allon, Howard | 1,923 |
| 31 | Jan 1 | | (h) | Hull City | D | 1 - 1 | Beech | 1,944 |
| 32 | 11 | | (a) | Chester City | D | 0 - 0 | | 1,885 |
| 33 | 18 | | (h) | Doncaster Rovers | L | 2 - 4 | Howard, Cooper (pen) | 1,708 |
| 34 | 25 | | (a) | Northampton Town | L | 0 - 3 | | 5,039 |
| 35 | Feb 1 | | (h) | Scarborough | W | 1 - 0 | Cooper | 1,843 |
| 36 | 8 | | (a) | Brighton & Hove Albion | L | 0 - 5 | | 8,412 |
| 37 | 11 | | (h) | Cardiff City | L | 2 - 3 | Beech 2 | 1,120 |
| 38 | 15 | | (h) | Torquay United | D | 1 - 1 | Beech | 1,548 |
| 39 | 22 | | (a) | Cardiff City | L | 0 - 2 | | 2,971 |
| 40 | Mar 1 | | (h) | Scunthorpe United | L | 0 - 1 | | 1,300 |
| 41 | 4 | | (a) | Wigan Athletic | D | 2 - 2 | Halliday, Howard | 3,229 |
| 42 | 8 | | (a) | Lincoln City | L | 1 - 2 | Allon | 2,915 |
| 43 | 15 | | (h) | Rochdale | L | 1 - 2 | Beech | 1,448 |
| 44 | 22 | | (a) | Fulham | L | 0 - 1 | | 7,222 |
| 45 | 29 | | (h) | Colchester United | W | 1 - 0 | Beech | 2,725 |
| 46 | 31 | | (a) | Mansfield Town | L | 0 - 1 | | 2,229 |
| 47 | Apr 5 | | (h) | Leyton Orient | W | 3 - 1 | Bradley, Baker, Halliday | 2,576 |
| 48 | 12 | | (h) | Cambridge United | L | 0 - 2 | | 3,186 |
| 49 | 19 | | (a) | Darlington | W | 2 - 1 | Brown, Allon | 4,662 |
| 50 | 26 | | (h) | Barnet | W | 4 - 0 | Allon 2, Baker, Halliday | 3,070 |
| 51 | May 3 | | (a) | Swansea City | D | 2 - 2 | Howard 2 | 5,423 |

Final Position : 20th in Division Three

Apps.
Sub.Apps.
Goals

**FA Cup**

| Match No. | Date | Round | Venue | Opponents | Result | | Scorers | Attendance |
|---|---|---|---|---|---|---|---|---|
| 21 | Nov 16 | R1 | (h) | York City | D | 0 - 0 | | 3,011 |
| 23 | 26 | R1r | (a) | York City | L | 0 - 3 | | 3,257 |

Apps.
Sub.Apps.
Goals

**League Cup**

| Match No. | Date | Round | Venue | Opponents | Result | | Scorers | Attendance |
|---|---|---|---|---|---|---|---|---|
| 2 | Aug 20 | R1/1 | (h) | Lincoln City | D | 2 - 2 | Bos (o.g.), Allon | 2,073 |
| 6 | Sep 3 | R1/2 | (a) | Lincoln City | L | 2 - 3 | Allon, Beech | 2,389 |

Apps.
Sub.Apps.
1 own goal Goals

| Pears | Ingram | McAuley | Beech | Davies | McDonald | Allon | Cooper | Howard | Halliday | Clegg | Tait | McGuckin | Houchen | Barron | Hislop | Lee | Mike | Horace | O'Connor | Irvine | Homer | Sunderland | Walton | Winstanley | Elliott | Bradley | Proctor | Knowles | Lucas | Cullen | Baker | Brown |
|---|---|---|---|---|---|---|---|---|---|---|---|---|---|---|---|---|---|---|---|---|---|---|---|---|---|---|---|---|---|---|---|---|
| 1 | 2 | 3 | 4 | 5 | 6 | 7 | 8 | 9 | 10 | 11 | | | | | | | | | | | | | | | | | | | | | | |
| | | | | | | | | | | | | | | | | | | | | | | | | | | | | | | | | |
| | | | | | | | | | | | | | | | | | | | | | | | | | | | | | | | | |
| 1 | 2 | 3 | 4 | 5 | 6 | 7 | 8 | 9 | 10 | *11* | *12* | | | | | | | | | | | | | | | | | | | | | |
| 1 | 2 | 3 | 7 | 4 | *6* | | 8 | | 10 | *12* | 11 | 5 | 9 | | | | | | | | | | | | | | | | | | | |
| 1 | 2 | 3 | 6 | 4 | | 7 | 8 | | 10 | *9* | 11 | 5 | *12* | | | | | | | | | | | | | | | | | | | |
| 1 | 2 | 3 | *9* | 4 | 6 | 7 | 8 | | 10 | **13** | **11** | 5 | *12* | | | | | | | | | | | | | | | | | | | |
| 1 | 2 | 3 | 11 | *4* | 6 | 7 | 8 | | 10 | 9 | | *12* | | 5 | | | | | | | | | | | | | | | | | | |
| 1 | 2 | 3 | 11 | 4 | 6 | **7** | 8 | *12* | 10 | *9* | | | **13** | 5 | | | | | | | | | | | | | | | | | | |
| 1 | 2 | 3 | 11 | *4* | 6 | | 8 | *12* | 10 | 7 | | | 9 | 5 | | | | | | | | | | | | | | | | | | |
| 1 | 2 | 3 | 11 | 4 | *6* | **7** | 8 | 9 | 10 | *12* | | | | 5 | **13** | | | | | | | | | | | | | | | | | |
| 1 | | 3 | 6 | 4 | | 7 | 8 | 9 | 10 | *11* | 2 | | | 5 | *12* | | | | | | | | | | | | | | | | | |
| 1 | **13** | 3 | 6 | 4 | | 7 | 8 | 9 | 10 | 11 | **2** | | | 5 | *12* | | | | | | | | | | | | | | | | | |
| 1 | 2 | 3 | 7 | | 6 | | 8 | | 10 | | | | | 5 | 11 | 4 | 9 | | | | | | | | | | | | | | | |
| 1 | 2 | 3 | 7 | | | | 8 | **13** | 10 | *12* | | 6 | | 5 | **11** | *4* | 9 | | | | | | | | | | | | | | | |
| 1 | 2 | 3 | *7* | | | **13** | 8 | *12* | 10 | 4 | | 6 | | 5 | 11 | | **9** | | | | | | | | | | | | | | | |
| 1 | *12* | 3 | 4 | 2 | 6 | | 8 | | 10 | *7* | | | | 5 | 11 | | 9 | | | | | | | | | | | | | | | |
| 1 | 2 | 3 | | 4 | | | 8 | 7 | 10 | | 6 | | | 5 | 11 | | 9 | | | | | | | | | | | | | | | |
| 1 | *2* | 3 | 4 | | | | **8** | **13** | 10 | ***7*** | *12* | 6 | | 5 | 11 | | 9 | ***14*** | | | | | | | | | | | | | | |
| | | 3 | *4* | 6 | | 7 | 8 | 10 | **13** | *12* | 2 | | | 5 | 11 | | **9** | | 1 | | | | | | | | | | | | | |
| | | 3 | 4 | | | | 8 | 9 | 10 | 7 | | 6 | | 5 | 11 | 2 | | | 1 | | | | | | | | | | | | | |
| | 2 | 3 | 4 | | | 7 | 8 | | *10* | 9 | | 6 | | | 11 | 5 | | | 1 | *12* | | | | | | | | | | | | |
| | 2 | 3 | 4 | | | 7 | | | | *9* | | 6 | | 8 | 11 | 5 | | | 1 | 10 | *12* | | | | | | | | | | | |
| | 2 | 3 | 4 | 5 | | | | 9 | | 7 | | | | 8 | 11 | 6 | | | 1 | 10 | | | | | | | | | | | | |
| | 2 | 3 | 4 | 6 | | 7 | 8 | 9 | | 10 | | | | | 11 | 5 | | | 1 | | | | | | | | | | | | | |
| | 2 | 3 | 4 | *10* | | 7 | 8 | 9 | | | | 6 | | | 11 | 5 | | | 1 | | | *2* | | | | | | | | | | |
| | 2 | 3 | 4 | 6 | | 7 | 8 | 9 | | | | | | | 11 | 5 | | | 1 | | | 10 | *12* | | | | | | | | | |
| | 2 | | 4 | *3* | | 7 | 8 | 9 | | **10** | *12* | 6 | | | 11 | 5 | | | 1 | | | **13** | | | | | | | | | | |
| | 2 | 3 | 4 | | | 7 | 8 | 9 | | 10 | | 6 | | | 11 | 5 | | | 1 | | | | | | | | | | | | | |
| | 2 | 3 | 4 | 6 | | 7 | 8 | 9 | | *10* | | | | | 11 | 5 | | | 1 | | | *12* | | | | | | | | | | |
| | 2 | 3 | 4 | 6 | | 7 | 8 | 9 | | 10 | | | | | | 5 | | | 1 | | | 11 | | | | | | | | | | |
| | 2 | 3 | 4 | *12* | | 7 | 8 | *9* | | **10** | | 6 | | | | 5 | | | 1 | | | 11 | | **13** | | | | | | | | |
| | 2 | 3 | 4 | | | 7 | 8 | 9 | | | 10 | 6 | | | | 5 | | | 1 | | | 11 | | | | | | | | | | |
| | 2 | 3 | 4 | | | 7 | 8 | 9 | | *12* | *10* | 6 | | | | 5 | | | 1 | | | 11 | | | | | | | | | | |
| | 2 | 3 | 4 | 5 | | | | 9 | | 8 | 10 | 6 | | | | | | | 1 | | | | 11 | | | 7 | | | | | | |
| | 2 | 3 | 4 | | | *12* | | *9* | | 8 | 10 | | | | **11** | 5 | | | 1 | | | **13** | | | 7 | 6 | | | | | | |
| | 2 | 3 | | | | | 8 | | 10 | **7** | *9* | 6 | | | 11 | 5 | | | 1 | | | **13** | | | *12* | 4 | | | | | | |
| | 2 | 3 | 9 | | | 7 | 8 | | 10 | | | *6* | | | 11 | 5 | | | 1 | | | | | | *12* | 4 | | | | | | |
| | 2 | 3 | 7 | 6 | | | | 9 | 10 | | 8 | | | | | 5 | | | 1 | | | | 11 | | | 4 | | | | | | |
| | 2 | 3 | 10 | 6 | | 7 | | 9 | | *12* | **8** | | | | | 5 | | | 1 | | | **13** | *11* | | | 4 | | | | | | |
| | 2 | 3 | 8 | **6** | | 7 | | 9 | 10 | 11 | 5 | | | | *12* | | | | 1 | | | **13** | | | | 4 | | | | | | |
| | 2 | 3 | 8 | 6 | | | | **9** | ***10*** | *12* | 5 | | | | 11 | | | | 1 | **13** | | | ***14*** | | | *4* | 7 | | | | | |
| | | | 4 | 6 | | | | | *12* | | | | | | 11 | **13** | | | 1 | | | | | | | 5 | 8 | **2** | 3 | *7* | 9 | 10 |
| | | | 4 | 6 | | | | **13** | *12* | | | | | | 11 | | | | 1 | | | | | | | 5 | *8* | 2 | 3 | 7 | **9** | 10 |
| | | | | | | 7 | 8 | | *10* | *12* | | | | | | 6 | | | 1 | | | | | | | 5 | | 2 | 3 | 4 | 9 | 11 |
| | | | | *12* | | 7 | 8 | | 10 | **13** | | | | | | 6 | | | 1 | | | | | | | 5 | | 2 | **3** | 4 | 9 | 11 |
| | *12* | | 7 | 4 | | ***14*** | | ***9*** | 10 | | | 6 | | | | | | | 1 | | | | | | | *5* | 8 | 2 | 3 | **13** | | **11** |
| | | | 4 | 5 | | 7 | | | 10 | | | 6 | | | | | | | 1 | | | | | | | | 8 | 2 | 3 | | 9 | 11 |
| | | | *4* | 5 | | | | 11 | 10 | *12* | | 6 | | | | | | | 1 | | | | | | | | 8 | 2 | 3 | 7 | 9 | |
| 16 | 34 | 38 | 42 | 30 | 9 | 27 | 33 | 26 | 28 | 24 | 16 | 21 | 2 | 16 | 23 | 23 | 7 | | 30 | 2 | | 6 | 2 | | 2 | 12 | 6 | 7 | 7 | 5 | 6 | 6 |
| | 3 | | | 2 | | 3 | | 6 | 3 | 11 | 3 | 1 | 3 | | 4 | 1 | 1 | 1 | | 2 | 1 | 7 | 2 | 1 | 2 | | | | | 1 | | |
| | 1 | 1 | 8 | 1 | | 9 | 9 | 7 | 8 | 2 | | | | | | | | | | 1 | | 1 | | | | 1 | | | | | 2 | 1 |

| Pears | Ingram | McAuley | Beech | Davies | McDonald | Allon | Cooper | Howard | Halliday | Clegg | Tait | McGuckin | Houchen | Barron | Hislop | Lee | Mike | Horace | O'Connor | Irvine | Homer | Sunderland | Walton | Winstanley | Elliott | Bradley | Proctor | Knowles | Lucas | Cullen | Baker | Brown |
|---|---|---|---|---|---|---|---|---|---|---|---|---|---|---|---|---|---|---|---|---|---|---|---|---|---|---|---|---|---|---|---|---|
| | 2 | 3 | 4 | | | | 8 | 9 | 10 | 7 | | 6 | | | 11 | 5 | | | 1 | | | | | | | | | | | | | |
| 1 | 2 | 3 | 4 | | | 7 | | | *10* | 9 | 8 | 6 | | | 11 | 5 | | | | *12* | | | | | | | | | | | | |
| 1 | 2 | 2 | 2 | | | 1 | 1 | 1 | 2 | 2 | 1 | 2 | | | 2 | 2 | | | 1 | | | | | | | | | | | | | |
| | | | | | | | | | | | | | | | | | | | | 1 | | | | | | | | | | | | |
| | | | | | | | | | | | | | | | | | | | | | | | | | | | | | | | | |

| Pears | Ingram | McAuley | Beech | Davies | McDonald | Allon | Cooper | Howard | Halliday | Clegg | Tait | McGuckin | Houchen | Barron | Hislop | Lee | Mike | Horace | O'Connor | Irvine | Homer | Sunderland | Walton | Winstanley | Elliott | Bradley | Proctor | Knowles | Lucas | Cullen | Baker | Brown |
|---|---|---|---|---|---|---|---|---|---|---|---|---|---|---|---|---|---|---|---|---|---|---|---|---|---|---|---|---|---|---|---|---|
| 1 | 2 | 3 | 4 | 5 | **6** | ***7*** | 8 | 9 | 10 | | *11* | *12* | **13** | | | ***14*** | | | | | | | | | | | | | | | | |
| 1 | 2 | 3 | 10 | 4 | *6* | 7 | 8 | | *12* | 11 | | 5 | 9 | | | | | | | | | | | | | | | | | | | |
| 2 | 2 | 2 | 2 | 2 | 2 | 2 | 2 | 1 | 1 | 1 | 1 | 1 | 1 | | | | | | | | | | | | | | | | | | | |
| | | | | | | | | | 1 | | | 1 | 1 | | | 1 | | | | | | | | | | | | | | | | |
| | | | 1 | | | 2 | | | | | | | | | | | | | | | | | | | | | | | | | | |

## League Table

| | P | W | D | L | F | A | Pts |
|---|---|---|---|---|---|---|---|
| Wigan Athletic | 46 | 26 | 9 | 11 | 84 | 51 | 87 |
| Fulham | 46 | 25 | 12 | 9 | 72 | 38 | 87 |
| Carlisle United | 46 | 24 | 12 | 10 | 67 | 44 | 84 |
| Northampton Town | 46 | 20 | 12 | 14 | 67 | 44 | 72 |
| Swansea City | 46 | 21 | 8 | 17 | 62 | 58 | 71 |
| Chester City | 46 | 18 | 16 | 12 | 55 | 43 | 70 |
| Cardiff City | 46 | 20 | 9 | 17 | 56 | 54 | 69 |
| Colchester United | 46 | 17 | 17 | 12 | 62 | 51 | 68 |
| Lincoln City | 46 | 18 | 12 | 16 | 70 | 69 | 66 |
| Cambridge United | 46 | 18 | 11 | 17 | 53 | 59 | 65 |
| Mansfield Town | 46 | 16 | 16 | 14 | 47 | 45 | 64 |
| Scarborough | 46 | 16 | 15 | 15 | 65 | 68 | 63 |
| Scunthorpe United | 46 | 18 | 9 | 19 | 59 | 62 | 63 |
| Rochdale | 46 | 14 | 16 | 16 | 58 | 58 | 58 |
| Barnet | 46 | 14 | 16 | 16 | 46 | 51 | 58 |
| Leyton Orient | 46 | 15 | 12 | 19 | 50 | 58 | 57 |
| Hull City | 46 | 13 | 18 | 15 | 44 | 50 | 57 |
| Darlington | 46 | 14 | 10 | 22 | 64 | 78 | 52 |
| Doncaster Rovers | 46 | 14 | 10 | 22 | 52 | 66 | 52 |
| Hartlepool United | 46 | 14 | 9 | 23 | 53 | 66 | 51 |
| Torquay United | 46 | 13 | 11 | 22 | 46 | 62 | 50 |
| Exeter City | 46 | 12 | 12 | 22 | 48 | 73 | 48 |
| Brighton & Hove Albion | 46 | 13 | 10 | 23 | 53 | 70 | 47 |
| Hereford United | 46 | 11 | 14 | 21 | 50 | 65 | 47 |

# 1997-98

## Division Three

Manager: Mick Tait

### Did you know that?

Tommy Miller made his debut for the club on 4 October at Chester City, a 3–1 defeat, when he came on as substitute for Steven Halliday.

Joe Allon played the last of his 194 games for the club on 30 August against Macclesfield Town when he came on as a substitute for Graeme Lee.

'Pools drew half their League games – 12 at home and 11 away.

| Match No. | Date | Round | Venue | Opponents | Result | | Scorers | Attendance |
|---|---|---|---|---|---|---|---|---|
| 1 | Aug 9 | | (a) | Exeter City | D | 1 - 1 | Cullen | 3,409 |
| 3 | 16 | | (h) | Colchester United | W | 3 - 2 | Baker, Allon 2 | 2,174 |
| 4 | 23 | | (a) | Rotherham United | L | 1 - 2 | Cullen | 3,086 |
| 6 | 30 | | (h) | Macclesfield Town | D | 0 - 0 | | 2,283 |
| 7 | Sep 2 | | (h) | Notts County | D | 1 - 1 | Howard | 2,010 |
| 8 | 7 | | (a) | Scarborough | D | 1 - 1 | Cullen | 3,027 |
| 9 | 13 | | (h) | Torquay United | W | 3 - 0 | Baker, Cullen, Lee | 1,927 |
| 10 | 20 | | (a) | Darlington | D | 1 - 1 | Cullen | 3,169 |
| 11 | 27 | | (h) | Shrewsbury Town | W | 2 - 1 | Ingram (pen), Cullen | 2,253 |
| 12 | Oct 4 | | (a) | Chester City | L | 1 - 3 | Baker | 2,163 |
| 13 | 11 | | (a) | Doncaster Rovers | D | 2 - 2 | Cullen, Lucas | 1,526 |
| 14 | 18 | | (h) | Leyton Orient | D | 2 - 2 | Howard, Ingram | 2,108 |
| 15 | 21 | | (h) | Peterborough United | W | 2 - 1 | Howard 2 | 1,990 |
| 16 | 25 | | (a) | Cardiff City | D | 1 - 1 | Baker | 3,383 |
| 17 | Nov 1 | | (h) | Brighton & Hove Albion | D | 0 - 0 | | 2,561 |
| 18 | 4 | | (a) | Swansea City | W | 2 - 0 | Cullen, Baker | 2,949 |
| 19 | 8 | | (a) | Scunthorpe United | D | 1 - 1 | Knowles | 3,272 |
| 21 | 18 | | (h) | Rochdale | W | 2 - 0 | Beech, Halliday | 1,666 |
| 22 | 22 | | (h) | Barnet | W | 2 - 0 | Cullen 2 | 2,225 |
| 23 | 29 | | (a) | Cambridge United | L | 0 - 2 | | 2,513 |
| 24 | Dec 2 | | (h) | Hull City | D | 2 - 2 | Beech, Lucas | 1,933 |
| 26 | 13 | | (a) | Lincoln City | D | 1 - 1 | Cullen | 2,849 |
| 27 | 20 | | (h) | Mansfield Town | D | 2 - 2 | Halliday, Howard | 2,309 |
| 28 | 26 | | (h) | Scarborough | W | 3 - 0 | Halliday 2, Clark | 3,905 |
| 29 | 28 | | (a) | Notts County | L | 0 - 2 | | 6,073 |
| 30 | Jan 3 | | (a) | Colchester United | W | 2 - 1 | Clark, Howard | 2,885 |
| 32 | 10 | | (h) | Exeter City | D | 1 - 1 | Clark | 2,507 |
| 33 | 17 | | (a) | Macclesfield Town | L | 1 - 2 | Cullen | 2,334 |
| 34 | 24 | | (h) | Rotherham United | D | 0 - 0 | | 2,375 |
| 35 | 28 | | (a) | Torquay United | L | 0 - 1 | | 2,238 |
| 36 | Feb 7 | | (h) | Darlington | D | 2 - 2 | Pedersen, Clark | 3,212 |
| 37 | 14 | | (h) | Chester City | D | 0 - 0 | | 2,186 |
| 38 | 21 | | (a) | Shrewsbury Town | L | 0 - 1 | | 2,160 |
| 39 | 24 | | (a) | Leyton Orient | L | 1 - 2 | Clark | 3,713 |
| 40 | 28 | | (h) | Doncaster Rovers | W | 3 - 1 | Clark, Bradley, Howard | 1,920 |
| 41 | Mar 3 | | (h) | Scunthorpe United | L | 0 - 1 | | 1,588 |
| 42 | 7 | | (a) | Brighton & Hove Albion | D | 0 - 0 | | 2,811 |
| 43 | 14 | | (h) | Swansea City | W | 4 - 2 | Halliday, Lee 2, Beech | 1,727 |
| 44 | 21 | | (a) | Rochdale | L | 1 - 2 | Clark | 1,395 |
| 45 | 28 | | (a) | Barnet | D | 1 - 1 | Midgley | 2,344 |
| 46 | Apr 4 | | (h) | Cambridge United | D | 3 - 3 | Miller, Di Lella 2 | 1,867 |
| 47 | 11 | | (a) | Hull City | L | 1 - 2 | Midgley | 3,343 |
| 48 | 13 | | (h) | Lincoln City | D | 1 - 1 | Beech | 1,997 |
| 49 | 18 | | (a) | Mansfield Town | D | 2 - 2 | Beech 2 | 2,047 |
| 50 | 25 | | (h) | Cardiff City | W | 2 - 0 | Midgley, Ingram (pen) | 2,817 |
| 51 | May 2 | | (a) | Peterborough United | D | 0 - 0 | | 4,724 |

Final Position : 17th in Division Three

Apps.
Sub.Apps.
Goals

**FA Cup**

| Match No. | Date | Round | Venue | Opponents | Result | | Scorers | Attendance |
|---|---|---|---|---|---|---|---|---|
| 20 | Nov 15 | R1 | (h) | Macclesfield Town | L | 2 - 4 | Beech, Pedersen | 3,165 |

Apps.
Sub.Apps.
Goals

**League Cup**

| Match No. | Date | Round | Venue | Opponents | Result | | Scorers | Attendance |
|---|---|---|---|---|---|---|---|---|
| 2 | Aug 12 | R1/1 | (a) | Tranmere Rovers | L | 1 - 3 | Howard | 3,878 |
| 5 | 26 | R1/2 | (h) | Tranmere Rovers | W | 2 - 1 | Baker, Lee | 1,626 |

Apps.
Sub.Apps.
Goals

| Davis | Knowles | Lucas | Ingram | Davies | Bradley | Allon | Cullen | Baker | Beech | Howard | Halliday | Barron | Dobson | Lee | Harper | Elliott | McDonald | Gavin | Miller | Irvine | Clark | Pedersen | Hollund | Larsen | Connor | Hutt | Nash | Midgley | Di Lella | Stephenson |
|---|---|---|---|---|---|---|---|---|---|---|---|---|---|---|---|---|---|---|---|---|---|---|---|---|---|---|---|---|---|---|
| 1 | 2 | 3 | 4 | 5 | 6 | 7 | *8* | 9 | 10 | 11 | *12* |  |  |  |  |  |  |  |  |  |  |  |  |  |  |  |  |  |  |  |
| 1 | 2 | 3 | 4 | 5 | 6 | *7* | 8 | 9 |  | 11 | *12* | 10 |  |  |  |  |  |  |  |  |  |  |  |  |  |  |  |  |  |  |
|  | 2 | 3 | 4 | *5* | 6 | **7** | 8 | ***9*** | 11 | ***14*** | **13** | 10 | 1 | *12* |  |  |  |  |  |  |  |  |  |  |  |  |  |  |  |  |
|  | 2 | 3 | 4 |  | 6 | *12* | 8 | 9 |  | 11 | 10 | 7 |  | *5* | 1 |  |  |  |  |  |  |  |  |  |  |  |  |  |  |  |
|  | 2 | 3 | 4 |  | 6 |  | *8* | 9 | 11 | *12* | 10 | 7 |  | 5 | 1 |  |  |  |  |  |  |  |  |  |  |  |  |  |  |  |
|  | 2 | 3 | 4 |  | 6 |  | 8 | *9* | 11 | *12* | **10** | 7 |  | 5 | 1 | **13** |  |  |  |  |  |  |  |  |  |  |  |  |  |  |
|  | 2 | 3 | *4* |  | 6 |  | 8 | 9 | 11 | *12* | **10** | 7 |  | 5 | 1 | **13** |  |  |  |  |  |  |  |  |  |  |  |  |  |  |
|  | 2 | 3 | 4 |  | 6 |  | 8 | **9** | 11 | **13** | *10* | *7* |  | 5 | 1 | ***14*** | *12* |  |  |  |  |  |  |  |  |  |  |  |  |  |
|  | 2 | 3 | 4 |  | 6 |  | 8 | 9 |  | 11 | 10 |  |  | 5 | 1 |  | 7 |  |  |  |  |  |  |  |  |  |  |  |  |  |
|  | 2 | 3 | 4 |  | 6 |  | 8 | 9 |  | 11 | **10** |  |  | 5 | 1 |  | *7* | *12* | **13** |  |  |  |  |  |  |  |  |  |  |  |
|  | 2 | 3 | 4 | *12* | 6 |  | 8 | 9 |  | **11** | **13** |  |  | *5* | 1 |  |  | ***14*** | 7 | ***10*** |  |  |  |  |  |  |  |  |  |  |
|  | 2 | 3 | 4 | 7 | 6 |  | 8 | *9* | 10 | 11 |  |  |  | 5 | 1 |  |  |  |  | *12* |  |  |  |  |  |  |  |  |  |  |
|  | *2* | 3 | 4 | 7 | 6 |  | 8 |  | 11 | 9 | 10 |  |  | 5 | 1 |  |  | *12* |  |  |  |  |  |  |  |  |  |  |  |  |
|  | 2 | 3 | 4 | 7 | 6 |  | 8 | 9 | 11 | 10 |  |  |  | 5 | 1 |  |  |  |  |  |  |  |  |  |  |  |  |  |  |  |
|  | 2 | 3 | 4 | 7 | 6 |  | 8 | *9* | 11 | **10** | *12* |  |  | 5 | 1 |  |  |  |  |  | **13** |  |  |  |  |  |  |  |  |  |
|  | 2 | 3 | 4 | 7 | 6 |  | 8 | 9 |  | 10 |  |  |  | 5 | 1 |  |  |  |  |  |  | 11 |  |  |  |  |  |  |  |  |
|  | 2 | 3 | 4 | 7 | *6* |  | **8** | ***9*** | **13** | 10 | ***14*** | *12* |  | 5 | 1 |  |  |  |  |  |  | 11 |  |  |  |  |  |  |  |  |
|  | 2 | 3 | 4 |  | 6 |  | 8 |  | 11 |  | 10 | 7 |  | 5 | 1 |  |  |  |  |  |  | 9 |  |  |  |  |  |  |  |  |
|  | 2 | 3 | 4 |  | 6 |  | 8 |  | 7 |  | 10 | 11 |  | 5 |  |  |  |  |  |  |  | 9 | 1 |  |  |  |  |  |  |  |
|  | 2 | 3 |  | 4 | 6 |  | **8** |  | 7 | *12* | *10* | 11 |  | 5 |  |  |  |  |  |  | **13** | 9 | 1 |  |  |  |  |  |  |  |
|  | 2 | 3 |  |  | 6 |  | 8 |  | 7 | *12* | 10 | 11 |  | 5 |  |  |  |  |  |  | *4* | 9 | 1 |  |  |  |  |  |  |  |
|  | 2 | 3 |  |  | 6 |  | 8 |  | 7 | 11 | 10 | 4 |  | 5 |  |  |  |  |  |  |  | 9 | 1 |  |  |  |  |  |  |  |
|  | 2 | 3 | *12* |  | *6* |  | 8 |  | 7 | 11 | 10 | **4** |  | 5 |  |  |  |  |  |  |  | 9 | 1 | **13** |  |  |  |  |  |  |
|  | 2 | 3 | 6 |  |  |  | 8 |  | 7 | *11* | 10 | 4 |  |  |  |  | 5 |  |  |  | *12* | 9 | 1 |  |  |  |  |  |  |  |
|  | *2* | 3 | 6 |  |  |  | 8 |  | 7 | ***11*** | **10** | 4 |  | *12* |  |  | 5 |  |  |  | **13** | 9 | 1 | ***14*** |  |  |  |  |  |  |
|  | 2 | *3* |  |  | 6 |  | 8 |  | 7 | 11 |  | 4 |  | 5 |  |  |  |  |  |  | 10 | 9 | 1 | *12* |  |  |  |  |  |  |
|  | 2 | 3 | 4 |  | 6 |  | 8 |  | 7 | 11 | *12* |  |  | 5 |  |  |  |  |  |  | *10* | 9 | 1 |  |  |  |  |  |  |  |
|  | 2 | 3 | 4 |  | 6 |  | 8 |  | 7 | *12* | *10* |  |  | 5 |  |  |  |  |  |  | **11** | 9 | 1 | **13** |  |  |  |  |  |  |
|  | 2 | 3 | 8 |  | 6 |  |  |  | 7 | 11 |  | 4 |  | 5 |  |  |  |  |  |  | 10 | 9 | 1 |  |  |  |  |  |  |  |
|  | 2 | 3 | 8 |  | 6 |  |  |  |  | 11 | *10* | 4 |  | 5 |  |  |  |  |  | *12* | 7 | 9 | 1 |  |  |  |  |  |  |  |
|  | 2 | 3 | 8 | 5 | 6 |  |  |  |  | 11 | *12* | 4 |  |  |  |  |  |  |  |  | 7 | 9 | 1 |  | 10 |  |  |  |  |  |
|  | 2 | 3 |  | 5 | 6 |  |  |  | 8 | 11 |  | 4 |  |  |  |  |  |  |  | *12* | 7 | 9 | 1 |  | *10* |  |  |  |  |  |
|  | 2 | 3 |  | *4* | 6 |  |  |  |  | 9 |  | 11 |  | 5 |  |  |  |  | *12* | **13** | ***7*** |  | 1 |  | **10** | 8 | ***14*** |  |  |  |
|  | 2 | 3 | 8 |  | 6 |  |  |  |  | 9 | *12* | 4 |  | 5 |  |  |  |  |  |  | 7 |  | 1 |  | *10* | 11 |  |  |  |  |
|  | 2 | 3 | 8 |  | 6 |  |  |  | 10 | 9 |  | 4 |  | 5 |  |  |  |  |  |  | 7 |  | 1 |  |  | 11 |  |  |  |  |
|  | 2 | 3 | 8 | *12* | ***6*** |  |  |  | 10 | 9 | **13** | 4 |  | *5* |  |  |  |  |  |  | 7 |  | 1 |  | ***14*** | **11** |  |  |  |  |
|  | 2 | 3 |  | 5 | 6 |  |  |  | 11 | 9 | 10 | 4 |  |  |  |  |  |  | 8 |  | 7 |  | 1 |  |  |  |  |  |  |  |
|  | 2 | 3 |  | 5 | 6 |  |  |  | 11 |  | 10 | *4* |  | 7 |  | *12* |  |  | 8 |  |  |  | 1 |  |  |  |  | 9 |  |  |
|  | 2 | 3 |  | 5 | 6 |  |  |  | 11 | **13** | 10 | 4 |  | **7** |  |  |  |  | *8* |  | ***14*** |  | 1 |  |  |  |  | ***9*** | *12* |  |
|  | 2 | 3 |  |  | 6 |  |  |  | 11 | 10 |  | 4 |  | 5 |  |  |  |  | 8 |  | 7 |  | 1 |  |  |  |  | 9 |  |  |
|  | 2 | 3 | 6 |  |  |  |  |  | *11* | 10 |  | 4 |  | 5 |  |  | *12* |  | 8 | ***14*** | **7** |  | 1 |  |  |  |  | ***9*** | **13** |  |
|  | 2 | 3 | 7 |  | 6 |  |  |  | *12* | 10 |  | 4 |  | 5 |  |  |  |  | 8 |  |  |  | 1 |  |  |  |  | 9 | *11* |  |
|  | 2 |  | 7 |  | 6 |  |  |  | 11 | 10 |  | 4 |  | *5* |  |  |  |  | 8 |  | 3 |  | 1 |  |  |  |  | 9 | *12* |  |
|  | 2 |  | 4 | 5 | 6 |  |  |  | 7 | 10 |  |  |  |  |  |  |  |  | 8 | *12* | 3 |  | 1 |  |  |  |  | *9* |  | 11 |
|  | 2 |  | *4* | 5 | 6 |  |  |  | 7 | 10 |  |  |  |  |  |  |  |  | 8 | **13** | 3 |  | 1 |  |  |  |  | 9 | *12* | **11** |
|  | 2 |  | 4 |  | 6 |  |  |  | 7 | 10 |  | 5 |  |  |  |  |  |  | 8 | *12* | 3 |  | 1 |  |  |  |  | *9* |  | 11 |
| 2 | 46 | 42 | 35 | 18 | 43 | 3 | 28 | 16 | 34 | 34 | 21 | 32 | 1 | 35 | 15 |  | 4 |  | 11 | 1 | 19 | 17 | 28 |  | 4 | 4 |  | 9 | 1 | 3 |
|  |  |  | 1 | 2 |  | 1 |  |  | 2 | 9 | 10 | 1 |  | 2 |  | 4 | 2 | 3 | 2 | 8 | 5 |  |  | 4 | 1 |  | 1 |  | 4 |  |
|  | 1 | 2 | 3 |  | 1 | 2 | 12 | 5 | 6 | 7 | 5 |  |  | 3 |  |  |  |  | 1 |  | 7 | 1 |  |  |  |  |  | 3 | 2 |  |
|  |  |  |  |  |  |  |  |  |  |  |  |  |  |  |  |  |  |  |  |  |  |  |  |  |  |  |  |  |  |  |
|  | 2 | 3 | 4 | ***7*** |  |  | **8** |  | 10 | *9* | *12* | 6 | 1 | 5 |  | ***14*** |  |  |  |  | **13** | 11 |  |  |  |  |  |  |  |  |
|  | 1 | 1 | 1 | 1 |  |  | 1 |  | 1 | 1 |  | 1 | 1 | 1 |  |  |  |  |  |  |  | 1 |  |  |  |  |  |  |  |  |
|  |  |  |  |  |  |  |  |  |  |  | 1 |  |  |  |  | 1 |  |  |  |  | 1 |  |  |  |  |  |  |  |  |  |
|  |  |  |  |  |  |  |  |  | 1 |  |  |  |  |  |  |  |  |  |  |  |  | 1 |  |  |  |  |  |  |  |  |
|  |  |  |  |  |  |  |  |  |  |  |  |  |  |  |  |  |  |  |  |  |  |  |  |  |  |  |  |  |  |  |
| 1 | 2 | 3 | 4 | 5 | 6 | 7 | 8 | 9 | 10 | 11 | *12* |  |  |  |  |  |  |  |  |  |  |  |  |  |  |  |  |  |  |  |
|  | 2 | 3 | 4 |  | 6 |  | 8 | 9 |  | 11 | 10 | 7 | 1 | 5 |  |  |  |  |  |  |  |  |  |  |  |  |  |  |  |  |
| 1 | 2 | 2 | 2 | 1 | 2 | 1 | 2 | 2 | 1 | 2 | 1 | 1 | 1 | 1 |  |  |  |  |  |  |  |  |  |  |  |  |  |  |  |  |
|  |  |  |  |  |  |  |  |  |  |  | 1 |  |  |  |  |  |  |  |  |  |  |  |  |  |  |  |  |  |  |  |
|  |  |  |  |  |  |  |  | 1 |  | 1 |  |  |  | 1 |  |  |  |  |  |  |  |  |  |  |  |  |  |  |  |  |

## League Table

|  | P | W | D | L | F | A | Pts |
|---|---|---|---|---|---|---|---|
| Notts County | 46 | 29 | 12 | 5 | 82 | 43 | 99 |
| Macclesfield Town | 46 | 23 | 13 | 10 | 63 | 44 | 82 |
| Lincoln City | 46 | 20 | 15 | 11 | 60 | 51 | 75 |
| Colchester United | 46 | 21 | 11 | 14 | 72 | 60 | 74 |
| Torquay United | 46 | 21 | 11 | 14 | 68 | 59 | 74 |
| Scarborough | 46 | 19 | 15 | 12 | 67 | 58 | 72 |
| Barnet | 46 | 19 | 13 | 14 | 61 | 51 | 70 |
| Scunthorpe United | 46 | 19 | 12 | 15 | 56 | 52 | 69 |
| Rotherham United | 46 | 16 | 19 | 11 | 67 | 61 | 67 |
| Peterborough United | 46 | 18 | 13 | 15 | 63 | 51 | 67 |
| Leyton Orient | 46 | 19 | 12 | 15 | 62 | 47 | 66 |
| Mansfield Town | 46 | 16 | 17 | 13 | 64 | 55 | 65 |
| Shrewsbury Town | 46 | 16 | 13 | 17 | 61 | 62 | 61 |
| Chester City | 46 | 17 | 10 | 19 | 60 | 61 | 61 |
| Exeter City | 46 | 15 | 15 | 16 | 68 | 63 | 60 |
| Cambridge United | 46 | 14 | 18 | 14 | 63 | 57 | 60 |
| Hartlepool United | 46 | 12 | 23 | 11 | 61 | 53 | 59 |
| Rochdale | 46 | 17 | 7 | 22 | 56 | 55 | 58 |
| Darlington | 46 | 14 | 12 | 20 | 56 | 72 | 54 |
| Swansea City | 46 | 13 | 11 | 22 | 49 | 62 | 50 |
| Cardiff City | 46 | 9 | 23 | 14 | 48 | 52 | 50 |
| Hull City | 46 | 11 | 8 | 27 | 56 | 83 | 41 |
| Brighton & Hove Albion | 46 | 6 | 17 | 23 | 38 | 66 | 35 |
| Doncaster Rovers | 46 | 4 | 8 | 34 | 30 | 113 | 20 |

# 1998-99

## Division Three

Managers: Mick Tait, Paul Baker & Brian Honour and Chris Turner

### Did you know that?

North East football legend Peter Beardsley joined 'Pools on a free transfer and played 22 League games, scoring twice. He made a major contribution in helping the club avoid relegation to the Conference.

The 'Beardsley factor' had a positive effect on attendances, with 5,098 witnessing a 3–0 win over Scarborough, who were eventually relegated to the Conference.

Average home attendances of 2,686 were 20 per cent up on the previous season.

| Match No. | Date | Round | Venue | Opponents | Result | | Scorers | Attendance |
|---|---|---|---|---|---|---|---|---|
| 1 | Aug 8 | | (h) | Cardiff City | D | 1 - 1 | Beech | 2,591 |
| 3 | 15 | | (a) | Barnet | W | 2 - 0 | Midgley, Beech | 2,049 |
| 4 | 22 | | (h) | Scunthorpe United | L | 1 - 2 | Ingram (pen) | 2,697 |
| 6 | 29 | | (a) | Cambridge United | W | 2 - 1 | Howard, Lee | 2,825 |
| 7 | 31 | | (h) | Hull City | W | 1 - 0 | Di Lella | 3,277 |
| 8 | Sep 4 | | (a) | Halifax Town | L | 1 - 2 | Beech | 3,820 |
| 9 | 8 | | (a) | Darlington | L | 0 - 2 | | 5,899 |
| 10 | 12 | | (h) | Exeter City | W | 4 - 3 | Beech 2, Blake (o.g.), Lee | 2,107 |
| 11 | 19 | | (a) | Rotherham United | L | 0 - 3 | | 3,769 |
| 12 | 26 | | (h) | Peterborough United | L | 1 - 2 | Heckingbottom | 2,389 |
| 13 | Oct 3 | | (a) | Leyton Orient | D | 1 - 1 | Midgley (pen) | 3,745 |
| 14 | 10 | | (h) | Shrewsbury Town | D | 1 - 1 | Beech | 1,897 |
| 15 | 17 | | (a) | Brentford | L | 1 - 2 | Miller | 4,085 |
| 16 | 20 | | (a) | Chester City | D | 1 - 1 | Beech | 2,100 |
| 17 | 24 | | (h) | Torquay United | W | 4 - 1 | Stephenson, Howard, Lee, Beech | 1,593 |
| 18 | 31 | | (a) | Brighton & Hove Albion | L | 2 - 3 | Beech, Midgley | 2,765 |
| 19 | Nov 7 | | (h) | Plymouth Argyle | W | 2 - 0 | Wooton (o.g.), Midgley | 2,121 |
| 20 | 10 | | (h) | Mansfield Town | L | 1 - 2 | Ingram (pen) | 1,779 |
| 22 | 21 | | (a) | Scarborough | W | 2 - 1 | Midgley, Brightwell | 1,775 |
| 23 | 28 | | (h) | Swansea City | L | 1 - 2 | Midgley | 2,052 |
| 26 | Dec 12 | | (a) | Carlisle United | L | 1 - 2 | Ingram (pen) | 3,025 |
| 27 | 19 | | (h) | Southend United | L | 2 - 4 | Di Lella, Howard | 1,898 |
| 28 | 26 | | (a) | Scunthorpe United | L | 0 - 1 | | 3,621 |
| 29 | 28 | | (h) | Rochdale | L | 0 - 1 | | 2,218 |
| 30 | Jan 2 | | (h) | Cambridge United | D | 2 - 2 | Beardsley, Barron | 3,788 |
| 31 | 9 | | (a) | Cardiff City | L | 1 - 4 | Clark | 7,766 |
| 32 | 16 | | (h) | Barnet | D | 2 - 2 | Midgley, Miller | 2,233 |
| 34 | 23 | | (a) | Hull City | L | 0 - 4 | | 5,808 |
| 36 | 30 | | (a) | Rochdale | W | 1 - 0 | Clark | 1,942 |
| 37 | Feb 6 | | (h) | Halifax Town | W | 2 - 0 | Howard 2 | 2,374 |
| 38 | 13 | | (h) | Darlington | L | 2 - 3 | Irvine, Miller | 3,980 |
| 39 | 20 | | (a) | Exeter City | L | 1 - 2 | Ingram (pen) | 2,997 |
| 40 | 27 | | (h) | Rotherham United | D | 0 - 0 | | 2,681 |
| 41 | Mar 6 | | (a) | Peterborough United | D | 1 - 1 | Miller | 4,854 |
| 42 | 13 | | (a) | Plymouth Argyle | D | 0 - 0 | | 4,441 |
| 43 | 20 | | (h) | Brighton & Hove Albion | D | 0 - 0 | | 2,261 |
| 44 | 27 | | (a) | Torquay United | L | 0 - 3 | | 1,927 |
| 45 | Apr 3 | | (h) | Brentford | L | 0 - 1 | | 2,719 |
| 46 | 5 | | (a) | Shrewsbury Town | W | 1 - 0 | Baker | 3,187 |
| 47 | 10 | | (h) | Chester City | W | 2 - 0 | Freestone, Jones | 2,413 |
| 48 | 13 | | (a) | Swansea City | L | 0 - 1 | | 4,429 |
| 49 | 17 | | (h) | Scarborough | W | 3 - 0 | Freestone 2 (1 pen), Baker | 5,098 |
| 50 | 24 | | (a) | Mansfield Town | L | 0 - 2 | | 3,337 |
| 51 | 27 | | (h) | Leyton Orient | W | 1 - 0 | Beardsley | 3,152 |
| 52 | May 1 | | (h) | Carlisle United | D | 0 - 0 | | 4,468 |
| 53 | 8 | | (a) | Southend United | D | 1 - 1 | Stephenson | 4,865 |

Final Position : 22nd in Division Three

Apps.
Sub.Apps.
2 own goals — Goals

**FA Cup**

| Match No. | Date | Round | Venue | Opponents | Result | | Scorers | Attendance |
|---|---|---|---|---|---|---|---|---|
| 21 | Nov 14 | R1 | (h) | Carlisle United | W | 2 - 1 | Howard, Miller | 2,845 |
| 24 | Dec 5 | R2 | (a) | Fulham | L | 2 - 4 | Midgley, Miller | 6,358 |

Apps.
Sub.Apps.
Goals

**League Cup**

| Match No. | Date | Round | Venue | Opponents | Result | | Scorers | Attendance |
|---|---|---|---|---|---|---|---|---|
| 2 | Aug 11 | R1/1 | (a) | Bolton Wanderers | L | 0 - 1 | | 6,429 |
| 5 | 25 | R1/2 | (h) | Bolton Wanderers | L | 0 - 3 | | 3,185 |

Apps.
Sub.Apps.
Goals

| Hollund | Knowles | Ingram | Barron | Lee | Beech | Stephenson | Di Lella | Irvine | Midgley | Clark | Brightwell | Howard | Miller | Pamberton | McDonald | Evans | Rush | Smith | Davies | Stokoe | Heckingbottom | Hutt | Baker | McGuckin | Miotto | Beardsley | Elliott | McKinnon | Strodder | Jones | Hughes | Westwood | Freestone | Dunwell |
|---|---|---|---|---|---|---|---|---|---|---|---|---|---|---|---|---|---|---|---|---|---|---|---|---|---|---|---|---|---|---|---|---|---|---|
| 1 | 2 | 3 | 4 | 5 | 6 | *7* | 8 | 9 | **10** | 11 | *12* | **13** | | | | | | | | | | | | | | | | | | | | | | |
| 1 | 2 | 3 | 4 | 5 | 6 | *10* | | 9 | 8 | 11 | | *12* | 7 | | | | | | | | | | | | | | | | | | | | | |
| 1 | 2 | 3 | 4 | 5 | 6 | | | *9* | 8 | 11 | | 10 | 7 | *12* | | | | | | | | | | | | | | | | | | | | |
| 1 | 2 | **3** | 4 | 5 | 6 | | **13** | *12* | ***8*** | 11 | | *10* | 7 | ***14*** | 9 | | | | | | | | | | | | | | | | | | | |
| 1 | 2 | | 4 | 5 | 6 | | *3* | *12* | 8 | **11** | | 10 | 7 | **13** | 9 | | | | | | | | | | | | | | | | | | | |
| 1 | 2 | 3 | 4 | 5 | 6 | | | *12* | **8** | *11* | | 10 | 7 | **13** | ***9*** | ***14*** | | | | | | | | | | | | | | | | | | |
| 1 | 2 | 3 | 4 | 5 | 6 | | | | 8 | 11 | | 10 | 7 | | *9* | | *12* | | | | | | | | | | | | | | | | | |
| 1 | 2 | 3 | 4 | 5 | 6 | ***11*** | | | *8* | **9** | | 10 | 7 | | | | | *12* | **13** | ***14*** | | | | | | | | | | | | | | |
| 1 | 2 | 3 | 4 | | 6 | *11* | **13** | | 8 | *12* | | ***14*** | 7 | | 5 | | | | ***9*** | **10** | | | | | | | | | | | | | | |
| 1 | 2 | 3 | 4 | | 6 | *11* | *12* | | 8 | **13** | | | | | | | 7 | | **9** | 10 | 5 | | | | | | | | | | | | | |
| 1 | 2 | | 4 | 5 | 6 | | 11 | | *12* | | | 9 | 8 | | | | *7* | | | 10 | 3 | | | | | | | | | | | | | |
| 1 | 2 | 4 | | 5 | 6 | | | *12* | 11 | | | 9 | *8* | | | | 7 | | | 10 | 3 | | | | | | | | | | | | | |
| 1 | 2 | 5 | 4 | | 6 | 11 | | *7* | 9 | 3 | *12* | | 8 | | | | | | | 10 | | | | | | | | | | | | | | |
| 1 | 2 | 7 | 4 | 5 | 6 | 11 | | | *12* | | | 9 | 8 | | | | | | | *10* | 3 | | | | | | | | | | | | | |
| 1 | 2 | 7 | 4 | 5 | 6 | *11* | | | 10 | **13** | *12* | ***9*** | 8 | | | | ***14*** | | | | **3** | | | | | | | | | | | | | |
| 1 | 2 | 4 | | 5 | 6 | 11 | | | *10* | 3 | 7 | 9 | 8 | | | | *12* | | | | | | | | | | | | | | | | | |
| 1 | 2 | 4 | | 5 | | **11** | *6* | *12* | 10 | 3 | 7 | ***9*** | 8 | | | | **13** | | | | | ***14*** | | | | | | | | | | | | |
| 1 | 2 | 4 | | 5 | | 11 | 6 | | 10 | 3 | 7 | 9 | 8 | | | | | | | | | | | | | | | | | | | | | |
| 1 | 2 | 4 | | 5 | | 11 | 6 | | 10 | 3 | 7 | 9 | | | | | | | | 8 | | | | | | | | | | | | | | |
| 1 | 2 | 4 | | 5 | | 11 | 6 | | 10 | 3 | 7 | 9 | *12* | | | | | | | *8* | | | | | | | | | | | | | | |
| 1 | 2 | 6 | 4 | 5 | | 11 | 8 | | 10 | **3** | *12* | | | | | | *9* | | | 7 | | | **13** | | | | | | | | | | | |
| 1 | 2 | 3 | 4 | 5 | | 11 | 8 | *12* | **10** | | *7* | 9 | | | | | | | | **13** | | | | 6 | | | | | | | | | | |
| | 2 | | 4 | 5 | | | | | 10 | | | 9 | 7 | | | | | 3 | | 8 | | 11 | | 6 | 1 | | | | | | | | | |
| | 2 | | 4 | 5 | | 11 | 7 | *10* | | | *12* | 9 | | | | | | 3 | | 8 | | | | 6 | 1 | | | | | | | | | |
| | 2 | 6 | 4 | **5** | | 11 | 10 | | | 3 | *12* | 9 | **13** | | | | | | | *8* | | | | | 1 | 7 | | | | | | | | |
| | *2* | 6 | 4 | | | 11 | **10** | | *12* | 3 | | 9 | 8 | | | | | | | | | **13** | | 5 | 1 | 7 | | | | | | | | |
| | 2 | | 4 | | | *11* | 6 | | 10 | 3 | *12* | 9 | **13** | | | | | | | **8** | | | | 5 | 1 | 7 | | | | | | | | |
| 1 | 2 | 11 | | 5 | | *12* | **13** | **9** | ***10*** | 3 | ***14*** | | *8* | | | | | | | | | 4 | | 6 | | 7 | | | | | | | | |
| 1 | *2* | 3 | 4 | | | 7 | | **13** | **10** | 11 | | 9 | *12* | | | | | | | | | | | 5 | | 8 | 6 | | | | | | | |
| 1 | 2 | 3 | 4 | | | 7 | | *12* | *10* | | 11 | 9 | | | | | | | | | | | | 5 | | 8 | 6 | | | | | | | |
| 1 | 2 | 5 | 4 | | | *7* | | 10 | | 11 | | 9 | *12* | | | | | | | | | | | | | 8 | 6 | 3 | | | | | | |
| 1 | 2 | 5 | 4 | | | *12* | | 10 | | *11* | | 9 | 7 | | | | | | | | | | | | | 8 | 6 | 3 | | | | | | |
| 1 | 2 | | 4 | | | | | | *9* | 11 | | | 7 | | | | **10** | | | *12* | | | **13** | | | 8 | 6 | 3 | 5 | | | | | |
| 1 | 2 | 6 | 4 | | | | | *10* | | 11 | | | 7 | | | | *12* | | | | | | 9 | | | 8 | | 3 | 5 | | | | | |
| 1 | 2 | **6** | 4 | *12* | | | | | | 11 | | | 7 | | | | | | | | | | 9 | | | 8 | | 3 | 5 | *10* | **13** | | | |
| 1 | 2 | | 4 | | | 6 | | *10* | | 11 | | | **7** | | | | | | | | | | *12* | | | 8 | | 3 | 5 | 9 | **13** | | | |
| 1 | 2 | | | | | 6 | | | | *11* | *12* | | 7 | | | | | | | | | | **9** | | | 8 | | 3 | 5 | 10 | | 4 | **13** | |
| 1 | *2* | *12* | 4 | | | | 7 | | | 3 | ***11*** | | | | | | | | | **13** | | | ***14*** | | | **8** | | | 5 | 10 | 6 | | 9 | |
| 1 | 2 | 3 | 4 | | | | **7** | | | 11 | | | | | | | | | | **13** | | | *12* | | | 8 | | | 5 | *10* | 6 | | 9 | |
| 1 | 2 | 3 | 4 | | | | | | | 11 | | | | | | | | | | 7 | | | | | | 8 | | | | 10 | 6 | 5 | 9 | |
| 1 | 2 | 3 | 4 | | | | | | | 11 | | | | | | | | | | 7 | | | *12* | | | 8 | | | 5 | 10 | *6* | | 9 | |
| 1 | 2 | 3 | 4 | | | | *12* | | | *11* | | | 7 | | | | | | | | | | **13** | | | 8 | | | 5 | **10** | 6 | | 9 | |
| 1 | 2 | 3 | 4 | | | | | | | 11 | | | 7 | | | | | | | | | | *12* | | | *8* | | | 5 | 10 | 6 | | 9 | |
| 1 | 2 | 3 | 4 | | | | 6 | | | 11 | | | 7 | | | | | | | | | | *12* | | | 8 | | | 5 | *10* | | | 9 | |
| 1 | 2 | 3 | 4 | | | | 6 | | | 11 | | | 7 | | | | | | | | | | | | | 8 | | | 5 | 10 | | *12* | 9 | |
| 1 | 2 | 3 | 4 | | | *12* | 6 | | | 11 | | | | | | | | | | | | | **13** | | | 8 | | | 5 | ***10*** | | *7* | **9** | ***14*** |
| 41 | 46 | 37 | 38 | 23 | 16 | 24 | 18 | 10 | 26 | 36 | 8 | 25 | 29 | | 5 | | 5 | 2 | 2 | 15 | 5 | 2 | 3 | 8 | 5 | 22 | 5 | 7 | 13 | 12 | 6 | 3 | 9 | |
| | | 1 | | 1 | | 3 | 5 | 8 | 3 | 3 | 9 | 3 | 5 | 4 | | 1 | 5 | 1 | 1 | 5 | | 2 | 10 | | | | | | | | 2 | 1 | 1 | 1 |
| | | 4 | 1 | 3 | 9 | 2 | 2 | 1 | 7 | 2 | 1 | 5 | 4 | | | | | | | | 1 | | 2 | | | 2 | | | | 1 | | | 3 | |

| Hollund | Knowles | Ingram | Barron | Lee | Beech | Stephenson | Di Lella | Irvine | Midgley | Clark | Brightwell | Howard | Miller | Pamberton | McDonald | Evans | Rush | Smith | Davies | Stokoe | Heckingbottom | Hutt |
|---|---|---|---|---|---|---|---|---|---|---|---|---|---|---|---|---|---|---|---|---|---|---|
| 1 | 2 | 4 | | 5 | | 11 | 6 | | 10 | 3 | 7 | 9 | **8** | | | | *12* | | | **13** | | |
| 1 | 2 | 5 | 4 | | | **11** | *6* | | 10 | 3 | **13** | 9 | 8 | | | | | | | **7** | | *12* |
| 2 | 2 | 2 | 1 | 1 | | 2 | 2 | | 2 | 2 | 1 | 2 | 2 | | | | | | | 1 | | |
| | | | | | | | | | | | 1 | | | | | | 1 | | | 1 | | 1 |
| | | | | | | | | | 1 | | | 1 | 2 | | | | | | | | | |

| Hollund | Knowles | Ingram | Barron | Lee | Beech | Stephenson | Di Lella | Irvine | Midgley | Clark | Brightwell | Howard | Miller | Pamberton | McDonald |
|---|---|---|---|---|---|---|---|---|---|---|---|---|---|---|---|
| 1 | 2 | 3 | 4 | 5 | 6 | *12* | *8* | **9** | 10 | 11 | | **13** | 7 | | |
| 1 | 2 | 3 | 4 | 5 | 6 | | | **13** | **8** | 11 | *12* | 10 | *7* | | 9 |
| 2 | 2 | 2 | 2 | 2 | 2 | | 1 | 1 | 2 | 2 | | 1 | 2 | | 1 |
| | | | | | | 1 | | 1 | | | 1 | 1 | | | |
| | | | | | | | | | | | | | | | |

## League Table

| | P | W | D | L | F | A | Pts |
|---|---|---|---|---|---|---|---|
| Brentford | 46 | 26 | 7 | 13 | 79 | 56 | 85 |
| Cambridge United | 46 | 23 | 12 | 11 | 78 | 48 | 81 |
| Cardiff City | 46 | 22 | 14 | 10 | 60 | 39 | 80 |
| Scunthorpe United | 46 | 22 | 8 | 16 | 69 | 58 | 74 |
| Rotherham United | 46 | 20 | 13 | 13 | 79 | 61 | 73 |
| Leyton Orient | 46 | 19 | 15 | 12 | 68 | 59 | 72 |
| Swansea City | 46 | 19 | 14 | 13 | 56 | 48 | 71 |
| Mansfield Town | 46 | 19 | 10 | 17 | 60 | 58 | 67 |
| Peterborough United | 46 | 18 | 12 | 16 | 72 | 56 | 66 |
| Halifax Town | 46 | 17 | 15 | 14 | 58 | 56 | 66 |
| Darlington | 46 | 18 | 11 | 17 | 69 | 58 | 65 |
| Exeter City | 46 | 17 | 12 | 17 | 47 | 50 | 63 |
| Plymouth Argyle | 46 | 17 | 10 | 19 | 58 | 54 | 61 |
| Chester City | 46 | 13 | 18 | 15 | 57 | 66 | 57 |
| Shrewsbury Town | 46 | 14 | 14 | 18 | 52 | 63 | 56 |
| Barnet | 46 | 14 | 13 | 19 | 54 | 71 | 55 |
| Brighton & Hove Albion | 46 | 16 | 7 | 23 | 49 | 66 | 55 |
| Southend United | 46 | 14 | 12 | 20 | 52 | 58 | 54 |
| Rochdale | 46 | 13 | 15 | 18 | 42 | 55 | 54 |
| Torquay United | 46 | 12 | 17 | 17 | 47 | 58 | 53 |
| Hull City | 46 | 14 | 11 | 21 | 44 | 62 | 53 |
| Hartlepool United | 46 | 13 | 12 | 21 | 52 | 65 | 51 |
| Carlisle United | 46 | 11 | 16 | 19 | 43 | 53 | 49 |
| Scarborough | 46 | 14 | 6 | 26 | 50 | 77 | 48 |

# 1999-2000

## Division Three

Manager: Chris Turner

### Did you know that?

Hartlepool-born Adam Boyd made his debut for the club on 2 November when he came on as substitute for Tommy Miller, who had scored a hat-trick, in the 3–0 home defeat of Barnet.

United won 16 home games in finishing seventh, their best since the 1956–57 season.

The second leg Play-off game at Darlington was 'beamed' back to the Victoria Park and watched by several thousand fans. This was the first occasion such an event was staged at the ground.

| Match No. | Date | Round | Venue | Opponents | Result | | Scorers | Attendance |
|---|---|---|---|---|---|---|---|---|
| 1 | Aug 7 | | (a) | Peterborough United | L | 1 - 2 | Jones | 5,886 |
| 3 | 14 | | (h) | Halifax Town | L | 0 - 2 | | 2,719 |
| 4 | 21 | | (a) | Carlisle United | W | 3 - 0 | Freestone 2, Miller | 4,033 |
| 6 | 28 | | (h) | Cheltenham Town | L | 0 - 1 | | 2,390 |
| 7 | 31 | | (a) | Shrewsbury Town | D | 0 - 0 | | 1,803 |
| 8 | Sep 4 | | (h) | Southend United | L | 1 - 2 | Stephenson | 1,980 |
| 9 | 11 | | (a) | Northampton Town | L | 1 - 2 | Miller | 4,724 |
| 10 | 18 | | (h) | Plymouth Argyle | W | 3 - 0 | Freestone, Lee, Henderson | 2,242 |
| 11 | 25 | | (a) | Leyton Orient | L | 1 - 2 | Stephenson | 3,889 |
| 12 | Oct 2 | | (h) | Darlington | W | 2 - 0 | Shilton, Fitzpatrick | 3,957 |
| 13 | 9 | | (h) | Hull City | W | 2 - 0 | Miller, Freestone | 3,114 |
| 14 | 16 | | (a) | Mansfield Town | W | 3 - 2 | Shilton, Stephenson, Miller | 2,612 |
| 15 | 19 | | (a) | Rotherham United | L | 0 - 3 | | 2,623 |
| 16 | 23 | | (h) | Leyton Orient | W | 1 - 0 | Henderson | 2,397 |
| 18 | Nov 2 | | (h) | Barnet | W | 3 - 0 | Miller 3 | 2,290 |
| 19 | 6 | | (a) | Brighton & Hove Albion | L | 0 - 1 | | 5,746 |
| 20 | 13 | | (h) | Chester City | W | 1 - 0 | Miller | 2,266 |
| 22 | 23 | | (a) | Torquay United | D | 0 - 0 | | 2,080 |
| 23 | 27 | | (a) | Macclesfield Town | D | 3 - 3 | Clark 2 (1 pen), Lee | 2,351 |
| 24 | Dec 4 | | (h) | Peterborough United | W | 1 - 0 | Jones | 2,404 |
| 26 | 11 | | (h) | Swansea City | L | 0 - 1 | | 2,397 |
| 27 | 18 | | (a) | Exeter City | W | 2 - 1 | Jones 2 | 2,261 |
| 28 | 26 | | (h) | York City | W | 2 - 1 | Henderson 2 | 4,668 |
| 29 | 28 | | (a) | Lincoln City | W | 2 - 1 | Clark, Miller | 3,480 |
| 30 | Jan 3 | | (h) | Rochdale | W | 3 - 2 | Miller (pen), Jones, Clark | 4,498 |
| 31 | 8 | | (a) | Swansea City | L | 1 - 2 | Henderson | 7,163 |
| 33 | 15 | | (a) | Halifax Town | D | 1 - 1 | Jones | 3,546 |
| 34 | 22 | | (h) | Carlisle United | W | 1 - 0 | Miller | 3,530 |
| 35 | 29 | | (a) | Cheltenham Town | L | 1 - 2 | Lee | 3,630 |
| 36 | Feb 5 | | (h) | Shrewsbury Town | W | 1 - 0 | Boyd | 2,933 |
| 37 | 12 | | (a) | Southend United | L | 1 - 2 | Lee | 3,337 |
| 38 | 19 | | (h) | Macclesfield Town | L | 1 - 4 | Miller | 2,823 |
| 40 | 26 | | (a) | Plymouth Argyle | D | 1 - 1 | Shilton | 3,917 |
| 41 | Mar 4 | | (h) | Northampton Town | W | 2 - 1 | Stephenson, Lee | 2,878 |
| 42 | 7 | | (h) | Brighton & Hove Albion | D | 0 - 0 | | 2,734 |
| 43 | 11 | | (a) | Barnet | D | 1 - 1 | Coppinger | 2,925 |
| 44 | 18 | | (h) | Torquay United | W | 2 - 0 | Stephenson, Lee | 2,766 |
| 45 | 21 | | (a) | Chester City | D | 1 - 1 | Fitzpatrick | 1,816 |
| 46 | 25 | | (a) | York City | L | 1 - 2 | Coppinger | 4,079 |
| 47 | Apr 1 | | (h) | Exeter City | W | 2 - 1 | Arnison, Clark | 2,668 |
| 48 | 8 | | (a) | Rochdale | L | 0 - 2 | | 2,332 |
| 49 | 15 | | (h) | Lincoln City | W | 2 - 0 | Henderson, Miller | 2,777 |
| 50 | 22 | | (h) | Mansfield Town | W | 1 - 0 | Henderson | 3,473 |
| 51 | 24 | | (a) | Darlington | D | 1 - 1 | Miller | 6,746 |
| 52 | 29 | | (h) | Rotherham United | L | 1 - 2 | Clark | 4,673 |
| 53 | May 6 | | (a) | Hull City | W | 3 - 0 | Lee, Coppinger, Henderson | 7,620 |

Final Position : 7th in Division Three

Apps.
Sub.Apps.
Goals

**Play-offs**

| | | | | | | | | |
|---|---|---|---|---|---|---|---|---|
| 54 | May 14 | SFl1 | (h) | Darlington | L | 0 - 2 | | 6,995 |
| 55 | 18 | SFl2 | (a) | Darlington | L | 0 - 1 | | 8,238 |

Apps.
Sub.Apps.
Goals

**FA Cup**

| | | | | | | | | |
|---|---|---|---|---|---|---|---|---|
| 17 | Oct 31 | R1 | (h) | Millwall | W | 1 - 0 | Jones | 2,847 |
| 21 | Nov 21 | R2 | (a) | Hereford United | L | 0 - 1 | | 4,914 |

Apps.
Sub.Apps.
Goals

**League Cup**

| | | | | | | | | |
|---|---|---|---|---|---|---|---|---|
| 2 | Aug 10 | R1/1 | (h) | Crewe Alexandra | D | 3 - 3 | Miller, Di Lella, Stephenson | 1,836 |
| 5 | 24 | R1/2 | (a) | Crewe Alexandra | L | 0 - 1 | | 5,095 |

Apps.
Sub.Apps.
Goals

| 13 Dibble | 2 Knowles | 3 Perkins | 4 Barron | 18 Lee | 6 Ingram | 7 Di Lella | 8 Miller | 9 Jones | 10 Freestone | 17 Stephenson | 11 Clark | 5 Strodder | 12 Midgley | 14 Henderson | 29 Tennebo | 1 Hollund | 16 Westwood | 33 Vindheim | 32 Fitzpatrick | 31 Shilton | 30 Boyd | 34 Mason | 35 McAvoy | 34 West | 27 Coppinger | 7 Arnison | 3 Beavers |
|---|---|---|---|---|---|---|---|---|---|---|---|---|---|---|---|---|---|---|---|---|---|---|---|---|---|---|---|
| 1 | 2 | 3 | 4 | 5 | 6 | *7* | 8 | 9 | 10 | 11 | *12* | | | | | | | | | | | | | | | | |
| 1 | 2 | 3 | **4** | | 6 | *7* | 8 | 9 | ***10*** | 11 | *12* | 5 | **13** | ***14*** | | | | | | | | | | | | | |
| 1 | 2 | | *4* | 6 | *12* | | 8 | **9** | ***10*** | 11 | 3 | 5 | **13** | ***14*** | 7 | | | | | | | | | | | | |
| 1 | *2* | *12* | 4 | | 6 | **8** | | 9 | 10 | 11 | 3 | 5 | **13** | ***14*** | ***7*** | | | | | | | | | | | | |
| | | 3 | | | 6 | | 8 | 9 | | 11 | 2 | 5 | 10 | | 7 | 1 | 4 | | | | | | | | | | |
| | | 3 | 4 | | 6 | | *8* | **9** | 10 | 11 | 2 | 5 | *12* | **13** | 7 | 1 | | | | | | | | | | | |
| | *12* | 3 | 4 | | 6 | | 8 | **13** | **10** | 11 | ***2*** | *5* | ***14*** | | 7 | 1 | 9 | | | | | | | | | | |
| | 2 | 3 | **4** | 5 | | | 8 | 9 | *10* | ***11*** | 7 | | | *12* | | 1 | **13** | 6 | ***14*** | | | | | | | | |
| | 2 | ***3*** | 4 | 5 | | | 8 | *9* | 10 | **7** | 11 | | | *12* | | 1 | | 6 | **13** | ***14*** | | | | | | | |
| | 2 | | 4 | 5 | | | 8 | 9 | | 11 | *12* | | | *10* | | 1 | **13** | 6 | **3** | 7 | | | | | | | |
| | 2 | | 4 | 5 | | | 8 | *9* | *12* | 11 | | | | 10 | | 1 | **13** | 6 | **7** | 3 | | | | | | | |
| | 2 | | 4 | 5 | | | 8 | 9 | *12* | 11 | **13** | | | *10* | | 1 | | 6 | **7** | 3 | | | | | | | |
| 1 | 2 | | 4 | 5 | | | 8 | *9* | *12* | 11 | **13** | | | 10 | | | | 6 | **7** | 3 | | | | | | | |
| | 2 | | 4 | 5 | | | 8 | *12* | *9* | ***11*** | **13** | | | 10 | | 1 | ***14*** | 6 | **7** | 3 | | | | | | | |
| | 2 | | 4 | 5 | | | ***8*** | 9 | *10* | 11 | **7** | | *12* | | | 1 | 6 | | **13** | 3 | ***14*** | | | | | | |
| | 2 | | 4 | 5 | | | 8 | | 10 | ***11*** | 7 | | **12** | *9* | | 1 | 6 | | ***14*** | 3 | **13** | | | | | | |
| | 2 | | 4 | 5 | | | 8 | 9 | **10** | 11 | *12* | | | **13** | | 1 | 6 | | *7* | 3 | | | | | | | |
| | 2 | | 4 | 5 | | | 8 | 9 | *12* | 11 | 3 | | | *10* | | 1 | 6 | | | | | 7 | | | | | |
| | 2 | | 4 | 5 | | | | *9* | *12* | 11 | 3 | | **13** | 10 | ***14*** | 1 | 6 | | | | | **7** | ***8*** | | | | |
| | 2 | | 4 | 5 | | | 8 | 9 | | 11 | 3 | | | *10* | | 1 | 6 | | | | | 7 | *12* | | | | |
| | 2 | | 4 | 5 | | | 8 | 9 | | 11 | **3** | | *12* | | | 1 | 6 | | | **13** | | *7* | 10 | | | | |
| | 2 | | 4 | 5 | | | 8 | *9* | *12* | 11 | 3 | **13** | | **7** | | 1 | 6 | | | | | | 10 | | | | |
| | 2 | | | 4 | | | ***8*** | *9* | *12* | 11 | 3 | 5 | | 7 | | 1 | 6 | | | **13** | | **10** | ***14*** | | | | |
| | 2 | | | 4 | | | 8 | 9 | | 11 | 3 | 5 | | *7* | | 1 | 6 | | | 10 | | | *12* | | | | |
| | 2 | | | 4 | | | 8 | **9** | *12* | 11 | 7 | 5 | **13** | *10* | | 1 | 6 | | | ***3*** | | ***14*** | | | | | |
| | 2 | | | 4 | | | 8 | 9 | *12* | 11 | 7 | 5 | | *10* | | 1 | 6 | | | 3 | | | | | | | |
| | 2 | | 7 | 4 | | | 8 | *9* | | 11 | 3 | 5 | 10 | | | 1 | 6 | | | | | | *12* | | | | |
| | **2** | | 4 | 7 | | | 8 | 9 | | 11 | *3* | 5 | **13** | ***10*** | | 1 | 6 | | | *12* | | | ***14*** | | | | |
| | 2 | | 4 | 6 | | | 8 | *9* | *12* | **11** | | 5 | ***14*** | | | 1 | 7 | | **13** | 3 | | | ***10*** | | | | |
| | 2 | | 4 | 6 | | | 8 | | ***9*** | 11 | *12* | 5 | | | | 1 | **7** | | *10* | 3 | ***14*** | | **13** | | | | |
| | 2 | | | 4 | | | 8 | *9* | | 11 | *12* | 5 | | **13** | ***14*** | 1 | 6 | | ***7*** | 3 | | | **10** | | | | |
| 1 | 2 | | 4 | 6 | | | 8 | *12* | | 11 | 10 | 5 | | *9* | **7** | | | | | 3 | | | **13** | | | | |
| | 2 | | 4 | 6 | | | 8 | **9** | | 11 | *12* | 5 | | | | 1 | 7 | | *10* | 3 | | | **13** | | | | |
| | 2 | | 4 | 6 | | | 8 | *9* | | 11 | 3 | 5 | | | | 1 | 7 | | 10 | | | | *12* | | | | |
| | 2 | | 4 | 5 | | | 8 | ***9*** | | 11 | 3 | | | **10** | | 1 | 6 | | *7* | | *12* | | **13** | ***14*** | | | |
| | 2 | | 4 | 6 | | | 8 | | | ***11*** | 3 | 5 | | **9** | *12* | 1 | 7 | | *10* | | | | | | **13** | ***14*** | |
| | 2 | | 4 | 10 | | | 8 | | *12* | 11 | 3 | 5 | | | **13** | 1 | 6 | | **7** | | | | | | *9* | | |
| | 2 | | 4 | **10** | | | 8 | | *12* | 11 | 3 | 5 | | **13** | | 1 | 6 | | 7 | | | | | | *9* | | |
| | 2 | | 4 | | | | 8 | | *9* | 11 | 3 | 5 | | *12* | **13** | 1 | 6 | | **7** | | | | | | ***10*** | | ***14*** |
| | 2 | | 4 | | | | 8 | | **9** | 11 | 3 | 5 | | *12* | | 1 | 6 | | ***7*** | | | | | | *10* | ***14*** | **13** |
| | 2 | | 4 | | | | 8 | | | 11 | **3** | 5 | *12* | ***14*** | | 1 | 6 | | | **13** | | | | | *10* | 7 | ***9*** |
| | 2 | | 4 | ***10*** | | | 8 | | | *11* | 3 | 5 | | **9** | | 1 | 6 | | *12* | | | | | | **13** | 7 | ***14*** |
| | 2 | | 4 | 5 | | | 8 | | | 11 | 3 | | **12** | *10* | | 1 | 6 | | **13** | | | | | | ***14*** | 7 | ***9*** |
| | 2 | | 4 | 10 | | | 8 | | | 11 | 3 | 5 | | 9 | | 1 | *6* | | | | | | | | | 7 | *12* |
| | ***2*** | | 4 | **10** | | | 8 | | | 11 | 3 | 5 | | 9 | | 1 | 6 | | *12* | | | | | | ***14*** | 7 | **13** |
| | ***2*** | | 4 | 10 | | | 8 | | | 11 | 3 | 5 | *12* | **9** | | 1 | 6 | | | | | | **13** | | *7* | ***14*** | |
| 6 | 43 | 7 | 40 | 38 | 6 | 3 | 44 | 30 | 15 | 46 | 34 | 28 | 2 | 23 | 6 | 40 | 33 | 7 | 16 | 16 | | 5 | 5 | | 6 | 5 | 2 |
| | 1 | 1 | | | 1 | | | 3 | 12 | | 10 | 1 | 15 | 12 | 5 | | 4 | | 8 | 5 | 4 | 1 | 11 | 1 | 4 | 3 | 5 |
| | | | | 7 | | | 14 | 6 | 4 | 5 | 6 | | | 8 | | | | | 2 | 3 | 1 | | | | 3 | 1 | |

| 13 Dibble | 2 Knowles | 3 Perkins | 4 Barron | 18 Lee | 6 Ingram | 7 Di Lella | 8 Miller | 9 Jones | 10 Freestone | 17 Stephenson | 11 Clark | 5 Strodder | 12 Midgley | 14 Henderson | 29 Tennebo | 1 Hollund | 16 Westwood | 33 Vindheim | 32 Fitzpatrick | 31 Shilton | 30 Boyd | 34 Mason | 35 McAvoy | 34 West | 27 Coppinger | 7 Arnison | 3 Beavers |
|---|---|---|---|---|---|---|---|---|---|---|---|---|---|---|---|---|---|---|---|---|---|---|---|---|---|---|---|
| *12* | | | 4 | 5 | | | 8 | ***14*** | | 11 | 3 | | 10 | | | 1 | 6 | | | | | | **13** | | **7** | *2* | ***9*** |
| 1 | | | 4 | 7 | | | 8 | *10* | 9 | **11** | 3 | 5 | | | | | 6 | | **13** | | | | *12* | | | 2 | |
| 1 | | | 2 | 2 | | | 2 | 1 | 1 | 2 | 2 | 1 | 1 | | | 1 | 2 | | | | | | | | 1 | 2 | 1 |
| 1 | | | | | | | | 1 | | | | | | | | | | | 1 | | | | 2 | | | | |
| | | | | | | | | | | | | | | | | | | | | | | | | | | | |

| 13 Dibble | 2 Knowles | 3 Perkins | 4 Barron | 18 Lee | 6 Ingram | 7 Di Lella | 8 Miller | 9 Jones | 10 Freestone | 17 Stephenson | 11 Clark | 5 Strodder | 12 Midgley | 14 Henderson | 29 Tennebo | 1 Hollund | 16 Westwood | 33 Vindheim | 32 Fitzpatrick | 31 Shilton | 30 Boyd | 34 Mason | 35 McAvoy | 34 West | 27 Coppinger | 7 Arnison | 3 Beavers |
|---|---|---|---|---|---|---|---|---|---|---|---|---|---|---|---|---|---|---|---|---|---|---|---|---|---|---|---|
| | 7 | | 4 | 5 | | | 8 | 9 | 10 | 11 | 6 | | | | | 1 | 2 | | | 3 | | | | | | | |
| | 2 | | 4 | 5 | | | 8 | ***9*** | 10 | *12* | ***14*** | | | **13** | | 1 | 11 | *6* | | 3 | | **7** | | | | | |
| | 2 | | 2 | 2 | | | 2 | 2 | 2 | 1 | 1 | | | | | 2 | 2 | 1 | | 2 | | 1 | | | | | |
| | | | | | | | | | | 1 | 1 | | | 1 | | | | | | | | | | | | | |
| | | | | | | | | 1 | | | | | | | | | | | | | | | | | | | |

| 13 Dibble | 2 Knowles | 3 Perkins | 4 Barron | 18 Lee | 6 Ingram | 7 Di Lella | 8 Miller | 9 Jones | 10 Freestone | 17 Stephenson | 11 Clark | 5 Strodder | 12 Midgley | 14 Henderson | 29 Tennebo | 1 Hollund | 16 Westwood | 33 Vindheim | 32 Fitzpatrick | 31 Shilton | 30 Boyd | 34 Mason | 35 McAvoy | 34 West | 27 Coppinger | 7 Arnison | 3 Beavers |
|---|---|---|---|---|---|---|---|---|---|---|---|---|---|---|---|---|---|---|---|---|---|---|---|---|---|---|---|
| 1 | 2 | 3 | 4 | 5 | 6 | 7 | 8 | 9 | *10* | 11 | | | *12* | | | | | | | | | | | | | | |
| 1 | 2 | | 4 | *5* | **12** | ***14*** | ***8*** | 9 | 10 | 11 | 3 | 6 | | **13** | 7 | | | | | | | | | | | | |
| 2 | 2 | 1 | 2 | 2 | 1 | 1 | 2 | 2 | 2 | 2 | 1 | 1 | | | 1 | | | | | | | | | | | | |
| | | | | | 1 | 1 | | | | | | | 1 | 1 | | | | | | | | | | | | | |
| | | | | | | 1 | 1 | | | 1 | | | | | | | | | | | | | | | | | |

## League Table

| | P | W | D | L | F | A | Pts |
|---|---|---|---|---|---|---|---|
| Swansea City | 46 | 24 | 13 | 9 | 51 | 30 | 85 |
| Rotherham United | 46 | 24 | 12 | 10 | 72 | 36 | 84 |
| Northampton Town | 46 | 25 | 7 | 14 | 63 | 45 | 82 |
| Darlington | 46 | 21 | 16 | 9 | 66 | 36 | 79 |
| Peterborough United | 46 | 22 | 12 | 12 | 63 | 54 | 78 |
| Barnet | 46 | 21 | 12 | 13 | 59 | 53 | 75 |
| Hartlepool United | 46 | 21 | 9 | 16 | 60 | 49 | 72 |
| Cheltenham Town | 46 | 20 | 10 | 16 | 50 | 42 | 70 |
| Torquay United | 46 | 19 | 12 | 15 | 62 | 52 | 69 |
| Rochdale | 46 | 18 | 14 | 14 | 57 | 54 | 68 |
| Brighton & Hove Albion | 46 | 17 | 16 | 13 | 64 | 46 | 67 |
| Plymouth Argyle | 46 | 16 | 18 | 12 | 55 | 51 | 66 |
| Macclesfield Town | 46 | 18 | 11 | 17 | 66 | 61 | 65 |
| Hull City | 46 | 15 | 14 | 17 | 43 | 43 | 59 |
| Lincoln City | 46 | 15 | 14 | 17 | 67 | 69 | 59 |
| Southend United | 46 | 15 | 11 | 20 | 53 | 61 | 56 |
| Mansfield Town | 46 | 16 | 8 | 22 | 50 | 65 | 56 |
| Halifax Town | 46 | 15 | 9 | 22 | 44 | 58 | 54 |
| Leyton Orient | 46 | 13 | 13 | 20 | 47 | 52 | 52 |
| York City | 46 | 12 | 16 | 18 | 39 | 53 | 52 |
| Exeter City | 46 | 11 | 11 | 24 | 46 | 72 | 44 |
| Shrewsbury Town | 46 | 9 | 13 | 24 | 40 | 67 | 40 |
| Carlisle United | 46 | 9 | 12 | 25 | 42 | 75 | 39 |
| Chester City | 46 | 10 | 9 | 27 | 44 | 79 | 39 |

# 2000-01

## Division Three

Manager: Chris Turner

### Did you know that?

Tommy Miller played his final game for the club on 16 May in the Play-off semi-final against Blackpool, a 3–1 defeat. He was transferred to Ipswich Town in the close season for a club record £750,000 fee.

'Pools finished fourth, their highest position since the 1990–91 promotion season, and again featured in the Play-offs, losing both games to Blackpool.

| Match No. | Date | Round | Venue | Opponents | Result | | Scorers | Attendance |
|---|---|---|---|---|---|---|---|---|
| 1 | Aug 12 | | (a) | Lincoln City | W | 2 - 0 | Fitzpatrick 2 | 3,588 |
| 2 | 19 | | (h) | Chesterfield | L | 1 - 2 | Henderson | 3,583 |
| 4 | 26 | | (a) | Exeter City | D | 1 - 1 | Henderson | 2,967 |
| 5 | 28 | | (h) | Cheltenham Town | D | 0 - 0 | | 2,870 |
| 6 | Sep 2 | | (h) | Shrewsbury Town | L | 1 - 3 | Lormor | 2,710 |
| 8 | 9 | | (a) | Blackpool | W | 2 - 1 | Miller, Henderson | 4,562 |
| 9 | 12 | | (a) | Torquay United | L | 0 - 1 | | 1,538 |
| 10 | 16 | | (h) | Macclesfield Town | D | 2 - 2 | Miller (pen), Shilton | 2,589 |
| 11 | 23 | | (a) | Mansfield Town | L | 3 - 4 | Shilton, Lormor, Henderson | 2,135 |
| 12 | 30 | | (h) | York City | W | 1 - 0 | Henderson | 2,130 |
| 13 | Oct 7 | | (h) | Darlington | W | 2 - 1 | Henderson, Miller | 2,365 |
| 14 | 14 | | (a) | Rochdale | L | 1 - 2 | Lormor | 2,813 |
| 15 | 18 | | (a) | Brighton & Hove Albion | L | 2 - 4 | Kuipers (o.g.), Sperrevik | 6,528 |
| 16 | 21 | | (h) | Plymouth Argyle | D | 1 - 1 | Henderson | 2,581 |
| 17 | 24 | | (a) | Hull City | D | 0 - 0 | | 5,294 |
| 18 | 28 | | (h) | Leyton Orient | W | 2 - 1 | Miller, Stephenson | 2,133 |
| 19 | Nov 4 | | (a) | Scunthorpe United | L | 0 - 3 | | 3,241 |
| 20 | 11 | | (h) | Kidderminster Harriers | W | 3 - 1 | Westwood, Midgley, Miller | 2,726 |
| 22 | 25 | | (a) | Cardiff City | L | 2 - 3 | Henderson, Miller | 6,251 |
| 23 | Dec 2 | | (h) | Southend United | W | 1 - 0 | Miller (pen) | 2,638 |
| 25 | 16 | | (a) | Halifax Town | W | 1 - 0 | Midgley | 2,042 |
| 26 | 23 | | (h) | Barnet | W | 6 - 1 | Stephenson, Midgley 3, Henderson, Tinkler | 3,133 |
| 27 | Jan 6 | | (h) | Exeter City | W | 2 - 0 | Miller 2 (1 pen) | 3,016 |
| 29 | 13 | | (a) | Cheltenham Town | W | 2 - 1 | Henderson, Sharp | 3,574 |
| 30 | 16 | | (a) | Chesterfield | D | 0 - 0 | | 4,240 |
| 31 | 20 | | (h) | Carlisle United | D | 2 - 2 | Midgley, Arnison | 4,473 |
| 32 | 27 | | (a) | Barnet | W | 3 - 1 | Henderson 2, Shilton | 2,565 |
| 34 | Feb 3 | | (a) | Shrewsbury Town | D | 1 - 1 | Seabury (o.g.) | 2,528 |
| 35 | 10 | | (h) | Blackpool | W | 3 - 1 | Henderson 2, Miller (pen) | 3,973 |
| 36 | 13 | | (a) | Carlisle United | W | 3 - 2 | Miller (pen), Shilton, Fitzpatrick | 4,159 |
| 37 | 17 | | (a) | Macclesfield Town | W | 1 - 0 | Tinkler | 2,228 |
| 38 | 20 | | (h) | Torquay United | W | 3 - 1 | Henderson, Fitzpatrick, Midgley | 3,932 |
| 39 | 24 | | (h) | Mansfield Town | D | 1 - 1 | Lormor | 3,699 |
| 40 | Mar 3 | | (a) | York City | D | 1 - 1 | Henderson | 4,553 |
| 41 | 6 | | (h) | Rochdale | D | 1 - 1 | Lormor | 3,492 |
| 42 | 10 | | (a) | Darlington | D | 1 - 1 | Knowles | 6,107 |
| 43 | 17 | | (h) | Brighton & Hove Albion | D | 2 - 2 | Lormor, Henderson | 4,410 |
| 44 | 24 | | (a) | Plymouth Argyle | W | 2 - 0 | Miller, Lormor | 4,226 |
| 45 | 27 | | (h) | Lincoln City | W | 1 - 0 | Miller | 3,584 |
| 46 | 31 | | (h) | Halifax Town | D | 1 - 1 | Mawson (o.g.) | 4,198 |
| 47 | Apr 7 | | (a) | Southend United | L | 1 - 2 | Tinkler | 3,759 |
| 48 | 14 | | (h) | Hull City | L | 0 - 1 | | 4,364 |
| 49 | 16 | | (a) | Leyton Orient | L | 1 - 3 | Miller | 5,359 |
| 50 | 21 | | (h) | Scunthorpe United | W | 1 - 0 | Miller | 3,897 |
| 51 | 28 | | (a) | Kidderminster Harriers | W | 1 - 0 | Sharp | 3,748 |
| 52 | May 5 | | (h) | Cardiff City | W | 3 - 1 | Midgley, Lormor, Miller | 5,324 |

Final Position : 4th in Division Three

Apps.
Sub.Apps.
3 own goals — Goals

**Play-offs**

| Match No. | Date | Round | Venue | Opponents | Result | | Scorers | Attendance |
|---|---|---|---|---|---|---|---|---|
| 53 | May 13 | SFl1 | (a) | Blackpool | L | 0 - 2 | | 5,720 |
| 54 | 16 | SFl2 | (h) | Blackpool | L | 1 - 3 | Henderson | 5,836 |

Apps.
Sub.Apps.
Goals

**FA Cup**

| Match No. | Date | Round | Venue | Opponents | Result | | Scorers | Attendance |
|---|---|---|---|---|---|---|---|---|
| 21 | Nov 18 | R1 | (a) | Scunthorpe United | L | 1 - 3 | Midgley | 3,552 |

Apps.
Sub.Apps.
Goals

**League Cup**

| Match No. | Date | Round | Venue | Opponents | Result | | Scorers | Attendance |
|---|---|---|---|---|---|---|---|---|
| 3 | Aug 22 | R1/1 | (a) | Burnley | L | 1 - 4 | Miller | 3,319 |
| 7 | Sep 5 | R1/2 | (h) | Burnley | W | 3 - 2 | Miller, Fitzpatrick, Stephenson | 1,090 |

Apps.
Sub.Apps.
Goals

| 1 Holland | 2 Knowles | 21 Robinson | 24 Ferguson | 16 Westwood | 13 Sharp | 6 Fitzpatrick | 8 Miller | 9 Lormor | 14 Henderson | 17 Stephenson | 3 Shilton | 12 Midgley | 19 McAvoy | 10 Sperrevik | 5 Strodder | 7 Arnison | 23 Williams | 15 Tennebo | 18 Lee | 26 Baker | 11 Clark | 27 Tinkler | 20 Boyd | 4 Barron | 29 Aspin | 26 Easter |
|---|---|---|---|---|---|---|---|---|---|---|---|---|---|---|---|---|---|---|---|---|---|---|---|---|---|---|
|1|2|3|4|5|6|7|8|9|10|11|12||||||||||||||||
|1|2|3|4|5|6|7|8|9|10|11|12|13|14||||||||||||||
|1|2|3|4|5|6|7|8|9|10|11|12|13||14|||||||||||||
|1|2||4|5|6|12|8|9|10|11|3|7|||13|14|||||||||||
|1|2|||5||12|8|9|10|11|3|7||13|6|4|||||||||||
||12|||5|6|7|8|9|10|11|3|13||14|4|2|1||||||||||
|||||5|6|7|8|9|10|11|3|12||13|4|2|1|14|||||||||
|||||5|6|7|8|9|10|11|3|12||13|4|2|1|14|||||||||
||2|||5|6||8|9|10|11|3|12||14|4|7|1||13||||||||
||2|13||5|||8|9|10|11|3|12||14|4|7|1|||6|||||||
||2|||5||12|8|9|10|11|3|||13|4|7|1|||6|||||||
||2|||5||12|8|9||11|3||13|10|4|7|1|||6|||||||
||2|||5|10|7|8|9||11|3|||12|4||1|||6|||||||
||2|||5||7|8||10|11|3|||9|4||1|||6|||||||
|||||5||7|8||10|11|3|12|13|9|4|2|1|||6|||||||
|||||5||7|8|||11|3|12|10|9|4|2|1|||6|13||||||
|||||5||12|8|||11|3|9|10||4|2|1|||6|13|7|14||||
|||||5|||8|||11|3|9|||4|2|1|||6|12|7|10|13|||
|||||5|||8||10|11||9|||4|2|1||||3|7||6|||
|||||5|||8||10|11||9||12|4|2|1||||3|7||6|||
|||||5|6||8||10|11||9||||2|1||||3|7||4|||
|||||5|6||8|12|10|11||9||13||2|1||||3|7||4|||
|||||5|6||8||10|11|12|9||||2|1||||3|7||4|||
|||||5|6||8|12|10|11||9||||2|1||||3|7||4|||
|||||5|6|12|8||10|11||9||||2|1||||3|7||4|||
|||||5|6||8|12|10|11||9||||2|1||||3|7||4|||
|||||5|6||8||10|11|3|9||||2|1|||||7||4|||
|||||5|6||8|12|10|11|3|9||||2|1|||||7||4|13||
||12|||5|6|13|8||10|11|3|9||||2|1|||||7||4|14||
||2|||5|6|12|8||10|11|3|9|||||1|||||7||4|13||
||2|||5|6||8||10|11|3|9|||||1|||||7||4|12||
||12|||5|6|11|8|13|10||3|9|||||1||||14|7||4|2||
|||||5|6|11|8|12|10||3|9|||||1||||13|7|14|4|2||
|||||5|6|12|8|13|10||3|9|||||1||||14|7|11|4|2||
||2|||5|6|12|8|13|10||3|9|||||1||||14|7|11||4||
||2|||5|6||8|9|10||3|12|||||1||||11|7||4|||
||2|||5|6||8|9|10|11|3|12|||||1|||||7||4|||
||2|3||5|6||8|9|10|11||12|||||1||||7|||4|13||
|||3||5|6||8|9|10|11||13|||12||1||||7|||4|2||
||2|||5|6||8|9|10|11||12|||||1||||3|7||4||13|
||2|||5|6|12|8||10||3|9||||11|1||||13|7||4||14|
|||||5|6||8|9|10|11|3|12||||2|1||13|||7||4||14|
|||||5|||8|12|10|11|3|9|||6|2|1||14||13|7||4|||
||2|||5|12||8|9|10|11||13|||||1||6||3|7||4|||
||2|||5|12||8|9|10|11||13|||||1||6||3|7||4|||
||2|||5|12||8|9||11||10|||||1||6||3|7||4||13|
|5|22|5|4|46|31|12|46|22|40|40|29|24|2|4|17|26|41||3|9|15|28|3|27|5||
||3|1|||3|11||9|||4|17|3|11|2|1||2|3||9||2|1|5|4|
||1|||1|2|4|16|8|17|2|4|8||1||1||||||3|||||

| 1 Holland | 2 Knowles | 21 Robinson | 24 Ferguson | 16 Westwood | 13 Sharp | 6 Fitzpatrick | 8 Miller | 9 Lormor | 14 Henderson | 17 Stephenson | 3 Shilton | 12 Midgley | 19 McAvoy | 10 Sperrevik | 5 Strodder | 7 Arnison | 23 Williams | 15 Tennebo | 18 Lee | 26 Baker | 11 Clark | 27 Tinkler | 20 Boyd | 4 Barron | 29 Aspin | 26 Easter |
|---|---|---|---|---|---|---|---|---|---|---|---|---|---|---|---|---|---|---|---|---|---|---|---|---|---|---|
||2|||5|12||8|9|13|11||10|||||1||6||3|7||4||14|
||2|||5|6||8|9|10|11|||||||1||12||3|7||4||13|
||2|||2|1||2|2|1|2||1|||||2||1||2|2||2|||
||||||1||||1||||||||||1|||||||2|
||||||||||1||||||||||||||||||

| 1 Holland | 2 Knowles | 21 Robinson | 24 Ferguson | 16 Westwood | 13 Sharp | 6 Fitzpatrick | 8 Miller | 9 Lormor | 14 Henderson | 17 Stephenson | 3 Shilton | 12 Midgley | 19 McAvoy | 10 Sperrevik | 5 Strodder | 7 Arnison | 23 Williams | 15 Tennebo | 18 Lee | 26 Baker | 11 Clark | 27 Tinkler | 20 Boyd | 4 Barron | 29 Aspin | 26 Easter |
|---|---|---|---|---|---|---|---|---|---|---|---|---|---|---|---|---|---|---|---|---|---|---|---|---|---|---|
|||||5|||8||10|11|3|9|||4|2|1||||6||12|7|||
|||||1|||1||1|1|1|1|||1|1|1||||1|||1|||
||||||||||||||||||||||||1||||
|||||||||||||1||||||||||||||

| 1 Holland | 2 Knowles | 21 Robinson | 24 Ferguson | 16 Westwood | 13 Sharp | 6 Fitzpatrick | 8 Miller | 9 Lormor | 14 Henderson | 17 Stephenson | 3 Shilton | 12 Midgley | 19 McAvoy | 10 Sperrevik | 5 Strodder | 7 Arnison | 23 Williams | 15 Tennebo | 18 Lee | 26 Baker | 11 Clark | 27 Tinkler | 20 Boyd | 4 Barron | 29 Aspin | 26 Easter |
|---|---|---|---|---|---|---|---|---|---|---|---|---|---|---|---|---|---|---|---|---|---|---|---|---|---|---|
|1|2|3|4|5|6|7|8|9|10|11|12|13|14||||||||||||||
|1|12|||5|6|7|8||10|11|3|||9|4|2||13|||||||||
|2|1|1|1|2|2|2|2|1|2|2|1|||1|1|1|||||||||||
||1||||||||||1|1|1|||||1|||||||||
|||||||1|2|||1||||||||||||||||

## League Table

| | P | W | D | L | F | A | Pts |
|---|---|---|---|---|---|---|---|
| Brighton & Hove Albion | 46 | 28 | 8 | 10 | 73 | 35 | 92 |
| Cardiff City | 46 | 23 | 13 | 10 | 95 | 58 | 82 |
| Chesterfield | 46 | 25 | 14 | 7 | 79 | 42 | 80 |
| Hartlepool United | 46 | 21 | 14 | 11 | 71 | 54 | 77 |
| Leyton Orient | 46 | 20 | 15 | 11 | 59 | 51 | 75 |
| Hull City | 46 | 19 | 17 | 10 | 47 | 39 | 74 |
| Blackpool | 46 | 22 | 6 | 18 | 74 | 58 | 72 |
| Rochdale | 46 | 18 | 17 | 11 | 59 | 48 | 71 |
| Cheltenham Town | 46 | 18 | 14 | 14 | 59 | 52 | 68 |
| Scunthorpe United | 46 | 18 | 11 | 17 | 62 | 52 | 65 |
| Southend United | 46 | 15 | 18 | 13 | 55 | 53 | 63 |
| Plymouth Argyle | 46 | 15 | 13 | 18 | 54 | 61 | 58 |
| Mansfield Town | 46 | 15 | 13 | 18 | 64 | 72 | 58 |
| Macclesfield Town | 46 | 14 | 14 | 18 | 51 | 62 | 56 |
| Shrewsbury Town | 46 | 15 | 10 | 21 | 49 | 65 | 55 |
| Kidderminster Harriers | 46 | 13 | 14 | 19 | 47 | 61 | 53 |
| York City | 46 | 13 | 13 | 20 | 42 | 63 | 52 |
| Lincoln City | 46 | 12 | 15 | 19 | 58 | 66 | 51 |
| Exeter City | 46 | 12 | 14 | 20 | 40 | 58 | 50 |
| Darlington | 46 | 12 | 13 | 21 | 44 | 56 | 49 |
| Torquay United | 46 | 12 | 13 | 21 | 52 | 77 | 49 |
| Carlisle United | 46 | 11 | 15 | 20 | 42 | 65 | 48 |
| Halifax Town | 46 | 12 | 11 | 23 | 54 | 68 | 47 |
| Barnet | 46 | 12 | 9 | 25 | 67 | 81 | 45 |

# 2001-02

## Division Three

Manager: Chris Turner

### Did you know that?

Richie Humphreys made his debut on 11 August against Mansfield Town. He set an all-time club record by appearing in every League game for the next five seasons.

Jermaine Easter made 12 League appearances as a substitute, scoring two goals. In total he played 30 games for 'Pools, all as a substitute, and after leaving the club in 2004 went on to play for Wales at full international level.

| Match No. | Date | Round | Venue | Opponents | Result | | Scorers | Attendance |
|---|---|---|---|---|---|---|---|---|
| 1 | Aug 11 | | (h) | Mansfield Town | D | 1 - 1 | Clark | 3,534 |
| 2 | 18 | | (a) | Shrewsbury Town | W | 3 - 1 | Clark (pen), Henderson, Tinkler | 2,783 |
| 4 | 25 | | (h) | Darlington | L | 1 - 2 | Tinkler | 4,842 |
| 5 | 27 | | (a) | Leyton Orient | L | 0 - 2 | | 3,719 |
| 6 | Sep 8 | | (a) | Scunthorpe United | L | 0 - 1 | | 3,206 |
| 7 | 15 | | (a) | Southend United | D | 0 - 0 | | 3,933 |
| 8 | 18 | | (h) | Cheltenham Town | L | 0 - 1 | | 2,599 |
| 9 | 22 | | (h) | Kidderminster Harriers | D | 1 - 1 | Watson | 3,130 |
| 10 | 25 | | (a) | Lincoln City | L | 0 - 2 | | 2,306 |
| 11 | 29 | | (h) | Carlisle United | W | 3 - 1 | Tinkler, Watson, Boyd | 3,854 |
| 12 | Oct 5 | | (a) | Rushden & Diamonds | L | 1 - 2 | Watson | 3,929 |
| 13 | 13 | | (h) | York City | W | 3 - 0 | Tinkler, Boyd 2 | 3,603 |
| 15 | 20 | | (a) | Torquay United | L | 0 - 1 | | 2,148 |
| 16 | 23 | | (a) | Macclesfield Town | W | 1 - 0 | Boyd | 1,356 |
| 17 | 27 | | (h) | Oxford United | L | 0 - 1 | | 3,595 |
| 18 | Nov 3 | | (a) | Plymouth Argyle | L | 0 - 1 | | 5,723 |
| 19 | 6 | | (h) | Hull City | W | 4 - 0 | Watson 3, Barron | 3,183 |
| 20 | 10 | | (h) | Exeter City | W | 2 - 0 | Watson, Lormor | 3,222 |
| 22 | 20 | | (h) | Halifax Town | W | 3 - 0 | Watson, Tinkler, Widdrington | 2,963 |
| 23 | 23 | | (a) | Swansea City | W | 1 - 0 | Smith | 4,161 |
| 24 | 30 | | (h) | Rochdale | D | 1 - 1 | Bass | 4,162 |
| 25 | Dec 8 | | (h) | Luton Town | L | 1 - 2 | Humphreys | 3,585 |
| 26 | 22 | | (a) | Luton Town | D | 2 - 2 | Clarke 2 | 6,739 |
| 27 | 29 | | (h) | Leyton Orient | W | 3 - 1 | Watson, Smith, Tinkler | 3,832 |
| 28 | Jan 12 | | (h) | Shrewsbury Town | D | 2 - 2 | Watson, Lee | 3,447 |
| 29 | 19 | | (a) | Mansfield Town | L | 0 - 3 | | 4,349 |
| 30 | 26 | | (h) | Rushden & Diamonds | W | 5 - 1 | Watson 2, Humphreys, Widdrington, Coppinger | 3,513 |
| 31 | 29 | | (h) | Scunthorpe United | W | 3 - 2 | Tinkler, Watson, Smith | 3,294 |
| 32 | Feb 5 | | (a) | Hull City | D | 1 - 1 | Boyd | 8,419 |
| 33 | 9 | | (h) | Torquay United | W | 4 - 1 | Boyd 2, Lee, Easter | 3,658 |
| 34 | 12 | | (a) | Bristol Rovers | W | 1 - 0 | Boyd | 6,482 |
| 35 | 16 | | (a) | York City | L | 0 - 1 | | 4,823 |
| 36 | 19 | | (a) | Darlington | D | 1 - 1 | Tinkler | 6,339 |
| 37 | 23 | | (h) | Southend United | W | 5 - 1 | Humphreys 2, Coppinger, Smith, Easter | 3,609 |
| 38 | 26 | | (a) | Cheltenham Town | L | 0 - 3 | | 3,257 |
| 39 | Mar 2 | | (a) | Kidderminster Harriers | L | 2 - 3 | Humphreys, Tinkler | 2,894 |
| 40 | 5 | | (h) | Lincoln City | D | 1 - 1 | Clarke | 3,126 |
| 41 | 9 | | (h) | Bristol Rovers | D | 1 - 1 | Watson | 3,699 |
| 42 | 16 | | (a) | Rochdale | D | 0 - 0 | | 3,219 |
| 43 | 19 | | (a) | Carlisle United | W | 2 - 0 | Lee, Watson | 3,147 |
| 44 | 22 | | (h) | Macclesfield Town | L | 1 - 2 | Westwood | 3,819 |
| 45 | 30 | | (a) | Oxford United | W | 2 - 1 | E.Williams 2 | 5,767 |
| 46 | Apr 1 | | (h) | Plymouth Argyle | W | 1 - 0 | Clarke | 3,725 |
| 47 | 6 | | (a) | Halifax Town | W | 2 - 0 | Watson, Lee | 1,838 |
| 48 | 13 | | (h) | Swansea City | W | 7 - 1 | Clarke 3, E.Williams, Boyd, Watson (pen), Henderson | 4,033 |
| 49 | 20 | | (a) | Exeter City | W | 2 - 0 | Watson, E.Williams | 3,595 |

Final Position : 7th in Division Three

Apps.
Sub.Apps.
Goals

**Play-offs**

| Match No. | Date | Round | Venue | Opponents | Result | | Scorers | Attendance |
|---|---|---|---|---|---|---|---|---|
| 50 | Apr 27 | SFl1 | (h) | Cheltenham Town | D | 1 - 1 | E.Williams | 7,135 |
| 51 | 30 | SFl2 | (a) | Cheltenham Town | D | 1 - 1* | Arnison | 7,165 |

* Lost 5 - 4 on penalties.

Apps.
Sub.Apps.
Goals

**FA Cup**

| Match No. | Date | Round | Venue | Opponents | Result | | Scorers | Attendance |
|---|---|---|---|---|---|---|---|---|
| 21 | Nov 17 | R1 | (a) | Swindon Town | L | 1 - 3 | Clarke | 4,766 |

Apps.
Sub.Apps.
Goals

**League Cup**

| Match No. | Date | Round | Venue | Opponents | Result | | Scorers | Attendance |
|---|---|---|---|---|---|---|---|---|
| 3 | Aug 20 | R1 | (h) | Nottingham Forest | L | 0 - 2 | | 3,938 |

Apps.
Sub.Apps.
Goals

| 21 Hollund | 15 Bass | 11 Clark | 4 Barron | 5 Lee | 6 Westwood | 7 Tinkler | 8 Humphreys | 10 Henderson | 14 Widdrington | 17 Stephenson | 20 Sharp | 9 Lormor | 16 Clarke | 12 Easter | 1 Williams, A. | 2 Arnison | 3 Robinson | 18 Simms | 23 Watson | 24 Ormerod | 19 Boyd | 25 Sweeney | 26 Smith | 27 Parkin | 24 Coppinger | 11 Williams, E. |
|---|---|---|---|---|---|---|---|---|---|---|---|---|---|---|---|---|---|---|---|---|---|---|---|---|---|---|
| 1 | 2 | 3 | 4 | 5 | 6 | 7 | 8 | 9 | 10 | 11 | 12 | 13 | | | | | | | | | | | | | | |
| 1 | 2 | 3 | 4 | 5 | 6 | 7 | 8 | 9 | 10 | 11 | 12 | 13 | 14 | | | | | | | | | | | | | |
| 1 | 2 | 3 | 4 | 5 | 6 | 7 | 9 | 10 | 8 | 11 | | 12 | 13 | 14 | | | | | | | | | | | | |
| | 2 | 3 | 4 | | 5 | 7 | 8 | | 10 | 11 | 6 | 9 | 12 | 13 | 1 | 14 | | | | | | | | | | |
| | 2 | | | 5 | | 7 | 9 | 10 | 8 | 11 | 6 | 12 | 4 | | 1 | | 3 | | | | | | | | | |
| | 2 | | | 5 | | 7 | 9 | 10 | 8 | 11 | 6 | 12 | 4 | | 1 | | 3 | 13 | | | | | | | | |
| | 2 | 12 | | 5 | | 7 | 9 | 10 | 8 | 11 | 6 | | 4 | 13 | 1 | | 3 | 14 | | | | | | | | |
| | 2 | 12 | | | | 7 | 13 | | | 11 | 6 | 9 | 4 | | 1 | | 3 | 5 | 10 | 8 | | | | | | |
| | 2 | 4 | | | | 8 | 12 | | | 11 | 6 | 9 | | | 1 | | 3 | 5 | 10 | 7 | | | | | | |
| | 2 | | 4 | 12 | | 7 | 13 | 9 | 8 | 11 | 6 | | | | 1 | | 3 | 5 | 10 | | 14 | | | | | |
| | 2 | | 4 | 5 | | 7 | 12 | 9 | 8 | 11 | 6 | | | 13 | 1 | | 3 | | 10 | | 14 | | | | | |
| | | | 4 | 5 | | 7 | 8 | | 11 | | 6 | | | | 1 | 2 | 3 | | 10 | | 9 | 12 | | | | |
| | | | 4 | 5 | | 7 | 8 | | 11 | | 6 | 12 | | | 1 | 2 | 3 | | 10 | | 9 | 13 | | | | |
| | | | 4 | 5 | | 7 | 8 | 9 | 11 | 12 | 6 | | | | 1 | 2 | 3 | 13 | 10 | | 14 | | | | | |
| | | | 4 | 5 | | 7 | 8 | 13 | 11 | 14 | 6 | 12 | | | 1 | 2 | 3 | | 10 | | 9 | | | | | |
| | 2 | | 4 | | 5 | 8 | 9 | | | 11 | 6 | 12 | 7 | | 1 | | 3 | 13 | 10 | | | | 14 | | | |
| | 2 | | 4 | | 5 | | 9 | 12 | 8 | | | | 7 | | 1 | | 3 | 6 | 10 | | 13 | | 11 | | | |
| | 2 | | 4 | | 5 | 12 | 9 | | 8 | | | 13 | 7 | | 1 | | 3 | 6 | 10 | | 14 | | 11 | | | |
| | 2 | | 4 | 5 | 6 | 8 | 9 | | 11 | | | 12 | 7 | | 1 | | 13 | | 10 | | 14 | | 3 | | | |
| | 2 | | 4 | 5 | 6 | 8 | 9 | | 11 | | | 12 | 7 | | 1 | | | | 10 | | | | 3 | | | |
| | 2 | | 4 | 5 | 6 | 8 | 9 | | 11 | | | | 7 | | 1 | | | | 10 | | 12 | | 3 | | | |
| | 2 | | 4 | | 5 | 8 | 10 | | 11 | | | 9 | 7 | | 1 | 12 | 14 | 6 | | | 13 | | 3 | | | |
| | | | 2 | 4 | 5 | 8 | 9 | | 6 | | | | 7 | | 1 | | 3 | | 10 | | 12 | | 11 | | | |
| | 12 | | 2 | 4 | 5 | 8 | 9 | | 6 | | | | 7 | | 1 | | 3 | | 10 | | 13 | | 11 | | | |
| | | | 2 | 4 | 5 | 8 | 9 | | 6 | 12 | | | 7 | | 1 | | 3 | | 10 | | 13 | | 11 | 14 | | |
| | 2 | | 4 | 5 | 6 | 8 | 9 | | | | | | 7 | | 1 | 12 | 3 | | 10 | | 13 | | 11 | | | |
| | | | 2 | 4 | 5 | 8 | 9 | | 6 | 12 | | | | | 1 | 13 | 3 | | 10 | | 14 | | 11 | | 7 | |
| | | | 2 | 4 | 5 | 8 | 9 | | 6 | | | 14 | | | 1 | 12 | 3 | | 10 | | 13 | | 11 | | 7 | |
| | | | 2 | 4 | 5 | 6 | 9 | 12 | | | | | | | 1 | | 3 | | 10 | | 8 | | 11 | | 7 | |
| | | | | 4 | 5 | 6 | 9 | 10 | | 12 | | 13 | | 14 | 1 | 2 | 3 | | | | 8 | | 11 | | 7 | |
| | | | 2 | 4 | 5 | 6 | 9 | 10 | | 7 | | | 12 | 13 | 1 | 3 | | | | | 8 | | 11 | | | |
| | | | 2 | 4 | 5 | 6 | 9 | 10 | | | | | | 12 | 1 | | 3 | | | | 8 | | 11 | | 7 | |
| | | | 2 | 4 | 5 | 6 | 9 | 12 | | 8 | | | 13 | 14 | 1 | | 3 | | | | 10 | | 11 | | 7 | |
| | | | 2 | 4 | 5 | 6 | 9 | | | 8 | | | 12 | 14 | 1 | 13 | 3 | | | | 10 | | 11 | | 7 | |
| | | | 2 | 4 | 5 | 6 | 9 | | | 8 | | | 12 | 13 | 1 | | 3 | | | | 10 | | 11 | | 7 | |
| | | | 2 | 4 | 5 | 6 | 9 | 10 | | 8 | | | 12 | 13 | 1 | | 3 | | 14 | | | | 11 | | 7 | |
| | | | 2 | 4 | 5 | 6 | 9 | | | 8 | | | 12 | 13 | 1 | | 3 | | 10 | | | | 11 | | 7 | |
| | | | 2 | 4 | 5 | 6 | 9 | | | 8 | | | 7 | | 1 | 12 | 3 | | 10 | | | | 11 | | | 13 |
| | | | 2 | 4 | 5 | 6 | 9 | | | 8 | | | 7 | | 1 | 3 | | | 10 | | | | 11 | | | |
| | | | 4 | 5 | 6 | 8 | 9 | 12 | | 11 | | | 7 | | 1 | 2 | | | 10 | | | | 3 | | | 13 |
| | | | 4 | 5 | 6 | 8 | 9 | | | 11 | | | 7 | | 1 | 2 | 12 | | 10 | | 13 | | 3 | | | 14 |
| | | | 4 | 5 | 6 | | 8 | 12 | | 11 | | | 7 | | 1 | 2 | 13 | | 10 | | | | 3 | | | 9 |
| | | | 2 | 4 | 5 | | 8 | 12 | | | | | 6 | | 1 | | 3 | | 10 | | 13 | | 11 | | 7 | 9 |
| | | | 2 | 4 | 5 | | 8 | 12 | | | | | 6 | | 1 | | 3 | | 10 | | 13 | | 11 | | 7 | 9 |
| | | | 2 | 4 | 5 | | 8 | 12 | | | | | 6 | | 1 | 13 | 3 | | 10 | | 14 | | 11 | | 7 | 9 |
| | | | | 4 | 5 | | 8 | 12 | | 13 | | | 6 | | 1 | 2 | 3 | | 10 | | 14 | | 11 | | 7 | 9 |
| 3 | 19 | 5 | 39 | 38 | 35 | 39 | 42 | 13 | 24 | 23 | 13 | 4 | 24 | | 43 | 11 | 33 | 6 | 31 | 2 | 10 | | 30 | | 14 | 5 |
| | 1 | 2 | | 1 | | 1 | 4 | 10 | | 6 | 2 | 13 | 9 | 12 | | 8 | 4 | 4 | 1 | | 19 | 2 | 1 | 1 | | 3 |
| | 1 | 2 | 1 | 4 | 1 | 9 | 5 | 2 | 2 | | | 1 | 7 | 2 | | | | | 18 | | 9 | | 4 | | 2 | 4 |

| 21 Hollund | 15 Bass | 11 Clark | 4 Barron | 5 Lee | 6 Westwood | 7 Tinkler | 8 Humphreys | 10 Henderson | 14 Widdrington | 17 Stephenson | 20 Sharp | 9 Lormor | 16 Clarke | 12 Easter | 1 Williams, A. | 2 Arnison | 3 Robinson | 18 Simms | 23 Watson | 24 Ormerod | 19 Boyd | 25 Sweeney | 26 Smith | 27 Parkin | 24 Coppinger | 11 Williams, E. |
|---|---|---|---|---|---|---|---|---|---|---|---|---|---|---|---|---|---|---|---|---|---|---|---|---|---|---|
| | | | 2 | 4 | 5 | | 8 | 13 | | 12 | | | 6 | | 1 | | 3 | | 10 | | 7 | | 11 | | | 9 |
| | | | 2 | 4 | 5 | | 7 | 12 | | 8 | | | 6 | | 1 | 3 | | | 10 | | | | 11 | | | 9 |
| | | | 2 | 2 | 2 | | 2 | | | 1 | | | 2 | | 2 | 1 | 1 | | 2 | | 1 | | 2 | | | 2 |
| | | | | | | | | 2 | | 1 | | | | | | | | | | | | | | | | |
| | | | | | | | | | | | | | | | | 1 | | | | | | | | | | 1 |

| 21 Hollund | 15 Bass | 11 Clark | 4 Barron | 5 Lee | 6 Westwood | 7 Tinkler | 8 Humphreys | 10 Henderson | 14 Widdrington | 17 Stephenson | 20 Sharp | 9 Lormor | 16 Clarke | 12 Easter | 1 Williams, A. | 2 Arnison | 3 Robinson | 18 Simms | 23 Watson | 24 Ormerod | 19 Boyd | 25 Sweeney | 26 Smith | 27 Parkin | 24 Coppinger | 11 Williams, E. |
|---|---|---|---|---|---|---|---|---|---|---|---|---|---|---|---|---|---|---|---|---|---|---|---|---|---|---|
| | 2 | | 4 | 12 | 5 | 8 | 9 | | 7 | | | | 6 | | 1 | | | 3 | 10 | | | | 11 | | | |
| | 1 | | 1 | | 1 | 1 | 1 | | 1 | | | | 1 | | 1 | | | 1 | 1 | | | | 1 | | | |
| | | | | 1 | | | | | | | | | | | | | | | | | | | | | | |
| | | | | | | | | | | | | | 1 | | | | | | | | | | | | | |

| 21 Hollund | 15 Bass | 11 Clark | 4 Barron | 5 Lee | 6 Westwood | 7 Tinkler | 8 Humphreys | 10 Henderson | 14 Widdrington | 17 Stephenson | 20 Sharp | 9 Lormor | 16 Clarke | 12 Easter | 1 Williams, A. | 2 Arnison | 3 Robinson | 18 Simms | 23 Watson | 24 Ormerod | 19 Boyd | 25 Sweeney | 26 Smith | 27 Parkin | 24 Coppinger | 11 Williams, E. |
|---|---|---|---|---|---|---|---|---|---|---|---|---|---|---|---|---|---|---|---|---|---|---|---|---|---|---|
| 1 | 2 | 3 | 4 | 5 | 6 | 7 | 9 | 10 | 8 | 11 | | 13 | 12 | | | | | | | | | | | | | |
| 1 | 1 | 1 | 1 | 1 | 1 | 1 | 1 | 1 | 1 | 1 | | | | | | | | | | | | | | | | |
| | | | | | | | | | | | | 1 | 1 | | | | | | | | | | | | | |
| | | | | | | | | | | | | | | | | | | | | | | | | | | |

## League Table

| | P | W | D | L | F | A | Pts |
|---|---|---|---|---|---|---|---|
| Plymouth Argyle | 46 | 31 | 9 | 6 | 71 | 28 | 102 |
| Luton Town | 46 | 30 | 7 | 9 | 96 | 48 | 97 |
| Mansfield Town | 46 | 24 | 7 | 15 | 72 | 60 | 79 |
| Cheltenham Town | 46 | 21 | 15 | 10 | 66 | 49 | 78 |
| Rochdale | 46 | 21 | 15 | 10 | 65 | 52 | 78 |
| Rushden & Diamonds | 46 | 20 | 13 | 13 | 69 | 53 | 73 |
| Hartlepool United | 46 | 20 | 11 | 15 | 74 | 48 | 71 |
| Scunthorpe United | 46 | 19 | 14 | 13 | 74 | 56 | 71 |
| Shrewsbury Town | 46 | 20 | 10 | 16 | 64 | 53 | 70 |
| Kidderminster Harriers | 46 | 19 | 9 | 18 | 56 | 47 | 66 |
| Hull City | 46 | 16 | 13 | 17 | 57 | 51 | 61 |
| Southend United | 46 | 15 | 13 | 18 | 51 | 54 | 58 |
| Macclesfield Town | 46 | 15 | 13 | 18 | 41 | 52 | 58 |
| York City | 46 | 16 | 9 | 21 | 54 | 67 | 57 |
| Darlington | 46 | 15 | 11 | 20 | 60 | 71 | 56 |
| Exeter City | 46 | 14 | 13 | 19 | 48 | 73 | 55 |
| Carlisle United | 46 | 12 | 16 | 18 | 49 | 56 | 52 |
| Leyton Orient | 46 | 13 | 13 | 20 | 55 | 71 | 52 |
| Torquay United | 46 | 12 | 15 | 19 | 46 | 63 | 51 |
| Swansea City | 46 | 13 | 12 | 21 | 53 | 77 | 51 |
| Oxford United | 46 | 11 | 14 | 21 | 53 | 62 | 47 |
| Lincoln City | 46 | 10 | 16 | 20 | 44 | 62 | 46 |
| Bristol Rovers | 46 | 11 | 12 | 23 | 40 | 60 | 45 |
| Halifax Town | 46 | 8 | 12 | 26 | 39 | 84 | 36 |

# 2002-03

## Division Three

Managers: Chris Turner, Colin West and Mike Newell

### Did you know that?

'Pools' away fixture against Hull City on Boxing Day drew a sell-out 22,319 crowd to mark the opening of the new Kingston Communications Stadium. Hull won the game 2–0.

After the 4–0 home win over Swansea, United were 14 points clear at the top of the table; however, a run of only three wins in their final 13 games handed the title to Rushden & Diamonds.

| Match No. | Date | Round | Venue | Opponents | Result | | Scorers | Attendance |
|---|---|---|---|---|---|---|---|---|
| 1 | Aug 10 | | (a) | Carlisle United | W | 3 - 1 | Tinkler 2, Humphreys | 10,862 |
| 2 | 13 | | (h) | Boston United | W | 2 - 0 | Watson 2 (1 pen) | 4,861 |
| 3 | 17 | | (h) | Macclesfield Town | L | 0 - 2 | | 4,684 |
| 4 | 24 | | (a) | Torquay United | D | 1 - 1 | Humphreys | 2,403 |
| 5 | 26 | | (h) | Hull City | W | 2 - 0 | E.Williams, Watson | 4,236 |
| 6 | 31 | | (a) | Oxford United | W | 1 - 0 | Watson | 4,768 |
| 7 | Sep 7 | | (a) | Swansea City | D | 2 - 2 | Tinkler, Watson | 3,370 |
| 9 | 14 | | (h) | Darlington | W | 4 - 1 | E.Williams 2, Humphreys, Tinkler | 6,360 |
| 10 | 17 | | (h) | Lincoln City | W | 2 - 1 | Boyd, E.Williams | 4,248 |
| 11 | 21 | | (a) | Bury | D | 1 - 1 | Boyd | 3,547 |
| 12 | 28 | | (h) | Rushden & Diamonds | L | 1 - 2 | Boyd | 5,502 |
| 13 | Oct 5 | | (a) | Shrewsbury Town | W | 1 - 0 | E.Williams | 3,142 |
| 14 | 13 | | (a) | Bournemouth | L | 1 - 2 | E.Williams | 5,998 |
| 15 | 19 | | (h) | Wrexham | W | 4 - 3 | Tinkler 3, Richardson | 4,506 |
| 17 | 25 | | (a) | Southend United | W | 1 - 0 | E.Williams | 5,168 |
| 18 | 29 | | (h) | Bristol Rovers | W | 2 - 0 | Arnison, E.Williams | 3,889 |
| 19 | Nov 1 | | (h) | York City | D | 0 - 0 | | 5,789 |
| 20 | 9 | | (a) | Exeter City | W | 2 - 1 | Tinkler, Richardson | 2,778 |
| 22 | 23 | | (a) | Leyton Orient | W | 2 - 1 | E.Williams 2 | 4,009 |
| 24 | 30 | | (h) | Kidderminster Harriers | W | 2 - 1 | Humphreys, Tinkler | 4,296 |
| 25 | Dec 14 | | (a) | Rochdale | L | 0 - 4 | | 3,059 |
| 26 | 20 | | (h) | Scunthorpe United | D | 2 - 2 | McCombe (o.g.), Henderson | 4,089 |
| 27 | 26 | | (a) | Hull City | L | 0 - 2 | | 22,319 |
| 28 | 28 | | (h) | Cambridge United | W | 3 - 0 | E.Williams, Tinkler, Clarke (pen) | 4,805 |
| 29 | Jan 1 | | (h) | Carlisle United | W | 2 - 1 | Lee, E.Williams | 5,071 |
| 30 | 4 | | (a) | Boston United | W | 1 - 0 | Clarke | 3,081 |
| 31 | 18 | | (h) | Oxford United | W | 3 - 1 | Humphreys, Richardson 2 | 5,049 |
| 32 | 21 | | (a) | Macclesfield Town | W | 1 - 0 | E.Williams | 1,576 |
| 33 | 25 | | (a) | Cambridge United | D | 0 - 0 | | 4,543 |
| 34 | Feb 1 | | (h) | Torquay United | W | 3 - 2 | Clarke 2, Richardson | 4,975 |
| 35 | 8 | | (h) | Exeter City | W | 2 - 1 | Humphreys, Boyd | 5,058 |
| 36 | 15 | | (a) | York City | D | 0 - 0 | | 5,953 |
| 37 | 22 | | (h) | Swansea City | W | 4 - 0 | Humphreys 3, Widdrington | 4,629 |
| 38 | Mar 1 | | (a) | Darlington | D | 2 - 2 | Boyd (pen), Clarke | 5,832 |
| 39 | 4 | | (a) | Lincoln City | L | 0 - 3 | | 3,409 |
| 40 | 7 | | (h) | Bury | D | 0 - 0 | | 5,734 |
| 41 | 15 | | (h) | Southend United | W | 2 - 1 | Humphreys 2 | 4,868 |
| 42 | 18 | | (a) | Wrexham | L | 0 - 2 | | 4,658 |
| 43 | 22 | | (a) | Bristol Rovers | L | 0 - 1 | | 6,557 |
| 44 | 29 | | (h) | Bournemouth | D | 0 - 0 | | 5,625 |
| 45 | Apr 5 | | (a) | Kidderminster Harriers | D | 2 - 2 | Clarke, E.Williams | 2,900 |
| 46 | 12 | | (h) | Leyton Orient | W | 4 - 1 | Tinkler 2 (1 pen), Lee, Clarke | 4,795 |
| 47 | 19 | | (a) | Scunthorpe United | L | 0 - 4 | | 5,280 |
| 48 | 21 | | (h) | Rochdale | D | 2 - 2 | Widdrington 2 | 5,408 |
| 49 | 26 | | (h) | Shrewsbury Town | W | 3 - 0 | E.Williams, Tinkler, Henderson | 5,384 |
| 50 | May 3 | | (a) | Rushden & Diamonds | D | 1 - 1 | Westwood | 6,291 |

Final Position: 2nd in Division Three - Promoted

Apps.
Sub.Apps.
1 own goal — Goals

**FA Cup**

| | | | | | | | | |
|---|---|---|---|---|---|---|---|---|
| 21 | Nov 16 | R1 | (a) | Southend United | D | 1 - 1 | Barron | 4,984 |
| 23 | 26 | R1r | (h) | Southend United | L | 1 - 2 | Richardson | 4,080 |

Apps.
Sub.Apps.
Goals

**League Cup**

| | | | | | | | | |
|---|---|---|---|---|---|---|---|---|
| 8 | Sep 10 | R1 | (h) | Tranmere Rovers | L | 1 - 2 | E.Williams | 2,778 |

Apps.
Sub.Apps.
Goals

| 1 Williams, A. | 4 Barron | 3 Robinson | 5 Lee | 6 Westwood | 23 Sweeney | 11 Clarke | 7 Tinkler | 9 Williams, E. | 10 Watson | 8 Humphreys | 2 Arnison | 14 Henderson | 19 Easter | 12 Smith | 15 Widdrington | 16 Boyd | 22 Simms | 26 Richardson | 28 Istead | 29 Barry-Murphy | 18 Bass |
|---|---|---|---|---|---|---|---|---|---|---|---|---|---|---|---|---|---|---|---|---|---|
| 1 | 2 | 3 | 4 | 5 | *6* | 7 | 8 | **9** | ***10*** | 11 | *12* | **13** | ***14*** | | | | | | | | |
| 1 | 6 | 3 | 4 | 5 | *12* | 7 | 8 | **9** | ***10*** | 11 | *2* | **13** | ***14*** | | | | | | | | |
| 1 | 6 | *3* | 4 | 5 | | 7 | 8 | **9** | 10 | 11 | ***2*** | *12* | **13** | ***14*** | | | | | | | |
| 1 | 6 | *3* | 4 | 5 | | 7 | 8 | 9 | 10 | 11 | 2 | | | *12* | | | | | | | |
| 1 | *2* | 3 | 4 | 5 | | 7 | 8 | ***9*** | 10 | 11 | *12* | | | **6** | **13** | ***14*** | | | | | |
| 1 | 2 | 3 | 4 | 5 | | **7** | 8 | 9 | *10* | 11 | **13** | *12* | | ***6*** | ***14*** | | | | | | |
| 1 | 2 | 3 | 4 | 5 | | 6 | 8 | *9* | **10** | 11 | 7 | *12* | | | | **13** | | | | | |
| 1 | 2 | 3 | 4 | 5 | | **7** | 8 | *9* | ***10*** | 11 | **13** | *12* | | | 6 | ***14*** | | | | | |
| 1 | 2 | 3 | 4 | 5 | | 7 | 8 | 9 | | 11 | | | | | 6 | 10 | *12* | | | | |
| 1 | 6 | | 4 | 5 | *12* | 7 | 8 | 9 | | 11 | *2* | | | | 3 | 10 | | | | | |
| 1 | 2 | *3* | 4 | 5 | | 7 | 8 | 9 | | 11 | | **13** | | *12* | 6 | **10** | | | | | |
| 1 | 2 | *3* | 4 | 5 | | 7 | 8 | 9 | | 11 | | | | *12* | 6 | **10** | | **13** | | | |
| 1 | 2 | 3 | 4 | 5 | | 7 | 8 | *9* | | 11 | | *12* | | **13** | **6** | ***10*** | | ***14*** | | | |
| 1 | 2 | 3 | 4 | 5 | | 7 | 6 | *9* | | 8 | | *12* | | **11** | **13** | ***14*** | | ***10*** | | | |
| 1 | 2 | 3 | 4 | 5 | | **7** | 6 | ***9*** | | 8 | **13** | | ***14*** | *11* | *12* | | | 10 | | | |
| 1 | | 3 | 4 | 5 | | **7** | 6 | *9* | | 8 | 2 | | *12* | 11 | | | | 10 | **13** | | |
| 1 | | 3 | 4 | 5 | | *7* | 6 | 9 | | 8 | 2 | | | 11 | | | | 10 | *12* | | |
| 1 | 6 | | 4 | 5 | | 2 | 8 | 9 | | 7 | | | | **11** | | *12* | | *10* | **13** | 3 | |
| 1 | 2 | | 4 | 5 | | 7 | 6 | *9* | | 8 | | | | 11 | | *12* | | 10 | | 3 | |
| 1 | 2 | | 4 | 5 | | **7** | 6 | 9 | | 8 | | | | *11* | *12* | | | 10 | | 3 | **13** |
| 1 | | | 4 | 5 | | | 8 | 9 | | 11 | 2 | | | | 7 | *12* | | *10* | **13** | 3 | **6** |
| 1 | 2 | | 4 | 5 | | **7** | 6 | 9 | | 8 | | *12* | | 11 | | | | *10* | **13** | 3 | |
| 1 | 2 | | 4 | 5 | | **7** | 6 | 9 | | 8 | | ***10*** | | *11* | *12* | | | ***14*** | **13** | 3 | |
| 1 | 2 | | 4 | 5 | | 7 | 6 | *9* | | 11 | | *12* | | | 8 | **13** | | **10** | | 3 | |
| 1 | **2** | 3 | 4 | 5 | | 7 | 6 | 9 | | 11 | | | *12* | | 8 | | | *10* | | | **13** |
| 1 | 2 | 3 | 4 | 5 | | 7 | 6 | *9* | | 11 | | *12* | | | 8 | | | 10 | | | |
| 1 | 4 | 3 | | 5 | | 7 | 6 | 9 | | 11 | | | | | 8 | | | 10 | | | 2 |
| 1 | 2 | 3 | 4 | 5 | | 7 | 6 | 9 | | 11 | | | | | 8 | | | 10 | | | |
| 1 | 2 | 3 | 4 | 5 | | 7 | 6 | *9* | | 11 | | | | | 8 | *12* | | 10 | | | |
| 1 | 2 | 3 | 4 | 5 | 6 | 7 | | **9** | | 11 | | *12* | | | 8 | **13** | | *10* | | | |
| 1 | 2 | 3 | 4 | 5 | | 7 | 6 | | | 11 | | *12* | | | 8 | 9 | | *10* | | | |
| 1 | 2 | 3 | 4 | 5 | | 7 | 6 | 9 | | 11 | | *12* | | | 8 | *10* | | | | | |
| 1 | 2 | 3 | 4 | 5 | | 7 | 6 | ***9*** | | 11 | *12* | **13** | | | *8* | **10** | | ***14*** | | | |
| 1 | 2 | 3 | 4 | 5 | | 7 | **6** | 9 | | 11 | **13** | *12* | | | 8 | *10* | | | | | |
| 1 | 2 | 3 | 4 | 5 | | 7 | 6 | 9 | | 11 | | *12* | | | 8 | *10* | | | | | |
| 1 | 2 | 3 | 4 | 5 | | 7 | 6 | *9* | *12* | 11 | | **13** | | | 8 | **10** | | | | | |
| 1 | 2 | 3 | 4 | 5 | | 7 | 6 | *9* | | **11** | *12* | ***14*** | | **13** | 8 | | | ***10*** | | | |
| 1 | 2 | 3 | 4 | 5 | | 7 | 6 | *9* | *12* | 11 | | **13** | | ***14*** | ***8*** | | | **10** | | | |
| 1 | 2 | 3 | 4 | 5 | | 7 | 6 | 9 | | 11 | | *12* | | **13** | **8** | | | *10* | | | |
| 1 | **2** | 3 | 4 | 5 | | 7 | 6 | *9* | 10 | 8 | **13** | *12* | | 11 | | | | | | | |
| 1 | | 3 | 4 | 5 | | 7 | 6 | *12* | *9* | 8 | 2 | 10 | | 11 | | | | | | | |
| 1 | 2 | 3 | 4 | 5 | | 7 | 6 | **9** | *12* | 11 | | *10* | **13** | | 8 | | | | | | |
| 1 | 2 | *3* | 4 | 5 | | 7 | 6 | 9 | *12* | 11 | | 10 | | | 8 | | | | | | |
| 1 | 2 | 3 | 4 | 5 | | 7 | 6 | *9* | *12* | 11 | | 10 | | **13** | **8** | | | | | | |
| 1 | 2 | 3 | 4 | 5 | | 7 | *6* | **9** | ***10*** | 8 | *12* | **13** | | 11 | | ***14*** | | | | | |
| 1 | 2 | 3 | 4 | 5 | | **7** | 6 | 9 | *10* | 8 | | *12* | **13** | 11 | | | | | | | |
| 46 | 42 | 38 | 45 | 46 | 2 | 45 | 45 | 44 | 12 | 46 | 9 | 5 | | 15 | 26 | 11 | | 20 | | 7 | 2 |
| | | | | | 2 | | | 1 | 5 | | 10 | 25 | 8 | 9 | 6 | 11 | 1 | 4 | 6 | | 2 |
| | | | 2 | 1 | | 7 | 13 | 15 | 5 | 11 | 1 | 2 | | | 3 | 5 | | 5 | | | |

| 1 Williams, A. | 4 Barron | 3 Robinson | 5 Lee | 6 Westwood | 23 Sweeney | 11 Clarke | 7 Tinkler | 9 Williams, E. | 10 Watson | 8 Humphreys | 2 Arnison | 14 Henderson | 19 Easter | 12 Smith | 15 Widdrington | 16 Boyd | 22 Simms | 26 Richardson | 28 Istead | 29 Barry-Murphy | 18 Bass |
|---|---|---|---|---|---|---|---|---|---|---|---|---|---|---|---|---|---|---|---|---|---|
| 1 | 2 | | 4 | 5 | | 7 | 6 | 9 | | 8 | *12* | | | **11** | **13** | | | 10 | | 3 | |
| 1 | 2 | | 4 | 5 | | | 6 | **9** | | 8 | *7* | | | 11 | | **13** | | 10 | *12* | 3 | |
| 2 | 2 | | 2 | 2 | | 1 | 2 | 2 | | 2 | 1 | | | 2 | | | | 2 | | 2 | |
| | | | | | | | | | | | 1 | | | | 1 | 1 | | | 1 | | |
| | 1 | | | | | | | | | | | | | | | | | 1 | | | |

| 1 Williams, A. | 4 Barron | 3 Robinson | 5 Lee | 6 Westwood | 23 Sweeney | 11 Clarke | 7 Tinkler | 9 Williams, E. | 10 Watson | 8 Humphreys | 2 Arnison | 14 Henderson | 19 Easter | 12 Smith | 15 Widdrington | 16 Boyd | 22 Simms | 26 Richardson | 28 Istead | 29 Barry-Murphy | 18 Bass |
|---|---|---|---|---|---|---|---|---|---|---|---|---|---|---|---|---|---|---|---|---|---|
| 1 | 2 | 3 | 4 | 5 | | 6 | 8 | *9* | | 11 | 7 | *12* | | | | 10 | | | | | |
| 1 | 1 | 1 | 1 | 1 | | 1 | 1 | 1 | | 1 | 1 | | | | | 1 | | | | | |
| | | | | | | | | | | | | 1 | | | | | | | | | |
| | | | | | | | | 1 | | | | | | | | | | | | | |

## League Table

| | P | W | D | L | F | A | Pts |
|---|---|---|---|---|---|---|---|
| Rushden & Diamonds | 46 | 24 | 15 | 7 | 73 | 47 | 87 |
| Hartlepool United | 46 | 24 | 13 | 9 | 71 | 51 | 85 |
| Wrexham | 46 | 23 | 15 | 8 | 84 | 50 | 84 |
| Bournemouth | 46 | 20 | 14 | 12 | 60 | 48 | 74 |
| Scunthorpe United | 46 | 19 | 15 | 12 | 68 | 49 | 72 |
| Lincoln City | 46 | 18 | 16 | 12 | 46 | 37 | 70 |
| Bury | 46 | 18 | 16 | 12 | 57 | 56 | 70 |
| Oxford United | 46 | 19 | 12 | 15 | 57 | 47 | 69 |
| Torquay United | 46 | 16 | 18 | 12 | 71 | 71 | 66 |
| York City | 46 | 17 | 15 | 14 | 52 | 53 | 66 |
| Kidderminster Harriers | 46 | 16 | 15 | 15 | 62 | 63 | 63 |
| Cambridge United | 46 | 16 | 13 | 17 | 67 | 70 | 61 |
| Hull City | 46 | 14 | 17 | 15 | 58 | 53 | 59 |
| Darlington | 46 | 12 | 18 | 16 | 58 | 59 | 54 |
| Boston United | 46 | 15 | 13 | 18 | 55 | 56 | 54 |
| Macclesfield Town | 46 | 14 | 12 | 20 | 57 | 63 | 54 |
| Southend United | 46 | 17 | 3 | 26 | 47 | 59 | 54 |
| Leyton Orient | 46 | 14 | 11 | 21 | 51 | 61 | 53 |
| Rochdale | 46 | 12 | 16 | 18 | 63 | 70 | 52 |
| Bristol Rovers | 46 | 12 | 15 | 19 | 50 | 57 | 51 |
| Swansea City | 46 | 12 | 13 | 21 | 48 | 65 | 49 |
| Carlisle United | 46 | 13 | 10 | 23 | 52 | 78 | 49 |
| Exeter City | 46 | 11 | 15 | 20 | 50 | 64 | 48 |
| Shrewsbury Town | 46 | 9 | 14 | 23 | 62 | 92 | 41 |

# 2003-04

## Division Two

Manager: Neale Cooper

### Did you know that?

Chris Turner's prophecy of 5,000-plus home attendances came true with average gates of 5,431, an increase for the 10th successive season and the highest since the 1967–68 promotion campaign.

In the third-round FA Cup tie at Sunderland, a narrow 1–0 defeat, 'Pools played in front of their biggest-ever gate at the time – 40,813.

| Match No. | Date | Round | Venue | Opponents | Result | | Scorers | Attendance |
|---|---|---|---|---|---|---|---|---|
| 1 | Aug 9 | | (a) | Peterborough United | W | 4 - 3 | Strachan, P.Robinson, Robson, Nelson | 5,965 |
| 3 | 16 | | (h) | Tranmere Rovers | D | 0 - 0 | | 5,357 |
| 4 | 23 | | (a) | Bristol City | D | 1 - 1 | Gabbiadini | 10,730 |
| 5 | 25 | | (h) | Port Vale | W | 2 - 0 | P.Robinson, Gabbiadini (pen) | 5,314 |
| 6 | 30 | | (a) | Luton Town | L | 2 - 3 | Clarke, P.Robinson (pen) | 5,515 |
| 7 | Sep 6 | | (h) | Oldham Athletic | D | 0 - 0 | | 5,728 |
| 8 | 12 | | (h) | Grimsby Town | W | 8 - 1 | Groves (o.g.), P.Robinson 3 (1 pen), Strachan, Humphreys, Gabbiadini, E.Williams | 5,528 |
| 9 | 16 | | (a) | Stockport County | W | 2 - 1 | E.Williams, Gabbiadini | 4,028 |
| 10 | 20 | | (a) | Brentford | L | 1 - 2 | Tinkler | 4,501 |
| 12 | 27 | | (h) | Brighton & Hove Albion | D | 0 - 0 | | 5,443 |
| 13 | 30 | | (h) | Wrexham | W | 2 - 0 | Clarke 2 | 4,677 |
| 14 | Oct 4 | | (a) | Bournemouth | D | 2 - 2 | Tinkler, Strachan | 6,342 |
| 15 | 10 | | (h) | Sheffield Wednesday | D | 1 - 1 | Gabbiadini | 7,448 |
| 17 | 18 | | (a) | Blackpool | L | 0 - 4 | | 6,871 |
| 18 | 21 | | (a) | Chesterfield | W | 2 - 1 | Evatt (o.g.), P.Robinson | 3,411 |
| 19 | 25 | | (h) | Wycombe Wanderers | D | 1 - 1 | Barron | 5,153 |
| 20 | Nov 1 | | (a) | Notts County | L | 0 - 1 | | 5,011 |
| 22 | 15 | | (h) | Rushden & Diamonds | W | 2 - 1 | Strachan (pen), Wilkinson | 4,923 |
| 23 | 22 | | (a) | Plymouth Argyle | L | 0 - 2 | | 9,000 |
| 24 | 29 | | (h) | Swindon Town | W | 2 - 0 | Strachan (pen), Wilkinson | 4,493 |
| 26 | Dec 13 | | (a) | Queen's Park Rangers | L | 1 - 4 | E.Williams | 15,003 |
| 27 | 20 | | (h) | Colchester United | D | 0 - 0 | | 4,135 |
| 28 | 26 | | (h) | Barnsley | L | 1 - 2 | E.Williams | 6,520 |
| 29 | 28 | | (a) | Oldham Athletic | W | 2 - 0 | E.Williams, Porter | 6,243 |
| 31 | Jan 10 | | (h) | Peterborough United | W | 1 - 0 | E.Williams | 4,855 |
| 32 | 17 | | (a) | Tranmere Rovers | D | 0 - 0 | | 7,418 |
| 33 | 24 | | (h) | Bristol City | L | 1 - 2 | Tinkler | 5,375 |
| 34 | 27 | | (a) | Port Vale | W | 5 - 2 | Shuker, Humphreys, Nelson, E.Williams, Clarke | 4,845 |
| 35 | Feb 7 | | (a) | Barnsley | D | 2 - 2 | E.Williams, Tinkler | 9,220 |
| 36 | 15 | | (a) | Sheffield Wednesday | L | 0 - 1 | | 20,732 |
| 37 | 20 | | (h) | Blackpool | D | 1 - 1 | Robertson | 5,497 |
| 38 | 28 | | (a) | Wycombe Wanderers | W | 4 - 3 | E.Williams 2, Robertson, Tinkler (pen) | 4,731 |
| 39 | Mar 2 | | (h) | Chesterfield | W | 2 - 0 | E.Williams, Tinkler | 4,976 |
| 40 | 6 | | (a) | Colchester United | W | 2 - 1 | Nelson, Istead | 3,348 |
| 41 | 13 | | (h) | Queen's Park Rangers | L | 1 - 4 | Porter | 6,519 |
| 42 | 16 | | (h) | Stockport County | D | 2 - 2 | E.Williams, Porter | 4,674 |
| 43 | 20 | | (a) | Grimsby Town | W | 2 - 0 | Boyd 2 | 4,303 |
| 44 | 27 | | (h) | Brentford | L | 1 - 2 | Boyd | 5,206 |
| 45 | Apr 3 | | (a) | Brighton & Hove Albion | L | 0 - 2 | | 6,257 |
| 46 | 6 | | (h) | Luton Town | W | 4 - 3 | Sweeney, Boyd 2 (1 pen), Robertson | 4,484 |
| 47 | 10 | | (h) | Bournemouth | W | 2 - 1 | Boyd 2 | 5,544 |
| 48 | 12 | | (a) | Wrexham | W | 2 - 1 | Clarke, Danns | 3,786 |
| 49 | 17 | | (h) | Notts County | W | 4 - 0 | Humphreys, Boyd 2, Robertson | 5,629 |
| 50 | 24 | | (a) | Rushden & Diamonds | W | 2 - 0 | E.Williams, Boyd | 4,568 |
| 51 | May 1 | | (h) | Plymouth Argyle | L | 1 - 3 | Boyd | 7,437 |
| 52 | 8 | | (a) | Swindon Town | D | 1 - 1 | Boyd | 11,627 |

Final Position : 6th in Division Two

Apps.
Sub.Apps.
2 own goals — Goals

**Play-offs**

| Match No. | Date | Round | Venue | Opponents | Result | | Scorers | Attendance |
|---|---|---|---|---|---|---|---|---|
| 53 | May 15 | SFl1 | (h) | Bristol City | D | 1 - 1 | Porter | 7,211 |
| 54 | 19 | SFl2 | (a) | Bristol City | L | 1 - 2 | Sweeney | 18,434 |

Apps.
Sub.Apps.
Goals

**FA Cup**

| Match No. | Date | Round | Venue | Opponents | Result | | Scorers | Attendance |
|---|---|---|---|---|---|---|---|---|
| 21 | Nov 8 | R1 | (h) | Whitby Town | W | 4 - 0 | Gabbiadini 2, Humphreys, Brackstone | 5,294 |
| 25 | Dec 7 | R2 | (a) | Burton Albion | W | 1 - 0 | Porter | 3,132 |
| 30 | Jan 3 | R3 | (a) | Sunderland | L | 0 - 1 | | 40,813 |

Apps.
Sub.Apps.
Goals

**League Cup**

| Match No. | Date | Round | Venue | Opponents | Result | | Scorers | Attendance |
|---|---|---|---|---|---|---|---|---|
| 2 | Aug 13 | R1 | (a) | Sheffield Wednesday | W | 2 - 2* | Robinson (pen), Istead | 13,410 |
| 11 | Sep 23 | R2 | (h) | West Bromwich Albion | L | 1 - 2 | Robinson (pen) | 5,265 |

* After extra-time. Won 5 - 4 on penalties.

Apps.
Sub.Apps.
Goals

| 1 Williams, A. | 14 Arnison | 22 Robson | 5 Nelson | 6 Westwood | 24 Jordan | 7 Clarke | 8 Humphreys | 9 Williams, E. | 23 Robinson, P. | 25 Strachan | 21 Istead | 11 Henderson | 19 Provett | 2 Barron | 4 Tinkler | 10 Gabbiadini | 27 Foley | 15 Boyd | 17 Easter | 28 McCann | 3 Robinson, M. | 20 Brackstone | 16 Richardson | 18 Sweeney | 29 Craddock | 31 Wilkinson | 33 Byrne | 32 Porter | 11 Shuker | 16 Robertson | 33 Walker | 12 Carson | 14 Danns |
|---|---|---|---|---|---|---|---|---|---|---|---|---|---|---|---|---|---|---|---|---|---|---|---|---|---|---|---|---|---|---|---|---|---|
|1|2|3|4|5|6|7|8|9|10|11|12|13||||||||||||||||||||||
|||3|4|5|6|7|8|9|10|11|12||1|2|13|14||||||||||||||||||
|||12|4|5|6|7|3||10|11|14|9|1|2|8|13||||||||||||||||||
|||3|4|5|12|7|8||9|11|13||1|2|6|10|14|||||||||||||||||
|||3|4|5||7|8||9|11|12|13|1|2|6|10||14|||||||||||||||
||2|3|4|5|||8|12|9|11|13||1|6|7|10||14|||||||||||||||
|||3|4|5||12|7|9|8|11|||1|2|6|10|||13|14|||||||||||||
|||12|4|5|3||7|9|8|11|14||1|2|6|10||||13|||||||||||||
|||3|4|5|||7|9|8|11|12||1|2|6|10||||13|||||||||||||
||||4|5||7|6|9|8|11|12||1|2|3|10|||13||||||||||||||
||||4|5||7|8|9|10|11|12||1|2|6|||13||14|3||||||||||||
||||4|5||7|8|9|10|11|||1|2|6|12||13|||3||||||||||||
||12||4|||7|8|9|2|11|||1|5|6|10||13|||3||||||||||||
||||4|5||7|8||9|11|||1|2|6|10||12|13||3|14|||||||||||
||12||4|5||7|8|9|13|11|||1|2|6|||14||||3|10||||||||||
||||4|5||7|8|9|12|11|||1|2|6|13||||||3|10|14|||||||||
||||4|5||7|8|9|12|11|||1|2|6|13||||||3|10||||||||||
|||3|4|2||7|8|9||11|||1||6|||||||||12|5|10|||||||
|||3|4|5||7|8|9|12|11|||1||6|13||||||||14|5|10|||||||
|||3|4|5|||8|9||11|||1|2|6|||||||||||12|7|10|||||
|||3|4|5|||8|9|12|11|||1|2||||||||||||6|10|7||||
|||3|4|5|||8|9|12|11|||1|2|6||||||||||13||10|7||||
||||4|5||12|8|9|13|11|14||1|2|6||||||3|||||||10|7||||
|||3|4|5|||8|9|10|11|13||1|2|6|||||||||||||12|7||||
|||12|4|5|||8|9|13|11|14||1|2|6||||||3|||||||10|7||||
|||3|4|5||13|8|9||11|12||1|2|6|||||||||||||10|7||||
|||3|4|5||12|8|9|13|11|14||1|2|6|||||||||||||10|7||||
|||3|4|5||12|8|9|10|11|14||1|2|6|||||||||||||13|7||||
|||12|4|2|||8|9|10|11|13||1||6|||||||||||||14|7|3|5||
||||4|5||12|8|9|10|11|||1|2|6|||||||||||||13|7|3|14||
||||4|5||11|8|9|10||||1|2|6|||||||||||||12|7|3||13|
|||13||5||11|8|9|||12||1|2|6||||||||||14|||10|7|3|4||
|||12|4|5|||8|9||11|13||1|2|6|||||||||||||10|7|3|||
|||11|4|5||12|8|9|||13||1|2|8|||||||||||||10|7|3||14|
||||4|5|||11|9|12||13||1|2|8|||||||||||||10||3||7|6|
||||2|5||13|11|9|||8||1||6|||12||||||||||10||3|4||7|
||||2|5|||11|9|||12||1||6|||7||||||||||10||3|8||4|
||||4|2||13|11|9||12|14||1||6|||8||||||||||10||3|5||7|
|||||5||7|8|9||11|12||1||2|||6||||||10|4|||13||3||||
|||||5||7|8|12||11|13||1||6|||10||||||4|2|||9||3||||
|||||5||7|8||13|11|12||1||6|||10||||||4|2|||9||3|||14|
|||||5||7|11|9|||12||1||6|||10||||||4|2|||13||3|||8|
|||||5||7|11|9||13|12||1||6|||10||||||4|2|||14||3|||8|
||||12|5||7|11|9|||13||1||6|||10||||||4|2|||14||3|||8|
||||12|5||13|11|9|||14||1||6|||8||||||4|2|||10||3|||7|
||||4|5|||11|9|12||||1|2|6|||8||||||7||||10||3||||
|1|2|17|38|45|4|23|46|39|19|34|1|1|45|32|43|9||10|||4|5|3|8|9|2|2|18|14|18|5|1|8|
||2|6|2||1|10||2|12|2|30|2|||1|6|1|8|3|4||1||3|1|2||9|||1|2|1|
|||1|3|||5|3|13|7|5|1|||1|6|5||12|||||1||2||3|1|4|||1|
||||4|5||12|11|9|14||||1|2|6|||8||||||7||||10||3|||13|
||||4|5||12|11|9|14||||1|2|6|||8||||||7||||10||3|||13|
||||2|2|||2|2|||||2|2|2|||2||||||2||||2||2||||
|||||||2|||2||||||||||||||||||||||||2|
|||||||||||||||||||||||||1||||1||||||
|||4|5||14|7|9|8|11|||1|2|6|10||||||3|||12|13||||||||
||3|4|5|||8|9|12|11|||1|2|6|||||||||||13|7|10||||||
||3|4|5||12|8|9|10|11|13||1|2|6|||||||||||||14|7||||||
||2|3|3|||3|3|2|3|||3|3|3|1||||||1|||||1|1|1||||||
||||||2|||1||1||||||||||||||1|2||1||||||
|||||||1|||||||||2||||||1||||||1||||||
||6|4|5|2|7|11|9|10|3|14|12|1|13|8||||||||||||||||||||
|||4|5||3|7|9|8|11|12||1|2|6|10||||13||||||||||||||
||1|2|2|1|2|2|2|2|2|||2|1|2|1||||||||||||||||||
|||||||||||2|1||1||||||1||||||||||||||
|||||||||2||1|||||||||||||||||||||||

## League Table

| | P | W | D | L | F | A | Pts |
|---|---|---|---|---|---|---|---|
| Plymouth Argyle | 46 | 26 | 12 | 8 | 85 | 41 | 90 |
| Queen's Park Rangers | 46 | 22 | 17 | 7 | 80 | 45 | 83 |
| Bristol City | 46 | 23 | 13 | 10 | 58 | 37 | 82 |
| Brighton & Hove Albion | 46 | 22 | 11 | 13 | 64 | 43 | 77 |
| Swindon Town | 46 | 20 | 13 | 13 | 76 | 58 | 73 |
| Hartlepool United | 46 | 20 | 13 | 13 | 76 | 61 | 73 |
| Port Vale | 46 | 21 | 10 | 15 | 73 | 63 | 73 |
| Tranmere Rovers | 46 | 17 | 16 | 13 | 59 | 56 | 67 |
| Bournemouth | 46 | 17 | 15 | 14 | 56 | 51 | 66 |
| Luton Town | 46 | 17 | 15 | 14 | 69 | 66 | 66 |
| Colchester United | 46 | 17 | 13 | 16 | 52 | 56 | 64 |
| Barnsley | 46 | 15 | 17 | 14 | 54 | 58 | 62 |
| Wrexham | 46 | 17 | 9 | 20 | 50 | 60 | 60 |
| Blackpool | 46 | 16 | 11 | 19 | 58 | 65 | 59 |
| Oldham Athletic | 46 | 12 | 21 | 13 | 66 | 60 | 57 |
| Sheffield Wednesday | 46 | 13 | 14 | 19 | 48 | 64 | 53 |
| Brentford | 46 | 14 | 11 | 21 | 52 | 69 | 53 |
| Peterborough United | 46 | 12 | 16 | 18 | 58 | 58 | 52 |
| Stockport County | 46 | 11 | 19 | 16 | 62 | 70 | 52 |
| Chesterfield | 46 | 12 | 15 | 19 | 49 | 71 | 51 |
| Grimsby Town | 46 | 13 | 11 | 22 | 55 | 81 | 50 |
| Rushden & Diamonds | 46 | 13 | 9 | 24 | 60 | 74 | 48 |
| Notts County | 46 | 10 | 12 | 24 | 50 | 78 | 42 |
| Wycombe Wanderers | 46 | 6 | 19 | 21 | 50 | 75 | 37 |

# 2004-05

## League One

Managers: Neale Cooper and Martin Scott

### Did you know that?

An estimated 17,000 Hartlepool supporters travelled to Cardiff for the Play-off Final against Sheffield Wednesday, over three times the average home attendance of 5,200!

Chris Westwood had the misfortune of being sent off in his final game for the club, the pivotal moment in the Play-off Final against Sheffield Wednesday on 29 May.

| Match No. | Date | Round | Venue | Opponents | Result | | Scorers | Attendance |
|---|---|---|---|---|---|---|---|---|
| 1 | Aug 7 | | (h) | Bradford City | W | 2 - 1 | Boyd (pen), Robertson | 6,032 |
| 2 | 10 | | (a) | Tranmere Rovers | L | 1 - 2 | Robertson | 8,128 |
| 3 | 18 | | (a) | Huddersfield Town | W | 2 - 0 | Betsy, Tinkler | 9,968 |
| 4 | 21 | | (h) | Blackpool | D | 1 - 1 | Williams | 5,144 |
| 6 | 28 | | (a) | Swindon Town | L | 0 - 3 | | 5,365 |
| 7 | 30 | | (h) | Colchester United | W | 2 - 1 | Williams, Boyd | 4,371 |
| 8 | Sep 4 | | (h) | Barnsley | D | 1 - 1 | Boyd | 5,119 |
| 9 | 11 | | (a) | Oldham Athletic | L | 2 - 3 | Westwood, Griffin (o.g.) | 5,805 |
| 10 | 18 | | (h) | Torquay United | W | 4 - 1 | Porter, Sweeney, Tinkler, Humphries | 4,485 |
| 12 | 25 | | (a) | Milton Keynes Dons | L | 2 - 4 | Boyd 2 | 3,685 |
| 14 | Oct 2 | | (h) | Hull City | W | 2 - 0 | Porter, Boyd | 5,768 |
| 15 | 8 | | (a) | Luton Town | L | 0 - 3 | | 7,865 |
| 16 | 16 | | (h) | Chesterfield | W | 3 - 2 | Sweeney 3 | 4,617 |
| 17 | 19 | | (a) | Brentford | L | 1 - 2 | Robson | 4,797 |
| 18 | 23 | | (a) | Peterborough United | L | 0 - 3 | | 3,841 |
| 19 | 30 | | (h) | Port Vale | W | 1 - 0 | Williams | 4,755 |
| 21 | Nov 6 | | (h) | Doncaster Rovers | W | 2 - 1 | Porter 2 | 5,495 |
| 23 | 20 | | (a) | Sheffield Wednesday | L | 0 - 2 | | 19,919 |
| 24 | 27 | | (h) | Bournemouth | W | 3 - 2 | Westwood, Nelson, Appleby | 4,376 |
| 27 | Dec 7 | | (a) | Walsall | L | 1 - 2 | Boyd | 5,522 |
| 28 | 11 | | (h) | Stockport County | W | 3 - 1 | Westwood 2, Porter | 4,572 |
| 29 | 18 | | (a) | Wrexham | W | 5 - 1 | Humphreys, Sweeney 2, Porter, Boyd | 3,582 |
| 30 | 26 | | (h) | Oldham Athletic | W | 2 - 1 | Boyd 2 (2 pens) | 6,520 |
| 31 | 28 | | (a) | Bristol City | D | 0 - 0 | | 13,034 |
| 32 | Jan 1 | | (a) | Barnsley | D | 0 - 0 | | 9,595 |
| 33 | 3 | | (h) | Milton Keynes Dons | W | 5 - 0 | Sweeney, Boyd 2, Porter, Appleby | 5,060 |
| 35 | 15 | | (a) | Torquay United | W | 2 - 1 | Porter, Sweeney | 2,543 |
| 37 | 22 | | (h) | Bristol City | W | 2 - 1 | Boyd (pen), Sweeney | 5,399 |
| 39 | Feb 5 | | (a) | Chesterfield | W | 1 - 0 | Boyd | 4,606 |
| 41 | 15 | | (h) | Luton Town | L | 2 - 3 | Davis (o.g.), Robson | 5,542 |
| 42 | 19 | | (a) | Port Vale | W | 1 - 0 | Porter | 4,366 |
| 43 | 22 | | (h) | Brentford | W | 3 - 1 | Boyd (pen), Williams, Sweeney | 4,206 |
| 44 | 26 | | (a) | Stockport County | L | 0 - 1 | | 4,548 |
| 45 | Mar 5 | | (h) | Wrexham | L | 4 - 6 | Strachan, Porter 2, Boyd | 4,707 |
| 46 | 8 | | (a) | Hull City | L | 0 - 1 | | 17,112 |
| 47 | 12 | | (h) | Tranmere Rovers | L | 0 - 1 | | 4,887 |
| 48 | 19 | | (a) | Bradford City | W | 2 - 1 | Williams, Porter | 7,509 |
| 49 | 25 | | (h) | Huddersfield Town | L | 0 - 1 | | 6,205 |
| 50 | 28 | | (a) | Blackpool | D | 2 - 2 | Boyd 2 | 6,853 |
| 51 | Apr 2 | | (h) | Swindon Town | W | 3 - 0 | Porter, Butler, Humphreys | 4,936 |
| 52 | 5 | | (h) | Peterborough United | D | 2 - 2 | Porter, Sweeney | 4,579 |
| 53 | 9 | | (a) | Colchester United | D | 1 - 1 | Sweeney | 3,148 |
| 54 | 15 | | (h) | Sheffield Wednesday | W | 3 - 0 | Boyd 3 | 6,429 |
| 55 | 23 | | (a) | Doncaster Rovers | L | 0 - 2 | | 7,024 |
| 56 | 30 | | (h) | Walsall | L | 1 - 3 | Boyd (pen) | 6,389 |
| 57 | May 7 | | (a) | Bournemouth | D | 2 - 2 | Daly, Sweeney | 8,620 |

Final Position : 6th in League One — Apps.

Sub.Apps.

1 own goal — Goals

**Play-offs**

| Match No. | Date | Round | Venue | Opponents | Result | | Scorers | Attendance |
|---|---|---|---|---|---|---|---|---|
| 58 | May 13 | SFl1 | (h) | Tranmere Rovers | W | 2 - 0 | Boyd 2 | 6,604 |
| 59 | 17 | SFl2 | (a) | Tranmere Rovers | L | 0 - 2* | Aggregate 2 - 2. Won 6 - 5 on penalties. | 13,356 |
| 60 | 29 | F | (a)# | Sheffield Wednesday | L | 2 - 4* | Williams, Daly | 59,808 |

# Played at Millenium Stadium, Cardiff *After extra-time — Apps.

Sub.Apps.

Goals

**FA Cup**

| Match No. | Date | Round | Venue | Opponents | Result | | Scorers | Attendance |
|---|---|---|---|---|---|---|---|---|
| 22 | Nov 13 | R1 | (h) | Lincoln City | W | 3 - 0 | Williams, Robson, Porter | 4,533 |
| 26 | Dec 4 | R2 | (h) | Aldershot Town | W | 5 - 1 | Westwood 2, Boyd 2, Tinkler | 4,556 |
| 34 | Jan 8 | R3 | (h) | Boston United | D | 0 - 0 | | 5,342 |
| 36 | 19 | R3r | (a) | Boston United | W | 1 - 0 | Boyd | 3,652 |
| 38 | 29 | R4 | (a) | Brentford | D | 0 - 0 | | 8,967 |
| 40 | Feb 12 | R4r | (h) | Brentford | L | 0 - 1 | | 7,580 |

Apps.

Sub.Apps.

Goals

**League Cup**

| Match No. | Date | Round | Venue | Opponents | Result | | Scorers | Attendance |
|---|---|---|---|---|---|---|---|---|
| 5 | Aug 23 | R1 | (h) | Macclesfield Town | W | 2 - 1 | Boyd, Sweeney | 2,883 |
| 11 | Sep 21 | R2 | (a) | Crystal Palace | L | 1 - 2* | Williams | 4,322 |

* After extra-time — Apps.

Sub.Apps.

Goals

| 1 Provett | 12 Ross | 3 Robertson | 5 Nelson | 6 Westwood | 4 Tinkler | 9 Williams | 15 Sweeney | 14 Porter | 10 Boyd | 8 Humphreys | 17 Betsy | 20 Istead | 19 Brackstone | 11 Strachan | 21 Konstantopoulos | 18 Robson | 25 Appleby | 22 Craddock | 16 Woods | 17 Pouton | 27 Foley | 2 Barron | 30 Turnbull | 17 Clark | 23 Wilkinson | 29 Maidens | 16 Gobern | 16 Daly | 32 Butler | 42 Howey |
|---|---|---|---|---|---|---|---|---|---|---|---|---|---|---|---|---|---|---|---|---|---|---|---|---|---|---|---|---|---|---|
| 1 | 2 | 3 | 4 | 5 | 6 | 7 | 8 | 9 | 10 | 11 | 12 | 13 | | | | | | | | | | | | | | | | | | |
| 1 | 2 | 3 | 4 | 5 | 6 | 7 | 8 | 9 | 10 | 11 | 12 | | | | | | | | | | | | | | | | | | | |
| 1 | 2 | 3 | 4 | 5 | 6 | 7 | 8 | | 10 | 11 | 9 | | | | | | | | | | | | | | | | | | | |
| 1 | 2 | 3 | 4 | 5 | 6 | 7 | 8 | 12 | 10 | 11 | 9 | 13 | 14 | | | | | | | | | | | | | | | | | |
| 1 | 2 | 3 | 4 | 5 | 6 | 7 | 8 | 9 | 10 | 11 | 12 | | | 13 | | | | | | | | | | | | | | | | |
| | 2 | | 4 | 5 | | 7 | 8 | | 10 | 11 | 9 | | | 6 | 1 | 3 | | | | | | | | | | | | | | |
| 1 | 2 | | 4 | 5 | | 7 | 8 | 9 | 10 | 11 | | 12 | | 6 | | 3 | 13 | | | | | | | | | | | | | |
| 1 | | | 4 | 5 | 12 | | 8 | | 10 | 11 | | 13 | | | | 3 | 14 | 2 | 6 | 7 | 9 | | | | | | | | | |
| 1 | | | 4 | | 5 | 12 | 8 | 9 | 10 | 11 | | 13 | | 6 | | 3 | | 2 | 14 | 7 | | | | | | | | | | |
| 1 | | | 4 | 5 | 6 | 9 | 8 | 12 | 10 | 11 | | | | 13 | | 3 | | | 2 | 7 | | | | | | | | | | |
| 1 | | | 4 | 12 | 5 | 7 | | 9 | 10 | 11 | | 13 | | 6 | | 3 | | | 14 | 8 | | 2 | | | | | | | | |
| 1 | | | 4 | | 5 | 7 | | 9 | 10 | 11 | | | | 6 | | 3 | | | | 8 | | 2 | | | | | | | | |
| 1 | | | 4 | | 5 | 7 | 8 | 9 | 10 | 11 | | | | 6 | | 3 | | | 12 | | | 2 | 13 | | | | | | | |
| 1 | | | 4 | 5 | 6 | 12 | 8 | 9 | 10 | 11 | | | | | | 3 | | | 7 | | | 2 | | | | | | | | |
| 1 | | | 4 | 5 | 6 | 12 | 8 | 9 | 10 | 11 | | | | 7 | | 3 | | | | | | 2 | | 13 | 14 | | | | | |
| | 12 | | | 5 | 6 | 7 | 8 | 9 | | 11 | | | | | 1 | 3 | | | | | | 2 | 13 | 4 | 10 | 14 | | | | |
| | 12 | | 13 | 5 | 6 | 7 | 8 | 14 | 10 | 11 | | | | | 1 | 3 | | | | | | 2 | | 4 | | | 9 | | | |
| | 2 | | 4 | 5 | 6 | 7 | 8 | 9 | 10 | 11 | | | | | 1 | 3 | | | | | 13 | 12 | | | 14 | | | | | |
| | | | 4 | 5 | 6 | | 8 | 9 | 10 | 11 | | | 3 | 7 | 1 | | 12 | | | | | 2 | | | | | | | | |
| | 2 | 12 | | 5 | 6 | | 8 | 9 | 10 | 11 | | | 3 | 7 | 1 | | 13 | | | | | | | 4 | | | | | | |
| | 2 | 3 | | 5 | 6 | 12 | 8 | 9 | 10 | 11 | | 13 | | 7 | 1 | | 14 | | | | | | | 4 | | | | | | |
| | 2 | 3 | 4 | 5 | 6 | 7 | 8 | 9 | 10 | 11 | | 13 | | 12 | 1 | | 14 | | | | | | | | | | | | | |
| | 2 | 3 | 4 | 5 | 6 | 7 | 8 | 9 | 10 | 11 | | 12 | | 13 | 1 | | 14 | | | | | | | | | | | | | |
| | 2 | 3 | 4 | 5 | 6 | 7 | 8 | 9 | 10 | 11 | | 12 | | 13 | 1 | | 14 | | | | | | | | | | | | | |
| | 2 | 3 | 4 | 5 | 6 | 7 | 8 | 9 | 10 | 11 | | 13 | | | 1 | | 12 | | | | | | | | | | | | | |
| | 2 | 3 | 4 | 5 | 6 | 7 | 8 | 9 | 10 | 11 | | | | 12 | 1 | | 14 | | | | | | | 13 | | | | | | |
| | 2 | | 4 | 5 | 6 | 7 | 8 | 9 | 10 | 11 | | 12 | | 13 | 1 | | 14 | | | | | | | 3 | | | | | | |
| | 2 | 3 | 4 | 5 | 6 | | 8 | 9 | 10 | 11 | | 12 | | | 1 | | 13 | | | | | | | 7 | | | | | | |
| | 2 | 3 | 4 | 5 | 6 | 12 | 8 | 9 | 10 | 11 | | | | | 1 | | | | | | | | | 7 | | | | | | |
| | 12 | | 4 | 5 | 6 | 13 | 8 | 9 | 10 | 11 | | | | 3 | 1 | 14 | | | | | | | | 2 | | | | 7 | | |
| | 2 | | 4 | | | 7 | 8 | 9 | 10 | 11 | | | 3 | 6 | 1 | | 12 | | | | | | | 5 | | | | | | |
| | 2 | | 4 | | | 7 | 8 | 9 | 10 | 11 | | | 3 | 6 | 1 | 12 | | | | | | | | 5 | | | | | | |
| | 2 | | 4 | | | 7 | 8 | 9 | 10 | 11 | | | 3 | 6 | 1 | | | | | | | 12 | | 5 | | | | 13 | | |
| | | | 4 | | | 7 | 8 | 9 | 10 | 11 | | | 3 | 6 | 1 | 12 | | | | | | 2 | | 5 | | | | 13 | | |
| 1 | | | 4 | | | 7 | 8 | 9 | 10 | 11 | | | 3 | 6 | | 12 | | 14 | | | | 2 | | 5 | | | | 13 | | |
| 1 | | | 4 | | | 7 | 8 | 9 | 10 | 11 | | 12 | 3 | 6 | | 13 | | 2 | | | | | | 5 | | | | | | |
| 1 | | 3 | 4 | 5 | 6 | 7 | 8 | 9 | 12 | 11 | | 13 | | | | 10 | | 2 | | | | | | 14 | | | | | | |
| 1 | | 3 | 4 | 5 | 6 | 7 | 8 | 9 | 12 | 11 | | | | | | 10 | | 2 | | | | | | 13 | | | | | 14 | |
| 1 | | 3 | 4 | 5 | | | 8 | 9 | 10 | 11 | | | | | | 7 | | 2 | | | | | | 6 | | | | 12 | 13 | |
| 1 | | 12 | 4 | 5 | | | 8 | 9 | 10 | 11 | | | | | | 3 | | 2 | | | | | | 7 | | | | 13 | 6 | |
| 1 | | | 4 | 5 | | | 8 | 9 | 10 | 11 | | 12 | | | | 3 | | 2 | | | | | | 6 | | | | 13 | 7 | |
| | | 3 | 4 | 5 | | | 8 | | 10 | 11 | | 12 | | 6 | 1 | | 13 | | | | | | | 2 | | | | 9 | 7 | 14 |
| | | | 4 | 5 | 12 | 13 | 8 | 9 | 10 | 11 | | | | 6 | 1 | 3 | | | | | | | | 2 | | | | 14 | 7 | |
| | | | 4 | 5 | | 9 | 8 | | 10 | 11 | | | | 6 | 1 | 3 | 13 | | | | | | | 2 | | | | 12 | 7 | |
| | | 13 | 4 | 5 | 6 | 7 | 8 | | 10 | 11 | | | | 12 | 1 | 3 | | 2 | | | | | | | | | | 9 | 14 | |
| | | | 4 | 5 | 12 | 7 | 8 | | 10 | 11 | | | | 6 | 1 | 3 | | | | | | 13 | | 2 | | | | 9 | 14 | |
| 21 | 21 | 17 | 42 | 36 | 30 | 31 | 44 | 36 | 43 | 46 | 3 | | 8 | 21 | 25 | 22 | | 9 | 3 | 5 | 1 | 10 | | 21 | 1 | | 1 | 4 | 5 | |
| | 3 | 3 | 1 | 1 | 3 | 7 | | 3 | 2 | | 3 | 17 | 1 | 8 | | 5 | 15 | 1 | 3 | | 1 | 3 | 2 | 4 | 2 | 1 | | 8 | 4 | 1 |
| | | 2 | 1 | 4 | 2 | 5 | 13 | 14 | 22 | 3 | 1 | | | 1 | | 2 | 2 | | | | | | | | | | | 1 | 1 | |

| 1 Provett | 12 Ross | 3 Robertson | 5 Nelson | 6 Westwood | 4 Tinkler | 9 Williams | 15 Sweeney | 14 Porter | 10 Boyd | 8 Humphreys | 17 Betsy | 20 Istead | 19 Brackstone | 11 Strachan | 21 Konstantopoulos | 18 Robson | 25 Appleby | 22 Craddock | 16 Woods | 17 Pouton | 27 Foley | 2 Barron | 30 Turnbull | 17 Clark | 23 Wilkinson | 29 Maidens | 16 Gobern | 16 Daly | 32 Butler | 42 Howey |
|---|---|---|---|---|---|---|---|---|---|---|---|---|---|---|---|---|---|---|---|---|---|---|---|---|---|---|---|---|---|---|
| | | | 4 | 5 | 13 | 7 | 8 | 12 | 10 | 11 | | | | 6 | 1 | 3 | | | | | | 2 | | | | | | 9 | | |
| | | | 4 | 5 | 12 | 7 | 8 | 13 | 10 | 11 | | | | 6 | 1 | 3 | | | | | | 2 | | | | | | 9 | 14 | |
| | | | 4 | 5 | | 13 | 8 | 9 | 10 | 11 | | | | 6 | 1 | 3 | | 12 | | | | 2 | | | | | | 14 | 7 | |
| | | | 3 | 3 | | 2 | 3 | 1 | 3 | 3 | | | | 3 | 3 | 3 | | | | | | 3 | | | | | | 2 | 1 | |
| | | | | | 2 | 1 | | 2 | | | | | | | | | | 1 | | | | | | | | | | 1 | 1 | |
| | | | | | | 1 | | | 2 | | | | | | | | | | | | | | | | | | | 1 | | |

| 1 Provett | 12 Ross | 3 Robertson | 5 Nelson | 6 Westwood | 4 Tinkler | 9 Williams | 15 Sweeney | 14 Porter | 10 Boyd | 8 Humphreys | 17 Betsy | 20 Istead | 19 Brackstone | 11 Strachan | 21 Konstantopoulos | 18 Robson | 25 Appleby | 22 Craddock | 16 Woods | 17 Pouton | 27 Foley | 2 Barron | 30 Turnbull | 17 Clark | 23 Wilkinson | 29 Maidens | 16 Gobern | 16 Daly | 32 Butler | 42 Howey |
|---|---|---|---|---|---|---|---|---|---|---|---|---|---|---|---|---|---|---|---|---|---|---|---|---|---|---|---|---|---|---|
| | 2 | | 4 | 5 | | 7 | 8 | 9 | 10 | 11 | | 12 | | 14 | 1 | 3 | | | | | 13 | | | 6 | | | | | | |
| 1 | 12 | | | 5 | 6 | | 8 | 9 | 10 | 11 | | 13 | 3 | 7 | | 14 | | | | | | 2 | | 4 | | | | | | |
| | 2 | 3 | 4 | 5 | 6 | 7 | 8 | 9 | 10 | 11 | | 13 | | | 1 | | 14 | | | | | | | 12 | | | | | | |
| | 2 | 3 | 4 | 5 | 6 | | 8 | | 10 | 11 | | 12 | | | 1 | | 9 | | | | | | | 7 | | | | | | |
| | 2 | 3 | 4 | 5 | 6 | | 8 | 9 | 10 | 11 | | 12 | | | 1 | | 13 | | | | | | | 7 | | | | | | |
| | 2 | 3 | 4 | 5 | 6 | 12 | 8 | 9 | 10 | 11 | | 13 | | | 1 | | | | | | | | | 7 | | | | | | |
| 1 | 5 | 4 | 5 | 6 | 5 | 2 | 6 | 5 | 6 | 6 | | | 1 | 1 | 5 | 1 | 1 | | | | | 1 | | 5 | | | | | | |
| | 1 | | | | | 1 | | | | | | 6 | | 1 | | 1 | 2 | | | | 1 | | | 1 | | | | | | |
| | | | | 2 | 1 | 1 | | 1 | 3 | | | | | | | 1 | | | | | | | | | | | | | | |

| 1 Provett | 12 Ross | 3 Robertson | 5 Nelson | 6 Westwood | 4 Tinkler | 9 Williams | 15 Sweeney | 14 Porter | 10 Boyd | 8 Humphreys | 17 Betsy | 20 Istead | 19 Brackstone | 11 Strachan | 21 Konstantopoulos | 18 Robson | 25 Appleby | 22 Craddock | 16 Woods | 17 Pouton | 27 Foley | 2 Barron | 30 Turnbull | 17 Clark | 23 Wilkinson | 29 Maidens | 16 Gobern | 16 Daly | 32 Butler | 42 Howey |
|---|---|---|---|---|---|---|---|---|---|---|---|---|---|---|---|---|---|---|---|---|---|---|---|---|---|---|---|---|---|---|
| | | | 4 | 5 | 6 | 12 | 8 | 13 | 9 | 11 | 10 | | | 7 | 1 | 3 | | 2 | | | | | | | | | | | | |
| 1 | | | 4 | 5 | 6 | 14 | 7 | 9 | 10 | 11 | | 12 | | 8 | | 3 | | | 2 | | | | | | | 13 | | | | |
| 1 | | | 2 | 2 | 2 | | 2 | 1 | 2 | 2 | 1 | | | 2 | 1 | 2 | | 1 | 1 | | | | | | | | | | | |
| | | | | | | 2 | | 1 | | | | 1 | | | | | | | | | | | | | | 1 | | | | |
| | | | | | | 1 | 1 | | 1 | | | | | | | | | | | | | | | | | | | | | |

## League Table

| | P | W | D | L | F | A | Pts |
|---|---|---|---|---|---|---|---|
| Luton Town | 46 | 29 | 11 | 6 | 87 | 48 | 98 |
| Hull City | 46 | 26 | 8 | 12 | 80 | 53 | 86 |
| Tranmere Rovers | 46 | 22 | 13 | 11 | 73 | 55 | 79 |
| Brentford | 46 | 22 | 9 | 15 | 57 | 60 | 75 |
| Sheffield Wednesday | 46 | 19 | 15 | 12 | 77 | 59 | 72 |
| Hartlepool United | 46 | 21 | 8 | 17 | 76 | 66 | 71 |
| Bristol City | 46 | 18 | 16 | 12 | 74 | 57 | 70 |
| Bournemouth | 46 | 20 | 10 | 16 | 77 | 64 | 70 |
| Huddersfield Town | 46 | 20 | 10 | 16 | 74 | 65 | 70 |
| Doncaster Rovers | 46 | 16 | 18 | 12 | 65 | 60 | 66 |
| Bradford City | 46 | 17 | 14 | 15 | 64 | 62 | 65 |
| Swindon Town | 46 | 17 | 12 | 17 | 66 | 68 | 63 |
| Barnsley | 46 | 14 | 19 | 13 | 69 | 64 | 61 |
| Walsall | 46 | 16 | 12 | 18 | 65 | 69 | 60 |
| Colchester United | 46 | 14 | 17 | 15 | 60 | 50 | 59 |
| Blackpool | 46 | 15 | 12 | 19 | 54 | 59 | 57 |
| Chesterfield | 46 | 14 | 15 | 17 | 55 | 62 | 57 |
| Port Vale | 46 | 17 | 5 | 24 | 49 | 59 | 56 |
| Oldham Athletic | 46 | 14 | 10 | 22 | 60 | 73 | 52 |
| Milton Keynes Dons | 46 | 12 | 15 | 19 | 54 | 68 | 51 |
| Torquay United | 46 | 12 | 15 | 19 | 55 | 79 | 51 |
| Wrexham | 46 | 13 | 14 | 19 | 62 | 80 | 43 |
| Peterborough United | 46 | 9 | 12 | 25 | 49 | 73 | 39 |
| Stockport County | 46 | 6 | 8 | 32 | 49 | 98 | 26 |

# 2005-06

## League One

Managers: Martin Scott and Paul Stephenson

### Did you know that?

Eifion Williams was leading goalscorer with seven League goals, the lowest individual total since the 1947–48 season when Fred Richardson and Jimmy Sloan jointly shared the 'record'.

United lost 2–1 in the FA Cup second round to Tamworth, managed by former player Martin Cooper.

| Match No. | Date | Round | Venue | Opponents | Result | | Scorers | Attendance |
|---|---|---|---|---|---|---|---|---|
| 1 | Aug 6 | | (h) | Bradford City | L | 0 - 2 | | 6,271 |
| 2 | 9 | | (a) | Bournemouth | D | 1 - 1 | Bullock | 5,406 |
| 3 | 13 | | (a) | Doncaster Rovers | W | 1 - 0 | Daly | 5,061 |
| 4 | 20 | | (h) | Walsall | D | 1 - 1 | Sweeney | 5,060 |
| 6 | 27 | | (a) | Huddersfield Town | L | 1 - 2 | Boyd | 11,241 |
| 7 | 29 | | (h) | Scunthorpe United | D | 3 - 3 | Proctor, E.Williams, Boyd (pen) | 5,044 |
| 8 | Sep 3 | | (h) | Yeovil Town | L | 0 - 1 | | 4,572 |
| 9 | 10 | | (a) | Blackpool | W | 2 - 1 | Sweeney, Istead | 5,494 |
| 10 | 17 | | (h) | Swansea City | D | 2 - 2 | Humphreys, Sweeney | 4,743 |
| 12 | 24 | | (a) | Chesterfield | L | 1 - 3 | Proctor | 4,078 |
| 13 | 27 | | (h) | Rotherham United | D | 0 - 0 | | 4,309 |
| 14 | Oct 1 | | (a) | Bristol City | W | 1 - 0 | Proctor | 11,365 |
| 15 | 15 | | (a) | Nottingham Forest | L | 0 - 2 | | 17,586 |
| 17 | 22 | | (h) | Milton Keynes Dons | W | 2 - 1 | Lewington (o.g.), Bullock | 4,337 |
| 18 | 29 | | (a) | Port Vale | W | 2 - 1 | E.Williams, Butler | 4,550 |
| 19 | Nov 1 | | (h) | Gillingham | W | 3 - 1 | Daly, Sweeney, Bullock | 4,522 |
| 21 | 12 | | (h) | Brentford | L | 1 - 2 | Sweeney | 4,811 |
| 22 | 19 | | (a) | Gillingham | L | 0 - 1 | | 6,092 |
| 23 | 26 | | (a) | Bradford City | W | 1 - 0 | Tinkler | 7,449 |
| 25 | Dec 6 | | (h) | Colchester United | L | 0 - 1 | | 3,375 |
| 26 | 10 | | (h) | Bournemouth | W | 2 - 1 | Istead, McDonald | 3,755 |
| 27 | 17 | | (a) | Walsall | L | 0 - 1 | | 4,293 |
| 28 | 26 | | (a) | Barnsley | D | 1 - 1 | E.Williams | 9,715 |
| 29 | 28 | | (h) | Southend United | L | 1 - 2 | E.Williams | 3,929 |
| 30 | 31 | | (a) | Oldham Athletic | L | 1 - 2 | E.Williams | 5,047 |
| 31 | Jan 2 | | (h) | Swindon Town | D | 1 - 1 | Strachan | 4,169 |
| 32 | 7 | | (a) | Yeovil Town | L | 0 - 2 | | 5,480 |
| 33 | 14 | | (h) | Tranmere Rovers | D | 0 - 0 | | 4,181 |
| 34 | 21 | | (a) | Swansea City | D | 1 - 1 | E.Williams | 13,960 |
| 35 | 28 | | (h) | Blackpool | L | 0 - 3 | | 4,421 |
| 36 | Feb 4 | | (a) | Rotherham United | D | 0 - 0 | | 5,960 |
| 37 | 11 | | (h) | Chesterfield | W | 1 - 0 | Robson | 4,596 |
| 38 | 14 | | (a) | Tranmere Rovers | D | 0 - 0 | | 6,301 |
| 39 | 25 | | (h) | Doncaster Rovers | D | 1 - 1 | Boyd | 5,459 |
| 40 | Mar 11 | | (h) | Huddersfield Town | W | 3 - 1 | Boyd, Maidens, Porter | 5,468 |
| 41 | 14 | | (a) | Scunthorpe United | L | 0 - 2 | | 4,550 |
| 42 | 18 | | (h) | Barnsley | D | 1 - 1 | Porter | 5,122 |
| 43 | 25 | | (a) | Southend United | L | 0 - 3 | | 8,496 |
| 44 | 31 | | (h) | Oldham Athletic | D | 1 - 1 | Bullock | 5,259 |
| 45 | Apr 8 | | (a) | Swindon Town | D | 1 - 1 | Humphreys | 5,225 |
| 46 | 11 | | (a) | Colchester United | L | 0 - 2 | | 3,916 |
| 47 | 15 | | (h) | Bristol City | L | 1 - 2 | E.Williams | 5,039 |
| 48 | 17 | | (a) | Milton Keynes Dons | L | 1 - 2 | Proctor | 6,472 |
| 49 | 22 | | (h) | Nottingham Forest | W | 3 - 2 | Porter, Nelson, Proctor | 5,336 |
| 50 | 29 | | (a) | Brentford | D | 1 - 1 | Nelson | 8,725 |
| 51 | May 6 | | (h) | Port Vale | D | 1 - 1 | Brown | 6,895 |

Final Position: 21st in League One - Relegated

Apps.
Sub.Apps.
1 own goal — Goals

**FA Cup**

| Match No. | Date | Round | Venue | Opponents | Result | | Scorers | Attendance |
|---|---|---|---|---|---|---|---|---|
| 20 | Nov 5 | R1 | (h) | Dagenham & Redbridge | W | 2 - 1 | Nelson, Butler | 3,655 |
| 24 | Dec 3 | R2 | (h) | Tamworth | L | 1 - 2 | Llewellyn (pen) | 3,786 |

Apps.
Sub.Apps.
Goals

**League Cup**

| Match No. | Date | Round | Venue | Opponents | Result | | Scorers | Attendance |
|---|---|---|---|---|---|---|---|---|
| 5 | Aug 23 | R1 | (h) | Darlington | W | 3 - 1 | Daly, Proctor 2 | 6,163 |
| 11 | Sep 21 | R2 | (a) | Charlton Athletic | L | 1 - 3 | Daly | 10,328 |

Apps.
Sub.Apps.
Goals

| 1 Konstantopoulos | 16 Clark | 8 Humphreys | 23 Williams, D. | 5 Nelson | 22 Bullock | 7 Llewellyn | 15 Sweeney | 6 Proctor | 10 Boyd | 24 Butler | 12 Strachan | 14 Daly | 11 Williams, E. | 32 Collins | 18 Robson | 29 Jones | 4 Tinkler | 34 Maidens | 36 Turnbull | 25 Istead | 33 Foley | 20 Craddock | 37 McDonald | 19 Brackstone | 2 Barron | 3 Robertson | 17 Clarke | 37 Walker | 32 Nash | 38 Pittman | 9 Porter | 28 Brown |
|---|---|---|---|---|---|---|---|---|---|---|---|---|---|---|---|---|---|---|---|---|---|---|---|---|---|---|---|---|---|---|---|---|
| 1 | 2 | 3 | 4 | 5 | *6* | **7** | 8 | 9 | 10 | ***11*** | *12* | **13** | ***14*** | | | | | | | | | | | | | | | | | | | |
| 1 | 2 | 3 | 4 | 5 | 6 | *12* | 8 | **9** | **13** | *11* | | 10 | 7 | | | | | | | | | | | | | | | | | | | |
| 1 | | 3 | 4 | 5 | 6 | | 8 | *9* | *12* | 11 | | 10 | 7 | 2 | | | | | | | | | | | | | | | | | | |
| 1 | | 3 | 2 | 5 | *6* | **13** | 8 | **9** | ***14*** | 11 | *12* | 10 | ***7*** | 4 | | | | | | | | | | | | | | | | | | |
| 1 | | ***11*** | 2 | 5 | *12* | ***14*** | 8 | 9 | **13** | 7 | *6* | **10** | | 4 | 3 | | | | | | | | | | | | | | | | | |
| 1 | *12* | **11** | 2 | 5 | *6* | ***7*** | 8 | 9 | 10 | | | **13** | ***14*** | 4 | 3 | | | | | | | | | | | | | | | | | |
| 1 | 4 | 11 | 2 | 5 | *12* | | 8 | 9 | **10** | 7 | | ***14*** | ***13*** | | 3 | 6 | | | | | | | | | | | | | | | | |
| 1 | | 3 | 2 | 5 | | | 8 | ***9*** | | 11 | | 10 | | 4 | | | *6* | **7** | *12* | **13** | ***14*** | | | | | | | | | | | |
| 1 | | 3 | 2 | 5 | | | 8 | ***9*** | | 11 | | 10 | | 4 | | | *6* | **7** | *12* | **13** | ***14*** | | | | | | | | | | | |
| 1 | | 3 | 2 | 5 | 10 | *12* | 8 | ***9*** | | 11 | | | | 4 | | | **6** | *7* | **13** | | ***14*** | | | | | | | | | | | |
| 1 | | 3 | 2 | 5 | ***10*** | **7** | 8 | 9 | | 11 | | | | 4 | | | *6* | 13 | *12* | | ***14*** | | | | | | | | | | | |
| 1 | | 3 | 2 | 5 | 11 | 7 | **8** | *9* | | | | ***10*** | *12* | 6 | | | **13** | ***14*** | 4 | | | | | | | | | | | | | |
| 1 | | 3 | 2 | 5 | 11 | 7 | 8 | **9** | | *12* | | 10 | **13** | 6 | | | ***14*** | | ***4*** | | | | | | | | | | | | | |
| 1 | | 3 | 4 | | *12* | ***7*** | 8 | | | 11 | | *10* | 9 | 5 | | | **13** | ***14*** | **6** | | | 2 | | | | | | | | | | |
| 1 | | 3 | 4 | | 6 | **7** | 8 | *12* | | *11* | | 10 | 9 | 5 | | | | **13** | | | | 2 | | | | | | | | | | |
| 1 | | 3 | 2 | 5 | **6** | ***7*** | 8 | *12* | | 11 | | 10 | *9* | 4 | | | | ***14*** | **13** | | | | | | | | | | | | | |
| 1 | | 3 | 2 | 5 | | | 8 | *9* | | 11 | | 10 | 7 | 4 | | | 6 | *12* | | | | | | | | | | | | | | |
| 1 | *12* | 3 | 2 | 5 | | | 8 | | | 11 | | 10 | ***9*** | 4 | | | *6* | **7** | | **13** | | | ***14*** | | | | | | | | | |
| 1 | | *11* | 2 | 5 | | 7 | 8 | | | | | *12* | 9 | 4 | | | 6 | | | **13** | | | **10** | 3 | | | | | | | | |
| 1 | *12* | 3 | | 5 | | 9 | 8 | **13** | | **11** | | ***14*** | 7 | 4 | | | *6* | | | | | | 10 | | ***2*** | | | | | | | |
| 1 | *6* | 11 | *12* | 5 | | 9 | 8 | | | | | **13** | | 4 | | | | | | ***7*** | | | **10** | | 2 | 3 | ***14*** | | | | | |
| 1 | 4 | 3 | *12* | 5 | | 9 | 8 | | | 11 | | **13** | | 6 | | | | | | ***7*** | | | **10** | | *2* | | ***14*** | | | | | |
| 1 | 4 | 3 | | 5 | | 10 | 8 | | | 11 | | *12* | *9* | 6 | | | | | | **7** | | 2 | | | | | **13** | | | | | |
| 1 | 4 | 3 | | 5 | | *10* | 8 | | | **11** | | *12* | ***9*** | 6 | | | | **13** | | ***14*** | | 2 | | | | | 7 | | | | | |
| 1 | *4* | 11 | *12* | 5 | | 10 | 8 | | | | **13** | ***14*** | 9 | 6 | | | | | | | | | | ***3*** | **2** | | 7 | | | | | |
| 1 | *12* | 3 | 4 | 5 | **13** | 10 | **8** | | | | *6* | | 9 | | | | | 7 | | | | | | | 2 | | ***11*** | ***14*** | | | | |
| 1 | 8 | 11 | 4 | 5 | *12* | 10 | | | | | *6* | **13** | 9 | | **3** | | | *7* | | | | | | | 2 | | | ***14*** | | | | |
| 1 | *4* | 3 | | 5 | *12* | 11 | 8 | | | | 7 | 10 | | | | | | | | | | | | | 2 | | | **9** | 6 | **13** | | |
| 1 | ***4*** | 3 | | 5 | *12* | | 8 | | | **11** | *7* | 10 | **13** | | | | | | | | | | | | 2 | | | ***14*** | 6 | 9 | | |
| 1 | **4** | 3 | | 5 | *12* | | 8 | | **13** | | *11* | 10 | 7 | | | | | | | | ***14*** | | | | 2 | | | | 6 | ***9*** | | |
| 1 | 5 | 3 | 2 | | *12* | | 8 | | | | | 10 | **9** | | 4 | | 6 | ***7*** | *11* | | **13** | | | | | | ***14*** | | | | | |
| 1 | 4 | 3 | 2 | 5 | | 10 | ***8*** | | 9 | | | *12* | | | **13** | | **6** | | 7 | | *11* | | | | | | ***14*** | | | | | |
| 1 | 4 | 3 | 2 | 5 | 6 | *7* | | | **9** | | | 10 | | | 11 | | | *12* | 8 | | **13** | | | | | | | | | | | |
| 1 | 4 | 3 | 2 | 5 | 6 | *7* | *12* | | **10** | | | | 9 | | ***14*** | | **13** | | 8 | | | | | | | | ***11*** | | | | | |
| 1 | 4 | 3 | 2 | 5 | 6 | 11 | | | *10* | | | | ***9*** | | **13** | | | **7** | 8 | | *12* | | | | | | | | | | ***14*** | |
| 1 | 4 | 3 | 2 | 5 | 6 | *11* | | | 10 | | | | ***9*** | | **13** | | | **7** | 8 | | *12* | | | | | | | | | | ***14*** | |
| 1 | 4 | 3 | 2 | 5 | 6 | 11 | | | *10* | | | | *12* | | **13** | | | **7** | 8 | | ***14*** | | | | | | | | | | ***9*** | |
| 1 | 4 | 3 | 2 | 5 | 6 | | | 9 | *12* | 11 | | | **13** | | *7* | | | | 8 | | | | | | | | | | | | **10** | |
| 1 | 4 | 3 | 2 | 5 | 6 | | | *9* | **13** | ***11*** | | | *12* | | 7 | | | ***14*** | 8 | | | | | | | | | | | | **10** | |
| 1 | 2 | 3 | 4 | 5 | 6 | | | 9 | *10* | 11 | | | *12* | | 7 | | | | **8** | | | | | | **13** | | | | | | | |
| 1 | 2 | 3 | 4 | 5 | 6 | | | *9* | **10** | ***11*** | | | *12* | | | | | 7 | 8 | | | | | | **13** | | | | | | | ***14*** |
| 1 | 2 | 3 | | 5 | **6** | | | *12* | ***10*** | 11 | | | 9 | | **13** | | | | 8 | | | | | | 4 | *7* | | | | | | ***14*** |
| 1 | 4 | 3 | *12* | 5 | | **13** | | 9 | | | | | 11 | | 2 | | **6** | | ***8*** | 10 | | | | | *7* | | ***14*** | | | | | |
| 1 | 4 | 3 | *12* | 5 | | | *8* | 9 | | | | | ***11*** | | 2 | | | | | **13** | | | | | 7 | | 6 | | | | **10** | ***14*** |
| 1 | 4 | 11 | *12* | 5 | | | 8 | 9 | **13** | ***14*** | | | **7** | | 3 | | | | | | | | | | *2* | | ***6*** | | | | 10 | |
| 1 | 4 | 3 | 2 | 5 | *6* | | ***8*** | **9** | *12* | 11 | | | **13** | | 7 | | | | | | | | | | | | | | | | 10 | ***14*** |
| 46 | 28 | 46 | 33 | 43 | 22 | 24 | 34 | 22 | 12 | 26 | 6 | 18 | 24 | 22 | 13 | 1 | 11 | 11 | 16 | 4 | 1 | 4 | 4 | 2 | 13 | 2 | 6 | 1 | 3 | 2 | 6 | |
| | 4 | | 6 | | 9 | 5 | 1 | 4 | 9 | 2 | 3 | 12 | 12 | | 6 | | 4 | 9 | 5 | 6 | 10 | | 1 | | 2 | | 6 | 3 | | 1 | 2 | 4 |
| | | 2 | | 2 | 4 | | 5 | 5 | 4 | 1 | 1 | 2 | 7 | | 1 | | 1 | 1 | | 2 | | | 1 | | | | | | | | 3 | 1 |

| 1 Konstantopoulos | 16 Clark | 8 Humphreys | 23 Williams, D. | 5 Nelson | 22 Bullock | 7 Llewellyn | 15 Sweeney | 6 Proctor | 10 Boyd | 24 Butler | 12 Strachan | 14 Daly | 11 Williams, E. | 32 Collins | 18 Robson | 29 Jones | 4 Tinkler | 34 Maidens | 36 Turnbull | 25 Istead | 33 Foley | 20 Craddock | 37 McDonald | 19 Brackstone |
|---|---|---|---|---|---|---|---|---|---|---|---|---|---|---|---|---|---|---|---|---|---|---|---|---|
| 1 | *12* | 3 | 4 | 5 | *6* | | 8 | ***14*** | | 11 | | ***10*** | 9 | | | | | **7** | | **13** | | 2 | | |
| 1 | | 11 | 4 | *5* | | 10 | 8 | | | 7 | | | **13** | | | | **6** | | | *12* | | 2 | 9 | 3 |
| 2 | | 2 | 2 | 2 | 1 | 1 | 2 | | | 2 | | 1 | 1 | | | | 1 | 1 | | | | 2 | 1 | 1 |
| | 1 | | | | | | | 1 | | | | | 1 | | | | | | | 2 | | | | |
| | | | | 1 | | 1 | | | | 1 | | | | | | | | | | | | | | |

| 1 Konstantopoulos | 16 Clark | 8 Humphreys | 23 Williams, D. | 5 Nelson | 22 Bullock | 7 Llewellyn | 15 Sweeney | 6 Proctor | 10 Boyd | 24 Butler | 12 Strachan | 14 Daly | 11 Williams, E. | 32 Collins | 18 Robson | 29 Jones | 4 Tinkler | 34 Maidens | 36 Turnbull | 25 Istead | 33 Foley |
|---|---|---|---|---|---|---|---|---|---|---|---|---|---|---|---|---|---|---|---|---|---|
| 1 | | 11 | 4 | 5 | *12* | | 8 | **13** | **10** | 7 | 6 | *9* | | 2 | 3 | | | | | | |
| 1 | | 3 | 4 | 5 | | **13** | 8 | 9 | | 11 | | ***10*** | | 2 | | | *6* | | *12* | **7** | ***14*** |
| 2 | | 2 | 2 | 2 | | | 2 | 1 | 1 | 2 | 1 | 2 | | 2 | 1 | | 1 | | | 1 | |
| | | | | | 1 | 1 | | 1 | | | | | | | | | | | 1 | | 1 |
| | | | | | | | | 2 | | | | 2 | | | | | | | | | |

## League Table

| | P | W | D | L | F | A | Pts |
|---|---|---|---|---|---|---|---|
| Southend United | 46 | 23 | 13 | 10 | 72 | 43 | 82 |
| Colchester United | 46 | 22 | 13 | 11 | 58 | 40 | 79 |
| Brentford | 46 | 20 | 16 | 10 | 72 | 52 | 76 |
| Huddersfield Town | 46 | 19 | 16 | 11 | 72 | 59 | 73 |
| Barnsley | 46 | 18 | 18 | 10 | 62 | 44 | 72 |
| Swansea City | 46 | 18 | 17 | 11 | 78 | 55 | 71 |
| Nottingham Forest | 46 | 19 | 12 | 15 | 67 | 52 | 69 |
| Doncaster Rovers | 46 | 20 | 9 | 17 | 55 | 51 | 69 |
| Bristol City | 46 | 18 | 11 | 17 | 66 | 62 | 65 |
| Oldham Athletic | 46 | 18 | 11 | 17 | 58 | 60 | 65 |
| Bradford City | 46 | 14 | 19 | 13 | 51 | 49 | 61 |
| Scunthorpe United | 46 | 15 | 15 | 16 | 68 | 73 | 60 |
| Port Vale | 46 | 16 | 12 | 18 | 49 | 54 | 60 |
| Gillingham | 46 | 16 | 12 | 18 | 50 | 64 | 60 |
| Yeovil Town | 46 | 15 | 11 | 20 | 54 | 62 | 56 |
| Chesterfield | 46 | 14 | 14 | 18 | 63 | 73 | 56 |
| Bournemouth | 46 | 12 | 19 | 15 | 49 | 53 | 55 |
| Tranmere Rovers | 46 | 13 | 15 | 18 | 50 | 52 | 54 |
| Blackpool | 46 | 12 | 17 | 17 | 56 | 64 | 53 |
| Rotherham United | 46 | 12 | 16 | 18 | 52 | 62 | 52 |
| Hartlepool United | 46 | 11 | 17 | 18 | 44 | 59 | 50 |
| Milton Keynes Dons | 46 | 12 | 14 | 20 | 45 | 66 | 50 |
| Swindon Town | 46 | 11 | 15 | 20 | 46 | 65 | 48 |
| Walsall | 46 | 11 | 14 | 21 | 47 | 70 | 47 |

# 2006-07

## League Two

Manager: Danny Wilson

### Did you know that?

Mickey Barron played the last of his 374 games for the club on 30 March, a 3–0 home win against Chester City, before retiring and becoming reserve-team coach.

Following the 2–1 win at Accrington Stanley on 18 November, 'Pools did not lose a League game until the 2–1 reverse at Barnet on 7 April, a total of 24 games, of which 20 were won.

| Match No. | Date | Round | Venue | Opponents | Result | | Scorers | Attendance |
|---|---|---|---|---|---|---|---|---|
| 1 | Aug 5 | | (h) | Swindon Town | L | 0 - 1 | | 4,690 |
| 2 | 8 | | (a) | Macclesfield Town | D | 0 - 0 | | 1,843 |
| 3 | 12 | | (a) | Walsall | L | 0 - 2 | | 5,637 |
| 4 | 19 | | (h) | Torquay United | D | 1 - 1 | Bullock | 3,688 |
| 6 | 26 | | (a) | Hereford United | L | 1 - 3 | Brown | 3,156 |
| 7 | Sep 1 | | (h) | Boston United | W | 2 - 1 | Sweeney, Daly | 4,054 |
| 8 | 9 | | (a) | Milton Keynes Dons | D | 0 - 0 | | 5,630 |
| 9 | 12 | | (h) | Mansfield Town | W | 2 - 0 | Porter 2 | 3,899 |
| 10 | 16 | | (h) | Shrewsbury Town | L | 0 - 3 | | 4,291 |
| 12 | 23 | | (a) | Peterborough United | W | 5 - 3 | Liddle 2, Robson, Daly 2 | 3,916 |
| 13 | 26 | | (a) | Grimsby Town | W | 4 - 1 | Liddle, Daly 2, Porter | 3,486 |
| 14 | 30 | | (h) | Wrexham | W | 3 - 0 | Daly 3 | 4,452 |
| 15 | Oct 6 | | (a) | Lincoln City | L | 0 - 2 | | 5,532 |
| 16 | 14 | | (h) | Stockport County | D | 1 - 1 | Robson | 4,372 |
| 18 | 20 | | (a) | Chester City | L | 1 - 2 | Porter | 2,580 |
| 19 | 28 | | (h) | Darlington | D | 0 - 0 | | 7,458 |
| 21 | Nov 4 | | (h) | Barnet | L | 0 - 1 | | 3,778 |
| 23 | 18 | | (a) | Accrington Stanley | W | 2 - 1 | E.Williams, Humphreys | 1,787 |
| 25 | 25 | | (h) | Wycombe Wanderers | W | 2 - 0 | Duffy 2 | 3,711 |
| 27 | Dec 5 | | (a) | Notts County | W | 1 - 0 | Monkhouse | 3,546 |
| 28 | 9 | | (a) | Bristol Rovers | W | 2 - 0 | Clark, Duffy | 4,906 |
| 29 | 15 | | (h) | Rochdale | W | 1 - 0 | Duffy | 3,659 |
| 30 | 23 | | (a) | Bury | W | 1 - 0 | Sweeney | 2,839 |
| 31 | 26 | | (h) | Grimsby Town | W | 2 - 0 | Daly, Monkhouse | 5,290 |
| 32 | 30 | | (h) | Peterborough United | W | 1 - 0 | Duffy | 4,654 |
| 33 | Jan 1 | | (a) | Mansfield Town | W | 1 - 0 | Monkhouse | 3,531 |
| 34 | 6 | | (a) | Shrewsbury Town | D | 1 - 1 | Brown | 4,334 |
| 35 | 13 | | (h) | Milton Keynes Dons | W | 1 - 0 | Sweeney | 4,851 |
| 36 | 20 | | (a) | Wrexham | D | 1 - 1 | Barker | 3,828 |
| 37 | 27 | | (h) | Bury | W | 2 - 0 | Brown, Sweeney | 4,901 |
| 38 | Feb 3 | | (a) | Swindon Town | W | 1 - 0 | Monkhouse | 6,841 |
| 39 | 10 | | (h) | Walsall | W | 3 - 1 | Nelson, Humphreys, Barker | 5,847 |
| 40 | 17 | | (a) | Torquay United | W | 1 - 0 | E.Williams | 2,194 |
| 41 | 20 | | (h) | Macclesfield Town | W | 3 - 2 | Brown, Barker, Morley (o.g.) | 5,242 |
| 42 | 24 | | (a) | Boston United | W | 1 - 0 | Humphreys | 2,120 |
| 43 | Mar 3 | | (h) | Hereford United | W | 3 - 2 | Clark, Brown, E.Williams | 5,535 |
| 44 | 9 | | (h) | Lincoln City | D | 1 - 1 | Barker (pen) | 6,903 |
| 45 | 17 | | (a) | Stockport County | D | 3 - 3 | Monkhouse, Barker 2 (1 pen) | 7,860 |
| 46 | 25 | | (a) | Darlington | W | 3 - 0 | Williams 2, Monkhouse | 10,121 |
| 47 | 30 | | (h) | Chester City | W | 3 - 0 | Barker, Monkhouse, Clark | 6,059 |
| 48 | Apr 7 | | (a) | Barnet | L | 1 - 2 | E.Williams | 2,906 |
| 49 | 9 | | (h) | Accrington Stanley | W | 1 - 0 | Barker (pen) | 5,867 |
| 50 | 14 | | (a) | Wycombe Wanderers | W | 1 - 0 | Barker | 5,540 |
| 51 | 20 | | (h) | Notts County | D | 1 - 1 | Brown | 6,174 |
| 52 | 27 | | (a) | Rochdale | L | 0 - 2 | | 5,846 |
| 53 | May 5 | | (h) | Bristol Rovers | L | 1 - 2 | Porter | 7,629 |

Final Position: 2nd in League Two - Promoted

Apps.
Sub.Apps.
1 own goal — Goals

**FA Cup**

| Match No. | Date | Round | Venue | Opponents | Result | | Scorers | Attendance |
|---|---|---|---|---|---|---|---|---|
| 22 | Nov 11 | R1 | (a) | Rochdale | D | 1 - 1 | Brown | 2,098 |
| 24 | 20 | R1r | (h) | Rochdale | W | 0 - 0* | | 2,788 |
| 26 | Dec 2 | R2 | (a) | Macclesfield Town | L | 1 - 2 | Regan (o.g.) | 1,992 |

* After extra-time. Won 4 - 2 on penalties.

Apps.
Sub.Apps.
1 own goal — Goals

**League Cup**

| Match No. | Date | Round | Venue | Opponents | Result | | Scorers | Attendance |
|---|---|---|---|---|---|---|---|---|
| 5 | Aug 22 | R1 | (a) | Burnley | W | 1 - 0 | Porter | 3,853 |
| 11 | Sep 19 | R2 | (a) | Hull City | L | 0 - 0* | | 6,392 |

* After extra-time. Lost 2 - 3 on penalties.

Apps.
Sub.Apps.
Goals

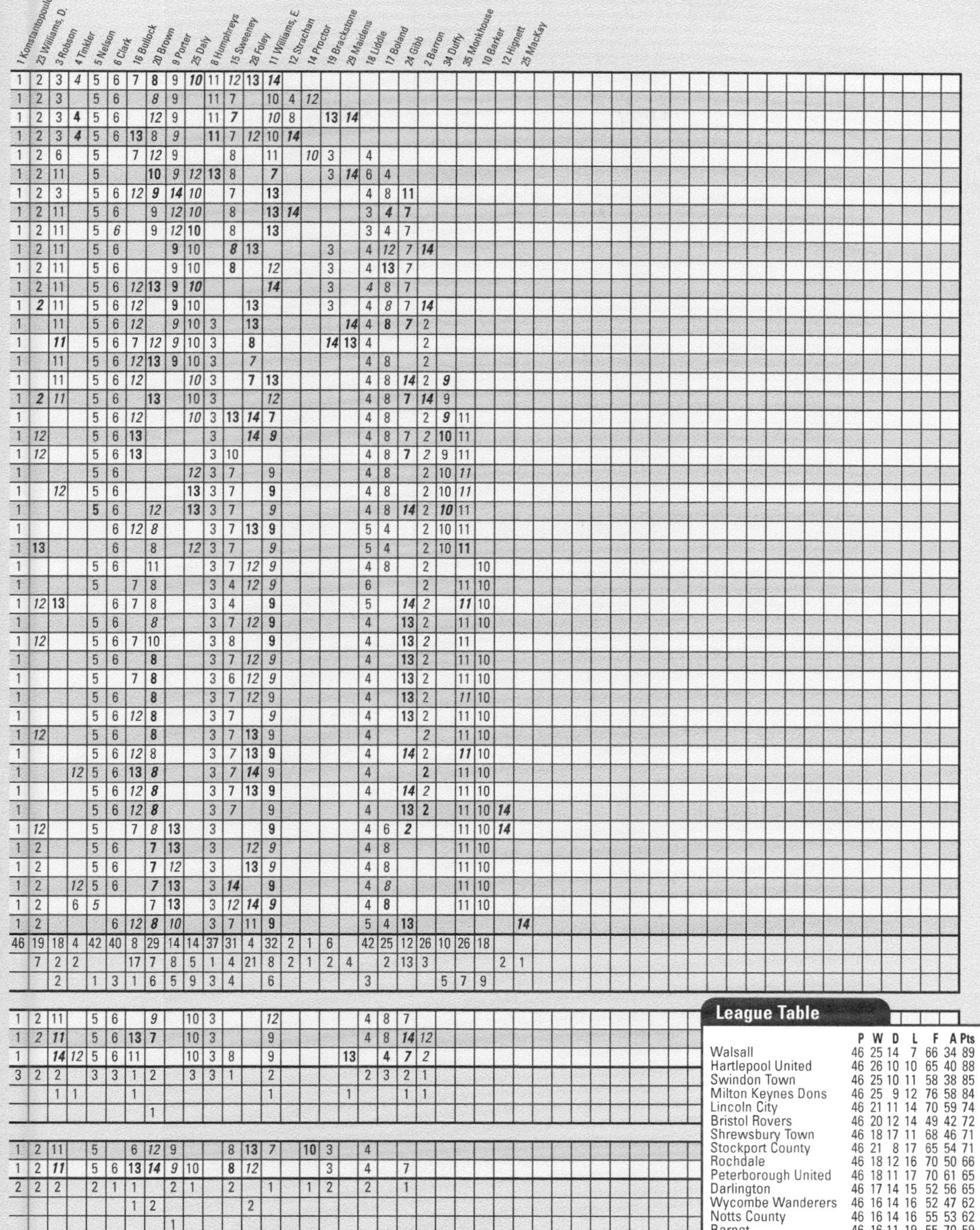

| 1 Konstantopoulos | 23 Williams, D. | 3 Robson | 4 Tinkler | 5 Nelson | 6 Clark | 16 Bullock | 20 Brown | 9 Porter | 25 Daly | 8 Humphreys | 15 Sweeney | 28 Foley | 11 Williams, E. | 12 Strachan | 14 Proctor | 19 Brackstone | 29 Maidens | 18 Liddle | 17 Boland | 24 Gibb | 2 Barron | 34 Duffy | 35 Monkhouse | 10 Barker | 12 Hignett | 25 MacKay |
|---|---|---|---|---|---|---|---|---|---|---|---|---|---|---|---|---|---|---|---|---|---|---|---|---|---|---|
| 1 | 2 | 3 | *4* | 5 | 6 | 7 | **8** | 9 | ***10*** | 11 | *12* | **13** | ***14*** | | | | | | | | | | | | | |
| 1 | 2 | 3 | | 5 | 6 | | *8* | 9 | | 11 | 7 | | 10 | 4 | *12* | | | | | | | | | | | |
| 1 | 2 | 3 | **4** | 5 | 6 | | *12* | 9 | | 11 | ***7*** | | *10* | 8 | | **13** | ***14*** | | | | | | | | | |
| 1 | 2 | 3 | ***4*** | 5 | 6 | **13** | 8 | *9* | | **11** | 7 | *12* | 10 | ***14*** | | | | | | | | | | | | |
| 1 | 2 | 6 | | 5 | | 7 | *12* | 9 | | | 8 | | 11 | | *10* | 3 | | 4 | | | | | | | | |
| 1 | 2 | 11 | | 5 | | | **10** | *9* | *12* | **13** | 8 | | ***7*** | | | 3 | ***14*** | 6 | 4 | | | | | | | |
| 1 | 2 | 3 | | 5 | 6 | *12* | ***9*** | ***14*** | *10* | | 7 | | **13** | | | | | 4 | 8 | **11** | | | | | | |
| 1 | 2 | 11 | | 5 | 6 | | 9 | *12* | *10* | | 8 | | **13** | ***14*** | | | | 3 | ***4*** | **7** | | | | | | |
| 1 | 2 | 11 | | 5 | *6* | | 9 | *12* | **10** | | 8 | | **13** | | | | | 3 | 4 | 7 | | | | | | |
| 1 | 2 | 11 | | 5 | 6 | | | **9** | 10 | | ***8*** | 13 | | | | 3 | | 4 | *12* | *7* | ***14*** | | | | | |
| 1 | 2 | 11 | | 5 | 6 | | | 9 | 10 | | **8** | | *12* | | | 3 | | 4 | **13** | *7* | | | | | | |
| 1 | 2 | 11 | | 5 | 6 | *12* | **13** | **9** | ***10*** | | | | ***14*** | | | 3 | | *4* | 8 | 7 | | | | | | |
| 1 | ***2*** | 11 | | 5 | 6 | *12* | | **9** | 10 | | | 13 | | | | 3 | | 4 | *8* | 7 | ***14*** | | | | | |
| 1 | | 11 | | 5 | 6 | *12* | | *9* | 10 | 3 | | 13 | | | | | ***14*** | 4 | **8** | ***7*** | 2 | | | | | |
| 1 | | ***11*** | | 5 | 6 | 7 | *12* | *9* | 10 | 3 | | **8** | | | | ***14*** | 13 | 4 | | | 2 | | | | | |
| 1 | | 11 | | 5 | 6 | *12* | **13** | **9** | 10 | 3 | | *7* | | | | | | 4 | 8 | | 2 | | | | | |
| 1 | | 11 | | 5 | 6 | *12* | | | *10* | 3 | | **7** | **13** | | | | | 4 | 8 | ***14*** | 2 | ***9*** | | | | |
| 1 | ***2*** | *11* | | 5 | 6 | | **13** | | 10 | 3 | | | *12* | | | | | 4 | 8 | **7** | ***14*** | 9 | | | | |
| 1 | | | | 5 | 6 | *12* | | | *10* | 3 | **13** | ***14*** | **7** | | | | | 4 | 8 | | 2 | ***9*** | 11 | | | |
| 1 | *12* | | | 5 | 6 | **13** | | | | 3 | | ***14*** | ***9*** | | | | | 4 | 8 | 7 | *2* | **10** | 11 | | | |
| 1 | *12* | | | 5 | 6 | **13** | | | | 3 | 10 | | | | | | | 4 | 8 | **7** | *2* | 9 | 11 | | | |
| 1 | | | | 5 | 6 | | | | *12* | 3 | 7 | | 9 | | | | | 4 | 8 | | 2 | 10 | *11* | | | |
| 1 | | *12* | | 5 | 6 | | | | **13** | 3 | 7 | | **9** | | | | | 4 | 8 | | 2 | 10 | *11* | | | |
| 1 | | | | **5** | 6 | | *12* | | **13** | 3 | 7 | | *9* | | | | | 4 | 8 | ***14*** | 2 | ***10*** | 11 | | | |
| 1 | | | | | 6 | *12* | *8* | | | 3 | 7 | **13** | **9** | | | | | 5 | 4 | | 2 | 10 | 11 | | | |
| 1 | **13** | | | | 6 | | 8 | | *12* | 3 | 7 | | *9* | | | | | 5 | 4 | | 2 | 10 | **11** | | | |
| 1 | | | | 5 | 6 | | 11 | | | 3 | 7 | *12* | *9* | | | | | 4 | 8 | | 2 | | | 10 | | |
| 1 | | | | 5 | | 7 | 8 | | | 3 | 4 | *12* | *9* | | | | | 6 | | | 2 | | 11 | 10 | | |
| 1 | *12* | **13** | | | 6 | 7 | 8 | | | 3 | 4 | | **9** | | | | | 5 | | ***14*** | *2* | | ***11*** | 10 | | |
| 1 | | | | 5 | 6 | | *8* | | | 3 | 7 | *12* | **9** | | | | | 4 | | **13** | 2 | | 11 | 10 | | |
| 1 | *12* | | | 5 | 6 | 7 | 10 | | | 3 | 8 | | **9** | | | | | 4 | | **13** | *2* | | 11 | | | |
| 1 | | | | 5 | 6 | | **8** | | | 3 | 7 | *12* | *9* | | | | | 4 | | **13** | 2 | | 11 | 10 | | |
| 1 | | | | 5 | | 7 | **8** | | | 3 | 6 | *12* | *9* | | | | | 4 | | **13** | 2 | | 11 | 10 | | |
| 1 | | | | 5 | 6 | | **8** | | | 3 | 7 | *12* | 9 | | | | | 4 | | **13** | 2 | | *11* | 10 | | |
| 1 | | | | 5 | 6 | *12* | **8** | | | 3 | 7 | | *9* | | | | | 4 | | **13** | 2 | | 11 | 10 | | |
| 1 | *12* | | | 5 | 6 | | **8** | | | 3 | 7 | **13** | 9 | | | | | 4 | | | *2* | | 11 | 10 | | |
| 1 | | | | 5 | 6 | *12* | 8 | | | 3 | 7 | **13** | **9** | | | | | 4 | | ***14*** | 2 | | ***11*** | 10 | | |
| 1 | | | *12* | 5 | 6 | **13** | ***8*** | | | 3 | *7* | ***14*** | 9 | | | | | 4 | | | **2** | | 11 | 10 | | |
| 1 | | | | 5 | 6 | *12* | ***8*** | | | 3 | 7 | **13** | **9** | | | | | 4 | | ***14*** | *2* | | 11 | 10 | | |
| 1 | | | | 5 | 6 | *12* | ***8*** | | | 3 | 7 | | 9 | | | | | 4 | | **13** | **2** | | 11 | 10 | ***14*** | |
| 1 | *12* | | | 5 | | 7 | *8* | **13** | | 3 | | | **9** | | | | | 4 | 6 | ***2*** | | | 11 | 10 | ***14*** | |
| 1 | 2 | | | 5 | 6 | | **7** | **13** | | 3 | | *12* | *9* | | | | | 4 | 8 | | | | 11 | 10 | | |
| 1 | 2 | | | 5 | 6 | | **7** | *12* | | 3 | | **13** | *9* | | | | | 4 | 8 | | | | 11 | 10 | | |
| 1 | 2 | | *12* | 5 | 6 | | ***7*** | **13** | | 3 | ***14*** | | **9** | | | | | 4 | *8* | | | | 11 | 10 | | |
| 1 | 2 | | 6 | *5* | | | 7 | **13** | | 3 | *12* | ***14*** | ***9*** | | | | | 4 | **8** | | | | 11 | 10 | | |
| 1 | 2 | | | | 6 | *12* | ***8*** | *10* | | 3 | 7 | 11 | **9** | | | | | 5 | 4 | **13** | | | | | | ***14*** |
| 46 | 19 | 18 | 4 | 42 | 40 | 8 | 29 | 14 | 14 | 37 | 31 | 4 | 32 | 2 | 1 | 6 | | 42 | 25 | 12 | 26 | 10 | 26 | 18 | | |
| | 7 | 2 | 2 | | | 17 | 7 | 8 | 5 | 1 | 4 | 21 | 8 | 2 | 1 | 2 | 4 | | 2 | 13 | 3 | | | | 2 | 1 |
| | | 2 | | 1 | 3 | 1 | 6 | 5 | 9 | 3 | 4 | | 6 | | | | | 3 | | | | 5 | 7 | 9 | | |

| 1 Konstantopoulos | 23 Williams, D. | 3 Robson | 4 Tinkler | 5 Nelson | 6 Clark | 16 Bullock | 20 Brown | 9 Porter | 25 Daly | 8 Humphreys | 15 Sweeney | 28 Foley | 11 Williams, E. | 12 Strachan | 14 Proctor | 19 Brackstone | 29 Maidens | 18 Liddle | 17 Boland | 24 Gibb | 2 Barron | 34 Duffy | 35 Monkhouse | 10 Barker | 12 Hignett | 25 MacKay |
|---|---|---|---|---|---|---|---|---|---|---|---|---|---|---|---|---|---|---|---|---|---|---|---|---|---|---|
| 1 | 2 | 11 | | 5 | 6 | | *9* | | 10 | 3 | | | *12* | | | | | 4 | 8 | 7 | | | | | | |
| 1 | *2* | ***11*** | | 5 | 6 | **13** | ***7*** | | 10 | 3 | | | 9 | | | | | 4 | 8 | ***14*** | *12* | | | | | |
| 1 | | ***14*** | *12* | 5 | 6 | 11 | | | 10 | 3 | 8 | | 9 | | | | **13** | | **4** | ***7*** | *2* | | | | | |
| 3 | 2 | 2 | | 3 | 3 | 1 | 2 | | 3 | 3 | 1 | | 2 | | | | | 2 | 3 | 2 | 1 | | | | | |
| | | 1 | 1 | | | 1 | | | | | | | 1 | | | | 1 | | | 1 | 1 | | | | | |
| | | | | | | | 1 | | | | | | | | | | | | | | | | | | | |

| 1 Konstantopoulos | 23 Williams, D. | 3 Robson | 4 Tinkler | 5 Nelson | 6 Clark | 16 Bullock | 20 Brown | 9 Porter | 25 Daly | 8 Humphreys | 15 Sweeney | 28 Foley | 11 Williams, E. | 12 Strachan | 14 Proctor | 19 Brackstone | 29 Maidens | 18 Liddle | 17 Boland | 24 Gibb | 2 Barron | 34 Duffy | 35 Monkhouse | 10 Barker | 12 Hignett | 25 MacKay |
|---|---|---|---|---|---|---|---|---|---|---|---|---|---|---|---|---|---|---|---|---|---|---|---|---|---|---|
| 1 | 2 | 11 | | 5 | | 6 | *12* | 9 | | | 8 | **13** | *7* | | **10** | 3 | | 4 | | | | | | | | |
| 1 | 2 | ***11*** | | 5 | 6 | **13** | ***14*** | *9* | 10 | | **8** | *12* | | | | 3 | | 4 | | 7 | | | | | | |
| 2 | 2 | 2 | | 2 | 1 | 1 | | 2 | 1 | | 2 | | 1 | | 1 | 2 | | 2 | | 1 | | | | | | |
| | | | | | | 1 | 2 | | | | | 2 | | | | | | | | | | | | | | |
| | | | | | | | | 1 | | | | | | | | | | | | | | | | | | |

## League Table

| | P | W | D | L | F | A | Pts |
|---|---|---|---|---|---|---|---|
| Walsall | 46 | 25 | 14 | 7 | 66 | 34 | 89 |
| Hartlepool United | 46 | 26 | 10 | 10 | 65 | 40 | 88 |
| Swindon Town | 46 | 25 | 10 | 11 | 58 | 38 | 85 |
| Milton Keynes Dons | 46 | 25 | 9 | 12 | 76 | 58 | 84 |
| Lincoln City | 46 | 21 | 11 | 14 | 70 | 59 | 74 |
| Bristol Rovers | 46 | 20 | 12 | 14 | 49 | 42 | 72 |
| Shrewsbury Town | 46 | 18 | 17 | 11 | 68 | 46 | 71 |
| Stockport County | 46 | 21 | 8 | 17 | 65 | 54 | 71 |
| Rochdale | 46 | 18 | 12 | 16 | 70 | 50 | 66 |
| Peterborough United | 46 | 18 | 11 | 17 | 70 | 61 | 65 |
| Darlington | 46 | 17 | 14 | 15 | 52 | 56 | 65 |
| Wycombe Wanderers | 46 | 16 | 14 | 16 | 52 | 47 | 62 |
| Notts County | 46 | 16 | 14 | 16 | 55 | 53 | 62 |
| Barnet | 46 | 16 | 11 | 19 | 55 | 70 | 59 |
| Grimsby Town | 46 | 17 | 8 | 21 | 57 | 73 | 59 |
| Hereford United | 46 | 14 | 13 | 19 | 45 | 53 | 55 |
| Mansfield Town | 46 | 14 | 12 | 20 | 58 | 63 | 54 |
| Chester City | 46 | 13 | 14 | 19 | 40 | 48 | 53 |
| Wrexham | 46 | 13 | 12 | 21 | 43 | 65 | 51 |
| Accrington Stanley | 46 | 13 | 11 | 22 | 70 | 81 | 50 |
| Bury | 46 | 13 | 11 | 22 | 46 | 61 | 50 |
| Macclesfield Town | 46 | 12 | 12 | 22 | 55 | 77 | 48 |
| Boston United | 46 | 12 | 10 | 24 | 51 | 80 | 46 |
| Torquay United | 46 | 7 | 14 | 25 | 36 | 63 | 35 |

# 2007-08

## League One

Manager: Danny Wilson

### Did you know that?

Joel Porter became the first substitute in 'Pools' history to score a hat-trick when he netted a treble in the 5–2 win against Lincoln City in the Johnstone's Paint Trophy.

Former Hartlepool United player Paul Bielby, who made 107 appearances, scoring 11 goals, between 1975 and 1978, was awarded an MBE in the New Year's Honours list for services to Youth Football Development.

| Match No. | Date | Round | Venue | Opponents | Result | | Scorers | Attendance |
|---|---|---|---|---|---|---|---|---|
| 1 | Aug 11 | | (a) | Luton Town | L | 1 - 2 | Barker (pen) | 6,013 |
| 3 | 18 | | (h) | Doncaster Rovers | W | 2 - 1 | Antwi-Birago, Barker (pen) | 5,544 |
| 4 | 25 | | (a) | Port Vale | W | 2 - 0 | Robson, Brown | 3,978 |
| 6 | Sep 1 | | (h) | Oldham Athletic | W | 4 - 1 | Moore, Brown, Barker (pen), Porter | 5,015 |
| 8 | 8 | | (a) | Leeds United | L | 0 - 2 | | 26,877 |
| 9 | 15 | | (h) | Swindon Town | D | 1 - 1 | Porter | 4,943 |
| 10 | 22 | | (a) | Leyton Orient | W | 4 - 2 | Moore 2, Brown, Monkhouse | 5,325 |
| 11 | 29 | | (h) | Walsall | L | 0 - 1 | | 4,948 |
| 12 | Oct 2 | | (h) | Carlisle United | D | 2 - 2 | Barker, Mackay | 5,359 |
| 13 | 6 | | (a) | Nottingham Forest | L | 1 - 2 | Barker | 17,520 |
| 15 | 12 | | (h) | Bristol Rovers | W | 1 - 0 | Brown | 4,963 |
| 16 | 27 | | (h) | Brighton & Hove Albion | L | 1 - 2 | Barker (pen) | 5,619 |
| 17 | Nov 3 | | (a) | Millwall | W | 1 - 0 | Sweeney | 7,731 |
| 18 | 6 | | (a) | Huddersfield Town | L | 0 - 2 | | 8,154 |
| 21 | 18 | | (h) | Bournemouth | D | 1 - 1 | Moore | 3,496 |
| 22 | 24 | | (a) | Gillingham | L | 1 - 2 | Brown | 5,488 |
| 23 | 27 | | (a) | Swansea City | L | 0 - 1 | | 11,421 |
| 25 | Dec 4 | | (h) | Tranmere Rovers | W | 3 - 1 | Liddle, Brown, Porter | 3,583 |
| 26 | 8 | | (a) | Yeovil Town | L | 1 - 3 | Mackay | 4,694 |
| 27 | 15 | | (h) | Crewe Alexandra | W | 3 - 0 | Nelson, Barker 2 (1 pen) | 3,915 |
| 28 | 22 | | (a) | Swindon Town | L | 1 - 2 | Moore | 5,875 |
| 29 | 26 | | (h) | Leeds United | D | 1 - 1 | Nelson | 7,784 |
| 30 | 29 | | (h) | Leyton Orient | D | 1 - 1 | Moore | 4,379 |
| 31 | Jan 1 | | (a) | Carlisle United | L | 2 - 4 | Humphreys 2 | 7,496 |
| 32 | 12 | | (a) | Northampton Town | D | 1 - 1 | Clark | 4,639 |
| 33 | 18 | | (h) | Cheltenham Town | L | 0 - 2 | | 4,120 |
| 34 | 22 | | (h) | Southend United | W | 4 - 3 | Barker (pen), Brown 2, Sweeney | 3,217 |
| 35 | 29 | | (a) | Doncaster Rovers | L | 0 - 2 | | 6,442 |
| 36 | Feb 2 | | (h) | Luton Town | W | 4 - 0 | Barker 2 (1 pen), Thompson, Porter | 3,913 |
| 37 | 9 | | (a) | Southend United | L | 1 - 2 | Sweeney | 7,436 |
| 38 | 12 | | (h) | Port Vale | W | 3 - 2 | Barker 2, Sweeney | 3,630 |
| 39 | 16 | | (a) | Cheltenham Town | D | 1 - 1 | Porter | 3,583 |
| 40 | 22 | | (h) | Northampton Town | L | 0 - 1 | | 3,945 |
| 41 | Mar 1 | | (a) | Bournemouth | L | 0 - 2 | | 3,984 |
| 42 | 4 | | (a) | Oldham Athletic | W | 1 - 0 | Mackay | 3,765 |
| 43 | 8 | | (h) | Gillingham | W | 4 - 0 | Monkhouse, Porter, Collins, McCunnie | 4,055 |
| 44 | 11 | | (h) | Huddersfield Town | W | 2 - 1 | Collins, Mackay | 3,650 |
| 45 | 15 | | (a) | Tranmere Rovers | L | 1 - 3 | Humphreys | 5,608 |
| 46 | 22 | | (a) | Crewe Alexandra | L | 1 - 3 | Porter | 4,412 |
| 47 | 24 | | (h) | Yeovil Town | W | 2 - 0 | Brown, Porter | 3,808 |
| 48 | 29 | | (h) | Swansea City | L | 1 - 3 | Liddle | 4,484 |
| 49 | Apr 5 | | (a) | Bristol Rovers | D | 0 - 0 | | 5,526 |
| 50 | 12 | | (h) | Millwall | L | 0 - 1 | | 4,077 |
| 51 | 19 | | (a) | Brighton & Hove Albion | L | 1 - 2 | Porter | 6,178 |
| 52 | 26 | | (h) | Nottingham Forest | L | 0 - 1 | | 5,206 |
| 53 | May 3 | | (a) | Walsall | D | 2 - 2 | Mackay, Brown | 5,021 |

Final Position: 15th in League One

Apps.
Sub.Apps.
Goals

**FA Cup**

| Match No. | Date | Round | Venue | Opponents | Result | | Scorers | Attendance |
|---|---|---|---|---|---|---|---|---|
| 19 | Nov 11 | R1 | (a) | Gainsborough Trinity | W | 6 - 0 | Barker 2, Liddle, Moore, Brown, Porter | 2,402 |
| 24 | Dec 1 | R2 | (a) | Hereford United | L | 0 - 2 | | 3,801 |

Apps.
Sub.Apps.
Goals

**League Cup**

| Match No. | Date | Round | Venue | Opponents | Result | | Scorers | Attendance |
|---|---|---|---|---|---|---|---|---|
| 2 | Aug 14 | R1 | (a) | Scunthorpe United | W | 2 - 1 | Foley 2 | 2,965 |
| 5 | 28 | R2 | (a) | Sheffield Wednesday | L | 1 - 2* | Moore | 8,751 |

* After extra-time

Apps.
Sub.Apps.
Goals

| 21 Lee-Barratt | 2 McCunnie | 20 Antwi-Birago | 3 Elliott | 5 Nelson | 7 Liddle | 4 Boland | 14 Brown | 9 Barker | 22 Moore | 8 Humphreys | 10 Porter | 15 Sweeney | 1 Budtz | 19 Robson | 6 Clark | 17 Foley | 11 Monkhouse | 18 Gibb | 24 Mackay | 27 Coles | 26 Nolan | 16 Bullock | 28 Thompson | 23 Turnbull | 27 Collins | 16 Lee | 22 Craddock |
|---|---|---|---|---|---|---|---|---|---|---|---|---|---|---|---|---|---|---|---|---|---|---|---|---|---|---|---|
| 1 | 2 | 3 | 4 | 5 | 6 | **7** | 8 | 9 | 10 | *11* | *12* | **13** | | | | | | | | | | | | | | | |
| | 2 | 3 | 4 | 5 | 6 | 7 | 8 | 9 | *10* | | *12* | | 1 | 11 | **13** | | | | | | | | | | | | |
| | 2 | 6 | | 5 | 4 | 7 | 8 | ***9*** | **10** | 3 | ***14*** | *12* | 1 | 11 | | **13** | | | | | | | | | | | |
| | 2 | 6 | 3 | 5 | 4 | | **7** | 9 | 10 | *12* | **13** | *8* | 1 | | | ***14*** | ***11*** | | | | | | | | | | |
| | 2 | 6 | *3* | 5 | 4 | | 8 | 9 | **10** | 11 | **13** | | 1 | | | | 7 | *12* | | | | | | | | | |
| | 2 | 6 | *3* | 5 | 4 | | 8 | 9 | **10** | 11 | **13** | | 1 | | ***14*** | | 7 | *12* | | | | | | | | | |
| | 2 | 6 | | 5 | 4 | **7** | *8* | ***9*** | 10 | 3 | *12* | | 1 | | **13** | | 11 | | ***14*** | | | | | | | | |
| | 2 | 6 | | 5 | 4 | 7 | 8 | 9 | | 3 | **10** | *12* | 1 | | ***14*** | | ***11*** | | **13** | | | | | | | | |
| | 2 | 6 | | 5 | 4 | 7 | ***8*** | 9 | **10** | 3 | *12* | | 1 | **13** | | *11* | | | ***14*** | | | | | | | | |
| | *12* | 6 | | 5 | 4 | 7 | **8** | 9 | 10 | 3 | ***14*** | | 1 | | | **13** | ***11*** | | | *2* | | | | | | | |
| | **13** | | | 5 | 4 | 7 | *8* | 9 | 10 | 3 | **11** | | 1 | | 6 | *12* | | | | 2 | | | | | | | |
| | ***3*** | | | 5 | 4 | 7 | 8 | 9 | | 11 | **10** | ***14*** | 1 | | *6* | | *12* | | **13** | 2 | | | | | | | |
| | | | | 5 | 6 | | 8 | 9 | *12* | 3 | *10* | 7 | 1 | | 4 | | 11 | 2 | | | | | | | | | |
| | | | | 5 | 6 | | ***7*** | 9 | **13** | 3 | *10* | 8 | 1 | | 4 | ***14*** | **11** | 2 | *12* | | | | | | | | |
| | 2 | | | 5 | | **8** | 11 | 9 | 10 | 3 | 7 | **13** | 1 | | 6 | *12* | | 4 | | | | | | | | | |
| | 7 | 6 | | 5 | | 8 | 11 | 9 | **10** | 3 | **13** | | 1 | | | *12* | | *4* | | | 2 | | | | | | |
| | 7 | 6 | | 5 | | **4** | 11 | *9* | **10** | 3 | *12* | 8 | 1 | | | **13** | | | | | 2 | | | | | | |
| | | 6 | | 5 | 4 | | ***7*** | *12* | 10 | 3 | *9* | 8 | 1 | **13** | | ***14*** | **11** | | | | 2 | | | | | | |
| | | 6 | 3 | 5 | 4 | | 7 | *12* | *10* | **11** | | 8 | 1 | | | **13** | | | 9 | | 2 | | | | | | |
| | | 6 | 3 | 5 | **4** | 8 | ***7*** | *12* | 10 | 11 | | **13** | 1 | | | ***14*** | | | *9* | | 2 | | | | | | |
| | | 3 | 4 | 5 | 6 | **8** | ***7*** | *12* | 10 | 11 | | **13** | 1 | | | ***14*** | | | *9* | | 2 | | | | | | |
| | | 6 | 3 | 5 | 4 | 7 | *8* | 9 | 10 | 11 | | *12* | 1 | | | | | | | | 2 | | | | | | |
| | | 6 | 3 | 5 | 4 | | | 9 | 10 | 11 | | 8 | 1 | | | **7** | | | **13** | | *2* | *12* | | | | | |
| | | 6 | 3 | 5 | 4 | | *12* | 9 | 10 | **11** | | 8 | 1 | **13** | | *7* | | | | | 2 | | | | | | |
| 1 | | | **3** | 5 | 4 | 8 | *12* | ***9*** | 10 | 11 | ***14*** | | | **13** | 6 | *7* | | | | | 2 | | | | | | |
| 1 | | | *3* | 5 | 4 | **8** | 7 | 9 | 10 | 11 | **13** | | | *12* | 6 | | | | | | 2 | | | | | | |
| 1 | 2 | 6 | | 5 | 4 | | 7 | 9 | | 3 | 10 | *12* | | 11 | | | | | | | | | *8* | | | | |
| 1 | ***7*** | 6 | | 5 | 4 | | 8 | *12* | | 3 | **10** | 2 | | | | 9 | | | **13** | | | | *11* | ***14*** | | | |
| | ***14*** | | | 5 | 4 | ***8*** | 7 | 9 | | 3 | 10 | 2 | 1 | | | *12* | **13** | | | | | | **11** | | 6 | | |
| | | 2 | | 5 | 4 | ***8*** | | 9 | | 3 | **10** | 7 | 1 | | | *12* | ***14*** | | **13** | | | | *11* | | 6 | | |
| | **13** | 6 | | 5 | 4 | ***8*** | | 9 | | *3* | 10 | 2 | 1 | *12* | | 7 | | | ***14*** | | | | 11 | | | | |
| | **13** | 6 | | | 4 | **8** | | 9 | | 3 | 10 | 2 | 1 | | | 7 | | | | | | | *11* | | | 5 | *12* |
| | *12* | 2 | | 5 | 6 | **8** | | 9 | | 3 | 10 | 7 | 1 | | | **13** | | | | | | | ***11*** | | | 4 | ***14*** |
| 1 | | 2 | | 5 | 6 | *8* | | 9 | | 3 | ***14*** | 7 | | | | ***11*** | *12* | | **13** | | | | | | | 4 | **10** |
| 1 | 2 | | | 5 | 6 | 8 | | *10* | | 3 | *12* | 7 | | | | **13** | 11 | | **9** | | | | | | 4 | | |
| 1 | 2 | | ***14*** | 5 | 6 | *8* | | | | ***3*** | 10 | 7 | | **13** | | *12* | **11** | | 9 | | | | | | 4 | | |
| 1 | 2 | | | 5 | 6 | 8 | | | | 3 | 10 | 7 | | | | | 11 | | 9 | | | | | | 4 | | |
| 1 | 2 | | | 5 | 6 | 8 | | | | 3 | ***10*** | 7 | | | *12* | ***14*** | 11 | | **9** | | | | | | *4* | | **13** |
| 1 | | 6 | | 5 | 4 | *8* | **13** | | | ***3*** | 10 | 7 | | ***14*** | | *12* | 11 | | **9** | | | | | | 2 | | |
| 1 | 2 | | | *12* | 6 | ***8*** | **13** | **9** | | 3 | 10 | 7 | | | 4 | ***14*** | 11 | | | | | | | | *5* | | |
| 1 | 2 | | | 5 | ***6*** | ***14*** | *9* | | | **3** | 10 | 7 | | 8 | 4 | **13** | 11 | | *12* | | | | | | | | |
| 1 | 2 | | | 5 | | 8 | | | | 3 | 9 | 7 | | 6 | 4 | *10* | 11 | | *12* | | | | | | | | |
| 1 | 2 | | *3* | 5 | | 4 | ***10*** | | | *12* | 9 | 7 | | **8** | 6 | **13** | 11 | | ***14*** | | | | | | | | |
| 1 | | | | 5 | 4 | *8* | 7 | | | 3 | 10 | 2 | | *12* | 6 | **13** | 11 | | **9** | | | | | | | | |
| 1 | | | | 5 | 6 | | 9 | | | 3 | *10* | 7 | | **13** | 4 | **8** | 11 | | *12* | | | | | | 2 | | |
| 1 | | | | 5 | *6* | *12* | 10 | | | **3** | | 2 | | **13** | 8 | 7 | 11 | | 9 | | | | | | 4 | | |
| 18 | 23 | 27 | 14 | 44 | 42 | 32 | 31 | 31 | 22 | 43 | 24 | 27 | 28 | 6 | 14 | 11 | 21 | 3 | 10 | 3 | 11 | | 7 | | 10 | 3 | 1 |
| | 6 | | 1 | 1 | | 2 | 4 | 5 | 2 | 2 | 15 | 9 | | 11 | 5 | 21 | 4 | 2 | 14 | | | 1 | | 1 | | | 3 |
| | 1 | 1 | | 2 | 2 | | 10 | 13 | 6 | 3 | 9 | 4 | | 1 | 1 | | 2 | | 5 | | | | 1 | | 2 | | |

| 21 Lee-Barratt | 2 McCunnie | 20 Antwi-Birago | 3 Elliott | 5 Nelson | 7 Liddle | 4 Boland | 14 Brown | 9 Barker | 22 Moore | 8 Humphreys | 10 Porter | 15 Sweeney | 1 Budtz | 19 Robson | 6 Clark | 17 Foley | 11 Monkhouse | 18 Gibb | 24 Mackay | 27 Coles | 26 Nolan |
|---|---|---|---|---|---|---|---|---|---|---|---|---|---|---|---|---|---|---|---|---|---|
| | 2 | **13** | | 5 | **4** | | 7 | ***9*** | 10 | 3 | *12* | 8 | 1 | | 6 | | ***14*** | | *11* | | |
| | *4* | *6* | | 5 | *12* | 8 | 11 | 9 | **10** | 3 | | 7 | 1 | | | | ***14*** | | **13** | | ***2*** |
| | 2 | 1 | | 2 | 1 | 1 | 2 | 2 | 2 | 2 | | 2 | 2 | | 1 | | | | 1 | | 1 |
| | | 1 | | | 1 | | | | | | 1 | | | | | | 2 | | 1 | | |
| | | | | | 1 | | 1 | 2 | 1 | | 1 | | | | | | | | | | |

| 21 Lee-Barratt | 2 McCunnie | 20 Antwi-Birago | 3 Elliott | 5 Nelson | 7 Liddle | 4 Boland | 14 Brown | 9 Barker | 22 Moore | 8 Humphreys | 10 Porter | 15 Sweeney | 1 Budtz | 19 Robson | 6 Clark | 17 Foley | 11 Monkhouse | 18 Gibb |
|---|---|---|---|---|---|---|---|---|---|---|---|---|---|---|---|---|---|---|
| | *2* | 6 | | 5 | 4 | 8 | 7 | ***9*** | **10** | | ***14*** | 11 | 1 | 3 | | **13** | | *12* |
| | 2 | 6 | | 5 | 4 | *8* | 7 | **9** | ***10*** | 3 | ***14*** | | 1 | 11 | | *12* | **13** | |
| | 2 | 2 | | 2 | 2 | 2 | 2 | 2 | 2 | 1 | | 1 | 2 | 2 | | | | |
| | | | | | | | | | | | 2 | | | | | 2 | 1 | 1 |
| | | | | | | | | | 1 | | | | | | | 2 | | |

## League Table

| | P | W | D | L | F | A | Pts |
|---|---|---|---|---|---|---|---|
| Swansea | 46 | 27 | 11 | 8 | 82 | 42 | 92 |
| Nottingham Forest | 46 | 22 | 16 | 8 | 64 | 32 | 82 |
| Doncaster Rovers | 46 | 23 | 11 | 12 | 68 | 41 | 80 |
| Carlisle United | 46 | 23 | 11 | 12 | 64 | 46 | 80 |
| Leeds United | 46 | 27 | 10 | 9 | 72 | 38 | 76 |
| Southend United | 46 | 22 | 10 | 14 | 70 | 55 | 76 |
| Brighton & Hove Albion | 46 | 19 | 12 | 15 | 57 | 49 | 69 |
| Oldham Athletic | 46 | 18 | 13 | 15 | 58 | 46 | 67 |
| Northampton Town | 46 | 17 | 15 | 14 | 60 | 55 | 66 |
| Huddersfield Town | 46 | 20 | 6 | 20 | 50 | 62 | 66 |
| Tranmere Rovers | 46 | 18 | 11 | 17 | 52 | 47 | 65 |
| Walsall | 46 | 16 | 16 | 14 | 51 | 45 | 64 |
| Swindon Town | 46 | 16 | 13 | 17 | 62 | 56 | 61 |
| Leyton Orient | 46 | 16 | 12 | 18 | 49 | -13 | 60 |
| Hartlepool United | 46 | 15 | 9 | 22 | 63 | 66 | 54 |
| Bristol Rovers | 46 | 12 | 17 | 17 | 45 | 56 | 53 |
| Millwall | 46 | 14 | 10 | 22 | 45 | 60 | 52 |
| Yeovil Town | 46 | 14 | 10 | 22 | 38 | 59 | 52 |
| Cheltenham Town | 46 | 13 | 12 | 21 | 42 | 64 | 51 |
| Crewe Alexandra | 46 | 12 | 14 | 20 | 47 | 65 | 50 |
| Bournemouth | 46 | 17 | 7 | 22 | 62 | 72 | 48 |
| Gillingham | 46 | 11 | 13 | 22 | 44 | 73 | 46 |
| Port Vale | 46 | 9 | 11 | 26 | 47 | 81 | 38 |
| Luton Town | 46 | 11 | 10 | 25 | 43 | 63 | 33 |

# 2008-09

## League One

Manager: Danny Wilson (to 15 December 2008); Chris Turner (from 16 December 2008)

### Did you know that?

In their centenary season, Hartlepool United recorded two Cup victories over Premiership sides by defeating West Bromwich Albion in the Football League (Carling) Cup and Stoke City in the FA Cup. These successes go alongside the victory over Crystal Palace in the 1992–93 FA Cup competition.

Joel Porter, one of Hartlepool's most-popular players of the past decade, played the last of his 209 games against Leeds United on 25 April. In all games he scored 66 goals for the club, including 23 in his final season.

| Match No. | Date | Round | Venue | Opponents | Result | | Scorers | Attendance |
|---|---|---|---|---|---|---|---|---|
| 1 | Aug 9 | | (h) | Colchester United | W | 4 - 2 | Brown 2, Boland, Jones | 3,831 |
| 3 | 16 | | (a) | Tranmere Rovers | L | 0 - 1 | | 5,418 |
| 4 | 23 | | (h) | Stockport County | L | 0 - 1 | | 3,945 |
| 6 | 30 | | (a) | Peterborough United | W | 2 - 1 | Monkhouse, Barker | 5,728 |
| 8 | Sep 6 | | (a) | Millwall | L | 0 - 2 | | 7,207 |
| 9 | 12 | | (h) | Cheltenham Town | W | 4 - 1 | Brown, Gallinagh (own goal), Monkhouse, Mackay | 3,637 |
| 10 | 20 | | (h) | Oldham Athletic | D | 3 - 3 | Monkhouse, Sweeney, Porter (pen) | 4,507 |
| 12 | 27 | | (a) | Leicester City | L | 0 - 1 | | 18,578 |
| 13 | Oct 3 | | (h) | Swindon Town | D | 3 - 3 | Porter 3 | 4,018 |
| 14 | 10 | | (a) | Northampton Town | L | 0 - 1 | | 5,277 |
| 15 | 18 | | (a) | Walsall | W | 3 - 2 | Sweeney, Robson, Brown | 4,142 |
| 16 | 21 | | (h) | Huddersfield Town | W | 5 - 3 | Kyle 2, Brown, Porter 2 | 3,771 |
| 17 | 25 | | (h) | Brighton & Hove Albion | W | 1 - 0 | Kyle | 3,962 |
| 18 | 28 | | (a) | Carlisle United | W | 1 - 0 | Brown | 5,637 |
| 19 | Nov 1 | | (a) | Leyton Orient | L | 0 - 1 | | 3,638 |
| 21 | 15 | | (h) | Milton Keynes Dons | L | 1 - 3 | O'Hanlon (own goal) | 4,021 |
| 23 | 22 | | (a) | Leeds United | L | 1 - 4 | Porter | 21,182 |
| 24 | 25 | | (h) | Bristol Rovers | D | 1 - 1 | Nelson | 3,171 |
| 26 | Dec 6 | | (h) | Yeovil Town | D | 0 - 0 | | 3,393 |
| 27 | 13 | | (a) | Hereford United | D | 1 - 1 | Beckwith (own goal) | 2,490 |
| 28 | 19 | | (h) | Southend United | W | 3 - 0 | Kyle 2, Robson | 3,123 |
| 29 | 26 | | (a) | Scunthorpe United | L | 0 - 3 | | 5,347 |
| 30 | 28 | | (h) | Crewe Alexandra | L | 1 - 4 | Porter | 3,877 |
| 32 | Jan 12 | | (a) | Oldham Athletic | L | 1 - 2 | Lomax (own goal) | 4,211 |
| 33 | 16 | | (h) | Northampton Town | W | 2 - 0 | Porter 2 | 3,814 |
| 35 | 27 | | (h) | Carlisle United | D | 2 - 2 | Monkhouse, Porter | 3,765 |
| 36 | 31 | | (a) | Brighton & Hove Albion | L | 1 - 2 | Nelson | 5,784 |
| 37 | Feb 3 | | (a) | Huddersfield Town | D | 1 - 1 | Jones | 9,294 |
| 38 | 7 | | (h) | Walsall | D | 2 - 2 | Gerrard (own goal), Porter | 3,286 |
| 39 | 14 | | (a) | Milton Keynes Dons | L | 1 - 3 | Lange | 8,657 |
| 40 | 17 | | (h) | Leicester City | D | 2 - 2 | Porter (pen), Monkhouse | 4,068 |
| 41 | 21 | | (h) | Leyton Orient | L | 0 - 1 | | 3,678 |
| 42 | 24 | | (a) | Swindon Town | W | 1 - 0 | Clark (pen) | 6,010 |
| 43 | 28 | | (a) | Colchester United | D | 1 - 1 | Nelson | 5,158 |
| 44 | Mar 3 | | (h) | Tranmere Rovers | W | 2 - 1 | Nelson, Clark (pen) | 3,033 |
| 45 | 7 | | (h) | Peterborough United | L | 1 - 2 | Monkhouse | 3,722 |
| 46 | 10 | | (a) | Stockport County | L | 1 - 2 | Mackay | 4,790 |
| 47 | 14 | | (a) | Cheltenham Town | L | 0 - 2 | | 2,945 |
| 48 | 21 | | (h) | Millwall | L | 2 - 3 | Sweeney 2 | 3,601 |
| 49 | 27 | | (a) | Southend United | L | 2 - 3 | Porter (pen), Jones | 7,227 |
| 50 | Apr 4 | | (h) | Hereford United | W | 4 - 2 | Porter 2 (1 pen), Collins, Sweeney | 3,579 |
| 51 | 11 | | (a) | Crewe Alexandra | D | 0 - 0 | | 4,477 |
| 52 | 13 | | (h) | Scunthorpe United | L | 2 - 3 | Nelson, Nardiello | 3,998 |
| 53 | 18 | | (a) | Yeovil Town | W | 3 - 2 | Porter 2, Nardiello | 4,232 |
| 54 | 25 | | (h) | Leeds United | L | 0 - 1 | | 6,402 |
| 55 | May 2 | | (a) | Bristol Rovers | L | 1 - 4 | Nardiello | 7,363 |

Final Position: 19th in League One — Apps.

Sub.Apps.

5 Own goals — Goals

**FA Cup**

| Match No. | Date | Round | Venue | Opponents | Result | | Scorers | Attendance |
|---|---|---|---|---|---|---|---|---|
| 20 | Nov 8 | R1 | (a) | Brighton & Hove Albion | D | 3 - 3 | Hawkins (own goal), Brown, Monkhouse | 2,545 |
| 22 | 18 | R1r | (h) | Brighton & Hove Albion | W | 2 - 1 | Porter (pen), Liddle | 3,288 |
| 25 | 29 | R2 | (a) | Fleetwood Town | W | 3 - 2 | MacKay 2, Porter | 3,280 |
| 31 | Jan 3 | R3 | (h) | Stoke City | W | 2 - 0 | Nelson, Foley | 5,367 |
| 34 | 24 | R4 | (h) | West Ham United | L | 0 - 2 | | 6,849 |

Apps.

Sub.Apps.

1 Own goal — Goals

**League Cup**

| Match No. | Date | Round | Venue | Opponents | Result | | Scorers | Attendance |
|---|---|---|---|---|---|---|---|---|
| 2 | Aug 12 | R1 | (h) | Scunthorpe United | W | 3 - 0 | Porter, Foley, Brown | 2,076 |
| 5 | 26 | R2 | (h) | West Bromwich Albion | W | 3 - 1* | Porter, Foley, Barker | 3,387 |
| 11 | Sep 23 | R3 | (a) | Leeds United | L | 2 - 3 | Monkhouse, Porter | 14,599 |

* After extra time. Score at 90 mins 1 - 1 — Apps.

Sub.Apps.

Goals

| 21 Lee-Barratt | 15 Sweeney | 3 Humphreys | 4 Boland | 5 Nelson | 6 Collins | 7 Liddle | 8 Jones | 10 Porter | 14 Brown | 11 Monkhouse | 17 Foley | 19 Robson | 9 Barker | 18 Mackay | 2 McCunnie | 16 Power | 22 Rowell | 34 Kyle | 12 Clark | 1 Budtz | 34 Henderson | 20 Nardiello | 23 Lange | 28 Guy | 29 Parker | 34 Skartz |
|---|---|---|---|---|---|---|---|---|---|---|---|---|---|---|---|---|---|---|---|---|---|---|---|---|---|---|
| 1 | 2 | 3 | 4 | 5 | 6 | 7 | 8 | ***9*** | *10* | **11** | *12* | **13** | ***14*** | | | | | | | | | | | | | |
| 1 | 2 | 3 | ***4*** | 5 | 6 | 7 | *8* | 9 | 10 | **11** | *12* | | **13** | | ***14*** | | | | | | | | | | | |
| 1 | 2 | 3 | *4* | 5 | 6 | 7 | **8** | 9 | 10 | ***11*** | **13** | | ***14*** | | | *12* | | | | | | | | | | |
| 1 | 4 | 3 | | 5 | 6 | 7 | 8 | **9** | *10* | ***11*** | **13** | ***14*** | *12* | | 2 | | | | | | | | | | | |
| 1 | 4 | 3 | | *5* | 6 | 7 | | 9 | 10 | ***11*** | **13** | **8** | ***14*** | | 2 | *12* | | | | | | | | | | |
| 1 | 4 | 3 | | 5 | 6 | 7 | 8 | **9** | ***10*** | *11* | | *12* | **13** | ***14*** | 2 | | | | | | | | | | | |
| 1 | 4 | 3 | | 5 | 6 | 7 | 8 | 9 | ***10*** | **11** | *12* | | **13** | ***14*** | *2* | | | | | | | | | | | |
| 1 | **4** | 3 | | 5 | 6 | ***7*** | 8 | *9* | 10 | 11 | | ***14*** | *12* | **13** | 2 | | | | | | | | | | | |
| 1 | **13** | 3 | | 5 | 6 | 7 | *4* | 9 | 10 | 11 | | *12* | | | **2** | | | 8 | | | | | | | | |
| 1 | 2 | *3* | | 5 | 6 | | 7 | 9 | 10 | **11** | | *12* | | **13** | | | | 8 | 4 | | | | | | | |
| 1 | 2 | 3 | | 5 | 6 | | 7 | *9* | 10 | **11** | **13** | *12* | | | | | | 8 | 4 | | | | | | | |
| 1 | **2** | 3 | | 5 | 6 | **13** | 7 | 9 | 10 | *11* | | *12* | | | | | | 8 | 4 | | | | | | | |
| 1 | 2 | 3 | | 5 | 6 | *12* | 7 | 9 | *10* | 11 | | | | | | | | 8 | 4 | | | | | | | |
| 1 | 2 | 3 | | 5 | 6 | **13** | 7 | **9** | 10 | *11* | | *12* | | | | | | 8 | 4 | | | | | | | |
| 1 | 2 | **3** | | 5 | 6 | *12* | 7 | ***9*** | 10 | 11 | ***14*** | **13** | | | | | | 8 | 4 | | | | | | | |
| 1 | ***2*** | 3 | | 5 | 6 | **13** | 7 | **9** | 10 | *11* | ***14*** | *12* | | | | | | 8 | 4 | | | | | | | |
| 1 | 2 | *12* | | 5 | *6* | **13** | 7 | 9 | 10 | **11** | | 3 | | | | | | 8 | 4 | | | | | | | |
| 1 | 2 | **13** | | 5 | | 4 | 7 | 9 | *10* | **11** | *12* | 3 | | | | | | 8 | 6 | | | | | | | |
| | 2 | 11 | | 5 | 6 | 4 | 7 | *9* | | | *12* | 3 | | 10 | | | | 8 | | 1 | | | | | | |
| | **2** | 11 | | 5 | 6 | 4 | | | | ***14*** | *12* | 3 | | *9* | **13** | | 7 | 8 | ***10*** | 1 | | | | | | |
| | 2 | 3 | | 5 | 6 | 4 | 7 | *9* | | **13** | | 11 | | *12* | | | | 8 | **10** | 1 | | | | | | |
| 1 | 2 | 3 | | 5 | 6 | | 7 | **9** | | 11 | | | | **13** | *12* | | *4* | 8 | 10 | | | | | | | |
| 1 | 2 | 3 | | 5 | 6 | 4 | 7 | 9 | | **11** | ***14*** | | | **13** | *12* | | | ***8*** | *10* | | | | | | | |
| 1 | | 3 | | 5 | 6 | 4 | **7** | | | *12* | *10* | 11 | | 9 | 2 | | **13** | | 8 | | | | | | | |
| 1 | | 3 | | 5 | | 4 | ***7*** | **9** | | 8 | | *11* | | 10 | 2 | *12* | ***14*** | | 6 | | **13** | | | | | |
| 1 | 2 | 3 | | 5 | | 4 | 7 | 9 | | 8 | *12* | 11 | | | | | | | 6 | | *10* | | | | | |
| 1 | *2* | 3 | | 5 | | 4 | 7 | 9 | | 8 | | 11 | | | *12* | | | | 6 | | | 10 | | | | |
| 1 | 8 | 3 | | 5 | | 4 | 7 | *9* | | | | 11 | | | 2 | | | | 6 | | *12* | 10 | | | | |
| 1 | 8 | 3 | | 5 | | 4 | | 9 | | 7 | | 11 | | *10* | 2 | | | | 6 | | | | *12* | | | |
| 1 | 2 | 3 | | 5 | 6 | 4 | | | | 11 | *7* | | | *12* | | **13** | **8** | | | | 10 | | 9 | | | |
| 1 | 2 | 3 | | 5 | 6 | 4 | | 9 | | 7 | ***12*** | *11* | | | | | | | 8 | | **13** | | 10 | | | |
| 1 | 2 | 3 | | 5 | 6 | 4 | | *9* | | 11 | **13** | | | | | | | | 8 | | *12* | **10** | | 7 | | |
| 1 | 2 | 3 | | 5 | 6 | 4 | | | | 11 | **13** | | | **9** | | | | | 8 | | *12* | *10* | | 7 | | |
| 1 | 2 | 3 | | 5 | 6 | 4 | *10* | | | 11 | *12* | | | 9 | | | | | 8 | | | | | 7 | | |
| 1 | 2 | 3 | | 5 | 6 | 4 | **10** | | | 11 | | | | *12* | | | | | 8 | | **13** | | | *7* | 9 | |
| 1 | 2 | 3 | | 5 | 6 | 4 | | *12* | | 11 | 7 | | | *10* | | | | | 8 | | | | | | 9 | |
| 1 | 2 | 3 | | 5 | 6 | 4 | | 9 | | 11 | *7* | | | *12* | | | | | 8 | | | | | | 10 | |
| 1 | 2 | 3 | | 5 | 6 | 4 | | **9** | | 11 | *12* | **13** | | *7* | | | | | 8 | | | | | | 10 | |
| 1 | 8 | 3 | | 5 | 6 | 4 | 7 | 9 | | 11 | | | | | | | | | 2 | | | *12* | | | 10 | |
| 1 | *8* | ***3*** | | 5 | 6 | 4 | **7** | 9 | | 11 | | | | | | | | | 2 | *12* | | **13** | | | 10 | ***14*** |
| | 8 | *3* | | 5 | 6 | 4 | **7** | 9 | | 11 | | ***14*** | | | | | | | 2 | 1 | | **13** | | | ***10*** | *12* |
| | 8 | **13** | | 5 | 6 | 4 | 7 | | | 11 | | | | *12* | | | | | 2 | 1 | | **9** | | | *10* | 3 |
| | 8 | | | 5 | 6 | 4 | ***7*** | *9* | | 11 | | **13** | | ***14*** | | | | | 2 | 1 | | *12* | | | **10** | 3 |
| | 8 | *12* | | 5 | 6 | 4 | 7 | **9** | | 11 | | | | **13** | | | | | *2* | 1 | | 10 | | | | 3 |
| | 8 | *12* | | ***5*** | 6 | 4 | 7 | **9** | | 11 | | ***14*** | | **13** | | | | | 2 | 1 | | 10 | | | | 3 |
| | 8 | *12* | | *5* | 6 | 4 | **7** | | | 11 | | 10 | | | | | **13** | | 2 | 1 | | 9 | | | | 3 |
| 37 | 43 | 39 | 3 | 46 | 40 | 37 | 36 | 37 | 18 | 41 | 4 | 14 | | 9 | 10 | | 3 | 15 | 35 | 9 | 2 | 8 | 2 | 4 | 9 | 5 |
| | 1 | 6 | | | | 6 | | 1 | | 3 | 19 | 15 | 8 | 14 | 5 | 4 | 3 | | | 1 | 6 | 5 | 1 | | | 2 |
| | 5 | | 1 | 5 | 1 | | 3 | 18 | 6 | 6 | | 2 | 1 | 2 | | | | 5 | 2 | | | 3 | 1 | | | |

| 21 Lee-Barratt | 15 Sweeney | 3 Humphreys | 4 Boland | 5 Nelson | 6 Collins | 7 Liddle | 8 Jones | 10 Porter | 14 Brown | 11 Monkhouse | 17 Foley | 19 Robson | 9 Barker | 18 Mackay | 2 McCunnie | 16 Power | 22 Rowell | 34 Kyle | 12 Clark | 1 Budtz | 34 Henderson | 20 Nardiello | 23 Lange | 28 Guy | 29 Parker | 34 Skartz |
|---|---|---|---|---|---|---|---|---|---|---|---|---|---|---|---|---|---|---|---|---|---|---|---|---|---|---|
| 1 | 2 | *3* | | 5 | 6 | ***14*** | 8 | 9 | ***10*** | 11 | **13** | *12* | | **7** | | | | | 4 | | | | | | | |
| 1 | 2 | *3* | | 5 | | 4 | 8 | 9 | 10 | *12* | **7** | 11 | | **13** | | | | | 6 | | | | | | | |
| 1 | 4 | 8 | | 5 | | 7 | | 9 | | 11 | | 3 | | 10 | 2 | | | | 6 | | | | | | | |
| 1 | *2* | 3 | | 5 | 6 | 7 | ***8*** | 9 | | ***14*** | **13** | 11 | | **10** | *12* | | | | 4 | | | | | | | |
| 1 | 2 | 3 | | 5 | | 4 | **7** | 9 | | 8 | **13** | 11 | | *10* | | | | | 6 | | *12* | | | | | |
| 5 | 5 | 5 | | 5 | 2 | 4 | 4 | 5 | 2 | 3 | 1 | 4 | | 4 | 1 | | | | 5 | | | | | | | |
| | | | | | | 1 | | | | 2 | 3 | 1 | | 1 | 1 | | | | | | 1 | | | | | |
| | | | | 1 | | 1 | | 2 | 1 | 1 | 1 | | | 2 | | | | | | | | | | | | |

| 21 Lee-Barratt | 15 Sweeney | 3 Humphreys | 4 Boland | 5 Nelson | 6 Collins | 7 Liddle | 8 Jones | 10 Porter | 14 Brown | 11 Monkhouse | 17 Foley | 19 Robson | 9 Barker | 18 Mackay | 2 McCunnie | 16 Power | 22 Rowell | 34 Kyle | 12 Clark | 1 Budtz | 34 Henderson | 20 Nardiello | 23 Lange | 28 Guy | 29 Parker | 34 Skartz |
|---|---|---|---|---|---|---|---|---|---|---|---|---|---|---|---|---|---|---|---|---|---|---|---|---|---|---|
| 1 | *2* | 3 | 4 | 5 | 6 | 7 | | *9* | **10** | | 8 | 11 | *12* | **13** | | | | | | | | | | | | |
| 1 | 2 | 3 | | 5 | 6 | 7 | 8 | **9** | ***10*** | *11* | ***14*** | *12* | **13** | | 4 | | | | | | | | | | | |
| 1 | *4* | 3 | | 5 | 6 | 7 | 8 | 9 | ***10*** | **11** | | **13** | *12* | ***14*** | 2 | | | | | | | | | | | |
| 3 | 3 | 3 | 1 | 3 | 3 | 3 | 2 | 3 | 3 | 2 | 1 | 1 | | | 2 | | | | | | | | | | | |
| | | | | | | | | | | | 1 | 2 | 3 | 2 | | | | | | | | | | | | |
| | | | | | | | | 3 | 1 | 1 | 2 | | 1 | | | | | | | | | | | | | |

## League Table

| | P | W | D | L | F | A | Pts |
|---|---|---|---|---|---|---|---|
| Leicester City | 46 | 27 | 15 | 4 | 84 | 39 | 96 |
| Peterborough United | 46 | 26 | 11 | 9 | 78 | 54 | 89 |
| Milton Keynes Dons | 46 | 26 | 9 | 11 | 83 | 47 | 87 |
| Leeds United | 46 | 26 | 6 | 14 | 77 | 49 | 84 |
| Millwall | 46 | 25 | 7 | 14 | 63 | 53 | 82 |
| Scunthorpe United | 46 | 22 | 10 | 14 | 82 | 63 | 76 |
| Tranmere Rovers | 46 | 21 | 11 | 14 | 62 | 49 | 74 |
| Southend United | 46 | 21 | 8 | 17 | 58 | 61 | 71 |
| Huddersfield Town | 46 | 18 | 14 | 14 | 62 | 65 | 68 |
| Oldham Athletic | 46 | 16 | 17 | 13 | 66 | 65 | 65 |
| Bristol Rovers | 46 | 17 | 12 | 17 | 79 | 61 | 63 |
| Colchester United | 46 | 18 | 9 | 19 | 58 | 58 | 63 |
| Walsall | 46 | 17 | 10 | 19 | 61 | 66 | 61 |
| Leyton Orient | 46 | 15 | 11 | 20 | 45 | 57 | 56 |
| Swindon Town | 46 | 12 | 17 | 17 | 68 | 71 | 53 |
| Brighton & Hove Albion | 46 | 13 | 13 | 20 | 54 | 69 | 52 |
| Yeovil Town | 46 | 12 | 15 | 19 | 41 | 66 | 51 |
| Stockport County | 46 | 16 | 12 | 18 | 59 | 57 | 50 |
| Hartlepool United | 46 | 13 | 11 | 22 | 66 | 79 | 50 |
| Carlisle United | 46 | 12 | 14 | 20 | 56 | 69 | 50 |
| Northampton Town | 46 | 12 | 13 | 21 | 60 | 64 | 49 |
| Crewe Alexandra | 46 | 12 | 10 | 24 | 59 | 82 | 46 |
| Cheltenham Town | 46 | 9 | 12 | 25 | 51 | 91 | 39 |
| Hereford United | 46 | 9 | 7 | 30 | 42 | 79 | 34 |

# 2009-10

## League One

Manager: Chris Turner

### Did you know that?

The attendance of 30,191 at Elland Road against Leeds United was the second highest for any Football League game involving Hartlepool United.

The three-point deduction for fielding an ineligible player, Gary Liddle, was the first time that Hartlepool United had suffered such a penalty since entering the Football League in 1921.

| Match No. | Date | Round | Venue | Opponents | Result | | Scorers | Attendance |
|---|---|---|---|---|---|---|---|---|
| 1 | Aug 8 | | (a) | Milton Keynes Dons | D | 0 - 0 | | 8,965 |
| 3 | 15 | | (h) | Charlton Athletic | L | 0 - 2 | | 4,408 |
| 4 | 18 | | (h) | Bristol Rovers | L | 1 - 2 | Behan | 3,137 |
| 5 | 22 | | (a) | Gillingham | W | 1 - 0 | Brown | 4,969 |
| 7 | 29 | | (h) | Norwich City | L | 0 - 2 | | 4,470 |
| 8 | Sep 4 | | (a) | Oldham Athletic | W | 3 - 0 | Brown, McSweeney, Behan | 4,014 |
| 9 | 12 | | (h) | Wycombe Wanderers | D | 1 - 1 | Boyd | 3,326 |
| 10 | 19 | | (a) | Colchester United | L | 0 - 2 | | 4,259 |
| 11 | 26 | | (h) | Walsall | W | 3 - 0 | Monkhouse 2, Larkin | 3,334 |
| 12 | 29 | | (a) | Stockport County | D | 2 - 2 | Boyd, Behan | 3,780 |
| 13 | Oct 3 | | (a) | Exeter City | L | 1 - 3 | Behan | 4,706 |
| 15 | 10 | | (h) | Brentford | D | 0 - 0 | | 3,105 |
| 16 | 17 | | (a) | Swindon Town | W | 2 - 0 | Brown, Monkhouse | 7,096 |
| 17 | 24 | | (h) | Tranmere Rovers | W | 1 - 0 | Hartley | 3,428 |
| 18 | 31 | | (a) | Brighton & Hove Albion | D | 3 - 3 | Boyd, Monkhouse, Jones | 5,694 |
| 20 | Nov 14 | | (h) | Leyton Orient | W | 1 - 0 | Boyd | 3,119 |
| 21 | 21 | | (a) | Huddersfield Town | L | 1 - 2 | Liddle | 14,836 |
| 22 | 24 | | (h) | Southampton | L | 1 - 3 | Monkhouse | 3,818 |
| 23 | Dec 1 | | (a) | Carlisle United | L | 2 - 3 | Bjornsson, Monkhouse | 4,109 |
| 24 | 5 | | (h) | Millwall | W | 3 - 0 | Hartley, Boyd, Bjornsson | 3,153 |
| 25 | 12 | | (a) | Southend United | L | 2 - 3 | Boyd, Grant (own goal) | 7,737 |
| 26 | 19 | | (h) | Yeovil Town | D | 1 - 1 | Monkhouse | 2,778 |
| 27 | 26 | | (a) | Leeds United | L | 1 - 3 | Bjornsson | 30,191 |
| 28 | Jan 2 | | (h) | Oldham Athletic | W | 2 - 1 | Jones, Monkhouse | 2,634 |
| 29 | 16 | | (h) | Milton Keynes Dons | L | 0 - 5 | | 3,211 |
| 30 | 19 | | (a) | Charlton Athletic | L | 1 - 2 | Behan (pen) | 14,636 |
| 31 | 23 | | (a) | Bristol Rovers | L | 0 - 2 | | 5,794 |
| 32 | 26 | | (h) | Gillingham | D | 1 - 1 | Austin | 2,465 |
| 33 | 30 | | (a) | Norwich City | L | 1 - 2 | Austin | 25,506 |
| 34 | Feb 6 | | (h) | Leeds United | D | 2 - 2 | Boyd, Sweeney | 5,115 |
| 35 | 20 | | (h) | Huddersfield Town | L | 0 - 2 | | 4,452 |
| 36 | 23 | | (h) | Carlisle United | W | 4 - 1 | Jones 2, Sweeney, Gamble | 2,975 |
| 37 | 27 | | (a) | Millwall | L | 0 - 1 | | 10,818 |
| 38 | Mar 6 | | (h) | Southend United | W | 3 - 0 | O'Donovan 3 | 3,299 |
| 39 | 13 | | (a) | Yeovil Town | L | 0 - 4 | | 4,169 |
| 40 | 19 | | (a) | Tranmere Rovers | D | 0 - 0 | | 5,409 |
| 41 | 23 | | (a) | Southampton | L | 2 - 3 | Monkhouse, Austin | 18,972 |
| 42 | 27 | | (h) | Swindon Town | L | 0 - 1 | | 3,536 |
| 43 | Apr 3 | | (a) | Leyton Orient | W | 3 - 1 | Liddle 2, O'Donovan | 3,604 |
| 44 | 5 | | (h) | Brighton & Hove Albion | W | 2 - 0 | O'Donovan, Monkhouse | 3,466 |
| 45 | 10 | | (a) | Wycombe Wanderers | L | 0 - 2 | | 4,342 |
| 46 | 13 | | (h) | Stockport County | W | 3 - 0 | Gamble, Monkhouse, O'Donovan | 2,869 |
| 47 | 17 | | (h) | Colchester United | W | 3 - 1 | Brown, O'Donovan 2 (1 pen) | 3,126 |
| 48 | 24 | | (a) | Walsall | L | 1 - 3 | O'Donovan | 3,457 |
| 49 | May 1 | | (h) | Exeter City | D | 1 - 1 | Behan | 3,983 |
| 50 | 8 | | (a) | Brentford | D | 0 - 0 | | 6,893 |

Final Position: 20th in League One

Apps.
Sub.Apps.
1 Own goal — Goals

**FA Cup**

| | | | | | | | | |
|---|---|---|---|---|---|---|---|---|
| 19 | Nov 7 | R1 | (h) | Kettering Town | L | 0 - 1 | | 2,645 |

Apps.
Sub.Apps.
Goals

**League Cup**

| | | | | | | | | |
|---|---|---|---|---|---|---|---|---|
| 2 | Aug 12 | R1 | Away | Coventry City | W | 1 - 0* | Boyd | 6,055 |
| 6 | 25 | R2 | Home | Burnley | L | 1 - 2* | Boyd | 3,501 |

* After extra time.

Apps.
Sub.Apps.
Goals

**Johnstone's Paint Trophy**

| | | | | | | | | |
|---|---|---|---|---|---|---|---|---|
| 14 | Oct 6 | R2 | Home | Grimsby Town | L | 0 - 2 | | 1,675 |

Apps.
Sub.Apps.
Goals

| 9 Behan | 7 McSweeney | 11 Monkhouse | 12 Brown | 14 Rowell | 23 Larkin | 10 Boyd | 2 Austin | 17 Foley | 26 Bjornsson | 3 Humphreys | 24 Greulich | 6 Clark | 27 Cherel | 30 Gamble | 32 O'Donovan | 20 Power | | | | | | | | |
|---|---|---|---|---|---|---|---|---|---|---|---|---|---|---|---|---|---|---|---|---|---|---|---|---|
| 1 | 2 | 3 | 4 | 5 | 6 | 7 | **8** | 9 | 10 | 11 | *12* | **13** | | | | | | | | | | | | |
| 1 | 2 | **3** | 4 | 5 | 6 | | ***8*** | 9 | 7 | 11 | *12* | **13** | | *10* | ***14*** | | | | | | | | | |
| 1 | 2 | 3 | 4 | 5 | 6 | | ***8*** | 9 | **7** | 11 | *10* | ***14*** | | *12* | | **13** | | | | | | | | |
| 1 | 2 | 3 | 4 | 5 | 6 | *12* | *8* | **9** | 7 | 11 | ***10*** | | | **13** | ***14*** | | | | | | | | | |
| 1 | 2 | 3 | 4 | 5 | 6 | ***8*** | ***14*** | 9 | **7** | 11 | *12* | | *10* | **13** | | | | | | | | | | |
| 1 | 2 | 3 | 4 | 5 | 6 | **8** | **13** | 9 | ***7*** | 11 | *10* | | *12* | ***14*** | | | | | | | | | | |
| 1 | 2 | ***3*** | 4 | 5 | 6 | 8 | | **9** | 7 | 11 | *10* | | | *12* | ***14*** | | **13** | | | | | | | |
| 1 | 2 | 3 | 4 | 5 | 6 | 8 | | ***9*** | 7 | **11** | 10 | | | ***14*** | | | *12* | **13** | | | | | | |
| 1 | 2 | 3 | ***4*** | 5 | 6 | | | *9* | | 11 | 7 | ***14*** | **13** | **10** | | | *12* | 8 | | | | | | |
| 1 | | 3 | 4 | 5 | 6 | | | **9** | | 11 | *7* | | *12* | 10 | 2 | | **13** | 8 | | | | | | |
| 1 | 2 | | 4 | 5 | 6 | | **13** | 9 | | **11** | *7* | | *12* | ***10*** | 3 | | ***14*** | 8 | | | | | | |
| 1 | | 3 | 4 | 5 | 6 | | | *9* | | 11 | 7 | | *12* | **10** | 2 | | **13** | 8 | | | | | | |
| 1 | | 3 | | 5 | 6 | 4 | | *9* | ***14*** | 11 | ***7*** | | **13** | **10** | 2 | | *12* | 8 | | | | | | |
| 1 | | 3 | ***14*** | 5 | 6 | 4 | | ***9*** | **13** | 11 | **7** | | | *10* | 2 | | | 8 | *12* | | | | | |
| 1 | | 3 | **13** | 5 | 6 | **4** | | ***9*** | *7* | 11 | | | *12* | 10 | 2 | | | 8 | ***14*** | | | | | |
| 1 | | 3 | | 5 | 6 | 4 | | *12* | | 11 | *10* | | *7* | 9 | 2 | | | 8 | | | | | | |
| 1 | | 3 | | 5 | 6 | 4 | | **13** | *12* | 11 | 10 | | *7* | **9** | 2 | | | 8 | | | | | | |
| 1 | | 3 | | 5 | 6 | 4 | | *9* | | 11 | 7 | | | 10 | 2 | | | 8 | *12* | | | | | |
| 1 | | 3 | 4 | 5 | 6 | | **13** | | 7 | 11 | | | | *10* | 2 | *12* | **9** | ***8*** | | ***14*** | | | | |
| 1 | | 3 | 4 | 5 | 6 | | *12* | | *7* | 11 | | | | **10** | 2 | | 9 | ***8*** | **13** | ***14*** | | | | |
| 1 | | 3 | 2 | 5 | 6 | 4 | **13** | | **7** | *11* | | | | 10 | | | 9 | 8 | | *12* | | | | |
| 1 | | 3 | 2 | 5 | 6 | 4 | | | *7* | 11 | | *12* | | 10 | | | 9 | 8 | | | | | | |
| 1 | | 3 | 7 | 5 | *6* | 4 | **13** | | ***11*** | | | | ***14*** | 10 | 2 | | 9 | **8** | | *12* | | | | |
| 1 | | 3 | 7 | | | 4 | ***14*** | | ***13*** | 11 | | | *12* | **10** | 2 | | *9* | 8 | | 6 | 5 | | | |
| 1 | | | 2 | | 6 | **7** | | *12* | | 11 | | | **13** | 10 | 3 | | *9* | 8 | | 5 | | 4 | | |
| 1 | 2 | | 4 | 5 | 6 | **13** | | *9* | | 11 | | | 7 | *12* | 3 | | | **10** | | | | 8 | | |
| 1 | 2 | | 4 | 5 | 6 | **13** | | *9* | | 11 | | | 7 | *12* | 3 | | | **10** | | | | 8 | | |
| 1 | | 3 | 4 | 5 | 6 | *12* | | **9** | | 11 | | | 7 | **13** | 2 | | | *10* | | | | 8 | | |
| 1 | | 3 | 4 | 5 | 6 | *12* | | **9** | | 11 | | | 7 | **13** | 2 | | | *10* | | | | 8 | | |
| 1 | | 3 | 4 | 5 | 6 | **13** | | *12* | | 11 | | | 7 | 9 | 2 | | | **10** | | | | 8 | | |
| 1 | | 3 | ***4*** | 5 | 6 | 7 | | *9* | | 11 | **13** | | *12* | **10** | 2 | | ***14*** | | | | | 8 | | |
| 1 | | 3 | 4 | 5 | 6 | 7 | | | ***14*** | | *12* | | **11** | *10* | 2 | | | **13** | | | | 8 | ***9*** | |
| 1 | | 3 | ***4*** | 5 | 6 | 7 | | **13** | | | ***14*** | | *11* | **10** | 2 | | | *12* | | | | 8 | 9 | |
| 1 | | 3 | 4 | 5 | 6 | 7 | | **13** | | 11 | | | | **10** | 2 | | | *12* | | | | *8* | 9 | |
| 1 | | 3 | 4 | 5 | 6 | 7 | | | **13** | ***11*** | *12* | | | **10** | 2 | | | ***14*** | | | | 8 | 9 | |
| 1 | | 3 | 4 | 5 | | **13** | | | *12* | 11 | **7** | | | | *2* | | | 10 | | 6 | | 8 | 9 | |
| 1 | | *3* | 4 | 5 | | *12* | | | 7 | 11 | **13** | | | | 2 | | | **10** | | 6 | | 8 | 9 | |
| 1 | | | ***4*** | 5 | | **7** | | | 2 | *11* | *12* | **13** | | ***14*** | 3 | | | 10 | | 6 | | 8 | 9 | |
| 1 | 2 | | **13** | 5 | 6 | | | | 7 | 11 | *12* | | | | 3 | | 10 | **8** | | | | ***4*** | *9* | ***14*** |
| 1 | 2 | | **13** | 5 | 6 | | | | 11 | *7* | *12* | | | | 3 | | *10* | **8** | | | | 4 | ***9*** | ***14*** |
| 1 | 2 | | **13** | 5 | | | | | ***11*** | 7 | *12* | | ***14*** | | 3 | | *10* | 8 | | 6 | | **4** | 9 | |
| 1 | 2 | 6 | ***14*** | *5* | | | | | ***7*** | 11 | **10** | | | **13** | 3 | | | 8 | | *12* | | 4 | 9 | |
| 1 | | 3 | *12* | 5 | 6 | **13** | | | 7 | 11 | ***10*** | | | ***14*** | 2 | | | *8* | | | | **4** | 9 | |
| 1 | | 3 | *12* | 5 | 6 | **13** | | | 7 | 11 | ***10*** | | | ***14*** | 2 | | | *8* | | | | **4** | 9 | |
| 1 | | 3 | **13** | 5 | 6 | | | *12* | *7* | 11 | ***10*** | | | ***14*** | 2 | | | 8 | | | | **4** | 9 | |
| 1 | | 3 | ***14*** | 5 | 6 | *12* | | **13** | *7* | 11 | | | | **10** | 2 | | | 8 | | | | ***4*** | 9 | |
| 46 | 16 | 38 | 32 | 44 | 40 | 22 | 4 | 21 | 24 | 43 | 19 | | 10 | 25 | 35 | | 10 | 33 | | 6 | 1 | 22 | 15 | |
| | | | 10 | | | 11 | 8 | 8 | 7 | | 12 | 6 | 12 | 15 | 3 | 2 | 8 | 5 | 4 | 5 | | | | 2 |
| | | 2 | 2 | | 3 | 4 | | 6 | 1 | 11 | 4 | | 1 | 7 | 3 | | 3 | | | | | 2 | 9 | |

| | | | | | | | | | | | | | | | | | | | | |
|---|---|---|---|---|---|---|---|---|---|---|---|---|---|---|---|---|---|---|---|---|
| 1 | | 3 | 4 | 5 | 6 | **13** | | *9* | | 7 | | | 11 | **10** | 2 | | | 8 | *12* | |
| 1 | | 1 | 1 | 1 | 1 | | | 1 | | 1 | | | 1 | 1 | 1 | | | 1 | | |
| | | | | | | 1 | | | | | | | | | | | | | 1 | |
| | | | | | | | | | | | | | | | | | | | | |

| | | | | | | | | | | | | | | |
|---|---|---|---|---|---|---|---|---|---|---|---|---|---|---|
| 1 | 2 | 3 | 4 | 5 | 6 | 7 | **8** | ***9*** | *10* | 11 | *12* | | **13** | ***14*** |
| 1 | 2 | 3 | **4** | 5 | 6 | 8 | **13** | 9 | 7 | 11 | | | *12* | *10* |
| 2 | 2 | 2 | 2 | 2 | 2 | 2 | 1 | 2 | 2 | 2 | | | | 1 |
| | | | | | | | 1 | | | | 1 | | 2 | 1 |
| | | | | | | | | | | | | | | 2 |

| | | | | | | | | | | | | | | | | | | |
|---|---|---|---|---|---|---|---|---|---|---|---|---|---|---|---|---|---|---|
| 1 | 2 | | 4 | 5 | 6 | | | *12* | **7** | 11 | | | 10 | **13** | 3 | | *9* | 8 |
| 1 | 1 | | 1 | 1 | 1 | | | | 1 | 1 | | | 1 | | 1 | | 1 | 1 |
| | | | | | | | | 1 | | | | | | 1 | | | | |
| | | | | | | | | | | | | | | | | | | |

## League Table

| | P | W | D | L | F | A | Pts |
|---|---|---|---|---|---|---|---|
| Norwich City | 46 | 29 | 8 | 9 | 89 | 47 | 95 |
| Leeds United | 46 | 25 | 11 | 10 | 77 | 44 | 86 |
| Millwall | 46 | 24 | 13 | 9 | 76 | 44 | 85 |
| Charlton Athletic | 46 | 23 | 15 | 8 | 71 | 48 | 84 |
| Swindon Town | 46 | 22 | 16 | 8 | 73 | 57 | 82 |
| Huddersfield Town | 46 | 23 | 11 | 12 | 82 | 56 | 80 |
| Southampton | 46 | 23 | 14 | 9 | 85 | 47 | 73 |
| Colchester United | 46 | 20 | 12 | 14 | 64 | 52 | 72 |
| Brentford | 46 | 14 | 20 | 12 | 55 | 52 | 62 |
| Walsall | 46 | 16 | 14 | 16 | 60 | 63 | 62 |
| Bristol Rovers | 46 | 19 | 5 | 22 | 59 | 70 | 62 |
| Milton Keynes Dons | 46 | 17 | 9 | 20 | 60 | 68 | 60 |
| Brighton & Hove Albion | 46 | 15 | 14 | 17 | 56 | 60 | 59 |
| Carlisle United | 46 | 15 | 13 | 18 | 63 | 66 | 58 |
| Yeovil Town | 46 | 13 | 14 | 19 | 55 | 59 | 53 |
| Oldham Athletic | 46 | 13 | 13 | 20 | 39 | 57 | 52 |
| Leyton Orient | 46 | 13 | 12 | 21 | 53 | 63 | 51 |
| Exeter City | 46 | 11 | 18 | 17 | 48 | 60 | 51 |
| Tranmere Rovers | 46 | 14 | 9 | 23 | 45 | 72 | 51 |
| Hartlepool United | 46 | 14 | 11 | 21 | 59 | 67 | 50 |
| Gillingham | 46 | 12 | 14 | 20 | 48 | 64 | 50 |
| Wycombe | 46 | 10 | 15 | 21 | 56 | 76 | 45 |
| Southend United | 46 | 10 | 13 | 23 | 51 | 72 | 43 |
| Stockport County | 46 | 5 | 10 | 31 | 35 | 95 | 25 |

# 2010-11

## League One

Managers : Chris Turner (to 19th August); Chris Wadsworth (from 19th August)

### Did you know that?

The home game against Notts County on 2 November was sensationally abandoned by referee Carl Boyeson after a mere 2 minutes and 50 seconds due to adverse weather conditions. The game was later replayed.

In the last minute of the final home game of the season Scott Flinders became the first Hartlepool United goalkeeper to score when he headed Fabian Yantorno's centre powerfully home.

| Match No. | Date | Round | Venue | Opponents | Result | | Scorers | Attendance |
|---|---|---|---|---|---|---|---|---|
| 1 | Aug 7 | | (a) | Rochdale | D | 0 - 0 | | 3,706 |
| 3 | 14 | | (h) | Swindon Town | D | 2 - 2 | Boyd, Sweeney | 2,893 |
| 4 | 21 | | (a) | Yeovil Town | W | 2 - 0 | Liddle, Monkhouse | 3,537 |
| 6 | 28 | | (h) | Sheffield Wednesday | L | 0 - 5 | | 4,084 |
| 8 | Sep 4 | | (a) | Milton Keynes Dons | L | 0 - 1 | | 7,656 |
| 9 | 11 | | (h) | Exeter City | L | 2 - 3 | Humphries, Sweeney | 2,641 |
| 10 | 18 | | (a) | Brentford | D | 0 - 0 | | 4,710 |
| 11 | 25 | | (h) | Walsall | W | 2 - 1 | Sweeney,Monkhouse | 2,552 |
| 12 | 28 | | (h) | Carlisle United | L | 0 - 4 | | 3,419 |
| 13 | Oct 2 | | (a) | Plymouth Argyle | W | 1 - 0 | McSweeney | 7,333 |
| 15 | 9 | | (h) | Peterborough United | W | 2 - 0 | Hartley, Liddle | 3,047 |
| 16 | 16 | | (a) | Leyton Orient | L | 0 - 1 | | 3,605 |
| 17 | 23 | | (h) | Bristol Rovers | D | 2 - 2 | Gamble, Sweeney | 2,792 |
| 18 | 30 | | (a) | Dagenham & Redbridge | D | 1 - 1 | Arber (own goal) | 2,464 |
| 21 | Nov 13 | | (h) | Brighton & Hove Albion | W | 3 - 1 | Austin, Liddle, Poole | 3,073 |
| 23 | 20 | | (a) | Colchester United | L | 2 - 3 | Murray, Horwood | 3,640 |
| 24 | 23 | | (a) | Tranmere Rovers | W | 1 - 0 | Gulacsi (own goal) | 4,340 |
| 25 | Dec 11 | | (a) | AFC Bournemouth | W | 1 - 0 | Brown | 6,129 |
| 27 | 26 | | (a) | Huddersfield Town | W | 1 - 0 | McSweeney | 14,813 |
| 28 | Jan 1 | | (h) | Oldham Athletic | W | 4 - 2 | Austin (pen), Hartley, Humphries, Sweeney | 3,411 |
| 29 | 3 | | (a) | Notts County | L | 0 - 3 | | 6,285 |
| 31 | 15 | | (h) | Dagenham & Redbridge | L | 0 - 1 | | 2,939 |
| 32 | 18 | | (a) | Bristol Rovers | D | 0 - 0 | | 5,285 |
| 33 | 22 | | (a) | Peterborough United | L | 0 - 4 | | 5,800 |
| 34 | 25 | | (h) | Notts County | D | 1 - 1 | Liddle | 2,545 |
| 35 | Feb 1 | | (a) | Oldham Athletic | L | 0 - 4 | | 3,056 |
| 36 | 5 | | (h) | Colchester United | W | 1 - 0 | Sweeney | 2,646 |
| 37 | 12 | | (a) | Brighton & Hove Albion | L | 1 - 4 | Sweeney | 7,296 |
| 38 | 15 | | (h) | Charlton Athletic | W | 2 - 1 | Monkhouse, Liddle | 2,289 |
| 39 | 19 | | (h) | Milton Keynes Dons | L | 0 - 1 | | 2,620 |
| 40 | 22 | | (h) | Southampton | D | 0 - 0 | | 3,301 |
| 41 | 26 | | (a) | Exeter City | W | 2 - 1 | Monkhouse 2 | 4,931 |
| 42 | Mar 1 | | (h) | Huddersfield Town | L | 0 - 1 | | 2,857 |
| 43 | 5 | | (h) | Brentford | W | 3 - 0 | Monkhouse 2, Liddle | 2,936 |
| 44 | 8 | | (a) | Carlisle United | L | 0 - 1 | | 3,898 |
| 45 | 12 | | (h) | Plymouth Argyle | W | 2 - 0 | Sweeney, Collins | 3,059 |
| 46 | 15 | | (h) | Leyton Orient | L | 0 - 1 | | 2,313 |
| 47 | 19 | | (a) | Walsall | L | 2 - 5 | Larkin 2 | 4,234 |
| 48 | 25 | | (h) | Rochdale | L | 0 - 2 | | 3,081 |
| 49 | Apr 2 | | (a) | Swindon Town | D | 1 - 1 | Horwood | 7,146 |
| 50 | 9 | | (h) | Yeovil Town | W | 3 - 1 | Boyd, Collins, Larkin | 2,834 |
| 51 | 16 | | (a) | Sheffield Wednesday | L | 0 - 2 | | 16,358 |
| 52 | 22 | | (h) | Tranmere Rovers | D | 1 - 1 | Sweeney | 2,969 |
| 53 | 25 | | (a) | Southampton | L | 0 - 2 | | 24,210 |
| 54 | 30 | | (h) | AFC Bournemouth | D | 2 - 2 | Boyd (pen), Flinders | 3,159 |
| 55 | May 7 | | (a) | Charlton Athletic | D | 0 - 0 | | 15,804 |

Final Position: 16th in League One

Apps.
Sub.Apps.
2 Own goals Goals

**FA Cup**

| Match No. | Date | Round | Venue | Opponents | Result | | Scorers | Attendance |
|---|---|---|---|---|---|---|---|---|
| 19 | Nov 6 | R1 | (h) | Vauxhall Motors | D | 0 - 0 | | 2,381 |
| 22 | 16 | R1r | (a) | Vauxhall Motors | W | 1 - 0 | Brown | 2,406 |
| 26 | Dec 14 | R2 | (h) | Yeovil Town | W | 4 - 2 | Sweeney 3, Humphries | 1,914 |
| 30 | Jan 8 | R3 | (a) | Watford | L | 1 - 4 | Sweeney | 8,950 |

Apps.
Sub.Apps.
Goals

**League Cup**

| Match No. | Date | Round | Venue | Opponents | Result | | Scorers | Attendance |
|---|---|---|---|---|---|---|---|---|
| 2 | Aug 10 | R1 | (h) | Sheffield United | W | 2 - 0 | Brown, Boyd (pen) | 2,520 |
| 5 | 24 | R2 | (h) | Wigan Athletic | L | 0 - 3 | | 3,197 |

Apps.
Sub.Apps.
Goals

**Johnstone's Paint Trophy**

| Match No. | Date | Round | Venue | Opponents | Result | | Scorers | Attendance |
|---|---|---|---|---|---|---|---|---|
| 7 | Aug 31 | R1 | (h) | Northampton Town | W | 4 - 0 | Horwood, Sweeney, Monkhouse, Behan | 1,359 |
| 14 | Oct 5 | R2 | (h) | Bradford City | W | 1 - 0 | McSweeney | 1,728 |
| 20 | Nov 9 | R3 | (a) | Sheffield Wednesday | L | 1 - 4 | Yantorno | 10,909 |

Apps.
Sub.Apps.
Goals

| 1 Flinders | 2 Austin | 6 Horwood | 15 Sweeney | 5 Collins | 29 Hartley | 14 Brown | 8 Gamble | 22 Bjornsson | 20 Murray | 11 Monkhouse | 10 Boyd | 7 McSweeney | 16 Haslam | 4 Liddle | 12 Yantorno | 19 Fredriksen | 9 Behan | 23 Larkin | 3 Humphreys | 32 Kean | 34 Poole | 36 Donaldson | 18 Mackay | 21 Rafferty | 38 Rowbotham | 37 Holden | 26 Johnson |
|---|---|---|---|---|---|---|---|---|---|---|---|---|---|---|---|---|---|---|---|---|---|---|---|---|---|---|---|
| 1 | 2 | 3 | 4 | 5 | 6 | 7 | 8 | 9 | 10 | 11 | 12 | 13 | 14 | | | | | | | | | | | | | | |
| 1 | | 3 | 4 | 5 | | 7 | 8 | | 10 | 11 | 9 | 13 | 2 | 6 | 12 | | | | | | | | | | | | |
| 1 | | 3 | 4 | 5 | 13 | 7 | 8 | | 10 | 11 | 9 | 14 | 2 | 6 | | 12 | | | | | | | | | | | |
| 1 | | 3 | 4 | 5 | 13 | 7 | 8 | | 10 | 11 | 9 | 14 | 2 | 6 | 12 | | | | | | | | | | | | |
| 1 | | 3 | 4 | 5 | | | | | 8 | 11 | 9 | 13 | 2 | 6 | 7 | | 12 | 14 | 10 | | | | | | | | |
| 1 | 2 | 3 | 4 | 5 | | | | | 8 | 11 | 13 | 14 | | 6 | 7 | | 12 | 9 | 10 | | | | | | | | |
| | 2 | 3 | 4 | 5 | | | | | 8 | 11 | | 13 | 12 | 6 | 7 | | 14 | 9 | 10 | 1 | | | | | | | |
| | 2 | 3 | 4 | 5 | | | 13 | | 8 | 11 | | 14 | | 6 | 7 | | 12 | 9 | 10 | 1 | | | | | | | |
| | 2 | 3 | 4 | 5 | | | 7 | 13 | 8 | 11 | 14 | 12 | | 6 | | | 9 | 10 | | 1 | | | | | | | |
| | 2 | 3 | | 5 | 6 | | 10 | 14 | 8 | 11 | | 7 | 13 | 4 | | | 12 | 9 | | 1 | | | | | | | |
| | 2 | 3 | | 5 | 6 | | 10 | 14 | 8 | 11 | | 7 | 13 | 4 | | | 12 | 9 | | 1 | | | | | | | |
| | 2 | 3 | 13 | 5 | 6 | | 10 | 14 | 8 | 11 | | 7 | | 4 | 12 | | | 9 | | 1 | | | | | | | |
| | 2 | 3 | 13 | 5 | 6 | | 10 | 12 | 8 | 11 | | 7 | | 4 | | | | 9 | | 1 | 14 | | | | | | |
| | 2 | | 4 | 5 | 3 | | 8 | 12 | 10 | 11 | | 7 | | 6 | | | 13 | 9 | | 1 | 14 | | | | | | |
| | 2 | 3 | 7 | 5 | 6 | 9 | 8 | | 10 | 11 | | 12 | 14 | 4 | | | | | | 1 | 13 | | | | | | |
| | 2 | 3 | 7 | 5 | 6 | 9 | | 13 | 10 | 11 | | 14 | | 4 | 8 | | | | 12 | 1 | | | | | | | |
| | 2 | 3 | 8 | 5 | 6 | 12 | 10 | 13 | 14 | 11 | | 7 | | 4 | | | | | 9 | 1 | | | | | | | |
| | 2 | 3 | 8 | 5 | 6 | 9 | 13 | 14 | 10 | 11 | | 7 | | 4 | | | | | 12 | 1 | | | | | | | |
| | 2 | 3 | 8 | 5 | 6 | 9 | | 14 | 10 | 11 | | 7 | 13 | 4 | | | | 12 | | 1 | | | | | | | |
| | 2 | 3 | 8 | 5 | 6 | 9 | | 14 | 10 | | | 7 | 12 | 4 | | | | 13 | 11 | 1 | | | | | | | |
| | 2 | 3 | 8 | | 6 | 12 | 10 | 14 | | 11 | 13 | 7 | 5 | 4 | | | | | 9 | 1 | | | | | | | |
| | 2 | 3 | 8 | | 6 | 9 | | 5 | 10 | 11 | 14 | 7 | | 4 | 13 | | | | 12 | 1 | | | | | | | |
| | 2 | 3 | 8 | | 6 | | 10 | 5 | | 9 | | 7 | | 4 | | | 12 | | 11 | 1 | | | | | | | |
| | 2 | 3 | 8 | 5 | 6 | | 10 | 12 | | 9 | | 7 | | 4 | | | | | 11 | 1 | | | | | | | |
| | 2 | 3 | 8 | 5 | 6 | 13 | 12 | | 10 | 11 | 14 | 7 | | 4 | | | | | | 1 | | 9 | | | | | |
| 1 | 2 | 3 | 8 | 5 | 6 | 9 | | | 10 | 11 | | 13 | | 4 | | | | | 12 | | | 7 | | | | | |
| 1 | | 3 | 8 | 5 | 6 | 9 | | | 10 | 12 | 7 | 14 | 2 | 4 | | | | 13 | 11 | | | | | | | | |
| 1 | | 3 | 8 | 5 | 6 | 13 | 7 | | 10 | 11 | | 12 | 2 | 4 | | | | 9 | 14 | | | | | | | | |
| 1 | | 3 | 8 | 5 | 6 | 9 | | | 10 | 11 | | 14 | 2 | 4 | | | | 12 | 13 | | | 7 | | | | | |
| 1 | | 3 | 8 | 5 | 6 | 12 | | | 10 | 11 | | 14 | 2 | 4 | | | | 13 | 9 | | | 7 | | | | | |
| 1 | | 3 | 8 | 5 | 6 | 9 | | | 10 | 11 | 14 | 13 | 2 | 4 | | | | 12 | | | | 7 | | | | | |
| 1 | | 3 | 8 | 5 | 6 | | 10 | | | 11 | | 7 | 2 | 4 | | | | 9 | 13 | | | 12 | | | | | |
| 1 | | 3 | 8 | 5 | 6 | 13 | | | 10 | 11 | | 7 | 2 | 4 | | | | 12 | | | | 9 | | | | | |
| 1 | | 3 | 8 | 5 | 6 | 14 | | | 10 | 11 | | 7 | 2 | 4 | | | | 12 | 13 | | | 9 | | | | | |
| 1 | | 3 | 8 | 5 | 6 | 14 | | | 10 | 11 | | 7 | 2 | 4 | | | | 13 | 12 | | | 9 | | | | | |
| 1 | | 3 | 8 | 5 | 6 | 10 | 14 | | | 11 | | 7 | 2 | 4 | 13 | | | 12 | | | | 9 | | | | | |
| 1 | | 3 | | 5 | 6 | 10 | 13 | | 8 | 11 | 14 | 7 | 2 | 4 | | | | 12 | | | | 9 | | | | | |
| 1 | | 3 | | 5 | 6 | | 8 | 12 | 10 | 11 | | 7 | 2 | 4 | 14 | | | 9 | 13 | | | | | | | | |
| 1 | | 3 | | 5 | 6 | | 8 | | | 11 | 12 | 14 | 2 | 4 | 7 | | 13 | 10 | | | | 9 | | | | | |
| 1 | | 3 | | 5 | 6 | | 8 | 13 | 10 | 11 | | 7 | 2 | 4 | | | | 9 | 12 | | | | | | | | |
| 1 | | 3 | 8 | 5 | 6 | | 4 | | 7 | 11 | 9 | 12 | 2 | | 14 | | | 13 | 10 | | | | | | | | |
| 1 | | 3 | 8 | 5 | 6 | | 4 | | 10 | 11 | 9 | 12 | 2 | | 7 | | 13 | | | | | | 14 | | | | |
| | | 12 | 8 | 5 | 6 | | 4 | | | 11 | 9 | 7 | | | | | 13 | 14 | | | | | 10 | 1 | 2 | 3 | |
| 1 | | 3 | 8 | 5 | 6 | | 7 | | | 11 | | 12 | 2 | 4 | 10 | | | | 9 | | | | 13 | | | | |
| 1 | 2 | 3 | 8 | | 6 | 10 | | | | | 9 | 7 | | 4 | 14 | | 13 | 12 | 11 | | | | | | | | 5 |
| 1 | 2 | 3 | 8 | 5 | 6 | 12 | 7 | | | 11 | 14 | 13 | | 4 | 10 | | | 9 | | | | | | | | | |
| 26 | 24 | 44 | 38 | 42 | 38 | 17 | 25 | 3 | 35 | 43 | 9 | 24 | 22 | 42 | 9 | 0 | 1 | 15 | 14 | 19 | 0 | 11 | 1 | 1 | 1 | 1 | 1 |
| 0 | 0 | 1 | 2 | 0 | 2 | 9 | 5 | 15 | 1 | 1 | 10 | 22 | 7 | 0 | 8 | 1 | 12 | 15 | 11 | 0 | 3 | 1 | 2 | 0 | 0 | 0 | 0 |
| 1 | 2 | 2 | 9 | 2 | 2 | 1 | 1 | 0 | 1 | 7 | 3 | 2 | 0 | 6 | 0 | 0 | 0 | 3 | 2 | 0 | 1 | 0 | 0 | 0 | 0 | 0 | 0 |

| 1 Flinders | 2 Austin | 6 Horwood | 15 Sweeney | 5 Collins | 29 Hartley | 14 Brown | 8 Gamble | 22 Bjornsson | 20 Murray | 11 Monkhouse | 10 Boyd | 7 McSweeney | 16 Haslam | 4 Liddle | 12 Yantorno | 19 Fredriksen | 9 Behan | 23 Larkin | 3 Humphreys | 32 Kean | 34 Poole |
|---|---|---|---|---|---|---|---|---|---|---|---|---|---|---|---|---|---|---|---|---|---|
| | 2 | 3 | 8 | 5 | 6 | | 10 | 14 | | 11 | | 7 | | 4 | | | | 9 | 13 | 1 | 12 |
| | 2 | 3 | 8 | 5 | 6 | 12 | 13 | 9 | | 11 | | 7 | | 4 | | | | | | 1 | 10 |
| | 2 | 3 | 8 | 5 | 6 | | 10 | | | 11 | 13 | 7 | 12 | 4 | 14 | | | | 9 | 1 | |
| | 2 | 3 | 4 | | 6 | 12 | 8 | | 10 | 11 | | 7 | | 5 | 14 | | | 13 | 9 | 1 | |
| | 4 | 4 | 4 | 3 | 4 | 0 | 3 | 1 | 1 | 4 | 0 | 4 | 0 | 4 | 0 | | | 1 | 2 | 4 | 1 |
| | 0 | 0 | 0 | 0 | 0 | 2 | 1 | 1 | 0 | 0 | 1 | 0 | 1 | 0 | 2 | | | 1 | 1 | 0 | 1 |
| | 0 | 0 | 4 | 0 | 0 | 1 | 0 | 0 | 0 | 0 | 0 | 0 | 0 | 0 | 0 | | | 0 | 1 | 0 | 0 |

| 1 Flinders | 2 Austin | 6 Horwood | 15 Sweeney | 5 Collins | 29 Hartley | 14 Brown | 8 Gamble | 22 Bjornsson | 20 Murray | 11 Monkhouse | 10 Boyd | 7 McSweeney | 16 Haslam | 4 Liddle | 12 Yantorno | 19 Fredriksen | 9 Behan | 23 Larkin |
|---|---|---|---|---|---|---|---|---|---|---|---|---|---|---|---|---|---|---|
| 1 | | 3 | 4 | 5 | | 7 | 8 | | 10 | 11 | 9 | 12 | 2 | 6 | | 13 | 14 | |
| 1 | | 3 | 4 | 5 | | 7 | 8 | | 10 | 11 | 9 | 14 | 2 | 6 | | | 13 | 12 |
| 2 | | 2 | 2 | 2 | | 2 | 2 | | 2 | 2 | 2 | 0 | 2 | 2 | | 0 | 0 | 0 |
| 0 | | 0 | 0 | 0 | | 0 | 0 | | 0 | 0 | 0 | 2 | 0 | 0 | | 1 | 2 | 1 |
| 0 | | 0 | 0 | 0 | | 1 | 0 | | 0 | 0 | 1 | 0 | 0 | 0 | | 0 | 0 | 0 |

| 1 Flinders | 2 Austin | 6 Horwood | 15 Sweeney | 5 Collins | 29 Hartley | 14 Brown | 8 Gamble | 22 Bjornsson | 20 Murray | 11 Monkhouse | 10 Boyd | 7 McSweeney | 16 Haslam | 4 Liddle | 12 Yantorno | 19 Fredriksen | 9 Behan | 23 Larkin | 3 Humphreys | 32 Kean | 34 Poole |
|---|---|---|---|---|---|---|---|---|---|---|---|---|---|---|---|---|---|---|---|---|---|
| 1 | | 3 | 4 | 5 | | 7 | 8 | | 10 | 11 | 9 | | 2 | 6 | 12 | | 13 | | 14 | | |
| | 2 | 3 | | | 6 | | 14 | 5 | | 13 | 10 | 11 | 8 | 4 | 7 | | 9 | 12 | | 1 | |
| | 2 | 3 | 4 | 5 | 12 | | 8 | 9 | 10 | 11 | | 13 | | 6 | 7 | | | | | 1 | 14 |
| 1 | 2 | 3 | 2 | 2 | 1 | 1 | 2 | 2 | 2 | 2 | 2 | 1 | 2 | 3 | 2 | | 1 | 0 | 0 | 2 | 0 |
| 0 | 0 | 0 | 0 | 0 | 1 | 0 | 1 | 0 | 0 | 1 | 0 | 1 | 0 | 0 | 1 | | 1 | 1 | 1 | 0 | 1 |
| 0 | 0 | 1 | 1 | 0 | 0 | 0 | 0 | 0 | 0 | 1 | 0 | 1 | 0 | 0 | 1 | | 1 | 0 | 0 | 0 | 0 |

## League Table

| | P | W | D | L | F | A | Pts |
|---|---|---|---|---|---|---|---|
| Brighton & Hove Albion | 46 | 28 | 11 | 7 | 85 | 40 | 95 |
| Southampton | 46 | 28 | 8 | 10 | 86 | 38 | 92 |
| Huddersfield Town | 46 | 25 | 12 | 9 | 77 | 48 | 87 |
| Peterborough United | 46 | 23 | 10 | 13 | 106 | 75 | 79 |
| Milton Keynes Dons | 46 | 23 | 8 | 15 | 67 | 60 | 77 |
| Bournemouth | 46 | 19 | 14 | 13 | 75 | 54 | 71 |
| Leyton Orient | 46 | 19 | 13 | 14 | 71 | 62 | 70 |
| Exeter City | 46 | 20 | 10 | 16 | 66 | 73 | 70 |
| Rochdale | 46 | 18 | 14 | 14 | 63 | 55 | 68 |
| Colchester United | 46 | 16 | 14 | 16 | 57 | 63 | 62 |
| Brentford | 46 | 17 | 10 | 19 | 55 | 62 | 61 |
| Carlisle United | 46 | 16 | 11 | 19 | 60 | 62 | 59 |
| Charlton Athletic | 46 | 15 | 14 | 17 | 62 | 66 | 59 |
| Yeovil Town | 46 | 16 | 11 | 19 | 56 | 66 | 59 |
| Sheffield Wednesday | 46 | 16 | 10 | 20 | 67 | 67 | 58 |
| Hartlepool United | 46 | 15 | 12 | 19 | 47 | 65 | 57 |
| Tranmere Rovers | 46 | 15 | 11 | 20 | 53 | 60 | 56 |
| Oldham Athletic | 46 | 13 | 17 | 16 | 53 | 60 | 56 |
| Notts County | 46 | 14 | 8 | 24 | 46 | 60 | 50 |
| Walsall | 46 | 12 | 12 | 22 | 56 | 75 | 48 |
| Dagenham & Redbridge | 46 | 12 | 11 | 23 | 52 | 70 | 47 |
| Bristol Rovers | 46 | 11 | 12 | 23 | 48 | 82 | 45 |
| Plymouth Argyle | 46 | 15 | 7 | 24 | 51 | 74 | 42 |
| Swindon Town | 46 | 9 | 14 | 23 | 50 | 72 | 41 |

# 2011-12

## League One

Managers : Chris Wadsworth, Mickey Barron and Neale Cooper

### Did you know that?

'Pools made a record start to the season with a nine game unbeaten run with five wins.

Luke James became 'Pools youngest goalscorer aged 17 years, 64 days when he volleyed home the second goal in the 2–0 home win against Rochdale.

| Match No. | Date | Round | Venue | Opponents | Result | | Scorers | Attendance |
|---|---|---|---|---|---|---|---|---|
| 1 | Aug 6 | | (a) | Milton Keynes Dons | D | 2 - 2 | Boyd, Poole | 7,287 |
| 3 | 13 | | (h) | Walsall | D | 1 - 1 | Nish | 5,170 |
| 4 | 16 | | (h) | Huddersfield Town | D | 0 - 0 | | 5,506 |
| 5 | 20 | | (a) | Stevenage Borough | D | 2 - 2 | Hartley, Boyd (pen) | 2,831 |
| 6 | 27 | | (a) | Rochdale | W | 3 - 1 | Boyd, Poole 2 | 2,600 |
| 8 | Sep 3 | | (h) | Exeter City | W | 2 - 0 | Liddle, Luscombe | 5,152 |
| 9 | 10 | | (a) | Carlisle United | W | 2 - 1 | Liddle, Boyd | 4,765 |
| 10 | 17 | | (h) | Bury | W | 3 - 0 | Solano, Nish 2 | 5,343 |
| 11 | 24 | | (a) | AFC Bournemouth | W | 2 - 1 | Solano, Horwood | 5,275 |
| 12 | Oct 1 | | (h) | Sheffield Wednesday | L | 0 - 1 | | 6,800 |
| 13 | 9 | | (a) | Notts County | L | 0 - 3 | | 6,172 |
| 14 | 15 | | (h) | Wycombe Wanderers | L | 1 - 3 | Boyd (pen) | 5,421 |
| 15 | 22 | | (a) | Chesterfield | W | 3 - 2 | Poole 2, Murray | 5,937 |
| 16 | 25 | | (h) | Tranmere Rovers | L | 0 - 2 | | 5,200 |
| 17 | 29 | | (h) | Charlton Athletic | L | 0 - 4 | | 5,333 |
| 18 | Nov 5 | | (a) | Leyton Orient | D | 1 - 1 | Austin (pen) | 4,424 |
| 20 | 19 | | (a) | Scunthorpe United | W | 2 - 0 | Monkhouse, Sweeney | 3,861 |
| 21 | 26 | | (h) | Yeovil Town | L | 0 - 1 | | 4,604 |
| 22 | 29 | | (h) | Preston North End | L | 0 - 1 | | 4,156 |
| 23 | Dec 10 | | (a) | Brentford | L | 1 - 2 | Collins | 6,352 |
| 24 | 17 | | (h) | Colchester United | L | 0 - 1 | | 4,029 |
| 25 | 26 | | (a) | Oldham Athletic | W | 1 - 0 | Poole | 4,459 |
| 26 | 31 | | (a) | Sheffield United | L | 1 - 3 | Hartley | 20,372 |
| 27 | Jan 2 | | (h) | Scunthorpe United | L | 1 - 2 | Monkhouse | 5,289 |
| 28 | 7 | | (h) | Rochdale | W | 2 - 0 | Brown, James | 4,663 |
| 29 | 14 | | (a) | Exeter City | D | 0 - 0 | | 4,016 |
| 30 | 21 | | (a) | Sheffield Wednesday | D | 2 - 2 | Hartley, Sweeney | 17,469 |
| 31 | 28 | | (h) | Carlisle United | W | 4 - 0 | James 2, Sweeney, Nish | 5,995 |
| 32 | 11 | | (h) | AFC Bournemouth | D | 0 - 0 | | 4,548 |
| 33 | 14 | | (a) | Preston North End | L | 0 - 1 | | 14,191 |
| 34 | 18 | | (h) | Notts County | W | 3 - 0 | Sweeney 2, Monkhouse | 4,718 |
| 35 | 25 | | (a) | Wycombe Wanderers | L | 0 - 5 | | 4,408 |
| 36 | 28 | | (a) | Bury | W | 2 - 1 | Humphreys, Boyd | 2,072 |
| 37 | Mar 3 | | (h) | Milton Keynes Dons | D | 1 - 1 | Poole | 4,955 |
| 38 | 6 | | (a) | Huddersfield Town | L | 0 - 1 | | 12,316 |
| 39 | 10 | | (a) | Walsall | D | 0 - 0 | | 3,751 |
| 40 | 17 | | (h) | Stevenage Borough | D | 0 - 0 | | 4,484 |
| 41 | 20 | | (h) | Oldham Athletic | L | 0 - 1 | | 4,109 |
| 42 | 24 | | (a) | Yeovil Town | W | 1 - 0 | Noble | 4,033 |
| 43 | 31 | | (h) | Sheffield United | L | 0 - 1 | | 5,825 |
| 44 | Apr 6 | | (a) | Colchester United | D | 1 - 1 | Sweeney | 3,921 |
| 45 | 9 | | (h) | Brentford | D | 0 - 0 | | 4,292 |
| 46 | 14 | | (h) | Chesterfield | L | 1 - 2 | Liddle | 4,004 |
| 47 | 21 | | (a) | Tranmere Rovers | D | 1 - 1 | Sweeney | 4,757 |
| 48 | 28 | | (h) | Leyton Orient | W | 2 - 1 | Sweeney, Noble | 4,502 |
| 49 | May 5 | | (a) | Charlton Athletic | L | 2 - 3 | Hartley, Liddle | 26,749 |

Final Position: 13th in League One

Apps.
Sub.Apps.
Goals

**FA Cup**

| | | | | | | | | |
|---|---|---|---|---|---|---|---|---|
| 19 | Nov 5 | R1 | (h) | Stevenage Borough | L | 0 - 1 | | 2,744 |

Apps.
Sub.Apps.
Goals

**League Cup**

| | | | | | | | | |
|---|---|---|---|---|---|---|---|---|
| 2 | Aug 9 | R1 | (h) | Sheffield United | L | 1 - 1* | Sweeney | 2,774 |

* After extra time. Lost 4 - 5 on penalties

Apps.
Sub.Apps.
Goals

**Johnstone's Paint Trophy**

| | | | | | | | | |
|---|---|---|---|---|---|---|---|---|
| 7 | Aug 30 | R1 | (a) | Scunthorpe United | L | 0 - 2 | | 1,768 |

Apps.
Sub.Apps.
Goals

| 1 Flinders | 2 Austin | 6 Horwood | 4 Liddle | 5 Collins | 29 Hartley | 24 Solano | 15 Sweeney | 9 Nish | 10 Boyd | 11 Monkhouse | 14 Luscombe | 20 Murray | 8 Poole | 3 Humphreys | 27 Larkin | 7 Brown | 16 Haslam | 12 Wright | 21 Rafferty | 18 Baldwin | 33 James | 23 Hassan | 17 Adjei | 28 Rowbotham | 34 Hawkins | 35 Noble | 19 Richards | 36 Rutherford | 30 Holden |
|---|---|---|---|---|---|---|---|---|---|---|---|---|---|---|---|---|---|---|---|---|---|---|---|---|---|---|---|---|---|
| 1 | 2 | 3 | 4 | 5 | 6 | 7 | 8 | 9 | 10 | 11 | 12 | 13 | 14 | | | | | | | | | | | | | | | | |
| 1 | 2 | 3 | 4 | 5 | 6 | 7 | | 9 | 10 | 11 | 12 | 8 | 13 | 14 | | | | | | | | | | | | | | | |
| 1 | 2 | 3 | | 5 | 6 | | | 9 | 13 | 11 | | 8 | 7 | 4 | 10 | 12 | 14 | | | | | | | | | | | | |
| 1 | 2 | 3 | | 5 | 6 | | | 9 | 7 | 11 | | 8 | 12 | 4 | 10 | 13 | 14 | | | | | | | | | | | | |
| 1 | 2 | 3 | 4 | | 6 | | | 9 | 10 | 11 | | 8 | 12 | 7 | | 13 | 5 | | | | | | | | | | | | |
| 1 | 2 | | 4 | | 6 | 7 | 11 | 9 | 10 | 13 | 14 | 8 | 12 | 3 | | | | 5 | | | | | | | | | | | |
| 1 | 2 | | 4 | 12 | 6 | 7 | 11 | 9 | 10 | 13 | 14 | 8 | | 3 | | | | 5 | | | | | | | | | | | |
| 1 | 2 | | 4 | 5 | 6 | 7 | 11 | 9 | 10 | 12 | | 8 | 13 | 14 | | | | 3 | | | | | | | | | | | |
| 1 | 2 | 14 | 4 | 5 | 6 | 7 | 11 | 9 | 10 | 12 | | 8 | 13 | 3 | | | | | | | | | | | | | | | |
| 1 | 2 | 12 | 4 | 5 | 6 | 7 | 11 | 9 | 10 | 13 | | 8 | 14 | 3 | | | | | | | | | | | | | | | |
| 1 | 2 | 12 | 4 | 5 | 6 | 7 | 11 | 9 | 10 | 13 | | 8 | 14 | 3 | | | | | | | | | | | | | | | |
| 1 | 2 | 10 | 4 | 5 | 6 | | 7 | 13 | 14 | 11 | 12 | 8 | 9 | | | | | 3 | | | | | | | | | | | |
| 1 | 2 | 10 | 4 | 5 | 6 | | | 13 | | 11 | 7 | 8 | 9 | 14 | | 12 | | 3 | | | | | | | | | | | |
| 1 | 2 | 10 | 4 | 5 | 6 | | | 13 | | 11 | 7 | 8 | 9 | | | 12 | | 3 | | | | | | | | | | | |
| 1 | 2 | 3 | 4 | 5 | 6 | | | 9 | 10 | 11 | 13 | 8 | 7 | | | 12 | | | | | | | | | | | | | |
| 1 | 7 | 10 | 12 | 5 | 6 | | 4 | | | 11 | 14 | 8 | 9 | 3 | | 13 | | 2 | | | | | | | | | | | |
| | 2 | 3 | 4 | | 6 | 7 | 8 | | 14 | 11 | | 10 | 9 | 12 | | | 13 | 5 | 1 | | | | | | | | | | |
| 1 | 2 | 3 | 4 | | 6 | 7 | 8 | | 12 | 11 | 13 | 10 | 9 | 14 | | | | 5 | | | | | | | | | | | |
| 1 | 2 | 3 | 12 | | 6 | 7 | 4 | | 10 | 11 | 13 | 8 | 9 | 14 | | | | 5 | | | | | | | | | | | |
| 1 | 2 | 3 | 4 | 5 | 6 | 13 | 8 | | 12 | 11 | 14 | 10 | 9 | | | 7 | | | | | | | | | | | | | |
| 1 | 2 | 3 | 4 | 5 | | 13 | 8 | | 14 | 11 | | 10 | 9 | | | 7 | | | | 6 | 12 | | | | | | | | |
| 1 | 2 | 3 | 4 | 5 | 6 | | 8 | | | 11 | | 10 | 9 | | | | | | | 7 | 12 | | | | | | | | |
| 1 | 2 | 3 | 4 | 5 | 6 | | 8 | | | 11 | | 10 | | 9 | | 12 | | | | 7 | 13 | | | | | | | | |
| 1 | 2 | 3 | 4 | | 5 | 13 | 8 | | 9 | 11 | 7 | | | 6 | | 12 | | | | | 10 | | | | | | | | |
| 1 | 2 | 3 | 4 | 5 | 6 | | 8 | | | 11 | | 10 | | 13 | | 12 | | | | 7 | 9 | | | | | | | | |
| 1 | 2 | 3 | 4 | 5 | 6 | | 8 | | | | | 11 | | | | 10 | 12 | | | 7 | 9 | 13 | | | | | | | |
| 1 | 2 | 3 | 4 | 5 | 6 | | 8 | | | 11 | | 10 | | 12 | | 13 | 7 | | | | 9 | | | | | | | | |
| 1 | 2 | 3 | 4 | 5 | 6 | | 8 | 13 | | 11 | | 10 | | | | 7 | 12 | | | 14 | 9 | | | | | | | | |
| 1 | 2 | 3 | 4 | 5 | 6 | | 8 | 12 | | 11 | | 10 | | | | 7 | | | | | 9 | | | | | | | | |
| 1 | 2 | 3 | 4 | 5 | 6 | | 8 | 13 | | 11 | | 10 | | | | 7 | 12 | | | | 9 | | | | | | | | |
| 1 | 2 | 3 | 4 | 5 | 6 | | 8 | | 13 | 11 | | 10 | | 14 | | 7 | 12 | | | | 9 | | | | | | | | |
| 1 | 2 | 3 | | 5 | 6 | | 8 | 14 | 12 | 11 | | 10 | | | | 7 | 4 | | | 13 | 9 | | | | | | | | |
| 1 | 2 | 3 | | 5 | 6 | | 8 | | 12 | 11 | | 10 | | 7 | | 9 | | | | 4 | | | | | | | | | |
| 1 | 2 | 3 | | 5 | 6 | | 8 | | 14 | 11 | | 10 | 9 | 4 | | 7 | | | | 13 | | | 12 | | | | | | |
| 1 | 2 | 3 | | 5 | 6 | | 8 | 14 | 13 | 11 | | 10 | 9 | 4 | | 12 | | | | 7 | | | | | | | | | |
| 1 | 2 | 3 | | | 6 | | 8 | | 13 | 11 | | 10 | | 7 | | 12 | | | | 4 | | | | 5 | 9 | | | | |
| 1 | 2 | 3 | 4 | 5 | 6 | | 8 | | 13 | 11 | | 10 | 12 | 9 | | | | | | 7 | | | | | | | | | |
| 1 | 2 | 3 | 4 | 5 | 6 | | 8 | | 12 | 11 | | 10 | 7 | | | | | | | | | | | | | 9 | 13 | | |
| 1 | 2 | 3 | 4 | 5 | 6 | | 8 | | 13 | 11 | | 10 | | 12 | | | | | | 7 | | | | | | 9 | | | |
| 1 | 2 | 3 | 4 | 5 | 6 | | 8 | | 13 | 11 | | 10 | | | | 12 | | | | | 7 | | | | | 9 | | | |
| 1 | 2 | 3 | 4 | 5 | | | 8 | | | 11 | | 10 | | 6 | | | | | | 7 | 12 | | | | | 9 | | | |
| 1 | 2 | 3 | 4 | 5 | 6 | | 8 | | 13 | 11 | | 10 | | 7 | | | | | | | 12 | | | | | 9 | | | |
| 1 | 2 | 3 | 4 | 5 | 6 | | 8 | | 12 | 11 | | 10 | | | | | | | | | 7 | | | | | 9 | | 13 | |
| 1 | 2 | | 5 | | 6 | | 8 | | | 11 | | 10 | | | | | | | | 3 | 7 | | | | | 9 | 4 | | 12 |
| 1 | 2 | 3 | 4 | | 6 | | 8 | | | 11 | | 10 | 13 | | | | | | | 5 | 12 | | | | | 9 | | | 7 |
| 1 | 2 | | 4 | | 6 | | 8 | | | 11 | | 10 | 13 | 7 | | | | | | 5 | 12 | | | | | 9 | | | 3 |
| 45 | 46 | 38 | 37 | 35 | 44 | 11 | 39 | 12 | 13 | 39 | 3 | 44 | 15 | 19 | 2 | 10 | 3 | 10 | 1 | 14 | 12 | 0 | 0 | 1 | 1 | 9 | 1 | 0 | 2 |
| 0 | 0 | 3 | 2 | 1 | 0 | 3 | 0 | 8 | 18 | 6 | 10 | 1 | 12 | 10 | 0 | 14 | 7 | 0 | 0 | 3 | 7 | 1 | 1 | 0 | 0 | 0 | 1 | 1 | 1 |
| 0 | 1 | 1 | 4 | 1 | 4 | 2 | 8 | 4 | 6 | 3 | 1 | 1 | 7 | 1 | 0 | 1 | 0 | 0 | 0 | 0 | 3 | 0 | 0 | 0 | 0 | 2 | 0 | 0 | 0 |

| | | | | | | | | | | | | | | | | | | | |
|---|---|---|---|---|---|---|---|---|---|---|---|---|---|---|---|---|---|---|---|
| 1 | 2 | 10 | 4 | | 6 | 7 | 8 | | 13 | 11 | 12 | | 9 | 3 | | | | 5 | 15 |
| 1 | 1 | 1 | 1 | | 1 | 1 | 1 | | | 1 | | | 1 | 1 | | | | 1 | |
| | | | | | | | | | 1 | | 1 | | | | | | | | 1 |
| | | | | | | | | | | | | | | | | | | | |

| | | | | | | | | | | | | | |
|---|---|---|---|---|---|---|---|---|---|---|---|---|---|
| 1 | 2 | 3 | 4 | 5 | 6 | 7 | 8 | 9 | 10 | 11 | 13 | 14 | 12 |
| 1 | 1 | 1 | 1 | 1 | 1 | 1 | 1 | 1 | 1 | 1 | | | |
| | | | | | | | | | | | 1 | 1 | 1 |
| | | | | | | | 1 | | | | | | |

| | | | | | | | | | | | | | | | | | |
|---|---|---|---|---|---|---|---|---|---|---|---|---|---|---|---|---|---|
| 1 | 2 | 3 | 4 | | 6 | | 13 | | 9 | 11 | 8 | | 7 | 10 | 12 | 14 | 5 |
| 1 | 1 | 1 | 1 | | 1 | | | | 1 | 1 | 1 | | 1 | 1 | | | 1 |
| | | | | | | | 1 | | | | | | | | 1 | 1 | |
| | | | | | | | | | | | | | | | | | |

## League Table

| | P | W | D | L | F | A | Pts |
|---|---|---|---|---|---|---|---|
| Charlton | 46 | 30 | 11 | 5 | 82 | 36 | 101 |
| Sheffield Wed | 46 | 28 | 9 | 9 | 81 | 48 | 93 |
| Sheffield Utd | 46 | 27 | 9 | 10 | 92 | 51 | 90 |
| Huddersfield | 46 | 21 | 18 | 7 | 79 | 47 | 81 |
| MK Dons | 46 | 22 | 14 | 10 | 84 | 47 | 80 |
| Stevenage | 46 | 18 | 19 | 9 | 69 | 44 | 73 |
| Notts County | 46 | 21 | 10 | 15 | 75 | 63 | 73 |
| Carlisle | 46 | 18 | 15 | 13 | 65 | 66 | 69 |
| Brentford | 46 | 18 | 13 | 15 | 63 | 52 | 67 |
| Colchester | 46 | 13 | 20 | 13 | 61 | 66 | 59 |
| Bournemouth | 46 | 15 | 13 | 18 | 48 | 52 | 58 |
| Tranmere | 46 | 14 | 14 | 18 | 49 | 53 | 56 |
| Hartlepool | 46 | 14 | 14 | 18 | 50 | 55 | 56 |
| Bury | 46 | 15 | 11 | 20 | 60 | 79 | 56 |
| Preston | 46 | 13 | 15 | 18 | 54 | 68 | 54 |
| Oldham | 46 | 14 | 12 | 20 | 50 | 66 | 54 |
| Yeovil Town | 46 | 14 | 12 | 20 | 59 | 80 | 54 |
| Scunthorpe | 46 | 10 | 22 | 14 | 55 | 59 | 52 |
| Walsall | 46 | 10 | 20 | 16 | 51 | 57 | 50 |
| Leyton Orient | 46 | 13 | 11 | 22 | 48 | 75 | 50 |
| Wycombe | 46 | 11 | 10 | 25 | 65 | 88 | 43 |
| Chesterfield | 46 | 10 | 12 | 24 | 56 | 81 | 42 |
| Exeter City | 46 | 10 | 12 | 24 | 46 | 75 | 42 |
| Rochdale | 46 | 8 | 14 | 24 | 47 | 81 | 38 |

# The Football League Trophy 1981-2009

## 1981-82 Football League Group Cup

| Match No. | Date | Round | Venue | Opponents | Result | | Scorers | Attendance |
|---|---|---|---|---|---|---|---|---|
| 1 | Aug 15 | GrpB/1 | (h) | Rotherham United | L | 0 - 1 | | 2,031 |
| 2 | 19 | GrpB/2 | (h) | Bradford City | L | 0 - 1 | | 1,221 |
| 3 | 22 | GrpB/3 | (a) | Hull City | L | 0 - 1 | | 1,621 |
| | | | | | | | | Apps. |
| | | | | | | | | Sub.Apps. |
| | | | | | | | | Goals |

## 1982-83 Football League Trophy

| Match No. | Date | Round | Venue | Opponents | Result | | Scorers | Attendance |
|---|---|---|---|---|---|---|---|---|
| 1 | Aug 14 | R1/1 | (h) | Hull City | L | 1 - 2 | Lawrence | 962 |
| 2 | 18 | R1/2 | (h) | Bradford City | L | 0 - 4 | | 655 |
| 3 | 21 | R1/3 | (a) | Halifax Town | L | 0 - 3 | | 938 |
| | | | | | | | | Apps. |
| | | | | | | | | Sub.Apps. |
| | | | | | | | | Goals |

## 1983-84 Football League Associate Members Cup

| Match No. | Date | Round | Venue | Opponents | Result | | Scorers | Attendance |
|---|---|---|---|---|---|---|---|---|
| 34 | Feb 22 | R1 | (a) | Bradford City | L | 2 - 3 | Dobson, A.Linighan | 1,179 |
| | | | | | | | | Apps. |
| | | | | | | | | Sub.Apps. |
| | | | | | | | | Goals |

## 1984-85 Freight Rover Trophy

| Match No. | Date | Round | Venue | Opponents | Result | | Scorers | Attendance |
|---|---|---|---|---|---|---|---|---|
| 29 | Jan 23 | R1/1 | (h) | Lincoln City | W | 2 - 1 | Waddle, Brown | 1,202 |
| 31 | Feb 6 | R1/2 | (a) | Lincoln City | L | 0 - 4 | | 1,316 |
| | | | | | | | | Apps. |
| | | | | | | | | Sub.Apps. |
| | | | | | | | | Goals |

This competition was launched in season 1981–82 to replace the Anglo-Scottish Cup and lasted just two seasons. In 1982–83 it was renamed the Football League Trophy. The current LDV Vans Trophy was launched in the 1983–84 season as the Associate Members Cup (AMC) for teams in the old Third and Fourth Divisions. The competition is currently sponsored by Johnstone Paints. The AMC was initially organised into mini-leagues of three clubs, who played each other in knock-out stages, and it was split into two regions (North and South). In 1996–97 the competition became a straight knock-out tournament. In 2000–01 seven clubs from the Nationwide Conference also played in the competition.

| Burleigh | Brown | Stimpson | Hogan | Bird | Linighan, A. | Kerr | Sweeney | Staff | Houchen | Harding | Hampton | Johnson | Linacre, J. | Howard |
|---|---|---|---|---|---|---|---|---|---|---|---|---|---|---|
| 1 | 2 | 3 | 4 | 5 | 6 | 8 | | | 9 | *11* | 10 | | 7 | *12* |
| 1 | 2 | 3 | 4 | 5 | 6 | 7 | 8 | **13** | 10 | | *11* | *12* | | **9** |
| 1 | 2 | **3** | 4 | 5 | 6 | 7 | 8 | *9* | 10 | 11 | *12* | | | **13** |
| 3 | 3 | 3 | 3 | 3 | 3 | 3 | 2 | 1 | 3 | 2 | 2 | | 1 | 1 |
| | | | | | | | | 1 | | | 1 | 1 | | 2 |
| | | | | | | | | | | | | | | |

| Watson | Brown | Stimpson | Hogan | Bird | Linighan, A. | Bainbridge | Lawrence | Smith | Staff | Johnson | Newton | Linacre | Lowe | Taylor | Wright | Linighan, D. | Gollogly | Fagan |
|---|---|---|---|---|---|---|---|---|---|---|---|---|---|---|---|---|---|---|
| 1 | 6 | 3 | 4 | | | **13** | 8 | | *12* | 11 | 9 | 10 | *2* | | | **7** | | 5 |
| 1 | 6 | 3 | 4 | | 5 | | 8 | | *12* | 11 | 9 | *10* | | 2 | | | | 7 |
| | 6 | 3 | *4* | 5 | | 7 | **8** | 10 | | 11 | 9 | | *12* | 2 | 1 | | **13** | |
| 2 | 3 | 3 | 3 | 1 | 1 | 1 | 3 | 1 | | 3 | 3 | 2 | 1 | 2 | 1 | 1 | | 2 |
| | | | | | | 1 | | | 2 | | | | 1 | | | | 1 | |
| | | | | | | | 1 | | | | | | | | | | | |

| Blackburn | Brown | Linighan, A. | Johnson | Lowe | Barker | Kennedy | Hogan | Dobson | Smithies | Linacre, P. |
|---|---|---|---|---|---|---|---|---|---|---|
| 1 | 6 | 5 | 11 | 8 | 3 | 7 | 4 | 10 | 2 | 9 |
| 1 | 1 | 1 | 1 | 1 | 1 | 1 | 1 | 1 | 1 | 1 |
| | | | | | | | | | | |
| | | | | | | | | | | |
| | | 1 | | | | | | 1 | | |

| Brownlie | Hedley | Smith | Brown | Taylor | Dixon | Linighan | Robinson | Hogan | Stevenson | Stimpson | Pollard | Waddle | Blackburn | Venus |
|---|---|---|---|---|---|---|---|---|---|---|---|---|---|---|
| | 4 | 5 | 6 | 11 | 9 | | 2 | 10 | 1 | 3 | 7 | 8 | | |
| **3** | *4* | 5 | 6 | 11 | 9 | 7 | 2 | 10 | | | *12* | 8 | 1 | **13** |
| 1 | 2 | 2 | 2 | 2 | 2 | 1 | 2 | 2 | 1 | 1 | 1 | 2 | 1 | |
| | | | | | | | | | | | 1 | | | 1 |
| | | | 1 | | | | | | | | | 1 | | |

## 1985-86

## Freight Rover Trophy

| Match No. | Date | Round | Venue | Opponents | Result | | Scorers | Attendance |
|---|---|---|---|---|---|---|---|---|
| 31 | Jan 21 | R1/1 | (a) | Rotherham United | L | 0 - 3 | | 1,309 |
| 33 | 28 | R1/2 | (h) | York City | W | 3 - 2 | Honour 2, Lester | 1,080 |
| | | | | | | | | Apps. |
| | | | | | | | | Sub.Apps. |

## 1986-87

## Freight Rover Trophy

| Match No. | Date | Round | Venue | Opponents | Result | | Scorers | Attendance |
|---|---|---|---|---|---|---|---|---|
| 22 | Dec 2 | PR | (a) | Scunthorpe United | L | 0 - 1 | | 952 |
| 23 | 6 | PR | (h) | Lincoln City | D | 0 - 0 | | 938 |
| | | | | | | | | Apps. |
| | | | | | | | | Sub.Apps. |
| | | | | | | | | Goals |

## 1987-88

## Sherpa Van Trophy

| Match No. | Date | Round | Venue | Opponents | Result | | Scorers | Attendance |
|---|---|---|---|---|---|---|---|---|
| 18 | Oct 27 | PR | (a) | Mansfield Town | L | 2 - 3 | Smith, Kennedy | 2,710 |
| 24 | Nov 24 | PR | (h) | Doncaster Rovers | W | 1 - 0 | Stokes | 782 |
| 37 | Feb 3 | R1 | (a) | Carlisle United | W | 2 - 0 | Baker, Borthwick | 1,433 |
| 39 | 9 | QF | (a) | Sunderland | W | 1 - 0 | Honour | 8,976 |
| 45 | Mar 9 | SFN | (h) | Preston North End | L | 0 - 2 | | 4,989 |
| | | | | | | | | Apps. |
| | | | | | | | | Sub.Apps. |
| | | | | | | | | Goals |

## 1988-89

## Sherpa Van Trophy

| Match No. | Date | Round | Venue | Opponents | Result | | Scorers | Attendance |
|---|---|---|---|---|---|---|---|---|
| 21 | Nov 29 | PR | (a) | Burnley | L | 0 - 3 | | 3,748 |
| 24 | Dec 13 | PR | (h) | York City | L | 0 - 2 | | 1,396 |
| | | | | | | | | Apps. |
| | | | | | | | | Sub.Apps. |
| | | | | | | | | Goals |

## 1989-90

## Leyland Daf Cup

| Match No. | Date | Round | Venue | Opponents | Result | | Scorers | Attendance |
|---|---|---|---|---|---|---|---|---|
| 18 | Nov 7 | PR | (a) | York City | L | 1 - 7 | McEwan (pen) | 1,444 |
| 22 | 28 | PR | (h) | Rotherham United | L | 1 - 4 | Baker | 818 |
| | | | | | | | | Apps. |
| | | | | | | | | Sub.Apps. |
| | | | | | | | | Goals |

| Blackburn | Nobbs | Kelly | Smith | Linighan | Shoulder | Honour | Newton | Walker | Hogan | Borthwick | Dobson | Robinson | Taylor | Chambers | Lester | Wilson | Hewitt | Proudlock |
|---|---|---|---|---|---|---|---|---|---|---|---|---|---|---|---|---|---|---|
| 1 | 2 | | 5 | | | 7 | *9* | 10 | 4 | *12* | 8 | 6 | | 3 | 11 | | | |
| | 2 | 3 | 5 | 6 | **8** | 7 | | | 4 | 9 | | | *10* | | 11 | 1 | *12* | **13** |
| 1 | 2 | 1 | 2 | 1 | 1 | 2 | 1 | 1 | 2 | 1 | 1 | 1 | 1 | 1 | 2 | 1 | | |
| | | | | | | | | | | 1 | | | | | | | 1 | 1 |

| Blackburn | McKinnon | Hogan | Smith | Sword | Honour | Shoulder | Borthwick | Walker | Lowe | Dixon, K. | Gibb | Nobbs | Little |
|---|---|---|---|---|---|---|---|---|---|---|---|---|---|
| 1 | 3 | | 5 | 6 | 7 | *8* | **9** | 10 | *12* | 11 | 4 | 2 | **13** |
| 2 | 2 | 1 | 2 | 2 | 2 | 2 | 2 | 2 | | 2 | 1 | 2 | |
| | | | | | | | | | 2 | | | | 1 |
| | | | | | | | | | | | | | |
| | | | | | | | | | | | | | |

| Barratt | Nobbs | Haigh | Smith | Stokes | Honour | Toman | Baker | Gibb | McKinnon | Borthwick | Kennedy | Carr | Tinkler | Hall | Whellans | Stokle |
|---|---|---|---|---|---|---|---|---|---|---|---|---|---|---|---|---|
| *2* | 4 | 11 | 5 | 6 | | 8 | 9 | 10 | 3 | **14** | *12* | 1 | | **7** | | |
| 11 | 4 | 2 | 5 | 6 | 7 | 8 | 9 | *12* | 3 | *10* | | 1 | | | | |
| 2 | 4 | 6 | 5 | | 7 | 8 | 9 | | 3 | 11 | | 1 | 10 | | | |
| 2 | 4 | 6 | 5 | | 7 | 8 | 9 | | 3 | 11 | | 1 | 10 | | | |
| *2* | 4 | | 5 | | 7 | 8 | **9** | *12* | 3 | 11 | | 1 | 10 | | **14** | 6 |
| 5 | 5 | 4 | 5 | 2 | 4 | 5 | 5 | 1 | 5 | 4 | | 5 | 3 | 1 | | 1 |
| | | | | | | | | 2 | | 1 | 1 | | | | 1 | |
| | | | 1 | 1 | 1 | | 1 | | | 1 | 1 | | | | | |

| McKinnon | Smith | Stokes | Honour | Toman | Borthwick | Barratt | Grayson | Doig | Atkinson | Baker | Ogden | Muggleton | Allon | Nobbs |
|---|---|---|---|---|---|---|---|---|---|---|---|---|---|---|
| 3 | 5 | | 7 | 8 | | | 10 | 4 | *11* | 6 | *12* | 1 | 9 | 2 |
| 3 | | 5 | 7 | 8 | *12* | 2 | *10* | **4** | **14** | 6 | 11 | 1 | 9 | |
| 2 | 1 | 1 | 2 | 2 | | 1 | 2 | 2 | 1 | 2 | 1 | 2 | 2 | 1 |
| | | | | | 1 | | | | 1 | | 1 | | | |
| | | | | | | | | | | | | | | |

| McKinnon | Tinkler | Atkinson, P.D. | Baker | Dalton | Davies | Allon | McEwan | Plaskett | Lamb | Smith | Trewick | Hutchison | Williams | Moverley |
|---|---|---|---|---|---|---|---|---|---|---|---|---|---|---|
| 3 | 4 | *12* | 6 | 11 | | 7 | 5 | 2 | *9* | | 8 | 10 | | 1 |
| 3 | 4 | *12* | 9 | 11 | 8 | 7 | | 2 | *10* | 5 | | | 6 | 1 |
| 2 | 2 | | 2 | 2 | 1 | 2 | 1 | 2 | 2 | 1 | 1 | 1 | 1 | 2 |
| | | 2 | | | | | | | | | | | | |
| | | | 1 | | | | 1 | | | | | | | |

# 1990-91

## Leyland Daf Cup

| Match No. | Date | Round | Venue | Opponents | Result | | Scorers | Attendance |
|---|---|---|---|---|---|---|---|---|
| 22 | Nov 28 | PR | (a) | Huddersfield Town | W | 4 - 1 | Dalton 2, Allon, Olsson | 1,405 |
| 26 | Dec 18 | PR | (h) | Bradford City | L | 0 - 4 | | 1,147 |
| 31 | Jan 22 | R1 | (a) | Bradford City | L | 2 - 3 | Baker, Allon | 2,308 |
| | | | | | | | | Apps. |
| | | | | | | | | Sub.Apps. |
| | | | | | | | | Goals |

# 1991-92

## Autoglass Trophy

| Match No. | Date | Round | Venue | Opponents | Result | | Scorers | Attendance |
|---|---|---|---|---|---|---|---|---|
| 22 | Nov 19 | PR | (a) | Bradford City | D | 3 - 3 | Tinkler, Baker, Fletcher | 1,562 |
| 32 | Jan 7 | PR | (h) | Hull City | W | 2 - 0 | Dalton, Baker | 1,550 |
| 36 | 21 | R1 | (h) | Scunthorpe United | W | 2 - 1 | Honour, Tinkler | 1,351 |
| 38 | Feb 4 | R2 | (a) | Stockport County | L | 0 - 3 | | 2,255 |
| | | | | | | | | Apps. |
| | | | | | | | | Sub.Apps. |
| | | | | | | | | Goals |

# 1992-93

## Autoglass Trophy

| Match No. | Date | Round | Venue | Opponents | Result | | Scorers | Attendance |
|---|---|---|---|---|---|---|---|---|
| 24 | Dec 8 | PR | (h) | Scarborough | W | 4 - 1 | Olsson, Johnson, Honour, Saville | 1,193 |
| 26 | 15 | PR | (a) | Carlisle United | L | 0 - 2 | | 859 |
| 32 | Jan 12 | R1 | (a) | Stockport County | L | 0 - 1 | | 2,383 |
| | | | | | | | | Apps. |
| | | | | | | | | Sub.Apps. |
| | | | | | | | | Goals |

# 1993-94

## Autoglass Trophy

| Match No. | Date | Round | Venue | Opponents | Result | | Scorers | Attendance |
|---|---|---|---|---|---|---|---|---|
| 13 | Sep 28 | PR | (h) | Darlington | D | 1 - 1 | Honour | 1,454 |
| 22 | Nov 9 | PR | (a) | York City | L | 0 - 2 | | 1,630 |
| | | | | | | | | Apps. |
| | | | | | | | | Sub.Apps. |
| | | | | | | | | Goals |

# 1994-95

## Auto Windscreens Shield

| Match No. | Date | Round | Venue | Opponents | Result | | Scorers | Attendance |
|---|---|---|---|---|---|---|---|---|
| 17 | Oct 18 | PR | (a) | Carlisle United | L | 0 - 2 | | 2,563 |
| 21 | Nov 8 | PR | (h) | Darlington | L | 0 - 2 | | 1,211 |
| | | | | | | | | Apps. |
| | | | | | | | | Sub.Apps. |

| Cox | Olsson | McKinnon | Tinkler | Bennyworth | Allon | Tupling | Baker | Fletcher | Dalton | Honour | Nobbs | MacPhail | Davies, A. |
|---|---|---|---|---|---|---|---|---|---|---|---|---|---|
| 1 | 2 | 3 | *4* | 8 | 7 | *12* | **9** | **13** | 11 | 10 |  | 5 | 6 |
| 1 | *12* | 3 | *4* | 6 | 7 | 8 | 9 |  | 11 | 10 | 2 | 5 |  |
| 1 |  | 3 | 4 | 6 | 7 | 8 | 9 |  | 11 |  | 2 | 5 | 10 |
| 3 | 1 | 3 | 3 | 3 | 3 | 2 | 3 |  | 3 | 2 | 2 | 3 | 2 |
|  | 1 |  |  |  |  | 1 |  | 1 |  |  |  |  |  |
|  | 1 |  |  |  | 2 |  | 1 |  | 2 |  |  |  |  |

| Hodge | McKinnon | Nobbs | Olsson | Baker | Honour | Dalton | McPhail | Tinkler | Fletcher | Gabbiadini | Tupling | Smith, M. | Southall | Smith, A. | Thompson |
|---|---|---|---|---|---|---|---|---|---|---|---|---|---|---|---|
| 1 | 3 | 2 | 8 | 9 | 10 | 11 |  | 4 | *12* |  | 6 | 5 | *7* |  |  |
| 1 |  | 2 | 8 | 9 |  | 11 | 5 | 4 | 10 |  | 6 |  | 7 | 3 |  |
| 1 |  | 2 | 8 | *9* | 10 | 11 | 5 | 4 | 7 |  | 6 |  | *12* | 3 |  |
| 1 |  | 2 | 8 | 9 | 10 | 11 | 5 | 4 |  | *12* | 6 |  | 3 |  | *7* |
| 4 | 1 | 4 | 4 | 4 | 3 | 4 | 3 | 4 | 2 |  | 4 | 1 | 3 | 2 | 1 |
|  |  |  |  |  |  |  |  |  | 1 | 1 |  |  | 1 |  |  |
|  |  |  |  | 2 | 1 | 1 |  | 2 | 1 |  |  |  |  |  |  |

| Hodge | Cross, R. | Cross, P. | McPhail | Emerson | Johnrose | Olsson | Saville | Honour | Gallacher | Southall | McGuckin | Johnson | Gilchrist | Peverell | Talia |
|---|---|---|---|---|---|---|---|---|---|---|---|---|---|---|---|
| 1 | 2 | 3 | 5 | *6* | 7 | 8 | 9 | 10 |  | *12* | 4 | **11** |  | **13** |  |
| 1 | 2 | 3 | 5 | 6 | 7 | 8 | 9 | 10 |  |  |  | *11* | 4 | *12* |  |
|  | 2 | 3 | 5 | 6 | 7 | 8 | 9 | 10 | *12* | *11* |  |  | 4 |  | 1 |
| 2 | 3 | 3 | 3 | 3 | 3 | 3 | 3 | 3 |  | 1 | 1 | 2 | 2 |  | 1 |
|  |  |  |  |  |  |  |  |  | 1 | 1 |  |  |  | 2 |  |
|  |  |  |  |  |  | 1 | 1 | 1 |  |  |  | 1 |  |  |  |

| Carter | Cross, R. | Cross, P. | McGuckin | MacPhail | Emerson | Wratten | West | Honour | Peverell | Gilchrist | Johnrose | Houchen | Olsson | Halliday |
|---|---|---|---|---|---|---|---|---|---|---|---|---|---|---|
| 1 | 2 | 3 | 4 | 5 | 6 | 8 | *12* | 10 | 7 |  | 9 |  | *11* |  |
| 1 | 2 | 3 | 4 | 5 | **14** | **8** | 11 |  |  | 7 | 10 | 9 | *6* | *12* |
| 2 | 2 | 2 | 2 | 2 | 1 | 2 | 1 | 1 | 1 | 1 | 2 | 1 | 2 |  |
|  |  |  |  |  | 1 |  | 1 |  |  |  |  |  |  | 1 |
|  |  |  |  |  |  |  |  | 1 |  |  |  |  |  |  |

| Horne | Ingram | Gilchrist | McGuckin | Oliver | Ainsley | Sloan | Houchen | Southall | Thompson | Halliday | Walsh | Foster |
|---|---|---|---|---|---|---|---|---|---|---|---|---|
| 1 | 2 | 4 | 5 | 8 | 6 | 7 | *9* | 11 | *12* |  | 3 | 10 |
| 1 | 2 | 4 | 5 | 7 | 6 |  | 9 | 11 |  | 8 | 3 | 10 |
| 2 | 2 | 2 | 2 | 2 | 2 | 1 | 2 | 2 |  | 1 | 2 | 2 |
|  |  |  |  |  |  |  |  |  | 1 |  |  |  |

# 1995-96

## Auto Windscreens Shield

| Match No. | Date | Round | Venue | Opponents | Result | | Scorers | Attendance |
|---|---|---|---|---|---|---|---|---|
| 17 | Oct 17 | PR | (a) | Crewe Alexandra | L | 0 - 8 | | 2,344 |
| 22 | Nov 7 | PR | (h) | Blackpool | W | 3 - 2 | Howard 2, Allon | 888 |

Apps.
Sub.Apps.
Goals

# 1996-97

## Auto Windscreens Shield

| Match No. | Date | Round | Venue | Opponents | Result | | Scorers | Attendance |
|---|---|---|---|---|---|---|---|---|
| 26 | Dec 10 | R1 | (h) | Burnley | L | 0 - 2 | | 921 |

Apps.
Sub.Apps.
Goals

# 1997-98

## Auto Windscreens Shield

| Match No. | Date | Round | Venue | Opponents | Result | | Scorers | Attendance |
|---|---|---|---|---|---|---|---|---|
| 25 | Dec 6 | R1 | (a) | Shrewsbury Town | W | 2 - 1 | Beech, Pedersen | 1,130 |
| 31 | Jan 6 | R2 | (h) | Scunthorpe United | L | 1 - 2 | Lee | 1,491 |

Apps.
Sub.Apps.
Goals

# 1998-99

## Auto Windscreens Shield

| Match No. | Date | Round | Venue | Opponents | Result | | Scorers | Attendance |
|---|---|---|---|---|---|---|---|---|
| 25 | Dec 8 | R1 | (a) | Chester City | W | 2 - 1* | Howard, Brightwell | 908 |
| 33 | Jan 19 | R2 | (h) | Preston North End | D | 2 - 2** | Miller 2 | 1,205 |
| 35 | 26 | QF | (h) | Lincoln City | L | 0 - 3 | | 1,370 |

* After extra-time **Won 4 - 3 on penalties

Apps.
Sub.Apps.
Goals

# 1999-2000

## Auto Windscreens Shield

| Match No. | Date | Round | Venue | Opponents | Result | | Scorers | Attendance |
|---|---|---|---|---|---|---|---|---|
| 25 | Dec 7 | R1 | (h) | Halifax Town | W | 1 - 0 | Henderson | 1,482 |
| 32 | Jan 10 | R2 | (a) | Preston North End | W | 2 - 1 | Midgley, Miller | 3,635 |
| 39 | Feb 22 | QF | (h) | Carlisle United | L | 1 - 2 | Lee | 2,399 |

Apps.
Sub.Apps.
Goals

| Jones | Ingram | McAuley | Billing | McGuckin | Howard | Halliday | Tait | Henderson | Canham | Horne | Lynch | Oliver | Sloan | Homer | Allon | Roberts | Lee | Allinson |
|---|---|---|---|---|---|---|---|---|---|---|---|---|---|---|---|---|---|---|
| 1 | 2 | 3 | 4 | 5 | 11 | *10* | 8 | 9 | 6 | | | | | *12* | 7 | | | |
| | 2 | 11 | 4 | | 9 | 10 | | 5 | | *12* | 6 | 8 | ***14*** | | ***7*** | *1* | **13** | **3** |
| 1 | 2 | 2 | 2 | 1 | 2 | 2 | 1 | 2 | 1 | | 1 | 1 | | | 2 | 1 | | 1 |
| | | | | | | | | | | 1 | | | 1 | 1 | | | 1 | |
| | | | | | 2 | | | | | | | | | | 1 | | | |

| Ingram | McAuley | Beech | Davies | Allon | Cooper | Howard | Clegg | Hislop | Lee | O'Connor | Irvine | Hutt | Gallagher |
|---|---|---|---|---|---|---|---|---|---|---|---|---|---|
| ***2*** | 3 | **4** | 6 | 7 | 8 | 9 | 10 | *11* | 5 | 1 | *12* | **13** | ***14*** |
| 1 | 1 | 1 | 1 | 1 | 1 | 1 | 1 | 1 | 1 | 1 | | | |
| | | | | | | | | | | | 1 | | |
| | | | | | | | | | | | | | |

| Knowles | Lucas | Bradley | Cullen | Beech | Howard | Halliday | Barron | Lee | Clark | Pedersen | Hollund | Larsen |
|---|---|---|---|---|---|---|---|---|---|---|---|---|
| 2 | 3 | 6 | 8 | 7 | 11 | 10 | 4 | 5 | | 9 | 1 | |
| 2 | | 6 | 8 | 7 | 11 | *10* | 4 | 5 | 3 | 9 | 1 | *12* |
| 2 | 1 | 2 | 2 | 2 | 2 | 2 | 2 | 2 | 1 | 2 | 2 | |
| | | | | | | | | | | | | 1 |
| | | | | 1 | | | | 1 | | 1 | | |

| Hollund | Knowles | Ingram | Barron | Lee | Stephenson | Di Lella | Irvine | Midgley | Clark | Brightwell | Howard | Miller | Rush | Smith | Stokoe | Hutt | Baker | Beardsley |
|---|---|---|---|---|---|---|---|---|---|---|---|---|---|---|---|---|---|---|
| 1 | 2 | 6 | 4 | 5 | 11 | | | **10** | 3 | ***14*** | 9 | *8* | **13** | | 7 | | *12* | |
| 1 | 2 | *11* | 4 | | | 6 | *12* | 10 | 3 | | 9 | 8 | | | | 5 | | 7 |
| 1 | 2 | 5 | 4 | 9 | *7* | | *12* | 10 | 3 | | | 6 | | 11 | | | | 8 |
| 3 | 3 | 3 | 3 | 2 | 2 | 1 | | 3 | 3 | | 2 | 3 | | 1 | 1 | 1 | | 2 |
| | | | | | | | 2 | | | 1 | | | 1 | | | | 1 | |
| | | | | | | | | | | 1 | 1 | 2 | | | | | | |

| 13 Dibble | 2 Knowles | 4 Barron | 18 Lee | 8 Miller | 9 Jones | 10 Freestone | 17 Stephenson | 11 Clark | 5 Strodder | 12 Midgley | 14 Henderson | 29 Tennebo | 1 Hollund | 16 Westwood | 32 Fitzpatrick | 31 Shilton | 30 Boyd | 34 Mason | 35 McAvoy | 34 West |
|---|---|---|---|---|---|---|---|---|---|---|---|---|---|---|---|---|---|---|---|---|
| | 2 | 4 | 5 | | | *9* | 11 | 3 | | **13** | 10 | | 1 | 6 | | | *12* | 7 | **8** | |
| 1 | 2 | 4 | | 8 | **13** | **9** | ***11*** | *12* | 5 | 10 | | 7 | | 6 | | *3* | ***14*** | | | |
| | 2 | *4* | 10 | 8 | 9 | | 11 | *12* | **5** | | | | 1 | 6 | ***7*** | 3 | | | ***14*** | **13** |
| 1 | 3 | 3 | 2 | 2 | 1 | 2 | 3 | 1 | 2 | 1 | 1 | 1 | 2 | 3 | 1 | 2 | | 1 | 1 | |
| | | | | | 1 | | | 2 | | 1 | | | | | | | 2 | | 1 | 1 |
| | | | 1 | 1 | | | | | | 1 | 1 | | | | | | | | | |

# 2000-01

## LDV Vans Trophy

| Match No. | Date | Round | Venue | Opponents | Result | | Scorers | Attendance |
|---|---|---|---|---|---|---|---|---|
| 24 | Dec 11 | R1 | (h) | Scunthorpe United | W | 3 - 2 | Henderson, Arnison, Miller | 1,538 |
| 28 | Jan 9 | R2 | (h) | Doncaster Rovers | W | 3 - 1 | Tinkler, Clark, Miller | 2,466 |
| 33 | 30 | QF | (a) | Lincoln City | L | 0 - 1 | | 1,357 |
| | | | | | | | | Apps. |
| | | | | | | | | Sub.Apps. |
| | | | | | | | | Goals |

# 2001-02

## LDV Vans Trophy

| Match No. | Date | Round | Venue | Opponents | Result | | Scorers | Attendance |
|---|---|---|---|---|---|---|---|---|
| 14 | Oct 16 | R1 | (h) | Bury | L | 0 - 1* | | 2,190 |
| | | | | | | | | Apps. |
| | | | | | | | | Sub.Apps. |
| | | | | | | | | Goals |

* After extra-time

# 2002-03

## LDV Vans Trophy

| Match No. | Date | Round | Venue | Opponents | Result | | Scorers | Attendance |
|---|---|---|---|---|---|---|---|---|
| 16 | Oct 22 | R1 | (a) | Tranmere Rovers | L | 0 - 5 | | 3,387 |
| | | | | | | | | Apps. |
| | | | | | | | | Sub.Apps. |
| | | | | | | | | Goals |

# 2003-04

## LDV Vans Trophy

| Match No. | Date | Round | Venue | Opponents | Result | | Scorers | Attendance |
|---|---|---|---|---|---|---|---|---|
| 16 | Oct 14 | R1 | (a) | Oldham Athletic | D | 3 - 3* | E.Williams, Clarke 2 | 3,575 |
| | | | | | | | | Apps. |
| | | | | | | | | Sub.Apps. |
| | | | | | | | | Goals |

*After extra-time. Lost 5 - 3 on penalties.

# 2004-05

## LDV Vans Trophy

| Match No. | Date | Round | Venue | Opponents | Result | | Scorers | Attendance |
|---|---|---|---|---|---|---|---|---|
| 13 | Sep 28 | R1 | (h) | Hull City | D | 3 - 3* | Strachan (pen), Pouton, Porter | 1,535 |
| 20 | Nov 2 | R2 | (a) | Carlisle United | W | 1 - 0 | Sweeney | 2,871 |
| 25 | 30 | QF | (a) | Oldham Athletic | L | 1 - 3 | Boyd | 2,835 |
| | | | | | | | | Apps. |
| | | | | | | | | Sub.Apps. |
| | | | | | | | | Goals |

* After extra-time. Won 4 - 1 on penalties.

| 16 Westwood | 13 Sharp | 6 Fitzpatrick | 8 Miller | 9 Lormor | 14 Henderson | 17 Stephenson | 3 Shilton | 12 Midgley | 10 Sperrevik | 7 Arnison | 23 Williams | 11 Clark | 27 Tinkler | 4 Barron | 29 Aspin |
|---|---|---|---|---|---|---|---|---|---|---|---|---|---|---|---|
| 5 | 6 | ***14*** | 8 | **13** | **10** | ***11*** | | *9* | *12* | 2 | 1 | 3 | 7 | 4 | |
| 5 | 6 | ***14*** | 8 | **13** | **10** | ***11*** | *12* | 9 | | 2 | 1 | *3* | 7 | 4 | |
| *5* | 6 | **13** | 8 | ***14*** | 10 | ***11*** | 3 | **9** | | 2 | 1 | | 7 | 4 | *12* |
| 3 | 3 | | 3 | | 3 | 3 | 1 | 3 | | 3 | 3 | 2 | 3 | 3 | |
| | | 3 | | 3 | | | 1 | | 1 | | | | | | 1 |
| | | | 2 | | 1 | | | | | 1 | | 1 | 1 | | |

| 4 Barron | 5 Lee | 7 Tinkler | 8 Humphreys | 14 Widdrington | 20 Sharp | 1 Williams, A. | 2 Arnison | 3 Robinson | 23 Watson | 19 Boyd |
|---|---|---|---|---|---|---|---|---|---|---|
| 4 | 5 | 7 | 8 | 11 | 6 | 1 | 2 | 3 | 10 | 9 |
| 1 | 1 | 1 | 1 | 1 | 1 | 1 | 1 | 1 | 1 | 1 |
| | | | | | | | | | | |
| | | | | | | | | | | |

| 23 Sweeney | 12 Arnison | 14 Henderson | 19 Easter | 15 Widdrington | 16 Boyd | 22 Simms | 21 Provett | 25 Robson | 20 Sharp | 27 McKenzie | 18 Bass |
|---|---|---|---|---|---|---|---|---|---|---|---|
| 11 | 7 | *9* | *12* | 4 | 10 | 5 | 1 | 3 | 6 | 8 | 2 |
| 1 | 1 | 1 | | 1 | 1 | 1 | 1 | 1 | 1 | 1 | 1 |
| | | | 1 | | | | | | | | |
| | | | | | | | | | | | |

| 1 Williams, A. | 5 Nelson | 6 Westwood | 7 Clarke | 8 Humphreys | 9 Williams, E. | 23 Robinson, P. | 25 Strachan | 2 Barron | 4 Tinkler | 10 Gabbiadini | 15 Boyd | 3 Robinson, M. |
|---|---|---|---|---|---|---|---|---|---|---|---|---|
| 1 | 4 | 5 | 7 | 8 | *9* | *12* | 11 | 2 | 6 | **10** | **13** | 3 |
| 1 | 1 | 1 | 1 | 1 | 1 | | 1 | 1 | 1 | 1 | | 1 |
| | | | | | | 1 | | | | | 1 | |
| | | | 2 | | 1 | | | | | | | |

| 12 Ross | 5 Nelson | 6 Westwood | 4 Tinkler | 9 Williams | 15 Sweeney | 14 Porter | 10 Boyd | 8 Humphreys | 20 Istead | 19 Brackstone | 11 Strachan | 21 Konstantopoulos | 18 Robson | 25 Appleby | 22 Craddock | 16 Woods | 17 Pouton | 27 Foley | 2 Barron | 17 Clark | 16 Gobern |
|---|---|---|---|---|---|---|---|---|---|---|---|---|---|---|---|---|---|---|---|---|---|
| | 4 | | | 9 | | 10 | **13** | ***14*** | **6** | 5 | 8 | 1 | 3 | | *12* | 11 | ***7*** | | *2* | | |
| *2* | 8 | 5 | 6 | 7 | 10 | **9** | | ***11*** | | | | 1 | 3 | | *12* | | | ***14*** | | 4 | **13** |
| | 4 | 5 | 6 | | 8 | ***9*** | 10 | 11 | **13** | 3 | **7** | 1 | | ***14*** | *12* | | | | *2* | | |
| 1 | 3 | 2 | 2 | 2 | 2 | 3 | 1 | 2 | 1 | 2 | 2 | 3 | 2 | | | 1 | 1 | | 2 | 1 | |
| | | | | | | | 1 | 1 | 1 | | | | | 1 | 3 | | | 1 | | | 1 |
| | | | | | 1 | 1 | 1 | | | | 1 | | | | | | 1 | | | | |

# 2005-06

## Football League Trophy

| Match No. | Date | Round | Venue | Opponents | Result | | Scorers | Attendance |
|---|---|---|---|---|---|---|---|---|
| 16 | Oct 18 | R1 | (a) | Scunthorpe United | L | 0 - 1 | | 2,028 |
| | | | | | | | | Apps. |
| | | | | | | | | Sub.Apps. |
| | | | | | | | | Goals |

# 2006-07

## Johnstone's Paint Trophy

| Match No. | Date | Round | Venue | Opponents | Result | | Scorers | Attendance |
|---|---|---|---|---|---|---|---|---|
| 17 | Oct 17 | R1 | (h) | Rotherham United | W | 3 - 1 | Bullock, Foley, Humphreys | 1,832 |
| 20 | 31 | R2 | (h) | Doncaster Rovers | L | 1 - 3 | Liddle | 1,853 |
| | | | | | | | | Apps. |
| | | | | | | | | Sub.Apps. |
| | | | | | | | | Goals |

# 2007-08

## Johnstone's Paint Trophy

| Match No. | Date | Round | Venue | Opponents | Result | | Scorers | Attendance |
|---|---|---|---|---|---|---|---|---|
| 7 | Sep 4 | R1 | (a) | Chesterfield | W | 3 - 1 | Foley, Brown 2 | 2,127 |
| 14 | Oct 9 | R2 | (a) | Lincoln City | W | 5 - 2 | Porter 3, Mackay, Moore | 936 |
| 20 | Nov 13 | R3 | (h) | Morecambe | L | 1 - 1* | Barker | 2,776 |
| * Lost 2 - 4 on penalties | | | | | | | | Apps. |
| | | | | | | | | Sub.Apps. |
| | | | | | | | | Goals |

# 2008-09

## Johnstone's Paint Trophy

| Match No. | Date | Round | Venue | Opponents | Result | | Scorers | Attendance |
|---|---|---|---|---|---|---|---|---|
| 7 | Sep 2 | R1 | (h) | Leicester City | L | 0 - 3 | | 2,807 |
| | | | | | | | | Apps. |
| | | | | | | | | Sub.Apps. |
| | | | | | | | | Goals |

| 1 Konstantopoulos | 16 Clark | 22 Bullock | 7 Llewellyn | 15 Sweeney | 24 Butler | 11 Williams, E. | 32 Collins | 29 Jones | 4 Tinkler | 34 Maidens | 25 Istead | 20 Craddock | 19 Brackstone |
|---|---|---|---|---|---|---|---|---|---|---|---|---|---|
| 1 | **13** | 10 | ***7*** | 8 | 11 | 9 | 5 | *4* | **6** | *12* | ***14*** | 2 | 3 |
| 1 |  | 1 | 1 | 1 | 1 | 1 | 1 | 1 | 1 |  |  | 1 | 1 |
|  | 1 |  |  |  |  |  |  |  |  | 1 | 1 |  |  |
|  |  |  |  |  |  |  |  |  |  |  |  |  |  |

| 23 Williams, D. | 3 Robson | 5 Nelson | 6 Clark | 16 Bullock | 20 Brown | 9 Porter | 25 Daly | 8 Humphreys | 28 Foley | 11 Williams, E. | 12 Strachan | 19 Brackstone | 29 Maidens | 18 Liddle | 21 Provett | 27 Turnbull, P. |
|---|---|---|---|---|---|---|---|---|---|---|---|---|---|---|---|---|
|  | *11* | 5 | 6 | 8 | ***9*** | **13** | **10** | *12* | 7 |  | 4 | 3 | ***14*** |  | 1 | 2 |
| 2 | *12* | 5 | 6 | 8 | **13** | ***9*** | **10** | 11 |  | ***14*** |  | *3* | 7 | 4 | 1 |  |
| 1 | 1 | 2 | 2 | 2 | 1 | 1 | 2 | 1 | 1 |  | 1 | 2 | 1 | 1 | 2 | 1 |
|  | 1 |  |  |  | 1 | 1 |  | 1 |  | 1 |  |  | 1 |  |  |  |
|  |  |  |  | 1 |  |  |  | 1 | 1 |  |  |  |  | 1 |  |  |

| 21 Lee-Barratt | 2 McCunnie | 20 Antwi-Birago | 3 Elliott | 5 Nelson | 7 Liddle | 4 Boland | 14 Brown | 9 Barker | 22 Moore | 8 Humphreys | 10 Porter | 15 Sweeney | 1 Budtz | 19 Robson | 6 Clark | 17 Foley | 18 Gibb | 24 Mackay |
|---|---|---|---|---|---|---|---|---|---|---|---|---|---|---|---|---|---|---|
|  | ***14*** | 6 |  | 5 | 4 |  | ***7*** | **9** |  | 3 | 10 |  | 1 | *11* | 8 | *12* | 2 | **13** |
| 1 | 2 | 6 | 3 |  | **4** |  | ***7*** | *9* | 10 |  | *12* | 8 |  | 11 | 5 |  | **13** | ***14*** |
|  | 2 | 6 |  | 5 |  | **4** |  | 9 | 10 | 3 | ***14*** | 7 | 1 | *11* |  | *12* | **13** | ***8*** |
| 1 | 2 | 3 | 1 | 2 | 2 | 1 | 2 | 3 | 2 | 2 | 1 | 2 | 2 | 3 | 2 |  | 1 | 1 |
|  | 1 |  |  |  |  |  |  |  |  |  | 2 |  |  |  |  | 2 | 2 | 2 |
|  |  |  |  |  |  |  | 2 | 1 | 1 |  | 3 |  |  |  |  | 1 |  | 1 |

| 21 Lee-Barratt | 15 Sweeney | 3 Humphreys | 5 Nelson | 6 Collins | 7 Liddle | 10 Porter | 14 Brown | 17 Foley | 19 Robson | 9 Barker | 2 McCunnie | 16 Power | 22 Rowell |
|---|---|---|---|---|---|---|---|---|---|---|---|---|---|
| 1 | **13** | 3 | 5 | 6 | 7 | ***14*** | ***10*** | **8** | 11 | 9 | 2 | *4* | *12* |
| 1 |  | 1 | 1 | 1 | 1 |  | 1 | 1 | 1 | 1 | 1 | 1 |  |
|  | 1 |  |  |  |  | 1 |  |  |  |  |  |  | 1 |
|  |  |  |  |  |  |  |  |  |  |  |  |  |  |

# Hartlepool United in the Football League

## Position

*Highest:* Second in the Third Division North – 1956–57
*Lowest:* Bottom of the Football League – 1959–60, 1962–63

## Points

*Most:* 60 – 1967–68 (two points for a win), 88 – 2006–07 (three points for a win)
*Most at home:* 40 – 1956–57 (two points for a win), 53 – 2002–03 (three points for a win)
*Most away:* 23 – 1967–68 (two points for a win), 41 – 2006–07 (three points for a win)
*Fewest:* 25 twice – 1923–24, 1962–63 (two points for a win), 36 – 1993–94 (three points for a win)
*Fewest at home:* 17 three times – 1923–24, 1961–62, 1962–63 (two points for a win), 24 – 2011–12 (three points for a win)
*Fewest away:* 4 twice – 1928–29, 1937–38 (two points for a win), 9 – 1993–94 (three points for a win)

## Wins

*Most:* 26 twice – 1955–56 and 2006–07
*Most at home:* 18 twice – 1955–56 and 1956–57
*Most away:* 12 – 2006–07
*Fewest:* 7 twice – 1923–24 (42 games) and 1962–63 (46 games)
*Fewest at home:* 5 twice – 1923–24 (21 games) and 1962–63 (23 games)
*Fewest away:* 0 twice – 1922–23 (19 games) and 1937–38 (23 games)

## Defeats

*Fewest:* 9 – 2002–03
*Fewest at home:* 1 four times – 1925–26 (21 games), 1956–57, 1967–68, 1997–98 (23 games)
*Fewest away:* 6 – 2006–07
*Most:* 29 – 1959–60
*Most at home:* 12 twice – 1959–60, 1993–94
*Most away:* 19 twice – 1950–51, 1970–71

## Draws

*Most:* 23 – 1997–98
*Most at home:* 12 three times – 1968–69, 1978–79, 1997–98
*Most away:* 11 – 1997–98
*Fewest:* 5 four times – 1931–32 (40 games), 1949–50 (42 games), 1954–55, 1955–56 (46 games)
*Fewest at home:* 1 twice – 1936–37, 1999–2000
*Fewest away:* 1 – 1931–32

## Goals in a season

*Most scored:* 90 – 1956–57
*Most scored at home:* 59 – 1925–26 (21 games)
*Most scored away:* 37 – 2003–04
*Fewest scored:* 33 – 1923–24 (42 games)

*Fewest scored at home:* 17 –1972–73
*Fewest scored away:* 6 – 1970–71
*Fewest conceded:* 39 – 1921–22 (38 games)
*Fewest conceded at home:* 11 – 1921–22 (19 games)
*Fewest conceded away:* 23 – 2006–07
*Most conceded:* 116 – 1932–33 (42 games)
*Most conceded at home:* 41 twice – 1958–59, 1959–60
*Most conceded away:* 87 – 1932–33

## Individual matches

*Highest score for:* 10 – 10–1 v Barrow (h) 4 April 1959
*Highest score for at home:* 10 – As above
*Highest score for away:* 6 – 6–1 v Southport 4 September 1956
*Highest score against:* 10 – 10–1 v Wrexham (a) 3 March 1962
*Highest score against at home:* 8 twice – 8–2 v Rochdale 21 April 1930, 8–1 v Plymouth Argyle 7 May 1994
*Highest score against away:* 10 – As above
*Biggest winning margin:* 9 – 10–1 v Barrow (h) 4 April 1959
*Biggest winning margin at home:* 9 – As above
*Biggest winning margin away:* 5 – 6–1 v Southport 4 September 1956
*Biggest losing margin:* 9 – 10–1 v Wrexham (a) 3 March 1962
*Biggest losing margin at home:* 7 – 8–1 v Plymouth Argyle 7 May 1994
*Biggest losing margin away:* 9 – As above
*Highest aggregate score:* 12 – 9–3 v Walsall (h) 23 January 1926
*Highest scoring draw:* 5–5 – v Darlington (a) 21 November 1936

## Sequences

*Consecutive wins:* 9 – 18 November 2006 to 1 January 2007
*Consecutive home wins:* 12 twice – 18 February 1933 to 7 October 1993, 17 March 1951 to 13 October 1951
*Consecutive away wins:* 5 twice – 19 March 2002 to 10 August 2002, 18 November 2006 to 1 January 2007
*Consecutive games unbeaten:* 23 – 18 November 2006 to 30 March 2007
*Consecutive games unbeaten at home:* 28 – 19 October 2002 to 20 December 2003
*Consecutive games unbeaten away:* 12 – 18 November 2006 to 25 March 2007
*Consecutive defeats:* 8 three times – 8 April 1950 to 26 August 1950, 28 March 1970 to 15 August 1970, 27 January 1993 to 27 February 1993
*Consecutive home defeats:* 8 – 1 October 2011 to 2 January 2012
*Consecutive away defeats:* 18 – 9 January 1971 to 16 October 1971
*Consecutive games without a win:* 18 – 9 January 1993 to 3 April 1993
*Consecutive home games without a win:* 8 three times – 27 March 1984 to 15 September 1984, 26 April 1986 to 1 November 1986, 16 January 1993 to 27 March 1993
*Consecutive away games without a win:* 31 – 26 March 1937 to 8 October 1938
*Consecutive games without conceding a goal:* 8 – 25 November 2006 to 1 January 2007
*Consecutive home games without conceding a goal:* 10 – 22 December 1973 to 27 March 1974
*Consecutive away games without conceding a goal:* 5 – 6 April 1968 to 6 May 1968
*Consecutive scoring games:* 27 – 18 November 2006 to 20 April 2007
*Consecutive non-scoring games:* 11 – 9 January 1993 to 2 March 1993
*Consecutive games with an unchanged team:* 14 – 26 January 1974 to 12 April 1974 (Watling; Potter, Shoulder; Dawes, Goad, Honour; Heath, Gauden, Moore, McMahon, Ward).

# Summary of League Seasons

| No. | Season | Division | Final Position | Games Played | Home W | Home D | Home L | Home F | Home A | Away W | Away D | Away L | Away F | Away A |
|---|---|---|---|---|---|---|---|---|---|---|---|---|---|---|
| 1 | 1921–22 | Div 3 North | 4th | 38 | 10 | 6 | 3 | 33 | 11 | 7 | 2 | 10 | 19 | 28 |
| 2 | 1922–23 | Div 3 North | 15th | 38 | 10 | 6 | 3 | 34 | 14 | 0 | 6 | 13 | 14 | 40 |
| 3 | 1923–24 | Div 3 North | 21st | 42 | 5 | 7 | 9 | 22 | 24 | 2 | 4 | 15 | 11 | 46 |
| 4 | 1924–25 | Div 3 North | 20th | 42 | 9 | 8 | 4 | 28 | 21 | 3 | 3 | 15 | 17 | 42 |
| 5 | 1925–26 | Div 3 North | 6th | 42 | 15 | 5 | 1 | 59 | 23 | 3 | 3 | 15 | 23 | 50 |
| 6 | 1926–27 | Div 3 North | 17th | 42 | 11 | 4 | 6 | 43 | 26 | 3 | 2 | 16 | 23 | 55 |
| 7 | 1927–28 | Div 3 North | 15th | 42 | 10 | 3 | 8 | 41 | 35 | 6 | 3 | 12 | 28 | 46 |
| 8 | 1928–29 | Div 3 North | 21st | 42 | 9 | 4 | 8 | 35 | 38 | 1 | 2 | 18 | 24 | 74 |
| 9 | 1929–30 | Div 3 North | 8th | 42 | 13 | 4 | 4 | 50 | 24 | 4 | 7 | 10 | 31 | 50 |
| 10 | 1930–31 | Div 3 North | 20th | 42 | 10 | 2 | 9 | 47 | 37 | 2 | 4 | 15 | 20 | 49 |
| 11 | 1931–32 | Div 3 North | 13th | 40 | 10 | 4 | 6 | 47 | 37 | 6 | 1 | 13 | 31 | 63 |
| 12 | 1932–33 | Div 3 North | 14th | 42 | 15 | 3 | 3 | 56 | 29 | 1 | 4 | 16 | 31 | 87 |
| 13 | 1933–34 | Div 3 North | 11th | 42 | 14 | 3 | 4 | 54 | 24 | 2 | 4 | 15 | 35 | 69 |
| 14 | 1934–35 | Div 3 North | 12th | 42 | 12 | 4 | 5 | 52 | 34 | 5 | 3 | 13 | 28 | 44 |
| 15 | 1935–36 | Div 3 North | 8th | 42 | 13 | 6 | 2 | 41 | 18 | 2 | 6 | 13 | 16 | 43 |
| 16 | 1936–37 | Div 3 North | 6th | 42 | 16 | 1 | 4 | 53 | 21 | 3 | 6 | 12 | 22 | 48 |
| 17 | 1937–38 | Div 3 North | 20th | 42 | 10 | 8 | 3 | 36 | 20 | 0 | 4 | 17 | 17 | 60 |
| 18 | 1938–39 | Div 3 North | 21st | 42 | 10 | 4 | 7 | 36 | 33 | 2 | 3 | 16 | 19 | 61 |
| 19 | 1946–47 | Div 3 North | 13th | 42 | 10 | 5 | 6 | 36 | 26 | 5 | 4 | 12 | 28 | 47 |
| 20 | 1947–48 | Div 3 North | 19th | 42 | 10 | 6 | 5 | 34 | 23 | 4 | 2 | 15 | 17 | 50 |
| 21 | 1948–49 | Div 3 North | 16th | 42 | 10 | 5 | 6 | 34 | 25 | 4 | 5 | 12 | 11 | 33 |
| 22 | 1949–50 | Div 3 North | 18th | 42 | 10 | 3 | 8 | 37 | 35 | 4 | 2 | 15 | 15 | 44 |
| 23 | 1950–51 | Div 3 North | 16th | 46 | 14 | 5 | 4 | 55 | 26 | 2 | 2 | 19 | 9 | 40 |
| 24 | 1951–52 | Div 3 North | 9th | 46 | 17 | 3 | 3 | 47 | 19 | 4 | 5 | 14 | 24 | 46 |
| 25 | 1952–53 | Div 3 North | 17th | 46 | 14 | 6 | 3 | 39 | 16 | 2 | 8 | 13 | 18 | 45 |
| 26 | 1953–54 | Div 3 North | 18th | 46 | 10 | 8 | 5 | 40 | 21 | 3 | 6 | 14 | 19 | 44 |
| 27 | 1954–55 | Div 3 North | 5th | 46 | 16 | 3 | 4 | 39 | 20 | 9 | 2 | 12 | 25 | 29 |
| 28 | 1955–56 | Div 3 North | 4th | 46 | 18 | 2 | 3 | 47 | 15 | 8 | 3 | 12 | 34 | 45 |
| 29 | 1956–57 | Div 3 North | 2nd | 46 | 18 | 4 | 1 | 56 | 21 | 7 | 5 | 11 | 34 | 42 |
| 30 | 1957–58 | Div 3 North | 17th | 46 | 11 | 6 | 6 | 45 | 26 | 5 | 6 | 12 | 28 | 50 |
| 31 | 1958–59 | Div 4 | 19th | 46 | 11 | 4 | 8 | 50 | 41 | 4 | 6 | 13 | 24 | 47 |
| 32 | 1959–60 | Div 4 | 24th | 46 | 9 | 2 | 12 | 40 | 41 | 1 | 5 | 17 | 19 | 68 |
| 33 | 1960–61 | Div 4 | 23rd | 46 | 10 | 4 | 9 | 46 | 40 | 2 | 4 | 17 | 25 | 63 |
| 34 | 1961–62 | Div 4 | 22nd | 44 | 6 | 5 | 11 | 27 | 35 | 2 | 6 | 14 | 25 | 66 |
| 35 | 1962–63 | Div 4 | 24th | 46 | 5 | 7 | 11 | 33 | 39 | 2 | 4 | 17 | 23 | 65 |
| 36 | 1963–64 | Div 4 | 23rd | 46 | 8 | 7 | 8 | 30 | 36 | 4 | 2 | 17 | 24 | 57 |
| 37 | 1964–65 | Div 4 | 15th | 46 | 11 | 10 | 2 | 44 | 28 | 4 | 3 | 16 | 17 | 57 |
| 38 | 1965–66 | Div 4 | 18th | 46 | 13 | 4 | 6 | 44 | 22 | 3 | 4 | 16 | 19 | 53 |
| 39 | 1966–67 | Div 4 | 8th | 46 | 15 | 3 | 5 | 44 | 29 | 7 | 4 | 12 | 22 | 35 |
| 40 | 1967–68 | Div 4 | 3rd | 46 | 15 | 7 | 1 | 34 | 12 | 10 | 3 | 10 | 26 | 34 |
| 41 | 1968–69 | Div 3 | 22nd | 46 | 6 | 12 | 5 | 25 | 29 | 4 | 7 | 12 | 15 | 41 |
| 42 | 1969–70 | Div 4 | 23rd | 46 | 7 | 7 | 9 | 31 | 30 | 3 | 3 | 17 | 11 | 52 |
| 43 | 1970–71 | Div 4 | 23rd | 46 | 6 | 10 | 7 | 28 | 27 | 2 | 2 | 19 | 6 | 47 |

| Goals Scored | Goals Against | Players Used | Top Goalscorers (League) | Total | Aggregate League | Average League |
|---|---|---|---|---|---|---|
| 52 | 39 | 34 | P. Robertson | 12 | 137,536 | 7,239 |
| 48 | 54 | 31 | C. Hardy | 11 | 85,394 | 4,494 |
| 33 | 70 | 32 | W.E. Smith | 9 | 79,973 | 3,808 |
| 45 | 63 | 30 | W.E. Smith | 12 | 86,589 | 4,123 |
| 82 | 73 | 22 | H. Wensley | 21 | 94,510 | 4,500 |
| 66 | 81 | 26 | H. Wensley | 16 | 63,411 | 3,020 |
| 69 | 81 | 25 | W.A. Robinson | 28 | 74,829 | 3,563 |
| 59 | 112 | 24 | W. Richardson | 19 | 70,565 | 3,360 |
| 81 | 74 | 24 | A.A. Pape | 21 | 98,781 | 4,704 |
| 67 | 86 | 27 | H.R. Simmons | 17 | 72,206 | 3,438 |
| 78 | 100 | 26 | S. Lumley | 18 | 79,197 | 3,960 |
| 87 | 116 | 21 | J.J. Hewitt | 23 | 78,535 | 3,740 |
| 89 | 93 | 22 | J.J. Hewitt | 20 | 77,423 | 3,687 |
| 80 | 78 | 22 | D.M. Lindsay | 21 | 65,398 | 3,114 |
| 57 | 61 | 27 | J. Wigham | 16 | 90,084 | 4,290 |
| 75 | 69 | 21 | S. English | 18 | 120,540 | 5,740 |
| 53 | 80 | 32 | S. English and J. Wigham | 9 | 109,585 | 5,218 |
| 55 | 94 | 27 | T. McGarry | 12 | 87,446 | 4,164 |
| 64 | 73 | 26 | S. Scott | 12 | 158,794 | 7,562 |
| 51 | 73 | 30 | F. Richardson and J. Sloan | 7 | 157,185 | 7,485 |
| 45 | 58 | 26 | F. Richardson | 9 | 175,538 | 8,359 |
| 52 | 79 | 29 | T.L. Owens | 12 | 161,795 | 7,705 |
| 64 | 66 | 22 | L.E. Wildon | 26 | 173,328 | 7,536 |
| 71 | 65 | 20 | L.E. Wildon | 19 | 212,698 | 9,248 |
| 57 | 61 | 19 | L.E. Wildon | 11 | 185,713 | 8,074 |
| 59 | 65 | 26 | L.E. Wildon | 15 | 170,789 | 7,426 |
| 64 | 49 | 19 | T. McGuigan | 18 | 180,126 | 7,832 |
| 81 | 60 | 21 | K. Johnson | 21 | 170,474 | 7,412 |
| 90 | 63 | 19 | K. Johnson | 24 | 212,178 | 9,225 |
| 73 | 76 | 25 | P. Thompson | 16 | 180,616 | 7,853 |
| 74 | 88 | 25 | H.M. Clark | 12 | 126,477 | 5,499 |
| 59 | 109 | 24 | H.M. Clark | 21 | 83,860 | 3,646 |
| 71 | 103 | 27 | R. Folland and K. Johnson | 12 | 94,104 | 4,091 |
| 52 | 101 | 23 | J. Edgar | 20 | 95,054 | 4,321 |
| 56 | 104 | 22 | J. Edgar and J. D. McLean | 11 | 89,921 | 3,910 |
| 54 | 93 | 23 | P. Thompson | 8 | 95,897 | 4,169 |
| 61 | 85 | 19 | P. Thompson | 16 | 135,326 | 5,884 |
| 63 | 75 | 26 | E.R. Phythian | 17 | 111,363 | 4,842 |
| 66 | 64 | 21 | E.R. Phythian | 23 | 132,921 | 5,779 |
| 60 | 46 | 24 | T.J. Bell | 14 | 142,362 | 6,190 |
| 40 | 70 | 27 | P. Blowman | 8 | 96,611 | 4,200 |
| 42 | 82 | 28 | T.J. Bell | 12 | 58,946 | 2,563 |
| 34 | 74 | 26 | D. Sharkey | 8 | 56,568 | 2,459 |

| Final | | | Games | Home | | | Away | | | | | Goals | | |
|---|---|---|---|---|---|---|---|---|---|---|---|---|---|---|
| No. | Season | Division | Position | Played | W | D | L | F | A | W | D | L | F | A |
| 44 | 1971–72 | Div 4 | 18th | 46 | 14 | 2 | 7 | 39 | 25 | 3 | 4 | 16 | 19 | 44 |
| 45 | 1972–73 | Div 4 | 20th | 46 | 8 | 10 | 5 | 17 | 15 | 4 | 7 | 12 | 17 | 34 |
| 46 | 1973–74 | Div 4 | 11th | 46 | 11 | 4 | 8 | 29 | 16 | 5 | 8 | 10 | 19 | 31 |
| 47 | 1974–75 | Div 4 | 13th | 46 | 13 | 6 | 4 | 40 | 24 | 3 | 5 | 15 | 12 | 38 |
| 48 | 1975–76 | Div 4 | 14th | 46 | 10 | 6 | 7 | 37 | 29 | 6 | 4 | 13 | 25 | 49 |
| 49 | 1976–77 | Div 4 | 22nd | 46 | 8 | 9 | 6 | 30 | 20 | 2 | 3 | 18 | 17 | 53 |
| 50 | 1977–78 | Div 4 | 21st | 46 | 12 | 4 | 7 | 34 | 29 | 3 | 3 | 17 | 17 | 55 |
| 51 | 1978–79 | Div 4 | 13th | 46 | 7 | 12 | 4 | 35 | 28 | 6 | 6 | 11 | 22 | 38 |
| 52 | 1979–80 | Div 4 | 19th | 46 | 10 | 7 | 6 | 36 | 28 | 4 | 3 | 16 | 23 | 36 |
| 53 | 1980–81 | Div 4 | 9th | 46 | 14 | 3 | 6 | 42 | 22 | 6 | 6 | 11 | 22 | 39 |
| 54 | 1981–82 | Div 4 | 14th | 46 | 9 | 8 | 6 | 39 | 34 | 4 | 8 | 11 | 34 | 50 |
| 55 | 1982–83 | Div 4 | 22nd | 46 | 11 | 5 | 7 | 30 | 24 | 2 | 4 | 17 | 16 | 52 |
| 56 | 1983–84 | Div 4 | 23rd | 46 | 7 | 8 | 8 | 31 | 28 | 3 | 2 | 18 | 16 | 57 |
| 57 | 1984–85 | Div 4 | 18th | 46 | 10 | 6 | 7 | 34 | 29 | 4 | 4 | 15 | 20 | 38 |
| 58 | 1985–86 | Div 4 | 6th | 46 | 15 | 6 | 2 | 41 | 20 | 5 | 4 | 14 | 27 | 47 |
| 59 | 1986–87 | Div 4 | 18th | 46 | 6 | 11 | 6 | 24 | 30 | 5 | 7 | 11 | 20 | 35 |
| 60 | 1987–88 | Div 4 | 16th | 46 | 9 | 7 | 7 | 25 | 25 | 6 | 7 | 10 | 25 | 32 |
| 61 | 1988–89 | Div 4 | 19th | 46 | 10 | 6 | 7 | 33 | 33 | 4 | 4 | 15 | 17 | 45 |
| 62 | 1989–90 | Div 4 | 19th | 46 | 12 | 4 | 7 | 45 | 33 | 3 | 6 | 14 | 21 | 55 |
| 63 | 1990–91 | Div 4 | 3rd | 46 | 15 | 5 | 3 | 35 | 15 | 9 | 5 | 9 | 32 | 33 |
| 64 | 1991–92 | Div 3 | 11th | 46 | 12 | 5 | 6 | 30 | 21 | 6 | 6 | 11 | 27 | 36 |
| 65 | 1992–93 | Div 2 | 16th | 46 | 8 | 6 | 9 | 19 | 23 | 6 | 6 | 11 | 23 | 37 |
| 66 | 1993–94 | Div 2 | 23rd | 46 | 8 | 3 | 12 | 28 | 40 | 1 | 6 | 16 | 13 | 47 |
| 67 | 1994–95 | Div 3 | 18th | 42 | 9 | 5 | 7 | 33 | 32 | 2 | 5 | 14 | 10 | 37 |
| 68 | 1995–96 | Div 3 | 20th | 46 | 8 | 9 | 6 | 30 | 24 | 4 | 4 | 15 | 17 | 43 |
| 69 | 1996–97 | Div 3 | 20th | 46 | 8 | 6 | 9 | 33 | 32 | 6 | 3 | 14 | 20 | 34 |
| 70 | 1997–98 | Div 3 | 17th | 46 | 10 | 12 | 1 | 40 | 22 | 2 | 11 | 10 | 21 | 31 |
| 71 | 1998–99 | Div 3 | 22nd | 46 | 8 | 7 | 8 | 33 | 27 | 5 | 5 | 13 | 19 | 38 |
| 72 | 1999–00 | Div 3 | 7th | 46 | 16 | 1 | 6 | 32 | 17 | 5 | 8 | 10 | 28 | 32 |
| 73 | 2000–01 | Div 3 | 4th | 46 | 12 | 8 | 3 | 40 | 23 | 9 | 6 | 8 | 31 | 31 |
| 74 | 2001–02 | Div 3 | 7th | 46 | 12 | 6 | 5 | 53 | 23 | 8 | 5 | 10 | 21 | 25 |
| 75 | 2002–03 | Div 3 | 2nd | 46 | 16 | 5 | 2 | 49 | 21 | 8 | 8 | 7 | 22 | 30 |
| 76 | 2003–04 | Div 2 | 6th | 46 | 10 | 8 | 5 | 39 | 24 | 10 | 5 | 8 | 37 | 37 |
| 77 | 2004–05 | FL 1 | 6th | 46 | 15 | 3 | 5 | 51 | 30 | 6 | 5 | 12 | 25 | 36 |
| 78 | 2005–06 | FL 1 | 21st | 46 | 6 | 10 | 7 | 28 | 30 | 5 | 7 | 11 | 16 | 29 |
| 79 | 2006–07 | FL 2 | 2nd | 46 | 14 | 5 | 4 | 34 | 17 | 12 | 5 | 6 | 31 | 23 |
| 80 | 2007–08 | FL 1 | 15th | 46 | 11 | 5 | 7 | 40 | 26 | 4 | 4 | 15 | 23 | 40 |
| 81 | 2008–09 | FL 1 | 19th | 46 | 8 | 7 | 8 | 45 | 40 | 5 | 4 | 14 | 21 | 39 |
| 82 | 2009/10* | FL 1 | 20th | 46 | 10 | 6 | 7 | 33 | 26 | 4 | 5 | 14 | 26 | 41 |
| 83 | 2010/11 | FL 1 | 16th | 46 | 9 | 6 | 8 | 32 | 32 | 6 | 6 | 11 | 15 | 33 |
| 84 | 2011/12 | FL 1 | 13th | 46 | 6 | 6 | 11 | 21 | 22 | 8 | 8 | 7 | 29 | 33 |

***Note:** 3 points deducted for playing an ineligible player, Gary Liddle, in the game against Brighton & Hov

| Goals Scored | Players Against | Used | Aggregate Top Goalscorers (League) | Total | Average League | League |
|---|---|---|---|---|---|---|
| 58 | 69 | 26 | R. Young | 18 | 87,235 | 3,793 |
| 34 | 49 | 22 | J.D. Coyne | 9 | 84,887 | 3,691 |
| 48 | 47 | 20 | A. Gauden | 12 | 62,578 | 2,721 |
| 52 | 62 | 23 | M. Moore | 14 | 60,578 | 2,634 |
| 62 | 78 | 27 | M. Moore and D. B. Smith | 13 | 50,194 | 2,182 |
| 47 | 73 | 31 | M. Poskett | 10 | 43,953 | 1,911 |
| 51 | 84 | 28 | W. Ayre | 12 | 65,157 | 2,833 |
| 57 | 66 | 23 | K.M. Houchen | 13 | 68,921 | 2,997 |
| 59 | 64 | 30 | K.M. Houchen | 14 | 67,055 | 2,915 |
| 64 | 61 | 25 | K.M. Houchen | 17 | 71,637 | 3,115 |
| 73 | 84 | 25 | K.M. Houchen | 17 | 47,259 | 2,055 |
| 46 | 76 | 33 | P. Dobson | 8 | 31,474 | 1,368 |
| 47 | 85 | 37 | P. Dobson | 12 | 33,495 | 1,456 |
| 54 | 67 | 27 | K.L. Dixon | 12 | 54,011 | 2,348 |
| 68 | 67 | 24 | A. Shoulder | 17 | 59,641 | 2,593 |
| 44 | 65 | 31 | K.L. Dixon | 9 | 37,964 | 1,651 |
| 50 | 57 | 27 | D.P. Baker | 20 | 48,963 | 2,129 |
| 50 | 78 | 28 | S.D. Grayson | 13 | 47,104 | 2,048 |
| 66 | 88 | 41 | J.B. Allon | 17 | 57,565 | 2,503 |
| 67 | 48 | 26 | J.B. Allon | 28 | 73,133 | 3,180 |
| 57 | 57 | 28 | D.P. Baker and P. Dalton | 13 | 73,627 | 3,201 |
| 42 | 60 | 25 | A.V. Saville | 13 | 72,195 | 3,139 |
| 41 | 87 | 25 | L.N. Southall | 9 | 47,742 | 2,076 |
| 43 | 69 | 33 | K.M. Houchen | 13 | 41,013 | 1,953 |
| 47 | 67 | 34 | J.B. Allon | 8 | 47,659 | 2,072 |
| 53 | 66 | 33 | J.B. Allon and M.N. Cooper | 9 | 48,459 | 2,107 |
| 61 | 53 | 31 | D.J. Cullen | 12 | 51,560 | 2,242 |
| 52 | 65 | 35 | C. Beech | 9 | 61,786 | 2,686 |
| 60 | 49 | 28 | T. Miller | 14 | 68,577 | 2,982 |
| 71 | 54 | 27 | K. Henderson | 17 | 77,820 | 3,383 |
| 74 | 48 | 27 | G. Watson | 18 | 82,027 | 3,566 |
| 71 | 51 | 21 | E. Williams | 15 | 113,861 | 4,950 |
| 76 | 61 | 34 | E. Williams | 13 | 124,915 | 5,431 |
| 76 | 66 | 31 | A. Boyd | 22 | 119,593 | 5,200 |
| 44 | 59 | 33 | E. Williams | 7 | 110,673 | 4,812 |
| 65 | 40 | 27 | R. Barker and J. Daly | 9 | 117,004 | 5,087 |
| 63 | 66 | 28 | R. Barker | 13 | 103,653 | 4,507 |
| 66 | 79 | 27 | J. Porter | 18 | 88,202 | 3,835 |
| 59 | 67 | 25 | A.Monkhouse | 11 | 79,207 | 3,444 |
| 47 | 65 | 28 | A.Sweeney | 9 | 67,460 | 2,933 |
| 50 | 55 | 30 | A.Sweeney | 8 | 114,098 | 4,961 |

on 5 April 2010.

# League Record Against Other Clubs

Up to and including 2011-12 season

| | *First* | *Home* | | | | | | *Away* | | | | | |
|---|---|---|---|---|---|---|---|---|---|---|---|---|---|
| ***Club*** | ***Played*** | ***P*** | ***W*** | ***D*** | ***L*** | ***F*** | ***A*** | ***P*** | ***W*** | ***D*** | ***L*** | ***F*** | ***A*** |
| Accrington Stanley | 1921–22 | 32 | 21 | 6 | 5 | 63 | 30 | 32 | 9 | 6 | 17 | 43 | 70 |
| Aldershot | 1958–59 | 27 | 11 | 8 | 8 | 35 | 33 | 27 | 6 | 4 | 17 | 28 | 58 |
| Ashington | 1921–22 | 8 | 4 | 0 | 4 | 12 | 10 | 8 | 1 | 1 | 6 | 8 | 17 |
| Barnet | 1993–94 | 9 | 5 | 2 | 2 | 19 | 6 | 9 | 2 | 2 | 5 | 11 | 18 |
| Barnsley | 1932–33 | 19 | 5 | 4 | 10 | 24 | 34 | 19 | 1 | 5 | 13 | 21 | 41 |
| Barrow | 1921–22 | 42 | 25 | 8 | 9 | 91 | 44 | 42 | 9 | 11 | 22 | 46 | 80 |
| Birmingham City | 1991–92 | 1 | 1 | 0 | 0 | 1 | 0 | 1 | 0 | 0 | 1 | 1 | 2 |
| Blackpool | 1981–82 | 11 | 4 | 3 | 4 | 13 | 14 | 11 | 3 | 3 | 5 | 13 | 19 |
| Bolton Wanderers | 1987–88 | 3 | 0 | 1 | 2 | 0 | 6 | 3 | 2 | 1 | 0 | 6 | 4 |
| Boston United | 2002–03 | 2 | 2 | 0 | 0 | 4 | 1 | 2 | 2 | 0 | 0 | 2 | 0 |
| Bournemouth | 1968–69 | 19 | 7 | 9 | 3 | 21 | 16 | 19 | 4 | 4 | 11 | 16 | 34 |
| Bradford City | 1937–38 | 37 | 14 | 12 | 11 | 42 | 40 | 37 | 13 | 8 | 16 | 39 | 58 |
| Bradford Park Avenue | 1922–23 | 23 | 11 | 4 | 8 | 40 | 30 | 23 | 7 | 3 | 13 | 25 | 57 |
| Brentford | 1962–63 | 20 | 10 | 5 | 5 | 26 | 15 | 20 | 3 | 4 | 13 | 12 | 35 |
| Brighton & Hove Albion | 1963–64 | 15 | 4 | 8 | 3 | 20 | 18 | 15 | 0 | 5 | 10 | 14 | 38 |
| Bristol City | 1982–83 | 5 | 2 | 1 | 2 | 9 | 8 | 5 | 1 | 2 | 2 | 2 | 5 |
| Bristol Rovers | 1968–69 | 9 | 4 | 3 | 2 | 12 | 9 | 9 | 2 | 3 | 4 | 6 | 10 |
| Burnley | 1985–86 | 8 | 4 | 4 | 0 | 16 | 7 | 8 | 0 | 3 | 5 | 1 | 13 |
| Bury | 1971–72 | 15 | 6 | 4 | 5 | 19 | 14 | 15 | 3 | 7 | 5 | 14 | 20 |
| Cambridge United | 1970–71 | 17 | 4 | 8 | 5 | 25 | 26 | 17 | 2 | 3 | 12 | 11 | 35 |
| Cardiff City | 1986–87 | 9 | 4 | 2 | 3 | 14 | 10 | 9 | 0 | 3 | 6 | 7 | 20 |
| Carlisle United | 1928–29 | 44 | 22 | 10 | 12 | 75 | 65 | 44 | 11 | 6 | 27 | 53 | 90 |
| Charlton Athletic | 2009–10 | 3 | 1 | 0 | 2 | 2 | 7 | 3 | 0 | 1 | 2 | 3 | 5 |
| Cheltenham Town | 1999–2000 | 5 | 1 | 1 | 3 | 4 | 5 | 5 | 1 | 1 | 3 | 4 | 9 |
| Chester City | 1931–32 | 48 | 25 | 11 | 12 | 77 | 56 | 48 | 7 | 12 | 29 | 43 | 100 |
| Chesterfield | 1921–22 | 38 | 20 | 6 | 12 | 65 | 41 | 38 | 8 | 5 | 25 | 39 | 87 |
| Colchester United | 1961–62 | 28 | 15 | 6 | 7 | 42 | 32 | 28 | 4 | 7 | 17 | 26 | 61 |
| Coventry City | 1925–26 | 2 | 2 | 0 | 0 | 5 | 3 | 2 | 0 | 0 | 2 | 3 | 9 |
| Crewe Alexandra | 1921–22 | 62 | 34 | 14 | 14 | 119 | 83 | 62 | 10 | 8 | 44 | 51 | 127 |
| Crystal Palace | 1958–59 | 3 | 1 | 0 | 2 | 6 | 6 | 3 | 1 | 1 | 1 | 6 | 8 |
| Darlington | 1921–22 | 67 | 35 | 12 | 20 | 117 | 77 | 67 | 21 | 14 | 32 | 72 | 126 |
| Dagenham & Redbridge | 2010–11 | 1 | 0 | 0 | 1 | 0 | 1 | 1 | 0 | 1 | 0 | 1 | 1 |
| Derby County | 1955–56 | 2 | 2 | 0 | 0 | 4 | 1 | 2 | 0 | 0 | 2 | 2 | 5 |

| Club | First Played | Home P | W | D | L | F | A | Away P | W | D | L | F | A |
|---|---|---|---|---|---|---|---|---|---|---|---|---|---|
| Doncaster Rovers | 1925–26 | 46 | 22 | 14 | 10 | 72 | 56 | 46 | 8 | 13 | 25 | 46 | 90 |
| Durham City | 1921–22 | 7 | 4 | 2 | 1 | 10 | 4 | 7 | 2 | 1 | 4 | 5 | 9 |
| Exeter City | 1958–59 | 37 | 16 | 14 | 7 | 58 | 46 | 37 | 5 | 8 | 24 | 30 | 68 |
| Fulham | 1991–92 | 6 | 3 | 0 | 3 | 6 | 7 | 6 | 1 | 1 | 4 | 5 | 8 |
| Gateshead | 1930–31 | 23 | 10 | 6 | 7 | 46 | 34 | 23 | 3 | 5 | 15 | 21 | 49 |
| Gillingham | 1958–59 | 17 | 10 | 5 | 2 | 30 | 14 | 17 | 1 | 3 | 13 | 8 | 39 |
| Grimsby Town | 1921–22 | 19 | 12 | 4 | 3 | 39 | 17 | 19 | 4 | 2 | 13 | 13 | 33 |
| Halifax Town | 1921–22 | 54 | 30 | 12 | 12 | 104 | 53 | 54 | 10 | 5 | 39 | 44 | 104 |
| Hereford United | 1972–73 | 19 | 10 | 4 | 5 | 31 | 19 | 19 | 2 | 4 | 13 | 15 | 41 |
| Huddersfield Town | 1975–76 | 15 | 6 | 4 | 5 | 19 | 18 | 15 | 2 | 2 | 11 | 10 | 26 |
| Hull City | 1930–31 | 24 | 9 | 8 | 7 | 41 | 31 | 24 | 2 | 5 | 17 | 16 | 52 |
| Kidderminster Harriers | 2000–01 | 3 | 2 | 1 | 0 | 6 | 3 | 3 | 1 | 1 | 1 | 5 | 5 |
| Leeds United | 2007–08 | 3 | 0 | 2 | 1 | 3 | 4 | 3 | 0 | 0 | 3 | 2 | 9 |
| Leicester City | 2008–09 | 1 | 0 | 1 | 0 | 2 | 2 | 1 | 0 | 0 | 1 | 0 | 1 |
| Leyton Orient | 1968–69 | 21 | 10 | 5 | 6 | 32 | 24 | 21 | 6 | 4 | 11 | 24 | 35 |
| Lincoln City | 1921–22 | 49 | 26 | 15 | 8 | 85 | 54 | 49 | 9 | 7 | 33 | 53 | 116 |
| Luton Town | 1965–66 | 8 | 6 | 0 | 2 | 18 | 10 | 8 | 1 | 1 | 6 | 8 | 16 |
| Macclesfield Town | 1997–98 | 6 | 1 | 2 | 3 | 7 | 12 | 6 | 3 | 2 | 1 | 7 | 5 |
| Maidstone United | 1989–90 | 2 | 2 | 0 | 0 | 5 | 2 | 2 | 1 | 0 | 1 | 6 | 5 |
| Mansfield Town | 1932–33 | 39 | 19 | 12 | 8 | 73 | 46 | 39 | 6 | 2 | 31 | 32 | 102 |
| Millwall | 1958–59 | 8 | 4 | 1 | 3 | 13 | 9 | 8 | 1 | 1 | 6 | 7 | 18 |
| Milton Keynes Dons | 1977–78 | 11 | 5 | 2 | 4 | 16 | 15 | 11 | 0 | 3 | 8 | 7 | 25 |
| Nelson | 1921–22 | 9 | 5 | 1 | 3 | 29 | 17 | 9 | 1 | 1 | 7 | 14 | 26 |
| New Brighton | 1923–24 | 21 | 15 | 3 | 3 | 53 | 21 | 21 | 3 | 5 | 13 | 22 | 41 |
| Newport County | 1962–63 | 18 | 5 | 6 | 7 | 22 | 19 | 18 | 4 | 3 | 11 | 17 | 32 |
| Northampton Town | 1958–59 | 28 | 18 | 5 | 5 | 52 | 28 | 28 | 1 | 8 | 19 | 24 | 58 |
| Norwich City | 2009–10 | 1 | 0 | 0 | 1 | 0 | 2 | 1 | 0 | 0 | 1 | 1 | 2 |
| Nottingham Forest | 2005–06 | 2 | 1 | 0 | 1 | 3 | 3 | 2 | 0 | 0 | 2 | 1 | 4 |
| Notts County | 1959–60 | 12 | 7 | 4 | 1 | 27 | 12 | 12 | 2 | 1 | 9 | 4 | 19 |
| Oldham Athletic | 1935–36 | 31 | 14 | 9 | 8 | 53 | 31 | 31 | 8 | 3 | 20 | 36 | 70 |
| Oxford United | 1962–63 | 5 | 2 | 1 | 2 | 7 | 6 | 5 | 2 | 0 | 3 | 6 | 15 |
| Peterborough United | 1960–61 | 27 | 10 | 5 | 12 | 29 | 31 | 27 | 6 | 6 | 15 | 34 | 61 |
| Plymouth Argyle | 1968–69 | 10 | 5 | 3 | 2 | 15 | 15 | 10 | 2 | 3 | 5 | 6 | 14 |
| Portsmouth | 1978–79 | 2 | 0 | 1 | 1 | 1 | 4 | 2 | 0 | 0 | 2 | 1 | 5 |
| Port Vale | 1929–30 | 23 | 13 | 6 | 4 | 40 | 29 | 23 | 5 | 6 | 12 | 22 | 43 |
| Preston North End | 1985–86 | 7 | 3 | 2 | 2 | 8 | 6 | 7 | 2 | 1 | 4 | 7 | 10 |
| Queen's Park Rangers | 2003–04 | 1 | 0 | 0 | 1 | 1 | 4 | 1 | 0 | 0 | 1 | 1 | 4 |
| Reading | 1968–69 | 12 | 4 | 3 | 5 | 20 | 21 | 12 | 2 | 2 | 8 | 7 | 29 |
| Rochdale | 1921–22 | 68 | 33 | 20 | 15 | 126 | 77 | 68 | 17 | 13 | 38 | 67 | 131 |
| Rotherham United | 1923–24 | 31 | 14 | 8 | 9 | 56 | 43 | 31 | 6 | 6 | 19 | 35 | 79 |
| Rushden & Diamonds | 2001–02 | 3 | 2 | 0 | 1 | 8 | 4 | 3 | 1 | 1 | 1 | 4 | 3 |

| | First | Home | | | | | | Away | | | | | |
|---|---|---|---|---|---|---|---|---|---|---|---|---|---|
| **Club** | **Played** | **P** | **W** | **D** | **L** | **F** | **A** | **P** | **W** | **D** | **L** | **F** | **A** |
| Scarborough | 1987–88 | 9 | 7 | 2 | 0 | 21 | 6 | 9 | 3 | 3 | 3 | 13 | 16 |
| Scunthorpe United | 1950–51 | 39 | 18 | 8 | 13 | 62 | 52 | 39 | 5 | 10 | 24 | 29 | 74 |
| Sheffield United | 1981–82 | 2 | 0 | 0 | 2 | 2 | 4 | 2 | 0 | 1 | 1 | 2 | 4 |
| Sheffield Wednesday | 2003–04 | 4 | 1 | 1 | 2 | 4 | 7 | 4 | 0 | 1 | 3 | 2 | 7 |
| Shrewsbury Town | 1950–51 | 12 | 5 | 4 | 3 | 16 | 15 | 12 | 5 | 4 | 3 | 13 | 10 |
| Southend United | 1969–70 | 21 | 11 | 3 | 7 | 37 | 28 | 21 | 2 | 5 | 14 | 18 | 39 |
| Southampton | 2009–10 | 2 | 0 | 1 | 1 | 1 | 3 | 2 | 0 | 0 | 2 | 2 | 5 |
| Southport | 1921–22 | 47 | 28 | 10 | 9 | 91 | 55 | 47 | 8 | 16 | 23 | 47 | 80 |
| South Shields | 1928–29 | 2 | 1 | 0 | 1 | 2 | 6 | 2 | 1 | 1 | 0 | 6 | 4 |
| Stalybridge Celtic | 1921–22 | 2 | 1 | 0 | 1 | 4 | 1 | 2 | 1 | 1 | 0 | 4 | 2 |
| Stockport County | 1921–22 | 63 | 31 | 18 | 14 | 114 | 63 | 63 | 14 | 12 | 37 | 64 | 130 |
| Stoke City | 1991–92 | 3 | 0 | 1 | 2 | 3 | 6 | 3 | 1 | 0 | 2 | 4 | 6 |
| Stevenage Borough | 2011–12 | 1 | 0 | 1 | 0 | 0 | 0 | 1 | 0 | 1 | 0 | 2 | 2 |
| Swansea City | 1967–68 | 20 | 7 | 4 | 9 | 30 | 26 | 20 | 3 | 6 | 11 | 17 | 36 |
| Swindon Town | 1968–69 | 13 | 3 | 6 | 4 | 16 | 14 | 13 | 3 | 4 | 6 | 13 | 20 |
| Torquay United | 1958–59 | 38 | 16 | 13 | 9 | 59 | 43 | 38 | 9 | 9 | 20 | 34 | 56 |
| Tranmere Rovers | 1921–22 | 55 | 26 | 14 | 15 | 92 | 61 | 55 | 10 | 10 | 35 | 59 | 122 |
| Walsall | 1921–22 | 25 | 11 | 9 | 5 | 51 | 32 | 25 | 6 | 7 | 12 | 30 | 56 |
| Watford | 1958–59 | 6 | 4 | 1 | 1 | 10 | 7 | 6 | 0 | 1 | 5 | 4 | 18 |
| West Bromwich Albion | 1991–92 | 2 | 0 | 2 | 0 | 2 | 2 | 2 | 1 | 0 | 1 | 3 | 4 |
| Wigan Athletic | 1978–79 | 9 | 3 | 4 | 2 | 13 | 11 | 9 | 1 | 5 | 3 | 12 | 13 |
| Wigan Borough | 1921–22 | 10 | 4 | 5 | 1 | 15 | 6 | 10 | 2 | 1 | 7 | 8 | 17 |
| Wolverhampton Wanderers | 1923–24 | 3 | 0 | 1 | 2 | 0 | 2 | 3 | 0 | 0 | 3 | 2 | 8 |
| Workington | 1951–52 | 22 | 11 | 4 | 7 | 33 | 28 | 22 | 5 | 10 | 7 | 17 | 26 |
| Wrexham | 1921–22 | 50 | 28 | 9 | 13 | 103 | 62 | 50 | 10 | 8 | 32 | 63 | 117 |
| Wycombe Wanderers | 2003–04 | 4 | 1 | 2 | 1 | 5 | 5 | 4 | 2 | 0 | 2 | 5 | 10 |
| Yeovil Town | 2005–06 | 6 | 2 | 2 | 2 | 6 | 4 | 6 | 3 | 0 | 3 | 7 | 11 |
| York City | 1929–30 | 47 | 26 | 10 | 11 | 91 | 60 | 47 | 8 | 13 | 26 | 41 | 91 |
| Total | | 1,880 | 909 | 478 | 493 | 3,171 | 2,210 | 1,880 | 366 | 392 | 1,122 | 1,823 | 3,748 |

Notes:

1. Games against Wimbledon and Rotherham County are included in the records of MK Dons and Rotherham United respectively.
2. The three games of the 1939–40 season were officially expunged from the records and are therefore excluded.

# ATTENDANCES

Attendance records have been divided into North Eastern League and Football League periods including Cup competitions. It should be noted that the North Eastern League figures were often based on contemporary estimates.

## NORTH EASTERN LEAGUE

**Highest – Home**

| | | |
|---|---|---|
| 1. | 12,000 (est.) | v South Shields (FAC), 29 November 1913 |
| 2. | 10,000 (est.) | v Sunderland 'A', 2 January 1909 |
| 3. | 8,000 (est.) | v Darlington (FAC), 16 October 1909 |
| 4. | 7,743 | v Houghton Rovers (FAC), 20 November 1920 |
| 5. | 7,000 (est.) | v South Shields Adelaide, 5 March 1910 |

**Lowest – Home**

| | | |
|---|---|---|
| 1. | 500 (est.) | v Spennymoor United, 24 April 1912 |
| 2. | 800 (est.) | v Carlisle United, 13 April 1921 |
| 3. | 987 | v Carlisle United, 13 February 1915 |
| 4. | 1,000 (est.) | v Shildon Athletic, 23 April 1910 |
| 5. | 1,500 (est.) | v Sunderland Royal Rovers, 28 April 1909 |

**Highest – Away**

| | | |
|---|---|---|
| 1. | 8,000 (est.) | v Middlesbrough Reserves, 25 December 1912 |
| 2. | 7,000 (est.) | v West Hartlepool (FAC), 3 October 1908 (played at the Victoria Ground) |
| 3. | 7,000 (est.) | v South Shields, 8 March 1913 |
| 4. | 6,000 (est.) | v Middlesbrough A, 25 March 1910 |
| 5. | 5,000 (est.) | v Bishop Auckland (FAC), 15 December 1920 |

**Lowest – Away**

| | | |
|---|---|---|
| 1. | 800 (est.) | v Newcastle United A, 5 April 1909 |
| 2. | 1,000 (est.) | v Hebburn Argyle, 4 September 1909 |
| 3. | 1,300 (est.) | v Sunderland Reserves, 7 November 1914 |
| 4. | 1,500 (est.) | v North Shields Athletic, 9 March 1912 |
| 5. | 2,000 (est.) | v Darlington, 19 September 1908 |

**Note:** The above attendances are based on contemporary estimates and are intended to illustrate the progression prior to joining the Football League. Later estimates of the same value have been excluded.

## FOOTBALL LEAGUE

**Highest – Home**

| | | |
|---|---|---|
| 1. | 17,264 | v Manchester United (FAC), 5 January 1957 |
| 2. | 17,200 | v Nottingham Forest (FAC), 29 January 1955 |
| 3. | 17,118 | v Hull City, 9 October 1948 |
| 4. | 16,862 | v Chelsea (FAC), 7 January 1956 |
| 5. | 16,000 | v Leeds United (FAC), 18 January 1979 |

| | | |
|---|---|---|
| 6. | 15,360 | v Oldham Athletic (FAC), 9 December 1950 |
| 7. | 15,176 | v Darlington, 26 August 1957 |
| 8. | 15,064 | v Grimsby Town (FAC), 11 January 1936 |
| 9. | 14,813 | v Aldershot (FAC), 11 December 1954 |
| 10. | 14,585 | v Darlington, 30 August 1948 |

**Note:** Since the redevelopment of Victoria Park the highest attendance is 7,784 v Leeds United on 26 December 2007.

**Highest – Away**

| | | |
|---|---|---|
| 1. | 59,808 | v Sheffield Wednesday (POF), 29 May 2005 (played at Cardiff) |
| 2. | 40,813 | v Sunderland (FAC), 3 January 2004 |
| 3. | 38,608 | v Burnley (FAC), 12 January 1952 |
| 4. | 36,632 | v Newcastle United (FAC), 10 January 1925 |
| 5. | 35,357 | v Hull City, 5 March 1949 |
| 6. | 30,191 | v Leeds United, 26 December 2009 |
| 7. | 30,064 | v Hull City, 26 December 1947 |
| 8. | 27,194 | v Arsenal (FLC), 3 October 1995 |
| 9. | 26,877 | v Leeds United, 8 September 2007 |
| 10. | 26,863 | v Manchester City (FAC), 3 January 1976 |

**Lowest – Home**

| | | |
|---|---|---|
| 1. | 655 | v Bradford City (FLT), 18 August 1982 |
| 2. | 700 | v Gateshead (D3NC), 15 March 1939 |
| 3. | 782 | v Doncaster Rovers (SVT), 24 November 1987 |
| 4. | 790 | v Stockport County, 5 May 1984 |
| 5. | 804 | v Colchester United, 2 May 1983 |
| 6. | 818 | v Rotherham United (LDC), 28 November 1989 |
| 7. | 823 | v Hereford United, 7 May 1988 |
| 8. | 844 | v Scunthorpe United, 22 December 1973 |
| 9. | 853 | v Crewe Alexandra, 7 March 1931 |
| 10. | 888 | v Blackpool (AWS), 7 November 1995 |

**Lowest – Away**

| | | |
|---|---|---|
| 1. | 290 | v Gateshead (D3NC), 8 March 1939 |
| 2. | 300 | v York City (D3NC), 13 January 1934 |
| 3. | 858 | v Rochdale, 2 April 1977 |
| 4. | 859 | v Carlisle United (AGT), 15 December 1992 |
| 5. | 876 | v Halifax Town, 23 April 1988 |
| 6. | 880 | v Southport, 7 May 1977 |
| 7. | 908 | v Chester City (AWS), 8 December 1998 |
| 8. | 910 | v Rochdale, 30 April 1985 |
| 9. | 936 | v Lincoln City (JPT), 9 October 2007 |
| 10. | 38 | v Halifax Town (FLT), 21 August 1982 |

**Note:** Unless otherwise indicated games are Football League fixtures.

# Individual Goalscoring Records

**Players who have scored 5 goals in a game:**

| | |
|---|---|
| Harry Simmons | 1930–31 v Wigan Borough in Division 3 North, won 6–1 |
| Bobby Folland | 1960–61 v Oldham Athletic in Division 4, won 5–1. |

**Players who have scored 4 goals in a game:**

| | |
|---|---|
| Ken Johnson | 1955–56 v Crewe Alexandra in Division 3 North, won 6–1 |
| | 1956–57 v Southport in Division 3 North, won 6–1 |
| | 1956–57 v Tranmere Rovers in Division 3 North, won 5–1 |
| Paul Baker | 1989–90 v Stockport County in Division 4, won 5–1 |
| Leo Harden | 1953–54 v Rochdale in Division 3 North, won 6–0 |
| Mark Lawrence | 1978–79 v Halifax Town in Division 4, won 4–2 |
| Les Owens | 1949–50 v Chester in Division 3 North, won 5–1 |
| Jimmy Sloan | 1946–47 v North Shields in FA Cup first round, won 6–0 |
| Peter Thompson | 1958–58 v Prescott Cables in FA Cup first round, won 5–0 |
| Eric Wildon | 1950–51 v Wrexham in Division 3 North, won 4–1 |

**The following 2 players have recorded 3 hat-tricks in League and Cup games:**
Josh Hewitt and Billy Robinson

**The following 10 players have recorded 2 hat-tricks in League and Cup games:**
Paul Baker, Keith Houchen, Ken Johnson, Syd Lumley, Tommy McGuigan, Joel Porter, Jack Scott, Jackie Smith, Antony Sweeney and Eric Wildon

**The following 40 players have recorded 1 hat-trick in a League and Cup game:**
Joe Allon, Terry Bell, Albert Bonass, Adam Boyd, Darryl Clarke, George Crowther, Paul Dalton, John Daly, Bobby Dixon, Paul Dobson, Johnny Edgar, Bob Folland, Terry Francis, Stephen Halliday, Cecil Hardy, Johnny Langland, Jimmy McCambridge, Billy McClure, Craig Midgley, Tommy Miller, Malcolm Moore, Jimmy Mulvaney, Barry Parkes, Ralph Pedwell, Ernie Phythian, Malcolm Poskett, Harry Proctor, Fred Richardson, Paul Robinson, Andy Saville, Billy Smith, Nicky Southall, Tony Sweeney, Jimmy Thompson, John Tinkler, Horace Waller, Gordon Watson, Harry Wensley, Johnny Wigham and Joe Willetts

**Players who have scored 50 or more career goals:**

| | Season | Total | League | FA Cup | FL Cup | Other |
|---|---|---|---|---|---|---|
| Ken Johnson | 1949–64 | 108 | 98 | 6 | 2 | 0 |
| Johnny Wigham | 1931–39 | 108 | 95 | 7 | 0 | 4 |
| Keith Houchen | 1977–97 | 94 | 92 | 0 | 2 | 0 |
| Paul Baker | 1987–98 | 92 | 76 | 6 | 5 | 5 |
| Eric Wildon | 1947–55 | 89 | 87 | 2 | 0 | 0 |
| Tommy McGuigan | 1950–58 | 79 | 75 | 4 | 0 | 0 |
| Joe Allon | 1988–97 | 79 | 67 | 5 | 4 | 3 |
| Adam Boyd | 1999–2012 | 79 | 69 | 3 | 4 | 3 |

| | | | | | | |
|---|---|---|---|---|---|---|
| Ralph Pedwell | 1929–34 | 68 | 66 | 2 | 0 | 0 |
| George Luke | 1953–60 | 68 | 60 | 8 | 0 | 0 |
| Joel Porter | 2003–09 | 66 | 52 | 5 | 4 | 5 |
| Bob Newton | 1977–86 | 62 | 50 | 10 | 2 | 0 |
| Peter Thompson | 1957–66 | 61 | 56 | 5 | 0 | 0 |
| Antony Sweeney | 2001–12 | 60 | 51 | 4 | 2 | 3 |
| Eifion Williams | 2001–07 | 56 | 50 | 2 | 1 | 3 |
| Josh Hewitt | 1930–34 | 55 | 53 | 2 | 0 | 0 |
| Ernie Phythian | 1965–68 | 55 | 51 | 1 | 3 | 0 |
| Leo Harden | 1946–56 | 52 | 47 | 5 | 0 | 0 |
| Jackie Smith | 1953–60 | 50 | 49 | 1 | 0 | 0 |

**Players who have scored 20 or more goals in a season:**

| | **Season** | **Total** | **League** | **FA Cup** | **FL Cup** | **Other** |
|---|---|---|---|---|---|---|
| Harold Wensley | 1925–26 | 22 | 21 | 1 | 0 | 0 |
| Billy Robinson | 1927–28 | 28 | 28 | 0 | 0 | 0 |
| Albert Pape | 1929–30 | 21 | 21 | 0 | 0 | 0 |
| Josh Hewitt | 1932–33 | 24 | 23 | 1 | 0 | 0 |
| Josh Hewitt | 1933–34 | 21 | 20 | 1 | 0 | 0 |
| Ralph Pedwell | 1933–34 | 20 | 18 | 2 | 0 | 0 |
| Duncan Lindsay | 1934–35 | 26 | 21 | 1 | 0 | 4 |
| Albert Bonass | 1934–35 | 23 | 20 | 2 | 0 | 1 |
| Sam English | 1936–37 | 20 | 18 | 2 | 0 | 0 |
| Eric Wildon | 1950–51 | 27 | 26 | 1 | 0 | 0 |
| Tommy McGuigan | 1954–55 | 20 | 18 | 2 | 0 | 0 |
| George Luke | 1955–56 | 23 | 19 | 4 | 0 | 0 |
| Ken Johnson | 1955–56 | 21 | 21 | 0 | 0 | 0 |
| Ken Johnson | 1956–57 | 26 | 24 | 2 | 0 | 0 |
| George Luke | 1956–57 | 20 | 19 | 1 | 0 | 0 |
| Peter Thompson | 1957–58 | 20 | 16 | 4 | 0 | 0 |
| Harry Clark | 1959–60 | 21 | 21 | 0 | 0 | 0 |
| Johnny Edgar | 1961–62 | 20 | 20 | 0 | 0 | 0 |
| Ernie Phythian | 1966–67 | 26 | 23 | 1 | 2 | 0 |
| Ron Young | 1971–72 | 20 | 18 | 2 | 0 | 0 |
| Paul Baker | 1987–88 | 25 | 20 | 3 | 1 | 1 |
| Andy Toman | 1987–88 | 20 | 17 | 3 | 0 | 0 |
| Joe Allon | 1990–91 | 35 | 28 | 3 | 2 | 2 |
| Andy Saville | 1992–93 | 20 | 13 | 5 | 1 | 1 |
| Tommy Miller | 2000–01 | 20 | 16 | 0 | 2 | 2 |
| Adam Boyd | 2004–05 | 29 | 22 | 3 | 1 | 3 |
| Joel Porter | 2008–09 | 23 | 18 | 2 | 3 | 0 |

# Oldest and Youngest Players

## Oldest Players –

**Mick Tait, Midfielder – born 30 September 1956**

Much-travelled midfield player who made his debut for 'Pools at the start of the 1992–93 season aged 35 years, 10 months and 15 days. Tait had two spells with the club as a player, culminating in him making his final appearance on 22 March 1997 against Fulham at the age of 40 years, 5 months and 22 days. He later had a spell as manager.

Mick Tait also became Hartlepools' oldest goalscorer when he netted against Rochdale in a Division Three fixture on 3 February 1996 at the age of 39 years, 4 months and 3 days.

**John MacPhail, Defender – born 7 December 1955**

Aged 39 years, 87 days when he played his final game against Lincoln City on 4 March 1995. Originally signed by Cyril Knowles, MacPhail made 196 appearances scoring five goals and managed the club from 1993 to 1994.

**Jacky Carr, Forward – born 26 November 1892**

Made his final appearance on 21 November 1931 against York City at the age of 38 years, 11 months and 26 days. Carr, who had a distinguished playing career, joined the club at the start of the season as player-manager, making 10 appearances before retiring to concentrate on his management duties.

**John Henry (Jack) Brown, Goalkeeper – born 19 March 1899**

Debut 1937–38 season v Gateshead at home on 18 September 1937, a 1–3 defeat. Aged 38 years and 6 months, this was Brown's only appearance for the club. He spent virtually all his career with Sheffield Wednesday, for whom he made 465 League appearances and played six times for England, as well as gaining Football League honours. Brown died in 1962.

**Craig Hignett, Midfielder – born 12 January 1970**

Made his debut as a substitute on 30 March 2007 against Chester City, aged 37 years, 2 months and 17 days. A much-travelled player, primarily with Crewe Alexandra, Middlesbrough and Barnsley, he was a short-term signing to support the promotion campaign and after one further appearance was released at the end of that season.

**Neil McBain, Goalkeeper – born 15 November 1895**

Played in an emergency at the 'Vic' for New Brighton, for whom he was manager, on 15 March 1947 at the age of 52 years, 4 months. This made McBain the oldest player ever to appear in a Football League game. 'Pools won 3–0.

McBain had previously had a distinguished career as a wing half-back for Everton, Liverpool and Manchester United, among others, and was capped three times by Scotland. He died in 1974.

The oldest team to represent Hartlepool United played at Chester in a Division Three North fixture on 20 September 1947, with an average age of 31 years and 2 months.

The team, with individual ages in brackets was:

Theaker (34 years, 9 months); Brown (38 years, 6 months), Hooper (36 years, 9 months); Hughes (26 years, 11 months), Tootill (33 years, 11 months), Jones (28 years, 11 months); Isaac (30 years, 10 months), Baines (28 years, 0 months), Wilkinson (23 years, 4 months), Price (29 years, 0 months), Simpson (32 years, 0 months).

# Youngest Players

**David Foley, Forward – born 12 May 1987**

Debut 2003–04 season v Port Vale at home on 25 August 2003 as a substitute for Paul Robinson, aged 16 years, 3 months and 13 days. 'Pools won 2–0.

**Steven Istead, Forward – born 23 April 1986**

Debut 2002–03 season v Bristol Rovers at home on 29 October 2002 as a substitute for Darrell Clarke, aged 16 years, 6 months and 6 days. 'Pools won 2–0. Despite making 81 appearances and scoring 4 goals, Istead only started in 7 games; the remaining 74 were as a substitute.

**John McGovern, Midfielder – born 28 October 1949**

Debut 1965–66 season v Bradford City at home on 21 May 1966, a 1–1 draw, aged 16 years, 6 months and 23 days.

**Luke James, Forward – born 4 November 1994**

Became 'Pools youngest goalscorer v Rochdale at home on 7 January 2012, scoring the second goal in a 2–0 win, aged 17 years and 64 days.

The youngest team to represent Hartlepool United played at Chester in a Division 4 fixture on 4 December 1982, with an average age of 21 years, 3 months.

The team with individual ages in brackets was – Wright (18 years, 2 months); Smith (23 years, 8 months), Stimpson (18 years, 9 months); Hogan (22 years, 2 months), Barker (26 years, 9 months), A. Linighan (20 years, 5 months); Staff (20 years, 3 months), Dobson (19 years, 11 months), Linacre (20 years, 6 months), Brown (23 years, 6 months), Bainbridge (19 years, 11 months).

# Televised Live Games

| Date | Comp | Opponents | Venue | Result | TV Channel |
|---|---|---|---|---|---|
| 4 September 1998 | Division 3 | Halifax Town | Away | L 1–2 | Sky Sports |
| 21 November 1999 | FA Cup R2 | Hereford United | Away | L 0–1 | Sky Sports |
| 20 August 2001 | FL Cup R1 | Nottingham Forest | Home | L 0–2 | Sky Sports |
| 13 October 2002 | Division 3 | Bournemouth | Away | L 1–2 | Sky Sports |
| 1 November 2002 | Division 3 | York City | Home | D 0–0 | Sky Sports |
| 7 December 2003 | FA Cup R2 | Burton Albion | Away | W 1–0 | BBC1 |
| 15 May 2004 | POSF1 leg | Bristol City | Home | D 1–1 | Sky Sports |
| 19 May 2004 | POSF2 leg | Bristol City | Away | L 1–2 | Sky Sports |
| 18 August 2004 | League 1 | Huddersfield Town | Away | W 2–0 | Sky Sports |
| 13 May 2005 | POSF1 leg | Tranmere Rovers | Home | W 2–0 | Sky Sports |
| 17 May 2005 | POSF2 leg | Tranmere Rovers | Away | L 0–2 | Sky Sports |
| 29 May 2005 | PO Final | Sheffield Wednesday | Away | L 2–4 | Sky Sports |
| 20 November 2006 | FA Cup R1r | Rochdale | Home | D 0–0 | Sky Sports |
| 18 November 2007 | League 1 | Bournemouth | Home | D 1–1 | Sky Sports |
| 24 January 2009 | FA Cup R4 | West Ham United | Home | L 2–0 | ITV1 |
| 4 September 2010 | League 1 | MK Dons | Away | L 0–1 | Sky Sports |
| 9 October 2011 | League 1 | Notts County | Away | L 0–3 | Sky Sports |

# Hartlepools United during World War Two

## 1939-40

Manager : Jimmy Hamilton

### FL North East Regional Division

| Match | Date | | Venue | Opponents | Result | Score | Scorers | Gate |
|---|---|---|---|---|---|---|---|---|
| 1 | Oct | 21 | (h) | Newcastle United | L | 1 - 2 | Wilson | 4,000 |
| 2 | | 28 | (a) | Hull City | W | 3 - 2 | Maguire 2, Stephens | 2,500 |
| 3 | Nov | 11 | (h) | Halifax Town | W | 3 - 2 | Stephens, Morton, West | 2,000 |
| 4 | | 18 | (a) | Leeds United | L | 1 - 2 | Stephens | 4,000 |
| 5 | | 25 | (h) | Bradford City | W | 4 - 1 | Stephens 3, West | 1,100 |
| 6 | Dec | 2 | (a) | Darlington | L | 0 - 4 | | 2,536 |
| 7 | | 25 | (h) | York City | L | 1 - 2 | Scrimshaw | 2,000 |
| 8 | Feb | 10 | (a) | Newcastle United | L | 0 - 3 | | 4,333 |
| 9 | | 24 | (h) | Hull City | W | 3 - 2 | Stephens 3 | 1,500 |
| 10 | Mar | 2 | (a) | Middlesbrough | L | 0 - 2 | | 1,480 |
| 11 | | 9 | (a) | Halifax Town | L | 1 - 3 | Marshall | 2,000 |
| 12 | | 16 | (h) | Leeds United | W | 2 - 1 | Howe (pen), West | 1,500 |
| 13 | | 22 | (h) | Bradford Park Avenue | L | 0 - 4 | | 2,500 |
| 14 | | 23 | (a) | Bradford City | L | 0 - 4 | | 2,500 |
| 15 | | 25 | (a) | Huddersfield Town | L | 1 - 4 | West | 4,326 |
| 16 | | 30 | (h) | Darlington | W | 3 - 1 | Armes, Middleton, Glassey | 1,300 |
| 17 | May | 18 | (a) | York City | L | 1 - 2 | West | |
| 18 | | 20 | (a) | Bradford Park Avenue | L | 0 - 2 | | 469 |
| 19 | | 25 | (h) | Middlesbrough | L | 1 - 2 | Middleton | 1,000 |
| 20 | June | 1 | (h) | Huddersfield Town | D | 2 - 2 | Carr 2 | 1,000 |

### FL North War Cup

| Match | Date | | Venue | Opponents | Result | Score | Scorers | Gate |
|---|---|---|---|---|---|---|---|---|
| 17 | Apr 13 | PR | (h) | Halifax Town | W | 2 - 1 | Heslop, Gallon | 1,000 |
| 18 | 20 | R1 | (a) | Barnsley | L | 0 - 3 | | 2,000 |
| 19 | 27 | R2 | (h) | Barnsley | D | 1 - 1 | Dawson | 1,000 |

**Appearances:** Agar 1; Armes* 2; Blenkinsop* 8; Brown 1; Carr* 1; Carter* 6; Copping* 1; Daniels 1; Dawson* 1; Deacon 3; Docking* 6; Dodds 4; Douglas 3; Earl 6; Fairhurst 3; Finlay* 1; Foreman 3; Fowler* 3; Gallon 1; Glassey 6; Gorman* 1; Hall J.* 3; Hall J.L.* 13; Hastings* 1; Hepplewhite* 4; Heslop 1; Heywood* 2; Hodgson* 1; Howe* 13; Isaac* 2; Johnston* 16; Laidler* 6; Laurence* 1; Leadman* 1; Logan* 2; Love 2; Maguire* 3; Mantle 2; Marshall* 5; McDermott* 1; McMahon* 6; McPhillips* 1; Middleton 5; Molloy* 1; Mordue* 8; Morton* 1; Nealle* 1; Neowe* 3; Nicholson* 1; Price 1; Robinson J. 2; Robinson J.* 1; Scrimshaw* 3; Shanks* 1; Smailes* 1; Smith* 6; Sphuler* 2; Stephens* 6; Thomas 16; Turner 3; Wallace 1; Wardle* 13; West 19; Wilson 4; Wright 3.

* Guest player.

**Goals:** 30; Stephens 9, West 5, Carr 2, Maguire 2, Middleton 2, Armes 1, Dawson 1, Gallon 1, Glassey 1, Heslop 1, Howe 1, Marshall 1, Morton 1, Scrimshaw 1, Wilson 1.

# 1943-44

Manager : Fred Westgarth

## FL North First Championship

| Match | Date | Venue | Opponents | Result | Score | Scorers | Gate |
|---|---|---|---|---|---|---|---|
| 1 | Aug 28 | (h) | Middlesbrough | W | 1 - 0 | Scrimshaw | 2,584 |
| 2 | Sep 4 | (a) | Middlesbrough | L | 2 - 3 | Bamford (pen), Mullen | 4,000 |
| 3 | 11 | (h) | Sunderland | L | 0 - 3 | | 6,208 |
| 4 | 18 | (a) | Sunderland | L | 0 - 3 | | 9,840 |
| 5 | 25 | (a) | Gateshead | D | 3 - 3 | Barrett (pen), Adams, Short | 3,000 |
| 6 | Oct 2 | (h) | Gateshead | W | 5 - 0 | Johnson 2, Adams 2, Robinson | 4,649 |
| 7 | 9 | (a) | York City | L | 0 - 2 | | 5,868 |
| 8 | 16 | (h) | York City | W | 4 - 1 | Robinson, Phillips, Corbett, Johnson | 5,241 |
| 9 | 23 | (a) | Newcastle United | W | 1 - 0 | Barrett (pen) | 10,065 |
| 10 | 30 | (h) | Newcastle United | W | 5 - 4 | Short 2, Scott, Mullen, Adams | 7,472 |
| 11 | Nov 6 | (h) | Darlington | W | 2 - 1 | Short, Bamford (pen) | 7,200 |
| 12 | 13 | (a) | Darlington | D | 2 - 2 | Robinson, Short | 7,009 |
| 13 | 20 | (a) | Middlesbrough | W | 3 - 1 | Adams, Robinson, Short | 4,000 |
| 14 | 27 | (h) | Middlesbrough | L | 3 - 4 | Adams, Short, Mullen | 7,000 |
| 15 | Dec 4 | (a) | Sunderland | W | 2 - 1 | Short, Johnson | 6,000 |
| 16 | 11 | (h) | Sunderland | D | 1 - 1 | Skinner | 6,585 |
| 17 | 18 | (h) | Darlington | W | 5 - 1 | Short 3, Robinson, Adams | 4,492 |
| 18 | 25 | (a) | Darlington | W | 5 - 1 | Corbett, Robinson 2, Drake, Skinner | 8,890 |

## FL North Second Championship

| Match | Date | Venue | Opponents | Result | Score | Scorers | Gate |
|---|---|---|---|---|---|---|---|
| 19 | Dec 27 | (a) | Middlesbrough | D | 1 - 1 | Robinson | 8,500 |
| 20 | Jan 1 | (h) | Middlesbrough | D | 1 - 1 | Skinner | 9,100 |
| 21 | 8 | (h) | Newcastle United | L | 1 - 2 | Short | 6,326 |
| 22 | 15 | (a) | Newcastle United | L | 1 - 5 | Robinson | 13,835 |
| 23 | 22 | (a) | Sunderland | W | 4 - 3 | Bamford 2, Adams, Ward | 7,500 |
| 24 | 29 | (h) | Sunderland | W | 4 - 2 | Farrington 2, Wardle, Hamilton | 7,000 |
| 25 | Feb 5 | (h) | Darlington | W | 2 - 1 | Short, Skinner | 8,000 |
| 26 | 12 | (a) | Darlington | W | 4 - 2 | Tooze 2 (2 own goals), Robinson, Farrington | 10,000 |
| 27 | 19 | (h) | Gateshead | L | 5 - 6 | Short 2 (1 pen), Scott, Smallwood 2 | 7,000 |
| 28 | 26 | (a) | Gateshead | D | 2 - 2 | Short 2 (1 pen) | 2,000 |
| 29 | Mar 4 | (h) | Newcastle United | W | 3 - 1 | Scott, Short, Bamford | 8,432 |
| 30 | 11 | (a) | Newcastle United | L | 0 - 3 | | 26,110 |
| 31 | 18 | (a) | Sunderland | L | 0 - 3 | | 3,000 |
| 32 | 25 | (h) | Sunderland | W | 2 - 1 | Short, Scott | 4,835 |
| 33 | Apr 1 | (a) | Gateshead | L | 2 - 3 | Short, Farrington | 2,000 |
| 34 | 8 | (h) | Gateshead | D | 3 - 3 | Baines 2, Drake | 5,419 |
| 35 | 15 | (h) | Middlesbrough | L | 2 - 6 | Bamford, Short | 3,670 |
| 36 | 22 | (a) | Middlesbrough | W | 5 - 0 | Scott, Nettleton 2, Baines, Own Goal | 2,000 |
| 37 | Apr 29 | (a) | Gateshead | L | 1 - 3 | Baines | 500 |
| 38 | May 6 | (h) | Gateshead | W | 6 - 2 | Baines 3, Farrington, Scott, Short | 2,000 |

**Note:** The following games counted towards the various Cup competitions as follows -Games 19–28 Football League North Cup Qualifying competition; Games 29–34 Football League Cup KO competition played on a two-legged basis; Games 35–38 The Tyne-Tees Cup played on a two-legged basis.

**Appearances:** Adams* 12; Atkinson 10; Baines* 7; Bamford* 13; Barrett* 19; Batey* 1; Beresford 1; Corbett 3; Cox* 1; Daniels 4; Dawes* 5; Deacon* 1; Delaney* 1; Drake 5; Farrington* 16; Forde* 9; Frazer* 1;Gledson 1; Hamilton* 4; Harrison* 1; Heal 1; Heywood* 38; Hipkin* 1; Howe* 2; Hyslop* 2; Johnston 3; Levitt 1; Makepeace* 23; Malpass* 4; Martin* 1; Milne 3; Mitchell 3; Mullen 20; Nettleton* 2; Phillips* 20; Robinson* 31; Rookes* 5; Rudkin* 1; Scott* 38; Scrimshaw* 2; Short* 31; Skinner* 21; Slack 3; Smallwood* 8; Tabram* 11; Thomas 1; Toothill* 3; Tracey* 1; Tunney* 16; Ward 1; Wardle* 2; Wilson* 2; Woodgate* 1; Woods* 1.

* Guest player.

**Goals:** 93; Short 22, Robinson 10, Adams 8, Baines 7, Bamford 6, Scott 6, Farrington 5, Johnston 4, Skinner 4, Mullen 3, Barrett 2, Corbett 2, Drake 2, Nettleton 2, Smallwood 2, Hamilton 1, Phillips 1, Scrimshaw 1, Ward 1, Wardle 1, own-goals 3.

# 1944-45

Manager : Fred Westgarth

## FL North First Championship

| Match | Date | Venue | Opponents | Result | Score | Scorers | Gate |
|---|---|---|---|---|---|---|---|
| 1 | Aug 26 | (a) | York City | L | 1 - 3 | Nettleton | 4,000 |
| 2 | Sept 2 | (h) | York City | W | 5 - 0 | Horton 3, Copeland, Short | 2,500 |
| 3 | 9 | (h) | Darlington | W | 4 - 2 | Horton 2, Copeland, Smallwood | 6,240 |
| 4 | 16 | (a) | Darlington | L | 1 - 2 | Horton | 6,736 |
| 5 | 23 | (a) | Gateshead | W | 3 - 1 | Horton, Nettleton, Smallwood | 2,000 |
| 6 | 30 | (h) | Gateshead | L | 2 - 5 | Barrett (pen), Short | 6,000 |
| 7 | Oct 7 | (h) | Bradford Park Avenue | D | 0 - 0 | | 8,057 |
| 8 | 14 | (a) | Bradford Park Avenue | L | 1 - 4 | Nettleton | 7,184 |
| 9 | 21 | (h) | Sunderland | L | 2 - 6 | Catterick, Short | 8,484 |
| 10 | 28 | (a) | Sunderland | L | 2 - 4 | Scott, West | 10,000 |
| 11 | Nov 4 | (h) | Middlesbrough | L | 2 - 3 | Harrison 2 | 4,784 |
| 12 | 11 | (a) | Middlesbrough | W | 3 - 0 | West, Short, Turney | 6,000 |
| 13 | 18 | (a) | Leeds United | L | 2 - 6 | Cochrane, Copeland | 8,000 |
| 14 | 25 | (h) | Leeds United | W | 3 - 0 | Nettleton, Scott, Cochrane | 4,940 |
| 15 | Dec 2 | (h) | Newcastle United | L | 2 - 3 | Nettleton, Cochrane | 7,204 |
| 16 | 9 | (a) | Newcastle United | L | 0 - 3 | | 12,000 |
| 17 | 16 | (a) | Bradford City | W | 4 - 2 | Horton, Cochrane (pen), Harrison 2 | 2,000 |
| 18 | 23 | (h) | Bradford City | W | 4 - 3 | Brown 3, Wardle | 5,500 |

## FL North Second Championship

| Match | Date | Venue | Opponents | Result | Score | Scorers | Gate |
|---|---|---|---|---|---|---|---|
| 19 | Dec 26 | (a) | Middlesbrough | D | 0 - 0 | | 10,000 |
| 20 | 30 | (h) | Middlesbrough | W | 6 - 4 | Short, Cochrane 2, Brown 2, Harrison | 8,000 |
| 21 | Jan 6 | (a) | Gateshead | W | 2 - 1 | Harrison, Brown | 3,000 |
| 22 | 13 | (h) | Gateshead | D | 1 - 1 | Brown | 6,756 |
| 23 | 20 | (a) | Darlington | L | 2 - 3 | Brown, Cochrane | 4,199 |
| 24 | Feb 10 | (a) | Newcastle United | L | 1 - 4 | Short | 15,467 |
| 25 | 17 | (a) | Sunderland | L | 2 - 6 | Short, Robinson | 12,200 |
| 26 | 24 | (h) | Sunderland | W | 3 - 1 | Adams, Brown 2 | 9,817 |
| 27 | Mar 3 | (h) | Newcastle United | W | 2 - 1 | Douglas, Brown | 9,523 |
| 28 | 10 | (h) | York City | D | 1 - 1 | Brown | 5,590 |
| 29 | 17 | (h) | Darlington | L | 0 - 3 | | 11,869 |
| 30 | 24 | (h) | Middlesbrough | W | 3 - 0 | Short, Brown 2 | 4,132 |
| 31 | 31 | (a) | Middlesbrough | W | 3 - 1 | Lyons 2, Skinner | 3,000 |
| 32 | Apr 7 | (h) | Huddersfield Town | L | 1 - 6 | Lyons | 6,046 |
| 33 | 14 | (a) | Huddersfield Town | L | 3 - 6 | Williams 2, Howe (own goal) | 2,210 |
| 34 | 21 | (a) | Sunderland | L | 0 - 5 | | 10,000 |
| 35 | 28 | (h) | Sunderland | L | 0 - 2 | | 3,275 |
| 36 | May 5 | (h) | Darlington | W | 2 - 0 | Bainbridge, Skinner | 2,000 |
| 37 | 12 | (a) | Darlington | L | 0 - 3 | | 3,173 |
| 38 | 19 | (a) | Middlesbrough | W | 2 - 1 | Short, Robertson | 2,500 |
| 39 | 21 | (h) | Darlington | L | 0 - 5 | | 2,500 |

**Note:**The following games counted towards the various cup competitions as follows – Games 19–28 Football League North Cup Qualifying competition; Games 29–34 Football League Cup KO competition played on a two-legged basis; Games 36–37 The Tyne-Tees Cup played on a two-legged basis.

**Appearances:** Adams* 7; Atkinson 25; Bainbridge T. 1; Bainbridge W.* 3; Barrett* 14; Birse* 1; Brown* 14; Catterick* 1; Chilton* 13; Cochrane* 11; Copeland 16; Coughlan 2; Cross* 6; Douglas 6; Dunn* 2; Forde* 36; Harrison* 22; Harvey* 2; Havlin 6; Hetherington* 1; Horton* 12; Jackson 1; James* 2; Keeys 5; Lilley* 1; Lloyd* 6; Lyon 3; Makepeace* 5; Male 1; Mitchell 1; Morris 3; Mullen 6; Murphy* 1; Nesbit* 1; Nettleton 12; Porter 5; Price 1; Purvis* 1; Robertson 4; Robinson G.H.* 3; Robinson J. 2; Rutherford* 30; Saxton 2; Scott F.* 1; Scott W.R.* 33; Shore* 1; Short* 24; Skinner* 22; Smallwood* 4; Spelman* 10; Tabram* 6; Tomlinson 7; Tootill* 8; Troman 1; Turney 4; Wardle* 2; West 7; Wharton 1; Williams 1.

* Guest player

**Goals:** 75; Brown 14, Short 9, Horton 8, Cochrane 7, Harrison 6, Nettleton 5, Copeland 3, Lyons 3, Scott W. 2, Skinner 2, Smallwood 2, West 2, Williams 2, Adams 1, Bainbridge W. 1, Barrett 1, Catterick 1, Douglas 1, Robertson 1, Robinson G. 1, Turney 1, Wardle 1, own goal 1.

# 1945-46

Manager : Fred Westgarth

## FL 3 North East Championship

| Match | Date | Venue | Opponents | Result | Score | Scorers | Gate |
|---|---|---|---|---|---|---|---|
| 1 | Aug 25 | (h) | Doncaster Rovers | D | 1 - 1 | Short | 5,997 |
| 2 | Sept 1 | (a) | Doncaster Rovers | L | 0 - 2 | | 7,000 |
| 3 | 8 | (a) | Rotherham United | L | 0 - 3 | | 7,000 |
| 4 | 15 | (h) | Rotherham United | L | 2 - 4 | Dryden, Robertson | 5,000 |
| 5 | 22 | (h) | Bradford City | W | 3 - 2 | Baines, Robertson, Short | 3,754 |
| 6 | 29 | (a) | Bradford City | L | 0 - 2 | | 7,647 |
| 7 | Oct 6 | (a) | Carlisle United | W | 3 - 1 | Short 2, Robertson | 6,000 |
| 8 | 13 | (h) | Carlisle United | W | 3 - 2 | Short 2 (1 pen), Robertson | 5,813 |
| 9 | 20 | (h) | Gateshead | L | 0 - 2 | | 6,000 |
| 10 | 27 | (a) | Gateshead | L | 1 - 3 | Harrison | 5,613 |
| 11 | Nov 3 | (h) | York City | L | 0 - 2 | | 4,000 |
| 12 | 10 | (a) | York City | L | 2 - 5 | Morris 2 | 4,000 |
| 15 | Dec 1 | (a) | Halifax Town | L | 2 - 3 | Robinson, McMahon | 4,000 |
| 16 | 8 | (h) | Halifax Town | D | 0 - 0 | | 3,000 |
| 17 | 22 | (a) | Lincoln City | L | 2 - 4 | McMahon, Johnson | 5,000 |
| 18 | 25 | (h) | Darlington | D | 0 - 0 | | 5,961 |
| 19 | 26 | (a) | Darlington | L | 2 - 5 | Johnson, McMahon | 8,518 |
| 20 | Jan 1 | (a) | Lincoln City | L | 1 - 4 | Price | 4,689 |

## FL 3 North East Cup Qualifying

| Match | Date | | Venue | Opponents | Result | Score | Scorers | Gate |
|---|---|---|---|---|---|---|---|---|
| 21 | Jan 5 | Q1 | (a) | Halifax Town | W | 5 - 2 | Copeland 2, Johnson, McMahon, Wooletts | 3,000 |
| 22 | 12 | Q2 | (a) | Rotherham United | D | 1 - 1 | McMahon | 8,436 |
| 23 | 19 | Q3 | (h) | Rotherham United | L | 2 - 3 | Short, Johnson | 5,000 |
| 24 | 26 | Q4 | (a) | Darlington | L | 1 - 3 | Johnson | 5,161 |
| 25 | Feb 2 | Q5 | (h) | Darlington | W | 5 - 1 | McMahon 2 (1 pen), Copeland, Short, Johnson | 4,596 |
| 26 | 9 | Q6 | (h) | Carlisle United | W | 5 - 3 | Johnson 4, Short | 5,238 |
| 27 | 16 | Q7 | (a) | Carlisle United | W | 3 - 1 | Johnson 3 | 7,000 |
| 28 | 23 | Q8 | (h) | Bradford City | D | 0 - 0 | | 5,144 |
| 29 | Mar 2 | Q9 | (a) | Bradford City | L | 2 - 6 | Short 2 | 5,000 |
| 30 | 9 | Q10 | (h) | Halifax Town | D | 1 - 1 | Moses | 5,874 |

## FL 3 North East Cup Proper

| Match | Date | | Venue | Opponents | Result | Score | Scorers | Gate |
|---|---|---|---|---|---|---|---|---|
| 31 | Mar 23 | R1/1 | (a) | Crewe Alexandra | W | 2 - 1 | Price, Oakes | 5,000 |
| 32 | 30 | R1/2 | (h) | Crewe Alexandria | D | 3 - 3 | Tabram, McMahon, Price | 6,000 |
| 33 | Apr 6 | R2/1 | (h) | Southport | L | 1 - 2 | Copeland | 7,122 |
| 34 | 13 | R2/2 | (a) | Southport | D | 1 - 1 | Price | 5,000 |

## FL North Second Championship

| Match | Date | Venue | Opponents | Result | Score | Scorers | Gate |
|---|---|---|---|---|---|---|---|
| 35 | Apr 19 | (h) | Barrow | W | 3 - 1 | Harden, McMahon, Copeland | 5,837 |
| 36 | 20 | (a) | Darlington | L | 1 - 4 | Tabram | 3,372 |
| 37 | 22 | (a) | Barrow | L | 1 - 2 | Spelman (pen) | 3,600 |
| 38 | 27 | (a) | York City | W | 3 - 2 | Price 2, Harden | 2,000 |
| 39 | May 4 | (h) | York City | W | 6 - 2 | Price 2, McMahon 2, Scott, Spelman (pen) | 4,150 |

**Appearances:** Baines* 3; Barkas* 1; Beardshaw* 1; Brunskill* 1; Copeland 23; Daniels 3; Dryden 6; Fenton* 1; Flatley* 1; Flinton* 2; Flood 1; Flynn 1; Forde* 8; Foreman 1; Gorman 2; Harden 5; Harrison* 3; Hesford* 6; Heywood 25; Holland 2; Hooper* 2; Howe* 1; Jarrie 2, Johnson 11; Johnstone 1; Jones* 1; Keeys 26; Lloyd* 10; Makepeace 4; Mason 1; McKinley 1; McMahon 27; Morris 13; Moses 3; Mullen 1; Mulroy 1; Nash* 1; Nettleton* 1; Newton* 1; Oakes* 1; Parker* 1; Porter 24; Price 11; Roberts 1; Robertson 14; Robinson* 4; Russell* 3; Scott S. 12; Scott W.R.* 3; Short* 12; Sidlow* 3; Simpson* 1; Skinner* 4; Spelman* 34; Tabram 8; Tootill* 17; Troman 6; Turney 5; Weir* 1; West 4; Wheatman 4; Willetts 20; Woods 9; Woollett* 1.

* Guest player

**Goals:** 68; Johnson 13, McMahon 11, Short 11, Price 8, Copeland 5, Robertson 4, Harden 2, Morris 2, Spelman 2, Tabram 2, Baines 1, Dryden 1, Harrison 1, Moses 1, Oakes 1, Robinson 1, Scott 1, Wooletts 1.

# Player Career Records

| Surname | Forenames | Position | Career | | Football League | | | Play-offs | | | FA Cup | | | FL Cup | | | Other | | | Total | | |
|---|---|---|---|---|---|---|---|---|---|---|---|---|---|---|---|---|---|---|---|---|---|---|
| | | | Start | Finish | Apps | Sub | Gls | Apps | Sub | Gls | Apps | Sub | Gls | Apps | Sub | Gls | Apps | Sub | Gls | Apps | Sub | Gls |
| Abdallah | Tewfik | Inside-Right | 1923 | 1924 | 11 | 0 | 1 | 0 | 0 | 0 | 0 | 0 | 0 | 0 | 0 | 0 | 0 | 0 | 0 | 11 | 0 | 1 |
| Adamson | Terence (Terry) | Right-Half-Back | 1967 | 1968 | 1 | 0 | 0 | 0 | 0 | 0 | 0 | 0 | 0 | 0 | 0 | 0 | 0 | 0 | 0 | 1 | 0 | 0 |
| Adjel | Samuel (Sammy) | Forward | 2011 | 2012 | 0 | 1 | 0 | 0 | 0 | 0 | 0 | 0 | 0 | 0 | 0 | 0 | 0 | 0 | 0 | 0 | 1 | 0 |
| Ainsley | Jason | Defender/Midfielder | 1994 | 1995 | 14 | 1 | 1 | 0 | 0 | 0 | 1 | 0 | 0 | 2 | 0 | 0 | 2 | 0 | 0 | 19 | 1 | 1 |
| Aitken | Andrew Liddell | Goalkeeper | 1935 | 1936 | 1 | 0 | 0 | 0 | 0 | 0 | 0 | 0 | 0 | 0 | 0 | 0 | 0 | 0 | 0 | 1 | 0 | 0 |
| Albeson | Brian | Left-Half-Back | 1975 | 1976 | 0 | 0 | 0 | 0 | 0 | 0 | 0 | 0 | 0 | 1 | 0 | 0 | 0 | 0 | 0 | 1 | 0 | 0 |
| Allan | William (Billy) | Left-Back | 1931 | 1932 | 1 | 0 | 0 | 0 | 0 | 0 | 0 | 0 | 0 | 0 | 0 | 0 | 0 | 0 | 0 | 1 | 0 | 0 |
| Allen | James Thomas (Jack) | Right-Back | 1924 | 1925 | 29 | 0 | 3 | 0 | 0 | 0 | 5 | 0 | 0 | 0 | 0 | 0 | 0 | 0 | 0 | 34 | 0 | 3 |
| Allen | Kenneth Richard (Kenny) | Goalkeeper | 1968 | 1969 | 7 | 0 | 0 | 0 | 0 | 0 | 0 | 0 | 0 | 0 | 0 | 0 | 0 | 0 | 0 | 7 | 0 | 0 |
| Allinson | Jamie | Centre-Half-Back | 1995 | 1996 | 3 | 1 | 0 | 0 | 0 | 0 | 0 | 1 | 0 | 0 | 0 | 0 | 1 | 0 | 0 | 4 | 2 | 0 |
| Allison | John Joseph | Half-Back/Inside-Forward | 1946 | 1947 | 13 | 0 | 0 | 0 | 0 | 0 | 0 | 0 | 0 | 0 | 0 | 0 | 0 | 0 | 0 | 13 | 0 | 0 |
| Allison | William Martin Laws (Bill) | Left-Back | 1935 | 1938 | 107 | 0 | 0 | 0 | 0 | 0 | 12 | 0 | 0 | 0 | 0 | 0 | 3 | 0 | 0 | 122 | 0 | 0 |
| Allon | Joseph Ball (Joe) | Centre-Forward/Outside-Right | 1988 | 1997 | 164 | 4 | 67 | 0 | 0 | 0 | 7 | 1 | 5 | 8 | 0 | 4 | 10 | 0 | 3 | 189 | 5 | 79 |
| Anderson | Christopher (Chris) | Centre/Wing-Half-Back | 1946 | 1947 | 2 | 0 | 0 | 0 | 0 | 0 | 0 | 0 | 0 | 0 | 0 | 0 | 0 | 0 | 0 | 2 | 0 | 0 |
| Anderson | James Ballantine (Jimmy) | Right-Half-Back | 1922 | 1923 | 13 | 0 | 0 | 0 | 0 | 0 | 0 | 0 | 0 | 0 | 0 | 0 | 0 | 0 | 0 | 13 | 0 | 0 |
| Anderson | William Boston (Billy) | Half-Back/Inside-Forward | 1955 | 1961 | 179 | 0 | 11 | 0 | 0 | 0 | 8 | 0 | 0 | 0 | 0 | 0 | 0 | 0 | 0 | 187 | 0 | 11 |
| Antwi-Birago | Godwin | Central Defender | 2007 | 2008 | 27 | 0 | 1 | 0 | 0 | 0 | 1 | 1 | 0 | 2 | 0 | 0 | 3 | 0 | 0 | 33 | 1 | 1 |
| Appleby | Andrew (Andy) | Midfielder | 2004 | 2005 | 0 | 15 | 2 | 0 | 0 | 0 | 1 | 2 | 0 | 0 | 0 | 0 | 0 | 1 | 0 | 1 | 18 | 2 |
| Arch | William Henry (Harry) | Right-Back | 1926 | 1927 | 23 | 0 | 0 | 0 | 0 | 0 | 1 | 0 | 0 | 0 | 0 | 0 | 0 | 0 | 0 | 24 | 0 | 0 |
| Arnison | Paul Simon | Right-Back | 1999 | 2003 | 53 | 24 | 3 | 3 | 0 | 1 | 2 | 0 | 1 | 2 | 0 | 0 | 5 | 0 | 1 | 65 | 24 | 6 |
| Ashurst | Leonard (Len) | Left-Back/Wing-Half-Back | 1970 | 1973 | 42 | 4 | 2 | 0 | 0 | 0 | 5 | 0 | 0 | 2 | 0 | 0 | 0 | 0 | 0 | 49 | 4 | 2 |
| Ashworth | Barry | Right-Half-Back | 1964 | 1966 | 45 | 0 | 4 | 0 | 0 | 0 | 2 | 0 | 0 | 2 | 0 | 0 | 0 | 0 | 0 | 49 | 0 | 4 |
| Aston | Stanley (Stan) | Centre-Half-Back | 1966 | 1968 | 20 | 1 | 0 | 0 | 0 | 0 | 0 | 0 | 0 | 0 | 0 | 0 | 0 | 0 | 0 | 20 | 1 | 0 |
| Atkinson | Charles Brown Clayton (Charlie) | Centre-Half-Back | 1959 | 1964 | 47 | 0 | 0 | 0 | 0 | 0 | 1 | 0 | 0 | 1 | 0 | 0 | 0 | 0 | 0 | 49 | 0 | 0 |
| Atkinson | David John | Outside-Right | 1968 | 1969 | 8 | 0 | 1 | 0 | 0 | 0 | 0 | 0 | 0 | 0 | 0 | 0 | 0 | 0 | 0 | 8 | 0 | 1 |
| Atkinson | Patrick Darren (Paddy) | Forward | 1988 | 1990 | 9 | 12 | 3 | 0 | 0 | 0 | 2 | 1 | 0 | 0 | 1 | 0 | 1 | 3 | 0 | 12 | 17 | 3 |
| Atkinson | Paul | Outside-Left | 1989 | 1990 | 5 | 6 | 1 | 0 | 0 | 0 | 0 | 0 | 0 | 0 | 0 | 0 | 0 | 0 | 0 | 5 | 6 | 1 |
| Austin | Neil Jeffrey | Right-Back | 2009 | 2012 | 105 | 3 | 6 | 0 | 0 | 0 | 6 | 0 | 0 | 1 | 0 | 0 | 4 | 0 | 0 | 116 | 3 | 6 |
| Ayre | William (Billy) | Central Defender | 1977 | 1981 | 141 | 0 | 27 | 0 | 0 | 0 | 8 | 0 | 1 | 6 | 0 | 0 | 0 | 0 | 0 | 155 | 0 | 28 |
| Bain | William Clark (Billy) | Centre-Forward | 1950 | 1951 | 2 | 0 | 0 | 0 | 0 | 0 | 0 | 0 | 0 | 0 | 0 | 0 | 0 | 0 | 0 | 2 | 0 | 0 |

| | | | Career | | Football League | | | Play-offs | | | FA Cup | | | FL Cup | | | Other | | | Total | | |
|---|---|---|---|---|---|---|---|---|---|---|---|---|---|---|---|---|---|---|---|---|---|---|
| Surname | Forenames | Position | Start | Finish | Apps | Sub | Gls | Apps | Sub | Gls | Apps | Sub | Gls | Apps | Sub | Gls | Apps | Sub | Gls | Apps | Sub | Gls |
| Bainbridge | Terence (Terry) | Wing-Half-Back/Wing-Forward | 1981 | 1984 | 34 | 3 | 1 | 0 | 0 | 0 | 1 | 0 | 0 | 4 | 0 | 1 | 1 | 1 | 0 | 40 | 4 | 2 |
| Baines | Cecil Peter | Centre/Inside-Forward | 1947 | 1948 | 9 | 0 | 1 | 0 | 0 | 0 | 0 | 0 | 0 | 0 | 0 | 0 | 0 | 0 | 0 | 9 | 0 | 1 |
| Baker | David Paul | Centre-Forward | 1987 | 1998 | 217 | 15 | 76 | 0 | 0 | 0 | 16 | 0 | 6 | 14 | 0 | 5 | 16 | 0 | 5 | 263 | 15 | 92 |
| Baldwin | Jack | Midfielder | 2011 | 2012 | 14 | 3 | 0 | 0 | 0 | 0 | 0 | 0 | 0 | 0 | 0 | 0 | 0 | 0 | 0 | 14 | 3 | 0 |
| Ballantyne | John Dixon (Dick) | Left-Back | 1950 | 1952 | 13 | 0 | 0 | 0 | 0 | 0 | 0 | 0 | 0 | 0 | 0 | 0 | 0 | 0 | 0 | 13 | 0 | 0 |
| Bannister | Neville | Wing-Forward | 1964 | 1965 | 41 | 0 | 8 | 0 | 0 | 0 | 2 | 0 | 0 | 0 | 0 | 0 | 0 | 0 | 0 | 43 | 0 | 8 |
| Barker | Allan Michael (Mickey) | Left-Back | 1982 | 1984 | 59 | 1 | 1 | 0 | 0 | 0 | 3 | 0 | 0 | 2 | 0 | 2 | 1 | 0 | 0 | 65 | 1 | 3 |
| Barker | Richard Ian (Richie) | Centre-forward | 2007 | 2009 | 49 | 13 | 23 | 0 | 0 | 0 | 2 | 0 | 2 | 2 | 3 | 1 | 4 | 0 | 1 | 57 | 16 | 27 |
| Barlow | Peter | Inside/Wing-Forward | 1970 | 1971 | 8 | 2 | 0 | 0 | 0 | 0 | 0 | 0 | 0 | 0 | 0 | 0 | 0 | 0 | 0 | 8 | 2 | 0 |
| Barras | Anthony (Tony) | Left-Half-Back | 1988 | 1990 | 9 | 3 | 0 | 0 | 0 | 0 | 1 | 0 | 0 | 2 | 0 | 0 | 0 | 0 | 0 | 12 | 3 | 0 |
| Barratt | Anthony (Tony) | Right-Back/Outside-Left | 1986 | 1989 | 93 | 5 | 4 | 0 | 0 | 0 | 8 | 0 | 0 | 4 | 0 | 0 | 6 | 0 | 0 | 111 | 5 | 4 |
| Barron | Michael James | Defender | 1996 | 2008 | 315 | 10 | 3 | 11 | 0 | 0 | 13 | 1 | 1 | 8 | 1 | 0 | 15 | 0 | 0 | 362 | 12 | 4 |
| Barry-Murphy | Brian | Left-Back | 2002 | 2003 | 7 | 0 | 0 | 0 | 0 | 0 | 2 | 0 | 0 | 0 | 0 | 0 | 0 | 0 | 0 | 9 | 0 | 0 |
| Barson | Frank | Centre-Half-Back | 1929 | 1930 | 9 | 0 | 2 | 0 | 0 | 0 | 0 | 0 | 0 | 0 | 0 | 0 | 0 | 0 | 0 | 9 | 0 | 2 |
| Bass | Jonathan David (Jon) | Right-Back | 2001 | 2003 | 21 | 3 | 1 | 0 | 0 | 0 | 1 | 0 | 0 | 1 | 0 | 0 | 1 | 0 | 0 | 24 | 3 | 1 |
| Bassett | Graham Raymond | Forward | 1983 | 1984 | 4 | 3 | 0 | 0 | 0 | 0 | 2 | 0 | 0 | 0 | 0 | 0 | 0 | 0 | 0 | 6 | 3 | 0 |
| Bates | John Wilfred | Outside-Right | 1965 | 1966 | 11 | 0 | 0 | 0 | 0 | 0 | 0 | 0 | 0 | 0 | 0 | 0 | 0 | 0 | 0 | 11 | 0 | 0 |
| Beavers | Paul Mark | Forward | 1999 | 2000 | 2 | 5 | 0 | 1 | 0 | 0 | 0 | 0 | 0 | 0 | 0 | 0 | 0 | 0 | 0 | 3 | 5 | 0 |
| Beech | Christopher Stephen (Chris) | Midfielder | 1996 | 1998 | 92 | 3 | 23 | 0 | 0 | 0 | 3 | 0 | 1 | 3 | 0 | 1 | 3 | 0 | 1 | 101 | 3 | 26 |
| Behan | Denis | Centre-Forward | 2009 | 2011 | 22 | 20 | 6 | 0 | 0 | 0 | 1 | 0 | 0 | 2 | 2 | 0 | 1 | 2 | 1 | 26 | 24 | 7 |
| Bell | Edward Dorman | Left-Half-Back | 1929 | 1930 | 4 | 0 | 0 | 0 | 0 | 0 | 1 | 0 | 0 | 0 | 0 | 0 | 0 | 0 | 0 | 5 | 0 | 0 |
| Bell | John James (Johnnie) | Inside/Centre/Wing-Forward | 1923 | 1924 | 12 | 0 | 4 | 0 | 0 | 0 | 0 | 0 | 0 | 0 | 0 | 0 | 0 | 0 | 0 | 12 | 0 | 4 |
| Bell | Terence John (Terry) | Centre/Inside-Forward | 1966 | 1970 | 111 | 6 | 34 | 0 | 0 | 0 | 4 | 0 | 3 | 2 | 0 | 1 | 0 | 0 | 0 | 117 | 6 | 38 |
| Bennyworth | Ian Robert | Central Defender | 1989 | 1991 | 81 | 1 | 3 | 0 | 0 | 0 | 2 | 0 | 0 | 8 | 0 | 0 | 3 | 0 | 0 | 94 | 1 | 3 |
| Beresford | John Turner | Left-Half-Back | 1966 | 1967 | 3 | 0 | 0 | 0 | 0 | 0 | 0 | 0 | 0 | 0 | 0 | 0 | 0 | 0 | 0 | 3 | 0 | 0 |
| Berryman | Stephen Christopher (Steve) | Goalkeeper | 1989 | 1990 | 1 | 0 | 0 | 0 | 0 | 0 | 0 | 0 | 0 | 0 | 0 | 0 | 0 | 0 | 0 | 1 | 0 | 0 |
| Best | Robert (Bobby) | Outside-Right | 1924 | 1927 | 72 | 0 | 4 | 0 | 0 | 0 | 8 | 0 | 1 | 0 | 0 | 0 | 0 | 0 | 0 | 80 | 0 | 5 |
| Betsy | Kevin Eddie Lewis | Forward | 2004 | 2005 | 3 | 3 | 1 | 0 | 0 | 0 | 0 | 0 | 0 | 1 | 0 | 0 | 0 | 0 | 0 | 4 | 3 | 1 |
| Bielby | Paul Anthony | Outside-Left | 1975 | 1978 | 74 | 21 | 8 | 0 | 0 | 0 | 8 | 0 | 2 | 4 | 0 | 1 | 0 | 0 | 0 | 86 | 21 | 11 |
| Bilcliff | Raymond (Ray) | Full-Back | 1960 | 1964 | 117 | 0 | 0 | 0 | 0 | 0 | 5 | 0 | 0 | 3 | 0 | 0 | 0 | 0 | 0 | 125 | 0 | 0 |
| Billing | Peter Graham | Defender/Midfielder | 1995 | 1996 | 35 | 1 | 0 | 0 | 0 | 0 | 1 | 0 | 0 | 4 | 0 | 0 | 2 | 0 | 0 | 42 | 1 | 0 |
| Bircham | Walter Clive | Outside-Right | 1959 | 1963 | 105 | 0 | 15 | 0 | 0 | 0 | 3 | 0 | 0 | 4 | 0 | 1 | 0 | 0 | 0 | 112 | 0 | 16 |
| Bircumshaw | Anthony (Tony) | Right-Back | 1966 | 1971 | 182 | 3 | 11 | 0 | 0 | 0 | 7 | 0 | 0 | 2 | 0 | 0 | 0 | 0 | 0 | 191 | 3 | 11 |
| Bird | John Charles | Centre-Half-Back | 1980 | 1985 | 139 | 2 | 16 | 0 | 0 | 0 | 4 | 0 | 0 | 6 | 0 | 0 | 4 | 0 | 0 | 153 | 2 | 16 |
| Birnie | John (Jack) | Left-Half-Back | 1923 | 1924 | 5 | 0 | 0 | 0 | 0 | 0 | 0 | 0 | 0 | 0 | 0 | 0 | 0 | 0 | 0 | 5 | 0 | 0 |

| | | | Career | | Football League | | | Play-offs | | | FA Cup | | | FL Cup | | | Other | | | Total | | |
|---|---|---|---|---|---|---|---|---|---|---|---|---|---|---|---|---|---|---|---|---|---|---|
| Surname | Forenames | Position | Start | Finish | Apps | Sub | Gls | Apps | Sub | Gls | Apps | Sub | Gls | Apps | Sub | Gls | Apps | Sub | Gls | Apps | Sub | Gls |
| Birtles | Frederick (Fred) | Inside-Right | 1925 | 1926 | 15 | 0 | 6 | 0 | 0 | 0 | 0 | 0 | 0 | 0 | 0 | 0 | 0 | 0 | 0 | 15 | 0 | 6 |
| Bjornsson | Armann Smari | Centre-Forward | 2009 | 2011 | 13 | 23 | 3 | 0 | 0 | 0 | 1 | 1 | 0 | 0 | 0 | 0 | 3 | 0 | 0 | 17 | 24 | 3 |
| Blackburn | Edwin Huitson (Eddie) | Goalkeeper | 1982 | 1987 | 161 | 0 | 0 | 0 | 0 | 0 | 3 | 0 | 0 | 6 | 0 | 0 | 5 | 0 | 0 | 175 | 0 | 0 |
| Blowman | Peter | Forward | 1967 | 1970 | 57 | 9 | 15 | 0 | 0 | 0 | 3 | 0 | 0 | 0 | 1 | 0 | 0 | 0 | 0 | 60 | 10 | 15 |
| Blythe | John David | Inside-Right | 1969 | 1970 | 1 | 0 | 0 | 0 | 0 | 0 | 0 | 0 | 0 | 0 | 0 | 0 | 0 | 0 | 0 | 1 | 0 | 0 |
| Boam | Stuart William | Centre-Half-Back | 1982 | 1983 | 1 | 0 | 0 | 0 | 0 | 0 | 0 | 0 | 0 | 0 | 0 | 0 | 0 | 0 | 0 | 1 | 0 | 0 |
| Boland | George (Dicky) | Outside-Left | 1925 | 1928 | 64 | 0 | 9 | 0 | 0 | 0 | 1 | 0 | 0 | 0 | 0 | 0 | 0 | 0 | 0 | 65 | 0 | 9 |
| Boland | William John (Willie) | Midfielder | 2006 | 2009 | 60 | 4 | 1 | 0 | 0 | 0 | 4 | 0 | 0 | 2 | 0 | 0 | 1 | 0 | 0 | 67 | 4 | 1 |
| Bonass | Albert Edward | Outside-Left | 1934 | 1936 | 77 | 0 | 31 | 0 | 0 | 0 | 9 | 0 | 4 | 0 | 0 | 0 | 3 | 0 | 1 | 89 | 0 | 36 |
| Borthwick | John Robert | Forward | 1982 | 1989 | 96 | 21 | 14 | 0 | 0 | 0 | 6 | 0 | 1 | 3 | 0 | 0 | 7 | 3 | 1 | 112 | 24 | 16 |
| Borthwick | John Walter | Right-Back | 1922 | 1923 | 2 | 0 | 0 | 0 | 0 | 0 | 0 | 0 | 0 | 0 | 0 | 0 | 0 | 0 | 0 | 2 | 0 | 0 |
| Boulton | John William Charles | Left-Back | 1923 | 1924 | 4 | 0 | 0 | 0 | 0 | 0 | 0 | 0 | 0 | 0 | 0 | 0 | 0 | 0 | 0 | 4 | 0 | 0 |
| Bowling | Ian | Goalkeeper | 1989 | 1990 | 1 | 0 | 0 | 0 | 0 | 0 | 0 | 0 | 0 | 0 | 0 | 0 | 0 | 0 | 0 | 1 | 0 | 0 |
| Bowron | Stephen (Steve) | Full-Back | 1929 | 1934 | 194 | 0 | 0 | 0 | 0 | 0 | 8 | 0 | 0 | 0 | 0 | 0 | 1 | 0 | 0 | 203 | 0 | 0 |
| Boyd | Adam Mark | Forward | 1999 | 2012 | 136 | 98 | 69 | 6 | 0 | 2 | 7 | 2 | 3 | 8 | 1 | 4 | 6 | 5 | 1 | 163 | 106 | 79 |
| Boylan | Anthony (Tony) | Forward | 1969 | 1972 | 9 | 1 | 0 | 0 | 0 | 0 | 0 | 0 | 0 | 0 | 0 | 0 | 0 | 0 | 0 | 9 | 1 | 0 |
| Brackstone | John | Left-Back | 2004 | 2007 | 21 | 4 | 0 | 0 | 0 | 0 | 3 | 0 | 1 | 2 | 0 | 0 | 5 | 0 | 0 | 31 | 4 | 1 |
| Bradbury | Allen | Left-Half-Back | 1970 | 1971 | 7 | 0 | 0 | 0 | 0 | 0 | 0 | 0 | 0 | 0 | 0 | 0 | 0 | 0 | 0 | 7 | 0 | 0 |
| Bradford | James R. (Jimmy) | Full-Back | 1935 | 1937 | 9 | 0 | 0 | 0 | 0 | 0 | 0 | 0 | 0 | 0 | 0 | 0 | 0 | 0 | 0 | 9 | 0 | 0 |
| Bradley | Russell | Central Defender | 1996 | 1998 | 55 | 0 | 2 | 0 | 0 | 0 | 0 | 0 | 0 | 2 | 0 | 0 | 2 | 0 | 0 | 59 | 0 | 2 |
| Bradley | William (Willie) | Wing-Forward | 1963 | 1966 | 98 | 0 | 15 | 0 | 0 | 0 | 5 | 0 | 0 | 2 | 0 | 0 | 0 | 0 | 0 | 105 | 0 | 15 |
| Braidford | Lowington (Lowe) | Centre-Forward | 1922 | 1923 | 29 | 0 | 9 | 0 | 0 | 0 | 0 | 0 | 0 | 0 | 0 | 0 | 0 | 0 | 0 | 29 | 0 | 9 |
| Brass | Robert Albert (Bobby) | Left-Half-Back | 1964 | 1966 | 27 | 1 | 0 | 0 | 0 | 0 | 2 | 0 | 1 | 0 | 0 | 0 | 0 | 0 | 0 | 29 | 1 | 1 |
| Bratt | William (Bill) | Inside/Right-Half-Back | 1921 | 1922 | 15 | 0 | 2 | 0 | 0 | 0 | 3 | 0 | 0 | 0 | 0 | 0 | 0 | 0 | 0 | 18 | 0 | 2 |
| Briggs | Harold (Harry) | Outside-Right | 1928 | 1929 | 18 | 0 | 3 | 0 | 0 | 0 | 1 | 0 | 0 | 0 | 0 | 0 | 0 | 0 | 0 | 19 | 0 | 3 |
| Briggs | Walter (Wally) | Goalkeeper | 1949 | 1952 | 44 | 0 | 0 | 0 | 0 | 0 | 0 | 0 | 0 | 0 | 0 | 0 | 0 | 0 | 0 | 44 | 0 | 0 |
| Broadbent | Albert Henry | Inside-Forward | 1966 | 1968 | 25 | 0 | 3 | 0 | 0 | 0 | 0 | 0 | 0 | 2 | 0 | 1 | 0 | 0 | 0 | 27 | 0 | 4 |
| Brooks | Stephen Michael (Steve) | Centre-Half-Back | 1978 | 1980 | 62 | 1 | 2 | 0 | 0 | 0 | 2 | 0 | 0 | 4 | 0 | 0 | 0 | 0 | 0 | 68 | 1 | 2 |
| Brown | Charles Marshall (Charlie) | Full/Half-Back | 1938 | 1939 | 5 | 0 | 0 | 0 | 0 | 0 | 0 | 0 | 0 | 0 | 0 | 0 | 0 | 0 | 0 | 5 | 0 | 0 |
| Brown | George A. | Half-Back | 1933 | 1936 | 51 | 0 | 0 | 0 | 0 | 0 | 9 | 0 | 0 | 0 | 0 | 0 | 2 | 0 | 0 | 62 | 0 | 0 |
| Brown | James | Midfielder | 2004 | 2012 | 124 | 50 | 29 | 0 | 0 | 0 | 6 | 2 | 4 | 7 | 3 | 2 | 5 | 2 | 2 | 142 | 57 | 37 |
| Brown | James (Jimmy) | Right-Back | 1923 | 1924 | 1 | 0 | 0 | 0 | 0 | 0 | 0 | 0 | 0 | 0 | 0 | 0 | 0 | 0 | 0 | 1 | 0 | 0 |
| Brown | John (Jack) | Goalkeeper | 1927 | 1928 | 5 | 0 | 0 | 0 | 0 | 0 | 0 | 0 | 0 | 0 | 0 | 0 | 0 | 0 | 0 | 5 | 0 | 0 |
| Brown | John Henry (Jack) | Goalkeeper | 1937 | 1938 | 1 | 0 | 0 | 0 | 0 | 0 | 0 | 0 | 0 | 0 | 0 | 0 | 0 | 0 | 0 | 1 | 0 | 0 |
| Brown | John Thomas (Jock) | Left-Back/Centre-Forward | 1962 | 1964 | 68 | 0 | 10 | 0 | 0 | 0 | 2 | 0 | 0 | 3 | 0 | 0 | 0 | 0 | 0 | 73 | 0 | 10 |

| Surname | Forenames | Position | Career | | Football League | | | Play-offs | | | FA Cup | | | FL Cup | | | Other | | | Total | | |
|---|---|---|---|---|---|---|---|---|---|---|---|---|---|---|---|---|---|---|---|---|---|---|
| | | | Start | Finish | Apps | Sub | Gls | Apps | Sub | Gls | Apps | Sub | Gls | Apps | Sub | Gls | Apps | Sub | Gls | Apps | Sub | Gls |
| Brown | Michael Robert | Midfielder | 1996 | 1997 | 6 | 0 | 1 | 0 | 0 | 0 | 0 | 0 | 0 | 0 | 0 | 0 | 0 | 0 | 0 | 6 | 0 | 1 |
| Brown | Philip (Phil) | Defender/Midfielder | 1979 | 1985 | 210 | 7 | 8 | 0 | 0 | 0 | 11 | 0 | 0 | 12 | 0 | 0 | 9 | 0 | 1 | 242 | 7 | 9 |
| Brown | Robert Beresford (Berry) | Goalkeeper | 1951 | 1956 | 126 | 0 | 0 | 0 | 0 | 0 | 13 | 0 | 0 | 0 | 0 | 0 | 0 | 0 | 0 | 139 | 0 | 0 |
| Brown | William (Billy) | Inside-Left | 1931 | 1932 | 13 | 0 | 3 | 0 | 0 | 0 | 0 | 0 | 0 | 0 | 0 | 0 | 0 | 0 | 0 | 13 | 0 | 3 |
| Brown | William Hutchinson (Billy) | Right-Back | 1946 | 1948 | 80 | 0 | 0 | 0 | 0 | 0 | 6 | 0 | 0 | 0 | 0 | 0 | 0 | 0 | 0 | 86 | 0 | 0 |
| Brownlie | John Jack | Full-Back | 1984 | 1985 | 19 | 0 | 1 | 0 | 0 | 0 | 2 | 0 | 0 | 2 | 0 | 0 | 1 | 0 | 0 | 24 | 0 | 1 |
| Brownlow | John Martin (Jackie) | Outside-Right | 1948 | 1949 | 3 | 0 | 0 | 0 | 0 | 0 | 0 | 0 | 0 | 0 | 0 | 0 | 0 | 0 | 0 | 3 | 0 | 0 |
| Buckley | Michael John (Mick) | Right-Half-Back | 1983 | 1984 | 6 | 0 | 0 | 0 | 0 | 0 | 0 | 0 | 0 | 2 | 0 | 0 | 0 | 0 | 0 | 8 | 0 | 0 |
| Budtz | Jan | Goalkeeper | 2007 | 2009 | 37 | 1 | 0 | 0 | 0 | 0 | 2 | 0 | 0 | 2 | 0 | 0 | 2 | 0 | 0 | 43 | 1 | 0 |
| Buller | Joseph (Joe) | Wing-Half-Back | 1929 | 1932 | 86 | 0 | 2 | 0 | 0 | 0 | 0 | 0 | 0 | 0 | 0 | 0 | 0 | 0 | 0 | 86 | 0 | 2 |
| Bullock | Lee | Midfielder | 2005 | 2008 | 30 | 27 | 5 | 0 | 0 | 0 | 2 | 1 | 0 | 1 | 2 | 0 | 3 | 0 | 1 | 36 | 30 | 6 |
| Burgess | David John | Right-Back | 1994 | 1995 | 11 | 0 | 0 | 0 | 0 | 0 | 0 | 0 | 0 | 2 | 0 | 0 | 0 | 0 | 0 | 13 | 0 | 0 |
| Burleigh | Martin Stewart | Goalkeeper | 1979 | 1982 | 84 | 0 | 0 | 0 | 0 | 0 | 5 | 0 | 0 | 4 | 0 | 0 | 3 | 0 | 0 | 96 | 0 | 0 |
| Burlison | Thomas Henry (Tommy) | Midfielder | 1957 | 1964 | 148 | 0 | 5 | 0 | 0 | 0 | 6 | 0 | 1 | 3 | 0 | 0 | 0 | 0 | 0 | 157 | 0 | 6 |
| Burluraux | Frederick (Fred) | Right-Back | 1932 | 1933 | 1 | 0 | 0 | 0 | 0 | 0 | 0 | 0 | 0 | 0 | 0 | 0 | 0 | 0 | 0 | 1 | 0 | 0 |
| Burn | Frederick (Fred) | Outside-Left | 1921 | 1922 | 9 | 0 | 1 | 0 | 0 | 0 | 0 | 0 | 0 | 0 | 0 | 0 | 0 | 0 | 0 | 9 | 0 | 1 |
| Burnett | William John (Billy) | Outside-Right | 1948 | 1954 | 194 | 0 | 17 | 0 | 0 | 0 | 10 | 0 | 2 | 0 | 0 | 0 | 0 | 0 | 0 | 204 | 0 | 19 |
| Butler | Arthur | Inside/Centre-Forward | 1921 | 1922 | 2 | 0 | 0 | 0 | 0 | 0 | 0 | 0 | 0 | 0 | 0 | 0 | 0 | 0 | 0 | 2 | 0 | 0 |
| Butler | Ernest (Ernie) | Wing-Forward | 1924 | 1926 | 58 | 0 | 4 | 0 | 0 | 0 | 5 | 0 | 1 | 0 | 0 | 0 | 0 | 0 | 0 | 63 | 0 | 5 |
| Butler | Kenneth (Ken) | Outside-Left | 1959 | 1961 | 20 | 0 | 2 | 0 | 0 | 0 | 0 | 0 | 0 | 1 | 0 | 0 | 0 | 0 | 0 | 21 | 0 | 2 |
| Butler | Paul John | Outside-Left | 1987 | 1988 | 6 | 3 | 0 | 0 | 0 | 0 | 1 | 0 | 0 | 2 | 0 | 0 | 0 | 0 | 0 | 9 | 3 | 0 |
| Butler | Thomas Anthony | Midfielder | 2004 | 2006 | 31 | 6 | 2 | 1 | 1 | 0 | 2 | 0 | 1 | 2 | 0 | 0 | 1 | 0 | 0 | 37 | 7 | 3 |
| Byron | Paul | Left-Half-Back | 1986 | 1987 | 1 | 0 | 0 | 0 | 0 | 0 | 0 | 0 | 0 | 0 | 0 | 0 | 0 | 0 | 0 | 1 | 0 | 0 |
| Cain | James Patrick (Jimmy) | Wing-Half-Back | 1960 | 1962 | 30 | 0 | 0 | 0 | 0 | 0 | 2 | 0 | 0 | 2 | 0 | 0 | 0 | 0 | 0 | 34 | 0 | 0 |
| Cairns | John Greenfield (Jackie) | Inside-Left | 1947 | 1950 | 16 | 0 | 2 | 0 | 0 | 0 | 0 | 0 | 0 | 0 | 0 | 0 | 0 | 0 | 0 | 16 | 0 | 2 |
| Calder | John H. | Full/Half-Back | 1938 | 1939 | 4 | 0 | 0 | 0 | 0 | 0 | 0 | 0 | 0 | 0 | 0 | 0 | 0 | 0 | 0 | 4 | 0 | 0 |
| Cameron | Jack (Jock) | Right-Back | 1953 | 1960 | 175 | 0 | 0 | 0 | 0 | 0 | 18 | 0 | 0 | 0 | 0 | 0 | 0 | 0 | 0 | 193 | 0 | 0 |
| Campbell | Paul John | Inside-Left | 1983 | 1984 | 1 | 2 | 0 | 0 | 0 | 0 | 0 | 0 | 0 | 0 | 0 | 0 | 0 | 0 | 0 | 1 | 2 | 0 |
| Canham | Anthony (Tony) | Midfielder | 1995 | 1996 | 25 | 4 | 1 | 0 | 0 | 0 | 0 | 0 | 0 | 3 | 0 | 0 | 1 | 0 | 0 | 29 | 4 | 1 |
| Carney | Stephen (Steve) | Left-Half-Back | 1985 | 1986 | 7 | 0 | 0 | 0 | 0 | 0 | 0 | 0 | 0 | 0 | 0 | 0 | 0 | 0 | 0 | 7 | 0 | 0 |
| Carr | Graham Gordon | Goalkeeper | 1989 | 1990 | 1 | 0 | 0 | 0 | 0 | 0 | 0 | 0 | 0 | 2 | 0 | 0 | 0 | 0 | 0 | 3 | 0 | 0 |
| Carr | John (Jackie) | Inside-Forward | 1931 | 1932 | 10 | 0 | 1 | 0 | 0 | 0 | 0 | 0 | 0 | 0 | 0 | 0 | 0 | 0 | 0 | 10 | 0 | 1 |
| Carr | Kevin | Goalkeeper | 1987 | 1988 | 31 | 0 | 0 | 0 | 0 | 0 | 4 | 0 | 0 | 0 | 0 | 0 | 5 | 0 | 0 | 40 | 0 | 0 |
| Carr | Peter | Defender | 1979 | 1980 | 22 | 0 | 0 | 0 | 0 | 0 | 1 | 0 | 0 | 0 | 0 | 0 | 0 | 0 | 0 | 23 | 0 | 0 |
| Carr | Thomas (Tommy) | Inside-Right/Right-Back | 1924 | 1929 | 131 | 0 | 13 | 0 | 0 | 0 | 4 | 0 | 0 | 0 | 0 | 0 | 0 | 0 | 0 | 135 | 0 | 13 |

| | | | Career | | Football League | | | Play-offs | | | FA Cup | | | FL Cup | | | Other | | | Total | | |
|---|---|---|---|---|---|---|---|---|---|---|---|---|---|---|---|---|---|---|---|---|---|---|
| Surname | Forenames | Position | Start | Finish | Apps | Sub | Gls | Apps | Sub | Gls | Apps | Sub | Gls | Apps | Sub | Gls | Apps | Sub | Gls | Apps | Sub | Gls |
| Carson | Stephen | Midfielder | 2003 | 2004 | 1 | 2 | 0 | 0 | 0 | 0 | 0 | 0 | 0 | 0 | 0 | 0 | 0 | 0 | 0 | 1 | 2 | 0 |
| Carswell | Robert | Centre-Forward | 1923 | 1924 | 2 | 0 | 0 | 0 | 0 | 0 | 0 | 0 | 0 | 0 | 0 | 0 | 0 | 0 | 0 | 2 | 0 | 0 |
| Carter | Timothy (Tim) | Goalkeeper | 1993 | 1994 | 18 | 0 | 0 | 0 | 0 | 0 | 1 | 0 | 0 | 4 | 0 | 0 | 2 | 0 | 0 | 25 | 0 | 0 |
| Catton | Edwin | Inside-Right | 1933 | 1934 | 8 | 0 | 3 | 0 | 0 | 0 | 0 | 0 | 0 | 0 | 0 | 0 | 1 | 0 | 0 | 9 | 0 | 3 |
| Chambers | Philip Martin (Phil) | Left-Back | 1985 | 1986 | 29 | 0 | 0 | 0 | 0 | 0 | 2 | 0 | 0 | 0 | 0 | 0 | 1 | 0 | 0 | 32 | 0 | 0 |
| Chape | George Edward | Right-Half-Back | 1924 | 1925 | 4 | 0 | 0 | 0 | 0 | 0 | 0 | 0 | 0 | 0 | 0 | 0 | 0 | 0 | 0 | 4 | 0 | 0 |
| Chapman | John | Right-Half-Back | 1938 | 1939 | 9 | 0 | 0 | 0 | 0 | 0 | 2 | 0 | 0 | 0 | 0 | 0 | 0 | 0 | 0 | 11 | 0 | 0 |
| Charlton | Harold (Harry) | Outside-Right | 1975 | 1976 | 2 | 1 | 0 | 0 | 0 | 0 | 0 | 0 | 0 | 0 | 0 | 0 | 0 | 0 | 0 | 2 | 1 | 0 |
| Chatterton | Walter | Centre-Forward | 1935 | 1936 | 2 | 0 | 1 | 0 | 0 | 0 | 0 | 0 | 0 | 0 | 0 | 0 | 0 | 0 | 0 | 2 | 0 | 1 |
| Cherel | Julian | Centre Half | 2009 | 2010 | 1 | 0 | 0 | 0 | 0 | 0 | 0 | 0 | 0 | 0 | 0 | 0 | 0 | 0 | 0 | 1 | 0 | 0 |
| Chesser | James Monteith (Jimmy) | Half-Back | 1922 | 1923 | 41 | 0 | 0 | 0 | 0 | 0 | 0 | 0 | 0 | 0 | 0 | 0 | 0 | 0 | 0 | 41 | 0 | 0 |
| Chilton | Anthony Julian Thomas (Tony) | Left-Back | 1985 | 1986 | 3 | 0 | 0 | 0 | 0 | 0 | 0 | 0 | 0 | 0 | 0 | 0 | 0 | 0 | 0 | 3 | 0 | 0 |
| Christon | Leonard (Len) | Centre-Forward | 1928 | 1929 | 2 | 0 | 0 | 0 | 0 | 0 | 0 | 0 | 0 | 0 | 0 | 0 | 0 | 0 | 0 | 2 | 0 | 0 |
| Clark | Benjamin (Ben) | Central Defender | 2004 | 2010 | 144 | 18 | 6 | 0 | 0 | 0 | 14 | 2 | 0 | 1 | 0 | 0 | 5 | 1 | 0 | 164 | 21 | 6 |
| Clark | Harold Maurice (Harry) | Inside-Forward | 1958 | 1961 | 118 | 0 | 43 | 0 | 0 | 0 | 5 | 0 | 0 | 1 | 0 | 0 | 0 | 0 | 0 | 124 | 0 | 43 |
| Clark | Ian David | Left-Back | 1997 | 2002 | 109 | 29 | 17 | 4 | 0 | 0 | 4 | 2 | 0 | 4 | 0 | 0 | 7 | 2 | 1 | 128 | 33 | 18 |
| Clark | Neville | Left-Half-Back | 1953 | 1954 | 2 | 0 | 0 | 0 | 0 | 0 | 0 | 0 | 0 | 0 | 0 | 0 | 0 | 0 | 0 | 2 | 0 | 0 |
| Clarke | Darrell James | Midfielder | 2001 | 2007 | 98 | 25 | 19 | 2 | 2 | 0 | 2 | 2 | 1 | 3 | 1 | 0 | 1 | 0 | 2 | 106 | 30 | 22 |
| Clarke | Henry (Harry) | Inside-Right | 1981 | 1982 | 5 | 2 | 1 | 0 | 0 | 0 | 0 | 1 | 0 | 0 | 0 | 0 | 0 | 0 | 0 | 5 | 3 | 1 |
| Clarke | James Henry (Harry) | Centre-Forward | 1949 | 1950 | 7 | 0 | 1 | 0 | 0 | 0 | 2 | 0 | 1 | 0 | 0 | 0 | 0 | 0 | 0 | 9 | 0 | 2 |
| Clarke | Malcolm McQueen | Forward | 1970 | 1972 | 29 | 4 | 0 | 0 | 0 | 0 | 1 | 0 | 0 | 3 | 0 | 0 | 0 | 0 | 0 | 33 | 4 | 0 |
| Clegg | David Lee | Midfielder | 1996 | 1997 | 24 | 11 | 2 | 0 | 0 | 0 | 2 | 0 | 0 | 1 | 0 | 0 | 1 | 0 | 0 | 28 | 11 | 2 |
| Cleugh | William (Billy) | Left-Half-Back | 1934 | 1935 | 1 | 0 | 0 | 0 | 0 | 0 | 0 | 0 | 0 | 0 | 0 | 0 | 0 | 0 | 0 | 1 | 0 | 0 |
| Cliff | John | Right-Half-Back | 1945 | 1946 | 0 | 0 | 0 | 0 | 0 | 0 | 1 | 0 | 0 | 0 | 0 | 0 | 0 | 0 | 0 | 1 | 0 | 0 |
| Clydesdale | William (Bill) | Left-Back | 1960 | 1961 | 14 | 0 | 0 | 0 | 0 | 0 | 0 | 0 | 0 | 1 | 0 | 0 | 0 | 0 | 0 | 15 | 0 | 0 |
| Coates | Walter Albert | Outside-Right | 1928 | 1929 | 2 | 0 | 0 | 0 | 0 | 0 | 0 | 0 | 0 | 0 | 0 | 0 | 0 | 0 | 0 | 2 | 0 | 0 |
| Cochrane | George Terence (Terry) | Forward | 1986 | 1987 | 2 | 0 | 0 | 0 | 0 | 0 | 0 | 0 | 0 | 0 | 0 | 0 | 0 | 0 | 0 | 2 | 0 | 0 |
| Coles | Daniel (Danny) Richard | Central Defender | 2007 | 2008 | 3 | 0 | 0 | 0 | 0 | 0 | 0 | 0 | 0 | 0 | 0 | 0 | 0 | 0 | 0 | 3 | 0 | 0 |
| Collins | Neill William | Defender | 2005 | 2006 | 22 | 0 | 0 | 0 | 0 | 0 | 0 | 0 | 0 | 2 | 0 | 0 | 1 | 0 | 0 | 25 | 0 | 0 |
| Collins | Samuel (Sam) Jason | Central Defender | 2007 | 2012 | 171 | 1 | 6 | 0 | 0 | 0 | 6 | 0 | 0 | 8 | 0 | 0 | 4 | 0 | 0 | 189 | 1 | 6 |
| Colquhoun | Duncan Morton | Outside-Left | 1934 | 1935 | 0 | 0 | 0 | 0 | 0 | 0 | 0 | 0 | 0 | 0 | 0 | 0 | 1 | 0 | 1 | 1 | 0 | 1 |
| Common | John (Jack) | Centre/Inside-Forward/Half-Back | 1923 | 1924 | 32 | 0 | 4 | 0 | 0 | 0 | 0 | 0 | 0 | 0 | 0 | 0 | 0 | 0 | 0 | 32 | 0 | 4 |
| Conlon | Bryan | Centre-Forward/Centre-Half-Back | 1972 | 1974 | 38 | 3 | 3 | 0 | 0 | 0 | 0 | 0 | 0 | 1 | 0 | 0 | 0 | 0 | 0 | 39 | 3 | 3 |
| Conlon | Paul Robert | Forward | 1995 | 1996 | 11 | 4 | 4 | 0 | 0 | 0 | 0 | 0 | 0 | 0 | 0 | 0 | 0 | 0 | 0 | 11 | 4 | 4 |
| Connell | David | Right-Half-Back | 1922 | 1923 | 15 | 0 | 0 | 0 | 0 | 0 | 2 | 0 | 0 | 0 | 0 | 0 | 0 | 0 | 0 | 17 | 0 | 0 |

| | | | Career | | Football League | | | Play-offs | | | FA Cup | | | FL Cup | | | Other | | | Total | | |
|---|---|---|---|---|---|---|---|---|---|---|---|---|---|---|---|---|---|---|---|---|---|---|
| Surname | Forenames | Position | Start | Finish | Apps | Sub | Gls | Apps | Sub | Gls | Apps | Sub | Gls | Apps | Sub | Gls | Apps | Sub | Gls | Apps | Sub | Gls |
| Connor | Paul | Forward | 1997 | 1998 | 4 | 1 | 0 | 0 | 0 | 0 | 0 | 0 | 0 | 0 | 0 | 0 | 0 | 0 | 0 | 4 | 1 | 0 |
| Cook | James Alexander (Alec) | Inside/Centre/Wing-Forward | 1922 | 1925 | 28 | 0 | 3 | 0 | 0 | 0 | 6 | 0 | 3 | 0 | 0 | 0 | 0 | 0 | 0 | 34 | 0 | 6 |
| Cook | Mitchell Christopher (Mitch) | Left-Back | 1994 | 1995 | 22 | 2 | 0 | 0 | 0 | 0 | 0 | 0 | 0 | 0 | 0 | 0 | 0 | 0 | 0 | 22 | 2 | 0 |
| Cooper | Douglas (Doug) | Centre-Forward | 1960 | 1961 | 16 | 0 | 6 | 0 | 0 | 0 | 1 | 0 | 1 | 0 | 0 | 0 | 0 | 0 | 0 | 17 | 0 | 7 |
| Cooper | James Thomson (Jim) | Outside-Right | 1965 | 1966 | 19 | 0 | 1 | 0 | 0 | 0 | 1 | 0 | 0 | 2 | 0 | 1 | 0 | 0 | 0 | 22 | 0 | 2 |
| Cooper | Mark Nicholas | Forward | 1996 | 1997 | 33 | 0 | 9 | 0 | 0 | 0 | 1 | 0 | 0 | 2 | 0 | 0 | 1 | 0 | 0 | 37 | 0 | 9 |
| Copeland | Edward (Teddy) | Outside-Right | 1938 | 1948 | 38 | 0 | 9 | 0 | 0 | 0 | 2 | 0 | 0 | 0 | 0 | 0 | 2 | 0 | 0 | 42 | 0 | 9 |
| Copeman | Robert (Bobby) | Right-Back | 1937 | 1938 | 1 | 0 | 0 | 0 | 0 | 0 | 0 | 0 | 0 | 0 | 0 | 0 | 0 | 0 | 0 | 1 | 0 | 0 |
| Coppinger | James | Forward | 1999 | 2002 | 20 | 4 | 5 | 1 | 0 | 0 | 0 | 0 | 0 | 0 | 0 | 0 | 0 | 0 | 0 | 21 | 4 | 5 |
| Corbett | Alexander McLennan (Alex) | Goalkeeper | 1953 | 1954 | 7 | 0 | 0 | 0 | 0 | 0 | 0 | 0 | 0 | 0 | 0 | 0 | 0 | 0 | 0 | 7 | 0 | 0 |
| Coulthard | Frank R. | Outside-Left | 1934 | 1935 | 4 | 0 | 0 | 0 | 0 | 0 | 0 | 0 | 0 | 0 | 0 | 0 | 0 | 0 | 0 | 4 | 0 | 0 |
| Cowan | William Duncan (Billy) | Inside-Left | 1930 | 1931 | 3 | 0 | 2 | 0 | 0 | 0 | 0 | 0 | 0 | 0 | 0 | 0 | 0 | 0 | 0 | 3 | 0 | 2 |
| Cowell | William (Billy) | Goalkeeper | 1924 | 1926 | 78 | 0 | 0 | 0 | 0 | 0 | 9 | 0 | 0 | 0 | 0 | 0 | 0 | 0 | 0 | 87 | 0 | 0 |
| Cox | Brian Roy | Goalkeeper | 1990 | 1991 | 34 | 0 | 0 | 0 | 0 | 0 | 2 | 0 | 0 | 4 | 0 | 0 | 3 | 0 | 0 | 43 | 0 | 0 |
| Coyne | John David | Forward | 1972 | 1974 | 47 | 8 | 10 | 0 | 0 | 0 | 3 | 0 | 0 | 2 | 0 | 0 | 0 | 0 | 0 | 52 | 8 | 10 |
| Craddock | Darren | Right-Back | 2004 | 2006 | 22 | 2 | 0 | 0 | 1 | 0 | 2 | 1 | 0 | 1 | 0 | 0 | 1 | 3 | 0 | 26 | 7 | 0 |
| Craddock | Thomas (Tom) | Forward | 2007 | 2008 | 1 | 3 | 0 | 0 | 0 | 0 | 0 | 0 | 0 | 0 | 0 | 0 | 0 | 0 | 0 | 1 | 3 | 0 |
| Craig | John | Inside-Right | 1925 | 1927 | 30 | 0 | 6 | 0 | 0 | 0 | 1 | 0 | 0 | 0 | 0 | 0 | 0 | 0 | 0 | 31 | 0 | 6 |
| Creamer | Peter Anthony | Full-Back/Midfielder | 1976 | 1978 | 63 | 0 | 3 | 0 | 0 | 0 | 3 | 0 | 0 | 0 | 0 | 0 | 0 | 0 | 0 | 66 | 0 | 3 |
| Crilly | Thomas (Tommy) | Left-Back | 1921 | 1922 | 37 | 0 | 0 | 0 | 0 | 0 | 11 | 0 | 0 | 0 | 0 | 0 | 0 | 0 | 0 | 48 | 0 | 0 |
| Crook | Leslie Ronald (Les) | Forward | 1970 | 1971 | 23 | 2 | 3 | 0 | 0 | 0 | 1 | 0 | 0 | 1 | 0 | 0 | 0 | 0 | 0 | 25 | 2 | 3 |
| Cross | Paul | Left-Back | 1991 | 1994 | 73 | 1 | 1 | 0 | 0 | 0 | 4 | 0 | 0 | 8 | 0 | 0 | 5 | 0 | 0 | 90 | 1 | 1 |
| Cross | Ryan | Right-Back | 1992 | 1994 | 49 | 1 | 2 | 0 | 0 | 0 | 5 | 0 | 0 | 8 | 0 | 0 | 5 | 0 | 0 | 67 | 1 | 2 |
| Crowther | George L. | Centre-Forward | 1921 | 1923 | 25 | 0 | 10 | 0 | 0 | 0 | 1 | 0 | 0 | 0 | 0 | 0 | 0 | 0 | 0 | 26 | 0 | 10 |
| Crowther | Stephen John (Steve) | Full-Back | 1975 | 1976 | 3 | 0 | 0 | 0 | 0 | 0 | 0 | 0 | 0 | 2 | 0 | 0 | 0 | 0 | 0 | 5 | 0 | 0 |
| Crumplin | Ian | Forward | 1978 | 1979 | 25 | 4 | 5 | 0 | 0 | 0 | 3 | 0 | 0 | 3 | 0 | 0 | 0 | 0 | 0 | 31 | 4 | 5 |
| Cullen | David Jonathan (Jon) | Midfielder | 1996 | 1998 | 33 | 1 | 12 | 0 | 0 | 0 | 1 | 0 | 0 | 2 | 0 | 0 | 2 | 0 | 0 | 38 | 1 | 12 |
| Cummings | Robert Douglas (Bobby) | Centre-Forward | 1967 | 1969 | 48 | 4 | 12 | 0 | 0 | 0 | 1 | 0 | 0 | 1 | 0 | 0 | 0 | 0 | 0 | 50 | 4 | 12 |
| Cunningham | David (Dave) | Forward | 1976 | 1977 | 10 | 2 | 1 | 0 | 0 | 0 | 0 | 0 | 0 | 0 | 0 | 0 | 0 | 0 | 0 | 10 | 2 | 1 |
| Cunningham | Kenneth Rankin (Ken) | Centre-Forward | 1963 | 1964 | 2 | 0 | 0 | 0 | 0 | 0 | 0 | 0 | 0 | 1 | 0 | 0 | 0 | 0 | 0 | 3 | 0 | 0 |
| Curry | Sean Patrick | Centre-Forward | 1989 | 1990 | 0 | 1 | 0 | 0 | 0 | 0 | 0 | 0 | 0 | 0 | 0 | 0 | 0 | 0 | 0 | 0 | 1 | 0 |
| Curtis | Ernest Robert (Ernie) | Inside-Forward/Half-Back | 1937 | 1938 | 16 | 0 | 1 | 0 | 0 | 0 | 0 | 0 | 0 | 0 | 0 | 0 | 0 | 0 | 0 | 16 | 0 | 1 |
| Dalton | Paul | Outside-Left | 1988 | 1992 | 140 | 11 | 37 | 0 | 0 | 0 | 7 | 0 | 1 | 10 | 0 | 2 | 9 | 0 | 3 | 166 | 11 | 43 |
| Daly | Jonathan Marvin (Jon) | Centre-Forward | 2004 | 2007 | 36 | 25 | 12 | 2 | 1 | 1 | 4 | 0 | 0 | 3 | 0 | 2 | 1 | 1 | 0 | 46 | 27 | 15 |
| Danskin | Jason | Outside-Right | 1987 | 1988 | 3 | 0 | 0 | 0 | 0 | 0 | 0 | 0 | 0 | 0 | 0 | 0 | 0 | 0 | 0 | 3 | 0 | 0 |

| | | | Career | | Football League | | | Play-offs | | | FA Cup | | | FL Cup | | | Other | | | Total | | |
|---|---|---|---|---|---|---|---|---|---|---|---|---|---|---|---|---|---|---|---|---|---|---|
| Surname | Forenames | Position | Start | Finish | Apps | Sub | Gls | Apps | Sub | Gls | Apps | Sub | Gls | Apps | Sub | Gls | Apps | Sub | Gls | Apps | Sub | Gls |
| Darling | Malcolm | Outside-Left | 1977 | 1978 | 2 | 2 | 0 | 0 | 0 | 0 | 0 | 0 | 0 | 0 | 0 | 0 | 0 | 0 | 0 | 2 | 2 | 0 |
| Daughtry | Paul William | Midfielder | 1994 | 1995 | 14 | 1 | 0 | 0 | 0 | 0 | 0 | 0 | 0 | 0 | 0 | 0 | 0 | 0 | 0 | 14 | 1 | 0 |
| Davidson | David Leighton (Dave) | Centre-Half-Back | 1937 | 1938 | 6 | 0 | 0 | 0 | 0 | 0 | 0 | 0 | 0 | 0 | 0 | 0 | 0 | 0 | 0 | 6 | 0 | 0 |
| Davies | Andrew Jonathan (Andy) | Midfielder | 1990 | 1992 | 4 | 3 | 0 | 0 | 0 | 0 | 1 | 0 | 0 | 0 | 0 | 0 | 2 | 0 | 0 | 7 | 3 | 0 |
| Davies | Geoffrey Peter (Geoff) | Centre-Forward | 1976 | 1977 | 5 | 0 | 1 | 0 | 0 | 0 | 0 | 0 | 0 | 0 | 0 | 0 | 0 | 0 | 0 | 5 | 0 | 1 |
| Davies | Glen | Central Defender/Midfielder | 1996 | 1998 | 48 | 4 | 1 | 0 | 0 | 0 | 1 | 0 | 0 | 3 | 0 | 0 | 1 | 0 | 0 | 53 | 4 | 1 |
| Davies | Kenneth Frank (Kenny) | Midfielder | 1989 | 1991 | 4 | 2 | 0 | 0 | 0 | 0 | 0 | 0 | 0 | 3 | 0 | 0 | 1 | 0 | 0 | 8 | 2 | 0 |
| Davis | Kelvin Geoffrey | Goalkeeper | 1997 | 1998 | 2 | 0 | 0 | 0 | 0 | 0 | 0 | 0 | 0 | 1 | 0 | 0 | 0 | 0 | 0 | 3 | 0 | 0 |
| Davison | Edward (Ted) | Centre-Half-Back | 1953 | 1954 | 1 | 0 | 0 | 0 | 0 | 0 | 0 | 0 | 0 | 0 | 0 | 0 | 0 | 0 | 0 | 1 | 0 | 0 |
| Dawes | Malcolm | Full-Back/Midfielder | 1970 | 1976 | 193 | 2 | 12 | 0 | 0 | 0 | 5 | 1 | 0 | 12 | 0 | 0 | 0 | 0 | 0 | 210 | 3 | 12 |
| Dearden | Kevin Charles | Goalkeeper | 1989 | 1990 | 10 | 0 | 0 | 0 | 0 | 0 | 0 | 0 | 0 | 0 | 0 | 0 | 0 | 0 | 0 | 10 | 0 | 0 |
| Debont | Andrew Cornelius | Goalkeeper | 1995 | 1996 | 1 | 0 | 0 | 0 | 0 | 0 | 0 | 0 | 0 | 0 | 0 | 0 | 0 | 0 | 0 | 1 | 0 | 0 |
| Denham | Charles (Charlie) | Outside-Right | 1958 | 1959 | 5 | 0 | 3 | 0 | 0 | 0 | 0 | 0 | 0 | 0 | 0 | 0 | 0 | 0 | 0 | 5 | 0 | 3 |
| Denham | John William | Left-Back | 1949 | 1950 | 1 | 0 | 0 | 0 | 0 | 0 | 0 | 0 | 0 | 0 | 0 | 0 | 0 | 0 | 0 | 1 | 0 | 0 |
| Derbyshire | Thomas (Tommy) | Goalkeeper | 1950 | 1951 | 1 | 0 | 0 | 0 | 0 | 0 | 0 | 0 | 0 | 0 | 0 | 0 | 0 | 0 | 0 | 1 | 0 | 0 |
| Desmond | Peter | Inside-Left | 1953 | 1954 | 1 | 0 | 0 | 0 | 0 | 0 | 0 | 0 | 0 | 0 | 0 | 0 | 0 | 0 | 0 | 1 | 0 | 0 |
| Di Lella | Gustavo Martin | Forward | 1997 | 2000 | 22 | 9 | 4 | 0 | 0 | 0 | 2 | 0 | 0 | 2 | 1 | 1 | 1 | 0 | 0 | 27 | 10 | 5 |
| Diamond | John James (Jack) | Centre-Forward | 1938 | 1939 | 9 | 0 | 1 | 0 | 0 | 0 | 0 | 0 | 0 | 0 | 0 | 0 | 1 | 0 | 4 | 10 | 0 | 5 |
| Dibble | Andrew Gerard | Goalkeeper | 1999 | 2000 | 6 | 0 | 0 | 1 | 1 | 0 | 0 | 0 | 0 | 2 | 0 | 0 | 1 | 0 | 0 | 10 | 1 | 0 |
| Dickenson | James (Jimmy) | Half-Back | 1930 | 1931 | 23 | 0 | 1 | 0 | 0 | 0 | 1 | 0 | 1 | 0 | 0 | 0 | 0 | 0 | 0 | 24 | 0 | 2 |
| Dixon | Andrew Paul | Forward | 1987 | 1996 | 10 | 7 | 1 | 0 | 0 | 0 | 0 | 0 | 0 | 0 | 2 | 0 | 0 | 0 | 0 | 10 | 9 | 1 |
| Dixon | Charles (Charlie) | Left-Back | 1922 | 1926 | 66 | 0 | 0 | 0 | 0 | 0 | 5 | 0 | 0 | 0 | 0 | 0 | 0 | 0 | 0 | 71 | 0 | 0 |
| Dixon | Colin | Left-Half-Back | 1983 | 1984 | 1 | 0 | 0 | 0 | 0 | 0 | 0 | 0 | 0 | 0 | 0 | 0 | 0 | 0 | 0 | 1 | 0 | 0 |
| Dixon | John William (Johnny) | Full-Back/Half-Back | 1958 | 1961 | 35 | 0 | 2 | 0 | 0 | 0 | 5 | 0 | 0 | 0 | 0 | 0 | 0 | 0 | 0 | 40 | 0 | 2 |
| Dixon | Kevin Lynton | Forward | 1983 | 1989 | 123 | 4 | 33 | 0 | 0 | 0 | 4 | 0 | 1 | 6 | 2 | 1 | 4 | 0 | 0 | 137 | 6 | 35 |
| Dixon | Robert Hall (Bobby) | Inside-Left/Wing-Forward | 1928 | 1933 | 114 | 0 | 27 | 0 | 0 | 0 | 3 | 0 | 1 | 0 | 0 | 0 | 0 | 0 | 0 | 117 | 0 | 28 |
| Dobbing | Robert (Bobby) | Left-Back | 1969 | 1970 | 34 | 0 | 1 | 0 | 0 | 0 | 2 | 0 | 0 | 2 | 0 | 0 | 0 | 0 | 0 | 38 | 0 | 1 |
| Dobell | Donald (Danny) | Centre-Forward/Half-Back | 1926 | 1930 | 62 | 0 | 5 | 0 | 0 | 0 | 0 | 0 | 0 | 0 | 0 | 0 | 0 | 0 | 0 | 62 | 0 | 5 |
| Dobson | Paul | Forward | 1981 | 1986 | 83 | 28 | 32 | 0 | 0 | 0 | 5 | 1 | 1 | 3 | 0 | 0 | 2 | 0 | 1 | 93 | 29 | 34 |
| Dobson | Warren Edward | Goalkeeper | 1997 | 1998 | 1 | 0 | 0 | 0 | 0 | 0 | 1 | 0 | 0 | 1 | 0 | 0 | 0 | 0 | 0 | 3 | 0 | 0 |
| Doig | Russell | Forward | 1987 | 1990 | 22 | 11 | 2 | 0 | 0 | 0 | 0 | 1 | 0 | 1 | 1 | 0 | 2 | 0 | 0 | 25 | 13 | 2 |
| Don | Robert Perrett | Right-Half-Back | 1938 | 1939 | 4 | 0 | 0 | 0 | 0 | 0 | 0 | 0 | 0 | 0 | 0 | 0 | 0 | 0 | 0 | 4 | 0 | 0 |
| Donald | Robert Stephenson (Bob) | Outside-Left | 1921 | 1922 | 8 | 0 | 0 | 0 | 0 | 0 | 1 | 0 | 0 | 0 | 0 | 0 | 0 | 0 | 0 | 9 | 0 | 0 |
| Donaldson | Robert Steve (Bobby) | Inside-Forward/Half-Back | 1947 | 1952 | 131 | 0 | 4 | 0 | 0 | 0 | 7 | 0 | 0 | 0 | 0 | 0 | 0 | 0 | 0 | 138 | 0 | 4 |
| Donaldson | Ryan Mark | Forward | 2010 | 2011 | 11 | 1 | 0 | 0 | 0 | 0 | 0 | 0 | 0 | 0 | 0 | 0 | 0 | 0 | 0 | 11 | 1 | 0 |

| | | | Career | | Football League | | | Play-offs | | | FA Cup | | | FL Cup | | | Other | | | Total | | |
|---|---|---|---|---|---|---|---|---|---|---|---|---|---|---|---|---|---|---|---|---|---|---|
| Surname | Forenames | Position | Start | Finish | Apps | Sub | Gls | Apps | Sub | Gls | Apps | Sub | Gls | Apps | Sub | Gls | Apps | Sub | Gls | Apps | Sub | Gls |
| Dougherty | Joseph (Joe) | Right/Left-Half-Back | 1921 | 1922 | 32 | 0 | 0 | 0 | 0 | 0 | 0 | 0 | 0 | 0 | 0 | 0 | 0 | 0 | 0 | 32 | 0 | 0 |
| Douglas | James Stewart (Jimmy) | Centre-Forward | 1962 | 1963 | 13 | 0 | 4 | 0 | 0 | 0 | 0 | 0 | 0 | 0 | 0 | 0 | 0 | 0 | 0 | 13 | 0 | 4 |
| Douglas | John Stewart | Inside-Forward/Half-Back | 1938 | 1950 | 32 | 0 | 1 | 0 | 0 | 0 | 0 | 0 | 0 | 0 | 0 | 0 | 0 | 0 | 0 | 32 | 0 | 1 |
| Downing | Derrick Graham | Full-Back/Midfielder | 1977 | 1978 | 40 | 0 | 4 | 0 | 0 | 0 | 5 | 0 | 1 | 2 | 0 | 0 | 0 | 0 | 0 | 47 | 0 | 5 |
| Dowson | Francis | Left-Half-Back | 1922 | 1923 | 18 | 0 | 0 | 0 | 0 | 0 | 2 | 0 | 1 | 0 | 0 | 0 | 0 | 0 | 0 | 20 | 0 | 1 |
| Dreyer | Gordon | Right-Half-Back | 1934 | 1937 | 41 | 0 | 0 | 0 | 0 | 0 | 4 | 0 | 0 | 0 | 0 | 0 | 3 | 0 | 0 | 48 | 0 | 0 |
| Drysdale | Brian | Left-Back | 1965 | 1969 | 169 | 1 | 2 | 0 | 0 | 0 | 7 | 0 | 0 | 5 | 0 | 0 | 0 | 0 | 0 | 181 | 1 | 2 |
| Duggan | Andrew James (Andy) | Central Defender/Midfielder | 1990 | 1991 | 2 | 0 | 0 | 0 | 0 | 0 | 0 | 0 | 0 | 0 | 1 | 0 | 0 | 0 | 0 | 2 | 1 | 0 |
| Dunbar | Ian | Midfielder | 1989 | 1991 | 1 | 2 | 0 | 0 | 0 | 0 | 0 | 0 | 0 | 0 | 0 | 0 | 0 | 0 | 0 | 1 | 2 | 0 |
| Dunn | Brian James | Outside-Left | 1958 | 1961 | 27 | 0 | 1 | 0 | 0 | 0 | 1 | 0 | 0 | 0 | 0 | 0 | 0 | 0 | 0 | 28 | 0 | 1 |
| Dunn | Richard (Dick) | Inside-Forward | 1949 | 1950 | 13 | 0 | 2 | 0 | 0 | 0 | 0 | 0 | 0 | 0 | 0 | 0 | 0 | 0 | 0 | 13 | 0 | 2 |
| Dunwell | Michael (Mike) | Forward | 1998 | 1999 | 0 | 1 | 0 | 0 | 0 | 0 | 0 | 0 | 0 | 0 | 0 | 0 | 0 | 0 | 0 | 0 | 1 | 0 |
| Duthie | John Flett | Inside-Forward | 1923 | 1924 | 3 | 0 | 0 | 0 | 0 | 0 | 1 | 0 | 1 | 0 | 0 | 0 | 0 | 0 | 0 | 4 | 0 | 1 |
| Dyson | James (Jim) | Goalkeeper | 1954 | 1959 | 63 | 0 | 0 | 0 | 0 | 0 | 5 | 0 | 0 | 0 | 0 | 0 | 0 | 0 | 0 | 68 | 0 | 0 |
| Easter | Jermaine Maurice | Forward | 2000 | 2004 | 0 | 27 | 2 | 0 | 2 | 0 | 0 | 0 | 0 | 0 | 0 | 0 | 0 | 1 | 0 | 0 | 30 | 2 |
| Edgar | Edward (Eddie) | Goalkeeper | 1976 | 1979 | 75 | 0 | 0 | 0 | 0 | 0 | 6 | 0 | 0 | 2 | 0 | 0 | 0 | 0 | 0 | 83 | 0 | 0 |
| Edgar | John (Johnny) | Inside-Forward | 1961 | 1963 | 72 | 0 | 31 | 0 | 0 | 0 | 1 | 0 | 0 | 3 | 0 | 0 | 0 | 0 | 0 | 76 | 0 | 31 |
| Edwards | Edward (Ted) | Left-Back | 1957 | 1958 | 1 | 0 | 0 | 0 | 0 | 0 | 0 | 0 | 0 | 0 | 0 | 0 | 0 | 0 | 0 | 1 | 0 | 0 |
| Edwards | Richard (Richie) | Goalkeeper | 1986 | 1987 | 1 | 0 | 0 | 0 | 0 | 0 | 0 | 0 | 0 | 0 | 0 | 0 | 0 | 0 | 0 | 1 | 0 | 0 |
| Elder | Alexander Yeoman Pirrie (Alex) | Inside-Right | 1951 | 1953 | 65 | 0 | 20 | 0 | 0 | 0 | 4 | 0 | 2 | 0 | 0 | 0 | 0 | 0 | 0 | 69 | 0 | 22 |
| Elliott | Andrew (Andy) | Centre-Forward | 1996 | 1998 | 2 | 6 | 0 | 0 | 0 | 0 | 0 | 1 | 0 | 0 | 0 | 0 | 0 | 0 | 0 | 2 | 7 | 0 |
| Elliott | Kevan | Forward/Midfielder | 1975 | 1977 | 24 | 3 | 1 | 0 | 0 | 0 | 1 | 0 | 0 | 1 | 1 | 0 | 0 | 0 | 0 | 26 | 4 | 1 |
| Elliott | Robert James (Robbie) | Full Back | 2007 | 2008 | 14 | 1 | 0 | 0 | 0 | 0 | 0 | 0 | 0 | 0 | 0 | 0 | 1 | 0 | 0 | 15 | 1 | 0 |
| Ellis | Kenneth (Ken) | Forward/Midfielder | 1971 | 1972 | 32 | 2 | 4 | 0 | 0 | 0 | 1 | 0 | 1 | 2 | 0 | 0 | 0 | 0 | 0 | 35 | 2 | 5 |
| Ellison | Anthony Lee | Forward | 1992 | 1993 | 3 | 1 | 1 | 0 | 0 | 0 | 0 | 0 | 0 | 0 | 0 | 0 | 0 | 0 | 0 | 3 | 1 | 1 |
| Ellison | William Roy | Inside-Forward | 1970 | 1971 | 5 | 0 | 0 | 0 | 0 | 0 | 0 | 0 | 0 | 0 | 0 | 0 | 0 | 0 | 0 | 5 | 0 | 0 |
| Embleton | David | Full-Back/Midfielder | 1973 | 1976 | 24 | 2 | 0 | 0 | 0 | 0 | 0 | 0 | 0 | 1 | 0 | 0 | 0 | 0 | 0 | 25 | 2 | 0 |
| Embleton | Edward (Eddie) | Inside-Forward | 1937 | 1938 | 22 | 0 | 6 | 0 | 0 | 0 | 2 | 0 | 1 | 0 | 0 | 0 | 2 | 0 | 1 | 26 | 0 | 8 |
| Emerson | Dean | Central Defender | 1992 | 1994 | 44 | 1 | 1 | 0 | 0 | 0 | 3 | 0 | 0 | 7 | 0 | 0 | 4 | 1 | 0 | 58 | 2 | 1 |
| Endean | Barry | Forward | 1975 | 1977 | 24 | 1 | 5 | 0 | 0 | 0 | 0 | 0 | 0 | 2 | 0 | 0 | 0 | 0 | 0 | 26 | 1 | 5 |
| English | Samuel (Sam) | Centre-Forward | 1936 | 1938 | 69 | 0 | 27 | 0 | 0 | 0 | 3 | 0 | 3 | 0 | 0 | 0 | 3 | 0 | 1 | 75 | 0 | 31 |
| Entwhistle | Robert Peter (Bobby) | Centre/Inside-Forward | 1964 | 1965 | 14 | 0 | 3 | 0 | 0 | 0 | 2 | 0 | 2 | 0 | 0 | 0 | 0 | 0 | 0 | 16 | 0 | 5 |
| Entwhistle | Wayne Peter | Inside-Left | 1989 | 1990 | 2 | 0 | 0 | 0 | 0 | 0 | 0 | 0 | 0 | 0 | 0 | 0 | 0 | 0 | 0 | 2 | 0 | 0 |
| Errington | Albert (Darkie) | Left-Back | 1926 | 1931 | 81 | 0 | 0 | 0 | 0 | 0 | 1 | 0 | 0 | 0 | 0 | 0 | 0 | 0 | 0 | 82 | 0 | 0 |
| Evans | David Thom (Dave) | Centre-Forward | 1978 | 1980 | 2 | 2 | 0 | 0 | 0 | 0 | 0 | 0 | 0 | 0 | 0 | 0 | 0 | 0 | 0 | 2 | 2 | 0 |

| | | | Career | | Football League | | | Play-offs | | | FA Cup | | | FL Cup | | | Other | | | Total | | |
|---|---|---|---|---|---|---|---|---|---|---|---|---|---|---|---|---|---|---|---|---|---|---|
| Surname | Forenames | Position | Start | Finish | Apps | Sub | Gls | Apps | Sub | Gls | Apps | Sub | Gls | Apps | Sub | Gls | Apps | Sub | Gls | Apps | Sub | Gls |
| Evans | Nicholas Andrew (Nicky) | Forward | 1998 | 1999 | 0 | 1 | 0 | 0 | 0 | 0 | 0 | 0 | 0 | 0 | 0 | 0 | 0 | 0 | 0 | 0 | 1 | 0 |
| Fagan | Michael Jeffrey (Mike) | Central Defender | 1979 | 1983 | 36 | 1 | 1 | 0 | 0 | 0 | 0 | 0 | 0 | 4 | 0 | 0 | 2 | 0 | 0 | 42 | 1 | 1 |
| Fairhurst | Richard (Dick) | Left-Back/Centre-Half | 1934 | 1935 | 11 | 0 | 0 | 0 | 0 | 0 | 0 | 0 | 0 | 0 | 0 | 0 | 1 | 0 | 0 | 12 | 0 | 0 |
| Fairhurst | William Shaw (Bill) | Left-Back | 1933 | 1935 | 58 | 0 | 0 | 0 | 0 | 0 | 6 | 0 | 0 | 0 | 0 | 0 | 1 | 0 | 0 | 65 | 0 | 0 |
| Farnaby | Craig | Inside-Forward | 1984 | 1985 | 5 | 0 | 0 | 0 | 0 | 0 | 0 | 0 | 0 | 0 | 0 | 0 | 0 | 0 | 0 | 5 | 0 | 0 |
| Fell | John William (Jackie) | Wing-Forward | 1928 | 1929 | 21 | 0 | 0 | 0 | 0 | 0 | 1 | 0 | 0 | 0 | 0 | 0 | 0 | 0 | 0 | 22 | 0 | 0 |
| Fenton | Isaac | Outside-Right | 1937 | 1938 | 1 | 0 | 0 | 0 | 0 | 0 | 0 | 0 | 0 | 0 | 0 | 0 | 0 | 0 | 0 | 1 | 0 | 0 |
| Ferguson | George Clifford (Cliff) | Inside-Right | 1930 | 1931 | 1 | 0 | 0 | 0 | 0 | 0 | 0 | 0 | 0 | 0 | 0 | 0 | 0 | 0 | 0 | 1 | 0 | 0 |
| Finch | Michael (Mike) | Goalkeeper | 1983 | 1985 | 3 | 0 | 0 | 0 | 0 | 0 | 0 | 0 | 0 | 1 | 0 | 0 | 0 | 0 | 0 | 4 | 0 | 0 |
| Finnigan | Joseph | Right-Half-Back | 1933 | 1934 | 3 | 0 | 0 | 0 | 0 | 0 | 0 | 0 | 0 | 0 | 0 | 0 | 0 | 0 | 0 | 3 | 0 | 0 |
| Firman | John R. | Outside-Left | 1935 | 1936 | 2 | 0 | 0 | 0 | 0 | 0 | 0 | 0 | 0 | 0 | 0 | 0 | 1 | 0 | 1 | 3 | 0 | 1 |
| Fitzpatrick | Lee Gareth | Midfielder | 1999 | 2001 | 28 | 19 | 6 | 0 | 1 | 0 | 0 | 0 | 0 | 2 | 0 | 1 | 1 | 3 | 0 | 31 | 23 | 7 |
| Flanders | Frederick (Fred) | Left-Back | 1922 | 1923 | 3 | 0 | 0 | 0 | 0 | 0 | 0 | 0 | 0 | 0 | 0 | 0 | 0 | 0 | 0 | 3 | 0 | 0 |
| Fletcher | Steven Mark (Steve) | Forward | 1990 | 1992 | 19 | 13 | 4 | 0 | 0 | 0 | 1 | 2 | 0 | 0 | 2 | 1 | 2 | 2 | 1 | 22 | 19 | 6 |
| Flinders | Scott Liam | Goalkeeper | 2009 | 2012 | 117 | 0 | 1 | 0 | 0 | 0 | 2 | 0 | 0 | 5 | 0 | 0 | 3 | 0 | 0 | 127 | 0 | 1 |
| Fogarty | Ambrose Gerald (Amby) | Midfielder | 1963 | 1967 | 127 | 0 | 22 | 0 | 0 | 0 | 7 | 0 | 3 | 4 | 0 | 0 | 0 | 0 | 0 | 138 | 0 | 25 |
| Foggon | Alan | Inside-Left | 1977 | 1978 | 18 | 0 | 2 | 0 | 0 | 0 | 0 | 0 | 0 | 0 | 0 | 0 | 0 | 0 | 0 | 18 | 0 | 2 |
| Foley | David John | Forward | 2003 | 2010 | 21 | 75 | 0 | 0 | 0 | 0 | 1 | 4 | 1 | 1 | 6 | 4 | 2 | 3 | 2 | 25 | 88 | 7 |
| Folland | Robert (Bobby) | Centre-Forward | 1959 | 1963 | 58 | 0 | 24 | 0 | 0 | 0 | 4 | 0 | 4 | 2 | 0 | 0 | 0 | 0 | 0 | 64 | 0 | 28 |
| Ford | Gary | Forward | 1995 | 1996 | 2 | 1 | 0 | 0 | 0 | 0 | 0 | 0 | 0 | 0 | 1 | 0 | 0 | 0 | 0 | 2 | 2 | 0 |
| Forrest | Keith | Inside-Right | 1969 | 1971 | 4 | 2 | 0 | 0 | 0 | 0 | 0 | 0 | 0 | 0 | 0 | 0 | 0 | 0 | 0 | 4 | 2 | 0 |
| Forster | Geoffrey Patrick (Geoff) | Forward | 1980 | 1981 | 10 | 4 | 4 | 0 | 0 | 0 | 0 | 0 | 0 | 2 | 0 | 1 | 0 | 0 | 0 | 12 | 4 | 5 |
| Foster | John Henry (Jack) | Centre-Half-Back | 1924 | 1927 | 54 | 0 | 2 | 0 | 0 | 0 | 3 | 0 | 0 | 0 | 0 | 0 | 0 | 0 | 0 | 57 | 0 | 2 |
| Foster | Lee | Midfielder | 1995 | 1996 | 0 | 1 | 0 | 0 | 0 | 0 | 0 | 0 | 0 | 0 | 0 | 0 | 0 | 0 | 0 | 0 | 1 | 0 |
| Foster | Wayne Paul | Forward | 1994 | 1995 | 4 | 0 | 1 | 0 | 0 | 0 | 0 | 0 | 0 | 0 | 0 | 0 | 2 | 0 | 0 | 6 | 0 | 1 |
| Fowler | Martin | Right-Half-Back | 1979 | 1980 | 6 | 0 | 0 | 0 | 0 | 0 | 0 | 0 | 0 | 0 | 0 | 0 | 0 | 0 | 0 | 6 | 0 | 0 |
| Fox | Alan | Centre-Half-Back | 1964 | 1966 | 58 | 0 | 0 | 0 | 0 | 0 | 3 | 0 | 0 | 3 | 0 | 0 | 0 | 0 | 0 | 64 | 0 | 0 |
| Francis | Terence (Terry) | Inside-Left | 1963 | 1965 | 18 | 0 | 4 | 0 | 0 | 0 | 0 | 0 | 0 | 1 | 0 | 0 | 0 | 0 | 0 | 19 | 0 | 4 |
| Franks | Anthony (Tony) | Right-Back | 1921 | 1923 | 45 | 0 | 0 | 0 | 0 | 0 | 5 | 0 | 0 | 0 | 0 | 0 | 0 | 0 | 0 | 50 | 0 | 0 |
| Fraser | Andrew McKnight (Andy) | Wing-Half-Back | 1961 | 1964 | 82 | 0 | 2 | 0 | 0 | 0 | 2 | 0 | 0 | 1 | 0 | 0 | 0 | 0 | 0 | 85 | 0 | 2 |
| Fredriksen | Jon Andre | Midfielder | 2009 | 2011 | 4 | 9 | 0 | 0 | 0 | 0 | 0 | 0 | 0 | 1 | 2 | 0 | 0 | 0 | 0 | 5 | 11 | 0 |
| Freestone | Christopher Mark (Chris) | Centre-Forward | 1998 | 2000 | 24 | 13 | 7 | 1 | 0 | 0 | 2 | 0 | 0 | 2 | 0 | 0 | 2 | 0 | 0 | 31 | 13 | 7 |
| Gabbiadini | Marco | Centre-Forward | 2003 | 2004 | 9 | 6 | 5 | 0 | 0 | 0 | 1 | 0 | 2 | 1 | 0 | 0 | 1 | 0 | 0 | 12 | 6 | 7 |
| Gabbiadini | Riccardo | Forward | 1990 | 1992 | 2 | 12 | 2 | 0 | 0 | 0 | 0 | 0 | 0 | 4 | 0 | 1 | 0 | 1 | 0 | 6 | 13 | 3 |
| Gadsby | Michael David (Mick) | Goalkeeper | 1971 | 1972 | 21 | 0 | 0 | 0 | 0 | 0 | 2 | 0 | 0 | 2 | 0 | 0 | 0 | 0 | 0 | 25 | 0 | 0 |

| | | | Career | | Football League | | | Play-offs | | | FA Cup | | | FL Cup | | | Other | | | Total | | |
|---|---|---|---|---|---|---|---|---|---|---|---|---|---|---|---|---|---|---|---|---|---|---|
| Surname | Forenames | Position | Start | Finish | Apps | Sub | Gls | Apps | Sub | Gls | Apps | Sub | Gls | Apps | Sub | Gls | Apps | Sub | Gls | Apps | Sub | Gls |
| Gadstone | Joseph Edward (Joe) | Centre-Forward | 1972 | 1973 | 1 | 0 | 0 | 0 | 0 | 0 | 0 | 0 | 0 | 0 | 0 | 0 | 0 | 0 | 0 | 1 | 0 | 0 |
| Gaffney | Terence (Terry) | Forward | 1977 | 1978 | 10 | 3 | 2 | 0 | 0 | 0 | 0 | 0 | 0 | 0 | 2 | 0 | 0 | 0 | 0 | 10 | 5 | 2 |
| Gallacher | John | Outside-Left | 1992 | 1994 | 18 | 5 | 2 | 0 | 0 | 0 | 1 | 0 | 0 | 3 | 0 | 0 | 0 | 1 | 0 | 22 | 6 | 2 |
| Gallagher | Ian | Midfielder | 1995 | 1997 | 1 | 0 | 0 | 0 | 0 | 0 | 0 | 0 | 0 | 0 | 0 | 0 | 0 | 0 | 0 | 1 | 0 | 0 |
| Gamble | Joseph (Joe) | Midfielder | 2009 | 2011 | 47 | 5 | 3 | 0 | 0 | 0 | 3 | 1 | 0 | 2 | 0 | 0 | 2 | 1 | 0 | 54 | 7 | 3 |
| Garrett | Scott | Right-Back | 1993 | 1995 | 14 | 1 | 0 | 0 | 0 | 0 | 0 | 0 | 0 | 0 | 0 | 0 | 0 | 0 | 0 | 14 | 1 | 0 |
| Gate | Kenneth Bruce (Ken) | Right-Back | 1968 | 1969 | 1 | 0 | 0 | 0 | 0 | 0 | 0 | 0 | 0 | 0 | 0 | 0 | 0 | 0 | 0 | 1 | 0 | 0 |
| Gauden | Allan | Forward | 1973 | 1975 | 63 | 0 | 15 | 0 | 0 | 0 | 4 | 0 | 0 | 10 | 0 | 5 | 0 | 0 | 0 | 77 | 0 | 20 |
| Gavin | Mark Wilson | Midfielder | 1984 | 1998 | 7 | 3 | 1 | 0 | 0 | 0 | 0 | 0 | 0 | 0 | 0 | 0 | 0 | 0 | 0 | 7 | 3 | 1 |
| Gibb | Alistair Stuart (Ali) | Full Back | 2006 | 2008 | 15 | 15 | 0 | 0 | 0 | 0 | 2 | 1 | 0 | 1 | 1 | 0 | 1 | 2 | 0 | 19 | 19 | 0 |
| Gibb | Dean Alan | Forward | 1986 | 1988 | 32 | 16 | 3 | 0 | 0 | 0 | 2 | 0 | 1 | 2 | 0 | 0 | 2 | 2 | 0 | 38 | 18 | 4 |
| Gibb | Thomas (Tommy) | Right-Half-Back | 1977 | 1978 | 40 | 0 | 4 | 0 | 0 | 0 | 5 | 0 | 0 | 2 | 0 | 0 | 0 | 0 | 0 | 47 | 0 | 4 |
| Gibbon | Arthur Thomas | Left-Back | 1958 | 1959 | 13 | 0 | 0 | 0 | 0 | 0 | 0 | 0 | 0 | 0 | 0 | 0 | 0 | 0 | 0 | 13 | 0 | 0 |
| Gilchrist | Philip Alexander (Phil) | Midfielder | 1992 | 1995 | 77 | 5 | 0 | 0 | 0 | 0 | 4 | 0 | 0 | 4 | 1 | 0 | 5 | 0 | 0 | 90 | 6 | 0 |
| Gill | George Arthur | Goalkeeper | 1921 | 1924 | 65 | 0 | 0 | 0 | 0 | 0 | 17 | 0 | 0 | 0 | 0 | 0 | 0 | 0 | 0 | 82 | 0 | 0 |
| Gill | John Barry Anthony | Centre-Half-Back | 1965 | 1971 | 201 | 3 | 1 | 0 | 0 | 0 | 7 | 0 | 0 | 6 | 0 | 0 | 0 | 0 | 0 | 214 | 3 | 1 |
| Gill | Joseph (Joe) | Goalkeeper | 1968 | 1969 | 4 | 0 | 0 | 0 | 0 | 0 | 0 | 0 | 0 | 0 | 0 | 0 | 0 | 0 | 0 | 4 | 0 | 0 |
| Goad | Alan Michael | Defender | 1967 | 1978 | 366 | 9 | 11 | 0 | 0 | 0 | 20 | 0 | 0 | 23 | 0 | 0 | 0 | 0 | 0 | 409 | 9 | 11 |
| Gobern | Lewis Thomas | Centre-Forward | 2004 | 2005 | 1 | 0 | 0 | 0 | 0 | 0 | 0 | 0 | 0 | 0 | 0 | 0 | 0 | 1 | 0 | 1 | 1 | 0 |
| Godbold | Harold (Harry) | Outside-Left | 1960 | 1963 | 65 | 0 | 8 | 0 | 0 | 0 | 3 | 0 | 0 | 2 | 0 | 0 | 0 | 0 | 0 | 70 | 0 | 8 |
| Goldthorpe | Wayne | Forward | 1976 | 1980 | 49 | 5 | 9 | 0 | 0 | 0 | 3 | 0 | 1 | 1 | 0 | 1 | 0 | 0 | 0 | 53 | 5 | 11 |
| Gollogly | John | Forward/Midfielder | 1984 | 1987 | 29 | 2 | 5 | 0 | 0 | 0 | 1 | 0 | 0 | 2 | 0 | 0 | 1 | 0 | 0 | 33 | 2 | 5 |
| Gorman | James | Right-Back | 1945 | 1946 | 0 | 0 | 0 | 0 | 0 | 0 | 2 | 0 | 0 | 0 | 0 | 0 | | | | 2 | 0 | 0 |
| Gorry | Martin Christopher | Left-Back | 1978 | 1980 | 59 | 0 | 0 | 0 | 0 | 0 | 4 | 0 | 0 | 4 | 0 | 0 | 0 | 0 | 0 | 67 | 0 | 0 |
| Gourlay | Archibald Murdoch (Archie) | Forward | 1994 | 1995 | 0 | 1 | 0 | 0 | 0 | 0 | 0 | 0 | 0 | 0 | 0 | 0 | 0 | 0 | 0 | 0 | 1 | 0 |
| Graham | Jack | Right-Half-Back | 1934 | 1935 | 5 | 0 | 0 | 0 | 0 | 0 | 0 | 0 | 0 | 0 | 0 | 0 | 0 | 0 | 0 | 5 | 0 | 0 |
| Graham | James Arthur (Jimmy) | Centre-Forward | 1935 | 1936 | 18 | 0 | 3 | 0 | 0 | 0 | 2 | 0 | 0 | 0 | 0 | 0 | 0 | 0 | 0 | 20 | 0 | 3 |
| Graham | Samuel J. (Sam) | Left-Half-Back | 1936 | 1937 | 12 | 0 | 0 | 0 | 0 | 0 | 0 | 0 | 0 | 0 | 0 | 0 | 0 | 0 | 0 | 12 | 0 | 0 |
| Grant | Brian Patrick | Right-Back | 1965 | 1967 | 35 | 0 | 0 | 0 | 0 | 0 | 1 | 0 | 0 | 2 | 0 | 0 | 0 | 0 | 0 | 38 | 0 | 0 |
| Granycombe | Neal | Inside-Left | 1980 | 1981 | 1 | 0 | 0 | 0 | 0 | 0 | 0 | 0 | 0 | 0 | 0 | 0 | 0 | 0 | 0 | 1 | 0 | 0 |
| Gray | Thomas (Tom) | Right-Back | 1924 | 1925 | 11 | 0 | 0 | 0 | 0 | 0 | 0 | 0 | 0 | 0 | 0 | 0 | 0 | 0 | 0 | 11 | 0 | 0 |
| Grayson | Simon Darrell | Forward | 1987 | 1990 | 39 | 5 | 13 | 0 | 0 | 0 | 5 | 0 | 0 | 2 | 1 | 2 | 2 | 0 | 0 | 48 | 6 | 15 |
| Green | Leslie (Les) | Goalkeeper | 1965 | 1967 | 34 | 0 | 0 | 0 | 0 | 0 | 0 | 0 | 0 | 0 | 0 | 0 | 0 | 0 | 0 | 34 | 0 | 0 |
| Green | William (Bill) | Central Defender | 1969 | 1973 | 128 | 3 | 9 | 0 | 0 | 0 | 1 | 1 | 0 | 4 | 0 | 0 | 0 | 0 | 0 | 133 | 4 | 9 |
| Gregory | Charles Frederick (Fred) | Left-Back | 1946 | 1947 | 21 | 0 | 0 | 0 | 0 | 0 | 2 | 0 | 0 | 0 | 0 | 0 | 0 | 0 | 0 | 23 | 0 | 0 |

| | | | Career | | Football League | | | Play-offs | | | FA Cup | | | FL Cup | | | Other | | | Total | | |
|---|---|---|---|---|---|---|---|---|---|---|---|---|---|---|---|---|---|---|---|---|---|---|
| Surname | Forenames | Position | Start | Finish | Apps | Sub | Gls | Apps | Sub | Gls | Apps | Sub | Gls | Apps | Sub | Gls | Apps | Sub | Gls | Apps | Sub | Gls |
| Gregson | William Cameron Smart (Bill) | Inside-Left | 1921 | 1922 | 1 | 0 | 0 | 0 | 0 | 0 | 0 | 0 | 0 | 0 | 0 | 0 | 0 | 0 | 0 | 1 | 0 | 0 |
| Greulich | Billy | Forward | 2009 | 2010 | 0 | 4 | 0 | 0 | 0 | 0 | 0 | 1 | 0 | 0 | 0 | 0 | 0 | 0 | 0 | 0 | 5 | 0 |
| Gribbin | Brian Thomas | Left-Back | 1972 | 1973 | 1 | 0 | 0 | 0 | 0 | 0 | 0 | 0 | 0 | 0 | 0 | 0 | 0 | 0 | 0 | 1 | 0 | 0 |
| Griffiths | Stephen (Steve) | Inside-Right | 1974 | 1975 | 0 | 1 | 0 | 0 | 0 | 0 | 0 | 0 | 0 | 0 | 0 | 0 | 0 | 0 | 0 | 0 | 1 | 0 |
| Guthrie | Ralph | Goalkeeper | 1956 | 1958 | 78 | 0 | 0 | 0 | 0 | 0 | 3 | 0 | 0 | 0 | 0 | 0 | 0 | 0 | 0 | 81 | 0 | 0 |
| Guy | Edward Frederick (Eddie) | Goalkeeper | 1974 | 1975 | 1 | 0 | 0 | 0 | 0 | 0 | 0 | 0 | 0 | 0 | 0 | 0 | 0 | 0 | 0 | 1 | 0 | 0 |
| Guy | Keith | Outside-Left | 1978 | 1979 | 7 | 3 | 0 | 0 | 0 | 0 | 0 | 0 | 0 | 2 | 0 | 0 | 0 | 0 | 0 | 9 | 3 | 0 |
| Guy | Lewis | Forward | 2008 | 2009 | 4 | 0 | 0 | 0 | 0 | 0 | 0 | 0 | 0 | 0 | 0 | 0 | 0 | 0 | 0 | 4 | 0 | 0 |
| Haigh | Paul | Full/Wing-Half-Back | 1987 | 1989 | 49 | 1 | 0 | 0 | 0 | 0 | 5 | 0 | 0 | 4 | 0 | 0 | 4 | 0 | 0 | 62 | 1 | 0 |
| Hall | Anthony David (Tony) | Outside-Right | 1987 | 1988 | 0 | 1 | 0 | 0 | 0 | 0 | 0 | 1 | 0 | 0 | 0 | 0 | 1 | 0 | 0 | 1 | 2 | 0 |
| Hall | Bertie | Right-Half-Back | 1926 | 1929 | 88 | 0 | 3 | 0 | 0 | 0 | 2 | 0 | 0 | 0 | 0 | 0 | 0 | 0 | 0 | 90 | 0 | 3 |
| Halliday | Robert | Inside-Left | 1938 | 1939 | 0 | 0 | 0 | 0 | 0 | 0 | 0 | 0 | 0 | 0 | 0 | 0 | 2 | 0 | 0 | 2 | 0 | 0 |
| Halliday | Stephen William (Steve) | Forward | 1993 | 1998 | 111 | 19 | 25 | 0 | 0 | 0 | 4 | 1 | 1 | 8 | 3 | 0 | 5 | 1 | 0 | 128 | 24 | 26 |
| Halstead | Fred D. | Centre-Half-Back | 1922 | 1923 | 8 | 0 | 0 | 0 | 0 | 0 | 0 | 0 | 0 | 0 | 0 | 0 | 0 | 0 | 0 | 8 | 0 | 0 |
| Hamilton | Hugh Hare (Hughie) | Outside-Right | 1963 | 1966 | 38 | 1 | 7 | 0 | 0 | 0 | 0 | 0 | 0 | 2 | 0 | 0 | 0 | 0 | 0 | 40 | 1 | 7 |
| Hamilton | James (Jimmy) | Half-Back | 1931 | 1933 | 48 | 0 | 2 | 0 | 0 | 0 | 3 | 0 | 0 | 0 | 0 | 0 | 0 | 0 | 0 | 51 | 0 | 2 |
| Hamilton | James (Jimmy) | Forward | 1982 | 1983 | 2 | 1 | 0 | 0 | 0 | 0 | 1 | 0 | 0 | 0 | 0 | 0 | 0 | 0 | 0 | 3 | 1 | 0 |
| Hampson | Walker | Wing/Centre-Half-Back | 1922 | 1923 | 22 | 0 | 4 | 0 | 0 | 0 | 0 | 0 | 0 | 0 | 0 | 0 | 0 | 0 | 0 | 22 | 0 | 4 |
| Hampton | Derek | Centre-Forward/Outside-Left | 1979 | 1982 | 66 | 8 | 18 | 0 | 0 | 0 | 2 | 0 | 1 | 3 | 0 | 0 | 2 | 1 | 0 | 73 | 9 | 19 |
| Harbron | Andrew | Centre-Half-Back | 1990 | 1991 | 0 | 0 | 0 | 0 | 0 | 0 | 0 | 0 | 0 | 1 | 0 | 0 | 0 | 0 | 0 | 1 | 0 | 0 |
| Harden | Leo | Outside-Left | 1946 | 1956 | 169 | 0 | 47 | 0 | 0 | 0 | 11 | 0 | 5 | 0 | 0 | 0 | 0 | 0 | 0 | 180 | 0 | 52 |
| Harding | Alan | Forward/Midfielder | 1978 | 1983 | 79 | 5 | 8 | 0 | 0 | 0 | 1 | 0 | 0 | 3 | 0 | 1 | 2 | 0 | 0 | 85 | 5 | 9 |
| Hardy | Cecil | Inside-Left | 1921 | 1927 | 124 | 0 | 45 | 0 | 0 | 0 | 11 | 0 | 3 | 0 | 0 | 0 | 0 | 0 | 0 | 135 | 0 | 48 |
| Hardy | Lawrence Richard (Dick) | Inside/Wing-Forward | 1931 | 1937 | 150 | 0 | 26 | 0 | 0 | 0 | 14 | 0 | 1 | 0 | 0 | 0 | 4 | 0 | 0 | 168 | 0 | 27 |
| Hardy | Sydney (Sid) | Outside-Left | 1924 | 1928 | 62 | 0 | 19 | 0 | 0 | 0 | 10 | 0 | 2 | 0 | 0 | 0 | 0 | 0 | 0 | 72 | 0 | 21 |
| Harland | Thomas W. (Tommy) | Full-Back | 1928 | 1934 | 39 | 0 | 0 | 0 | 0 | 0 | 0 | 0 | 0 | 0 | 0 | 0 | 0 | 0 | 0 | 39 | 0 | 0 |
| Harley | Richard John | Centre-Forward | 1976 | 1977 | 4 | 0 | 1 | 0 | 0 | 0 | 0 | 0 | 0 | 0 | 0 | 0 | 0 | 0 | 0 | 4 | 0 | 1 |
| Harper | Stephen Alan (Steve) | Goalkeeper | 1997 | 1998 | 15 | 0 | 0 | 0 | 0 | 0 | 0 | 0 | 0 | 0 | 0 | 0 | 0 | 0 | 0 | 15 | 0 | 0 |
| Harrington | Paul | Inside-Right | 1983 | 1984 | 0 | 2 | 0 | 0 | 0 | 0 | 0 | 0 | 0 | 0 | 0 | 0 | 0 | 0 | 0 | 0 | 2 | 0 |
| Harris | George | Centre-Forward | 1935 | 1936 | 1 | 0 | 1 | 0 | 0 | 0 | 0 | 0 | 0 | 0 | 0 | 0 | 0 | 0 | 0 | 1 | 0 | 1 |
| Harris | John | Outside-Left | 1927 | 1928 | 1 | 0 | 0 | 0 | 0 | 0 | 0 | 0 | 0 | 0 | 0 | 0 | 0 | 0 | 0 | 1 | 0 | 0 |
| Harris | John (Jack) | Half-Back | 1921 | 1922 | 4 | 0 | 0 | 0 | 0 | 0 | 0 | 0 | 0 | 0 | 0 | 0 | 0 | 0 | 0 | 4 | 0 | 0 |
| Harris | Martin | Wing-Forward | 1977 | 1978 | 0 | 1 | 0 | 0 | 0 | 0 | 0 | 0 | 0 | 0 | 0 | 0 | 0 | 0 | 0 | 0 | 1 | 0 |
| Harrison | Eric George | Left-Half-Back | 1964 | 1966 | 81 | 0 | 4 | 0 | 0 | 0 | 6 | 0 | 0 | 3 | 0 | 0 | 0 | 0 | 0 | 90 | 0 | 4 |
| Harrison | Henry (Harry) | Goalkeeper | 1926 | 1928 | 68 | 0 | 0 | 0 | 0 | 0 | 2 | 0 | 0 | 0 | 0 | 0 | 0 | 0 | 0 | 70 | 0 | 0 |

| | | | Career | | Football League | | | Play-offs | | | FA Cup | | | FL Cup | | | Other | | | Total | | |
|---|---|---|---|---|---|---|---|---|---|---|---|---|---|---|---|---|---|---|---|---|---|---|
| **Surname** | **Forenames** | **Position** | **Start** | **Finish** | **Apps** | **Sub** | **Gls** | **Apps** | **Sub** | **Gls** | **Apps** | **Sub** | **Gls** | **Apps** | **Sub** | **Gls** | **Apps** | **Sub** | **Gls** | **Apps** | **Sub** | **Gls** |
| Harrison | Walter | Right-Half-Back/Inside-Right | 1929 | 1931 | 10 | 0 | 2 | 0 | 0 | 0 | 0 | 0 | 0 | 0 | 0 | 0 | 0 | 0 | 0 | 10 | 0 | 2 |
| Hartley | Peter | Left-Back | 2009 | 2012 | 120 | 2 | 8 | 0 | 0 | 0 | 6 | 0 | 0 | 3 | 0 | 0 | 2 | 1 | 0 | 131 | 3 | 8 |
| Hartnett | James Benedict (Jimmy) | Outside-Left | 1957 | 1958 | 7 | 0 | 1 | 0 | 0 | 0 | 0 | 0 | 0 | 0 | 0 | 0 | 0 | 0 | 0 | 7 | 0 | 1 |
| Harvey | David | Outside-Right | 1970 | 1971 | 3 | 2 | 0 | 0 | 0 | 0 | 0 | 0 | 0 | 0 | 0 | 0 | 0 | 0 | 0 | 3 | 2 | 0 |
| Haslam | Steven | Right-Back | 2009 | 2012 | 41 | 14 | 0 | 0 | 0 | 0 | 0 | 1 | 0 | 4 | 0 | 0 | 4 | 0 | 0 | 49 | 15 | 0 |
| Hassan | Emmanuel Oluwaseun (Callum) | Forward | 2011 | 2012 | 0 | 1 | 0 | 0 | 0 | 0 | 0 | 0 | 0 | 0 | 0 | 0 | 0 | 0 | 0 | 0 | 1 | 0 |
| Hawkes | Barry | Inside/Outside-Left | 1961 | 1962 | 9 | 0 | 0 | 0 | 0 | 0 | 0 | 0 | 0 | 0 | 0 | 0 | 0 | 0 | 0 | 9 | 0 | 0 |
| Hawkins | George Harry | Inside-Forward | 1947 | 1949 | 30 | 0 | 4 | 0 | 0 | 0 | 1 | 0 | 0 | 0 | 0 | 0 | 0 | 0 | 0 | 31 | 0 | 4 |
| Hawkins | Lewis Henry | Forward | 2011 | 2012 | 1 | 0 | 0 | 0 | 0 | 0 | 0 | 0 | 0 | 0 | 0 | 0 | 0 | 0 | 0 | 1 | 0 | 0 |
| Healey | William Richard Ernest (Bill) | Half-Back | 1955 | 1956 | 6 | 0 | 0 | 0 | 0 | 0 | 0 | 0 | 0 | 0 | 0 | 0 | 0 | 0 | 0 | 6 | 0 | 0 |
| Heaney | Neil Andrew | Outside-Left | 1990 | 1991 | 2 | 1 | 0 | 0 | 0 | 0 | 0 | 0 | 0 | 0 | 0 | 0 | 0 | 0 | 0 | 2 | 1 | 0 |
| Heath | Donald (Don) | Outside-Right | 1973 | 1975 | 36 | 1 | 2 | 0 | 0 | 0 | 1 | 0 | 0 | 6 | 0 | 0 | 0 | 0 | 0 | 43 | 1 | 2 |
| Hedley | Graeme | Midfielder | 1984 | 1985 | 32 | 0 | 9 | 0 | 0 | 0 | 2 | 0 | 0 | 2 | 0 | 1 | 2 | 0 | 0 | 38 | 0 | 10 |
| Henderson | Damian Michael | Forward/Defender | 1994 | 1996 | 45 | 3 | 6 | 0 | 0 | 0 | 1 | 0 | 0 | 3 | 1 | 0 | 2 | 0 | 0 | 51 | 4 | 6 |
| Henderson | George | Centre-Forward | 1970 | 1971 | 1 | 0 | 0 | 0 | 0 | 0 | 0 | 0 | 0 | 0 | 0 | 0 | 0 | 0 | 0 | 1 | 0 | 0 |
| Henderson | Kevin Malcolm | Forward | 1999 | 2003 | 82 | 49 | 29 | 1 | 2 | 1 | 1 | 1 | 0 | 3 | 3 | 0 | 5 | 0 | 2 | 92 | 55 | 32 |
| Henderson | Lauchlan | Left-Half-Back | 1921 | 1922 | 2 | 0 | 0 | 0 | 0 | 0 | 0 | 0 | 0 | 0 | 0 | 0 | 0 | 0 | 0 | 2 | 0 | 0 |
| Henderson | Liam | Forward | 2008 | 2009 | 2 | 6 | 0 | 0 | 0 | 0 | 0 | 1 | 0 | 0 | 0 | 0 | 0 | 0 | 0 | 2 | 7 | 0 |
| Henderson | Thomas (Tommy) | Left-Half-Back | 1925 | 1926 | 1 | 0 | 0 | 0 | 0 | 0 | 0 | 0 | 0 | 0 | 0 | 0 | 0 | 0 | 0 | 1 | 0 | 0 |
| Hepple | John Andrew | Right-Back | 1988 | 1989 | 1 | 1 | 0 | 0 | 0 | 0 | 0 | 0 | 0 | 0 | 0 | 0 | 0 | 0 | 0 | 1 | 1 | 0 |
| Hepplewhite | Wilson | Midfielder | 1967 | 1969 | 52 | 0 | 2 | 0 | 0 | 0 | 3 | 0 | 0 | 3 | 0 | 0 | 0 | 0 | 0 | 58 | 0 | 2 |
| Herd | George | Inside/Outside-Right | 1970 | 1971 | 10 | 4 | 0 | 0 | 0 | 0 | 0 | 0 | 0 | 1 | 0 | 0 | 0 | 0 | 0 | 11 | 4 | 0 |
| Herring | David Harry | Outside-Right | 1958 | 1959 | 2 | 0 | 0 | 0 | 0 | 0 | 0 | 0 | 0 | 0 | 0 | 0 | 0 | 0 | 0 | 2 | 0 | 0 |
| Heward | Harold Aubrey | Left-Half-Back | 1935 | 1936 | 28 | 0 | 0 | 0 | 0 | 0 | 2 | 0 | 0 | 0 | 0 | 0 | 0 | 0 | 0 | 30 | 0 | 0 |
| Hewitt | Charles William (Chuck) | Outside-Right | 1921 | 1922 | 6 | 0 | 0 | 0 | 0 | 0 | 11 | 0 | 3 | 0 | 0 | 0 | 0 | 0 | 0 | 17 | 0 | 3 |
| Hewitt | John Joseph (Josh) | Centre-Forward | 1930 | 1934 | 110 | 0 | 53 | 0 | 0 | 0 | 6 | 0 | 2 | 0 | 0 | 0 | 1 | 0 | 0 | 117 | 0 | 55 |
| Hewitt | Martin (Marty) | Inside-Right | 1985 | 1987 | 11 | 3 | 2 | 0 | 0 | 0 | 1 | 0 | 0 | 0 | 0 | 0 | 0 | 1 | 0 | 12 | 4 | 2 |
| Heywood | Albert Edwards (Napper) | Goalkeeper | 1946 | 1947 | 39 | 0 | 0 | 0 | 0 | 0 | 2 | 0 | 0 | 0 | 0 | 0 | 0 | 0 | 0 | 41 | 0 | 0 |
| Hick | William Morris (Billy) | Inside-Left | 1921 | 1922 | 1 | 0 | 0 | 0 | 0 | 0 | 0 | 0 | 0 | 0 | 0 | 0 | 0 | 0 | 0 | 1 | 0 | 0 |
| Hickman | Joseph (Joe) | Goalkeeper | 1926 | 1929 | 27 | 0 | 0 | 0 | 0 | 0 | 0 | 0 | 0 | 0 | 0 | 0 | 0 | 0 | 0 | 27 | 0 | 0 |
| Higgins | Andrew Martin (Andy) | Centre-Forward | 1982 | 1983 | 3 | 1 | 1 | 0 | 0 | 0 | 0 | 0 | 0 | 0 | 0 | 0 | 0 | 0 | 0 | 3 | 1 | 1 |
| Higgins | Robert James (Bob) | Centre-Half-Back | 1979 | 1980 | 2 | 0 | 0 | 0 | 0 | 0 | 1 | 0 | 0 | 0 | 0 | 0 | 0 | 0 | 0 | 3 | 0 | 0 |
| Hignett | Craig John | Midfielder | 2006 | 2007 | 0 | 2 | 0 | 0 | 0 | 0 | 0 | 0 | 0 | 0 | 0 | 0 | 0 | 0 | 0 | 0 | 2 | 0 |
| Hill | Reginald (Reg) | Half-Back | 1932 | 1937 | 139 | 0 | 6 | 0 | 0 | 0 | 13 | 0 | 0 | 0 | 0 | 0 | 5 | 0 | 0 | 157 | 0 | 6 |
| Hillyard | Ronald William (Ron) | Goalkeeper | 1971 | 1972 | 23 | 0 | 0 | 0 | 0 | 0 | 0 | 0 | 0 | 0 | 0 | 0 | 0 | 0 | 0 | 23 | 0 | 0 |

| | | | Career | | Football League | | | Play-offs | | | FA Cup | | | FL Cup | | | Other | | | Total | | |
|---|---|---|---|---|---|---|---|---|---|---|---|---|---|---|---|---|---|---|---|---|---|---|
| Surname | Forenames | Position | Start | Finish | Apps | Sub | Gls | Apps | Sub | Gls | Apps | Sub | Gls | Apps | Sub | Gls | Apps | Sub | Gls | Apps | Sub | Gls |
| Hinchcliffe | John (Jackie) | Wing-Half-Back | 1961 | 1964 | 88 | 0 | 8 | 0 | 0 | 0 | 4 | 0 | 0 | 3 | 0 | 1 | 0 | 0 | 0 | 95 | 0 | 9 |
| Hinshelwood | William Douglas (Willie) | Left-Half-Back | 1963 | 1964 | 17 | 0 | 3 | 0 | 0 | 0 | 1 | 0 | 0 | 1 | 0 | 0 | 0 | 0 | 0 | 19 | 0 | 3 |
| Hird | Thomas (Tommy) | Outside-Right | 1933 | 1935 | 84 | 0 | 22 | 0 | 0 | 0 | 6 | 0 | 0 | 0 | 0 | 0 | 4 | 0 | 2 | 94 | 0 | 24 |
| Hislop | Terence Kona | Midfielder | 1996 | 1997 | 23 | 4 | 0 | 0 | 0 | 0 | 2 | 0 | 0 | 0 | 0 | 0 | 1 | 0 | 0 | 26 | 4 | 0 |
| Hodge | Martin John | Goalkeeper | 1991 | 1993 | 69 | 0 | 0 | 0 | 0 | 0 | 6 | 0 | 0 | 8 | 0 | 0 | 6 | 0 | 0 | 89 | 0 | 0 |
| Hodgson | Michael (Mike) | Outside-Right | 1964 | 1965 | 1 | 0 | 0 | 0 | 0 | 0 | 0 | 0 | 0 | 0 | 0 | 0 | 0 | 0 | 0 | 1 | 0 | 0 |
| Hodgson | William (Bill) | Wing-Half-Back/Centre-Forward | 1928 | 1929 | 4 | 0 | 1 | 0 | 0 | 0 | 1 | 0 | 0 | 0 | 0 | 0 | 0 | 0 | 0 | 5 | 0 | 1 |
| Hogan | John Terence (Terry) | Inside-Right | 1957 | 1958 | 9 | 0 | 0 | 0 | 0 | 0 | 1 | 0 | 0 | 0 | 0 | 0 | 0 | 0 | 0 | 10 | 0 | 0 |
| Hogan | Roy David | Forward/Midfielder | 1977 | 1987 | 271 | 13 | 32 | 0 | 0 | 0 | 10 | 1 | 2 | 11 | 1 | 2 | 12 | 0 | 0 | 304 | 15 | 36 |
| Hold | Ronald (Ronnie) | Centre-Forward | 1968 | 1969 | 0 | 0 | 0 | 0 | 0 | 0 | 1 | 0 | 0 | 0 | 0 | 0 | 0 | 0 | 0 | 1 | 0 | 0 |
| Holden | Darren | Full-back | 2010 | 2012 | 3 | 1 | 0 | 0 | 0 | 0 | 0 | 0 | 0 | 0 | 0 | 0 | 0 | 0 | 0 | 3 | 1 | 0 |
| Holland | J. | Inside-Right | 1945 | 1946 | 0 | 0 | 0 | 0 | 0 | 0 | 1 | 0 | 1 | 0 | 0 | 0 | 0 | 0 | 0 | 1 | 0 | 1 |
| Hollund | Martin | Goalkeeper | 1997 | 2002 | 117 | 0 | 0 | 1 | 0 | 0 | 4 | 0 | 0 | 5 | 0 | 0 | 7 | 0 | 0 | 134 | 0 | 0 |
| Holmes | Stanley (Stan) | Right-Back | 1949 | 1950 | 1 | 0 | 0 | 0 | 0 | 0 | 0 | 0 | 0 | 0 | 0 | 0 | 0 | 0 | 0 | 1 | 0 | 0 |
| Holmes | Steven Peter (Steve) | Defender | 1994 | 1995 | 5 | 0 | 2 | 0 | 0 | 0 | 0 | 0 | 0 | 0 | 0 | 0 | 0 | 0 | 0 | 5 | 0 | 2 |
| Homer | Christopher (Chris) | Forward | 1994 | 1997 | 2 | 5 | 0 | 0 | 0 | 0 | 0 | 0 | 0 | 0 | 1 | 0 | 0 | 1 | 0 | 2 | 7 | 0 |
| Honour | Brian | Midfielder | 1984 | 1995 | 301 | 18 | 26 | 0 | 0 | 0 | 21 | 1 | 2 | 21 | 3 | 3 | 19 | 0 | 6 | 362 | 22 | 37 |
| Honour | John | Forward/Midfielder | 1972 | 1976 | 107 | 5 | 6 | 0 | 0 | 0 | 8 | 0 | 1 | 7 | 0 | 0 | 0 | 0 | 0 | 122 | 5 | 7 |
| Hooper | Harry Reed | Full-Back | 1947 | 1950 | 66 | 0 | 4 | 0 | 0 | 0 | 0 | 0 | 0 | 0 | 0 | 0 | 0 | 0 | 0 | 66 | 0 | 4 |
| Hope | John William March | Goalkeeper | 1975 | 1976 | 23 | 0 | 0 | 0 | 0 | 0 | 4 | 0 | 0 | 1 | 0 | 0 | 0 | 0 | 0 | 28 | 0 | 0 |
| Hopkins | William (Pop) | Centre-Half-Back | 1921 | 1923 | 53 | 0 | 1 | 0 | 0 | 0 | 3 | 0 | 0 | 0 | 0 | 0 | 0 | 0 | 0 | 56 | 0 | 1 |
| Horace | Alain | Midfielder | 1996 | 1997 | 0 | 1 | 0 | 0 | 0 | 0 | 0 | 0 | 0 | 0 | 0 | 0 | 0 | 0 | 0 | 0 | 1 | 0 |
| Horne | Brian Simon | Goalkeeper | 1994 | 1996 | 73 | 0 | 0 | 0 | 0 | 0 | 2 | 0 | 0 | 4 | 0 | 0 | 2 | 1 | 0 | 81 | 1 | 0 |
| Horwood | Evan David | Left-Back | 2010 | 2012 | 82 | 4 | 3 | 0 | 0 | 0 | 5 | 0 | 0 | 3 | 0 | 0 | 4 | 0 | 1 | 94 | 4 | 4 |
| Houchen | Keith Morton | Centre-Forward | 1977 | 1997 | 264 | 15 | 92 | 0 | 0 | 0 | 6 | 1 | 0 | 17 | 1 | 2 | 6 | 0 | 0 | 293 | 17 | 94 |
| Howard | David Frederick | Centre-Forward | 1980 | 1982 | 6 | 3 | 4 | 0 | 0 | 0 | 0 | 0 | 0 | 0 | 0 | 0 | 1 | 2 | 0 | 7 | 5 | 4 |
| Howard | Steven John (Steve) | Forward | 1995 | 1998 | 117 | 25 | 26 | 0 | 0 | 0 | 3 | 0 | 0 | 6 | 0 | 1 | 5 | 0 | 2 | 131 | 25 | 29 |
| Howe | John Robert (Jack) | Left-Back | 1934 | 1936 | 24 | 0 | 0 | 0 | 0 | 0 | 0 | 0 | 0 | 0 | 0 | 0 | 2 | 0 | 0 | 26 | 0 | 0 |
| Howells | Peter | Outside-Left | 1956 | 1957 | 1 | 0 | 0 | 0 | 0 | 0 | 0 | 0 | 0 | 0 | 0 | 0 | 0 | 0 | 0 | 1 | 0 | 0 |
| Howey | Stephen Norman | Centre-Half-Back | 2004 | 2005 | 0 | 1 | 0 | 0 | 0 | 0 | 0 | 0 | 0 | 0 | 0 | 0 | 0 | 0 | 0 | 0 | 1 | 0 |
| Huberry | Robert (Bob) | Right-Back | 1921 | 1922 | 1 | 0 | 0 | 0 | 0 | 0 | 0 | 0 | 0 | 0 | 0 | 0 | 0 | 0 | 0 | 1 | 0 | 0 |
| Huggins | Albert | Inside/Centre-Forward | 1934 | 1936 | 11 | 0 | 2 | 0 | 0 | 0 | 0 | 0 | 0 | 0 | 0 | 0 | 2 | 0 | 0 | 13 | 0 | 2 |
| Hughes | Daniel Paul (Danny) | Midfielder | 1998 | 1999 | 6 | 2 | 0 | 0 | 0 | 0 | 0 | 0 | 0 | 0 | 0 | 0 | 0 | 0 | 0 | 6 | 2 | 0 |
| Hughes | James (Jimmy) | Centre-Forward | 1935 | 1936 | 8 | 0 | 3 | 0 | 0 | 0 | 0 | 0 | 0 | 0 | 0 | 0 | 0 | 0 | 0 | 8 | 0 | 3 |
| Hughes | John (Jack) | Left-Half-back | 1937 | 1938 | 36 | 0 | 1 | 0 | 0 | 0 | 2 | 0 | 0 | 0 | 0 | 0 | 2 | 0 | 0 | 40 | 0 | 1 |

| Surname | Forenames | Position | Career | | Football League | | | Play-offs | | | FA Cup | | | FL Cup | | | Other | | | Total | | |
|---|---|---|---|---|---|---|---|---|---|---|---|---|---|---|---|---|---|---|---|---|---|---|
| | | | Start | Finish | Apps | Sub | Gls | Apps | Sub | Gls | Apps | Sub | Gls | Apps | Sub | Gls | Apps | Sub | Gls | Apps | Sub | Gls |
| Hughes | William Henry (Billy) | Centre-Half-Back | 1946 | 1950 | 124 | 0 | 2 | 0 | 0 | 0 | 7 | 0 | 0 | 0 | 0 | 0 | 0 | 0 | 0 | 131 | 0 | 2 |
| Humphreys | Derek John Beattie | Goalkeeper | 1969 | 1970 | 4 | 0 | 0 | 0 | 0 | 0 | 0 | 0 | 0 | 0 | 0 | 0 | 0 | 0 | 0 | 4 | 0 | 0 |
| Humphreys | Richard John (Ritchie) | Defender/Midfielder | 2001 | 2012 | 412 | 38 | 33 | 7 | 0 | 0 | 28 | 1 | 2 | 12 | 0 | 0 | 10 | 3 | 1 | 469 | 42 | 36 |
| Hunt | Thomas Richardson (Tom) | Outside-Right | 1923 | 1924 | 2 | 0 | 0 | 0 | 0 | 0 | 0 | 0 | 0 | 0 | 0 | 0 | 0 | 0 | 0 | 2 | 0 | 0 |
| Hunter | Albert | Centre-Forward | 1925 | 1926 | 1 | 0 | 0 | 0 | 0 | 0 | 2 | 0 | 1 | 0 | 0 | 0 | 0 | 0 | 0 | 3 | 0 | 1 |
| Hunter | Philip (Phil) | Outside-Right | 1969 | 1970 | 1 | 0 | 0 | 0 | 0 | 0 | 0 | 0 | 0 | 0 | 0 | 0 | 0 | 0 | 0 | 1 | 0 | 0 |
| Hunter | Robert (Bob) | Inside-Right | 1970 | 1971 | 1 | 0 | 0 | 0 | 0 | 0 | 0 | 0 | 0 | 0 | 0 | 0 | 0 | 0 | 0 | 1 | 0 | 0 |
| Hutchison | Donald (Don) | Midfielder | 1989 | 1991 | 19 | 5 | 2 | 0 | 0 | 0 | 2 | 0 | 0 | 1 | 1 | 0 | 1 | 0 | 0 | 23 | 6 | 2 |
| Hutt | Stephen Graham (Steve) | Forward | 1995 | 1998 | 6 | 3 | 0 | 0 | 0 | 0 | 0 | 0 | 0 | 0 | 0 | 0 | 0 | 1 | 0 | 6 | 4 | 0 |
| Hyson | Matthew Alexander (Matty) | Forward | 1994 | 1995 | 1 | 4 | 0 | 0 | 0 | 0 | 0 | 0 | 0 | 0 | 1 | 0 | 0 | 0 | 0 | 1 | 5 | 0 |
| Ingram | Stuart Denevan (Denny) | Full Back | 1993 | 2000 | 192 | 7 | 10 | 0 | 0 | 0 | 7 | 0 | 0 | 13 | 2 | 0 | 8 | 0 | 0 | 220 | 9 | 10 |
| Irvine | Stuart Christopher | Forward | 1996 | 1999 | 13 | 18 | 2 | 0 | 0 | 0 | 0 | 1 | 0 | 1 | 1 | 0 | 0 | 3 | 0 | 14 | 23 | 2 |
| Isaac | James (Jimmy) | Inside/Wing-Forward | 1947 | 1949 | 56 | 0 | 9 | 0 | 0 | 0 | 4 | 0 | 2 | 0 | 0 | 0 | 0 | 0 | 0 | 60 | 0 | 11 |
| Istead | Steven Brian | Forward | 2002 | 2006 | 5 | 59 | 3 | 0 | 0 | 0 | 0 | 10 | 0 | 1 | 3 | 1 | 1 | 2 | 0 | 7 | 74 | 4 |
| Jacques | Joseph (Joe) | Central Defender | 1975 | 1976 | 5 | 0 | 0 | 0 | 0 | 0 | 0 | 0 | 0 | 0 | 0 | 0 | 0 | 0 | 0 | 5 | 0 | 0 |
| James | Luke Myers | Midfielder | 2011 | 2012 | 12 | 7 | 3 | 0 | 0 | 0 | 0 | 0 | 0 | 0 | 0 | 0 | 0 | 0 | 0 | 12 | 7 | 3 |
| Jarps | Joseph Henry (Joe) | Goalkeeper | 1931 | 1932 | 2 | 0 | 0 | 0 | 0 | 0 | 0 | 0 | 0 | 0 | 0 | 0 | 0 | 0 | 0 | 2 | 0 | 0 |
| Jarrie | Frederick (Fred) | Goalkeeper | 1945 | 1948 | 1 | 0 | 0 | 0 | 0 | 0 | 2 | 0 | 0 | 0 | 0 | 0 | 0 | 0 | 0 | 3 | 0 | 0 |
| Jobson | John Thomas (Jack) | Right/Centre-Half-Back | 1924 | 1927 | 102 | 0 | 2 | 0 | 0 | 0 | 10 | 0 | 0 | 0 | 0 | 0 | 0 | 0 | 0 | 112 | 0 | 2 |
| Johnrose | Leonard (Lenny) | Forward | 1991 | 1994 | 59 | 7 | 11 | 0 | 0 | 0 | 5 | 0 | 1 | 5 | 1 | 4 | 5 | 0 | 0 | 74 | 8 | 16 |
| Johnson | David | Inside-Left | 1974 | 1975 | 1 | 0 | 0 | 0 | 0 | 0 | 0 | 0 | 0 | 0 | 0 | 0 | 0 | 0 | 0 | 1 | 0 | 0 |
| Johnson | David Alan | Forward | 1991 | 1993 | 10 | 0 | 2 | 0 | 0 | 0 | 2 | 0 | 1 | 0 | 0 | 0 | 2 | 0 | 1 | 14 | 0 | 4 |
| Johnson | Dennis | Inside-Left | 1957 | 1958 | 2 | 0 | 0 | 0 | 0 | 0 | 0 | 0 | 0 | 0 | 0 | 0 | 0 | 0 | 0 | 2 | 0 | 0 |
| Johnson | Henry (Harry) | Full-Back | 1938 | 1939 | 24 | 0 | 0 | 0 | 0 | 0 | 2 | 0 | 0 | 0 | 0 | 0 | 1 | 0 | 0 | 27 | 0 | 0 |
| Johnson | John James (Jack) | Goalkeeper | 1933 | 1935 | 52 | 0 | 0 | 0 | 0 | 0 | 3 | 0 | 0 | 0 | 0 | 0 | 3 | 0 | 0 | 58 | 0 | 0 |
| Johnson | Kenneth (Ken) | Forward/Midfielder | 1949 | 1964 | 384 | 0 | 98 | 0 | 0 | 0 | 26 | 0 | 6 | 3 | 0 | 2 | 0 | 0 | 0 | 413 | 0 | 106 |
| Johnson | Kevin Peter | Midfielder | 1974 | 1984 | 134 | 14 | 11 | 0 | 0 | 0 | 6 | 1 | 1 | 11 | 1 | 2 | 4 | 1 | 0 | 155 | 17 | 14 |
| Johnson | Matthew Harrison (Matt) | Outside-Left | 1933 | 1934 | 6 | 0 | 0 | 0 | 0 | 0 | 0 | 0 | 0 | 0 | 0 | 0 | 0 | 0 | 0 | 6 | 0 | 0 |
| Johnson | Paul | Central Defender | 2010 | 2011 | 1 | 0 | 0 | 0 | 0 | 0 | 0 | 0 | 0 | 0 | 0 | 0 | 0 | 0 | 0 | 1 | 0 | 0 |
| Johnson | Thomas O. (Tom) | Goalkeeper | 1937 | 1938 | 12 | 0 | 0 | 0 | 0 | 0 | 0 | 0 | 0 | 0 | 0 | 0 | 0 | 0 | 0 | 12 | 0 | 0 |
| Jones | Carl | Central Defender | 2005 | 2007 | 1 | 0 | 0 | 0 | 0 | 0 | 0 | 0 | 0 | 0 | 0 | 0 | 1 | 0 | 0 | 2 | 0 | 0 |
| Jones | Gary | Centre-Forward | 1998 | 2000 | 42 | 3 | 7 | 1 | 1 | 0 | 2 | 0 | 1 | 2 | 0 | 0 | 1 | 1 | 0 | 48 | 5 | 8 |
| Jones | Henry (Jerry) | Left-Half-Back | 1946 | 1949 | 75 | 0 | 1 | 0 | 0 | 0 | 2 | 0 | 0 | 0 | 0 | 0 | 0 | 0 | 0 | 77 | 0 | 1 |
| Jones | Kenneth (Ken) | Left-Back | 1960 | 1962 | 33 | 0 | 0 | 0 | 0 | 0 | 1 | 0 | 0 | 1 | 0 | 0 | 0 | 0 | 0 | 35 | 0 | 0 |
| Jones | Richard Glynn (Ritchie) | Midfielder | 2008 | 2010 | 58 | 11 | 7 | 0 | 0 | 0 | 4 | 1 | 0 | 4 | 0 | 0 | 0 | 0 | 0 | 66 | 12 | 7 |

| | | | Career | | Football League | | | Play-offs | | | FA Cup | | | FL Cup | | | Other | | | Total | | |
|---|---|---|---|---|---|---|---|---|---|---|---|---|---|---|---|---|---|---|---|---|---|---|
| Surname | Forenames | Position | Start | Finish | Apps | Sub | Gls | Apps | Sub | Gls | Apps | Sub | Gls | Apps | Sub | Gls | Apps | Sub | Gls | Apps | Sub | Gls |
| Jones | Steven (Steve) | Goalkeeper | 1991 | 1996 | 45 | 3 | 0 | 0 | 0 | 0 | 2 | 0 | 0 | 4 | 0 | 0 | 1 | 0 | 0 | 52 | 3 | 0 |
| Jordan | Andrew Joseph (Andy) | Central Defender | 2003 | 2004 | 4 | 1 | 0 | 0 | 0 | 0 | 0 | 0 | 0 | 1 | 0 | 0 | 0 | 0 | 0 | 5 | 1 | 0 |
| Joyce | John | Outside-Right | 1966 | 1969 | 4 | 0 | 0 | 0 | 0 | 0 | 0 | 0 | 0 | 0 | 0 | 0 | 0 | 0 | 0 | 4 | 0 | 0 |
| Kean | Jacob Kendall (Jake) | Goalkeeper | 2010 | 2011 | 19 | 0 | 0 | 0 | 0 | 0 | 4 | 0 | 0 | 0 | 0 | 0 | 2 | 0 | 0 | 25 | 0 | 0 |
| Keenlyside | George J. | Inside/Wing-Forward | 1923 | 1924 | 24 | 0 | 1 | 0 | 0 | 0 | 3 | 0 | 1 | 0 | 0 | 0 | 0 | 0 | 0 | 27 | 0 | 2 |
| Keeys | Frederick (Fred) | Centre-Half-Back | 1945 | 1946 | 0 | 0 | 0 | 0 | 0 | 0 | 1 | 0 | 0 | 0 | 0 | 0 | 0 | 0 | 0 | 1 | 0 | 0 |
| Kell | George | Right/Left-Back | 1925 | 1928 | 71 | 0 | 1 | 0 | 0 | 0 | 4 | 0 | 0 | 0 | 0 | 0 | 0 | 0 | 0 | 75 | 0 | 1 |
| Kelly | James Patrick (Jimmy) | Left-Back | 1971 | 1972 | 5 | 0 | 0 | 0 | 0 | 0 | 0 | 0 | 0 | 0 | 0 | 0 | 0 | 0 | 0 | 5 | 0 | 0 |
| Kelly | Thomas John (Tom) | Left-Back | 1985 | 1986 | 14 | 1 | 0 | 0 | 0 | 0 | 0 | 0 | 0 | 2 | 0 | 0 | 1 | 0 | 0 | 17 | 1 | 0 |
| Kennedy | Alan Philip | Left-Back | 1987 | 1988 | 4 | 1 | 0 | 0 | 0 | 0 | 0 | 0 | 0 | 0 | 0 | 0 | 0 | 1 | 1 | 4 | 2 | 1 |
| Kennedy | Raymond (Ray) | Outside-Right | 1983 | 1984 | 18 | 5 | 3 | 0 | 0 | 0 | 0 | 0 | 0 | 0 | 0 | 0 | 1 | 0 | 0 | 19 | 5 | 3 |
| Kerr | Peter | Right-Half-Back/Outside-Right | 1949 | 1950 | 2 | 0 | 0 | 0 | 0 | 0 | 0 | 0 | 0 | 0 | 0 | 0 | 0 | 0 | 0 | 2 | 0 | 0 |
| Kerr | Robert (Bobby) | Midfielder | 1980 | 1982 | 48 | 1 | 2 | 0 | 0 | 0 | 2 | 0 | 0 | 3 | 0 | 0 | 3 | 0 | 0 | 56 | 1 | 2 |
| Kessler | Laurie P. | Outside-Left | 1921 | 1922 | 13 | 0 | 0 | 0 | 0 | 0 | 11 | 0 | 3 | 0 | 0 | 0 | 0 | 0 | 0 | 24 | 0 | 3 |
| Key | Lance William | Goalkeeper | 1995 | 1996 | 1 | 0 | 0 | 0 | 0 | 0 | 0 | 0 | 0 | 0 | 0 | 0 | 0 | 0 | 0 | 1 | 0 | 0 |
| King | Alan | Wing-Forward | 1967 | 1968 | 0 | 1 | 0 | 0 | 0 | 0 | 0 | 0 | 0 | 0 | 0 | 0 | 0 | 0 | 0 | 0 | 1 | 0 |
| Kirk | Henry Joseph (Harry) | Outside-Left | 1969 | 1971 | 42 | 3 | 5 | 0 | 0 | 0 | 2 | 0 | 1 | 0 | 0 | 0 | 0 | 0 | 0 | 44 | 3 | 6 |
| Knowles | Darren Thomas | Right-Back | 1996 | 2001 | 164 | 4 | 2 | 2 | 0 | 0 | 5 | 0 | 0 | 7 | 1 | 0 | 8 | 0 | 0 | 186 | 5 | 2 |
| Knox | Thomas (Tommy) | Goalkeeper | 1933 | 1934 | 25 | 0 | 0 | 0 | 0 | 0 | 3 | 0 | 0 | 0 | 0 | 0 | 1 | 0 | 0 | 29 | 0 | 0 |
| Konstantopoulos | Dimitrios (Dimi) | Goalkeeper | 2004 | 2007 | 117 | 0 | 0 | 3 | 0 | 0 | 10 | 0 | 0 | 5 | 0 | 0 | 4 | 0 | 0 | 139 | 0 | 0 |
| Kyle | Kevin Alistair | Forward | 2008 | 2009 | 15 | 0 | 5 | 0 | 0 | 0 | 0 | 0 | 0 | 0 | 0 | 0 | 0 | 0 | 0 | 15 | 0 | 5 |
| Lackenby | George | Full/Centre-Half-Back | 1960 | 1963 | 86 | 0 | 1 | 0 | 0 | 0 | 3 | 0 | 0 | 1 | 0 | 0 | 0 | 0 | 0 | 90 | 0 | 1 |
| Lamb | Alan | Inside-Left | 1989 | 1991 | 4 | 10 | 0 | 0 | 0 | 0 | 0 | 1 | 0 | 0 | 0 | 0 | 1 | 1 | 0 | 5 | 12 | 0 |
| Lambert | Eric Victor | Centre-Half-Back | 1946 | 1947 | 16 | 0 | 0 | 0 | 0 | 0 | 2 | 0 | 0 | 0 | 0 | 0 | 0 | 0 | 0 | 18 | 0 | 0 |
| Lange | Rune | Forward | 2008 | 2009 | 2 | 1 | 1 | 0 | 0 | 0 | 0 | 0 | 0 | 0 | 0 | 0 | 0 | 0 | 0 | 2 | 1 | 1 |
| Langland | John (Johnny) | Inside/Wing-Forward | 1958 | 1960 | 38 | 0 | 11 | 0 | 0 | 0 | 3 | 0 | 0 | 0 | 0 | 0 | 0 | 0 | 0 | 41 | 0 | 11 |
| Langridge | John | Inside-Left | 1982 | 1983 | 5 | 1 | 0 | 0 | 0 | 0 | 0 | 0 | 0 | 0 | 0 | 0 | 0 | 0 | 0 | 5 | 1 | 0 |
| Larkin | Colin | Midfielder | 2009 | 2012 | 27 | 27 | 4 | 0 | 0 | 0 | 2 | 1 | 0 | 0 | 3 | 0 | 1 | 2 | 0 | 30 | 33 | 4 |
| Larkin | Gordon Thomas | Outside-Left | 1977 | 1980 | 5 | 9 | 1 | 0 | 0 | 0 | 0 | 0 | 0 | 0 | 1 | 0 | 0 | 0 | 0 | 5 | 10 | 1 |
| Larsen | Stig Olav | Forward | 1997 | 1998 | 0 | 4 | 0 | 0 | 0 | 0 | 0 | 0 | 0 | 0 | 0 | 0 | 0 | 1 | 0 | 0 | 5 | 0 |
| Lawrence | Mark | Forward/Midfielder | 1977 | 1984 | 155 | 13 | 24 | 0 | 0 | 0 | 8 | 0 | 0 | 7 | 1 | 1 | 3 | 0 | 1 | 173 | 14 | 26 |
| Lealman | Fred | Outside-Right | 1938 | 1939 | 7 | 0 | 2 | 0 | 0 | 0 | 0 | 0 | 0 | 0 | 0 | 0 | 1 | 0 | 0 | 8 | 0 | 2 |
| Lee | Bert | Centre-Forward | 1921 | 1922 | 3 | 0 | 1 | 0 | 0 | 0 | 0 | 0 | 0 | 0 | 0 | 0 | 0 | 0 | 0 | 3 | 0 | 1 |
| Lee | Graeme Barry | Central Defender | 1995 | 2007 | 211 | 11 | 19 | 5 | 1 | 0 | 8 | 1 | 0 | 7 | 2 | 1 | 8 | 1 | 2 | 239 | 16 | 22 |
| Lee | John William (Jack) | Outside-Left | 1924 | 1925 | 2 | 0 | 0 | 0 | 0 | 0 | 0 | 0 | 0 | 0 | 0 | 0 | 0 | 0 | 0 | 2 | 0 | 0 |

| | | | Career | | Football League | | | Play-offs | | | FA Cup | | | FL Cup | | | Other | | | Total | | |
|---|---|---|---|---|---|---|---|---|---|---|---|---|---|---|---|---|---|---|---|---|---|---|
| Surname | Forenames | Position | Start | Finish | Apps | Sub | Gls | Apps | Sub | Gls | Apps | Sub | Gls | Apps | Sub | Gls | Apps | Sub | Gls | Apps | Sub | Gls |
| Lee | Thomas Joseph (Tommy) | Forward | 1969 | 1970 | 6 | 0 | 0 | 0 | 0 | 0 | 0 | 0 | 0 | 1 | 0 | 0 | 0 | 0 | 0 | 7 | 0 | 0 |
| Lee-Barratt | Aran | Goalkeeper | 2007 | 2009 | 55 | 0 | 0 | 0 | 0 | 0 | 5 | 0 | 0 | 3 | 0 | 0 | 2 | 0 | 0 | 65 | 0 | 0 |
| Lees | Norman | Forward/Midfielder | 1970 | 1971 | 20 | 0 | 1 | 0 | 0 | 0 | 0 | 0 | 0 | 0 | 0 | 0 | 0 | 0 | 0 | 20 | 0 | 1 |
| Leonard | Henry (Harry) | Right-Back | 1948 | 1949 | 2 | 0 | 0 | 0 | 0 | 0 | 1 | 0 | 0 | 0 | 0 | 0 | 0 | 0 | 0 | 3 | 0 | 0 |
| Lester | Michael John Anthony (Mike) | Outside-Left | 1985 | 1986 | 11 | 0 | 1 | 0 | 0 | 0 | 0 | 0 | 0 | 0 | 0 | 0 | 2 | 0 | 0 | 13 | 0 | 1 |
| Lewis | L. | Centre-Forward | 1945 | 1946 | 0 | 0 | 0 | 0 | 0 | 0 | 1 | 0 | 0 | 0 | 0 | 0 | 0 | 0 | 0 | 1 | 0 | 0 |
| Liddle | Bryan | Left-Back | 1984 | 1985 | 12 | 1 | 0 | 0 | 0 | 0 | 0 | 0 | 0 | 0 | 0 | 0 | 0 | 0 | 0 | 12 | 1 | 0 |
| Liddle | Gary Daniel | Defender | 2006 | 2012 | 240 | 8 | 18 | 0 | 0 | 0 | 13 | 2 | 2 | 12 | 0 | 0 | 9 | 0 | 1 | 274 | 10 | 21 |
| Liddle | Isaac | Inside-Right | 1926 | 1928 | 12 | 0 | 2 | 0 | 0 | 0 | 0 | 0 | 0 | 0 | 0 | 0 | 0 | 0 | 0 | 12 | 0 | 2 |
| Lilley | Thomas (Tom) | Right-Back | 1924 | 1926 | 60 | 0 | 0 | 0 | 0 | 0 | 3 | 0 | 0 | 0 | 0 | 0 | 0 | 0 | 0 | 63 | 0 | 0 |
| Linacre | John Edward | Forward/Midfielder | 1977 | 1984 | 207 | 4 | 12 | 0 | 0 | 0 | 11 | 1 | 1 | 7 | 0 | 0 | 1 | 0 | 0 | 226 | 5 | 13 |
| Linacre | Philip (Phil) | Forward/Full-Back | 1980 | 1984 | 78 | 4 | 17 | 0 | 0 | 0 | 6 | 0 | 3 | 1 | 1 | 0 | 3 | 0 | 0 | 88 | 5 | 20 |
| Linacre | William (Billy) | Outside-Right | 1953 | 1956 | 89 | 0 | 10 | 0 | 0 | 0 | 12 | 0 | 2 | 0 | 0 | 0 | 0 | 0 | 0 | 101 | 0 | 12 |
| Lindsay | Duncan Morton | Centre-Forward | 1934 | 1935 | 37 | 0 | 21 | 0 | 0 | 0 | 3 | 0 | 1 | 0 | 0 | 0 | 3 | 0 | 0 | 43 | 0 | 22 |
| Linighan | Andrew (Andy) | Central Defender | 1980 | 1984 | 110 | 0 | 4 | 0 | 0 | 0 | 8 | 0 | 0 | 7 | 1 | 1 | 5 | 0 | 4 | 130 | 1 | 9 |
| Linighan | David | Central Defender | 1981 | 1986 | 84 | 7 | 5 | 0 | 0 | 0 | 4 | 0 | 0 | 3 | 1 | 1 | 3 | 0 | 1 | 94 | 8 | 7 |
| Lister | James (Jimmy) | Centre-Forward | 1921 | 1922 | 8 | 0 | 2 | 0 | 0 | 0 | 7 | 0 | 6 | 0 | 0 | 0 | 0 | 0 | 0 | 15 | 0 | 8 |
| Lithgo | Gordon | Inside-Forward/Outside-Right | 1960 | 1964 | 37 | 0 | 8 | 0 | 0 | 0 | 0 | 0 | 0 | 2 | 0 | 1 | 0 | 0 | 0 | 39 | 0 | 9 |
| Little | Alan | Midfielder | 1985 | 1987 | 12 | 0 | 1 | 0 | 0 | 0 | 0 | 0 | 0 | 1 | 0 | 0 | 0 | 1 | 0 | 13 | 1 | 1 |
| Little | Robert A. | Goalkeeper | 1926 | 1927 | 4 | 0 | 0 | 0 | 0 | 0 | 0 | 0 | 0 | 0 | 0 | 0 | 0 | 0 | 0 | 4 | 0 | 0 |
| Livingstone | Allan McKenzie | Inside-Forward | 1924 | 1925 | 3 | 0 | 1 | 0 | 0 | 0 | 0 | 0 | 0 | 0 | 0 | 0 | 0 | 0 | 0 | 3 | 0 | 1 |
| Livingstone | Joseph (Joe) | Forward | 1965 | 1967 | 15 | 0 | 5 | 0 | 0 | 0 | 0 | 0 | 0 | 2 | 0 | 1 | 0 | 0 | 0 | 17 | 0 | 6 |
| Livsey | Gordon William | Goalkeeper | 1977 | 1978 | 6 | 0 | 0 | 0 | 0 | 0 | 0 | 0 | 0 | 0 | 0 | 0 | 0 | 0 | 0 | 6 | 0 | 0 |
| Llewellyn | Christopher (Chris) Mark | Forward | 2005 | 2006 | 24 | 5 | 0 | 0 | 0 | 0 | 1 | 0 | 1 | 0 | 1 | 0 | 1 | 0 | 0 | 26 | 6 | 1 |
| Loadwick | Derek | Outside-Left | 1978 | 1980 | 49 | 2 | 1 | 0 | 0 | 0 | 4 | 0 | 0 | 2 | 0 | 0 | 0 | 0 | 0 | 55 | 2 | 1 |
| Locker | Stephen | Centre-Half-Back | 1988 | 1989 | 0 | 1 | 0 | 0 | 0 | 0 | 0 | 0 | 0 | 0 | 0 | 0 | 0 | 0 | 0 | 0 | 1 | 0 |
| Lockhart | Keith Samuel | Outside-Left | 1986 | 1987 | 2 | 0 | 0 | 0 | 0 | 0 | 0 | 0 | 0 | 0 | 0 | 0 | 0 | 0 | 0 | 2 | 0 | 0 |
| Longmore | Samuel James (Jimmy) | Right-Back | 1922 | 1923 | 12 | 0 | 0 | 0 | 0 | 0 | 0 | 0 | 0 | 0 | 0 | 0 | 0 | 0 | 0 | 12 | 0 | 0 |
| Lonie | Arthur | Right-Half-Back | 1923 | 1924 | 10 | 0 | 0 | 0 | 0 | 0 | 3 | 0 | 2 | 0 | 0 | 0 | 0 | 0 | 0 | 13 | 0 | 2 |
| Lonsdale | Joseph Stanley (Stan) | Left-Back/Outside-Right | 1960 | 1961 | 9 | 0 | 0 | 0 | 0 | 0 | 0 | 0 | 0 | 0 | 0 | 0 | 0 | 0 | 0 | 9 | 0 | 0 |
| Lormor | Anthony (Tony) | Centre-Forward | 2000 | 2002 | 26 | 22 | 9 | 2 | 0 | 0 | 0 | 0 | 0 | 1 | 1 | 0 | 0 | 3 | 0 | 29 | 26 | 9 |
| Love | Robert William (Bob) | Centre/Inside-Forward | 1938 | 1939 | 13 | 0 | 2 | 0 | 0 | 0 | 0 | 0 | 0 | 0 | 0 | 0 | 2 | 0 | 1 | 15 | 0 | 3 |
| Lowe | Kenneth (Kenny) | Midfielder | 1981 | 1996 | 63 | 4 | 6 | 0 | 0 | 0 | 2 | 0 | 0 | 3 | 1 | 0 | 2 | 1 | 0 | 70 | 6 | 6 |
| Lowe | Simon John | Inside/Outside-Right | 1986 | 1987 | 12 | 2 | 1 | 0 | 0 | 0 | 0 | 0 | 0 | 1 | 1 | 0 | 0 | 2 | 0 | 13 | 5 | 1 |
| Lucas | Richard | Left-Back | 1996 | 1998 | 49 | 0 | 2 | 0 | 0 | 0 | 1 | 0 | 0 | 2 | 0 | 0 | 1 | 0 | 0 | 53 | 0 | 2 |

| Surname | Forenames | Position | Career Start | Career Finish | Football League Apps | Football League Sub | Football League Gls | Play-offs Apps | Play-offs Sub | Play-offs Gls | FA Cup Apps | FA Cup Sub | FA Cup Gls | FL Cup Apps | FL Cup Sub | FL Cup Gls | Other Apps | Other Sub | Other Gls | Total Apps | Total Sub | Total Gls |
|---|---|---|---|---|---|---|---|---|---|---|---|---|---|---|---|---|---|---|---|---|---|---|
| Luckett | Paul | Left-Back | 1975 | 1977 | 19 | 0 | 0 | 0 | 0 | 0 | 0 | 0 | 0 | 0 | 0 | 0 | 0 | 0 | 0 | 19 | 0 | 0 |
| Luke | George Thomas | Outside-Left | 1953 | 1960 | 186 | 0 | 60 | 0 | 0 | 0 | 19 | 0 | 8 | 0 | 0 | 0 | 0 | 0 | 0 | 205 | 0 | 68 |
| Lumley | Robert (Bobby) | Inside-Forward | 1954 | 1961 | 145 | 0 | 25 | 0 | 0 | 0 | 7 | 0 | 1 | 1 | 0 | 0 | 0 | 0 | 0 | 153 | 0 | 26 |
| Lumley | Sydney (Sid) | Centre-Forward | 1931 | 1932 | 25 | 0 | 18 | 0 | 0 | 0 | 1 | 0 | 0 | 0 | 0 | 0 | 0 | 0 | 0 | 26 | 0 | 18 |
| Luscombe | Nathan John | Midfielder | 2011 | 2012 | 3 | 10 | 1 | 0 | 0 | 0 | 0 | 1 | 0 | 0 | 1 | 0 | 1 | 0 | 0 | 4 | 12 | 1 |
| Lynch | Christopher John (Chris) | Defender/Midfielder | 1992 | 1996 | 38 | 12 | 2 | 0 | 0 | 0 | 0 | 1 | 0 | 3 | 4 | 0 | 1 | 0 | 0 | 42 | 17 | 2 |
| McAndrew | Anthony (Tony) | Left-Half-Back | 1988 | 1989 | 4 | 0 | 0 | 0 | 0 | 0 | 0 | 0 | 0 | 0 | 0 | 0 | 0 | 0 | 0 | 4 | 0 | 0 |
| McAuley | Sean | Left-Back | 1995 | 1997 | 84 | 0 | 1 | 0 | 0 | 0 | 3 | 0 | 0 | 6 | 0 | 0 | 3 | 0 | 0 | 96 | 0 | 1 |
| McAvoy | Andrew David (Andy) | Midfielder | 1999 | 2001 | 7 | 14 | 0 | 0 | 2 | 0 | 0 | 0 | 0 | 0 | 1 | 0 | 1 | 1 | 0 | 8 | 18 | 0 |
| McBurney | Michael Leslie (Mike) | Inside-Right | 1974 | 1975 | 5 | 1 | 1 | 0 | 0 | 0 | 0 | 0 | 0 | 0 | 0 | 0 | 0 | 0 | 0 | 5 | 1 | 1 |
| McCaffery | Aidan | Wing-Half-Back | 1986 | 1987 | 6 | 0 | 0 | 0 | 0 | 0 | 0 | 0 | 0 | 0 | 0 | 0 | 0 | 0 | 0 | 6 | 0 | 0 |
| MacCallum | Stewart | Right-Half-Back | 1956 | 1957 | 2 | 0 | 0 | 0 | 0 | 0 | 0 | 0 | 0 | 0 | 0 | 0 | 0 | 0 | 0 | 2 | 0 | 0 |
| McCambridge | James (Jimmy) | Forward/Left-Half-Back | 1936 | 1937 | 16 | 0 | 4 | 0 | 0 | 0 | 0 | 0 | 0 | 0 | 0 | 0 | 1 | 0 | 0 | 17 | 0 | 4 |
| McCann | Ryan Patrick | Midfielder | 2003 | 2004 | 0 | 4 | 0 | 0 | 0 | 0 | 0 | 0 | 0 | 0 | 1 | 0 | 0 | 0 | 0 | 0 | 5 | 0 |
| McCarthy | Jonathan David (Jon) | Inside-Left | 1987 | 1988 | 0 | 1 | 0 | 0 | 0 | 0 | 0 | 0 | 0 | 0 | 0 | 0 | 0 | 0 | 0 | 0 | 1 | 0 |
| McClure | William (Willie) | Outside-Left | 1950 | 1953 | 118 | 0 | 24 | 0 | 0 | 0 | 6 | 0 | 2 | 0 | 0 | 0 | 0 | 0 | 0 | 124 | 0 | 26 |
| McCluskey | Andrew (Andy) | Midfielder | 1969 | 1970 | 4 | 2 | 0 | 0 | 0 | 0 | 0 | 0 | 0 | 0 | 0 | 0 | 0 | 0 | 0 | 4 | 2 | 0 |
| McCready | Thomas (Tommy) | Inside-Forward | 1949 | 1950 | 34 | 0 | 3 | 0 | 0 | 0 | 2 | 0 | 0 | 0 | 0 | 0 | 0 | 0 | 0 | 36 | 0 | 3 |
| McCreery | David | Defender/Midfielder | 1991 | 1995 | 34 | 5 | 0 | 0 | 0 | 0 | 4 | 0 | 0 | 2 | 1 | 0 | 0 | 0 | 0 | 40 | 6 | 0 |
| McCubbin | Robert (Bert) | Outside-Right | 1963 | 1964 | 2 | 0 | 0 | 0 | 0 | 0 | 0 | 0 | 0 | 0 | 0 | 0 | 0 | 0 | 0 | 2 | 0 | 0 |
| McCunnie | James (Jamie) | Defender/Midfielder | 2007 | 2009 | 33 | 11 | 1 | 0 | 0 | 0 | 3 | 1 | 0 | 4 | 0 | 0 | 3 | 1 | 0 | 43 | 13 | 1 |
| McDonald | Christopher William (Chris) | Central Defender | 1996 | 1998 | 18 | 2 | 0 | 0 | 0 | 0 | 0 | 0 | 0 | 2 | 0 | 0 | 0 | 0 | 0 | 20 | 2 | 0 |
| McDonald | Dean | Forward | 2005 | 2006 | 4 | 1 | 1 | 0 | 0 | 0 | 1 | 0 | 0 | 0 | 0 | 0 | 0 | 0 | 0 | 5 | 1 | 1 |
| MacDonald | Garry | Right-Back | 1989 | 1991 | 10 | 8 | 1 | 0 | 0 | 0 | 0 | 0 | 0 | 0 | 1 | 0 | 0 | 0 | 0 | 10 | 9 | 1 |
| McEwan | Stanley (Stan) | Defender/Midfielder | 1989 | 1990 | 14 | 0 | 2 | 0 | 0 | 0 | 1 | 0 | 0 | 1 | 0 | 0 | 1 | 0 | 1 | 17 | 0 | 3 |
| McGarry | Thomas (Tommy) | Centre-Forward | 1938 | 1939 | 20 | 0 | 12 | 0 | 0 | 0 | 2 | 0 | 0 | 0 | 0 | 0 | 2 | 0 | 2 | 24 | 0 | 14 |
| McGeough | James (Jimmy) | Inside-Left | 1972 | 1973 | 1 | 1 | 0 | 0 | 0 | 0 | 0 | 0 | 0 | 0 | 0 | 0 | 0 | 0 | 0 | 1 | 1 | 0 |
| McGinley | John | Outside-Left | 1986 | 1987 | 2 | 0 | 0 | 0 | 0 | 0 | 0 | 0 | 0 | 0 | 0 | 0 | 0 | 0 | 0 | 2 | 0 | 0 |
| McGlen | James (Jim) | Outside-Left | 1926 | 1927 | 20 | 0 | 3 | 0 | 0 | 0 | 1 | 0 | 0 | 0 | 0 | 0 | 0 | 0 | 0 | 21 | 0 | 3 |
| McGovern | John Prescott | Outside-Right | 1965 | 1969 | 69 | 3 | 5 | 0 | 0 | 0 | 2 | 0 | 0 | 2 | 0 | 2 | 0 | 0 | 0 | 73 | 3 | 7 |
| MacGregor | James Peter | Left-Half-Back/Inside-Left | 1953 | 1955 | 2 | 0 | 0 | 0 | 0 | 0 | 0 | 0 | 0 | 0 | 0 | 0 | 0 | 0 | 0 | 2 | 0 | 0 |
| MacGregor | Terence James (Terry) | Inside-Forward/Half-Back | 1956 | 1963 | 47 | 0 | 2 | 0 | 0 | 0 | 1 | 0 | 0 | 0 | 0 | 0 | 0 | 0 | 0 | 48 | 0 | 2 |
| McGuckin | Thomas Ian | Central Defender | 1991 | 1999 | 155 | 5 | 8 | 0 | 0 | 0 | 6 | 0 | 0 | 13 | 1 | 1 | 6 | 0 | 0 | 180 | 6 | 9 |
| McGuigan | Thomas (Tommy) | Inside-Forward | 1950 | 1958 | 325 | 0 | 75 | 0 | 0 | 0 | 25 | 0 | 4 | 0 | 0 | 0 | 0 | 0 | 0 | 350 | 0 | 79 |
| Mackay | Michael | Centre-forward | 2007 | 2011 | 20 | 30 | 7 | 0 | 0 | 0 | 5 | 2 | 2 | 0 | 2 | 0 | 1 | 2 | 1 | 26 | 36 | 10 |

| Surname | Forenames | Position | Career Start | Career Finish | Football League Apps | Football League Sub | Football League Gls | Play-offs Apps | Play-offs Sub | Play-offs Gls | FA Cup Apps | FA Cup Sub | FA Cup Gls | FL Cup Apps | FL Cup Sub | FL Cup Gls | Other Apps | Other Sub | Other Gls | Total Apps | Total Sub | Total Gls |
|---|---|---|---|---|---|---|---|---|---|---|---|---|---|---|---|---|---|---|---|---|---|---|
| McKellar | David | Goalkeeper | 1988 | 1989 | 5 | 0 | 0 | 0 | 0 | 0 | 0 | 0 | 0 | 2 | 0 | 0 | 0 | 0 | 0 | 7 | 0 | 0 |
| McKenna | Francis (Frank) | Centre-Forward/Outside-Right | 1959 | 1960 | 32 | 0 | 5 | 0 | 0 | 0 | 1 | 0 | 0 | 0 | 0 | 0 | 0 | 0 | 0 | 33 | 0 | 5 |
| McKeown | Joseph Francis (Joe) | Inside-Right | 1950 | 1951 | 46 | 0 | 7 | 0 | 0 | 0 | 2 | 0 | 0 | 0 | 0 | 0 | 0 | 0 | 0 | 48 | 0 | 7 |
| Mackey | Thomas Scott (Tom) | Half-Back | 1928 | 1930 | 30 | 0 | 1 | 0 | 0 | 0 | 2 | 0 | 0 | 0 | 0 | 0 | 0 | 0 | 0 | 32 | 0 | 1 |
| Mackie | James (Jimmy) | Outside-Left | 1937 | 1939 | 6 | 0 | 2 | 0 | 0 | 0 | 0 | 0 | 0 | 0 | 0 | 0 | 1 | 0 | 0 | 7 | 0 | 2 |
| McKinnon | Robert (Rob) | Left-Back | 1986 | 1999 | 253 | 1 | 7 | 0 | 0 | 0 | 15 | 0 | 0 | 15 | 0 | 0 | 15 | 0 | 0 | 298 | 1 | 7 |
| McLaughlin | James Charles (Jimmy) | Outside-Left | 1953 | 1954 | 13 | 0 | 2 | 0 | 0 | 0 | 0 | 0 | 0 | 0 | 0 | 0 | 0 | 0 | 0 | 13 | 0 | 2 |
| McLean | David John | Right-Half-Back | 1986 | 1987 | 6 | 0 | 0 | 0 | 0 | 0 | 0 | 0 | 0 | 0 | 0 | 0 | 0 | 0 | 0 | 6 | 0 | 0 |
| McLean | John Derek | Inside/Outside-Right | 1961 | 1964 | 89 | 0 | 16 | 0 | 0 | 0 | 5 | 0 | 1 | 2 | 0 | 0 | 0 | 0 | 0 | 96 | 0 | 17 |
| McLean | Robert | Centre-Forward | 1937 | 1938 | 1 | 0 | 0 | 0 | 0 | 0 | 0 | 0 | 0 | 0 | 0 | 0 | 0 | 0 | 0 | 1 | 0 | 0 |
| McLeod | Robert Alexander (Bobby) | Central Defender | 1965 | 1969 | 23 | 5 | 0 | 0 | 0 | 0 | 1 | 0 | 0 | 0 | 0 | 0 | 0 | 0 | 0 | 24 | 5 | 0 |
| McMahon | Francis Gerard (Frank) | Left-Half-Back | 1973 | 1974 | 7 | 0 | 0 | 0 | 0 | 0 | 0 | 0 | 0 | 0 | 0 | 0 | 0 | 0 | 0 | 7 | 0 | 0 |
| McMahon | Hugh (Hughie) | Outside-Left | 1945 | 1948 | 28 | 0 | 7 | 0 | 0 | 0 | 4 | 0 | 3 | 0 | 0 | 0 | 0 | 0 | 0 | 32 | 0 | 10 |
| McMahon | Kevin | Forward | 1973 | 1976 | 104 | 3 | 29 | 0 | 0 | 0 | 7 | 0 | 1 | 12 | 0 | 4 | 0 | 0 | 0 | 123 | 3 | 34 |
| McMaster | Christopher (Chris) | Forward | 1976 | 1978 | 3 | 1 | 0 | 0 | 0 | 0 | 0 | 0 | 0 | 0 | 0 | 0 | 0 | 0 | 0 | 3 | 1 | 0 |
| McMordie | Alexander (Eric) | Inside/Outside-Right | 1976 | 1978 | 46 | 1 | 2 | 0 | 0 | 0 | 2 | 0 | 0 | 2 | 0 | 0 | 0 | 0 | 0 | 50 | 1 | 2 |
| McNamee | Gerard (Ged) | Inside/Outside-Right | 1979 | 1983 | 2 | 2 | 0 | 0 | 0 | 0 | 0 | 0 | 0 | 0 | 0 | 0 | 0 | 0 | 0 | 2 | 2 | 0 |
| McNamee | John | Centre-Half-Back | 1973 | 1974 | 2 | 0 | 0 | 0 | 0 | 0 | 0 | 0 | 0 | 0 | 0 | 0 | 0 | 0 | 0 | 2 | 0 | 0 |
| McPartland | Desmond (Des) | Goalkeeper | 1969 | 1971 | 56 | 0 | 0 | 0 | 0 | 0 | 1 | 0 | 0 | 1 | 0 | 0 | 0 | 0 | 0 | 58 | 0 | 0 |
| MacPhail | John | Centre-Half-Back | 1990 | 1995 | 159 | 4 | 4 | 0 | 0 | 0 | 11 | 0 | 0 | 11 | 0 | 1 | 11 | 0 | 0 | 192 | 4 | 5 |
| McPheat | William (Willie) | Inside-Left | 1965 | 1966 | 13 | 2 | 2 | 0 | 0 | 0 | 2 | 0 | 2 | 0 | 0 | 0 | 0 | 0 | 0 | 15 | 2 | 4 |
| McStay | William John (Willie) | Right-Back | 1989 | 1990 | 3 | 0 | 0 | 0 | 0 | 0 | 0 | 0 | 0 | 0 | 0 | 0 | 0 | 0 | 0 | 3 | 0 | 0 |
| McSweeney | Leon | Winger | 2009 | 2011 | 48 | 29 | 3 | 0 | 0 | 0 | 4 | 0 | 0 | 2 | 2 | 0 | 2 | 1 | 1 | 56 | 32 | 4 |
| Maddison | William Hartley | Outside-Right | 1973 | 1975 | 3 | 1 | 0 | 0 | 0 | 0 | 0 | 0 | 0 | 0 | 0 | 0 | 0 | 0 | 0 | 3 | 1 | 0 |
| Maggiore | Anthony (Tony) | Full-Back/Midfielder | 1975 | 1977 | 24 | 4 | 0 | 0 | 0 | 0 | 1 | 0 | 0 | 2 | 0 | 0 | 0 | 0 | 0 | 27 | 4 | 0 |
| Maidens | Michael Douglas | Midfielder | 2004 | 2008 | 11 | 14 | 1 | 0 | 0 | 0 | 1 | 1 | 0 | 0 | 1 | 0 | 1 | 2 | 0 | 13 | 18 | 1 |
| Makepeace | Ralph | Half-Back | 1932 | 1934 | 45 | 0 | 2 | 0 | 0 | 0 | 3 | 0 | 0 | 0 | 0 | 0 | 1 | 0 | 0 | 49 | 0 | 2 |
| Malley | Philip (Phil) | Inside-Right | 1983 | 1984 | 0 | 1 | 0 | 0 | 0 | 0 | 0 | 0 | 0 | 0 | 0 | 0 | 0 | 0 | 0 | 0 | 1 | 0 |
| Malone | Richard Philip (Dick) | Right-Back | 1977 | 1979 | 36 | 0 | 2 | 0 | 0 | 0 | 2 | 0 | 0 | 4 | 0 | 0 | 0 | 0 | 0 | 42 | 0 | 2 |
| Marshall | William (Billy) | Full-Back | 1964 | 1966 | 57 | 0 | 0 | 0 | 0 | 0 | 0 | 0 | 0 | 3 | 0 | 0 | 0 | 0 | 0 | 60 | 0 | 0 |
| Mason | Arthur | Full-Back | 1929 | 1932 | 18 | 0 | 0 | 0 | 0 | 0 | 1 | 0 | 0 | 0 | 0 | 0 | 0 | 0 | 0 | 19 | 0 | 0 |
| Mason | Gary Ronald | Midfielder | 1999 | 2000 | 5 | 1 | 0 | 0 | 0 | 0 | 1 | 0 | 0 | 0 | 0 | 0 | 1 | 0 | 0 | 7 | 1 | 0 |
| Mason | Robert (Bobby) | Centre-Half-Back | 1928 | 1929 | 13 | 0 | 1 | 0 | 0 | 0 | 1 | 0 | 0 | 0 | 0 | 0 | 0 | 0 | 0 | 14 | 0 | 1 |
| Mason | Thomas Mason (Tom) | Right-Half-Back | 1946 | 1947 | 5 | 0 | 0 | 0 | 0 | 0 | 0 | 0 | 0 | 0 | 0 | 0 | 0 | 0 | 0 | 5 | 0 | 0 |
| Mathison | George | Left-Half-Back | 1937 | 1938 | 0 | 0 | 0 | 0 | 0 | 0 | 0 | 0 | 0 | 0 | 0 | 0 | 1 | 0 | 0 | 1 | 0 | 0 |

| Surname | Forenames | Position | Career Start | Career Finish | Football League Apps | Football League Sub | Football League Gls | Play-offs Apps | Play-offs Sub | Play-offs Gls | FA Cup Apps | FA Cup Sub | FA Cup Gls | FL Cup Apps | FL Cup Sub | FL Cup Gls | Other Apps | Other Sub | Other Gls | Total Apps | Total Sub | Total Gls |
|---|---|---|---|---|---|---|---|---|---|---|---|---|---|---|---|---|---|---|---|---|---|---|
| Melville | Alan Allistair | Centre-Half-Back | 1960 | 1962 | 5 | 0 | 0 | 0 | 0 | 0 | 0 | 0 | 0 | 1 | 0 | 0 | 0 | 0 | 0 | 6 | 0 | 0 |
| Middleton | Charles William (Charlie) | Inside-Left | 1936 | 1937 | 1 | 0 | 0 | 0 | 0 | 0 | 0 | 0 | 0 | 0 | 0 | 0 | 0 | 0 | 0 | 1 | 0 | 0 |
| Midgley | Craig Steven | Forward | 1997 | 2001 | 61 | 35 | 18 | 2 | 0 | 0 | 3 | 0 | 2 | 2 | 2 | 0 | 7 | 1 | 1 | 75 | 38 | 21 |
| Mike | Adrian Roosevelt (Adie) | Centre-Forward | 1996 | 1997 | 7 | 0 | 1 | 0 | 0 | 0 | 0 | 0 | 0 | 0 | 0 | 0 | 0 | 0 | 0 | 7 | 0 | 1 |
| Millar | John McVey (Jock) | Outside-Left/Right | 1929 | 1930 | 18 | 0 | 5 | 0 | 0 | 0 | 1 | 0 | 0 | 0 | 0 | 0 | 0 | 0 | 0 | 19 | 0 | 5 |
| Miller | Lumley Robert (Bob) | Inside/Wing-Forward | 1962 | 1963 | 9 | 0 | 2 | 0 | 0 | 0 | 0 | 0 | 0 | 0 | 0 | 0 | 0 | 0 | 0 | 9 | 0 | 2 |
| Miller | Thomas William (Tommy) | Midfielder | 1997 | 2001 | 130 | 7 | 35 | 4 | 0 | 0 | 5 | 0 | 2 | 6 | 0 | 3 | 8 | 0 | 5 | 153 | 7 | 45 |
| Miller | Walter | Right-Half-Back | 1949 | 1950 | 1 | 0 | 0 | 0 | 0 | 0 | 0 | 0 | 0 | 0 | 0 | 0 | 0 | 0 | 0 | 1 | 0 | 0 |
| Mills | William E. | Centre-Forward | 1923 | 1924 | 2 | 0 | 0 | 0 | 0 | 0 | 0 | 0 | 0 | 0 | 0 | 0 | 0 | 0 | 0 | 2 | 0 | 0 |
| Mitchell | John George | Centre-Forward | 1946 | 1947 | 3 | 0 | 2 | 0 | 0 | 0 | 0 | 0 | 0 | 0 | 0 | 0 | 0 | 0 | 0 | 3 | 0 | 2 |
| Mitchell | Norman | Outside-Right | 1957 | 1959 | 23 | 0 | 6 | 0 | 0 | 0 | 0 | 0 | 0 | 0 | 0 | 0 | 0 | 0 | 0 | 23 | 0 | 6 |
| Mitchell | Thomas (Tommy) | Outside-Left | 1922 | 1924 | 35 | 0 | 1 | 0 | 0 | 0 | 0 | 0 | 0 | 0 | 0 | 0 | 0 | 0 | 0 | 35 | 0 | 1 |
| Mittell | James Lyons (Jimmy) | Goalkeeper | 1935 | 1937 | 65 | 0 | 0 | 0 | 0 | 0 | 10 | 0 | 0 | 0 | 0 | 0 | 0 | 0 | 0 | 75 | 0 | 0 |
| Monkhouse | Andrew William (Andy) | Winger | 2007 | 2012 | 213 | 14 | 36 | 0 | 0 | 0 | 9 | 4 | 1 | 7 | 1 | 1 | 4 | 1 | 1 | 233 | 20 | 39 |
| Moore | Ian Ronald | Forward | 2007 | 2008 | 22 | 2 | 6 | 0 | 0 | 0 | 2 | 0 | 1 | 2 | 0 | 1 | 2 | 0 | 1 | 28 | 2 | 9 |
| Moore | Malcolm | Centre-Forward | 1973 | 1976 | 127 | 2 | 34 | 0 | 0 | 0 | 7 | 1 | 3 | 12 | 0 | 5 | 0 | 0 | 0 | 146 | 3 | 42 |
| Moore | Watson Evans (Watty) | Centre-Half-Back | 1948 | 1960 | 447 | 0 | 3 | 0 | 0 | 0 | 25 | 0 | 0 | 0 | 0 | 0 | 0 | 0 | 0 | 472 | 0 | 3 |
| Moore | William Riddell (Bill) | Goalkeeper | 1936 | 1937 | 16 | 0 | 0 | 0 | 0 | 0 | 0 | 0 | 0 | 0 | 0 | 0 | 0 | 0 | 0 | 16 | 0 | 0 |
| Mordue | John (Jack) | Inside-Forward/Outside-Right | 1927 | 1932 | 131 | 0 | 31 | 0 | 0 | 0 | 4 | 0 | 0 | 0 | 0 | 0 | 0 | 0 | 0 | 135 | 0 | 31 |
| Mordue | Thomas (Tucker) | Centre/Inside-Forward | 1928 | 1931 | 101 | 0 | 26 | 0 | 0 | 0 | 3 | 0 | 1 | 0 | 0 | 0 | 0 | 0 | 0 | 104 | 0 | 27 |
| Mordue | William Michael (Billy) | Inside/Wing-Forward | 1922 | 1930 | 111 | 0 | 18 | 0 | 0 | 0 | 5 | 0 | 0 | 0 | 0 | 0 | 0 | 0 | 0 | 116 | 0 | 18 |
| Morrell | Robert Ian (Bobby) | Right-Half-Back | 1963 | 1965 | 34 | 0 | 0 | 0 | 0 | 0 | 3 | 0 | 0 | 1 | 0 | 0 | 0 | 0 | 0 | 38 | 0 | 0 |
| Morris | Douglas (Doug) | Outside-Right | 1945 | 1951 | 19 | 0 | 3 | 0 | 0 | 0 | 2 | 0 | 0 | 0 | 0 | 0 | 0 | 0 | 0 | 21 | 0 | 3 |
| Morris | Henry (Harry) | Centre-Half-Back | 1923 | 1924 | 7 | 0 | 2 | 0 | 0 | 0 | 0 | 0 | 0 | 0 | 0 | 0 | 0 | 0 | 0 | 7 | 0 | 2 |
| Morrison | George Charles | Centre-Half-Back/Centre-Forward | 1951 | 1952 | 2 | 0 | 0 | 0 | 0 | 0 | 0 | 0 | 0 | 0 | 0 | 0 | 0 | 0 | 0 | 2 | 0 | 0 |
| Moses | George | Forward/Half-Back | 1946 | 1947 | 19 | 0 | 4 | 0 | 0 | 0 | 2 | 0 | 0 | 0 | 0 | 0 | 0 | 0 | 0 | 21 | 0 | 4 |
| Moses | Jack (Jackie) | Inside-Left | 1934 | 1937 | 21 | 0 | 3 | 0 | 0 | 0 | 0 | 0 | 0 | 0 | 0 | 0 | 3 | 0 | 3 | 24 | 0 | 6 |
| Moverley | Robert (Rob) | Goalkeeper | 1988 | 1990 | 29 | 0 | 0 | 0 | 0 | 0 | 5 | 0 | 0 | 0 | 0 | 0 | 2 | 0 | 0 | 36 | 0 | 0 |
| Muggleton | Carl David | Goalkeeper | 1988 | 1989 | 8 | 0 | 0 | 0 | 0 | 0 | 0 | 0 | 0 | 0 | 0 | 0 | 2 | 0 | 0 | 10 | 0 | 0 |
| Mulholland | Thomas S. (Tom) | Inside-Right | 1921 | 1922 | 5 | 0 | 1 | 0 | 0 | 0 | 6 | 0 | 2 | 0 | 0 | 0 | 0 | 0 | 0 | 11 | 0 | 3 |
| Mulvaney | James | Inside/Outside-Left | 1965 | 1968 | 67 | 2 | 31 | 0 | 0 | 0 | 3 | 0 | 1 | 2 | 0 | 1 | 0 | 0 | 0 | 72 | 2 | 33 |
| Murray | Joseph (Joe) | Goalkeeper | 1934 | 1936 | 7 | 0 | 0 | 0 | 0 | 0 | 0 | 0 | 0 | 0 | 0 | 0 | 0 | 0 | 0 | 7 | 0 | 0 |
| Murray | Paul | Midfielder | 2010 | 2012 | 79 | 2 | 2 | 0 | 0 | 0 | 1 | 0 | 0 | 2 | 1 | 0 | 2 | 0 | 0 | 84 | 3 | 2 |
| Musgrave | Joseph William (Joe) | Half-Back | 1938 | 1939 | 20 | 0 | 3 | 0 | 0 | 0 | 0 | 0 | 0 | 0 | 0 | 0 | 1 | 0 | 0 | 21 | 0 | 3 |
| Mutrie | Leslie Alan (Les) | Inside-Right | 1984 | 1985 | 18 | 0 | 4 | 0 | 0 | 0 | 2 | 0 | 0 | 2 | 0 | 0 | 0 | 0 | 0 | 22 | 0 | 4 |

| Surname | Forenames | Position | Career Start | Career Finish | Football League Apps | Football League Sub | Football League Gls | Play-offs Apps | Play-offs Sub | Play-offs Gls | FA Cup Apps | FA Cup Sub | FA Cup Gls | FL Cup Apps | FL Cup Sub | FL Cup Gls | Other Apps | Other Sub | Other Gls | Total Apps | Total Sub | Total Gls |
|---|---|---|---|---|---|---|---|---|---|---|---|---|---|---|---|---|---|---|---|---|---|---|
| Myers | Ernest Colin | Inside-Left | 1926 | 1927 | 22 | 0 | 0 | 0 | 0 | 0 | 8 | 0 | 0 | 0 | 0 | 0 | 0 | 0 | 0 | 30 | 0 | 0 |
| Nardiello | Daniel Antony (Danny) | Forward | 2008 | 2009 | 8 | 5 | 3 | 0 | 0 | 0 | 0 | 0 | 0 | 0 | 0 | 0 | 0 | 0 | 0 | 8 | 5 | 3 |
| Nash | Gerard Thomas | Defender | 2005 | 2006 | 3 | 0 | 0 | 0 | 0 | 0 | 0 | 0 | 0 | 0 | 0 | 0 | 0 | 0 | 0 | 3 | 0 | 0 |
| Nash | Marc | Forward | 1997 | 1998 | 0 | 1 | 0 | 0 | 0 | 0 | 0 | 0 | 0 | 0 | 0 | 0 | 0 | 0 | 0 | 0 | 1 | 0 |
| Nelson | Michael John | Centre-Half-Back | 2003 | 2009 | 255 | 4 | 14 | 5 | 0 | 0 | 20 | 0 | 2 | 13 | 0 | 0 | 9 | 0 | 0 | 302 | 4 | 16 |
| Nesbitt | Edward (Eddie) | Goalkeeper | 1971 | 1972 | 1 | 0 | 0 | 0 | 0 | 0 | 0 | 0 | 0 | 0 | 0 | 0 | 0 | 0 | 0 | 1 | 0 | 0 |
| Nesbitt | Mark Thomas | Right-Back | 1990 | 1992 | 2 | 0 | 0 | 0 | 0 | 0 | 0 | 0 | 0 | 0 | 0 | 0 | 0 | 0 | 0 | 2 | 0 | 0 |
| Nevin | William (Billy) | Centre-Forward | 1937 | 1938 | 4 | 0 | 2 | 0 | 0 | 0 | 0 | 0 | 0 | 0 | 0 | 0 | 1 | 0 | 0 | 5 | 0 | 2 |
| Nevins | Lawrence (Laurie) | Outside-Left | 1947 | 1949 | 18 | 0 | 8 | 0 | 0 | 0 | 1 | 0 | 0 | 0 | 0 | 0 | 0 | 0 | 0 | 19 | 0 | 8 |
| Newton | John Lochinvar | Wing-Half-Back | 1946 | 1958 | 332 | 0 | 15 | 0 | 0 | 0 | 29 | 0 | 4 | 0 | 0 | 0 | 0 | 0 | 0 | 361 | 0 | 19 |
| Newton | Robert (Bob) | Centre-Forward | 1977 | 1986 | 158 | 3 | 50 | 0 | 0 | 0 | 11 | 0 | 10 | 8 | 0 | 2 | 4 | 0 | 0 | 181 | 3 | 62 |
| Nicholson | Benjamin Cummings (Ben) | Half-Back | 1921 | 1925 | 17 | 0 | 0 | 0 | 0 | 0 | 2 | 0 | 0 | 0 | 0 | 0 | 0 | 0 | 0 | 19 | 0 | 0 |
| Nicholson | Stanley (Stan) | Inside-Left | 1958 | 1959 | 7 | 0 | 1 | 0 | 0 | 0 | 1 | 0 | 0 | 0 | 0 | 0 | 0 | 0 | 0 | 8 | 0 | 1 |
| Nish | Colin John | Centre-Forward | 2011 | 2012 | 12 | 8 | 4 | 0 | 0 | 0 | 0 | 0 | 0 | 1 | 0 | 0 | 0 | 0 | 0 | 13 | 8 | 4 |
| Nobbs | Alan Keith | Defender/Midfielder | 1985 | 1994 | 274 | 6 | 1 | 0 | 0 | 0 | 12 | 1 | 0 | 16 | 1 | 0 | 16 | 0 | 0 | 318 | 8 | 1 |
| Nobbs | Harold | Half-Back | 1929 | 1932 | 68 | 0 | 1 | 0 | 0 | 0 | 1 | 0 | 0 | 0 | 0 | 0 | 0 | 0 | 0 | 69 | 0 | 1 |
| Nobbs | Walter | Right-Half-Back | 1935 | 1937 | 21 | 0 | 1 | 0 | 0 | 0 | 0 | 0 | 0 | 0 | 0 | 0 | 1 | 0 | 0 | 22 | 0 | 1 |
| Noble | Barry | Goalkeeper | 1971 | 1972 | 1 | 0 | 0 | 0 | 0 | 0 | 0 | 0 | 0 | 0 | 0 | 0 | 0 | 0 | 0 | 1 | 0 | 0 |
| Noble | Ryan | Forward | 2011 | 2012 | 9 | 0 | 2 | 0 | 0 | 0 | 0 | 0 | 0 | 0 | 0 | 0 | 0 | 0 | 0 | 9 | 0 | 2 |
| Nolan | Edward (Eddie) | Full Back | 2007 | 2008 | 11 | 0 | 0 | 0 | 0 | 0 | 1 | 0 | 0 | 0 | 0 | 0 | 0 | 0 | 0 | 12 | 0 | 0 |
| Normanton | Graham Stephen | Full-Back/Midfielder | 1979 | 1981 | 17 | 1 | 0 | 0 | 0 | 0 | 0 | 0 | 0 | 0 | 0 | 0 | 0 | 0 | 0 | 17 | 1 | 0 |
| Norton | David John (Dave) | Full-Back/Midfielder | 1978 | 1980 | 14 | 3 | 2 | 0 | 0 | 0 | 1 | 0 | 0 | 1 | 0 | 0 | 0 | 0 | 0 | 16 | 3 | 2 |
| Norton | Paul | Goalkeeper | 1988 | 1989 | 5 | 0 | 0 | 0 | 0 | 0 | 1 | 0 | 0 | 0 | 0 | 0 | 0 | 0 | 0 | 6 | 0 | 0 |
| Oakley | Norman | Goalkeeper | 1958 | 1964 | 182 | 0 | 0 | 0 | 0 | 0 | 8 | 0 | 0 | 3 | 0 | 0 | 0 | 0 | 0 | 193 | 0 | 0 |
| O'Connor | Paul Daniel | Goalkeeper | 1995 | 1997 | 31 | 0 | 0 | 0 | 0 | 0 | 1 | 0 | 0 | 0 | 0 | 0 | 1 | 0 | 0 | 33 | 0 | 0 |
| O'Connor | Vincent John (Jackie) | Wing-Forward | 1948 | 1949 | 2 | 0 | 0 | 0 | 0 | 0 | 0 | 0 | 0 | 0 | 0 | 0 | 0 | 0 | 0 | 2 | 0 | 0 |
| Odams | James Richard | Goalkeeper | 1933 | 1934 | 1 | 0 | 0 | 0 | 0 | 0 | 0 | 0 | 0 | 0 | 0 | 0 | 0 | 0 | 0 | 1 | 0 | 0 |
| O'Donnell | John (Jack) | Left-Back | 1932 | 1933 | 28 | 0 | 2 | 0 | 0 | 0 | 2 | 0 | 0 | 0 | 0 | 0 | 0 | 0 | 0 | 30 | 0 | 2 |
| O'Donnell | Jonathan David (Jon) | Right-Back/Half-Back | 1976 | 1977 | 30 | 1 | 1 | 0 | 0 | 0 | 1 | 0 | 0 | 2 | 0 | 0 | 0 | 0 | 0 | 33 | 1 | 1 |
| O'Donovan | Roy | Centre-Forward | 2009 | 2010 | 15 | 0 | 9 | 0 | 0 | 0 | 0 | 0 | 0 | 0 | 0 | 0 | 0 | 0 | 0 | 15 | 0 | 9 |
| Ogden | Paul | Midfielder | 1988 | 1990 | 9 | 3 | 0 | 0 | 0 | 0 | 1 | 0 | 0 | 0 | 1 | 0 | 1 | 1 | 0 | 11 | 5 | 0 |
| Oldham | Eric | Left-Back | 1959 | 1960 | 12 | 0 | 0 | 0 | 0 | 0 | 0 | 0 | 0 | 0 | 0 | 0 | 0 | 0 | 0 | 12 | 0 | 0 |
| Oliver | Henry Spoors (Harry) | Left-Back | 1938 | 1939 | 9 | 0 | 0 | 0 | 0 | 0 | 0 | 0 | 0 | 0 | 0 | 0 | 0 | 0 | 0 | 9 | 0 | 0 |
| Oliver | Howard Derek | Wing-Forward | 1968 | 1969 | 0 | 1 | 0 | 0 | 0 | 0 | 0 | 0 | 0 | 0 | 0 | 0 | 0 | 0 | 0 | 0 | 1 | 0 |
| Oliver | Keith | Midfielder | 1993 | 1996 | 25 | 7 | 0 | 0 | 0 | 0 | 0 | 1 | 0 | 5 | 3 | 0 | 3 | 0 | 0 | 33 | 11 | 0 |

| | | | Career | | Football League | | | Play-offs | | | FA Cup | | | FL Cup | | | Other | | | Total | | |
|---|---|---|---|---|---|---|---|---|---|---|---|---|---|---|---|---|---|---|---|---|---|---|
| Surname | Forenames | Position | Start | Finish | Apps | Sub | Gls | Apps | Sub | Gls | Apps | Sub | Gls | Apps | Sub | Gls | Apps | Sub | Gls | Apps | Sub | Gls |
| Ollerenshaw | John | Right-Back | 1950 | 1951 | 2 | 0 | 0 | 0 | 0 | 0 | 0 | 0 | 0 | 0 | 0 | 0 | 0 | 0 | 0 | 2 | 0 | 0 |
| Olsson | Paul | Midfielder | 1989 | 1994 | 162 | 9 | 13 | 0 | 0 | 0 | 10 | 0 | 0 | 11 | 2 | 0 | 10 | 1 | 1 | 193 | 12 | 14 |
| Ormerod | Anthony | Forward | 2001 | 2002 | 2 | 0 | 0 | 0 | 0 | 0 | 0 | 0 | 0 | 0 | 0 | 0 | 0 | 0 | 0 | 2 | 0 | 0 |
| Osmond | Joseph Edward (Joe) | Left-Back | 1924 | 1925 | 1 | 0 | 0 | 0 | 0 | 0 | 0 | 0 | 0 | 0 | 0 | 0 | 0 | 0 | 0 | 1 | 0 | 0 |
| Owbridge | Charles Richard (Charlie) | Goalkeeper | 1931 | 1933 | 19 | 0 | 0 | 0 | 0 | 0 | 0 | 0 | 0 | 0 | 0 | 0 | 0 | 0 | 0 | 19 | 0 | 0 |
| Owens | Richard | Inside-Left | 1935 | 1936 | 1 | 0 | 0 | 0 | 0 | 0 | 0 | 0 | 0 | 0 | 0 | 0 | 0 | 0 | 0 | 1 | 0 | 0 |
| Owens | Thomas Leslie (Les) | Centre-Forward | 1949 | 1950 | 28 | 0 | 12 | 0 | 0 | 0 | 3 | 0 | 1 | 0 | 0 | 0 | 0 | 0 | 0 | 31 | 0 | 13 |
| Owers | Philip (Phil) | Goalkeeper | 1987 | 1988 | 2 | 0 | 0 | 0 | 0 | 0 | 0 | 0 | 0 | 2 | 0 | 0 | 0 | 0 | 0 | 4 | 0 | 0 |
| Oxley | George | Centre-Forward | 1936 | 1937 | 0 | 0 | 0 | 0 | 0 | 0 | 0 | 0 | 0 | 0 | 0 | 0 | 1 | 0 | 0 | 1 | 0 | 0 |
| Pape | Albert Arthur | Centre-Forward | 1929 | 1930 | 37 | 0 | 21 | 0 | 0 | 0 | 1 | 0 | 0 | 0 | 0 | 0 | 0 | 0 | 0 | 38 | 0 | 21 |
| Park | Oswald (Ossie) | Centre-Half-Back | 1934 | 1938 | 104 | 0 | 1 | 0 | 0 | 0 | 15 | 0 | 1 | 0 | 0 | 0 | 4 | 0 | 0 | 123 | 0 | 2 |
| Park | Robert Clydesdale (Bobby) | Midfielder | 1974 | 1975 | 14 | 3 | 0 | 0 | 0 | 0 | 0 | 0 | 0 | 1 | 1 | 0 | 0 | 0 | 0 | 15 | 4 | 0 |
| Parker | Keigan | Forward | 2008 | 2009 | 9 | 0 | 0 | 0 | 0 | 0 | 0 | 0 | 0 | 0 | 0 | 0 | 0 | 0 | 0 | 9 | 0 | 0 |
| Parkes | Barry Joseph | Inside-Left | 1960 | 1963 | 29 | 0 | 7 | 0 | 0 | 0 | 2 | 0 | 1 | 0 | 0 | 0 | 0 | 0 | 0 | 31 | 0 | 8 |
| Parkes | Sidney (Sid) | Goalkeeper | 1946 | 1948 | 6 | 0 | 0 | 0 | 0 | 0 | 2 | 0 | 0 | 0 | 0 | 0 | 0 | 0 | 0 | 8 | 0 | 0 |
| Parkin | Jonathan (Jon) | Forward | 2001 | 2002 | 0 | 1 | 0 | 0 | 0 | 0 | 0 | 0 | 0 | 0 | 0 | 0 | 0 | 0 | 0 | 0 | 1 | 0 |
| Parkinson | John | Left-Half-Back | 1971 | 1972 | 1 | 0 | 0 | 0 | 0 | 0 | 0 | 0 | 0 | 0 | 0 | 0 | 0 | 0 | 0 | 1 | 0 | 0 |
| Parkinson | Thomas Oswald (Tot) | Inside-Forward | 1921 | 1925 | 60 | 0 | 19 | 0 | 0 | 0 | 1 | 0 | 0 | 0 | 0 | 0 | 0 | 0 | 0 | 61 | 0 | 19 |
| Parry | Anthony John (Tony) | Midfielder | 1965 | 1972 | 181 | 8 | 5 | 0 | 0 | 0 | 7 | 0 | 0 | 7 | 1 | 0 | 0 | 0 | 0 | 195 | 9 | 5 |
| Parsons | David (Davie) | Centre/Wing-Forward | 1921 | 1922 | 2 | 0 | 0 | 0 | 0 | 0 | 0 | 0 | 0 | 0 | 0 | 0 | 0 | 0 | 0 | 2 | 0 | 0 |
| Patterson | George Thomas | Wing-Half-Back | 1960 | 1961 | 18 | 0 | 1 | 0 | 0 | 0 | 0 | 0 | 0 | 1 | 0 | 0 | 0 | 0 | 0 | 19 | 0 | 1 |
| Peake | Jason William | Midfielder | 1991 | 1992 | 5 | 1 | 1 | 0 | 0 | 0 | 0 | 0 | 0 | 0 | 0 | 0 | 0 | 0 | 0 | 5 | 1 | 1 |
| Pears | Stephen (Steve) | Goalkeeper | 1996 | 1997 | 16 | 0 | 0 | 0 | 0 | 0 | 1 | 0 | 0 | 2 | 0 | 0 | 0 | 0 | 0 | 19 | 0 | 0 |
| Pearson | John | Inside-Right | 1968 | 1969 | 1 | 0 | 0 | 0 | 0 | 0 | 0 | 0 | 0 | 0 | 0 | 0 | 0 | 0 | 0 | 1 | 0 | 0 |
| Pearson | John George | Right-Back | 1952 | 1953 | 1 | 0 | 0 | 0 | 0 | 0 | 0 | 0 | 0 | 0 | 0 | 0 | 0 | 0 | 0 | 1 | 0 | 0 |
| Peart | Ronald (Ron) | Centre-Half-Back | 1938 | 1939 | 8 | 0 | 0 | 0 | 0 | 0 | 0 | 0 | 0 | 0 | 0 | 0 | 0 | 0 | 0 | 8 | 0 | 0 |
| Pederson | Jan Ove | Forward | 1997 | 1998 | 17 | 0 | 1 | 0 | 0 | 0 | 1 | 0 | 1 | 0 | 0 | 0 | 2 | 0 | 1 | 20 | 0 | 3 |
| Pedwell | Ralph | Outside-Left | 1929 | 1934 | 156 | 0 | 66 | 0 | 0 | 0 | 7 | 0 | 2 | 0 | 0 | 0 | 1 | 0 | 0 | 164 | 0 | 68 |
| Peek | James (Jim) | Full-Back | 1959 | 1960 | 7 | 0 | 0 | 0 | 0 | 0 | 0 | 0 | 0 | 0 | 0 | 0 | 0 | 0 | 0 | 7 | 0 | 0 |
| Perkins | Christopher Peter (Chris) | Left-Back | 1999 | 2000 | 7 | 1 | 0 | 0 | 0 | 0 | 0 | 0 | 0 | 1 | 0 | 0 | 0 | 0 | 0 | 8 | 1 | 0 |
| Peverell | Nicholas John (Nicky) | Forward | 1992 | 1995 | 14 | 22 | 3 | 0 | 0 | 0 | 1 | 1 | 1 | 0 | 1 | 0 | 1 | 2 | 0 | 16 | 26 | 4 |
| Phythian | Ernest Rixon (Ernie) | Centre-Forward | 1965 | 1968 | 124 | 0 | 51 | 0 | 0 | 0 | 5 | 0 | 1 | 6 | 0 | 3 | 0 | 0 | 0 | 135 | 0 | 55 |
| Pickard | Frank | Outside-Right | 1935 | 1936 | 3 | 0 | 1 | 0 | 0 | 0 | 0 | 0 | 0 | 0 | 0 | 0 | 0 | 0 | 0 | 3 | 0 | 1 |
| Pickering | Archibald (Archie) | Left-Half-Back | 1937 | 1939 | 1 | 0 | 0 | 0 | 0 | 0 | 0 | 0 | 0 | 0 | 0 | 0 | 0 | 0 | 0 | 1 | 0 | 0 |
| Pimblett | Francis Roy (Frank) | Outside-Left | 1979 | 1980 | 3 | 0 | 0 | 0 | 0 | 0 | 0 | 0 | 0 | 0 | 0 | 0 | 0 | 0 | 0 | 3 | 0 | 0 |

| Surname | Forenames | Position | Career Start | Career Finish | Football League Apps | Football League Sub | Football League Gls | Play-offs Apps | Play-offs Sub | Play-offs Gls | FA Cup Apps | FA Cup Sub | FA Cup Gls | FL Cup Apps | FL Cup Sub | FL Cup Gls | Other Apps | Other Sub | Other Gls | Total Apps | Total Sub | Total Gls |
|---|---|---|---|---|---|---|---|---|---|---|---|---|---|---|---|---|---|---|---|---|---|---|
| Pittman | Jon-Paul | Centre-Forward | 2005 | 2006 | 2 | 1 | 0 | 0 | 0 | 0 | 0 | 0 | 0 | 0 | 0 | 0 | 0 | 0 | 0 | 2 | 1 | 0 |
| Plaskett | Stephen Colin (Steve) | Right-Back | 1988 | 1990 | 19 | 1 | 0 | 0 | 0 | 0 | 0 | 0 | 0 | 0 | 0 | 0 | 2 | 0 | 0 | 21 | 1 | 0 |
| Platt | James Archibald (Jim) | Goalkeeper | 1978 | 1979 | 13 | 0 | 0 | 0 | 0 | 0 | 0 | 0 | 0 | 0 | 0 | 0 | 0 | 0 | 0 | 13 | 0 | 0 |
| Pollard | Brian Edward | Outside-Right | 1984 | 1985 | 2 | 0 | 0 | 0 | 0 | 0 | 0 | 0 | 0 | 0 | 0 | 0 | 1 | 1 | 0 | 3 | 1 | 0 |
| Poole | James Alexander | Forward | 2010 | 2012 | 15 | 15 | 8 | 0 | 0 | 0 | 2 | 1 | 0 | 0 | 1 | 0 | 1 | 1 | 0 | 18 | 18 | 8 |
| Poole | Kevin | Goalkeeper | 1990 | 1991 | 12 | 0 | 0 | 0 | 0 | 0 | 0 | 0 | 0 | 0 | 0 | 0 | 0 | 0 | 0 | 12 | 0 | 0 |
| Porter | Joel William | Centre-Forward | 2003 | 2009 | 135 | 38 | 52 | 3 | 2 | 1 | 11 | 2 | 5 | 6 | 3 | 4 | 5 | 4 | 4 | 160 | 49 | 66 |
| Porter | William (Bill) | Left-Back | 1945 | 1947 | 2 | 0 | 0 | 0 | 0 | 0 | 2 | 0 | 0 | 0 | 0 | 0 | 0 | 0 | 0 | 4 | 0 | 0 |
| Poskett | Malcolm | Forward | 1976 | 1986 | 54 | 2 | 20 | 0 | 0 | 0 | 3 | 0 | 1 | 2 | 0 | 0 | 0 | 0 | 0 | 59 | 2 | 21 |
| Potter | George Ross | Defender | 1971 | 1977 | 212 | 1 | 4 | 0 | 0 | 0 | 13 | 0 | 1 | 16 | 0 | 1 | 0 | 0 | 0 | 241 | 1 | 6 |
| Pouton | Alan | Midfielder | 2004 | 2005 | 5 | 0 | 0 | 0 | 0 | 0 | 0 | 0 | 0 | 0 | 0 | 0 | 1 | 0 | 1 | 6 | 0 | 1 |
| Power | Alan | Midfielder | 2008 | 2010 | 0 | 6 | 0 | 0 | 0 | 0 | 0 | 0 | 0 | 0 | 0 | 0 | 1 | 0 | 0 | 1 | 6 | 0 |
| Powton | Brian | Goalkeeper | 1952 | 1953 | 4 | 0 | 0 | 0 | 0 | 0 | 0 | 0 | 0 | 0 | 0 | 0 | 0 | 0 | 0 | 4 | 0 | 0 |
| Poyntz | William Ivor (Billy) | Half-Back | 1927 | 1928 | 31 | 0 | 0 | 0 | 0 | 0 | 1 | 0 | 0 | 0 | 0 | 0 | 0 | 0 | 0 | 32 | 0 | 0 |
| Price | John (Jack) | Forward/Right-Half-Back | 1938 | 1948 | 90 | 0 | 12 | 0 | 0 | 0 | 5 | 0 | 1 | 0 | 0 | 0 | 3 | 0 | 1 | 98 | 0 | 14 |
| Price | Kenneth Edward (Ken) | Forward | 1961 | 1962 | 8 | 0 | 3 | 0 | 0 | 0 | 0 | 0 | 0 | 0 | 0 | 0 | 0 | 0 | 0 | 8 | 0 | 3 |
| Priestley | Jason Aaron | Goalkeeper | 1989 | 1990 | 16 | 0 | 0 | 0 | 0 | 0 | 0 | 0 | 0 | 0 | 0 | 0 | 0 | 0 | 0 | 16 | 0 | 0 |
| Pringle | Brian | Outside-Right | 1972 | 1973 | 1 | 0 | 0 | 0 | 0 | 0 | 0 | 0 | 0 | 0 | 0 | 0 | 0 | 0 | 0 | 1 | 0 | 0 |
| Proctor | John Roxby (Jack) | Right-Back | 1934 | 1938 | 149 | 0 | 20 | 0 | 0 | 0 | 13 | 0 | 2 | 0 | 0 | 0 | 9 | 0 | 1 | 171 | 0 | 23 |
| Proctor | Mark Gerard | Midfielder | 1996 | 1997 | 6 | 0 | 0 | 0 | 0 | 0 | 0 | 0 | 0 | 0 | 0 | 0 | 0 | 0 | 0 | 6 | 0 | 0 |
| Proctor | Michael | Forward | 2005 | 2007 | 23 | 5 | 5 | 0 | 0 | 0 | 0 | 1 | 0 | 2 | 1 | 2 | 0 | 0 | 0 | 25 | 7 | 7 |
| Proctor | Michael Henry (Harry) | Half-Back/Forward | 1932 | 1933 | 61 | 0 | 14 | 0 | 0 | 0 | 3 | 0 | 0 | 0 | 0 | 0 | 1 | 0 | 0 | 65 | 0 | 14 |
| Proudlock | Paul | Forward | 1984 | 1993 | 11 | 10 | 0 | 0 | 0 | 0 | 1 | 0 | 0 | 0 | 0 | 0 | 0 | 1 | 0 | 12 | 11 | 0 |
| Provett | Robert James | Goalkeeper | 2003 | 2007 | 66 | 0 | 0 | 2 | 0 | 0 | 4 | 0 | 0 | 3 | 0 | 0 | 3 | 0 | 0 | 78 | 0 | 0 |
| Prudham | Charles Edward (Eddie) | Inside-Left | 1976 | 1977 | 3 | 0 | 0 | 0 | 0 | 0 | 0 | 0 | 0 | 0 | 0 | 0 | 0 | 0 | 0 | 3 | 0 | 0 |
| Prudhoe | Mark | Goalkeeper | 1983 | 1988 | 16 | 0 | 0 | 0 | 0 | 0 | 0 | 0 | 0 | 0 | 0 | 0 | 0 | 0 | 0 | 16 | 0 | 0 |
| Race | Henry (Harry) | Inside-Right | 1938 | 1939 | 3 | 0 | 0 | 0 | 0 | 0 | 0 | 0 | 0 | 0 | 0 | 0 | 0 | 0 | 0 | 3 | 0 | 0 |
| Race | William (Billy) | Outside-Right | 1929 | 1931 | 19 | 0 | 2 | 0 | 0 | 0 | 0 | 0 | 0 | 0 | 0 | 0 | 0 | 0 | 0 | 19 | 0 | 2 |
| Rafferty | Andrew (Andy) | Goalkeeper | 2010 | 2012 | 2 | 0 | 0 | 0 | 0 | 0 | 0 | 1 | 0 | 0 | 0 | 0 | 0 | 0 | 0 | 2 | 1 | 0 |
| Ramsden | Bernard (Barney) | Right-Back | 1949 | 1950 | 13 | 0 | 0 | 0 | 0 | 0 | 0 | 0 | 0 | 0 | 0 | 0 | 0 | 0 | 0 | 13 | 0 | 0 |
| Ray | Philip (Phil) | Right-Back | 1983 | 1984 | 5 | 0 | 1 | 0 | 0 | 0 | 2 | 0 | 0 | 0 | 0 | 0 | 0 | 0 | 0 | 7 | 0 | 1 |
| Rayment | Joseph (Joe) | Outside-Right | 1927 | 1928 | 19 | 0 | 2 | 0 | 0 | 0 | 1 | 0 | 0 | 0 | 0 | 0 | 0 | 0 | 0 | 20 | 0 | 2 |
| Rayment | Joseph Watson (Joe) | Outside-Right | 1955 | 1958 | 63 | 0 | 17 | 0 | 0 | 0 | 2 | 0 | 0 | 0 | 0 | 0 | 0 | 0 | 0 | 65 | 0 | 17 |
| Reddish | Shane | Defender/Midfielder | 1994 | 1996 | 41 | 2 | 0 | 0 | 0 | 0 | 0 | 0 | 0 | 1 | 0 | 0 | 0 | 0 | 0 | 42 | 2 | 0 |
| Reed | Hugh Dennett | Centre-Forward | 1976 | 1977 | 6 | 0 | 1 | 0 | 0 | 0 | 0 | 0 | 0 | 0 | 0 | 0 | 0 | 0 | 0 | 6 | 0 | 1 |

| | | | Career | | Football League | | | Play-offs | | | FA Cup | | | FL Cup | | | Other | | | Total | | |
|---|---|---|---|---|---|---|---|---|---|---|---|---|---|---|---|---|---|---|---|---|---|---|
| Surname | Forenames | Position | Start | Finish | Apps | Sub | Gls | Apps | Sub | Gls | Apps | Sub | Gls | Apps | Sub | Gls | Apps | Sub | Gls | Apps | Sub | Gls |
| Reid | Thomas Stewart (Tom) | Centre-Half-Back | 1937 | 1938 | 7 | 0 | 0 | 0 | 0 | 0 | 0 | 0 | 0 | 0 | 0 | 0 | 2 | 0 | 0 | 9 | 0 | 0 |
| Reilly | Peter | Inside-Right | 1924 | 1925 | 1 | 0 | 0 | 0 | 0 | 0 | 0 | 0 | 0 | 0 | 0 | 0 | 0 | 0 | 0 | 1 | 0 | 0 |
| Reilly | William J. (Billy) | Left-Half-Back | 1933 | 1934 | 7 | 0 | 0 | 0 | 0 | 0 | 0 | 0 | 0 | 0 | 0 | 0 | 0 | 0 | 0 | 7 | 0 | 0 |
| Richards | Jordan | Midfielder | 2011 | 2012 | 1 | 1 | 0 | 0 | 0 | 0 | 0 | 0 | 0 | 0 | 0 | 0 | 0 | 0 | 0 | 1 | 1 | 0 |
| Richardson | Frederick (Fred) | Centre-Forward | 1947 | 1956 | 149 | 0 | 35 | 0 | 0 | 0 | 16 | 0 | 8 | 0 | 0 | 0 | 0 | 0 | 0 | 165 | 0 | 43 |
| Richardson | George Edward Holland | Outside-Right | 1927 | 1928 | 3 | 0 | 0 | 0 | 0 | 0 | 0 | 0 | 0 | 0 | 0 | 0 | 0 | 0 | 0 | 3 | 0 | 0 |
| Richardson | George William | Left-Half-Back | 1924 | 1928 | 106 | 0 | 13 | 0 | 0 | 0 | 6 | 0 | 0 | 0 | 0 | 0 | 0 | 0 | 0 | 112 | 0 | 13 |
| Richardson | Graham Charles | Goalkeeper | 1975 | 1981 | 89 | 0 | 0 | 0 | 0 | 0 | 3 | 0 | 0 | 5 | 0 | 0 | 0 | 0 | 0 | 97 | 0 | 0 |
| Richardson | Marcus Glenroy | Forward | 2002 | 2003 | 23 | 4 | 5 | 0 | 0 | 0 | 2 | 0 | 1 | 0 | 0 | 0 | 0 | 0 | 0 | 25 | 4 | 6 |
| Richardson | William (Billy) | Centre-Forward | 1928 | 1929 | 29 | 0 | 19 | 0 | 0 | 0 | 0 | 0 | 0 | 0 | 0 | 0 | 0 | 0 | 0 | 29 | 0 | 19 |
| Richley | Lionel (Len) | Left-Half-Back | 1951 | 1954 | 72 | 0 | 0 | 0 | 0 | 0 | 4 | 0 | 0 | 0 | 0 | 0 | 0 | 0 | 0 | 76 | 0 | 0 |
| Ridley | James (Jimmy) | Outside-Right | 1932 | 1933 | 8 | 0 | 1 | 0 | 0 | 0 | 0 | 0 | 0 | 0 | 0 | 0 | 0 | 0 | 0 | 8 | 0 | 1 |
| Rimmington | Norman | Goalkeeper | 1947 | 1952 | 124 | 0 | 0 | 0 | 0 | 0 | 7 | 0 | 0 | 0 | 0 | 0 | 0 | 0 | 0 | 131 | 0 | 0 |
| Rivers | James Embleton (Jimmy) | Goalkeeper | 1928 | 1933 | 129 | 0 | 0 | 0 | 0 | 0 | 4 | 0 | 0 | 0 | 0 | 0 | 0 | 0 | 0 | 133 | 0 | 0 |
| Robbins | Patrick (Paddy) | Inside/Wing-Forward | 1938 | 1939 | 24 | 0 | 5 | 0 | 0 | 0 | 1 | 0 | 0 | 0 | 0 | 0 | 4 | 0 | 1 | 29 | 0 | 6 |
| Roberts | Benjamin James (Ben) | Goalkeeper | 1995 | 1996 | 4 | 0 | 0 | 0 | 0 | 0 | 0 | 0 | 0 | 0 | 0 | 0 | 1 | 0 | 0 | 5 | 0 | 0 |
| Roberts | Jeremy | Goalkeeper | 1983 | 1984 | 1 | 0 | 0 | 0 | 0 | 0 | 2 | 0 | 0 | 0 | 0 | 0 | 0 | 0 | 0 | 3 | 0 | 0 |
| Roberts | Winston (Windy) | Inside-Left | 1958 | 1959 | 3 | 0 | 0 | 0 | 0 | 0 | 3 | 0 | 0 | 0 | 0 | 0 | 0 | 0 | 0 | 6 | 0 | 0 |
| Robertson | Alexander (Alec) | Inside-Left | 1935 | 1938 | 79 | 0 | 16 | 0 | 0 | 0 | 11 | 0 | 3 | 0 | 0 | 0 | 6 | 0 | 1 | 96 | 0 | 20 |
| Robertson | Hugh Scott | Left-Back | 2003 | 2005 | 37 | 3 | 6 | 2 | 0 | 0 | 4 | 0 | 0 | 0 | 0 | 0 | 0 | 0 | 0 | 43 | 3 | 6 |
| Robertson | Leonard Verdun | Inside-Forward | 1945 | 1946 | 0 | 0 | 0 | 0 | 0 | 0 | 2 | 0 | 0 | 0 | 0 | 0 | 0 | 0 | 0 | 2 | 0 | 0 |
| Robertson | Peter | Inside/Wing-Forward | 1921 | 1923 | 36 | 0 | 18 | 0 | 0 | 0 | 2 | 0 | 0 | 0 | 0 | 0 | 0 | 0 | 0 | 38 | 0 | 18 |
| Robertson | Thomas (Tommy) | Full-Back | 1927 | 1929 | 35 | 0 | 0 | 0 | 0 | 0 | 1 | 0 | 0 | 0 | 0 | 0 | 0 | 0 | 0 | 36 | 0 | 0 |
| Robinson | Anthony (Tony) | Outside-Left | 1986 | 1987 | 1 | 1 | 0 | 0 | 0 | 0 | 0 | 0 | 0 | 0 | 0 | 0 | 0 | 0 | 0 | 1 | 1 | 0 |
| Robinson | Arthur | Inside-Right | 1931 | 1932 | 1 | 0 | 0 | 0 | 0 | 0 | 0 | 0 | 0 | 0 | 0 | 0 | 0 | 0 | 0 | 1 | 0 | 0 |
| Robinson | David Alan | Right-Back | 1983 | 1986 | 64 | 2 | 1 | 0 | 0 | 0 | 3 | 0 | 0 | 2 | 0 | 0 | 3 | 0 | 0 | 72 | 2 | 1 |
| Robinson | Henry | Outside-Right | 1930 | 1932 | 6 | 0 | 1 | 0 | 0 | 0 | 0 | 0 | 0 | 0 | 0 | 0 | 0 | 0 | 0 | 6 | 0 | 1 |
| Robinson | John | Left-Half-Back | 1959 | 1960 | 9 | 0 | 0 | 0 | 0 | 0 | 0 | 0 | 0 | 0 | 0 | 0 | 0 | 0 | 0 | 9 | 0 | 0 |
| Robinson | Joseph (Joe) | Goalkeeper | 1938 | 1939 | 11 | 0 | 0 | 0 | 0 | 0 | 0 | 0 | 0 | 0 | 0 | 0 | 0 | 0 | 0 | 11 | 0 | 0 |
| Robinson | Joseph William (Billy) | Outside-Right | 1955 | 1958 | 43 | 0 | 11 | 0 | 0 | 0 | 4 | 0 | 1 | 0 | 0 | 0 | 0 | 0 | 0 | 47 | 0 | 12 |
| Robinson | Mark | Left-Back | 2000 | 2004 | 80 | 5 | 0 | 1 | 0 | 0 | 0 | 0 | 0 | 2 | 0 | 0 | 2 | 0 | 0 | 85 | 5 | 0 |
| Robinson | Mark William | Forward | 1982 | 1984 | 34 | 1 | 4 | 0 | 0 | 0 | 2 | 0 | 0 | 2 | 0 | 0 | 0 | 0 | 0 | 38 | 1 | 4 |
| Robinson | William Atkin (Billy) | Inside/Centre-Forward | 1924 | 1928 | 62 | 0 | 38 | 0 | 0 | 0 | 1 | 0 | 1 | 0 | 0 | 0 | 0 | 0 | 0 | 63 | 0 | 39 |
| Robson | Cuthbert (Cud) | Outside-Right | 1927 | 1928 | 20 | 0 | 5 | 0 | 0 | 0 | 0 | 0 | 0 | 0 | 0 | 0 | 0 | 0 | 0 | 20 | 0 | 5 |
| Robson | David Mark | Outside-Left | 1986 | 1987 | 1 | 0 | 0 | 0 | 0 | 0 | 0 | 0 | 0 | 0 | 0 | 0 | 0 | 0 | 0 | 1 | 0 | 0 |

| Surname | Forenames | Position | Career | | Football League | | | Play-offs | | | FA Cup | | | FL Cup | | | Other | | | Total | | |
|---|---|---|---|---|---|---|---|---|---|---|---|---|---|---|---|---|---|---|---|---|---|---|
| | | | Start | Finish | Apps | Sub | Gls | Apps | Sub | Gls | Apps | Sub | Gls | Apps | Sub | Gls | Apps | Sub | Gls | Apps | Sub | Gls |
| Robson | Frederick E. (Fred) | Left-Back | 1925 | 1926 | 12 | 0 | 0 | 0 | 0 | 0 | 3 | 0 | 0 | 0 | 0 | 0 | 0 | 0 | 0 | 15 | 0 | 0 |
| Robson | Lancelot (Lance) | Centre-Forward | 1969 | 1970 | 8 | 0 | 2 | 0 | 0 | 0 | 0 | 0 | 0 | 0 | 0 | 0 | 0 | 0 | 0 | 8 | 0 | 2 |
| Robson | Matthew James (Matty) | Left-Back | 2003 | 2009 | 90 | 45 | 8 | 3 | 0 | 0 | 9 | 3 | 1 | 9 | 2 | 0 | 8 | 1 | 0 | 119 | 51 | 9 |
| Robson | Percy T. | Inside-Left | 1930 | 1931 | 3 | 0 | 1 | 0 | 0 | 0 | 0 | 0 | 0 | 0 | 0 | 0 | 0 | 0 | 0 | 3 | 0 | 1 |
| Rodger | John James (Jimmy) | Half-Back | 1937 | 1938 | 12 | 0 | 0 | 0 | 0 | 0 | 0 | 0 | 0 | 0 | 0 | 0 | 1 | 0 | 0 | 13 | 0 | 0 |
| Rose | Leslie Eric Ronald (Les) | Left-Half-Back | 1938 | 1939 | 12 | 0 | 0 | 0 | 0 | 0 | 2 | 0 | 0 | 0 | 0 | 0 | 0 | 0 | 0 | 14 | 0 | 0 |
| Ross | John (Jack) James | Right-Back | 2004 | 2005 | 21 | 3 | 0 | 0 | 0 | 0 | 5 | 1 | 0 | 0 | 0 | 0 | 1 | 0 | 0 | 27 | 4 | 0 |
| Ross | William Eric | Left-Half-Back | 1971 | 1972 | 2 | 0 | 0 | 0 | 0 | 0 | 0 | 0 | 0 | 0 | 0 | 0 | 0 | 0 | 0 | 2 | 0 | 0 |
| Rowbotham | Joshua James (Josh) | Full-back | 2010 | 2012 | 2 | 0 | 0 | 0 | 0 | 0 | 0 | 0 | 0 | 0 | 0 | 0 | 0 | 0 | 0 | 2 | 0 | 0 |
| Rowe | George William | Outside-Left | 1921 | 1923 | 28 | 0 | 1 | 0 | 0 | 0 | 2 | 0 | 0 | 0 | 0 | 0 | 0 | 0 | 0 | 30 | 0 | 1 |
| Rowell | Jonathan | Midfielder | 2008 | 2010 | 3 | 9 | 0 | 0 | 0 | 0 | 0 | 0 | 0 | 0 | 0 | 0 | 0 | 1 | 0 | 3 | 10 | 0 |
| Rowlands | John Henry | Central Defender | 1975 | 1977 | 47 | 2 | 10 | 0 | 0 | 0 | 5 | 0 | 1 | 0 | 0 | 0 | 0 | 0 | 0 | 52 | 2 | 11 |
| Rush | David | Forward | 1991 | 1999 | 13 | 5 | 2 | 0 | 0 | 0 | 0 | 1 | 0 | 0 | 0 | 0 | 0 | 1 | 0 | 13 | 7 | 2 |
| Russell | William Howie (Bill) | Inside-Forward | 1946 | 1948 | 13 | 0 | 1 | 0 | 0 | 0 | 0 | 0 | 0 | 0 | 0 | 0 | 0 | 0 | 0 | 13 | 0 | 1 |
| Rutherford | Greg | Midfielder | 2011 | 2012 | 0 | 1 | 0 | 0 | 0 | 0 | 0 | 0 | 0 | 0 | 0 | 0 | 0 | 0 | 0 | 0 | 1 | 0 |
| Rutherford | John (Jack) | Goalkeeper | 1937 | 1938 | 4 | 0 | 0 | 0 | 0 | 0 | 1 | 0 | 0 | 0 | 0 | 0 | 2 | 0 | 0 | 7 | 0 | 0 |
| Rylands | David Robert (Dave) | Centre-Half-Back | 1975 | 1976 | 11 | 0 | 0 | 0 | 0 | 0 | 0 | 0 | 0 | 0 | 0 | 0 | 0 | 0 | 0 | 11 | 0 | 0 |
| Sales | Ronald Duncan (Ronnie) | Centre-Half-Back | 1950 | 1951 | 3 | 0 | 0 | 0 | 0 | 0 | 0 | 0 | 0 | 0 | 0 | 0 | 0 | 0 | 0 | 3 | 0 | 0 |
| Saville | Andrew Victor (Andy) | Centre-Forward | 1991 | 1993 | 37 | 0 | 13 | 0 | 0 | 0 | 4 | 0 | 5 | 4 | 0 | 1 | 1 | 0 | 1 | 46 | 0 | 20 |
| Scaife | Robert Henry (Bobby) | Wing-Forward | 1975 | 1978 | 77 | 3 | 10 | 0 | 0 | 0 | 5 | 0 | 2 | 2 | 0 | 0 | 0 | 0 | 0 | 84 | 3 | 12 |
| Scorgie | John | Outside-Left | 1921 | 1922 | 4 | 0 | 0 | 0 | 0 | 0 | 2 | 0 | 0 | 0 | 0 | 0 | 0 | 0 | 0 | 6 | 0 | 0 |
| Scott | Jack | Outside Left/Right | 1936 | 1938 | 70 | 0 | 20 | 0 | 0 | 0 | 6 | 0 | 2 | 0 | 0 | 0 | 2 | 0 | 0 | 78 | 0 | 22 |
| Scott | Joseph Cumpson (Joe) | Inside/Outside-Right | 1958 | 1960 | 62 | 0 | 8 | 0 | 0 | 0 | 1 | 0 | 0 | 0 | 0 | 0 | 0 | 0 | 0 | 63 | 0 | 8 |
| Scott | Michael Ramsey (Mike) | Outside-Left | 1964 | 1965 | 2 | 0 | 0 | 0 | 0 | 0 | 0 | 0 | 0 | 1 | 0 | 0 | 0 | 0 | 0 | 3 | 0 | 0 |
| Scott | Robert William (Bobby) | Centre-Half-Back | 1976 | 1977 | 37 | 0 | 0 | 0 | 0 | 0 | 1 | 0 | 0 | 2 | 0 | 0 | 0 | 0 | 0 | 40 | 0 | 0 |
| Scott | Samuel (Sammy) | Centre/Inside-Forward | 1946 | 1948 | 49 | 0 | 17 | 0 | 0 | 0 | 2 | 0 | 2 | 0 | 0 | 0 | 0 | 0 | 0 | 51 | 0 | 19 |
| Scott | Thomas (Tom) | Outside-Right | 1936 | 1937 | 6 | 0 | 0 | 0 | 0 | 0 | 0 | 0 | 0 | 0 | 0 | 0 | 1 | 0 | 0 | 7 | 0 | 0 |
| Scrimshaw | Stanley (Stan) | Inside-Forward | 1935 | 1937 | 18 | 0 | 1 | 0 | 0 | 0 | 0 | 0 | 0 | 0 | 0 | 0 | 2 | 0 | 0 | 20 | 0 | 1 |
| Self | Edward Richard (Eddie) | Outside-Left | 1936 | 1939 | 114 | 0 | 16 | 0 | 0 | 0 | 8 | 0 | 5 | 0 | 0 | 0 | 7 | 0 | 0 | 129 | 0 | 21 |
| Sharkey | Dominic (Nick) | Forward | 1970 | 1972 | 55 | 5 | 12 | 0 | 0 | 0 | 1 | 1 | 0 | 1 | 0 | 1 | 0 | 0 | 0 | 57 | 6 | 13 |
| Sharp | James | Central Defender | 2000 | 2002 | 44 | 5 | 2 | 1 | 1 | 0 | 0 | 0 | 0 | 2 | 0 | 0 | 5 | 0 | 0 | 52 | 6 | 2 |
| Shaw | Robert A. | Inside/Wing-Forward | 1923 | 1924 | 12 | 0 | 0 | 0 | 0 | 0 | 0 | 0 | 0 | 0 | 0 | 0 | 0 | 0 | 0 | 12 | 0 | 0 |
| Sheridan | John | Right-Half-Back | 1966 | 1970 | 117 | 3 | 1 | 0 | 0 | 0 | 2 | 0 | 0 | 7 | 0 | 0 | 0 | 0 | 0 | 126 | 3 | 1 |
| Sherratt | James Aaron (Jimmy) | Centre/Inside-Forward | 1948 | 1949 | 20 | 0 | 4 | 0 | 0 | 0 | 0 | 0 | 0 | 0 | 0 | 0 | 0 | 0 | 0 | 20 | 0 | 4 |
| Shilton | Samuel Roger (Sam) | Full Back/Midfielder | 1999 | 2001 | 45 | 9 | 7 | 0 | 0 | 0 | 3 | 0 | 0 | 1 | 1 | 0 | 3 | 1 | 0 | 52 | 11 | 7 |

| | | | Career | | Football League | | | Play-offs | | | FA Cup | | | FL Cup | | | Other | | | Total | | |
|---|---|---|---|---|---|---|---|---|---|---|---|---|---|---|---|---|---|---|---|---|---|---|
| Surname | Forenames | Position | Start | Finish | Apps | Sub | Gls | Apps | Sub | Gls | Apps | Sub | Gls | Apps | Sub | Gls | Apps | Sub | Gls | Apps | Sub | Gls |
| Short | William (Billy) | Half-Back | 1921 | 1922 | 18 | 0 | 0 | 0 | 0 | 0 | 6 | 0 | 4 | 0 | 0 | 0 | 0 | 0 | 0 | 24 | 0 | 4 |
| Shotton | John | Midfielder | 1990 | 1991 | 0 | 1 | 0 | 0 | 0 | 0 | 0 | 0 | 0 | 0 | 0 | 0 | 0 | 0 | 0 | 0 | 1 | 0 |
| Shotton | Robert (Bob) | Left-Back | 1931 | 1932 | 33 | 0 | 0 | 0 | 0 | 0 | 1 | 0 | 0 | 0 | 0 | 0 | 0 | 0 | 0 | 34 | 0 | 0 |
| Shoulder | Alan | Forward | 1985 | 1988 | 66 | 0 | 24 | 0 | 0 | 0 | 3 | 0 | 2 | 4 | 0 | 0 | 3 | 0 | 0 | 76 | 0 | 26 |
| Shoulder | James (Jimmy) | Left-Back | 1973 | 1975 | 62 | 1 | 3 | 0 | 0 | 0 | 4 | 0 | 0 | 9 | 0 | 0 | 0 | 0 | 0 | 75 | 1 | 3 |
| Siddall | Barry Alfred | Goalkeeper | 1989 | 1990 | 11 | 0 | 0 | 0 | 0 | 0 | 0 | 0 | 0 | 0 | 0 | 0 | 0 | 0 | 0 | 11 | 0 | 0 |
| Simmons | Henry Richard (Harry) | Inside/Centre-Forward | 1930 | 1931 | 31 | 0 | 17 | 0 | 0 | 0 | 1 | 0 | 0 | 0 | 0 | 0 | 0 | 0 | 0 | 32 | 0 | 17 |
| Simms | Gordon Henry | Central Defender | 2001 | 2002 | 6 | 5 | 0 | 0 | 0 | 0 | 1 | 0 | 0 | 0 | 0 | 0 | 1 | 0 | 0 | 8 | 5 | 0 |
| Simpkin | Christopher John (Chris) | Left-Half-Back | 1976 | 1978 | 47 | 0 | 0 | 0 | 0 | 0 | 0 | 0 | 0 | 2 | 0 | 0 | 0 | 0 | 0 | 49 | 0 | 0 |
| Simpkins | Kenneth (Ken) | Goalkeeper/Centre-Forward | 1963 | 1968 | 121 | 0 | 1 | 0 | 0 | 0 | 8 | 0 | 0 | 5 | 0 | 0 | 0 | 0 | 0 | 134 | 0 | 1 |
| Simpson | Robert (Bobby) | Wing-Forward | 1947 | 1948 | 13 | 0 | 1 | 0 | 0 | 0 | 1 | 0 | 0 | 0 | 0 | 0 | 0 | 0 | 0 | 14 | 0 | 1 |
| Sinclair | Jade | Inside-Forward | 1989 | 1990 | 4 | 0 | 0 | 0 | 0 | 0 | 1 | 0 | 0 | 0 | 0 | 0 | 0 | 0 | 0 | 5 | 0 | 0 |
| Skarz | Joseph Peter (Joe) | Left-Back | 2008 | 2009 | 5 | 2 | 0 | 0 | 0 | 0 | 0 | 0 | 0 | 0 | 0 | 0 | 0 | 0 | 0 | 5 | 2 | 0 |
| Skedd | Anthony Stuart (Tony) | Defender/Midfielder | 1992 | 1995 | 39 | 7 | 1 | 0 | 0 | 0 | 1 | 1 | 0 | 1 | 1 | 0 | 0 | 0 | 0 | 41 | 9 | 1 |
| Skillen | Keith | Outside-Right | 1975 | 1976 | 4 | 2 | 1 | 0 | 0 | 0 | 0 | 0 | 0 | 1 | 0 | 1 | 0 | 0 | 0 | 5 | 2 | 2 |
| Slater | Darren | Midfielder | 1995 | 1996 | 0 | 1 | 0 | 0 | 0 | 0 | 0 | 0 | 0 | 0 | 0 | 0 | 0 | 0 | 0 | 0 | 1 | 0 |
| Sloan | James (Jimmy) | Centre/Inside-Forward | 1946 | 1952 | 83 | 0 | 28 | 0 | 0 | 0 | 5 | 0 | 4 | 0 | 0 | 0 | 0 | 0 | 0 | 88 | 0 | 32 |
| Sloan | Mark Scott | Forward | 1994 | 1996 | 27 | 8 | 2 | 0 | 0 | 0 | 1 | 1 | 1 | 2 | 1 | 0 | 1 | 1 | 0 | 31 | 11 | 3 |
| Small | John Hedley | Goalkeeper | 1965 | 1966 | 2 | 0 | 0 | 0 | 0 | 0 | 0 | 0 | 0 | 0 | 0 | 0 | 0 | 0 | 0 | 2 | 0 | 0 |
| Smith | Anthony (Tony) | Centre-Half-Back | 1984 | 1989 | 200 | 0 | 8 | 0 | 0 | 0 | 11 | 0 | 1 | 10 | 0 | 0 | 12 | 0 | 1 | 233 | 0 | 10 |
| Smith | Anthony (Tony) | Defender | 1991 | 1992 | 4 | 1 | 0 | 0 | 0 | 0 | 0 | 0 | 0 | 0 | 0 | 0 | 2 | 0 | 0 | 6 | 1 | 0 |
| Smith | Anthony (Tony) | Inside-Right | 1967 | 1968 | 2 | 0 | 1 | 0 | 0 | 0 | 0 | 0 | 0 | 0 | 0 | 0 | 0 | 0 | 0 | 2 | 0 | 1 |
| Smith | David Bryan (Dave) | Inside-Right | 1974 | 1976 | 42 | 0 | 13 | 0 | 0 | 0 | 4 | 0 | 1 | 2 | 0 | 0 | 0 | 0 | 0 | 48 | 0 | 14 |
| Smith | Edward (Ted) | Left-Back | 1923 | 1925 | 56 | 0 | 0 | 0 | 0 | 0 | 7 | 0 | 0 | 0 | 0 | 0 | 0 | 0 | 0 | 63 | 0 | 0 |
| Smith | George | Full-Back/Midfielder | 1977 | 1980 | 81 | 4 | 2 | 0 | 0 | 0 | 7 | 0 | 0 | 4 | 0 | 0 | 0 | 0 | 0 | 92 | 4 | 2 |
| Smith | George | Goalkeeper | 1928 | 1929 | 4 | 0 | 0 | 0 | 0 | 0 | 0 | 0 | 0 | 0 | 0 | 0 | 0 | 0 | 0 | 4 | 0 | 0 |
| Smith | George Henry | Goalkeeper | 1967 | 1970 | 112 | 0 | 0 | 0 | 0 | 0 | 5 | 0 | 0 | 5 | 0 | 0 | 0 | 0 | 0 | 122 | 0 | 0 |
| Smith | Ian Paul | Winger/Midfielder | 2001 | 2003 | 45 | 10 | 4 | 2 | 0 | 0 | 3 | 0 | 0 | 0 | 0 | 0 | 0 | 0 | 0 | 50 | 10 | 4 |
| Smith | Jeffrey (Jeff) | Midfielder | 1998 | 1999 | 2 | 1 | 0 | 0 | 0 | 0 | 0 | 0 | 0 | 0 | 0 | 0 | 1 | 0 | 0 | 3 | 1 | 0 |
| Smith | John (Jackie) | Centre/Inside-Forward | 1953 | 1960 | 119 | 0 | 49 | 0 | 0 | 0 | 5 | 0 | 1 | 0 | 0 | 0 | 0 | 0 | 0 | 124 | 0 | 50 |
| Smith | Michael (Mick) | Centre-Half-Back | 1989 | 1992 | 53 | 2 | 6 | 0 | 0 | 0 | 0 | 0 | 0 | 2 | 0 | 0 | 2 | 0 | 0 | 57 | 2 | 6 |
| Smith | Robert (Rob) | Full-Back/Wing-Half-Back | 1972 | 1976 | 141 | 11 | 4 | 0 | 0 | 0 | 11 | 0 | 0 | 13 | 0 | 0 | 0 | 0 | 0 | 165 | 11 | 4 |
| Smith | Robert William (Bobby) | Inside-Right | 1971 | 1973 | 67 | 2 | 7 | 0 | 0 | 0 | 5 | 0 | 0 | 2 | 0 | 1 | 0 | 0 | 0 | 74 | 2 | 8 |
| Smith | T. Potter | Inside-Forward | 1924 | 1925 | 30 | 0 | 7 | 0 | 0 | 0 | 5 | 0 | 1 | 0 | 0 | 0 | 0 | 0 | 0 | 35 | 0 | 8 |
| Smith | Trevor Martin | Midfielder | 1976 | 1983 | 57 | 8 | 4 | 0 | 0 | 0 | 7 | 0 | 1 | 4 | 0 | 1 | 1 | 0 | 0 | 69 | 8 | 6 |

| | | | Career | | Football League | | | Play-offs | | | FA Cup | | | FL Cup | | | Other | | | Total | | |
|---|---|---|---|---|---|---|---|---|---|---|---|---|---|---|---|---|---|---|---|---|---|---|
| **Surname** | **Forenames** | **Position** | **Start** | **Finish** | **Apps** | **Sub** | **Gls** | **Apps** | **Sub** | **Gls** | **Apps** | **Sub** | **Gls** | **Apps** | **Sub** | **Gls** | **Apps** | **Sub** | **Gls** | **Apps** | **Sub** | **Gls** |
| Smith | William (Billie) | Half-Back | 1937 | 1938 | 28 | 0 | 1 | 0 | 0 | 0 | 2 | 0 | 0 | 0 | 0 | 0 | 3 | 0 | 0 | 33 | 0 | 1 |
| Smith | William E. (Billy) | Centre/Inside-Forward | 1923 | 1925 | 44 | 0 | 21 | 0 | 0 | 0 | 3 | 0 | 9 | 0 | 0 | 0 | 0 | 0 | 0 | 47 | 0 | 30 |
| Smithies | Michael Howard (Mike) | Right-Back | 1982 | 1987 | 32 | 3 | 0 | 0 | 0 | 0 | 1 | 0 | 0 | 0 | 0 | 0 | 1 | 0 | 0 | 34 | 3 | 0 |
| Solan | Kenneth (Ken) | Inside-Left | 1968 | 1969 | 6 | 0 | 1 | 0 | 0 | 0 | 2 | 0 | 0 | 0 | 0 | 0 | 0 | 0 | 0 | 8 | 0 | 1 |
| Solano | Nolberto Albino (Nobby) | Midfielder | 2011 | 2012 | 11 | 3 | 2 | 0 | 0 | 0 | 1 | 0 | 0 | 1 | 0 | 0 | 0 | 0 | 0 | 13 | 3 | 2 |
| Somers | Michael Robert (Mickey) | Outside-Left | 1966 | 1969 | 63 | 3 | 3 | 0 | 0 | 0 | 0 | 0 | 0 | 5 | 0 | 0 | 0 | 0 | 0 | 68 | 3 | 3 |
| Southall | Leslie Nicholas (Nicky) | Midfielder | 1991 | 1995 | 118 | 20 | 24 | 0 | 0 | 0 | 4 | 4 | 0 | 6 | 1 | 3 | 7 | 2 | 0 | 135 | 27 | 27 |
| Speirs | Walter Gardner | Forward | 1989 | 1990 | 0 | 1 | 0 | 0 | 0 | 0 | 0 | 0 | 0 | 1 | 0 | 0 | 0 | 0 | 0 | 1 | 1 | 0 |
| Spelman | Isaac | Right-Half-Back | 1946 | 1947 | 25 | 0 | 0 | 0 | 0 | 0 | 2 | 0 | 0 | 0 | 0 | 0 | 0 | 0 | 0 | 27 | 0 | 0 |
| Spelman | Michael Thomas (Mike) | Forward/Midfielder | 1971 | 1977 | 115 | 6 | 4 | 0 | 0 | 0 | 8 | 0 | 0 | 12 | 0 | 0 | 0 | 0 | 0 | 135 | 6 | 4 |
| Spencer | John Thomas | Outside-Right | 1922 | 1923 | 1 | 0 | 0 | 0 | 0 | 0 | 0 | 0 | 0 | 0 | 0 | 0 | 0 | 0 | 0 | 1 | 0 | 0 |
| Spencer | Tim | Half-Back | 1938 | 1939 | 0 | 0 | 0 | 0 | 0 | 0 | 0 | 0 | 0 | 0 | 0 | 0 | 2 | 0 | 1 | 2 | 0 | 1 |
| Sperrevik | Tim | Forward | 2000 | 2001 | 4 | 11 | 1 | 0 | 0 | 0 | 0 | 0 | 0 | 1 | 0 | 0 | 0 | 1 | 0 | 5 | 12 | 1 |
| Spraggon | Frank | Centre-Half-Back | 1976 | 1977 | 1 | 0 | 0 | 0 | 0 | 0 | 0 | 0 | 0 | 0 | 0 | 0 | 0 | 0 | 0 | 1 | 0 | 0 |
| Spry | William Hedley (Billy) | Outside-Right | 1928 | 1929 | 15 | 0 | 2 | 0 | 0 | 0 | 0 | 0 | 0 | 0 | 0 | 0 | 0 | 0 | 0 | 15 | 0 | 2 |
| Staff | Paul | Forward | 1979 | 1984 | 88 | 10 | 14 | 0 | 0 | 0 | 4 | 0 | 0 | 4 | 0 | 1 | 1 | 3 | 0 | 97 | 13 | 15 |
| Stalker | John Alexander Hastie Inglis | Centre-Forward | 1982 | 1983 | 3 | 1 | 0 | 0 | 0 | 0 | 0 | 0 | 0 | 0 | 0 | 0 | 0 | 0 | 0 | 3 | 1 | 0 |
| Stamper | Frank Fielden Thorpe | Inside-Forward/Half-Back | 1949 | 1958 | 301 | 0 | 26 | 0 | 0 | 0 | 25 | 0 | 4 | 0 | 0 | 0 | 0 | 0 | 0 | 326 | 0 | 30 |
| Stephenson | John R. (Jackie) | Inside-Right | 1929 | 1930 | 11 | 0 | 0 | 0 | 0 | 0 | 0 | 0 | 0 | 0 | 0 | 0 | 0 | 0 | 0 | 11 | 0 | 0 |
| Stephenson | Paul | Winger/Midfielder | 1997 | 2002 | 136 | 9 | 9 | 5 | 1 | 0 | 4 | 1 | 0 | 5 | 1 | 2 | 8 | 0 | 0 | 158 | 12 | 11 |
| Stevenson | Alan | Goalkeeper | 1984 | 1985 | 35 | 0 | 0 | 0 | 0 | 0 | 2 | 0 | 0 | 1 | 0 | 0 | 1 | 0 | 0 | 39 | 0 | 0 |
| Stewart | Charles David (Dave) | Inside-Right | 1982 | 1983 | 5 | 3 | 0 | 0 | 0 | 0 | 0 | 0 | 0 | 0 | 0 | 0 | 0 | 0 | 0 | 5 | 3 | 0 |
| Stimpson | Barrie George | Left-Back | 1980 | 1985 | 85 | 1 | 2 | 0 | 0 | 0 | 5 | 0 | 0 | 6 | 0 | 0 | 7 | 0 | 0 | 103 | 1 | 2 |
| Stokes | Wayne Darren | Central Defender | 1987 | 1990 | 62 | 0 | 1 | 0 | 0 | 0 | 6 | 0 | 0 | 4 | 0 | 0 | 3 | 0 | 1 | 75 | 0 | 2 |
| Stokle | David | Left-Half-Back | 1986 | 1990 | 9 | 0 | 0 | 0 | 0 | 0 | 0 | 0 | 0 | 1 | 0 | 0 | 1 | 0 | 0 | 11 | 0 | 0 |
| Stokoe | Graham Lloyd | Midfielder | 1995 | 1999 | 23 | 5 | 0 | 0 | 0 | 0 | 1 | 1 | 0 | 0 | 0 | 0 | 1 | 0 | 0 | 25 | 6 | 0 |
| Stonehouse | Derek | Left-Back | 1963 | 1965 | 34 | 0 | 0 | 0 | 0 | 0 | 4 | 0 | 0 | 0 | 0 | 0 | 0 | 0 | 0 | 38 | 0 | 0 |
| Storer | Charles (Charlie) | Centre-Half-Back | 1924 | 1926 | 31 | 0 | 0 | 0 | 0 | 0 | 5 | 0 | 1 | 0 | 0 | 0 | 0 | 0 | 0 | 36 | 0 | 1 |
| Storey | John | Full-Back | 1923 | 1924 | 13 | 0 | 0 | 0 | 0 | 0 | 0 | 0 | 0 | 0 | 0 | 0 | 0 | 0 | 0 | 13 | 0 | 0 |
| Storton | Stanley Eugene (Stan) | Right-Back | 1964 | 1966 | 72 | 0 | 0 | 0 | 0 | 0 | 6 | 0 | 0 | 3 | 0 | 0 | 0 | 0 | 0 | 81 | 0 | 0 |
| Strachan | Gavin David | Midfielder | 2003 | 2007 | 63 | 15 | 7 | 3 | 0 | 0 | 4 | 1 | 0 | 5 | 0 | 0 | 4 | 0 | 1 | 79 | 16 | 8 |
| Strodder | Gary | Centre-Half-Back | 1998 | 2000 | 58 | 3 | 0 | 1 | 0 | 0 | 1 | 0 | 0 | 2 | 0 | 0 | 2 | 0 | 0 | 64 | 3 | 0 |
| Strong | George James (Jimmy) | Goalkeeper | 1933 | 1934 | 1 | 0 | 0 | 0 | 0 | 0 | 0 | 0 | 0 | 0 | 0 | 0 | 0 | 0 | 0 | 1 | 0 | 0 |
| Summerfield | William Henry (Harry) | Goalkeeper | 1921 | 1925 | 59 | 0 | 0 | 0 | 0 | 0 | 9 | 0 | 0 | 0 | 0 | 0 | 0 | 0 | 0 | 68 | 0 | 0 |
| Sunderland | Jonathan Paul (Jon) | Midfielder | 1996 | 1997 | 6 | 7 | 1 | 0 | 0 | 0 | 0 | 0 | 0 | 0 | 0 | 0 | 0 | 0 | 0 | 6 | 7 | 1 |

| Surname | Forenames | Position | Career | | Football League | | | Play-offs | | | FA Cup | | | FL Cup | | | Other | | | Total | | |
|---|---|---|---|---|---|---|---|---|---|---|---|---|---|---|---|---|---|---|---|---|---|---|
| | | | Start | Finish | Apps | Sub | Gls | Apps | Sub | Gls | Apps | Sub | Gls | Apps | Sub | Gls | Apps | Sub | Gls | Apps | Sub | Gls |
| Sunley | Mark | Right-Back | 1994 | 1995 | 1 | 1 | 0 | 0 | 0 | 0 | 0 | 0 | 0 | 0 | 0 | 0 | 0 | 0 | 0 | 1 | 1 | 0 |
| Sutcliffe | Percy | Centre-Half-Back | 1923 | 1924 | 19 | 0 | 0 | 0 | 0 | 0 | 3 | 0 | 0 | 0 | 0 | 0 | 0 | 0 | 0 | 22 | 0 | 0 |
| Sweeney | Alan | Right-Back | 1979 | 1982 | 97 | 0 | 2 | 0 | 0 | 0 | 4 | 0 | 0 | 3 | 0 | 0 | 2 | 0 | 0 | 106 | 0 | 2 |
| Sweeney | Antony Thomas | Midfielder | 2001 | 2012 | 298 | 34 | 51 | 5 | 0 | 1 | 22 | 0 | 4 | 15 | 0 | 2 | 9 | 2 | 2 | 349 | 36 | 60 |
| Sweeney | Paul Martin | Left-Back | 1994 | 1995 | 1 | 0 | 0 | 0 | 0 | 0 | 0 | 0 | 0 | 1 | 0 | 0 | 0 | 0 | 0 | 2 | 0 | 0 |
| Swift | Arnold | Goalkeeper | 1930 | 1931 | 3 | 0 | 0 | 0 | 0 | 0 | 0 | 0 | 0 | 0 | 0 | 0 | 0 | 0 | 0 | 3 | 0 | 0 |
| Sword | Thomas William (Tommy) | Left-Half-Back | 1986 | 1987 | 18 | 0 | 0 | 0 | 0 | 0 | 1 | 0 | 0 | 2 | 0 | 0 | 2 | 0 | 0 | 23 | 0 | 0 |
| Sykes | Kenneth (Ken) | Left-Back | 1949 | 1950 | 1 | 0 | 0 | 0 | 0 | 0 | 0 | 0 | 0 | 0 | 0 | 0 | 0 | 0 | 0 | 1 | 0 | 0 |
| Tait | Michael Paul (Mick) | Defender/Midfielder | 1992 | 1997 | 134 | 5 | 3 | 0 | 0 | 0 | 4 | 0 | 0 | 11 | 0 | 1 | 1 | 0 | 0 | 150 | 5 | 4 |
| Talia | Francesco (Frank) | Goalkeeper | 1992 | 1993 | 14 | 0 | 0 | 0 | 0 | 0 | 0 | 0 | 0 | 0 | 0 | 0 | 1 | 0 | 0 | 15 | 0 | 0 |
| Taylor | Allan | Goalkeeper | 1937 | 1938 | 25 | 0 | 0 | 0 | 0 | 0 | 1 | 0 | 0 | 0 | 0 | 0 | 1 | 0 | 0 | 27 | 0 | 0 |
| Taylor | George Leslie | Goalkeeper | 1953 | 1955 | 34 | 0 | 0 | 0 | 0 | 0 | 3 | 0 | 0 | 0 | 0 | 0 | 0 | 0 | 0 | 37 | 0 | 0 |
| Taylor | Mark | Right-Back | 1982 | 1983 | 1 | 0 | 0 | 0 | 0 | 0 | 0 | 0 | 0 | 0 | 0 | 0 | 2 | 0 | 0 | 3 | 0 | 0 |
| Taylor | Peter Mark Richard | Outside-Left | 1983 | 1986 | 42 | 5 | 4 | 0 | 0 | 0 | 2 | 0 | 1 | 0 | 1 | 0 | 3 | 0 | 0 | 47 | 6 | 5 |
| Telford | Robert (Bob) | Inside/Centre-Forward | 1926 | 1927 | 3 | 0 | 0 | 0 | 0 | 0 | 0 | 0 | 0 | 0 | 0 | 0 | 0 | 0 | 0 | 3 | 0 | 0 |
| Telling | Hubert | Left-Half-Back | 1937 | 1938 | 2 | 0 | 0 | 0 | 0 | 0 | 0 | 0 | 0 | 0 | 0 | 0 | 0 | 0 | 0 | 2 | 0 | 0 |
| Tennebo | Thomas | Midfielder | 1999 | 2000 | 6 | 7 | 0 | 0 | 0 | 0 | 0 | 0 | 0 | 1 | 1 | 0 | 1 | 0 | 0 | 8 | 8 | 0 |
| Thayne | William (Billy) | Half-Back | 1930 | 1934 | 101 | 0 | 8 | 0 | 0 | 0 | 6 | 0 | 0 | 0 | 0 | 0 | 1 | 0 | 0 | 108 | 0 | 8 |
| Theaker | Clarence Alfred (Cam) | Goalkeeper | 1947 | 1948 | 14 | 0 | 0 | 0 | 0 | 0 | 1 | 0 | 0 | 0 | 0 | 0 | 0 | 0 | 0 | 15 | 0 | 0 |
| Thomas | Ernest (Ernie) | Half-Back | 1937 | 1939 | 62 | 0 | 0 | 0 | 0 | 0 | 2 | 0 | 0 | 0 | 0 | 0 | 3 | 0 | 0 | 67 | 0 | 0 |
| Thomas | John William | Forward | 1991 | 1992 | 5 | 2 | 1 | 0 | 0 | 0 | 0 | 0 | 0 | 0 | 0 | 0 | 0 | 0 | 0 | 5 | 2 | 1 |
| Thompson | Alan | Winger | 2007 | 2008 | 7 | 0 | 1 | 0 | 0 | 0 | 0 | 0 | 0 | 0 | 0 | 0 | 0 | 0 | 0 | 7 | 0 | 1 |
| Thompson | Alfred Stanley (Stan) | Outside-Right | 1935 | 1936 | 34 | 0 | 11 | 0 | 0 | 0 | 4 | 0 | 0 | 0 | 0 | 0 | 1 | 0 | 1 | 39 | 0 | 12 |
| Thompson | James E. (Jimmy) | Inside/Centre-Forward | 1929 | 1932 | 67 | 0 | 22 | 0 | 0 | 0 | 0 | 0 | 0 | 0 | 0 | 0 | 0 | 0 | 0 | 67 | 0 | 22 |
| Thompson | Kevin John | Forward | 1969 | 1971 | 6 | 0 | 1 | 0 | 0 | 0 | 0 | 0 | 0 | 0 | 0 | 0 | 0 | 0 | 0 | 6 | 0 | 1 |
| Thompson | Malcolm George | Centre-Forward | 1968 | 1970 | 43 | 3 | 9 | 0 | 0 | 0 | 0 | 1 | 0 | 2 | 0 | 0 | 0 | 0 | 0 | 45 | 4 | 9 |
| Thompson | Norman | Centre-Forward | 1937 | 1938 | 1 | 0 | 0 | 0 | 0 | 0 | 0 | 0 | 0 | 0 | 0 | 0 | 0 | 0 | 0 | 1 | 0 | 0 |
| Thompson | Paul Derek Zetland | Forward | 1991 | 1995 | 44 | 12 | 9 | 0 | 0 | 0 | 1 | 0 | 0 | 4 | 1 | 1 | 1 | 1 | 0 | 50 | 14 | 10 |
| Thompson | Peter | Forward | 1957 | 1966 | 138 | 0 | 56 | 0 | 0 | 0 | 6 | 0 | 5 | 1 | 0 | 0 | 0 | 0 | 0 | 145 | 0 | 61 |
| Thompson | Raymond (Ray) | Left-Back | 1946 | 1958 | 396 | 0 | 2 | 0 | 0 | 0 | 27 | 0 | 0 | 0 | 0 | 0 | 0 | 0 | 0 | 423 | 0 | 2 |
| Thompson | Robert | Centre-Forward | 1926 | 1927 | 4 | 0 | 3 | 0 | 0 | 0 | 0 | 0 | 0 | 0 | 0 | 0 | 0 | 0 | 0 | 4 | 0 | 3 |
| Thompson | Thomas Russell (Tommy) | Outside-Right | 1921 | 1923 | 10 | 0 | 0 | 0 | 0 | 0 | 0 | 0 | 0 | 0 | 0 | 0 | 0 | 0 | 0 | 10 | 0 | 0 |
| Thompson | William T. (Billy) | Outside-Right | 1921 | 1922 | 1 | 0 | 0 | 0 | 0 | 0 | 0 | 0 | 0 | 0 | 0 | 0 | 0 | 0 | 0 | 1 | 0 | 0 |
| Thoms | Henry (Harry) | Half-Back | 1921 | 1922 | 33 | 0 | 1 | 0 | 0 | 0 | 11 | 0 | 2 | 0 | 0 | 0 | 0 | 0 | 0 | 44 | 0 | 3 |
| Thomson | Kenneth Gordon (Kenny) | Centre-Half-Back | 1962 | 1963 | 28 | 0 | 2 | 0 | 0 | 0 | 1 | 0 | 0 | 0 | 0 | 0 | 0 | 0 | 0 | 29 | 0 | 2 |

| | | | Career | | Football League | | | Play-offs | | | FA Cup | | | FL Cup | | | Other | | | Total | | |
|---|---|---|---|---|---|---|---|---|---|---|---|---|---|---|---|---|---|---|---|---|---|---|
| Surname | Forenames | Position | Start | Finish | Apps | Sub | Gls | Apps | Sub | Gls | Apps | Sub | Gls | Apps | Sub | Gls | Apps | Sub | Gls | Apps | Sub | Gls |
| Thomson | Robert (Bobby) | Midfielder | 1987 | 1988 | 2 | 1 | 0 | 0 | 0 | 0 | 0 | 0 | 0 | 1 | 0 | 0 | 0 | 0 | 0 | 3 | 1 | 0 |
| Thornton | Percy | Half-Back | 1929 | 1933 | 97 | 0 | 10 | 0 | 0 | 0 | 4 | 0 | 2 | 0 | 0 | 0 | 0 | 0 | 0 | 101 | 0 | 12 |
| Tinkler | John | Midfielder | 1986 | 1992 | 153 | 17 | 7 | 0 | 0 | 0 | 10 | 1 | 1 | 8 | 2 | 1 | 12 | 0 | 2 | 183 | 20 | 11 |
| Tinkler | Mark | Midfielder | 2000 | 2007 | 200 | 11 | 34 | 4 | 2 | 0 | 12 | 0 | 2 | 7 | 0 | 0 | 8 | 0 | 1 | 231 | 13 | 37 |
| Tither | John | Left-Half-Back | 1929 | 1933 | 15 | 0 | 1 | 0 | 0 | 0 | 0 | 0 | 0 | 0 | 0 | 0 | 0 | 0 | 0 | 15 | 0 | 1 |
| Todd | Alexander (Alex) | Left-Half-Back | 1952 | 1954 | 4 | 0 | 0 | 0 | 0 | 0 | 0 | 0 | 0 | 0 | 0 | 0 | 0 | 0 | 0 | 4 | 0 | 0 |
| Toman | James Andrew (Andy) | Inside/Outside-Right | 1986 | 1989 | 112 | 0 | 28 | 0 | 0 | 0 | 9 | 0 | 4 | 4 | 0 | 0 | 7 | 0 | 0 | 132 | 0 | 32 |
| Tootill | George Albert (Alf) | Centre-Half-Back | 1947 | 1948 | 18 | 0 | 0 | 0 | 0 | 0 | 0 | 0 | 0 | 0 | 0 | 0 | 0 | 0 | 0 | 18 | 0 | 0 |
| Towse | Thomas (Tom) | Centre-Forward | 1921 | 1923 | 13 | 0 | 5 | 0 | 0 | 0 | 1 | 0 | 0 | 0 | 0 | 0 | 0 | 0 | 0 | 14 | 0 | 5 |
| Trail | Derek John Falconer | Midfielder | 1969 | 1970 | 36 | 3 | 2 | 0 | 0 | 0 | 2 | 0 | 0 | 0 | 0 | 0 | 0 | 0 | 0 | 38 | 3 | 2 |
| Tremain | Sidney (Sid) | Goalkeeper | 1932 | 1933 | 16 | 0 | 0 | 0 | 0 | 0 | 0 | 0 | 0 | 0 | 0 | 0 | 0 | 0 | 0 | 16 | 0 | 0 |
| Trewick | John | Inside-Right | 1989 | 1990 | 8 | 0 | 0 | 0 | 0 | 0 | 0 | 0 | 0 | 0 | 0 | 0 | 1 | 0 | 0 | 9 | 0 | 0 |
| Troman | James | Centre/Wing-Half-Back | 1945 | 1946 | 0 | 0 | 0 | 0 | 0 | 0 | 2 | 0 | 0 | 0 | 0 | 0 | 0 | 0 | 0 | 2 | 0 | 0 |
| Tunks | Roy William | Goalkeeper | 1988 | 1989 | 5 | 0 | 0 | 0 | 0 | 0 | 0 | 0 | 0 | 0 | 0 | 0 | 0 | 0 | 0 | 5 | 0 | 0 |
| Tunstall | Eric Walter | Midfielder | 1968 | 1969 | 0 | 1 | 0 | 0 | 0 | 0 | 0 | 0 | 0 | 0 | 0 | 0 | 0 | 0 | 0 | 0 | 1 | 0 |
| Tupling | Stephen (Steve) | Midfielder | 1989 | 1992 | 83 | 6 | 3 | 0 | 0 | 0 | 4 | 0 | 0 | 5 | 1 | 0 | 6 | 1 | 0 | 98 | 8 | 3 |
| Turnbull | Philip | Right-Back | 2006 | 2007 | 0 | 0 | 0 | 0 | 0 | 0 | 0 | 0 | 0 | 0 | 0 | 0 | 1 | 0 | 0 | 1 | 0 | 0 |
| Turnbull | Stephen | Midfielder | 2004 | 2008 | 16 | 8 | 0 | 0 | 0 | 0 | 0 | 0 | 0 | 0 | 1 | 0 | 0 | 0 | 0 | 16 | 9 | 0 |
| Turnbull | Terence Michael (Terry) | Centre-Forward | 1976 | 1977 | 13 | 0 | 3 | 0 | 0 | 0 | 0 | 0 | 0 | 1 | 0 | 1 | 0 | 0 | 0 | 14 | 0 | 4 |
| Turner | Richard | Right-Back | 1937 | 1938 | 1 | 0 | 0 | 0 | 0 | 0 | 1 | 0 | 0 | 0 | 0 | 0 | 0 | 0 | 0 | 2 | 0 | 0 |
| Turner | Robert Peter (Robbie) | Centre-Forward | 1986 | 1987 | 7 | 0 | 1 | 0 | 0 | 0 | 0 | 0 | 0 | 0 | 0 | 0 | 0 | 0 | 0 | 7 | 0 | 1 |
| Underwood | William Kenneth (Bill) | Outside-Right | 1947 | 1948 | 1 | 0 | 0 | 0 | 0 | 0 | 0 | 0 | 0 | 0 | 0 | 0 | 0 | 0 | 0 | 1 | 0 | 0 |
| Vass | Stephen (Steve) | Full-Back | 1979 | 1981 | 4 | 0 | 0 | 0 | 0 | 0 | 0 | 0 | 0 | 1 | 0 | 0 | 0 | 0 | 0 | 5 | 0 | 0 |
| Veart | Robert (Bobby) | Forward | 1970 | 1973 | 59 | 12 | 12 | 0 | 0 | 0 | 4 | 1 | 4 | 0 | 2 | 0 | 0 | 0 | 0 | 63 | 15 | 16 |
| Veitch | Thomas (Tommy) | Forward | 1976 | 1977 | 10 | 0 | 0 | 0 | 0 | 0 | 0 | 0 | 0 | 0 | 0 | 0 | 0 | 0 | 0 | 10 | 0 | 0 |
| Venus | Mark | Left-Back | 1984 | 1985 | 4 | 0 | 0 | 0 | 0 | 0 | 0 | 0 | 0 | 0 | 0 | 0 | 0 | 1 | 0 | 4 | 1 | 0 |
| Vindheim | Rune | Midfielder | 1999 | 2000 | 7 | 0 | 0 | 0 | 0 | 0 | 1 | 0 | 0 | 0 | 0 | 0 | 0 | 0 | 0 | 8 | 0 | 0 |
| Vitty | Ronald (Ron) | Right-Back | 1949 | 1950 | 7 | 0 | 0 | 0 | 0 | 0 | 0 | 0 | 0 | 0 | 0 | 0 | 0 | 0 | 0 | 7 | 0 | 0 |
| Waddell | William (Willie) | Outside-Right | 1971 | 1974 | 43 | 5 | 9 | 0 | 0 | 0 | 4 | 0 | 0 | 2 | 0 | 0 | 0 | 0 | 0 | 49 | 5 | 9 |
| Waddle | Alan Robert | Centre-Forward | 1983 | 1985 | 16 | 0 | 2 | 0 | 0 | 0 | 0 | 0 | 0 | 1 | 0 | 0 | 2 | 0 | 1 | 19 | 0 | 3 |
| Waite | George Henry | Inside/Outside-Right | 1926 | 1927 | 26 | 0 | 7 | 0 | 0 | 0 | 0 | 0 | 0 | 0 | 0 | 0 | 0 | 0 | 0 | 26 | 0 | 7 |
| Walker | James | Forward | 2005 | 2006 | 1 | 3 | 0 | 0 | 0 | 0 | 0 | 0 | 0 | 0 | 0 | 0 | 0 | 0 | 0 | 1 | 3 | 0 |
| Walker | James McIntyre (Jim) | Inside-Forward | 1969 | 1970 | 10 | 0 | 0 | 0 | 0 | 0 | 0 | 0 | 0 | 0 | 0 | 0 | 0 | 0 | 0 | 10 | 0 | 0 |
| Walker | John Robert | Right-Back | 1922 | 1924 | 24 | 0 | 0 | 0 | 0 | 0 | 2 | 0 | 0 | 0 | 0 | 0 | 0 | 0 | 0 | 26 | 0 | 0 |
| Walker | Nigel Stephen | Inside-Left | 1985 | 1987 | 77 | 5 | 8 | 0 | 0 | 0 | 3 | 0 | 0 | 4 | 0 | 0 | 3 | 0 | 0 | 87 | 5 | 8 |

| | | | Career | | Football League | | | Play-offs | | | FA Cup | | | FL Cup | | | Other | | | Total | | |
|---|---|---|---|---|---|---|---|---|---|---|---|---|---|---|---|---|---|---|---|---|---|---|
| **Surname** | **Forenames** | **Position** | **Start** | **Finish** | **Apps** | **Sub** | **Gls** | **Apps** | **Sub** | **Gls** | **Apps** | **Sub** | **Gls** | **Apps** | **Sub** | **Gls** | **Apps** | **Sub** | **Gls** | **Apps** | **Sub** | **Gls** |
| Wallace | John (Jack) | Goalkeeper | 1938 | 1939 | 31 | 0 | 0 | 0 | 0 | 0 | 2 | 0 | 0 | 0 | 0 | 0 | 4 | 0 | 0 | 37 | 0 | 0 |
| Waller | Horace | Centre-Forward | 1930 | 1932 | 10 | 0 | 7 | 0 | 0 | 0 | 1 | 0 | 1 | 0 | 0 | 0 | 0 | 0 | 0 | 11 | 0 | 8 |
| Wallis | Derek | Centre-Forward | 1963 | 1964 | 2 | 0 | 0 | 0 | 0 | 0 | 0 | 0 | 0 | 0 | 0 | 0 | 0 | 0 | 0 | 2 | 0 | 0 |
| Walsh | Alan | Left-Back | 1994 | 1995 | 4 | 0 | 1 | 0 | 0 | 0 | 1 | 0 | 0 | 2 | 0 | 0 | 2 | 0 | 0 | 9 | 0 | 1 |
| Walsh | William (Billy) | Half-Back | 1923 | 1925 | 28 | 0 | 0 | 0 | 0 | 0 | 5 | 0 | 0 | 0 | 0 | 0 | 0 | 0 | 0 | 33 | 0 | 0 |
| Walton | James (Jimmy) | Left-Half-Back | 1926 | 1927 | 2 | 0 | 0 | 0 | 0 | 0 | 0 | 0 | 0 | 0 | 0 | 0 | 0 | 0 | 0 | 2 | 0 | 0 |
| Walton | Paul Anthony | Forward | 1995 | 1997 | 3 | 7 | 0 | 0 | 0 | 0 | 0 | 0 | 0 | 0 | 0 | 0 | 0 | 0 | 0 | 3 | 7 | 0 |
| Wann | John Dennis | Forward | 1975 | 1976 | 2 | 0 | 0 | 0 | 0 | 0 | 0 | 0 | 0 | 0 | 0 | 0 | 0 | 0 | 0 | 2 | 0 | 0 |
| Ward | William (Billy) | Outside-Right/Left | 1971 | 1975 | 87 | 8 | 10 | 0 | 0 | 0 | 3 | 0 | 0 | 1 | 2 | 1 | 0 | 0 | 0 | 91 | 10 | 11 |
| Wardrobe | Thomas Barrie | Centre-Forward | 1984 | 1985 | 23 | 4 | 2 | 0 | 0 | 0 | 0 | 0 | 0 | 0 | 0 | 0 | 0 | 0 | 0 | 23 | 4 | 2 |
| Warnock | Neil | Outside-Left | 1971 | 1973 | 58 | 2 | 5 | 0 | 0 | 0 | 2 | 0 | 1 | 4 | 0 | 0 | 0 | 0 | 0 | 64 | 2 | 6 |
| Warren | Ernest Thorne (Ernie) | Left-Half-Back | 1934 | 1935 | 15 | 0 | 0 | 0 | 0 | 0 | 0 | 0 | 0 | 0 | 0 | 0 | 0 | 0 | 0 | 15 | 0 | 0 |
| Watling | Barry John | Goalkeeper | 1972 | 1976 | 139 | 0 | 0 | 0 | 0 | 0 | 7 | 0 | 0 | 12 | 0 | 0 | 0 | 0 | 0 | 158 | 0 | 0 |
| Watson | Gordon William George | Forward | 2001 | 2003 | 43 | 6 | 23 | 2 | 0 | 0 | 1 | 0 | 0 | 0 | 0 | 0 | 1 | 0 | 0 | 47 | 6 | 23 |
| Watson | John | Goalkeeper | 1978 | 1982 | 44 | 0 | 0 | 0 | 0 | 0 | 3 | 0 | 0 | 6 | 0 | 0 | 2 | 0 | 0 | 55 | 0 | 0 |
| Waugh | Kenneth (Ken) | Right-Back | 1956 | 1962 | 195 | 0 | 0 | 0 | 0 | 0 | 9 | 0 | 0 | 2 | 0 | 0 | 0 | 0 | 0 | 206 | 0 | 0 |
| Wayman | Brian O. | Inside-Left | 1924 | 1925 | 5 | 0 | 0 | 0 | 0 | 0 | 0 | 0 | 0 | 0 | 0 | 0 | 0 | 0 | 0 | 5 | 0 | 0 |
| Weatherspoon | Charles William (Charlie) | Centre-Forward | 1952 | 1953 | 3 | 0 | 2 | 0 | 0 | 0 | 0 | 0 | 0 | 0 | 0 | 0 | 0 | 0 | 0 | 3 | 0 | 2 |
| Weir | Alan | Wing-Half-Back | 1983 | 1984 | 9 | 1 | 0 | 0 | 0 | 0 | 0 | 0 | 0 | 1 | 0 | 0 | 0 | 0 | 0 | 10 | 1 | 0 |
| Welford | William Frederick (Bill) | Right-Half-Back | 1958 | 1959 | 8 | 0 | 0 | 0 | 0 | 0 | 4 | 0 | 0 | 0 | 0 | 0 | 0 | 0 | 0 | 12 | 0 | 0 |
| Welsh | Eric | Outside-Right | 1971 | 1972 | 13 | 2 | 2 | 0 | 0 | 0 | 2 | 0 | 0 | 2 | 0 | 0 | 0 | 0 | 0 | 17 | 2 | 2 |
| Welsh | William (Billy) | Centre/Half-Back | 1933 | 1934 | 3 | 0 | 0 | 0 | 0 | 0 | 0 | 0 | 0 | 0 | 0 | 0 | 0 | 0 | 0 | 3 | 0 | 0 |
| Wensley | Harold (Harry) | Centre-Forward | 1925 | 1927 | 76 | 0 | 37 | 0 | 0 | 0 | 4 | 0 | 1 | 0 | 0 | 0 | 0 | 0 | 0 | 80 | 0 | 38 |
| West | Colin | Centre-Forward | 1999 | 2000 | 0 | 1 | 0 | 0 | 0 | 0 | 0 | 0 | 0 | 0 | 0 | 0 | 0 | 0 | 0 | 0 | 1 | 0 |
| West | Colin William | Forward | 1993 | 1994 | 29 | 7 | 5 | 0 | 0 | 0 | 1 | 0 | 0 | 4 | 0 | 1 | 1 | 1 | 0 | 35 | 8 | 6 |
| West | Norman | Inside-Left | 1937 | 1946 | 19 | 0 | 7 | 0 | 0 | 0 | 2 | 0 | 0 | 0 | 0 | 0 | 1 | 0 | 0 | 22 | 0 | 7 |
| Westmoreland | William (Bill) | Left-Back/Inside-Forward | 1934 | 1935 | 7 | 0 | 0 | 0 | 0 | 0 | 0 | 0 | 0 | 0 | 0 | 0 | 0 | 0 | 0 | 7 | 0 | 0 |
| Westwood | Christopher John (Chris) | Central Defender | 1999 | 2005 | 244 | 6 | 7 | 11 | 0 | 0 | 15 | 0 | 2 | 8 | 0 | 0 | 9 | 0 | 0 | 287 | 6 | 9 |
| Whellans | Robert (Robbie) | Inside-Left | 1987 | 1988 | 8 | 3 | 1 | 0 | 0 | 0 | 1 | 0 | 0 | 0 | 0 | 0 | 0 | 1 | 0 | 9 | 4 | 1 |
| White | Dennis | Full-Back | 1967 | 1973 | 55 | 3 | 0 | 0 | 0 | 0 | 0 | 1 | 0 | 4 | 0 | 0 | 0 | 0 | 0 | 59 | 4 | 0 |
| Whitelock | Arthur | Right-Back | 1950 | 1951 | 6 | 0 | 0 | 0 | 0 | 0 | 0 | 0 | 0 | 0 | 0 | 0 | 0 | 0 | 0 | 6 | 0 | 0 |
| Whitfield | Michael (Mick) | Inside-Right | 1983 | 1984 | 15 | 1 | 0 | 0 | 0 | 0 | 2 | 0 | 0 | 2 | 0 | 0 | 0 | 0 | 0 | 19 | 1 | 0 |
| Whyte | Crawford | Left-Back | 1937 | 1938 | 5 | 0 | 0 | 0 | 0 | 0 | 1 | 0 | 0 | 0 | 0 | 0 | 3 | 0 | 0 | 9 | 0 | 0 |
| Widdrington | Thomas (Tommy) | Midfielder | 2001 | 2003 | 50 | 6 | 5 | 0 | 0 | 0 | 1 | 1 | 0 | 1 | 0 | 0 | 2 | 0 | 0 | 54 | 7 | 5 |
| Wiggett | David Jonathan (Dave) | Left-Back | 1976 | 1978 | 54 | 0 | 1 | 0 | 0 | 0 | 4 | 0 | 0 | 2 | 0 | 0 | 0 | 0 | 0 | 60 | 0 | 1 |

| Surname | Forenames | Position | Career | | Football League | | | Play-offs | | | FA Cup | | | FL Cup | | | Other | | | Total | | |
|---|---|---|---|---|---|---|---|---|---|---|---|---|---|---|---|---|---|---|---|---|---|---|
| | | | Start | Finish | Apps | Sub | Gls | Apps | Sub | Gls | Apps | Sub | Gls | Apps | Sub | Gls | Apps | Sub | Gls | Apps | Sub | Gls |
| Wigham | John (Johnny) | Centre/Inside-Forward | 1931 | 1939 | 264 | 0 | 95 | 0 | 0 | 0 | 23 | 0 | 7 | 0 | 0 | 0 | 4 | 0 | 4 | 291 | 0 | 106 |
| Wildon | Leslie Eric | Centre/Inside-Forward | 1947 | 1955 | 200 | 0 | 87 | 0 | 0 | 0 | 15 | 0 | 2 | 0 | 0 | 0 | 0 | 0 | 0 | 215 | 0 | 89 |
| Wilkie | Derrick | Centre-Half-Back | 1961 | 1964 | 74 | 0 | 0 | 0 | 0 | 0 | 3 | 0 | 0 | 1 | 0 | 0 | 0 | 0 | 0 | 78 | 0 | 0 |
| Wilkinson | Jack | Forward | 2003 | 2005 | 3 | 4 | 2 | 0 | 0 | 0 | 0 | 2 | 0 | 0 | 0 | 0 | 0 | 0 | 0 | 3 | 6 | 2 |
| Wilkinson | Joseph (Joe) | Goalkeeper | 1959 | 1962 | 74 | 0 | 0 | 0 | 0 | 0 | 3 | 0 | 0 | 2 | 0 | 0 | 0 | 0 | 0 | 79 | 0 | 0 |
| Wilkinson | Kenneth (Ken) | Centre-Forward/Half-Back | 1946 | 1949 | 53 | 0 | 5 | 0 | 0 | 0 | 3 | 0 | 0 | 0 | 0 | 0 | 0 | 0 | 0 | 56 | 0 | 5 |
| Wilkinson | Thomas (Tommy) | Wing-Half-Back | 1953 | 1958 | 22 | 0 | 0 | 0 | 0 | 0 | 1 | 0 | 0 | 0 | 0 | 0 | 0 | 0 | 0 | 23 | 0 | 0 |
| Wilks | Fred | Goalkeeper | 1932 | 1933 | 15 | 0 | 0 | 0 | 0 | 0 | 2 | 0 | 0 | 0 | 0 | 0 | 0 | 0 | 0 | 17 | 0 | 0 |
| Willetts | Joseph (Joe) | Full-Back | 1946 | 1956 | 239 | 0 | 20 | 0 | 0 | 0 | 19 | 0 | 2 | 0 | 0 | 0 | 0 | 0 | 0 | 258 | 0 | 22 |
| Williams | Anthony Simon | Goalkeeper | 2000 | 2004 | 131 | 0 | 0 | 4 | 0 | 0 | 4 | 0 | 0 | 1 | 0 | 0 | 5 | 0 | 0 | 145 | 0 | 0 |
| Williams | Darren | Defender | 2005 | 2007 | 52 | 13 | 0 | 0 | 0 | 0 | 4 | 0 | 0 | 4 | 0 | 0 | 1 | 0 | 0 | 61 | 13 | 0 |
| Williams | Eifion Wyn | Forward | 2001 | 2007 | 175 | 33 | 50 | 6 | 1 | 2 | 10 | 3 | 1 | 4 | 2 | 2 | 4 | 1 | 1 | 199 | 40 | 56 |
| Williams | John Thomas (Johnny) | Left-Back/Centre-Half | 1927 | 1929 | 41 | 0 | 1 | 0 | 0 | 0 | 2 | 0 | 0 | 0 | 0 | 0 | 0 | 0 | 0 | 43 | 0 | 1 |
| Williams | Paul Andrew | Left-Half-Back | 1989 | 1990 | 7 | 1 | 0 | 0 | 0 | 0 | 1 | 0 | 0 | 0 | 0 | 0 | 1 | 0 | 0 | 9 | 1 | 0 |
| Willis | John George | Inside/Wing-Forward | 1954 | 1959 | 25 | 0 | 7 | 0 | 0 | 0 | 0 | 0 | 0 | 0 | 0 | 0 | 0 | 0 | 0 | 25 | 0 | 7 |
| Willox | Alexander (Sandy) | Centre-Forward | 1951 | 1952 | 6 | 0 | 0 | 0 | 0 | 0 | 0 | 0 | 0 | 0 | 0 | 0 | 0 | 0 | 0 | 6 | 0 | 0 |
| Wilson | Harry | Left-Back | 1983 | 1984 | 16 | 0 | 0 | 0 | 0 | 0 | 2 | 0 | 0 | 2 | 0 | 0 | 0 | 0 | 0 | 20 | 0 | 0 |
| Wilson | John | Left-Back | 1930 | 1931 | 1 | 0 | 0 | 0 | 0 | 0 | 0 | 0 | 0 | 0 | 0 | 0 | 0 | 0 | 0 | 1 | 0 | 0 |
| Wilson | John Ball (Jack) | Left-Back | 1938 | 1939 | 25 | 0 | 0 | 0 | 0 | 0 | 2 | 0 | 0 | 0 | 0 | 0 | 4 | 0 | 0 | 31 | 0 | 0 |
| Wilson | Philip Michael (Phil) | Central Defender | 1989 | 1990 | 0 | 1 | 0 | 0 | 0 | 0 | 0 | 0 | 0 | 0 | 0 | 0 | 0 | 0 | 0 | 0 | 1 | 0 |
| Wilson | Stuart | Goalkeeper | 1985 | 1986 | 0 | 0 | 0 | 0 | 0 | 0 | 0 | 0 | 0 | 0 | 0 | 0 | 1 | 0 | 0 | 1 | 0 | 0 |
| Winn | Stephen (Steve) | Inside-Left | 1982 | 1983 | 1 | 0 | 0 | 0 | 0 | 0 | 0 | 0 | 0 | 0 | 0 | 0 | 0 | 0 | 0 | 1 | 0 | 0 |
| Winstanley | Craig Jason | Midfielder | 1996 | 1997 | 0 | 1 | 0 | 0 | 0 | 0 | 0 | 0 | 0 | 0 | 0 | 0 | 0 | 0 | 0 | 0 | 1 | 0 |
| Woffinden | Richard Shaw | Left-Half-Back | 1938 | 1939 | 15 | 0 | 1 | 0 | 0 | 0 | 0 | 0 | 0 | 0 | 0 | 0 | 0 | 0 | 0 | 15 | 0 | 1 |
| Woods | Cyril | Inside-Right | 1938 | 1939 | 25 | 0 | 6 | 0 | 0 | 0 | 1 | 0 | 1 | 0 | 0 | 0 | 0 | 0 | 0 | 26 | 0 | 7 |
| Woods | Martin Paul | Midfielder | 2004 | 2005 | 3 | 3 | 0 | 0 | 0 | 0 | 0 | 0 | 0 | 1 | 0 | 0 | 1 | 0 | 0 | 5 | 3 | 0 |
| Woods | Patrick B. (Paddy) | Left-Half-Back | 1945 | 1946 | 0 | 0 | 0 | 0 | 0 | 0 | 1 | 0 | 0 | 0 | 0 | 0 | 0 | 0 | 0 | 1 | 0 | 0 |
| Woof | William (Billy) | Forward | 1983 | 1984 | 0 | 0 | 0 | 0 | 0 | 0 | 0 | 2 | 0 | 0 | 0 | 0 | 0 | 0 | 0 | 0 | 2 | 0 |
| Worthington | Peter Robert (Bob) | Left-Back | 1974 | 1975 | 6 | 0 | 0 | 0 | 0 | 0 | 0 | 0 | 0 | 0 | 0 | 0 | 0 | 0 | 0 | 6 | 0 | 0 |
| Wratten | Paul | Midfielder | 1992 | 1994 | 52 | 5 | 1 | 0 | 0 | 0 | 2 | 1 | 0 | 4 | 1 | 0 | 2 | 0 | 0 | 60 | 7 | 1 |
| Wright | Gary | Goalkeeper | 1982 | 1983 | 12 | 0 | 0 | 0 | 0 | 0 | 0 | 0 | 0 | 0 | 0 | 0 | 1 | 0 | 0 | 13 | 0 | 0 |
| Wright | George Clifford (Cliff) | Forward | 1964 | 1970 | 178 | 6 | 31 | 0 | 0 | 0 | 8 | 0 | 2 | 8 | 1 | 1 | 0 | 0 | 0 | 194 | 7 | 34 |
| Wright | James (Jim) | Right-Back | 1938 | 1939 | 34 | 0 | 0 | 0 | 0 | 0 | 0 | 0 | 0 | 0 | 0 | 0 | 4 | 0 | 0 | 38 | 0 | 0 |
| Wright | Ralph Lawrence | Forward | 1970 | 1971 | 23 | 1 | 3 | 0 | 0 | 0 | 0 | 0 | 0 | 1 | 0 | 0 | 0 | 0 | 0 | 24 | 1 | 3 |
| Wright | Stephen John | Full-Back/Centre-Half-Back | 2011 | 2012 | 10 | 0 | 0 | 0 | 0 | 0 | 1 | 0 | 0 | 0 | 0 | 0 | 0 | 0 | 0 | 11 | 0 | 0 |

| | | | Career | | Football League | | | Play-offs | | | FA Cup | | | FL Cup | | | Other | | | Total | | |
|---|---|---|---|---|---|---|---|---|---|---|---|---|---|---|---|---|---|---|---|---|---|---|
| Surname | Forenames | Position | Start | Finish | Apps | Sub | Gls | Apps | Sub | Gls | Apps | Sub | Gls | Apps | Sub | Gls | Apps | Sub | Gls | Apps | Sub | Gls |
| Wrightson | John Mawson | Inside-Left | 1923 | 1924 | 1 | 0 | 0 | 0 | 0 | 0 | 0 | 0 | 0 | 0 | 0 | 0 | 0 | 0 | 0 | 1 | 0 | 0 |
| Yantorno Blengio | Fabian Rodrigo | Midfielder | 2010 | 2011 | 9 | 8 | 0 | 0 | 0 | 0 | 0 | 2 | 0 | 0 | 0 | 0 | 2 | 1 | 1 | 11 | 11 | 1 |
| Yews | Thomas Peace (Tommy) | Outside-Right | 1921 | 1923 | 39 | 0 | 3 | 0 | 0 | 0 | 8 | 0 | 0 | 0 | 0 | 0 | 0 | 0 | 0 | 47 | 0 | 3 |
| Young | Alfred (Alf) | Wing/Centre-Half-Back | 1923 | 1928 | 123 | 0 | 1 | 0 | 0 | 0 | 8 | 0 | 0 | 0 | 0 | 0 | 0 | 0 | 0 | 131 | 0 | 1 |
| Young | John | Inside-Right | 1927 | 1929 | 19 | 0 | 4 | 0 | 0 | 0 | 0 | 0 | 0 | 0 | 0 | 0 | 0 | 0 | 0 | 19 | 0 | 4 |
| Young | John | Midfielder | 1968 | 1969 | 3 | 0 | 0 | 0 | 0 | 0 | 0 | 0 | 0 | 0 | 0 | 0 | 0 | 0 | 0 | 3 | 0 | 0 |
| Young | Matthew Spratt (Matty) | Outside-Right | 1923 | 1924 | 29 | 0 | 3 | 0 | 0 | 0 | 3 | 0 | 0 | 0 | 0 | 0 | 0 | 0 | 0 | 32 | 0 | 3 |
| Young | Ronald (Ron) | Inside/Wing-Forward | 1968 | 1973 | 177 | 9 | 40 | 0 | 0 | 0 | 7 | 1 | 3 | 5 | 0 | 3 | 0 | 0 | 0 | 189 | 10 | 46 |
| Young | Roy | Outside-Left | 1969 | 1970 | 0 | 0 | 0 | 0 | 0 | 0 | 0 | 0 | 0 | 1 | 0 | 0 | 0 | 0 | 0 | 1 | 0 | 0 |
| Younger | William (Billy) | Inside/Outside-Left | 1962 | 1963 | 37 | 0 | 4 | 0 | 0 | 0 | 1 | 0 | 0 | 2 | 0 | 1 | 0 | 0 | 0 | 40 | 0 | 5 |

ND - #0160 - 090625 - C0 - 234/156/37 - PB - 9781780910307 - Gloss Lamination